Skilled interpersonal communication

Fifth edition

There is a fundamental, powerful and universal desire amongst humans to interact with others. People have a deep-seated need to communicate, and the greater their ability in this regard the more satisfying and rewarding their lives will be. The contribution of skilled interpersonal communication to success in both personal and professional contexts is now widely recognised and extensively researched. As such, knowledge of various types of skills, and of their effects in social interaction, is crucial for effective interpersonal functioning.

Previous editions have established *Skilled Interpersonal Communication* as the foremost textbook on communication. This thoroughly revised and expanded fifth edition builds on this success to provide a comprehensive and up-to-date review of the current research, theory and practice in this burgeoning field of study. The first two chapters introduce the reader to the nature of skilled interpersonal communication and review the main theoretical perspectives. Subsequent chapters provide detailed accounts of the 14 main skill areas, namely: nonverbal communication; reinforcement; questioning; reflecting; listening; explaining; self-disclosure; set induction and closure; assertiveness; influencing; negotiating; and interacting in and leading group discussions.

Written by one of the foremost international experts in the field and founded solidly on research, this book provides a key reference for the study of interpersonal communication. This theoretically informed, yet practically oriented text will be of interest both to students of interpersonal communication in general, and to qualified personnel and trainees in many fields.

Owen Hargie is Professor of Communication at the University of Ulster, and visiting Professor at Robert Gordon University Aberdeen and University of Chester. He is an elected Member of the prestigious Royal Norwegian Society of Sciences and Letters, and Associate Fellow of the British Psychological Society. He has published over 20 books and 120 book chapters and journal articles.

Skilled interpersonal communication

Research, theory and practice

Fifth edition

Owen Hargie

Routledge
Taylor & Francis Group

LONDON AND NEW YORK

Published in 2011
by Routledge
27 Church Road, Hove, East Sussex,
BN3 2FA

Simultaneously published in the USA
and Canada
by Routledge
270 Madison Avenue, New York, NY
10016

*Routledge is an imprint of the Taylor
& Francis Group, an Informa business*

Typeset in Century Old Style by
RefineCatch Limited, Bungay, Suffolk
Printed and bound in Great Britain by
TJ International Ltd, Padstow,
Cornwall
Cover design by Lisa Dynan

This publication has been produced
with paper manufactured to strict
environmental standards and with
pulp derived from sustainable forests.

*British Library Cataloguing in
Publication Data*
A catalogue record for this book is
available from the British Library

*Library of Congress Cataloging in
Publication Data*
Hargie, Owen.
Skilled interpersonal communication :
research, theory, and practice / Owen
Hargie.—5th ed.
    p. cm.
Includes bibliographical references
and index.
1. Interpersonal communication.
I. Title.
BF637.C45H33 2010
153.6—dc22
                                    2010010084

ISBN: 978–0–415–43203–0 (hbk)
ISBN: 978–0–415–43204–7 (pbk)

For my late colleague, co-author, and lifelong friend, David Dickson

Contents

CONTENTS

Figures

Boxes

Preface to the fifth edition

The contribution of effective interpersonal communication to success in both personal and professional contexts is now widely recognised. This topic is studied in its own right on many further and higher education courses. Interpersonal training programmes have also been reported in the literature for every professional group, and the contribution of communication to social and personal well-being has been extensively researched. It is clear that the ability to communicate effectively at an interpersonal level is a vital part of the human condition. As such, knowledge of various types of skills, and of their effects in social interaction, is crucial for interpersonal functioning. It is for this reason that interest in the study of skilled communication has mushroomed in the past few years.

In the intervening period since the fourth edition of this book was published, a considerable amount of feedback has been provided by tutors and trainees involved in interpersonal skills programmes, as well as from practising professionals. The result of this feedback has developed and shaped the current text. For example, the term 'social skill' tends to predominate within clinical contexts and in developmental/elementary educational fields. In academic and professional spheres, the more common usage is 'interpersonal skill' or 'communication skill'. The title of this book reflects the fact that its heartland lies in the academic domain of interpersonal communication, as applied to higher order contexts. It also reflects the fact that the treatment of skill in the book encompasses a comprehensive review of research findings and analyses of theoretical perspectives, as well as direct applications to practice in a range of settings.

The function of the book is to provide a key reference for the study of interpersonal communication per se. It is concerned with the identification, analysis and evaluation of a range of skills that are employed widely in interaction. As such, this text will be of interest both to students of interpersonal communication in general, and to qualified personnel and trainees in many fields in particular. Detailed accounts are provided of 14 areas, namely: the nature of interpersonal skill; nonverbal communication; reinforcement; questioning; reflecting; listening; explaining; self-disclosure; set induction; closure; assertiveness; influencing; negotiating; interacting in and leading group discussions.

However, from a personal perspective, the most significant change is the absence of my former co-author, colleague and close friend, David Dickson, who passed away on 24 May 2008. David and I were school pals, university friends and close work colleagues. He was a constant source of inspiration, wisdom, support, creativity and unending good humour. His untimely death meant that his absence was particularly deeply felt in this fifth edition. In fact, David had begun working on the new edition before his death and his contributions are evidenced throughout the book.

I also remember with great fondness and affection another close friend, and co-author of the first three editions of this text, the late Christine Saunders. As with David, Christine's contributions are widely reflected in this new edition. Working on this publication was a lonely task following the years of fun and camaraderie with Christine and David when producing the earlier editions. I miss them and think of them often. Their influence pervades the book and it has been a privilege for me to produce this new edition in their memory. However, while I recognise with gratitude and affection their role in forming and shaping this text, I also fully accept sole responsibility for any of its flaws.

I would also like to acknowledge the assistance provided by the School of Communication, University of Ulster. Thanks also to all those members of staff at the university, and at other centres, who have been involved in, and contributed to, the evolution of Communication programmes. The support, advice and encouragement of these colleagues are reflected throughout this book. The invaluable feedback provided by trainees enrolled on skills programmes is also recognised.

A special note of thanks is given to the editorial staff at Routledge for all their help, support and expertise. Words of appreciation are due to Philip Burch and David Barr, Graphic Design Technicians in the School of Communication at the University of Ulster for their skill in producing some of the more intricate diagrams. Finally, I am indebted to my wife, Patricia, who provided the necessary motivation and love to sustain me throughout the production of this text.

Owen Hargie
Jordanstown
June 2010

Chapter 1

Communicating effectively: the skills approach

INTRODUCTION

THERE IS A FUNDAMENTAL, powerful and universal desire amongst humans to interact with others. As expressed by Afifi and Guerrero (2000: 170): 'There is a long history of research establishing the importance that individuals place on connectedness . . . individuals' needs for initiating, developing and maintaining social ties, especially close ones, is reflected in a litany of studies and a host of theories.' The mere presence of another has been shown to be arousing and motivating and this in turn influences our behaviour – a process termed *compresence* (Burgoon *et al.*, 1996). We behave differently in the company of another person than when alone. When we meet others we are 'onstage' and so give a performance that differs from how we behave 'offstage'. We also enjoy interacting, and indeed the act of engaging in facilitative interpersonal communication has been shown to contribute to positive changes in emotional state (Gable and Shean, 2000). While our dealings with others can sometimes be problematic or even contentious, we also seek, relish and obtain great reward from social interaction. Conversely, if we are unable to engage meaningfully with others, or are ostracised by them, the result is often loneliness, unhappiness and depression (Williams and Zadiro, 2001).

The seemingly innate need for relationships with others has been termed *sociation* (Wolff, 1950). As Ryff and Singer (2000: 31) put it: 'Across time and settings, people everywhere have subscribed to the view that close, meaningful ties to others is an essential feature of what it means to be fully human.' In other words, individuals need to commune with others. Three core types of psychological need have been identified – competence, relatedness and autonomy – and the satisfaction of all three results in optimal well-being (Patrick *et al.*, 2007). The competence need involves a wish to feel confident and effective in carrying out actions, in order to achieve one's goals. The relatedness need reflects a desire to have close connections and positive relationships with significant others. The autonomy need involves wanting to feel in control of one's own destiny, rather than being directed by others.

In order to satisfy all three psychological needs it is necessary to have an effective repertoire of interpersonal skills. These skills have always been important. Our early ancestors who lived in groups were more likely to survive than those who lived alone, and so the skills involved in developing and maintaining social bonds assumed a central role in human evolution (Leary, 2001). Thus, Forgas and Williams (2001: 7) noted: 'Homo sapiens is a highly sociable species . . . our impressive record of achievements owes a great deal to the highly elaborate strategies we have developed for getting along with each other and co-ordinating our interpersonal behaviors.' Indeed, Levinson (2006) argued that the human mind is specifically adapted to enable us to engage in social interaction, and that we could therefore be more accurately referred to as *homo interagens*.

Another part of the reason for sociation is that: 'The essence of communication is the formation and expression of an identity. The formation of the self is not an independent event generated by an autonomous actor. Rather, the self emerges through social interaction' (Coover and Murphy, 2000: 125). In this way, 'a sense of personal identity is achieved through negotiation with others' (Postmes *et al.*, 2006: 226). In other words, we become the people we are as a result of our interchanges with others (this issue is further discussed in Chapter 2 and explored in more detail in Chapter 9). Interaction is the essential nutrient that nourishes and sustains the social milieu. Furthermore, since communication is a prerequisite for learning, without the capacity for sophisticated methods and channels for sharing knowledge, both within and between generations, our advanced human civilisation would simply not exist. Communication therefore represents the very essence of the human condition. Indeed, one of the harshest punishments available within most penal systems is that of solitary confinement – the removal of any possibility of interpersonal contact.

Thus, people have a deep-seated need to communicate, and the greater their ability in this regard the more satisfying and rewarding will be their existence. Research has shown that those with higher levels of interpersonal skill have many advantages in life (Burleson, 2007; Segrin and Taylor, 2007; Segrin *et al.*, 2007; Hybels and Weaver, 2009). They cope more readily with stress, adapt and adjust better to major life transitions, have higher self-efficacy in social situations, greater satisfaction in their close personal relationships, more friends, and are less likely to suffer from depression, loneliness or anxiety. One reason for this is that they are sensitive to the needs of other people, and this in turn leads to them being liked by others, who will seek out their company.

In a review of research, Segrin (2000) concluded that interactive skills have a 'prophylactic effect' in that socially competent people are resilient to the ill effects of life crises, whereas individuals with poor skills experience a worsening of psychosocial problems when faced with stressors in life. As summarised by Segrin and Taylor (2007: 645): 'Human beings seek and desire quality interpersonal relationships and experiences. Social skills appear to be an important mechanism for acquiring such relationships, and where they are experienced, obvious signs of positive psychological states are abundantly evident.' Many of the benefits here are, of course, interrelated, and so it is probable that the network of friendships developed by skilled individuals helps to buffer and support them in times of personal trauma. Those with high levels of skill also act as positive communication role models for others, and so they are more likely to be effective parents, colleagues or managers.

There are other tangible rewards to be gained from developing an effective interpersonal skill repertoire. These begin from an early age, since children who develop good interactive skills also perform better academically (McClelland *et al.*, 2006; Graziano, *et al.*, 2007). Skilled children know how to communicate effectively with the teacher and so are more likely to receive help and attention in the classroom. Their interactive flair also enables them to develop peer friendships and thereby make school a more enjoyable experience. The benefits then continue in many walks of life after school.

In the business sphere there are considerable advantages to be gained from good communication (Robbins and Judge, 2009), and effective managers have been shown to have a strong repertoire of interpersonal skills (Bambacas and Patrickson, 2008; Clampitt, 2010). Surveys of employers also consistently show that they rate the ability to communicate effectively as a key criterion in recruiting new staff (CBI, 2008). Individuals need to pay attention to their *social capital*, which refers to the benefits that accrue from being socially skilled, fostering a large network of conducive and committed relationships characterised by goodwill, trust and reciprocity, forging commitments, and developing a good social reputation (De Carolis and Saparito, 2006; McCallum and O'Connell, 2009).

The relationship between social capital and interpersonal skill has been compared to that between resource stock and resource flow in organisations, in that social capital can be regarded as an accumulated asset, while interpersonal skill is one of the key factors that determine the value of this asset (Baron and Markman, 2000). Entrepreneurs who possess high levels of interpersonal skill have advantages in a range of areas, such as obtaining funding, attracting quality employees, maintaining good relationships with co-founders of the business, and producing better results from customers and suppliers (Baum *et al.*, 2006). Not surprisingly, therefore, skilled communicators have been shown to be upwardly mobile and more likely to receive pay raises and gain promotions (Burleson, 2007).

Likewise, in health care, the importance for professionals of having a 'good bedside manner' has long been realised. In 400 BC, Hippocrates noted how the patient 'may recover his health simply through his contentment with the goodness of the physician'. In recent years, this belief in the power of communication to contribute to the healing process has been borne out by research. Di Blasi *et al.* (2001) carried out a systematic review of studies in Europe, the USA and Canada that investigated the effects of doctor–patient relationships. They found that practitioner interpersonal skills made a significant difference to patient well-being. Practitioners with good interpersonal skills, who formed a warm, friendly relationship with their patients and provided reassurance, were more effective in terms of patient well-being than those who kept consultations impersonal or formal. Similarly, Rider and Keefer (2006) and Tallman *et al.* (2007) have shown that high levels of practitioner interpersonal skill are positively correlated with increases in the quality of care and effective health outcomes, while ineffective skills are associated with decreased patient satisfaction and increased medication errors and malpractice claims. These findings are corroborated in the field of nursing, where effective interpersonal communication has been shown to be related to improved health outcomes, such as greater patient satisfaction and quality of life (Klakovich and dela Cruz, 2006).

Similar findings recur across professions. Thus, in teaching, interpersonal skills have been shown to be critical for optimum classroom performance (Worley *et al.*, 2007). As aptly summarised by Orbe and Bruess (2005: 6): 'The quality of our communication and the quality of our lives are directly related . . . Our lives are a direct reflection of the quality of the communication in them.' This means that interpersonal skills are at the very epicentre of our social existence. We ignore them at our peril.

But the good news is that we can improve our ability to communicate. A great deal is now known about the key constituents of the DNA of interactive life. Indeed, the academic study of interpersonal communication has a very long and rich tradition, spanning some 5000 years. Pedagogical Luddites of today who complain about the introduction of the 'new' discipline of Communication should pay attention to history. The oldest essay ever discovered, written about 3000 BC, consisted of advice to Kagemni, the eldest son of Pharaoh Huni, on speaking effectively in public. Similarly, the oldest book, the *Precepts*, written in Egypt by Ptah-Hotep circa 2675 BC, is a treatise on effective communication.

Given the early historical focus on communication, it is perhaps surprising that this area was subsequently largely neglected in terms of academic study in higher education, until its resurgence in the late twentieth century. As noted by Bull (2002: vii): 'Communication is of central importance to many aspects of human life, yet it is only in recent years that it has become the focus of scientific investigation.' For example, it was not until 1960 that the notion of communication as a form of skilled activity was first suggested (Hargie, 2006a).

In the intervening years, the fairly obvious observation that some individuals are better social interactors than others led to carefully formulated and systematic investigations into the nature and function of interpersonal interaction. Indeed Segrin (1992) pointed out that the concept of social skill has been investigated by researchers in virtually all fields of social science. This has occurred at three levels:

1   Theoretical analyses of how and why people behave as they do have resulted in various conceptualisations of skilled behaviour (see Hargie, 2006a).
2   Research has been conducted into the identification and effects of different types of social behaviour. It is this level that the present book addresses.
3   Several approaches to training in communication skills have been introduced in order to ascertain whether it is possible to improve the social performance of the individual (for a review of these see Hargie, 2006b).

Over the past 20 years there has been a vast outpouring of research in this field. An important part of this research and scholarship has involved an analysis of the exact nature of the skills process.

THE NATURE OF INTERPERSONAL SKILLS

In terms of nomenclature, different terms are used synonymously to describe this area. The terms 'social skills', 'interpersonal skills' and 'communication skills' are often used interchangeably. The latter, however, can encompass written as well as interpersonal skills, while the former is generally used to refer to developmental or clinical applications. In this text all three terms will be employed interchangeably but the main emphasis is upon the 'interpersonal' descriptor. Thus, interpersonal skills, in a global sense, can be defined as the skills we employ when interacting with other people. This definition is not very informative, however, since it really indicates what skills are used for rather than what they are. It is rather like defining an aeroplane as something that gets you from one country to another.

Attempts to define the term 'interpersonal skill' proliferate within the literature. In order to illustrate this point it is useful to examine some of the definitions that have been put forward by different theorists. In his early work in this area, Phillips (1978: 13) concluded that a person is skilled according to:

> the extent to which he or she can communicate with others, in a manner that fulfils one's rights, requirements, satisfactions, or obligations to a reasonable degree without damaging the other person's similar rights, requirements, satisfactions, or obligations, and hopefully shares these rights etc. with others in free and open exchange.

This definition emphasises the macro elements of social encounters, in terms of reciprocation between participants. This theme is also found in the definition given by Schlundt and McFall (1985: 23), who defined social skills as 'the specific component processes that enable an individual to behave in a manner that will be judged as "competent". Skills are the abilities necessary for producing behavior that will accomplish the objectives of a task.'

These definitions tend to view skill as an *ability* that the individual may possess to a greater or lesser extent. A somewhat different focus has been proffered by other theorists, who define skill in terms of the *behaviour* of the individual. For example, Robbins and Hunsaker (2009: 6) iterated that 'a skill is a system of behavior that can be applied in a wide range of situations', while Cameron (2000: 86) stated that 'the term *skill* connotes *practical expertise*, the ability to *do* something'. Proctor and Dutta (1995: 18) extended this behavioural emphasis, to encompass the *goals* of the individual: 'Skill is goal-directed, well-organized behavior', while Kelly (1982: 3) emphasised the dimension of *learning* by defining skills as 'those identifiable, learned behaviors that individuals use in interpersonal situations to obtain or maintain reinforcement from their environment'.

These elements were summarised by Robbins and Hunsaker (2009: 6), who argued that to gain competence in a skill 'people need to understand the skill conceptually and behaviourally, have opportunities to practice the skill, get feedback on how well they are performing the skill, and use the skill often enough to integrate it into their behavioral repertoires.'

In his review of definitions of skilled behaviour, Hargie (2006a: 13) defined interpersonal skill as 'a process in which the individual implements a set of goal-directed, inter-related, situationally appropriate social behaviours, which are learned and controlled'. This is the definition adopted in this book. It emphasises seven separate components of skill:

- Skilled performance is part of a transactional *process*.
- Skilled behaviours are *goal directed*.
- Skilled behaviours are *interrelated*.
- Skills should be *appropriate* to the *situation*.
- Skills are defined in terms of identifiable units of *behaviour*.
- Skilled behaviours are *learned*.
- Skills are under the cognitive control of the individual.

Skilled performance is part of a transactional process

Stewart *et al.* (2005) argued that interpersonal communication is characterised by an ongoing verbal and nonverbal process of collaborative meaning-making. In this sense, interaction requires considerable coordination, as each person regulates their actions in line with others (Gonzales *et al.*, 2010). This involves what Pickering (2006) referred to as 'the dance of dialogue', wherein individuals align their talk with one another, and construct shared meaning from the conversation. Balachandra *et al.* (2005) likened certain forms of interaction, such as negotiation, to the process of improvised performance (similar to improvised jazz or theatre) where those involved must pay attention to the moves of others and be flexible in how they respond. As will be discussed more fully in Chapter 2, skilled performance is indeed a *process* that involves:

- formulating appropriate goals
- devising related action plans
- implementing these plans
- monitoring the effects of behaviour
- being aware of, and interpreting, the responses of others
- taking cognisance of the context in which interaction occurs
- adjusting, adapting or abandoning goals and responses in the light of outcomes.

Skilled behaviours are goal directed

They are those behaviours the individual employs in order to achieve a desired outcome, and are therefore purposeful, as opposed to chance, or unintentional. As expressed by Carnevale and De Dreu (2006: 55), 'the human being is an *intentional system*', designed to pursue goals. In his review of the field, Wilson (2006: 100) demonstrated how most scholars 'view communication as a goal-driven process'. Likewise, Huang (2000: 111) noted that, 'the purposes people bring into communication have important consequences on communication processes'. Goals both motivate and navigate the interpersonal process (Berger, 2002; Oettingen *et al.*, 2004). For example, if A wishes to encourage B to talk freely, A will look at B, use head nods when B speaks, refrain from interrupting B, and utter 'guggles' ('Hmm, hmm', 'Uh, huh'; etc.) periodically. In this instance these *behaviours* are *directed* towards the *goal* of encouraging participation.

The goals we pursue are not always conscious, and indeed one feature of skilled performance is that behaviour is often executed automatically (Moors and De Houwer, 2007). Once responses are learned they tend to become hard-wired or habitual, and goal-directed behaviour is then under what Dijksterhuis *et al.* (2007) refer to as 'unconscious control'. In this way, people automatically and subconsciously regulate their behaviour in order to achieve their goals (Chen *et al.*, 2007). When we know how to drive, we no longer have to think about actions such as how to start the car, brake, reverse, and so on. Yet, when learning to drive, these actions are consciously monitored as they are performed.

In the successful learning of new skills we move through the stages of *unconscious incompetence* (we are totally unaware of the fact that we are behaving in an incompetent manner), *conscious incompetence* (we know what we should be doing and we know we are not doing it very well), *conscious competence* (we know we are performing at a satisfactory level) and finally *unconscious competence* (we just do it without thinking about it and we succeed). This is also true of interpersonal skills. During free-flowing social encounters, less than 200 milliseconds typically elapses between the responses of speakers and rarely do conversational pauses reach three seconds. As a result, some elements, such as exact choice of words used and use of gestures, almost always occur without conscious reflection (Wilson *et al.*, 2000). In relation to the negotiation context, McRae (1998: 123) explained: 'Expert negotiators become so proficient at certain skills in the negotiating process that they do not have to consciously think about using these skills. It's as if the responses become second nature.' However, an awareness of relevant goals does not ensure success. As expressed by Greene (2000: 147):

> Action may not be so readily instantiated in overt behavior . . . the inept athlete, dancer, actor or public speaker may well have a perfectly adequate abstract representation of what he or she needs to do, but what actually gets enacted is rather divergent from his or her image of that action.

Thus, skill involves not just the ability to formulate appropriate goals, it also necessitates being able to successfully implement them in practice. In other words, '*skill* refers to the degree to which a performed behavior proves successful' (Miczo *et al.*, 2001: 40). An important part of this, as will be discussed in more detail in Chapter 2, is the ability to accurately detect the goals being pursued by those with whom we interact (Palomares, 2009a).

Skilled behaviours are interrelated

Skilled behaviours are synchronised in order to achieve a particular goal. Thus the individual will employ several behaviours simultaneously. For example, as mentioned previously, when encouraging B to talk, A may smile, use head nods, look directly at B and utter guggles, and all of these signals will be interpreted by B as signs of encouragement to continue speaking. Each behaviour relates to this common goal, and so the behaviours are in this way interrelated and synchronised.

Skills should be appropriate to the situation

Our behaviour is influenced to a very large degree by situational demands (Snyder and Stukas, 2007), and skilled individuals employ context-relevant behaviours. Dickson and McCartan (2005) referred to this aspect of skilled performance as *contextual propriety*. In their review of this area, White and Burgoon (2001) concluded that the key feature of social interaction is that it necessitates adaptation. Indeed, linguistic conceptualisations purport that skill is mutually constructed through dialogue and so can only be understood by an interpretation of how narratives develop in any particular context (Holman, 2000).

From an interpersonal communication perspective, Wilson *et al.* (2000: 136–137) illustrated how effective interaction involves adaptation at all levels:

> Speakers coordinate their own behavior with that of their interactive partner. Interparty coordination is evident at microlevels, such as in the timing of mutual smiles . . . (and) . . . at more macrolevels, such as in the adjustment of one's own plans to the apparent plans of one's conversational partner.

In many routine situations, such as filling stations or fast food counters, participants have a good idea of one another's goals and so adaptation is easy. However, in more complex contexts, such as psychotherapy or negotiation, the interactors have to spend considerable time establishing one another's agendas and agreeing mutual goals for the encounter, so that they can adjust and adapt their responses accordingly (Berger, 2000).

Skills are defined in terms of identifiable units of behaviour

In this way, 'skill is reflected in the performance of communicative behaviors. It is the *enactment* of knowledge and motivation' (Cupach and Canary, 1997: 28). We judge whether or not people are skilled based upon how they actually *behave*. Verbal and nonverbal behaviour therefore represent the oxygen of the communicating organism. Skilled responses are hierarchically organised in such a way that large elements, like being interviewed, are comprised of smaller behavioural units such as looking at the interviewer and answering questions. The development of interpersonal skills can be facilitated by training the individual to acquire these smaller responses before combining them into larger repertoires. Indeed, this technique is also used in the learning of many motor skills.

Skilled behaviours are learned

The sixth aspect of the definition is that behaviours are learned. It is now generally accepted that most forms of behaviour displayed in social contexts are learned (Burton and Dimbleby, 2006). From the day of their birth, infants are communicated with as if they can understand. Parents and other carers talk to them and ascribe intentionality to their behaviour (e.g. 'You are hungry and are looking for some milk, aren't you?', 'There, you wanted your rattle, didn't you?'). The function here is to bring the infant into 'personhood' by treating it as a communicating being (Penman, 2000). This is a very important step in the social development of the individual. For example, as the child grows it is taught to read. This begins with the social process of slowly reading and speaking the words aloud, which eventually results in the child learning to read silently. The skill of talking to oneself in silence takes time to master, and is predicated upon the earlier social dynamic of reading with others. In this way, communication is central to the development of cognitive abilities.

Children reared in isolation miss out on these essential learning experiences. As a result they display distorted, socially unacceptable forms of behaviour (Newton, 2002). At a less extreme level, there is evidence to indicate that children from culturally richer home environments tend to develop more appropriate social behaviours than those from socially deprived backgrounds (Messer, 1995). Bandura's (1986) social cognitive theory purports that all repertoires of behaviour, with the exception of elementary reflexes (such as eye blinks), are learned. This process of social learning involves the *modelling* and *imitation* of the behaviour of significant others, such as parents, teachers, siblings or peers. By this process, from an early age, children may walk, talk and act like their same-sex parent. At a later stage, however, the child may develop the accent of his or her peers and begin to talk in a similar fashion – despite the accent of parents.

In addition to modelling and imitation, a second major element in the learning of social behaviour is the *reinforcement*, by significant others, of these behaviours when displayed by the individual. In childhood, for example, parents encourage, discourage or ignore various behaviours that the child displays. As a general rule, the child learns, and employs more frequently, those behaviours that are encouraged, while tending to display less often those that are discouraged or ignored. In this sense, feedback is crucial to effective performance (see Chapter 4 for a full discussion of reinforcement).

Skills are under the cognitive control of the individual

The final element in the definition of skills, and another feature of social cognitive theory, is that they are under the cognitive *control* of the individual. As expressed by Cameron (2000: 86):

> A 'skilled' person does not only know how to do certain things, but also understands *why* those things are done the way they are. S/he is acquainted with the general principles of the activity s/he is skilled in, and so is able to modify what s/he does in response to the exigencies of any specific situation.

Thus a socially inadequate individual may have learned the basic elements of skills but may not have developed the appropriate thought processes necessary to control the utilisation of these elements in interpersonal encounters. An important dimension of control relates to the timing of behaviours. Skilled behaviour involves implementing behaviours at the most apposite juncture. Learning *when* to employ behaviours is just as crucial as learning *what* these behaviours are and *how* to use them. As expressed by Wolvin and Coakley (1996: 52): 'Communication skills combine with communicator *knowledge* – information and understanding – to influence the entire process.'

Zimmerman (2000) identified four key stages in the learning of skills.

1   ***Observation.*** Here the person watches others perform the skill, and also pays attention to other dimensions such as the motivational orientation, values and performance standards of the actors, as well as how the repertoires used vary across target persons.
2   ***Emulation.*** At this stage the individual is able to execute a behavioural display to approximate that observed. The display is emulated but not replicated. For example, the *style* of praise used may be similar but the *actual words used* will differ.
3   ***Self-control.*** This involves the actor beginning to *master* the skill. Thus, the tennis player will practise serving until this is fully developed, while a barrister will likewise practise questioning technique.
4   ***Self-regulation.*** Finally, the person learns to use the skill appropriately across different personal and contextual conditions. To continue the analogies, here the tennis player is concerned with placing the serve where it is likely to find the opponent's weak point, while the barrister will consider appropriate questions to achieve the best outcomes from different witnesses.

The acronym CLIPS is useful for remembering the key features of interpersonal skill. Skilled performance is:

- Controlled by the individual.
- Learned behaviour that improves with practice and feedback.
- Integrated and interrelated verbal and nonverbal responses.
- Purposive and goal directed.
- Smooth in the manner in which the performance is executed.

OVERVIEW

Simon (1999) illustrated how our identity and sense of purpose depend on us finding a 'place' in our social world. The ability to achieve this 'place' in turn is dependent to a very large extent upon one's interactive skills. The fluent application of skill is a crucial feature of effective social interaction. In Chapter 2 a model is presented, which sets the study of skill within the wider context of the social milieu. This illustrates how the appropriateness of behaviour is determined by a number of variables relating to the context of the interaction, the roles of those involved and their goals, as well as personal features of the interactors (age, sex, personality, etc.). It is, therefore, impossible to legislate in advance for every situation in terms of what behaviours will be most successful to employ. The information about skills contained in this book should rather be regarded as providing resource material for the reader. How these resources are employed is a decision for the reader, given the situation in which any particular interaction is taking place.

There are 14 main skill areas covered in this text, beginning with nonverbal communication (NVC) in Chapter 3. This aspect of interaction is the first to be examined, since all of the areas that follow contain nonverbal elements and so an understanding of the main facets of this channel facilitates the examination of all the other skills. Chapter 4 incorporates an analysis of reinforcement, while questioning is reviewed in Chapter 5. In Chapter 6, an alternative strategy to questioning, namely reflecting, is investigated. Reflection consists of concentrating on what another person is saying and reflecting back the central elements of that person's statements.

The skill of listening is explored in Chapter 7, where the active nature of listening is emphasised, while explaining is focused upon in Chapter 8. In Chapter 9, self-disclosure is examined from two perspectives; first, the appropriateness of self-disclosure by the professional, and second, methods for promoting maximum self-disclosure from clients. Two important episodes in any action – the opening and closing sequences – are reviewed in Chapter 10. Techniques for protecting personal rights are discussed in Chapter 11 in terms of the skill of assertiveness. The skill area of influencing and persuading has attracted growing interest in recent years and this is covered in Chapter 12, and the related skill of negotiation is addressed in Chapter 13. Finally, in Chapter 14 the skills involved in interacting in and leading small group discussions are examined.

It should be realised that research in the field of social interaction is progressing rapidly and it is anticipated that, as our knowledge of this area increases, other important skill areas may be identified. The skills contained in this book do not represent a completely comprehensive list, but they are generally regarded as being the central aspects of interpersonal communication. In addition, it is recognised that, while these skills are studied separately, in practice they overlap and complement one another. What is definitely the case is that knowledge of the repertoire of skilled behaviours covered in this text will enable readers to extend and refine their own pattern or style of interaction.

Chapter 2

A conceptual model of skilled interpersonal communication

INTRODUCTION

NUMEROUS CONTRASTING THEORIES and models have been formulated in an attempt to represent and make sense of what happens when people engage in social interchange (see, for example, Antos *et al.*, 2008; Griffin, 2008; Berger *et al.*, 2010; Smith and Wilson, 2010). In the previous chapter, one such theoretical framework was introduced, wherein communication was conceptualised as a form of skilled performance. The present chapter builds on this framework to develop a skills-based model of interpersonal communication. Before examining this model in more depth, the initial issue that needs to be addressed is what precisely is meant by the terms 'communication' and 'interpersonal communication'. The first part of this chapter focuses upon this area. Having done so, a skill-based theoretical model of the communicative process is then discussed. This illustrates how what takes place when two people interact involves a process that is undergirded by a complex of perceptual, cognitive, affective and performative operations, all of which function within and are influenced by the contextual framework. The activity is held to be energised and given direction by the desire to achieve set goals and is accomplished by the ongoing monitoring of personal, social and environmental circumstances.

COMMUNICATION AND INTERPERSONAL COMMUNICATION

As a concept, communication is notoriously difficult to pin down. It represents a phenomenon that is at one and the same time ubiquitous yet elusive, prosaic yet mysterious, straightforward yet frustratingly prone to failure. It has been portrayed as 'both complex and brittle, composed of several series of sometimes very subtle actions and behaviours, which as a rule are felicitous but quite often less than completely successful' (Rosengren, 2000: 37). This has created difficulties when it comes to reaching agreement over matters of formal definition. Holli *et al.* (2008) attributed the problem to the vast range of activities that can be legitimately subsumed under this label. Traced back to its Latin roots the verb 'to communicate' means 'to share', 'to make common', meanings reflected in much of the current literature. Hewes (1995) identified two central themes at the core of communication:

1   *intersubjectivity* – which has to do with striving to understand others and being understood in turn
2   *impact* – which represents the extent to which a message brings about change in thoughts, feelings or behaviour.

Accordingly, Hamilton (2008: 5) defined communication as 'the process of people sharing thoughts, ideas, and feelings with each other in commonly understandable ways'.

In this book the focus is largely restricted to interpersonal communication. In his review of the field, and while recognising that there are wide variations in how the concept has been interpreted, Burleson (2010a: 151) preferred this definition: 'Interpersonal communication is a complex situated social process in which people who have established a communicative relationship exchange messages in an effort to generate shared meanings and accomplish social goals.' The main elements of this definition will be explored later in this chapter. Three further key features of the process were identified by Hartley (1999) in that the focus is upon communication that:

- is essentially nonmediated (or face to face)
- takes place in a dyadic (one-to-one) or small group setting
- in form and content is shaped by and conveys something of the personal qualities of the interactors as well as their social roles and relationships.

Others have embellished this list (e.g. Adler *et al.*, 2006). When compared with other forms of communication, this subcategory is typified by the following:

- the uniqueness of each interpersonal exchange – people are dealt with as individuals
- the physical closeness of the interaction
- the multiplicity of communication channels that are available
- the irreplaceability of the relationship that results
- the interdependence of the interactors
- the instantaneity of feedback available

- the extent of self-disclosure engendered
- the intrinsic nature of rewards stemming from intensive person-to-person contact.

In simple terms, Brooks and Heath (1993: 7) defined interpersonal communication as 'the process by which information, meanings and feelings are shared by persons through the exchange of verbal and nonverbal messages'. With this in mind, the tasks carried out by Ms Bodie, the chief executive of a major retail corporation (see Box 2.1), involving letters, reports, newspapers, files, email, television, etc., fall outside this remit. Rather, it is the sorts of processes that characterise her encounters with her PA, executive team, financial adviser, director of store marketing and design and communications director with which this book is concerned. This leads on to the first defining feature of communication.

Communication is a process

A distinct tradition within communication theory is that of conceptualising what takes place as a process of sending and receiving messages (Stewart, *et al.*, 2005; DeVito, 2008a). Communication requires that at least two contributors are involved in an ongoing and dynamic sequence of events, in which each affects and is affected by the other in a system of reciprocal determination. Each at the same time perceives the other in context, makes some sort of sense of what is happening, comes to a decision as to how to react, and responds accordingly. Being more specific, the

---

Box 2.1 Ms Bodie communicates

Ms Bodie is chief executive of a major retail corporation. Let us take a typical day in her life. Before leaving for work she checks the messages on her Blackberry and answers the most urgent. Her first task, upon arrival at work, is spent with her PA dealing with recent electronic and snail mail, and telephone messages. She then dictates replies on matters arising, emails the director of human resources about a pending case of harassment by a member of staff, faxes some urgent documents to suppliers in the USA and makes several telephone calls before chairing the first meeting of the day with her executive team. After lunch, she and her financial director discuss the quarterly financial statement. At 2.30 pm, her PA informs her that the director of store marketing and design has just arrived for his appraisal interview. That over, she meets with the director of communications. An article which she read in the local paper on her way to work that morning had troubled her. It suggested that the company may be on the verge of shedding up to 25 per cent of its workforce. A press release is prepared and it is decided that Ms Bodie should go on local television that evening to quash the rumour. Before leaving she prepares for an online presentation that she will deliver first thing next morning to members of the National Confederation of Retail Management. A truly busy day and all of it communication centred – but communication in many and diverse forms.

components of the communicative process, in its simplest form, have been identified as including *communicators, message, medium, channel, code, noise, feedback* and *context* (Proctor and Adler, 2007). Each of these will now be examined in turn.

Communicators

The indispensability of communicators to the process is fairly obvious. In early linear models of how communication took place (e.g. Shannon and Weaver, 1949), one was designated the *source*, the other the *receiver*, and the process was held to commence when the former transmitted a message to the latter. This is a good example of what Clampitt (2010) called 'arrow' communication, that is, communication that goes in one direction only. More recently the oversimplicity of this thinking about face-to-face interaction has been recognised. Communicators are, at one and the same time, senders and receivers of messages. While person A is speaking, he or she is usually also monitoring the effects of the utterance, requiring information from B to be simultaneously received. Correspondingly, person B, in listening to A, is also reacting to A's contribution. The notion of 'source–receiver' is therefore a more accurate representation of the role of each participant (DeVito, 2008b).

Message

The message can be thought of as the content of communication embodying whatever it is that communicators wish to share. Gouran (1990: 6) described it as 'a pattern of thought, configuration of ideas, or other response to internal conditions about which individuals express themselves'. Such expression, however, presupposes some form of behavioural manifestation: thoughts and feelings, to be made known, must be encoded or organised into a physical form capable of being transmitted to others. Decoding is the counterpart of encoding whereby recipients attach meaning to what they have just experienced (O'Hair *et al.*, 2007).

Medium

The medium is the particular means of conveying the message. In a seminal contribution, Fiske (1990) described three types of media:

1   *presentational* – e.g. voice, face, body
2   *representational* – e.g. books, paintings, architecture, photographs
3   *technological/mechanical* – e.g. internet, phone, MP3, television, radio, CD.

The first of these is pivotal to interpersonal communication. Media differ in the levels of *social presence* afforded. As explained by Stevens-Long and McClintock (2008: 22) this is 'the degree to which the medium is experienced as sociable, warm, sensitive, or personal, creating the impression that the person communicating is *real*'. *Media richness* is a similar concept suggesting that media differ in the richness of information that they carry. Actually talking to someone face to face provides a greater richness of social cues and a fuller experience of the individual than for example texting or emailing. Choices as to the most suitable medium to use depend upon a range of factors (Picot *et al.*, 2008; Sears and Jacko, 2008). In organisations, face-to-face rather than mediated (telephone, letters, email, etc.) communication is the medium consistently preferred by employees (Hargie and Tourish, 2009).

Channel

Differences between channel and medium are sometimes blurred in the literature, and indeed the two terms are often used interchangeably. 'Channel' refers to that which 'connects' communicators and accommodates the medium. DeVito (2005) described it as operating like a bridge between the sender and receiver. Fiske (1990) gave as examples light waves, sound waves, radio waves as well as cables of different types, capable of carrying pulses of light or electrical energy. Likewise, DeVito (2005) distinguished between different channels:

- the *vocal-auditory* channel which carries speech
- the *gestural-visual* channel which facilitates much nonverbal communication
- the *chemical-olfactory* channel accommodating smell
- the *cutaneous-tactile* channel which enables us to make interpersonal use of touch.

These different channels are typically utilised simultaneously in the course of face-to-face communication.

Code

A code is a system of meaning shared by a group. It designates signs and symbols peculiar to that code and specifies rules and conventions for their use. The English language, for example, is a code in accordance with which the accepted meaning of 'dog' is an animal with four legs that barks. Other codes are Morse, French, Braille, etc.

Noise

Here the word 'noise' has a rather special meaning which is more than mere sound. It refers to any interference with the success of the communicative act that distorts or degrades the message so that the meaning taken is not that intended. As such, noise may originate in the source, the channel, the receiver, or the context within which participants interact. It may be external and take the form of intrusive sound, which masks what is being said, or it may be internal, stemming from intrapersonal distractions. Ethnic or cultural differences can cause communication 'noise', in that meanings attached to particular choices of word or forms of expression can vary considerably, causing unintended confusion, misunderstanding, insult or hurt (Holliday *et al.*, 2004).

Feedback

By means of feedback, the sender is able to judge the extent to which the message has been successfully received and the impact that it has had. Monitoring receiver reactions enables subsequent communications to be adapted and regulated to achieve a desired effect. Feedback, therefore, is vitally important to successful social outcomes. It plays a central role in the model of skilful interaction to be elaborated later in this chapter and more will be said about it then.

Context

As noted by Adler and Elmhorst (2008: 9): 'Communication always takes place in some setting, and the context in which it occurs can have a powerful effect on what happens.' To be more accurate, communication takes place within intermeshing frameworks. Contexts identified include the physical, social, chronological and cultural, although a relational context could be added as well. An inescapable instance, geographical location, provides a physical setting for what takes place. To take one example, people in lifts often behave in rather restrained ways that match the physical constraints of their surroundings. In addition, all encounters occur within a temporal context. A college seminar may be held late on a Friday afternoon or early on Monday morning and the vigour and enthusiasm of the discussion can be influenced as a result. Relationship provides a further framework for interaction. For example, unmarried males tend to react more positively to touch from a significant other than unmarried females, but this pattern is reversed for married individuals (Hanzal *et al.*, 2008). It is also possible to envisage a range of psychosocial factors such as status relationship that constitute a different but equally significant framework for communication.

So far, context has been depicted as exerting an influence upon communication. But it should not be overlooked that, in many respects, interactors can also serve to shape aspects of their situation through communication. The concept of context features prominently in the model to be developed shortly and will be returned to there.

Communication is transactional

As already noted, earlier models of communication as a fundamentally linear process, where a message is formulated by the source and sent to the receiver, have now given way to a more transactional conceptualisation that stresses dynamic interplay and the changing and evolving nature of the process. Communicators continually affect and are affected by each other, in a system of reciprocal influence (Adler *et al.*, 2006).

Communication is inevitable

This is a contentious point. Communication has long been held, by those theorists who adopt a broad view of what constitutes the phenomenon (e.g. Watzlawick *et al.*,

1967; Scheflen, 1974), to be inevitable in social situations where each is aware of the other's presence and is influenced in what is done as a result. Watzlawick *et al.* (1967: 49) were responsible for the much quoted maxim that, under such circumstances 'one cannot *not* communicate'. Imagine the situation where shy boy and attractive girl are seated opposite each other in a railway carriage. Attractive girl sees shy boy looking at her legs. She eases her skirt over her knees. Their eyes meet, shy boy blushes and they both look away in embarrassment. Has communication taken place between them or can their reactions be at best described as merely expressive or informative? Are all actions communication? What if I display behaviour that I have little control over and do not mean to display, am I communicating?

For some theorists, unless conditions are imposed, then all behaviour becomes communication, so rendering the term largely redundant (Trenholm and Jensen, 2007). Some nonverbal behaviour may best be described as informative rather than communicative. The debate concerns issues such as communicative behaviour being intentional, performed with conscious awareness, and being code based (Knapp and Hall, 2010). Applying such conditions in their most extreme form would confine communication to those acts:

- performed with the intention of sharing meaning
- perceived as such by the recipient
- performed by both in the full glare of conscious awareness
- accomplished by means of a shared arbitrary code. Arbitrary in this sense means that the relationship between the behaviour and what it represents is entirely a matter of agreed convention.

But does the encoder have to be consciously aware of the intention? What if the decoder fails to recognise that the witnessed behaviour was enacted intentionally and reacts (or fails to act) accordingly?

For many, these impositions are too extreme and create particular problems for the concept of *nonverbal* communication. Different sets of more relaxed restrictions have been suggested. Burgoon *et al.* (1996: 13–14), for instance, advocated that those actions be accepted as communicative that '(a) are typically sent with intent, (b) are used with regularity among members of a given social community, society or culture, (c) are typically interpreted as intentional, and (d) have consensually recognised meaning'. As such, an unconscious, unintentional facial expression could still be accepted as communicative. Remland (2009) additionally argued that communication does not have to rely upon an arbitrary code. Such codes are made up of symbols whose relationship to the thing in the world that they represent is merely a matter of agreed convention. Taking a previous example, there is no obvious reason why 'dog' should be the word symbol that represents the animal to which it refers. Indeed, the Spanish use 'perro'. Intrinsic codes that are biologically rather than socially based are also acceptable. This would include blushes being recognised as symptoms of embarrassment, despite the fact that they do not share this same type of arbitrary relationship.

Communication is purposeful

Another commonly cited characteristic of communication is its purposefulness (Dickson and McCartan, 2005). Those who take part do so with some end in mind; they want to effect some desired outcome. According to this functional view of the phenomenon, communication is far from idle or aimless but is conducted to make something happen – to achieve a goal of some sort. As expressed by Westmyer and Rubin (1998: 28):

> To understand why people engage in interpersonal communication, we must remember that communication is goal directed. Interpersonal needs establish expectations for communication behaviour. Communicators are mindful in that they are capable of acknowledging their needs and motives, and realize that they can choose particular communication behaviors to fulfil these needs.

It is this that both adds impetus to and provides direction for the transaction. A pivotal implication of casting communication as purposeful activity is that it must also be thought of as 'adjusted' (Kellermann, 1992). That is, communicators fashion what they say and do, on an ongoing basis, in response to the goals that they are pursuing and the likelihood of their attainment (Wilson, 2006; Palomares, 2008). Adjusted performance presupposes the possibility of selection and choice amongst alternative courses of action. In other words, communication is a strategic enterprise. Dillard (1998) claimed that even the affective dimension of communication is in some respects managed strategically. While not denying an expressive element that may be more difficult to control, Planalp (1998: 44) agreed:

> People communicate their emotions to others for some purpose, whether intentionally or unintentionally ... They may communicate emotion in order to get support (e.g. sadness, loneliness), negotiate social roles (anger, jealousy), deflect criticism (shame, embarrassment), reinforce social bonds (love), or for any number of other reasons.

Does attributing purposefulness to the communicative act presuppose consciousness? For some the answer is in the affirmative; purposive behaviour implies conscious awareness. Klinger *et al.* (1981: 171) believed that convictions of the existence of unconscious goals do not match the evidence, concluding that 'life would be far more chaotic than it is if substantial portions of people's goal strivings were for goals about which the striver was unconscious'. Emmons (1989) summarised this thinking by suggesting that it is commonly accepted that people have considerable access to their goals and can readily report them but are less aware of the underlying motivational basis upon which they are founded.

On the other hand, Langer *et al.* (1978) argued that much of communication is 'mindless'. They distinguished between *mindful* activity where 'people attend to their world and derive behavioral strategies based upon current incoming information' and *mindlessness* where 'new information is not actually being processed. Instead prior scripts, written when similar information was once new, are stereotypically reenacted' (p. 363). Burgoon and Langer (1995) explored the various ways in which language itself can predispose to mindlessness in its capacity to mould thought. Similarly, Monahan (1998) demonstrated how interactors' evaluations of others can be influenced by nonconscious feelings derived from information sources of which they have little awareness. Consistent with this thesis, Kellermann (1992) argued that communication is at one and the same time purposeful/strategic and also primarily automatic. Likewise, Lakin (2006: 63) concluded that 'consciousness is not required for behavior to be either strategic or adaptive'. As stressed by Burgoon (2005: 238) in relation to acting deceptively, 'strategic activity should not be construed as requiring a high degree of cognitive awareness or mindfulness'.

Circumstances under which we tend to become aware of customarily nonconscious encoding decisions (Motley, 1992; Burgoon and Langer, 1995) include the following:

- novel situations
- situations where carrying out a routinely scripted performance becomes effortful
- conflict between two or more message goals
- anticipations of undesirable consequences for a formulated or preformulated version of a message, thus requiring reformulation
- some unexpected intervention (perhaps due to a failed attempt to 'take the floor' or experiencing the 'tip-of-the-tongue' phenomenon) between the initial decision to transmit a message and the opportunity so to do
- the goals of the communication being difficult to actualise or the situation being troublesome in some other way.

In sum, describing communication as purposeful does not imply that the entirety of the communicative act must necessarily be prominent in the ongoing stream of consciousness. While intention, control and awareness are central to general conceptualisations of communication as skilled activity, it seems that many well-rehearsed sequences can be enacted with only limited awareness. When skills are well honed, they can often be executed on the 'back burner' of conscious thought. But the success of an encounter may be compromised as a result. This aspect of the goal-related nature of communication will be further explored later in the chapter.

Communication is multidimensional

Another significant feature of communication is its multidimensionality: messages exchanged are seldom unitary or discrete. Communication scholars have long concurred about two separate but interrelated levels to the process (Watzlawick *et al.*, 1967; Adler and Elmhorst, 2008). One concerns *content* and has to do with substantive matters (e.g. discussing last night's television programme; explaining the theory of relativity). These issues form the topic of conversation and usually spring to mind when thinking about what we do when communicating. But this is seldom, if ever, all that we do when communicating. Another level, although less conspicuous, addresses the *relationship* between the interactors. Furthermore, such matters as identity projection and confirmation are also part and parcel of the interchange.

21

Identity projection and confirmation

In their choice of topic for discussion (and topics avoided), particular words and forms of expression adopted, manicured accents, speed of speech and a whole complex of nonverbal behaviours and characteristics, interactors work at designing the messages they send about themselves. These messages are to do with who and what they are, and how they wish to be received and reacted to by others. According to Wetherell (1996: 305): 'As people live their lives they are continually making themselves as characters or personalities through the ways in which they reconcile and work with the raw material of their social situation.' Communication is at the forefront of this endeavour. Our identity is formulated and evolves as a result of our interactions with others (McConnell and Strain, 2007). In this sense, identity is not only something that we convey but a reality that is created in our dealings with others (this is further discussed in Chapter 9).

Impression management and *self-presentation* are the terms used to refer to the process of behaving in such a way as to get others to ratify the particular image of self offered (Guerrero *et al.*, 2007). A direct approach is talking about oneself and strategies for introducing self as a topic into conversation have been analysed by Bangerter (2000). For the quest to be successful, however, it has to be carried out with subtlety. Being seen as boastful and self-opinionated could well spoil the effect. Less conspicuous ways are therefore frequently utilised, often relying on the nonverbal channel (see Chapter 3). If the attempt is seen (or seen through) as a flagrant attempt at self-aggrandisement or ingratiation, it will backfire and a less than attractive impression be created.

Succeeding in conveying the right impression can confer several sorts of possible advantage (Leary, 1996). It can lead to material rewards as well as social benefits such as approval, friendship and power. Goffman (1959) emphasised the importance of social actors maintaining *face*, which can be thought of as a statement of the positive value claimed for self – a public expression of self-worth. He observed that actors characteristically engage not only in self-focused facework but are also careful not to invalidate the face being presented by their partner. In a highly influential book chapter, Brown and Levinson (1978) analysed how politeness operates as a strategy intended to reduce the likelihood of this being thought to have happened. Giving criticism is an example of a face-threatening situation. Metts and Cupach (2008) outlined how both verbal and nonverbal cues of politeness help to mitigate the possible negative effects of verbal criticism.

Relationship negotiation

Communication also serves relational ends in other ways by helping to determine how participants define their association (Foley and Duck, 2006). It is widely agreed that relationships are shaped around two main dimensions that have to do with *affiliation* (or liking) and *dominance*, although a third concerning level of involvement or the *intensity* of the association also seems to be important (Tusing and Dillard, 2000). Status differences are often negotiated and maintained by subtle (and not so subtle) means. The two directives 'Shut that damned window!' and 'I wonder would you mind closing the window, please?' are functionally equivalent on the content dimension (i.e. the speaker obviously wishes the person addressed to close the window), but a different type of relationship is presupposed in each case.

Power is also an important factor in human relationships (Fiske and Berdahl, 2007). When people with relatively little social power, occupying inferior status positions, interact with those enjoying power over them, the former have been shown (Berger, 1994; Burgoon *et al.*, 1996) to manifest their increased 'accessibility' by, among other things:

- initiating fewer topics for discussion
- being more hesitant in what they say
- being asked more questions
- providing more self-disclosures
- engaging in less eye contact while speaking
- using politer forms of address
- using more restrained touch.

Sets of expectations are constructed around these parameters. It is not only the case that people with little power behave in these ways; there are norms or implicit expectations that they should do so.

These two communicative dimensions, content and relationship, are complexly interwoven and interrelated (Knapp and Vangelisti, 2009). Statements have relational significance and the orchestrating of relationships is typically achieved in this 'indirect' way. Indeed, Hanna and Wilson (1998) argued that every communication episode represents some defining element of the relationship. While the relationship itself may become the topic of conversation (i.e. form the content of talk), this usually only happens if it has become problematic.

Communication is irreversible

Simply put, once something is said it cannot be 'taken back'. In this sense, communication is like a tube of glue – once it is out it cannot easily be retracted and there is usually mess involved in trying to do so. It could be perhaps a confidence that was broken by a secret being revealed, but once that revelation has taken place it cannot be undone. This is not to deny that efforts can be made to mitigate the personal and relational consequences of the act. We can work at redefining what has taken place in order to make it more palatable and ourselves less blameworthy. The *account* is one mechanism used to this end. Accounts in this sense can be regarded as explanations for troublesome acts (Cody and McLaughlin, 1988; Buttny and Morris, 2001). Possibilities include apologies, justifications and excuses (Bousfield, 2008). In the case of the latter, the untoward action is attributed to the intervention of some external influence (e.g. that the information was extracted under threat or torture). Nevertheless, once information is in the public domain it cannot be reprivatised.

A SKILL MODEL OF INTERPERSONAL COMMUNICATION

The key characteristics of interpersonal communication covered above provide a necessary foundation for the components and processes underpinning skilled dyadic (two-person) interaction. The model covered in this chapter builds upon skill models developed, inter alia, by Dickson *et al.* (1997), Bull (2006) and Hargie (2006c), based upon earlier theorising by Argyle (1983). The model, as presented in Figure 2.1, identifies six elements of skilled interpersonal interaction:

1   person–situation context
2   goal
3   mediating processes
4   response
5   feedback
6   perception.

By way of an overview, the model rests upon three basic assumptions. The first is that, as has already been claimed, people act purposefully; second, that they are sensitive to the effects of their action; third, that they take steps to modify subsequent action in the light of this information. In keeping with the model, dyadic interaction is depicted within a person–situation framework. What takes place when people come together and engage in communication is partly a feature of the particular attributes and characteristics that make each a unique individual, and partly due to the parameters of the shared situation within which they find themselves.

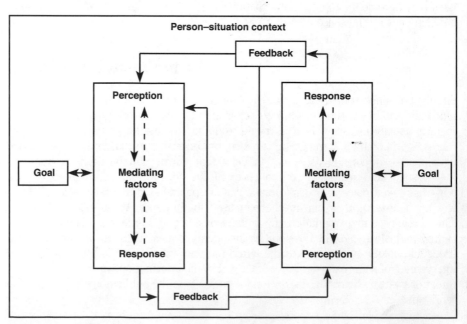

Figure 2.1   Skill model of interpersonal communication

As already discussed, a widely agreed feature of social activity is that it is goal directed. People establish and pursue goals in the situations within which they interact. What transpires is entered into in order to achieve some end-state, even if this amounts to little more than the pleasure to be had from conversing. In a quest to realise the adopted goal, mediating processes are operationalised. Accordingly, possible strategies for actualising these outcomes may be formulated, their projected effects evaluated, and a decision on a plan of action derived. The implementation of this course of action will, in turn, be acted out in the responses made. The interactive nature of the process is such that each interactor, in reacting to the other, provides as feedback information of relevance in arriving at decisions on goal attainment. Additional to this mediated facility, each has a direct channel of feedback on performance, enabling monitoring of self to take place.

While feedback makes information available, it can only be acted upon if it is actually received by the recipient. Perception is therefore central to skilful interaction, yet its intrinsically selective and subjective nature often results in perceptual inaccuracy and miscommunication (Hinton, 1993; Hanna and Wilson, 1998). Notwithstanding, and to recapitulate, information stemming from perceptions of self, the situation and the other interactor, is considered in accordance with a complex of mediating processes, the outcome of which is a plan to govern action. This plan of action, deemed to maximise opportunities for goal attainment under the prevailing circumstances, is represented in strategies to be actioned, thereby determining individual responses. The model also recognises the interrelationship between goals and mediation, perception and responses. In this way, our mediating processes may cause us to evaluate our current goals as unattainable and so we will formulate new ones. Furthermore, the way in which we perceive others is influenced by our prevailing emotional state and cognitive structure, and our responses play a part in shaping our thoughts and feelings (as shown by the dotted arrows in Figure 2.1).

To sum up, and in keeping with cognitive theories of interpersonal communication in general, 'people are assumed to be actors and to have goals . . . these actors are endowed with complex mental machinery. The machinery is deployed in pursuit of those goals' (Hewes, 1995: 164). It should be remembered that due to the dynamic and changing character of communication, both participants are, at one and the same time, senders and receivers of information. Each is, even when silent, acting and reacting to the other. Furthermore, potential barriers to successful communication exist at each of the different stages outlined. A more detailed consideration of each of these components of the model will now be presented.

Person–situation context

Participants bring considerable personal 'baggage' to social encounters. This includes their knowledge, motives, values, emotions, attitudes, expectations and dispositions. The way in which they have come to regard themselves (*self-concept*) and the beliefs that they have formed about their abilities to succeed in various types of enterprise (*self-efficacy*) will determine the sorts of encounters contemplated, goals selected, how these are pursued, and anticipated rewards derivable from them.

Interaction is also codetermined by parameters of the situation within which individuals find themselves, including role demands and the rules that pertain. Take, for example, a priest and a parishioner in the confessional. Each is personally unique, yet the respective roles inherent in this highly restricted situation dictate that, regardless of the individuals involved, much the same sort of activity will be entered into by priests, on the one hand, and parishioners, on the other. The implicit rules governing how both parties should conduct themselves under these circumstances will, by condoning certain actions and disapproving others, regulate the interaction that unfolds. The physical setting of space and place is a further constraining feature of the environment that has potential effects on interaction. The location of the encounter and the physical layout both have a significant influence upon the communicative process (Beaulieu, 2004; Li and Li, 2007).

There has long been debate about whether our behaviour is determined by the types of people we are or by the situation in which we find ourselves. It is now generally recognised that personal and situational sources of influence are bidirectional (Cervone *et al.*, 2008; Fleeson and Noftle, 2008). As summarised by Hirsh (2009: 755): 'Although researchers examining the situational and dispositional determinants of behaviour have traditionally been at odds with one another, contemporary models acknowledge the importance of adopting an interactionist framework.' Furthermore, it is not only the case that personal characteristics and situational factors combine to determine behaviour. What transpires during social contact can also effect changes in interactors. Involvement with others can lead to modifications in individual knowledge, beliefs and attitudes (indeed the success of educational and counselling interventions depends on it) and can also, within limits, serve to redefine the social situation (Smith and Boster, 2009). Thus, participants may decide to dispense with the customary formality surrounding situations such as the selection interview, summit meetings, etc., and turn them into much more relaxed occasions. While acknowledging the interactive nature of the person–situation context, it is useful to examine each separately.

Personal characteristics

A complex of personal factors, including knowledge, motives, attitudes, personality and emotions, shape the interactive process in respect of goals pursued, perceptions and interaction patterns.

Knowledge

A distinction can be made between what is known, on the one hand, and the cognitive processes by means of which information is decoded, stored and retrieved from memory, on the other (Greene, 1995; Meyer, 1997; Roskos-Ewoldsen and Monahan, 2007). While closely interrelated, it is only the latter that is relevant at this point. The former will be addressed in relation to mediating processes.

Knowledge of our social world and how it operates, of people and the circumstances in which they find themselves, together with shared communication codes, is fundamental to any contemplation of skilled interpersonal activity. Having relevant information upon which to draw is invaluable when deciding courses of action and pursuing them. Indeed, it is drawn upon at every stage of the communication process – from identifying goals that are likely to be within reach, through making sense of the situation and the actions of the other, to selecting and implementing a considered strategy.

Psychologists and communication scholars have made use of the notion of schema in explaining how information is organised into a framework representing the world as experienced by the individual, and used to interpret current events. A schema can be thought of as a 'mental structure which contains general expectations and knowledge of the world. This may include general expectations about people, social roles, events and how to behave in certain situations' (Augoustinos and Walker, 1995: 32). Different types of schema (or schemata) have been identified (Fiske and Taylor, 2008). These include:

- *self schemas* – concern our knowledge of ourselves
- *event schemas or scripts* – represent the sequences of events that characterise particular, frequently encountered, social occasions such as ordering a meal or buying a newspaper
- *role schemas* – involve concepts according to which we expect people, based upon occupation, gender, race and so forth, to abide by certain norms and behave within set parameters of appropriate conduct
- *causal schemas* – enable us to form judgements about cause–effect relationships in our physical and social environment, and to adopt courses of action based upon the anticipations which such schemata make possible
- *person schemas* – facilitate, as organised sets of knowledge about features and characteristics, the social categorisation of others.

The related concept *category* has also been used to explain how we structure information about others and impose meaning on the social world in which we operate. Fiedler and Bless (2001: 123) defined a category as a 'grouping of two or more distinguishable objects that are treated in a similar way'. 'Party', for instance, is a category that you may use to group particular social events with features that distinguish them in important ways from other social events such as lectures, concerts or public meetings. The complexity of our social worlds makes categorising people, occasions and happenings inescapable. It would simply be chaotically impossible to treat everything we encountered in life as separate, uniquely different and distinct. We would find it impossible to function in this way. Categorising others, and our social world, is therefore inevitable. Some people though have more highly elaborated category systems than others to represent areas of their social lives.

But placing people in categories can have a negative side. It may lead to the application of *stereotypes*, whereby individual characteristics tend to be neglected and all members of the group are regarded in an undifferentiated manner, as sharing a set of generalised attributes (Schneider, 2005; Nelson, 2009). Under these circumstances individuality suffers and people or events are regarded as being largely interchangeable. The cost of this type of generalising 'is that we fail to appreciate the complete uniqueness of the whole person, ensuring that our stereotypes sometimes lead us into judgements that are both erroneous and biased' (Tourish, 1999: 193).

Stereotypes may be widely held (social stereotypes) or peculiar to an individual (personal stereotypes). They can also become self-fulfilling. If we regard all red-haired people as aggressive, we may act towards them in a belligerent way and so precipitate an aggressive reaction that confirms our stereotype (this is further discussed in Chapter 10).

Motives

Why do people do all of the things suggested as elaborated in this model of skilled interaction? Why, indeed, take part in interaction at all? A full consideration of these matters would extend well beyond the scope of this chapter. For present purposes, however, they can be scaled down to two vital and related issues:

1   Why do people adopt the goals that they do?
2   Having done so, why do they continue to behave in accordance with them?

The second question is probably easier to answer than the first. Goals are taken to contribute both direction and impetus to the interactive process and therefore have inherent motivational implications (Maes and Gebhardt, 2000). They have been described as 'attractors' in that 'people spend much of their time doing things that keep their behavior in close proximity to their goals' (Carver and Scheier, 2000: 70). Persistence to achievement is an important characteristic of goal-directed behaviour and this motivational effect is perhaps the one that has received most attention from researchers.

Not all goal aspirations, of course, are necessarily translated into action. Whether or not they are depends upon an appreciation of a variety of external and internal factors. They include assessments of how conducive environmental circumstances are at that time to goal achievement together with judgements of self-efficacy (Bandura, 1997), which determine the extent to which individuals believe that they have the abilities and resources at hand to succeed.

The proposed reasons why goals are formulated in the first place have already been referred to. Many accounts highlight the notion of need (e.g. Ryan *et al.*, 1996). Guirdham (2002) regarded motives as the internal responses to needs. Dillard (1990) believed, in turn, that goals reflect broad underlying motives. But what are these underlying needs that impel us to establish goals in directing our activities with others? As mentioned in Chapter 1, there are three core concerns:

1   the need to feel in control and to be able to predict events of which one is part (*autonomy*)
2   the need to have a sense of belonging to and intimate involvement with others, making possible approval from them (*relatedness*)
3   the need to exercise mastery and display competence in one's strivings, thereby experiencing a sense of self-worth (*competence*).

On a broader front, a range of physiological and safety needs can also be thought of as determining what we seek from our environment (Maslow, 1954). We are obviously motivated to meet our biological needs for food, drink, sex, etc., and to protect ourselves from physical harm.

Attitudes

Our attitudes are another highly significant personal characteristic that impacts upon interaction. Just how these attitudes are structured and the extent to which they determine what we do are topics of ongoing debate (Albarracin *et al.*, 2005; Crano and Prislin, 2008). A long-standing way of thinking about attitudes (Katz and Stotland, 1959) is in terms of three constituent elements, sometimes referred to as ABC:

1   *Affective* – how one feels about the target, either positive or negative, in liking or disliking. Indeed for some this is the most important attribute.
2   *Behavioural* – one's predisposition to behave in a certain way towards the target.
3   *Cognitive* – one's knowledge or beliefs about the target.

For example, I may have a particular attitude towards my next-door neighbour such that I believe that he is jealous of me and out to do me down (cognitive), which makes me dislike him (affective) so I avoid his company (behavioural). Note, however, that attitudes only define a tendency to behave in a particular way in respect of an attitude object. According to the *theory of planned behaviour* (Ajzen, 1991), additional considerations such as *perceived behavioural control* (the ease with which we feel we can accomplish the behaviour) and *subjective norms* (our appreciation of the prevailing expectations regarding that behaviour and our motivation to comply) are likely to shape our intentions to behave accordingly. It is these intentions that directly lead to behaviour in line with attitudes (the relationship between attitudes and behaviour is explored further in Chapter 12).

In any situation therefore there may not be a direct correspondence between attitude and actual behaviour. Attitudes interact with other personal characteristics including motives, values and other attitudes, together with situational forces, to influence behaviour (Albarracin *et al.*, 2005). Furthermore, not all attitudes are equally accessible or held with the same strength of feeling (Haddock and Maio, 2008).

Personality

Personality is the complex of unique traits and characteristics of an individual that shapes interaction with the environment and the ability to relate to oneself and others. A large number of personality traits has been identified. However, there is now wide consensus regarding the validity of what has been termed the 'five factor model', or 'big five' traits of extraversion, openness, neuroticism, agreeableness and conscientiousness (Chamorro-Premuzic, 2007). To take just the first of these, extraversion–introversion is one dimension along which individuals can be placed that has implications for communicative behaviour. There is evidence that introverts tend to speak less, make more frequent use of pauses, engage in lower frequencies of gaze at their partners, are less accurate at encoding emotion and prefer to interact at greater interpersonal distances (John *et al.*, 2008; Knapp and Hall, 2010).

Emotion

Affect is central to interpersonal life and has attracted considerable attention from scholars of communication (Tiedens and Leach, 2004; Philippot and Feldman, 2005). Just how emotion operates though, and the contributions of, for instance, physiological constituents, on the one hand, and social, moral and cultural determinants, on the other, is a matter of ongoing debate (Porter and Samovar, 1998; Metts and Planalp, 2002; Frijda, 2006). Regardless, it is widely acknowledged that we cannot completely separate the affective and the cognitive – how we feel from how and what we think (Demetriou and Wilson, 2008). As expressed by Bless (2001: 392): 'Affective states have been shown to influence encoding, storage, retrieval, judgmental processes, and style of information processing. These processes are, of course, highly intertwined.'

Dillard (1998) identified three ways in which emotions can be involved in the communication process:

1   *Emotion-motivated communication* is behaviour caused by underlying emotion (e.g. one driver swears at another and acts threateningly in a fit of road rage).
2   *Emotion-manifesting communication* provides insights into a person's underlying emotional state (e.g. a patient's downcast look enables the nurse to make judgements about that person's 'spirits').
3   *Emotion-inducing communication* involves words and actions that trigger emotion in others (e.g. someone cries after being told a sad story).

Age

The relative ages of participants will influence their behaviour and the expectations that each has of the other. Particular ways in which communication is used by and towards older people and issues surrounding intergeneration talk has attracted considerable research interest (Nussbaum and Coupland, 2004). Older people are frequently subjected to simplified forms of speech that can be seen as patronising (Dickson and McCartan, 2005; Lin *et al.*, 2008). Examples of some of these are presented in Box 2.2.

Negative stereotypes of older people seem to be at the bottom of this way of relating. Picking up on cues denoting advanced years can activate a stereotype suggesting incompetence, decline or senility, such that younger speakers may tailor what they say in keeping with this set of beliefs. One example of this is a tendency to use simplified or partonising talk with mature adults. Older people tend to have frequent contact with health workers. Does communication in this context, therefore, reveal these same trends? The answer is yes. In working with institutionalised older people, 'secondary baby talk' or 'elderspeak' has been found to be a feature of carers' com-

---

Box 2.2 Examples of patronising communication with older people

- *Simplification strategies* – using a simplified register as one might with a child (e.g. basic vocabulary, short sentences, simple sentence structure, more restricted range of sentence patterns).
- *Clarification strategies* – ways of making yourself heard and understood (e.g. speaking more loudly, slowly and with exaggerated intonation, using repetition).
- *Diminutives* – being dismissively familiar or patronising; includes calling the person 'honey', 'love' or 'dear', etc., or describing some thing or event, such as a nap, as 'little' (e.g. 'It's time for a little nap, dear').
- *Demeaning emotional tone* – acting superciliously.
- *Secondary babytalk* – talking as one would to a baby (e.g. 'Just a teensy-weensy bit more?').
- *Avoidance* – discussing the older person in their presence with a relative rather than addressing them directly.
- *Overly controlling* – being impatient or assuming the person's needs are already known.

---

munication, and often regardless of the level of personal competence of the receiver (Nussbaum *et al.*, 2005; Carpiac-Claver and Levy-Storms, 2007). However, older people tend to rate carers more favourably when nonpatronising speech is used (Draper, 2005). There is a caveat here, however, in that the lower the older person's level of cognitive functioning, the more favourably this type of elderspeak is rated (Roter and Hall, 2006).

Gender

Numerous studies have documented differences in how males and females communicate verbally and nonverbally (Dindia and Canary, 2006; Knapp and Hall, 2010). These, however, should not be overstated, nor should it be assumed that they apply to each and every individual (Dow and Wood, 2006; Blakemore *et al.*, 2008). With that in mind (and other things being equal), females compared with males typically tend to:

- interact at closer interpersonal distances
- be more tolerant of spatial intrusion
- make greater use of eye contact and touch
- smile more and are more facially, gesticularly and vocally expressive
- be more adept at both encoding and decoding nonverbal messages
- have deeper insights into their relational goals.

Males and females express themselves differently in language. Researchers commonly report that 'women are more likely than men to use language to form and maintain connections with others (i.e. affiliation), whereas men are more likely to use language to assert dominance and to achieve utilitarian goals (i.e. self-assertion)'

(Leaper and Ayres, 2007: 328–329). This was shown by Tannen (1995), who analysed how males and females typically respond to 'trouble talk' – being told about some personal problem or difficulty. When women disclose personal predicaments, they primarily expect (and tend to get from other women) a listening ear, confirmation of their concerns and an understanding reaction. Indeed, this type of talk serves, in part, to strengthen interpersonal bonds between friends. Men, however, instinctively respond by tackling the problem head-on in an attempt to solve it through giving information or offering advice. Miscommunication is such that men see women wallowing in their problems rather than discussing practical steps to solve them. Women, on the other hand, feel that men don't understand them and are not prepared to make the effort to do so. Frustration is shared equally. This issue of gender differences is further discussed in several chapters, particularly Chapter 9.

Situational factors

It will be recalled that personal characteristics and situational factors operate to provide a contextual backdrop for communication. Acting conjointly they determine how people conceive of social episodes, formulate goals, attach meanings to events and exchange patterns of conduct. Both features of the person and the situation may, within limits, be subject to change as a result of interaction. Several attempts have been made to delineate the essential constituents of situations (Miller *et al.*, 1994; Gosling *et al.*, 2008). Perhaps the simplest categorisation is that by Pervin (1978) who proposed that the key constituents are:

- who is involved
- what is happening
- where the action is taking place.

A more highly differentiated analysis of social situations, derived from extensive research, is that offered by Argyle *et al.* (1981) and elaborated by Hargie (2006c). They identified eight key features of the situations within which people interact:

1   *Goal structure.* Situations have goal implications. Not only do we seek out situations with goal satisfaction in mind, but particular situations will also place constraints on the goals that can be legitimately pursued.
2   *Roles.* In most situations individuals act in accordance with more or less clearly recognised sets of expectations centring upon their social position and status.
3   *Rules.* Situations are rule governed. There are (often implicit) stipulations that govern what is acceptable conduct for participants. It is perfectly acceptable for two friends at a party to sing, shout, dance and drink alcohol from a bottle. Were such behaviour transferred to a lecture it would be in strict contravention of the contrasting rules that prevail.
4   *Repertoire of elements.* This refers to the range of behaviours that may be called upon for the situation to be competently handled.
5   *Sequences of behaviour.* In many situations interaction unfolds in a quite

predictable sequence of acts on the part of participants. As already mentioned, people often function in highly routine instances according to scripts.

6   **Situational concepts.** The idea of individuals possessing knowledge which enables them to make sense of situations and perform appropriately in them was discussed in relation to the notion of a schema.

7   **Language and speech.** There are linguistic variations associated with social situations. Some, for example public speaking, require a more formal speech style than others, such as having a casual conversation.

8   **Physical environment.** The physical setting, including furniture, decor, lighting, layout, etc., often influences who talks to whom, how they feel, how much they say and how the talk is regulated.

Culture

At a broader level, cultural background is a highly significant contextualising factor. Culture can be regarded as the way of life, customs and script of a group of people. Cultural and subcultural variables have a bearing on the different features of the communicative process. In turn, communication shapes culture (Conway and Schaller, 2007). Intercultural differences therefore run much deeper than possible differences in language, encompassing not only much of the nonverbal channel of communication but beyond to the underlying social order itself and the meanings and values that give it form (Asante *et al.*, 2007). When two people from radically different cultures come together, not only may they be attempting to use different language codes to represent a shared world, but the respective social worlds themselves may have little overlap.

Cultural influences permeate values, beliefs and cherished practices. Indeed, so pervasive are cultural effects that they can be thought to shape individuals' entire understanding of their social worlds. A classic study conducted by Hofstede (1980) exposed four underlying dimensions along which a large sample of different national groups could be plotted in respect of fundamental values espoused. These dimensions were:

- **power distance** – the amount of respect and deference displayed by those in different positions on a status hierarchy
- **individualism–collectivism** – the extent to which one's identity is shaped by individual choices and achievements or a feature of the collective group to which one belongs
- **uncertainty avoidance** – the degree to which life's uncertainties can be controlled through planning and foresight
- **masculinity–femininity** – this has to do with the relative focus upon competitive, task-centred achievement versus cooperation and harmonious relationships.

European and North American cultures scored high on individualism and low on power distance, while those from Latin American and Asian countries were low on individualism but high on power distance. These cultural dimensions have been shown to influence communication in myriad ways (Gudykunst and Matsumoto, 1996).

At another level, culturally prescribed norms govern how people conduct themselves during social encounters. These norms determine punctuality, interpersonal distance, touch, use of gestures, facial expressions, gaze patterns – indeed all the nonverbal codes (Manusov and Patterson, 2006; Remland, 2006). Machismo in Hispanic cultures, for example, imposes display rules that forbid male expressions of pain. In Muslim cultures there are gender difficulties surrounding touch by a male health worker in the course of a physical examination of a female patient. Aspects of culture are explored in future chapters, and particularly in Chapter 11.

Having considered the person–situation context of communication in some detail, the other components of the model will now be explored.

Goals

As discussed earlier in the chapter and in Chapter 1, goals are central to skilled performance. Dillard (2008: 66) defined goals as 'future states of affairs that an individual is committed to achieving or maintaining'. Put another way, the goals that we have in mind are mental representations of future end-states that we would like to make happen (Fishbach and Ferguson, 2007). Three telltale qualities of behaviour in pursuit of such outcomes were identified by Oettingen and Gollwitzer (2001):

- *persistence* – a course of action will be continued until the goal is achieved (or abandoned, under exceptional circumstances)
- *appropriateness* – courses of action adopted are ones likely to reduce the difference between existing and desired states and effect a successful outcome
- *selectivity* – the individual is attuned to stimuli associated with the goal in initiating and directing behaviour.

Different ways of analysing and categorising human goals have been documented (e.g. Moskowitz and Grant, 2009; Brataas *et al.*, 2010; Caughlin and Scott, 2010). Some of the most significant elements will now be examined.

Content and process elements

Maes and Gebhardt (2000) specified that goals have *content* and *process* properties. The former defines *what* is to be attained, the latter addresses *how* this is to be effected and commitment to the objective.

Task and relational goals

One of the assumptions underlying many goal-based accounts of human endeavour is that individuals are typically striving to actualise a multiplicity of outcomes in their dealings with their material and interpersonal environs, and often concurrently (Dillard, 2008). Austin and Vancouver (1996: 338), in their comprehensive review, argued that 'single goals cannot be understood when isolated from other goals'. Indeed, Samp and Solomon (1998) identified seven categories of goal behind communicative responses to problematic events in close relationships:

1   to maintain the relationship
2   to accept fault for the event
3   to ensure positive face
4   to avoid addressing the event
5   to manage the conversation
6   to cope with emotion
7   to restore negative face.

Referring back to what was said earlier about the multidimensionality of communication, Tracy and Coupland (1990) identified one of the most basic distinctions as that between task goals and face or relational goals. In certain situations it may be difficult to satisfy both and yet be vitally important to do so. For example, health care presents myriad occasions when face can be compromised (Brataas *et al.*, 2010). Instances of humour being used as a face-giving strategy to stave off awkward embarrassment have been reported in medical contexts (Foot and McCreaddie, 2006). As aptly summarised by Lawler (1991: 195): 'Skill is required by the nurse to construct a context in which it is permissible to see other people's nakedness and genitalia, to undress others, and to handle other people's bodies.'

Instrumental and consummatory goals

Along similar lines, Ruffner and Burgoon (1981) distinguished between goals that are *instrumental* and those that are *consummatory*. Instrumental goals are carried out in order to achieve some further outcome (e.g. a supervisor may reward effort to increase productivity). Consummatory communication, on the other hand, satisfies the communicator's goal without the *active* intervention of another (e.g. the supervisor may reward in order to experience the feeling of satisfaction or power when distributing largesse).

Implicit and explicit goals

Some of the goals that we try to achieve in interaction are readily available to us. We are consciously aware of them and, if asked, could articulate them with little effort. Not all goals are like this but rather many operate in a reflexive, automatic manner (Bargh, 2005). While influential in what we do, we would find these more difficult to account for. As explained by Berger (1995: 144): 'Given that conscious awareness is a relatively scarce cognitive resource, it is almost a certainty that, in any social-interaction situation, several goals will be implicit for the actors involved, and that goals at the focal point of conscious awareness will change during the course of most social-interaction episodes.' Furthermore, Carver and Scheier (1999) suggested that we may even be pre-programmed to automatically follow certain courses of action when faced with particular sets of circumstances, as a default option. What communication scholars need to address are issues of 'when goals exist in consciousness, how they arrive there, how long they stay, and by what mechanisms this movement occurs' (Dillard, 1997: 51). At the moment there are few answers to such questions.

Hierarchical organisation

Goals are hierarchically structured, with some being more widely encompassing than others (Oettingen and Gollwitzer, 2001). This theme is common in the literature although some authors have countenanced more complex arrangements than others. Dillard (1990) believed that a three-level structure was adequate, with broad motives leading to goals that, in turn, governed subgoals. Berger (1995) also identified *meta-goals* that overarch more specific instances. These include quests for *efficiency* – a requirement to achieve the objective by the most economical means, and *social appropriateness* – a stipulation not to violate prevailing norms and expectations.

Furthermore, primary and secondary goals may be at work in specific interactive episodes (Wilson, 2010). *Primary goals* are the ostensible reason for the interaction taking place; they give it meaning and establish expectations and responsibilities. *Secondary goals* span different episodes, shaping and placing constraints around the pursuit of primary goals (e.g. maintaining face or reducing anxiety).

Goal importance

Austin and Vancouver (1996) highlighted importance and commitment as factors in goal setting. More weight is attached to some goals than others. It is these that have most impact upon action at any particular juncture. Decisions reached about goal selection and commitment depend very much on the psychological value attached to the accomplishment of that outcome, estimates of the likelihood of various antici-pated courses of action being successful in this respect, projected immediacy of gratification, possible costs which may ensue, and so on (Locke and Latham, 1990; Shah and Kruglanski, 2000). One implication of recognising that goals differ in importance, coupled with the assertion that interactors are typically pursuing several goals at the same time, is the need for a prioritising mechanism to regulate goal selection. There must be some form of ongoing assessment and reprioritising as certain outcomes are achieved, others possibly abandoned or alternative means contemplated, and as circumstances alter (Bandura, 1997; Brataas *et al.*, 2009). These circumstances, of course, include the participation of the interactive partner. In their investigation of goal management during contrived conversations between mainly strangers, one of the most striking outcomes reported by Waldron *et al.* (1990) was the greater importance of ongoing adjustment to changing circumstances rather than the deployment of fixed, predetermined plans.

Temporal perspective

Dillard (1997) charted a temporal dimension to goals. This, together with hierarchical orderings, is in keeping with the views of Hargie (2006a) when talking about long-term and short-term goals. He gave the example of an employment interviewer interviewing a job applicant. The principal goal directing this activity is, of course, to reach a proper decision as to the suitability of the interviewee. An appropriate short-term goal might be to welcome the candidate, make introductions and ask relevant questions. Actions are generally under the immediate control of goals at this level although long-term goals must not be lost sight of.

Level of precision

Carver and Scheier (2000) noted that goals differ in their level of concreteness/abstraction. Some may be quite specific and precise, others more vague and indeterminate. Thus, a junior nurse may have as a goal to be more assertive in transactions with other staff, or to politely but firmly refuse to swap shifts with Jo the next time the request is made. In the context of the identification of objectives for educational or therapeutic interventions, one of the commonly accepted recommendations is that they be precisely articulated in assessable terms (Millar *et al.*, 1992).

Goal compatibility

How the goals of interactors relate has obvious and extremely important implications for the encounter and what transpires. Goals may be:

* ***similar*** – here both are striving to achieve the same or similar goal but in so doing each may coincidentally thwart the other (e.g. both friends want to offload about their partner trouble)
* ***complementary*** – here goals are compatible (e.g. one wants to offload, the other to listen)
* ***opposed*** – one's goal may be in direct opposition to that of the other (e.g. A wants to find out about B, while B is determined not to reveal personal information).

In terms of the individual, conflict can also take place between goals at a similar level and between goals at one hierarchical level and the next (Maes and Gebhardt, 2000). In discussing metagoals in the strategic management of embarrassment, for example, Sharkey (1997) explained how social appropriateness may be forfeited in favour of efficiency when it is the intention of someone to deliberately cause embarrassment to another. Efficiency refers to how quickly and easily one can accomplish one's goal, while social appropriateness refers to being able to do so without causing loss of face for others. Sharkey gave the example of someone hogging the conversation among a group of friends and one of the group saying, 'Do your parents realise you talk as much as this?' Here, the response may be efficient in getting the person to stop talking, but it is low in social appropriateness as it may anger the speaker as well as causing embarrassment for everyone present.

Mediating processes

These processes mediate between the goal being pursued, our perceptions of events and what we decide to do about them. They also, as we have seen, play a part in the formulation of goals, influence how people and events are perceived and reflect the capacity of the individual to assimilate, deal with and respond to the circumstances of social encounters. It will be recalled that, in keeping with the thinking of Hewes and Planalp (1987) and Greene (1995), a differentiation was made between these processes and the sorts of knowledge structures discussed in the earlier section as instances of personal characteristics.

Cognitive processes

Discussions of the cognitive processes that make interpersonal communication possible can be readily found in the literature (e.g. Roskos-Ewoldsen and Monahan, 2007; Strack and Förster, 2009). In the sequence of steps leading to a particular course of action being generated, Kreps (1988) outlined: information organisation, processing and evaluation; decision making; and the selecting of action strategies. It is these action strategies, or plans for action, that Argyle (1994) regarded as the essential contribution of this stage to interaction.

Wyer and Gruenfeld (1995) identified five key cognitive elements that guide information processing in interpersonal encounters:

1 *semantic encoding* – the interpretation of messages in keeping with available semantic concepts and structures
2 *organisation* – the arranging of information into mental representations of the person, thing or event
3 *storage and retrieval* – the storage of these representations in memory and their subsequent selective access as and when required
4 *inference processes* – decisions to respond are shaped by inferences about the implications and consequences of that action. Assumptions and implications about the nature of the encounter, the communicators and their relationship are also important
5 *response generation* – of overriding importance here are the strategies selected to bring about targeted goals and objectives. Possibilities of responses sometimes being 'mindless' must also be acknowledged, as must the influence of emotion on performance.

Some of the processes that lead to the pursuit of a certain course of action are more cognitively demanding than others. Those involving 'mindful' problem solving or decision making are particularly challenging, and deserve further attention. A distinction can be made between descriptive and prescriptive models of problem solving and decision making, or between how decisions are arrived at and how they should be arrived at. Nelson-Jones (1996) recommended a seven-stage framework for rational decision making:

1   ***Confront*** – this includes recognising the need for a decision to be taken, clarifying what exactly it is that is hoped to be achieved, and being open to the circumstances, both internal and external, of the decision.

2   ***Generate options and gather information*** – try to think of as many options as possible, without any attempt at this point to evaluate their chances of success. This may involve, time permitting, gathering additional information which can be drawn upon.

3   ***Assess the predicted consequences of options*** – projected advantages and disadvantages of each need to be thought through. One important consequence, of course, is the probability of that course of action successfully achieving the goal being pursued. Others have to do with judgements of self-efficacy – the belief in one's ability to successfully implement that strategy; implications for face – how one might be seen by the other or others; and personal costs – including the amount of difficulty and effort required. By reflecting upon the positive and negative features of each option according to these criteria, the best option under the circumstances can be logically and systematically revealed.

4   ***Commit to the decision*** – here resolve to the course of action selected should be strengthened.

5   ***Plan how to implement the decision*** – a plan should be formulated in which goals and subgoals are clearly stated, constituent tasks broken down, difficulties anticipated and sources of support identified.

6   ***Implement the decision*** – timing of implementation is one of the important factors to bear in mind. Other features of implementation will be taken up when the *Response* element of the model is explicated.

7   ***Assess consequences of implementation*** – reflecting upon outcomes leads to improved future performance.

The complexities involved at this stage of cognitive processing are still the subject of much speculation (Matlin, 2009). For instance, *metacognitions* play a part. In order to interact successfully, we must be able to think about and form an opinion on how others think and how they go about making sense of the world that they experience. The way in which messages are encoded by skilled communicators will reflect judgements along these lines.

Affective processes

Emotions were discussed earlier in relation to personal factors, but they also play a key role in the mediation process. Various theoretical perspectives on how and when emotion is experienced, and the role of interpersonal schemata in the process, have been posited. Hargie (2006c) charted the role of both cognitive and affective elements that serve a mediating capacity in interaction, and demonstrated the close interrelationship between the two systems. It is clear that the meanings we attach to events are often coloured by how we feel at the time (Demetriou and Wilson, 2008). Forgas (1994) discovered that people who were happy tended to locate causes of relational conflict in external and unstable sources while those who were sad looked to internal and stable alternatives. The former responded with active strategies for coping while the latter were more passive. Wyer and Gruenfeld (1995: 38) highlighted reciprocity as a further mediating role of emotion on behaviour, in that 'individuals appear to reciprocate the affect or emotion that they perceive a communicator has conveyed to them' (this is further discussed in Chapter 3 in relation to the phenomenon of emotional contagion).

While the important end product of mediating processes is a strategy or plan of action designed with goal achievement in mind, this plan must always be tentative and open to revision. Given the inherent fluidity of interaction, Berger (1995: 149) argued persuasively that 'reducing the actions necessary to reach social goals to a rigid, script-like formula may produce relatively ineffective social action'. Unfortunately this is what sometimes characterises encounters with professionals, where interactions become ossified in repetitive, stereotyped rituals, merely carried out in a mechanical way with little affective warmth or care shown for the client. Skilled communication must always be adaptively and reflexively responsive to the emotional needs of the other.

Responses

Plans and strategies decided upon are implemented at this stage. There can be no guarantee, of course, that their translation into action will be flawless or indeed successful. Jordan (1998) identified two of the main errors that can occur: *slips* are actions that are not part of the plan, or are planned but performed out of sequence; *lapses* are planned actions that are omitted rather than enacted.

According to the *hierarchy principle* (Knowlton and Berger, 1997), when people fail to achieve an interactional goal but persist, they tend first to adjust low-level elements of the plan (e.g. volume or speed of speech) rather than more abstract higher order elements (e.g. general strategy).

A common categorisation of social action is that of *verbal* and *nonverbal* communication. While closely connected, verbal communication has to do with the purely linguistic message, with the actual words used. Nonverbal behaviour encompasses a whole range of body movements and facial expressions, together with vocal aspects of speech (nonverbal communication is discussed in depth in the next chapter).

Feedback

The concept of feedback has long been the subject of investigation in the social sciences (Hattie and Timperley, 2007; van de Ridder *et al.*, 2008). Feedback enables us to assess the effects of our communications. It is a fundamental feature of communication and without it skilled engagement would not be possible. For Heath and Bryant (2000: 76), who emphasised the interpretive dimension of the process, 'Feedback stresses the strategic and interactive nature of communication'. Having acted, individuals rely on knowledge of their performance together with outcomes that may have accrued in order to reach decisions as to what to do next and alter subsequent responses accordingly.

In the model in Figure 2.1, two sources of feedback are depicted. First, we have access, through internal receptors in muscles and joints, as well as visually (to a certain extent) and aurally (albeit with distortion), to what we do and say when communicating with others. Second, as interaction takes place, each person is, in what they say and do, providing the other with information which can act as feedback. Convergence towards mutual understanding and shared meaning is proportional to the degree to which feedback is put to effective use. Limited provision and/or reception increase the chances of divergence and misunderstanding.

Corresponding to the different aspects of responding, feedback can be provided verbally or nonverbally. Although both are typically implicated, nonverbal modes may be particularly salient when it comes to affective or evaluative matters, while cognitive or substantive feedback relies more heavily upon the verbal.

Perception

Not all information potentially available via feedback is perceived, and not all information received is perceived accurately. But it is only through the perceptual apparatus that information about the internal and external environment, including other people and the messages that they transmit, can be decoded and acted upon through making judgements and decisions in relation to the goals being sought.

In their review of this area, Skowronski *et al.* (2008: 313) pointed out that 'perceptions of others are relevant to virtually every human endeavour'. How we perceive others is fundamental to skilful interaction, yet perception is a profoundly precarious activity (Teiford, 2007). Generally speaking, perception is an *active* and highly *selective* process (Eysenck, 1998). These qualities tend to be emphasised in particular with reference to social interaction (Zebrowski, 2007). We are actively involved in the perceptions that we make, rather than being merely passive recipients (Hess *et al.*, 2008). We seldom attend to all the stimuli available in any situation, but rather filter out the less conspicuous, less interesting or less personally involving elements. As such, perception is subjective. Despite naive assumptions, the belief that we perceive and observe other people in a correct, factual, unbiased, objective way is a myth. Rather, what we observe typically owes as much, if not more, to ourselves in perceiving, as it does to the other person in being perceived. As expressed by Wilmot (1995: 150):

> There is no 'immutable reality' of the other person awaiting our discovery. We attribute qualities to the other based on the cues we have available, and the unique way we interpret them. Our perception of the other, while seeming certain, is grounded in permanent uncertainty.

A consequence of the essentially selective and inferential nature of social perception and its heavy dependence upon the knowledge structures, expectations and attributional processes of the perceiver often results in perceptual inaccuracy and hence miscommunication (Hinton, 1993).

In addition to perceptions of others, skilled interpersonal behaviour also requires *metaperception*, which refers to 'predictions of others' judgments of oneself' (Malloy *et al.*, 2007: 603). Skilled communicators have the ability to make accurate perceptions of self and how one is being perceived by others. People differ in the extent to which they monitor their performance and under what conditions (Snyder, 1987). While high self-monitors endeavour to create and maintain an impression in keeping with the situation and to earn approval, low self-monitors are much less preoccupied by these concerns. Nevertheless, lax self-monitoring is likely to diminish one's communicative effectiveness (Metts and Mikucki, 2008).

OVERVIEW

The ability to communicate is not unique to humans, but we have a sophistication that far surpasses all other species. It enables us to move beyond events taking place at this time. We can share knowledge, beliefs and opinions about happenings in the distant past and possibilities for the future; about events here or in some other place; about the particular or the general; the concrete or the abstract. It also enables us to make deep, meaningful and lasting contact with others through establishing, maintaining and terminating relationships (Parks, 2006).

Despite its significance, communication is a notoriously difficult concept to define precisely. Nevertheless, a number of attributes are readily recognised by many, if not all, of those who have deliberated on the topic. Interpersonal communication can be thought of as a process that is transactional, purposeful, multidimensional, irreversible and (possibly) inevitable. Skilled interpersonal involvement can be accounted for accordingly in terms of notions of personal-situation context, goals, mediating processes, responses, feedback and perception.

All communication is context bound. We can think of spatial, temporal, relational and sometimes organisational frameworks within which it is embedded. The personal characteristics of the participants together with features of the shared situation act to shape the interaction that transpires and both may be influenced, to some extent, in consequence. Likewise, goals pursued are determined by personal and situational factors. Plans and strategies to accomplish these derive from mediating processes and resulting tactics are enacted in manifested responses. A central premise of the model outlined is that, in interactive arrangements, participants are at one and the same time, in what they say and do, providing each other with information of relevance to decisions about the extent of goal attainment. Without such feedback, skilled interaction would be impossible but it can only be acted upon if it is perceived. In this way, personal perception, although inherently subjective, plays a pivotal role in interpersonal transactions.

Throughout the remaining chapters of this book, the central features of each skill area under focus will be examined in terms of relevant aspects of goals, mediating factors, response repertoires, feedback, perception and central aspects of the person–situation context.

Chapter 3

Communicating without words: skilled nonverbal behaviour

INTRODUCTION

THE ACT OF COMMUNICATING usually conjures up images of what people variously say, text or email one other: that is, of the content exchanged in the delivery of messages. But communication is a more inclusive process. Studies of how much the average person talks per day show that the large majority of interaction time is not taken up by speech but by nonverbal communication (NVC). As such, relating interpersonally demands the ability to display skilled nonverbal behaviour and to be sensitive to the body language of others. This chapter is, accordingly, concerned with those forms and functions of face-to-face interaction that do not rely primarily upon the content of what we say. Rather, the focus is upon how we communicate through, for example, a glance, gesture, postural shift or facial expression. The look on our faces, the direction and duration of our eye gaze, the nature of our gestures, the posture we adopt and so forth can often be more telling than the accompanying words. Interestingly, from an early age most of us are taught to 'watch what we say', and so develop a high level of awareness and control over our message content. By contrast, we are not taught to 'watch' our body language, and so we are often unaware of how we are behaving nonverbally during interactions with others. Yet there is evidence that our patterns of nonverbal behaviour remain more consistent over time than our verbal behaviour (Weisbuch *et al.*, 2010).

At the same time, distinguishing between verbal and nonverbal communication is not as conceptually straightforward as it might at first seem. Neither is it useful to think of the two as being operationally discrete (Jones and LeBaron, 2002), and particularly when it comes to hand/arm gestures (Beattie, 2004). While some theorists support the conceptualisation of nonverbal behaviour as skill (e.g. Friedman, 1979), others have argued that it is not a discrete skilled area. Thus, Riggio (1992: 6) pointed out that while 'the communication skill framework separates skills in verbal and nonverbal communication, in reality, verbal and nonverbal skills are complexly intertwined'. However, nonverbal behaviour is undoubtedly a distinct form of communication which can be utilised alone or as part of other skills. For the most part, in our everyday social contact, verbal and nonverbal codes are indeed intermeshed, each to varying degrees defining and qualifying the other in the overall process of conveying meaning (Sidnell, 2006; DeVito, 2008a).

Fascination with nonverbal aspects of social intercourse can be traced back to scholars such as Aristotle, Cicero and Quintilian in the West and Confucius in the East. In classical and medieval times, forms of specific gesture were identified in the teaching of rhetoric along with their planned effects on audiences (Gordon *et al.*, 2006). The concerted attention by social scientists to nonverbal matters has been shown to be much more recent, having a starting point in the 1960s (Knapp, 2006). This followed a long period during which the topic was deprecated as inconsequential, and those interested in it as academically suspect. For example, Aldous Huxley (1954: 77) described nonverbal education as a subject which was 'for academic and ecclesiastical purposes, non-existent and may be safely ignored altogether or left, with a patronising smile, to those whom the Pharisees of verbal orthodoxy call cranks, quacks, charlatans and unqualified amateurs'. Such milestones in the evolution of the subject as Charles Darwin's *The Expression of Emotion in Man and Animals* (Darwin, 1872/1955) only began to receive serious social scientific recognition in the past few decades (Ekman and Keltner, 1997).

But developments since then have been immense. Growth of interest has burgeoned, leading to significant theoretical, conceptual and empirical advances in the field as witnessed by countless publications of books, book chapters and journal articles. What was once described by Burgoon (1980: 179) as the 'foundling child of the social sciences – disdained, neglected, even nameless' is now a well-established member of the family, and indeed has outgrown it. The multifaceted study of nonverbal communication currently draws inspiration from disciplines such as neurophysiology which lie well beyond the established boundaries of the social sciences. Thus, Segerstrale and Molnar (1997) identified NVC as one of the foremost sites of a rapprochement between biology and social science, with respective researchers investigating such fundamental issues as the extent to which nonverbal behaviour is culturally prescribed or naturally determined. Indeed, a bio-evolutionary paradigm, which attempts to explain aspects of nonverbal behaviour in terms of Darwinian concepts of heritability and survival value, has generated much interest amongst those theorising in the area (Floyd, 2006).

VERBAL AND NONVERBAL COMMUNICATION

At first sight, crafting a sharp definition of 'nonverbal' might seem like an easy task, but things are less than simple. Although the division between verbal and nonverbal communication defies any sharp delineation, NVC is often thought of broadly as 'communication without words' (DeVito, 2005: 105). In a piece of early but still relevant work, Laver and Hutcheson (1972) distinguished between verbal and nonverbal, and vocal and nonvocal communication. As shown below, vocal behaviour refers to all aspects of speech, including content and accompanying expressions such as tone of voice, rate of speech and accent. Nonvocal behaviour, by contrast, refers to all other bodily activities that serve a communicative purpose, such as facial expressions, gestures and movements. These are often referred to as body language. Verbal communication, on the other hand, refers to the content of what is said – the actual words and language used, while nonverbal behaviour refers to all vocal and nonvocal behaviour that is not verbal in the sense defined above (Box 3.1).

This system seems therefore to insert a sharp and clearly recognisable division between the verbal and the nonverbal, until it is realised that verbal communication has a nonvocal element. It encompasses types of gestural communication such as formal sign language that one may have expected to find listed as nonverbal. Correspondingly, and just as counter-intuitively, 'subtle aspects of speech frequently have been included in discussions of nonverbal phenomena' (Mehrabian, 2007: 1). Framing precise definitions based upon hard and fast distinctions between verbal and nonverbal communication, therefore, presents difficulties. Instead, some have teased the two forms apart by pointing up broad differences (Richmond and McCroskey, 2000; Andersen, 2008). As such, and by comparison with the nonverbal, verbal messages:

- rely much more heavily upon symbols (i.e. words) as part of an arbitrary code
- tend to be discretely packaged in separate words (i.e. in digital form) rather than represented in continuous behaviour (i.e. in analogue form) as when gazing or holding a certain posture
- make use of the vocal/aural channel of communication (at least in face-to-face interaction)
- for the most part carry meaning explicitly rather than implicitly
- typically address cognitive/propositional rather than emotional/relational matters
- are processed primarily by different hemispheric regions of the brain.

Remland (2006) further noted that verbal interchanges must take place sequentially (i.e. participants must take turns) but interactors can communicate simultaneously using a nonverbal code.

In this chapter, therefore, the focus is upon communication by, for instance, tone

---

Box 3.1 Verbal and vocal communication

	Verbal communication	**Nonverbal communication**
Vocal	Content of talk.	Intonation, pitch, volume, accent, rate of speech, etc.
Nonvocal	Sign language, writing, etc.	Body language (gestures, posture, facial expressions, gaze, etc.).

of voice, volume of speech and intonation. In addition to these nonverbal aspects of speech, information is transmitted and received through a whole range of body movements such as posture adopted. When seated is the posture stiff, upright and symmetrical suggesting tension or anxiety, or is the person sprawled out in the chair suggesting a feeling of relaxation or familiarity? Faces too play an important role in social encounters by at times giving expression to our inner thoughts, such as showing delight when presented with an unexpected gift or displaying sadness when told about the death of a friend. A smile can also suggest approachability and availability for interaction.

Before we open our mouths to speak, our physical appearance conveys a great deal of information about our age, sex, occupation, status (if a certain uniform is worn) and personality. For someone with the unnerving perceptual acuity of a Sherlock Holmes in matters of social observation, such cues may become the veritable words of biography; Arthur Conan Doyle (2001: 20) placed the following words in the mouth of his great sleuth: 'By a man's finger-nails, by his coat-sleeve, by his boot, by his trouser-knees, by the callosities of his forefinger and thumb, by his expression, by his shirt-cuffs – by each of these things a man's calling is plainly revealed.' As a manifestation of a physical-attractiveness stereotype, the powerful effects of appearance on favourable judgements of such attributes as intelligence, warmth, friendliness and social confidence are well documented (Myers, 2008).

Not only are we concerned with the appearance and behaviour of the people involved in communication, but in addition, environmental factors such as architecture, furniture, decoration, colour and texture can provide insight into the nature of those inhabiting that space, and in turn shape interpersonal contact. These examples give some idea of the categories to which nonverbal behaviour attends. A more comprehensive range will be presented later in the chapter.

THE IMPORTANCE OF NONVERBAL COMMUNICATION

There is a reduced prospect of successful face-to-face interaction in situations where interactors have little appreciation of their own NVC, or a lack of sensitivity to the other person's body language. This is as applicable to work as it is to everyday social situations. Hamilton (2008: 127) asserted that 'The impact of nonverbal communication on your success in business cannot be overemphasized'. The role of NVC has been acknowledged, inter alia, in management (Hargie *et al.*, 2004), education (McCroskey, *et al.*, 2006), nursing (Dickson and McCartan, 2005), law (Brodsky *et al.*, 1999), pharmacy (Berger, 2005) and medicine (Robinson, 2006a). In relation to the latter, for example, a study by Rosenblum *et al.* (1994) found that the academic grades assigned to medical students by their clinical supervisors were predictable from ratings of their nonverbal behaviour while interacting with patients.

Relative contribution of NVC and verbal communication

Difficulties in sharply separating the verbal from the nonverbal have already been noted. Attempting to treat each as distinct and independent with a view to making differential judgements about relative value is not particularly fruitful. Nevertheless, the verbal medium has often been set as a benchmark for assessing the significance of the nonverbal. Consider a situation where a person is saying something but conveying an altogether different message through NVC. Which holds sway? What are the relative contributions of the two to the overall message received? In early research, still frequently cited, it was estimated that overall communication was made up of body language (55 per cent), paralanguage (the nonverbal aspects of speech) (38 per cent) and the verbal content (7 per cent) (Mehrabian, 1972). It may come as something of a surprise to learn that *what* we say may contribute a mere 7 per cent to the overall message received. These proportions, however, should not be regarded as absolute and seriously underrepresent the contribution of verbal communication in circumstances where information from all three channels is largely congruent. Guerrero and Floyd (2006) offered a more modest estimate of 60 to 65 per cent of meaning carried nonverbally during social exchanges. While likewise questioning the veracity of the Mehrabian figures, a review by Burgoon *et al.* (1996) nevertheless still identified a general trend favouring the primacy of meaning carried nonverbally, with a particular reliance upon visual cues. But qualifying conditions apply. The finding holds more for adults in situations of message incongruity and where the message has to do with emotional, relational or impression-forming outcomes. It should also be emphasised, of course, that in any case NVC does not have to be shown to be more important than the verbal in order to be significant.

Trustworthiness and NVC

As mentioned earlier, we tend to be less aware of the nonverbal accompaniment to much of what we say than we are of the actual words spoken. While we often carefully monitor what is said to achieve the desired effect, how we are saying it may escape censor such that the reality of the situation is 'leaked' despite our best efforts. In this way, NVC can be thought of as a more 'truthful' form of communication through the insights that it affords into what may lie behind the verbal message. This is the 'window on the soul' assumption. It is only true to a point. Even in the case of facial expressions, it would be wrong to assume a simple, direct and unerring cause–effect relationship with underlying emotional states. Certain facial displays are regulated in keeping with the social context, making them more or less likely to be exhibited (Chovil, 1997). Social intentions and motives can be at the root of such behaviour rather than these expressions being the simple, reflexive manifestation of emotional states (Izard, 1997; Scherer and Grandjean, 2007).

Skilled interactors can learn to control what their bodies say, as well as the messages sent in words. The work of 'spin doctors' with politicians and other influential people in the public eye does not stop merely at verbal manicure. Appropriate facial expressions, looks, gestures and tone of voice are all included in the 'branded' end product. Part of the 'repackaging' of the former UK Prime Minster Mrs Thatcher, as she became one of the most formidable politicians of her generation, included the use of a lower vocal register (Yeates and Wakefield, 2004). Formerly, her rather high-pitched voice had appeared to create an unfavourable impression of feminine hysteria rather than the assured gravitas of a to-be-respected, international statesperson.

Phylogeny and NVC

Phylogeny concerns the evolution of a species. Taking an evolutionary view of our origins, NVC is undoubtedly an earlier, more primitive form of communication than language. According to Leakey (1994), particularly telling evolutionary changes took place in the emergence of modern humankind during a period stretching between from half a million to some 35,000 years ago. The outcome was people with similar appearances and abilities to those we see around us today. The precise point at which language emerged and whether it developed rapidly or more slowly over a period extending beyond half a million years ago is a matter for debate. However, its emergence seems to have been associated with an increase in brain size, advances in toolmaking skills, the first appearance of art and living in extended social collectives. A complex and sophisticated system of communication enabled individuals to become part of larger groups and to successfully plan and execute collaborative projects such as hunting. Indeed, this ability has been mooted as one reason behind the eventual displacement of Neanderthal in Europe by Homo sapiens, around about 30,000 years ago (Pitts and Roberts, 1997).

Earlier hominid species would, of course, have had basic ways of making themselves known. Some suggest that this was most likely in the form of body movements together with a range of vocalisations similar perhaps to those of the present-day non-human primates (Papousek *et al.*, 2008). Lieberman (1998: 84–85) proposed that 'the earliest form of protolanguage used manual gestures, facial expressions (grin, lip protrusion, etc.) and posture – a sort of body language'. As such, it would be essentially restricted to expressing emotional states such as anger or fear, and perhaps fixing relational bonds as in grooming. Here, therefore, we have NVC enabling our early ancestors to regulate social life in small groups, albeit in less sophisticated ways than that made possible by the advent of modern language.

Ontogeny and NVC

Ontogeny refers to the development of the individual, and here again we find NVC, especially through visual, tactile and vocal cues, pre-dating language as a rudimentary means of making contact with others. As noted by Feldman and Tyler (2006: 182), 'as early as the first few days of life, infants appear to possess some instinctive capacity for nonverbal communication'. They are particularly attuned to observed facial expressions even within hours of birth and react differently to a stimulus resembling a face. Important early interaction between mother and child takes place not only through touch but also synchronised exchanges of patterns of gaze and vocalisation. Increased levels of gaze between mother and child are associated with heightened vocal activity (Giles and Le Poire, 2006). In addition to synchronising early vocal exchanges with carers in ways that mimic conversational turn-taking, infants a few months old display facial expressions that closely resemble those of adults in conveying emotions such as joy, surprise and interest, but especially pain (Oster *et al.*, 1992). Once again we rely upon NVC when language is unavailable, this time in the evolution of the individual rather than the species.

Substance of nonverbal messages

Language is particularly suited to conveying ideas and information about our environment, together with our understandings and intentions in respect of it. Through the use of language we have succeeded in such spectacular feats of joint endeavour as building the pyramids and putting a man on the moon. Only through language can we access and meaningfully discuss the philosophy of Wittgenstein, plays of Shakespeare, songs of the Beatles, poetry of Keats or novels of Tolstoy. Nonverbal behaviour, in contrast, tends to convey information of a different type (although not exclusively so), to do with such matters as feelings and our attitudes towards those whom we meet (Adler and Elmhorst, 2008). Included are impression management and the projection of personal and social identity. It is largely through drawing upon such raw material that interpersonal relationships are built, sustained and sometimes terminated. These relationships, in turn, are the bedrock of institutions such as marriage, family and work, which go to make up society.

Universality of NVC

We can often make ourselves known in a rudimentary way through signs and gestures when communicating with people from differing cultural backgrounds who do not share a common language. NVC therefore has a greater universality than language. This is particularly so when it comes to the expression of primary emotions such as fear or anger (Andersen, 2008). But it would be misguided to assume that all NVC is similar. Failure to appreciate the nonverbal nuances of cultural diversity can lead to miscommunication and interaction breakdown (Matsumoto, 2006), which is just as real as failure to use the proper words. Axtell (1991) identified a range of examples of the myriad ways in which body language and gestures are used in dramatically different forms as we move from culture to culture. For instance, while in most of Europe and North America shaking the head signals refusal and disagreement, in parts of India it indicates the opposite. There nodding the head means 'no'. However, in Japan nodding the head may mean neither agreement nor disagreement but merely ongoing attention to the speaker. A common mistake made by business people travelling abroad, and often to their cost, is to assume that those whom they meet will more or less observe the same social conventions with which they are accustomed (Hamilton, 2008).

PURPOSES OF NONVERBAL COMMUNICATION

Just why we should make use of NVC is an intriguing question. We are the only species with this marvellously abstract and sophisticated means of communicating that we call language. Other species display various forms of nonverbal behaviour. Through changes in, for example, real or apparent size, posture and movement, odour and skin colour, and in myriad grunts, screams and roars, they convey information about bodily and emotional states, signal mating readiness, claim social status and announce territorial ownership. But language is different. It frees us from the here and now, from the physical and actual. Without it we would find it difficult or impossible to refer to, never mind take into account, abstract concepts such as love, loyalty or honour; happenings at this point in time in another place; happenings in the past; happenings in the future; things that have never happened and probably never will (including the whole literary genre of fiction).

The bulk of this chapter will be devoted to mapping different forms of nonverbal behaviour. Before doing so, however, it is necessary to address the question as to why we make use of NVC. In answering the question, some of the points raised in the previous section will be extended by examining the commonly identified purposes of NVC (Richmond and McCroskey, 2000; Burgoon *et al.*, 2010; Knapp and Hall, 2010). These are summarised in Box 3.2.

Replacing verbal communication

Some NVC, especially in the form of gestures, is used as a direct substitute for words under circumstances where speech is either not feasible or desirable. It may be that participants have neither hearing nor speech, relying entirely on the use of hand, arm or mouth movements as part of recognised signing systems allowing communication to take place. Sometimes, on the other hand, individuals are temporarily denied a suitable channel to facilitate speech, and so resort to some form of gesture-based contact (e.g. divers under water). In other situations, excessive ambient noise may make talking impossible. Alternatively, interactors may find themselves too far apart to have a normal conversation, necessitating some alternative such as semaphore or the tic-tac system of signalling used by racecourse bookmakers. Secrecy may be a further reason for not wishing to talk publicly. In different sports, team members can be seen using nonverbal cues to signal the proposed play at different stages of the game.

Box 3.2 Purposes of nonverbal communication (NVC)

NVC is used to achieve a number of interpersonal goals, including:

1 *to replace verbal communication* in situations where it may be impossible or inappropriate to talk
2 *to complement verbal communication*, thereby enhancing the overall message
3 *to modify the spoken word*
4 *to contradict*, either intentionally or unintentionally, what is said
5 *to regulate conversation* by helping to mark speech turns
6 *to express emotions and interpersonal attitudes*
7 *to negotiate relationships* in respect of, for instance, dominance, control and liking
8 *to convey personal and social identity* through such features as dress and adornments
9 *to contextualise interaction* by creating a particular social setting.

Complementing the spoken word

Nonverbal behaviour is often used alongside what is said in a way that is consistent with it. In so doing, the verbal message may be clarified, extended or enhanced. Some material, such as giving elaborate directions or describing an irregular shape, can be difficult to get across in words alone. In order to facilitate the overall message an imaginary map or outline is sometimes drawn in the air while describing the route or object. These gestures are known as illustrators (Friesen *et al.*, 1980) and they will be examined later in the chapter when discussing gestures. These accompanying movements actually facilitate speech where it is difficult to describe aspects of space and shape in purely verbal terms. Such gesticulations have been found to be less prevalent when both conversationalists are familiar with an object referred to than when only one is (Gerwing and Bavelas, 2004). They may also assist in the tasks of learning and remembering (Goldin-Meadow, 1997).

Not only has gesturing been found to aid the receiver's comprehension of the message, but it also enhances the speaker's levels of fluency and retrieval of information in delivering it (Goldin-Meadow and Wagner, 2005; Harrigan, 2005). Nonverbal cues can also complement language in other ways involving propositional and emotional messages. Expressions of sympathy are much more convincing when the sympathiser's overall demeanour mirrors what is said.

Modifying talk

The verbally delivered message can be either nonverbally accentuated or attenuated. This is a further example of accompanying nonverbal cues serving to qualify what is said. Such behaviour can sometimes help to emphasise parts of the verbal messages. When a speaker puts more stress on certain words than others, uses pauses between words to convey gravity or interest, varies the tone and speed of utterances, the importance of certain words or phrases is underlined in the mind of the listener. In a sense it is analogous to the writer who puts words in italics or underlines them. In addition, body movements are frequently used to add more weight to the verbal message. Take, for example, the mother who in wanting to ensure that her son is listening closely and taking her seriously, swings him round to face her closely, puts both arms on his shoulders and looks at him straight in the eyes before beginning to speak. Alternatively, a benign smile may temper the overall message received in the context of a stern parental rebuke. All are examples of NVC working to deliver a more or less extreme message.

Contradicting the spoken word

There are occasions where a person says one thing but conveys an incongruous message nonverbally: where the two modes are at odds. This may or may not be done intentionally. Forms of discourse ranging from sarcasm to humour often rely upon something being said 'in a particular way'. The words suggest one interpretation but tone of voice and body language something different. The NVC, as it were, provides a frame for interpreting what was said. Such subtlety may, however, be missed by children who have been found, when compared with adults, to place a more negative interpretation on a critical comment by an adult said with a smile (Knapp and Hall, 2010). According to Leathers (1979), when exposed to contradictory verbal and nonverbal signals we follow a three-step sequence. We typically become confused and uncertain, then we look for extra information to resolve the discrepancy and finally, if unsuccessful, we react negatively with displeasure or withdrawal.

Another aspect here is that when it is deemed that the discrepancy is unintentional, it may be construed as an attempt to deceive. Lying is a common if unpalatable feature of much of everyday discourse (Ford, 2006). It is often sparked by such self-serving motives as achieving goals, gaining influence and creating favourable impressions, but we can also resort to lying in the interests of others, in order to protect or support them (Ennis *et al.*, 2008). Despite popular belief, there is no one telling cue or pattern of cues that directly, uniquely and unambiguously signals deception (DePaulo *et al.*, 2003). While there is some research to indicate that in high-stake contexts where people have a lot to lose (such as during interrogation) they tend to avoid eye contact and speak with a higher pitched voice when lying (Gray, 2008), other studies have shown no difference between liars and truth-tellers in patterns of eye gaze (Burgoon and Levine, 2010). The reality is that 'there is nothing like Pinocchio's nose' to enable us to readily identify deception (Vrij *et al.*, 2000: 241). Indeed, when consistencies have been found between nonverbal cues and lying, those cues have been interpreted as due to the underlying processes that accompany deception and attempts at control (such as physiological arousal, negative affect, cognitive demand), rather than by the deceit itself (Burgoon, 2005).

As such, lying can manifest itself in different ways including increased autonomic arousal suggesting heightened stress (e.g. raised heart rate and sweating); conspicuous attempts to control performance (e.g. appearing 'wooden' or having a slow deliberate delivery); displaying emotion which may either be caused by the deception (e.g. signs of anxiety and guilt) or the basis of it (e.g. pretending to be happy when sad); and increased cognitive processing of information (e.g. more concentrated thinking revealed in gaze avoidance). There is some research, albeit based upon replies to forced-choice questions on computer, to suggest that when people lie their responses are longer than when they are being truthful (Gregg, 2007). The hypothesis here is that while truth-telling involves only the processing of true beliefs, deception necessitates two further processes – the decision to lie and the composition of the fabrication, and these two additional processes result in longer response times.

However, the extent to which dissembling triggers these processes depends upon such factors as the complexity of the deceit and the risks involved in being caught out. Furthermore, the processes just mentioned are not unique to deception and can emerge during interaction for other reasons. Again, some people may be less fazed or challenged than others at having to dissemble (Rogers, 2008). Machiavellian types are extremely proficient at most forms of nonverbal deception and tend, for instance, not to avoid gaze when being untruthful (Anderson *et al.*, 1999). Small wonder that our success is limited when it comes to relying upon nonverbal behaviour to detect deceit (Vrij, 2006). While Strömwall and Granhag (2007) found that adults could detect lying in children with a 62.5 per cent success rate, inconsistencies and contradictions in their statements (i.e. verbal cues) were the most telling giveaways. Verbal aspects of deception will be further discussed in Chapter 9.

It is important to reiterate, though, that when receiving mixed messages, where there is inconsistency between the verbal and the nonverbal channels, the latter normally holds sway. This is in keeping with the assumption that NVC is a more 'truthful' channel. In some early studies reviewed by Remland (2009), vocal and facial cues, in particular, were relied upon heavily in forming judgements in such mixed message situations.

Regulating conversations

How do we manage to conduct conversations so that we don't keep interrupting each other but at the same time there are no awkward silences between speech turns? The highly coordinated nature of interaction is an inescapable feature of the process (Cappella and Schreiber, 2006). Detailed analyses have revealed some of the strategies used to prevent over-talk, handle it when it occurs, and generally manage turn-taking (Schegloff, 2000). NVC is an important part of this process. Conversationalists are able to anticipate when they will have an opportunity to take the floor. Duncan and Fiske (1977) identified a number of nonverbal indices that offer a speaking turn to the other person. These include a rise or fall in pitch at the end of a clause, a drop in voice volume, termination of hand gestures and change in gaze pattern. In addition, they found that if a speaker persisted with a gesticulation even when not actually talking at that point, it essentially eliminated attempts by the listener to take over the turn.

Hence, someone (but depending on their culture) coming to the end of a speech turn will typically introduce a downward vocal inflection (unless they have just asked a question), stop gesticulating and look at their partner (Argyle, 1994). This information can, of course, be made use of in situations where one is keen not to hand over the floor. Since high status and interpersonal influence are usually positively correlated with extent of verbal contribution, those with higher power are less likely to employ turn-yielding cues.

Nonverbal cues have also been implicated in the broader work of organising the interactive episode. In a detailed analysis of doctor–patient consultations in a general practice setting, Robinson (1998) revealed how gaze and shifts in body orientation were used to mark sequences of engagement with and disengagement from particular tasks, in preparation for patients' disclosure of the complaint that brought them along.

Expressing emotions and interpersonal attitudes

Expressing emotion is tightly bound up with managing relationships (Graham *et al.*, 2008). NVC is a crucial source of information on how we feel, and how we feel about others. Furthermore, relating successfully depends upon competence in both encoding (sending) and decoding (interpreting) NVC. In relation to the latter point, Bryon *et al.* (2007) found that salespersons who were better at recognising emotion from nonverbal cues sold more and recorded higher average annual salary increases. However, the extent to which affective information is managed intentionally and with awareness can vary (Bull, 2002). Some emotional indices, such as pupil dilation in response to heightened arousal or sweating when anxious, are largely outside our control (Collett, 2003). Others suggesting anger or sadness are more manageable. Facial expressions represent an important emotional signalling system, although body movements and gestures are also implicated. Six basic emotional states that can be reliably read from facial patterns are sadness, anger, disgust, fear, surprise and happiness (Ekman and Friesen, 2003). Contempt may be a possible seventh. A substantial body of evidence, following the earlier work of Charles Darwin, claimed that these are reasonably universal across cultures (Ekman and O'Sullivan, 1991). Nevertheless, questions have been raised over the extent to which facial expressions can be thought of as the direct products of underlying biologically determined affective states, unaffected by social and cultural influences in their expression, perception and interpretation (Scherer and Grandjean, 2007). An alternative way of viewing them is as a means of signalling behavioural intent. This issue will be returned to later, in the section on facial expressions.

We also reveal attitudes about others in our nonverbal behaviour towards them. For example, direct displays of positive affect have been shown to be communicated through smiles, eye contact, facial expressiveness, touch, posture and voice (Guerrero and Floyd, 2006).

Negotiating relationships

As shown in Chapter 2, communication is a multifaceted activity. Two people discussing an issue are doing other interpersonal things at the same time, both in what they say and how they say it. One of these 'other things' that can become the topic of conversation, but seldom does outside of intimate partnerships or problematic encounters (e.g. a conflict about role responsibilities at work), is the nature of the relationship itself. Aspects of social power, dominance and affiliation are conveyed through nonverbal channels. Amount of talk (talk time), loudness of speech, seating location, posture, touch, gestures and proximity are instrumental in conveying who is controlling the situation as the dominant party in an interaction (Collett, 2003; Burgoon and Dunbar, 2006). In all these ways actions can speak louder than words.

Through largely nonverbal means, people establish, sustain, strengthen or indeed terminate a relational position. This can be done on an ongoing basis, as adjustments are made to ensure that levels of involvement are acceptable. *Immediacy* or psychological closeness is a feature of interaction that is regulated in part nonverbally, and indeed has been singled out as arguably the most important function of NVC (Andersen and Andersen, 2005). Immediacy has to do with warmth, depth of involvement or degree of intensity characterising an encounter. It is expressed through a range of indices including eye contact, interpersonal distance, smiling and touch, and must be appropriate to the encounter. Violating expectations in respect of these, for example by coming too close, gazing too much, leaning too far forward or orienting too directly, can lead to discomfort on the part of the recipient, compensatory shifts by that person and negative evaluations of the violator (Burgoon, 1995; Houser, 2005).

These compensatory behavioural adjustments re-establish the status quo, thereby maintaining a level of involvement that is both predictable and comfortable. More generally, and according to *communication accommodation theory* (e.g. Giles and Ogay, 2007), interlocutors convey their attitudes about one another and indicate their relational aspirations by the extent to which they tailor aspects of their communicative performance to make these more compatible with those of the other. They may adjust their initial discrepant speech rate, for instance, to find a balanced compromise or alternatively accentuate difference if they find they have little desire to promote commonality, reduce social distance or seek approval. When individuals are actively managing personal relationships it would often be too disturbing to state openly that the other was not liked or thought to be inferior. Nonverbal cues can be exchanged about these states but without the message ever being made explicit. In addition, initial relationships can change over time so that an original dominant–submissive relationship can become more egalitarian. Change would not come about as readily if it had been explicitly stated at the beginning how each felt towards the other.

Conveying personal and social identity

In a complex of ways involving habitat, dress, deportment, accent, etc., we send messages about ourselves including the groups and social categories to which we belong. In so doing we also implicitly suggest how we would like to be perceived, received and related to. This is a further role for NVC (Afifi, 2006). While not all nonverbal behaviour is strategically deployed in this quest, among those cues that are, those promoting judgements of physical attractiveness, warmth and pleasantness, likability, credibility and power are particularly salient. In business organisations with steep hierarchical structures of authority, projecting suitable images of status forms an inevitable part of dealing with others both within and outwith the company. Features such as size of office and opulence of furnishings take on special significance in this process. Organisations often have standards stipulating the minimum size and type of office for employees at a particular level in the management pecking order.

Contextualising interaction

Finally, in the ways that people interact and communicate they create social situations. Through chosen dress code, arrangement of office space and so on, opportunities are created for a meeting to become a very formal interview or a more casual chit-chat. Appropriate forms of conduct will be correspondingly suggested. All social settings, from the familiar such as Sunday lunch, staff meeting or a visit to the dentist, to the more elaborate such as a graduation ceremony or a funeral, carry with them acceptable codes of conduct. Someone who deviates from these common patterns of behaviour and so upsets the social order may be called upon either to apologise or offer an excuse or explanation for their wayward behaviour.

These various purposes of NVC do not always occur independently, nor are they separately served by specific behavioural cues. It is quite possible for several to be exercised simultaneously. The remainder of this chapter examines more closely the various forms that nonverbal behaviour can take. These are presented in Box 3.3.

HAPTICS

Touch is a primitive form of communication in respect of both evolutionary (phylogenic) and personal (ontogenic) development. It is one of the earliest and most basic forms of stimulation that we experience, even when still in the womb. It is widely recognised that physical contact is crucial to the psychological and biological well-being of infants and to their subsequent social and intellectual development (Richmond and McCroskey, 2000). Benefits of massage in accelerating growth and weight gain among premature babies have been reported (Adler, 1993). The profound effects of tactile stimulation extend throughout life (Jones, 2005). Apart from its specialised therapeutic use ('the healing touch') in a health context, touch has been found to affect heart rate, blood pressure and nutritional intake of patients. It can also have a comforting or calming effect (Routasalo, 1999). In more specific circumstances a number of beneficial outcomes have been documented in research studies. In situations where it is used appropriately, the person touching is more likely:

- to be more positively evaluated (Erceau and Guéguen, 2007)
- to have others comply with requests (Willis and Hamm, 1980)
- to receive preferential treatment (Guéguen and Fisher-Lokou, 2003)
- to have money returned (Kleinke, 1977)
- to receive tips from customers when waiting at table (Ebesu-Hubbard *et al.*, 2003).

But tactile contact is not always well received. *Touch avoidance* is a general predisposition distinguishing those who like this form of contact and engage in it from others who devalue and largely shun tactile communication (Andersen, 2005). That apart, physical contact can be an extremely ambiguous act frequently suffused with

---

Box 3.3 Types of nonverbal communication (NVC)

NVC can take the following forms:

- *haptics* – communication through physical touch
- *kinesics* – communication through body movement (e.g. gestures, head nods, posture, eye contact, facial expression)
- *proxemics* – messages conveyed through the perception and use of personal and social space (e.g. interpersonal distance, territoriality)
- *physical characteristics* – information revealed through body shape, size and adornments
- *environmental factors* – messages carried by features of the social surroundings such as furniture, décor and lighting
- *vocalics* – communication by means of the nonverbal elements of speech (e.g. voice pitch, resonance and so on).

---

sexual possibilities and the potential for violence. Probably for this reason it is strictly rule bound and taboo ridden. One cannot go touching anyone, anywhere, at any time, in any place – at least not without getting into trouble. In an early and frequently cited study, students reported that they were touched most often on the hands and arms, although who was doing the touching also made a difference (Jourard, 1966).

Touching is used to achieve a number of goals relating to both the context in which it occurs and the relationship of the interactors. Heslin and Alper (1983) identified five such purposes:

- *Functional/professional.* A number of professionals touch people in the normal course of their work: nurses, dentists, doctors, opticians, chiropodists, airport security staff and hairdressers, to name but a few. A common distinction here is between *instrumental* and *expressive* touch (Tutton, 1991; Dickson *et al.*, 1997). The former happens in the normal course of carrying out a task and does not carry any further connotations (e.g. a nurse taking a patient's pulse). Expressive touching, on the other hand, conveys interpersonal messages to do with emotion, attitude or association (e.g. a nurse holding a child's hand during an uncomfortable procedure conducted by a doctor).
- *Social/polite.* We have different culturally prescribed forms of contact used as part of the greeting ritual. They serve to acknowledge the other and ascribe to that person a social involvement. In Western culture a handshake is typically used in formal situations. In other cultures kissing, embracing or nose rubbing may be more common. Being in direct, ongoing contact may also signal to others that these two are together: that they form a pair (or couple). Examples of these *tie signs* include linking arms and holding hands, which express a certain shared relational intimacy (Afifi and Johnson, 2005).
- *Friendship/warmth.* This includes contacts such as a friendly pat, or a comforting touch on the hand, aimed at establishing amicable relationships. It is a way of showing interest in others and positive feelings towards them. This can be very rewarding in terms of giving encouragement, expressing care and concern, and showing emotional support and understanding. It has been pointed out that in standard Western culture friends are unlikely to engage in much touching when alone, because it tends to be more associated with sexual motives (Richmond and McCroskey, 2000).
- *Love/intimacy.* In close relationships touching is a very profound way of conveying depth of feeling. This love of course may be that for a child, spouse or parent. Even with a partner, love can take on different guises from the passion of early romance to the enduring commitment of old age. Each set of circumstances will be marked quite differently through type and extent of physical contact. Again there may be close friendships that we could describe as intimate but not necessarily involving love, as such. Once more, touching is likely to be one of the features that sets these apart from mere acquaintances.
- *Sexual arousal.* The famous sex therapists Masters and Johnson (1970) claimed that sex is the ultimate form of human communication. Here we have touch being used in its most intense form involving parts of the body only accessible to certain others and typically when in private.

Several other types of contact, as identified by Jones (1999), can be added to the above list. They include touch:

- in the context of play (e.g. tickling)
- as an expression of negative feelings (e.g. hitting or slapping)
- as a way of managing interaction (e.g. placing a hand on someone's shoulder to get attention)
- to gain influence and control (e.g. touching someone lightly as we ask a favour)
- as a symbolic or ritualistic act (e.g. two heads of state shaking hands to symbolise accord between their nations)
- that is accidental (e.g. bumping into someone).

Various factors including culture, status, gender and age shape who touches whom, under what circumstances, how much and where (Knapp and Hall, 2010). Touch features much more extensively in social encounters in some parts of the world than in others (DiBiase and Gunnoe, 2004). So called *contact* cultures where touching is more prevalent include southern Europe, the Middle East and Central America, while among noncontact counterparts can be listed northern Europe, North America and Japan.

Issues of status also influence touching. Powerful individuals, when interacting with subordinates, tend to indulge in more non-reciprocated touch (Burgoon and Bacue, 2003). Those displaying such behaviour also attract higher ratings of power and dominance than the recipients of that contact (Major and Heslin, 1982). In a study by Hall (1996) of actual touching at academic meetings, while there was no evidence that high-status participants touched low-status participants with greater frequency than vice versa, differences did emerge in the type of contact initiated. High-status academics tended to touch arms and shoulders in what was judged to be a sign of affection. Low-status counterparts were more likely to shake hands, which was regarded as essentially a formal expression. Implications of power and control could also be the basis of some findings suggesting that female patients react more favourably than males to expressive touch by nurses (Dickson, 1999). That said, Andersen (2008) concluded from his review of the evidence that touch had actually more to do with conveying immediacy and intimacy than with status and dominance. Certainly touch was one of the principal components of the expression of immediacy reviewed by Guerrero (2005).

Males and females differ in how they communicate by tactile means, at least in Western societies. Generally men are less touch oriented and when they do make physical contact are more likely to engage in hand touching than non-hand touching (DiBiase and Gunnoe, 2004). This trend extends to professional interaction, with male nurses touching less and male patients being touched less (Routasalo, 1999). However, the social setting within which touch occurs is an important factor. Sporting contexts, for example, seem to be largely exempt from the normal trend downplaying male touch. Again, it should be noted that most of this research has focused on 'friendly or at least innocuous touches' (Hall, 2006: 206). We know a lot less about the uses of other forms of touch to do with, for instance, aggression.

Finally, haptic communication seems to change across the lifespan. Younger men (under 30 years) and those in dating relationships (rather than being married) have been found to touch more than females (Willis and Dodds, 1998). As noted in Chapter 2, marital status is also important in that unmarried men have more favourable reactions to touch than unmarried women, while for married males and females this pattern is reversed. In old age, there may be a blurring of functional and expressive forms of touch due to declining health with increased care needs. However, when hospitalised, there is evidence that older people receive the least amount of tactile contact; Hollinger and Buschmann (1993) showed that their perception of being touched, when it did occur, was found to be most positive when it:

- was appropriate to the situation
- did not impose a greater level of intimacy than desired
- was not condescending
- did not detract from their sense of independence and autonomy.

KINESICS

Kinesics, as the name suggests, addresses communication through bodily motion. When observing individuals or groups interacting one is often struck by the sheer dynamism of what goes on. Even if seated, arms and hands are typically busy; heads and perhaps bodies turning to follow the conversation; eyes darting from one to another in the group, lingering here and there, including some in the ongoing discourse, excluding others, monitoring reactions; and all the while facial expressions conveying continued interest, boredom or liking. The five main areas of kinesics to be focused upon in this section are gestures, head nods, posture, eye gaze and facial expressions.

Gestures

Here the focus is upon movements of hands and arms. These vary depending upon such factors as culture and situation. Italians are notorious users while British newscasters, it would seem, find little need for them at all. Different attempts have been made to classify behaviour of this type. Beattie (2004), drawing on earlier contributions by McNeil (1992), referred to three main classes of gesture directly linked to speech: *iconic* gestures are essentially pictorial and bear a physical resemblance to the concrete thing or act talked about; *metaphoric* gestures are similar but refer to ideas or other abstract entities; and *beats* are used to mark out the rhythm of speech. Alternatively, Ekman and Friesen (1969), in pioneering work, identified five main types: *emblems*, *illustrators*, *regulators*, *affect displays* and *adaptors*.

Emblems

Emblems are one of the few nonverbal cues that function, to all intents and purposes, like words. These would include the signs used by police officers to direct the flow of traffic, by those communicating with deaf people, and by producers of television programmes. While emblems have a direct verbal translation this can differ from culture to culture. Since some have obscene meanings in a specific context, one must be careful. The sign with the thumb touching the tip of the index finger to form a ring, palm facing out, that in the UK means exquisite, in France and Belgium means that the thing referred to is worthless. In Turkey and Malta the gesture is an obscene insult with the ring representing an orifice – invariably the anus. Further examples of emblems from around the world are well documented (e.g. Axtell, 1991; Hogg and Vaughn, 2008).

Illustrators

These accompany speech and are linked to it. Not only are they linked to speech but they also co-occur in a tightly synchronised manner (Bavelas and Chovil, 2006). On their own they make little sense but take their meaning from the conversational context. Such hand gestures, in a variety of forms, can be used to enhance and facilitate what is said. Providing emphasis is one example. When teachers are asking pupils to remember some important information, they may enumerate with their fingers the number of points to be remembered. This is borne out by research into teachers' use of nonverbal skills in the classroom where it was shown that hand gestures, gazing and mild facial expressions were the most commonly used nonverbal behaviours (Kadunc, 1991). It was also found that teachers' gestures most often comprised illustrators and least often emblems.

In addition, hand gestures can provide illustrations of the verbal content of a message. Lausberg *et al.* (2007) noted that *ideographic gestures*, as well as enunciating abstract concepts or ideas (e.g. cupped hands when explaining love), can be used to trace the pattern of thought as it unfolds. *Pantomimes* act out some occurrence, or imagined subject or circumstance. On the other hand, pointing to an object or place while referring to it involves *deictic gestures*. These can also be self-focused (*self-deictics*).

Regulators

These orchestrate conversation and ensure that turn taking is switched smoothly. As speakers finish a speech turn they will probably drop their hand as they bring a gesture to an end. Not to do so, despite the fact that they may have stopped speaking, is usually enough to signal that they still have something left to say and have not conceded the floor. *Baton gestures* (also referred to as *beats*) are a slightly different type used by the speaker, among other things, to mark out the beat of the delivery. They can be thought of as regulating an individual's contributions rather than the to-and-fro of exchange. It is as if the speaker is conducting the orchestra of his or her own voice with an invisible baton.

Affect displays

Hand movements also convey emotional states, although the face is a richer source of such information. Gestures can reveal emotional dispositions such as embarrassment (e.g. hand over the mouth); anger (e.g. white knuckles); aggression (e.g. fist clenching); shame (e.g. hands covering the eyes); nervousness (e.g. nail and finger biting); boredom (e.g. hair preening); and despair (e.g. hand wringing). Professionals should be sensitive to these hand signals, which, because of their often spontaneous nature, may reveal more about the client's feelings than words would permit.

Adaptors

Feldman *et al.* (1991) distinguished between gestures that are linked with speech (*illustrators*) and directed towards objects or events, and those which are more socially related. The latter involve four main types:

1   *object-adaptors* – fiddling with something (e.g. playing with a pen or paper cup)
2   *self-adaptors* – these are more self-focused, involving one part of the body such as a hand or arm coming into moving contact with another part (e.g. scratching or hand wringing)
3   *alter-adaptors* – gestures used in a defensive, self-protective manner (e.g. clasping hands or folding arms in front of chest)
4   *other-adaptors* – these are targeted towards another (e.g. picking lint off someone's clothing or a mother stroking a child).

The first two, in particular, act as a form of tension release and are characteristically performed unintentionally and with little awareness. These are thought to be the echoes of early childhood attempts to satisfy needs. One school of thought suggests that they are signs of anxiety or unease (Bernieri, 2005). They may also be associated with negative feelings towards self or others (Knapp and Hall, 2010). Alternatively, it has been found that self-adaptors can create impressions of honesty, genuineness and warmth (Harrigan, 2005).

Gestures aiding communication

Those who supplement their dialogue with good use of hand and arm movements usually arouse and maintain the attention of their listeners, indicate their interest and enthusiasm, and tend to make the interaction sequence a stimulating and enjoyable experience for all participants. Kendon (1984) focused on the various conditions under which individuals use the gestural expressive mode and concluded that the speaker divides the task of conveying meaning between words and gestures in such a way as to achieve either economy of expression or a particular effect on the listener. For instance, a gesture can be used as a device for completing a sentence that, if spoken, might prove embarrassing to the speaker. It can also be used as a means of telescoping what one wants to say, when the available time is shorter than one would like. Gestures can also be employed to clarify some potentially ambiguous word or as an additional component when the verbal account is inadequate to truly represent the information being shared. Feyereisen and Havard (1999) discovered that adults made greater use of representational gestures when responding to questions requiring them to draw upon mental images that were motor (e.g. 'Could you explain how to wrap a box in a paper for a present?') rather than visual (e.g. 'Could you describe the room in which you live most often?').

It has been found that receivers benefit from the use of gestures in aiding the clarity and comprehension of an explanation or description (Goldin-Meadow and Wagner, 2005). Evidence that accuracy of understanding can be increased when gesticulations complemented the spoken word was provided in three studies by Riseborough (1981). First, she showed that persons were better able to identify objects from descriptions accompanied by appropriate gestures than those without gestures. Second, she found that subjects could recall a story more accurately when accompanying gestural behaviours were employed. Third, when the sound channel was obstructed by white noise, illustrative gestures increased comprehension. But we often see speakers gesticulate, such as when on the telephone, even when they cannot be seen by listeners and therefore under circumstances where gesticulations can have no evident communicative advantage for the audience. It has been found that doing so can benefit *speakers* in facilitating speech and cognition (Stevanoni and Salmon, 2005).

Head nods

Head movements are a particular form of gesture and as such can replace or be associated with talk. Head nodding and shaking are a ubiquitous feature of the interactive process and are related to the role of speaker and listener in quite involved ways (McClave, 2000). In relation to the listener's role, interest shown towards a speaker can be communicated by a tilting of the head to one side. Positive associations have also been found between ratings of physicians' head nodding when interacting with patients and impressions of their levels of rapport (Robinson, 2006a). Conversely, in work with marriage partners in conflict, Feeney *et al.* (1999) discovered that periods of withdrawal from discussion of issues that primarily exercised their partners were marked by the head being down. Husbands also turned the head away during these phases. In keeping with this finding, head nodding is an important 'back-channel' signal from the listener indicating that the speaker should continue talking.

As mentioned earlier, NVC serves to regulate turn taking during conversation. Based upon fine-grained analysis of doctor–patient interaction, Robinson (2006a) reported that physicians tended to head nod at junctures where it seemed that patients were completing or could potentially complete their speech turn. Examining the role of the speaker, Duncan and Fiske (1977) found that two cues, head turning away from the other person and beginning to gesture, were significantly associated with taking the role of speaker. This was confirmed by Thomas and Bull (1981), examining conversations between mixed-sex pairs of British students, who found that prior to asking a question the students typically either raised the head or turned the head towards the listener. Just before answering a question the speaker turned the head away from the listener. This last finding may be due to the effects of cognitive planning on the part of the listener prior to taking up the speaker's role.

Posture

Posture can be revealing of status, emotion, interpersonal attitudes and gender. Heller (1997) charted four main categories of human posture: standing, sitting, squatting and lying. Everyday interpersonal communication, of course, predominantly concerns the first two. In a study of tipping behaviour by restaurant clientele in the US Midwest, Leodoro and Lynn (2007) reported that the waitress was more successful when she either sat down at or leaned over the table.

Status

Posture is one of the cues used to make decisions about the relative status of those we observe and deal with, at least when status is accompanied by power and the potential for dominance. The degree of relaxation exuded seems to be a telling feature (Andersen, 2008). High-status individuals characteristically adopt a more relaxed position when they are seated (e.g. body tilting sideways; lying slumped in a chair) than low-status subjects who are more upright and rigid. When standing, people in a position of power and influence again appear more relaxed, often with arms crossed or hands in pockets, than those in subordinate positions who are generally 'straighter' and 'stiffer'. Those with high status are also likely to take up more expansive postures, standing at their full height, chest expanded and with hands on hips (Argyle, 1988).

Interpersonal attitudes

A seated person who leans forward towards the other is deemed to have a more positive attitude towards both the person and the topic under discussion than when leaning backwards (Siegel, 1980). The reason is probably that forward leaning is a component of the complex of interpersonal behaviour already mentioned called immediacy that signals close psychological contact (Guerrero, 2005). It is also interesting to note that most prolonged interactions are conducted with both participants either sitting or standing, rather than one standing, and the other sitting. Where this situation does occur, communication is usually cursory (e.g. information desks) or strained (e.g. interrogation sessions).

Relative posture adopted is a significant marker of how interactors feel about each other and of the relationship between them. *Postural congruence* or *mirroring* occurs when similar or mirror-image postures are taken up, with ongoing adjustments to maintain synchrony. Common matched behaviours include leg positions, leaning forward, head propping, facial expressions and hand and arm movements. This form of 'mimicry', which is usually carried out subconsciously, is taken as a positive sign that the exchange is harmonious. Research findings show that 'mimicry serves an important *social* function in that it facilitates the smoothness of interactions and increases liking between interaction partners' (Karremans and Verwijmeren, 2008: 940). The evidence also indicates that we are more likely to mimic the verbal and nonverbal behaviour of people whom we like or are attracted to (Gonzales *et al.*, 2010). This means that we are in turn more likely to be attracted to those who mirror our behaviours. Thus, therapists who use matching postures are perceived by clients to be affiliative and empathic, and this in turn encourages greater interviewee disclosure (Hess *et al.*, 1999). Indeed, Ivey *et al.* (1987) recommended what they termed 'movement symmetry' in therapy as a way of facilitating empathy. Likewise, in positive doctor–patient exchanges, nonverbal mirroring has been shown to be prevalent, particularly in relation to reciprocation of head nods and smiles (Duggan and Bradshaw, 2008).

Emotions

Based upon earlier findings, bodily posture was thought to reveal the degree of intensity of emotion, rather than the specific emotional state which was held to be the domain of facial expressions (Ekman, 1985). In a series of experiments, Bull and Frederikson (1995) illustrated how particular listener attitudes and emotions are encoded in this way, so that boredom was shown to be associated with a backward lean, legs outstretched, and head dropped and supported on one hand. Adults have also been found to successfully identify emotions depicted by actors playing emotional scenes on videotape, even when facial and voice cues were denied them (Montepare *et al.*, 1999). Approached from the opposite direction, there are fascinating findings to suggest that manipulating expressive behaviour such as posture and facial expressions can influence subsequent emotional feelings (Flack *et al.*, 1999).

Personality

Dysphoria (sadness or depression) has been shown to be characterised by distinctive gait and postural patterns (Michalak *et al.*, 2009). The typical gait of depressed individuals involves reduced walking speed, vertical head movements and arm swing. Moreover, depressed and sad walkers displayed greater sideways swaying movements of the upper body and a more slumped posture. The diagnostic value of NVC in the clinical/therapeutic setting has been commented upon by Knapp and Hall (2010) who affirmed the validity of much of the popular stereotype of the depressed person as being downcast and generally sluggish in movement. Focusing on patient behaviour, Fisch *et al.* (1983) found that posture was a significant indicator when differentiating between severely depressed and nearly recovered patients during doctor–patient interviews.

Eye gaze

Obsession with gaze, looking and being looked at, together with its potent effects on social behaviour is deep rooted in the human condition (Seppänen, 2006). It has been graphically documented down through the ages, epitomised in the celebrated eye gaze of the Mona Lisa that has fascinated for centuries, and in aphorisms such as 'The eyes are the windows of the soul.' Gaze refers primarily to looking at another in the facial area. *Mutual gaze* happens when the other reciprocates. This is sometimes also referred to as *eye contact* when the eyes are the specific target, although just how accurately we can judge whether someone is looking us directly in the eye or merely in that region of the face is open to debate. Associated terms are *gaze omission* where gaze is absent and *gaze avoidance* where it is intentionally being withheld. When gaze becomes fixed and focused in an intrusive way that may infringe norms of politeness, it becomes a *stare* and is associated with a different set of social meanings and potential reactions.

Gazing during social interaction can serve a variety of purposes. In an early analysis, Kendon (1967) suggested these were primarily to do with expressing emotional information, regulating interaction, revealing cognitive activity and monitoring feedback from the other. More recent classifications (e.g. Richmond and McCroskey, 2000; Knapp and Hall, 2010) are elaborate differentiations of these core functions, but add the further purpose of marking the relationship.

Expressing emotional information

The region of the eyes is a particularly significant part of the face when it comes to expressing fear and surprise (Ekman and Friesen, 2003). The direction of gaze also shapes judgements about emotion revealed facially (Adams and Kleck, 2003). In an experiment into nonverbal manifestations of pain, involving four different procedures – electric shock, cold, pressure and muscle ischemia – Prkachin (1997) found that closing the eyes was a consistent pain expression, while other signals were narrowing of the eyes and blinking.

Initiating and regulating interaction

Catching someone's eye is the necessary first step to opening up channels of communication and seeking contact with them. In a group discussion, patterns of gazing are used to orchestrate the flow of conversation, with members being brought into play at particular points. In dyads, a typical interactive sequence would be person A coming towards the end of an utterance looking at person B to signal that it is B's turn to speak. B, in turn, looks away after a short period of mutual gaze to begin responding, especially if intending to speak for a long time, or if the message is difficult to formulate in words. Person A will continue to look reasonably consistently while B, as speaker, will have a more broken pattern of glances (Argyle, 1994).

Revealing cognitive activity

Eye behaviour can be used to infer underlying thought processes (Gray and Ambady, 2006). What we do with our eyes can reveal how cognitively taxed we are at that point in time. We tend to avoid gaze when processing difficult material in order to minimise distractions. Thus, there is a greater likelihood of gaze being avoided when attempting to answer more difficult questions (Glenberg *et al.*, 1998). By examining patterns of eye movements, Mogg *et al.* (2000) showed how the hypervigilance of anxious subjects predisposed them to quickly shift their gaze towards angry faces.

Monitoring feedback

In Western society people in general look more as they listen than as they speak, and the duration of looking is longer during listening than talking (Kleinke, 1986). But speakers gaze periodically to obtain feedback and make judgements about how their message is being received and adjustments that may need to be made to their delivery.

Culture and gender are two highly significant determinants of levels and patterns of social looking. Culture helps to shape expectations of eye behaviour, especially the frequency and target of gazing (Schofield *et al.*, 2008), although duration may also be pertinent (Matsumoto, 2006). While Swedes gaze less frequently than the English, they do so for longer. At a general level, Arab culture tends to be more gaze oriented than either English or North American. Even within the latter it seems that Afro-Americans, compared to whites, look more while speaking and away when listening. In India, gaze avoidance is a mark of deference when talking to someone of much higher status.

Women tend to look and be looked at more than men. Based on a review of studies involving children and adults, Hall (2006) found that females gazed more in conversations than did males, with the difference more pronounced amongst adults. Different explanations for this phenomenon include the view that women display a greater need for inclusion and affiliation than men, and that desire for affiliation promotes more looking (Argyle and Cook, 1976). Alternatively, it is contended that eye contact is seen as less threatening to females than males, with the result that they are less likely to break eye contact in similar situations. A further explanation is along the lines that these gender differences are really a reflection of traditional differences in dominance/submissiveness.

Marking the relationship

The extent of our involvement with another is reflected in our eye behaviour. We make more and longer eye contact with people we regard positively and from whom we expect a positive reaction, leading Andersen and Andersen (2005: 115) to assert: 'Eye contact is at the heart of the immediacy construct, as it can signal interest, approach, involvement, warmth, and connection simultaneously.' Professionals such as counsellors are encouraged to make use of eye contact to signal not only positive affect but also attention to and interest in the client (Ivey *et al.*, 2010). Reduced levels of eye contact amongst couples can be variously interpreted as disapproval, less power and dominance or lowered levels of intimacy, depending upon the context (Feeney *et al.*, 1999). Paradoxically, we also sometimes look extensively at those with whom we are in conflict (e.g. staring or glaring). Noller (1980) documented how marital couples in conflict gazed more at each other during episodes of disagreement.

In addition to conveying relational information in respect of liking, affiliation and interest, gaze also signals differences in status, power and dominance. It has been reported to be associated with high-status people who indulge more extensively in this type of eye behaviour (Dunbar and Burgoon, 2005). Likewise, dominant individuals have been shown to engage in greater levels of mutual gaze (Kalma, 1992). However, the ratio of looking while speaking to when listening is a more telling indicator of dominance than absolute levels of this type of behaviour. According to this visual dominance ratio, those in higher-status positions look about the same while speaking and listening while their subordinates gaze much more while listening (Burgoon and Bacue, 2003).

Facial expressions

Studies of facial expressions have a long history, spanning at least two centuries (e.g. Bell, 1806). This is because the face is an incredibly powerful source of information about us, our attitudes towards others and how we relate to them (Ekman and Friesen, 2003). At present it probably attracts more research and scholarly debate than any other aspect of NVC. For instance, counsellor facial expressions have been found to be predictive of clients' perceptions of rapport during helping interviews (Sharpley et al., 2006). Over 20 different muscles responsible for producing in excess of 1000 distinct expressions make the face a rich source of detail, particularly to do with emotion. There are three key parts: the brows and forehead, the eyes and bridge of the nose, and the cheeks and mouth. Variations here are highly salient, as in Figure 3.1 where emotional states (such as sadness and happiness) can readily be interpreted from basic schematic facial representations (as evidenced by the ubiquitous happy/sad emoticons included in emails and texts). The traditional view, which can be traced back to Charles Darwin, emphasises facial *affect displays* as biologically based, direct expressions of underlying emotional states that have some sort of adaptive value. He wrote 'that in the case of the chief expressive actions they are not learned but are present from the earliest days and throughout life are quite beyond our control' (Darwin, 1872/1955: 352).

Consistent with this thinking is an emphasis on the universality of emotional expression: people reveal and recognise the same states in the same way regardless of where they live. As previously mentioned, the six basic emotions consistently decodable are sadness, anger, disgust, fear, surprise and happiness, with contempt as a possible seventh. There is evidence that we may be specially attuned to process certain types of emotional information leading to the rapid recognition of anger and threat (Esteves, 1999; Fox et al., 2000). Of course our emotional experiences are not confined to the above seven. How other emotions such as shame, guilt, pride, embarrassment and amusement are depicted has also attracted considerable interest (Keltner, 1997). Some of these states may be revealed in fleeting, *micromomentary expressions* that pass with little conscious awareness in a fraction of a second and are particularly difficult to control (Ekman and Rosenberg, 2005). The complexity of the face is also witnessed in *affect blends* or configurations that convey more than one basic emotion at the same time: the mouth may be smiling while the eyes are sad.

However, the orthodox view of the face as mainly a direct, biologically based system for revealing emotion has not gone unchallenged (Russell and Fernandez-Dols, 1997). Rather than arguing in favour of the primacy of discrete categories of emotion (e.g. sadness, anger, etc.), Russell (1997) advanced a view that first we process emotional NVC in terms of the dimensions of pleasure and arousal. Any specific emotions attributed are secondary and in keeping with situational and additional detail about the person observed. Recent developments in this area also accentuate social signalling functions over the purely biological. A view of facial expressions has been proposed

Figure 3.1 Effects of eyebrow and mouth variations on facial expressions

as culturally determined, circumstantially sensitive ways of communicating that are shaped by social motives and intentions (Kupperbusch *et al.*, 1999; Fridlund and Russell, 2006). Perhaps both views can be accommodated. Buck (1994) argued that spontaneous and deliberate (symbolic) expressions represent two parallel systems, both of which are important.

But of course we do not always reveal what we might feel, as a matter of course. The fact that showing emotion on the face is regulated by *display rules* is well established (Ekman and Friesen, 1969; Afifi, 2006). Social pressures mean that it is not always acceptable to make affective states public, particularly in certain cultures. The inscrutable face is often associated with the Japanese stereotype. In an often-cited experiment, Friesen (1972) had American and Japanese students watch alone a gruesome piece of film while being videotaped. Similar expressions of disgust, etc. were revealed but when later asked about the film, only the American students persisted with these negative facial displays. The Japanese are also less approving of showing disgust and sadness in the company of close friends. More recent cross-cultural work revealed that Russian and South Korean participants reported higher levels of control over their emotional expressions compared with the Japanese, while American subjects were the least censorious (Matsumoto, 2006). Apart from cross-cultural differences in display rules, Craig *et al.* (1997) found that patients with chronic lower back trouble attenuated their expressions of pain in the presence of the physiotherapist, even when told not to.

Emotional contagion, a process whereby emotion spreads from one person to another, is a further interesting interpersonal feature of facial signalling (Lishner *et al.*, 2008). Laughing is infectious, it is said. When you see someone smiling, do you tend to do likewise? Do you feel happier as a result? One view of emotional contagion (Hatfield *et al.*, 1994) suggests a two-step process. First, we mimic the expression of the other. Such mimicry can be carried out automatically. Dimberg *et al.* (2000) found that subjects who were not conscious of being exposed to happy and sad faces, still registered reactions in the facial muscles corresponding to happy and sad configurations. Second, feedback from our facial (and other) muscles leads to experiences of those corresponding emotions – we feel as the other person feels (Blairy *et al.*, 1999). In the organisational setting, emotional contagion has been shown to be implicated as the mechanism linking leader affect with follower affect (Johnson, 2008).

Smiles

These are one of the most common and easily recognised forms of facial expression, yet smiles have many and diverse meanings (LaFrance and Hecht, 1999). While enjoyment is one obvious interpretation, smiling may also signal appeasement or even contempt. Indeed, people sometimes smile in response to distressing circumstances, although doing so may lead to them being judged negatively by others (Ansfield, 2007). Spontaneous as opposed to contrived (or social) smiles can be readily differentiated, with the former, *Duchenne* smile, involving not only the mouth but also the eyes. Interestingly, Matsumoto and Willingham (2009) found no differences in the winning and losing facial expressions of noncongenitally blind, congenitally blind and sighted athletes. All of them used a social smile when they lost, but a Duchenne smile when they won. This study indicates that such facial expressions are not dependent on observational learning, and that other learning modalities, including reinforcement not involving the visual channel, may be sufficient for learning the facial display rules in this context. The other alternative is that there may be an evolved, possibly genetic, basis for these responses. The fact that the blind newborn child uses smiles lends support to this latter perspective (Jones, 2008).

Duchenne smiles are preferred in social contexts. Peace *et al.* (2006) found that fashion models displaying genuine smiles had their outfits judged more favourably than those with posed or no smiles. Gender and status are factors here, with females smiling more and low-status people seemingly more pressured into it (Hecht and LaFrance, 1998). Gender and information on job status of the person have also been found to have a significant impact on interpretations of facial expressions of emotion (Algoe *et al.*, 2000). Among men, there is some evidence that those with higher testosterone levels have less pronounced smiles (Dabbs, 1997).

While this subsection has been about the fluidity of the face as a means of communicating, fixed features can also be informative and influential. A key factor in recognising gender from photographs is the distance from eyelid to brow, which is smaller in men (Campbell *et al.*, 1999). Additionally, personality attributes can be made from features etched on the face. Size of eyes was found by Paunonen *et al.* (1999) to be associated with judged personality traits based mainly upon perceptions of masculinity/femininity, babyfacedness and to a lesser extent attractiveness. Finally, faces that are symmetrical are regarded as more attractive in both males and females (Koehler *et al.*, 2002).

PROXEMICS

Proxemics refers to the process whereby we perceive and make use of personal and social space. In particular, there are three broad aspects: territoriality, personal space and interpersonal distance; orientation; and seating arrangements. All of these have a direct bearing on the interactive process.

Territoriality

Territory refers to a geographical area over which individuals claim some particular set of rights for a period of time by way of access, occupancy or utilisation. It invokes associated concepts such as encroachment, invasion and defence. There are four main subdivisions here:

1   ***Primary territory*** is associated with the occupier who has exclusive use of it. This could be a house, or even a bedroom, which others may not enter without seeking permission and through invitation. It is an area of privacy that one can retreat to and where one has control. Omata (1996) reported that few Japanese women could lay claim to spaces at home that were exclusively theirs although most had personalised areas where they could go to be alone, relax or entertain friends. Those who had such private space showed better levels of adaptation. One study found that an increase in the number of students sharing a room was associated with more territorial behaviour, including creating barriers and arranging the room to make it less amenable to open interaction (Gress and Heft, 1998). Similarly, Sinha and Mukherjee (1996) discovered that students under such conditions of increased crowding required larger personal space and disliked the sharing arrangement more, although these effects were attenuated somewhat when room-mates were highly cooperative.

2   ***Secondary territory*** is less strongly linked with an individual or group. People may, out of habit, sit in the same seat in a lecture room or in the pub, but this cannot be backed up by claims of 'ownership' and exclusivity.

3   ***Public territory*** is space that is available to all to make use of for limited periods of time and is therefore particularly difficult to control. Park benches,

library seats and parking spaces are examples. Nevertheless, we have a tendency to claim more rights here than we are entitled to: we often relinquish our occupancy begrudgingly. Leaving *markers* that delineate boundaries is one way of defending one's 'patch' and preventing occupancy. By way of an example, Afifi (2006) observed how students place books or personal belongings on the seat next to them to stop others from sitting there.

4   *Interaction territory* is a special type of space that is created by others when interacting (e.g. a group having a conversation on the footpath). It lasts only as long as the interaction, but during that period others tend to walk around rather than through the gathering. Schiavo *et al.* (1995) noted that this is more likely in the overall context of public space (e.g. students in conversation in a corridor in the library) rather than secondary territory to which the interactors have limited claims (e.g. nonresident students in conversation in the corridor of the halls of residence). In the latter case, resident students were less likely to acknowledge the nonresidents' interaction territory.

Personal space and interpersonal distance

Personal space can be thought of as mobile and changing, yet ever-present personal territory. It is an area of space immediately surrounding the body, and slightly larger at the front, that 'travels' with us as we move around. It can grow or shrink depending upon our personality, the situation in which we find ourselves or our relationship with the person with whom we are dealing – but we feel very uncomfortable when it is encroached upon (Li and Li, 2007). Introverts, violent offenders, Type A personalities (i.e. very driven, time-conscious, competitive individuals) and the highly anxious tend to claim larger personal spaces (Argyle, 1988), although no significant sex differences have been consistently found (Akande, 1997). Violations of personal space may be not only disturbing but can also adversely affect our ability to function effectively. Those with a larger personal space were most negatively affected by high social density conditions on recall performance in a task requiring high levels of information processing (Sinha *et al.*, 1999).

Linked to personal space is interpersonal distance. This is the distance that interactors maintain when having a conversation. The possibilities extend from a situation of touching to essentially the limits of hearing. Within this range a particular distance will be established which may be thought to be a completely arbitrary factor and of no particular matter. However, this would be mistaken on both counts. Interpersonal distance is shaped by a nexus of factors such as social setting, culture, gender, age, status, topic of conversation, relationship shared and physical features of interactors (Knapp and Hall, 2010). In turn it has implications for how comfortable we feel about the encounter as well as our interpersonal attitudes towards, and relationship with, the other (McCall *et al.*, 2009). Contact cultures, as well as engaging in more haptic communication, tend to sanction closer interpersonal distances. Females also are more likely to get closer when having a conversation under normal circumstances. When hints of threat or discomfort are introduced, though, larger distances may be taken up than those characterising males (Hall, 1984). This could possibly account for the finding that females waiting to use an ATM approached males less closely than vice versa (Kaya and Erkip, 1999). Interpersonal distance has also been found to be closer in same-sex interactions (Jacobson, 1999; Kaya and Erkip, 1999). Interestingly, Uzell and Horne (2006) discovered that gender, as a personality factor, was a more important determinant of this measure than biological sex, per se, with those men and women sharing more feminine traits communicating at closer distances.

Young children tend to pay scant regard to conventions of interpersonal distance but are looked upon more negatively when older if they remain negligent. A generalisation cited by Richmond and McCroskey (2000) is that we probably interact at closer distances with people of the same age, although they caution that little systematic research has been conducted. In addition, both status differences and the topic of conversation must be taken into account here. Interactors of equal status tend to take up a closer distance than those of unequal status (Zahn, 1991). In fact, where a status differential exists, lower-status individuals will typically permit those of higher status to approach more closely than they would feel privileged to do. As the topic of conversation shifts to become more intimate than is comfortable for the other, that person may increase distance. Interpersonal distance is, therefore, part of this dynamic of nonverbal cues, including gaze and orientation, serving to regulate levels of intimacy and involvement. As expressed by Andersen and Andersen (2005: 114): 'Immediacy can be signaled through several proxemic or spatial channels. Most primary is interpersonal distance (i.e. proxemics). Closer distances can be both an indication and a cause of closer interpersonal relationships.' Presenting a fuller picture, evidence is cited by Andersen *et al.* (2006) that closer distances only lead to greater immediacy when the other is positively experienced as being rewarding.

Relationships shared have a further determining role in marking out physical closeness in situations. The anthropologist Edward Hall (1966), whose work in this area is seminal, found that four distinct categories of distance characterised the range of interpersonal contacts engaged in by predominantly white, middle-class American males from business and professional backgrounds:

- *intimate*, ranging from touching to about 18 inches (45 cm) – reserved for very close friends and family
- *casual-personal*, from 18 inches to 4 feet (45 centimetres to 1.2 metres) – typifies informal conversations with friends and acquaintances
- *social-consultative*, from 4 to 12 feet (1.2 to 3.7 metres) – used for more impersonal professional transactions
- *public*, from 12 feet (3.7 metres) to the range of sound and vision – used for making speeches and addressing large groups at formal gatherings.

Finally, physical characteristics of participants also determine, to some extent, the distance between interactors. For example, research studies have shown that people select greater distances for interactions with those with physical deformities (Kleck and Strenta, 1985) or facial disfigurement (Houston and Bull, 1994).

Orientation and seating arrangements

Orientation refers to body angles adopted when people talk face to face, such as directly facing or shoulder to shoulder. As such it concerns the position of the trunk, rather than head, and marks the degree of intimacy in the conversation and levels of friendship (Andersen *et al.*, 2006). It is useful to look at proximity and orientation together since it has been found that there can be an inverse relationship between them: that is, direct face-to-face alignment is linked to greater interpersonal distance and sideways angling to closer distance. This would be expected in situations where orientation was being used to compensate for excessive closeness (Andersen *et al.*, 1998). Orientation can also be used to include or exclude others from the group during discussion.

Early studies of seating behaviour by Sommer (1969) in North America, replicated by Cook (1970) in the UK, pointed to some interesting differences in seating arrangements when individuals are given a choice of where to sit when involved in different sorts of activities. Cook asked a sample including civil servants, school teachers and secretaries how they would position themselves at a rectangular table if asked to carry out a series of tasks with a friend of the same sex. The tasks were:

- *conversation* (sitting chatting for a few minutes before work)
- *cooperation* (sitting doing a crossword or such like)
- *co-action* (sitting at the same table individually reading)
- *competition* (competing to see who would be first to solve a number of puzzles).

As Figure 3.2 shows, a side-by-side position was considered to be cooperative in nature, while a face-to-face orientation was regarded as competitive. A 90-degree

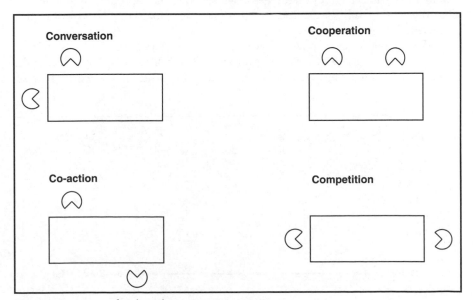

Figure 3.2 Types of task and seating arrangements

angle in relation to one other was selected for conversations, while for co-action (studying or working independently) a location across the table but at the opposite ends was chosen.

Finally, seating can be arranged in such a way as to encourage or discourage interaction. A layout that promotes interchange is called *sociopetal*; one that has the opposite effect *sociofugal*. It is important, therefore, that seating for a group discussion is arranged using a sociopetal pattern to make it easier for open interchange and sharing. On the other hand, a sociofugal variant would be more suited if the intention is for a presenter to play a centrally dominant role by making more use of one-way communication. Examples of types of seating varying along the sociopetal–sociofugal dimension are shown in Figure 3.3. Further elements of spatial arrangement in respect of office design will be presented later, in the section on environmental factors (p. 77).

PHYSICAL CHARACTERISTICS

This encompasses a vast array of bodily features some of which are more easily altered than others, but all of which are used to make judgements about the person in respect of, for instance, ethnicity, gender, age, occupation, status and attraction. This can include body shape and size, height, hair colour and style, dress and adornments such as jewellery. Physical characteristics, as a potent aspect of the nonverbal channel, cannot be overemphasised, particularly in initiating some form of social contact. Before we even know what people sound like or what they have to say we begin to form impressions based on physical appearance. At the centre of most of these will be evaluations of physical attraction. As shown by Myers (2008: 390), 'there is now a file cabinet full of research studies showing that appearance *does* matter. The consistency and pervasiveness of this effect is astonishing. Good looks are a great asset.'

The importance of physical attractiveness is abundantly evident in both the amount and variety of artefacts sold annually, such as designer clothes, false nails, perfume, after-shave, expensive shoes and so forth. To the extent that we

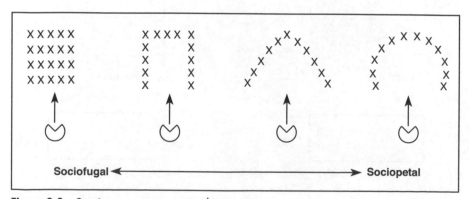

Figure 3.3 Seating arrangements and interaction

can make ourselves more attractive in the way that we present ourselves, we have a distinct advantage in most walks of life. In their review of this area, Zebrowitz and Montepare (2008: 176) concluded: 'People with more attractive faces are perceived as more likable, outgoing, and socially competent as well as higher in sexual responsiveness, social power, intelligence, and health.' In a large-scale meta-analysis of over 900 separate studies, Langlois *et al.* (2000) confirmed this finding, concluding that 'attractiveness is a significant advantage for both children and adults in almost every domain of judgment' (p. 404). Equating beauty with goodness has become known as the *physical attractiveness bias,* wherein physically attractive people are seen as more personable, popular, intelligent, persuasive, happy, interesting, confident and outgoing (Wilson and Nias, 1999; Harris and Garris, 2008; Patry, 2008). They are also more likely to be trusted with secrets, have their work assessed favourably, be selected for jobs and start work on a higher initial salary (Swami and Furnham, 2007a). Mehrabian and Blum (1997) derived several factors to account for ratings of physical attraction by both males and females from photographs of young adults of both sexes; the main ones were *masculinity* (determined by features to do with strength, larger chest, broader chin), *femininity* (based upon larger and rounder eyes, make-up, longer hair), *self-care* (suggested by shapely figure, well groomed, well-fitting clothes) and *pleasantness* (based upon perceptions of friendliness, happiness, babyish features).

Body size and shape

Present-day estimations of female physical attraction based upon body size and shape favour the slender. In a study by Swami *et al.* (2007a) in which males in three European countries (Britain, Spain and Portugal) rated images of women, body mass index (BMI), a measure of weight in relation to height, was the most important factor in judgements of the females' physical attractiveness. Those with low BMIs were rated as more appealing. According to Margo (1997), 'Barbie doll' features are universally beautiful and represent stereotyped features of the human form that have become more prevalent during recent evolutionary history. Indeed, being underweight seems an attractive feature in men as well as women (Henss, 1996).

But perhaps this preference has a larger cultural component than has been suggested. It has often been reported that men favour women with a low waist-to-hip ratio (WHR), ideally around 0.7, and particularly as romantic partners in one-off encounters (Singh, 1993; Braun and Bryan, 2006). This preference, though, could be more typical of male choice in affluent, developed Western society. What about those in subsistence economies? Marlowe and Westman (2001) found that Hazda men in Tanzania, who were hunter-gatherers, preferred heavier women with higher WHRs (i.e. with fuller waists). These researchers argued that in subsistence situations such as these where women's work is physically demanding and energy sapping, thinness could indicate poor health or inability to cope with the harsh conditions. From an evolutionary perspective such women would be less likely to conceive and successfully raise children. The topic of attractiveness will be returned to in Chapter 10.

Height

It is well established that tall people are regarded more positively than short people (Hensley and Cooper, 1987). Thus, those American presidents polled as the greatest were almost four inches taller than those regarded as failures (Young and French, 1996). These expectations can influence job success (Case *et al.*, 2009). For example, Melamed and Bozionelos (1992) discovered that height was a key determinant of promotion among British civil service managers. In terms of earnings, Judge and Cable (2004) found that in the US workplace those who were six feet tall could expect to earn $166,000 more over a 30-year career span than those who were seven inches shorter. Similarly, Case and Paxson (2008) showed that in both the US and UK for every additional 10 centimetre (4 inches) height advantage, males earned between 4 to 10 per cent more, and females between 5 and 8 per cent more. These results were confirmed in a large Australian study, where Kortt and Leigh (2010) illustrated how a 10-centimetre increase in height was linked to a 3 per cent increase in pay for men, and a 2 per cent increase for women.

Dress

In addition to attractiveness, we make assumptions about occupation, status and credibility from how someone is dressed and react accordingly. Several studies have shown that people are more inclined to take orders from, accept the lead given by and comply with requests made by someone in authority wearing an appropriate uniform or 'high-status' clothing. As expressed by Smith and Mackie (2007: 374): 'Medical doctors wear white lab coats and sling stethoscopes around their necks; police officers, firefighters, and paramedics wear uniforms and identification badges. These symbols are usually enough to activate the norm of obedience to authority.'

In a corporate context, how employees are attired has a well-recognised significance for their organisation's image (Hargie *et al.*, 2004). Some companies have returned to a more formal dress code, perhaps as a reaction to the general confusion that has grown up over what constitutes casual dress at work (Egodigwe, 2003). Those in sectors such as financial services and public administration are particularly subject to more conservative expectations over how they dress for the office (Adler and Elmhorst, 2008). From a traditional perspective, Molloy (1975) believed men in business and managerial positions commanded greatest credibility when wearing ideally a dark blue suit. In the often-cited television debate between Richard Nixon and John F. Kennedy as part of the 1960 US presidential campaign, Nixon appeared in a grey suit that contrasted poorly with the drab grey background of the studio. Kennedy, on the other hand, wore a stylist dark suit. While Nixon's failure to win the battle of image in this debate has been commonly put down to his infamous 'seven o'clock shadow', this sartorial contrast is also thought to have played a key part.

As far as colour is concerned, the general maxim 'the darker the suit, the greater the authority' is widely cited (Golden, 1986; Greenleaf, 1998). There is also some evidence of a 'red effect', in that in a study by Elliot and Niesta (2008) the colour red resulted in higher ratings by males of attractiveness and sexually desirablility of females. However, red did not affect the ratings of females for other females, nor did red increase male ratings of the female's likeability, kindness or intelligence.

Interestingly there is evidence of a causal relationship between dress and displays of attractiveness. Lõhmus *et al.* (2009) carried out a study in which they photographed the faces of 25 women wearing clothes that the females themselves regarded as attractive, unattractive or comfortable. They then had these facial photographs (the clothes were not visible) rated by males and significant differences emerged. The results showed that the men rated the faces of the females wearing attractive clothes most highly, followed by those wearing the comfortable clothes, while those wearing the unattractive clothes were rated as least attractive. The effects of their feelings about their attire seemed to have a direct impact upon the emotions of the females; this affected their facial expressions, which in turn influenced the way in which they were evaluated by males.

For women, dress choices at work are more complex and possible interpretations more varied than with men (Kaiser, 1999). Apart from suits, Hamilton (2008) suggested that dresses and skirts worn with blazers or matching jackets in conservative colours are most impactful. Suitability, though, will probably depend ultimately upon the type of profession and the corresponding image cultivated. Three broad categories have been identified (Wallach, 1986; Larson, 2010b):

- *Corporate.* The corporate woman wants to be seen as competent, rational and objective (e.g. banker, accountant, lawyer), and so dresses more formally, for example wearing suits in grey or blue colours. Women wearing a jacket rather than a dress or skirt and blouse tend to be perceived as more powerful (Temple and Loewen, 1993).
- *Communicator.* This woman wants to project an image of warmth, sincerity and approachability (e.g. personnel, marketing, teaching, social work, media), and so dresses in a practical, relaxed style.
- *Creative.* Here the image is one of flair, originality and innovation (e.g. musician, artist, writer, fashion designer, advertising), involving dramatic colours and exaggerated design.

Before leaving this section, it should again be repeated that the effects of physical attraction are more pronounced in situations where there have been few opportunities to interact with the target person over an extended period.

ENVIRONMENTAL FACTORS

The physical setting can influence our mood, how we perceive the social situation, and judgements about the person who occupies or has responsibility for that space. It can also help to determine our likelihood of interacting with others, the form that interaction will take and how long it is likely to last. Hall (1966) distinguished between *fixed-feature* and *semifixed-feature* elements of the environment. The former includes everything that is relatively permanent or not easily changed, like the architectural layout of a house, size and shape of rooms, and materials used in their construction. Semifixed features are much easier to move around or modify, and include furniture, lighting, temperature and colour of decor. Based upon such characteristics, we form impressions of our surroundings, organised around six dimensions (Knapp and Hall, 2010):

1   *formality* – concerns cues leading to decisions about how casual one can be in what is said and done or if a more ritualised or stylised performance is demanded
2   *warmth* – here one feels more or less comfortable, secure and at ease in what are regarded as convivial surroundings
3   *privacy* – has to do with the extent to which interactors feel that they have the space to themselves or whether others may intrude or eavesdrop
4   *familiarity* – involves impressions of having encountered this type of setting before and knowing how to deal with it (or not, as the case may be)
5   *constraint* – concerns perceptions of how easy it is to enter and leave the situation
6   *distance* – addresses how close, either physically or psychologically, we feel to those with whom we share the space.

These perceptions will in turn shape the types of interaction we engage in and how we experience them. The ways in which work space is arranged and utilised can send strong signals about the status and authority of occupants, the sorts of tasks and activities being implicitly proposed, and indeed the desirability and appropriateness of communication in that situation.

Those in authority and control in organisations commonly have their status acknowledged by the way that they position themselves vis-à-vis others with whom they associate. As a rule they tend to adopt positions that are more central and elevated than their lesser ranking colleagues. They are also privileged with greater space and more privacy (Guerrero and Floyd, 2006). It is common for the seats of power in organisations to be located in palatial surroundings on the top floors of buildings. Chief executive officers of large corporations rarely occupy small, dark rooms in the basement. It was said of Harry Cohen, one-time president of Columbia Pictures, that he had his desk placed on a raised platform at the far end of a long, spacious room as a way of not only marking status but also intimidating those who came to do business with him.

How office design conveys messages about the position and personality of the manager deserves further attention. According to Korda (1975), one of the factors that determines the power afforded by an office arrangement is the extent to which the manager can control space and readily restrict access to visitors. Furthermore, he believed that the organisation and use of office space are more impactful in this sense than the size of the office per se or how it is furnished. Other factors, such as having access monitored on one's behalf by someone of lesser status such as a gate-keeping secretary, not being exposed, being able to look directly at visitors and see them before being seen, are also held to be important. In relation to the latter points, from the office plans in Figure 3.4, it can be seen that person A communicates most power and control, B next, with C the least.

In larger offices, separate areas are often set side for distinct purposes, enabling temporary adjustments to be made to suggest power and control. What Korda (1975)

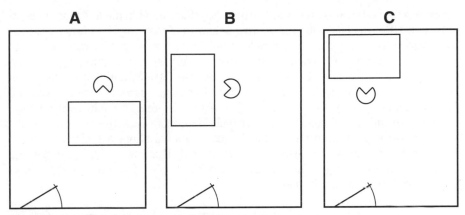

Figure 3.4 Office designs communicating power

called the *pressure area* is centred on the desk and is the site of formal business transactions. It is here that hard bargaining and difficult decision making takes place. The *semisocial area* is furnished differently with, for example, a sofa or easy chairs, coffee table, drinks cabinet, etc., and can be used to stall, ingratiate or mollify a visitor, as necessary.

Furthermore, it seems that apart from impressions of power and authority, personality judgements are frequently based upon how office space is utilised. Comfort in dealing with others, friendliness and extraversion tend to be attributed to occupants of more open office arrangements in which, for example, the desk, as with B and C in Figure 3.4, is moved against a wall rather than used as a barrier. The more effective professional will select that area of the office more appropriate to the task to be carried out with a particular client or colleague. Additionally, variations in the arrangements of environmental factors such as architectural style, interior decor, lighting conditions, colours, sounds and so on can be extremely influential on the outcome of interpersonal communication (Burgoon *et al.*, 1996; Pollack, 1998).

VOCALICS

Nonverbal communication, it will be recalled, includes aspects of speech as well as body language. These are the parts that accompany the spoken word, but are not verbal. The general term *paralinguistics* includes such features as speech rate and intensity; pitch, modulation and quality of voice; and articulation and rhythm control. Using the acronym VAPER, Nelson-Jones (2005a) cited five nonverbal dimensions of voice messages as important for counsellors in helping interviews: Volume, Articulation, Pitch, Emphasis and Rate.

Knapp and Hall (2010) reviewed evidence to show that judgements are made from paralanguage (with varying degrees of accuracy) about different elements of the communication process. These have to do with the speaker, how the message is presented and how it should be received. Speech rate, for instance, has been linked to messages about emotions, relationships and social influence, although how it is used between conversational partners rather than by either individually is a more important feature (Buller, 2005). Other nonverbal sounds like moaning and sighing, speech dysfluencies and vocalisations such as 'uh-huh', 'er' and 'ahh' are also included under the general heading of vocalics. Our preference for aspects of paralanguage can change across the life cycle. For example, Saxton *et al.* (2009) found that pre-teen girls (11 years) favoured higher pitched rather than deep male voices, but from the age of 13 years, and especially with the onset of puberty, this preference had been reversed and the older girls found a deeper, mature male voice more attractive.

Prosody is the term used to refer to those vocal variations associated with the words that help convey the meaning of what is said. This can be exemplified in the statement: 'John's lending me his guitar.' If we decide to place more vocal emphasis on certain words we can alter its meaning:

- JOHN's lending me his guitar (*John* is the one giving the guitar; no one else).
- John's LENDING me his guitar (John's *lending*, not giving, swopping or selling his guitar).
- John's lending ME his guitar (*I* am the recipient and no one else)
- John's lending me HIS guitar (the guitar being lent does not belong to anyone but *John*).
- John's lending me his GUITAR (nothing else is being loaned, only his *guitar*).

Accent is an important marker of social identity and a rich source of opinions and value judgements about people. It is a readily accessible cue that can be used to place an individual in a particular social category. As explained by Wigboldus *et al.* (1999: 153): 'Even when communicating with a total stranger, information about a recipient's most relevant social category memberships, such as gender, age and origin, is mostly directly available from the recipient's tone of voice, looks or accent.' Once a person is located, by accent, according to ethnic background, culture or class, corresponding stereotypes are triggered that in turn can evoke favourable or unfavourable attributions. Accent is indeed a powerful catalyst for prejudice on occasion. Accordingly, popular stereotypes portray Glaswegians as aggressive, London cockneys as crafty and devious, Yorkshire men as doggedly determined but unimaginative, and so on.

Accent is a speech characteristic that we sometimes modify in line with that of our conversational partner. According to *communication accommodation theory*, it will be recalled from earlier in the chapter that we tend to bring our speech more into line with that of our partner when we are seeking approval, creating a positive association or signalling in-group membership (Giles and Ogay, 2007). For example, Willemyns *et al.* (1997) found that interviewees in an Australian study used broader accents when interviewed by someone with a broad Australian rather than a more cultivated accent.

The speaker

From accompanying vocalic indices, impressions can be formed, with varying degrees of veracity, about age, gender, size, personality, emotional state and, to some extent, occupation (Scherer *et al.*, 2003; Ko *et al.*, 2006; Imhof, 2010). Indeed, Drahota *et al.*

(2008) found that subjects could tell from listening to audio recordings whether the speaker was smiling or not, and could judge with a high level of accuracy what type of smile the speaker was using (the types employed were Duchenne smile, non-Duchenne smile, suppressed smile, non-smile). Drahota *et al.* noted that their findings regarding the affective quality of speech have many implications, not least for the development of synthetic speech, since 'effective emotional speech programs have yet to be developed. Although the present computerized voices are clear, they lack the emotional qualities which make human speech so meaningful and naturalistic' (p. 286).

Scherer (1979) claimed that rate of speech can be directly related to anger: 'hot' anger has a notably fast tempo while 'cool' anger is more moderate in pace. Mean amplitude (associated closely with loudness) and the extent to which amplitude varies around a mean value have been shown to be positively related to perceived dominance of the speaker (Tusing and Dillard, 2000). Speech rate, on the other hand, was negatively associated (i.e. the faster the rate, the lower the estimation of dominance). Anxiety is an emotional state likely to produce speech errors (Knapp and Hall, 2010). In the early stages of interaction with others, participants can be beset by speech dysfluencies. However, as participants become more familiar with the situation, the frequency of speech errors decreases (Scott *et al.*, 1978).

The presentation of the message

Decisions are taken about the message in respect of levels of enthusiasm, excitement or competence, from accompanying paralanguage. We have all had experience of speeches delivered in such a dreary monotone that the most interesting material seems boring. Conversely, quite boring material can become interesting if delivered by someone who stimulates interest, through changing the pitch, tone, speed and volume of vocal pattern. Politicians and good public orators use these vocal techniques in order to emphasise points, stimulate feelings and generally obtain and sustain the interest of their audiences.

How the message should be received

The vocalics sometimes contain a meta-message that lets the listener know how the verbal content is to be taken (e.g. 'tongue in cheek', soberly, respectfully, etc.). In *The Selling of the President 1968*, it is related how before a broadcast the announcer who was about to do the introduction asked if his voice was too shrill. 'Yeah, we don't want it like a quiz show,' he was told. 'He's going to be presidential tonight so announce presidentially' (McGinniss, 1988: 155).

But it isn't just about image and personal impressions. How information is delivered paralinguistically has important consequences for how much of the message is understood, recalled and acted upon. Verbal fluency was one of two strongest predictors of persuasiveness to emerge from a study by Burgoon *et al.* (1990).

OVERVIEW

When we think about the communicative process and how it operates, the nonverbal tends to be overshadowed by the verbal. Little wonder that the contribution of nonverbal elements is often downplayed in our estimation of their role in the overall activity. Their very ubiquity and prosaic quality often, and paradoxically, render them in many respects invisible to the eyes of the naive observer looking in on interaction from the outside. The case is very different on the inside for those who are actually acting and reacting to one another. Much of what they do is nonverbal and is in response to nonverbal cues picked up from the other. Yet it would be a mistake to assume that the verbal and nonverbal are two distinct systems of communication (Beattie, 2004). Nothing could be further from the truth. As stressed by Wagner and Lee (1999: 262–263): 'Nonverbal behavior in real settings is inextricably bound up with the verbal behavior that it usually accompanies and cannot be understood without reference to that verbal communication.' Even reaching neatly defined conceptual distinctions is difficult. In broad terms, though, NVC compared to language tends to rely less on a symbolic code, is often represented in continuous behaviour, carries meaning less explicitly and typically conveys emotional/relational rather than cognitive/propositional information.

Riggio (2005) noted that being nonverbally skilful involved an expressive element, an element of sensitivity and one of regulation or control over performance. By means of NVC we can replace, complement, modify or contradict the spoken word. When it is suspected that the latter was done unintentionally and deceit is possible, nonverbal cues are often regarded as more truthful. We also regulate conversations through gestures, gaze and vocal inflection. Revealing emotions and interpersonal attitudes, negotiating relationships, signalling personal and social identity and contextualising interaction are further uses served by means of haptics, proxemics, kinesics and vocalics, together with physical characteristics of the person and the environment. We need information about other people's qualities, attributes, attitudes and values in order to know how to deal with them. We often infer personality, attitudes, emotions and social status from the behavioural cues presented to us. Of course the situation also works in reverse: not only do we gather information about others from the way they present themselves to us, but we ourselves go to great lengths to present others with a certain type of picture of ourselves.

The potency of the nonverbal aspects of interaction must be recognised by professionals who should be sensitive to the kind of atmosphere they are creating, the scene they are setting and the parameters they are placing on an interaction, often before they even begin to speak. Knowledge of the various facets of NVC, and of their effects in social interaction, can enable us to improve our ability to successfully deal with others. The skilled use of nonverbal behaviour is a key facet of success in interpersonal encounters. It must also be stressed, however, that much of nonverbal meaning is inferred and can be easily misconstrued. It only suggests possibilities and must be interpreted in the overall context of not only verbal but also personal and circumstantial information. Many of the elements of NVC that have been discussed in this chapter will be returned to in the remaining chapters of this book.

Chapter 4

Rewarding others:
the skill of reinforcing

INTRODUCTION

$\mathbf{F}$ROM EARLY CHILDHOOD THE role of social rewards, in the form of verbal and nonverbal reinforcement, is crucial. The smiles, hugs and soothing vocalisations of a mother are important reinforcers for her child. Likewise the eye contact, smiles and paralinguistic messages of the infant are key rewards for the mother during the mother–child bonding process. In addition, the mother's social reinforcement is usually directly related to the satisfaction of the child's biological needs (food, heat, etc.), and so an associative link is formed. When the child is being changed, kept warm or fed it is simultaneously receiving social reinforcers (smiles, etc.). Thus, the connection between social and material reinforcers is established from the earliest stage of development. In this way, the power of social reinforcement begins to be learned by the child, who quickly learns to shape the behaviour of the mother or caregiver. Goldstein *et al.* (2007: 2) showed that by the age of five months infants 'have learned that their vocalizations produce changes in caregivers' behavior. Infants have linked their babbling with the expectation of a social response.'

Throughout life, a fundamental principle governing behaviour is that people tend to do things associated with positively valued outcomes for them. By contrast, they usually do not persist with actions that from past experience have produced little of positive consequence, or even unwanted negative effects. As noted by Skinner (1971: 199), reinforcement is based 'on the simple principle that whenever something reinforces a particular activity of an organism, it increases the chances that the organism will repeat that behavior'. This is summarised by the maxim in the business world: 'What gets rewarded gets done.' Positively valued outcomes can of course take many forms. Some (e.g. obtaining food, water and shelter) are necessary for physical survival, while others (e.g. attractive company) are less basic but still important. Events that are even less tangible, yet highly valued just the same, include positive features of interpersonal contact, as shown in Box 4.1. Friendly smiles, words of praise, warm congratulations, generous applause or an enthusiastic response from an attentive listener are all reactions that are generally desired. Not only do we find them appealing, but we also tend to act in ways that bring them about. The fact that these positive reactions can influence what we do, by making it more likely that we will engage in such behaviours in preference to others, is central to the concept of reinforcement as an interpersonal skill.

It will be recalled from Chapter 1 that the ability to obtain and provide rewards features prominently in attempts to define interpersonal skill. Deficits in this respect can have negative personal and interpersonal consequences. Reviews of the area have shown correlations between interpersonal skill deficits, inability to gain positive reinforcement and poor psychological well-being (Segrin *et al.*, 2007; Segrin and Taylor, 2007). Interpersonal inadequacy also seems to be associated with loneliness and social anxiety. Having the potential to reward (i.e. *rewardingness*) is a key dimension of interaction that plays a central role in friendship formation and personal attraction (Foley and Duck, 2006; Smith and Mackie, 2007). Faraone and Hurtig (1985) examined what those regarded as highly socially skilled actually did compared to their low social skill counterparts when in conversation with a stranger of the opposite sex. The highly skilled were more rewarding in the way in which they reduced uncertainty, and therefore possible unease in the situation, and were more positive towards the other through what was said and topics introduced. Rewards in social situations serve 'to keep others in the relationship, to increase the other's attraction to ego, and to

---

Box 4.1 Everyday examples of reinforcement

- An infant makes its first attempt at the word 'Mummy' and the adoring mother responds with enraptured smiles, hugs and kisses.
- A pupil who has been struggling with quadratic equations gets them all right for the first time and the attentive teacher lavishes generous praise.
- The striker for the home team scores a goal and is mobbed by his team mates while the frenetic fans chant his name in exultation.
- Someone in the group tells a funny story and the other members erupt in laughter.
- A sales executive beats the monthly target and earns the heart-felt congratulations of the sales team.
- A learner driver manages to complete a U-turn for the first time and the instructor smiles in recognition and gives a 'thumbs-up' sign.

In all of these cases it is likely that the person reacted to in each of these positive ways will be influenced subsequently to strive to do similar things in future situations. When they do so their actions (scoring goals, telling funny stories, saying 'Mummy', etc.) are said to have been reinforced.

---

make greater influence possible, when reinforcement is contingent upon the desired behaviour' (Argyle, 1995: 82). Likewise, in professional circles the ability to reinforce effectively during dealings with those availing themselves of the service on offer has been heavily stressed (Dickson *et al.*, 1997; Arnold and Boggs, 2006).

REINFORCEMENT AND PROFESSIONAL PRACTICE

In their analysis of generic communication styles, de Vries *et al.* (2009) found that one of the core dimensions was that of 'supportiveness', which involved complimenting, praising, encouraging and comforting others. This style is important since, in his research into 'comforting communication', Burleson (2010b: 161) has shown that 'people who are skilled at providing emotional support are more popular, better liked, and have more lasting friendships and intimate relationships'. More generally, a core skill common to professional practice in a range of settings involves responding positively to others so as to reward and reinforce appropriately. In education, for instance, reinforcement is seen as a powerful tool to be used by teachers to improve pupils' social behaviour in class and promote academic achievement (Sutherland and Wehby, 2001; Woolfolk, 2005). Indeed, in their pioneering research into teaching skills, Turney *et al.* (1983) charted how through reinforcement teachers could increase pupils' attention and motivation, improve classroom behaviour and promote achievement by various verbal and nonverbal means including:

- praise and encouragement
- gestures
- adjusting physical proximity
- opportunities to take part in other activities such as playing class games with peers.

Shifting the focus from teaching to psychotherapy, a view has been advanced of the psychotherapist as a powerful source of social reinforcement that is used during the consultation to shape change (Castonquay and Beutler, 2005). For Beier and Young (1998), while clients' maladaptive patterns of relating may elicit painful responses from others, those same patterns may also meet a more compelling need for predictability and consistency in dealings with them. In this way dysfunctional behaviour is sustained through interpersonal reinforcement. The therapist's task is to reshape more productive and satisfying styles of interaction. Likewise, the role of reinforcement in parent–child interaction therapy has been highlighted (Boothe and Borrego, 2004), as has the crucial role of the therapist as a purveyor of reinforcement therein (Borrego and Urquiza, 1998).

In the related field of counselling, Ivey and Ivey (2007) attributed special status to 'attending' in their taxonomy of constituent microskills, going so far as to label it 'the foundation skill' (p. 63) of the interviewing and counselling process. Attending to the client in this sense involves:

- following the conversational lead offered
- adopting appropriate body language

- engaging visually
- being vocally responsive.

Ivey and Ivey (2007: 62) pointed out that:

> Attending behavior encourages the client to talk. You will want to use attending behavior to help clients tell their stories and to reduce interviewer talk. Conversely, their lack of attending behavior can also serve a useful function. Through non-attention you can help other people talk less about topics that are destructive or nonproductive.

Based on the premise that people will only talk about what others are prepared to listen to, clients can be encouraged to disclose issues of concern through the judicious use of attending behaviour and the reinforcing effects of selective listening on the part of the counsellor or interviewer.

Reinforcement has also been identified as playing a prominent role in physiotherapists' interactions with patients (Adams *et al.*, 1994). In this study, physiotherapy sessions involving both adults and children in outpatient, obstetrics and gynaecology, neurology and paediatric departments were videotaped for fine-grained analysis. Reinforcement was identified as an important element of the task-oriented dimension of practice. It featured in work with both adults and children and comprised, for example, praise, acknowledging increased effort, positive feedback, smiling and eye contact. This piece of research was closely based upon earlier work by Saunders and Caves (1986), who used a similar methodology to unearth the key communication skills of a different professional group – speech and language therapists. 'Using positive reinforcement' was one of the categories to emerge from interactions with children and adults. Verbal and nonverbal subtypes were specified. Using the same approach, Hargie *et al.* (2000) not only established key communication skills of the community pharmacist, but also asked participants to differentiate in terms of importance between the 11 types to emerge. Reinforcement, in the context of explaining to patients, was rank ordered second after rapport building.

In other areas of health care, health worker social rewards in the form of attention, praise, approval, compliments and so on can increase patient satisfaction and improve adherence to prescribed drug regimens and recommended courses of action. This may include sticking to a set diet and maintaining healthy eating patterns (Holli *et al.*, 2008). By taking steps to monitor patient behaviour and reinforce adherence when it does take place, health professionals can go some way to ensuring that patients cooperate fully in their treatment. This may have a particular impact in cases of difficult or unpleasant courses of action. In controlling diabetes mellitus, according to Warren and Hixenbaugh (1998: 441): 'It is the role of the doctor to convince the patient that the discomfort or inconvenience in the short-term will bring rewards (by avoiding complications) in the long-term . . . In order to achieve this, reinforcements, such as praise for appropriate behaviour, must be immediate.'

Fisher (2001) emphasised that influencing change along these lines presupposes the prior establishment of a relationship of trust, acceptance and respect. It is only in this context that praise and approval are likely to be valued. Extending this thinking, Buckmann (1997) argued that using rewards like selective positive feedback, benevolent behaviour and acceptance statements which convey to patients that they are held in high regard can act indirectly to enhance adherence. These ways of relating strengthen health professionals' referent power (i.e. the social power bestowed upon them as people to be identified with or 'looked up to'). This, together with their expert power (i.e. the influence they command due to their expertise), serves to strengthen patients' self-esteem and sense of self-efficacy (these aspects of influence are further addressed in Chapter 12). Following the argument through, patients who have a better sense of their own worth and a greater belief in their ability to succeed in the task are more likely to cooperate in their treatment.

Rewards, including praise, make a potentially beneficial contribution to other and diverse areas of professional activity such as management and organisational operations. Those intent on building effectively functioning teams in the workplace have been advised to be particularly attentive to the power of social rewards (Hargie et al., 2004). When systematically applied, improvements in staff absenteeism, motivation, job satisfaction, productivity and safety can result (for reviews see, for example, Austin and Carr, 2000; Pershing, 2006). The findings were summarised by Reid and Parsons (2000: 281), with reference to human service settings, as follows:

> A variety of consequences have been demonstrated through OBM [Organizational Behavior Management] research to have reinforcing effects on desired staff performance including, for example money, free meals, commercial trading stamps, discount coupons, and work duties, trips away form the work site, and special recognition ceremonies.

However, as always, reinforcement is a two-way street and in the workplace rewards work both ways, as employees attempt to influence and shape the behaviour of managers. As shown by Hargie et al. (2004: 85–86):

> Subordinates influence managers through rewards such as social approval (praise, nonverbal acknowledgment, etc.), and by their work rate and volume of output. Conversely they can punish managers by withdrawing verbal and nonverbal rewards and by reducing their work efforts.

Finally, sports coaches who employ rewarding techniques have been found to be popular and have also been shown to enhance levels of skill and improve results (Smith and Smoll, 2007; Freeman et al., 2009). Furthermore, Justine and Howe (1998) reported that among adolescent female field hockey players frequent praise from the coach was associated with greater perceptions of self-competence and satisfaction with both the coach and general team involvement.

BEHAVIOUR AND ITS CONSEQUENCES

Since Ivan Pavlov, the eminent Russian physiologist, introduced the term (Pavlov, 1927), the concept of reinforcement has been the subject of much heated debate in psychology. One psychologist who was at the forefront of much of this was B. F. Skinner (1953). Skinner preferred the term 'reinforcement' to 'reward' due to the greater semantic precision which it afforded, together with its lack of mentalistic trappings. As such, a reinforcer, by definition, has the effect of increasing the probability of the preceding behaviour. The application of reinforcement procedures in keeping with Skinnerian principles is known as *instrumental* or *operant conditioning*. The central tenet of this process focuses on the ability of the consequences of behaviour to increase the probability of subsequent manifestations of that behaviour, relative to some preconditioned level (Lieberman, 2000).

For any particular piece of behaviour we can think, first, of environmental stimuli that precede or accompany it and, second, of others taking place subsequently. Consider the classroom example of a teacher asking the class a question, to which Mary raises her hand. As far as the child's act is concerned, the most conspicuous antecedent stimulus is obviously the posed question. The pupil's response also takes place within the context of a plethora of accompanying stimuli which constitute the classroom environment. Other stimuli follow on from it and are made available as a consequence of the behaviour having been performed (e.g. the teacher may react enthusiastically, the child may be offered the opportunity to display knowledge by answering, other classmates may marvel at her brilliance, etc). Further significant factors have to do with, for instance, how hungry Mary is for this sort of attention. The role of antecedent stimuli will be returned to, but for the moment let us stay with the outcomes of performance. In broadest terms, the relationship between a response and its consequences may lead to that response subsequently being:

- increased in frequency
- decreased in frequency, or
- left largely unchanged.

As to the first of these eventualities, reinforcement is the process taking place. Reinforcers serve to make preceding actions more likely to recur. Reinforcement can take a positive or a negative form, as will be explained shortly. Before doing so though, it is useful to consider outcomes that serve to reduce the likelihood of similar future actions.

Punishment

Punishment has the effect of suppressing behaviour so that it is less likely that those acts leading to it will be repeated. Indeed, it too can operate in either a positive or a negative way. *Positive punishment* involves the introduction of something unpleasant (a noxious stimulus) such as a physical blow or hurtful criticism, contingent upon the appearance of the targeted behaviour. *Negative punishment* requires withdrawing some benefit that, had the individual not acted in such a way, would have continued to be enjoyed. Removing privileges such as access to the television or computer is an example.

Attempts at control and influence through punishment are common in everyday interaction and may be subtly exercised. They can involve sarcasm, ridicule, derision, reprimands and threats, to specify but a few. However, a number of undesirable side-effects have been associated with punishment (Martin *et al.*, 2007). It can produce negative emotional reactions such as fear and avoidance, which may generalise beyond the response being punished to the punishing agent, for example a teacher, and then have a further dysfunctional impact upon attitude to the subject being taught and even to school itself. In most contexts it is clear that the carrot is better than the stick.

Extinction

When actions previously reinforced cease, for whatever reason, to produce customary outcomes that are positively valued, the likely long-term effect will also be a reduction in those activities. This occurs through the phenomenon of extinction. Thus, while there are important differences between punishment and extinction, both serve to reduce the likelihood of a response (Newman and Newman, 2007).

Positive reinforcement

So reinforcement can be engineered through positive or negative means. The positive reinforcement principle states that 'if, in a given situation, somebody does something that is followed immediately by a positive reinforcer, then that person is more likely to do the same thing again when he or she next encounters a similar situation' (Martin and Pear, 2007: 30). As noted by Nicholas (2008: 122): 'A positive reinforcer could be an event, a privilege, a material object, or a behaviour that strengthens the response.' Mary, the pupil in the earlier example, may have had her contribution to the lesson enthusiastically endorsed by the teacher, making her more prepared to offer further contributions, given the opportunity. It is positive reinforcement and rewards that are commonly acknowledged when reinforcement is talked of as an interpersonal skill, and it is therefore this type around which much of the analysis in this chapter will be based.

Before moving on, the relationship between positive reinforcement and reward needs to be clarified. For some, such as Martin and Pear (2007), the terms are roughly synonymous. Indeed, Nelson-Jones (1996), operating within a counselling framework, declared a preference for 'reward', believing it to be more in keeping with the language of helping. Technically speaking, however, a reinforcer must, by definition, act to increase the frequency of the behaviour upon which it is contingent. In contrast, for Kazdin (2008) a reward is something given and received in return for something done. While it may act as a reinforcer, whether or not it actually does is an empirical question. On this point, and in the classroom context, Zirploi and Melloy (2001: 165) stressed that 'teachers cannot assume that an item, activity, or other stimulus will be reinforcing to a student'. Indeed, Capstick (2005) showed that there are often marked differences between what teachers and pupils perceive to be the most potent forms of reward.

Negative reinforcement

Here an act is associated with the avoidance, termination or reduction of an aversive stimulus that would have either occurred or continued at some level had the response not taken place. Negative reinforcement and punishment should not be confused. Although both involve aversive states, in the case of punishment this state is made contingent on the occurrence of the behaviour under focus and has the effect of making that behaviour less likely to recur. With negative reinforcement, behaviour resulting in the noxious stimulus being reduced, eliminated or avoided will be more probable in future.

Examples of negative reinforcement in everyday life are common. We have a headache, take FeelFine analgesic and the pain disappears, making it more likely that we will take FeelFine the next time a headache strikes. The television becomes uncomfortably loud when the adverts come on, spurring us to grab the remote control to turn down the volume. One theory is that habit-forming behaviours like drinking alcohol or smoking are maintained through their effect in reducing tension (Stroebe, 2000). Experimental evidence was produced by Craighead *et al.* (1996) that college women with bulimia nervosa and past depression had higher rates of learning on a computerised mental maze task when provided with negative social feedback for errors made, rather than positive feedback for correct responses. It was thought that avoidance or minimisation of negative reactions was the key factor.

Much of our interpersonal interaction is shaped in a similar way through negative reinforcement (Cipani and Schock, 2007). Bringing to an end as quickly as possible an interchange with someone found unpleasant, uninteresting or just difficult to relate to could be accounted for in this way. A similar explanation may explain why we speak back in defence of our position in conversations where it has been challenged. An argument can be thought of as a logical, reasoned debate or, alternatively, as a quarrel between two people each of whom is out to vanquish the other (Billing, 2001). Contemporary society is increasingly typified by arguments, with associated confrontation and threats to face (Tannen *et al.*, 2007). As such, disagreement with our point of view and the prospect of being shown to be wrong can make us feel vulnerable, threatened and humiliated. Having the chance to successfully defend our beliefs and opinions often brings relief and therefore makes responding more likely.

Conversational repair is a further feature of talk (Hutchby and Wooffitt, 2008). Corrections, apologies and disclaimers are brought into play when participants unwittingly break a conversational or societal rule, thereby running the risk of causing confusion or even losing face (Bull, 2002). Viewed as the application of negative reinforcement, breaking the rule may cause embarrassment or discomfort, assuaged by an apology or disclaimer, thereby making it likely that these forms of repair will be relied upon again in similar situations.

Allen and Stokes (1987) reported a more formal application of negative reinforcement in managing the disruptive and uncooperative behaviour of children receiving restorative dental treatment. In this case, children were asked to be 'Big Helpers' by lying still and being quiet while the dentist worked. This led to the temporary suspension of treatment. Gradually children had to be 'Big Helpers' for longer periods of time in order to have the dentist suspend treatment for a period. Not only were children markedly more compliant by the last visit but, from readings of heart rate and blood pressure, were significantly less stressed by the experience. The different types of behavioural consequence outlined in this section are summarised in Box 4.2.

Box 4.2 Consequences of behaviour

- *Punishment* – suppresses targeted behaviour.
- *Positive punishment* – involves the introduction of something unpleasant (e.g. being scolded, slapped, made to feel uncomfortable, etc.).
- *Negative punishment* – involves the removal of something desired (e.g. television confiscated, credit card withdrawn, car keys taken away, etc.).
- *Extinction* – eliminates targeted behaviour (e.g. you will stop putting a coin in a particular dispensing machine that consistently fails to deliver a can of soft drink).
- *Reinforcement* – promotes targeted behaviour.
- *Positive reinforcement* – involves the introduction of something pleasant (e.g. receiving praise, chocolate, attention, money; playing a favourite computer game; etc.).
- *Negative reinforcement* – involves the removal of something undesirable (e.g. stopping pain, boredom, embarrassment, stress, etc.).

CATEGORIES OF POSITIVE REINFORCEMENT

The vast range of things that we do as we go about our daily lives gives rise to a multiplicity of differing outcomes, both physical and social. Many of these exert a controlling influence through the operation of positive reinforcement. Psychologists have proposed different systems of classification. Sherman (1990) suggested five core reinforcement categories – primary, conditioned, social, sensory and activity.

Primary reinforcers

These can be thought of as stimuli that are inherently valued, the positive value and reinforcing potential of which do not rely upon a process of prior learning. Ones that spring most readily to mind include food, drink, shelter, air, sex and so on. These are things that we depend on for survival, due to our biological make-up. Despite their fundamental indispensability, the limitations of these as a direct means of influencing the complexities of everyday person-to-person interaction will be appreciated. Here the rewards tend to be more subtle.

Conditioned reinforcers

This grouping, also called *secondary reinforcers*, is in sharp contrast to the previous one. It includes events that have no intrinsic worth but whose power to control behaviour is ultimately derived from an earlier association with primary reinforcers. We have *learned* to value conditioned reinforcers. Tokens, stickers, vouchers, medals, stamps, badges, stars and such like have been incorporated into organised programmes called *token economies* where they are earned for engaging in particular tasks and subsequently exchanged for more basic back-up reinforcers (Kazdin, 2008). Under certain circumstances, an originally neutral stimulus can become associated with a number of primary reinforcers. Money, to cite one example, can be used to obtain food, drink, shelter, heat, sex, etc. Skinner (1953) called this special class *generalised reinforcers*. Since these are particularly applicable in relation to social reinforcement they are discussed further under the next subheading.

Social reinforcers

Lieberman (2000: 208) defined social reinforcers, in broad terms, as 'stimuli whose reinforcing properties derive uniquely from the behaviour of other members of the same species'. Social behaviour, by definition, presupposes the involvement of others. In the main, the types of rewards that govern and shape it are also contributed by those with whom we mix and intermingle and are a powerful, though often subtle, influence on our actions. Buss (1983) further categorised these rewards as either process or content.

Social process rewards

These are an inherent part of interpersonal contact and include, in order of increasing potency, the mere presence of others, attention from them, and their conversational responsivity. An interesting observation is that too much or too little of these activities can be aversive; it is only at a notional intermediate level that they become reinforcing. The attention given by a teacher to a pupil in the same environment may well change from being reinforcing to punishing if it is either withdrawn totally or, at the other extreme, becomes intrusively persistent.

Social content rewards

What takes place within interaction also has rewarding ramifications. Here Buss (1983) paid particular heed to the acts of showing deference, praising, extending sympathy and expressing approval, confirmation or affection. Unlike their process equivalents, these presuppose a certain type of interpersonal relationship to be relevant and effective. Thus, we seldom show affection to complete strangers.

As well as process and content rewards, individuals can find variously reinforcing opportunities to compare themselves to others, compete, dominate or self-disclose, and may seek out situations and occasions to indulge themselves accordingly.

Generalised reinforcers

Individuals are moulded as social beings through the influence of the social milieu of which they are a part. As we have seen, the subtleties of the process involve the judicious distribution, by significant others, of such mechanisms as attention, interest, approval and affection. It is these sorts of activities that lie at the heart of positive responding conceived of as an interpersonal skill. Through them one person can influence what another does without using actual or threatened physical force.

According to Skinner, positive social reactions can be used to shape interpersonal behaviour because they serve as generalised reinforcers. The approval and attention of others are examples. Of approval, he wrote: 'A common generalised reinforcer is approval ... It may be little more than a nod of the head or a smile on the part of someone who characteristically supplies a variety of reinforcers. Sometimes ... it has a verbal form "Right!" or "Good!" ' (Skinner, 1957: 53). In the case of attention, he noted: 'The attention of people is reinforcing because it is a necessary condition for other reinforcements from them. In general, only those who are attending to us reinforce our behaviour' (Skinner, 1953: 78).

For Lieberman (2000), among others, these aspects of social performance, in that they can be thought of at all as reinforcers in the Skinnerian sense, embrace both learned and unlearned dimensions. To be more specific, the suggestion is that some of the nonverbal features, such as smiles and hugs, may not depend upon prior experience to be positively valued. In others words, they are a blend of primary and conditioned reinforcers.

Sensory reinforcers

Listening to beautiful music, looking at a striking painting, attending the theatre or watching an exciting sporting event are all attractive possibilities, albeit to varying extents for different individuals. We need only think of the costs and inconveniences that devotees will endure to indulge themselves in these ways to appreciate that certain quantities and qualities of sensory stimulation can be highly rewarding.

This fact was exploited by Mizes (1985) in treating an adolescent girl who was hospitalised following complaints of chronic lower-back pain. The extent of this pain was such that she was virtually bedridden. Tests and examinations failed to locate any physical cause and the case was treated as an abnormal behaviour disorder, which was being inadvertently held in place through operant conditioning. When opportunities to watch television, have access to the telephone and receive parental visits were made conditional upon demonstrably increased mobility, symptoms gradually subsided.

Activity reinforcers

For Premack (1965), activities rather than things are reinforcing. It is eating and drinking that is of significance, rather than food or drink, as such. Stated formally, the *Premack principle* proposes that activities of low probability can be increased in likelihood if activities of high probability are made contingent upon them. Activity reinforcement can be a powerful means of organising work routines and maximising commitment in a diversity of professional settings, including management, health care, sport and education. Holli *et al.* (2008) highlighted the benefits in the management of patients with eating disorders of walking, gardening or reading (or whatever the client finds attractive) as rewards to be earned by sticking to agreed dietary habits. In sport, the example is given by Martin and Pear (2007) of a swimming coach who produced a 150 per cent improvement in the practice of racing turns at both ends of the pool together with the number of swimming sets completed without stopping. The reinforcing activity was being allowed to take part in a final ten-minute fun activity in the pool, which was made contingent upon these elements of training.

In school, pupils may prefer, for example, more practical classes to didactic instruction. Lessons can be arranged in such a way that to get to do practical activities the theory must be understood. The 'Good Behaviour Game', for use with younger pupils, has been employed as a way of improving behaviour in class (Rathvon, 2008). If the group record fewer than, say, five tally marks for breaking classroom rules during the day, they win privileges such as a period of 'free time' before going home. More generally, Burden and Byrd (2009) pointed out that being permitted to carry out classroom tasks such as operating equipment, taking a note to the office or checking attendance can be prized activities in the classroom.

The potential for these principles to enhance managerial effectiveness and raise output has been recognised for some time (e.g. Komaki, 1982). Increasing productivity was demonstrated in an early study by Gupton and Le Bow (1971) through an internal rearrangement of the various types of task that workers carried out. In this case the workers were part-time telephone sales personnel in industry who sold both new and renewal service contracts. On average, the success rate for attempts at renewals was more than twice that for new sales, so sales personnel tended to devote most of their energies to the former. As far as the firm was concerned this resulted in a general failure to attract new customers. A new regime was imposed whereby five new calls were required before the representatives had an opportunity to make attempts at renewal sales. This contingency resulted in a substantial increase not only in the number of new contracts sold, but renewals as well.

It should not be assumed, however, that only certain activities can reinforce. Premack (1965) stressed that any behaviour can increase the likelihood of any other provided that the former tends to occur more frequently and, in order to perform it, the latter has to be carried out. In a subsequent modification of this principle, though, Timberlake and Allison (1974) produced evidence in support of their *response deprivation hypothesis*. Thought of in this light, it is having been prevented from engaging in an activity at its optimum level that bestows reinforcing potential upon it. The more we have been deprived of an activity in this way, the more powerful it will become.

STIMULUS CONTROL

It was mentioned earlier in the chapter that behaviour can be set in a context of, on the one hand, preceding and accompanying stimuli and, on the other, consequent events. When a certain action only succeeds in eliciting reinforcement in the presence of particular accompanying stimuli, then that piece of behaviour is said to be under *stimulus control* and those stimuli have become *discriminating stimuli* in respect of it (Leslie and O'Reilly, 1999). They signal the availability of a reinforcer for behaving in that way. When the overall context acts in this way then *contextual control* is in operation (Sarafino, 2004).

Many examples of stimulus control spring to mind. The doctor–patient consultation is traditionally a one-sided affair, especially with male doctors (Dickson and McCartan, 2005; Imber, 2008). This high control style involves interrupting frequently, asking almost all of the questions (see Chapter 5) and setting the agenda. Attempts by patients to negotiate their own agendas usually meet with little success. In this setting, doctor questions may serve as discriminative stimuli indicating to patients when their contributions will be welcomed and when not. Hooper (1995) analysed differences between expert and novice nurses when taking the pulse and blood pressure of senior citizens. She discovered that discriminative stimuli such as casual conversation, client comfort and health-related information differentiated between the two groups in respect of such elements of practice as eye contact, verbal interaction, use of touch, attending to the client and obtaining the measurement. In the business sphere, the perspicacious employee who learns to read the subtle cues that suggest the likelihood of the manager being receptive to new ideas, and accordingly picks an opportunity to propose some innovation, is also being influenced by stimulus control. Discriminative stimuli therefore signal the occasion for particular behaviours to be reinforced and must not be confused with reinforcing stimuli. The latter always function as a consequence of the targeted behaviour.

VICARIOUS REINFORCERS

So far the focus has been upon the direct impact of a positive outcome on the acquisition and regulation of the behaviour that brought it about. But the influence of rewards is wide ranging and can be indirect. Vicarious reinforcement is the process whereby individuals are more likely to adopt particular behaviours if they see others being rewarded for engaging in them (Kazdin, 2008). Through observing the actions of others we learn not only what to do but also how to do it; we benefit from their successes (Bandura, 2006). Rewards, vicariously experienced, can influence learning, motivation and emotions. Seeing others rewarded for some behaviour (e.g. observing other pupils being rewarded by the teacher for answering questions in the classroom) can act as a strong inducement for the observer to do likewise when it is inferred that similar outcomes will accrue by behaving in the same way.

Furthermore, when the consequences of actions are socially mediated, a basis is established for reassessing the attractiveness of experienced outcomes through witnessing what happens to others under comparable conditions. Receiving recognition from a supervisor will probably mean much more once it is realised, from observations of interactions with others, that this person rarely acknowledges effort. Receiving rewards and punishments is associated with the creation of pleasant and unpleasant emotional states. Awareness of these states and circumstances in other people can be emotionally arousing and this facility is believed to account for empathic responsivity to them (Bandura, 1986). The ability to engage empathically with others is, of course, fundamental to effective counselling (Egan, 2007).

The consequences here are far-reaching. For example, Rebellon (2006: 403), in a study of adolescent delinquency, illustrated the potency of vicarious reinforcement, finding that 'a delinquent attracts the attention of peers, that audience members take note of this phenomenon, and that they therefore increase their delinquency in proportion to their own desire for peer attention'. Vicarious reinforcement has important implications for professional practice. A teacher in a large and busy classroom may find difficulty in providing reinforcement on an individual basis for appropriate behaviour and accomplishments. Under these circumstances much of the teacher-based reinforcement that pupils receive is likely to be vicarious, as they observe other pupils being rewarded for particular responses. In relation to management, the maxim of 'praise publicly–punish privately' articulates the potentially vicarious benefits of bestowing rewards in the presence of others (Prue and Fairbank, 1981). This practice was used effectively by O'Reilly and Puffer (1989) to enhance expressed motivation, satisfaction and productivity among a group of retail sales clerks when the basis of reward allocation was seen to be fair. On a more cautionary note, however, two possible downsides of vicarious reinforcement are as follows:

- Praising in public can cause embarrassment for some and so may produce negative rather than positive effects (Giacolone and Rosenfeld, 1987).
- Watching others persistently rewarded for something that the observer has done equally competently, but without comparable recompense, may cause resentment and demotivation. This has been referred to as the implicit effects of observed consequences and, as such, distinguished from vicarious facets (Bandura, 1986).

INTERPERSONAL EFFECTS OF SOCIAL REWARDS AND REINFORCERS

A range of goals tends to be served by social rewards and reinforcers (Dickson *et al.*, 1993; Cairns, 2006). These are summarised in Box 4.3, and will now be examined in more detail.

Box 4.3 Purposes of reinforcement

The main goals served by the skill of reinforcement are:

1 to promote interaction and maintain relationships
2 to increase the participation of the interactive partner
3 to influence the nature and content of the contribution of the other person
4 to demonstrate a genuine interest in the ideas, thoughts and feelings of the other
5 to make interaction interesting and enjoyable
6 to create an impression of warmth and understanding
7 to increase one's own social attractiveness as the source of rewards
8 to improve the confidence and self-esteem of the other person
9 to display one's own power as the controller of rewards.

Promoting interaction and maintaining relationships

During social encounters we not only welcome but demand a certain basic level of reward. If it is not forthcoming we may treat this as sufficient grounds for abandoning the relationship in favour of more attractive alternatives. One review of friendship and peer relations in children found that the characteristics that distinguished between popular and unpopular children included being rewarding and supportive (Erwin, 1993). Conversely, Jones *et al.* (1982) discovered that college students who were lonely, in comparison to their more gregarious peers, were found to be strikingly less attentive to conversational partners. More extremely, Argyle (1995) noted the marked lack of reinforcement typifying the interpersonal performance of certain categories of patients with mental disorders such as schizophrenia and depression. He described them as unrewarding to the point of being 'socially bankrupt'. Actual conversational deficits of depressives include less fluent, more monotonous speech and poor eye contact. These individuals do not show interest and attention, with the result that interacting with them is unrewarding (Hammen, 1997). Impoverished social contact may produce a further deterioration in mental state with fewer opportunities for inter-personal involvement, thus creating a debilitating downward spiral: 'As the individual becomes more depressed, social avoidance leads to further reductions in exposure to positive reinforcement and the problem is compounded' (Walker, 2001: 162).

Increasing active involvement of the interactive partner

For professionals who work mainly with other people, it is important that recipients of the service are encouraged to be fully involved in what takes place if the goals of the encounter are to be achieved. Promoting active participation in the classroom is a good example. Costs incurred by pupils in the form of energy expended, lack of opportunity to devote time to competing activities and fear of getting it wrong, amongst others, must be offset by the availability of rewards. In some learning situations (e.g. acquiring a novel skill), intrinsic rewards from efficient task performance may be limited initially. Teacher reinforcement is therefore one method of increasing pupil commitment to what is taking place.

Influencing the nature and content of contribution

Apart from extending the general level of participation, rewards can be administered in a planned and systematic fashion to selectively reinforce and shape contributions along particular lines. Interviewees can be influenced by selective interviewer reinforcement to continue with the detailed exploration of certain topics or issues to the exclusion of others regarded by the interviewer as being of lesser relevance or even counterproductive. In a medical setting, for instance, White and Saunders (1986) demonstrated how patients suffering from chronic pain conversationally focused more on their pain when the interviewer responded with attention and praise. Selectively reinforcing 'well talk', on the other hand, had the opposite effect.

Martin and Pear (2007) gave a more spectacular example of a young girl who began complaining of headaches. This attracted considerable attention in the form of concern from parents and eventually, as the migraine-like condition worsened, from health workers. No organic cause could be found for her complaint. A behaviour treatment programme was introduced in which all those with whom she came in contact agreed to ignore 'pain behaviour' (e.g. complaining, taking tablets, going to bed, etc.) and praise 'well behaviour' whenever it was manifested. Over a 12-week period, the mean number of pain behaviours dropped from eight to less than one per day. Using the same principles, teachers can increase the incidence of appropriate pupil behaviour in class (Zirploi and Melloy, 2001; Woolfolk, 2005).

Before progressing, it should be acknowledged that when worded in this way there is little which is either original or profound in the proposition that people are inclined to do things that lead to positive outcomes and avoid other courses of action that produce unwanted consequences. This much is widely known. Indeed, the statement may seem so obvious as to be trivial. But Lieberman (2000) makes the telling observation that, despite this general awareness, individuals are often remarkably unsuccessful in bringing about behavioural change in both themselves and other people. It has been found that partners of drug abusers often unwittingly encourage the very behaviour that they are trying to eliminate through their inconsistent use of reinforcement and punishment (LePoire et al., 2000). The conclusion drawn by Lieberman (2000: 193) is that 'Clearly the principle of reward cannot be quite as simple as it sounds.'

Many professionals make surprisingly poor use of this interpersonal skill. Cannell et al. (1977), investigating the performance of survey interviewers, found that adequate or appropriate responses received proportionately less positive interviewer reinforcement than did less desirable reactions. Refusal to respond, the least desirable response, received proportionately the highest levels of reinforcement. Furthermore, during investigative interviews, interviewer reinforcement can distort the information-gathering process, leading to false accounts of what took place (Milne and Bull, 1999). For example, Garven et al. (1998) analysed several hundred interview transcripts conducted with children as part of an inquiry into alleged child abuse by seven Californian teachers. They found evidence of several suggestive techniques employed, including praising or rewarding children when they said or did something that fitted in with interviewers' assumptions (see Chapter 5 for a further discussion of interviews with children).

Teachers have also been criticised for failing to make proper use of praise in the classroom. Reviewing a number of studies, Brophy (1981: 8) concluded that its use is 'typically infrequent, noncontingent, global rather than specific, and determined more by students' personal qualities or teachers' perceptions of students' need for praise than by the quality of student conduct or achievement'. Likewise, educators have been accused of praising on the basis of answers they expect to receive rather than those actually given (Eggen and Kauchak, 1999).

Conveying information about the source: interpersonal attraction

In addition to influencing what recipients say or do, bestowing rewards also conveys information about the giver. Providers of substantial amounts of social reinforcement are usually perceived to be keenly interested in those with whom they interact and what they have to say. They also typically create an impression of being warm, accepting and understanding. Teacher praise and encouragement have been associated with pupil ratings of teacher attraction, trustworthiness, expertness and potency (Kelly and Daniels, 1997) and of satisfaction with the course (Worland, 1998). By contrast, those who dispense few social rewards are often regarded as cold, aloof, depressed or bored – as well as boring.

Extending this thinking, some investigators such as Clore and Byrne (1974) have made use of the concept of reinforcement in attempting to account for inter-personal attraction. Responses and pleasurable feelings that stem from receiving rewards become associated, it is proposed, with the provider, or even with a third party who happens to be consistently present when they are dispensed. Such attraction, however, is neither universal nor unconditional, depending as it does upon how what is taking place is construed by the recipient. The source is more likely to be found to be attractive if the action being praised is regarded by the recipient as praiseworthy. Praise from that individual is valued and may reflect a positive change from a more negative disposition by the source towards the recipient (Raven and Rubin, 1983). If, on the other hand, it is thought that there are ulterior motives for lavish praise or compliments, and ingratiation or manipulation are suspected, liking for the source will deteriorate (Aronson, 2008).

Influencing perceptions of self

Positive reactions may not only produce more favourable impressions towards those who offer them, but can also result in heightened feelings of self-esteem and self-efficacy in the recipient. Self-esteem refers to the sense of personal worth that an individual holds, ranging from love and acceptance to hate and rejection. Self-efficacy is a belief in one's ability to successfully accomplish a task or reach a goal (Bandura, 1997). Being given positive information about levels of skill possessed can make us think differently about tackling some task drawing upon that capacity. More generally, Sullivan (1953) believed that one's concept of self develops out of the reflected appraisals of significant others. Thus, positive rewarding experiences with parents and other key adults lead to positive views of self, while experienced negativity, including blame, constant reprimands and ridicule, results in feelings of worthlessness. Does this mean then that those receiving praise invariably assume that they are better or more able than those who do not? This is an important question to be returned to shortly.

Self-enhancement versus self-verification

People are not merely passive recipients of the reactions of others. Rather, they often make a deliberate effort to present themselves in such a way as to attract a particular type of evaluative response. One motive for this is *self-enhancement*. Through a process of *impression management* or *self-presentation* individuals go out of their way to make themselves as appealing as possible to others (Hogg and Vaughn, 2008). The importance of promoting a positive assessment of self in this way and being looked upon favourably has been stressed (Pilkington and Smith, 2000; Tesser, 2001). Attention, praise, approval and various other rewards will be valued on these grounds. But what if such reactions clash with our existing perceptions of self and the suggested positive self-evaluations are inconsistent with how we already see ourselves? For some, under certain circumstances, *self-verification* rather than self-enhancement is what counts (Gómez *et al.*, 2007; Swann, 2009). Here, it is not necessarily a positive evaluation that is being sought, but rather one that is consistent with the individual's existing self-referenced views and beliefs. According to Taylor *et al.* (1995), a range of factors including personality and culture, as well as situational aspects, will make self-enhancement rather than self-verification salient. For those with negative views of themselves, receiving information from others that backs up these perceptions (i.e. self-verification) seems to be stressed (Swann *et al.*, 2007). These findings have interesting and significant ramifications for rewarding and reinforcing. For those with a poor self-concept and low self-esteem, praise and other positive reactions incongruent with how they regard themselves may not be appreciated and fail to have a reinforcing influence. Indeed, the opposite may be the case. Before leaving the topic though, it should be mentioned that people vary, more generally, in the extent to which their sense of self-esteem is contingent upon external factors such as praise or criticism (Wolfe, 2007).

Locus of control

A further dimension of personality that is of functional relevance to social rewards is *locus of control*. This term refers to the extent to which individuals regard themselves, rather than powerful others or mere chance, as having control over what happens to them. The originator of the term locus of control, Rotter (1966), developed the following formula to determine the behaviour potential of a response – that is the likelihood of a particular response being chosen in a specific situation:

behaviour potential = reinforcement value × expectancy

Here, reinforcement value refers to one's personal evaluation of the reward, while expectancy refers to one's subjective estimation of the likelihood of actually receiving the reinforcement in this context. Those who believe that they can personally influence the extent to which they will receive reinforcement have a high internal locus of control. These individuals believe that rewards gained are contingent upon their own performance and a reflection of their relatively enduring characteristics and qualities. At the other extreme, those who think that reinforcement is determined by external forces have a high external locus of control. This is typified by the idea that any successes which may occasionally happen are due largely to chance, luck or some external influence rather than to their own efforts. Those with an internal locus of control tend to attain higher levels of reward (Kormanik, and Rocco, 2009). In their review of research in a range of areas such as physical and mental well-being, educational attainment and organisational achievement, Maltby *et al.* (2007: 93) concluded: 'With very few exceptions, it appears that internals are more successful than externals in most situations.'

Manifesting power

Finally, the distribution of rewards can be conceptualised as an exercise in power and authority. Being in a position to determine whether or not another receives something of value confers on the bestower the ability to exert influence, and the power to set the conditions to be met for the rewards to be bestowed. When the allocation of rewards is viewed by the recipient as an attempt at control, however, resistance to such manipulation may result. This can be a manifestation of *psychological reactance*, and an attempt to assert personal freedom and autonomy when these are threatened (see Chapter 12 for a fuller discussion of power and reactance).

BEHAVIOURAL COMPONENTS OF SOCIAL REINFORCEMENT

It will be recalled that, in theory, anything that increases the frequency of the preceding piece of behaviour can be considered a reinforcer. Even if this list is restricted to elements of interpersonal behaviour, the resulting number of potential reinforcers could be extensive. Coverage will, therefore, be restricted to the more widely recognised elements featured in the literature. In doing so, a conceptual distinction will be made between components that are essentially verbal and those that are nonverbal. While this is a convenient way of structuring the section, as noted in Chapter 3 in practice these two channels are closely interwoven.

Verbal components

The verbal channel of communication is a powerful source of social reinforcement. Things said can provide feedback, validate self-views and strengthen feelings of self-esteem and self-worth, or have the opposite effect. Verbal components of reinforcement range in sophistication from simple expressions such as 'okay', to more elaborate responses that relate to some aspect of the functioning of the other.

Acknowledgement/confirmation

This category contains expressions, words and phrases that acknowledge, confirm or agree with what has been said or done. Examples include verbalisations such as 'Okay', 'Yes', 'Right', 'Fine', 'I see', 'That's it', as well as nonlexical vocalisations like 'Mm-hmm' and 'Uh-huh' (strictly speaking the latter would be more appropriately listed under the nonverbal heading, but since they have often been grouped along with the other verbal utterances exemplified it is more convenient to include them here). These listener responses are a common feature of conversations, since they signal that the listener is paying attention to the speaker (Brownell, 1995). They have also been shown to be crucial to the regulation of interaction when people talk over the telephone (Hargie *et al.*, 2004).

Within the sphere of nursing, Balzer Riley (2008) illustrated the importance of phrases such as 'Mm-hmm', 'Yeah', 'I see' as signals of attention to patients and colleagues. From a counselling perspective, Ivey *et al.* (2010) referred to these types of responses as 'minimal verbal utterances' (p. 157) and described them as one way of encouraging the client to continue with their explication of personal concern during interviews. Together with nonverbal responses such as head nods and smiles, they have also been termed 'minimal encouragers', which 'work by using the "minimal" amount of feedback necessary to encourage clients to keep talking' (Blonna and Water, 2005: 62).

The reinforcing consequences of these attending utterances have been revealed in a number of classic experimental investigations, one of the most widely reported of which was that conducted by Greenspoon (1955) in which he simply asked subjects to produce as many individual words as they could think of. By responding with 'Mm-hmm' each time a subject gave a plural noun and ignoring all other types of words, the number of plural nouns mentioned by subjects increased considerably over the course of the experiment. Not all subsequent investigations, though, have produced such positive outcomes. Rosenfeld (1987) suggests that at least some of these failures could be accounted for by the fact that social reinforcers were administered on a noncontingent basis (subjects were exposed to them regardless of whether they were engaging in lengthy speech turns). For a stimulus to serve as a reinforcer for any specific piece of behaviour and conditioning to take place, it must occur in conjunction with that behaviour (Lieberman, 2000). Thus, the lack of contingent application was also one of the reasons offered by Nelson-Gray *et al.* (1989) to explain why, in their experimental investigation, no discernible increase in interviewee problem-related statements was brought about by increasing the frequency of interviewer minimal encouragers.

Praise/encouragement

Unlike the previous category, here listener reactions go beyond the simple acknowledgement and confirmation of, or agreement with, what has been said or done, to overtly express praise or support. Instances of this category of reward range from one-word utterances, for example, 'Good', 'Excellent' (and various other superlatives), through phrases like 'Well done', 'How interesting', 'Keep it up', to more elaborate avowals of appreciation as circumstances warrant. These are commonly employed by a broad spectrum of professionals when interacting with those to whom a service is offered. When appropriately administered, reinforcing consequences can be achieved. Professional areas where such effects have been examined are as diverse as organisational management, interviewing and coaching. Martin and Pear (2007) presented, as an example, the case of a basketball coach who used praise to increase the number of supportive comments made by players to other team members, thereby strengthening team spirit. Practice drills were also enhanced in this way. Alternatively, Thompson and Born (1999) demonstrated how praise and verbal prompting could be effective with older people suffering from dementia or brain injury in getting them to take part correctly in exercise sessions while attending an adult daycare programme.

Teaching is an activity where opportunities abound for putting praise and approval to good use in rewarding effort and accomplishment in the classroom (Zirploi and Melloy, 2001). It represents probably the most extensively researched area of application of this type of social reinforcer and several reviews are available (Brophy, 1981; Wheldall and Glynn, 1989; Cameron and Pierce, 1996; Hancock, 2000; Cairns, 2006). Through the judicious use of reinforcement, significant and beneficial changes can be brought about in:

- student attentiveness (Taylor, 1997)
- on-task behaviour in class (Sutherland *et al.*, 2000)
- student time spent on homework assignments (Hancock, 2000)
- motivation to learn, particularly when good performance is linked to effort rather than intelligence or ability (Dweck, 2007)
- levels of academic achievement (McCowan *et al.*, 1995; Merrett and Thorpe, 1996)
- pupils' and students' evaluations of praise (Elwell and Tiberio, 1994; Bardine, 1999) and of the teachers that use it (Kelly and Daniels, 1997).

As a general conclusion, therefore, it would appear that praise in the classroom can pay dividends. In practice though, there is evidence that:

- teachers put praise to a number of uses apart from rewarding and reinforcing
- pupils are aware of this
- praise is not always administered effectively
- some pupils are more appreciative than others of praise and respond to it differentially.

Good and Brophy (2008) questioned the extent to which techniques such as praise are a prominent feature of the day-to-day classroom discourse of teachers and are used with reinforcing effect. Alternative purposes of praise include encouraging, directing and gaining rapport. Whether teacher praise acts as an effective reinforcer depends upon a number of qualifying variables such as:

- features of the pupils, such as reinforcement history
- the type of task undertaken
- the pupil's actual performance
- the nature of the praise
- the manner in which the praise is administered
- characteristics of the source.

Pupils are also sensitive to the plurality of uses to which teachers put praise and interpret it accordingly. Taylor (1997) found that they applied labels such as deserved (when the performance was good) versus instructional. The latter included (a) encouraging, (b) signalling to others to do the same and (c) increasing cooperation and participation.

The success of praise as a reinforcer can be increased (Hancock, 2000; Burden and Byrd, 2009) by ensuring that it:

- is applied contingently
- specifies clearly the particular behaviour being reinforced
- is offered soon after the targeted behaviour

- is credible to the recipient
- is restricted to those students who respond best to it – not all do, with some finding this type of reward patronising or embarrassing when delivered in the presence of peers.

Praise and children's culture and socioeconomic status

The influence of factors such as culture and socioeconomic status on children's susceptibility to reinforcers has been the subject of concerted enquiry. There are clear cultural differences in reinforcement (Cairns, 2006). For example, in eastern cultures such as Japan and Taiwan, teacher reinforcement in classrooms is much less prevalent than in American classrooms (Weirzbicka, 2004). Furthermore, Weirzbicka showed how the expressions 'good girl' and 'good boy', which are widely used in Anglo parental speech to praise children for their actions, do not have equivalents in other European languages. She argues that these terms have their roots in the English and American puritanical past. Weirzbicka also noted that in some cultures, such as China and the Gusii culture in Kenya, parents tend not to praise their children. In the latter context, praise is eschewed because it is felt that it would make the child disobedient, rude and conceited.

Socioeconomic status attracted the attention of researchers some years ago, leading Russell (1971: 39) to conclude: 'One of the most consistent findings is that there is a social class difference in response to reinforcement.' Middle-class children have been held to respond better to less tangible reinforcers, including praise and approval, when compared with their lower-class compatriots. The latter, it is assumed, are less likely to be exposed to this type of reinforcement, especially for academic achievement, and are therefore unlikely to attach much value to it, favouring instead tangible rewards such as money, food or toys. However, Schultz and Shemman (1976), having undertaken a comprehensive review of the area, were quite adamant that this view was ill-founded.

Relationships between these variables, if they do exist, are likely to be much more convoluted than those intimated by Russell. Miller and Eller (1985), for instance, reported significant increases in subsequent intelligence test scores among lower- and middle-class white children following the praising of initial test performance, but gender differences played a part as well. Thus middle-class females were more susceptible to praise than their male counterparts. In comparison, praise improved the performance of lower-class males but not females. Elwell and Tiberio (1994) reported that male pupils expressed a greater preference for teachers to praise 'all the time' and 'praise loudly'. Perhaps as a result of the growing 'classlessness' of much of contemporary society, there has been a reduced interest in this line of research in recent years.

Praise and age

Marisi and Helmy (1984) found age differences to be implicated in determining how praise is reacted to. Comparing the effects of this incentive on performances of 6-year-old boys with those of 11- and 17-year-olds on a motor task, they discovered that it was only with the youngest group that praise proved beneficial. Likewise, Bracken and Lombard (2004) reported computer-mediated praise leading to enhanced learning in young children. Shifting the focus to perceptions and attitudes towards the praised, Miller and Hom (1997) replicated some earlier findings to the effect that older pupils (eighth grade) compared to younger (fourth and sixth grades) generally see praised children as being less able. On the other hand, Wheldall and Glynn (1989) have shown that the behaviour of adolescents in class can be effectively managed by the teacher praising acceptable conduct in keeping with rules previously agreed by members, and largely ignoring minor infringements. Here, however, praise was contingently administered, unlike the procedure followed by Marisi and Helmy (1984). Differences in the nature of the behaviour focused upon should also be appreciated. The boys in the study by Marisi and Helmy were engaged in the acquisition of a motor skill.

Praise and personality

Several personality factors have been found to mediate the reinforcing impact of praise. The first of these is pupils' locus of control (Kennelly and Mount, 1985). As previously mentioned, people who are essentially internally set hold a belief in their own ability to extract reinforcers from the environment, whereas externals are inclined to put any rewards that come their way down to chance or luck. Kennelly and Mount found that internality of control and an appreciation of the contingency of teacher rewards were predictive of good academic achievement and teacher ratings of pupil competence. By contrast, Baron *et al.* (1974) and Henry *et al.* (1979) associated an external orientation with receptivity to verbal reinforcement.

Self-efficacy, it will be remembered, refers to a belief in one's ability to succeed at some task or undertaking. Kang (1998) reported a complex relationship between praise, age, gender, academic status and self-efficacy. Praise was positively related to self-efficacy among regular students, but negatively so for those at the bottom end in classes with a large spread of ability. This pattern was reversed in groups with a narrow spread of ability. Generally, girls and students at the bottom of the class had lower levels of self-efficacy.

There is good reason to believe, at least with older individuals, that the personality dimension extraversion/introversion may play a further salient role. In particular it seems that extraverts may be more receptive to the effects of praise, while for introverts the punishment of inappropriate responses can produce better results (Boddy *et al.*, 1986; Gupta and Shukla, 1989). Susceptibility to such interpersonal rewards from others seems to be strengthened among those who display a heightened need for approval, and therefore have a predilection to act in ways that will increase the chances of others reacting favourably towards them.

Praise: a possible downside

While praise is undoubtedly a potent force in social interaction, as already alluded to in this chapter, there can be dark sides to this phenomenon. The claims that praise boosts motivation for the rewarded activity, results in more of it, promotes learning and improves self-image, have been challenged (Lepper *et al.*, 1996; Deci *et al.*, 1999). One reason put forward for this criticism is that intrinsic motivation to engage in a task may suffer when external rewards are offered (McLean, 2009). This perspective purports that by having the motivational basis for completing an activity switched from an intrinsic interest in it to some external gratuity such as money, we may gradually come to carry out that activity only for the remuneration. Once the reward ceases, it is argued, so too will the behaviour. Internal motivators, such as a sense of satisfaction or pride, are powerful impellents to action and anything that minimises their influence can seriously undermine long-term commitment. Consider the scenario in Box 4.4.

So far it has been assumed that praise, among other things, strengthens belief in ability and promotes self-esteem. Meyer *et al.* (1986) argued that just the opposite may sometimes occur and showed that those subjects praised for success at an easy task and not blamed for failure at a difficult task inferred that their ability for that type of work was low, when they had few other cues upon which to base judgements. When praise for success at the easy task was withheld and failure at the difficult task blamed, subjects assessed their ability as being much higher. Other studies have reported that children can attribute teacher praise to low ability on their part (Miller and Hom, 1997). Black students who were praised for a good academic performance by a white evaluator, who lacked knowledge of their level, assumed that the evaluator had lower expectations of them and rated the evaluator less favourably than black students not praised (Lawrence, 2001). Furthermore, Derevensky and Leckerman (1997) discovered that pupils in special education classes tended to receive more praise and positive reinforcement than those in regular classes. Similarly, weaker pupils in classrooms have been shown to receive more praise from teachers (Hattie and Timperley, 2007). Praise does not always carry positive messages, therefore, as far as inferences about ability levels are concerned. In particular, this type of support 'may be ineffective, or even associated with negative outcomes if it reduces the recipient's sense of autonomy, control, or self-efficacy' (Freeman *et al.*, 2009: 197). Pupils' understanding of the reason for praise being given will determine what they make of it.

Another possible downside of praise was highlighted by Twenge (2006), who argued that many parents overpraise their children to the extent that their offspring

---

Box 4.4 An example of intrinsic rewards driving performance

A group of cross-country runners meets up each lunchtime to cover a four-mile course before getting quickly showered and returning to work. It means that they only have time to grab a quick snack and the lunch hour is one endless rush – but they enjoy it. One winter's day they meet up as usual. By the end of the second mile, the weather turns very cold and they find themselves facing driving rain while underfoot the mud is ankle deep. The usual banter gradually dies as the group struggles up a steep rise with two miles still to go. They begin to get colder, wetter and more exhausted. One of the runners is finally heard to grumble through chattering teeth, 'If I was being paid to do this, I would be asking for a wage increase!'

---

then develop a misguided sense of their actual abilities. This attitude can also be evidenced more generally in some school systems where there is a reluctance to fail pupils. Likewise, many elementary schools in the UK employ a token economy system, whereby teachers distribute stickers as rewards to children for good behaviour. However, research has shown that these are often allocated freely and for minimal efforts (such as sitting in your seat) in an attempt to allocate approval to all children, with the result that they lose their rewarding potential (MacLure and Jones, 2009). As one four-year-old pupil put it, 'What's the point of doing anything if you're praised for just sitting' (Henry, 2009). As a result of research findings in this area, one journalist wrote an article entitled 'Beware the Carrot: Rewards Don't Work' (Bloom, 2009). It is argued that these classroom reward systems seem to be guided by the maxim of the Dodo in *Alice's Adventures in Wonderland*, whose decision at the end of a race was that 'EVERYBODY has won, and all must have prizes' (Phillips, 1998). As a result of such parental and educational over-allocation of reward, these young people can face later disappointment and disillusionment as they crash on the hard rock of reality when confronted with some of the harsher difficulties in life. A reward for doing very little provides no useful feedback and does not increase the individual's sense of competence. In addition, receiving such a reward can convey to the child that the activity has been carried out just to please the teacher – the child feels less in control and so less committed to the activity.

There seem to be differences across ages and gender in relation to differential forms of praise with children. Corpus and Lepper (2007) compared four forms of reinforcement:

1   ***product praise*** – for what someone has produced (e.g. 'This is a very good essay.')
2   ***process praise*** – for effort expended (e.g. 'You have worked really well on this essay.')
3   ***person praise*** – for a particular trait (e.g. 'You are very clever.')
4   ***neutral feedback*** – (e.g. a positive sounding 'Okay.').

Results showed that four- and five-year-old children demonstrated increased motivation after receiving any of the first three types of praise, but not the fourth (neutral). However, girls aged 9 to 11 years actually showed decreased motivation after person praise, whereas boys in this age group reacted well to all four types of praise. Dweck (2000, 2007) and her co-workers also carried out a series of studies examining the effects of these types of praise. Their work showed that children praised for their ability (person praise) rather than effort (process praise) were less likely to want to tackle tasks that would have greater learning potential but would not guarantee success in favour of those that they knew they could do successfully. Receiving praise for ability also created vulnerability; when faced with failure, such children expressed least enjoyment with the activity, showed less perseverance and found the experience most aversive. Children praised for their ability were also more likely to regard intelligence as a fixed trait rather than something that could be enhanced.

The extent to which praise can undermine intrinsic motivation and be detrimental to performance has, however, been the subject of considerable debate (Sansone and Harackiewicz, 2000; Bronson and Merryman, 2009). In an extensive review of some 100 experiments, Cameron and Pierce (1994: 394) concluded: 'Our overall findings suggest that there is no detrimental effect [of extrinsic rewards] on intrinsic motivation.' Nevertheless, Good and Brophy (2008) cautioned that, in the classroom, reinforcement must always be applied in such a way as to complement natural outcomes of performance and not undermine intrinsic interest. According to Lieberman (2000), praise and other social rewards are less likely to have this negative effect than are material alternatives.

In order to overcome some of the potential downsides of reinforcement, the research findings suggest a number of guidelines to follow when using reinforcement in the classroom. It is better to use praise rather than material rewards and to attribute the praise to the child's own motivation. Rather than praising the child just for carrying out a task, make the reward contingent upon the attainment of a certain level or standard. Link the praise directly to improvements in performance and include specific feedback information on improvement as part of the reward. Finally, encourage pupils to reflect on why they are being praised. For example, an English teacher could reward a child by saying: 'Well done! Your essay has improved from a C grade to a B grade [attainment of higher level]. The overall structure is much better, as is your use of grammar and spelling [feedback information]. Your enjoyment in writing this really comes across [reward linked to internal motivation]. How do you feel about the essay this time? [encouraging child to reflect on reasons for the reward].'

Response development

There is a progressive sequence of rewards, which commences with the mere acknowledgement of a response, continues with the positive evaluation of it through praise, and proceeds to the further exploration and development of the content. In this way, having an idea or action accepted as part of the agenda for the ongoing discourse may be looked upon as the highest form of praise. It is quite easy for a teacher, manager, interviewer or coach to express a few perfunctory words of acknowledgement or commendation before continuing on a completely different tack. However, the development of one's response indicates: (a) that the listener must have been carefully attending; (b) that the content must have been considered worthy of the listener's time and effort to make it part of 'the talk'.

A response can be developed in a number of ways. In the classroom, Burden and Byrd (2009) recommended that teachers should follow up pupils' contributions by encouraging them to elucidate their initial response, develop it, move their ideas to higher levels and provide support for their opinions. This is a powerful means of providing reinforcement during a lesson, even if it is less frequently used than alternatives already considered. On the other hand, teachers may develop a pupil's contribution by elaborating upon it themselves. The potential reward for pupils of having their ideas form part of the lesson will be readily appreciated. In a group, members may be asked to contribute their suggestions and be reinforced by having their responses further explored by other members. In a coaching context, certain individuals can be selected to demonstrate a skill or technique to the other participants for them to develop. If tactfully handled, this form of response development can be highly motivating and positively valued.

Clearly there is a whole range of possibilities for developing responses. Dickson *et al.* (1993), in reviewing some conditioning type studies, suggested that reflective statements (see Chapter 6) and self-disclosures (see Chapter 9) may function in this way. In general though, research concerning the reinforcing effects of response development is less prevalent than that involving reinforcers included in the previous two categories.

Nonverbal components

The administration of reinforcement is not solely dependent upon the verbal channel of communication. It has been established that a number of nonverbal behaviours, such as a warm smile or an enthusiastic nod of the head, can also have a reinforcing impact on the behaviour of the other person during interaction. For instance, Rosenfarb (1992: 343) believed that positive change in client behaviour during psychotherapy can be accounted for in this way. He explained how this might operate:

> Often, subtle therapeutic cues serve to reinforce selected aspects of client behavior. A therapist's turn of the head, a change in eye contact, or a change in voice tone may reinforce selected client behavior . . . One therapist, for example, may lean forward in her chair whenever a client begins to discuss interpersonal difficulties with his mother. Another therapist may begin to nod his head as clients begin to discuss such material. A third may maintain more eye contact. In all three cases, each therapist's behavior may be serving as both a reinforcing stimulus for previous client behavior and as a discriminative stimulus for the further discussion of such relevant material.

The fact that nonverbal cues can operate to influence behaviour should not surprise us unduly as it will be remembered from Chapter 3 that the nonverbal channel of communication is frequently more important than the verbal channel with regard to the conveying of information of an emotional or attitudinal nature. The nonverbal channel is particularly adept at communicating states and attitudes such as friendliness, interest, warmth and involvement.

Gestural reinforcement

This category includes relatively small movements of specific parts of the body. 'Gestural' in this sense is broadly defined to encompass not only movements of the hands, arms and head, but also the facial region. Concerning the latter, two of the most frequently identified reinforcers are smiles and eye contact.

Smiles

In carrying out a satisfaction survey of the quality of school life, Furst and Criste (1997) noted that the boys who took part valued teacher smiles. Some research evidence also suggests that smiles can have a reinforcing effect. In one experiment, Showalter (1974) succeeded in conditioning affect statements through the selective use of smiles by the interviewer. Many studies have combined smiles with other nonverbal and verbal reinforcers. Krasner (1958) combined smiles with head nods and 'mm-hmm' to increase the use of the word 'mother' by subjects. Pansa (1979) increased the incidence of self-referenced affect statements provided by a group of reactive schizophrenics using a comparable procedure, although Saigh (1981) obtained less positive results. This lack of consistency could be due to smiles being interpreted differently by subjects. LaFrance and Hecht (1999: 45) stated: 'There may be no gesture with more diverse meanings and more varied forms than the human smile. Smiles convey delight and happiness, but people also smile when they feel anything but enjoyment.'

Eye contact

This is an important element of interpersonal interaction. The establishment of eye contact is usually a preparatory step when initiating interaction. During a conversation, continued use of this behaviour is an indicator of our responsiveness to the other, and level of involvement in the exchange. Its selective use can, therefore, have reinforcing potential. A positive relationship between interviewer eye contact and subjects' verbal productivity was documented by O'Brien and Holborn (1979). Goldman (1980) also reported that verbal encouragement could be used to reinforce expressed attitudes more effectively when coupled with eye contact. The overuse of eye contact or gaze, though, can also be threatening and cause discomfort or distress.

Gestures

Certain movements of the hands and arms can signal appreciation and approval. Probably the most frequently used gestures of this type are applause and the 'thumbs-up' sign. Head nods are gestures that have a wider relevance. Their frequent use can be seen during practically any interactive episode, being commonly used to indicate acknowledgement, agreement and understanding. As such, they belong to a group of attention-giving behaviours know as 'back-channel' communication (Bowe and Martin, 2007). Matarazzo and Wiens (1972) found that the use of head nods by an interviewer had the effect of increasing the average duration of utterance given by an interviewee. Although total verbal output of subjects increased significantly, Scofield (1977) obtained a disproportionately higher number of self-referenced statements following contingent application of interviewer head nods combined with a paraphrase, restatement or verbal encouragement.

Proximity reinforcement

Unlike the previous category, the present one includes gross movements of the whole body or substantial parts of it. Proximity reinforcement refers to potential reinforcing effects that can accrue from altering the distance between oneself and another during interaction. A reduction in interpersonal distance usually accompanies a desire for greater intimacy and involvement. However, while someone who adopts a position at some distance from the other participant may be seen as being unreceptive and detached, a person who approaches too closely may be regarded as overfamiliar, dominant or even threatening. In the study by Goldman (1980), already referred to, attitudes of subjects were more successfully modified by means of verbal reinforcers when the interviewer stood at a moderate (four to five feet) rather than a close (two to three feet) interpersonal distance.

With participants who are seated, as professionals often are during encounters, it is obviously much more difficult to effect sizeable variations in interpersonal distance. However, this can be accomplished, to a certain extent, by adopting forward or backward leaning postures. Mehrabian (1972) reported that a forward leaning posture was one component of a complex of behaviours which he labelled 'immediacy' and which denotes a positive attitude towards the other person. Similarly, Nelson-Jones (2005a) believed that this type of posture conveys acceptance and receptivity when used in counselling. As with some other nonverbal reinforcers, studies conducted in part to establish the reinforcing effects of a forward leaning posture have combined it with several other reinforcers. However, there is also some research evidence supporting the reinforcing effects which a forward leaning posture per se can have (Banks, 1972).

Touch

Used appropriately, touch can be a powerful form of reinforcement. According to Jones and Yarbrough (1985), it can be construed in a number of ways to convey, among other things, affection, appreciation and support. As such, the relevance of touch to care delivery is evident and its rewarding effects in the nursing setting have been well documented (Routasalo, 1999; Connor and Howett, 2009). In the classroom, Wheldall *et al.* (1986) found that when teachers of mixed-gender infant classes used positive contingent touch when praising good 'on-task' classroom behaviour, rates of this type of behaviour rose by some 20 per cent. Nevertheless, as with many forms of nonverbal behaviour, 'touch and the lack of touch are intriguing and complex entities because the meaning of touch can vary from one situation to the next' (Davidhizar and Giger, 1997: 204). In many contexts, of course, touch is inappropriate, even socially forbidden, and must be used with discretion (see Chapter 3).

HOW DO REINFORCERS REINFORCE?

The key feature of reinforcement is that it modifies the future probability of the behaviour that led to it. There is much less agreement, however, about just how this is brought about. Three main possibilities will be briefly considered here: reinforcement as a direct modifier of behaviour; as motivation; and as information.

Reinforcement as a direct modifier of behaviour

Favoured by theorists such as Skinner (1953), this view is that essentially reinforcers function directly and automatically to bring about behavioural change. Two important implications stem from this view. The first is that the individual's awareness of what is taking place is not a prerequisite for reinforcement. According to Martin and Pear (2007: 39): 'For a reinforcer to increase an individual's behavior, it is not necessary that that individual be able to talk about or indicate an understanding of why he or she was reinforced.' While reporting findings substantiating this proposition, Lieberman (2000) nevertheless concluded that the circumstances under which reinforcement without awareness takes place tend to be rather contrived or extraordinary.

The second implication concerns the nature of the relationship between the targeted response and the reinforcing event. Does reinforcement depend on the behaviour in question bringing about a positive outcome (*contingency*) or simply being followed in time by it (*contiguity*)? A belief in contiguity as a necessary and sufficient condition for reinforcement to take place is commonly associated with its unconscious operation. Skinner (1977: 4), for instance, wrote: 'Coincidence is the heart of operant conditioning. A response is strengthened by certain kinds of consequences, but not necessarily because they are actually produced by it.' The precise nature of the relationship between behaviour and subsequent events in respect of contingency and contiguity is not entirely clear. Wasserman and Neunaber (1986) demonstrated how subjects could be influenced to respond in the mistaken belief that it increased the frequency of a light coming on, which was associated with points being earned, even though this was in fact not the case. A causal relationship can sometimes be inferred where none exists.

Reinforcement as motivation

A second possibility is that reinforcers serve largely to motivate. In this way, the expectation of receiving a reward for succeeding in a task spurs on further efforts in that direction and makes it more likely that this type of task will be undertaken again. Such incentives may be external and represent the projected attainment of a tangible outcome (e.g. money, food, praise, etc.), or as Bandura (1989) stressed, be internal and derivable from anticipated positive self-evaluations at the prospect of succeeding in the task at hand.

Reinforcement as information

The third possibility adopts the cognitive stance that reinforcers function, in the main, by providing information on task performance. Sarafino (2004) pointed out that feedback is implicit in many of the forms of reward that we obtain. Thus, if we receive a material reward or praise for some action, this in itself also tells us that we performed well. However, Hattie and Timperley (2007) and Cairns (2006) have argued that the two are inherently different processes. Cairns noted: 'Reinforcement implies some changes and learning in a behavioural sense . . . Feedback implies an information loop which may or may not have links in the learning sense or in effecting any possible repetition of the behaviour' (p. 150).

Conditioning studies are often arranged so that response-contingent points are allocated which can then be exchanged by subjects for back-up reinforcers such as food or money. The material value of these reinforcers is usually quite small. Wearden (1988) drew attention to the fact that, in some instances, subjects work diligently for paltry financial remuneration. Likewise, when food is the reward, it is often left unconsumed, indeed sometimes discarded without being tasted, and yet at the same time subjects continue to work for more. These findings are difficult to reconcile in motivational terms, if money or food are thought of as the key inducements. Wearden argued that perceiving the conditioning procedure as a problem-solving exercise in the eyes of the subjects is the more plausible explanation. Points received for an appropriate move are prized not hedonistically through association with money or food, but on account of the information they contribute to finding a solution to the 'puzzle'. In this way, conditioning results have been explained in terms of subjects trying to figure out the connection between what they do and the outcomes they experience in a sort of puzzle-solving exercise (Dulany, 1968).

While conclusive proof to resolve these differences in position is lacking, the present consensus of opinion appears to be that, as far as social performance in everyday situations is concerned, probably little instrumental conditioning takes place without at least some minimal level of conscious involvement (Lieberman, 2000). The effects of reinforcement seem to rely more upon a contingent than a mere contiguous association between behaviour and reward (Schwartz, 1989). Furthermore, recipients' understanding of why they received the reward also seems to matter (Miller and Hom, 1997).

GUIDELINES FOR THE USE OF THE SKILL OF REINFORCEMENT

Sets of recommendations for enhancing the effectiveness of reinforcing procedures can be found in different sources (e.g. Zirploi and Melloy, 2001; Maag, 2003; Cairns 2006; Burden and Byrd, 2009). The main aspects will now be highlighted.

Appropriateness of rewards

Throughout this chapter an attempt has been made to stress the fact that stimuli which may have reinforcing properties in some situations may not have the same effects in others. Bearing in mind the model discussed in Chapter 2, it is important that one remains sensitive to the characteristics of the situation, including the other people involved, when choosing the type of reinforcement to use. Thus, some forms of praise that would be quite appropriate when used with a child would seem extremely patronising if used with an adult. Attention should, in addition, be paid to the reinforcement history of the individual. Not all rewards will be prized equally. Different people may prefer certain reinforcers to others, and the same individual on different occasions may find the same reinforcer differentially attractive.

Reinforcement given should also be appropriate to the task undertaken and the degree of success achieved. A consideration here has to do with the recipient's perception of equity. Lawler (1983) produced evidence that, at least with material rewards, less satisfaction is expressed when there are discrepancies between what is received and what is felt to be deserved, even when the inequity results in higher recompense than was thought to be merited. Furthermore, people who receive praise for completing a relatively easy task may, if they have little else to go on, conclude they have low ability at this type of work. This is also the case with the well-known expression 'damned with faint praise', where the reinforcement proffered actually indicates a lack of ability on the part of the recipient (e.g. where a teacher says to a pupil 'That's not too bad for you, John.').

Genuineness of application

It is important that social rewards are perceived as genuinely reflecting the source's reaction to the targeted person or performance. If not, they may come across as sarcasm, veiled criticism or perhaps as bored habit. Complementarity of verbal and nonverbal behaviour is important in this regard. When seen as an attempt at cynical manipulation, rewards are also likely to be counterproductive (Aronson, 2008). This is exemplified by the phrase 'too sweet to be wholesome', which refers to someone who over-reinforces, well beyond the subcultural norm, and so is viewed as having ulterior motives – the rewards are then not regarded as genuine and the person is viewed with suspicion.

Contingency of reinforcement

In order for the various social behaviours reviewed in this chapter to function as effective reinforcers it is important that their application be made contingent upon the particular action it is intended to modify. As expressed by Martin and Pear (2007: 42), 'reinforcers must be contingent on specific behaviors in order for those behaviors to improve'. This does not mean that the random use of such behaviour will fail to produce an effect. It may well serve to create a particular impression of the provider or the situation, or put the recipient at ease. It is highly improbable, however, that it will selectively reinforce as desired. In many situations, it may be prudent to specify, quite precisely, the behavioural focus of attention.

Frequency of reinforcement

It is not necessary to reinforce constantly each and every instance of a specific response for that class of response to be increased. It has been found that, following an initial period of continual reinforcement to establish the behaviour, the frequency of reinforcement can be reduced without resulting in a corresponding reduction in target behaviour. This is called *intermittent reinforcement*, and many real-life activities (such as gambling) are maintained in this way. Frequencies of performance do not decline in the face of intermittent reinforcement, but rather they actually increase and become more resistant to extinction (Leslie and O'Reilly, 1999). Accordingly, Maag (2003) recommended that rewards should be used sparingly to maximise their reinforcing efficacy. A related recommendation is that recipients have access to these only after performing the desired behaviour. Along similar lines, *gain/loss theory* predicts that when the receipt of a reward is set against a backdrop of a general paucity of positive reaction from that source, its effect will be enhanced (Aronson, 2008).

Variety of reinforcement

The continual and inflexible use of a specific reinforcer will quickly lead to that reinforcer losing its reinforcing properties. The recipient will become satiated. If an interviewer responds to each interviewee statement with, for example, 'Good', this utterance will gradually become denuded of any evaluative connotations, and consequently will rapidly cease to have reinforcing effects. An attempt should therefore be made to employ a variety of reinforcing expressions and behaviours while ensuring that they do not violate the requirement of appropriateness.

Timing of reinforcement

A broadly agreed recommendation is that a reinforcing stimulus should be applied directly following the target response. As expressed by Zirploi and Melloy (2001: 166): 'As the interval between the behavior and reinforcement increases, the relative effectiveness of the reinforcer decreases.' If reinforcement is delayed, there is a danger that other responses may intervene between the one to be promoted and the presentation of the reinforcer. Making the individual aware of the basis upon which the reinforcer, when it is delivered, is gained may help to reduce the negative effects of delay. This is not to overlook the fact that, from a motivational viewpoint, the availability of immediate payoff is likely to have greater incentive value than the prospect of having to wait for some time for personal benefits to materialise.

Selective reinforcement

In this context, selective reinforcement refers to the fact that it is possible to reinforce selectively certain elements of a response without necessarily reinforcing it in total. This can be effected during the actual response. Nonverbal reinforcers such as head nods and verbal reinforcers like 'Mm-hmm' are of particular relevance in this respect since they can be used without interrupting the speaker. Selective reinforcement can also be applied following the termination of a response. Thus, a teacher may partially reinforce a pupil who has almost produced the correct answer to a question with, 'Yes, John, you are right, Kilimanjaro is a mountain, but is it in the Andes?' By so doing, the teacher reinforces that portion of the answer which is accurate, while causing the pupil to rethink the element which is not.

Allied to this process, *shaping* permits nascent attempts at an ultimately acceptable end performance to be rewarded. By systematically demanding higher standards for rewards to be granted, performances can be shaped to attain requisite levels of excellence. The acquisition of most everyday skills like swimming, driving a car, or playing a violin involve an element of shaping. If reinforcers were withheld until the full-blown activity was performed in accordance with more advanced criteria of excellence, learning could take a long time and be an extremely thankless task for the learner.

OVERVIEW

As a social skill, reinforcement is central to interpersonal interaction. What people do, what they learn, the decisions that they take, their feelings and attitudes towards themselves and others, indeed the sorts of individuals they become, can be shaped and moulded by the reactions of others. While the basic notion that people tend to behave in ways that bring about positive outcomes for them is scarcely iconoclastic, it does seem that in many professional circles reinforcement as a social skill is not well used. Good and Brophy (2008), for example, question whether teachers routinely use praise in the classroom in such a way as to be maximally reinforcing of desired behaviour and achievement.

The types of social reinforcers concentrated upon in this chapter were divided into verbal and nonverbal for the purpose of analysis. In practice, however, these two channels intermesh. Verbal reinforcers include such reactions as acknowledging, confirming, praising, supporting and developing the other's responses in a variety of ways. Nonverbally, gestures such as smiles, head nods and eye contact, together with larger body movements, including reducing interpersonal distance, forward posture leans and touch, have been found to have reinforcing potential.

When utilised in accordance with the guidelines outlined above, reinforcement can serve to promote interaction and maintain relationships; increase the involvement of the interactive partner; make interaction interesting and enjoyable, demonstrate a genuine interest in the ideas, thoughts and feelings of the other; create an impression of warmth and understanding; enhance the interpersonal attractiveness of the source; and improve the confidence and self-esteem of the recipient. At the same time, the effectiveness of reinforcement is determined by a complex array of interwoven factors, including those to do with the source, the recipient, the context, the nature of the reward itself and the way in which it is delivered.

Chapter 5

Finding out about others:
the skill of questioning

INTRODUCTION

THE QUESTION IS A key constituent of the DNA of interactional
life. In one of my communication classes I use an exercise in which I
ask four volunteers to come to the front of the class. I then instruct them
to carry on a conversation about 'the events of the week'. The only rule
is that no one is allowed to ask a question. Two things happen. First, the
interaction is very stilted and difficult. Second, someone very quickly
asks a question. To continue with the above analogy, in the absence of
questioning DNA, the communication organism often becomes unstable
and eventually dies.

Questions are at the heart of most interpersonal encounters.
Information seeking is a core human activity that is central to learning,
decision making and problem solving (Mokros and Aakhus, 2002). As
Waterman *et al.* (2001: 477) argued: 'Asking questions is a fundamental
part of communication, and as such will be an important factor in the
work of many professionals.' In most social encounters, questions are
asked and responses reinforced – this is the method whereby information is gathered and conversation encouraged. Thus, questioning is
one of the most widely used interactive skills and one of the easiest
to identify in general terms. However, as cautioned by Dickson and
Hargie (2006: 121): 'While at a surface level questioning seems to be a
straightforward feature of communication, deeper analysis, at functional, structural, and textual levels, reveals questioning to be a complex
and multifaceted phenomenon.'

Society is fascinated by questions and answers. Those involved in
public question and answer sessions have become the gladiators of the

117

electronic era. Let us take a few examples. Contestants in television quiz shows can win fame and fortune just by knowing the answers to questions they are asked. Their 'hosts', or interrogators, on these shows are already household names. Television and radio interviewers also become celebrities because they are good at asking the right questions, albeit in an entertaining fashion. Courtroom dramas, in which lawyers thrust rapier-like questions at innocent and guilty defendants or witnesses, are ubiquitous. So too with police films where the skilled detective eventually breaks down the recalcitrant suspect through insightful and incisive questioning. Question Time in the UK House of Commons and Senate Investigations in the USA, both of which involve hard and often harsh questioning, have a special type of fascination for viewers.

The above examples underline the ultimate power and potential of questions as contributors to success or failure across different contexts. They also reflect the fact that this is a core interpersonal skill. This chapter examines the nature, function and effects of various forms and types of questions across a range of social contexts.

DEFINITION OF QUESTION

The first question we need to ask is, perhaps paradoxically, what exactly is a question? There is no simple answer here, since a question can be defined in grammatical, sociolinguistic or semantic terms. In analysing definitional issues, Wang (2006) noted that grammatically a question is interrogative in form, syntactically it is a sentence in which the subject and the first verb in the verb phrase are inverted, and semantically it communicates a desire for further information. The latter meaning is in line with the skills perspective, wherein a question is defined as a request for information, whether factual or otherwise. This request for information can be verbal or nonverbal. As delineated by Stewart and Cash (2008: 51): 'A question is *any statement or nonverbal act that invites an answer or response.*' For example, a high-pitched 'guggle' such as 'Hmmm?' after someone has made a statement is a form of request to the speaker to continue speaking. Similarly, a directional nod of the head, after asking one member of a group a question, can indicate to another member that the question is being redirected and a response expected. Questions, then, may be nonverbal signals urging another to respond. They may also be statements uttered in an inquisitive fashion, for example:

- 'Tell me more.'
- 'You do realise what will happen.'

Statements that request information are termed *prosodic questions* and defined as 'declarative sentences containing question cues that may be intonational, or these utterances are marked as questions by means of a variety of contextual cues' (Woodbury, 1984: 203). In the legal context, prosodic questions are widely used by attorneys (e.g. 'You were still in your home at that time?'), especially during the cross-examination of witnesses (Dillon, 1990). Conversely, as these examples given by Wang (2006: 533) illustrate, what seem like questions may in fact be statements:

- Who cares? (I don't care.)
- What difference does it make? (It makes no difference.)

Although a question can be posed nonverbally, most questions in social interaction are verbal in nature. At the same time, there are certain nonverbal signals that should accompany the verbal message, if a question is to be recognised as such. One paralinguistic signal is the raising or lowering of the vocal inflection on the last syllable of the question. Other nonverbal behaviours include head movements, rapidly raising or lowering the eyebrows and direct eye contact at the end of the question accompanied by a pause. The function of these nonverbal behaviours is to emphasise to the other person that a question is being asked and a response expected.

QUESTIONS IN CONTEXT

The skill of questioning is to be found at every level in social interaction. Young children, exploring a new environment, seem to be naturally inquisitive, always seeking answers to an ever increasing number of questions. At this stage, questions play a crucial role in their learning and maturation process, as they attempt to assimilate information in order to make sense of their surroundings. It is very important for the child's development that parents take time to answer these questions (Cook, 2009). This rewards the child for asking questions, inculcates a sense of curiosity and provides answers to what are perceived to be important issues.

Investigations into the use of questions in various professional contexts have been carried out for decades. In the educational context, Margutti (2006: 314) pointed out: 'Questions and answers are the most prevalent instructional tools in a long standing pedagogic tradition in which the centrality of questions in teaching is widely recognized ... and which is claimed, by some, to have come down all the way from Socrates.' A large volume of research into the effects of teacher questions in the classroom has now been accumulated (Gayle *et al.*, 2006). An early study was conducted by Corey (1940), in which she had an expert stenographer make verbatim records of all classroom talk in six classes. It was found that, on average, the teacher asked a question once every 72 seconds. Some 30 years later, Resnick (1972), working with teachers and pupils in an infant school (serving five- to seven-year-old children) in south-east London, found that 36 per cent of all teacher remarks were questions. Furthermore, this figure increased to 59 per cent when only extended interactions were analysed. More recently, this rapid rate of teacher questioning was confirmed in the preschool setting by Siraj-Blatchford and Manni (2008), who discovered that over an observation period of 400 hours, the 28 teachers being recorded asked a total of 5808 questions.

In a review of such studies, Dillon (1982) reported results to show that teachers ask about two questions per minute, while their pupils taken as a whole only ask around two questions per hour, giving an average of one question per pupil per month. When the teachers were surveyed about their use of questions, it was found that they actually asked three times as many questions as they estimated they had and received only one-sixth the number of pupil questions estimated. However, as previously mentioned, reticence at asking questions is not the general norm for children. For example, Tizard *et al.* (1983) radio-recorded four-year-old girls at home and at school and found that on average per hour the children asked 24 questions at home and only 1.4 at school. Interestingly, one major reason given by students for their reluctance to ask questions in class is fear of a negative reaction from classmates (Dillon, 1988). Daly *et al.* (1994), in a US study, found a significant and negative correlation between question asking and age in pupils aged between 13 and 16 years. As pupils got older they felt less comfortable about asking questions in class. Daly *et al.* also found that in terms of question asking the following felt more at ease:

- males
- whites
- higher-income groups
- those with higher self-esteem
- those who felt accepted by the teacher.

Smith *et al.* (2006) illustrated how a three-part *Initiation–Response–Follow-up* (*IRF*) pattern has long been the norm in classrooms. This consists of a teacher *Initiation*, usually a question, followed by a brief pupil *Response*, and a teacher *Follow-up* where some type of feedback or evaluation is given to the pupil's answer. As summarised by Smith *et al.* (2006), this IRF structure 'often consists of closed teacher questions, brief pupil answers which teachers do not build upon, superficial praise rather than diagnostic feedback, and an emphasis on recalling information rather than genuine exploration of a topic' (p. 444). Such findings indicate that teachers need to be more aware of the many nuances pertaining to classroom questioning.

An analysis of the use of questions by doctors reveals parallel findings. As Brashers *et al.* (2002: 259), in their review of information exchange in the consultation, put it: 'Physicians ask most of the questions and patients provide most of the information.' Indeed, West (1983) found that out of a total of 773 questions identified in 21 doctor–patient consultations, only 68 (9 per cent) were initiated by patients. Furthermore, when patients did ask questions nearly half of these were marked by speech disturbances, indicating discomfort at requesting information from the doctor. Likewise, Sanchez (2001) cited a study in which, during an average consultation time per patient of 2.1 minutes, doctors asked 27.3 questions. Such a pattern and volume of doctor questions means that patients have little scope to reply, let alone formulate a question. Yet one of the key elements rated most highly by patients when receiving bad news is the opportunity to ask questions (Hind, 1997).

The difficulties faced by patients in asking questions have been well documented (Katz *et al.*, 2007). When asked, the main reason given by patients for not asking questions of doctors is a fear of appearing to be ignorant (Roter and Hall, 2006). In particular, less-well-educated and lower-income patients have been shown to ask fewer questions of doctors (Siminoff *et al.*, 2006). Skelton and Hobbs (1999) found that patients often prefaced their questions with the phrase 'I was wondering ...'. Doctors never used this expression with patients. Interestingly, the only time they did use it was when they telephoned colleagues. Similarly, Wynn (1996) discovered that medical students quickly learned how to handle patient-initiated questions – by adopting the strategy of asking unrelated doctor-initiated ones. In this way, they maintained control of the consultation. However, Parrott *et al.* (1992), in a study of paediatrician–patient communication, showed that while paediatricians generally asked more questions than patients, during consultations in which they specifically addressed concerns raised by patients more questions were subsequently asked by the latter. It would therefore seem that patient questions can be encouraged (and of course discouraged) by the approach of the doctor.

In relation to community pharmacy, Morrow *et al.* (1993) carried out a UK study in which they recorded a series of community pharmacist–patient consultations. They found that patients asked on average 2.5 questions per consultation compared to an average of 4.1 for pharmacists. This ratio of patient questions is much higher than that found in doctor–patient consultations. Interestingly, a number of the questions asked by these patients related to requests for clarification about what the doctor had previously told them. This suggests that either they felt more at ease asking questions of the pharmacist than indicating lack of understanding to the doctor, or that they had subsequently thought of questions they would have liked to have been able to ask the doctor. Morrow *et al.* (1993) argued that the public may have a view that since pharmacies are readily and easily accessible, pharmacists are probably 'approachable' professionals. Furthermore, the fact that in most instances clients are paying directly for the services they receive may mean that they feel more empowered to ask questions in community pharmacies.

QUESTIONS AND CONTROL

The above findings reflect the control differential in relation to questioner and respondent. In a review of questions as a form of power, Wang (2006: 531) illustrated how 'the inborn features of questions make them naturally bound up with power in that questions possess the ability to dominate and control'. As shown by Gee *et al.* (1999), there is usually a considerable difference between interviewer and interviewee in terms of expertise, status and power. Indeed, this power imbalance was noted in a humorous fashion by Lewis Carroll in *Alice's Adventures in Wonderland* (1866/2003) where a father responds to his child's questions as follows:

'I have answered three questions and that is enough,'
Said his father. 'Don't give yourself airs!
Do you think I can listen all day to such stuff?
Be off, or I'll kick you down stairs.'

Bolden (2009: 122) noted that questions allow the questioner to control the conversation 'by requesting the addressee to engage with a specific topic and/or perform a particular responsive action'. Furthermore, in most contexts it is the person of higher status, or the person in control, who asks the questions. Thus, the majority of questions are asked by teachers in classrooms, doctors in surgeries, nurses on the ward, lawyers in court, detectives in interrogation rooms and so on. For this reason, some counselling theorists have long argued that counsellors should try not to ask any questions at all of clients, to avoid being seen as the controller of the interaction (Rogers, 1951). A related power factor here is the attitude of the questioner. For example, Baxter *et al.* (2006) found that when respondents were interviewed in a firm, formal manner they were more likely to alter their initial answers than when interviewed in a friendly, relaxed fashion. The manner in which interviewees are questioned also affects how they are judged by observers. As noted by Fiedler (1993: 362): 'The way in which a person is questioned may have a substantial effect on his or her credibility, regardless of what he/she actually says.' For example, witnesses in court or candidates at selection interviews may be treated with the utmost respect when being questioned, or alternatively dealt with in an offhand manner. As well as directly impacting upon the respondent's self-esteem and confidence, such treatment is in turn likely to have an impact upon how the jury or selection panel respectively evaluate the responses.

To compound the problem, the respondent in many instances feels under stress when being questioned. This is certainly true in the above examples where stress and anxiety are often experienced by patients on the ward or in the surgery, by suspects in police stations, by pupils in classrooms and by defendants in court. Furthermore, in the latter two cases, the person asking the questions already knows the answers, and this makes these situations even more stressful and removed from normal interaction. In everyday conversation we do not ask questions to which we already know the answers, or if we do we employ elaborate verbalisations to explain our behaviour ('I was surprised to discover something . . . Let me see if you can guess . . .').

In the courtroom, it is a long-known maxim that lawyers should only ask questions to which they already know the answers. In this context, the creation of stress in witnesses is regarded as a legitimate tactic, and this is developed by a rapid-fire questioning approach. Take the excerpt in Box 5.1, involving a sequence of questions posed by defence counsel Mr Bailey to Mark Fuhrman, one of the Los Angeles police detectives at the murder scene in the famous OJ Simpson trial in the USA. Such a sequence, where one question is asked every few seconds, the respondent does not know what to expect next and the answers are already known by the questioner, would undoubtedly put most people under pressure. In the classroom, however, the heightened anxiety of pupils may be dysfunctional and detrimental both to learning and to pupil–teacher attitudes. Teachers should bear this in mind when employing this skill. Professionals also need to be careful in relation to the overall volume of questions used since, as shown by Benn *et al.* (2008: 57), 'too many questions may inhibit the development of a collaborative relationship'.

PURPOSES OF QUESTIONS

Bolden (2009: 122) pointed out: 'Questions and answers are among the most readily recognizable and pervasive ways through which participants achieve and negotiate their communicative goals.' In fact, questions serve a range of purposes, depending upon the context of the interaction. For example, questions are asked by:

- salespeople to assess customer needs and relate their sales pitch to the satisfaction of these needs
- teachers to check for pupil understanding
- negotiators to slow the pace of the interaction and put pressure on their opponents
- doctors to facilitate diagnoses.

Box 5.1 Excerpt from the OJ Simpson trial

Q: When you entered the home, did you go directly out the front door to view the bodies once again or did you at that time begin to walk around and make observations?

A: No. I was led by Officer Riske.

Q: All right. The purpose in taking that route was to get back to where you had started, but in a different place, right?

A: Yes, sir.

Q: And to get there without walking through the pooling of blood that was around the area, that was your purpose, right?

A: Yes. Yes, sir.

Q: How long would you say you spent at the crime scene from that vantage point up on the steps I believe you told us on that occasion?

A: Once Officer Riske brought us out into the landing? Just long enough to point out a few items of evidence, show us the footprints and then walk us back along the right side of those shoeprints.

Q: Okay. Well, how long do you think you spent there?

A: Couple minutes.

Q: Maybe only two?

A: Two, three minutes.

Q: Okay. And you made the observations you described for us on direct examination about Mr Goldman, the other evidence that was lying around?

A: Officer Riske was pointing them out with his flashlight.

Q: Okay. These are things he had discovered and he was showing them to you. These were not things that you were discovering as a detective, right?

A: I was listening and he was pointing them out, yes, sir, that's correct.

Q: Were you?

A: No. We were quiet listening to his – his lead.

Q: And he told you that he had seen them there when he first came on the scene a little after midnight?

A: Yes.

Q: Now, after spending two, three minutes there, where did you go?

A: We walked down along the pathway that's on the north side of the residence, looked at the gate.

Q = Mr Bailey, Defence Counsel
A = Mark Fuhrman, LAPD Detective

The main general goals of questions are outlined in Box 5.2. However, it should be realised that the type of question asked influences the extent to which each of these various goals can be fulfilled. Indeed, it is the responses made to questions that determine whether or not the objective has been achieved. In this sense, a question is only as good as the answer it evokes.

Box 5.2 Goals of questioning

The main goals served by the skill of questioning are:
1 to obtain information
2 to initiate interaction
3 to maintain control of an interaction
4 to arouse interest and curiosity concerning a topic
5 to diagnose specific difficulties the respondent may have
6 to express an interest in the respondent
7 to ascertain the attitudes, feelings and opinions of the respondent
8 to encourage maximum participation from respondents
9 to assess the extent of the respondent's knowledge
10 to encourage critical thought and evaluation
11 to communicate, in group discussions, that involvement and overt participation by all group members is expected and valued
12 to encourage group members to comment on the responses of other members of the group
13 to maintain the attention of group members (e.g. by asking questions periodically without advance warning).

TYPES OF QUESTION

Several different classifications of question types have been proposed. Rudyard Kipling (1902) put forward the following early categorisation of questions:

> I keep six honest serving men
> (They taught me all I knew);
> Their names are What and Why and When,
> And How and Where and Who.

As will be seen, these lines reflect, to a fair degree, the different classifications of questions that have been identified.

Closed/open questions

The most common division of questions relates to the degree of freedom, or scope, given to the respondent in answering. Those that leave the respondent open to choose any one of a number of ways in which to reply are referred to as open questions, while those that require a short response of a specific nature are termed closed questions.

Closed questions

These usually have a correct answer, or can be answered with a short response selected from a limited number of possible options. There are three main types:

1   *Selection question.* Here the respondent is presented with two or more alternative responses from which to choose. As a result, this type is also known as an *alternative question* or *forced choice question.* Examples include:

  • 'Would you rather have Fyfe, Cameron or Rodgers as the next President?'
  • 'Do you want to travel by sea or by air?'

2   *Yes–no question.* As the name suggests, this question may be adequately answered by a 'yes' or 'no', or some equivalent affirmative or negative. Examples include:

  • 'Did you go to university?'
  • 'Has there been any bleeding?'

3   *Identification question.* This requires the respondent to identify the answer to a factual question and present this as the response. This may involve:

  • recall of information, e.g. 'Where were you born?'
  • identification of present circumstances, e.g. 'Where exactly is the pain occurring now?'
  • queries about future events, e.g. 'Where are you going on holiday?'

Closed questions are usually easy to answer, and so are useful in encouraging early participation in an interaction. They have a number of applications across contexts. In fact-finding encounters, they are of particular value and so are often used in a variety of research and assessment type interviews. In the research interview it is the responses of subjects that are of importance, and answers to closed questions are usually more concise and therefore easier to record and code than replies to open questions (Breakwell *et al.*, 2006). This in turn facilitates comparisons between the responses of different subjects. In many assessment interviews, the interviewer has to ascertain whether or not the client is suitable for some form of grant or assistance and so find out whether the person meets a number of specified requirements (e.g. a social welfare official has to ask a client about financial affairs, family background, etc. before deciding upon eligibility for state allowances). Here again, closed questions are of value.

In the medical sphere it has been shown that doctors are two to three times more likely to ask yes–no questions than any other type of question (Raymond, 2003). Likewise, Morrow *et al.* (1993) found that while almost all pharmacist questions were closed in nature, some 69 per cent of these were of the yes–no variety. They argued that pharmacists were following the clinical algorithm approach of eliminative questioning for diagnosis. While this approach, if carried out expertly, should result in the correct clinical conclusion, it is not without drawbacks in that important information may be missed. For example, one of the clients in their study was suffering from very severe toothache for which the pharmacist had recommended a product and was completing the sale when the client asked, 'What about if you've taken any other tablets? I've taken Paracodol.' This unsolicited enquiry provoked further questions and subsequently altered the pharmacist's dosage recommendations.

Closed questions can usually be answered adequately in one or a very few words. They are restricted in nature, imposing limitations on the possible responses that the respondent can make. They give the questioner a high degree of control over the interaction, since a series of such questions can be prepared in advance in order to structure the encounter, and the answers that the respondent may give can usually be anticipated. Where time is limited and a diagnosis has to be made, or information gathered, closed questions are often the preferred mode. Their potential for structured control is one of the reasons that teachers use significantly more closed than open questions in classrooms, and why this pattern is more marked in numeracy than in literacy classes (Smith *et al.*, 2006). This pattern of closed questioning in the classroom emerges at the initial stage of education, so that Siraj-Blatchford and Manni (2008: 7) found in a preschool setting that '94.5 per cent of all the questions asked by the early childhood staff were closed questions that required a recall of fact, experience or expected behaviour, decision between a limited selection of choices or no response at all'.

Open questions

These can be answered in a number of ways, with the response being left open to the respondent. Here, the respondent is given a higher degree of freedom in deciding which answer to give. Open questions are broad in nature and require more than one or two words for an adequate answer. In general they have the effect of 'encouraging clients to talk longer and more deeply about their concerns' (Hill, 2004: 118). They are useful in allowing a respondent to express opinions, attitudes, thoughts and feelings. They do not require any prior knowledge on the part of questioners, who can ask open questions about topics or events with which they are not familiar. They also encourage the respondent to talk, thereby leaving the questioner free to listen and observe. This means, of course, that the respondent has a greater degree of control over the interaction and can determine to a greater extent what is to be discussed. It also means that the questioner has to listen carefully to what is being said in order to follow up on responses.

An important advantage of open questions is that the respondent may reveal information that the questioner had not anticipated. Where a respondent has a body of specialised knowledge to relate, the use of open questions can facilitate the transmission of this knowledge. As noted by Kidwell (2009), closed questions merely require respondents to 'fill in' the specific detail requested, whereas open questions encourage them to 'fill out' whatever information they wish to provide. For this reason, however, where time is limited, or with overtalkative clients, they may be less appropriate. Answers to open questions may be time consuming and may also contain irrelevant or less vital information.

Open/closed sequences

Some open questions place more restriction upon respondents than others, depending upon the frame of reference subsumed in the question. Consider the following examples of open questions asked by a detective of a suspect:

1   'Tell me about your spare time activities.'
2   'What do you do in the evenings?'
3   'What do you do on Saturday evenings?'
4   'What did you do on the evening of Saturday, 19 January?'

In these examples, the focus of the questions has gradually narrowed from the initial very open question to the more restricted type of open question. This could then lead into more specific closed questions, such as:

5   'Who were you with on the evening of Saturday, 19 January?'
6   'Where were you at 7.00 pm that evening?'

This approach, of beginning an interaction with a very open question and gradually reducing the level of openness is termed a *funnel sequence* (Kahn and Cannell, 1957) (see Figure 5.1). This has been recommended in investigative interviewing, where there is evidence that a structure which begins by encouraging a free narrative response from interviewees ('Tell me all you know about X'), and then progressively narrowing the focus, is most effective (Powell *et al.*, 2007). A funnel structure is also common in counselling interviews, where the helper does not want to impose any restrictions on the helpee about what is to be discussed, and may begin a session by asking, 'What would you like to talk about?' or 'How have things been since we last met?' Once the helpee begins to talk, the helper may then want to focus in on certain aspects of the responses given. Likewise, in the medical interview, Cohen-Cole and Bird (1991: 13) pointed out:

> A considerable body of literature supports the use of open-ended questioning as an efficient and effective vehicle to gain understanding of patients' problems. To be sure, after an initial nondirective phase ... the doctor must ask progressively more focused questions to explore specific diagnostic hypotheses. This ... has been called an 'open-to-closed cone'.

An alternative approach to this sequencing of questions is to use an *inverted funnel* (or *pyramid*) *sequence*, whereby an interaction begins with very closed questions and gradually opens out to embrace wider issues. Such an approach is often adopted in careers guidance interviews in which the interviewer may want to build up a picture of the client (e.g. academic achievements, family background, interests) before progressing to possible choice of career and the reasons for this choice (e.g. 'Why do you think you would like to be a soldier?'). By using closed questions initially to obtain information, the careers interviewer may then be in a better position to help the client evaluate possible, and feasible, career options.

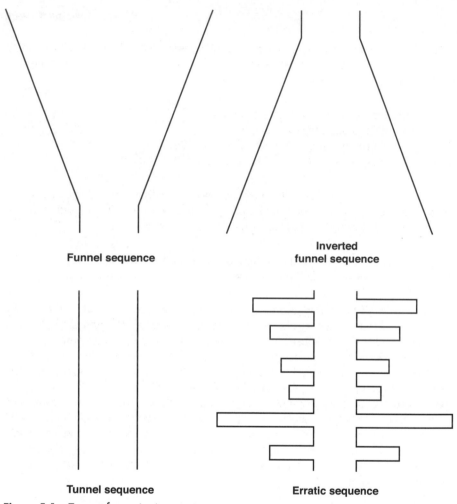

Funnel sequence

**Inverted
funnel sequence**

Tunnel sequence

Erratic sequence

Figure 5.1 Types of questioning sequence

A third type of questioning sequence is the *tunnel sequence*, also referred to as the 'string of beads' (Stewart and Cash, 2008). Here, all of the questions employed are at the same level and are usually closed. Such a sequence may be used in certain types of assessment interview, wherein the objective is to establish a set of factual responses. This type of closed tunnelling for information is often characteristic of screening interviews, where the respondent has to be matched against some pre-set criteria (e.g. eligibility for some form of state welfare benefit or grant). A closed tunnel sequence of questions is also used by lawyers in court when they wish to direct a witness along a predetermined set of answers (as can be seen from the transcript in Box 5.1).

There is research evidence to suggest that a consistent sequence of questions facilitates participation and understanding in respondents, whether the sequence be of a tunnel, funnel or inverted funnel nature. On the other hand, an *erratic sequence* of open and closed questions is likely to confuse the respondent and reduce the level of participation. Erratic sequences of questions (also known as rapid variations in the level of cognitive demand) are common in interrogative interviews where the purpose is to confuse suspects and 'throw them off guard' since they do not know what type of question to expect next. Indeed, in courtrooms, Kestler (1982: 156) recommended that when lawyers wish to trap witnesses they should use an erratic sequence, involving 'a quick change of focus designed to catch the witness off-balance, with thoughts out of context'.

Comparing open and closed questions

Several research studies have examined the relative effects of open and closed questions in different situations. In an early investigation, Dohrenwend (1965) found that, in research interviews, responses to open questions contained a higher proportion of self-revelation than did responses to closed questions when the subject matter under discussion was objective, and a lower proportion when the subject matter was subjective. This finding suggests that when concerned with self-disclosures, closed questions may be more effective in keeping the respondent to the topic of the question (for more information on self-disclosure see Chapter 9). Dohrenwend also found, however, that responses to open questions were about three times longer than those to closed ones, as measured by amounts of verbalisation. Again, responses to subjective open questions were significantly shorter than responses to objective open questions, whereas length of response to closed questions did not vary with subject matter. Dohrenwend concluded that closed questions offer more definite advantages than open questions in research interviews because they exert a tighter control over respondents' answers. Open questions, while answered in more detail, tended to result in responses that deviated from the topic of the question, whereas with closed questions the respondent was more likely to answer the question in a direct fashion.

However, although closed questions may facilitate control, they also have disadvantages in research interviews. Dillon (1997) illustrated how both types of question may result in missing or inaccurate information being gathered. He showed that, when asked the open question of what they preferred in a job, only half as many respondents mentioned a 'feeling of accomplishment' as those who selected it when it was presented as one of the alternatives in closed format. On the other hand, good pay was the most frequently volunteered answer to the open question, but the least frequently selected alternative in the closed question. Furthermore, some 60 per cent of responses to the open question did not appear in the five main alternatives to the closed one. If the factor a subject considers most important is missing from the list attached to a closed question, it is not likely to be mentioned and instead some of the presented factors will be offered as the answer. This is because the respondent perceives one of the 'rules' of the task to be that of having to make a choice from the presented list. Unless told otherwise, the subject assumes that the items on the list are the sole focus of the experimenter. On the other hand, if only the open question is used, the respondent may simply overlook one or more important factors. Dillon therefore recommended the use of open questions with a range of respondents in order to produce an exhaustive list of alternatives for later inclusion in closed question format in survey interviews.

Generalisations about the relative efficacy of open or closed questions are difficult, since the intellectual capacity of the respondent must be taken into consideration. It has long been known that open questions may not be as appropriate with respondents of lower intellect. Schatzman and Strauss (1956) compared respondents who had not gone beyond secondary school level with respondents who had spent at least one year at college. They found that open questions tended to be more effective with the latter group than with the former, as judged by the questioning behaviour of experienced interviewers who were given a certain degree of freedom about what type of questions to employ. The interviewers used more open questions with the respondents of higher education than with those of lower education.

Research comparing the use of open and closed questions in counselling (Dickson *et al.*, 1997) has found that open questions are more effective:

- in promoting interviewee self-disclosures
- in producing more accurate responses
- in increasing perceived counsellor empathy.

Thus, most texts in the area recommend that counsellors should concentrate on asking open questions that require a more extended response. As noted by Strong (2006: 1005): 'There is a common proverb in counseling that a good question is one that requires a lengthy pause to answer.' Likewise, Egan (2007: 124) proffered the following advice to helpers: 'As a general rule, ask open-ended questions ... Counselors who ask closed questions find themselves asking more and more questions. One closed question begets another.' Given this backdrop, Forrester *et al.* (2008) were surprised to discover that social workers, who are often perceived to have a counselling role, asked on average twice as many closed questions as open ones during interviews. The relevance of the advice given by Egan (2007) was substantiated by the fact that one of the social workers in the Forrester *et al.* (2008) study ended up asking ten times as many closed as open questions.

Likewise, in the medical sphere, research in the USA (where the consultation with the doctor is normally preceded by a consultation with a nurse or medical assistant) has shown that patients show significantly greater satisfaction with the relational aspect of doctors' communication when the physician begins the consultation with an open (e.g. 'How can I help?', 'What brings you in today?') as opposed to a closed (e.g. 'I see you have sinus problems', 'I understand you're having some leg problems') question (Robinson and Heritage, 2006). In addition, such initial open questions by doctors have been shown to result in significantly longer patient answers, which in turn reveal significantly more symptoms (Heritage and Robinson, 2006).

In a different context, Loftus (1982) found that in the questioning of eyewitnesses, open questions produced more accurate information, but less overall detail, than specific closed questions. As a result, she recommended that in this context, questions should be open initially ('Tell me what happened') to obtain accuracy of information, followed by specific closed questions ('What age was he?') to obtain a fuller picture. This recommendation has been consistently supported in studies of investigative interviewing (Memon and Bull, 1999; Wright and Powell, 2006).

Another feature that needs to be taken into consideration in any examination of the relative effects of open and closed questions is the length of the question itself.

There is evidence to indicate that duration of responses is related to length of questions, in that longer answers tend to be given to longer questions (Wilson, 1990). One explanation for this may be that as the length of a question increases it is likely to contain an increased number of propositions, each of which then needs to be addressed by the respondent. It could also be that the respondent judges the length of reply expected by the questioner in proportion to the duration of the question, and responds in line with this perceived implicit expectancy.

The linguistic context of questions is also important. For example, Allwinn (1991) demonstrated how closed questions could be elaborated on by skilled people through the use of pre-remarks (e.g. 'I'm not very knowledgeable about this so could I ask you . . .?') to indicate that a detailed response is required, despite the fact that the question could logically be answered in one or a few words. Also, the context and rules of the interaction may mean that although a question has been phrased in a closed fashion, it is clear that an open reply is expected. Thus, the perceived purpose of a question is influenced by a range of factors, each of which may influence how it is interpreted.

Recall/process questions

This categorisation refers to the cognitive level at which questions are pitched. Recall questions are also known as lower order cognitive questions, and process questions as higher order cognitive questions. The distinction between recall and process questions is most commonly made within education, and can be found primarily in classroom interaction research studies.

Recall questions

As the name suggests, these involve the simple recall of information. They are at a lower level of cognitive demand since they only test the ability of the respondent to recall facts, for example:

- 'Where were you born?'
- 'When was the Battle of Waterloo?'

Recall questions serve a number of useful purposes in different settings. A teacher may employ them at the beginning of a lesson to ascertain the extent of pupil knowledge about the topic. Such questions provide feedback for the teacher and also encourage pupil participation at the outset. They can also be used intermittently to check that the class has understood what has been covered so far and is ready to move on to the next stage. In this way their function is 'to share facts in order to establish a firm foundation for further work' (Morgan and Saxton, 2006: 48). Similarly, at the end of a lesson the teacher may use this type of question to determine the extent of pupil learning that has taken place as a result of the lesson, and also to highlight to pupils that such learning has occurred.

In interviewing contexts, recall questions may be employed at the beginning of an interview as a form of 'ice-breaker' to get the interviewee talking. As mentioned earlier, they are also important when questioning eyewitnesses to crimes. In medicine, recall questions are also of relevance in the diagnosis of an illness. Thus, a doctor will use questions such as:

- 'When did the pain first begin?'
- 'Have you had any dizzy spells?'

Process questions

These are so called because they require the respondent to use some *higher mental process* in order to respond. This may involve giving opinions, justifications, judgements or evaluations, making predictions, analysing information, interpreting situations or forming generalisations. In other words, the respondent is required to think at a higher order level about the answer. For example: 'How do you think you could improve your relationship with your wife?' Such questions require the respondent to go beyond the simple recall of information and usually there is no correct answer. Furthermore, they require longer responses and can seldom be answered in one or two words. They are employed in situations where someone is being encouraged to think more deeply about a topic. For this reason they are often utilised to assess the ability of an individual to think at a higher order level. In executive-type selection interviews, they are frequently used in this assessment function, for example:

- 'What can you offer this company that other applicants cannot?'
- 'What have been your main strengths and weaknesses as a manager?'

In teaching, they encourage pupils to reflect upon the material being presented. Research reviews of questioning in the classroom context have consistently found that teachers ask considerably more recall than process questions (Gall, 1970; Hargie, 1983; Dickson and Hargie, 2006; Morgan and Saxton, 2006). These are somewhat disconcerting findings, since the type of questions asked by teachers affects the degree of creativity or expressiveness available to pupils, and process questions provide more scope than recall questions. In a world where technological advances move at a rapid pace, facts can quickly become outdated and the ability to evaluate new information is of great importance. Morgan and Saxton (2006: 46) advised that if teachers want 'students to think about what they are learning so that learning becomes part of their view of themselves and their world, you have to ask questions that will help them understand . . . and help them think about the meanings being made'. For this reason, Hargie (1983: 190) argued that during training 'attention should be given to means whereby teachers can increase their use of thought-provoking questions as opposed to factual or recall questions'. There is firm research evidence to support such a proposal, since Rousseau and Redfield (1980: 52), in reviewing a total of 20 studies, showed that 'gains in achievement over a control group may be expected for groups of children who participate in programmes where teachers are trained in questioning skills . . . gains are greatest when higher cognitive questions are used during instruction'.

However, caution should be exercised in attempting to generalise about the use of process as opposed to recall questions. Research tends to suggest that process questions are more effective in increasing both participation and achievement of individuals of high intellectual ability, whereas recall questions appear to be more appropriate for individuals at lower ability levels. For example, Rubie-Davies (2007) found that teachers who held above average expectations for their pupils used more higher order questions than those with below average expectations. For teachers with mixed ability classes, there are some particular difficulties here, in that the consistent use of process questions is likely to stimulate pupils with a high IQ but be inappropriate for, or confuse, pupils with a low IQ.

At first sight, there would appear to be little difference between the recall/process and the closed/open categorisations of questions, and indeed many closed questions are of a recall nature, while many process questions are open. However, it is possible to have closed process questions and open recall questions. Consider a science teacher who has explained to pupils the properties of water and limestone and then asks, 'Will the water pass through the limestone?' While the question is process, it is also closed. Similarly, a question such as 'What did you do during the holidays?' is both open and recall. Thus, there are differences inherent in these two classifications of questions and both are useful in varying contexts.

Affective questions

These are questions that relate specifically to the emotions, attitudes, feelings or preferences of the respondent – that is to the *affective* domain. An affective question can be recall, process, open or closed, depending upon which aspect of feelings is being explored. Where an attempt is being made to ascertain reactions to a past event, a recall question may be employed (e.g. 'Who was your favourite teacher at school?'). On the other hand, when present feelings are being explored, a closed question may be used (e.g. 'Do you feel a little embarrassed talking about this?').

The utilisation of recall or closed questions, however, places restrictions upon respondents in terms of what they are expected to relate about their feelings. Where it is important that the client be given time and freedom to discuss emotions, open questions are more advantageous. Open affective questions facilitate the expression of feelings. These can relate to past emotions (e.g. 'How did you feel when your mother died?') or to the present emotional state ('What are your feelings towards your husband now?'). To encourage a respondent to think more deeply about feelings, and about the underlying reasons for these, process questions may be applicable. Rather than merely asking for feelings to be reported, they further tap into an evaluation of possible underlying causes (e.g. 'What caused you to hate your father so much?'). This type of question encourages the respondent to interpret reasons for feelings and perhaps become more rational in exploring them.

Affective questions are particularly relevant in counselling contexts where the discussion of feelings is very important. They are also important in health care, where it has been shown that skilled doctors use more questions that address the psychosocial aspects of the patient's condition than their less skilled colleagues (Ford and Hall, 2004; Tallman *et al.*, 2007).

Leading questions

All questions contain assumptions or presuppositions. Fiedler (2007: 15) defined presuppositions as 'silent implications or taken-for-granted inferences' within questions. As a very simple example, if I ask you 'What time is it?' the presuppositions are that: (a) you have access to this information; (b) you can read the time; and (c) you are willing to give me this information. Likewise you would usually assume that: (a) I genuinely do not know the time; (b) I do not have access to this information; and (c) I really wish to find out this information. However, if the interaction is between a pair of young adult strangers, the target might then make the assumption that the questioner is really attempting to open dialogue as the first step in relational development, and respond accordingly. If the target is the spouse of the questioner, both are at a party, and the hour is late, the question might be read as a signal that it is time to go home, as the babysitter will be ready to leave. Adler *et al.* (2006) termed these latter examples *counterfeit questions* in that they are not what they appear at first sight, since they carry hidden agendas. Question assumptions can also, of course, be true or false. For example, a detective, in attempting to trap a suspect who claims to have been at a particular cinema on the evening of a crime, may ask, 'What did you do when the power failed in the cinema at 8.45 pm?' There was no power failure and so this false assumption places the suspect in a difficult position if being deceitful.

Leading questions are assumption laden. By the way they are worded, they lead the respondent towards an expected response. The anticipated answer is implied or assumed within the question, and may or may not be immediately obvious to the respondent, depending upon the phrasing. For this reason, they have also been termed *misleading questions* or *suggestive questions* (Gee *et al.*, 1999). There are four different types: conversational leads; simple leads; implication leads; subtle leads.

Conversational leads

As the name suggests, these are used in common parlance. Everyday conversations typically contain comments that anticipate a certain type of response, for example:

- 'Isn't it a lovely day?'
- 'Wasn't that a terrible accident yesterday?'

These lubricate the flow of conversation since they anticipate the response that the other person would have been likely to give and so demonstrate shared understanding. In interviews, conversational leads convey the impression of friendliness and interest on the part of the interviewer, providing of course they accurately anticipate the respondent's answer. Correct conversational leading questions create the feeling amongst respondents that the interviewer is listening carefully and 'in tune' with them. This in turn stimulates them to continue developing their ideas, feeling confident that the interviewer is paying attention and understanding what they are saying.

Simple leads

These are unambiguously intended to lead the respondent to give an answer that the questioner expects to receive. Unlike the conversational lead, the simple lead assumes the answer the questioner expects, as opposed to the answer that the respondent would have given in any case. The simple lead, then, takes little cognisance of the respondent's thoughts and feelings, for example:

- 'Surely you don't support the communists?'
- 'You do, of course, go to church, don't you?'

The latter example includes a *tag question* ('don't you?'). This type of question, tagged on at the end, turns a statement into a leading question. As noted by Lester (2008: 306): 'The question created by adding the question tag is not usually a genuine request for information. It is typically a request for confirmation that the information in the main body of the sentence is correct'.

It has been known for some time that the use of simple leads that are obviously incorrect can induce respondents to participate fully in an interview, in order to correct any misconceptions inherent in the question. Beezer (1956), for example, conducted interviews with refugees from the then East Germany in which he found that simple leading questions that were clearly incorrect yielded more information from respondents than did questions that were not leading. Thus, when respondents were asked, 'I understand you don't have to pay very much for food in the East Zone because it is rationed?' most replied by trying to correct the interviewer's mistaken impressions about general living conditions.

The blatantly incorrect simple leading question serves to place the respondent in the position of expert vis-à-vis the misinformed interviewer. As a result, the respondent may feel obliged to provide information that will enlighten the interviewer. Some of this information may involve the introduction of new and insightful material. While they can be effective in encouraging participation, it is not possible to state how and in what contexts simple leading questions can be most gainfully employed. In certain situations, and with particular types of respondent, their use is counterproductive. Most authors of texts on interviewing have eschewed this form of questioning as bad practice. Furthermore, in the courtroom, leading questions are not permitted in the direct examination of a witness by the counsel for the side calling the witness, although they are allowed during cross-examination of the other side's witnesses.

Kestler (1982: 59) positively recommended the use of leading questions by lawyers during cross-examination since they 'permit control of the subject matter and scope of the response. The witness is constrained to answer "yes" or "no"'. They are also used by detectives to encourage suspects to confess to crimes. Here, what are known as *minimisation strategies* are employed to reduce the suspect's perceived responsibility for what happened. These involve 'offering legal or moral face-saving excuses for actions, conceptualizing actions as accidental, blaming the victim and underplaying the seriousness of the charges' (Klaver *et al.*, 2008: 73). Examples of leading questions using minimisation strategies with a suspect in a rape case are as follows:

- 'She led you on and on and look at the way she was dressed, what else would you have thought?
- 'She's a bit of a slag, she was asking for it really, wasn't she?'

Research findings show that minimisation strategies result in suspects believing that they will be treated more leniently if they confess, even when no such leniency is explicitly offered.

Implication leads

These lead the respondent to answer in a specific fashion, or accept a negative implication if the response given is contrary to that suggested. Implication leads exert a much greater degree of pressure on the respondent to reply in the expected manner than simple leads, and for this reason they are also known as *complex leading questions*. An example of this type of question is: 'Anyone who cared for their country would not want to see it destroyed in a nuclear attack or invaded by a foreign power, so don't you think any expenditure on an effective defensive deterrent is money well spent?' In this case, a negative answer places the respondent in the position of apparently being unpatriotic.

If a respondent disagrees with the assumed response, a justification is usually expected by the questioner. For this reason, implication leads are often used by radio and television interviewers when interviewing political or controversial individuals. Similarly, in arguments and debates they are employed in order to put opponents under pressure, and emphasise a certain point of view. Loftus (1982) provided another example of an implication lead, namely: 'Did you know that what you were doing was dishonest?' This type of 'trick question' puts the respondent under pressure either to accept the negative implication of dishonesty or respond at length. It is a variant of the well-known and oft-cited implication question, 'When did you stop beating your wife?'

There are some well-documented instances where leading questions have tripped up politicians. The late Canadian leader Pierre Trudeau was once asked in a television interview, 'If you were shaken awake in the night, would your first words be in English or French?' No matter what his reply he was going to alienate a considerable constituency. Likewise, the then UK Labour opposition leader Neil Kinnock, who supported nuclear disarmament, was asked whether he would send soldiers in a nuclear-free Britain into battle against a nuclear power. His dithering response resulted in the Conservatives producing a poster of a soldier with his arms raised in surrender with the caption 'Labour's policy on arms'. Finally, the former leader of the then UK Conservative opposition William Hague was asked in a radio interview the dual-negative implication lead, 'You are a grown-up. Do you really expect to win the next election?' Given that he was by stature a small person, the question had a doubly hurtful yet impactful resonance.

Subtle leads

A humorous example of the effects of subtle leads is the story about the Dominican and Jesuit priests who debated whether it was permissible to say their daily prayers and smoke their pipes at the same time. Unable to reach a definitive conclusion, each agreed to consult his superior for guidance. The Jesuit returned very satisfied saying he had obtained permission. The Dominican bemoaned this outcome, saying his superior had refused his request. 'What did you ask him?' enquired the Jesuit. 'Well obviously, if it was okay for me to smoke while praying.' 'Ah,' said the Jesuit, 'that was your mistake. I asked mine if it was permissible to pray while smoking.' As this story indicates, subtle leads may not be instantly recognisable as leading questions, but nevertheless they are worded in such a way as to elicit a certain type of response. They are also known as *directional questions* in that the respondent is being subtly directed towards a particular type of answer. This is because, as summarised by Loftus (2006: 3), 'just changing a single word or two in a question can sometimes have a sizeable effect on the answer'.

In the sphere of interrogation, Buckwalter (1983) illustrated that suspects of crimes are more forthcoming when asked to 'tell the truth' rather than 'confess your crime'. Similarly, in cases of murder, motives are given more readily to the question 'Why did you do it?' than to 'Why did you murder him?' Buckwalter advised interviewers to avoid terms such as kill, steal, rape, and replace them with words such as shoot, take, sex. In fact it is a myth that the key to effective interrogation is to accuse, confuse, hurt or embarrass the suspect. Such Gestapo-like techniques just do not work. Rather, they make the person afraid, resentful, reluctant, hostile and defensive – all of which reduces the likelihood of truthful disclosure. Texts on interrogation recommend that the best guide is not to think of oneself as asking questions, but as being questioned. Their advice is to put yourself in the position of the respondent and ask what would make you tell the truth in this context.

Research in interrogation consistently reveals that to be successful the interviewer must build up a rapport with the interviewee and appear to be nonjudgemental (Williamson, 2005). Good interrogators possess qualities such as genuineness, trustworthiness, concern, courtesy, tact, empathy, compassion, respect, friendliness, gentleness, receptivity, warmth and understanding. We disclose to such people – they seem to care and do not judge (see Chapter 9 for further discussion of disclosure). In media interviewing a similar style pays dividends. The television journalist Alan Whicker recommended a soft rather than a hard-hitting approach to interviewing, pointing out that a subtle style encourages maximum participation. As he expressed it, 'It's possible to ask practically any question provided you do so pleasantly. And you catch more flies with honey than you do with vinegar' (Craig, 2009).

Another example of how a subtle change in the wording of a question can influence the respondent to answer in a particular way was reported by Harris (1973). When subjects were asked either 'How tall was the basketball player?' or 'How short was the basketball player?' they guessed about 79 inches and 69 inches, respectively. Other questions asked by Harris along the same lines produced similar results – thus the question 'How long was the movie?' resulted in average estimates of 130 minutes, whereas 'How short was the movie?' produced an average of 100 minutes. Loftus (1975) reported similar findings. When subjects were asked either 'Do you get headaches frequently, and if so, how often?' or 'Do you get headaches occasionally, and if so, how often?' the respective reported averages were 2.2 and 0.7 headaches per week.

This is part of the *acquiescence effect* wherein respondents comply or acquiesce to the explicit or implicit direction of the question (Bhattacharya and Isen, 2008). Most people when asked 'How many animals of each kind did Moses take on the ark?' will reply 'two' even though they are aware that in the biblical story it was Noah who took animals on the ark. This phenomenon, termed the *The Moses Illusion* (Erickson and Mattson, 1981), illustrates how respondents attempt to gauge and anticipate the answer that the questioner is seeking and so demonstrate helpfulness by supplying it. Gibbs and Bryant (2008: 368) noted that part of the question–answer process involves 'understanding the questioner's plans and goals when formulating appropriate replies'. We are not just passive recipients of questions. Rather, we actively search for and interpret the meanings and assumptions behind the inquisitive words being used. Indeed, as Wänke (2007: 234) noted: 'Respondents will use any cue in the provided information to infer the intended meaning of a question . . . Previous questions, introductions, the question wording, answer formats, and any other information may serve this purpose.' The desire to give the 'right' answer is a powerful force in human nature. This is one of the reasons why 'researchers have long known that people tend to agree with one-sided statements, and that the same subject may agree to two opposite statements on different occasions' (Kunda and Fong, 1993: 65). A practical application of the acquiescence effect can be found in retail contexts, where staff are trained to ask directional questions. For example, in a fast-food outlet if a customer asks for a soft drink, the person taking the order will often be told to use a directional assumptive question: 'A large one?' The customer usually accepts the assumption, and so profits are maximised. Likewise, in restaurants waiting staff are trained to use subtle leads such as 'Are you enjoying your meal?' or 'Is everything okay?'

How questions are contextualised can also influence acquiescence. For example, Hirt *et al.* (1999) showed that low expectancy conditions (e.g. saying 'If you don't remember it's all right') as compared to high expectancy conditions (e.g. 'Tell me when you get an earlier memory') produced earliest reported life memories from respondents of 3.45 years and 2.28 years respectively. Furthermore, when college students were initially asked to report their earliest memory the mean recall age was 3.7 years. However, students were then told that most people could recall their second birthday, if they were willing to really let themselves go, focus and concentrate. When then asked for memories of second birthday and earlier memories, 59 per cent of subjects reported a memory of their second birthday, and the mean recall age fell to 1.6 years. In addition, when fed a piece of false information (i.e. getting lost in a shopping mall) together with three actual events (as supplied by parents or siblings) some 25 per cent then claimed to have memories of this false event.

An important related phenomenon here is what is known as *anchor bias* (Brewer *et al.*, 2007). This occurs when the initial question contains a suggested figure. For example, a subject is asked 'Do you think the chance that you will get the flu is more or less than 90 per cent?' Subjects are then asked the subsequent question 'What do you think the percentage chance is that you will get the flu?' The suggested anchor number of 90 per cent then influences the subject in formulating an answer to the second question, which as a result will be closer to this figure. The fact that this figure has been stated leads the respondent to make the assumption that it must somehow be close to the actuality. Otherwise why would the questioner cite it? Variations of this anchoring effect have been studied for decades. Thus, Loftus (1975) asked subjects either 'In terms of the total number of products, how many other products have you tried? 1? 2? 3?' or 'In terms of the total number of products, how many other products have you tried? 1? 5? 10?'. Responses to these questions averaged 3.3 and 5.2 other products respectively. Likewise, Gaskell *et al.* (1993) showed how when asked about annoyance with television adverts, subjects given high alternatives (every day, most days, once a week, once a month, less often, never) reported significantly higher frequencies than those given low alternatives (once a week or more often, once a month, about every few months, once a year, less often, never). The values in a given scale are assumed to reflect average, typical or normative, behaviour, and so respondents wishing to be seen as 'normal' choose a figure near the mid-point.

Furthermore, Bless *et al.* (1992) cited evidence to demonstrate that the more demanding the computation of a requested frequency response, the more likely it is that respondents are led by the alternatives suggested in the question. Interestingly, Hetsroni (2007) found that subjects given an open question format produced significantly higher estimates than those provided with fixed response alternatives. One reason for this may have been that the absence of possible answers meant there was no standard against which subjects could estimate normative responses. It has also been shown that the nature of the given response scale can affect perceived definitions of terms. Thus, in one study two groups of subjects were asked to report how often they felt 'really annoyed' (Wright *et al.*, 1997). Subjects received a set of either low response frequencies (from 'less than once a year' to 'more than every three months') or high response frequencies (from 'less than twice a week' to 'several times a day'). Respondents were then asked to define 'annoyed' and it was found that those in the low response frequency group described it as a more severe disturbance than those in the high frequency condition.

Another example of subtle leads lies in the use of implicit verb causality. Action verbs such as 'attack' or 'assist' imply that the subject is the initiator or cause of the behaviour. In contrast, state verbs such as 'admire' or 'abhor' suggest that the object of the statement is the cause of the event. Thus, 'Why did Stephen attack Helen?' suggests that Stephen is the aggressor, whereas 'Why did Stephen abhor Helen?' suggests that Helen was in some way responsible for Stephen's reaction. Research has shown (Fiedler, 2007) that the degree of guilt attributed to a defendant is lower when state rather than action verbs are used in questions. In addition, answering questions containing state verbs about whether someone depicted on video attacked or ridiculed others has been shown to induce greater negative judgements of the depicted person, even when the respondent denies that the event occurred. This is because the implicit verb causality in the phrasing of the question influences later judgements.

Another feature associated with subtle leads is the *misinformation effect*, which occurs when respondents are led by questions in such a way as to confirm aspects of an event that never happened. In their review of this field, Zaragoza *et al.* (2006: 35) concluded that the misinformation effect 'is one of the best-known and most influential findings in psychology'. In an early study, Loftus and Palmer (1974) had subjects view films of car accidents and then questioned them about what they had seen. The question 'About how fast were the cars going when they smashed into each other?' produced higher estimates of speed than when the verb 'smashed' was replaced by 'hit', 'bumped', 'collided' or 'contacted'. One week later those subjects who had been asked the former question were also more likely to say 'yes' to the question 'Did you see broken glass?' even though no glass was broken in the accident. In a related piece of research, Loftus and Zanni (1975) compared the effects of questions containing an indefinite article with the same questions containing a definite article. In this study 100 graduate students were shown a short film of a car accident and then asked questions about it. It was found that questions which contained a definite article (e.g. 'Did you see *the* broken headlight?') produced fewer uncertain or 'I don't know' responses, and more false recognition of events which never in fact occurred, than did questions which contained an indefinite article (e.g. 'Did you see *a* broken headlight?').

This *false recognition* was also reported in the Loftus (1975) study. She conducted four different experiments, each of which highlighted the way in which the wording of questions asked immediately after an event influenced the responses to questions asked considerably later. In one of these experiments, students were shown a videotape of a car accident and asked a number of questions about it. Half of the subjects were asked 'How fast was the white sports car going when it passed the barn while travelling along the country road?' while half were asked 'How fast was the white sports car going while travelling along the country road?' Although no barn appeared in the film, 17.3 per cent of those asked the former question responded 'Yes' when later asked 'Did you see a barn?' as opposed to only 2.7 per cent of those asked the latter question.

The concept of *recovered memory* has caused much debate in this area. Here, people are interviewed in depth until they eventually recall past experiences, often of abuse, which had previously been repressed. However, it has been argued that such recovered memory is often in fact *false memory* planted as a result of biased questioning (Pezdek and Banks, 1996). In particular, questions that encourage respondents to think about an event can lead to a process termed *imagination inflation*. As defined by Loftus (2001: 584), this is 'the phenomenon that imagining an event increases subjective confidence that the event actually happened'. Interestingly, getting people to write down their constructed experiences greatly increases their belief in the veracity of these fictitious events. Loftus further showed that certain people are more susceptible to such inflation, including those who:

- have a tendency to confuse fact with fiction
- more often experience lapses in attention and memory
- possess more acute powers of imagery.

The implications of the above findings have ramifications for anyone concerned with obtaining accurate information from others, but they are of particular import for those who have to interview children.

Effects of leading questions upon children

There is a growing volume of research to show that leading questions have a particularly distorting effect upon the responses of children (Walker, 1999; Zajac *et al.*, 2003; Krähenbühl and Blades, 2006; Pipe *et al.*, 2007). One reason for this is that the acquiescence effect is very strong with young children. Furthermore, Milne (1999: 175) showed how children with intellectual disabilities 'were significantly more likely to go along with misleading questions (i.e. questions which lead the child to the wrong answer)'. This finding was confirmed in a later study by Ternes and Yuille (2008). Furthermore, Hardy and van Leeuwen (2004) demonstrated that younger children (3 to 5.5 years) were less able to resist suggestion than older ones (5.5 to 8 years). Loukusa *et al.* (2008) also showed that the ability of children to interpret the contextual dimensions of questions developed over time between the ages of 3 and 9 years. Given the research findings in this area, they concluded: 'It is imperative that interviewers avoid contaminating children's statements through use of inappropriate interviewing techniques such as leading questions' (p. 155). During the 1990s there was a series of child abuse scandals in which children were clearly subjected to biased interviews. One such scandal was the 'Orkney Satanic Abuse' inquiry in which social services believed children had been subjected to sexual and satanic ritual abuse. This belief led to some suggestive, insistent and indeed insidious interviewing of very young children (see Box 5.3), and the inquiry was eventually discredited.

Leading questions need to be used with caution, or avoided altogether, by those who interview children. For those on the receiving end of such questions, Gee *et al.* (1999) showed how young people could be inoculated against the effects of misleading questions by receiving training in how to deal with them. Endres *et al.* (1999) similarly illustrated how giving children advance warning about 'tricky' questions, and explicitly allowing them to reject a question by saying 'I don't know' when unsure about the answer, led to a reduction in errors in responses to suggestive questions. These results were confirmed by Ghetti and Goodman (2001), who found that giving children clear prior instructions about how to deal with questions resulted in more accurate recall by them of events.

Research has also supported the use of open questions with children (Holliday and Albon, 2004). In their detailed work in this area, Waterman *et al.* (2001) showed how children were less accurate in reporting events they had experienced when answering closed questions than when answering open ones. They further found that yes–no questions could produce distorted responses. For example, when asked nonsensical yes–no questions (e.g. 'Is a fork happier than a knife?' 'Is red heavier than yellow?') 75 per cent of five- to eight-year-olds answered either 'yes' or 'no'. Yet, when later questioned about their responses it was clear that many children who answered 'no' were simply indicating that they did not agree with the assumption inherent in the question. But they did not say so at the time. The problem is that a yes–no question presupposes a predetermined response (either 'yes' or 'no') and the child acquiesces with this (Waterman *et al.*, 2004).

Furthermore, the social demands of the situation are such that children assume that adults will ask reasonable questions, and so they feel under pressure to respond to the expectations inherent in these questions (Okanda and Itakura, 2008). When asked open format nonsensical questions (e.g. 'What do feet have for breakfast?') 95 per cent of children said they did not understand the question. This was particularly the case when children were told that it was okay to say if they did not understand. In their review of this area, Powell and Snow (2007: 57) showed that the most effective approach for professionals interviewing children involved 'the use of non-leading open-ended questions and other prompts that encourage elaborate responses, but allow the interviewee flexibility to report what information they remember'. Likewise, in their analysis, Krähenbühl and Blades (2006: 326) concluded:

Box 5.3 Orkney satanic abuse crisis

Excerpt from an interview between a female social worker and four-year-old child

Q: Where are the dickies and the fannies?
A: Don't know.
Q: Can you write the word?
A: No.
Q: . . . a word for when a dickie goes into a fanny?
A: Don't know.
Q: Would you like to whisper?
A: No.
Q: Is it yuckie inside and outside . . . is there any other word?
A: [Anxious to please] Gooey?
Q: [Amid childish laughter] Oh that's a good word . . . what does gooey feel like?
A: Here, this [puts finger in mouth and pops].
Q: What happened to gooey?
A: Don't know.
Q: Has it got a colour?
A: [Begins to count slowly up to four.]
Q: I wonder what this gooey is. Can you tell me?
A: No.
Q: When you put the dickie into the fanny . . .
A: No. [Angry] Now can I play? I am going to get my red car. This is boring. [Gets the red car and begins to play.] Go and get me some toys.
Q: When you put the dickie into the fanny it's yucky and gooey and disgusting. Who hurt you the most?
A: No one did it to me . . .
Q: We won't write it down.
A: No one has been doing it to me [breaks into a scream]. NOBODY HAS BEEN DOING IT TO ME.
Q: You can play with the red car. We won't write it down if you want to whisper it . . .
A: [Shouting even louder] I AM NOT . . . AND I AM NOT GOING TO WRITE IT DOWN.
Q: If it's a name you can see written down you can point to it [She shows child a list of names.] Is it a name you see written down?
A: [Still shouting] No. I don't have to tell. No one has been doing that thing to me.

The room falls silent. The child is seen rocking in her chair, staring at her inquisitors.

Source: *Sunday Times Magazine* (27 February 1994)

'Researchers have found that the use of open-ended questions has indeed improved the accuracy levels in recall.'

Young children have a particular problem with the use of *embedded questions* such as 'Can you tell me who was there?' (Hardy and van Leeuwen, 2004). These are confusing for children because they contain two questions – in this case 'Are you able to tell me?' and 'Who was there?' Embedded questions are also known as *indirect probes*, and so those interviewing children should avoid these and use direct probes. In the latter example it is best just to use the direct probe – 'Who was there?' Likewise, hypothetical questions (e.g. 'What if I told you he wasn't tall enough to reach the window from the garden?') have been shown to confuse children, who until the age of about 11 years do not have the abstract reasoning abilities to deal with them (Sas, 2002). These findings have obvious implications for those involved in questioning children in forensic situations, such as child abuse investigations. Yet, in practice, children are often subjected to very difficult questioning routines. For example, in 2009 a court case at the London Old Bailey attracted immense media interest. A four-year-old girl (the youngest child ever to give evidence in this court) was required to testify against a man whom she claimed had raped her. She gave evidence from an adjoining room via a video link. It transpired that the accused, who was later found guilty, had previously been convicted of torturing and killing an 18-month-old child. However, what provoked particular outcry in this case was the way in which the barrister questioned the child. Among a series of leading questions, multiple questions and difficult tag questions that he asked her were the following:

- 'He didn't touch you, did he? Did he? I have to ask you one more time. We have to have an answer from you, he didn't touch you did he? . . . [and after a considerable delay] . . . I have to wait until I get your answer. He didn't touch you, did he?'
- 'Do you remember that you said to me, that you didn't tell fibs? Is that true or a fib? What is truth?'
- 'He didn't touch you with his willy, did he?'
- 'Was it something someone told you to say? Was it something you made up?'

Not surprisingly, one journalist reporting on this case concluded 'there has to be a better system for gaining justice for infants than cross-examination in court' (Anthony, 2008).

As summarised by Lamb *et al.* (1999: 261): 'Researchers agree that the manner in which children are questioned can have profound implications for what is "remembered".' The title of a book chapter by Walker and Hunt (1998) neatly sums it up, 'Interviewing Child Victim-Witnesses: How You Ask Is What You Get'. Yet it has been shown that closed questions predominate in many such interview contexts (Wright and Powell, 2006; Powell and Snow, 2007) and that children often respond to the assumptions in the questions they are asked without making their real answers clearly known. In their study into the experiences of young witnesses in court cases in England, Wales and Northern Ireland, Plotnikoff and Woolfson (2009) interviewed 182 children and 172 parents. They found that some 65 per cent of the young people interviewed reported problems relating to how they were questioned in court by lawyers, including the complexity of questions, a related lack of comprehension, a rapid or repetitive questioning style, having 'words put in their mouth', and having their answers interrupted. Among the key recommendations from this study was that when dealing with child witnesses steps need to be taken by the judicial system to improve standards of questioning overall, and in particular to control inappropriate questioning of children by lawyers. Useful advice on questioning child witnesses has been formulated by the Criminal Justice System (2007).

Probing questions

These are follow-up questions designed to encourage respondents to expand upon initial responses. Stewart and Cash (2008) referred to them as *secondary questions* in that they follow on from the main or primary question. They are ubiquitous, so that in group discussions some 90 per cent of all questions asked have been shown to be probes (Hawkins and Power, 1999). They are also very important in dyadic contexts, leading Bernard (2006: 217) to conclude: 'The key to successful interviewing is learning how to probe.' Once a respondent has given an initial answer it can be explored further by using one of the following types of probe: clarification probes; justification probes; relevance probes; exemplification probes; extension probes; accuracy probes; restatement probes; echo probes; nonverbal probes; consensensus probes; clearing-house probes.

Clarification probes

These are used to elicit a clearer, more concisely phrased response in situations where the questioner is either confused or uncertain about the content or meaning of the initial responses. Since an important purpose here is to obtain more detail, they are also known as *informational probes*. Examples include:

- 'What exactly do you mean?'
- 'Could you explain that to me again?'

As noted by Stewart *et al.* (2005: 167–168), this type of clarifying question is 'motivated by a need to understand more clearly'. In the medical context, Tallman *et al.* (2007) found that doctors who used this type of probing question in order to fully understand the patient's situation received higher ratings of patient satisfaction.

Justification probes

These require respondents to explain and expand upon initial responses by giving a justification and reasons for what they have said, for example:

- 'Why did you say that?'
- 'How did you reach that conclusion?'

Relevance probes

These give respondents an opportunity to reassess the appropriateness of a response and/or make its relevance to the main topic under consideration more obvious. This enables the questioner to ascertain which relationships are being made between objects, people or events, and in addition encourages the respondent to reflect on the validity of these. Relevance probes include:

- 'How does this relate to your home background?'
- 'Is this relevant to what we discussed earlier?'

Exemplification probes

These require respondents to provide concrete or specific instances of what they mean by what may, at first, appear to be a rather vague statement. Asking for an example to illustrate a general comment often helps to clarify it and provides further insight into the thoughts of the respondent. Included here are questions such as:

- 'Could you give me an instance of that?'
- 'Where have you shown leadership qualities in the past?'

Extension probes

These are used to encourage a respondent to expand upon an initial answer by providing further information pertinent to the topic under discussion. In classroom research these have been termed *uptake questions*, in that the teacher uses the pupil's answer in the follow-up question (Smith *et al.*, 2006). An extension question is best employed in situations where it is felt that a respondent should be able to make further responses that will facilitate the development of the discussion. Examples include:

- 'That's interesting, tell me more.'
- 'Is there anything else that you can remember about it?'

The simple, brief form of this type of question ('And . . .?' 'So . . .?' 'Go on') is referred to as a *nudging probe* (Stewart and Cash, 2008).

Accuracy probes

These questions draw the respondent's attention to a possible error in fact that has been made. This offers the respondent the option to adjust or restructure the response where necessary. As they afford an opportunity for the person to think about what has just been said they are also known as *reflective probes*. They are most useful in situations where either it is absolutely vital that the respondent is certain about the accuracy of responses (e.g. an eyewitness being cross-examined in court), or where the questioner knows the correct answer and wishes to give the respondent a chance to reflect upon an initial response (e.g. a teacher questioning pupils). Accuracy probes include:

- 'Are you quite sure about that?'
- 'It definitely happened before 3.00 pm?'

Restatement probes

These are used to encourage a respondent to give an adequate answer, following either an unrelated response, or no answer at all, to an initial question. This form of probe is also known as *prompting*. Depending upon the hypothesised cause of the respondent's failure, the questioner may prompt in different ways. If it is thought that the respondent did not correctly hear the initial question, the questioner may simply restate it. If it is thought that the person did not understand the initial phrasing of the question, it may be rephrased either in parallel fashion, or at a simpler level. It may, however, be deemed necessary to prompt the respondent either by reviewing information previously covered (e.g. 'You remember what we talked about last week') or by giving a clue which will help to focus attention in the right direction. An example of this latter type of prompt is included in the following excerpt from a radio 'phone-in' quiz:

> *Q:* With what country would you associate pasta?
> *A:* Spain
> *Q:* No, you might drink some Chianti with the pasta [prompt].
> *A:* Yes, of course, Italy.

Echo probes

These are so called because they are questions that 'echo' the words used by the respondent in the initial response, by repeating these in the follow-up probe. They are often employed in everyday interaction, but if overused they are counterproductive, since if every answer is parroted back, the respondent will soon become very aware of this and in all probability stop responding. As cautioned by Bernard (2006: 219): 'If you use the echo probe too often, though, you'll hear an exasperated informant asking, "Why do you keep repeating what I just said?".' Examples of echo probes are included in the following:

> *A:* After the meal he became very romantic, and told me that he loved me.
> *Q:* He told you that he loved you?
> *A:* Yes, and then he took my hand and asked me to marry him.
> *Q:* He asked you to *marry* him?

Nonverbal probes

These are behaviours employed in such a manner as to indicate to the respondent a desire for further information. Included here is the use of appropriate paralanguage to accompany expressions such as 'Ohh?!' or 'Never?!', together with inquisitive nonverbal behaviours (e.g. raising or lowering of eyebrows, sideways tilt of the head and eye contact). An attentive pause following an initial response can be used as a *silent probe*, indicating a desire for further responses. Indeed, interviewer pauses can put pressure on interviewees to respond in order to fill the silence.

Consensus probes

These give an opportunity for a group to pause in a discussion and for individual respondents to express their agreement or disagreement with an initial response. Asking consensus questions is a useful technique for a group leader to employ in order to gauge the extent of support within the group for any proposed idea or line of action. By asking 'Does everyone agree with that?' or 'Is there anyone not happy with that?' the level of group consensus can be evaluated.

Clearinghouse probes

The purpose of this type of probe was described by Stewart (2009: 191): 'A *clearinghouse* probe is designed to make sure all important information has been covered.' These are very open questions that allow the respondent to answer as they wish. Stewart and Cash (2008) recommended the use of clearinghouse probes at the end of interviews. For example, during the closing stage of a selection interview the interviewer may ask the candidate, 'Is there anything we haven't asked you that you would like to have been asked, or anything you would like to add before we finish?'

Probes must be used skilfully, and as a result of ineptitude or faulty listening by the questioner this is not always the case (see Excerpts 1 and 2 in Box 5.4). The ability to probe effectively is at the core of effective questioning. Fowler and Mangione (1990) illustrated how probing is one of the most difficult techniques for interviewers to acquire, while Millar *et al.* (1992: 131) noted: 'Novice interviewers often find that they have obtained a wealth of superficial information because they have failed to explore interviewee responses in any depth.'

In one study of groups, Hawkins and Power (1999) found that females used more probing questions than males. They speculated that this is because women value connection and cooperation more than men. Males may be more sensitive to what they see as 'intrusions' into their personal and private life. Indeed, Millar and Gallagher (2000) illustrated how some interviewees may resent interviewers who probe too deeply, especially about sensitive topics, since they then feel an increase in vulnerability and a need to defend themselves. Likewise, Egan (2007) underscored the importance of sensitivity when using probing questions in a helping context, and recommended they be employed as 'gentle nudges' to help keep the interviewee focused, rather than as a

Box 5.4 Examples of questioning by lawyers

Excerpt 1

Q: You say the stairs went down to the basement?
A: Yes.
Q: And these stairs, did they go up also?

Excerpt 2

Q: She had three children, right?
A: Yes.
Q: How many were boys?
A: None.
Q: Were there any girls?

Source: Sevilla (1999)

way of extorting information from reluctant clients. Therefore, probes must be used with care. When skilfully employed they invite elaboration of arguments, sharing of information and opinions, and result in increased respondent participation.

One interesting aspect here is what is known as the *probing effect*. This refers to the fact that a respondent who is probed is rated as being more honest, both by the questioner and by observers, as compared to someone who is not probed. This unusual finding has been well corroborated across a range of conditions and contexts (Levine and McCornack, 2001). There is no consensus about why this probing effect should occur. One explanation is that probing produces in respondents a heightened state of awareness, as they realise they are under scrutiny. As a result, they carefully monitor and adapt their verbal and nonverbal behaviours to make these appear more truthful, and thereby convey a greater impression of honesty. The probing effect has implications across many situations, not least for lawyers who have to make decisions about the questioning of individuals in the courtroom (Heller, 2006).

Rhetorical questions

These do not expect a response, either because the speaker intends to answer the question, or because the question is equivalent to a statement (as in 'Who would not wish their children well?' to mean 'Everyone wishes their children well.'). In the former case, rhetorical questions are often used by public speakers to stimulate interest in their presentation by encouraging the audience to 'think things through' with them. With large audiences, interactive questions are usually not appropriate since only a few people would be given a chance to answer, and the rest may have difficulty in hearing their responses. For this reason, lecturers, politicians and other individuals, when addressing large groups, often employ rhetorical questions. As Turk (1985: 75) put it: 'Asking questions is the best way to promote thought . . . We are so conditioned to provide answers to sentences in question form, that our minds are subconsciously aroused towards an answer, even if we remain silent.' In this way, rhetorical questions have been shown to impact upon the type of thinking engaged in by listeners (Whaley and Wagner, 2000). However, while they are useful devices for providing variation and generating interest, they do not seem to have any persuasive power in relation to the message being delivered (Gayle *et al.*, 1998).

Multiple questions

These are two or more questions phrased as one. While a multiple question may contain a number of questions of the same type, quite often it comprises an open question followed by a closed one to narrow the focus (e.g. 'How is the project progressing? Did you get the data collected?'). Multiple questions may be useful where time is limited and it is important to get some answer from a respondent. For this reason they are often used by radio and television interviewers who have a given (often brief) period of time in which to conduct the interview, and so just getting the interviewee to respond is the priority. In most situations, however, they are wasteful – especially where the questions subsumed within the multiple question are unrelated. In the clinical interview setting, Morrison (2008: 57) referred to these as *double questions* and noted that they 'may seem efficient but they are often confusing. The patient may respond to one part of the question and ignore the other without you realising it.' In essence, multiple questions are liable to confuse the respondent, and/or the responses given may confuse the questioner who may be unclear exactly which question has been answered. They can also cause frustration.

In an early classroom study, Wright and Nuthall (1970) found that the tendency on the part of a teacher to ask one question at a time was positively related to pupil achievement, whereas the tendency to ask more than one question at a time was negatively related to achievement. In the field of health, Dickson *et al.* (1997) showed how patients have difficulties in formulating a reply when asked multiple questions. They serve to pressurise and confuse the patient and they also decrease the probability of receiving accurate information. Despite this, they are often employed, such as in the following example taken from a medical context: 'So how are you feeling? Did the tablets help? Are you able to get some sleep now?'

RELATED ASPECTS OF QUESTIONING

Effective communicators are uniquely concerned with *how* they ask questions. In particular, they pay attention to the following issues.

Structuring

In certain social situations where a large number of questions will be used, it is useful to structure the interaction in such a way as to indicate to the respondent what questions are likely to be asked, and why it is necessary to ask them (e.g. 'In order to help me advise you about possible future jobs I would like to find out about your qualifications, experience and interests. If I could begin with your qualifications . . .').

By structuring the interaction in this way, the respondent knows why the questions are required, and what type of questions to expect. Once the respondent is aware of the immediate goals of the questioner and recognises these as acceptable, the interaction will flow more smoothly (see also the skill of set induction in Chapter 10 for a fuller discussion of this type of structuring).

Pausing

The function of pausing as a form of silent probe has already been mentioned. However, as well as pausing after receiving a response, pauses both before and after asking a question can be advantageous. By pausing before asking a question, the attention of the listener can be stimulated and the question given greater impact. For example, Margutti (2006) showed that in the classroom setting a long pause by the teacher was often the signal to pupils that a new question–answer sequence was about to begin, whereas during questioning–answer sequences teachers tended to use very brief 'micro-pauses'. By pausing after asking a question, the respondent is given the distinct impression of being expected to provide some form of response. The use of pauses after asking a question also overcomes the possibility of multiple questions. Finally, pausing after a respondent gives an initial answer encourages the person to continue talking.

The importance of pausing was investigated in studies by Rowe (1969, 1974a, 1974b). She found that when teachers increased the average 'wait-time' after pupil responses, the length of these responses increased from 7 words when the pause was 1 second to 28 words when the pause was 3 seconds. Other positive benefits were that:

- the teacher tended to ask more process questions
- pupils asked more questions
- those pupils who did not tend to say much started talking and produced novel ideas.

The benefits of teacher pauses of some 3 seconds were confirmed by Tobin (1987). Yet there is evidence to indicate that the average teacher pauses following a teacher question and a pupil response are 1.26 seconds and 0.55 seconds respectively (Swift et al., 1988). The disadvantages of such a short wait-time were highlighted by Dillon (1990: 221) who, in a review of research into the benefits of pausing across a range of professional contexts, concluded that pauses need to be of a minimum of 3 seconds duration in order 'to enhance the partner's participation and cognition'.

Distribution

In group contexts, leaders should try to involve as many respondents as possible in the discussion (see Chapter 14 for more information on group leadership). One method whereby this can be achieved is by distributing questions to all members, so that everyone's point of view is heard. This is a useful technique, especially with individuals who may be reluctant to express their views unless given a specific invitation. The redirection of a question from one group member to another may be of particular value in achieving a discrete distribution of questions, without exerting undue pressure, or embarrassing any one individual. Distribution has also been found to be important in the medical context. For example, in paediatric consultations, research has shown that the recipient of the initial physician question determines the extent to which the child is likely to participate in the encounter (Stivers, 2001). When this is addressed directly to the child (e.g. 'Well Patricia and how can I help you today?') rather than to the parent ('Well Mrs Jones and how is Patricia today?'), the child is likely to become a more active participant. Stivers and Majid (2007) extended this research to examine factors associated with the direction of questions to children rather than parents. They found that, in the US context, paediatricians were less likely to direct questions to black or Latino children of low-education parents as compared to their white peers. Professionals therefore need to be aware of possible implicit biases in their distribution of questions.

Responses

Jacobs and Coghlan (2005) illustrated how the study of questioning has taken primacy over the process of answering. Few theories of communication incorporate an explicit model of answering. Yet, just as there is a wide variation in types of questions that can be asked, so too is there a broad range of possible responses (Bolden, 2009). As shown by Hayashi (2009: 2122): 'Answering a question is not a simple matter of providing the information requested by the questioner ... respondents to questions have at their disposal a variety of ways to display their stance toward the question.' Responses to questions have been divided into *preferred*, where the reply fits with the expectations of the question, and *dispreferred*, where the answer runs contrary to these expectations (Raymond, 2003). The latter form is often communicated in subtle ways. For example, prefacing the answer to a question by 'Oh' can indicate that the question is perceived to be inapposite, unexpected or unwarranted. It may also signify that this is not a topic the respondent wishes to discuss at any length (Heritage, 1998). However, there is one context where the opposite is the case. This is in relation to the HAY ('How are you?') question, used as part of the greeting ritual, where no depth of reply is expected (see Chapter 10 for further discussion of the HAY question). Here, an Oh-prefaced response (e.g. 'Oh, fine.') tends to indicate that in fact the respondent does not really feel fine and wishes to discuss this further.

Replies to questions can also illuminate the perspective of the respondent. When St Paul's Cathedral was being built in London it is said that Sir Christopher Wren, the architect, visited the stoneyard one day and asked the first stonecutter he met what he was doing. 'I am cutting stone,' was the reply. When he asked the same question to a second stonecutter the reply was, 'I am helping to build a great cathedral.' Likewise, respondents often choose what questions, or parts thereof, to answer. This was exemplified in the following exchange between the television interviewer Michael Parkinson and Nelson Mandela:

> *Mandela:* Mr Parkinson, I have to tell you before we begin that I am deaf.
> *Parkinson:* I hope, sir, that you will be able to hear my questions.
> *Mandela:* [smiling] I will hear the ones I want to answer.

Dillon (1990) identified a large number of possible answers to questions, the main types of which can be summarised as follows:

1 *Silence.* The respondent may choose to say nothing.
2 *Overt refusal to answer.* For example, 'I'd rather not say.'
3 *Unconnected response.* The respondent may change the topic completely.
4 *Humour.* For example, to the question 'How old are you?' the respondent may reply 'Not as old as I feel.' The American baseball player Lawrence 'Yogi' Berra once replied to a question, 'I wish I had an answer to that, because I'm tired of answering that question.'
5 *Lying.* The respondent may simply give a false answer.
6 *Stalling.* Again, to the question 'How old are you?' the respondent may reply 'How old do you think I am?' Answering a question with a question is a classic stalling technique. For example, Bob Dylan once replied enigmatically to a reporter, 'How can I answer that question if you've got the nerve to ask it?'
7 *Evading.* Wilson (1990) discussed several techniques used by politicians to evade having to directly answer questions. These include questioning the question, attacking the interviewer, or stating that the question has already been answered. A good example of evasion occurred when the fiery former miners' union leader Arthur Scargill was being pressed by a television interviewer to 'answer this important question' and replied: 'Let me answer *my* important questions first, and then I'll answer yours.' Likewise, in terms of attacking the questioner, the fiery Ulster politician Rev. Ian Paisley evaded a question by implying a degree of journalist inebriation when he retorted, 'Let me smell your breath.'
8 *Selective ambiguity.* Thus, to the question about age the respondent may reply, 'Don't worry, I'll finish the marathon okay.' In other words, the respondent pretends to recognise the 'real' question, and answers it.
9 *Withholding and concealing.* In this instance, respondents attempt to avoid disclosing information that may be damaging to them or those close to them. This is a problem commonly faced by investigators (criminal, insurance, etc.), but is also applicable to those professionals who have to deal with sensitive or taboo issues such as child abuse, incest, drug abuse and so on.
10 *Distortion.* Respondents in many instances give the answers that they feel are socially desirable, often without consciously realising they are so doing. Thus, in survey interviews the respondents tend to overestimate behaviours such as voting, reading books and giving to charity and underestimate illnesses, financial status, illegal behaviour and money spent on gambling (Wood and Williams, 2007).
11 *Direct honest response.* Here, the respondent gives a direct, truthful answer to the question.

In any interaction, the professional needs to evaluate the responses received and make decisions about how to follow these up with appropriate probing questions if necessary.

OVERVIEW

Although at first sight questioning would seem to be a straightforward interpersonal skill, upon further examination it can be seen that in fact it is quite complex. While most of us employ a barrage of questions in everyday parlance without giving them a great deal of thought, in professional contexts this is not acceptable. As aptly summarised by Morgan and Saxton (2006: 12): 'We all know how to ask questions – after all, we have been doing it since we could talk – but as you likely realize, becoming an *effective* questioner is hard. It takes time and vigilance.'

As shown in this chapter, there is a large variety of different types of question that can be asked in any given situation, and the answers received are markedly affected by both the wording and the type of question asked. However, no hard-and-fast rules about which type of question to use in particular social encounters exist, since much more situation-specific research is needed in order to investigate the effects of aspects such as the nature of the respondent and the effects of the social context. Nevertheless, the categorisations of questions contained in this chapter provide a key template for the analysis of the effects of questions in social interaction. Furthermore, the examples given and the research reviewed provide the reader with insight into the different modes of usage, and the accompanying effects, of different types of question.

It is clear that questions are powerful tools for finding out about others. However, they can also constitute a useful and subtle method for regulating the participation levels of respondents, maintaining control of the conversation, getting the answers we want, and encouraging conformity. In other words, questions need to be used skilfully. There would therefore seem to be a great deal of truth in the advice given by Voltaire that we should 'Judge a man not by his answers but by his questions.'

Chapter 6

Showing understanding for others: the skill of reflecting

INTRODUCTION

A S WITH THE SKILL of questioning, reviewed in the previous chapter, the skill of reflecting is a way of encouraging participation and gaining information. However, the two skills differ in a number of important respects. To use a motoring analogy, when using questions the interviewer is driving the interaction with the interviewee as passenger, but the use of reflections encourages the interviewee to become the driver with the interviewer as a fellow traveller. Reflecting involves responding to the other in a nondirective manner, while at the same time conveying interest, understanding and engagement. Although some inconsistencies have been identified among the definitions which are presented in the literature (Dickson, 2006), reflections can be defined as statements, in the interviewer's own words, that encapsulate and represent the essence of the interviewee's previous message. As shown in Figure 6.1, when the emphasis is exclusively upon reflecting back the factual component, this is termed 'paraphrasing' (or 'reflection of content'); where it is solely upon the affective or feeling component, it is 'reflection of feeling'; and where both facts and feelings are involved, it is referred to as 'reflection'. Some theorists make a further distinction between *simple reflections*, which focus upon what the other person has just said, and *complex reflections*, which go beyond this to include some pertinent aspects of earlier interviewee responses beyond the previous speech turn (Moyers *et al.*, 2003; Forrester *et al.*, 2008).

Carl Rogers, the founder of person-centred counselling (Rogers, 1980, 1991), is commonly credited with coining the term, although the technique is, of course, used in other approaches to counselling (see

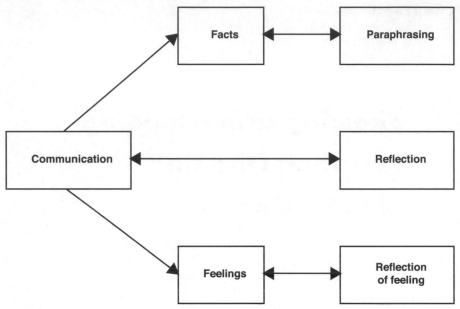

Figure 6.1 Types of reflection

Strong, 2006; Ivey *et al.*, 2010), and in a variety of settings that have nothing to do with counselling (Van der Molen and Gramsbergen-Hoogland, 2005). To take but one example, Rautalinko and Lisper (2004) reported positive results from a training programme designed to improve the reflective listening of insurance company personnel during conversations with clients.

STYLES OF INTERACTING

Before examining reflecting in detail, it is useful to consider the contrasting styles that people can adopt when dealing with others. While different models accounting for style can be found, they all share the premise that there are recurring patterns in a person's behaviour that are evident to others during interaction (Snavely and McNeil, 2008). Style, in this sense, refers to the characteristic manner in which the content of communication is delivered (Norton, 1983; Dinsbach *et al.*, 2007; de Vries *et al.*, 2009) or, more generally, how someone handles an interpersonal episode. It refers to *how* what is done is done. Cameron (2000) emphasised its expressive function in creating a particular 'aesthetic' presence for the other. As such, the importance of paying attention to communication style in business interactions has been stressed (Kenman, 2007). Conversational style includes aspects such as degree of formality (Mayer *et al.*, 2004), assumed dominance (Martin and Gayle, 2004), as well as elaboration and directness (Adler and Rodman, 2006).

The latter characteristic, directness, is most relevant here and has been commented upon in the contexts of business (Ding, 2006), social work (Seden, 2005), therapy (Corey, 2005), medicine (Roter and Hall, 2006) and interviewing (Stewart and

Cash, 2008). Directness involves the degree of explicit influence and control exercised or attempted and, correspondingly, the extent to which the conversational partner is constrained in responding (DeVito, 2008b). At one extreme of this dimension, the interviewer following a direct style will determine the form, content and pace of the encounter. At the other extreme these features will depend upon the concerns and predilections of the interviewee, with the interviewer staying conversationally much more in the background, guiding and facilitating lines of talk.

According to Benjamin (2001), a direct style is typified by the use of interviewer leads, an indirect style by responses. Although both terms are difficult to define unambiguously, responding has to do with reacting to the thoughts and feelings of interviewees, with exploring their worlds and keeping them at the centre of things. On the other hand, the interviewer who leads tends to replace the interviewee on centre stage and become the dominant feature in the interaction. Benjamin (2001: 206) explained it as follows: 'When leading, I make use of my own life space; when responding, I tend more to utilize the life space of the client. Responses keep the client at the center of things; leads make the interviewer central.'

Reflections are accordingly a type of response. As defined by Forrester *et al.* (2008: 43): 'A reflection is a hypothesis about what the client means or feels expressed as a statement.' When reflecting, the interviewer strives to capture the significant message in the respondent's previous contribution and re-presents this understanding. This has been described as the interviewer 'mirroring back' to interviewees what they have just said. As noted earlier, reflections can be contrasted with questions, which are often used to lead the conversation. It is useful, at this point, to consider some examples. Read the two short fictional scenarios in Boxes 6.1 and 6.2.

These two conversations with Karen differ markedly in the approaches adopted by Kate and Cheryl, respectively. In the first situation (Box 6.1), Kate probes for mainly factual information to do with Karen's book, her course, and what she intended to do after university. Kate and her agenda are very much the dominating features of the conversation with Karen doing little more than passively acting as the information source. Questioning is the tactic used exclusively to direct the interchange from one topic to the next, and each question does little to develop the previous response. There is minimal encouragement for Karen to furnish information other than what is directly relevant to Kate's line of enquiry. The second exchange (Box 6.2), in contrast, centres very much upon Karen and the difficulties she is experiencing, with Cheryl staying conversationally, much more in the background. Rather than directly leading Karen into areas that are not of her choosing, Cheryl gently guides the conversation in ways that facilitate Karen's discussion of personal issues that seem important for her to ventilate. Unlike the first exchange, in the second there are no questions asked by Cheryl, apart from her opening query. Rather, her interjections take the form of statements – these statements are reflections.

Apart from contributing examples of the technique of reflecting, the two contrasting conversational excerpts involving Karen serve to make two additional points. The first is that it is not always necessary to ask questions to get in-depth information from others. The second more general point is that verbal styles adopted during interaction can differ markedly. The particular style adopted by an interviewer is, in part, dependent upon the type of interview being conducted (Keats, 2000). A more direct, questioning style is most appropriate where:

- the interviewee has accepted the interviewer's role as interrogator
- the information required is, basically, factual in nature
- the amount of time to be devoted to the interview is limited
- a long-term relationship need not be established
- the information is directly for the benefit of the interviewer.

In contrast, a more indirect, responsive style is typically used to best advantage when:

- the interviewee is the participant who stands to gain from the encounter
- exchanges have a significant affective dimension
- the information is confused, fragmented and hazy – due, perhaps, to the fact that it involves a problem never fully thought through before
- it is important to build a harmonious, egalitarian relationship with the interviewee.

Despite this distinction it would be inappropriate to assume that a more direct style of operating is never used under the latter set of conditions, or that questions should not form part of the range of skills employed. Equally, it would be mistaken to conclude that in the former circumstances a reflective statement should never be contemplated. Indeed, counsellors vary in the directness of their style depending upon the particular school of counselling to which they subscribe so that some are likely to be more direct than others across a range of contexts. Nevertheless, as a generality, the above distinction holds.

Box 6.1 Strangers on a train: Scene 1

Karen is a first-year student travelling home by train for the weekend. During the journey she falls into conversation at different times with two fellow passengers, both of whom are strangers to her. The first one is with Kate and this is how the conversation progresses.

Kate: Good book, is it?
Karen: Sorry!
Kate: That book you're reading . . . Good is it?
Karen: No, not really.
Kate: Why are you reading it then?
Karen: I have to, in a way. It's part of my course.
Kate: Oh . . . are you a student?
Karen: Yes . . . at the university.
Kate: What are you studying?
Karen: Law . . . and I must have this book finished before my tutorial on Monday morning.
Kate: Enjoy it, do you . . . university?
Karen: I suppose so, in a way.
Kate: What do you intend to do then . . . when you finish?
Karen: I don't really know.

Box 6.2 Strangers on a train: Scene 2

After Kate leaves the train, Cheryl enters the carriage and joins Karen. Let us now eavesdrop on their conversation.

Cheryl: You're not really reading it, are you?

Karen: Pardon!

Cheryl: The book . . . you haven't turned a page in the last ten minutes.

Karen: [Smiling] No, I suppose I haven't. I need to get through it though, but I keep drifting away.

Cheryl: It doesn't really hold your interest?

Karen: No, not really. I wouldn't bother with it, to be honest, but I have to have it read for a tutorial. I'm at the university.

Cheryl: [Smiling] It's a labour of labour then, rather than a labour of love.

Karen: I should say! I don't enjoy it at all . . . Indeed, I'm getting to like the whole course less and less.

Cheryl: So it's not just the book, it's the whole programme as well.

Karen: Yes, in a way . . . although the course itself isn't really bad . . . some of it is pretty good, in fact, and the lecturers are fine. It's me, I suppose. You see, I wanted to do English rather than Law . . . but my parents talked me out of it.

Cheryl: So the course is okay, as such, it's just that, had it been left to you, you would have chosen a different one.

Karen: Oh, they had my best interests at heart, of course, my parents. They always do, don't they? They believed that my job prospects would have been limited with a degree in English. And they give me a really generous allowance . . . but, I'm beginning to feel that I'm wasting my time . . . and their money. They would be so disappointed, though, if I told them I was quitting my legal studies.

Some of the disadvantages of relying on questions have been pointed out in counselling (Inskipp, 2006; Egan, 2007), teaching (Dickson and Hargie, 2006; Smith *et al.*, 2006) and interviewing (Hartley, 1999; Stewart and Cash, 2008). Questions can:

- socialise the interviewee to speak only in response and to merely reveal information directly requested
- encourage the interviewee to let the interviewer take complete responsibility for the interaction, and for finding a satisfactory solution to the problems or difficulties presented by the interviewee
- inhibit the development of a warm, understanding relationship, conducive to the exploration of important, but perhaps intimate and, for the interviewee, potentially embarrassing details
- direct the conversation in ways that are shaped by the interviewer's underlying assumptions.

Despite these disadvantages, many professionals rely upon a predominantly questioning style (see Chapter 5). For example, in one study of interviewing skills employed by social workers, the number of questions used outnumbered reflections by a ratio of more than 15 to 1 (Forrester *et al.*, 2008).

FACTUAL AND AFFECTIVE COMMUNICATION

Reflecting has been regarded by some theorists as a unitary phenomenon and labelled accordingly, while others have conceived of it as encompassing a varying number of related processes, including *reflection of content* (Manthei, 1997), *reflecting experience* (Brammer and MacDonald, 2003), *reflection of meaning* (Freshwater, 2003; Ivey *et al.*, 2010) and *restatement* (Hill, 2004). Some have conceptualised reflection as a form of *dialogic practice* through which interviewer and interviewee co-construct meaning (Strong, 2006). However, the most commonly cited distinction is between *reflection of feeling* and *paraphrasing* (Dickson, 2006). Most of the messages that we both send and receive provide different types of information. One type of information is basically *factual* or *cognitive* concerning things, places, people, happenings and so on. A second is predominantly *feeling-based* or *affective* concerning our emotional states or attitudinal reactions to ourselves, to others or to our environment. As explained by Adler and Rodman (2006: 190), almost all statements have two types of message: 'Content messages, which focus on the subject being discussed, are the most obvious ... In addition, virtually all communication – both verbal and nonverbal – contains relational messages, which make statements about how the parties feel toward one another.'

Some messages are predominantly factual, others essentially affective. An example of the former would be 'It's 4.30 pm.' in response to a request for the correct time. An example of the latter would be 'Oh no!' uttered by someone who has just been informed of a tragic event. This is obviously an expression of shocked grief, rather than a challenging of the fact that the event occurred, and is therefore fundamentally affective. The majority of messages, however, contain elements of both types of information. Consider the following statement:

> Mornings could not come soon enough for me, that summer. I was always up well before the others. I could scarcely wait for them to rise and the fun to begin. Breakfast was eaten swiftly and we ran to the beach. Each day seemed to hold endlessly exciting possibilities. The time just flew past.

The factual parts of the message are that the person had a daily routine of getting up early, waiting for the others, grabbing some breakfast and heading for the beach. The affective part, of course, conveys the sense of happiness, excited anticipation and general joie de vivre.

The emotive component of a message can take three basic forms:

1   ***Explicitly stated.*** Here the feeling aspect is directly mentioned in the verbal content. For example, 'I was ecstatic.'
2   ***Implicitly mentioned.*** In this case, feelings are not directly stated but rather the affective information is implicitly contained in what is said. Egan (2007) distinguished between *discussed* and *expressed* feelings and emphasised that

emotional experience that is expressed 'is part of the message and needs to be identified and understood' (p. 104). Thus, take someone who has recently suffered loss and says listlessly, 'Most days I just don't even get up ... I don't have the energy to do anything. I can't concentrate ... not even think straight. I've lost all interest – everything just seems so pointless. I keep having these really black thoughts ...' Here, depression, while not explicitly mentioned, is a palpable emotional message carried by the words. In other instances, though, the implicit emotional message 'written between the lines', as it were, may be less certain.

3   *Inferred.* The affective component of a message can be inferred from the manner in which the verbal content is delivered – from the nonverbal and paralinguistic accompaniments. When the verbal and nonverbal/paralinguistic elements of an emotional or attitudinal message conflict as, for example, when someone says glumly 'I am overjoyed', the latter source of information usually holds sway in our decoding (Afifi, 2006). A main reason for this is that the nonverbal message is judged to be more credible and less easily faked (see Chapter 3).

It can be difficult trying to accurately decode affect when it has not been explicitly stated and, in these cases, care is recommended (Jones, 2005). This would seem to be particularly good advice in the case of some types of nonverbal behaviour. Indeed, the notion of a direct, invariable relationship between an underlying emotion and a particular corresponding facial display, for instance, has been challenged (Fernandez-Dols, 1999; Remland, 2006). Empathic handling of nebulous feelings expressed in less direct ways can often be difficult and uncertain. It can, however, be beneficial if it helps to put others in touch with feeling states of which they are largely unaware – and does so in a nonthreatening manner.

PURPOSES OF REFLECTING

Reflecting serves a number of purposes (Brammer and MacDonald, 2003; Hill, 2004; Dickson, 2006). Some of these were summarised by Forrester *et al.* (2008: 43): 'They are central to the expression of accurate empathy; they encourage deeper exploration of emotional content; and they allow the worker or counsellor sensitively to manage the interview, e.g. by summarizing one stage and opening up another.' The overall goals served by reflecting are presented in Box 6.3. While a number of these are common to both paraphrasing and reflection of feeling, some are more obviously relevant to one than the other.

PARAPHRASING

Paraphrasing, also referred to as *reflection of content* or *restatement*, can be defined as the process of feeding back to another, in your own words, the essential factual part of the other's message. The emphasis here is upon content (events, thoughts, ideas, descriptions, etc.) rather than affect. Paraphrasing is most appropriate when the

Box 6.3 Purposes of reflecting

The main goals served by the skill of reflecting are:

1 To demonstrate interest in and involvement with the other person.
2 To display close attention to what is being communicated.
3 To show that you are trying to understand fully what the other is saying.
4 To check your perceptions and ensure accuracy of understanding.
5 To facilitate the other person's comprehension of issues involved and clarity of thinking on these matters.
6 To focus attention upon particular aspects and encourage further exploration.
7 To communicate a deep concern for that which the other person considers to be important.
8 To place the major emphasis upon the interviewee, rather than the interviewer.
9 To indicate that it is acceptable for the other person to have and express feelings in this situation and so facilitate their ventilation.
10 To allow the other person to 'own' feelings expressed.
11 To enable the other person to realise that feelings can be an important cause of behaviour.
12 To help the other person to scrutinise underlying reasons and motives.
13 To operate from within the other's frame of reference and demonstrate empathy.

message received carries little emotion to be dealt with, or when it may be inappropriately premature to begin to explore the affective undertow in depth and so initially dealing with the facts is a safer option (Egan, 2007; Cormier *et al.*, 2008). Paraphrases, therefore, have three important prerequisites:

1 The focus is primarily upon the *factual information* received; the word 'primarily' is used purposefully, however, since it is often difficult to eliminate affective aspects entirely.

2 They should be couched, for the most part, *in the speaker's own words*. Adler and Rodman (2006: 131) characterised it as 'restating in your own words the message you thought the speaker had just sent, without adding anything new'. It is not concerned with simply repeating what has just been said. One type of probing technique, echoing, involves the straight repetition of the interviewee's previous statement, or a part of it (see Chapter 5). Such restatement, however, does not constitute a paraphrase. If, when paraphrasing, the interviewer continually repeats the interviewee's words it can quickly lead to the latter becoming frustrated. As aptly expressed by Inskipp (2006: 80): 'Paraphrasing is not parroting.' Instead, interviewers should respond using their own terms, perhaps using synonyms, while not violating or misrepresenting the original meaning (Wood, 2004).

3 They should contain the *essential* component of the previous message. This requires the speaker to identify the core of the statement embedded in the verbiage. The key question to consider is: 'What is this person really trying to communicate?' It should, therefore, not be assumed that the paraphrase must

encompass everything that has just been said, some of which may well be tangential.

In the conversation between James and Julie in Box 6.4, all of Julie's responses are paraphrases. These examples of paraphrasing manifest, 'in action', the defining characteristics of the skill, and help to illustrate some of its advantages. By demonstrating that she can accurately reproduce the fundamentally important parts of what James has just said, Julie demonstrates that she:

- is attending single-mindedly
- recognises that it is important to understand fully what James is striving to relate, hence conveying respect
- has accurately 'tuned in' to James' narrative.

By so doing, James is also made aware of the fact that Julie is interested in his present difficulty and quite prepared to become involved in helping him explore it further.

Box 6.4 James, Rebecca and the party that went wrong

James: I'm not sure whether or not to phone Rebecca, after what happened at the party on Saturday night . . . and the row, and that.

Julie: You had an argument with Rebecca at the weekend?

James: Yes. I didn't know Vicky would be there. There's nothing between Vicky and me now, but you know the way she always comes on strong . . . trying to make other girls jealous?

Julie: Ah, so Rebecca thought that you and Vicky had something going on?

James: Yes, and Rebecca started to talk to Andy and one thing led to another. Andy didn't know that we were together . . . and the next thing they were getting cosy on the sofa. Andy couldn't believe his luck! She only did it to get back at me, though.

Julie: Right, Rebecca didn't really fancy Andy, she was simply retaliating, as she saw it?

James: At the time though, I didn't realise what was going on. Andy and I are mates and I *thought* he was trying to make a move on my girl. So I grabbed him by the shirt and dragged him out . . . He thought I had gone mad. So he hit me and I hit him . . . Mind you we were both fairly drunk as well.

Julie: You thought that Andy was taking liberties, so you initiated a drunken row.

James: Yeah . . . when I think of it now, I feel so stupid . . . so embarrassed . . . neither Rebecca nor Andy has been in touch since. If I phone they might ring off, but the longer I leave it, the worse it could get. On the other hand, I suppose, waiting until the weekend could give everyone a chance to simmer down and forget it.

Julie: You are keen to mend fences with Rebecca and Andy but are unsure when is best to make a start?

According to Hill (2004: 131), responding with this type of reflective statement in a formal helping setting has an effect whereby 'clients can evaluate what they are thinking, add things they had forgotten, think about whether they actually believe what they have said, and think about things at a deeper level'.

One of the foremost uses of this type of reflective statement is to let clients know they are being listened to (Cormier *et al.*, 2008). Indeed, Orbe and Bruess (2005: 166) described as a 'great listener' someone who is capable of paraphrasing without changing the meaning of what has just been said. From the interviewer's point of view, the subsequent reaction of the interviewee to the paraphrase offered also confirms (assuming it is accurate) that the interviewer is on the proper 'wavelength'. Indeed, paraphrases are often used for this very purpose – as a check on accurate understanding. Broadcast journalists employ this skill frequently when interviewing – they paraphrase the interviewee's responses to clarify and check the precise meaning of these for both parties immediately involved, and also for the listeners. Likewise, in the classroom, teachers frequently paraphrase pupil contributions. By so doing they not only establish that they have fully understood what was said, but also clarify the information provided for the rest of the class. Again, it is not uncommon to hear someone who has just received directions to get to a particular place paraphrase back what was told, e.g. 'So I go to the end of the road, turn right, second on the left and then right again.' In this case, paraphrasing serves the dual purpose of checking accuracy and promoting the memorisation of the information.

By encapsulating and unobtrusively presenting to the interviewee in a clear and unambiguous manner a key facet of their previous communication, the speaker also gently guides and encourages the continuation of this theme and the exploration of it in greater depth. Interviewees' thoughts, especially when dealing with an apparently intractable problem, are often inchoate and ambiguous. An accurate paraphrase, by condensing and crystallising what has been said, can often help the interviewee to see more clearly the exigencies of the predicament (Lindon and Lindon, 2007). Paraphrasing also enables interviewers to keep interviewees and their concerns front stage, by responding and guiding rather than leading and directing. It indicates that interviewers, rather than insisting on imposing their own agenda, are actively trying to make sense of what is being heard from within the interviewee's frame of reference (Hough, 2006). In the sports context, it has often been said that a good referee is one who controls the game and lets it flow, while remaining in the background. In many situations the same holds true for a good interviewer. Paraphrasing is one method of accomplishing this. The emphasis is placed firmly upon the interviewee. Using Benjamin's (2001) terminology, the interviewer uses the interviewee's life space rather than that of the interviewer. By keeping the focus upon those issues which the interviewee wants to ventilate, the interviewer also says metaphorically that their importance is acknowledged. A tacit commitment personally to get involved with these concerns is also communicated by the interviewer when paraphrasing effectively.

REFLECTION OF FEELING

Reflection of feeling can be defined as the process of feeding back to another, in your own words, the essence of the feelings expressed in the other's previous communication. The similarity between this definition and that of paraphrasing will be noted and many of the features of the latter, outlined above, are applicable. The major difference between the two definitions is, of course, the concern with affective matters peculiar to reflection of feeling, including those messages conveyed nonverbally (Inskipp, 2006). The most important steps in the use of the skill are regarded by Brammer and MacDonald (2003) to be:

- recognising the feeling being expressed
- labelling and describing this feeling clearly and accurately
- observing the reaction of the other
- evaluating the extent to which the reflection was helpful.

Thus, a prerequisite for the successful use of this skill is the ability to identify accurately and name the feelings being expressed by the other. Unless this initial procedure can be accomplished, the likelihood that the subsequent reflection of those feelings will achieve its desired purpose is greatly reduced. A number of relevant distinctions to do with expressing feelings have been identified by Nelson-Jones (2005b). He pointed out that feelings can be simple or complex, and that sometimes what comes across is a jumble of mixed emotions. Two common combinations of affect identified by Teyber (2006) are:

- anger–sadness–shame
- sadness–anger–guilt.

In the first, predominating anger may be a reaction to hurt, invoking sadness with both combining to trigger shame. In the second, sadness is the primary emotion connected to repressed anger leading to guilt. In each case, the presenting feeling of anger or sadness is buttressed by a much more involved constellation of emotions and experiences, some of which are easier for the individual to recognise and discuss than others. This multidimensionality makes the task of identifying and reflecting feeling that much more demanding. Again, and with respect to the objects of feelings, they may be self-focused, directed towards the interviewer, or be vented on a third party, thing or event. Furthermore, feelings discussed may have been experienced in the past or be current in the here-and-now of the encounter. Concentrating upon the latter is referred to as *immediacy* (Egan, 2007). Present tense reflections of here-and-now states create more powerful experiencing and can often be most useful.

Turning to inferred emotional states, some are more readily identifiable than others from nonverbal cues such as facial expressions (Ekman and O'Sullivan, 1991; Remland, 2006) and vocal features (Banse and Scherer, 1996). In an early series of experiments, Davitz (1964) had actors read verbally neutral sentences in such a way as to convey different emotions. Tapes of these were presented to judges for decoding. Fear and anger were most readily recognisable. In general, however, positive emotions are more easily discerned than unpleasant ones, with females being more successful than males at reading such cues (Kirouac and Hess, 1999; Burgoon and Bacue, 2003). It is also possible to train individuals to improve their performance. As far as reflecting back feelings based solely upon nonverbal cues is concerned, Lindon and Lindon (2007) recommended a cautious approach. Until a certain level of familiarity and trust has been established, recipients may be made to feel embarrassingly transparent and quite vulnerable if feelings are reflected prematurely. Thus, in his research into actual counsellor–client exchanges, Strong (2006) found that counsellors used reflection later in the process, once rapport had been established.

While the terms 'feelings' and 'emotions' are sometimes used synonymously, feelings often refer to more subtle emotional or attitudinal states. For this reason they are typically more difficult to label accurately. It has been suggested that one cause of this difficulty, especially with the novice interviewer, is an insufficient repertoire of feeling terms, making fine discrimination and identification problematic. Cormier *et al.* (2008) advocated that interviewers have at their disposal a number of broad categories of feeling words. Each of these can be expressed at a mild, moderate or intense level. For example, 'petrified' could accurately describe someone in intense fear; 'alarmed' if that feeling is moderate; and 'frightened' if only mildly experienced. Other examples of feelings continuums are given in Box 6.5. By initially determining the broad category and then the intensity level, subtle feelings can more easily be deciphered, thereby facilitating the process of reflecting them back. Van der Molen and Gramsbergen-Hoogland (2005) stressed the importance of feelings expressed being reflected at the appropriate level of intensity, in order for the interviewer to be on the same wavelength as, and fully in touch with, the interviewee.

An excerpt from a helping interview is provided in Box 6.6. Compare the helper responses in this excerpt with the examples of paraphrases provided previously. Here, the interviewer's primary focus is upon exploration and understanding of the feelings being conveyed by the client. While these examples were drawn from a helping session, it should be realised that this skill has a much broader application. For instance, in the negotiating process the role of emotion in shaping proceedings is very important (Shapiro, 2000). Here, reflecting the feelings of the other assists in the process of exploring their needs, building rapport and mutual respect and preventing a build-up of emotional negativity (Gray, 2003; Hargie *et al.*, 2004; see Chapter 13 for further discussion of negotiation). Reflection of feeling is therefore appropriate across a range of social settings in promoting the examination of feelings, emotions and attitudes.

Reflecting feeling shares a number of features in common with the skill of paraphrasing. By responding in this way, attention to and interest in the other are demonstrated. It helps clients to feel understood, and to sense that both they and their

---

Box 6.5 Examples of continuum of feelings

Mild	*Moderate*	*Intense*
Surprised	Shocked	Stunned
Happy	Delighted	Ecstatic
Annoyed	Angry	Furious
Like	Love	Adore
Unhappy	Sad	Depressed
Joy	Delight	Jubilation
Dislike	Hate	Despise
Interested	Absorbed	Enthralled
Ignored	Rejected	Abandoned

Box 6.6 Examples of reflecting feeling

Client: Well my wife finally left. As you know, she had threatened this on and off for a while but I never dreamed she would actually walk out. But, to my amazement, she did. I can't believe it.

Helper: You are shocked.

Client: Yes. She was everything I ever wanted and although she had that affair last year, I had begun to put that behind me.

Helper: You had started to move on.

Client: More or less. It was very hurtful at the time but I know I had been taking her for granted. I was working all hours, trying to earn as much money as I could – for us. I tried to change and pay her more attention and this is the thanks I get.

Helper: You are clearly very upset.

Client: Yeah. I don't know where I go from here. I still care for her but part of me also is very angry at what she has done. That's the thanks I get. I'm not sure that I even want her back.

Helper: You have mixed feelings. You have affection for her but there is also a sense of betrayal.

Client: Indeed. She was my first love but she has treated me terribly . . . [client continues to discuss his situation].

---

concerns are important and respected. Burleson (2003) reviewed the beneficial effects on psychological, relational, physical and health outcomes of providing emotional support to those in distressed states. In a class of supportive response that encourages the further elaboration of difficult circumstances and associated feelings, he included 'reflections or restatements of the target's emotive expressions' (p. 566). Such messages are high in person centredness (HPC) and, as Burleson (2008: 208) pointed out, HPC messages 'explicitly recognize and legitimize the other's feelings, help the other to articulate those feelings, elaborate reasons why those feelings might be felt, and assist the other to see how those feelings fit in a broader context'. In this way, reflecting back the central feeling element of what they have just communicated can enable recipients to think more clearly and objectively about issues that previously were vague and confused.

Another key benefit of this skill is that it acts as a means whereby the speaker can check for accuracy of understanding (Wilkins, 2003). Going beyond aspects held in common with paraphrasing, reflection of feeling indicates to others that it is acceptable for them to have and express feelings in that situation – it validates their affective experiences (Hill, 2004). This is important, since in many everyday conversations the factual element of communication is stressed to the neglect, and even active avoidance, of the affective dimension. People often need to be 'given permission' before they will reveal emotionally laden detail. But when they do unburden themselves the release can heighten energy and promote a sense of well-being (Cormier *et al.*, 2008). By reflecting the other's feelings, a speaker acknowledges that person's right both to have and to disclose such emotions.

Another goal of reflection of feeling is to help people to 'own' their feelings – to appreciate that ultimately they are the source of, and can take responsibility for, their affective states. Various ploys commonly used by people to disown their feelings include speaking in the second person (e.g. '*You* get depressed being on your own all the time'), or third (e.g. '*One* gets depressed . . .'), rather than in the first person (e.g. '*I* get depressed . . .'). Sometimes a feeling state is depersonalised by referring to 'it' (e.g. '*It's* not easy being all alone', rather than, 'I find it difficult being all alone'). Lindon and Lindon (2007) recommended helping the other to personalise feelings through reflecting. Since reflective statements make explicit the other's affective experiences and label those statements as clearly belonging to them, they help them to acknowledge and come to terms with their emotions. Indeed, it has been contended that helping clients to progress towards maximum self-awareness and understanding is the primary aim of this skill (Manthei, 1997). Recipients are also encouraged to examine and identify underlying reasons and motives for behaviour of which they previously may not have been completely aware. Furthermore, they begin to realise that feelings can have important causal influences upon their actions.

The use of this skill can also serve to foster a facilitative relationship. Interviewers who reflect feeling accurately are more likely to be regarded as empathic (Lang and van der Molen, 1990; Hough, 2006). As shown by Teyber (2006: 53), clients experience a deep sense of being empathised with when 'the therapist can reflect the most basic feeling or capture the key issue in what the client has just said'. However, it should not be assumed that reflection of feeling and empathy are one and the same. Empathy is a broad concept involving several subprocesses (Chakrabarti and Baron-Cohen, 2008), and being empathic involves much more than reflecting feeling. Nevertheless, an appropriate, well-chosen reflection can be one way of manifesting empathic understanding and adopting the other's internal frame of reference (Irving and Dickson, 2006). Interviewees consequently feel deeply understood, sensing that the interviewer is with them and is able to perceive the world from their perspective. The interviewee in such a relationship is motivated to relate more freely to the interviewer and divulge information that has deep personal meaning.

Practices to avoid when reflecting feeling

Reflection of feeling is, therefore, a very useful skill for all interactors, professional or otherwise, to have in their repertoires. However, there are some problems associated with it, including the following:

1   *Inaccuracy.* Accuracy is important when labelling feelings expressed by the respondent. By reflecting feelings that were neither experienced nor expressed, the other's sense of confusion and failure to be understood can be heightened. This does not mean that failing occasionally to 'hit the nail on the head' is necessarily disastrous.

2   *Moving too quickly.* This happens when the reflection begins to surface sensed emotion that the listener is not yet ready either to acknowledge or perhaps to discuss in any depth in that situation or at that stage of the relationship.

3   *Emotional abandonment.* Interviewers should avoid bringing deep feelings

to the surface without assisting the interviewee to deal with them. This can sometimes happen at the end of an interview when the interviewer leaves the interviewee 'in mid-air' (see Chapter 10 for a discussion of effective closure techniques).

4   **Ossified expression.** There is a tendency among many inexperienced practitioners to consistently begin their reflection with a phrase such as 'You feel . . .'. While such a sentence structure may be a useful way of learning the skill, its monotonous use can appear mechanical and indeed 'unfeeling' over time and can have an adverse effect on the recipient. For this reason a greater variety of types of opening phrases should be developed.

5   **Parroting.** Another malpractice includes an over-reliance upon the feeling words of the interviewee, by simply repeating back what was said. This 'parroting' of emotional labels should be distinguished from reflecting feeling. Unlike the latter, 'parroting only irritates speakers and implies that you have not really processed or understood their situation and subsequent reaction' (Balzer Riley, 2008: 120). It tends to stunt conversations and can quickly become antagonising.

6   **Over-inclusion.** This occurs when the reflection goes beyond what was actually communicated by including unwarranted suppositions, or speculations. Conversely, the reflective statement should not neglect any important aspect of the affective message of the other.

7   **Emotional mismatch.** Perhaps one of the most difficult features of the skill is trying to match the depth of feeling included in the reflection to that initially expressed. If the level of feeling of the reflection is too shallow, the recipient is less likely to feel fully understood or inclined to examine these issues more profoundly. If it is too deep, the person may feel threatened and anxious, resulting in denial and alienation. More generally, the reflective statement should mirror the same type of language and forms of expression of the other, without being patronising. The latter, together with the other potential pitfalls mentioned above, can only be overcome by careful practice, coupled with a critical awareness of one's performance.

RESEARCH OUTCOMES OF A REFLECTIVE STYLE

Comparisons of the outcomes of an indirect, reflective style with a range of alternatives have been carried out in several well-established empirical studies over a number of years. Much of this research has an interviewing or counselling orientation. In some cases, attitudes of both interviewees and external judges to interviewers manifesting contrasting styles were sought. In early work by Silver (1970), low-status interviewees were reported to feel much more comfortable with interviewers who displayed a reflective rather than a judgemental approach. Ellison and Firestone (1974) found that subjects regarded a reflective interviewer, rather than an intrusive counterpart who controlled the direction and pace of the interview in a particularly assertive manner, as having a greater capacity to encourage the revelation of highly intimate details. The reflective interviewer was also perceived as passive, easygoing and nonassertive.

An interrogative approach in which further information was requested, and a predictive style which required the interviewer accurately to predict interviewees' reactions in situations yet to be discussed, were the alternatives to reflecting examined by Turkat and Alpher (1984). Although impressions were based upon written transcripts rather than actual interviews, those interviewers who used reflections were regarded as understanding their clients. Empathic understanding and positive regard (two of the core conditions for effective person-centred counselling) were related to the reflective style of interviewing, in a study by Zimmer and Anderson (1968). They drew upon the opinions of external judges who viewed a video-taped counselling session. From the painstaking analysis of therapy sessions undertaken by Hill and her colleagues (Hill et al., 1988; Hill, 1989), not only was reflecting discovered to be one of the most common of the identified techniques utilised by therapists, but clients reported that they found it one of the most helpful. They regarded it as providing support and seldom reacted negatively to its use. Such reflections assisted clients in becoming more deeply attuned to their emotional and personal experiences, leading to more profound levels of exploration and greater insights into their circumstances and difficulties. One of the most marked outcomes was an association with significantly reduced levels of anxiety. Incidentally, and by way of comparison, closed questions in particular were regarded by clients as decidedly unhelpful when used by therapists (see also Chapter 5).

Other researchers, rather than focusing upon attitudes, have investigated the effects of reflecting upon the actual behaviour of the interviewee. Some form of interviewee self-disclosure has commonly been measured (for further information on self-disclosure see Chapter 9). Powell (1968), for instance, carried out a study on the effects of reflections on subjects' positive and negative self-referent statements (i.e. statements about themselves). 'Approval-supportive' and 'open disclosure' were the comparative experimental conditions. The former included interviewer statements supporting subjects' self-references while the latter referred to the provision of personal detail by the interviewer. Reflections were found to produce a significant increase in the number of negative, but not positive, self-references. Kennedy et al. (1971) similarly reported an increase in interviewee self-statements attributable to the use of this technique.

Vondracek (1969) and Beharry (1976) looked at the effects of reflecting not only on the amount of subjects' self-disclosure but also on the degree of intimacy provided. More intimate detail was associated with the reflective style of interviewing in both cases. A similar result was reported by Mills (1983) in relation to rates rather than quality of self-disclosure. More recently, Forrester et al. (2008) also found a positive relationship between the use of reflections by social workers and client self-disclosure. Feigenbaum (1977) produced an interesting finding concerning sex differences of subjects. While females disclosed more, and at more intimate levels, in response to reflections, male subjects scored significantly higher on both counts in response to interviewer self-disclosure.

An investigation of marital therapists and couples undergoing therapy was conducted by Cline et al. (1984). A complex relationship emerged involving not only gender but also social status of subjects. Thus, the degree to which the therapist reflected was found to correlate positively with subsequent changes in positive social interaction for middle-class husbands but with negative changes for both lower-class husbands and wives. It also related positively to changes in expression of personal feeling for middle-class husbands and wives. When assessed three months after the termination of therapy, a positive relationship emerged between therapist reflections and outcome measures of marital satisfaction but for lower-class husbands only.

There seems to be little doubt now that there is a strong individual difference factor influencing reactions and outcomes to nondirective, reflective versus directive styles of engagement. In addition to demographic variables such as gender and class differences already mentioned, personality characteristics have also been researched. Some evidence reviewed by Hill (1992) suggests that locus of control, cognitive complexity and reactance of clients may be important. Locus of control, it will be recalled from Chapter 4, refers to a belief in personally significant events being shaped by either internal or external sources, while reactance is a predisposition to perceive and respond to events as restrictions on personal autonomy and freedom (see Chapter 12). Cognitive complexity relates to the conceptual differentiation and sophistication with which individuals make sense of their circumstances. Hill (1992) came to the conclusion that those high on internality of control and cognitive complexity and low on reactance were more suited to less directive interventions such as reflecting.

In sum, these findings suggest that attitudes towards interviewers who use a reflective style are largely positive. At a more behavioural level, this technique can produce increases in both the amount and intimacy of information which interviewees reveal about themselves. In the actual therapeutic context there is some evidence linking reflecting with positive outcome measures for certain clients. However, the intervening effects of individual differences in demographic and personality factors should not be overlooked. Research studies centred on the separate skills of paraphrasing and reflecting of feeling are limited. The majority of the suggestions and recommendations concerning the skills have been derived from adopted philosophical positions in respect of, for example, counselling and interviewing. Experiences of those practitioners who have employed and 'tested' the skills in the field have also been influential. Some research investigations into paraphrasing and reflection of feeling have been conducted. For the most part these have been experimental in design, conducted in laboratory settings and have sought to establish the effects upon various measures of interviewee verbal behaviour.

Paraphrasing research

In some research studies, paraphrases are defined in such a way as to include affective material (e.g. Hoffnung, 1969), while in others affective content is not explicitly excluded (e.g. Kennedy and Zimmer, 1968; Haase and Di Mattia, 1976; Weger *et al.*, 2010). Further definitional inconsistencies have also been noted by Dickson (2006) in reviewing research in the area and the point should be kept in mind when interpreting the following findings.

Kennedy and Zimmer (1968) reported an increase in subjects' self-referenced statements attributable to paraphrasing, while similar findings featuring self-referenced affective statements were noted by both Hoffnung (1969) and Haase and Di Mattia (1976). According to Citkowitz (1975), on the other hand, this skill had only limited effect in this respect, although there was a tendency for the association to be more pronounced when initial levels of self-referenced affect statements were relatively high. The subjects in this experiment were chronic schizophrenic inpatients and the data were collected during clinical-type interviews. The distinction between the affective and the factual has been more explicitly acknowledged by others who have researched paraphrasing. Waskow (1962), for instance, investigated the outcome of selective interviewer responding on the factual and affective aspects of subjects' communication in a therapeutic interview. It emerged that a significantly higher percentage of factual responses was given by those subjects who had their contributions paraphrased. Auerswald (1974) and Hill and Gormally (1977), however, produced more disappointing findings. In both cases, though, paraphrasing took place on an essentially random basis. Affective responses by subjects were also selected as the dependent variable.

The few studies considering the effects of this technique on attitudes towards the interviewer, rather than behavioural changes on the part of the interviewee, have reported largely favourable outcomes. A positive relationship was detailed by Dickson (1981) between the proportion of paraphrases to questions asked by employment advisory personnel and ratings of interviewer competency provided by independent, experienced judges. A comparable outcome emerged when client perceptions of interviewer effectiveness were examined by Nagata *et al.* (1983). Likewise, in a study of the effects of paraphrases upon interviewee responses, Weger *et al.* (2010) found that interviewers employing this technique received significantly higher ratings of likeability than when they simply used acknowledgements (e.g. 'Okay', 'That's great'). In this study, paraphrases did not lead to higher ratings by interviewees of conversational satisfaction or an increased perception of feeling understood. However, as Weger *et al.* (2010) acknowledge, this research had a number of limitations. It included only three interviewees, all of whom were university students; in addition, the interviewees were also university students, who were being interviewed about a putative (and unpopular with students) new system of comprehensive examination prior to graduation. This topic was likely to have influenced the overall attitudes of interviewees to the conversational experience.

It would therefore seem that when paraphrases are used contingently and focus upon factual aspects of communication, recipients' verbal performance can be modified accordingly. In addition, paraphrasing seems to promote favourable judgements of the interviewer by both interviewees and external judges. Counselling trainees have also indicated that this is one of the skills which they found most useful when conducting interviews (Spooner, 1976).

Reflection of feeling

Studies into reflection of feeling can be divided into three categories – two major and one minor:

1   experiments, largely laboratory-based, designed to identify effects of reflecting feeling on subjects' verbal behaviour
2   studies that have attempted to relate the use of the technique to judgements, by either interviewees or observers, of interviewers in terms of such attributes as empathy, warmth and respect. In many instances both types of dependent variable have featured in the same investigation

3   descriptive studies profiling the use of reflective statements by renowned
     counsellors, such as Carl Rogers.

In relation to the first category, the effects of reflections of feeling on interviewees'
affective self-reference statements were explored by Merbaum (1963), Barnabei *et al.*
(1974), Highlen and Baccus (1977) and Highlen and Nicholas (1978), among others.
With the exception of Barnabei *et al.* (1974), this interviewing skill was found to
promote substantial increases in affective self-talk by subjects. Highlen and Nicholas
(1978), however, combined reflections of feeling with interviewer self-referenced affect
statements (self-disclosures) in such a way that it is impossible to attribute the
outcome solely to the influence of the former. One possible explanation for the failure
by Barnabei *et al.* (1974) to produce a positive finding could reside in the fact that
reflections of feeling were administered in a random or noncontingent manner. It has
already been mentioned that paraphrases used in this indiscriminate way were
equally ineffective in producing increases in self-referenced statements.
    Switching attention to the effects of reflecting feeling on judgement of personal/
relational qualities, a significant relationship between reflection of feeling and ratings
of empathic understanding emerged in a piece of research conducted by Uhlemann
et al. (1976). These ratings were provided by external judges and based upon both
written responses and audio-recordings of actual interviews. Likewise, Ehrlich *et al.*
(1979) found that interviewers who reflected feelings that had not yet been named by
interviewees were regarded by the latter as being more expert and trustworthy. A
similar procedure, labelled 'sensing unstated feelings', by Nagata *et al.* (1983), emerged
as a significant predictor of counsellor effectiveness when assessed by surrogate
clients following a counselling-type interview. However, not all findings have been as
positive. Highlen and Baccus (1977) failed to reveal any significant differences in
clients' perceptions of counselling climate, counsellor comfort or personal satisfaction
between clients allocated to a reflection of feeling and to a probe treatment. Similarly,
Gallagher and Hargie (1992) found no significant relationships between ratings of
counsellors' reflections, on the one hand, and on the other, separate assessments by
counsellors, clients and judges of empathy, genuineness and acceptance displayed
towards clients. As acknowledged by the authors, the small sample size may have
been a factor in the outcome of this investigation.
    Finally, and referring to the third category of study, in an analysis of the
counselling session captured on film and entitled *Carl Rogers Counsels an Individual –
On Anger and Hurt*, Lietaer (2004) found that almost 53 per cent of Rogers's contributions took the form of reflections of expressed feeling by the client. A further
5.5 per cent were reflections of underlying feelings.

OVERVIEW

Reflection is a powerful skill when used appropriately. It puts respondents at centre
stage in the interaction, allows them to develop and evaluate their thoughts, ideas and
feelings, and helps to establish a close bond between the interactors. At first blush it
seems deceptively simple, but it is a skill that many novices find difficult to master.
This often only becomes evident to them when they attempt to put the skill into

practice. In the numerous training programmes that I have implemented in well over three decades, it is my view that this is the most difficult skill for trainees to acquire. During practicals trainees tend to revert to asking questions rather than reflecting. This is because in everyday life they use questions profusely but reflections rarely. To obtain optimum effect, the following points should be remembered when adopting a reflective style:

1   *Use your own words.* Reflecting is not merely a process of echoing back the words just heard. Speakers should strive rather to reformulate the message using their own terminology. In addition, Ivey *et al.* (2010) recommended using a sentence stem that includes, as far as possible, a word in keeping with the other's characteristic mode of receiving information. For example, assuming that the other is a 'visualiser' (i.e. someone who relies mainly upon visual images as a means of gathering and processing information and who uses expressions such as 'I *see* what you mean . . .'; 'The *picture* that I am getting . . .'), it would be more appropriate to begin a reflection with 'It *appears* that . . .' or 'It *looks* like . . .'. By contrast, with someone who prioritises the aural channel (and uses expressions like 'I *hear* what you are saying . . .'; 'I can't *tune in* to what she is saying . . .'), then reflections beginning with 'It *sounds* to me that . . .' or 'As I *listen* to you, what seems to be *coming through* is . . .' may be more apposite.

2   *Do not go beyond the information communicated by the addressee.* Remember, reflecting is a process of only feeding back information already given by the speaker. The reflection should not add to or take away from the meaning as presented. Reflections should not include speculations or suppositions which represent an attempt to impose meaning on what was communicated, and while based upon it may not be strictly warranted by it. The speaker, therefore, when reflecting, should not try to interpret or psychoanalyse. Interpretation may be useful on occasion, but it is not reflection. For example:

> *A:*   I suppose I have never had a successful relationship with men. I never seemed to get on with my father when I was a child . . . I always had problems with the male teachers when I was at school . . .
>
> *B:*   You saw the male teachers as extensions of your father.

Note that this statement by B is not a reflection. It is an interpretation that goes beyond what was said by A.

3   *Be concise.* The objective is not to include everything said but to select what appear to be the most salient elements of the preceding message. It is only the core or essence of what the other was trying to communicate that the speaker should strive to reflect. Reflections should be short statements rather than long, involved or rambling.

4   *Be specific.* It will be recalled that one of the goals of reflecting is to promote understanding. Frequently, interviewees, perhaps due to never having previously fully thought through that particular issue, will tend to express themselves in a rather vague, confused and abstract manner. It is more beneficial if, when reflecting, interviewers try to be as simple, concrete and specific as possible,

thereby ensuring that both they and indeed the interviewees successfully comprehend what is being said.

5   ***Be accurate.*** Accuracy depends upon careful listening (see Chapter 7). While person B is talking, person A should be listening single-mindedly, rather than considering what to say next, or entertaining other thoughts less directly relevant to the encounter. The inclusion of a 'check-out' statement as part of the reflective utterance has been advised as a means of assessing accuracy of understanding, when the affective message received has not been explicitly stated (Ivey *et al.*, 2010). For instance, 'Deep down I sense a feeling of relief, would you agree?' In addition to inviting corrective feedback, by offering the opportunity to comment on the accuracy of understanding, the speaker avoids giving the impression of assumed omniscience or of imposing meaning on the other. If a practitioner is frequently inaccurate in reflections proffered, the client will quickly realise that further prolongation of the interaction is pointless, since the practitioner does not seem able to appreciate what is being said. This certainly does not mean that an occasional inaccuracy by a generally and genuinely concerned interviewer will be disastrous. Rather, in such a case the recipient, realising the speaker's determination to grasp meaning, will generally be motivated to provide additional information and rectify the misconception. Indeed, Hill (2004: 158) advanced an argument that 'helpers should not be as concerned with assessing the accuracy of a particular reflection as with trying to understand clients and communicating to clients that they are struggling to understand'.

6   ***Do not overuse reflections.*** Not all contributions should be reflected. To attempt to do so would restrict rather than help the other person. Reflections need to be used in conjunction with the other skills that an interviewer should have available (e.g. questioning, reinforcing, self-disclosure, etc.). In some instances it is only after rapport has been established that reflection of feeling can be used without the interviewee feeling awkward or threatened.

7   ***Focus upon the immediately preceding message.*** Reflections typically reflect what is contained in the other's immediately preceding statement. It is possible, and indeed desirable on occasion, for reflections to be wider ranging and to cover a number of interjections. The interviewer may wish, for example, at the end of the interview, to reflect the facts and feelings expressed by the interviewee during its entire course. Reflections such as these that have a broader perspective are called *summaries of content* and *summaries of feeling*, and are a useful means of identifying themes expressed by the interviewee during the complete interview, or parts of it (see Chapter 10 for more detail on closure).

8   ***Combining facts and feelings.*** Reflection contains two essential component skills – reflection of feeling and paraphrasing. It is, of course, possible to combine both factual and feeling material in a single reflection if this is felt to be the most appropriate response. Indeed, this is often how the skill is used in practice. As an introductory tool for those unused to conveying empathic understanding, Egan (2007: 102–103) recommended what he called 'the basic formula': 'You feel . . . [here name the correct emotion expressed by the client] because . . . [here indicate the correct thoughts, experiences, and behaviors that give rise to the

feelings].' Feelings and facts are brought together in this format with one type of information complementing the other and enabling the recipient to perceive the relationship between them. Moreover, Ivey *et al.* (2010) identified how, in this way, deeper meanings underlying expressed experiences can be located and sensitively surfaced. They referred to this process as *reflection of meaning*.

Chapter 7

Paying attention to others: the skill of listening

INTRODUCTION

IN SOCIAL INTERACTION THE process of listening is of crucial importance. As Mark Twain famously observed: 'If we were supposed to talk more than we listen, we would have two tongues and one ear.' To respond appropriately to others, we must pay attention to the messages they are sending and link our responses to these. In Chapter 3 it was noted that the average person does not actually speak for long periods each day, and indeed several studies into the percentage of time spent in different forms of communication have found listening to be the predominant interpersonal activity. Adults spend about 70 per cent of their waking time communicating (Adler *et al.*, 2006). Of this, on average 45 per cent of communication time is spent listening, 30 per cent speaking, 16 per cent reading and 9 per cent writing. In the work context, for the average employee these figures have been calculated as 55 per cent listening, 23 per cent speaking, 13.3 per cent reading and 8.4 per cent writing, but for managers the listening figure increases to 63 per cent (Wolvin and Coakley, 1996).

The importance of listening is now widely recognised across many contexts (Rautalinko and Lisper, 2004; Moore, 2005; Gable, 2007; Flynn *et al.*, 2008; Hargie, 2009). Classroom research has shown that those students who score highest in listening ability achieve higher levels of academic attainment (Beall *et al.*, 2008). In her review of research in this area Jalongo (2010: 4) concluded: 'Listening comprehension, defined as the young child's ability to understand what he or she hears, is highly predictive of overall academic achievement.' In the business sphere, Bambacas and Patrickson (2008) found that senior human resource

177

executives rated the listening ability of candidates as a key criterion when recruiting prospective managers. Likewise, McCallum and O'Connell (2009) showed that listening ability is a key competency in organisational leadership. Peterson (2007: 286) highlighted how through listening, managers can 'attain information and insights that are needed for well-grounded decision making. In this regard, they can acquire overviews of the ongoing performance, plans, needs, personalities, and communication styles of others, both inside and outside of the organization.'

This was confirmed by Goby and Lewis (2000) in a study of the insurance industry, where staff at all levels, as well as customers (policyholders), regarded listening as the primary communication skill. Similarly, in a study of 1000 salespeople, Rosenbaum (2001) found that the ability to listen in depth to client needs was a defining characteristic of success. However, Stewart and Cash (2008: 35) reported that surveys of hundreds of companies in the USA 'reveal that poor listening skills create barriers in all positions from entry level to CEO'. Other recent research has confirmed that many managers are poor listeners, and that this is particularly the case in relation to receptiveness to difficult information being raised by employees. In their review of the area, Barwise and Meehan (2008: 22) argued that a main reason for this is that 'managers often unwittingly signal that they don't want to hear bad news – for instance, by changing the subject or avoiding interaction – and subordinates tend to censor themselves'.

For professionals in most fields, listening is therefore a core skill. Knowledge of and expertise in listening techniques are central to success in interactions with clients and other professionals. For example, in their empirical investigation of this area, Hargie et al. (2000) identified listening as a key skill in community pharmacy practice. In their study of medical skills, Rider and Keefer (2006: 626) illustrated how a core competency for doctors was the ability to 'demonstrate effective listening by hearing and understanding in a way that the patient feels heard and understood'. This was borne out in a major empirical study of doctor–patient communication by Tallman et al. (2007), where the ability to display active listening was found to be a key determinant of physician effectiveness. Likewise, studies have shown that patients rate listening as the most important skill they look for in health professionals (Channa and Siddiqi, 2008; Davis et al., 2008a; Boudreau et al., 2009). As summarised by Davis et al. (2008b: 168): 'Research indicates that when healthcare providers listen to patients, there is more compliance with medical regimens, patient satisfaction is increased, and physicians are less vulnerable to malpractice lawsuits.' More generally, for those whose job involves a helping or facilitative dimension, it has been argued that the capacity to be a good listener is the most fundamental of all skills (Nelson-Jones, 2005a).

In terms of personal well-being: 'Not only is listening a valuable skill, it is also conducive to good health. Studies have shown that when we talk our blood pressure goes up; when we listen it goes down' (Borisoff and Purdy, 1991a: 5). However, this may also depend upon the amount of effort we devote to listening. Galanes et al. (1998) reviewed research that showed how those who are actively trying to listen to, remember and understand what another person is saying show signs of concerted physical activity including accelerated heartbeat, whereas those not listening at all to the speaker have heart rates that often drop to the level of sleep.

Listening is a central skill at the earliest stage of personal development. The infant begins to respond to a new world by hearing and listening, with neonates showing a clear preference for listening to human speech (Vouloumanos and Werker, 2007). Newborns have also been shown to prefer speakers of their native language (Kinzler *et al.*, 2007). Wilding *et al.* (2000) illustrated how neonates are able to discriminate between their father's voice and that of a male stranger, and infants prefer to look at their mother's face rather than a stranger's. They showed how babies rapidly develop the ability to combine visual and auditory stimuli, so at age 6 to 12 weeks they become distressed when shown a video of their mother in which the speech and visual content are discrepant.

In fact, listening is at the heart of communicative development, since the child has to learn to listen before learning to speak, learns to speak before learning to read and learns to read before learning to write. In this sense, listening is a fundamental skill and the foundation for other communication skills. For this reason, listening can be regarded as a *prerequisite skill* upon which all other interactive skills are predicated. To ask the right questions, be assertive, give appropriate rewards, employ apposite self-disclosure, negotiate effectively, open and close interactions and so on, you must engage in concerted listening. As aptly expressed by Robbins and Hunsaker (2009: 89): 'If you aren't an effective listener, you're going to have consistent trouble developing all the other interpersonal skills.' Indeed, many of the problems encountered during social interchange are caused by ineffective listening. Not surprisingly, research studies have shown a range of benefits that accrue from effective listening in both personal and commercial contexts (see Box 7.1 for a summary of these).

DEFINING THE TERM

Academic interest in listening can be traced back to the mid-twentieth-century work of Wiksell (1946) and Nichols (1947). Since that time, the volume of literature in this area has expanded rapidly. But what is the exact meaning of the term 'listening'? In their analysis, Wolff *et al.* (1983) noted that the term 'listen' is based upon an amalgam of the Anglo-Saxon words: *hylstan* (hearing) and *hlosnian* (wait in suspense). However, there is a lack of consensus in the literature with regard to the precise meaning of the term (Bodie *et al.*, 2008). One reason for this is that listening is performed cognitively but evaluated behaviourally (Janusik, 2007). As a result, different definitions

Box 7.1 Benefits of effective listening	
At work	Personally
✓ Greater customer satisfaction	✓ Better family relationships
✓ Increased employee satisfaction	✓ Improved social network
✓ Higher levels of productivity	✓ Greater interpersonal enjoyment
✓ Fewer mistakes	✓ Improved self-esteem
✓ Improved sales figures	✓ Higher grades at school/college
✓ More information sharing	✓ More close friends
✓ Greater innovation and creativity	✓ An enriched life

emphasise either the covert cognitive aspect or the overt behavioural dimension. Thus, some theorists regard listening as a purely cognitive auditory activity, as 'a deliberate process through which we seek to understand and retain aural (heard) stimuli' (Gamble and Gamble, 2008: 182). In this sense it is 'the process of receiving and interpreting aural stimuli' (Pearson and Nelson, 2000: 99). More specifically, listening is viewed as 'the complex, learned human process of sensing, interpreting, evaluating, storing and responding to oral messages' (Steil, 1991: 203).

In terms of interpersonal interaction, the focus of study for those who hold this perspective has been upon 'the process by which spoken language is converted to meaning in the mind' (Lundsteen, 1971: 1). As Bostrom (2006) demonstrated in his systematic overview of the field, this approach emanated from the cognitive tradition and was significantly influenced by the supposition that reading and listening are different aspects of what are regarded as the same process – that of acquiring and retaining information. In this paradigm, listening is perceived as being parallel to, and the social equivalent of, reading. When we read we attempt to understand and assimilate the written word; when we listen we attempt to understand and assimilate the spoken word. Both are seen as cognitive linguistic abilities.

This cognitive, or information processing, perspective made an important distinction between hearing and listening, in that hearing was regarded as a physical activity and listening as a mental process. In this sense, we may use our visual pathways to see but we read with our brains (and indeed blind people read using tactile pathways and Braille), and we activate our neurosensory pathways to hear but we listen with our brains. As shown by Boudreau *et al.* (2009), the cortex is not simply a passive receiver of sensory input – it actively modulates it. We do not need to learn to see but we need to learn to read. Similarly, we do not have to learn how to hear, but we have to learn how to listen. As Roach and Wyatt (1999: 197) pointed out: 'Far from being a natural process, listening is clearly a consciously purposive activity for which we need systematic training and supervision to learn to do well.' An important distinction between hearing and listening is that 'whereas the former refers to a physiological receptivity at an individual level . . . the latter refers to an intersubjective orientation at a discursive, thus social level' (Jacobs and Coghlan, 2005: 120).

Aural definitions of listening ignore the important nonverbal cues emitted by the speaker. Yet such cues help to determine the actual meaning of the message being conveyed (see Chapter 3). For this reason, researchers in interpersonal communication have focused upon a communication competency model, underscoring the importance of *all* interactive behaviour in listening, encompassing both verbal and nonverbal responses (Bodie *et al.*, 2008). Thus, Bostrom (2006: 279) asserted that 'the best definition of listening is the *acquisition, processing, and retention of information in the interpersonal context'*. It is 'the process of becoming aware of all the cues that another person emits' (Van Slyke, 1999: 98). As such, it necessitates 'capturing and understanding the messages that clients communicate, either verbally or nonverbally, clearly or vaguely' (Hill, 2004: 100). This is similar to the definition recommended by the International Listening Association (2009): 'the process of receiving, constructing meaning from, and responding to spoken and/or nonverbal messages'. This is the perspective that is followed in this chapter, where listening is regarded as the process whereby one person pays careful overt and covert attention to, and attempts to assimilate, understand and retain, the verbal and nonverbal signals being emitted by another.

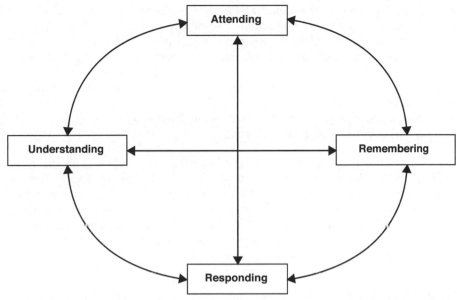

Figure 7.1 Main processes involved in listening

Scholars in this field also distinguish between two other usages of the term. The first sense emphasises the visible nature of the process, and is referred to as *active listening* (Weger *et al.*, 2010). This occurs when an individual displays behaviours that signal overt attention to another. The second usage emphasises the cognitive process of assimilating information. This does not imply anything about the overt behaviour of the individual, but rather is concerned with the covert aspects. An individual may be listening covertly without displaying outward signs of so doing, and so is engaged in *passive listening*. In terms of interpersonal skill, it is the former meaning of the term that is utilised, and it is therefore important to identify those verbal and nonverbal aspects of behaviour that convey the impression of active listening. Adler and Rodman (2006) identified the key subprocesses involved in listening as attending to the message, attempting to understand it, responding appropriately and remembering the key components. While listening is often portrayed as a linear activity, these subprocesses are in fact all interrelated (Figure 7.1). Thus, for example, we are less likely to attend to, respond appropriately to or remember messages we cannot understand.

PURPOSES OF LISTENING

The skill of listening serves a number of purposes in social interaction, as summarised in Box 7.2. The specific goals vary depending upon the context. For example, in the sphere of management, Alvesson and Sveningsson (2003) found that managers perceived listening as serving a range of purposes including, inter alia, as a way of:

- gathering, structuring and understanding information
- demonstrating interest in and respect for employees
- affirming the value of the individual and their right to 'be heard'
- making people feel included and respected, thereby increasing a sense of 'belonging'
- enabling the manager to ascertain and overcome negative employee experiences
- providing reassurance and reducing anxiety
- finding the appropriate emotional tone for an interaction
- facilitating the decision-making process.

One recurring problem is that we often listen with the goal of responding, rather than listening with the goal of understanding (Van Slyke, 1999). In other words, our main concern is with our own point of view rather than with gaining a deeper insight into the other person's perspective. As shown in Box 7.2, our objectives when listening should include conveying attention and interest, gaining a full, accurate insight into the perspectives held by others and encouraging an open interchange of views leading to agreed understanding and acceptance of goals.

ASSIMILATING INFORMATION

The processes of feedback, perception and cognition are all of importance in the assimilation of information during listening. In interpersonal interaction a constant stream of feedback impinges upon us, both from the stimuli received from other people and from the physical environment. Not all of this feedback is consciously perceived, since there is simply too much information for the person to cope with adequately. As a result, a *selective perception filter* (see Figure 7.2) is operative, and its main function is to filter only a limited amount of information into the conscious, while some of the remainder may be stored at a subconscious level. Evidence that such subconscious storage does occur can be found from studies into *subliminal perception*, which refers to the perception of stimuli below the threshold

---

Box 7.2 Purposes of listening

The main goals served by the skill of listening are:

1 to focus specifically upon the messages being communicated by the other person
2 to gain a full, accurate insight into the other person's communication
3 to critically evaluate what others are saying
4 to monitor the nonverbal signals accompanying the other person's verbal messages
5 to convey interest, concern and attention
6 to encourage full, open and honest expression
7 to develop an 'other-centred' approach during interaction
8 to reach a shared and agreed understanding and acceptance with others about both sides' goals and priorities.

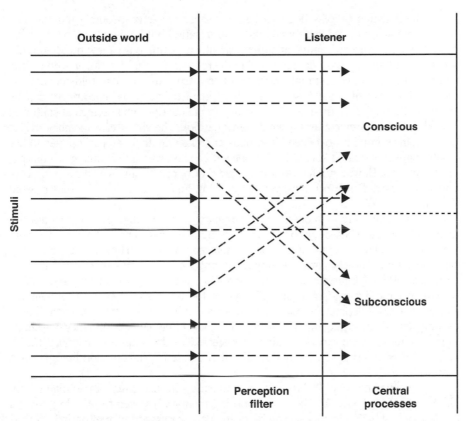

Figure 7.2 Selective perception process

of awareness (Karremans *et al.*, 2006). For example, information flashed onto a screen for a split second, so fast that it cannot be read consciously, can influence our behaviour.

Figure 7.2 illustrates how, from the large number of stimuli in the environment, a certain amount is presented as feedback. These are represented by the arrows on the extreme left of the figure. Some stimuli are not perceived at all, or are filtered into the subconscious at a very early stage. Within the physical environment, the ticking of clocks, the hum of central-heating systems, the pressure of one's body on the chair, etc. are usually filtered into the subconscious during social encounters, if these are interesting. If, however, one is bored during an encounter (e.g. sitting through a dull lecture) then these items may be consciously perceived, and the social 'noises' from the lecturer given less attention. Unfortunately, in interpersonal interaction, vital information can be filtered out, in that we may be insensitive to the social signals emitted by others. Where this occurs, effective listening skills are not displayed. In order to listen successfully we must be sensitive to verbal and nonverbal cues, and select the most relevant of these to focus upon. By observing closely the actions and reactions of others, it is possible to improve one's ability to demonstrate concerted and accurate listening.

The listening process begins when our senses register incoming stimuli. The sensory register receives large amounts of information but holds it for a brief period of time. Visual sensory storage is highly transitory, lasting only a few hundred milliseconds. Auditory sensory data are held in the register for slightly longer – up to four seconds. To be retained, stimuli must be filtered from the sensory register into the individual's level of consciousness and held in memory. Social encounters can be coded and stored in both semantic memory (remembering what someone said) and episodic memory (remembering what someone did). The short-term memory (STM) store retains stimuli for between 20 seconds and one minute. In an early paper, Miller (1956) suggested that STM could only cope with some seven units, plus or minus two, of information. However, later work indicated that remembering is a complex process and that it is difficult to quantify precisely how many 'units' can be remembered (Cowan *et al.*, 2007).

In remembering, a process of 'chunking' occurs, in that groups of data are arranged together based on previous learning patterns. Thus, the set of letters UNOPECNATO may at first sight look like ten separate units. However, it can readily be chunked into three separate acronyms by anyone who knows them – UN (United Nations), OPEC (Organization of the Petroleum Exporting Countries) and NATO (North Atlantic Treaty Organization), making the letter string easier to remember. Likewise, a new telephone number is retained for only a short period as each digit is assimilated as a separate unit; if this number is used frequently, it becomes one single unit (or chunk) of information and is transferred to the long-term memory (LTM) store. LTM is a permanent storage facility that can retain information literally for a lifetime.

Working memory (WM) is also important in listening. As explained by Gathercole *et al.* (2004: 2): 'The term "working memory" is used to refer to a mental workplace in which information can be stored and processed for brief periods of time in the course of demanding cognitive activities.' WM posits a duality system whereby both storage/memory and attentional/computational functions combine in the creation of meaning. These two functional components respectively enable the individual to retain information and manipulate this during complex cognitive tasks (Conway *et al.*, 2007). As expressed by Baddeley *et al.* (2009: 9), those with greater WM capacities have a higher ability to 'keep things in mind' during information processing. This means that they are better able to manage and deal with incoming verbal and visual information (Gathercole, 2008), which in turn facilitates listening (McInnes *et al.*, 2003; Janusik, 2007). In this way, people with high WM capacity have the ability to remember relevant details during interpersonal encounters and to bring these into play at apposite moments during interaction.

Bostrom (2006) reviewed a range of research studies that found a link between capacity for short-term listening (STL) and success in various contexts. Good short-term listeners asked more questions in interviews, performed better in oral presentations, were rated as being better managers and had a higher rate of upward mobility within their organisation. However, while the importance of STM for the listening process has been illustrated, the exact nature of any causal relationship between STM, listening ability and overt listening behaviour is unclear (Ohata, 2005; Bostrom, 2006). Thomas and Levine (1996) found a positive and significant correlation between recall ability and use of head nods, gaze duration and short backchannel behaviours ('uh hu', 'mmm', etc.), but concluded that 'there is more to listening than simply recall. The reverse is also true. There is obviously more to recall than listening' (p. 121). Likewise, Bostrom (2006: 274) concluded that although 'research indicates that STL is closely implicated in interpersonal activities . . . just how these abilities relate to one another is not known'. It should be noted that no link exists between long-term memory and listening ability. In other words, there is no relationship between having a good memory for distant events and being an effective listener. Fans of *The Simpsons* television cartoon series will be aware of the Grandpa Simpson character, who frequently regales the family with detailed memories of days of yore while blissfully ignoring what others are saying to him in the here and now.

TYPES OF LISTENING

There are six different types of listening: discriminative, comprehension, evaluative, appreciative, empathic and dialogic.

Discriminative listening

This is the most basic form of listening, where the goal is simply to scan and monitor auditory and/or visual stimuli (Wolvin, 2009). Examples include scrutinising an interactive partner's facial expressions to ascertain their reactions to what we have just said, or listening to hear if the baby is crying upstairs. In each case the objective is to focus upon or *discriminate* incoming stimuli for feedback purposes. For some professionals, of course, discriminative listening is vital. This is especially the case with health professionals in a hospital context who have to monitor the well-being of patients on a regular basis, and make crucial discriminative decisions based upon the stimuli received.

Comprehension listening

The emphasis here is upon listening for central facts, main ideas and critical themes so as to fully *comprehend* the messages being received. This occurs when we listen to informative or instructive messages in order to increase our understanding, enhance our experience and acquire data that will be of future use to us. We may practise this type of listening at the 'getting-to-know-you' stage of relationships, while attending lectures, conducting fact-finding interviews or watching radio or television documentaries. This form of listening has also been termed *content listening* (Kramer, 2001) and *informational listening* (Orbe and Bruess, 2005).

Evaluative listening

This takes place when a speaker is trying to persuade us, by attempting to influence our attitudes, beliefs or actions. We listen evaluatively to enable us to make appropriate judgements concerning such persuasive messages. As part of this, we listen for the spin or slant that the speaker puts on the message (Egan, 2007). We may practise this type of listening when dealing with salespeople, negotiating at meetings, listening to party political speeches, watching television adverts or even when deciding with friends which pub to go to for the evening. In all of these instances we have to listen to the available evidence and the supporting arguments, weigh these up and *evaluate* them before making a decision. The emphasis here is therefore upon listening for the central propositions being made, and being able to determine the strengths and weaknesses of each. Bostrom (2006) termed this form of listening *interpretive listening*. It has also been referred to as *critical listening* in that it 'challenges the speaker's message by evaluating its accuracy, meaningfulness, and utility' (Pearson *et al.*, 2006: 111).

Appreciative listening

This occurs when we seek out certain signals or messages in order to gain pleasure from, or *appreciate*, their reception (Brownell, 2005). We may listen appreciatively to relax and unwind, to enjoy ourselves, to gain inner peace, to increase emotional or cultural understanding, or to obtain spiritual satisfaction. This type of listening occurs when we play music which appeals to us, when we decide to attend a church service, when sitting in a park or walking in the country while assimilating the sounds of nature, and when we attend a public meeting in order to hear a charismatic speaker.

Empathic listening

Empathic listening takes place when we listen to someone who has a need to talk and be understood by another. Here the listener demonstrates a willingness to attend to and attempt to understand the thoughts, beliefs and feelings of the speaker. One in-depth study of listening dyads found that what speakers most wanted was for the listener to understand what they were saying, and to care about and empathise with them – their recommendation was to 'listen with your heart' (Halone and Pecchioni, 2001: 64). As Stewart and Cash (2008: 36) put it: 'Empathic listening is total and genuine response: reassuring, comforting, expressing warmth, and showing unconditional regard.' While the first four types of listening are intrinsic in that they are for the benefit of the listener, empathic listening is extrinsic in that the listener is seeking to help the speaker. This type of listening is common between close friends and spouses. It is at the core of formal helping situations, and hence has also been referred to as *therapeutic listening* (Wolvin, 2009) and *reflective listening* (Rautalinko and Lisper, 2004). Walker (1997) identified three elements of effective empathic listening:

1 ***Active emotional commitment.*** The listener has to set aside personal worries, thoughts or prejudices and be ready to fully engage with the thoughts ideas and feelings of the other person.
2 ***Acceptance of role-taking as a necessity.*** The listener has to attempt to understand as fully as possible the role of the speaker and see the world from this perspective.

3   *Identification with the other.* At this stage the listener can closely identify with the thoughts and feelings of the other person.

Dialogic listening

The term 'dialogue' comes from the Greek words *dia* ('through') and *logos* ('meaning', or 'understanding'). In dialogic listening, meaning emerges and is shaped from conversational interchange (Shotter, 2009). As summarised by Jacobs and Coghlan (2005: 115), this type of listening 'involves the constitution of a relational basis that allows for intersubjective meaning generation'. Here, listening is two-way and of benefit to both sides, as we share views with one another in an attempt to reach a mutually agreed position. For this reason it is also known as *relational listening* (Halone and Pecchioni, 2001). All of us carry large amounts of cultural, national, racial, etc. baggage with us when we enter into discussions. We also bring our own ethnocentric slant, which means that we tend to perceive and judge other viewpoints from the perspective of our own. In dialogic listening we need to adopt a more cosmopolitan attitude that does not assume that the values and beliefs of any particular group are the only possible alternative. Rather, we must suspend judgement and be open and receptive to the views of others. As Stewart *et al.* (2005: 176) expressed it: 'The first step towards dialogic listening is to recognize that each communication event is a ride on a tandem bicycle, and you may or may not be in the front seat.' This type of listening is central to negotiations, where to reach effective outcomes the needs and goals of both sides must be jointly explored (see Chapter 13).

Rehling (2008) argued that what she termed *compassionate listening* is a subset of dialogic listening for those who communicate in depth with the very seriously ill. As she describes it:

> Grounding our listening in compassion suggests listening to someone who is seriously ill with an openness and acceptance of human suffering, a hope to better understand that suffering and a desire to act to relieve the isolation and loneliness so often reported during serious illness.
>
> (Rehling, 2008: 87)

Compassionate listening involves developing a sense of 'we-ness' during dialogue, in which shared humanity is emphasised and there is recognition of the common struggles that characterise life (such as serious illness and death). The listener shares her or his own sense of vulnerability and mortality. Through discussion, a new sense of joint understanding is achieved. However, as emphasised by Rehling (2008), compassionate listening can only take place when both parties are ready to participate. For example, some seriously ill people may not want to engage at this level of depth of sharing.

While appreciative listening is not so applicable in the social context, knowledge of discriminative, comprehension, evaluative, empathic and dialogic listening skills is of key import. Bearing these types in mind, a useful acronym for effective interpersonal listening is **PACIER**:

Perceive the other person's verbal and nonverbal communication.
Attend carefully to gain maximum information.
Comprehend and assimilate the verbal message.
Interpret the meaning of the accompanying nonverbals.
Evaluate what is being said and, where appropriate, empathise.
Respond appropriately.

THE LISTENING PROCESS

At first sight listening may be regarded as a simple process (Figure 7.3) in which both sides take turns to respond and listen, but in fact this perspective needs to be extended to take full account of all of the processes involved (Figure 7.4). As we talk, at the same time we also scan for feedback to see how our messages are being received. When we listen, we evaluate what is being said, plan our response, rehearse this and then execute it. While the processes of evaluation, planning and rehearsal usually occur subconsciously, they are important because they can interfere with the pure listening activity. Thus, we may have decided what we are going to say before the other person has stopped speaking, and as a result may not be listening effectively. It is therefore important to ensure that those activities that mediate between listening and speaking do not interfere with the listening process itself. In terms of the verbal message being received, listening is influenced by three main factors: reductionism, rationalisation and change in the order of events

Reductionism

The human memory is notoriously fallible. On average, we have forgotten about half of what we hear immediately after hearing it, and within 8 hours we remember only

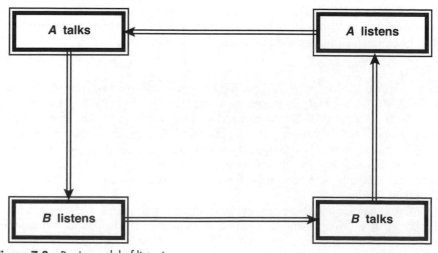

Figure 7.3 Basic model of listening

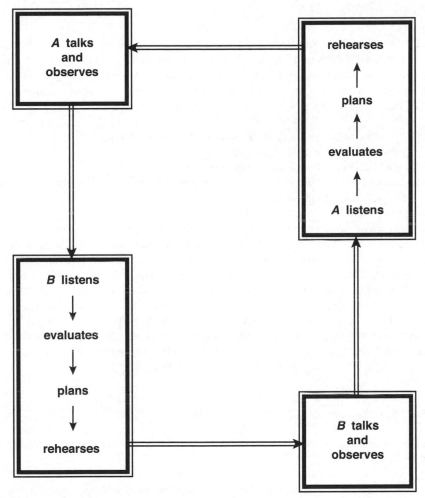

Figure 7.4 Extended model of listening

35 per cent of the message (Adler *et al.*, 2006). After 24 hours we have forgotten up to 80 per cent of the information received (Wilson, 2004). Since we can only assimilate a limited amount of data, the messages we receive have to be reduced, sometimes at the expense of vital information. For this reason it is important to attempt to ensure that the central information being conveyed is remembered. The following techniques can help to facilitate retention.

Recording

Obviously, where it is possible to video- or audio-record the interaction, this provides verbatim recall. However, this is not always feasible.

Note-taking

Retention can be facilitated by noting the main points emanating from the interaction. As Bostrom (1990: 29) pointed out: 'Notetaking may enhance memory by enabling the receiver to transform the message so that it corresponds more closely with his or her own cognitive structure.' Such transformation involves several subprocesses, including:

- increased mental activity involved in writing and listening
- selection and reduction of material
- repetition of the core features being presented
- adaptation or translation of the message into more personally meaningful and accessible terminology.

These processes involved in note-taking should enable the message to be more readily assimilated. Watson and Barker (1984) reported that note-taking interchanged rather than concurrent with listening was more effective in terms of remembering what has been said. It is also socially more appropriate if note-taking does not dominate the interaction, but is rather something that occurs sporadically and is explained to the speaker ('Can I just note down some details before I forget them?'). Care needs to be taken, however, since it has been shown that note-taking by doctors is regarded by patients as problematic. In particular, when the doctor consults medical records or makes notes therein, patients have been shown to become unsure about whether the doctor is actually listening or not (Ruusuvuori, 2001).

Memory devices

A range of techniques serve as aids to memory. Dickson *et al.* (1997) highlighted three main mnemonics:

1 **Acronyms.** For example, PAIL to remember the four types of skin cuts – Puncture, Abrasion, Incision, Laceration.
2 **Rhymes.** To remember names, such as 'Big Bobby Blair, very fat, red hair'.
3 **Visualisation.** The listener creates a mental picture of what the speaker is saying – for example, trying to visualise a client's home environment and relationships as they are being described.

In a review of this area, Gellatly (1986) illustrated how mnemonics were a key part of early Greek and Roman education, and pointed out that mnemonics work by imposing organisation or order on the information to be remembered. While there is some research evidence to vindicate the use of these memory aids (Gregg, 1986), it would appear that their success is dependent both upon the ability of the listener to use them and upon the nature of the message being communicated.

Organising material

Material should be organised into main themes, ideas and categories, and into a chronological sequence where possible. Such organisation must not, of course, interfere with the act of listening, but where time is available during interaction (as is usually the case), then this type of 'conceptual filing' can facilitate later recall.

Rationalisation

As we listen, we assimilate information in such a way as to make it fit with our own situation and experience. If it does not fit immediately we may rationalise what we hear in order to make it more acceptable, but by so doing distort the facts. This occurs in three main ways:

1   We attribute different causes to those presented. Thus, a patient may attribute a troublesome cough to the weather or argue that it 'runs in the family', rather than accept a practioner's explanation that it is due to heavy smoking.
2   Transformation of language is a common form of rationalisation. This is often due to what Gregg (1986) termed *acoustic confusions*, caused by close similarity in the sounds of certain words. In the medical field, products with similar sounding names can be mixed up by doctors, nurses and pharmacists, with potentially tragic consequences (for example, in one case a Belgian patient died after being given the diuretic Lasix® instead of the anti-ulcer drug Losec®).
3   Paradoxically given the aforementioned reductionism, there may be the *addition of material*. A classical instance of this occurs in everyday gossip, whereby a basic story is enlarged and embroidered upon during each retelling, until eventually it becomes a sensational story. Care needs to be taken in professional situations to avoid 'reading too much into' what the client has said.

Change in the order of events

This is a common occurrence in the assimilation of information, whereby data becomes jumbled and remembered in the wrong order. Thus, 'Take two tablets three times daily after meals' is remembered as 'Take three tablets twice daily before meals'; or 'He lost his job and then started to drink heavily' becomes 'He started to drink heavily and then lost his job as a result'. Such mistakes can be avoided by the careful conceptual organisation of material being received.

FACETS OF LISTENING

There are four main facets that need to be taken into consideration. These are the characteristics associated with the listener, the speaker, the message and the environment. From the available evidence, the following conclusions can be adduced (for fuller reviews, see Borisoff and Purdy, 1991b; Burley-Allen, 1995; Wolvin and Coakley, 1996; Bostrom, 2006).

The listener

Galanes *et al.* (2006) distinguished between four main types of listener (see Box 7.3). In addition, several positive correlations have been found between characteristics of the listener and ability to listen effectively.

Linguistic aptitude

Those with a wider vocabulary are better listeners, since they can more readily understand and assimilate a greater range of concepts. Academic achievement has also been shown to be associated with listening ability (although as might be expected, academic achievement is also usually highly correlated with linguistic aptitude).

Motivation

A listener who is highly motivated will remember more of the information presented. Such motivation can be caused by a variety of factors, ranging from a school pupil's fear of negative feedback from a demanding teacher, to the desire of a caring professional to help a particular client.

Box 7.3 Four types of listener

1 **People-oriented listeners.** Their primary concern is for others' feelings and needs. Can be distracted away from the task owing to this focus on psycho-emotional perspectives. We seek them out when we need a listening ear. Are good helpers.

2 **Task-oriented listeners.** Are mainly concerned with getting the business done. Do not like discussing what they see as irrelevant information or having to listen to 'long-winded' people or 'whingers'. Can be insensitive to the emotional needs of others.

3 **Content-oriented listeners.** These are analytical people who enjoy dissecting information and carefully scrutinising it. They often focus on the literal meaning of what has been said. They want to hear all sides and leave no stone unturned, however long the process. Can be slow to make decisions as they are never quite sure if they have garnered all the necessary information. Are good mediators.

4 **Time-oriented listeners.** Their main focus is upon getting tasks completed within set timeframes. They see time as a valuable commodity, not to be wasted. Are impatient with what they see as 'prevaricators' and can be prone to jump to conclusions before they have heard all of the information.

Organisational ability

As mentioned earlier, the ability to organise incoming information into appropriate categories facilitates learning. Good listeners identify the key elements of the messages received and store these in appropriate conceptual compartments.

Use of special concentration techniques

There are several such techniques employed by effective listeners. One of these is to attempt to put oneself in the speaker's position and try to see the world from this perspective. The memory aids mentioned previously are also useful here. A final approach is the use of intrapersonal dialogue, wherein the listener engages in covert self talk to heighten receptivity. Egan (2007: 93) referred to this as 'listening to oneself', or having an 'internal conversation'. This may involve the use of:

- covert coaching (e.g. 'I'm not paying enough attention. I need to listen more carefully.')
- self-reinforcement (e.g. 'I'm listening well and understanding what he is saying.')
- asking covert questions (e.g. 'Why is she telling me this now?').

There is some evidence that when listening to lectures, the latter technique of self-questioning may be most effective. King (1992) carried out a study in which she found that undergraduates trained to use self-questions (asking themselves questions during the lecture such as 'What is the main idea of . . .?' 'How is this related to what we studied earlier?') remembered more about the lecture content one week later than either those taught to summarise the lecture in writing or those who simply took notes.

Age

In his review of communication problems when dealing with older individuals, Giordano (2000) noted that a reduced capacity for information processing has been widely reported in this age group. However, he also highlighted how there are wide differences between older people so that some will be more adversely affected than others. Furthermore, age also brings positive changes, such as an increased vocabulary and a wealth of experience of dealing with people in various situations. Thus, listening faculties may be reduced or enhanced, depending upon the individual.

The reaction to noise by age is, however, relatively consistent. Most young people enjoy noisy, rapidly changing, environments with lots of stimulation and become bored if this is not available. With age, however, our need for such levels of arousal decreases. Older adults in general prefer quiet, peaceful and tranquil surroundings and find noise offputting. This is because they find it more difficult to cope with the cognitive interference caused by the intrusive stimuli. They are less able to manage divided attention, and so tend to be much more susceptible to distraction from the effects of extraneous noise. So, when dealing with this age group the importance of securing a quiet location should be borne in mind. Likewise, reaction time and speech discrimination decrease with age, so that older people tend to need more time to process information and respond. This means that a slower rate of speech may be desirable. Giordano (2000) also recommended the use of periods of silence to allow the older person time for reflection. However, as discussed in Chapter 2, when communicating with this age group, the dangers of *ageism* must be avoided.

Gender

There is now a substantial body of research to substantiate the view that females are more perceptive at recognising and interpreting nonverbal messages. Borisoff and Merrill (1991: 65), after reviewing the available evidence, concluded: 'Numerous studies have established women's superior abilities as both decoders and encoders of nonverbal messages when compared with men.' They suggested that part of the reason for these differences may be attributable to a status factor, in that lower-status people spend more time listening to higher-status people than vice versa and males may therefore conceptualise the listening role as being of lower status. However, this view is not in line with research findings by Johnson and Bechler (1998). They conducted a study at a Midwestern US university where undergraduate students met in leaderless groups and were rated on leadership skills and listening skills by separate teams of raters. Results showed that those rated high in listening behaviours by one set of coders were also rated high in leadership by a different set of coders. Interestingly, no differences were found in recall ability among subjects, and so it was the display of listening behaviour that was important. Johnson and Bechler concluded that their results confirm the general finding that leaders demonstrate more effective listening skills than other group members.

What may be the case is that each gender tends to tune in to different aspects of a message, and indeed Adler and Elmhorst (2008: 111) argued that often 'a man pays attention to the content of a message while a woman focuses on the relational dimension of the words'. Another difference is that males may be more likely to use head nods as a sign of *agreement*, whereas females often use them as indicators of *attention* but not necessarily agreement with the speaker (Stewart and Logan, 1998). This can lead to gender confusion if a male takes nods as agreement and then becomes annoyed when the female proceeds to express disagreement. A similar problem occurs in cross-cultural communication in that people from some cultures – e.g. Asian – may use nods as signs of listening but not necessarily concurring. However, much more research is required in order to chart the precise nature and extent of gender influence on listening ability.

Physical condition

Listening ability deteriorates as fatigue increases. Thus, someone who is extremely tired is less capable of displaying prolonged listening. Professionals with a heavy caseload need to attempt to ensure that they do not have to handle their most demanding case at the end of a tiring day.

Disposition

Introverts are usually better listeners than extraverts, since they are content to sit back and let the other person be the centre of attention. Furthermore, highly anxious individuals do not usually make good listeners since they tend to be too worried about factors apart from the speaker to listen carefully to what is being said. As noted by Beck (1999: 63): 'Anxiety makes the mind wander from the current communication situation.' Individuals who are high sensation-seekers also perform poorly if they are required to listen for long periods. Likewise, those who are more susceptible to distractions are not good listeners, an extreme example being the hyperactive child. Finally, what Adler *et al.* (2006) referred to as 'stage hogs' or 'conversational narcissists' are bad listeners. These are dominating, self-centred, egotistical individuals who only want to talk and have no real interest in what others have to say.

The speaker

A number of aspects pertaining to the speaker are of importance.

Speech rate

While the average rate of speech is between 125 and 175 words per minute, the average 'thought rate' at which information is cognitively processed is between 400 and 800 words per minute. The differential between speech and thought rate gives the listener an opportunity to assimilate, organise, retain and covertly respond to the speaker. However, this differential may also encourage the listener to fill up the spare time with other unrelated mental processes (such as daydreaming). Listening can be improved by using this spare thought time positively by, for example, asking covert questions such as:

* 'What are the main points being made?'
* 'What reasons are being given?'
* 'In what frame of reference should this be viewed?'
* 'What further information is necessary?'

Where a speaker exceeds 300 words per minute, listening can be problematic. It is difficult to listen effectively for an extended period to a very rapid speaker, since we cannot handle the volume of information being received. Wolff *et al.* (1983: 155), in reviewing the literature on speech rate, however, concluded that listeners:

> prefer to listen, can comprehend better, and are more likely to believe a message that is presented at the rate of 190 words or more per minute ... They demonstrate marked efficiency when listening to a speaker talking at 280 words per minute – twice the rate of normal speech.

Interestingly, as a result of such findings, television advertisers speeded up the rate of verbal presentation in their adverts, with positive results in terms of viewer comprehension and recall. However, here listeners are only exposed to short blasts of material, accompanied by other visual and audio stimulation. In social contexts, a word of caution was noted by Janse (2004) who, following experimental studies in this field, concluded that speakers should only increase their speech rate if they are sure that listeners are able and willing to exert considerable effort to listening. The current findings also suggest that we have problems paying attention for lengthy periods to people who talk at, or below, the normal rate of speech. Professionals who have to deal with depressed clients will be aware of the problems involved in maintaining concentration with someone who says very little. Thus, when long pauses and a slow speech rate are used by a client, concentrated listening is required from the professional.

However, the topic of conversation and its degree of difficulty need to be factored in to the equation. A slow speed may be appropriate with a complex issue whereas with more basic material a faster pace is usually the norm. This was confirmed in a study by Robinson *et al.* (1997), where undergraduates were presented with taped lectures delivered at slow, moderate or fast rates. The results indicated that students receiving the slower speed comprehended the lectures better and rated the material as more important than those receiving the faster delivery. As a result of their findings, Robinson *et al.* recommended that for lectures a speech rate of around 100 words per minute is most appropriate. One reason for this was identified by Dabbs (1985: 191), who observed: 'Long pauses are accepted by the participants in intellectual conversation as a normal result of trying to "figure things out", while long pauses in social conversation indicate things are not going well and will tend to be avoided.'

Speech delivery

The clarity, fluency and audibility of the speaker all have an influence on listener comprehension. Thus, it requires effort to listen to and comprehend someone who speaks English with a pronounced foreign accent, or who has a strong, unfamiliar, regional dialect. It is also difficult to listen to someone with a severe speech dysfluency, both because the message being delivered is disjointed and because the listener is preoccupied thinking about how to respond to the dysfluency. Finally, it is not easy to pay attention to an individual who speaks in a dull monotone (as most students will testify), or who mumbles and does not have good voice projection.

Emotionality

If the speaker displays high levels of emotion, the listener may be distracted by this and cease to listen accurately to the content of the verbal message. In situations where individuals are in extreme emotional states, their communication is inevitably highly charged. It is often necessary to sustain an interaction in these circumstances. Sustaining can be defined as the process whereby someone experiencing an extreme emotional state is encouraged to ventilate, talk about and understand their emotions. When faced with a person experiencing extreme emotions (e.g. of depression or aggression), it is often not advisable either to reinforce positively or to rebuke the individual for this behaviour, since such reactions may well be counterproductive. For example, by rebuking an individual who is displaying aggressive behaviour, it is likely that this will only serve to heighten the aggression. A more reasoned response is to react in a calm fashion, demonstrating an interest in, without overtly reinforcing, the emotional person, but also showing a willingness to listen and attempt to understand what exactly has caused this to occur.

Only when strong emotional feelings begin to decrease can a more rational discussion take place. Someone who is 'too emotional' about something is likely to be 'too worked up about it' to listen to reasoned arguments. When dealing with an individual who is displaying high levels of emotion, it may be necessary to be prepared to wait for a considerable period of time before this is ventilated. During this period the anxiety of the listener may interfere with the ability to listen carefully. Too much attention may be paid to the emotional message being conveyed, and as a result important information of a more factual nature may not be assimilated. Conversely, full concentration may be upon the factual content, with the emotional message being ignored. In both of these cases, message distortion occurs, in that the listener is not perceiving the total communication.

Status

If the speaker is regarded as an important person, or a recognised authority on a topic, listening comprehension is increased as more credence will be attached to what is being said. Also, more attention tends to be paid if the speaker is in a position of superiority. Attention is therefore greater if the listener has admiration and respect for a speaker of high credibility. In a study of interruptions in British and Italian management meetings, Bargiela-Chiappini and Harris (1996) found that those of lower status rarely interrupt. This was confirmed more recently in an experimental study by Farley (2008) who found that those who interrupted were perceived to be of higher status than those who had been interrupted. Furthermore, those who had been interrupted rated themselves as less influential than those who had not been interrupted. On the downside, the interrupters were rated as less likeable. This topic of interruptions will be returned to later in the discussion of active listening.

The message

The following aspects of the message itself need to be borne in mind: structure, significance and complexity.

Structure

A message that is unclear and lacking in any coherent structure is more difficult to listen to and comprehend (see Chapter 8 for a discussion of effective explanation). The speaker may be emphasising the trivial, being deliberately vague and evasive or speaking for a long time without a break. It is sometimes the goal of the speaker to confuse, distract or mislead the listener by distorting the message being conveyed (many politicians are quite adept in this field), or the speaker may simply be incapable of clarity of expression. In both of these cases, it is often necessary to interrupt, by asking questions in an attempt to understand what is being said.

Significance

The importance that we attach to an issue has been shown to affect the way in which we attend to it (Lecheler *et al.*, 2009). If the message is of particular interest, or of special significance, comprehension and recall are heightened. In an experimental study in this area, Schneider and Laurion (1993) investigated how well undergraduates listened to and recalled items on radio news. They found greatest recall for 'high-interest' items of particular relevance (e.g. student-related issues, stories about their university). In addition, when the message conveys similar values, attitudes or viewpoints to our own, listening is facilitated, since most of us like to have our beliefs and expectations confirmed. Paradoxically, however, it has also been found that if a message contains a significant disconfirmation of our expectations, listening can also be heightened, as we are then motivated to evaluate this unexpected message. Thus, Frick (1992), in an investigation of the concept of 'interestingness', discovered that people find most interesting those statements that change, or challenge confidence in, their existing beliefs. Results also suggested that statements that advance our understanding are attended to with particular interest. An example given by Frick was that 'a clinician would find most interesting those statements by a client that further the clinician's understanding of the client' (p. 126). In similar vein, a social worker who suspects a parent of child abuse is likely to pay concerted attention to both the parent and the child when they are discussing parent–child relationships. At the same time, it is also important to pay attention to those areas that a client does not initiate. Indeed, listening theorists often emphasise the importance of listening to what is *not* being said by the speaker. Thus, a child who steadfastly avoids or blocks any discussion about a parent may well be sending out an important message.

Complexity

The difficulty of the material being delivered also affects listening. As discussed in relation to speech rate, most people can cope more effectively with basic material delivered at a fast rate, but with complex information a slower speed of speech is required, to allow time for assimilation.

The environment

Three elements of the environment in which the interaction is taking place need to be considered: ventilation and temperature, noise and seating.

Ventilation and temperature

Kennedy *et al.* (2006) developed an instrument to measure perception of listening ease. They found that listening was perceived to be more difficult if the environment was either unpleasantly warm or cold. Optimum listening occurs when the room temperature is at a comfortable level.

Noise

In a study of the impact of music on performance, Ransdell and Gilroy (2001) investigated the effects of music upon students' ability to write essays on computer. They found that music disrupted writing fluency. However, in this study the (perhaps unusual) choice of music (slow ballads taken from a Nelson Riddle Orchestra tape) was not self-selected by the students. By contrast, Bowman *et al.* (2007) found that listening to slow (but not fast) Mozart music, as compared to listening to rock music, improved students' listening comprehension on a video-taped lecture they viewed. Again, however, the selection of rock music was not self-selected by subjects and was rather esoteric (Chuck Berry, Elton John, Billy Joel). Having discussed this issue with my own students and colleagues, it is clear that some people like to work to music (but music they like) while others do not. In terms of interpersonal encounters, comprehension deteriorates when there is loud, intrusive noise that interferes with the assimilation process (such as building work going on outside). However, it remains unclear whether nonintrusive or self-selected background noise has an adverse effect on listening or indeed facilitates it. For example, most pubs, restaurants and hotel lounges play background music to encourage conversation. The level of noise is important, since background noise may be filtered out whereas intrusive sounds cannot (see Figure 7.2). However, the nature of the interaction is also relevant, so that a lecturer would not encourage even background noise if total concentration from students was desired. Dentists, on the other hand, often play background music to encourage patients to relax while in surgery.

Seating

Perhaps not surprisingly, one empirical study of 123 interactive dyads found that being seated was regarded as a facilitator to effective listening (Halone and Pecchioni, 2001). If someone is expected to listen for a prolonged period, as in lecture theatres or classrooms, comfortable seating has been shown to be an important factor for listening effectiveness (Kennedy *et al.*, 2006). Yet most schools provide less than comfortable chairs for pupils and expect sustained, concerted attention from them throughout the school day. In group contexts, a compact seating arrangement is more effective than a scattered one. People pay more attention and recall more when they are brought close together physically, as opposed to when they are spread out around the room.

OBSTACLES TO EFFECTIVE LISTENING

The following factors have been identified as obstacles to listening (see Figure 7.5 for a summary of obstacles at the main stages of listening).

Dichotomous listening

This occurs when we attempt to assimilate information simultaneously from two different sources. Examples include trying to listen to two people in a group who are speaking at the same time, conducting a telephone conversation while carrying on a face-to-face interaction with another person, or when distracted by some form of extraneous noise. In all of these instances the dichotomous nature of the listening interferes with the ability of the listener to interact effectively, since messages may be either received inaccurately or not received at all. Effective listening is facilitated by paying attention to only one person at a time, and by manipulating the environment in order to ensure that extraneous distractions are minimised (e.g. by closing doors, switching off the television or having telephone calls intercepted).

Listening stage	Obstacles
Sensing	External noise (e.g. roadworks outside) Physical impairments (e.g. hard of hearing) Information overload
Attending	Poor speaker delivery (e.g. monotone) Overly long messages Lack of message coherence or structure Fatigue Uncomfortable environment Poor attending habits or disposition Negative attitudes to the speaker
Understanding	Low academic or linguistic ability Selective listening Mental set and biases of the listener Inability to empathise Different speaker/listener backgrounds
Remembering	Poor short-term listening ability Memory store limitations Proactive and retroactive inhibition

Figure 7.5   Obstacles to listening

Inattentiveness

Here the listener for some reason does not give full attention to the speaker. Someone who is self-conscious, and concerned with the personal impression being conveyed, is unlikely to be listening closely to others. In terms of research into memory, two identified problems relate to the process of inhibition (Quinlan and Dyson, 2008). Proactive inhibition occurs when something that has already been learned interferes with attempts to learn new material. A parallel problem is retroactive inhibition, which is where material that has already been learned is impaired as a result of the impact of, and interference from, recent material. In interpersonal encounters inhibition also occurs. *Retroactive listening inhibition* is where the individual is still pondering over the ramifications of something that happened in the recent past, at the expense of listening to the speaker in the present interaction. *Proactive listening inhibition* takes place when someone has an important engagement looming, and a preoccupation with this militates against listening in the present. The main mental focus then tends to be more about how to handle the future encounter than about what the speaker is currently saying.

Individual bias

Oscar Wilde clearly identified one of the pitfalls of listening when he said: 'Listening is a very dangerous thing. If one listens one may be convinced.' Our biases are like comfort blankets – we do not like them to be threatened and cannot contemplate losing them. One study of what individuals wanted from others in terms of listening showed that two key features were that the listener should put personal thoughts aside and be open minded (Halone and Pecchioni, 2001). Yet in reality it is almost impossible to listen to others in a totally unbiased way (Egan, 2007). The biases we have developed as part of our upbringing and socialisation are filters that often distort the messages we receive. This can occur in a number of contexts. Someone with limited time may not wish to get involved in lengthy dialogue and therefore may choose to 'hear' only the less provocative or unproblematic part of what was said. Similarly a person who does not want to recognise difficult realities may refuse to accept these when expressed by another – either by distorting the message or by refusing to listen to the speaker altogether (a common example where this occurs is in bereavement where the bereaved may initially not accept the fact that a loved one has actually died – the *denial stage* of bereavement). At another level, people may not respond accurately to questions or statements simply because they wish to make a separate point when given the floor. One example of this is politicians who want to ensure, at all costs, that they get their message across, and when asked questions in public meetings frequently do not answer these accurately, but rather take the opportunity to state their own point of view.

Mental set

We are all affected by previous experiences, attitudes, values and feelings, and these in turn influence the mental set for any given situation (see Chapter 10). We evaluate others based on their appearance, initial statements or what they said during previous encounters. These influence the way the speaker is heard, in that statements may be screened so that only those aspects that fit with specific expectations are perceived. The process of stereotyping acts as a form of cognitive short-cut that enables us to deal swiftly with others without having to make the effort to find out about them (see Chapter 2). Here all members of a particular group are regarded as homogeneous and having identical traits and behaviour patterns. By ascribing a stereotype to the speaker (e.g. racist, delinquent) we then become less objective. Judgements tend to be based on who is speaking, rather than on what is being said. While it is often important to attempt to evaluate the motives and goals of the speaker, this can only be achieved by a reasoned, rational process, rather than by an irrational or emotional reaction to a particular stereotype. Galanes *et al.* (2006) used the term *mind raping* to refer to the process whereby the listener enforces ascribed meaning to what the speaker has said. This involves forcefully imposing one's interpretation upon the other in statements such as: 'I heard what you *said*, but I know what you really *mean*.' It is therefore important to listen both carefully and objectively to everything that is being communicated.

Blocking

The process of blocking occurs when an individual does not wish to pursue a certain line of communication, and so employs various techniques to end or divert the conversation. The main blocking techniques are presented in Box 7.4. On occasions, some of these are quite legitimate. For example, a pharmacist would be expected to advise a patient to see a doctor immediately if a serious illness was suspected. However, it is where blocking is used negatively that it becomes a serious obstacle to effective listening.

ACTIVE LISTENING

Research has shown that speakers want listeners to respond appropriately to what they are saying rather than to 'just listen' (Halone and Pecchioni, 2001). In other words, they desire active listening in the form of both verbal and nonverbal behaviours. Active listening requires concerted effort and attention (Orbe and Bruess, 2005), as it involves showing that we have both heard and understood what the other person has communicated (Kagan, 2007). Duck and McMahan (2009) argue that what they term *engaged listening* is the key to relational success; this involves 'caring, trusting, wanting to know more, and feeling excited, enlightened, attached, and concerned' (p. 91). The importance of engaged listening was demonstrated in a study by Beukeboom (2009), who showed university students a neutral film clip about a kiosk owner and then had confederates interview them about what they had seen. Some

Box 7.4 Blocking tactics to listening	
Tactic	*Example*
Rejecting involvement	'I don't wish to discuss this with you.' 'That has nothing to do with me.'
Denial of feelings	'You've nothing to worry about.' 'You'll be all right.'
Selective responding	Focusing only on specific aspects of the speaker's message, while ignoring other parts of it.
Admitting insufficient knowledge	'I'm not really qualified to say.' 'I'm only vaguely familiar with that subject.'
Topic shift	Changing the topic away from that expressed by the speaker.
Referring	'You should consult your doctor about that.' 'Your course tutor will help you on that.'
Deferring	'Come back and see me if the pain persists.' 'We'll discuss that next week.'
Pre-empting any communication	'I'm in a terrible rush. See you later.' 'I can't talk now. I'm late for a meeting.'

interviewers used a positive listening style, with smiles, open posture and head nods, while others used a negative style involving frowns, unsmiling expression and closed posture. Results showed that listening style significantly affected how the subjects responded. Those interviewed with a positive listening style gave more of their own opinions and included more abstractions and interpretations (e.g. 'He doesn't trust people anymore.'), whereas those interviewed with the stern, negative style stuck to the descriptive and concrete facts of the film (e.g. 'He arranges newspapers in his stand.'). The process of emotional contagion (see Chapter 3) probably plays a part here. When the listener shows warmth and enthusiasm for what we are saying, this attitude influences us and so we are likely to become more expressive and expansive. By contrast, when the listener is cold and formal, we are more likely to provide basic, factual responses.

Although verbal responses are the main indicators of successful listening, if accompanying nonverbal behaviours are not displayed it is usually assumed that an individual is not paying attention, and ipso facto not listening. Thus, while these nonverbal signs may not be crucial to the assimilation of verbal messages, they are expected by others. The first part of listening can be viewed as a silent response that precedes the spoken reply, and has been described as a type of initial answer (Jacobs and Coghlan, 2005). Furthermore, the nonverbal information conveyed by the speaker adds to and provides emphasis for the verbal message (see Chapter 3). An early example of this was shown in a study by Strong *et al.* (1971) who asked college students to listen only or both view and listen to tapes of counsellors, and rate them on a 100-item checklist. Results indicated that when the counsellors were both seen and heard they were described as more cold, bored, awkward, unreasonable and disinterested than when they were heard only. This study highlighted the importance of attending to both verbal and nonverbal information in judging social responses.

Verbal indicators of listening are discussed in many of the skills reviewed throughout this book. As noted earlier, listening is a prerequisite skill that is part of all other skills. Within the skill of reinforcement, for example, *verbal reinforcers* are often regarded as being associated with attending (see Chapter 4). In terms of listening, however, it has long been known that caution is needed when employing verbal reinforcement. Thus, Rosenshine (1971) found that the curve of the relationship between amount of verbal reinforcement by teachers and degree of pupil participation in classroom lessons was bell-shaped. While verbal reinforcers (e.g. 'very good', 'yes') initially had the effect of increasing pupil participation, if this reinforcement was continued in its basic form, pupils began to regard it with indifference. Rosenshine pointed out that it is simple to administer positive reinforcers without much thought, but to demonstrate genuine listening some reasons have to be given for their use. Pupils need to be told why their responses are good for the reinforcement to be regarded as genuine.

Another aspect of reinforcement that is a potent indicator of effective listening is *reference to past statements*. This can range from simply remembering someone's name to remembering other details about facts, feelings or ideas they may have expressed in the past. This shows a willingness to pay attention to what was previously discussed and in turn is likely to encourage the person to participate more fully in the present interaction. This is part of the process of *verbal following*, whereby the listener matches verbal responses closely to those of the speaker, so that they 'follow on' in a coherent fashion. If the listener makes linked statements that build upon the ideas expressed by the speaker, this is an indication of attentiveness and interest.

However, a distinction needs to be made between *coherent topic shifts*, which occur once the previous topic has been exhausted, and *noncoherent topic shifts*, which are abrupt changes of conversation that are not explained. We often use *disjunct markers* to signal a change of topic ('Incidentally . . .', 'Can I ask you a different question?', 'Before I forget . . .'). In the early stages of a relationship, individuals usually ensure that a disjunct marker is used before making a noncoherent topic shift, whereas once a relationship has been developed, the need for such disjunct markers recedes. Thus, married couples often use unmarked noncoherent topic shifts during conversation without this unduly affecting their relationship. However, in professional interactions disjunct markers are advisable where verbal following does not take place.

It is also important to keep *interruptions* to a minimum. The words of the ancient Greek philosopher Xenocrates should be borne in mind: 'I have often regretted my speech, never my silence.' Research studies have shown that interruptions are not well received during interactive episodes (Halone and Pecchioni, 2001; Farley, 2008). In their study of doctor–patient consultations, Tallman *et al.* (2007) found that physician interruptions were related to patient dissatisfaction. Doctors who received low satisfaction ratings from patients interrupted after one or two sentences, whereas those who were given high ratings allowed the patient up to five uninterrupted sentences during storytelling. Interruptions often result in inattentive clients with unfinished business. As Tallman *et al.* (2007: 22) cautioned: 'An interrupted story doesn't simply drift away. It stays with the patient. Sometimes the patient's issue was not important medically, but it *so occupied the patient's attention* that the patient did not attend to what the doctor had to say.'

Within the skill of questioning (see Chapter 5), the use of *probing questions* is a direct form of listening, wherein the questioner follows up the responses of the respondent by asking related questions. What Kramer (2001) termed 'verbal door openers' are also useful (e.g. 'Would you like to talk about that a little bit more?'). Similarly, the skill of *reflecting* (see Chapter 6) represents a powerful form of response development. In order to reflect accurately the feeling or the content of what someone has said, it is necessary to listen carefully before formulating a succinct reflecting statement. The use of *summarisation* during periods of closure is also evidence of prolonged listening throughout an interaction sequence (see Chapter 10).

Nonverbal responses are also important during listening. A key feature of effective listening is the ability to combine the meaning from body language and paralanguage with the linguistic message (Burley-Allen, 1995). Certain nonverbal behaviours are associated with attending while others are associated with lack of listening. Thus, Rosenfeld and Hancks (1980) showed how head nods, forward leaning posture, visual attention and eyebrow raises were all correlated with positive ratings of listening responsiveness. They also found the most prevalent vocalisation to be the guggle 'Mm hmm', with the most frequent nonverbal listening indicator being the head nod. This latter finding was confirmed more recently by Duggan and Parrott (2001), who showed that head nods and smiles were very potent indicators of listening in doctor–patient interchanges. The main nonverbal listening responses are shown in Box 7.5.

Parallel and contrasting nonverbal cues have been identified as signs of inattentiveness or lack of listening (Duggan and Parrott, 2001). The most common of these are:

- inappropriate facial expressions
- lack of eye contact
- poor use of paralanguage (e.g. flat tone of voice, no emphasis)
- slouched or shifting posture
- absence of head nods
- the use of distracting behaviours (e.g. rubbing the eyes, yawning, writing or reading while the speaker is talking).

In fact, an effective technique to induce someone to stop talking is to use these indicators of nonlistening. These nonverbal signals can of course be deceiving, in that someone who is assimilating the verbal message may not appear to be listening. Most teachers have experienced the situation where a pupil appears to be inattentive and yet when asked a question is able to give an appropriate response. Conversely, people may engage in pretend listening, or *pseudo-listening*, where they show all of the overt signs of attending but are not actually listening at all (Sandow and Allen, 2005). This was referred to by Orbe and Bruess (2005: 181) as 'a masquerade for real listening'.

Box 7.5 Nonverbal signs of listening

1 **Smiles** used as indicators of willingness to follow the conversation or pleasure at what is being said.

2 **Direct eye contact.** In western society the listener usually looks more at the speaker than vice versa (in other cultures this may not be the case, and direct eye gaze may be viewed as disrespectful or challenging).

3 **Using appropriate paralanguage** to convey enthusiasm for the speaker's thoughts and ideas (e.g. tone of voice, emphasis on certain words, lack of interruption).

4 **Reflecting the facial expressions of the speaker**, in order to show sympathy and empathy with the emotional message being conveyed.

5 **Adopting an attentive posture**, such as a forward or sideways lean on a chair. Similarly a sideways tilt of the head (often with the head resting on one hand) is an indicator of listening. What is known as *sympathetic communication* involves the mirroring of overall posture, as well as facial expressions. Indeed, where problems arise in communication such mirroring usually ceases to occur (see Chapter 6 for a fuller discussion of mirroring).

6 **Head nods** to indicate agreement or willingness to listen.

7 **Refraining from distracting mannerisms**, such as doodling with a pen, fidgeting, or looking at a watch.

Although it is possible to listen without overtly so indicating, in most social settings it is important to demonstrate such attentiveness. Thus, both the verbal and nonverbal determinants of active listening play a key role in social interaction. In fact, these signs are integrated in such a fashion that, in most cases, if either channel signals lack of attention this is taken as an overall indication of poor listening.

OVERVIEW

There is a well-known story about the main difference between the two nineteenth-century UK prime ministers Benjamin Disraeli and William Gladstone. This purported that when you dined with Gladstone you left feeling he was the most intelligent, charming and wittiest person in England, but when you dined with Disraeli you left feeling that *you* were the most intelligent, charming and wittiest person in England. The difference was in the listening ability of the two individuals. Listening is a fundamental component of interpersonal communication. In a survey of attitudes to various communication behaviours, Glynn and Huge (2008: 564) concluded: 'There are obvious social costs for those who always talk more than they listen in conversation.' One of the dangers was aptly noted by the former US president Calvin Coolidge when he remarked: 'No man ever listened himself out of a job.' It is important to realise that listening is not something that just happens, but rather is an active process in which the listener decides to pay careful attention to the speaker. It involves focusing upon the speaker's verbal and nonverbal messages, while at the same time actively portraying verbal and nonverbal signs of listening. The following guidelines should be borne in mind:

1   *Get physically prepared to listen.* If the interaction is taking place in your own environment, provide an appropriate physical layout of furniture, ensure adequate temperature and ventilation, and keep intrusive noise and other distractions to a minimum.

2   *Be mentally prepared to listen objectively.* Try to remove all other thoughts from your mind, and concentrate fully. Be aware of your own biases, avoid preconceptions and do not stereotype the speaker.

3   *Use spare thought time positively.* Keep your thoughts entirely on the message being delivered, by asking covert questions, constructing mental images of what is being said or employing other concentration techniques.

4   *Do not interrupt.* There is a Native American Indian proverb that advises: 'Listen or your tongue will make you deaf.' It is therefore important to 'hold your tongue' and let the other person contribute fully. Develop a system of *mental banking*, where ideas you wish to pursue can be cognitively 'deposited' and 'withdrawn' later. This allows the speaker to have a continuous flow, and the fact that you can later refer back to what has been said is a potent indicator of active listening.

5   *Organise the speaker's messages* into appropriate categories and, where relevant, chronological order. Identify the main thrust and any supporting arguments. This process facilitates comprehension and recall of what was said.

6   *Do not overuse blocking tactics.* These are often employed subconsciously to prevent the speaker from controlling an interaction.

7   *Remember that listening is hard work.* Winston Churchill once remarked: 'Courage is what it takes to stand up and speak. Courage is also what it takes to sit down and listen.' It takes energy and commitment to listen actively. It has been said that the only place you will find easy listening is as a specialist section in a music store. Professionals who spend their working day listening will testify that it is an exhausting activity, and one that requires discipline and determination. Indeed, as Figley (2002) has shown, those who work in the therapeutic sphere (counsellors, health professionals, etc.) can suffer from the phenomenon of *compassion fatigue* as a result of concerted listening to accounts of traumatic experiences.

In concluding this chapter, it is useful to bear in mind one of the precepts proffered by Polonius to his son Laertes in Shakespeare's *Hamlet, Prince of Denmark*: 'Give every man thine ear, but few thy voice.'

Chapter 8

Getting your message across: the skill of explaining

INTRODUCTION

THE AMOUNT OF INFORMATION in circulation seems to grow like Topsy. The electronic blizzard of information technology, epitomised by the internet, produces an unending flow of material in the form of facts, theories, speculations and opinions intended to variously inform, entertain, sell, shock or persuade. Billions of texts and emails are also sent daily. At the same time, and despite predictions to the contrary, the volume of printed paper continues to increase exponentially. For example, about one million new books are published every year, and there are over 60,000 academic journals publishing numerous editions annually. Not surprisingly, information overload is a condition experienced by many. Being exposed in this way to a mish-mash of data, of course, does not automatically make us better informed. For this to happen, we need more than to have material simply 'dumped' upon us. Rather, it has to be delivered in such a way that we can sort it out and make sense of it. This chapter is devoted to the processes involved in delivering information in such a way as to maximise comprehension. The focus will be upon the task of sharing detail and educing understanding. Presentations that rely more upon emotion and are intended primarily to persuade (rather than enlighten) through creating changes in attitude or opinion (rather than knowledge) will be dealt with in Chapter 12.

Referring to communication within organisations, Clampitt (2010) highlighted three different dimensions: *data*, *information* and *knowledge*. While recognising difficulties in providing precise definitions of each, data are said to concern particular representations of reality, not all of which may be accurate or relevant to that person at that time. Information is created when certain elements are focused upon and isolated from background data, so enabling their potential contribution to decision making to be delineated. Finally, knowledge relies upon recognising patterns and consistencies in information, thereby making possible the development of theories that can be tested. It is only such knowledge that produces effective action. There is, therefore, a need to give thought to the organisation of material, how it is delivered and to whom if we are to benefit from what we read and hear, as well as successfully getting our own message across.

Explaining is a standard feature of everyday casual talk as well as forming the substance of more formal addresses to large gatherings attending lectures or public presentations. It is also a crucial part of skilled professional practice in areas such as education, health, medicine, technology, architecture, business and law (Brown, 2006). The importance of teachers being able to put across material in such a way that pupils readily grasp it is obvious and has long been an abiding concern of educationalists (Thyne, 1963). But patients too have a need for information about diagnosis, prognosis, condition or treatment to be delivered in ways that they can understand. Hajek *et al.* (2007) produced evidence linking patients' judgements of doctors' ability to explain matters in language familiar to them with patients' estimates of their likelihood of subsequently complying with received medical advice. Likewise in the world of law, advice and instruction that may be couched in arcane (indeed archaic) language has to be communicated clearly if recipients are not to be disadvantaged.

In the modern corporate environment, professionals must be effective communicators. It is pointless having good ideas if others cannot grasp or appreciate them. In their analysis, de Vries *et al.* (2009) found that one of the core generic communication styles was that of 'expressiveness'. This style involved being articulate, energetic, eloquent, fluent and assured. This obviously links directly to the ability to deliver effective explanations. However, explaining is an activity that is often performed poorly by many professionals. This was summarised in early work in the field of teaching by Gage *et al.* (1968: 3):

> Some people explain aptly, getting to the heart of the matter with just the right terminology, examples and organization of ideas. Other explainers, on the contrary, get us and themselves all mixed up, use terms beyond our level of comprehension, draw inept analogies and even employ concepts and principles that cannot be understood without an understanding of the very thing being explained.

But teachers need not be singled out for special attention. Instances of health worker–patient conversation have been pinpointed where deficiencies in information giving lie at the heart of poor levels of professional communication (Dickson and McCartan, 2005). Patients complain about not being told enough by doctors, and not understanding what is said when they are given explanations (Brataas *et al.*, 2009). This has been known for some time. The findings were summarised by the Audit Commission (1993: 1) as follows: 'A common complaint is that there is not enough information. Equally, information often exists but the quality is poor.' Nor are such deficits confined to the NHS. A comparable exercise by the Health Services Commissioner for Victoria, Australia identified poor communication as a source of patient complaint about hospitals (Office of the Health Services Commissioner, 2008). Likewise, Japanese doctors and patients do not always agree on the level of doctors' explanations that they feel are necessary, particularly in respect of information about diagnosis (Hagihara *et al.*, 2006a).

Moving from health to law, doubts have been expressed about how well the law system works in some US courts. At the centre of the process of criminal justice is a trial overseen by a judge, whose task it is to apply the appropriate law and make the jury familiar with it. The jury in turn is charged with applying that law to the evidence in reaching a verdict. The extent to which this is done effectively is limited by how successfully members fully grasp instructions received. Specific problems of comprehension have to do with vocabulary and the technical meaning of some terms that can be at odds with everyday interpretations. Additionally, instructional material can be poorly structured and awkwardly expressed (Tiersma, 2006). Referring specifically to jurors' difficulties in grasping the nuances of patent law, Caliendo (2004: 210) concluded that 'there exists a common failure to communicate to juries a statement of the law that is both clear and correct'.

In the world of management, the ability to get facts, ideas and judgements across in a clear and pithy way is no less valued. As summarised by Rowan (2003: 404):

> Just as good informative and explanatory communication is appreciated, the effects of poor informing and explaining are feared. At the workplace, poor informative and explanatory communication skills lead to frustration between shift employees, lost revenue, and misunderstood employee benefit provisions.

Managers can be expected to give on average 26 formal presentations a year (Adler and Elmhorst, 2008), and this aspect of the managerial role gains even greater prominence as careers progress. Employees prefer business communication to be direct, easily understood and succinct. The observation by Mandel (1987) still holds that oral briefings mostly fail because they are too long-winded, include too few examples, are unattractively delivered and have content that is poorly organised and contains too much technical jargon. The need to retain the interest of the audience emerged as the presentation skill ranked top by a variety of professionals (Engleberg, 2002). Survey evidence attests to the growing recognition of the importance of graduates entering the job market with skills of this type. A sample of 1500 corporate recruiters representing companies across the USA revealed that over 50 per cent of those responding placed good oral and written communication top of their list of skills required of business applicants (Moody *et al.*, 2002). When the actual skills that constitute this competency are distilled down, those to do with making presentations rank highly in both importance and frequency of use.

It is, therefore, essential that a broad range of professionals have the skills necessary to deliver effective explanations that are comprehensible to a variety of audiences. But first let us examine the nature of explanations per se.

WHAT IS AN EXPLANATION?

This is a deceptively simple question but one that has occupied philosophers and social scientists for some time (Achinstein, 1983; Risjord, 2005; Brown, 2006). One particular semantic knot to be unravelled is whether 'explaining' is essentially the same as other activities such as 'describing', 'instructing' and 'relating', involving the giving of information, or in some way different from these. A further difficulty centres upon whether anything has to be understood for an explanation to have occurred. But let us leave this matter aside for the moment and tackle the first issue.

Some take a very broad and inclusive approach to defining what represents an explanation, for example Hamilton (2008: 345) states: 'In an explanation, the speaker describes the relationship between certain items, defines a word or term, or gives instruction on how to do something or how to get somewhere.' Even more broadly defined by Martin (1970: 59): 'The job of someone who explains something to someone ... is to fill in the gap between his audience's knowledge or beliefs about some phenomena and what he takes to be the actual state of affairs.' Here we see that what counts is leaving the audience knowing or believing something of which they were previously ignorant. In a sense it does not really matter if information given is strictly accurate provided that the explainer takes what is told to be the case. At the other extreme, explaining has been thought of in a much more restrictive sense as a special type of 'telling'. Here an explanation is different from a description, instruction or speculation. What is peculiar about it is that it goes beyond mere description to give reasons or reveal causes for the facts or events under discussion. In other words, answering the question 'Why?' is an implicit or explicit feature. This defining characteristic was brought out by Pavitt (2000: 379), in discussing scientific explanations:

> A question such as, 'Why did she say that?' or 'Why will she say that?' demands a third type of answer, one that increases understanding by giving a reason for the content of her past or future utterance. We call this type of answer an 'explanation'.

One way around this definitional dilemma is to think of categories of explanation rather than just explanations versus non-explanations. Some but not all of these may have to do with presenting cause–effect relationships. One of the most pragmatic and robust typologies is that provided by Brown (2006), who outlined *descriptive*, *interpretive* and *reason-giving* varieties.

- *Descriptive explanations.* These are provided when presenting information about specific procedures, structures, processes or directions. They typically address the question 'How?' In a qualitative study of science lessons with elementary pupils in Canada, Rowell and Ebbers (2004) found the majority of explanations to be of this type.
- *Interpretive explanations.* These define or clarify issues, meanings or statements. Here it is the question 'What?' that is mainly being responded to.
- *Reason-giving explanations.* These specify the cause–effect relationships that account for some phenomenon or the reasons behind some action or event.

They are commonly occasioned by the question 'Why?' Within this category, Pavitt (2000) made a further distinction between *functional* and *causal* explanations:

— Functional explanations are required when the audience is confused about the purpose of some phenomenon.
— Causal explanations set out cause–effect relationships and often invoke laws or general principles.

Examples of these can be found in Box 8.1.

But the term 'to explain' has two further meanings, one referring to the intention of the speaker, the other the success of the outcome (Turney *et al.*, 1983). Adopting the former but not the latter, it makes sense to say, 'I explained it to him but he did not understand.' What counts for Achinstein (1983) in this respect is that:

• the speaker intends to answer the listener's question
• the speaker believes that what is said is a correct answer to the question
• the intention is to directly answer the question
• the listener appreciates the speaker's intentions in these respects.

Note that there is no mention here of the listener's consequent level of comprehension. In professional contexts, however, this usage is clearly not sufficient. Rather, when it is said that something has been explained by a teacher or doctor, not only is it an expectation but a requirement that it be understood by the pupil or patient.

Box 8.1 Examples of types of explanation

Descriptive
• Going over the steps of how to bath a baby.
• Outlining how to operate a new computer program.

Interpretive
• Making clear the significance of a white line on an X-ray of a damaged leg.
• Providing the meaning of the word 'oxymoron'.

Reason-giving
• Pointing out why wage rises that are not linked to productivity can trigger inflation.
• Explaining why some trees lose their leaves in winter.

Functional
• Explaining why flamingos have funny-shaped bills.
• Presenting reasons why racing cars have broad wheels and spoilers.

Causal
• Outlining why sunbathing can lead to skin cancer.
• Setting out the sequence of steps leading from turning the key in the ignition to a car engine firing up.

As such, the claim 'I explained it to them but they did not understand' would be inherently contradictory. This stipulation is partly reflected in the working definition proffered by Brown and Edmunds (2009: 76): 'Explaining is concerned with giving understanding to others.' This way of thinking also sits foursquare with the original meaning of the word as derived from the Latin verb *explanare*, 'to make plain'.

ABOUT EXPLAINING

Any particular explanation may involve elements that are descriptive, interpretive, causal or functional. It may also take place in the context of an impromptu encounter with another as, for instance, when a manager clarifies some aspect of the company's financial systems to a member of the office staff. Alternatively, it can be a well-prepared formal presentation to a group. The coverage in this chapter should be useful in both sets of circumstances.

Explanations can also take contrasting forms. We tend to think of the *monologue* approach with the explainer delivering a 'lecture' while the recipient listens. But the *Socratic technique* can be very effective when it comes to creating understanding. Named after the Greek philosopher renowned for his technique of responding with a whole series of questions when asked to explain some abstract idea such as 'justice', we can often lead others to understanding in a dialogue where we do most of the questioning (see Box 8.2). This approach has the advantage of affording the listener an active role in the learning process.

Three principal modes of explaining can be employed:

* **_verbal explanations_** rely exclusively upon the spoken (or written) word to carry meaning and create understanding
* **_illustrations_** supplement verbal presentations with pictures, models, graphs, videos and so on

---

Box 8.2 The Socratic technique

Why have camels got flat feet?

Mother:	Well Jane, where do camels live?
Jane:	In the desert.
Mother:	That's right. What is the ground like in the desert?
Jane:	It's all sandy.
Mother:	Where else can sand be found?
Jane:	At the beach.
Mother:	Yes, do you remember last summer on the beach when we played ball?
Jane:	Oh yes!
Mother:	What was it like trying to run on the soft sand?
Jane:	It was really hard. My feet dug in.
Mother:	Yes so did mine. What though if we had large, flat feet like a camel?
Jane:	Oh, so that is why camels have flat feet.

- *demonstrations* involve 'explaining by doing'. They are a very practical and applied way of getting information across, usually about some process or technique.

It is difficult to legislate for skilful explaining. Regardless of the particular topic, there is no one proper way of presenting it that guarantees success. Adequacy is directly related, for instance, to the recipient's age, background knowledge and ability. How finely should the concept be broken down? At what level should it be pitched? How can it be related to other material? What activities can the audience benefit from engaging in? These are the sorts of decisions faced by many professionals on a day-to-day basis. Lawyers, business people, engineers, doctors and nurses find themselves having to make clients and patients aware of complicated information and involved states of affairs, on the basis of which informed decisions have to be taken.

Even restricting recipients to the adult population, what may well work as a clear and concise outline for one individual may merely serve to get another person confused and frustrated, while an indignant third may find it insultingly patronising. The problem in explaining was cryptically highlighted by the American baseball player Lawrence 'Yogi' Berra, famous for his malapropisms and non sequiturs, when he said, 'There are some people who, if they don't already know, you can't tell them.' Perhaps the most fundamental rule is that explanations, as indeed with communication more generally, must be tailored to the needs, abilities and backgrounds of the audience. The onus is on the explainer to establish at what level an explanation should be pitched and how it can best be delivered.

PURPOSES OF EXPLAINING

The main goals of explaining are listed in Box 8.3. Some of these take precedence, depending upon the context of the interaction. Successfully meeting the needs and wants of recipients, particularly in professional contexts, is an important guiding principle. In health care, research reviews demonstrate that many patients positively value and benefit from the presentation of information by health professionals about

---

Box 8.3 Purposes of explaining

The main goals served by the skill of explaining are:

1 to provide others with information otherwise unavailable
2 to simplify complexity
3 to illustrate the essential features of particular phenomena
4 to clarify uncertainties revealed during interaction
5 to express opinions regarding particular attitudes, facts or values
6 to reach some common understanding
7 to demonstrate how to execute a specific skill or technique
8 to empower others thorough giving understanding and increased autonomy
9 to ensure learning.

---

their condition (Brown *et al.*, 2003; Dickson and McCartan, 2005). This is particularly so for 'monitors' – patients who actively search out and request such information. 'Blunters', by contrast, deliberately avoid this detail, especially when news may be unpleasant (Miller *et al.*, 1988; Klein and Knäuper, 2008). Moreover, Leydon *et al.* (2000) revealed that while all cancer patients in their study wanted basic information pertaining to diagnosis and treatment, some did not want further extensive detail at all stages of their illness.

Being able to impart information to patients in terms that they can readily grasp is a crucial communication skill for doctors (Schirmer *et al.*, 2005) and nurses (Klakovich and dela Cruz, 2006). Giving adequate and relevant information and explanation can result in tangible benefits to patients in terms of reduced pain and discomfort, anxiety and depression, and earlier recovery (Thompson, 1998; Carlson *et al.*, 2005). It can also promote patient adherence to treatment regimens (Hagihara *et al.*, 2006b) and reduce levels of non-attendance for medical appointments (Hamilton *et al.*, 1999). One study found that the explanation given by doctors before and after the procedure was a key determinant of patient satisfaction with endoscopy (Yanai *et al.*, 2008). However, Australian patients admitted to hospital for an operative procedure on their knee (knee arthroscopy) expressed dissatisfaction with the lack of information received on possible complications surrounding the investigation and post-operative care (McGaughey, 2004). Likewise, in a large-scale survey of patients with the eye condition glaucoma, 60 per cent of those who reported changing doctors did so due to poor communication (Herndon *et al.*, 2006).

Deficient explanations have doubtless contributed to findings such as that patients in general forget some 50 per cent of the information given by practitioners (Morrow and Hargie, 2001) and that some 50 per cent of patients in North America, Europe and Japan do not take their medication correctly (International Medical Benefit/ Risk Foundation, 1993). Usable information is an important source of social power (see Chapter 12). It follows that informing and training are ways of self-empowering others through enabling them to make more informed decisions over matters affecting their lives without having to seek help and guidance. Personal autonomy is promoted as a result.

As already discussed, explaining is a way of creating understanding on behalf of the audience. But having to explain material after being exposed to it can also be an effective way for the explainer to learn it. Hence the old maxim: 'The best way to learn something is to have to teach it.' This was demonstrated in an experiment by Coleman *et al.* (1997), who discovered that setting students the task of subsequently explaining Darwin's theory of evolution through natural selection produced more learning and understanding of that material than asking them to summarise it, or merely listening to it. Rittle-Johnson (2006) also discovered that self-explanation, or generating explanations for oneself, was effective in promoting learning among school pupils and in facilitating its subsequent transfer to the solving of new arithmetic problems.

THE EXPLAINING PROCESS

We can think of the key features of explaining in terms of the 5-Ps model – Pre-assessment, Planning, Preparation, Presentation and Postmortem. Each of these will be developed with the aid of a diagram (Figure 8.1) that extends the work of French (1994) and Kagan and Evans (1995). Although the first three are often overlooked in a rush to 'get on with it', when explanations go wrong it is often on account of inadequate forethought. Admittedly the unexpected can often knock off course even the most carefully crafted presentation. However, studies have shown that competent planning and preparation are linked to clarity of explanations (Brown, 2006). Someone who has a firm grasp of the material to be put across, and has given thought to how best to do so, is much more likely to explain effectively.

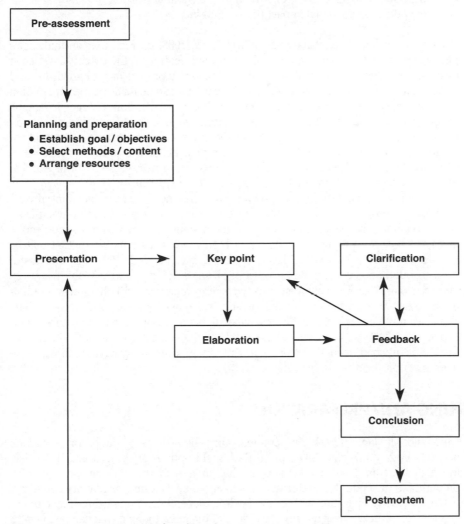

Figure 8.1 The 5-Ps model of explaining

PRE-ASSESSMENT

This has to do with finding out about the recipient and the circumstances that pertain before embarking on the mission to inform. Neglecting these considerations can result in much wasted effort – or worse. A quick checklist of things to assess includes:

- what the other wants or needs to know
- what they already know
- their ability to make sense of what they are about to hear
- the potential emotional impact of the material.

Referring to scientific explanations, Gilbert *et al.* (1998) claimed that an audience's judgement of the adequacy of an explanation is a feature of the extent to which it meets a need. This will depend on the degree to which prior relevant knowledge and understanding is taken into account, and the use that can be made of the explanation in the future. Professionals such as doctors (Thompson, 1998) and judges (Tiersma, 2006) often make the mistake of overestimating what patients and jurors already know. Health workers should establish, at the outset, whether what appears to be a request for information is indeed that, rather than perhaps a plea for reassurance (Brataas *et al.*, 2009). Nurses sometimes respond to the former with reassurance and to the latter with a factual explanation (Kagan and Evans, 1995).

Finding out what is already known makes sense not only from the point of view of avoiding needless repetition but also in establishing a suitable starting point from which to launch the explanation. Again, without some appreciation of the audience's linguistic code and cognitive abilities it is highly probable that information will be pitched at entirely the wrong level. Calderhead (1996) indicated that successful teachers build pupil understanding, other pupil characteristics and available resources into their planning. To explain effectively requires a certain empathic understanding of the other, in that the explainee's perspective must be taken into account. The explainer must develop a feel for how what is being proposed will be received and experienced. For example, in situations where the patient is not ready to receive further detail about a condition or treatment, attempting an explanation along these lines is a futile exercise (Berger, 2005).

PLANNING AND PREPARATION

Duck and McMahan (2009: 296) pointed out: 'The success of public presentations depends largely on what takes place during this phase of the process.' Likewise, Monarth and Kase (2007) made the point that, in general, the more time available for preparation, the better the performance is likely to be. But time available to plan and make adequate preparation will obviously differ depending upon settings and circumstances. Nevertheless, it is usually the case that the more thought that can be given to what needs to be covered and how best to do so, the better the end result. This seems to be realised by the more experienced professional. Carter (1990) noted that novice teachers tend to jump in without giving adequate thought and planning to the task in hand. The more expert, on the other hand, develop:

- *cognitive schemata*, which rely on the integration of specialised knowledge linked to specific situations
- *organisational knowledge* in terms of how concepts are related and form a pattern
- *tacit knowledge*, which is constructed or invented from repeated experiences over time.

Planning and preparation comprise several sequenced and interdependent subtasks.

Establish goals/objectives

An explanation may be triggered by a direct request from someone who needs or wants to know something. Alternatively it may be the explainer who initiates the exchange. In the latter case, an important first step may be to create a 'felt need' on the part of recipients. They should have a sense that listening to what is about to be said will be worthwhile (see the section on motivational set in Chapter 10, p. 291). Regardless of who initiates the episode, the explainer must have a firm grasp of the issue to be dealt with and what the explanation should achieve. Hamilton (2008) advocated committing this purpose to paper in a sentence at the outset of the preparatory process. A broad goal may be broken down into specific objectives and thought of in terms of changes brought about in recipients (Bradbury, 2006). These may relate to:

- what they should be able to *do* (*behavioural objective*)
- what they should *know and understand* (*cognitive objective*)
- *feelings* and *attitudes* that they should hold (*affective objective*).

Identify content and select methods

Here decisions are taken about the content of the explanation (the actual material to be put across) and how best to do so. Linked in turn to the material to be covered are the boundaries that circumscribe it, marking the relevant from the irrelevant. There is a logic that connects this set of judgements with those concerning goals and objectives. Each type of objective will suggest a somewhat different approach to giving information. For example, if the intention is that the audience should be able to complete some manual task, perhaps involving an element of skill, a demonstration coupled with practice opportunities may be required. A need simply to know, on the other hand, could probably be satisfied with a verbal explanation or illustration.

Organise content

In discussing the importance of preparing your presentation and structuring the content, Beagrie (2007) cautioned that without a 'map' both you and your audience, in trying to reach your destination, will probably only succeed in getting lost. Once subject matter is firmly located, several other processes come into play. They include:

- selecting the key elements
- determining how these key elements are related
- structuring and linking the explanation to the particular audience.

Any body of information will have key elements that really must be grasped. In identifying these, Adler and Elmhorst (2008) advocated teasing out no more than five such elements. A greater number poses problems for the audience's powers of memory and will most likely be quickly forgotten. But it is not just presenting the main points that matters, how they interrelate is also important. This in turn will suggest a sensible approach to structuring the explanation so that it moves, for instance, from the simple to the complex and is easy to follow. Research in the teaching context shows that the teacher's ability to prepare, structure, organise and sequence facts and ideas with the maximum of logical coherence is positively related to pupil achievement (Wragg and Brown, 2001). Some alternative strategies to be adopted when it comes to structuring material can be found in Box 8.4. When selecting, linking and structuring terms and ideas, the age, sex, background, experience and mental ability of the audience should not be forgotten. The length of time available for the task is also relevant.

Box 8.4 Strategies for organising content

1 **Topical arrangement.** Here the issue is analysed into related topics and subtopics to be presented – the key elements. These have no particular relationship to one another, apart from shared relevance. The order in which they are covered is typically shaped by going from (a) the known to the unknown, and (b) the simple to the complex.
2 **Chronological sequence.** In this case the key elements contained are ordered in relation to a timeline (e.g. describing how the company evolved to its present state, or outlining the steps involved in a manufacturing process).
3 **Logical sequence.** There are two alternatives here. The deductive sequence moves from general principles to what needs to be done in certain specific cases of relevance to the group. The converse, inductive sequence begins with specific cases and from them moves to the derivation of broad principles that should be accepted and applied.
4 **Causal pattern.** Here the material is ordered in terms of a sequence of cause–effect relationships that explains events and why they came about. It can be extended into the next possibility.
5 **Problem–solution.** This option structures the presentation into two sections. The first sketches the nature of the problem. The second maps the solution.
6 **Motivated sequence.** This is a more elaborate alternative than (5). It is particularly suited when the intention is to change attitudes, beliefs or practices. It follows the sequence of gaining attention, establishing need, outlining how that need can be satisfied, helping the audience to visualise the satisfied need and finally stipulating what has to be done to accomplish that state.

Arrange resources

This point is particularly apt in the context of a more formal presentation. Part of preparation is arranging for all the various resources drawn upon to be when and where you need them, and in working order. If possible, it is also worthwhile to check out the location of the presentation in advance and the actual room that has been set aside. The size and position of the room, type of furniture and facilities, and available equipment should be noted. These can all influence levels of comfort and be more or less conducive to learning. They will also shape what it is possible to do with the group.

PRESENTATION

While the potential of an explanation will be enhanced as a result of the above preparatory processes, effectiveness must ultimately depend upon the flow of the discourse and levels of clarity created. According to the model represented in Figure 8.1, sequenced and ordered key points should be presented one at a time. After making the point, it should be elaborated upon and understanding checked before moving on to the next. If necessary, clarification can be provided. Although relatively few studies have been concerned with the identification of effective planning and structuring aspects, a great deal of research attention has focused on presentation skills and tactics. An examination of these research findings has revealed a number of crucial features and these are discussed and analysed in the remainder of this chapter.

Clarity

Clear explanations tend to be understood – those that are unclear simply cause confusion. There is little doubt that clarity of speech is one of the most challenging features of effective explaining (Engleberg and Daly, 2004). Having the ability to get their message across clearly has been shown to be one of the interpersonal skills that senior human resource personnel look for in managers in supervisory positions (Bambacas and Patrickson, 2008). Of course, explainers need to know their subject, but while this may be necessary it is not a sufficient condition for success. Their knowledge base is only one part of the equation. The topic still has to be communicated to an audience in a clear, unambiguous and structured way. Consistently using language that patients can understand is widely recognised as one of the communication competencies required from doctors (Schirmer *et al.*, 2005). As analysed by Chesebro and McCroskey (2001), instructional clarity encompasses two interrelated elements: first, the structure of content and how different elements that make up the body of material are organised, and second, how that content is delivered. As far as the first element is concerned, Brown (2006) identified four structuring moves associated with clarity:

1   *Signposts.* These are statements that provide the listener with an advanced framework for structuring the information to come. As the name suggests, their function is to point the direction ahead and chart the path that will be taken.

For example, a fitness instructor may begin explaining why a pulse monitor is being used by saying, 'Let me first explain what a pulse monitor does in measuring your heart rate, then the importance of knowing how hard you are working when you train. Finally I will go over how this information can be used to work out different training schedules for you.' In essence, these comments are the equivalent of the introduction in a report or essay.

2   *Frames.* These are words or phrases that mark the beginnings and endings of sections within the body of the talk. They are used to indicate the boundaries of specific topics or subtopics contained in the explanation. Frames are particularly useful when the material is complex, with different embedded subelements. An example would be: 'Okay, that covers what the pulse monitor does in picking up an electrical signal from the heart, each time it beats. Moving on from there to why that information is useful to you as you train . . .'.

3   *Foci.* Foci statements highlight or emphasise key features of the explanation and help to make these 'stand out' from a backdrop of lesser material. Foci statements in relation to the ongoing example would be:

- 'Don't forget, you should always make sure someone is with you if you try to check your maximum pulse.'
- 'So remember, never turn training sessions into races.'
- 'It's very important that you include some recovery sessions in your regime as well.'

4   *Links.* Most talks or explanations cover a series of subtopics, each designed to contribute to the listener's overall knowledge of a subject. Links are important in two respects. First, clarity of comprehension is improved if the speaker links the subtopics into a meaningful whole. Second, speakers should try to link their explanation to the experience, previously acquired knowledge and observations of the audience. For instance: 'Now you see, given that the heart adapts to higher levels of demand, why it is important to organise training so that you are continually asking a little more of it each time, to notice improvements in your fitness level. It's just like any other muscle, in that sense. The pulse monitor lets you check accurately how hard your heart is working.'

There is classroom-based evidence that greater clarity of exposition is associated with increased liking by students of both teacher and course, lower levels of learner apprehension and heightened student motivation to learning. Moreover, students also tend to learn more under these circumstances (Chesebro and McCroskey, 2001; Comadena *et al.*, 2007). In the higher education sector, among the main sources of dissatisfaction that students have with lectures are incoherence and failure of the lecturer to pitch the material at a level appropriate to the group (Brown, 2006).

Concision

The old maxim that 'a little remembered is better than a lot forgotten' has much to commend it when it comes to giving information. An explanation that carries more detail than is necessary is just as defective as one that does not carry enough – a key feature of effective explanations is that they are succinct (Harper, 2004). Thus, one study of first-year college students found that the introduction of additional quantitative material, in the form of illustrations and formulae not directly germane to the task, produced less effective learning (Mayer and Jackson, 2005). It has long been known that, in relation to the lecture context in colleges, 'learning begins to diminish seriously after fifteen minutes' (Verner and Dickinson, 1967: 90). In health-care situations where patients may be distracted by pain or have little energy, the crucial time period will be considerably shorter. Indeed, providing too much detail has been shown to be a communication problem in community care (Groogan, 1999). Clampitt (2010: 122) in his analysis of organisations likened information to food. He asserted that 'there are far too many managers who have grown fat on information, but are starved for knowledge'. One way to 'diet' strongly advocated by Blundel (1998) is by embracing the KISS principle – 'Keep It Short and Simple'.

Fluency

Based upon over 30 years of personal experience in attending lectures and conferences, Bassnett (2007) concluded that the key to improving the quality of such events lay with enhancing delivery, by not speaking too fast, being fluent, having good voice projection and looking at the audience. For presentations to be successful, sloppy speech, poor enunciation and imprecise diction need to be rectified (Beaver, 2006). It is not only annoying to listen to garbled, rambling sentences punctuated all the way through with 'ums' and 'ahs', this annoyance can also very quickly lead to inattention. Christenfeld (1995), in a study of undergraduates, reported that impressions of quality were negatively affected when speakers used a profusion of 'ums', and attributed their overuse to anxiety or lack of preparation on the part of the speaker. In the school context, Wragg and Brown (2001) also found that a fluent delivery was associated with explaining effectiveness in terms of subsequent pupil achievement.

It is easier to appreciate what makes for a fluent presentation by considering the different ways in which dysfluency can be displayed. Some of the types noted in Box 8.5, such as a lisp or stammer, may require specialised treatment. Others can be occasioned by particular circumstances. As pointed out by Crystal (1997: 280): 'A certain amount of "normal non-fluency" is found in young children . . . and indeed everyone is prone to hesitation, especially in situations where they have to speak under pressure.' One of the causes of punctuating speech with sounds such as 'eh' or 'mm' is trying to put too many ideas or facts across in one sentence. It is better to use reasonably short crisp sentences, with pauses in between, than long rambling ones full of subordinate clauses. This will generally tend to eliminate speech hesitancies. Another cause of dysfluency is lack of adequate planning and forethought.

While the evidence points overwhelmingly to the need for a verbal presentation to be as fluent as possible, one area in which dysfluency might be positively encouraged was outlined by Heath (1984). He noted that when doctors in the medical interview explained new technical terms they tended to adopt a speech hesitation or dysfluency, which may actually gain the attention of the patient. In fact, doctors often combined an 'umm' or an 'ahh' with frame devices such as 'what we call . . .' or 'it's

---

Box 8.5 Ten ways to be dysfluent

1 *Filled pauses* – 'umm', 'ah', 'er'.
2 *Sloppy diction* – lack of clear enunciation of word sounds.
3 *Articulation handicaps* –e.g. lisp.
4 *Stammering* – difficulty in controlling the rhythm and timing of speech.
5 *False starts* – e.g. 'I must mention . . . well, maybe first I should say . . . of course, you may already know. . .'
6 *Poorly organised sentences* – e.g. 'Well we didn't intend when we left . . . see, John had this ticket . . . oh and Jane phoned me.'
7 *Repetitive phrases* – e.g. 'sort of', 'you know'.
8 *Hesitation* – 'Can I . . . say that . . .'.
9 *Cluttering* – abnormally fast rate of speech, with syllables running into each other.
10 *Lack of voice projection* – e.g. mumbling.

---

something like . . .', thereby helping the patient to locate and attend to the conversational moments in which medical terms were introduced.

Pausing

Pausing briefly to collect and organise thought processes before embarking on an explanation can also facilitate fluent speech patterns. Added to that, planned pausing can help to increase understanding of the explanation. Rosenshine (1968), in an early research review of those behaviours related to teacher effectiveness, found that teachers who used pauses following an explanation increased pupils' knowledge by ensuring that not too much material was covered too rapidly. Brown and Bakhtar (1988) provided further support for the use of pausing when presenting lengthy explanations in their study of lecturing styles. Their research showed that one of the five most common weaknesses of lecturers was speaking too quickly. Similarly, in the health context, a survey of 617 breast cancer patients found that one of the areas where they felt improvement was most needed in their care and treatment was that doctors need to take more time when giving explanations to patients (Oskay-Özcelik *et al.*, 2007).

Appropriate language

Any explanation must contain language appropriate to the intellectual capacity, background and language code of the listener. Professionals are bilingual. In addition to their native tongue, they learn the specialised and often highly technical language associated with their work. All professionals have a stock-in-trade of jargon. Indeed, in many respects it can serve them well as a means of facilitating communication within the group, acting as a very conspicuous marker of group identity, and denying information access to nongroup members. But jargon can also get in the way of understanding. In the medical sphere, Roter and Hall (2006: 127) noted: 'The use of "medicalese" and the various forms of medical jargon and code persists despite its problematic nature. Indeed, it is not unusual for a patient to feel alarmed and confused after leaving the doctor's office because of failures to understand what the doctor was talking about.'

Professionals sometimes forget that clients are excluded from the specialist language used by them. Blocks to communication occur when what linguists call *code switching* takes place and jargon forms part of the dialogue with patients or clients not privy to this lexicon. The problem is further compounded by the fact that the same words sometimes appear in the vocabularies of both, but with different meanings. Tiersma (2006) gave examples of everyday words such as 'burglary' and 'mayhem' that have somewhat different and much more precise legal interpretations as well as common meanings. He stressed the importance of explaining to jurors the precise legal meanings of such terms. Similarly, in medicine there is evidence that terms such as 'risk factor' are not particularly well understood by patients (Turton, 1998). In their analysis of how quantitative risk information (e.g. percentage chance of contracting a flu bug) can most effectively be explained to the public, Skubisz *et al.* (2009) emphasised that communicators should avoid jargon, and recommended that they should not only explain exactly what a term means but also explicitly state what it does not mean.

Of course, it is sometimes difficult for professionals to eliminate completely all technical terms, and to do so may indeed even jeopardise the client's full grasp of issues. It is how these terms are introduced that counts. Possibilities noted by Hopper *et al.* (1992), in an interesting study of naturally occurring telephone conversations to do with medical advice, included: giving a term and (as an aside) asking about the caller's familiarity with it; giving a paraphrase with the term; observing the caller's problems with terminology used and following up with a brief explanation; and applying a term to a condition that the caller described.

Language also reflects the culture of the people who use it. Differences are not only a matter of foreign word usage. Communication styles may additionally be at odds in levels of formality, precision and directness. An emphasis on maintaining harmony and not causing offence sometimes means that members of high-context cultures, such as Koreans, use elaborate forms of circumlocution in conflict situations to avoid responding with a direct refusal; to say 'no' could compromise the other's *kibun*, or sense of personal harmony, and threaten their face (Adler and Elmhorst, 2008).

Reducing vagueness

An explanation characterised by vague, indeterminate words and expressions will be less successful than one that employs precise terms to present specific information. With particular reference to good practices when nurses communicate with their patients and health colleagues, Balzer Riley (2008: 147) pointed out that 'being specific means being detailed and clear in the content of our speech. It means being concrete, so that our communication is focused and logical.' Language, though, is inherently ambiguous and prone to confusion. In a famous 1952 trial in England, 19-year-old Derek Bentley was sentenced to be hanged for the murder of a police officer, although the shooting was carried out by his accomplice, the 16-year-old Christopher Craig. Since the latter was a minor he could not be sentenced to death. The verdict, still controversial, depended upon the interpretation of Bentley's alleged directive that night to his partner when they were confronted by the police officer – 'Let him have it, Chris.' The prosecution's position was that Bentley had told his accomplice to shoot: the defence argued that Bentley was in fact telling him to hand over the gun.

This 'slipperiness' of language is captured in the well-known communication euphemism that 'Meanings are in people not in words.' Holli *et al.* (2008) ventured that much of the misunderstandings and breakdowns that plague communication can be laid at this particular door. In English even simple words can have multiple interpretations; 'fast' has some 15 dictionary definitions. For some patients, being told that an event is 'likely' may be translated by them numerically as a one in ten probability, for others, one in two (Edwards *et al.*, 2002). But confusions and imprecision creep into other languages as well, sometimes with disastrous consequences. Strong (2005) related how confusion over the Japanese word *mokusatsu* may have led to the atomic bomb attacks on Hiroshima and Nagasaki in 1945. The word was used by Prime Minister Suzuki to describe cabinet policy on the Potsdam Declaration that would have brought war to an end. *Mokusatsu* can mean either to ignore or to keep silent on something. Suzuki had the latter in mind. The cabinet was withholding comment, given their difficulties in breaking the news of surrender to the Japanese people. The Allied nations interpreted the broadcasted message as the Declaration being ignored by the Japanese, hence precipitating the attack on Hiroshima some eight days later.

Not all imprecision can be totally eliminated from verbal explanations on every occasion. Most people will have experienced a situation when they have groped to find the exact term, and failing to find it, have substituted a less precise, more general alternative. However, attempts should be made to remove vagueness if the goal is to promote understanding. Problematic words and phrases have been noted (Gage *et al.*, 1968; Miltz, 1972; Bradbury, 2006) and are listed in Box 8.6. Well-established findings

---

Box 8.6 Being precise about vagueness

The following are common forms of vagueness in an explanation:

- ***ambiguous designation*** – e.g. 'type of thing', 'all of this', 'sort of stuff'
- ***undefined comparisons*** – e.g. 'Our figures show a marked increase.'
- ***negative intensifiers*** – e.g. 'was not too', 'was not hardly', 'was not quite', 'not infrequently'
- ***approximation*** – e.g. 'about as much as', 'almost every', 'nearly'
- ***bluffing and recovery*** – e.g. 'they say that', 'and so on', 'to cut a long story short'
- ***indeterminate numbers*** – e.g. 'a couple of', 'a fair number', 'some'
- ***groups of items*** – e.g. 'kinds', 'aspects', 'factors', 'things'
- ***possibility and probability*** – e.g. 'are not necessarily', 'it could be that', 'probably'
- ***unattributed sources*** – 'There are findings to confirm that the product works.'

---

by Hiller *et al.* (1969: 674) into teachers' explanations revealed that 'the greater the number of words and phrases expressing haziness, qualification and ambiguity ("some", "things", "a couple", "not necessarily", "kind of") the less clear the communication'. From a sample of 84 undergraduate student lessons, Land (1984) found that students could accurately distinguish teacher clarity on the basis of presence or absence of vague terms. In particular, he noted that high-clarity lessons were significantly related to high student ratings on achievement tests along with high student ratings of perception of clarity.

Providing emphasis

Another telling feature when attempting to explain effectively is the need to provide emphasis. This helps to make prominent the key points and crucial features of content. By providing points of emphasis the speaker can direct the listener's attention to the most important or essential information in the presentation, while 'playing down' the inessential parts. Emphasis can be grouped into two categories, nonverbal and verbal.

Nonverbal emphasis

Effective public speakers, politicians and television presenters versed in the skills of oratory use purposeful variation in their voices to alert their audiences' attention to key issues. As well as the voice, skilful speakers also employ appropriate speech-related gestures and movements to underline key features of their explanations (Tierney, 1996). In particular, varied movements of the eyes, head, face, fingers, hands and whole body are used purposefully and in a focused manner to suit the information being stressed.

Verbal emphasis

Speakers employ three main verbal techniques to achieve emphasis: verbal cueing, mnemonics and planned repetition.

Verbal cueing

This occurs when an individual employs specific verbal 'markers' to preface that part of the message to which attention is drawn. These verbal markers can be individual words such as 'first, second, third', 'important', 'finally', 'major', 'fundamental', or phrases such as 'listen carefully', 'the important point to remember is', 'take time before you answer this question'. Verbal cueing helps to differentiate between the relevant and the irrelevant, the more important and the less important and the specific detail from the general background information.

Mnemonics

Perhaps not so common as verbal cueing but in a sense equally effective in acting as an aide-memoire to the listener is the use of a mnemonic. As pointed out in the previous chapter, these are useful devices to facilitate understanding. An example might take advantage of the fact that key words essential to the explanation all begin with the same letter of the alphabet, making it is easy to recall them when needed. One example is the '5-Ps' of the explaining process used in this chapter. An *acronym*, where the first letter of each point combines to make a word, can also be highly memorable; for example FARM-B for the five classes of vertebrate animals – *f*ish, *a*mphibian, *r*eptile, *m*ammal, *b*ird. Much more elaborate systems to accomplish prodigious feats of memory, such as memorising entire packs of playing cards, have been described by the illusionist Derren Brown (2007).

Planned repetition

A third technique is that of planned repetition of selected points during the presentation. Repetition enables the recipient to experience a 'feeling of familiarity' with the material, which in turns facilitates cognitive processing (this aspect of repetition is further discussed in Chapter 12). This is especially useful if a great deal of new or unfamiliar material is being explained. Ley (1988), from a research review of patient compliance with doctors' prescriptions, suggested that one major way a doctor can increase patient compliance is to repeat the important points of the instructions. Structured summaries judiciously placed at various points throughout a lengthy explanation appear to be beneficial to the recipient.

Aids to explanation

Where possible, the speaker should plan to include some kind of aid to improve the quality of an explanation. Most presentations benefit from aids in one form or other to visually support what is said. They can be an immensely powerful tool for helping to get the message across in an illuminating and attractive manner. The old adage often holds true that 'A picture is worth a thousand words.' Aids can range from physical objects and models to pictures, tables, charts, graphs and diagrams shown either via video, overhead projector, film, flipchart, or computer mediated. People assimilate information using different sensory channels. Some favour looking rather than listening and are particularly likely to appreciate the benefits of a multimedia approach. Visual representations can, therefore, support the spoken word and, by introducing greater variety, make for a more attractive experience for the group.

The advantages of presenters using visual aids include being perceived more favourably by their audiences, taking less time to present concepts, and producing greater retention of what is learned (Moody *et al.*, 2002; O'Hair *et al.*, 2007). Likewise, Downing and Garmon (2002) reviewed evidence attesting to the beneficial effects of technology-based presentations on ease of note-taking and grasping the organisation of content material. Visual images also tend to 'stick' in the mind. Bradbury (2006) estimated that audiences may remember as little as 10 per cent of a verbal presentation after three days, but as much as 66 per cent over the same timespan when the material is delivered in a mixed verbal/visual format. Additional benefits of visual material, identified by Pathak (2001), include:

- gaining and directing attention to key points
- providing a veridical representation of that being explained
- helping to organise material provided in text by contributing a visual framework displaying interrelationships, etc.
- offering an interpretation by illuminating the meaning of dense text
- compensating for limited reading skills.

Computer software packages have now become a popular medium for delivering an attractive message with impact. Perhaps the golden rule when making out such software-based presentations is to avoid the 'all bells-and-whistles' trap. In the hands of the overzealous, the huge range of options available for colour, design, font type and size, pictures, cartoons, animation and sound effects can quickly lead to a visual spectacular in which the core message gets lost amid the special effects, so that the presenter (and the core message) ends up sidelined. One study of the university sector found that a common failing is that lecturers whizz through far too many PowerPoint slides too rapidly with the result that students soon become disengaged, bored and switched off (Mann and Robinson, 2009). Another important facet here is that for aids to be effective they must be shared. Increasingly, explanations are mediated e.g. through telephone or computer helplines. Jucks *et al.* (2007) found that when the explainer has access to computer representations (such as graphics images and diagrams) relating to the topic being explained, but these are not available to the person making the enquiry, the quality of the explanation is impaired. In preparing visual aids, advice proffered (e.g. Hargie *et al.*, 2004; Beaver, 2007; Hamilton, 2008) includes avoiding:

- having too many
- cluttering slides with too much information – a general rule is no more than six lines of text per slide
- using long sentences rather than pithy phrases – a general rule is no more than six words per line
- employing a font size that is too small, or that is difficult to read (e.g. Song and Schwarz, 2010, found that the Arial font was easy to read and facilitated assimilation of material as compared to a more difficult-to-read font such as Mistral)
- including colour on an arbitrary basis, or hues that are difficult to distinguish at a distance
- letting the technology take over – remember these are just aids.

Aids may also facilitate the retrieval of information from memory. According to the *dual-coding hypothesis* (Paivio, 1971; Liaw, 2004), audiovisual information is coded in memory in two different but related ways – verbally and visually. Textual messages are only coded verbally. Support for this hypothesis was documented by Walma van der Molen and van der Voort (2000) in an investigation where children (a) watched news stories on television; (b) read a print version; (c) read a print version together with photographs; or (d) listened to an audio version. The television-mediated material was remembered most successfully. Further support for integrating text and diagrams is available from a series of experiments designed to examine the consequences of combining these two formats in an instructional package on the learning outcome of students (Chandler and Sweller, 1992). These researchers found that when mental integration between diagrams and text is essential in order to make sense of the material, then integrated formats should be adopted.

Verbal examples

The simplest aid to use in an explanation is the verbal example, analogy or case study. Like a bridge, a carefully selected example should span the space between what the listeners already know and what they are about to learn. To work, it must have a firm foundation in the experiences that the listener brings to the situation. It is usually best to provide more than one example at a time to clarify a point, or provide proof (Hamilton, 2008). By so doing, the chances are reduced of coincidentally creating strong semantic links between non-essential elements of the example and the concept under focus (Rowan, 2003). Concrete everyday scenarios make the subject 'come alive' for the listener. Rosenshine (1971) illustrated how explanations were more effective when a piece of information, principle or concept was followed by an example or examples, leading to a restatement of the initial detail. Thus, a concept should be introduced as follows:

Statement → Example → Statement

A nurse might say, 'Your blood pressure is the pressure of the blood against your artery walls as it flows. Anything that prevents that flow will increase the pressure [statement]. Think of turning on the garden hose and holding your thumb over the end. You could check the build-up of pressure by trying to press the hose in the middle [example]. In the same way the pressure of your blood is increased when a narrowing in the artery hinders the flow [statement].'

However, Brown and Armstrong (1989), in an analysis of 48 video-recorded and transcribed lessons, found that the rule/example/rule model was more appropriate to interpretive explanations of unfamiliar topics than for other types of explanation aiming at restructuring ideas. This suggests that the pattern of examples should be related both to the type of explanation given and to the listeners' previous knowledge.

Conclusion

Conclusions are opportunities to draw together the various strands of the explanation in a neat summary statement. This may be particularly important when the material has been gone through on a point-by-point basis, so ensuring that the links binding the various subelements are firmly in place and a successful synthesis is achieved.

On occasion, however, it may be appropriate to leave a 'loose thread' – perhaps an unanswered question, or some seeming inconsistency. This can motivate the group to continue reflecting on the issue, and can serve as a useful lead-in if it is intended to continue with the explanation at a later date. Widener (2005) also drew attention to opportunities when closing to add impact to what was related during the presentation and leave the audience with a lasting impression of its content (see Chapter 10 for further information on closure).

Managing anxiety

So far the discussion about explaining has concentrated upon the more cognitive/rational aspects of the task. But there is also a crucial visceral/emotional dimension that should not be ignored, especially when delivering formal presentations to large audiences. The fear of speaking in public, or *glossophobia*, is widespread. Public speaking anxiety (PSA) occurs when 'individuals experience physiological arousal (e.g. increased heart rate), negative self-focused cognitions (e.g. "I'm concerned I'll appear incompetent."), and/or behavioral concomitants (e.g., trembling) in response to an expected or actual presentation' (Bodie, 2010: 71). Surveys of the general population have consistently found that fear of public speaking ranks high in the list of most nerve-racking activities (Beagrie, 2007), being described by Beaver (2005) as one of the most prevalent of all fears. The phenomenon of *speech apprehension* (Gamble and Gamble, 2008) is a particular manifestation of a more general unease in relating to others, termed *communication apprehension* (Daly *et al.*, 1997). Such apprehension about speaking in public can be dysfunctional if not properly managed (Horwitz, 2001). In his review of research, Bodie (2010) identified the type of response patterns associated with PSA, the instruments available to measure these, and the effectiveness of the various types of intervention that have been employed to help remediate this problem.

While inability to handle dysfunctional anxiety can present difficulties, the point also needs to be made that experiencing some level of stress when about to present is neither abnormal nor dysfunctional and is familiar to even the most experienced speakers. Indeed it is often even desirable. Without it we probably would not be sufficiently on our toes to give of our best. Keeping stress positive and within constructive boundaries is what matters. PSA has four interwoven components (Monarth and Kase, 2007). These involve:

- *physiology* – increased blood pressure and heart rate, rapid breathing, trembling, feeling weak, sweating, etc.
- *mood* – feeling nervous, depressed, agitated, panicky, etc.
- *cognitions* – convincing yourself in advance that you can't do it, that it will go horribly wrong, that if you make the slightest slip it will be a disaster, etc.
- *behaviour* – avoiding presentations if possible, displaying nervous mannerisms, overcompensating by perhaps trying to memorise the speech thus eliminating all spontaneity, etc.

Steps to manage such dysfunctional affect include:

- ***Finding out how to present effectively and becoming more skilled at it.*** Often fear is a consequence of knowing or suspecting that you have not the resources to deliver a competent performance. The confidence that comes from planning and being well prepared also helps.
- ***Learning to relax.*** Anxiety is often learnt. This may be from being 'spooked' by listening to others or perhaps, as children, sensing their unease about speaking in public; watching others' faltering attempts; or giving a presentation that went horribly wrong and being humiliated in this way, so that a lot of trepidation and little self-confidence has formed around this activity. But relaxing can likewise be learned. It is always good advice that when preparing for a tense situation you should avoid those who might heighten your level of tension – panic can be very infectious. Rather, seek out more relaxed company.
- ***Desisting from talking yourself down.*** Often those who are cruelly tormented at the thought of having to talk in public engage in negative self-statements such as: 'I'll never be able to do this. I'll make a complete fool of myself. They will see right through me, and think that I'm stupid. I'll dry up in the middle of it. My mind will go blank. I'll never be able to face them again', and so forth. In other words, these people convincingly 'talk' themselves into believing that they are going to do poorly, and then get extremely agitated at the prospect. This serves to make them even more certain that failure is inevitable: and in truth under these circumstances a self-fulfilling prophecy comes into play, and so failure probably results. Negative ruminations should be replaced with constructive alternatives (McCarthy and Hatcher, 2002). Positive self-statements should be employed such as: 'I'm very well prepared for this talk. I have good visual aids that they will enjoy. I have answers to questions I may be asked. I'm looking forward to it.'

POSTMORTEM

So the explanation has been given, but the task is not yet over. Evaluating the outcome is indispensable. Taking pains to assess learning and doing so in a systematic way is a crucial part of the instructional process. Understanding can never be taken for granted, although in their study of health professionals, Baker *et al.* (2007) found that few actually took pains to check patients' understanding of what had been explained. The explainer must reflect upon what took place and evaluate to what extent the identified objectives were successfully achieved. If necessary, and as represented in Figure 8.1, the material may have to be gone over again once some thought has been given to what went wrong and why.

Obtaining feedback from the audience is important in checking both levels of understanding and, by association, the adequacy of the explanation (Dickson *et al.*, 1997). Completeness of feedback was shown by Schroth (1992) to significantly affect the speed at which complex concepts were initially acquired. Subjects who were given verbal feedback after each response, irrespective of whether the response was correct or incorrect, did better than subjects receiving feedback only after correct responses or those receiving feedback only after incorrect responses.

There are four main ways to check the efficacy of an explanation:

1   Note the nonverbal behaviour of the listener or listeners, since this is a rich source of evidence. Experienced and successful presenters constantly scan the faces and movements of explainees, both during and after the explanation, to detect signs of puzzlement, confusion or disinterest. However, since individuals vary in the amount and kind of behaviour they overtly display it is not always easy, or even possible, to deduce the efficacy of explanations by nonverbal means alone. Furthermore, some listeners may show nonverbal signs of attention and understanding out of politeness or not wanting to appear stupid, although they do not actually understand what is being said.

2   Another method of obtaining knowledge of comprehension is to ask a series of related questions. In the study by Baker *et al.* (2007), those health professionals who failed to check patient understanding through asking questions gave as a reason a lack of confidence in their ability to do so. They also reported failing to be convinced that using questions in this way was indeed an effective technique for improving patient understanding.

3   Alternatively, feedback can be gleaned by inviting listeners to ask questions on any aspect of an explanation they feel requires further clarification. This would appear to be more valid in terms of 'real' problems encountered by listeners, yet there is a danger that they may not respond for fear of seeming obtuse. In addition, where there is a status difference people are reluctant to ask questions of those of a higher status (see Chapter 5).

4   It is also possible to ask the listener to summarise what has been heard. Although this is often an effective technique with pupils in school it can sometimes be less so in situations with adults where an impression of 'being tested' would be inappropriate. This possible interpretation can be overcome by phrasing the request so it seems that the speaker is accepting responsibility for any failure (e.g. 'I'm not sure how well I have explained that, would you tell me what you understand from it?').

At a broader level, and taking feedback into account, there is advantage in adopting a reflective approach to presentations (Burton and Dimbleby, 2006). This involves setting time aside to think back over what parts went well or not so well, together with trying to pinpoint reasons for successes and failures. Why was the audience still confused and unsure at the end? How could this be improved upon next time? Are there general lessons to be learned about explaining this type of material to this type of audience? It is only by adopting this approach that ongoing improvement will be brought about.

DEMONSTRATIONS

Illustrations make use of the sorts of audiovisual aids already mentioned to supplement speech. Demonstrations go further. Here an activity or process is explained by being carried out. This is explaining through doing. When the material is of a practical nature (e.g. a new skill or technique) and the learning objective is behavioural or performative (i.e. the audience being able to carry out the skill or technique), then this form of explanation is often called for. If a picture is worth a thousand words, then a demonstration is worth a thousand pictures. 'Hear one, see one, do one' has a long tradition in medical training. The medical student is told about a procedure, sees it carried out and is then expected to attempt it.

If an explanation does require a demonstration there are several specific points that should be borne in mind in order to achieve effective results. They can be examined under three familiar headings: planning and preparation, presenting, and obtaining feedback.

Planning and preparation

First, before proceeding with the demonstration, it is important to check that all items of equipment needed are prepared and available for use. In addition, the chief steps involved in the demonstration should be listed in the sequence in which they are to be presented.

Presenting

Having devised the procedures to be used in the demonstration the next step is to present it in action. Initially, observers must be alerted to the purpose of the demonstration and what they will be expected to accomplish once it has been completed. When the viewers are prepared for the demonstration they should be guided step by step through the action with accompanying verbal descriptions of the essential features at each stage of the process (e.g. 'The first point to remember is keep your feet shoulder-width apart.'). In addition, the linkage between one step and the next should be clearly illustrated so that observers can see how each step fits into the overall action. Depending upon the complexity of the demonstration, it can be worked through completely, followed by a repeat performance emphasising the vital features at each stage. If, however, the skill or technique being explained is more complicated, the complete action can be broken down into coherent segments, which the observer can practise in parts.

Obtaining feedback

Finally, it is important to assess whether or not the demonstration has been enacted effectively. Feedback can be obtained by a number of methods:

- having the observer or observers repeat the demonstration
- repeating the demonstration slowly but requesting the onlookers to give the appropriate directions at each stage
- requesting viewers to verbalise the salient features of the demonstration following the initial enactment.

OVERVIEW

This chapter has explored the nature, functions and techniques of explaining in a variety of professional and social contexts. Explaining is an attempt to create understanding, thus going beyond the mere giving of information. Different types of explanation were identified including those that reveal causes, reasons, justifications and motives underlying the problem or event being analysed. While the bulk of research into the skill of explaining has its roots in educational settings it is by no means the sole prerogative of that profession. Other professions, both on a group or one-to-one basis, are also involved in providing relevant and interesting explanations for their consumers or colleagues. For example, the role and effectiveness of explanation has attracted considerable interest in health care and in legal settings. Likewise, the scientific community has begun to embark on the daunting quest of making knowledge of scientific advances accessible to a wider audience, with eminent UK scientists playing prominent roles. Stilgoe (2008) argued that upcoming scientific advances in contentious areas such as stem cell research, genetically modified food and human enhancement will require a better-informed public to become more fully engaged with the social and ethical concerns entailed.

The explaining process can be analysed using the 5-Ps model of pre-assessment, planning, preparation, presentation and postmortem. Studies have uncovered that well-planned or structured explanations result in greater understanding, that clear, unambiguous explanations are highly valued by listeners and that summaries or feedback checks are effective in aiding retention. In conclusion, it should be remembered that the success of an explanation is measured not by the amount of detail conveyed but by the degree of understanding demonstrated by the listener. As such, the activity must be built around the particular needs, capacities and resources of the audience.

Chapter 9

Telling others about yourself: the skill of self-disclosure

INTRODUCTION

T HE TERM SELF-DISCLOSURE is an amalgam of two elements. First, there is the intriguing entity of the 'self' and what exactly this comprises. Second, there is the process of 'disclosure' whereby the individual opens up some aspect of self to others. This chapter will examine both of these concepts, but with the main focus upon the latter. However, before exploring the fascinating world of how, what, when and why people disclose information about themselves, let us begin by examining the notion of self.

One major difference between Homo sapiens and other species is that humans possess a complex sense of self (Tracy and Robins, 2007). Not surprisingly, therefore, investigations of the self are as old as social science. Well over a century ago the psychologist James (1890, 1892), in attempting to map the terrain, made a distinction between two types of self:

1 the 'I' self, which he saw as a knowing self in that it generates all of the knowledge we have of ourselves
2 the 'me' self, which he viewed as being composed of three dimensions:

   * a material self, relating to our evaluations of our physical bodies and possessions (home, car, etc.)
   * a social self, concerned with how we see ourselves relating to and with others

- a spiritual self, which is comprised of our ideas, thoughts, values and beliefs.

More recently, the concept of self has attracted an enormous amount of attention. Different conceptualisations have been put forward as to what exactly constitute its main components (see Box 9.1). However, as MacDonald (2007) illustrated, agreement on the definition of 'self' has proven difficult. It takes many forms and can be analysed from myriad perspectives (Sedikides and Spencer, 2007). As an illustration of this, one conceptualisation of the different sides to self is presented in Figure 9.1.

Early notions about the existence of a self-contained, individual, unitary or

---

Box 9.1 Dimensions of self: two examples

1 ***Reflexive consciousness*** – the ability to think introspectively about who we are.
2 ***Interpersonal being*** – the self as it relates to and with other people.
3 ***Executive function*** – how the self makes plans and behaves in such a way as to attempt to exert control over the outside world.

(Adapted from Beaumeister, 1999)

1 ***Personal self*** – you as a unique individual, your ideas, emotions, values, beliefs, etc.
2 ***Social self*** – your social roles and how you 'fit' with others.
3 ***Cultural self*** – your identification with ethnic, religious, gender, social class or other grouping.

(Adapted from Stewart and Logan, 1998)

Me as:	Type of self:
I really am	True self
I would really like to be	Ideal self
I want others to think I am	Social self
I used to be	Past self
A new person	Reconstructed self
I should be	Ought self
I hope to become	Expected self
I am afraid of becoming	Feared self
I could have been	Missed self
Unwanted by one or more others	Rejected self

Figure 9.1 Types of self

'sovereign self' that reveals or leaks information about 'inner reality' through disclosure have been replaced by the concept of a social or dialogic self. While activity in certain regions of the brain has been associated with the functioning of the self (Heatherton *et al.*, 2007), it is the case that, as summarised by Carmichael *et al.* (2007: 285), 'the self is inextricably relational ... no satisfactory understanding of the self is possible without considering the social influences on, and interpersonal functions of, the self'. How we present our self is adaptable and varies from situation to situation in that 'the self is a dynamic entity that displays some flexibility in its interplay with the environment, notably by its capacity to change, to adapt to various situations, and to integrate new components' (Amiot *et al.*, 2007: 204). Indeed, some would argue that what we present is a 'reflected self' which is shaped by others, so that eventually we come to see ourselves as we think others see us (Tice and Wallace, 2005). In this way, self is constructed and reconstructed through interaction; it is 'fluid and emergent, characterised by fragmentation and multiplicity. Self cannot be separated from other; rather, other helps to construct self in an ongoing dialogue' (Baxter and Sahlstein, 2000: 293).

Thus, self can be thought of as a social construction and self-disclosure is a process between individuals in which selves are shared, shaped, negotiated and altered. In this way, identity is formed by a combination of how we see ourselves and by how others see us (Woodward, 2000). For example, when two people get married they do not have given roles to guide their behaviour as wife or husband. Rather, these are formulated, developed, adjusted and agreed, both as a result of interactions within marriage and following consultations with significant others.

Recent perspectives conceptualise the self as being composed of a number of context-dependent self-aspects (e.g. husband, mother, student, manager, church treasurer, golf club member), any of which may be activated by the social situation (McConnell and Strain, 2007). There is a considerable volume of research to show that people who play a large number of roles enjoy many benefits compared to those with only a few defining identities. The 'role-rich' cope more readily with change and stress, have better physical health and are more satisfied with their lot in life than the 'role-poor' (McKenna and Bargh, 2000). Given that the self is social, others (family, friends, work colleagues and so on) are almost always involved or in some way affected by our disclosures (Aron *et al.*, 2004). In this sense, information is often co-owned by a relevant circle of people, who need to be considered before it is revealed (Petronio, 2002). One example of this occurs following marriage when newly-weds have to take cognisance of the expectations of their in-laws, including rules to do with information sharing, family secrets and appropriate disclosure. In this instance, research shows that disclosure of the family's private information to the new in-law serves to signify that this person is accepted as a family member (Serewicz and Canary, 2008). Disclosure from in-laws has also been shown to be related to marital harmony (Serewicz *et al.*, 2008).

There are also inner tensions between what Rosenfeld (2000) termed 'integration versus separation' and 'expression versus privacy', in that part of us wants to engage fully with others and another part wishes to hold something back. Thus, there is a need to strike a balance between 'revealing and concealing' (Buslig and Burgoon, 2000). We like to have a group identity but at the same time have private aspects of ourselves that we keep from others. There is a unique essence to each person, such that 'the inner self may well be shaped by social communication, but the self is far from a passive acceptance of feedback. Instead, the self actively processes and selects (and sometimes distorts) information from the social world' (Beaumeister, 1999: 10). Furthermore, the notion of 'place identity' is also important. As Dixon and Durrheim (2004) point out, the term place identity 'denotes how individuals' sense of self arises in part through their transactions with material environments' (p. 457) in such a way that 'material environments not only underpin but also become *part of* the self' (p. 458). We use a variety of terms to express place identity, such as feeling 'out of place' or 'at home'. Place identity involves having a sense of 'insideness' (see Box 9.2).

A great deal of social interaction consists of participants making statements, or disclosures, about a wide variety of issues. These disclosures may be either objective statements about other people, places or events, or subjective disclosures about the self. This latter type of statement, whereby the speaker reveals some personal information to others, is referred to as self-disclosure. Self-disclosure is the cement that binds the parts together in the structure of interpersonal relationships (Guerrero *et al.*, 2007). Without disclosure, the whole relational edifice will collapse (Brehm *et al.*, 2006), and so knowledge of this field is of key importance for effective interpersonal functioning.

WHAT IS SELF-DISCLOSURE?

There is disagreement about the exact meaning of the term. Some definitions restrict the field of study to verbal disclosures only. Here, self-disclosure is defined as 'what individuals verbally reveal about themselves (including thoughts, feelings, and experiences) to others' (Dindia, 2000a: 148). A similar definition was proffered by Rosenfeld (2000), who added the further stipulation that the disclosure must be made to another person (and not one's self, or a pet, etc.): 'For a communicative act to be considered self-disclosing, it must contain personal information about the sender, the sender must communicate this information verbally, and another person must be the target' (p. 6). Some go even further to restrict the sphere of study to deeper levels of disclosure in terms of 'the revealing of intimate information about the self in conversation' (Cooks, 2000: 199).

Hoffman's definition (1995: 238) highlighted the issues of veracity and accessibility: 'the revelation of information about the self that is verbally delivered, truthful, significantly revealing, and difficult or impossible to attain through other means'. Others underscore the importance of intentionality on the part of the discloser, so that Greene *et al.* (2006: 411) defined self-disclosure as occurring when 'one intends to deliberately divulge something personal to another'. Indeed, Fisher (1984) argued that information disclosed unintentionally, or by mistake, is a *self-revelation* rather than

---

Box 9.2 Three 'sides' to place identity

1 *Physical insideness.* Knowing one's way around and being familiar with the physical details of one's environment. Having a sense of personal 'territory'.
2 *Social insideness.* Feeling a sense of being connected to and part of a place. Knowing other people and being known and accepted by them.
3 *Autobiographical insideness.* The idiosyncratic sense of 'having roots' to a place. Knowing 'where you come from' and 'who you are'.

---

a self-disclosure. Mader and Mader (1990: 210) further emphasised the aspect of relational consequences: 'You self-disclose when you (1) intentionally give another person information about yourself (2) that the other person is not likely to get on his own and (3) that you realize could significantly affect your relationship to this person.' Pearson and Spitzberg (1987: 142) limited the scope even further by defining self-disclosure as 'communication in which a person voluntarily and intentionally tells another person accurate information about himself or herself', thereby excluding disclosures made under any form of threat.

But these definitions tend to exclude the study of nonverbal self-disclosures, which can be an important channel for communicating personal information – especially about feelings and emotions. In this chapter a wider perspective is held and self-disclosure is defined as the process whereby person A verbally and/or nonverbally communicates to person B some item of personal information that was previously unknown to B. In this sense, telling a close friend your name would not be a self-disclosure since this information would already be known, whereas telling a complete stranger your name would be a self-disclosure. Likewise, nonverbal disclosures, whether intentional or not, are included since these are the main means whereby we provide information about our emotional state (see Chapter 3). One important difference between verbal and nonverbal self-disclosure is that we have greater control over the former than the latter.

The recognition of self-disclosure as a central interpersonal skill began with the pioneering work of Sidney Jourard (1964, 1971), who stressed the need for a high degree of openness between individuals in many contexts, and illustrated the potency of self-disclosure as a technique for encouraging deep levels of interpersonal sharing. Since that time, an enormous amount of interest has been generated, to the point where 'self-disclosure is one of the most researched topics of the past three decades in the fields of interpersonal communication, social psychology, and social and personal relationships' (Baxter and Sahlstein, 2000: 289). Indeed, as Tardy and Dindia, 2006: 229) state: 'The pervasiveness and importance of self-disclosure accounts for the intense interest in this phenomenon shown by social scientists. Literally thousands of quantitative studies have been conducted over a period extending forty years.'

Self-disclosure has been analysed and measured in various ways. Thus, McKay *et al.* (2009) identified four main disclosure categories:

1   ***Observations.*** Reporting what you have done or experienced: 'I graduated in 2004.'
2   ***Thoughts.*** These go beyond simple observations to reveal judgements about what has been experienced: 'If I had it to do again I would take the opportunity to study abroad as part of my degree.'
3   ***Feelings.*** The expression of affect: 'I really loved university – it was probably the happiest period of my life.'
4   ***Needs.*** Here the focus is upon needs and wants: 'I miss the challenges of academic life and feel that I want to take a postgraduate course now.'

Furthermore, there is a large number of pen-and-paper inventories designed to measure different aspects of self-disclosure, including:

- as a personality factor (Derlega and Chaikin, 1975)
- as varying across specific situations (Chelune, 1976)
- as a function of the target person (Miller *et al.*, 1983)
- specifically within feminist therapy (Simi and Mahalik, 1997)
- between spouses within marriage (Waring *et al.*, 1998).

An awareness of the nuances of self-disclosure is important in professional communication, for two main reasons. First, it is vital to be aware of contexts in which it is appropriate to self-disclose to clients. Second, professionals need to be aware of the benefits that accrue from and the methods whereby they can encourage, full, open and honest self-disclosures from clients.

FEATURES OF SELF-DISCLOSURE

There are four key features of self-disclosure: use of personal pronoun; self-disclosure can be about facts or feelings; the object of the disclosure can be about self or other; and disclosures can be about past, present or future events.

Use of personal pronoun

Verbal self-disclosures involve the use of the personal pronoun 'I', or some other personal self-reference pronoun such as 'my' or 'mine'. While these words may be implied from the context of the speaker's utterances, their presence serves to remove any ambiguity about whether or not the statement being made is intrapersonal (relating to personal experiences). Compare, for example, the statements:

A: Selection interviews can create a great amount of stress.
B: I find selection interviews very stressful.

In A it is not immediately clear whether the speaker is referring to selection interviews in general or to personal feelings about attending selection interviews. The use of the personal pronoun 'I' in B, however, serves to clarify the nature of the statement as a self-disclosure. A personal self-reference pronoun is often the criterion used in research investigations as evidence of disclosure (Harper and Harper, 2006). This is one of the following three methods used to measure the phenomenon:

1   observer or recipient estimates of disclosure
2   self-report measures such as inventories, self-ratings or sentence completion tasks
3   objective counts of actual disclosures made during interaction.

One problem is that different research investigations use a range of measures, some tailored specifically for a particular investigation. Some investigations focus on one dimension of disclosure while others examine several aspects. This makes gener-alisations across studies very difficult (Omarzu, 2000). Even studies that use the 'objective' approach may not be directly comparable owing to differing definitions about what exactly constitutes a self-disclosure. While the counting of self-reference pronouns is one measurement criterion, another definition of self-disclosure used in research studies is 'a verbal response (thought unit) which describes the subject in some way, tells something about the subject, or refers to some affect the subject experiences' (Tardy, 1988: 331). This definition obviously requires detailed training on the part of observers to ensure accuracy and agreement about instances of disclosure. Such differences need to be borne in mind when evaluating research findings in this field. Furthermore, much research on self-disclosure has been conducted in the artificial 'laboratory' situation and the results of these studies need to be treated with caution, since the extent to which they generalise to real-life contexts is unclear.

Disclosures can involve facts or feelings

When two people meet for the first time, it is more likely that they will focus upon factual disclosures (name, occupation, place of residence) while keeping any feeling disclosures at a fairly superficial level ('I hate crowded parties', 'I like rock music'). This is largely because the expression of personal feelings involves greater risk and places the discloser in a more vulnerable position. At the same time, deep levels of disclosure may be made to a stranger providing we feel sure that we will never meet the person again, and that we do not have friends or acquaintances in common. This is discussed later in the chapter in the section on length and commitment of interaction.

A gradual progression from low to high levels of self-disclosure leads to better relationship development. The expression of deep feeling or of high levels of factual disclosure (e.g. 'I was in prison for five years.') increases as a relationship develops. For this reason, professionals should expect clients to experience difficulties in self-disclosing at any depth at the early stage of an encounter. Even if the client has a deep-rooted need to 'tell someone', such an experience is inevitably embarrassing, or at least awkward, where the disclosures relate to very personal details. The skilled helper will be aware of this and employ techniques that help the client to overcome such initial feelings.

Factual and feeling disclosures at a deeper level can be regarded as a sign of commitment to a relationship. Two people who are in love usually expect to give and receive disclosures about their feelings – especially towards one another (Kassin *et al.*, 2008). They also want to know everything about one another. In such a relationship there is a high level of trust, just as there is in the confession box, a doctor's surgery or a counsellor's office (areas where disclosures are also high). *Social penetration theory* (Altman and Taylor, 1973; Taylor and Altman, 1987) postulates that relationships progress through a number of stages:

*   *Orientation.* When people meet for the first time, shallow information about self is disclosed more readily than intimate details. For the relationship to develop, disclosures must be reciprocal. Some estimate will be made of the likely rewards and costs of pursuing the relationship, and for progression to occur the anticipated rewards must outweigh the costs.

- *Exploratory affective exchange.* More intimate details, especially at the feeling level, begin to be reciprocated.
- *Affective exchange.* High levels of disclosure are exchanged as people get to know one another in depth.
- *Stable exchange.* Once a relationship has been firmly established, it should be characterised by continuing openness.
- *Depenetration.* If a relationship begins to fail as the costs start to outweigh the benefits, there begins a gradual process of withdrawal of disclosure, leading to relational termination.

The object of the disclosure

A self-disclosure can be about one's own personal experience, or it can be about one's personal reaction to the experiences being related by another. Consider the following interaction:

> *John:*   I haven't been sleeping too well recently. I work from early morning until after midnight every day, and yet nothing seems to sink in. I'm really worried about these exams. What would I do if I failed them?
>
> *Mary:*   You know John, I am very concerned about you. It seems to me that you are working too much, and not getting enough rest.

This is an example of a self-disclosure as a personal reaction to the experiences of another person, since Mary expresses concern and gives an opinion about the statements made by John. This is sometimes referred to as a *self-involving* statement, as opposed to a disclosure about one self (Knox *et al.*, 1997). In the example given, Mary could have chosen to give a parallel self-disclosure about her own experience by saying something like 'I remember when I was sitting my final exams. I was worried about them too. What I did was to make sure I stopped working in time to get out of the house and meet other people. This took my mind off the exams.'

Both of these types of approach are appropriate in different contexts, depending upon the nature of the interaction taking place and the goals of the interactors. If the objective is to give concerted attention to an individual and encourage full disclosure, then concentrating upon one's reactions to the feelings or thoughts of the other person would be most appropriate. If, however, the intention is to demonstrate that the person's feelings are not unusual, then the use of a parallel self-disclosure relating one's own experience would be more apposite.

Self-disclosure can be about past, present or future events

Self-disclosure can be about the past ('I was born in 1990.', 'I was really grief-stricken when my father died.'), present ('I am a vegetarian.', 'I am very happy.') or future ('I hope to get promotion.', 'I want to get married and have a family.'). One situation in which people are expected to self-disclose in terms of facts and feelings about the past, present and future is in the selection interview. Candidates will be asked to talk about their previous experience or education, to say why they have applied for the job and to outline their aspirations. Not only are interviewees expected to give details about themselves, but they will also more often than not be expected to relate their attitudes and feelings towards their experiences.

ELEMENTS OF SELF-DISCLOSURE

There are several important elements of self-disclosure that need to be taken into consideration. These relate to valence, informativeness, appropriateness, flexibility, accessibility, honesty and disclosure avoidance.

Valence

This is the degree to which the disclosure is positive or negative for both discloser and listener. In the early stages of relationship development, disclosures are mainly positive, and negative self-disclosures usually only emerge once a relationship has been established. This is another reason why some clients find difficulty in disclosing negative information to an unfamiliar professional. Negative self-disclosures have been shown to be marked by paralinguistic cues such as stuttering, stammering, repetition, mumbling and low 'feeble' voice quality, whereas positive disclosures tend to be characterised by rapid, flowing, melodious speech (Bloch, 1996).

Lazowski and Andersen (1991) found that negative disclosures were regarded as having more informative power than positive ones. They postulated one reason for this finding as being that, since it is less acceptable for people to disclose negative information, such disclosures are likely to be more heartfelt and revealing. This is also true of positive and negative attributions, in that we only make a positive attribution about a person after repeated observations, whereas we readily ascribe negative evaluations after only a single instance (Fiedler, 2007). For example, we may say that someone is dishonest after witnessing one lie, but we only say they are honest when we have had considerable experience of their response patterns. In addition, what is known as the *Pollyanna principle* (Matlin and Stang, 1978) means that we tend to seek out positive rather than negative stimuli, and expect and report more positive than negative experiences. In like vein, we expect others to make positive self-disclosures and so we become more alert upon receiving a negative disclosure. This is because what is known as the *negativity effect* means that negative information is attributed as possessing greater relevance than positive information (Yoo, 2009). Thus, the comparative rarity of negative disclosures, and their greater inferential power, mean that we need to use them with caution.

Research evidence shows that negative disclosures can be disadvantageous. Lazowski and Andersen (1991) carried out a study in which they had university undergraduates watch videotapes of an individual self-disclosing to someone off-camera. They found that the use of negative disclosures (e.g. 'I felt like telling him that I practically hated him, that I disliked him more than anyone I'd met in a long time.'), when compared to positive disclosures (e.g. 'I felt like telling him that he was really a pretty nice guy.'), led both male and female viewers to like the male speaker significantly less and to expect to be less comfortable when interacting with him. In a later study, Yoo (2009) confirmed this finding that the use of negative disclosures tends to lead to more negative evaluations of the discloser. These differences were illustrated in a study by Miller *et al.* (1992), who contrasted the relative effects of negative, positive and bragging disclosures. The latter contained more superlatives (e.g. 'best' rather than 'good'); reference to doing better than others or having power over them; less emphasis on working hard and more on being a 'wonderful' person; and less credit given to group efforts and more to personal achievements. Examples of each of the three categories used in this study were as follows.

- *Positive*: 'I even got the most valuable player award. Boy, was I surprised . . . I was pleased to get the award and the recognition. I was glad to help my team finish the season so well.'
- *Negative*: 'I didn't play well this season. I was embarrassed . . . I tried to look like I was having fun but I kept thinking how lousy I played and that I shouldn't have come.'
- *Bragging*: 'I was the leading player all summer. Actually, I'm the best all-round player this league has ever seen. I could have my choice to play in any team I want next year.'

The results indicated that to be rated as competent and successful the use of bragging disclosures was a better strategy than negative disclosures, whereas the latter were seen as being more socially sensitive. However, the highest overall evaluations were given for positive disclosures, which were viewed as being both successful and socially sensitive. Thus, the optimum approach would seem to be a mid-point between being self-deprecating at one extreme and boastful at the other. Bragging about accomplishments as a disclosure strategy was not popular in one study of dating behaviour among undergraduates, where other tactics such as emotional disclosure (e.g. 'I care about you.') were regarded as more appropriate (Wildermuth *et al.*, 2007). But one context where self-promotion and a degree of bragging is the expected social norm is the employment interview. The rules of this form of interview are such that interviewers expect candidates to sell themselves in the best possible light. Here, two particular behaviours are commonly employed:

1 **Entitlements** refer to attempts to associate oneself with successful events or people (e.g. 'I was at EagleAir when we developed the breakthrough XJ521 jet fighter.', 'I took my degree at London when Eysenck was Head of Department.'). This indirect self-presentation technique, known as 'association' or 'basking in reflected glory', can influence the perceptions of others if used skilfully (Carter and Sanna, 2006). However, it tends to be used more by males than females (Guadagno and Cialdini, 2007).

2 **Enhancements** are attempts to augment or exaggerate the importance of one's achievements (e.g. 'My degree programme was one of the hardest to gain entry to.', 'The senior manager was off ill quite a lot and so in reality I ran the department.').

While the continuous and indiscriminant use of negative self-disclosure is dysfunctional, the judicious application of such disclosures can actually facilitate relational development. For example, disclosing negative emotions when one is in need of support (such as being nervous before giving a talk) can be perceived as the sharing of an important experience and a mark of friendship (Graham *et al.*, 2008). It can indicate that the discloser perceives the recipient as someone to be trusted not to take advantage of a revealed weakness. It also highlights the discloser's needs and enables the recipient to reciprocate by showing concern for these, thereby enhancing the relational bond. However, for this to be effective Graham *et al.* noted that negative emotions should be expressed to those with whom one has a relationship, the depth of disclosed emotional state should be concomitant with the level of friendship, and the intensity of the disclosure should reflect the degree of emotional need. Given these parameters, Graham *et al.* showed that the disclosure of appropriate negative emotions increased ratings of likability, elicited offers of help and increased the level of relational intimacy.

Another interesting dimension of valence relates to the phenomenon of gossip, which has attracted increasing research attention (Brennan, 2009). An important function of self-disclosure is to influence and guide how others talk and gossip about us. Thus, we are aware of the wider implications regarding the valence of our disclosures beyond the immediate encounter. Gossip also serves a social comparison function in that it enables us to 'gain information about the validity of our opinions and abilities by talking with or about similar others' (Wert and Salovey, 2004: 132). This aspect of social comparison will be discussed later in the chapter.

Informativeness

Here, self-disclosure is assessed along three main dimensions:

1 **Breadth** – the total number of disclosures used. This is measured by counts of self-reference pronouns or topics covered, or by self-report instruments.
2 **Depth** – the level of intimacy of the disclosure. In general, emotionally intense, negative or embarrassing information tends to be rated as higher in intimacy (Omarzu, 2000). Depth is measured either using self-report instruments, or by rating actual disclosures made for intimacy level.
3 **Duration** – this is measured either by the total amount of time the person spends disclosing, or by a word count of disclosing statements.

The Derlega and Chaikin Inventory (1975) was designed to measure breadth and depth of disclosures. Examples of shallow levels of disclosure given in this inventory include: 'How often my aunts and uncles and family get together', 'Whether or not I have ever gone to a church other than my own', and examples of deeper levels include 'How frequently I like to engage in sexual activity' and 'The kinds of things I do that I don't want people to watch'.

In the Lazowski and Andersen (1991) study mentioned earlier, it was found that disclosures about thoughts and feelings were viewed as deeper and more informative than those concerned with actions and they surmised that this is because 'it is access to otherwise hidden cognitions and affects that gives listeners the feeling that they have heard something significant about the speaker' (p. 146). One topic that has been found to be difficult for most people to discuss is that of death. For example, a survey carried out by the US National Hospice Foundation found that parents find it easier to talk to their children about sex than to talk to their own parents about dying with dignity (Levy, 1999).

Appropriateness

This is perhaps the most crucial aspect of self-disclosure. Each disclosure needs to be evaluated in the light of the context in which it occurs. While there are no hard-and-fast rules about the exact appropriateness of self-disclosure, there are some general indicators. Self-disclosures are more appropriate as follows:

- *From low-status to high-status individuals but not vice versa.* Where there is a high degree of asymmetry in status, disclosure tends to be in one direction (Bochner, 2000). Thus, workers may disclose personal problems to their supervisors, but the reverse does not usually happen. This is because for a supervisor to disclose personal information to a subordinate would cause a loss of face, which would affect the status relationship. Research findings tend to suggest that self-disclosures are most often employed between people of equal status (Tardy and Dindia, 2006). However, Phillips *et al.* (2009) demonstrated that people make decisions about whether or not to disclose certain information to either underline existing status differences or serve to reduce them. For example, a senior manager in a corporation may attempt to reduce status differentials by disclosing to a shop floor employee details of a low socioeconomic family background.
- *When the listener is not flooded with them.* There would seem to be a relationship between psychological adjustment and self-disclosure in that individuals who are extremely high or low disclosers are regarded as less socially skilled.
- *When they are compatible with the roles of the interactors.* We may disclose information to our spouses that we would not disclose to our children. Similarly, clients will often discuss a problem with a 'neutral' counsellor that they would not wish to discuss with their spouses or with close friends. Patients disclose answers to highly personal questions from doctors, such as 'Do you take drugs?' or 'How often do you have sexual intercourse?' that they would be unlikely to tolerate in other contexts. Nor would they expect the doctor to reciprocate with similar information.
- *When acceptable in the particular social context.* We would be unlikely to disclose during an intimate dinner on a first date that we are suffering from painful haemorrhoids, but we would do so in a doctor's surgery.

Flexibility

Self-disclosure flexibility refers to the ability of an individual to vary the breadth and depth of disclosures across situations. Highly flexible disclosers are able to modify the nature and level of their self-disclosures whereas less flexible disclosers tend to disclose at the same level regardless of context. Miller and Kenny (1986) illustrated how 'blabber-mouths' who disclose in an undifferentiated fashion are not the recipients of high levels of disclosure from others. Such individuals (also known as *talkaholics*) who have a tendency to communicate compulsively have been the subject of academic inquiry and scales have been designed to measure this characteristic (Long *et al.*, 2000).

Accessibility

This refers to the ease with which self-disclosures can be obtained from an individual. Some people disclose freely while others are much more reluctant to reveal personal information. This may be due to personality, upbringing and culture in that the child may have grown up in a context where the norm is not to disclose too much. It may also be caused by lack of learning about how and what to disclose during social encounters. Quite often clients disclose a 'presenting' problem and only after they have established confidence in the professional will they reveal the real problem. This is particularly true where the problem is of an intimate or embarrassing nature.

Honesty

There is a joke that goes as follows:

> *Q:* What is the difference between Washington, Nixon and Clinton?
> *A:* Washington couldn't tell a lie. Nixon couldn't tell the truth. Clinton couldn't tell the difference!

This joke relates to the veracity of disclosures. Lies can be divided into three broad categories (Ennis *et al.*, 2008):

1 *self-centred lies* – used to protect oneself ('I was not there when it happened.')
2 *other-oriented lies* – employed to protect a second person in the interaction ('That dress suits you perfectly.')
3 *altrusitic lies* – used to protect a third party ('I was with James at that time, and so he could not have done that.').

More specifically, the main reasons for making dishonest disclosures have been shown (DePaulo *et al.*, 1996, 2003a, 2003b) to be:

- to create a favourable impression
- to influence and persuade others
- to save face
- to support and reassure others
- to avoid conflict
- to increase or reduce interaction with others.

Given the importance of these functions to the preservation of harmonious relationships, it is not surprising that deception is widespread (Granhag and Vrij, 2007). As Vrij (2007: 335) concluded, lies 'often serve as a social lubricant. Given this positive aspect of deception, it is not surprising that lying is a daily life event'. Indeed, some form of deception, often in the form of 'white lies', has been shown to occur in at least one quarter of all conversations (Buller and Burgoon, 1996). One example of this is research into what is known as *avoidance-avoidance conflict* (AAC; Bull, 2002). AAC occurs in a situation where the person has to choose between disclosing a hurtful truth, telling a face-saving lie or giving an equivocal response (Edwards and Bello, 2001). For example, a close friend produces a painting that her 13-year-old son has just finished and asks for your opinion. You could respond:

- 'I think it's really beautiful. He has an obvious talent and flair for art.' (Lie)
- 'I think it's very poor. The perspective is all wrong and there isn't enough contrast in the shading to give a three-dimensional feel to the painting.' (Truth)
- 'Oh, so he's interested in art. You must be very proud of him.' (Equivocation)

When faced with AAC, research shows that the overwhelming majority of people opt for equivocation (Rosenfeld, 2000). The truth may be unpleasant for the recipient and damaging for the relationship, a lie can cause stress for the discloser and may cause problems if unveiled later, while an equivocal response often saves face all round.

In specialised circumstances, such as police interviewing, disclosures need to be examined carefully. Gudjonsson (1999) illustrated how confessions made by suspects are disputed in court for one of three reasons:

1   It is claimed that the confession was never actually made, but was fabricated either by the police or by a third party to whom the defendant is alleged to have confessed.
2   The confession is retracted – the defendant claims that although a confession was made, this was done under some form of duress and is actually false.
3   The defence counsel disputes a confession that the defendant maintains is true, on grounds that the person is not fit to plead because of intellectual impairment or psychological incapacity.

Since deception is widely practised, it becomes rather difficult to detect. A common joke in comedy sketches goes as follows:

A: I always know when you're lying.
B: How do you know?
A: Your lips move!

As discussed in Chapter 3, in reality deceit is not always so easy to detect. In fact, research has consistently shown that people are on average only 47 per cent accurate in detecting deception – that is less than chance. Furthermore, there is a strong human propensity to judge messages as truthful – a process known as the *truth bias* (Burgoon and Levine, 2010). The truth bias is most marked during face-to-face encounters and with those with whom we have a close relationship. There is also a lack of consistency in the results of research studies into deception (Ali and Levine, 2008). In reviewing this area, Vrij (2000: 92) concluded: 'There is no such thing as typical deceptive behaviour – that is, there is no behaviour or set of behaviours that all liars exhibit. Deceptive behaviour depends on someone's personality and on the circumstances under which the lie is told.'

The deceiver's degree of motivation is important, in relation to the consequences of the lie being detected (Gray, 2008). If I tell you (falsely) that the bottle of wine you have brought to my house is one that I like and that I will enjoy drinking it at a later time, the costs associated with being found out are relatively small. On the other hand, a perpetrator trying to convince a detective of personal innocence following a brutal murder has a great deal at stake.

Knowledge of the baseline or 'normal' pattern of individual behaviour has been shown to be crucial before decisions about deviations therein can be made in judging the veracity of disclosures (Malone and DePaulo, 2001). In general terms, however, the following behaviours seem to be associated with deception (Dickson *et al.*, 1997; Vrij, 2000; Kassin and Gudjonsson, 2004):

- more indirect answers that do not specifically refer to self (e.g. replying to the question 'Do you drink?' with 'Nobody in my family takes drink.')
- increased use of negative statements ('I am not guilty.' rather than 'I am innocent.')
- greater degree of 'levelling' (use of terms such as 'all', 'every', 'none', 'nobody')
- fewer 'exclusive' words (e.g. without, but, except), which require cognitive effort
- more general statements with fewer specific details given.

Disclosure avoidance

The corollary of self-disclosure is self-suppression, and Hastings (2000a) illustrated how suppression, or avoidance, of certain talk and actions is culturally universal. She used the term *egocasting* to describe the intrapersonal process whereby the individual decides what side of self to display and portray to others (Hastings, 2000b). She argued that when the person has to decide whether to disclose something that could cause potential personal harm, the self (or 'ego') makes a decision based upon the probable reaction of others and how this will in turn impact upon self and self-image. One example of this is the phenomenon of *self-silencing*, wherein the individual consistently suppresses personal opinions because of the fear that self-expression would damage the relationship (Harper and Welsh, 2007). In identifying the main general aim of suppression as to protect the individual against harm, Afifi and Guerrero (2000) charted a number of more specific reasons for disclosure avoidance. These were later confirmed in a study by Derlega *et al.* (2008).

- need for privacy – as expressed by a young female in the Afifi and Guerrero (2000) study: 'My mom wants me to tell her everything. She thinks she has to know everything about me all the time. I get sick of it. Sometimes I want to tell her it's just not her business. I am almost an adult. I have my own life. I need my privacy' (p. 176)

- social inappropriateness of the disclosure (e.g. we do not discuss bowel movements at the dining table)
- futility (e.g. 'We've discussed this hundreds of times before and got nowhere.')
- wanting to avoid criticism, punishment or embarrassment. Fear of stigma has been shown to be a major determining feature here – particularly for those suffering from certain conditions, such as HIV/AIDS (Ostrom *et al.*, 2006)
- a desire to avoid conflict (so we may not tell aggressive others that we disagree with what they are saying)
- protection of the relationship (e.g. we would be unlikely to tell our partner that we found someone else more attractive)
- dissimilarity (nothing in common with the other person).

Research into the issue of secrecy has also been explored in relation to disclosure avoidance. Secrecy refers to information that someone consciously withholds from another. Afifi *et al.* (2007: 63) described a secret as 'the type of private information that is viewed as risky enough that it is worth intentionally concealing'. Secrets involve a *secret-keeper* and a *secret-target* – the person from whom the information is kept. For example, a wife (secret-keeper) tells her husband (secret-target) that their 18-year-old daughter is going steady with a boy at college, but does not tell him that they are sleeping together. Those in the secret-keeper position often have a benign attitude to secrecy, yet this usually changes to resentment when they find themselves in the secret-target position. This is because being in the former position tends to give one a feeling of control and power, while being 'kept in the dark' leads to feelings of exclusion, rejection or betrayal. However, secret-keepers experience stress as they undergo a process of *rumination*, whereby they are trying to suppress the information but at the same time find it difficult not to think (or ruminate) about it. Indeed, there is a paradox here in that while they may try not to think about the information, they must at the same time think about it so that they do not unwittingly reveal it (Afifi and Caughlin, 2006).

Individuals are more likely to reveal a secret where three conditions prevail: the target has a right or need to know this information, the discloser has a high need for catharsis, and others, including the target, are persuading the person to divulge the information (Afifi and Steuber, 2009). While, in general, secrecy can be damaging for relationships (Finkenauer *et al.*, 2005; Smetana *et al.*, 2006), under certain circumstances it is beneficial. For example, Vangelisti and Caughlin (1997) found that, within families, secrets kept to protect family members from hurt or pain were positively related to relational satisfaction, while secrets held as a result of poor intra-family communication or a desire to avoid evaluation had negative effects upon familial relationships. However, the distinction is not always easy to make and requires a deeper knowledge of those involved. In the earlier example, is the wife withholding the secret to protect her husband from pain, because she is afraid of how he will evaluate their daughter, or is it just one more instance of poor communications generally within the family? In their study of marriage, Finkenauer and Hazam (2000) found that both disclosure and secrecy were important potential sources of marital satisfaction, and it was the appropriate use and goal of each that was most important.

In therapy, it has been shown that many clients conceal certain types of information (Farber, 2003). Among the information that is less likely to be revealed to therapists are matters to do with sex, personal failures and aggression. By comparison, aspects of oneself and one's parents that are most disliked tend to be the topics most commonly discussed by clients. In the medical sphere, while open disclosure to patients about their condition is the norm, there are occasions where therapeutic nondisclosure (also referred to as therapeutic privilege or therapeutic exception) may be considered (Berger, 2005). This is where disclosure would be likely to cause emotional distress such that the patient's capacity for decision making would be impaired, or where it would violate the patient's expressed cultural requirements.

PURPOSES OF SELF-DISCLOSURE

The goals of the discloser appear to be of paramount importance in determining the amount, content and intimacy of disclosure in different contexts (Oguchi, 1991; Derlega *et al.*, 2008). For example, research has shown (Rosenfeld, 2000) that with friends the top two reasons for self-disclosure are: (a) relationship maintenance and enhancement; (b) self-clarification – to learn more about one's thoughts and feelings. With strangers, however, the top two purposes are: (a) reciprocity – to facilitate social interchange; (b) impression formation – to present oneself in the best light. The skilled use of self-disclosure can therefore facilitate goal achievement for both professionals and their clients. The main goals of self-disclosure by professionals are as follows.

To overcome fear

Many people have a fear of disclosing too much about their thoughts and feelings, since there is the risk of:

- being rejected, not understood, or subjected to ridicule
- causing embarrassment or offence to the listener
- expressing and presenting oneself so badly that a negative image of self is portrayed.

The fear of disclosure is so great in some people, termed 'inhibitors' or 'suppressors', that they avoid revealing anything negative to others (Kowalski, 1999). Indeed, in many subcultures self-disclosure is actively discouraged with the child being told 'Don't let others know your business.', 'Tell people only what they need to know.', or 'Whatever you say, say nothing.' This attitude then persists into later life where respect is often given to the person who 'plays cards close to the chest'. While in a game of poker it is wise not to disclose too much, either verbally or nonverbally, the attitude of avoiding self-disclosure can cause problems for people when they may have a need to talk about personal matters. Often, before we make a deep disclosure, there is a strategic process of *testing* (Kelly and McKillop, 1996) or *advance pre-testing* (Duck, 1999), whereby we 'trail' the topic with potential confidants and observe their reactions. If these are favourable, then we continue with the revelations; if not, we move on to a new topic.

However, the initial dangers of self-disclosure are such that we expect an equal commitment to this process from people with whom we may wish to develop a relationship (Greene *et al.*, 2006). For this reason, reciprocation is expected in the early stages of everyday interaction. In relation to the poker analogy it is a case of the individual wanting to see all of the cards on the table. The fear of self-disclosure can be overcome partially by a self-disclosure from the professional to the effect that this type of problem has been dealt with often, or that it is quite acceptable for the client to have the problem.

To encourage reciprocation

Self-disclosure is contagious. As noted by Harper and Harper (2006: 251): 'One feature of self-disclosure is its reciprocity; meaning that a person's disclosure increases the likelihood that the other party will also disclose.' In everyday interaction, reciprocation of self-disclosures is the norm. Three main theories have been proposed to explain this reciprocation effect (Archer, 1979):

1   *Trust-attraction.* The argument here is that when A discloses, B perceives this as conveying trust. As a result, B is likely to be more attracted to A and this increased liking in turn leads B to disclose to A.
2   *Social exchange.* Interpersonal encounters have been conceptualised as a form of joint economic activity or social exchange in which both sides seek rewards and try to minimise costs, which may be in the form of money, services, goods, status, love or affection (Kelley and Thibaut, 1978). Thus, when A discloses this is a form of investment in the relationship and a reciprocal return is expected. There also tends to be a norm of equity between people, which means that we do not like to feel in debt or beholden to others and so B feels under pressure to reciprocate the initial disclosure at a similar level of intimacy in order to return the investment.
3   *Modelling.* This approach purports that, by disclosing, A is providing B with a model of appropriate and perhaps expected behaviour in that context. B then follows the model as provided and so reciprocates the disclosure.

There is no firm evidence to support one of these theories over the other two and different studies have lent support to one or other. Indeed, it is likely that all three explanations can partially account for reciprocation and that the relative importance of each will vary across situations.

As Kowalski (1996) illustrated, reciprocation can sometimes take the form of one-upmanship. For example, if I tell you about my experience of being burgled and what I had stolen, you may top this by telling me about how when you were burgled you lost five times as much as me. Also, in everyday interaction, if A makes an intimate self-disclosure, this influences the depth of disclosure reciprocated by B. Indeed, there is evidence that the reciprocation effect holds even when the recipient of disclosure is a computer pre-programmed to respond in specific ways (Moon, 2000). Of course, social rules and norms must be followed for reciprocation to occur – the depth of disclosure needs to be gradual, beginning at a shallow level and slowly becoming more intimate (Aron *et al.*, 2006). People are also more likely to reciprocate fully if they believe they were individually sought out by the discloser to receive the initial disclosure, rather than being just another in a whole line of people being told the story (Omarzu, 2000). If these rules are broken then not only will the reciprocity effect not occur, but the relationship between disclosure and attraction is also broken.

Where reciprocation of self-disclosures does not occur, one of three types of situations prevails:

1   The person making the disclosures is not really interested in the listener. This type of person's need to tell all is so great that the effect on the listener is not considered. The speaker is simply using the listener as a receptacle into which to pour disclosures. This is quite common when someone is undergoing some form of inner turmoil and needs a friendly ear to encourage the ventilation of fears and emotions. To use another analogy, the listener becomes a 'wailing wall' for the speaker. In certain professional contexts this is acceptable, as in counselling and therapy (Farber, 2006).
2   The person who is receiving the disclosures does not care about the speaker. In this case the speaker is foolish to continue disclosing, since it is possible that the listener may use the disclosures against the speaker, either at the time of the disclosure or later.
3   Neither one cares about the disclosures of the other. In this case there is no real relationship. If one person discloses, it is a monologue; if both disclose, it is a dialogue in which exchanges are superficial. A great deal of everyday, fleeting conversation falls into the latter category.

In professional situations, clients can often be encouraged to 'open up' by receiving a self-disclosure from the professional. Such a disclosure can have a very potent effect on the client, who will then be more likely to begin to self-disclose more freely. However, in many fields there is a need for more self-disclosure from professionals. For example, Hargie et al. (2000) found that self-disclosure was recognised by pharmacists as a core skill, but in their study, which involved video-recording community pharmacist–patient interactions, few pharmacist disclosures actually occurred. Likewise, Fisher and Groce (1990) analysed 43 medical interviews and found that doctors rarely disclosed information about themselves. The pattern of low disclosure by health professionals seems to evolve at an early stage. Thus, Ashmore and Banks (2001) found that student nurses were less willing to disclose to patients than to any other target-person. Yet the use of some disclosures can help practitioners to present a more 'human' face to patients. Tallman et al. (2007) videotaped 92 primary care consultations and related the behaviour of doctors to patient satisfaction ratings. They found that physicians who received higher satisfaction ratings were also more likely to self-disclose. Examples of disclosure included female doctors telling patients that they too had children, and a physician telling a patient that her husband was on statins. However, disclosures need to be skilled, since in a study of 113 doctor–patient consultations, McDaniel et al. (2007) found that most disclosures by physicians were not really helpful for the patient, as they often switched the focus away from and failed to return to the patient topic that preceded the doctor's disclosure. Thus, in the Tallman et al. (2007) study, successful physicians used self-disclosure selectively, and they were always relevant to the patient's situation.

Self-disclosure by the professional can be advantageous in other contexts. For example, appropriate teacher disclosures have benefits in the classroom (Cayanus and Martin, 2008). When teachers use positive disclosures that are directly linked to the lesson material, these are well received by students and increase motivation, engagement and learning. In terms of valence, it can be acceptable for instructors to reveal some negative experiences. For example, a sports teacher may detail an instance of having played badly and lost a game, or an art teacher may describe the production of a painting that did not turn out as well as expected. Teacher disclosures that are mildly negative can have a number of advantages: they underline the fact than no one is perfect or flawless, but that we learn from our mistakes; they show a 'human' side to the teacher and this, in turn, can facilitate student liking and engagement; and if teachers only use positive disclosures they may be perceived as narcissistic and students may feel inferior (Cayanus *et al.*, 2009). However, teachers should avoid using too many negative disclosures. They should also definitely refrain from revealing deeply negative details (such as having stolen, told lies, or cheated in examinations), as these have an adverse impact on students (Cayanus and Martin, 2008). Thus, studies by McBride and Wahl (2005) and Hosek and Thompson (2009) showed that while instructors made self-disclosures about their personal histories, families and everyday activities, they did not reveal information on personal matters such as salary, or information that could damage their credibility or lead to negative evaluations (such as sexual activity or drug-taking).

In the field of therapy, Baldwin (2000) presented a comprehensive case in support of disclosures by therapist to client. Likewise, Bochner (2000) illustrated how the use of disclosure by therapists can help to achieve 'mutuality' (a greater degree of equality) with clients, while Knox *et al.* (1997) and Burkard *et al.* (2006) found that clients appreciated and benefited from appropriate counsellor disclosures. However, Hill (2004) demonstrated that, whereas clients tended to rate disclosures by the therapist as helpful, counsellors were more likely to rate them as unhelpful. In their study of clients currently in long-term therapy, at one extreme they identified a minority of clients who preferred no counsellor disclosures at all, while at the other some were voracious in their desire to know as much as possible about the helper – even to the extent of seeking out other clients of the same therapist to share information. A number of advantages of counsellor disclosures emerge from research findings (see Box 9.3). Knox *et al.* (1997) found that the most effective therapist disclosures occurred as follows:

Box 9.3 Advantages of counsellor disclosure

When used appropriately counsellor disclosures:

- act as a role model for clients to make changes in themselves
- make the helper seem more human and more real
- serve to balance the power differential between helper and helpee
- are beneficial for the overall relationship
- offer new insights to clients
- give clients a feeling of *universality*, through reassurance that they are not alone in how they feel and that their feelings are neither abnormal nor unexpected
- show clients that things can and do work out.

- when clients were discussing important personal issues
- the disclosures were personal as opposed to self-involving; they were often about past experiences, and none was concerned with feelings or opinions about the therapy relationship per se. Three main categories of disclosure emerged here – (i) *family* (e.g. one therapist revealed having a son); (ii) *leisure activities* (one talked about fly-fishing); (iii) *shared difficult experiences* (one revealed the problems she experienced with her family when she 'came out' as a lesbian)
- the clients felt that the helper had disclosed to offer reassurance that their feelings were understandable.

While it is recognised that helper disclosures can have advantages and disadvantages depending upon how they are employed, and that the decision to disclose depends upon the context and the therapeutic orientation of the therapist (Farber, 2006), it has been recommended (Knox and Hill, 2003; Burkard *et al.*, 2006; Egan, 2007) that helpers:

- let clients know at the outset if they intend to disclose their own experiences – this should form part of the initial 'contract'
- time the disclosures to fit with the flow and content of the interaction
- do not disclose too much or too often – any disclosures should be focused
- ensure that any disclosures are culturally appropriate, given the client's background
- disclose solely for the client's benefit – role reversal is not the purpose here and helpers should not burden the client with their problems
- do not disclose too much but be selective and focused; counsellor disclosures should be to the point rather than rambling
- be flexible – disclosure will be appropriate for some clients but not with others.

To open conversations

When two people meet for the first time they give and receive self-disclosures. In an early study in this field, Chaikin and Derlega (1976) identified three main stages or levels of relationship development:

1 *Awareness.* Here, people have not actually interacted but are aware of the presence of one another. At this stage, for example, a female may stand close to or walk slowly past a male in whom she is interested.
2 *Surface contact.* Here, individuals begin to communicate by exchanging superficial information about themselves, and make judgements about whether or not to pursue the relationship.
3 *Mutuality.* Finally, people begin to disclose and exchange personal feelings, and engage in deeper self-disclosures as the relationship develops.

Many professionals use self-disclosure to open interactions and establish surface contact. Such disclosures are usually directly related to the job role or to basic personal information. By comparison, mutuality occurs in intimate personal relationships.

To search for commonalities

At the surface contact stage of a relationship, people give self-disclosures in the hope that the other person may be able to identify with them. At this stage they search for shared interests or experiences to chart some common ground on which to build a conversation. This would usually occur in informal meetings between professionals and clients. It is also important in certain business contexts, such as selling, where the professional salesperson may want to establish a common frame of reference with the client, in order to facilitate the development of a relationship (and the likelihood of a successful outcome in terms of sales). On occasions, the professional may want to highlight commonalities. Thus, a health professional visiting a young mother who has just had her first child may say, 'I know the problems associated with becoming a parent since I have three children myself.', thereby establishing a common bond, and providing a foundation for a discussion of the particular problems faced by this mother.

To express concern for the other person

This is the type of self-disclosure in which the professional expresses feelings about the other person. Such disclosures can serve as a potent form of reinforcement (see Chapter 4). Disclosure is a skill employed by effective negotiators as a way of building trust with the other side (see Chapter 13 for further information on this aspect of negotiation).

To share experiences

In certain instances, the professional will have had similar experiences to the client, and can share these to underline the fact that there is a depth of understanding between the two. This also helps to portray the professional as 'human'. For example, one situation where this can be of immense benefit is where a client has recently been bereaved and the professional has also faced the pain of bereavement. The use of a self-disclosure here can be a valuable reassurance to the client that the pain will pass (e.g. 'I remember when my mother died I thought I would never get over it.'). However, this type of 'me too' approach needs to be used appropriately and should not be taken to the extreme of what Yager and Beck (1985) termed the 'we could have been twins' level.

To express one's point of view

In many contexts, such as at staff meetings, interviews and case conferences, the professional is expected to put forward personal thoughts, ideas and opinions. The ability to do so confidently and competently is therefore important. These are the main purposes of professional self-disclosure. However, self-disclosure by clients also serves a number of important goals. These will now be explored.

To facilitate self-expression

It can become a burden not being able to tell others about personal matters and having to keep things 'bottled up'. Self-disclosure can have a therapeutic effect, by enabling us to 'get it off our chest' or 'letting go' (Kassin and Gudjonsson, 2004), which is why counselling, the confessional or discussing something with a close friend can all make us feel better. There is indeed truth in the old maxim that 'A problem shared is a problem halved.' As summarised by Kim and Ko (2007: 325): 'Self-expression allows people to distinguish themselves from others, to reflect their own beliefs and needs, and validate their own self-concepts.' Stewart *et al.* (2005) referred to self-disclosure as part of a process of social *exhaling* (as opposed to listening, which they termed *inhaling*). Professionals should be aware both of the existence of the need for clients to exhale, and of ways to allow them to satisfy it. It is interesting to note that when people are not able to utilise interpersonal channels for disclosure, they often use substitutes such as keeping a personal diary, talking to a pet or conversing with God. Indeed, this need can be observed at an early stage in young children who often disclose to a teddy bear or doll.

After a traumatic event the victim may attempt to suppress or inhibit thoughts about it and avoid discussing it with others. However, the more disturbing the event, the greater is the need to talk about it and ventilate one's feelings. If this process is not facilitated, then adverse health effects are likely to occur, as the person continually ruminates about what has happened (Kowalski, 1999). Trying to keep it inside tends to result in thoughts and visions of the experience beginning to dominate – a phenomenon referred to as the *hyperaccessibility of suppressed thoughts* (Kircanski *et al.*, 2008). Interestingly, Kowalski (1999) illustrated how, while disclosure after a stressful event provides a necessary catharsis, disclosure before a stressful event may not be beneficial as it can serve to magnify feelings of anxiety.

In a comprehensive review of the research on a range of illnesses (such as cardiovascular diseases, HIV, cancer), Tardy (2000: 121) found considerable evidence to show that self-disclosure has positive effects upon health, concluding: 'Self-disclosure facilitates health by not only eliminating the deleterious consequences of inhibition but also by organising thoughts and memories in more productive ways.' One reason for this is that disclosure has been shown to boost immunological functioning (Petrie *et al.*, 1995). These findings are particularly important for health professionals, since it is clear that for patients to fully disclose, the most important prerequisite is the sensitivity shown by health caregivers who must be aware that 'the messages they convey – even when they are saying nothing at all – will guide patients in their decision making about whether to tell the whole truth, or only that part which the caregiver seems most receptive to hearing' (Parrott *et al.*, 2000: 147).

There is evidence that written disclosures are also beneficial. It would appear that writing about trauma can contribute to the healing process because the written task necessitates the person having to work through the event and come to terms with thoughts and feelings about it. As noted by Cresswell *et al.* (2007: 238):

Writing about major life events and traumatic experiences can have significant benefits for mental and physical health. Throughout the past two decades, a large literature has shown that expressive writing improves physical health in a variety of populations.

For example, Pennebaker and Francis (1996) found that first-year students who were asked to write about their thoughts and feelings about coming to college, in comparison to a control group, had a reduced level of illness visits to the health centre, coupled with improved grade point averages. Likewise, Warner *et al.* (2006) carried out a study of adolescents with asthma and found that those involved in written disclosure, compared to control subjects, experienced a number of benefits, including improved positive affect and decreased asthma symptoms and functional disability. However, in their review of the research, Stroebe *et al.* (2006) noted that while written disclosure has been shown to produce benefits over a wide range of medical and psychological conditions, there are also cases where it has not effected improvements. They concluded that written disclosure may be of greater benefit for more vulnerable, insecurely attached individuals who have fewer opportunities for disclosure in their everyday lives. By comparison, securely attached adults are less likely to benefit from written disclosure, as they have developed relationships in which they have regular opportunities for self-disclosure to facilitate their personal adjustment. On the other hand, Greenberg and Stone (1992) argued that the written expression of feelings on occasions can be superior to oral disclosures, since the recipient of interpersonal disclosures may respond inappropriately. They cited the example of how when incest victims tell their mothers about the event a high proportion of mothers respond by disbelieving or blaming them.

This occurs in other areas. Victims of abuse in childhood often face threats about what will happen if they disclose and may not be believed when they do tell (Walker and Antony-Black, 1999). Studies of the gay population reveal difficulties with disclosure or 'coming out', especially to family (Savin-Williams and Dube, 1998). In a study of 194 gay people between the ages of 14 and 21 years, living at home, D'Augelli *et al.* (1998) found that those who had disclosed that they were gay reported verbal or physical abuse from family members and higher levels of 'suicidality' (feelings and thoughts about suicide).

These findings are interesting for the process of therapy. People seem to benefit from discussing or writing about their deepest feelings, and this can be a key step in the process of coping with the trauma. As Tubbs (1998: 229) aptly summarised it: 'Part of returning to mental health involves sharing oneself with others.'

To heighten personal knowledge

An important function of disclosure is the process of *self-clarification* (Orbe and Bruess, 2005). This is exemplified by the saying 'How do I know what I think until I hear what I say?' The value of the 'talking cure' in therapy is a good example of how the process of allowing someone freely to express their thoughts, ideas, fears, problems, etc. actually facilitates the individual's self-awareness. The importance of self-disclosure in therapy was explained by Stricker (1990: 289):

> It is through the self-disclosure of the patient to the therapist that he can begin to recognize previously hidden and unacceptable aspects of himself, to recognize the acceptability of what had been experienced as forbidden secrets, and to grow in a healthier fashion.

Thus, self-disclosure can help people to clarify and understand their feelings and the reasons for them; in other words it encourages them to know themselves more fully. This view was confirmed in a study of adults (aged 33 to 48 years old) in Japan and the USA, where it was shown that in both countries levels of self-knowledge and self-disclosure were positively correlated (Asai and Barnlund, 1998).

To promote social comparison

A key process in interpersonal interaction is that of *social comparison*, in that we evaluate ourselves in terms of how we compare to others. In particular, we engage in two types of comparison (Adler *et al.*, 2006). First, we decide whether we are *superior or inferior* to others on certain dimensions (attractiveness, intelligence, popularity, etc.). Here, the important aspect is to compare with an appropriate reference group. For example, modest joggers should not compare their performance with Olympic standard marathon runners. Second, we judge the extent to which we are the *same or different* from others. At certain stages of life, especially adolescence, the pressure to fit in with and be seen as similar to peers is immense. Thus, wearing the right brand of clothes or shoes may be of the utmost importance. We also need to know whether our thoughts, beliefs and ideas are in line with and acceptable to those of other people. This is part of the process of *self-validation* whereby we employ self-disclosures to seek support for our self-concept (Orbe and Bruess, 2005: 64).

People who do not have access to a good listener may not only be denied the opportunity to heighten their self-awareness, but they are also denied valuable feedback as to the validity and acceptability of their inner thoughts and feelings. By discussing these with others, we receive feedback as to whether these are experiences which others have as well, or whether they are less common. Furthermore, by gauging the reactions to our self-disclosures we learn what types are acceptable or unacceptable with particular people and in specific situations. On occasions it is the fear that certain disclosures may be unacceptable to family or friends that motivates an individual to seek professional help. Counsellors will be familiar with client statements such as: 'I just couldn't talk about this to my husband.', 'I really can't let my mother know my true feelings.' Another aspect of social comparison in the counselling context relates to a technique mentioned earlier known as *normalising*. This is the process whereby helpers provide reassurance to clients that what they are experiencing is not abnormal or atypical, but is a normal reaction shared by others when facing such circumstances (Dickson *et al.*, 1997). Patient disclosure, facilitated by the therapist, seems also to facilitate the process of normalising (Munro and Randall, 2007).

To develop relationships

The appropriate use of self-disclosure is crucial to the development and maintenance of long-term relationships (Foley and Duck, 2006; Greene *et al.*, 2006). Those who disclose either too much or too little tend to have problems in establishing and sustaining relationships. Even in close relationships there can be dangers with deep disclosures, especially of a highly sensitive nature. This is shown in studies of the difficulties faced by those diagnosed with HIV/Aids in disclosing this to intimate partners (Derlega *et al.*, 2000; Allen *et al.*, 2008). Similarly, individuals who disclose at a deep level to relative strangers, or who make only negative disclosures, will find it difficult to make friends. In the therapeutic context, by encouraging clients to self-disclose and giving sensitive feedback, helpers can provide them with a valuable learning experience about how to use this skill.

To ingratiate and manipulate

Some clients use self-disclosures in an attempt to ingratiate themselves with the professional, for whatever reason. This type of client tends to disclose quite a lot and say very positive things about the professional ('You are the only person who understands me.', 'I don't know what I would do without you.'). In a sense, the client is 'coming on too strong' and this can be very difficult to deal with. The purpose may be to manipulate the professional for some form of personal gain. On the other hand, if this type of revelation is genuine, it can be a signal that the client is becoming overdependent. Either way, it is advisable to be aware of this function of manipulative disclosure.

These then are the main purposes of self-disclosure by both the professional and the client. A number of them can be illustrated with reference to the Johari window (Luft, 1970) developed by two psychologists, Joseph Luft and Harry Ingram (and named after the initial letters of both first names). As depicted in Figure 9.2, this indicates four dimensions of the self. There are aspects that are:

*   known both by self and by others (A), such as statements one has made
*   unknown by the self but known to others (B), including personal mannerisms, annoying habits and so on
*   personally known but not revealed to others (C), including embarrassing thoughts or feelings
*   unknown both to self and others (D), such as how one would behave in a particular crisis context.

One of the effects of self-disclosing is that the size of segment A is increased and the size of the segments B, C and D reduced. In other words by encouraging clients to self-disclose, not only do they find out more about themselves, but the professional also gains valuable knowledge about them and thereby understands them more fully.

	Known to self	*Unknown to self*
Known to others	A	B
Unknown to others	C	D

Figure 9.2 The Johari window

FACTORS INFLUENCING SELF-DISCLOSURE

A number of factors pertaining to the nature of the discloser, the recipient, the relationship and the context influence the extent to which self-disclosure is employed.

The discloser

The following characteristics of the discloser have been examined: age; gender; ethnic and religious group; personality; intoxication level.

Age

First-born children tend to disclose less than later-born children. This difference may be due to later-borns being more socially skilled because their parents have more experience of child-rearing and they have older siblings to interact with. It may also be the case that the eldest child has higher status and is therefore less likely to disclose to lower-status siblings. More generally, in a study of 212 undergraduates in the USA, Dolgin and Lindsay (1999) found that there was less disclosure to siblings who were five years younger. They also found that while younger siblings reported disclosure to seek advice and emotional support from older siblings, the latter reported more disclosures aimed at teaching their younger brothers or sisters. Another difference was that females reported making more disclosures for emotional support than did males. One important factor here is the nature of the relationship between siblings. Thus, Howe *et al.* (2000), in a study of Canadian fifth and sixth grade children (mean age 11.5 years), found that warmth of the relationship was a key determinant of sibling disclosure.

Disclosure tends to increase with age. As Archer (1979) pointed out, this finding has been reported in studies of children between the age of 6 and 12 years, and in college students between the ages of 17 and 55 years. However, Sinha (1972), in a study of adolescent females, found that 12- to 14-year-old girls disclosed most, followed by 17- to 18-year-olds, with 15- to 16-year-olds disclosing least. Sinha argued that at this latter stage the adolescent is at a stage of transition from girl to woman and may need more time to 'find herself'.

In a study of 174 adolescents in the USA, Papini *et al.* (1990) found that self-disclosures about emotional matters to best friends increased from 12 to 15 years of age. They also found that at the age of 12 years adolescents preferred to emotionally disclose to parents, but by the age of 15 years they preferred to disclose to friends. It was further discovered that adolescents with high self-esteem and the esteem of peers were more likely to disclose their emotional concerns to friends, whereas those who felt 'psychosocially adrift' did not communicate such worries in this way. The adolescents in this study disclosed more about their concerns to parents who were perceived to be open to discussion, warm and caring. Adolescents have been shown to decide not to disclose to parents in order to avoid criticism or punishment, to develop autonomy from them, or for emotional reasons (Smetana, 2008).

Coupland *et al.* (1991) conducted a series of studies on 'painful self-disclosure'

(PSD) in interactions between women aged 70 to 87 years and women in their mid-thirties. PSD refers to the revelation of intimate information on ill health, bereavement, immobility, loneliness, etc. They found that the older women revealed more PSDs, initiated more of them and were less likely to close such disclosing sequences. Since older women usually have experienced more painful events simply by virtue of longevity, it is perhaps not surprising that they disclose more of them than younger women. It could also be related to a reduced need for approval from others, in that the older individual may be less concerned with what other people think, and so more willing to voice an opinion. Coupland *et al.* (1991) suggested that PSDs can have positive effects for older women in terms of earning credit for having coped successfully with difficult life events. They speculated that such PSDs can help the older person to 'locate oneself in relation to past experiences, to one's own state of health, to chronological age and perhaps to projectable future decrement and death' (p. 191).

Many older people clearly enjoy and benefit from talking about their past and indeed such reminiscence is a positive method of therapy for this age group (Williams and Nussbaum, 2001). The experiences of loss are of particular import at this life stage (Suganuma, 1997). However, their greatest recall (the 'personal memory bump') is for life events that occur between the ages of 10 and 30 (Thorne, 2000). During this span, identity is shaped for adult life. It is also a time of highly charged emotional events, such as going to high school, dating, college, starting employment, finding a partner, setting up home, having children. Hence, many of the memories recalled are of 'firsts' (first love, first job, etc.).

Gender

Studies have been carried out to ascertain gender differences in talk. For example, in one study 396 students in the USA were fitted with digital devices, which, every 12.5 minutes, automatically recorded what they said for a 30-second period (Mehl *et al.*, 2007). Factoring up from these recorded samples, the researchers concluded that women used some 16,215 words and men 15,669 words over an assumed period of 17 waking hours per day. However, this study has been criticised both on the relatively small sample size and on the skewed nature of the sample, in that university students may well be more verbose than the remainder of the population. Furthermore, very large within-sample differences were also evident. For example, follow-up investigation revealed that the most talkative male was estimated to use 47,000 words per day and the least talkative male only 500 words (Science Daily, 2007). In their meta-analysis of research studies into gender differences in adults' language use, Leaper and Ayres (2007) found that women used more self-disclosures than men. Dindia (2000b), in an earlier meta-analytical study, also found that females disclosed more than males, but this was moderated by the gender of the recipient, so that:

- females do not disclose to males any more than males do to males
- females disclose more to females than males do to males
- females disclose more to females than males do to females
- females disclose more to males than males do to females.

Kowalski (1999) highlighted another gender difference, in that while men tend to be more careful with regard to the content of their self-disclosures, women are more concerned about the reciepient of their disclosures. There are several impinging variables that interact with gender to determine disclosure levels:

1   *Situational factors.* The topic, gender of recipient and relationship between discloser and recipient are all determinants of disclosure. For example, battered women specifically want to talk to another female about their experiences (Dieckmann, 2000).

2   *Gender role identity.* This relates to how strongly a person feels male or female. It would seem that individuals, either male or female, who regard themselves as possessing female attributes disclose more. Shaffer *et al.* (1992) ascertained that measures of sex role identity were better predictors of self disclosure to same-sex strangers than was gender per se (which failed to predict willingness to disclose). Both males and females high in femininity self-disclosed more. Masculinity had no effect upon disclosure levels, while androgynous subjects (high in both male and female traits) demonstrated high levels of intimacy and flexibility in their disclosures across various contexts.

3   *Gender role attitudes.* This refers to how one believes a male or female should behave. We learn to display what we feel are the appropriate behaviours for our gender role (Richardson and Hammock, 2007). These will have been influenced by same-sex parent and significant others. Thus, if a male believes his role to be the solid, strong, silent type he is unlikely to be a high discloser.

4   *Gender role norms of the culture or subculture.* Grigsby and Weatherley (1983) found that women were significantly more intimate in their disclosures than men. It would seem that it is more acceptable in Western society for females to discuss personal problems and feelings. Males disclose more about their traits, work and personal opinions while females disclose more about their tastes, interests and relationships. Males have also been shown to be less willing to disclose distressing information than females (Ward *et al.*, 2007). It is therefore important to be aware that males may find difficulty in discussing personal matters, and may need more help, support and encouragement to do so.

Ethnic and religious group

Differences in disclosure have been found between different ethnic groups (Asai and Barnlund, 1998; Harris *et al.*, 1999). In the USA, European Americans tend to disclose more than African Americans, who in turn disclose more than Latin Americans. In general, Americans have been found to be more disclosing than similar groups in Japan, Germany, Great Britain and the Middle East. Yet Wheeless *et al.* (1986), in a study of 360 students, found no difference in disclosure levels between American students and students of non-western cultural origin studying in the USA. Likewise, Rubin *et al.* (2000) compared 44 North Americans with 40 Chinese students studying in the USA for less than three years and found that target person and nature of topic were much more powerful determinants of disclosure than either gender or nationality.

In another study, Hastings (2000a) investigated disclosure among Asian Indian postgraduate students at university in the USA. She found clear cultural differences in nature and pattern of disclosure. Role relationships played a very large part in determining disclosure amongst Asian Indians. Hindus believe that God has decreed the roles occupied by individuals and so the hierarchy is sacred and one's position deserved. Therefore, subordinates should not question those in authority. As a result, the Indians found difficulties with the propensity for US students to make demands of, or challenge, those in authority (their professors). They also disliked perceived American traits of extensive talk, overt expressions of self and the direct, forcible statement of personal viewpoints. As summarised by Hastings: 'Whereas American friendship is enacted through expressing oneself, Indian friendship is enacted through suppressing oneself' (p. 105).

The traditional Japanese trait of humility has caused difficulty in the operation of effective focus groups (Flintoff, 2001). This is because it is almost impossible to get participants to express strong views, and if someone does so the other group members invariable concur with this opinion. Western companies operating in Japan consider focus groups an integral part of the business process. In an attempt to overcome prevailing disclosure norms they have asked participants to write down their views and then read them out. But this is far from ideal, removing as it does the dynamic interchange of ideas that characterises this method. Flintoff argued that if Japan wants Western companies to engage fully, changes may have to take place in their traditional pattern of avoiding disagreements.

There is little evidence regarding the effects of religious affiliation upon disclosure levels. One early study was conducted by Jourard (1961) at the University of Florida, in which he investigated differences between affiliates of the Baptist, Methodist, Catholic and Jewish faiths in relation to level of disclosures to parents and closest friends of both genders. No significant differences were found between denominations for females, although Jewish males were significantly higher disclosers than members of the other denominations, none of whom differed from one another. Jourard speculated that this difference may have been due to closer family ties in the Jewish community and therefore could have been a factor of subculture rather than religion per se.

In another American study, Long and Long (1976) found that attire (presence or absence of a habit) but not religious status (nun versus non-nun) produced significant differences in interviewee responses. Males were more open in the presence of an interviewer not in habit, whereas the opposite was true for females. Thus, religious dedication appeared to be less important than the impact of clothing whereby such dedication is usually signalled.

A similar 'identification' effect was reported by Chesner and Beaumeister (1985), in a study of disclosures by clients to counsellors who identified themselves as devout Christians or Jews compared to counsellors who did not disclose religious convictions. It was found that Jewish subjects disclosed significantly less to the counsellor who declared himself a devout Christian. Chesner and Beaumeister concluded that counsellor disclosure of religion does not facilitate client disclosure and may in fact reduce it.

In the Northern Ireland context, a study of Protestant (P) and Catholic (C) undergraduates revealed that both C and P students were significantly more likely to disclose to those of the same religion than to those of the other religion, as measured by the Miller *et al.* (1983) scale (Dickson *et al.*, 2000). Interestingly, gender differences emerged here, in that females were significantly more likely than males to disclose to those from the opposite religion. In another part of this study, actual interactions between same and opposite religion dyads revealed a greater breadth of disclosure (number of topics discussed) in same religion pairs. Also in the Northern Ireland context, Hargie *et al.* (2008) found that the decision of Ps and Cs to disclose to those from the outgroup was mediated by degree of trust held for that group.

Personality

Personality variables have been shown to relate to disclosure level (Reno and Kenny, 1992; Suganuma, 1997; Waldo and Kemp, 1997; Matsushima *et al.*, 2000; Omarzu, 2000). Shy, introverted types, those with low self-esteem and individuals with a high need for social approval disclose less, and social desirability is negatively related to depth of disclosure. Also those with an external locus of control (who believe their destiny is shaped by events 'outside' themselves over which they have no control) disclose less than those with an internal locus of control (who believe they can largely shape their own destiny). Lonely individuals have also been found to disclose less (Schwab *et al.*, 1998), while neurotics tend to have low self-disclosure flexibility, in that they disclose the same amount, regardless of the situation. Finally, a significant and positive correlation between machiavellianism and disclosure has been reported for females but not for males (O'Connor and Simms, 1990).

Intoxication level

There is a common conception that alcohol consumption has a positive effect upon disclosure level. In fact this has not been consistently shown to be the case. In their review of the area, Monahan and Lannutti (2000) found mixed results in relation to research into the effects of alcohol consumption on self-disclosure: some studies reported increased disclosure, some reported lower disclosure, while others produced no effects at all. The context of the interaction is the crucial variable. Thus, for example, Monahan and Lannutti found that, when sober, females with low social self-esteem (SSE) disclosed significantly less than those with high SSE when interacting with a flirtatious male but, when intoxicated, low SSE females disclosed at the same level as those with high SSE.

The recipient

A number of characteristics of the listener influence the amount of self-disclosure received including: acceptance/empathy; gender; status; attractiveness.

Acceptance/empathy

Accepting/empathic people receive more disclosures. Miller *et al.* (1983) identified certain individuals, whom they term 'openers', who are able to elicit intimate disclosures from others. They developed an 'opener scale' to measure this ability, containing items such as 'I'm very accepting of others.' and 'I encourage people to tell me how they are feeling.' The nonverbal behaviour of openers is very important. For example, Duggan and Parrott (2001) found that head nods and appropriate smiles and related facial expressions from physicians encouraged greater levels of disclosure from patients. Also in the medical sphere, in the Tallman *et al.* (2007) study mentioned earlier, it was found that doctors who encouraged patients to fully disclose their fears and concerns received higher patient satisfaction ratings. Forrester *et al.* (2008) reported similar findings with social workers. Stefanko and Ferjencik (2000) identified five dimensions that were characteristic of openers:

1   ***Communicativeness and reciprocity.*** The ability to readily engage with others and to reciprocate disclosure appropriately.
2   ***Emotional stability.*** Showing appropriate reactions and avoiding any rapid mood swings.
3   ***Perspective taking ability.*** Being able to see things from the other person's point of view.
4   ***Spontaneity in communication.*** Showing acceptance of disclosure, especially about intimate or embarrassing topics.
5   ***Being sympathetic.*** Showing understanding and concern for the other.

In her study of people who had survived a near-death experience, Hoffman (1995) found that the reaction of potential targets was crucial. If the discloser detected listener rejection or disinterest upon initially raising the issue, this stymied their future willingness to discuss what had been a pivotal life experience for them. Furthermore, Yeschke (1987) illustrated how acceptance is important in encouraging self-disclosure in the often stressful context of interrogations, giving the following advice to interrogators: 'Even if dealing with so called rag bottom, puke, scum bag type interviewees, select a positive accepting attitude' (p. 41).

Gender

While females in general tend to receive more disclosures than males, as discussed earlier this is influenced by the gender of the discloser. It is also dependent upon topic and context. For example, a male may prefer to discuss embarrassing personal health problems with a male rather than female doctor.

Status

As discussed above, individuals disclose more to those of the same status than to people of higher status, and disclose least to lower-status individuals.

Attractiveness

The attractiveness of the listener is another important element in encouraging self-disclosures. Part of the reason for this is simply that we like attractive people. Tardy and Dindia (2006) illustrated how self-disclosure is related to liking in three ways: 'We like people who self-disclose to us, we disclose more to people we like, and we like others as a result of having disclosed to them' (p. 237). Not surprisingly, therefore, more self-disclosures tend to be made to individuals who are perceived as being similar (in attitudes, values, beliefs, etc.), since such individuals are usually better liked. Evidence that this is a two-way link was found in a study by Vittengl and Holt (2000) where a positive correlation occurred between self-disclosure and ratings of attractiveness even in brief 'get acquainted' ten-minute conversations between strangers. It is therefore clear that appropriate disclosure is a key element in the establishment of positive relationships. Dress is also part of attractiveness. Thus, one study showed that patients were significantly more likely to disclose their sexual and psychological problems to doctors wearing 'professional' dress (i.e. a white coat), as this was their preferred mode of dress for physicians (Rehman *et al.*, 2005).

The relationship

The following features of the relationship between discloser and recipient influence the amount of self-disclosure used: trust; role relationships; anticipated length and commitment; physical proximity; voluntary involvement.

Trust

As noted by Fitness (2001: 75), in her review of the phenomenon of 'betrayal' in interpersonal relationships: 'Over the course of evolutionary history, humans have become finely attuned to the possibility of betrayal by others.' When we disclose certain matters we can make ourselves vulnerable. This means that we need to trust others before we will disclose. Interestingly, however, a paradox here is that self-disclosure requires trust, but also creates it. As the following rhyme, published in *Punch* in 1875, illustrates, if the discloser trusts the recipient to keep disclosures in confidence and not misuse them, then more self-disclosures will occur:

> There was an old owl liv'd in an oak
> The more he heard, the less he spoke;
> The less he spoke, the more he heard
> O if men were all like that wise bird!

In certain contexts the professional can be faced with an ethical dilemma when receiving self-disclosures. For example, if a client discloses having committed a crime of some sort, there may be a legal requirement for the professional to inform the police, yet to do so could well destroy the relationship of trust that has been developed. How such ethical dilemmas are resolved will, of course, depend upon the particular circumstances involved.

There is evidence to suggest that people regard trust as a relative dimension in relation to self-disclosure. Petronio and Bantz (1991) investigated the use of prior restraint phrases (PRPs) such as 'Don't tell anyone' or 'This is only between ourselves', on disclosures. Their study of 400 undergraduates revealed that a large percentage of both disclosers and receivers of such private disclosure anticipated that the recipient would pass on that information. This was confirmed in a survey of 1500 office workers by the company Office Angels (2000), where some 93 per cent admitted to imparting to others information that they had been asked specifically not to disclose to anyone else. This report, entitled *Forget Kissing . . . Everyone's Busy Telling!*, also revealed that over three-quarters (77 per cent) of workers would have told at least two others by the end of the working day in which they received the disclosure. The main reason (36 per cent) given for so doing was the attention and recognition obtained from having 'inside' information, although 20 per cent of staff had a more Machiavellian motive, reporting that they would use the new knowledge as a means of demonstrating power.

The use of PRPs is part of what Petronio (2002) termed 'communication privacy management' (CPM), whereby we attempt to place a border around who will have access to private information about self. CPM purports that individuals regulate access to personal information using a rule-based system guided by five key criteria: cultural norms; contextual aspects (the physical and social situation); gender; motivational expectations (e.g. relationship development); and risk-benefit analysis. This process is also known as 'communication boundary management' (CBM). As explained by Dillow *et al.* (2009: 206): 'CBM theory proposes that all individuals construct metaphorical boundaries around information that they con-sider private or sensitive'. These boundaries are important, given that when one self-discloses information of a highly private nature there is both the possibility and temptation of betrayal by the recipient, while for the discloser there is the external danger of being discovered and the internal danger of giving oneself away. This makes such disclosures particularly fascinating elements of interpersonal encounters.

Interestingly, a gender difference emerged in the Petronio and Bantz (1991) study, in that males were more likely to expect subsequent disclosure when a PRP was not used, whereas females were more likely to expect subsequent disclosure when a PRP was used. It was also found that the five types of people most likely to receive disclosures were (in order and for both genders):

- best female friend
- nonmarital significant other
- best male friend
- mutual friend
- spouse.

Those most unlikely to be told were strangers and the recipient's father. This latter finding is compatible with other research findings, which show that fathers are often the least likely recipients of disclosure (Mathews *et al.*, 2006; Derlega *et al.*, 2008). In addition, one study of parents' disclosures about their own lives and concerns to their late adolescent children (freshers at university) found that fathers disclosed less than mothers, and the self-stated purpose of their disclosures was more likely to relate to attempts at changing the behaviour of the children. Mothers, on the other hand, cited venting, seeking advice and looking for emotional support as their main reasons for disclosing (Dolgin, 1996). These findings were confirmed by the same author in a parallel survey of freshers themselves, who rated mothers as disclosing more than fathers, especially about their problems and emotions (Dolgin and Berndt, 1997).

Role relationships

In certain professional relationships the reciprocation norm does not hold, and it is the expectation that one person makes almost all of the disclosures. For instance, at a selection interview the candidate is expected to be the discloser.

Anticipated length and commitment

As previously indicated, an awareness of the entirely one-off nature of an encounter can actually encourage self-disclosure. This was initially termed the 'stranger-on-the-train phenomenon' (Thibaut and Kelley, 1959) and in later years, as travel preferences changed, 'in-flight intimacy' (De Vito, 1993). This phenomenon can also apply to some professional situations. For example, a client may be reluctant to return for a second visit, following an initial session in which deep self-disclosures have been made to the counsellor, who is in effect a complete stranger. Counsellors should therefore employ appropriate closure skills in order to help overcome this problem (see Chapter 10).

Physical proximity

Johnson and Dabbs (1976) found that there was less intimate disclosure at close inter-personal distances (18 inches) and more tension felt by the discloser than at a medium distance (36 inches). However, there is some evidence to suggest that it is males, but not females, who find close interpersonal distance a barrier to disclosure (Archer, 1979). A recent example of distal disclosure is via the internet. In cyberspace relationships, the anonymity afforded by the medium results in an increased rate of disclosure (Gibbs *et al.*, 2006; Schouten *et al.*, 2007). Graff (2007) argued that for effective online interaction, self-disclosure is essential. Studies have shown that within a short time people quickly disclose person problems, sexual preferences, etc. to their online partners (Whitty and Carr, 2006). Interestingly, online relationships are often rated more positively than face-to-face interactions. Possible reasons for this are that we may be more likely to idealise online partners, and also that people make more effort when composing messages online so that the recipient will like them. The internet also allows people to present a new 'self' to the world without upsetting existing 'offline' relationships. It can be very difficult for someone to make changes to existing aspects of self when the social environment stays the same. One's family, colleagues and friends may resist these new sides of self. Such problems do not occur in virtual relationships.

Voluntary involvement

There is more self-disclosure in relationships where the client has volunteered to talk about some issue. An extreme example of the negative effects of coercion upon self-disclosure is the individual who is 'helping police with their enquiries'. However, this can also be a problem where a client has been referred to the professional and is present under some degree of duress. In such a relationship greater efforts need to be made to encourage self-disclosure.

The situation

Finally, the situation in which the interaction is taking place influences the degree of self-disclosure. Thus, Wyatt *et al.* (2000) found that the two locations in which disclosure occurred most frequently were at home and at work. Other important dimensions of situation include the following: warmth; privacy; crisis; isolation.

Warmth

A 'warm' environment has been found to encourage self-disclosure, so that if there are soft seats, gentle lighting, pleasant decor and potted plants in an office, a client is more likely to open up. This finding is interesting, since interrogation sessions stereotypically take place in 'cold' environments (bare walls, bright lights, etc.). Presumably, the willingness of the person to self-disclose is an important factor in determining the type of environment for the interaction. One piece of research (Jensen, 1996) also found that background classical music had an effect upon the choice of topics for disclosure, and promoted self-expression among undergraduates, but more research is needed to chart the exact effects of different types of music upon various people across diverse settings.

Privacy

Solano and Dunnam (1985) showed that self-disclosure was greater in dyads than in triads, which in turn was greater than in a four-person group. They further found that this reduction applied regardless of the gender of the interactors and concluded that there may well be a linear decrease in self-disclosure as group size increases. Likewise, a study reported by Derlega *et al.* (1993) found that when student subjects were informed that their interaction with another subject (a confederate of the experimenter) was being video-recorded for later showing to an introductory psychology class, their depth of self-disclosures stayed at a superficial level, regardless of the intimacy of disclosures of the confederate subject. However, when no mention was made of being video-taped, the level of intimacy of disclosure from the confederate subject was reciprocated by the 'true' subject. This study highlighted the importance of privacy for encouraging self-disclosure.

One interesting exception to the privacy norm lies in the phenomenon of television chat or 'shock' shows, when people appear in front of what they know will be huge audiences and disclose sometimes excruciatingly embarrassing and often negative personal information (Peck, 1995). So why do they do this? Orrego *et al.* (2000) in researching this area found four main motives:

1   a desire to remedy negative views about themselves or their group and 'set the record straight'
2   a forum to enable them to hit back against those whom they feel have victimised them
3   wanting '15 minutes of fame'
4   the opportunity to promote some business venture.

Priest and Dominick (1994) in their study of people who had appeared on such shows found that most were from marginalised groups (gays, AIDS victims, transsexuals, etc.) or were a little on the 'outside' (e.g. plastic surgeons). Most were evangelical in wanting to disseminate their views to a wider audience and to serve as role models for others. There are therefore specific reasons behind this exception to the general rule of privacy and disclosure.

One variant of privacy is that of anonymous disclosure, sometimes achieved through the camouflage of an alternative identity or pseudonym. Anonymity occurs in a range of contexts, such as unsigned letters, leaks and whistle-blowing in organisations, the church confessional, radio call-in shows, police confidential telephone lines and computer-based bulletin boards and chat rooms. In his review of this field, Scott (using the byline Anonymous, 1998) illustrated how the rapid expansion in communication technologies resulted in a concomitant increase in anonymous messages being sent. In a study of disclosure in computer-mediated communication, Joinson (2001) also found that visually anonymous individuals disclosed significantly more information about themselves than did those who could be seen. Anonymity usually results in deeper levels and greater honesty of disclosure – the safety of remaining 'hidden' allows the individual to express intimate information or true feelings more readily. In this way, confidential telephone helplines such as the Samaritans encourage people to discuss very personal problems without undue embarrassment. This is because the physical distance and anonymity in such encounters facilitates the establishment of 'psychological proximity' (Hargie *et al.*, 2004).

Crisis

People are more likely to self-disclose in situations where they are undergoing some form of crisis, especially if this stress is shared by both participants. Thus, patients in a hospital ward who are awaiting operations generally disclose quite a lot to one another.

Isolation

If individuals are cut off from the rest of society they tend to engage in more self-disclosure. For example, two prisoners sharing a cell often share a high degree of personal information. Indeed, for this reason the police sometimes place a stooge in a cell along with a prisoner from whom they want some information. Likewise in cults, people are encouraged to fully disclose their most intimate details. As well as fostering a sense of bonding and belonging, this enables the cult leaders to exploit members' expressed weaknesses (Tourish and Wohlforth, 2000).

These then are the main findings relating to the influence which the characteristics of the discloser, the recipient, the relationship and the situation have upon the extent to which self-disclosure is employed during interpersonal interaction. From this review of research findings, it is obvious that self-disclosure is affected by a wide range of variables, many of which are operative in any particular encounter. It is important for professionals to be aware of the importance of these variables when making decisions about giving and receiving self-disclosures.

OVERVIEW

Self-disclosure is the cement that binds the bricks in any relationship edifice. Without it, relational structures are inherently unstable and prone to collapse. It is an important skill for professionals to be aware of from two perspectives. First, they need to be conscious of the likely effects of any self-disclosures they may make upon the clients with whom they come into contact. Second, many professionals operate in contexts wherein it is vital that they are able to encourage clients to self-disclose freely, and so a knowledge of factors that facilitate self-disclosure is very useful. Our impressions of other people can be totally wrong in many cases since we do not know what is 'going on inside them'. As Jourard (1964: 4) pointed out: 'Man, perhaps alone of all living forms, is capable of *being* one thing and *seeming* from his actions and talk to be something else.' The only method of attempting to overcome this problem of finding out what people are really like is to encourage them to talk about themselves openly and honestly. If we cannot facilitate others to self-disclose freely, then we will never really get to know them.

When giving and receiving self-disclosures, Stewart and Logan (1998) argued that three factors are important:

1   *Emotional timing.* Is the person in the right frame of mind to receive your disclosure? (e.g. someone who has just been fired may not be the best person to tell about your promotion.)
2   *Relevance timing.* Does the disclosure fit with the purpose and sequence of this conversation?
3   *Situational timing.* Is this environment suitable for discussion of this topic?

In addition, the following factors need to be considered:

- the total number of disclosures made
- the depth of these disclosures
- the nonverbal as well as verbal disclosures
- the age, gender and personality of the interactors
- the status and role relationships between the interactors

- how best to respond to client disclosures
- when it is best not to disclose.

The general importance of self-disclosure in everyday interaction reflects the fundamental value of this skill in many professional contexts. It is therefore useful to conclude with an early quotation from Chaikin and Derlega (1976: 178), which neatly encapsulates the central role that this aspect has to play:

> The nature of the decisions concerning self-disclosure that a person makes will have great bearing on his life. They will help determine the number of friends he has and what they are like: they will influence whether the discloser is regarded as emotionally stable or maladjusted by others: they will affect his happiness and the satisfaction he gets out of life. To a large extent, a person's decisions regarding the amount, the type, and the timing of his self-disclosures to others will even affect the degree of his own self-knowledge and awareness.

Chapter 10

Opening and closing interactions: the skills of set induction and closure

INTRODUCTION

Sᴇᴛ ɪɴᴅᴜᴄᴛɪᴏɴ ᴀɴᴅ ᴄʟᴏꜱᴜʀᴇ are the skills we employ to enter and exit social encounters. As summarised by Burgoon *et al.* (1996: 340): 'The first task for conversants is knowing how to start and stop interactions. Some conversations begin and end smoothly and effortlessly, others are difficult, uncomfortable, and problematic.' Firsts and lasts seem to be of special importance in life. This is reflected in the host of words we have to describe these periods – beginning and ending, opening and closing, hello and goodbye, salutation and farewell, arrival and departure, introduction and conclusion, alpha and omega, start and finish, etc. In psychological terms, one of the reasons for this is that we are much more likely to remember that which we encounter first (the *primacy effect*) and last (the *recency effect*) in any sequence. Events in between are less clearly recalled. Given that people are more likely to be influenced by what we said or did as they met us and just before they left us, we should give due consideration to how these interactional phases are handled. Not surprisingly, their role in the development and maintenance of relationships has been the subject of serious study for some considerable time (e.g. Roth, 1889).

Greetings and partings are therefore very important parameters within which social interaction takes place. They are structured, formalised sequences during which we have a greater opportunity to make important points or create an effective impact. Given their prevalence, Levinson (2006) referred to greetings and partings as 'strong universals' in human interaction. Humans have developed elaborate meeting and leave-taking rituals to mark these occasions, and parents overtly teach their children to engage in appropriate behaviours at both stages ('Say hello', 'Wave goodbye'). The greeting auto-pilot kicks in when we meet those who we know, even if we are just passing and do not intend to engage in conversation. As colleagues walk past one another they smile, engage in eye contact and make *adjacency pair* verbal responses where an utterance anticipates a related one from the other person (Cooren and Fairhurst, 2004), such as: 'Hi. How are you?' followed by the reply 'Good. And you?', and walk on. These responses are so much a part of our everyday lives that in fact we often only notice them when they are absent. Thus, if we meet a friend or colleague who does not engage in the process of salutation, or who leaves without any disengaging ritual, we become concerned. Indeed, if we cannot engage fully in greetings and partings, rules of interactional politeness deem that we provide some or all of: an apology ('Sorry'); a justification ('I can't stop now, I'm late for class') and a relational continuity indicator ('I'll phone you this evening').

Although in this chapter set induction and closure are discussed separately, these are complementary skills. There is truth in the old adage that to have a good ending you must first have a good beginning. The symbiotic relationship between the two can be exemplified by examining the behaviours initially identified by Kendon and Ferber (1973) as being associated with the three main phases of greetings and partings between friends:

A   **Distant phase.** When two friends are at a distance, but within sight, the behaviours displayed include hand waving, eyebrow flashing (raising both eyebrows), smiling, head tossing and direct eye contact.

B   **Medium phase.** When the friends are at a closer, interim distance, they avoid eye contact, smile and engage in a range of grooming (self-touching) behaviours.

C   **Close phase.** At this stage the friends again engage in direct eye contact, smile, make appropriate verbalisations and may touch one another (shake hands, hug or kiss).

During greetings the sequence is ABC, while during partings the reverse sequence CBA operates. At the greeting stage this signals the availability of the participants for interaction, whereas during parting it underlines the decreasing accessibility.

Greetings and partings are important relational events. Relationships have been conceptualised as mini-cultures with their own meanings, values, communication codes and traditions (Mittendorff *et al.*, 2006). Within them communicative symbols, often comprehensible only to those involved, are used as 'tie-signs' to create feelings of 'we-ness'. As part of this, different groups evolve their own special greeting and parting codes, for example:

• Steuten (2000) illustrated how bikers and rockers developed elaborate greeting rituals relevant to their type of group, which reflected their shared interests and helped to cement the bonds between members.

• Bell and Healey (1992), in their study of university students in the USA, found a special language of terms used between friends at greeting and parting.

• Williams (1997) charted the unique behaviours used at these stages by Saramakan Bushnegroes in the rain forest in Suriname, South America.

Opening and closing have been identified from a review of research studies in medicine as two of the 14 core skills that contribute to effective consultations (Lipkin, 1996). Interestingly, in the psychotherapeutic context, Flemmer *et al.* (1996) found that experienced therapists (>16 years' experience) rated the opening phase as being significantly more important than did less experienced therapists. This suggests that over time the import of the skill of set induction becomes even more apparent.

SET INDUCTION

Anyone familiar with the world of athletics will be aware of the instructions given to competitors before a race – 'On your marks. Get set. Go!' By telling the athletes to get set, the starter is preparing them for the final signal and allowing them to become both mentally and physically ready for the impending take-off. This simple example is a good introduction to the skill of set induction. Set induction was a term coined by psychologists to describe that which occurs when 'an organism is usually prepared at any moment for the stimuli it is going to receive and the responses it is going to make' (Woodworth and Marquis, 1949: 298). In other words, it establishes in the individual a state of readiness, involves gaining attention and arousing motivation, as well as providing guidelines about that which is to follow.

It is a skill that is widely used, in various forms, in interaction. At a simple level it may involve two people discussing local gossip, where, to stimulate the listener's attention, they may use phrases such as: 'Have you heard the latest?' At another level, on television and at the cinema, there are 'trailers' advertising forthcoming attractions in an exciting and dramatic fashion to arouse interest in what is to follow. Indeed, television programmes usually contain a fair degree of set induction in themselves, employing appropriate introductory music and accompanying action to stimulate the viewer.

The term 'set' has many applications in our everyday lives. For example, how a table is set reveals quite a lot about the forthcoming meal – how many people will be eating, how many courses there are and how formal the behaviour of the diners is likely to be. Other uses of the term 'set' include 'It's a set-up', 'Are you all set?' and 'Is the alarm set?' In all of these instances, preparation for some form of activity to follow is the central theme and this is the main thrust of the skill of set induction.

In relation to social interaction, the induction of an appropriate set can be defined as the initial strategy employed to establish a frame of reference, deliberately designed to facilitate the development of a communicative link between the expectations of the participants and the realities of the situation. Set induction can therefore be a long or a short process depending upon the context of the interaction.

Purposes of set induction

Set induction involves more than simply giving a brief introduction at the beginning of a social encounter. It may involve a large number of different activities, appropriate to the situation in which set is to be induced. The generic goals of the skill are shown in Box 10.1. However, the specific functions need to be tailored to the demands of the prevailing situation, and so varying techniques are employed to achieve them. Thus, a

Box 10.1 Goals of set induction

The main goals served by the skill of set induction are:

1 to induce in participants a state of readiness appropriate to the task to follow, through establishing rapport, arousing motivation and gaining attention
2 to establish links with previous encounters (during follow-up sessions)
3 to ascertain the expectations of participants
4 to discover the extent of participants' knowledge of the topic to be discussed
5 to indicate to or negotiate with participants reasonable objectives for the encounter
6 to explain what one's functions are and what limitations may accompany these functions.

helper uses different behaviours to open a counselling session from a professor introducing a lecture to a large university class. The process can take an infinite variety of forms both between and within contexts. The set used is influenced by, amongst other things, the subject matter to be discussed, the amount of time available, the time of day, the length of time since the last meeting, the location of the encounter, and the personality, experience and cultural background of those involved. Such factors should be borne in mind when evaluating the main techniques for inducing set. There is even some research to suggest that the approach used in greetings is influenced by the individual's testosterone level. In an interesting experimental study of greeting behaviour, Dabbs *et al.* (2001) discovered that high-testosterone males and females entered the room more quickly, were more businesslike and forward in their manner, focused directly on the other person and displayed less nervousness. In comparison, low-testosterone individuals were more responsive, attentive and friendly, but also more tense and nervous.

During professional encounters, set usually progresses through the four phases of:

MEETING → GREETING → SEATING → TREATING

At the meeting stage the initial *perceptions* gleaned of one another are very important. Greetings represent the *social* phase of welcome and salutation. During the seating stage the professional must demonstrate a *motivation* to become involved with the client. Finally, treating represents the transition to the *cognitive* or substantive business to be transacted. These stages do not always progress in a linear fashion, but rather they overlap and are interdependent. However, it is useful in terms of analysis to examine each separately.

Perceptual set

How we perceive others upon first meeting plays a crucial role in social interaction. The human brain is a predictive organ – it attempts to work out what to expect next. Thus, during social encounters we search out and evaluate cues that may enable us to predict with accuracy how others will behave towards us. Research on first impressions shows that the initial judgements we make upon meeting others are crucially important in influencing how we react to them and interpret their responses (Demarais and White, 2005; Ambady and Skowronski, 2008). There is now a considerable volume of research into the accuracy of first impressions (AFI). Those who score highly in terms of AFI tend to be more socially skilled, popular with peers, experience lower levels of loneliness, depression and anxiety, have higher quality of personal relationships, and achieve more senior positions and higher salaries at work. In their review of this area, Hall and Andrzejewski (2008: 98) concluded: 'A large amount of research shows that it is good to be able to draw accurate inferences about people based on first impressions.' This is not really surprising as AFI enables the individual to respond appropriately at the outset to different people, and to make informed decisions in a range of situations (e.g. Should I ask this person for a date? Should I appoint this person to this position?).

The fascinating recurring finding from research into first impressions is that we are often accurate in some of the snap judgements we make about others upon meeting them for the first time. What is referred to as 'zero-acquaintance' research, where individuals who have just met and have not interacted evaluate one another, has shown high levels of accuracy between judgements of personality and actual inventory scores of personality (Kenny and West, 2008). Likewise, there has also been research showing the potency of what is known as 'thin slices', or very short video segments, of behaviour in judging eventual outcomes. Curhan and Pentland (2007) illustrated how when people are shown such 'thin slices' of an interaction (ranging in different studies from between six seconds to three minutes), and especially of the opening sequence, they can make remarkably accurate judgements about how the encounter will progress. This has been found in a variety of diverse contexts including, inter alia, marital relationships (e.g. whether a couple will divorce), employment interview decisions, sales and negotiation outcomes, poker winners and losers, criminal trial deliberations, and ratings of professional competence. As noted by Pentland (2007: 192), we 'use these "thin slice" characterizations of others to quite accurately judge prospects for friendship, work relationship, negotiation, marital prospects, and so forth'.

These studies also show that we make evaluations of others at a very early stage and based upon minimal evidence. However, as Gray (2008) in her review of the field illustrated, first impressions can be accurate but they can also be inaccurate. Thus, Willis and Todorov (2006) demonstrated that after as little as one-tenth of a second we have made inferences based upon the facial appearance of the other person, and we then tend to become anchored on this initial judgement. Our early perceptions influence our expectations, and this in turn shapes our behaviour. Initial perceptions also impact upon subsequent processing, since we tend to adapt any conflicting information to make it fit more easily with our existing cognitive frame (Adler *et al.*, 2006). This is part of a process known as *selective distortion*, wherein we assimilate new material in such a way as to make it compatible with our established beliefs (Orbe and Bruess, 2005). Distortion can take the form of the *halo effect*, whereby if our initial perceptions are positive we then tend to view the person's future behaviour in a benevolent light. The corollary is the *horn effect*, where we form an early adverse opinion and then perceive the individual's future behaviour through this negative lens.

But why should first impressions be so important in social life? Some theorists argue that there is an evolutionary basis underpinning our seemingly visceral reaction of making instant decisions based upon initial impressions. Thus, Schaller (2008) argued that many aspects of human cognition evolved as a result of their contribution to our social and physical well-being. One such aspect is the capacity to rapidly judge others. For our distant ancestors this was often crucial. For example, upon meeting others they had to answer questions such as: Is this person likely to cause me serious harm? Do they appear to be carrying a potentially life-threatening and contagious disease? So, it is argued, the ability to make what could be life-saving decisions was learned and then evolved as society developed. We may be less worried today about whether someone will cause us bodily harm or be carrying a deadly disease, but we still need to ascertain whether the other person is likely to be a friend or foe. Thus, we may ask questions such as: Is this person trustworthy? On a more positive note, since time immemorial humans, upon first meeting potential partners, have also asked themselves a question such as: Does this person seem suitable as a romantic mate? But like all aspects of interpersonal communication, impression formation is a two-way street. We therefore know that others are also assessing us when we meet. Lamb (1988: 103) illustrated how:

> Infants develop fear of strangers at between seven and eight months, when they begin to make the distinction between who they know and who they do not. We never outgrow this uncertainty about people outside our established circle. As adults we worry about the first impressions we make, finding ourselves at the mercy of someone who is bound to form judgements on the basis of very little genuine knowledge about us.

It is therefore clear that initial perceptions matter a great deal. There is considerable wisdom in the aphorism 'You don't get a second chance to make a first impression.' Our perceptual set is determined by both the environment and the participants.

The nature of the environment

People organise their physical spaces to make statements about their identity. What is referred to as 'behavioural residue' provides information about the person living there (Gosling *et al.*, 2008). For example, a very tidy office with everything exactly in order and spotlessly clean, with a set of designer teacups placed neatly on a separate table, is one form of behavioural residue, while an office with irregular piles of paper and dusty books everywhere and stained coffee mugs here and there is evidence of a very different residue. Likewise, displays of hard rock posters, highly valuable original paintings, or sporting trophies provide evidence about the type of person with whom we will be interacting and the image they are presenting to others. As a result, we form impressions of individuals based on how they organise their spaces. Gosling *et al.* (2005a, 2005b) carried out studies in which they had observers make judgements about the personality traits of the occupants of 94 offices and 83 student bedrooms. They found that observers could make reasonably accurate judgements based solely on environmental cues.

Thus, the nature of the environment affects initial impressions. Dittmar (1992) carried out a study in which she filmed a young male and a young female individually in a relatively affluent and in a fairly impoverished environment. She found that when filmed in the wealthy environment the actors were rated as more intelligent, successful, educated and in control of their lives than when in the impoverished context, whereas when in the latter they were rated as warmer, friendlier and more self-expressive. Interestingly, close proximity to stigmatised others seems to increase the likelihood of the stigma 'rubbing off' on to oneself. Thus, Hebl and Mannix (2003) found that when a male job applicant was photographed sitting next to an overweight female the applicant was stigmatised, even when the raters were informed that there was no social relationship between the two individuals.

People also arrange their spaces in order to help them achieve their interactive goals. Thus, when we enter a room for the first time, the layout of tables, chairs and other furnishings are translated into a set of expectancies about the format for the interaction (for a full discussion of these aspects of nonverbal communication see Chapter 3). For example, a table and upright chairs usually convey an impression of a business-like environment, whereas a coffee table and easy chairs suggest a more social or conversational type of interaction. Thus, someone attending a selection interview may be somewhat taken aback if confronted with the latter type of setting since this is contrary to expectations.

Personal features of the participants

The age, sex, dress and general appearance of the other person all affect the initial perceptual set that is induced. It has been found that important decisions, such as whether or not to offer someone a job, are affected by initial impressions of the candidate gleaned by the interviewer (Millar and Tracey, 2006; Harris and Garris, 2008). In their review of this area, Whetzel and McDaniel (1999: 222) concluded: 'Interviewers' reactions to job candidates are strongly influenced by style of dress and grooming. Persons judged to be attractive or appropriately groomed or attired, received higher ratings than those judged to be inappropriately dressed or unattractive.'

Body features

We are judged on level of attractiveness from early childhood (Hawley *et al.*, 2007). Burnham and Phelan (2000) argued that some aspects of attractiveness are universal because they have a biological foundation. Clear skin is favoured because it is a sign of health, physical symmetry is viewed as the ideal and so is desirable and, as pointed out in Chapter 3, males from most cultures find females with a 0.7 waist-to-hip ratio (WHR, i.e. curvaceous body shape) most attractive. However, as also noted in Chapter 3, the latter finding has been queried in subsequent studies. Thus, Swami *et al.* (2006) found that female body mass index (BMI), a measure of height in relation to weight, was more important than WHR in determining ratings of attractiveness, and that this was more marked for Japanese than British males. In general, facial attractiveness and body weight seem to be the two key determining features in ratings of physical attraction, for both males and females (Swami *et al.*, 2007b). In relation to the latter aspect, in their review of the field Roehling *et al.* (2008: 392) concluded: 'Research indicates that overweight job applicants and employees are stereotypically viewed as being less conscientiousness, less agreeable, less emotionally stable, and less extraverted than their "normal-weight" counterparts.'

As discussed in Chapter 3, individuals rated high in attractiveness are viewed more positively by others. It has been shown that unattractive, when compared to attractive, females are regarded as more deceptive and are less likely to be believed when making a claim of sexual harassment (Seiter and Dunn, 2001). In line with the 'beauty is good' stereotype (Callan *et al.*, 2007), attractive people tend to receive more eye contact, more smiles, closer bodily proximity and greater body accessibility (openness of arms and legs) than those rated as being unattractive. It is likely that someone rated as being very attractive will also be seen as being popular, friendly and interesting to talk to. This in turn influences the way in which the attractive individual is approached, creating a *self-fulfilling prophecy* whereby: 'People have an expectation about what another person is like, which influences how they act towards that person, which causes that person to behave consistently with people's original expectations, making the expectations come true' (Aronson *et al.*, 2007: 67).

Ratings of attractiveness also seem to be influenced by a range of impinging factors. For example, one study found that hungry males preferred females with a higher body weight, while satiated males rated those with a lower body weight as more attractive (Swami and Tovée, 2006). Another study, into female ratings of attractiveness in males, found that their preferences changed across the menstrual cycle (Penton-Voak and Perrett, 2000). When presented with a choice of faces varying in masculinity and femininity, females preferred the masculine face during the follicular (fertile) phase of the cycle (days 6–14) but not at other times. Many of these judgements about attractiveness are, of course, subconscious but they nevertheless influence the way in which we respond.

However, decisions about interpersonal attractiveness are not just skin deep and involve more than mere physical features. Rather, there are three types of attractiveness: physical, social and task (Burgoon and Bacue, 2003). Physical attractiveness encompasses facial and body features. Social attractiveness refers to how well the individual communicates interpersonally in terms of factors such as friendliness, warmth and humour. Ratings of task attractiveness are related to how appealing individuals are as work partners. A physically less attractive professional may be successful and popular with clients by adopting a conducive interactive style (social attractiveness) together with a skilled, expert, approach (task attractiveness).

Dress

People are frequently evaluated on the basis of their mode of dress. The reason for this is that the style of dress which one adopts is often a sign of the image one wishes to project or group to which one belongs. Thus, certain professions have become associated with a particular style of dress, with the deliberate intention of conveying a definite public persona. This is exemplified by the adoption of uniforms by members of many institutions and organisations, who wish to present a consistent image, or be immediately identified in their job function. Police officers, soldiers, nurses, hospital doctors, clergy and traffic wardens all immediately induce a certain type of set in the observer. At another level, however, male business executives, civil servants, solicitors and estate agents have a less formal type of 'uniform' – usually a suit, shirt and tie. Indeed, the notion of 'dressing down days' at work proves the rule that dressing up is the expected norm. Forsythe (1990) found that female job applicants received more favourable hiring recommendations from experienced male and female business personnel when they were wearing more masculine clothing (e.g. a dark navy suit) than when wearing distinctly feminine attire (e.g. a soft beige dress).

The dress of professionals has an influence on client perceptions. One survey of patients in the USA showed that some 76 per cent preferred doctors to wear a white coat compared to under 5 per cent who favoured casual dress; in addition, perceptions of dress correlated significantly with ratings of trust and confidence in the physician (Rehman et al., 2005). These findings were confirmed in a survey of patients by Rowland et al. (2005) who concluded: 'It is clear that a physician's image is more than a facade. It is a mirror of competence, trust, expertise, and compassion' (p. 219). Numerous research studies have been conducted into determining the effects of dress and physical attractiveness upon evaluations of counsellors. In summarising the findings from these studies, Kleinke (1986) noted that counsellors who dress formally enough to portray an impression of competence and whose attire is in style rather than old-fashioned are preferred to those who dress very formally and are consequently seen as 'stuffy' or unapproachable. Likewise, more physically attractive counsellors are preferred.

Age

Initial judgements of others are also influenced by age (Ryan et al., 2007). Generally, older, more mature professionals are likely to be viewed as having greater experience, while newly qualified professionals are seen as having a more up-to-date knowledge base.

Gender

In terms of gender, males tend be more positively evaluated if they are regarded as being competent, assertive and rational, whereas females are viewed more positively if they portray traits such as gentleness, warmth and tact (Hargie, 2006b).

These are the main facets of perceptual set linked to personal attributes. However, as discussed in Chapter 3, our evaluations of individuals are influenced by a wide array of features, such as height, the use of cosmetics and perfumes, whether a male has a moustache or a beard, and whether or not glasses are worn. Such aspects all come together to influence the judgements we make of others. Although it is also true that first impressions can be deceptive, they are often accurate, which is why most of us judge a book to some extent by its cover.

Social set

Greetings have been shown to be ubiquitous across time and cultures (Tessonneau, 2005; Bowe and Martin, 2007). Before proceeding with the main business of the interaction, it is desirable to employ a number of social techniques. These serve to humanise the encounter, and often facilitate the achievement of the core task objectives. Indeed, one of the difficulties with telephone communication is what has been labelled the *coffee and biscuits problem* (Hargie *et al.*, 2004). In most business meetings, the first thing that happens is that refreshments are wheeled in. The process of getting to know one another then begins, as the participants engage in the universal shared human activity of drinking coffee and eating biscuits. As well as being a sign of basic civility, this has a deeper level of significance. In a sense, coffee can help to lubricate the business machine. Before progressing to the main task, it enables each side to make judgements about the likely formality of the occasion, and how personable and amenable the other is. On the telephone this cannot happen and so the social opportunies are lost.

What is known as *sociality communication* has been the focus of research attention across a range of contexts, and has been shown to be central to effective interaction (Koermer and Kilbane, 2008). Sociality communication refers to behaviour that facilitates smooth cooperative interaction. It incorporates four separate dimensions (Koermer and McCroskey, 2006):

1   *Courtesies* involve friendly greetings and a polite approach.
2   *Pleasantries* relate to small talk on aspects such as the weather or current events.
3   *Sociabilities* include jokes and disclosures pertaining to gossip.
4   *Privacies* are deeper disclosures about oneself.

Social set incorporates the first two of these dimensions and can also include elements of the third. The fourth dimension comes into play as relationships develop (see Chapter 9).

The induction of an appropriate social set is an important preliminary to the more substantive issues to follow, in that it serves to establish a good, amicable working relationship between the participants at the beginning of the interaction. Three techniques are employed here: receptivity, non-task comments and the provision of creature comforts.

Receptivity

The way that professionals receive their clients is of considerable importance. Robinson (1998) argued that the first stage is to negotiate a *participation framework* where both sides communicate their availability (or otherwise) to become involved. This is followed by an *engagement framework* where they move on to mutually collaborative communication. In the doctor–patient context, Robinson charted how degree of willingness to be involved was signalled nonverbally by the doctor, from an extreme of not looking at the patient, through eye gaze but not body asymmetry, and on to full engagement with the upper and lower torso and feet oriented towards the patient. Research by Tallman *et al.* (2007) has shown that doctors who receive higher ratings of patient satisfaction devote time and effort to the greeting stage. As discussed in Chapter 5, when the doctor begins the interaction with an open question there is significantly greater engagement from patients than when the encounter is opened with a closed question. Similarly, in paediatric encounters the degree of involvement of children is influenced by the physician's first question. This can be directed to the child (e.g. 'Right, Colin, how can I help you today?'), parent (e.g. 'So what can we do for Colin today?') or open to either (e.g. 'How can I help you today?'). When the opening query is directed to the child, there is a greater likelihood of the child becoming more actively involved in the consultation (Stivers, 2001).

The use of social reinforcement techniques (handshake, smile, welcoming remarks, tone of voice and eye contact) are important at the outset, since they serve to make the other person feel more at ease and responsive (see Chapter 4). While some form of nonverbal greeting ritual is universal across countries and cultures, considerable variation has been charted in the exact form this takes (Axtell, 1999; Migge, 2005). Indeed, some countries may or may not use some parts of the greeting ritual. For example, Germans have fewer conversational routines during opening and closing phases, and are much less likely to engage in polite conversation – to the extent that there is no German term for 'small talk' (House, 2005). Greetings across cultures range from Maori nose rubbing, Tibetan tribesmen sticking out their tongues at one another, Eskimos banging their hand on the other person's head or shoulders and East African tribes spitting at each other's feet. These behaviours all serve the same function – that of forming a human bond. They can also have important benefits.

Allday and Pakurar (2007) found that the use of teacher greetings at the start of lessons increased the amount of time spent by pupils in on-task behaviours. Similarly, Brown and Sulzerazaroff (1994), in a study of bank tellers, demonstrated how words of greeting, a smile and direct eye contact were all significantly correlated with ratings of customer satisfaction. In the counselling context, smiles and facial signal of interest by the counsellor have been shown to be important in engaging clients at the outset (Sharpley *et al.*, 2006). The importance of smiling was also evidenced in an experimental study by Monahan (1998), who found that the effect existed even at a subconscious level. Subjects shown slides at a subliminal level of a person smiling gave increased ratings of their likeability and attractiveness.

Another important aspect of receptivity is the use of the client's name. This leads to a more favourable evaluation of the speaker and has been shown to be important in the professional context (Hargie *et al.*, 2004). Whether formal or first names are used is a matter for sensitive judgement or negotiation. One major survey of patients in the USA revealed that the majority wanted physicians to greet them with a handshake and to use their first name, and preferred the doctor to introduce themselves using both first and last names (Makoul *et al.*, 2007). They also wanted the physician to smile, be warm, attentive, friendly and calm. Thus, Kahn (2008: 1988) developed the following checklist for doctors to follow in their initial meeting with patients in hospital:

1   Ask permission to enter the room and wait for an answer.
2   Introduce yourself, showing ID badge.

3   Shake hands (wear glove if needed).
4   Sit down. Smile if appropriate.
5   Briefly explain your role on the team.
6   Ask the patient how he or she is feeling about being in the hospital.

An important aspect here is how greeting behaviours are employed. Let us consider for a moment just one common greeting ritual – the handshake. A recurring aspect is that it is usually initiated by the person of higher status (Webster, 1984). However, the handshake is not a unitary behaviour but, as illustrated by Astrom and Thorell (1996), takes many forms (see Box 10.2 for the main ones). One Swedish study investigated the effects of handshakes and associated behaviour (e.g. direction of eye gaze) upon the rather eclectic mix of therapists, car salespeople and clergy – all selected because they were professional groups who regularly engage in handshaking. It was found that a strong handshake was clearly associated with ratings of extraversion and a weak one with introversion. The most satisfying greeting behaviour was direct eye gaze while a weak handshake was rated as the least satisfying. This latter finding confirmed other research showing that a limp, wet, 'dead fish' handshake is disliked and rated negatively whereas a firm handshake is viewed positively (Astrom, 1994).

This result was also confirmed in a detailed study by Chaplin *et al.* (2000), who noted that the handshake has historically been seen as a male greeting behaviour. They studied the handshake in relation to gender, personality and first impressions. Four trained coders shook hands twice with college undergraduates, and rated each handshake on a five-point scale along eight dimensions:

1   strength (weak–strong)
2   temperature (cold–warm)

Box 10.2 Handshake variations

The other person:

- clasps your hand more weakly than 'normal'
- clasps your hand more strongly than 'normal'
- retains your hand longer than 'normal'
- releases your hand immediately after touching it
- pulls your hand towards them
- pumps your hand up and down several times
- performs pumping and clenching movements
- proffers only the fingers
- proffers the whole hand in a sort of thumb grip
- rejects your hand
- grasps your hand with both of theirs
- clasps your hand from above
- clasps your hand from below
- clasps your hand with their palm turned downwards
- clasps your hand with their palm turned upwards.

---

3   dryness (damp–dry)
4   completeness of grip (very incomplete–full)
5   duration (brief–long)
6   vigour (low–high)
7   texture (soft–rough)
8   eye contact (none–direct).

These ratings were then correlated with the other variables. Among the main significant findings to emerge were that five of the above variables (strength, duration, completeness of grip, vigour and eye contact) combined to constitute the 'firm handshake', and male handshakes were firmer than females. Those with firm handshakes were more extraverted and less shy and neurotic, and also created better first impressions. Chaplin *et al.* (2000) highlighted the significance of these findings for females in professional contexts where 'giving a firm handshake may provide an effective initial form of self-promotion for women that does not have the costs associated with other less subtle forms of assertive self-promotion' (p. 117). This was corroborated in a study of employment interviews by Stewart *et al.* (2008), where a strong relationship was found between the quality of the handshake by candidates and hiring decisions. A firm handshake by females was shown to be especially important.

Gender differences have also been noted in greeting rituals. Thus, the eyebrow flash (both eyebrows raised briefly) is used more often by men, and is rated more positively when used with members of the opposite sex, and as a greeting with people we know (Martin, 1997; Noller, 2005). In a study of 152 greeting dyads at Kansas City International Airport, Greenbaum and Rosenfeld (1980) found that bodily contact was observed in 126 (83 per cent) of the greetings. The types of contact observed were:

- mutual lip kiss
- face kiss
- mutual face contact excluding kiss
- handshake
- handholding
- hand to upper body (touching the face, neck, arm, shoulder or back)
- embrace.

Female greeting behaviour was very similar with both males and females, whereas males used markedly different greetings with females as opposed to males. Male same-sex dyads had a significantly higher frequency of handshaking, whereas dyads containing a female had significantly more mutual lip kisses and embraces. In another study, females were shown to smile more and have closer interpersonal proximity during greetings (Astrom, 1994).

Non-task comments

A seemingly universal way of opening interaction involves what is known as the 'empty question' regarding the other's well-being. An example is the formal and slightly ridiculous 'How do you do?' Variants on this theme proliferate. For example, in inner city Belfast it is 'How's about you?' often reduced to ' 'bout ye?' In their analysis of *phatic communion*, or small talk, Coupland *et al.* (1992) highlighted how this type of HAY (How are you?) question serves to signal recognition for and acknowledgement of the other person, but is not expected to produce any self-revelations from the respondent. They used the following joke to illustrate this.

> *A:* How are you?
>
> *B:* I have bursitis; my nose is itching; I worry about my future; and my uncle is wearing a dress these days.

But although this type of question is in a sense redundant, it is nevertheless expected as a curtain raiser for the business to follow. To employ another metaphor, non-task comments are employed to 'break the ice' in social encounters and serve as a preliminary to the exchange of information at a more substantive level. Statements relating to the weather or non-controversial current affairs are quite common social openers, as are comments relating to the specific situation (e.g. 'Sorry about the mess. We're having some renovations carried out.'). This form of opening is also important in the health care setting (Stein *et al.*, 2005). As explained by Holli *et al.* (2003: 45): 'Although it may be time-consuming for the busy professional, the opening exchange of either information or pleasantries is important and should not be omitted.' Interestingly, in the medical setting the HAY question, when posed by a physician, can be interpreted by patients either as an ice-breaker, or as a request for them to provide details of their medical condition (Robinson, 2006b).

While non-task comments are useful in a range of situations, they need to be used judiciously. An early note of caution was sounded by the eminent psychiatrist Sullivan (1954), who warned against the use of non-task comments (which he termed *social hokum*) in the psychiatric interview. He argued that in this particular context it was more important to get into substantive issues as soon as possible. Also in the clinical context, Morrison (2008) supported this perspective when he advised against small talk, noting: 'In most cases your patient has come for treatment because of troubling problems. Comments about the weather, baseball, or television shows may seem at best a distraction, or at worst an expression of unconcern on your part.' Similarly, Millar and Gallagher (2000: 392) cautioned concerning selection interviews: 'Although non-task comments may help to reduce anxiety levels of nervous applicants, it is equally possible that the use of social chit-chat may introduce unwanted variations into the procedures.' Thus, non-task comments need to be appropriate to context.

Provision of creature comforts

Creature comforts refer to those items used to make someone feel more at ease. These include a soft or 'easy' chair, an offer of a drink, whether alcoholic or a cup of tea or coffee, and reasonable lighting and temperature in the room. All of these are important for rapport building. This is clearly demonstrated by the fact that they are often taken away in situations where an individual is being subjected to stress, such as in severe interrogation sessions. In some settings professionals have little control over the physical location of the encounter and so have to try to compensate for the dearth of creature comforts by optimising their use of interpersonal skills.

Motivational set

A key function of set induction is to gain attention and arouse motivation at the beginning of an interaction. The way individuals perceive and assimilate information is affected by their initial motivation to attend. To maximise client involvement, the professional must both be motivated and be motivating. Thus, the two core methods used to induce motivational set are showing personal commitment and dramatic techniques.

Showing personal commitment

A prerequisite to the successful motivation of others is that we show enthusiasm and commitment for the task ourselves. A professional who seems unprepared, uninterested, rushed or nervous is most unlikely to inspire confidence in or be able to motivate clients. The best gospel preachers display evangelical zeal in their perform-ance. Good counsellors adopt a caring style. Successful lawyers exude confidence and expertise. In the service sector, employers use the technique of *mystery shopper*, whereby an assessor pretending to be a client visits the service area, to check that staff are showing motivation when they meet clients (Hargie and Tourish, 2009). Looking and sounding the part are key aspects of motivational set. To fully engage clients, professionals must show concern, commitment, enthusiasm, interest, attention and expertise.

Dramatic techniques

In many situations, particularly in learning environments, it is very important to gain the attention of participants at the outset, so that the task may proceed as smoothly as possible. All good entertainers know the value of beginning a performance with a 'flash-bang' to immediately grab the attention of the audience. Indeed, Munter (2000) used the term *grabbers* to describe such techniques. The following four dramatic techniques can be employed to engage motivational set: novel stimuli; an intriguing problem; a provocative statement; behaviour change.

Novel stimuli

These are effective attention-gaining devices. Magicians have long recognised the power of rabbits being pulled from hats. Producers of television news programmes, aware of the value of stories involving violence in obtaining the attention of viewers, have a maxim regarding opening items of 'If it bleeds, it leads.' They also use 'teasers' to trail upcoming items, since it has been found that viewers pay more attention to news stories that have been teased and to commercials immediately following the teaser (Cameron *et al.*, 1991; Wittebols, 2004). The implications of these results are fairly obvious. There are many aids (diagrammatic, real objects, audio-visual recordings, etc.) that can be used in order to arouse motivation. By focusing on any of these at the outset, the learning environment can be enhanced.

A word of caution is needed here, however, in that to be effective in the longer term, the novel stimulus must be related to the task in hand. Otherwise this technique will be seen as gimmickry and all it will achieve is literally novelty value. In addition, it has been shown that the use of teasers can lead radio listeners to form premature judgements about culpability in relation to threatening stories (rape, murder, etc.). Dolinski and Kofta (2001) carried out an experiment whereby university students either heard stories as a whole, or as a headline followed by a break (the typical 'more on that story after this short break' approach) and then the full story. They found that listeners were consistently more likely to attribute culpability to the central person (e.g. a male arrested for suspected rape, or a hospital doctor who misdiagnosed a ruptured appendix as inflammation of the ovary after which a patient died) when the story was teased. It seems that we make judgements based on the information available and these then become resistant to change (see the discussion later in the chapter on *need for closure*). Dolinski and Kofta (2001: 255) concluded: 'Newspaper readers, radio listeners, and TV viewers should be aware that they are prone to make biased moral judgments on the basis of information provided in the headline part of the message.'

An intriguing problem

Employed at the beginning of an interaction sequence this can engage listeners' interest immediately, and hold it for a long time if they are required to solve the problem. This technique is equally applicable whether the problem posed is a technical or a social one. Furthermore, it does not really matter whether or not the problem has a correct solution. The idea here is to establish immediate involvement and participation at a cognitive or practical level. The use of case histories can be particularly relevant in this respect. Here, a tutor presents details of a particularly difficult case and asks trainees how they would have dealt with it.

A provocative statement

This method of inducing set must be carefully thought out, since the object of the exercise is to provoke comment, rather than aggression, on the part of the listener. With very sensitive topics or volatile audiences, great caution should be exercised.

Behaviour change

The adoption of unexpected or unusual behaviour can be a powerful method for gaining attention. This needs to depart from the normal behaviour pattern to be most effective. For example, a lecturer may sit with the audience or move about the room without speaking in order to grab attention. All humans have a basic cognitive structure that strives to accommodate new information of an unexpected nature. It is therefore the element of behavioural surprise that is central to the efficacy of this method, since it stimulates the individual's attentiveness.

Cognitive set

The main purpose of many encounters is concerned with substantive issues of fact. Before proceeding to these issues, however, it is important to check that the terms of reference are clearly understood at the outset. In order to achieve this objective, it is necessary to ensure that all parties are in clear agreement as to the nature and objectives of the ensuing interaction. In other words, it is important to induce an appropriate cognitive set in the participants, so that they are mentally prepared in terms of the background to, and likely progression of, the main business to follow. As Millar and Tracey (2006: 89), in their analysis of interviewing, noted: 'The interviewer must indicate what the objectives are, propose ideas about how the interview will proceed, and give an indication of the structure, content and duration of the interview.'

The functions of cognitive set can be summarised as the process of informing participants where they have been, what stage they are now at and where they are going. This involves five main components: providing prior instructions; reviewing previous information; ascertaining expectations; outlining functions; and goal setting.

Prior instructions

It has long been known that prior instructions, such as techniques to use in solving a problem or special items to be aware of, help to improve performance. In an early study in this field, Reid *et al.* (1960) found that serial learning was speeded up by providing instructions to subjects about how to approach the learning task. In reviewing research into prior instructions, Turk (1985) concluded that telling individuals what they will hear actually biases them to perceive what they have been encouraged to expect, regardless of what message they actually receive. As Turk (1985: 76) put it: 'Telling people what they are about to perceive will radically affect what they do perceive'. Park and Kraus (1992) had a group of subjects ask one question each to a person they did not know. They found that when the questioners were instructed to obtain as much information as possible about traits of the respondent such as intelligence, honesty, truthfulness and dependability, they were able to do so successfully. Park and Kraus concluded that it is possible to 'obtain a greater amount of verbal information relevant to difficult-to-judge dimensions when instructed to do so' (p. 445). On the basis of their results they recommended that personnel officers and selectors at employment interviews should be instructed in advance to search for specific information about candidates.

Even subtle aspects of prior instructions can have an impact. Thus, Song and Schwarz (2010) found that the font used in written instructions affected how an exercise described was perceived. In one experiment involving a physical exercise, when the easy-to-read Arial font was used, subjects estimated that the task would take 8.2 minutes to complete, whereas when the difficult-to-read Mistral font was employed for the same set of instructions, the anticipated time was 15.1 minutes. Respondents also viewed the task as being more difficult when Mistral was used as opposed to Arial. As a result, they were more willing to incorporate the exercise into their everyday routine when the easy-to-read font was employed. However, this effect can be mitigated by telling those subjects given the Mistral version that the instructions may be difficult to read owing to the font used. When this caveat is added to the prior instructions, the differential effect of the fonts is eliminated. It seems that the difficulty is then attributed to the font rather than the exercise per se (for a comparison of the two fonts see Box 10.3, where the first set of instructions is given in Arial and then replicated in Mistral, using the same font size).

Finally, Miller *et al.* (2001) found that our reactions to others in need can be mediated by prior instructions. In a meta-analysis of research studies in this field they found that subjects responded much more sympathetically and empathically when asked either to put themselves in the other person's situation, or to try hard to imagine how that person was actually feeling. Conversely, when asked only to focus objectively on the person's behaviour or the facts of the situation, feelings of empathy and sympathy were greatly reduced.

Reviewing previous information

It is important to ascertain the extent of knowledge participants may have regarding the subject to be discussed. This information, when gathered at an early stage, enables decisions to be made about the appropriate level for any ensuing explanations and whether or not to encourage contributions. These points are pertinent when addressing a new topic for the first time. The process of linking what is already known with the new material to follow has been shown to be an effective teaching procedure for facilitating the understanding and retention by pupils of new information (Burden and Byrd, 2009).

In many interpersonal transactions, one encounter is influenced by decisions made and commitments undertaken in the previous meeting. Again, it is important to establish that all parties are in agreement as to the main points arising from prior interactions and the implications of these for the present discussion. If there is

---

Box 10.3 Comparing instructions in Arial and Mistral fonts

Standing upright, hold a stick horizontally with both hands, keeping the palms down. Let the stick rest against the front of your thighs.
Now, with your good arm, push the injured arm out to the side and raise it up as far as you can, while keeping your elbows straight.
Hold this position for five seconds. Repeat the exercise ten times.

Standing upright, hold a stick horizontally with both hands, keeping the palms down. Let the stick rest against the front of your thighs.
Now, with your good arm, push the injured arm out to the side and raise it up as far as you can, while keeping your elbows straight.
Hold this position for five seconds. Repeat the exercise ten times.

---

disagreement or confusion at this stage, it is unlikely that the current encounter will be fruitful. This problem is formally overcome in many business settings where minutes of meetings are taken. The minutes from a previous meeting are reviewed and agreed at the outset, before the main agenda items for the current meeting are discussed. This procedure ensures that all participants are in agreement about what has gone before, and have therefore a common frame of reference for the forthcoming meeting. In addition, agenda items are usually circulated prior to the meeting, and this in itself is a form of cognitive set, allowing individuals to prepare themselves for the main areas to be discussed.

Dealing with expectations

Snyder and Stukas (2007: 363) noted: 'When people meet and interact with new acquaintances, they often use expectations about what these other people will be like to guide their interactions.' In this way, people approach social encounters with certain explicit or implicit expectations, which they expect to have fulfilled (Hamilton, 2005). If expectations are unrealistic or misplaced, it is important to discover this and make it clear at a very early stage. Otherwise the conversation may proceed for quite some time before these become explicit. This may result in frustration, embarrassment or even anger, if people feel their time has been wasted. It can also result in the discussion proceeding at dual purposes, or even terminating, with both parties reading the situation along different yet parallel lines. By ascertaining the immediate goals of those involved, such problems can be overcome. This can be achieved simply by asking what others expect from the present encounter. Once goals are clarified, behaviour is more easily understood.

The process of *priming* is important here, as there is now considerable research to show that how we have been primed to receive information does indeed influence our judgements (Weisbuch *et al.*, 2008). The effect was borne out in a classic study by Kelley (1950), who found that when subjects were told to expect a 'warm' or 'cold' instructor they developed a positive or negative mental set respectively. This influenced both their evaluations of instructors and the way in which they interacted with them. More recently, Singh *et al.* (1997) and Fiske *et al.* (2007) confirmed the importance of 'warm' and 'cold' as central traits, which once ascribed to someone trigger other positive or negative evaluations respectively.

This is linked to the *interpersonal expectancy effect* also known as the *Pygmalion effect*. This refers to the way in which our expectations of others influence how we perceive and respond to them, and how this in turn affects the way they respond to us (Harris and Garris, 2008). In the words of Baker (1994: 38): 'Expectations are self-fulfilling prophesies. What we expect of people is often what we get.' Hanna and Wilson (1998: 102) gave as an example: 'If you are subconsciously looking for evidence that another person is angry with you, you are likely to find that evidence in the person's behavior.' This process is known as the *perceptual confirmation effect*. In one classic study in the USA, researchers selected pupils at random and informed their teachers that these children had been identified as 'late bloomers' who would soon show marked improvements in their academic performance. Follow-up analyses revealed that these children had indeed outperformed their peers. This was attributed to the increased attention and reward they had received from teachers based upon the set expectations (Rosenthal and Jacobson, 1992). A range of follow-up studies confirmed how teacher expectations directly impact upon pupil performance (Rubie-Davies *et al.*, 2006). This effect has also been shown to be prevalent in a range of other social contexts (Rosenthal, 2006). If we are set to perceive others in either a positive or negative light, our behaviour towards them is likely to provoke the response we expected. As aptly summarised by Pratkanis (2007: 23): 'Expectations guide inter-pretations and perceptions to create a picture of reality that is congruent with expectations.'

The corollary of the Pygmalion effect is the *Galatea effect*, which refers to the expectations we hold of ourselves, and the fact that we are likely to realise these self-expectations (Carmeli and Schaubroeck, 2007). In analysing this area, Kirsch (1999) distinguished between two types of expectancy:

1 **Stimulus expectancy** does not affect the stimulus itself but rather the per-son's perception of it. For example, if I expect people of a certain race to be aggressive, when I interact with individuals of that race I am more likely to perceive their behaviour as aggressive regardless of whether it really is or not.
2 **Response expectancy** relates to one's anticipated responses in a situation. Thus, if I believe that I am going to really enjoy spending time with a particular individual, then when I am with that person I am more likely to behave in a way consistent with this expectation (smiling, laughing, paying attention to the other person, etc.). In fact this example is very pertinent since there is considerable research to show that people tend to behave in such a way as to ensure that their emotional expectations are confirmed (Catanzaro and Mearns, 1999).

Another distinction is between expectation-congruent (*assimilation effect*) stimuli that confirm what we had thought, and expectation-discrepant (*contrast effect*) stimuli that are contrary (Tormala and Petty, 2007). How the latter are perceived is crucial in shaping final opinions about the experience. The strength of expectations is central here. People spend months or years planning and looking forward to great occasions in their lives such as wedding ceremonies or holidays. The anticipation of success and enjoyment are very high, and this in turn is likely to lead to expectation-discrepant (negative) experiences being filtered out of the occasion itself.

Outlining functions

This may involve the outlining of professional job role and functions. If someone holds false expectations, as was discussed in the previous section, it is vital to make this clear and to point out what can and cannot be done within the limitation of professional parameters. Once this has been achieved the interaction should flow more smoothly, with both participants aware of their respective roles. This does not always occur. One study of doctor–patient interactions in a US hospital (Santen *et al.*, 2008) revealed that in 82 per cent of consultations the physicians introduced themselves as a doctor and only in 7 per cent of cases did they identify themselves as a resident (in training). Also in this study, in 64 per cent of instances, attending (supervising) physicians introduced themselves as a doctor, with only 6 per cent stating that they were in fact the supervising physician. Patients felt that it was very important for them to know the level of training of their doctor, yet most stated that they were unaware of this. Although the residents may fear a loss of perceived status (and the supervising physician may be sensitive to this), the patient has a right to know the stage of training of those responsible for their care.

Nelson-Jones (2005b) used the term *structuring* to refer to the process by which professionals make clients aware of one another's roles, and argued that a key juncture for outlining functions is at the contracting stage of the initial session. At this stage the professional often has to answer the implicit or explicit client question 'How are you going to help me?' Counsellors answer this question in different ways, depending upon their theoretical perspectives. A useful general approach for counsellors is to respond to this question by emphasising that their role involves helping and supporting people as they sort out their problems and reach eventual personal decisions, rather than offering instant solutions.

Goal setting

As discussed in Chapter 2, goals are at the very epicentre of interaction. They provide direction for action and serve as an interpretation filter through which the behaviour of others is judged. A key goal in new or relatively unfamiliar contexts is that of *uncertainty reduction* or *uncertainty management* (Afifi, 2010; Knobloch, 2010). When encountering new situations: 'We want to know what is expected of us, what the rules of the interaction are, what others think of us, what relationship we will have with them, and so on' (Hargie, 2006b: 42). Experienced professionals develop *cognitive schemas* to enable them to deal swiftly and efficiently with a range of persons and situations (see Chapter 2). These schemas, developed after repeated exposure to the same situation, are cognitive structures containing knowledge and information about how to behave in a particular context. They contain *scripts* that are readily enacted – for example, the same greeting ritual is often implemented automatically with every client. As shown by Balcetis (2008), we tend to be *cognitive misers*, using established schemas to guide our behaviour across different people and settings. However, for trainee professionals who have not acquired relevant schemas, interaction is much more difficult and uncertain.

Likewise, for clients the visit to a professional may be one in which no schema or script exists. Again, uncertainty will be high and so the stage of goal setting is crucial in helping the client to better understand what the interaction entails (Hargie *et al.*, 2009). Thus, in the medical field, orientation statements by the physician that explain to the patient the sequence and purpose of forthcoming activities which will be carried out are important (Stein *et al.*, 2005), as these have been shown to facilitate both the communication process and health-related outcomes (Robinson and Stivers, 2001). In the workplace, newly hired employees have been shown to use a range of techniques to decrease their uncertainty (Clampitt, 2010). At times of major change the information needs of all employees are heightened. If the organisation itself does not deal effectively with such uncertainty, the grapevine goes into overdrive and rumours proliferate. Interestingly, one exception here is that police interrogators deliberately increase uncertainty when they imply to suspects that they know a lot more about their activities than they are being told, thereby keeping the suspect off balance and so more vulnerable to 'cracking' under the pressure. This technique, whereby detectives exaggerate to suspects the evidence they have about them, is known as *maximisation* (Klaver *et al.*, 2008). However, the reduction of uncertainty should usually be a core goal of the opening phase of interaction. If it is not dealt with, the cognitive space of individuals is occupied with attempts to reduce it, often at the expense of what would be more profitable activities.

In many contexts (e.g. in person-centred counselling where the client is allowed to structure the interaction and decide what should be discussed) it is not feasible for the professional simply to state the goals. However, in those situations where it is appropriate, it is helpful to state clearly the goals for the interaction, and the stages that are likely to be involved in pursuit of these goals. This can be a useful method for structuring the encounter. For example, the ability of teachers to structure lesson material in a logical, coherent fashion has long been known to be a feature of effective teaching (Rosenshine, 1971). There are other situations where it is desirable to structure interaction by providing guidelines about that which is to be discussed and the stages through which the discussion will proceed. In the medical context, Cohen-Cole (1991: 53) pointed out: 'Effective interviews begin with an explicit statement or acknowledgement of goals. Sometimes these may need to be negotiated between the doctor and the patient if there are some differences in objectives.' Kurtz *et al.* (1998) also highlighted the importance of the *screening* process, whereby the doctor checks and confirms the list of problems raised by the patient, giving as an example: 'So that's headaches and tiredness. Is there anything else you'd like to discuss today?' (p. 23).

The importance of negotiating the agenda has been recognised in the counselling context. Lang and van der Molen (1990: 93) noted that as early as possible in the helping interview 'the helper is advised to inform the client straightaway about his way of working, and then see if the client agrees with that, or whether he has other expectations'. Similarly in the negotiation context, the stage of formulating an agenda is essential to success. One side cannot simply decide upon the goals of the encounter and impose them on the other, but rather the first act of the negotiation drama is that of deciding the nature and structure of play (see Chapter 13).

Goal setting allows participants to prepare themselves fully. They will therefore be mentally prepared for the topics to be discussed, and be thinking about possible contributions they may be able to make. It also means that the individual feels less uncertain and more secure in the situation, knowing in advance what the purpose of the interaction is, what the main themes are likely to be, how the sequence of discussion should proceed, and the anticipated duration of the interaction.

Overview of set induction

In *The Republic* the philosopher Plato argued: 'The beginning is the most important part of the work.' This also holds for interpersonal encounters. In their analysis of interviewing, Stewart and Cash (2008: 77) noted: 'The few seconds or minutes of the opening are critical. What you do and say, or fail to do and say, influences how the other party perceives self, you, and the situation.' Set induction is therefore a very important process – hence the expressions 'Well begun is half done' and 'Start off as you intend to go on.' It will vary in length, form and elaborateness depending on the context of the interaction. *Perceptual set* refers to the effects of the initial impression formed by people based upon the nature of the environment and the personal attributes of the interactors. *Social set* is the process of welcoming people, providing creature comforts and generally making them feel settled. *Motivational set* is concerned with showing personal commitment and encouraging clients to participate fully. *Cognitive set* involves establishing expectations and outlining goals for the interaction.

The acronym STEP can be used to describe the four main stages of the skill of set induction, as people step into a relationship:

- *Start.* This involves welcoming others, settling them down and gaining attention.
- *Transact.* Here, expectations are ascertained, and the functions of the participants outlined. Any links with previous encounters should be made.
- *Evaluate.* An analysis is then carried out of the relationship between the expectations of the participants and the realities of the present situation. Any discrepancies must be clarified before the interaction can progress fruitfully.
- *Progress.* This stage marks the end of the beginning, when the interaction moves on to the main body of the business to be conducted. It involves finalising and agreeing the goals for, and the nature, content and duration of, the forthcoming interaction.

CLOSURE

As mentioned earlier, closure is the parallel side to set induction. However, there are also differences between the two. First, in general social encounters while we may think about how we should welcome someone, we seldom give much thought to how we will disengage from them (unless the relationship is not going well and we want to extricate ourselves from it). Generally, closure is more of an impromptu event – it just happens. In professional contexts more care and attention needs to be paid to the closing phase. In his analysis of interviewing, Stewart (2009: 192–193) pointed out:

> Too often the closing is seen by both parties as merely a stopping point or way of saying goodbye, an unimportant appendage to the interview. The closing, however, is as important as the opening. An abrupt, brief, seemingly uncaring closing may destroy the relationship.

A second major difference, as noted by one of the first academics to seriously study this field, is that 'greetings mark a transition to increased access and farewells to a state of decreased access' (Goffman, 1972: 79). The fact that access is literally being closed down means that the ending of the encounter has to be managed in such a way that the relationship is maintained and no one feels a sense of being rejected. Burgoon *et al.* (1996: 343) noted: 'It would be very efficient to end conversations by just walking away. But social norms call for balancing efficiency with appropriateness.' In fact, these norms are learned at an early age. First (1994) illustrated how 'The Leaving Game' is one of the first examples of dramatic play enacted by children (at around the age of 2.3 years). In this game, the child shows knowledge of the ramifications of parting by giving the twin instructions to the role-playing other: 'I'm leaving. You cry.'

In their review of the area, Bowe and Martin (2007: 69) noted: 'A short and abrupt farewell seems to devalue the interaction in some way.' Indeed, abrupt closures usually indicate personal or relational dysfunction. For example, one study compared 24 autistic individuals with a group of 24 nonautistic persons with 'mental retardation' matched for chronological and mental age (Hobson and Lee, 1996). It was found that the autistic individuals were less likely to engage in greeting and parting behaviours. More generally, abrupt closures occur for a variety of reasons, including:

- *ending an undesired interaction* (e.g. the rejection of unwanted sexual advances)
- *testing affinity* (e.g. to see if the other person will come after you as you walk away)
- *when frustration reaches a certain point* ('This is hopeless, I'm leaving.')
- *avoiding possible conflict* (if discussion is becoming overheated it may be better to leave rather than risk verbal or physical abuse)
- *demonstrating power and status* (those with higher status can terminate interactions suddenly – they see their time as more important than anyone else's and so may decide unilaterally how it is used; for example, in her study of closure patterns in primary care visits, West (2006) found that it was the doctor who initiated the closure).

The nonverbal behaviours used in these abrupt endings range through breaking off all eye contact, stopping talking altogether, to the extreme of turning one's back and walking away. Verbal statements fall into three main types:

1 *rejection remarks* that indicate you do not want the conversation to continue ('Would you please go away.', 'Clear off.')
2 *departure injunctions* that are a sign of higher status and power ('Off you go now.', 'I'm stopping it there. Go and work on it.')
3 *exasperation exits* that show you feel any further communication is a waste of time ('This is going nowhere. I've had enough.', 'I can't take any more of this.').

In linguistic terminology, closure has been defined as a final speech turn that is recognised as such by both parties involving 'the simultaneous arrival of the conversationalists at a point where one speaker's completion will not occasion another speaker's talk, and that will not be heard as some speaker's silence' (Schegloff and Sacks, 1973: 295). This is achieved through 'a set of regularly occurring behaviors that provide a normative, mutually agreed-upon process for terminating interactions' (Kellerman *et al.*, 1991: 392). These behaviours in turn serve to bring the interaction 'to an orderly ending and pull together the issues, concerns, agreements, and information shared' (Stewart and Cash, 2008: 94). They also shift the perspective from the present to the future. Thus, closure involves directing attention to the termination of an encounter, highlighting the main issues discussed, making arrangements for future meetings and ending the interaction in such a way that the relationship is maintained.

The expression 'need for closure' has entered the everyday lexicon in relation to ending a particular episode – such as an argument between colleagues, the completion of a work project or agreeing a divorce settlement. It is also widely employed to refer to the process of coming to terms with the loss of a loved one. This is especially so where there are problems surrounding the death, and indeed the need for closure is particularly strong when the person's remains have not been located (e.g. following kidnapping or terrorist offences). In this latter context, the term refers to the strongly felt human need to go through a process that will lead to acceptance of the loss. Understanding exactly how and why someone died and being able to go through the normal rituals associated with burial are all involved in this process of 'putting it all to rest' as part of final closure. This psychological phenomenon in many ways underscores and reflects the importance of closure more generally in human relationships.

There has been a considerable amount of research into the psychological phenomenon of *need for closure*, which has been defined as 'a motivated need for certainty' (McKay *et al.*, 2006: 422). More specifically, it can be conceptualised as 'a desire for a firm answer to a question, and as an aversion toward ambiguity' (Chirumbolo and Leone, 2008: 1280). There are individual differences in the degree to which different people need to have issues sorted out and wrapped up quickly. Some can handle large amounts of uncertainty and try to put off making decisions for as long as possible, while others like to have things cut and dried and want decisions made as swiftly as is feasible. As shown by Mannetti *et al.* (2002), motivation for closure ranges along a continuum from a high need to secure closure at one end to a strong desire to avoid closure at the other. Related dimensions here are the concepts of *seizing* and *freezing*, in that individuals with a high need for closure seize upon early information to make judgements and then freeze their decision at that point, closing their minds to any further relevant information (Kruglanski, 2004). They use a process of *perceptual accentuation* so that in effect they see what they want to see (Orbe and Bruess, 2005). The *confirmation bias* also comes into play as the person with a high need for closure actively seeks data that confirm the early decision and filters out contradictory stimuli (Mojzisch *et al.*, 2008). Thus, in the courtroom context, Honess and Charman (2002: 74) have shown how 'once jurors have made up their mind, they stop thinking about the evidence too hard'.

Individuals with a high need for closure are more rigid in their style of thinking and are generally 'cognitively impatient' – they do not want to think about things for long periods. Those with a low need for closure are happier to accept that life may involve multiple interpretations and conflicting opinions, and will more readily suspend judgement and postpone decisions (Neale and Fragale, 2006). A *Need for Closure Scale* (Neuberg *et al.*, 1997) has been developed to measure this phenomenon. It includes items such as 'I think that having clear rules and order at work is essential for success' and 'I don't like to go into a situation without knowing what to expect'. However, the situational context is an important moderating variable here, so that as the costs of not making a decision escalate, the need for closure increases accordingly (Richter and Kruglanski, 2004). For example, if your child is very seriously ill and you have to make a decision about agreeing to surgery that could save its life, this decision is likely to be expedited regardless of degree of personal need for closure.

This concept has relevance for both interactional set and closure. Those with a high need for closure are more heavily influenced by first impressions as they search for aspects to seize upon in terms of decision making. They desire clearly structured interactions with transparent goals, and readily accept the need to bring an encounter to an end in a neat and tidy manner. On the other hand, individuals with a low need for closure are less likely to make judgements based upon initial information. They prefer interactions that are loosely structured with less clear-cut goals, and they can be difficult to persuade that it is time to terminate an interaction. As a result, with this type of person, closure can be more prolonged and messier.

PURPOSES OF CLOSURE

The main goals of closure are shown in Box 10.4. Not all of these are relevant in every context, since to be effective the closure must reflect the tone, tenor and overall purpose of the encounter. In addition, closure, like set induction, depends upon a range of variables, including location, time available, the type of people involved and the anticipated duration of separation. As with set induction, closure also progresses through four interrelated and overlapping sequential stages, in this case:

RETREATING → REVIEWING → REINFORCING → REBONDING

The retreating phase involves efforts to influence the *perceptions* of others in such a way that they fully realise that you are in the process of leaving. The stage of reviewing relates to *cognitive* issues pertaining to the substantive business conducted, when decisions taken are summarised. Third, clients should be reinforced or *motivated* to carry out certain actions. Finally, rebonding refers to the *social* dimension of ensuring that a good rapport is maintained as leave-taking occurs.

Box 10.4 Goals of closure

The main goals served by the skill of closure are:

1   to signal that the interaction is about to end
2   to summarise substantive issues covered and agreements reached
3   to consolidate any new material introduced in the session
4   to assess the effectiveness of the interaction
5   to motivate participants to carry out certain courses of action
6   to provide links with future events
7   to give participants a sense of achievement
8   to establish commitment to the future of the relationship
9   to formally mark the final termination of the encounter.

Perceptual closure

The first stage of closure is that of indicating to the client that it is time to close. This necessitates the use of closure indicators and markers to signal that the end of the interaction is approaching. These *preclosing behaviours* and *final closure markers* have been shown to occur in telephone conversations as well as in face-to-face encounters (Placencia, 1997). A wide range of behaviours has been identified within both categories (Wolvin and Coakley, 1996; West, 2006).

Preclosing

This involves the use of both verbal and nonverbal behaviours to signal the end of the encounter. These flag to clients that the time has come to start winding up, and help to steer the discussion gently and smoothly into the final termination. Dolden (2008. 100–101) highlighted how 'the sequence of preclosing moves . . . used to initiate leave-taking creates a structural space where unaddressed issues can be raised, ensuring that the closing is collaboratively achieved'. Closing indicators include elongated and emphasised words such as 'Soooo . . .', 'Oookaay.' In a study of telephone conversations, Bangerter *et al.* (2004) found that 'Okay' and 'All right' were the two most frequently used preclosing terms. These closure indicators can be followed by more direct phrases: 'In the last few minutes that we have . . .', 'We're coming to the end of our session . . .'. Another tactic here is that of *projection*, where the other person is portrayed as the one really wanting or needing to terminate the interaction, owing to fatigue, other commitments, etc. ('You have worked very hard. I'm sure you've had enough for today.', 'I know how busy you are so I don't want to take up any more of your time.'). Accompanying nonverbal signals should reinforce the preclosing message (see Box 10.5). O'Leary and Gallois (1999) found that the most common nonverbal signs of preclosing were placing the hands on the arms of the chair in a way that would assist standing up, a forward lean of 30 degrees or more from previous position, smiling, more movement while speaking, and looking away from the other person.

This step of preparing the client for closure is very important. In the context of interviewing, Stewart and Cash (2008: 93) illustrated how 'an abrupt or tactless closing may undo the relationship established during the interview and agreements reached

---

Box 10.5 Nonverbal closure indicators

- Breaking eye contact.
- Taking out car keys.
- Gathering papers together.
- Looking at a watch or clock.
- Placing both hands on the arms of the chair.
- Explosive hand movements on the thighs or desk.
- Changing seated posture to a more raised position.
- Nodding the head rapidly.
- Orientating one's posture and feet towards the exit.

---

by making the other party feel like a discarded container – important only as long as needed'. Using preclosing to shade into the final parting ritual is therefore well advised.

Clients also make closing indicators when they feel that the time has come to end an interaction, and professionals need to be sensitive to these. In certain areas such as selling and negotiating this is a key to success. For example, in the former context clients emit buying signals to convey that they are ready to close. These include receptive verbalisations such as 'It looks really nice', body language including approving nods and smiles, physical actions such as handling the sales item lovingly and possessively, and acceptance-indicative questions such as 'Do you have it in blue?' (Hargie *et al.*, 2004).

Closure markers

These are used to mark and underscore the final ending of the encounter. They take three forms:

- *formal markers*, usually used in business contexts – 'It was nice to meet you.', 'Goodbye.'
- *informal markers* used with friends and colleagues – 'Cheers.', 'See you later.' 'Bye.', 'All the best.'
- *departure announcements* – 'I've got to go now.', 'Right, I'm off.'

Likewise, accompanying nonverbal markers occur along a continuum of formality – on the formal end is the handshake, while on the informal side there may be not much more than a smile. In between there are waves, kisses and hugs. More formal parting rituals tend to occur with people of higher status, with those who are not kith and kin, and in business encounters. The duration and intensity of closure markers is also greater when the period of anticipated separation is longer.

The success of closure indicators and markers is dependent upon the client. Those with a low need for closure may blissfully ignore closure attempts and very direct methods may then be required (opening the door, walking slowly out of the office, etc.). Indeed, Kellerman *et al.* (1991) reported that although much research has focused upon mutually negotiated leave-taking, in fact some 45 per cent of all conversations have unilaterally desired endings. They found that when ending an encounter that the other side does not want to close, the most common tactic is the use of external and uncontrollable events, such as third party entrances. For example, where it is known that a particular client will be difficult to get to leave, an *orchestrated intervention* can be arranged. Examples of this include the secretary coming in to announce your next urgent appointment, a colleague calling in to accompany you to a meeting or someone calling on the telephone at a prearranged time.

Cognitive closure

As defined by Millar and Tracey (2006: 94), cognitive closure is 'a means of seeking agreement that the main themes of the communication have been accurately received and understood'. It involves three main strategies – summarisation, checking out, and continuity links.

Summarisation

Summaries offer both sides the opportunity to check out that they are in agreement about the meaning of what has been discussed. There is now a considerable body of research across a wide range of professional contexts, including community pharmacy (Hargie *et al.*, 2000), university lecturing (Saunders and Saunders, 1993), medicine (Stein *et al.*, 2005), psychotherapy (Flemmer *et al.*, 1996), physiotherapy (Adams *et al.*, 1994) and negotiating (Rackham, 2007), to attest to the fact that professionals see summarisation as a key part of their role. Interestingly, however, actual practice often differs from the ideal. Thus, in the above studies, university lecturers often closed lectures abruptly claiming to have 'run out of time', doctors frequently ended the consultation with the writing and handing over of a prescription and pharmacists had brief closing statements (e.g. 'Go and see your doctor if it persists.'). Time and effort therefore need to be allowed for summarisation.

Research has clearly shown that an explicit concluding summary increases the listener's comprehension (Cruz, 1998). It should certainly take place at the end of interaction, but in longer encounters *intermittent summaries* or *spaced reviews* can be used periodically. In essence, summaries are important at three points: at the end of discussion on a particular issue or topic; at the end of the session; and at the final termination of the professional relationships.

At the end of discussion on a particular issue or topic

Where there has been a detailed, involved or protracted exchange it is useful to provide a summary of what has been covered. Such transitional reviews help to map out the contours of the relational terrain. They enable both sides to reflect, and hopefully agree, on what was covered. In certain types of encounter (e.g. educational or medical) this also serves the purpose of consolidating learning, by cementing core material in the listener's memory. Another important function is that they enable the professional to bring that part of the discussion to a rational end and progress on to the next topic.

At the end of the session

At the parting stage, the summary should scan back over the main features of the interaction. The key issues that emerged should be crystallised and linked to previous sessions and future encounters. On the perceptual side, a session summary is also a very potent closure indicator, signalling that the interaction is now ending. For this reason, they were termed *historicizing acts* by Albert and Kessler (1976), since they treat the session as something that is now in the past. Part of this may also involve *contingency planning*. This involves giving advice to the client about coping with unexpected events, what to do if things do not work out according to plan, and when and how to seek help if required. Kurtz *et al.* (1998) emphasised the importance of this part of closure, which they referred to as *safety netting*, in doctor–patient interactions. Doctors who receive higher ratings of patient satisfaction have been found to underline the importance of providing summaries for patients at the end of the consultation (Tallman *et al.*, 2007).

At the final termination of the professional relationship

The summary at this stage must range back over all previous meetings, putting what has been covered into a final perspective. This is one of the most difficult periods of professional communication. Final endings of relationships are never easy. Once human bonds have been formed, we do not like to break them (Fine and Harvey, 2005). The impact upon clients of final termination has long been recognised within psychoanalytic theory (Ferraro and Garella, 1997). In his analysis of the psychoanalytic context, Schubert (2000) highlighted how clients at this 'mourning' stage of the loss of the relationship can experience separation anxiety and depressive affects. The role of the therapist is therefore crucial. An important function of final summarisation is what is known in relational communication theory as *grave dressing* (Duck and Wood, 2005). The relationship is dead but its 'grave', or memory, should be presented in a positive light. The relationship is thereby portrayed as having been worthwhile and not a waste of time. Thus, the summary at this juncture should give emphasis to client achievements.

Checking out

This is the process whereby the professional ensures that the client fully understands what has been covered, and that both parties are in agreement about what has been agreed. One of the identified weaknesses of health professionals is that they do not always check that patients fully comprehend the information they have been given (Dickson *et al.*, 1997). Indeed, studies have shown that when filling prescriptions community pharmacists are often asked by patients to re-explain what the doctor has already told them about how to use the prescribed medication (Morrow *et al.*, 1993). They had not understood, but this lack of comprehension was not picked up by the doctor.

Checks can be made in two ways. First, the professional can ask questions to test for understanding of the material covered. As discussed in Chapter 5, questions are widely used across every profession. However, while they are expected and accepted by pupils in classrooms or students in seminars, feedback questions need to be used with care in other contexts. It is not normal practice in social exchanges to 'test' others – it can be taken as a sign of being seen as somewhat slow or stupid. As explained in Chapter 8, a useful tactic is for the professional to accept responsibility for any failure in understanding, by prefacing such questions with statements like 'I don't know if I explained that very clearly, could I just ask you . . .?'. Questions can also be used to ascertain how the client feels about how the session went. This type of summative evaluation can provide very useful feedback for future encounters.

Second, the client can be invited to ask questions. Norms of professional–client interaction mean that clients often neither expect nor are encouraged to ask questions (see Chapter 5). This means that time, thought and effort may be needed to facilitate clients as they formulate relevant questions. One exception to this rule is in the employment interview where there is a definite 'invite questions' stage, when candidates are asked 'Is there anything you would like to ask us?' Here, interviewees are well advised to prepare informed questions and to ask these in an appropriate manner (Millar and Tracey, 2006).

Care also needs to be taken with this tactic of inviting questions. One problem is that the client may take the opportunity to introduce new material at this juncture. Those with a low need for closure are particularly prone to this tactic. In their oft-quoted study of doctor–patient consultations, Byrne and Long (1976) termed this the *by the way . . . syndrome*, later referred to in the counselling context as the *door handle phenomenon* (Lang and van der Molen, 1990). In the latter context, an extreme example of this is where a client, standing at the door and about to leave, lobs an interactional hand grenade back into the room in the form of a controversial statement (e.g. 'I've been thinking a lot lately about suicide.'). The door handle phenomenon causes problems for the professional in making a decision as to whether to continue with the encounter (not easy where appointments have been booked), or arrange to discuss the issue at a later time.

White *et al.* (1997) carried out a detailed study of audio-recordings of doctor–patient encounters. They found that new problems were introduced by patients at the end of the consultation in 23 per cent of cases. They termed such instances *interrupted closures*, which they defined as occurring when 'an attempt by one person to shift from present problems to a future orientation was not followed by a corresponding shift on the part of the other' (p. 159). To circumvent such problems they recommended a number of procedures. When combined with other findings, it is possible to formulate six main strategies to help prevent interrupted closures (see Box 10.6).

Continuity links

Most animals have greeting rituals, some of which are very elaborate. Indeed, nesting birds have greeting displays each time one of them returns to the nest with food. Chimpanzees are most similar to humans in that they touch hands, hug and kiss when they meet. However, in his analysis of greetings and partings, Lamb (1988: 103) noted that there is no ritual of parting among other animals since 'they presumably do not have any conception of the future of their relationships and therefore do not need to reassure each other that there will be such a future or that the past has been worthwhile'. For humans, however, the sense of temporal and relational continuity means that endings of interactions are seen as important. Bridges must be built at this stage to carry the interactors over to their next encounter. As summarised by Bolden (2008: 99): 'Leave-taking serves to project possible future encounters, and is, thereby, a practice for maintaining a continuous relationship across periods of separation.' Knapp *et al.* (1973) termed this stage of closure *futurism*.

Box 10.6 Techniques for circumventing the interrupted closure

1 Orient the client at the beginning of the session (see the section on cognitive set, p. 293) and continue this throughout the encounter, explaining what is going to happen next at each stage.
2 Explicitly ask clients to state *all* of their concerns early in the encounter, and secure their agreement on the identified list. Heritage *et al.* (2007) found that after the initial patient opening phase, the question 'Is there something else you want to address in the visit today?' was especially effective in eliciting additional concerns at the outset of doctor–patient consultations. By comparison, the question 'Is there anything else you want to address in the visit today?' was ineffective.
3 Address psychosocial and emotional as well as task concerns.
4 Allow the person to talk freely and without interruptions.
5 Do not invite questions during the final closing phase. A common reason for the 'by the way' interjections in the White *et al.* study was the tendency for doctors to finish with the 'Anything else?' question. This raises new expectations in the client's mind and may negate the closing ritual.
6 When new issues are raised at the end it is generally best to defer exploration of these to a future visit, rather than engage in a hurried discussion at the end.

In professional contexts, continuity links include reference to how the work covered in the current encounter will be carried on at the next one. In formal business meetings one aspect of futurism is the very simple task of agreeing or noting the date of the next meeting. At the same time, however, a good chairperson should relate the business transacted in the present meeting to the agenda for the next one. Relational bonds also need to be consolidated at this stage, in the form of social comments about future meetings (e.g. 'I look forward to seeing you again next week.').

Motivational closure

By employing this type of closure, individuals can be directed to reflect more carefully, consider in greater depth, and relate any new insights gained from the present encounter to more general issues in a wider context. Three principal methods are employed to effect motivational closure: motivational exhortations, thought-provoking aphorisms and interim tasks.

Motivational exhortations

In many interactions, an important function of this stage of closing is that of minimising the phenomenon of *cognitive dissonance*, initially identified by Festinger (1957), and widely researched since (Cooper, 2007). When individuals have to make decisions, they often experience doubts and anxiety – or dissonance – about whether their decision is the right one. The more important the decision, the greater will be the dissonance, or discomfort. Eventually, dissonance is overcome in one of two ways: either by convincing oneself that the decision is indeed a good one and embracing it warmly, or alternatively by abandoning the decision and reverting to the former state of affairs. Motivational exhortations are useful in helping to persuade clients that they have made the correct decision. For example, Hargie *et al.* (2004) illustrated how such exhortations (e.g. 'This is the best deal in the store – and you'll get years of enjoyment from it.') are of importance for salespersons in ensuring that clients stay committed to a buying decision. Likewise, after an initial counselling encounter a client may experience dissonance about whether the decision to seek help and reveal personal details to a stranger was justified. Here again, motivating exhortations can be used to reassure the client about the efficacy of their decision, and so encourage the person to return for another session ('You have taken the first step towards resolving this by coming here today.').

Another function of these exhortations is to secure maximum commitment from clients. They are used ubiquitously by sports coaches during 'pep' talks before their players go out to perform. Sometimes the imagery used can be quite violent – and indeed unprintable here! Expressions used include 'Go out and kill them.', 'Give them hell.', 'Let them know you mean business.', 'You have one chance. Don't blow it or you'll regret it for the rest of your life.' The purpose here is to ensure that the sportspeople are fully geed up to give of their utmost.

In their meta-analysis of research in motivational interviewing, Hettema *et al.* (2005) illustrated how securing *commitment* from clients to carry out a course of action is crucial. If this commitment is not there, then the behaviour is unlikely to follow. For example, research has shown that there is no point in explaining to clients the methods that they can employ to stop existing behaviour (such as smoking or drinking) unless they are fully committed to stopping (Gaume *et al.*, 2008). There is little advantage in knowing how to do something that you have no intention of doing. It is therefore important to secure overt client statements of high commitment to change. As noted by Hettema *et al.* (2005: 10): 'To say, "I'll think about it," or "I'll try," for example, reflects a much lower level of commitment than "I promise" or "I will".' Thus, time is most gainfully spent in these contexts at gearing motivational exhortations towards maximum commitment. Once a person has fully and irrevocably decided upon a course of action, the means will usually be found to effect it (for further discussion on commitment see Chapter 12).

Thought-provoking aphorisms

In certain types of situation, it is useful to end an interaction with a succinct and apt statement that encourages listeners to reflect upon the main theme covered. These can be self-produced or quotations from the great and the good. This strategy is very common in public presentations. Let us take two recent examples from the radio programme *Thought For Today*. Here, the presenter has a two- or three-minute slot in which to cover a topical issue. One speaker, discussing the issue of animal rights, finished with, 'When you're dying for a big steak remember that a cow just did.', while another talking about third world poverty ended, 'Live simply so that others can simply live.' This strategy is also relevant in other contexts.

Interviewers can use it to motivate clients to continue (or change) a certain course of action.

Interim tasks

Homework and assignments have a familiar ring for students. Although not always welcomed, they serve the important purpose of making them think more about the subject in between classes. This technique is used in many settings to motivate clients to carry out tasks relating to the issue under consideration after the interaction has ended. In therapy, clients may be encouraged to try out new techniques that have been discussed. In training, tasks are geared towards the process of optimising transfer from the training environment to the actual organisational setting. To effect maximum motivation, the task set should be one that is challenging but also manageable.

Social closure

If an interaction has been successful, the leave-taking is marked by mixed emotions – happiness with the encounter coupled with sadness at its ending. As aptly expressed by Juliet to Romeo in Shakespeare's *Romeo and Juliet*, this means that 'Parting is such sweet sorrow.' One function of social closure is to underline a 'feelgood' factor in terms of the relationship. How we leave an interaction influences our attitudes to it. If it ends on a relational high, we depart feeling that it has been an enjoyable and worthwhile venture. We are then more likely to contact the person again if required. Social closure encompasses both task and non-task elements.

Task rewards

These are used to underline for the client that they have achieved something of worth, and that this is recognised and valued (for a full discussion of the role of rewards see Chapter 4). They can be employed to reward the person individually using 'you' language ('You achieved a lot today. Well done.', 'Your work is really paying dividends. I wish everyone put in as much effort as you.'). Alternatively, they can emphasise the sense of 'working together' using 'we' language ('That was a good meeting. We work well together.', 'That's great. I think we've nearly cracked it.'). Where the interaction has involved a group, then whole-group rewards are appropriate. Thus, teachers and lecturers may reward an entire class for their work, or a chairperson in concluding a meeting can point out how well the members worked together. This technique helps to foster a sense of team spirit. Like summaries, task rewards are important at three stages:

1   *At significant points within a session.* When a major part of the work has been completed, statements such as 'We are really getting somewhere.' provide participants with a feeling that something is being achieved and encourage further effort. Rewards may also include a 'time-out' ('I think we deserve a break

and a coffee.') to mark such successes. Negotiators often signal and celebrate interim agreements on particular points in this way.

2   *At the end of a session.* Here, the client should be rewarded for major efforts made during the encounter.

3   *At the termination of the relationship.* As discussed above, 'grave dressing' is important as the final curtain falls, and so clients must be rewarded for the efforts they made and everything they achieved during the professional relationship.

Non-task comments

The final part of closure should emphasise the human moment. The main business is over, tasks have been completed, and it is time to acknowledge the client as a person. So, personal or welfare aspects of leave-taking enter the fray at this point. These fall into five main types:

1   *The expression of gratitude phase*, as the name suggests, involves thanking the person for their time and efforts ('Thanks for coming along.', 'I appreciate you giving up your time.').

2   *Social closing niceties.* Here we owe a considerable debt to the weather and traffic in formulating comments such as 'Oh dear, it's really pouring down. Good thing you brought your umbrella.', 'Hope you get home before the rush hour.'

3   *Reference to generic or specific social events.* This is commonplace – ranging from the ubiquitous 'Have a nice day.' in the US service sector to more tailored generalities ('Have a good weekend.'), or mention of specific occasions ('Enjoy the wedding.').

4   *Reference to future meetings.* These occur during continuity links ('Look forward to seeing you again next week.').

5   *Well-wishing comments.* These are statements of concern regarding the other person's well-being ('Look after yourself.', 'Take care now.').

At final termination, such statements not only reward the client, but they also underline the finality of the occasion – 'It was a pleasure working with you. If you need to talk with me at any time in the future, you know where I am.' These statements should of course be accompanied by appropriate nonverbal reinforcers (see Chapter 4).

Overview of closure

In *Julius Caesar*, Shakespeare summarised the overarching functions of closure:

> If we do meet again, why we shall smile!
> If not, why then, this parting was well made.

Closure serves to leave participants both feeling satisfied with an encounter, and happy to re-engage with one another as and when required. While introductions can be prepared, closures usually cannot. This is because the termination has to be directly related to the interaction that has gone before. However, knowing the stages through which closure progresses can greatly facilitate the implementation of the process.

Perceptual closure is used initially to signal that the encounter is entering the end-zone, and then to mark the final exchange. *Cognitive closure* allows agreements to be ratified regarding the main issues discussed and decisions made, as well as establishing links with the next meeting. *Motivational closure* is employed to encourage clients to continue to consider, and work on, issues further. Finally, *social closure* cements the relational bonds that have been established. It is important to remember that the closure is the last point of contact between interactors and therefore the one they are most likely to remember. The advice of Millar and Tracey (2006: 94) in their review of interviewing is pertinent here: 'It is important to plan and allocate time for ending the interview as both a business transaction and a social encounter.' Efforts made at this juncture can have very significant import, both on the impact of the current encounter and for the future of the relationship itself.

OVERVIEW

Greeting and parting skills represent the ties that bind interaction. Arrivals and departures are ubiquitous. Across countries and cultures people wish each other a good morning, afternoon, evening or night. We have all been taught the basics of these skills as part of the socialisation process, and so we often take them for granted. So much so, indeed, that we then proceed to ignore them by jumping quickly into and out of social encounters. As Irving and Hazlett (1999: 264/265) noted, the busy professional 'often feels that he or she is pressed for time and it is these very important elements at the beginning and end that are often rushed or overlooked'. But a cheap and clipped hello and goodbye is no substitute for a sincere, focused welcome, and a warm, thoughtful parting. Due to the primacy and recency effects, much of what we do at these two junctures remains imprinted upon the minds of those with whom we interact. Time and effort spent at the opening and closing phases should therefore be regarded as a key investment towards the effectiveness of relationships.

Chapter 11

Standing up for yourself: the skill of assertiveness

INTRODUCTION

ASSERTIVENESS IS AN AREA of study with a long history. It dates back to the pioneering work in the field of behaviour therapy by Salter (1949) and Wolpe (1958), highlighting the fact that certain individuals in society had specific problems in standing up for their rights. As a result, the skill of assertiveness was introduced during therapy in an attempt to help such people function more effectively in their everyday lives. Since then, the skill has attracted enormous interest, reflecting the importance of this aspect of social interaction across many areas. As noted by McCartan and Hargie (2004a: 707): 'The contribution of assertiveness to communication competence is now widely recognized.' A huge volume of research has been conducted, and assertion training (AT) programmes are widespread.

Professionals must possess the ability to be assertive and so AT programmes proliferate in this area. This is because a key feature of assertiveness is that it is an aspect of interpersonal communication that can be developed and improved. As McKay *et al.* (2009: 125) pointed out: 'Assertiveness is a skill you can acquire, not a personality trait that some people are born with and others not.' It is a skill that is of importance when dealing with family, friends, peers, superiors and subordinates. It is pertinent to interactions between different groups of professionals, especially where differences of power and status exist, and it is of relevance to interactions between professionals and clients (Back and Back, 2005).

Early definitions of assertiveness were fairly all-embracing in terms of interactional skills. Lazarus (1971), for example, regarded assertiveness as comprising four main components:

1   the ability to refuse requests
2   the ability to ask for favours and make requests
3   the ability to express positive and negative feelings
4   the ability to initiate, continue and terminate general conversations.

It is obvious that this conceptualisation of assertiveness is very broad, encompassing almost all forms of human interaction. Indeed, as Kelly (1982: 172) pointed out: 'The terms "assertion training" and "social skills training" were often used in interchangeable fashion; it was not recognized that assertiveness represents one specific kind of interpersonal competency.' It would seem that training in this field was introduced and found to be beneficial before the concept of assertiveness was defined with any precision. Dissatisfaction with this state of affairs led to a more focused study of assertion, based specifically upon the theme of standing up for one's rights in a sensitive, competent manner. This latter interpretation is the one given by most dictionaries and a perspective usually held by lay people, and it is the view adopted in this chapter.

While differing meanings of assertion proliferate within the literature, useful definitions of assertive behaviour can be found in two of the influential texts in this area. Thus, Lange and Jakubowski (1976: 38) stated: 'Assertion involves standing up for personal rights and expressing thoughts, feelings and beliefs in direct, honest, and appropriate ways which respect the rights of other people.' More recently, Alberti and Emmons (2008: 8) posited: 'Assertiveness enables us to act in our own best interests, to stand up for ourselves without undue anxiety, to exercise personal rights without denying the rights of others, and to express our feelings . . . honestly and comfortably.' Both of these definitions emphasise an important component of assertion, namely respect for the rights of other people. The skilled individual must therefore achieve a balance between defending personal rights while not infringing the rights of others.

Assertiveness can be conceptualised as comprising two broad response classes, one negative and the other positive (see Box 11.1). However, most research and training efforts have been devoted to the negative, or conflict, components, since this is the aspect of assertion many people find particularly difficult.

PURPOSES OF ASSERTIVENESS

The skill of assertion helps us to achieve nine main interpersonal goals (Box 11.2). Most of these relate to the ability of the individual to respond effectively in an assertive manner. However, linked to the behavioural repertoire are functions to do with protection of personal rights (1) and respect for the rights of others (5), as well as the development of feelings of confidence (8) and self-efficacy (9) in being able to respond in a self-protecting fashion. The type of assertiveness used can determine the extent to which each of these goals is fulfilled, and so knowledge of types of assertiveness is of vital importance during social encounters. Furthermore, personal and contextual factors also play a crucial role in determining the effectiveness of assertive responses.

Box 11.1 Negative and positive assertion

Negative or *conflict assertion* comprises six main components:

- making reasonable requests
- refusing unwanted or unreasonable requests
- asking others to change their behaviour
- giving personal opinions even if unpopular
- expressing disagreement or negative feelings
- responding to criticism from others.

Positive assertion also involves six main aspects:
- expressing positive feelings
- responding to positive feelings expressed by others
- giving compliments
- accepting compliments gracefully
- admitting mistakes or personal shortcomings
- initiating and sustaining interactions.

Box 11.2 Goals of assertiveness

The main goals served by the skill of assertiveness are:

1 to protect one's personal rights
2 to withstand unreasonable requests
3 to make reasonable requests
4 to deal effectively with unreasonable refusals
5 to recognise the personal rights of others
6 to change the behaviour of others
7 to avoid unnecessary conflicts
8 to confidently communicate one's real position on any issue
9 to develop and maintain a personal sense of self-efficacy.

SEQUENTIAL STAGES IN ASSERTIVENESS

A sequence of stages is involved in the decision-making process with regard to whether or not to implement an assertive approach (see Figure 11.1).

Self-focus

First, the individual must engage in self-focused attention. This process of self-focus involves monitoring and evaluating the behaviour of self and others (Panayiotou *et al.*, 2007). Without an awareness of the nuances of interpersonal communication, success in assertion, or indeed in any social skill, is unlikely. As will be seen later in

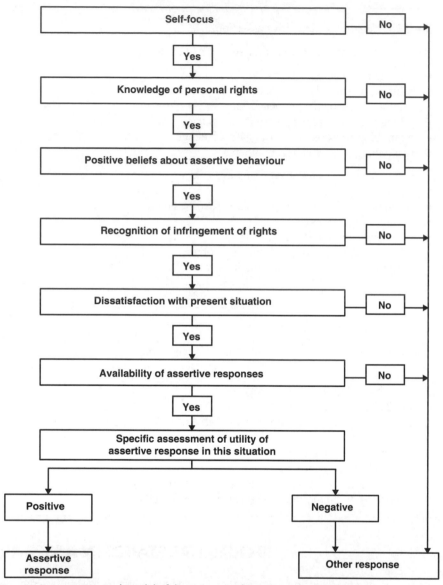

Figure 11.1 Sequential model of the assertion decision-making process

the chapter, at one extreme some (unassertive) people are blissfully unaware that they are being treated woefully, while at the other there are those (aggressive) who have no idea of how obnoxious they appear to others. As repeatedly emphasised in this book, skill necessitates acute perceptual acumen.

Knowledge of rights

Given that the individual has the capacity to self-focus, the next prerequisite is knowledge of personal rights. In order to protect our rights we must first know what they are. It is not always clear in many situations exactly what one's rights are, and it is therefore sometimes necessary to consult with others in order to gauge their views about whether personal rights have been infringed. This process of consultation is termed *reality testing*, which may involve asking other people for advice either about what exactly your rights are (e.g. 'Has he the right to ask me to do that?'), or about their perceptions of your behaviour (e.g. 'Have I upset you in some way?', 'Do you mind doing this?'). There is evidence to indicate that assertive individuals may have a greater awareness of what their job role actually entails. In a study of social workers in Israel, Rabin and Zelner (1992) found that assertiveness in the work setting was significantly and positively correlated to both role clarity and job satisfaction. Knowing the parameters of one's job would therefore seem to facilitate the protection of personal rights, which may in turn contribute to increased happiness in the work environment. In terms of actual rights, Zuker (1983) produced a general Assertive Bill of Rights for individuals, which included the right to:

✔ be treated with respect
✔ have and express personal feelings and opinions
✔ be listened to and taken seriously
✔ set one's own priorities
✔ say no without feeling guilty
✔ ask for what one wants
✔ get what one pays for
✔ make mistakes
✔ assert oneself even though it may inconvenience others
✔ choose not to assert oneself.

Positive beliefs about assertion

Our beliefs about assertive behaviour are very important. As expressed by Mnookin *et al.* (1996: 221): 'Assertiveness also presupposes the self-esteem or belief that one's interests are valid and that it is legitimate to satisfy them.' Arnes (2008) has shown that *assertive expectancies* are crucial in determining the extent to which an individual pursues an assertive response. He found that, based upon their expectations, people 'show dramatically different assertiveness due to different assumptions about behavioral consequences' (p. 1541). Take someone who believes that one should always do what one's superiors say or negative consequences will accrue. Before this person could effectively be assertive, this belief would have to be replaced with a new one, for example that it is always valid to ask for a good reason if requested to do anything that seems unreasonable. Piccinin *et al.* (1998) carried out a study with Canadian undergraduates on their ability to criticise others. They found that high as opposed to low assertives reported more confidence in their ability to criticise the behaviour of others effectively, believed that this was more likely to produce positive outcomes and were less worried about the possible negative consequences of so doing. From previous research, Piccinin *et al.* identified five behaviours as being associated with quality of criticism. These can be illustrated with examples relating to a work situation where one person is too cold:

1   using *'I'- language* (e.g. 'I see the window is wide open.' rather than 'You have left the window wide open.')
2   clearly *specifying the problem* ('I can't work because I'm freezing.' rather than 'It's cold.')
3   showing *empathy* ('I know you like fresh air.')
4   *bidirectionality* or 'roundedness' ('You are hardy and could survive an arctic expedition, but it's just too cold for me in here.')
5   suggesting *explicit change* ('Please close the window.').

Interestingly, using these criteria Piccinin *et al.* (1998) found no difference between high and low assertives on *quality* of responses. This result confirmed earlier research that a crucial determinant of assertion is *motivation to act* rather than lack of understanding of how to be assertive.

Those who are very socially anxious are more likely to be nonassertive, as they have a strong desire to make a good impression but also doubt their ability to achieve this desired state (Suzuki and Sleyman, 2006). This was confirmed in a study by Gudleski and Shean (2000), which found that depressed individuals rated themselves lower than nondepressed people on assertiveness, but significantly higher on measures of submissiveness and the need to please others. Anderson (1997) also found that those who experienced most anxiety were least assertive in terms of both verbal and nonverbal behaviours. Likewise, those high in the personality trait of *agreeableness* are less likely to assert themselves, since such individuals are altruistic, noncritical, trusting and helpful (Meriac and Villanova, 2006).

These research findings illustrate how changes in beliefs and expectations may well be a prerequisite for changes in assertive behaviour. The process of *cognitive restructuring* is important for people with inappropriate beliefs (Cavell and Malcolm, 2006). Such restructuring includes changes in *self-instructions*, those covert behaviour-guiding self-statements we employ when making decisions about which responses to carry out. Nonassertive individuals have a higher frequency of negative self-statements and a greater belief that their behaviour will lead to negative consequences. Thus, submissive individuals use self-statements such as 'She will not like me if I refuse.', rather than 'I have the right to refuse.'

In terms of intrapersonal dialogue, there would also seem to be a difference in the use of self-reinforcements, with nonassertive people again being more negative in their self-evaluations of performance. Submissive people are more likely to think: 'I sounded terrible, stuttering and stammering. She is probably laughing at me now.' Assertive individuals, on the other hand, tend to be more positive (e.g. 'I'm glad I said no. She is not likely to bother me again.'). In reviewing research in this field, Rakos (1991) illustrated how nonassertive individuals emit roughly equal numbers of positive and negative self-statements in conflict situations whereas assertive people generate about twice as many positive as negative self-statements. He concluded that 'direct training in autonomous self-instruction, apart from any other intervention, has resulted in significant gains in assertiveness' (p. 53).

Recognition of infringement of rights

The individual also has to recognise that personal rights have been infringed. One study found that nonassertive people tend to need more time to perceive and assimilate information and make decisions about how to respond, and concluded: 'If individuals fall behind at this early step in the process of asserting themselves, then they may be more likely to miss opportunities to be assertive' (Collins *et al.*, 2000: 931). Thus, by the time submissive individuals realise that their rights have indeed been violated, it is probably too late to rectify the situation. To quote the title of the Collins *et al.* article, it is a case of 'Those who hesitate lose.' Submissive individuals are also more likely to perceive the behaviour of others inaccurately by, for example, perceiving unreasonable requests as being reasonable. Such people are viewed as 'easy touches' in terms of borrowing items, doing extra work, etc., since they are always ready to be helpful. There comes a time when being helpful turns into being used, and people need to learn not only to be able to draw the line between these two, but also to actually learn to perceive the behaviour of others more accurately, in order to distinguish reasonable and unreasonable requests. Indeed, on occasions other people point out to us that this has happened – for whatever reason we have accepted unreasonable behaviour as reasonable.

Dissatisfaction with present situation

We must then experience dissatisfaction with this state of affairs. Two core features in determining an assertive response are the importance of the issue and the strength of negative feeling. These are related, in that with more important issues we are likely to feel more dissatisfied or aggrieved when our rights are negated. Thus, affect is crucial in assertiveness. For example, when standing in line outside a theatre we may notice someone jumping the queue, but if it is a warm evening and we are chatting happily with our date, our mood may be such that we think 'what the heck' and ignore it. Alternatively, if we have had to wait for a long time in the rain and have become annoyed, we may challenge the line jumper very assertively.

Availability of assertive responses

In order to be assertive, we must first be aware of what the available response alternatives are, and have learned how to use them. Much of this chapter is devoted to an analysis of assertive response components and their likely effects.

Assessment of response utility

Before we invoke an assertive response, we should assess the utility of so doing. The context is important in making a decision to be assertive, since the effectiveness of an assertive response depends upon its situational appropriateness (Ryan *et al.*, 2006). If we adjudge that assertion is a legitimate response in this context, and that it will produce a long-term positive benefit for the relationship (as opposed to merely a short-term behaviour change), then we are likely to choose this alternative. However, assertion is not always the most appropriate choice in every situation. From working with a range of professional groups, I have ascertained a number of contexts in which it is more difficult to be assertive. These include:

- in someone else's home or office
- in a strange country or subculture
- when alone as opposed to with friends or colleagues
- with superiors at work
- with other professionals of higher status and power
- when promoted to a position of authority over those who were formerly friends and colleagues
- with older people
- with the seriously or terminally ill and their relatives
- with those in poverty or in severe social deprivation
- with friends or close work colleagues
- with members of the opposite sex
- with those who are disabled.

The utility of assertion in these situations is more likely to be negatively evaluated. In addition, there are at least three broad contexts in which it may be more skilled to be nonassertive.

1   ***Interacting with a highly sensitive individual.*** If by being assertive someone is liable to burst into floods of tears, or physically attack you, it may be wise to be nonassertive, especially if the encounter is a one-off. Thus, in the example used earlier, if the queue jumper is a huge, inebriated male uttering expletives and waving a knife, we may justifiably decide that there is a negative utility for an assertive response.

2   ***Seeing that someone is in a difficult situation.*** If you are in a busy restaurant and know that a new waitress has just been employed, you are more likely to overlook certain issues, such as someone who came in later being served before you. Here it is appropriate to be nonassertive, since personal rights are not deliberately being denied, and to be assertive may cause undue stress to the other person. Equally, if the other person is from a different culture and may not fully understand the norms of the present situation, you may decide not to adopt an assertive stance (issues of culture are discussed later in the chapter).

3   ***Manipulating others.*** Some females may deliberately employ a helpless style in order to achieve their goals, for example to encourage a male to change a flat

tyre on their car. Equally, males may do likewise. If stopped by police following a minor traffic misdemeanour it is usually wise to be nonassertive ('I'm terribly sorry officer, but I've just bought this car ...'), since such behaviour is more likely to achieve positive benefits.

STYLES OF RESPONDING

In order to fully understand the concept of assertiveness, it is necessary to distinguish this style of responding from other approaches. Three core styles are of relevance here, namely nonassertion, assertion and aggression.

Nonassertion

Nonassertive responses involve expressing oneself in such a self-effacing, apologetic manner that one's thoughts, feelings and rights can easily be ignored. In this 'cap in hand' style, the person:

- hesitates and prevaricates
- speaks softly
- looks away
- tends to fidget nervously
- avoids issues
- agrees regardless of personal feelings
- does not express opinions
- values self below others
- lacks confidence
- suffers personal hurt to avoid any chance of hurting others.

The objective here is to appease others and avoid conflict at any cost. This can be described as the 'Uriah Heep' style, as epitomised in Charles Dickens' *David Copperfield* in which Uriah explains how he was brought up: 'to be umble to this person, and umble to that; and to pull our caps off here, and to make bows there; and always to know our place, and abase ourselves before our betters'. Nonassertive individuals:

- tend to avoid public attention
- use minimal self-disclosure or remain silent so as not to receive criticism for what they say
- are modest and self-deprecating
- use self-handicapping strategies whereby they underestimate potential future achievements so as to avoid negative evaluation if they fail
- if they have to engage with others, prefer to play a passive, friendly and very agreeable role.

Assertion

Assertive responses involve standing up for oneself, yet taking the other person into consideration. The assertive style involves:

- answering spontaneously
- speaking with a conversational yet firm tone and volume
- looking at the other person
- addressing the main issue
- openly and confidently expressing personal feelings and opinions
- valuing oneself equal to others
- being prepared to listen to the other's point of view
- hurting neither oneself nor others.

The objective here is to try to ensure fair play for everyone. Perhaps not surprisingly, Karagözoglu *et al.* (2007) found that there was a positive correlation between assertion and self-esteem. Furthermore, as shown by Lightsey and Barnes (2007: 32), assertiveness is 'incompatible with or inversely related to many negative psychological symptoms', such as anxiety, depression and low self-esteem. Assertive individuals have also been found to be high in the constructive trait of *argumentativeness*, which is the tendency to present and defend one's position while also challenging opposing views, whereas *verbal aggressiveness* is a destructive trait that involves a tendency to focus one's attacks upon the other person's self-concept (Johnson *et al.*, 2007; Avtgis *et al.*, 2008). A key aspect of assertion is taking cognisance of the other person's point of view (Sanchez, 2001). With this in mind, Williams and Akridge (1996) developed the *Responsible Assertion Scale* that measures the extent to which assertive responses are coupled with respect for others.

Aggression

Aggression has been defined as 'the delivery of an aversive stimulus from one person to another, with intent to harm and with an expectation of causing such harm, when the other person is motivated to escape or avoid the stimulus' (Geen, 2001: 3). These aversive stimuli involve more than just physical violence since in social situations verbal aggression is more prevalent. Verbal aggression has been defined as 'behavior that attacks an individual's self-concept in order to deliver psychological pain' (Myers and Bryant, 2008: 268). Such behaviours include attacks on one's ability, character or appearance, name calling, profanity, the use of demands, blunt directives and threats – all of which violate the rights of the other person. Using this style, the aggressor:

- interrupts and answers before the other is finished speaking
- talks loudly and abrasively
- glares at the other person
- speaks 'past' the issue (accusing, blaming, demeaning)
- vehemently and arrogantly states feelings and opinions in a dogmatic fashion

- values self above others
- hurts others to avoid personal hurt.

The objective is to win, regardless of the other person. It may involve belittling others through the tactic of *downward comparison*, whereby an attempt is made to demean the achievements of those with whom one may be compared (Unzueta *et al.*, 2008). This form of direct aggression is also known as *blasting*, which involves derogating others to make oneself appear superior (Guadagno and Cialdini, 2007). A variation of this tactic is a straight verbal attack on the other person. This is a strategy commonly used by politicians. In response to a critical question the then Bavarian Prime Minister Franz-Josef Strauss replied by asking whether the journalist had finished high school. In the cut-throat battle between politicians and journalists, such a response may be fair game, but in the general social world this is much less acceptable.

Comparing the three styles

Hargie *et al.* (2004), in their review of the management field, illustrated how in earlier times the aggressive style was often employed by autocratic managers in oppressive organisations. However, as a result of a range of changes, including a better-educated workforce, the flattening of managerial hierarchies and recognition by employees of their legal rights not to be bullied or harrassed, an aggressive style is no longer acceptable. Managers must be assertive, not aggressive. The former style should lead to harmony at work, the latter is likely to result in litigation in court. These three styles can be exemplified in relation to a situation in which you are asked for the loan of a book which you do not wish to lend:

1   'Um . . . How long would you need it for? It's just that . . . ah . . . I might need it for an assignment. But . . . if it wasn't for long . . .'. (Nonassertion)
2   'I'm sorry. I'd like to help you out, but I bought this book so I would always have it to refer to, so I never loan it to anyone.' (Assertion)
3   'No. Why don't you buy your own damn books!?' (Aggression)

Although some psychoanalytic perspectives conceptualise assertiveness and aggression as distinct entities belonging to two different types of motivational system (Fosshage, 1998), most theorists see these response classes as differing in intensity rather than in kind (McCartan, 2001). In this sense, they are regarded as points on the same continuum:

Nonassertion → Assertion → Aggression

Assertiveness forms the mid-point of this continuum and is usually the most appropriate response. Aggressive individuals tend to be viewed as intransigent, coercive, overbearing and lacking in self-control. They may initially get their own way by browbeating and creating fear in others, but they are usually disliked and avoided. Alternatively, this style may provoke a similar response from others, with the danger that the verbal aggression may escalate and lead to overt physical aggression.

Nonassertive individuals, on the other hand, are often viewed as weak, 'mealy-mouthed' creatures who can be easily manipulated, and as a result they frequently express dissatisfaction with their lives, owing to a failure to attain personal goals. They may be less likely to inspire confidence in others or may even be seen as incompetent. Assertive individuals, however, tend to feel more in control of their lives, derive more satisfaction from their relationships and achieve their goals more often. They also obtain more respect from, and inspire confidence in, those with whom they interact since they tend to be viewed as strong characters who are not easily swayed.

This is evident at an early stage, so that in junior high school Windschitl (2001) found that assertive pupils were more likely to voice their views, make suggestions and give directives to peers. Less assertive pupils, in turn, tended to acquiesce to these directives. Leaper (2000) linked the continuum of assertive–nonassertive to that of affiliative–nonaffiliative (Figure 11.2). This produces four styles of behaviour. Those who are assertive and affiliative are *collaborative* individuals who only use assertion when necessary, but place a high value on having good relationships with others. On the other hand, assertive individuals who are nonaffiliative do not care about being friendly and use assertive skills to *control* others and get their own way. Nonassertive people who are affiliative are *obliging* by nature and like to fit in and do what others want. Finally, those who are both nonassertive and nonaffiliative tend to *withdraw* from interaction with others and like to keep themselves to themselves.

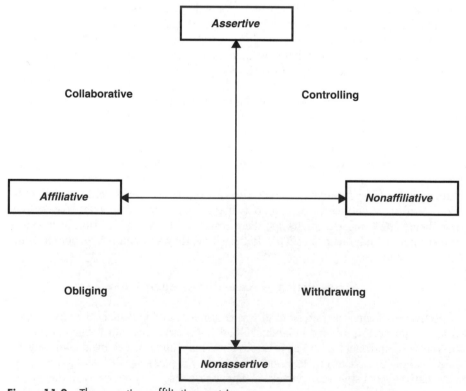

Figure 11.2 The assertion–affiliation matrix

Several research studies have verified the behavioural responses associated with these three styles. An early investigation by Rose and Tryon (1979) found that assertive behaviour was clearly associated with:

- louder voice (68 decibel (dB) level was viewed as nonassertive; 76dB level was the assertive ideal; 84dB level was towards the aggressive end of the continuum)
- reduced response latency (pauses of 16 seconds before responding were seen as nonassertive, whereas pauses of 3–4 seconds were viewed as assertive)
- greater use of gestures (although increased gestures coupled with approach behaviour were seen as aggressive)
- increased vocal inflection.

The relationship between amplitude of voice and perceptions of dominance (high amplitude) and submissiveness (low amplitude) was confirmed in a later study by Tusing and Dillard (2000). They postulated the reason for this relationship as being that 'during the course of evolutionary history, certain vocal cues became associated with dominance because they served as markers of organisms' aggressive potential' (p. 164). In other words, a loud bark was a signal of a deep bite.

McFall *et al.* (1982), in a detailed research investigation, identified what they termed *assertive body movements*, the most salient being hands, arms and overall body cues. The nonverbal behaviour of assertive individuals was controlled, smooth and purposive, whereas nonassertive people displayed shifty, shaky and fidgety body activity. Furthermore, Kolotkin *et al.* (1983) found that duration of eye contact was greater for assertive as opposed to nonassertive individuals. They also found that the use of smiles helps to convey that a response is meant to be assertive rather than aggressive. Interestingly, however, there is a relationship between laughter and dominance, in that submissive people laugh much more at the humour of dominant individuals than vice versa (Provine, 2000).

Types of aggression

Although most texts on assertion differentiate between three styles of responding, some theorists have made a distinction between different types of aggression. Buss and Perry (1992) developed an aggression inventory, which contains four factors, or subdivisions, of aggression. These are outlined below, with examples of actual items from the inventory.

1 *Physical aggression.* 'Given enough provocation, I may hit another person.' 'If I have to resort to violence to protect my rights, I will.'
2 *Verbal aggression.* 'I tell my friends openly when I disagree with them.' 'When people annoy me I may tell them what I think of them.'
3 *Anger.* 'I sometimes feel like a powder keg ready to explode.' 'Sometimes I fly off the handle for no good reason.'
4 *Hostility.* 'I am sometimes eaten up with jealousy.' 'When people are especially nice, I wonder what they want.'

The relationship between these elements is that they represent different dimensions of aggression: physical and verbal responses represent the instrumental or behavioural components; anger is the emotional or affective aspect; and hostility the cognitive element.

Another common distinction is that between open, direct aggression and passive, indirect aggression. Del Greco (1983) argued that these two types combine with nonassertion and assertion to form the two continua of coerciveness and directness, as shown in Figure 11.3. The passive, or indirect, aggressive style of responding seems to embrace a range of behaviours, including sulking, using emotional blackmail (such as crying in order to get your own way), pouting and being subtly manipulative. Del Greco developed an inventory to measure all four response styles. Indirect, or passive, aggressive items include: 'When I am asked for my preference I pretend I don't have one, but then I convince my friends of the advantages of my hidden preferences.' and 'When my friend asks me for my opinion I state that I have none, then I proceed to make my true preference seem the most attractive.' This type of Machiavellian approach is one clear example of indirect aggression. Another example is the *deflected aggression* scenario, where, for example, a person slams drawers and doors shut while refusing to discuss the reason for so doing. The four response styles can be illustrated with reference to alternative ways of responding to someone smoking in a 'No Smoking' area:

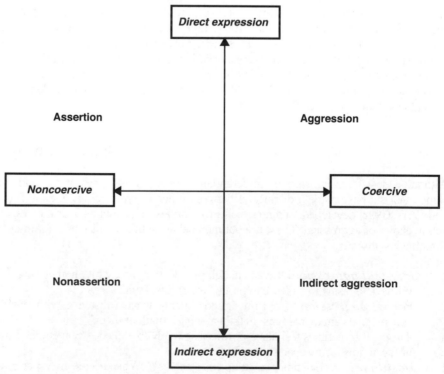

Figure 11.3 Four styles of responding

1   'Hey, you, there's no smoking allowed in this area. Either put out or get out!' (*Aggressive*)
2   'Excuse me, but do you realise that this is a No Smoking area? Cigarette smoke affects me quite badly, so I'd be grateful if you would not smoke here.' (*Assertive*)
3   Not mentioning your discomfort, and hoping that someone else will confront the smoker. (*Nonassertive*)
4   Coughing loudly and vigorously waving a hand towards the smoker as if to fan the smoke away. (*Indirectly aggressive*)

Once again, assertiveness is regarded as the optimum approach. While it is possible to be skilfully manipulative, there is always the danger of being found out, with resulting negative consequences. Similarly in the case of passive aggression, as in (4) above, this can also lead to a negative evaluation, or may simply be ignored by the other person.

A distinction has also been made between aggression and resort-to-aggression styles. In their study of assertion in relation to consumers' verbal behaviour following a failure of service, Swanson and McIntyre (1998) confirmed the two factors of aggression and assertion as originally measured by the *Consumer Assertiveness and Aggression Scales* (Richins, 1983). They further analysed the aggression factor in relation to aggression per se and resort-to-aggression. As illustrated in Figure 11.4

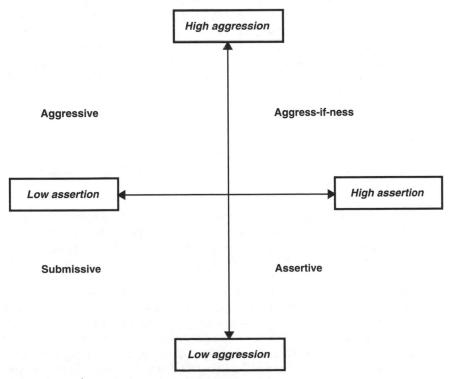

Figure 11.4   The aggression–assertion matrix

aggressive individuals are high on aggression but low on assertion – they do not use the assertive approach at all. By comparison, some individuals are high on both assertion and aggression. They employ an assertive style initially but are prepared to become aggressive if necessary (I have termed this the 'aggress-if-ness' style) to get what they want. An example of an item on the Richins Scale relating to the aggress-if-ness style is: 'Sometimes being nasty is the best way to get a complaint taken care of.' Swanson and McIntyre found that the two high assertive groups (assertive and resort-to-aggression) reported a greater likelihood of discussing an incident of poor customer service with family, friends and acquaintances than the low assertive groups (nonassertive and aggressive).

TYPES OF ASSERTIVENESS

There are five key types of assertive behaviour:

1   ***Basic assertion.*** This involves a simple expression of standing up for personal rights, beliefs, feelings or opinions. For example, when interrupted a basic assertive expression would be: 'Excuse me, I would like to finish what I was saying.'
2   ***Empathic assertion.*** This type of assertion conveys sensitivity to the other person, by making a statement that conveys some recognition of the other person's situation or feelings before making the assertive statement. Thus, an example of an empathic assertion to an interruption would be: 'I know you are keen to get your views across, but I would like to finish what I was saying.'
3   ***Escalating assertion.*** Here the individual begins by making a minimal assertive response and, if the other person fails to respond to this, gradually increases or escalates the degree of assertiveness employed. Someone visited at home by a 'pushy' salesperson may use escalating assertiveness as follows:

    *   'No, I've decided that I don't wish to purchase any of these products.'
    *   'No, as I've already said, I'm not buying any of them.'
    *   'Look, I've told you twice that the answer is no. I'm going to have to ask you to leave now.'

    There may come a time when assertion fails, and a stronger response is required. As Rakos (2006) pointed out, if your assertion attempts are repeatedly ignored, it may be necessary to escalate to the level of reasonable threats or actions. For example, someone who has been continually bullied or harassed at work despite assertive attempts to overcome this, may then refuse to speak to or deal with the bully, take the matter to higher levels of management, or initiate legal action.
4   ***Confrontive assertion.*** This is used when someone does not do what had been previously agreed. It involves clearly reminding the person what was agreed, and contrasting this with what actually happened. The speaker then firmly states what the other person must now do (e.g. 'You said you would have the report finished by Tuesday. It is now Thursday and you still haven't produced it. I want you to have it completed by 4.00 pm today.').

5   *I-language assertion.* Here the speaker objectively describes the behaviour of the other person, how this affects the speaker's life or feelings and why the other person should change this behaviour. In the case of being interrupted, an I-language assertive response would be: 'This is the fourth time you've interrupted me in the past few minutes. This makes me feel that you aren't interested in what I am saying, and I feel a bit hurt and annoyed. I would like you to let me finish what I want to say.' This statement also contains *You-language*, which tends to be perceived as blaming or accusing the other person and can result in defensive reactions. Compare the following two utterances.

- 'You are annoying me because you never pay for your fair share of these expenses.'
- 'I feel annoyed because I believe that I am paying more than my fair share of these expenses.'

The second statement is much less accusatory than the first and therefore less likely to provoke a hostile response. However, there is a danger, especially if overused, of I-language being perceived as selfish, self-centred and unconcerned with the other person. Indeed, I-language statements do not seem to be characteristic of most everyday conversations (Gervasio, 1987). For these reasons, the use of *We-language* can be an effective alternative. The use of We-language helps to convey the impression of partnership in and joint responsibility for any problems to be discussed. Continuing with the above exemplar, the We-language response would be:

- 'We need to talk about how we are both contributing to the payment of these expenses. It is important that neither of us feels annoyed about the present arrangement.'

Direct and indirect assertion

Linehan and Egan (1979) distinguished between direct and indirect styles of assertiveness. They argued that a direct, unambiguous assertive style may not always be most effective, especially for those individuals for whom it is important to be liked and regarded positively by others. Rather, a more ambiguous, indirect style of response seems more appropriate in some instances (despite the fact that many texts recommend a direct style). An example of these two styles can be seen in relation to the following question:

Q: Could you loan me that DVD you bought yesterday?
Direct: No, I never loan my DVDs to anyone.
Indirect: Oh, you mean *The Oceans Live* – you know, I'm still trying to get a chance to sit down and watch it myself. I usually take ages with a new DVD.

Here the direct approach may be seen as brusque or even offensive. In the indirect approach, however, there has been no refusal and so the other person may reply by attempting to obtain a commitment about borrowing the DVD in the future. However, as will be shown later, the direct style can be less abrasive if it is coupled with an embellishment to turn it into a complex-direct style and so soften the impact of direct assertion. Some theorists suggest that little white lies may be used here, but caution is required as not only does this pose an ethical dilemma, but it can also backfire if the lie is later unveiled. At the same time, as mentioned in Chapter 9, deception occurs in around one quarter of all conversations. Niikura (1999a), in a study of assertiveness across four cultures, found that the option of 'making an excuse' (a euphemism for telling a lie) when having to turn down a request from a senior colleague was very popular in all cultures. Another option was that of 'You tell the boss that you would do it but actually you don't, and tell him/her a lie about why you didn't do it' and again this was a not infrequent selection.

The goal is to lessen the impact of the refusal and so maintain the relationship. Thus, using the complex-direct approach, a response (whether truthful or not) to the above question would be:

Complex-direct: I know you would look after it really well, but I've recently had two DVDs that I loaned damaged, so I've just had to make the general decision never to loan my DVDs to anyone again. That way I hope no one will feel personally offended.

There is consistent research evidence to show that standard direct assertion is viewed as being as effective as and more socially desirable than aggressive behaviour, and more socially competent but distinctly less likeable than nonassertion (Wilson and Gallois, 1993). It seems that assertiveness is evaluated positively in theory, but when faced with the practical reality is rated less favourably than nonassertion (McCartan and Hargie, 2004a). As expressed by Dickson *et al.* (1997: 131): 'One interesting research finding, however, is that while people tend to respect assertive individuals, they often do not like to have to deal with assertive responses.' For example, Harwood *et al.* (1997) carried out a study in which subjects evaluated conversations between a bystander and the driver following a car accident. They found that an assertive style of response from the bystander was perceived to be more competent but less kind and less respectful than a nonassertive style. Equally, we may not like to be in the company of those who are continually assertive. In a review of research on complaining, Kowalski (1996) concluded that people who complain frequently are viewed more negatively than those who seldom do so. A similar dislike for assertion emerged in a Slovakian study, where Bugelova (2000) found an assertive style was perceived as unbecoming or impolite and regarded as a hindrance to friendship. In fact in their review of this phenomenon, Buslig and Burgoon (2000: 193) noted: 'Submissive behavior is often ineffective for reaching instrumental goals, but perceived more positively in terms of interpersonal impressions.' We like and probably have more empathy for nonassertive people. Thus, assertion needs to be used sensitively.

Assertiveness can provoke a number of adverse reactions. This may especially be the case when a change in style from submissiveness to assertiveness is made. It is useful to be aware of some of the possible negative reactions of others. Alberti and Emmons (2008) identified five main ones:

1   ***Backbiting.*** Making statements sotto voce, which the assertee ensures are overheard by the asserter ('Who does she think she is?', 'All of a sudden he's now Mr Bigfellow.').

2   ***Aggression.*** Others may try to negate the assertion by using threatening or hostile behaviour in an attempt to regain dominance. They may also use apologetic sarcasm as a form of aggression ('I'm so terribly, terribly, sorry. How unforgivably rude of me to even think of asking you.').

3   ***Over-apologising.*** Apologies can also be genuine. Some people may feel they have caused offence and as a result apologise profusely. In such instances reassurance by the asserter is needed, showing that the apology is accepted and the deed now in the past.

4   ***Emotionality.*** When someone who was formerly submissive becomes assertive, the recipient may react by becoming emotional. This can include temper tantrums, huffing or guilt-based accusations ('You don't love me any more.', 'You've become very selfish. Can't you think of me at all?'). In extreme cases, when the new behaviour signals a potential change in the relational power balance, it can also result in assertee psychosomatic reactions (headaches, stomach pains, feeling weak). Again, an assertive response is required to deal with these.

5   ***Revenge-seeking.*** The assertion may apparently be accepted but the person retains hidden resentment and a desire to 'get their own back'.

Protective assertion

Assertiveness is an important skill when one is coming under pressure from others (Dryden and Constantinou, 2004). This is particularly important in areas such as drug abuse and safe sex. Thus, assertion has been shown to be related to a reduced incidence of alcohol abuse (Epstein *et al.*, 2000), lower chronicity and quantity of alcohol, cocaine and heroin consumption (Torrecillas *et al.*, 2000), and greater condom use to prevent sexually transmitted disease (Zamboni *et al.*, 2000). Three types of protective assertion skills were identified by Fry (1983) as forms of verbal defence to be used against manipulation, nagging or rudeness:

1   ***Broken record.*** Here the person simply makes an assertive statement and keeps repeating it (analogous to the needle sticking on a broken vinyl record) until it is accepted by the other person. For example, to repeated pleas for a loan the individual may just keep using the refusal assertion response: 'No, I'm not going to give you any money.'

2   ***Fogging.*** Using this tactic the person verbally accepts negative criticism but clearly has no intention of changing behaviour. The idea here is that eventually the initiator becomes tired of getting no real response to the criticisms and eventually gives up. An example of a fogging sequence is:

A: You always look down in the dumps.
B: Yes, I probably do.
A: Could you not try to look a bit happier?

    B: I suppose I could.

    A: If you did, you would be a bit more pleasant to work with.

    B: Yes, you're probably right.

3   ***Metalevel assertion.*** As the name suggests, this involves an attempt to widen the perspective rather than sticking to a specific issue. One example of this approach, of moving from the particular to the general, would be where someone involved in an argument with a colleague says, 'We obviously are not going to agree about this, and I think this is typical of what is happening to our whole working relationship.'

COMPONENTS OF ASSERTIVENESS

In order to execute assertiveness skills effectively, three central components need to be mastered: content, process and nonverbal responses.

Content

The actual content of an assertive response should include both an expression of rights and a statement placing this within the context of socially responsible and appropriate behaviour. A number of accompanying elaboration components, or embellishments, have been identified (Linehan and Egan, 1979; Rakos, 2006). Box 11.3 presents a summary of these in relation to an assertive response to the refusal of an invitation. These content statements can obviously be combined to soften the assertion, and distinguish the response from aggression. They serve the important purpose of protecting mutual face and so maintaining the relationship: the asserter achieves the desired personal goal, but at the same time shows concern for the face needs of the assertee (Edwards and Bello, 2001). However, a note of caution was sounded by Rakos (2006), who pointed out that these embellishments are likely to be more consistent with a female than a male approach to, and expectations of, assertion.

One situation that can be difficult to cope with assertively is that of embarrassment. In their discussion of strategies for handling embarrassing predicaments, Cupach and Metts (1990) identified four main types of content responses:

1   ***Apology.*** Apologies range in complexity (Goei *et al.*, 2007). They can involve any or all of: a basic statement of apology ('I'm sorry.'); an expression of remorse ('I feel terrible about this.'); a statement accepting responsibility ('It was entirely my fault.'); a denial of intent ('It was an accident.'); an explanation ('I wasn't looking where I was going.'); self-castigation ('I'm so clumsy.'); an attempt at remediation or restitution (e.g. offering to replace a spilled drink); a request to be pardoned ('Please forgive me.'); and a promise of forbearance ('I'll be more careful in the future.'). Research shows that more complex apologies, involving more of these subelements, tend to have greater effects in terms of reducing negative outcomes (such as anger and aggression) and increasing positive benefits (such as liking).

Box 11.3 Elaboration components in assertion statements

Using the example of a refusal to an invitation from a colleague to go to the bar at lunchtime, the elaborations are as follows:

- A short *delay*, or brief *filled pause* ('Ahh'), before responding, so that the refusal is not seen as abrupt or brusque.
- An *expression of appreciation or praise* for the kindness and thoughtfulness of the other person in making the offer ('It's really nice of you to ask.'). The power of praise in conflict assertion was aptly noted by Mark Twain: 'I think a compliment ought always to precede a complaint, where one is possible, because it softens resentment and insures for the complaint a courteous and gentle reception.'
- A *cushioning* of the way the refusal itself is expressed, usually through an expression of regret at not being able to accept ('Much as I'd like to come, I'm afraid I won't be able to.').
- An *explanation* for the necessity to assert oneself ('I have work to finish off during the lunch break.').
- Showing *empathy* for the other person's situation ('I know you had been looking forward to it.').
- A short *apology* for any resulting consequence ('I'm sorry if you are on your own over lunch.').
- An attempt to identify a mutually acceptable *compromise* ('I haven't time to go out to the bar, but how about just having a quick bite in the canteen?').

---

2   ***Accounts.*** These can be either in the form of an *excuse*, which expresses denial of responsibility for an untoward act without negating its severity ('I know it is a mess, but it was an accident.'); or a *justification*, which expresses responsibility for the untoward act but denies the pejorative nature of the consequences ('Yes, I did spill it, but there's no real harm done.').

3   ***Humour.*** A joke can be one of the most effective methods for dealing with embarrassment, since it can convert a potential loss of social approval into a positive gain. In this sense, 'a well formed joke, especially one reflecting on the unintentional incompetence of the transgressor, can express remorse, guilt, and embarrassment as an apology would without unduly lowering the individual's status vis-à-vis others who are present' (Cupach and Metts, 1990: 329).

4   ***Avoidance.*** This strategy would include not mentioning sensitive topics to particular people, quickly changing an embarrassing topic, staying silent or simply leaving the room.

Obviously, two or more of these can be used at the same time. Thus, an assertive response might involve giving an excuse, apologising and offering restitution, while at the same time employing appropriate humour.

In her analysis of tactics used by those who are held publicly responsible for an event that has been evaluated negatively, Schutz (1998) identified six possible response strategies:

1   ***Denial.*** This is summarised by the 'It never happened.' response. The veracity and motives of those who claim that it did are then called into question.

2   ***Reframing.*** Here the essence is 'It was not like that.' The approach is to present the event in a new 'frame' – it did occur but it was not nearly as bad as portrayed.

3   ***Dissociation.*** This is the 'I was not to blame.' strategy. The event did occur but the person did not cause it. It was someone else's fault. One variation of this is in the use of pronominals to associate or dissociate oneself with what happened – here Shutz gave the example of supporters of sports teams when talking about victories saying '*We* won . . .' but when defeated saying '*They* lost . . .'.

4   ***Justification.*** The nub of this approach is 'It was the only thing to do'. Responsibility is accepted but the argument is that nothing else could have been done, or even that the response averted potentially more damaging events and so the public should be grateful.

5   ***Excuses.*** The typical statement here is 'I could not prevent it.' The main excuse tends to be that of extenuating or extraordinary circumstances – that no one could have foreseen the event.

6   ***Concessions, apologies and remediation.*** The response here is 'I accept full responsibility and wish to do whatever I can to compensate.' As Schutz illustrated, when remediation is offered as well as an apology, the impact is more positive in terms of public perceptions of the perpetrator's image.

Rose and Tryon (1979) made another important distinction between three general types of assertion content, which can be exemplified in relation to complaining about a meal in a restaurant, as follows:

1   ***Description of the behaviour*** – 'Excuse me, this meal is cold.'

2   ***Description of behaviour plus indication of your noncompliance*** – 'Excuse me, this meal is cold. I couldn't eat it.'

3   ***Description, noncompliance, plus request for behaviour change*** – 'Excuse me, this meal is cold. I couldn't eat it. Could you please replace it?'

Rose and Tryon found that ratings of assertiveness increased as individuals moved from simply giving a description through to using all the above three types of content.

Process

The way in which assertive responses are carried out can be crucial to their success (Townend, 2007). Thus, the correct timing of vocalisations and nonverbal responses is vital. Although a slight delay is important in refusing a genuine invitation (Holman, 2000), assertive responses should be given without long hesitations. On occasions, we may have our rights infringed because we are unsure about whether they actually have been violated. If we later discover this to be the case then it is necessary to reconstruct the situation in which the infringement occurred ('Yesterday you asked me to do X. I have since discovered that it is not my job to do X. I would therefore be grateful if you would not ask me to do this again.').

Stimulus control skills are also important. These refer to manipulations of the environment, or other people, to make the assertive response more successful. For example:

- Asking someone to come to your room where you will feel more in charge, rather than discussing an issue in the corridor. Humans, like all animals, are territorial and our sense of *place* is very important to how we respond (Dixon and Durrheim, 2004). We feel more comfortable in our own lairs, with familiar sights, sounds and smells. Conversely, we are more uncomfortable when on someone else's patch. To borrow a sporting analogy, it is always harder to get a result when playing away from home. Thus, it is easier to be assertive when we are on our own ground.
- Requesting that you seek the opinion of another person to help settle the matter, when you already know that the views of this third person concur with your own.
- Simply asking for time to consider a request, which allows you to think through the ramifications thereof.

The use of reinforcement (see Chapter 4) is also important, for three reasons. First, rewarding another person is actually a positive use of assertion; someone who has performed a task well has the right to expect reward. Second, the reward can help to minimise any negative feelings resulting from the assertion. Third, it encourages the other person to behave appropriately towards you in the future.

Nonverbal responses

The final component of assertiveness relates to the nonverbal behaviour of the asserter. The main nonverbal assertive behaviours are: medium levels of eye contact; avoidance of inappropriate facial expressions; smooth use of gestures while speaking, yet inconspicuous while listening; upright posture; direct body orientation; medium interpersonal distance; and appropriate paralinguistics (short response latency, medium response length, good fluency, medium volume and inflection, increased firmness).

PERSONAL AND CONTEXTUAL FACTORS

There are several factors that influence the degree, nature and effectiveness of assertion, namely: gender, cultural background, situation, age, disability and the assertive level of the assertee.

Gender

In a meta-analysis of research studies into gender difference in adult language use, Leaper and Ayres (2007) found that males were significantly more likely to use assertive speech while females were significantly more likely to employ affiliative language patterns. However, as this section will show, the relationship between gender and assertiveness is both complex and complicated. In an early review, Kahn (1981: 349) suggested that: 'People expect women to behave unassertively. Women may not only accept this judgment . . . but . . . may avoid behaviors that do not fit "the feminine role" and when they do engage in "masculine assertiveness", they are likely to encounter disbelief or even hostility.'

More recently, in their review of the literature on gender differences in behaviour in organisations, Guadagno and Cialdini (2007: 485) showed that not much had changed in the intervening quarter of a century, concluding that 'assertiveness in a man is seen as a gender "appropriate" behavior, whereas an assertive woman is seen as violating gender-based expectations for behavior and may be thought of in a derogatory manner'. Ongoing research reveals that males have significantly higher scores than females on tests of assertiveness (Sigler *et al.*, 2008).

Some feminist writers have argued that the entire concept of assertion is andro-centric (male-centred) and embued with demeaning portrayals of women for being 'weak' in this area (Cameron, 1994; Crawford, 1995). Despite such views, the main perspective within the feminist movement tends to be that this is a skill which women should possess (Rakos, 2006). Thus, females have consistently been advised to under-take AT (LaFrance and Harris, 2004). Likewise, several assertiveness books have been written specifically for women. This is not surprising given that females consistently report difficulties in being assertive. Indeed, the plethora of written material and self-help texts specifically designed for women and the popularity of women's AT programmes is in itself a form of evidence that females feel they need more help in this field. This is perhaps not surprising given that the most successful style for females seems to be one where they are perceived to be both competent and nice (Rudman and Glick, 2001) – not always an easy combination to sustain in conflict situations.

In reviewing the field of gender differences in language use, Mulac (2006: 223) posed the question as to whether men and women really use language differently. His answer was 'an unrestrained "Yes!" – meaningful differences in language behavior do exist. This conclusion is supported by a substantial number of empirical investiga-tions of actual male-female language use conducted in a variety of communication contexts'. However, he also noted that these differences should be read as *gender-indicative tendencies* since both genders can and do display the same language fea-tures. Indeed, questions have been raised regarding the validity of much of the research into gender differences in language (Cameron, 2009). Furthermore, context is very important. While overall women or men may have a higher mean differential level of production of certain linguistic features, their usage varies according to situation (LaFrance and Harris, 2004; Palomares, 2009b). As shown by Leaper and Smith (2004: 993): 'Although the pattern of gender differences in the use of language tends to be consistent when differences are reported, many studies find no significant differences.' In addition, specific individuals may use gender-opposite language styles. Three general, and in many ways complementary, explanations have been put forward to explain gender differences in language (Leaper and Ayers, 2007):

1   The *biological* perspective purports that gender differences were shaped by evolutionary necessities, whereby males were required to be assertive and

aggressive (e.g. as hunters or warriors) while females were affiliative and nurturing, especially in terms of child-rearing. This approach emphasises gender differences in brain functioning and organisation (Andersen, 2006). Thus, girls usually develop language earlier than boys, and achieve higher scores on verbal production measures. However, while biological influences may impact upon some aspects of language production, most analysts would now accept that social factors play a prominent role in gender variations in language use (Halpern, 2000).

2 In the *social constructionist* approach, gender is seen as being socially engineered. Here it is argued that females and males will behave similarly if they are placed in the same circumstances, with equal authority, and required to play the same roles. It is further posited that we can decide who we want to be in terms of gender identity, but at the same time we are also subjected to external situational and cultural demands and pressures to conform to certain expectations (Kimmel, 2004). This approach highlights the demand characteristics of the specific context as playing a key role in language variation. In particular, it accords considerable relevance to the role of structural power. It points to the higher power and status of males in society as an important influence on gender variations in behaviour. This perspective is therefore linked to the *gender-as-power* perspective, where differences in male and female language use are purported to reflect the relative dominance and submissiveness of the two genders.

3 The *social developmental* paradigm gives central importance to the cumulative impact of cognitive learning, practice and experience over time. This approach is also referred to as *gender-as-culture*, or the *two cultures hypothesis*. It argues that boys and girls to a large extent inhabit different 'worlds' at the formative stage of development (up to 15 years old). As a result of their repeated exposure to the same gender in-group, they adopt a specific type of either 'masculine' or 'feminine' language usage. For example, boys and girls engage in very different games (Wood, 2009). Boys play games that usually involve large numbers, are competitive, grounded in doing something, and emphasise achievement – the notion of being most valuable player (MVP) is highly regarded. Communication is used primarily to attract attention and assert one's ideas. By contrast, girls play games involving smaller groups, such as house or school, where the goals are less clear cut, and so negotiations have to take place about who does what. Communication is used to develop and sustain relationships, by ensuring that everyone is included. Opportunities for learning are central in terms of knowledge, expectations and skills, so that gender differentiated experiences are more likely to result in increased feelings of self-efficacy in the gender-specific role. Likewise, responses and roles that are regarded as having greater relevance to one's own gender become more salient than those perceived to belong to the other gender. Thus, Martin and Ruble (2004: 67) argued that children quickly become 'gender detectives who search for cues about gender – who should or should not engage in a particular activity, who can play with whom, and why girls and boys are different'.

In their review of research studies of language and gender, Mulac *et al.* (2001) found a number of main difference effects as shown in Box 11.4. These differences

---

Box 11.4 Gender differences in language

Males tend to make greater use of:

- references to quantity ('20 feet high', 'weighed at least a ton')
- judgemental adjectives (giving personal evaluations – 'That's stupid.')
- directives (telling another what to do – 'Put it over there.')
- locatives (indicate the position/location of objects – 'To the right of . . .')
- elliptical sentences (short or one-word sentences in which either the subject or predicate is understood, e.g. 'Awesome!' 'Great idea.')
- self-referenced statements ('My view is . . .').

Females tend to use more:

- intensive adverbs ('terribly', 'so', 'really')
- dependent clauses to qualify the primary meaning (e.g. 'I am Communications Manager, which involves a host of responsibilities.')
- reference to emotions ('cheerful', 'angry')
- sentences of greater mean length
- sentence initial adverbials ('Due to the lighting, the room seems . . .')
- uncertainty verbs ('It seems to be . . .', 'I might be able to . . .')
- hedges ('sort of', 'a bit like')
- negations (statements of what something is not, e.g. 'It is not a very deep shade of blue.')
- oppositions ('He looks happy yet also sad.')
- questions.

---

indicate why females may find it more difficult to be assertive. The male-preferred style reflects shorter, more directive, self-opinionated and explicit language use. Expressions of direct assertiveness will therefore not be so problematic. On the other hand, the preferred female style of longer and more indirect sentences, coupled with greater expressed uncertainty and qualification, does not lend itself so easily to assertion. Wood (2009) also identified differences between what was regarded as typical masculine and feminine nonverbal behaviour, in that females were expected to smile more, disengage eye contact if someone stares (males hold eye contact), show interest in others (males try to show confidence and control), and interact in such a way as to be nice to others (while males interact in such a way as to impress others). Again, these female-typical behaviours of being nice, smiling, avoiding prolonged gaze and showing interest rather than confidence or control mean that females can find it more difficult to communicate in an assertive style.

Some research has been carried out to ascertain whether assertion is learned at an early age. One study of four- to six-year-olds in eastern USA found no difference in assertive behaviour between boys and girls (Beneson *et al.*, 1998). However, confounding variables here included the facts that the study focused upon almost exclusively white, middle/upper-class children, the girls were in the presence of friends, and they knew the boys. All of these factors facilitate assertion displays. In contrast, Leaper (2000) analysed the assertion and affiliation behaviours of European American and

Latin American girls and boys (mean age 48 months) and their parents in their own homes. Each child played individually with mother or father, with a feminine stereo-typed toy (foods and plates) and a masculine stereotyped toy (track and cars). It was found that fathers were more assertive (e.g. giving directions, disagreeing) than mothers who, in turn, were more affiliative (e.g. praising, asking for the child's opin-ion). Furthermore, in general, children were more assertive than their mothers but less assertive than their fathers. Leaper argued that this latter finding may reflect the mother's willingness to let the child take control, but that it could also lead to a learned stereotype of women as being less powerful than men. Differences also emerged in relation to the play settings, in that the toy food scenario produced higher levels of both assertion and affiliation – in other words, it was a more collaborative encounter (see Figure 11.2).

Leaper (2000) argued that gender-typed play scenarios mean that girls learn to cooperate from an early age, whereas boys learn to compete. Another finding was that both fathers and mothers demonstrated less assertion than their sons but not their daughters in the toy track condition, while no such difference emerged in the food play. Leaper summarised these findings as showing a pattern of children being presented with role models of assertive fathers and affiliative mothers, and of boys but not girls being encouraged to be assertive and take control in masculine stereotyped activities. Overall, this study illustrated how gender differences in assertion can be shaped by a combination of parental role models, and reward for differential activities in stereotyped play activities.

Lewis and Gallois (1984) found that both males and females were more assertive towards those of the same gender; that expression of negative feeling was more acceptable from a member of the opposite sex; and that aggressive encounters were more prevalent in same-sex dyads. In another study, Nix et al. (1983) concluded that assertiveness is a masculine sex-role characteristic. They found that females achiev-ing high masculinity scores in the Bem Sex Role Inventory scored significantly higher on measures of assertiveness than those high in femininity. This finding is consistent with general trends wherein masculine sex-role characteristics tend to be attributed to assertive individuals; masculine or androgynous females are more likely to be assertive than feminine women; masculinity and conflict assertiveness are positively correlated; and direct assertiveness tends to be viewed as masculine (McCartan and Hargie, 2004b).

The situation in which assertion occurs may also be important. For example, both male and female university students evaluated a female speaker more favourably when using an assertive as opposed to a tentative style of speech (Hawkes et al., 1996). In the work context, there is evidence that females who use assertiveness are judged as less socially attractive, and as less competent than males who use similar behaviours (Rakos, 2006). One study of higher level managers found that female executives rated displays of warmth and support, and avoiding a direct 'no' in response to requests, higher than males (Dubrin, 1994). Likewise, Bugelova (2000) found that for both undergraduates and middle managers, levels of assertiveness were higher in males than in females. Other studies in organisations indicate that, while higher level female managers have moderate levels of argumentativeness (an assertive personality trait), female assertiveness is not usually well received by males (Schullery, 1997). A disparity in conflict styles was confirmed in a study by Swanson (1999), which found no difference between males and females on assertion but showed that males were more likely to be verbally aggressive. This latter result was also reported by Archer *et al.* (1995).

It has been suggested that, when dealing with disputes, males are more likely to operate on a 'one-up, one-down' basis, and so direct confrontation literally gives them the opportunity to achieve one-upmanship. Similarly, the *fight-or-flight response*, whereby the individual reacts to threats from others by either attacking the source of the threat or fleeing from it, has been portrayed as a male approach (Aronson *et al.*, 2007). Females, on the other hand, prefer a relational route to conflict resolution; they see the option of openly confronting the other person as leading to likely retaliation and harmful for the overall relationship (Dindia and Canary, 2006; Lundgren and Rudawsky, 2000). Accordingly it has been argued that they develop a *tend-and-befriend response* as an alternative to fight-or-flight. That is, they prefer nurturant activities that protect themselves and their loved ones (tending), and the development of strong social networks (befriending) to buffer the effects of threat. However, there is also evidence to indicate that females are more likely to be indirectly aggressive (Richardson and Green, 2006). In recognising this, Owens *et al.* (2000) carried out a study in Australia on the effects of peer indirect aggression (e.g. exclusion from the group, telling lies about the person) on teenage girls. They discovered that victims suffered a wide range of psychological effects, including loss of self-esteem, anxiety and depression. This in turn led to a range of ideas about how to escape the pain, ranging from a desire to leave the school to thoughts of suicide. The most vulnerable girls were those who had few friends, were new to the school or lacked assertiveness. Some responded by retaliating against the perpetrator. This is interesting, given that another study found that training in physical self-defence actually served to increase women's self-reported levels of assertiveness (Weitlauf *et al.*, 2000).

In a meta-analysis of research studies on gender effects on children's language use, Leaper and Smith (2004) found that boys used more assertive speech than girls, who in turn were more affiliative and talkative in their speech patterns than boys. However, these differences were small. Overall, there is no clear picture as to the exact nature of the relationship between the effects of different types of assertiveness, the situation in which they are employed and the gender of asserter and assertee. One problem here, as with all studies in the field of assertion, is that different investigators use differing measurements and methodologies. For example, subjects may be asked to respond to written, audio or video vignettes of assertiveness, engage in role plays, complete one of the large number of self-report assertion scales that now exist (see McCartan, 2001, for a review of these) or be confronted with an experimentally contrived assertive encounter they believe to be real. Ratings of assertion may be made by the subjects themselves, by those with whom they have interacted or by trained observers. These variations make comparisons between studies very difficult.

The final compounding factor is that the role of women in society has changed rapidly in recent years. Indeed, in terms of gender stereotypes we have gone through a 'transitional era' (Wood, 2007). In traditional fairy tales, portrayals of females were typically either 'submissive/beautiful' (e.g. Cinderella, Snow White, Goldilocks) or 'aggressive/ugly' (Ugly Sisters, Wicked Witch, Evil Stepmother). Similarly, in films familiar storylines were of the bold dashing knight in shining armour winning the hand of the shy fair maiden, or of the tough galloping cowboy in the white hat rescuing the defenceless damsel in distress. These stereotypes persisted for quite some time. For example, when the cult television series *Star Trek* began in the late 1960s, its futuristic interpretation of advanced human civilisation had only one female member as part of the elite group on the bridge of the *Enterprise*, and she was in essence a glorified telephonist who rarely got 'beamed' anywhere. More recently this has changed. The females on the programme are now centrally involved in the hard action, including as captain. The concept of 'ladette culture', replete with loud, hard-drinking, self-directed, often sexually predatory females, has also affected gender image and expectations. Furthermore, female entrants to the traditional professions (medicine, pharmacy, law, etc.) now often outnumber males, and within many churches there are now female priests. All such changes influence the attitudes of both males and females to assertive behaviour by the latter.

One specific problem faced by females is that of sexual assertiveness when negotiating sexual activity with a partner (Auslander *et al.*, 2007). To address this issue, Morokoff *et al.* (1997) developed the *Sexual Assertiveness Scale* for females. This measures responses to three areas of sexual activity as follows, with actual scale items given in parenthesis:

- initiation ('I begin sex with my partner if I want to.')
- refusal ('I have sex if my partner wants me to even if I don't want to.')
- pregnancy–STD prevention ('I refuse to have sex if my partner refuses to use a condom or latex barrier.').

In testing this scale with women from both university and the wider community, Morokoff *et al.* found that:

- the greater a woman's sexual experience the more likely she was to initiate sex
- the anticipation of a negative partner response reduced the level of assertiveness in refusing a sexual advance or requesting barrier precautions
- feelings of self-efficacy about how to use condoms were related to self-reported ability to refuse a sexual advance.

Also in this domain, Livingstone *et al.* (2007) demonstrated a significant link between low sexual assertiveness and subsequent sexual victimisation.

In a fascinating longitudinal meta-analysis of 385 studies dating from the 1920s to the 1990s, Twenge (1998) charted changes in assertiveness across these eight decades. She found no consistent changes in male scores over this period. However, female assertion scores mirrored their social status and roles at each era, showing an increase pre-war (1928–1945), a decrease post-war (1945–1967) and an increase thereafter. Interestingly, she also found a positive correlation between assertion scores and overall figures for educational attainment for women. This suggests that 'getting on' in society involves 'standing up' for one's rights. It also indicates that female assertive behaviour changes according to shifting societal expectations, whereas male assertion remains constant.

Cultural background

As discussed in Chapter 2, the context within which responses are employed is important. For example, a subculture of people with certain strong religious beliefs may actually eschew assertiveness as a valid modus operandi and be guided by Biblical maxims of submissiveness such as the following from Matthew 5: 'Blessed are the meek: for they shall inherit the earth.'; 'Whoever slaps you on your right cheek, turn the other to him also.'; and 'Give to him who asks you, and from him who wants to borrow from you do not turn away.' For such groups, obviously AT would not be either relevant or appropriate. One problem with early approaches to the study of cultural differences was that Western culture was regarded as 'universal' and other cultures were viewed as having 'special features' (Niikura, 1999a). This perspective no longer prevails and it is now accepted that no culture should be seen either explicitly or implicitly as being universal.

One of the most researched aspects of culture is that of individualism versus collectivism (Kim and Ko, 2007). In individualist cultures such as North America (Canada and USA) and some European countries (e.g. Norway and the UK), the emphasis tends to be upon the self as an independent entity with needs, wants and goals that are legitimate to pursue individually. As such, standing up for one's rights seems perfectly valid and indeed natural. In collectivist cultures, individual rights are subordinate to those of the group and so assertion is not so appropriate. Thus, in many eastern countries (e.g. China, Japan, Korea) and in Latin America (e.g. Brazil, Mexico) the emphasis is more upon an interdependent self. For example, in Hispanic culture the concept of *personalismo* is central. The difference between these two cultural styles, as highlighted in Box 11.5, was neatly summarised by Morris *et al.* (2001: 100) in the example that: 'Brazilians display stronger intentions to do what is expected of them, whereas North Americans display a stronger intention to do what they personally desire.' Likewise, Libby and Eibach (2007) noted that the differing positive and negative cultural expectations from assertive responses were

Box 11.5 Individualist and collectivist cultural differences	
Important in individualist cultures	*Important in collectivist cultures*
Needs	Duties
Rights	Norms
Concern for self ('I' orientation)	Concern for group ('we' orientation)
Being successful	Being accepted
Innovation	Respect for tradition
Equality	Given role
Privacy	Sharing
Competition	Cooperation
Informality	Formality
Directness	Indirectness
Being upfront	Protecting face
Assertion	Nonassertion

encapsulated in the saying in Western cultures that 'The squeaky wheel gets the grease.' and in Eastern cultures 'The nail that stands up gets pounded down.' In this way, 'American parents try to raise their children to be independent, self-reliant, and assertive (a "cut above the rest"), whereas Japanese children are raised to fit into their groups and community' (Kassin *et al.*, 2008: 64).

It should be noted that the differences between these two cultural styles is not so neat as it may at first seem. Thus, collectivist cultures differ in the ways in which they maintain intergroup relations and avoid conflicts. Latin Americans achieve this through open, warm, expressive, emotional displays. On the other hand, the Chinese tradition of *jen* and the Japanese one of *amae* emphasise the maintenance of harmony through a more passive, respectful and less overtly emotional approach in their dealings with one another. In addition, as Hargie (2006b) illustrated, aspects of collectivism can be found in individual cultures and vice versa so that 'at different times, in varying situations, and with different people, we may adopt either an individualistic or a more collective style of communicating' (p. 63). Reykowski (2001) and Iyengar and Brockner (2001) demonstrated how the individual's own position on the individualist–collectivist (I–C) continuum often plays a more influential role in determining responses than the I–C norms of the national or cultural group to which the person belongs. However, it is also clear that cultural differences make attempts to employ assertive behaviour with people from different subcultures fraught with difficulty. In particular, assertive responses are not appropriate where values of humility, tolerance or subservience are prevalent.

There is evidence that individuals take culture into account when choosing style of assertion. Thus, a study in Germany of the manner in which Turkish immigrants handled conflict situations found that the preferred style varied depending upon the target person (Klinger and Bierbraver, 2001). When dealing with someone from the Turkish community a more indirect, nonconfrontational approach, typical of this cultural group, was usually employed. However, when dealing with a German a more direct, instrumental style, again in keeping with the norms of this target group, was used.

Minorites and subcultures in the USA with a strong sense of separate identity, such as the Mexican, Japanese and Chinese communities, tend to report being less assertive than whites. These subcultures also emphasise respect for and obedience to elders and in particular parents, so that any form of assertion from child to parent is likely to be frowned upon. This again is different from the norm for Caucasians, where open disagreement and negotiated decisions are acceptable between parents and children. In similar vein, in some subcultures assertion may be associated with a macho male role model, with females being expected to play an acquiescent or subservient role.

There is evidence to indicate that cultural differences in assertion may be cognitively based, emanating from cultural values and norms rather than from assertive behaviour deficits, since in role-play situations people from these cultures are able to behave as assertively as whites. For example, Sue *et al.* (1990) found that second generation Chinese American female undergraduates were as assertive as Caucasian females on scores on the Rathus Assertiveness Scale and on role-play tests with either an Asian or a Caucasian experimenter. The only significant difference between the groups was that the Chinese Americans scored higher on the Fear of Negative

Evaluation Scale. It could therefore be the case that in real-life encounters such apprehension of disapproval from others may result in Chinese American females being less assertive. As Sue *et al.* (1990: 161) put it: 'Chinese-Americans are able to demonstrate assertiveness in laboratory settings, but do they inhibit this response in other situations?'

Hastings (2000a) investigated the behaviour of Asian Indian postgraduate students in the USA. She found that this cultural group disliked the American norm of extensive use of talk and their expression of direct, forceful opinions. The US students were perceived as pushy, verbally aggressive and showing a lack of respect for superiors (their professors). Indian culture places a very high value on acceptance, self-suppression and concern for the feelings of others. Hindu religion regards the role occupied by an individual as having been designated by God, and as such it has to be respected. The Indians in this study perceived the 'recipients' of their behaviour not to be just those immediately involved, but also their family and wider community which might eventually find out what had been said. Their decisions about assertive responses were guided by these factors. It was not the case that they did not know how to use assertive behaviours, but rather they recognised that these were not culturally acceptable.

One study compared assertive responses of African American, Hispanic and European American high school students (Yager and Rotheram-Borus, 2000). It was found that assertive responses were more frequent among European Americans, while aggressive and expressive responses were more common in the Hispanic and African American groups. Yager and Rotheram-Borus argued that these response patterns could be misperceived by the outgroup and thus be a potential source of cross-ethnic conflicts. Differences also emerged in a cross-cultural investigation of assertion in low-income 'thirty-something' women in the USA (Yoshioka, 2000). Here, African Americans, Hispanic Americans and Caucasians all agreed about appropriate assertive responses towards other females and towards children. However, in relation to assertion with males, the Hispanic group differed from the other two in that they were more affiliative in their reaction to male aggression.

Niikura (1999a, 1999b) carried out an investigation which compared the responses of white-collar workers in the USA, Japan, Malaysia and the Philippines on a self-expression questionnaire, and to hypothetical scenarios such as:

> Your boss asks you to do something personal for him/her on a holiday. You have always been on friendly terms with your boss and he/she has helped you in many ways. However, you have already made reservations at a resort hotel for you and your family for that same day.

Similarities were found between workers in Japan, Malaysia and the Philippines in terms of the psychological bonds they felt to relationships with superiors. The Japanese and Malayans showed a much higher reluctance to directly refuse an annoying request from a friend. By contrast, the Americans were more likely to directly turn down unwanted requests from either superiors or friends. The Japanese respondents differed from the other groups in their reluctance to ask questions in a public forum. In Japan there is a sense of shame attached to asking questions about matters one does not understand and indeed it is regarded as a sign of over-assertiveness to ask questions. The Japanese, Malaysian and Philippino subjects placed greater importance on group solidarity and respect for senior members of staff than did the Americans. Niikura (1999b: 697) speculated: 'The differences between the Asian and the U.S. perceptions of assertiveness in interpersonal relations and the conflicting views of how to maintain group harmony would be sources of misunderstanding and friction when such people interact.'

In the study by Leaper (2000) of parent–child interactions described earlier, it was found that there were higher levels of both assertion and affiliation in Latin American than European American families. While Leaper pointed out that this finding of collaborativeness or *familism* was consistent with other reports of Latino families, he also noted that care is needed in interpreting such findings, since other variables, including parent education and age, socioeconomic status, religion and family size impact upon behaviour patterns. For example, Mexican-descent parents with higher education levels have been shown to hold more gender-egalitarian attitudes (Leaper and Valin, 1996). Furthermore, in his review of this area, Rakos (1991: 13) concluded: 'Studies with diverse cultural groups generally find the normative level of self-reported assertive behavior generally approaches that of white Americans as the group's sociocultural similarity to mainstream American norms and values increases.'

The above results present an opaque image of the relationship between cultural group and appropriate assertion. While it is clear that culture is a very important variable in the assertion equation, no hard-and-fast guidelines can be offered about how best to respond in any particular cultural context. Thus, Cheng and Chun (2008) found that the nature of the request in terms of degree of reasonableness was an important factor in distinguishing differences between Caucasian American and Chinese adults. While there was no difference between the two groups in relation to rejection of very reasonable or very unreasonable requests, the Caucasian Americans were significantly more likely than the Chinese to reject requests of moderate legitimacy. As Yoshioka (2000) in her review of this area pointed out, a key dimension of AT for subcultural groups is that of *message matching*. This involves a careful assessment of both situation and assertee to decide how best to match the specific message being delivered, and whether a subcultural or mainstream cultural response is most appropriate.

Situation

It has long been known that the situation in which assertiveness is required is important. Following a detailed research investigation, Eisler *et al.* (1975: 339) concluded:

> An individual who is assertive in one interpersonal context may not be assertive in a different interpersonal environment. Furthermore, some individuals may have no difficulty responding with negative assertions but may be unable to respond when the situation requires positive expressions.

The old description of a person who is 'a lion inside the home and a lamb outside' is an example of this. Few individuals are assertive across all contexts. Most find it easier to assert themselves in some situations than in others. Attention needs to be devoted to situations in which the individual finds it difficult to be assertive, and strategies devised to overcome the particular problems.

In the context of the work environment, Bryan and Gallois (1992) carried out a study in which people who were all in employment in a variety of occupations, ranging from professionals to unskilled labourers, judged written vignettes of supervisors, subordinates and co-workers sending either positive or negative assertive messages to one another. Results indicated that positive messages were more favourably rated than negative ones, especially in relation to judgements concerning the likely outcome of the interaction and the probable effects on the relationship. The expression of a personal limitation was rated least favourably of the positive messages, while expressing displeasure was rated as the most negative message. The only difference to emerge between the status groupings was that subordinates were rated more favourably than supervisors or co-workers when using negative assertions. The judges in this study were also asked to generate rules that would apply to, or govern, these assertive interactions. The most common rules identified, in order of frequency, were maintaining eye contact, being polite, being friendly and being pleasant. These findings suggest the importance of using relationship maintenance skills when being assertive.

Certain types of assertiveness may well be more appropriate in some settings than in others. Cianni-Surridge and Horan (1983) found this to be the case in the job interview. They had 276 employers rate the efficacy of 16 'frequently advocated assertive job-seeking behaviours' in terms of whether or not each would enhance the applicant's chances of being offered employment. They found that some behaviours were advantageous and some disadvantageous. Thus, for example: 'Following an interview, an applicant writes you a letter thanking you for interviewing him/her and expressing his/her continued interest in the position' was regarded by 54 employers as greatly enhancing, by 176 as enhancing, by 46 as having no effect and by 0 as diminishing or greatly diminishing job prospects. On the other hand: 'An applicant feels his/her interview with you went poorly. He/she requests a second interview with another interviewer' was regarded by 44 employers as greatly diminishing, by 100 as diminishing, by 119 as having no effect, by 10 as enhancing and by 3 as greatly enhancing job prospects.

Age

This is another important factor in assertiveness. Pardeck *et al.* (1991), in a study of postgraduate students in the USA, found a significant and positive correlation between age and assertiveness. This may be because older people have gained more life experience, including situations where they have had to stand up for themselves, and so have developed more confidence in defending their rights. However, more research is needed in order to ascertain the exact nature of the relationship between assertiveness and maturation.

Disability

AT has been shown to be of benefit to physically disabled individuals. Glueckauf and Quittner (1992) in a Canadian study found that wheelchair users who received AT made significant increases in the number of assertive responses and concomitant decreases in passive responses during a role-play test as compared to a control group who received no AT. The AT group also reported significantly higher increases in assertiveness in both general and disability related situations. This result is of particular interest since previous research has shown that wheelchair users often experience discomfort in situations which involve refusing help, managing patronising remarks and giving directives. Furthermore, it has also been shown that nondisabled individuals experience difficulties (e.g. show more motoric inhibition, end interactions sooner and are more likely to express attitudes inconsistent with true beliefs) in interactions with wheelchair users (Glueckauf and Quittner, 1992). There is clearly a need for more research into the possible inhibiting effects of wheelchairs during interpersonal encounters and to ways in which such effects can be overcome.

The assertee

A key aspect of assertion is the target person. From the above reviews, it is clear that the gender and cultural background of the assertee are core determinants of the effectiveness of assertive responses. However, the assertion level of the assertee is also important. In two early studies, Gormally (1982) found that assertive behaviour was rated more favourably by assertive individuals, while Kern (1982) discovered that low assertive subjects reacted negatively to assertive behaviour whereas high assertive subjects generally devalued nonassertive behaviour. These findings suggest that decisions about when and how to apply assertion should be moderated by the assertive nature of the recipient.

Thus, the relationship with the other person is of vital import in deciding how to be assertive. An interesting dimension of relationships was explored by Dickson *et al.* (2009) in relation to teasing behaviour (banter). They illustrated how teasing can be interpreted either as playfulness/joking or as derogation/aggression since it usually has both friendly and hostile components. Between friends it is normally the former purpose that is served by banter and the humour is therefore two-way. In other contexts there would seem to be a dominance or control function prevalent, since high-status people can tease low-status people but not usually vice versa. Banter has been shown to be a common feature of relationships between work colleagues, and when used appropriately to contribute to the process of relational development. Alberts (1992) pointed out that decisions about how to react to teasing behaviour are made on the basis of four main elements: the perceived goal of the teaser; background knowledge of and relationship with this person; the context in which the tease is employed; and the paralinguistic tone with which it is delivered. Where banter is used as a form of sarcasm or 'put down', it is necessary to assertively indicate that such behaviour is unacceptable. This needs to be done skilfully to avoid accusations of not being able to take a joke.

Lewis and Gallois (1984) investigated the influence of friendship on assertiveness. They found that certain types of negative assertions (expression of anger, or difference of opinion) were more acceptable when made by friends as opposed to strangers. However, refusal of a request from a friend was perceived to be less socially skilled and more hurtful than refusal from a stranger. As a result, they recommended that with strangers it is 'wise to refrain from assertively expressing a difference of opinion or negative feelings, at least until the relationship is well established' (p. 366).

OVERVIEW

The three response styles reviewed in this chapter can be explained succinctly as follows.

* aggressive – *talking at* others
* assertive – *talking with* others
* submissive – *talking little to* others.

Assertiveness is a very important social skill both in professional contexts and in everyday interactions. We feel hurt, aggrieved and upset if our rights have been violated. Yet some individuals find it very difficult to be assertive. This is often related to upbringing in that they may have been raised under a very strict regime by parents in which as children they were seen and not heard, and learned in school that the quiet child who did as it was told was most approved of by the teacher. It can then be difficult in later life to overcome this residue of parental and educational upbringing. As summarised by Paterson (2000: 209) in his book on this topic:

> Assertiveness skills can be difficult to learn. Many of us grow up without learning to use them effectively. As well, assertiveness goes against our temptations. Sometimes we want to push other people to do our bidding. Sometimes we are desperately afraid of conflict. Assertiveness may mean holding back from our automatic ways of doing things.

One common pitfall is that individuals move from prolonged nonassertion straight into aggression, feeling they can no longer put up with being used, taken for granted or having their rights ignored. But such a sudden and unexpected explosion of anger is not the best approach, and indeed can destroy relationships. It is therefore important to employ assertiveness at an early stage, and in a skilled manner that recognises the rights of the other while also protecting one's own rights. Research evidence has clearly shown that assertion skills are not innate – they can be learned and improved. Once they are learned, it becomes easier to stand up for oneself, to say 'no' without undue concern, to make reasonable requests, and to regard oneself as equal to others. Our self-confidence and sense of self-worth are improved accordingly.

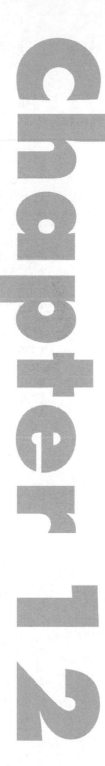

Chapter 12

Using your influence: the skill of persuasion

INTRODUCTION

A S FORGAS AND WILLIAMS (2001: 7) noted: 'The sophisticated ability of humans to influence, and be influenced, by each other is probably one of the cornerstones of the evolutionary success of our species, and the foundation of the increasingly complex forms of social organization we have been able to develop.' It is therefore not surprising that persuasion and influence are omnipresent in human society (Dillard, 2010). We meet these change agents many times every day and in different guises. As noted by Moons *et al.* (2009: 44): 'Persuasion is a pervasive and crucial component of social life.' Consumers are exposed to an unending stream of commercial messages daily (on websites, television, radio and newspaper adverts, billboard posters, etc.), all aimed at encouraging the target to adopt a service, idea or product. For example, the average American watches some 37,822 television commercials per year (Kassin *et al.*, 2008). At this level, the persuasion attempt is directed towards the masses. Consequently, a vast volume of literature has been produced in this field. Research into the effects of television and radio advertising, health promotion campaigns, posters, public relations (PR) interventions and so on has attracted enormous interest (Dillard *et al.*, 2007a).

However, Cody and Seiter (2001: 325) illustrated how 'scholarly interest in the process of persuasion has changed considerably in the last few decades from a focus on one-to-many influence attempts to the study of interpersonal or one-to-one influence attempts'. The main reason for this is the recognition that almost all exchanges between people involve some element of influence (Benoit and Benoit, 2008). As shown by Erb and Bohner (2007), influence is an integral part of human interaction. Even in the most informal encounters, such as when friends meet to 'hang out' together, they behave in such a way as to communicate liking for one another (through smiles, eye contact, verbal following, etc.). While these behaviours may be carried out without the goal consciously in mind, the purpose is clearly to influence the other person to maintain the friendship. In the work situation, persuasion is also endemic. Indeed, Mortensen (2008: 3) concluded: 'Regardless of our actual job title, we all persuade – we all sell – for a living.'

Given the ubiquity and pervasiveness of influence in the social milieu, it is not surprising that 'a long history of research has examined the methods we use to attempt to change someone's attitudes or behavior or to strengthen already established attitudes or behaviors' (Afifi, 2006: 53). Thus, Pratkanis (2007) identified a total of 125 tactics that we use to influence one another. These tactics have been found to be effective across a wide range of diverse social contexts (Levine, 2006). Knowledge of these is important, since it has been shown that: 'Individuals vary greatly in their ability to use such tactics. Research findings indicate that such differences are related to success in a wide variety of occupations' (Baron and Markman, 2000: 109). This chapter navigates the large and complex terrain of persuasion and identifies the central components thereof.

In terms of definition, while the terms influence and persuasion are often viewed as synonyms and used interchangeably, in fact there are four main differences between the two processes:

1   ***Resistance.*** Knowles and Riner (2007) argued that persuasion is used to attempt to overcome some level of resistance to the message, noting that: 'Persuasion is only required when people feel "I don't like it!", "I don't believe it!", or "I won't do it!" . . . All persuasion, therefore is implicitly aimed at resistance.' Likewise, Sanders and Fitch (2001) highlighted that persuasion is influence when there is resistance, whereas influence per se 'is achieved by offering inducements that make it expedient or self-interested in the moment for that particular target person to do what is being asked, given his or her existing convictions and dispositions' (p. 263). They also made the important point that 'not everything is a *persuadable*' (p. 268). Persuadable actions are those that are not obligatory, and as such there may well be resistance to what is being suggested. In similar vein, Johnston (1994: 7) defined persuasion as 'a voluntary change in beliefs, attitudes and/or behaviors'. Another feature here is that for actions to be persuadable they should not be proscribed, so that compliance is possible. For example, my head of school at university would not be expected to have to persuade me to come to work – it is part of my contractual obligations. The head would also be unlikely to try to persuade me carry out a proscribed action, such as robbing a bank in order to obtain finances to help improve the school's financial situation. However, persuasion techniques could be employed to try to encourage me to run a communication consultancy course for businesspersons to bring in additional income.

2   ***Conscious awareness.*** While it has been shown that a great deal of influence takes place at a subconscious level (Hogan and Speakman, 2006; Jarrett, 2008), persuasion attempts are carried out with clear and deliberate intent. For example,

a film star who wears a certain brand of tee-shirt on a television show may *influence* young people to purchase a similar product, without consciously intending so to do. However, if the same film star had agreed to appear in a television advert to promote this brand of tee-shirt, then it would have been quite clear that a *persuasion* attempt was being made. Given this aspect of intentionality, interpersonal persuasion has been defined as 'the conscious manipulation of face-to-face communication to induce others to take action' (Robbins and Hunsaker, 2009: 214). Taking this line of thought further, persuasion always involves influence, but influence does not always involve persuasion. This distinction was recognised in the definition proffered by Hybels and Weaver (2009: 399): '*Persuasion* is the process that occurs when a communicator (sender) influences the values, beliefs, attitudes or behaviour of another person (receiver).'

3   **Direction.** When we say that a persuasion attempt is being made, we usually assume that this process is one-way. Indeed, if both sides are simultaneously engaging in persuasive attempts, the interaction is usually a negotiation of some form. By contrast, interpersonal influence is a reciprocal process (Hsiung and Bagozzi, 2003). Thus, in a social encounter where Person A is trying to persuade Person B, both A and B will be concurrently engaged in a process of ongoing mutual influence.

4   **Success.** A final difference between the two terms is that persuasion is successful influence. As O'Keefe (2002: 3) pointed out: 'The notion of success is embedded in the concept of persuasion.' Thus, it does not make sense to say 'I persuaded them to do it but they didn't.' However, it is possible to say 'I influenced them but they still didn't do it.' Here, the person is indicating a shift or softening in attitude, but a failure at the behavioural level. In this way, influencing is often incremental leading to eventual change, whereas persuasion usually refers to a specific change attempt. Thus, when parents perceive someone to be a 'bad influence' on their child, they believe that over a period of time this person will effect negative changes and that their son or daughter will eventually be led astray.

A distinction has also been made between 'hard' and 'gentle' persuasion. Pratkanis (2001) illustrated how in democratic societies *deliberative persuasion* is central. This involves debate, discussion, deliberation, argument and analysis – the process is two-way. By contrast, in authoritarian or autocratic regimes, leaders assume they know what others should think or want, and persuasion in the form of propaganda is employed to convince them that this is the case. In this latter form of *dictatorial persuasion*, communication is one-way and debate or dissent is discouraged. Deliberative persuasion has been shown to have the benefits of stimulating creative problem solving, fostering relationships and trust between individuals, and developing greater consent for and commitment to what are regarded as group decisions. Dictatorial persuasion, on the other hand, results in an over-reliance on the leader to make decisions and give guidance, and a reduction in individual initiative. Members also have much less commitment to decisions imposed upon them to which they feel no sense of ownership. It also leads to hostility and distrust, making long-term group effort and relationships difficult to sustain. These findings have obvious ramifications for organisations, in that employees will respond more favourably to deliberative than dictatorial forms of persuasion.

PURPOSES OF PERSUASION

As shown by Johnston (1994), the goal of persuasion can take many forms. To take but five examples, it may include:

1   the elimination of an existing belief (e.g. that smoking is not bad for one's health)
2   a change in strength of an existing belief (from the position above to one where it is accepted that heavy smoking can be bad for one's health)
3   the creation of a new belief (moving further from (2) above to believing that smoking is definitely bad for one's health)
4   a change in intentions to carry out an action (saying 'I now definitely intend to stop smoking.')
5   a change in actual behaviour (stopping smoking).

In general terms, the six main goals of persuasion are as shown in Box 12.1.

THE PERSUASION PROCESS

Figure 12.1 illustrates how the process of persuasion involves one person, the influencing 'agent', attempting to alter the beliefs, feelings, knowledge or behaviour of another, the 'target'. This has four main outcomes:

1   ***Instant success.*** It can be immediately effective, resulting in the intended changes to the target's beliefs, feelings, knowledge or behaviour.
2   ***No change.*** The target may simply reject the persuasion attempt and continue with the current response.
3   ***Increased resistance.*** There may not only be no change, but the target may also become very resistant to any future persuasion attempts from this agent. This process is referred to as the *boomerang effect*, which occurs when a persuasion attempt produces the opposite effect to the one originally anticipated (Byrne and Hart, 2009). For example, a flawed effort to persuade can backfire by strengthening the original position rather than changing it. As pointed out earlier, some degree of resistance by the target is a common feature of persuasion attempts and ways of overcoming this must be formulated by the agent to ensure success (Knowles *et al.*, 2001). It should also be noted that resistance can take many forms. Yukl (2010) identified six main variants: overt refusal to carry out the request; explanations or excuses as to why the request cannot be complied with; attempts to persuade the agent to alter or withdraw the request; appeals to a higher authority to have the request removed; delays in responding so that the requested action is not carried out; and pretending to comply while secretly attempting to sabotage the assignment.

Box 12.1 The six main purposes of persuasion

The main goals served by the skill of persuasion are to achieve:

1 ***Adoption.*** Here the aim is to encourage targets to develop new responses – that is to persuade them to *start doing or believing something*. Thus, a doctor may encourage an overweight individual to begin a diet or start an exercise regime, and to accept that weight loss will lead to better health.

2 ***Continuance.*** The objective here is to encourage targets to *keep doing or believing something* at their current level of commitment. For example, if a sports team is top of their league, the main goal of persuasion would be maintenance of performance. Likewise, one goal of a Catholic priest should be to encourage devout members of his parish to maintain their faith.

3 ***Improvement.*** The objective here is to get targets to perform at a higher level than at present. In other words, to get them to *do something better or have an increased level of belief*. The former is a common key goal of most educationalists. Thus, one reason teachers give their students detailed feedback on coursework is so that their next assignment may improve accordingly.

4 ***Deterrence.*** Conversely, the objective may be to persuade targets not to develop a particular behaviour, so that they *do not start doing or believing something*. Indeed, this is the aim of many health education campaigns geared towards young people – to encourage them not to take up activities such as smoking, drug-taking or drink-driving, and not to form the view that such activities are 'cool'.

5 ***Discontinuance.*** In this instance the goal is to get targets to desist from a current response – to persuade them to *stop doing or believing something*. This can often be the most difficult task for the persuader. Once behaviour patterns and beliefs have been learned they become resistant to change. For example, before new patterns of working can be introduced in an organisation, old practices have to be stopped. This can often be the most difficult aspect of such change. Humans are creatures of habit, and it is hard to 'unlearn' habituated patterns of behaviour and established belief systems.

6 ***Reduction.*** Where it is deemed that targets may not be able to completely cease a certain action, the goal may be to encourage them to cut down and *do it less or believe it less strongly*. For example, it would be preferable if someone smoked ten cigarettes a day rather than 20, or drank three pints of beer as opposed to six.

---

4 ***Delayed success.*** There may be a time delay before the attempt proves successful. Here, a phenomenon known as the *sleeper effect* occurs. As described by Allen and Stiff (1998: 176): 'The term *sleeper* derives from an expectation that the long-term effect is larger than the short-term effect in some manner (the effect is asleep but awakes to be effective later).' Thus, a target may initially reject a persuasion attempt and yet some weeks or months later begin to accept it. In their meta-analysis of research studies, Allen and Stiff confirmed the

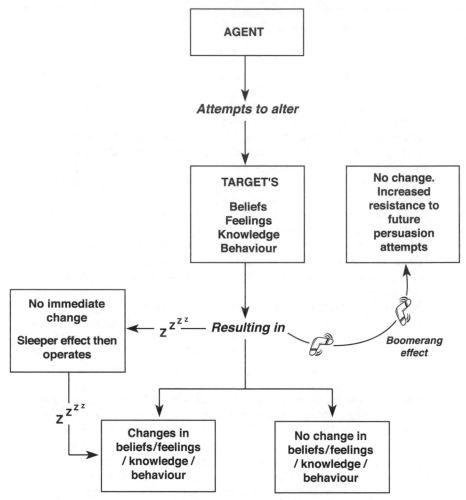

Figure 12.1 Persuasive communication: process and outcomes

existence of the sleeper effect. This process often involves a separation between source and message. For example, a message from a low credibility source is likely to be rejected at the outset. With the passage of time, however, the message is further processed and also becomes decoupled from its original source. The message content itself is remembered and becomes important – the source is now irrelevant. The target begins to say things like 'I've changed my mind on that.' or 'It's not quite so clear cut as I used to think.' However, if the message is from a low credibility source the sleeper effect is more potent when the target only discovers this after receiving the actual message (Kassin *et al.*, 2008). The sleeper effect may be more powerful when people believe that their defence against a persuasion attempt was weak. In such cases, there is evidence that they then become less certain of their initial views, and demonstrate an increased vulnerability to later persuasion attempts (Tormala *et al.*, 2006).

Another important aspect to note here is that even if persuasion attempts are not immediately successful in effecting actual changes in behaviour, they can still have a number of useful benefits. For example, Ohme (2001) itemised five positive effects of media influence attempts:

1   A clearer perception of reality. Thus, although many still smoke, most citizens of western countries (including smokers) are now aware of the health risks associated with smoking as a result of media campaigns.
2   An increased awareness of the issue in general, and a possible enhanced receptivity to future messages on this topic. If you are a heavy drinker, messages about possible liver damage may not stop you drinking immediately, but could make you listen more carefully to such messages in the future.
3   Self-initiated information seeking about the topic – the wish to know more about it. Opportunities to read articles or watch television programmes about the topic may be more likely to be taken once an initial interest has been stirred.
4   The stimulation of issue-related discussions with significant others. There can be an increased desire to ascertain what family, friends and work colleagues think of the issue.
5   The reinforcement of existing positive behaviour. For instance, health information messages about the importance of regular exercise reward those who currently take such exercise and encourage them to continue.

While the first four of these may not produce instant results, they can contribute to a 'slow burn' effect, resulting in later behavioural change.

Targets can also be encouraged to become more resistant to persuasion messages. There are two main methods whereby this can be achieved: forewarning and inoculation.

Forewarning

This relates to the process wherein the target audience is told something about the person or message they are about to encounter. The forewarning can come (a) from the speaker or (b) from someone who introduces this person, and so takes one of two forms respectively:

(a)   *A persuasion intent statement.* This tells the target that a persuasion attempt is about to be made (e.g. 'I am going to present evidence to support the view that all drugs should be decriminalised.').
(b)   *A topic and position statement.* This informs the target about the issue about to be presented and where the speaker stands on this (e.g. 'I now wish to introduce Jo Fleming, a well-known supporter of animal rights, who hopes to convince you of the view that not only is it unethical to kill animals for food, but also that as the dairy and other industries involve considerable cruelty you should adopt a vegan lifestyle.').

One issue that is linked to forewarning is whether or not there is any delay between warning and message delivery. In a meta-analysis of research in this field, the main conclusion reached by Benoit (1998: 146) was that: 'Forewarning an audience to expect a persuasive message tends to make that message less persuasive ... regardless of type of warning ... (or) presence of delay.' However, Benoit found that to be effective the warning must come *before* the persuasion attempt. A message does not lose its persuasiveness if the warning is given *after* it has been delivered. Thus, it is not the information per se that affects persuasiveness, it is the forewarning. In this sense, prevention is essential. It appears that when targets are forewarned they adopt a less receptive frame of mind and become more resistant to the perceived 'interference'. Overall, it is best not to have a forewarned target when making a persuasion attempt.

For people who have to address an audience that has been forewarned, Benoit recommended the following five compensatory techniques in attempting to overcome such resistance:

1   Be introduced by a credible third person.
2   Stress a lack of personal bias on the issue.
3   Ask the audience to keep an open mind.
4   Emphasise that both sides of the argument have been given due consideration.
5   State that the target's best interests were considered – not just the speaker's.

Four 'reverse psychology' approaches can also be employed in attempting to overcome resistance: co-opting; ironic effect; paradoxical suggestion; alternative choice double-bind.

Co-opting

This is a method for attempting to minimise rejection by openly acknowledging it in advance (e.g. by saying 'Your first reaction is likely to be to reject what I am about to say.'). As expressed by Knowles and Linn (2004: 138): 'One of the ways to turn resistance against itself is to acknowledge it.' In such instances an appeal for *suppression* is useful. Here, the target audience is asked to suppress the instinctive denial response (e.g. 'I would like you to try to avoid the natural impulse of immediately rejecting what I am about to say to you. Please hear me out and then make a judgement about what I have said.').

Ironic effect

It is possible to get targets to do what you want by telling them to do the opposite. If I say to you 'Don't think of a white bear.', you will find it difficult not to think of a white bear. In this way, 'thought suppression can actually increase the thoughts one wishes to suppress instead of subsiding them' (Soetens *et al.*, 2006: 656). One common example of this is that people on a diet who try not to think about food often begin to think much more about food. This process is therefore also known as the *rebound effect*. The ironic effect seems to be caused by the interplay of two related cognitive processes (Wegner, 1994). This dual-process system involves, first, an intentional operating process, which consciously attempts to locate thoughts unrelated to the suppressed ones. Second, and simultaneously, an unconscious monitoring process tests whether the operating system is functioning effectively. If the monitoring system encounters thoughts inconsistent with the intended ones, it prompts the intentional operating process to ensure that these are replaced by appropriate thoughts. However, it is argued that the intentional operating system can fail due to increased cognitive load caused by fatigue, stress, emotional factors, etc., and so the monitoring process filters the inappropriate thoughts into consciousness, making them highly accessible. They can then have a strong impact upon emotions, behaviour and even dreams (Kozak *et al.*, 2007).

Paradoxical suggestion

This involves making a suggestion about the target person's future behaviour, but then indicating that perhaps it would be expecting too much and that the person might not be up to the task just yet (e.g. 'I am not sure you have reached the point where you feel you could do this. I'm worried about asking too much of you.'). The rationale here is that when we are told that we may not be able to do something, paradoxically we often experience a stronger desire to do it (Knowles and Linn, 2004). This is a motivational technique in that the goal is to indirectly challenge the target to react to the perceived weakness by 'showing' the agent that the apparent lack of faith in their ability is misplaced. The target then becomes motivated to complete the suggested behaviour. This technique should be employed when a relationship has been established, so that the stated lack of belief in the target's ability is seen in a caring light. However, with people of low self-esteem or low self-efficacy this approach needs to be used with care, as they may take the apparent lack of belief in their capability as a confirmation of their low level of worth or ability.

Alternative choice double-bind

Using this technique, the agent devises 'creative' choices aimed at ensuring that targets carry out actions to which they may be initially resistant (Erickson and Rossi, 1975). For example, if a parent knows a child will resist going to bed, alternative choices can be introduced by saying to the child: 'Would you rather put on your pyjamas first or brush your teeth first?' The child is given a choice and has a desire to be the decision maker, but is in a double-bind in that both outcomes lead towards bedtime. Similarly, a salesperson may say to a customer: 'Would you prefer the blue or the red?' Here, the offer is dual-positive, in that both alternatives lead subtly in the direction of a sale.

There is a long history of using reverse psychology techniques in the therapeutic context (Dowd and Milne, 1986). However, while such techniques can be powerful, they are not without problems. The main problems are that they do not always work, and they are manipulative and indeed deceitful (Knowles and Riner, 2007). The target may take the agent's suggestions at face value and so act in the way opposite to that intended, or may refuse to participate at all. For reverse psychology to work, the agent must both have no moral qualms about engaging in subterfuge, and be fairly certain that the target will react as anticipated.

Inoculation

This is a stronger form of forewarning as it actively prepares targets to refute the messages that will be received (Lin and Pfau, 2007). Inoculation messages can be affective or cognitive (Ivanov *et al.*, 2009a). Emotional inoculation messages consist of 'affect-laden words, anecdotes, and opinionated statements' whereas cognitive inoculation messages are objective in tone with 'verifiable, falsifiable information, such as statistics, facts, and research findings' (Peau *et al.*, 2001: 217). Inoculation attempts consist of two main components, *threat* (targets the affective level) and *refutational pre-emption* (targets the cognitive level). The effectiveness of these two mechanisms in inoculation has been well documented in a wide range of research studies (Pfau *et al.*, 2009).

Threat

This involves warning the target about the imminent attack upon their attitudes or beliefs. All inoculation attempts have been shown to include threat, which in turn acts as a wake-up call for resistance. Thus, the objective is to mobilise targets to realise that their beliefs are about to be challenged, and to motivate them to pay attention to ways of dealing with it. This is the *anticipatory warning* stage of inoculation, when the emotions are stirred and the target is motivated towards action.

Refutational pre-emption

Here, the likely future arguments with which the target will be faced are detailed, and counter-arguments are provided to refute each of these. This is the *anticipatory coping* stage and is at the epicentre of inoculation. The success of inoculation is affected by two main processes – *delay* and *decay*. *Delay* refers to the time it takes the target to generate counter-arguments with which to resist the message, while *decay* relates to the extent to which these arguments lose their force over time (Ivanov *et al.*, 2009b). Techniques that reduce delay and protect against decay are therefore important in maximising the effectiveness of inoculation. Thus, it has been shown that the more effort that targets devote to the development of counter-arguments to possible future challenges by engaging in what has been termed *cognitive work*, the greater is their resistance to later counter-persuasion attempts (Pfau *et al.*, 2001). Another useful antidote to delay and decay is the technique of *rote learning*. Many religions and cults get members to rote learn sets of beliefs, prayers and key statements (e.g. biblical passages) so that they become embedded in their psyche, and as such very resistant to change. As part of this process, it is possible to get individuals to rote learn refutational arguments against future counter-messages. A related tactic here is that of *anchoring*, which involves connecting the forthcoming new message to an already established belief or set of values. It then becomes difficult to change one without the other. For example, a Roman Catholic priest discovers that a student in his parish will later hear a lecture from a pro-choice speaker on the rights of women to decide what to do with their own bodies. He may then attempt to 'anchor' the student by connecting the belief (a) that good and devout Catholics value the sanctity and sacredness of all life to (b) an opposition to the future message in support of abortion.

Another form of pre-emption has been termed *stealing thunder*, which involves disclosing incriminating evidence about oneself or one's client, rather than have this revealed by someone else. For instance, defence lawyers in court will tell the jury negative facts about their client rather than giving the prosecuting attorney the opportunity to capitalise on this later. This gives the impression of openness and honesty. It also inoculates the target and so draws much of the poison from the sting of the potentially harmful detail. In their analysis of this phenomenon, Williams and Dolnik (2001) pointed out that stealing thunder is part of the process of *dissuasion*, which involves persuading people not to be swayed by something that could otherwise be influential. Their review of research concluded that: 'Stealing thunder has been shown to be an effective method of minimizing the impact of damaging information in a variety of different contexts' (p. 228).

STEPS TO SUCCESSFUL PERSUASION

A number of what are known as *stage theories* have been put forward to explain the persuasion process (Weinstein and Sandman, 2002). These conceptualise a range of stages or steps that need to be gone through for the overall process to be successful. The most widely employed of these is the *transtheoretical model of change* initially developed by Prochaska and DiClemente (1992). This envisages five main stages:

1   *Precontemplation.* Here the person is not thinking about changing current behaviour or starting a new behaviour. There is no intention to change.
2   *Contemplation.* At this stage the person has been made aware of the issue and thought about the process of change, but is still ambivalent. No decision has been made about whether or not to act. Part of the person may want to change while another part does not. Change is always difficult (and even frightening), and so it does not happen without psychological upheaval.
3   *Preparing.* If the person decides that the benefits of change outweigh the costs, a decision is made to change. Preparations then have to be made to cope with this. Strategies need to be formulated about when, where and how the new response will be carried out. It may also involve publicly informing others about the intention to change.
4   *Action.* This is the implementation phase, when the person is actively involved in an overt attempt to carry out the behaviour. Others may need to be reminded that the new pattern of behaviour has deliberately been adopted, and is not an aberration.
5   *Maintenance.* Once a change has been made there is then the challenge of maintaining it. Behaviour change may meet with resistance from significant

others and the person has to deal with this – to the extent of even altering friendship patterns.

A sequential model of the five stages is shown in Figure 12.2. Here it can be seen that the main outcomes of either behaviour change or no behaviour change are dependent upon whether or not there is progression through each stage. It is also acknowledged that even after the response has been implemented relapse can take place. Where relapse occurs the individual either again prepares for action, or reverts to the former response pattern and abandons the new one. As explained in Chapter 10, after making an important decision individuals are affected by the process of *cognitive dissonance*, as doubts and anxiety are experienced about whether the decision was correct

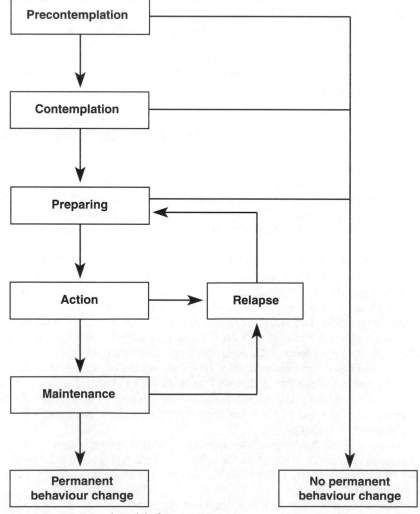

Figure 12.2   Sequential model of persuasion

(Aronson *et al.*, 2007). This dissonance is eventually resolved in one of two ways. People can either become convinced that the decision was correct and so stay with it, or alternatively decide that a wrong decision was made and relapse to the former state of affairs. For effective persuasion, the target must be convinced in the long term about the rectitude of the decision taken.

A more fine-grained 12-step sequential analysis of persuasion was presented by McGuire (1981), involving the following:

1   exposure to the message
2   attending to the message
3   becoming interested in it
4   understanding it
5   learning how to process and use it
6   yielding to it
7   memorising it
8   retrieving it when required
9   using it when making decisions
10   executing these decisions
11   reinforcing these actions
12   consolidating the decision based upon the success of the actions.

While each of these stages is important, they can be collapsed into five main steps (Figure 12.3). First, the message must be *attended to* if it is to have any impact. A message that is perceived to have a high level of direct relevance is more effective since 'this enhanced personal relevance promotes greater attention, elaboration, message processing, and, ultimately, persuasion' (Noar *et al.*, 2009: 113). Relevance therefore results in a higher degree of involvement by targets, and this has been shown to be a key factor in persuasion (Braverman, 2008). Those who are more actively involved pay more attention to the messages being delivered. However, as summarised by Buller and Hall (1998: 155) in their review of research into this stage:

> Attention to persuasive messages is far from guaranteed; it is unstable, fickle, and capricious. Persuasive messages compete for receiver's consideration with

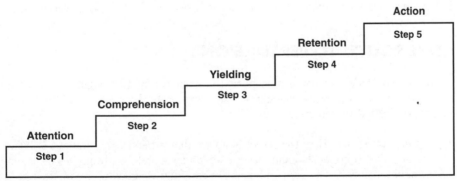

Figure 12.3 Five steps to successful persuasion

other messages, environmental cues, and internal responses. As a result some messages receive detailed examination, whereas others remain ignored or only partially processed.

Buller and Hall investigated two types of distraction:

1   ***Communication-irrelevant distractions.*** These are stimuli extraneous to the interactive process that shift attention away from the speaker (e.g. intrusive noise). These lessen the power of persuasive appeals.
2   ***Communication-relevant distractions.*** These are stimuli intrinsic to the communication process (e.g. speaker attributes). When the distraction focuses upon positive aspects (e.g. attractiveness), persuasion is enhanced. However, if attention is paid to negative features (e.g. poor speech pattern), persuasibility diminishes.

The second step in the model shown in Figure 12.3 is that the target person must understand fully what is being said. The importance of message delivery in ensuring *comprehension* will be discussed in more depth later in the chapter. Third, the message must be accepted, in that the person has to *yield* to it. This is at the heart of persuasion, and much of this chapter is concerned with techniques whereby acceptance can be encouraged. Fourth, the target has to *retain* or remember the message. Finally, the acid test is whether the person *carries out the action* and implements the recommended response. As discussed in Chapter 2, attitudes encompass three elements, often referred to as the ABC of attitudes:

Affect – one's feeling and emotions regarding the object of the attitude.
Behaviour – how one actually behaves towards the other.
Cognitions – the thoughts beliefs, knowledge, etc. one has concerning that under focus.

Long-term changes in behaviour usually necessitate changes in the other two aspects. An important distinction has been made between *private acceptance*, which produces attitude change, and *public compliance*, where the person complies with what is being recommended but does not really change inner beliefs or feelings (Hargie *et al.*, 2004). Retention and implementation of new responses are dependent on private acceptance.

COGNITIVE ROUTES TO PERSUASION

Dual process models of persuasion posit the existence of two cognitive routes in the processing of persuasive messages. The *elaboration likelihood model* (Petty and Cacioppo, 1986) identified these as follows:

1   ***Central route.*** Here the target is aware that a persuasion attempt is being made, and consciously examines the advantages and disadvantages of incoming information. The pros and cons are carefully weighed up in an attempt to process incoming information rationally before a final decision is taken (Griffin

(2008). The *cognitive-response model* (Wright, 1980) demonstrated how individuals using this rational approach relate incoming material to existing knowledge and beliefs. For a persuasion attempt to be successful the message must receive a favourable evaluation during this cognitive elaboration process.

2   ***Peripheral route.*** Here, information tends to be processed at a subconscious level, and the target is not aware that a persuasion attempt is being made. There is scant analysis or scrutiny of message content, and the response is more intuitive. The emotional state of the target is important, since as shown in Box 12.2 it has been found that people in a happy or positive mood are less likely to systematically process messages via the central route than are those in a sad or negative state (Mitchell, 2000). Thus, establishing a sense of 'feel-good' in the target encourages peripheral processing.

For example, a television advert may sell a particular brand of car by presenting details of its price and features and systematically comparing these to those of its rivals (*central route* strategy). An alternative approach would be to show lots of very attractive people having great fun as they drive the car past charming locations in bright sunshine under a blue cloudless sky, with a popular soundtrack playing in the background, and ending with a shot of the car and a voiceover stating: 'It's out there' (*peripheral route* strategy). The latter is an attempt to plant a subconscious association between the car, being happy and being part of the beautiful people 'set'. If this were processed centrally the viewer would be asking questions such as: 'What does it mean to say that it's out there?' or 'How does buying this car bring with it a guarantee that I will be driving it with a beautiful young person sitting beside me?' However, the fact is that most television adverts are not centrally processed, but rather are dealt with through the peripheral route. They are successful because they hit us at the more vulnerable subconscious level.

Message processing is moderated by a range of factors, including the cognitive ability and motivation of the target (O'Keefe, 2006). To take an example, there is a greater likelihood that those who have undergone third level education will centrally evaluate the arguments being presented by a politician, while those with a basic

---

Box 12.2 Negative and positive mood and persuasion

Negative mood is associated with:

- central processing of information
- a cognitive, systematic style of argument processing
- more time spent on the evaluation of persuasive appeals
- stronger arguments being more successful than weaker ones.

Positive mood is associated with:

- peripheral processing of persuasion attempts
- a passive, less rational approach to the evaluation of information
- much more rapid processing of incoming information
- no differential being made between weak and strong arguments.

education may be more influenced by a feeling of whether or not they like this person. However, if the better-educated target has no interest whatsoever in politics, then the likelihood of peripheral processing is increased. An important difference between the two routes is that attitudes formed via the central route are more persistent over time and more resistant to change (Haugtvedt and Petty, 1992). This is because the individual has thought through the process and made a conscious decision that is then likely to directly influence behaviour over a prolonged period. The inclusion in a message of rhetorical questions phrased in a leading manner (see Chapter 5) encourages greater engagement by the target. This, in turn, increases the likelihood of an elaborated consideration of the arguments, leading to greater resistance to opposing arguments (Blankenship and Craig, 2006). An example of this strategy would be the insertion of a rhetorical question such as the following into an argument encouraging greater government spending in the university sector: 'Wouldn't you agree therefore that money spent on higher education is a valuable investment that will have many positive benefits for society?'

Attempts to change attitudes that have been formed as a result of a cognitive elaboration process are more easily dealt with, as the counter-arguments will have already been given consideration. By contrast, decisions taken via the peripheral route have been made without careful thought, and so are more vulnerable to counter-arguments. As noted by Quine *et al.* (2002: 176): ' "Central route" processing produces attitudes that have temporal persistence and are predictive of behaviour and resistant to change, while peripheral route processing is typified by absence of argument scrutiny and produces only temporary attitude change.'

Having said this, it must also be noted that the peripheral route is ubiquitous in human encounters. Cialdini (2007) argued that the fixed-action patterns that guide the behaviour of most animals also occur in humans. In other words, our behaviour becomes hard-wired and we respond without thinking. We do not have the time or cognitive space to analyse and evaluate the hundreds of persuasion attempts that impinge upon us every day. As a result we make shortcut decisions to save time and energy. These decisions are, in turn, guided by a set of core processes, or *heuristics* (Burger, 2007), that directly influence our behaviour and are for the most part based upon valid reasoning. Such behaviour-guiding templates are the keys that can unlock the doors to persuasibility in others. To use another metaphor, they are the triggers that fire compliance behaviours. As such, people can be manipulated by their use. For example, the aphorism that 'you get what you pay for' is usually true. The more you pay for a car, a hotel room or a watch, the better it is likely to be. Thus, we expect to pay more for the best. Knowing that this is the case, a sharp operator may take advantage of the 'more-expensive-is-best' short circuit process in potential buyers by inflating the price of goods to make them appear to be of higher quality.

In interpersonal encounters much of what persuades us is processed peripherally. For example, we do not usually consciously rate others on their level of attractiveness, and are not aware on a moment-by-moment basis whether another person is smiling, is humorous, stands close to us, uses our first name, praises us and so on. These behaviours are processed via the peripheral route, but they all affect the outcome of persuasion attempts. Likewise, if we go to the bar with someone and they buy us a drink, we do not usually consciously think that we are in debt to this person and must reciprocate. Rather, we naturally feel this pressure and so the likelihood is that the reciprocation autopilot kicks in and we buy the next round. Indeed, if we become aware that a direct attempt is being made to persuade us to do something, we begin to process information centrally. Then we may become suspicious of the smiles and praise we are receiving or wonder why this person is offering us something with no obligation. Under such circumstances a compliance attempt is likely to boomerang.

PERSUASION PROOFS

The study of persuasion has a long tradition. The classical era of scholarship in this field ran from 500 BC to 300 AD, and included notable scholars such as Plato, Aristotle, Cicero and Quintellian. It was the Greek philosopher Aristotle who provided the first detailed analysis of persuasion. He identified three main persuasion categories:

1   *Ethos.* Here the credibility of the persuader is highlighted.
2   *Logos.* Here the rationality of the message is focused upon.
3   *Pathos.* This involves appeals to the emotions of the target.

These are now known respectively as *personal proofs*, *logical proofs* and *emotional proofs*, although it should be realised that they are not functionally discrete categories as there are areas of overlap between them, and they are interlinked. During persuasion attempts, techniques from each area can be used in combination, and indeed Aristotle believed that the most effective appeals contain a balanced mix of the three. However, for the purposes of analysis it is useful to examine each separately.

Personal proofs

One of the most important components in the persuasion equation is the nature of the agent. In order to be persuaded, first we have to be convinced of the bona fides of the person who is trying to persuade us. There are four main determinants of personal proof: power, the relationship, attractiveness and humour.

Power

The relationship between power and persuasion is reflected in the definition of power as 'the amount of influence that one person can exercise over another' (Georgesen and Harris, 1998: 185). The persuasive force of power has long been recognised. Henry Kissinger famously claimed that 'power is the great aphrodisiac', but whatever the truth of this particular assertion it is clear that power is a core determinant for gaining compliance in many contexts. Tourish and Wohlforth (2000: 23) illustrated that 'human behavior is driven by an impulse to *conform to authority*'. It is therefore hardly surprising that agents are likely to use any power they possess to ensure such conformity. Hargie *et al.* (2004) showed how 'The Iron Law of Power' means that people with greater power tend to use it as and when required to get their own way. Thus, while power may not be the first shot fired in a battle of wills, it will be brought into play at some stage to ensure compliance. Given its importance, it is not surprising that we are influenced by the power of the source. But how and in what ways?

This question can best be answered by examining the classic delineation of types of power initially identified by French and Raven (1959) that then became the accepted standard in the field (Raven, 1992). This includes six forms of power. The first three of these (*legitimate*, *reward* and *coercive*) emanate from the ability of the agent to determine and control the target person's outcomes. The last three (*information, referent* and *expert*) are purely to do with influence and here the target makes a willing decision to cooperate.

Legitimate power

In essence, the bases of this power are rights and duties. Some people, by virtue of their position, have a legitimate right to request certain types of compliance from others, who in turn have a duty to comply. The power resides in the position. The holder of the power is *in authority*. Thus, a police officer has considerable power over citizens. If requested by an officer in uniform to move our car we are much more likely to comply than if asked by someone dressed in casual clothes. But the power only remains while performing the job, so that when the officer is off duty or retired this is relinquished. Legitimate power is attached to the role, not the person. It is also limited to the functions of the role. For instance, the security guard in the building where we work may legitimately ask us for identification, but has no power to request that we work overtime. In addition, this is a two-way street. Both managers and subordinates wield legitimate power. While the former has the authority to direct and control the latter as they perform their job, the latter can insist that set procedures be carried out by the former in accordance with statutory requirements (e.g. selection or appraisal interviews). Indeed, the introduction of initiatives such as the Patients' Charter, Citizens' Charter and Bill of Rights have empowered those who formerly had little such formal, legitimate authority. Interestingly, people often excuse their behaviour on the basis that someone with legitimate power told them to carry it out. The ultimate example of this was the defence plea of the Nazi leaders at the Nuremberg war crime trials following World War II: 'I was only following orders.'

Reward power

Those who have control over the administration of rewards wield considerable power. As discussed in Chapter 4, the impact of reinforcement upon performance is both far-reaching and ubiquitous. This is learned from a very early age. Young children soon realise that parents have control over valued resources, and that they often have to carry out certain tasks in order to receive them. They also quickly learn that they too have similar power over parents and so begin to trade rewards (e.g. 'If I get an A-grade will you buy me a bicycle?'). Throughout life, those who are the controllers of the rewards that we seek have power over us. Thus, lecturers have reward power over students, as do employers over employees. However, again this is a two-way process. Employees can reward their employer by working harder, and students their professors by turning up for class and appearing motivated. Social rewards such as praise are potent forms of power.

Coercive power

Those who are able to administer punishments also have considerable power. To continue with the earlier example, police officers possess this form of power, and we are therefore likely to obey their request, for example, to move our car from a restricted parking zone. We know that if we do not we are likely to receive a fine. There is a symbiotic relationship between reward and coercive power. Usually someone who can reward us can ipso facto also punish us (e.g. by withholding the rewards). Thus, parents can both reward their children (e.g. by allowing them to stay up late to watch a television programme) and punish them (e.g. by sending them to bed early). However, we tend to like those who reward us and dislike those who threaten or punish us. It is therefore wise to remember the advice proffered by Machiavelli in *The Prince*, written in 1514, that those in power should 'delegate to others the enactment of unpopular measures and keep in their own hands the distribution of favours' (Machiavelli, 1514/1961: 106). One reason for this is that the norm of exchange means that those who have been punished are likely to seek retribution, while those who have been rewarded seek to reciprocate the favours they have received.

Information power

Here, the content of the message is the basis of the power. Those who are 'in the know' are in a privileged position. The holders of information that is 'inside', 'top secret', 'classified', etc. have considerable power – they can keep this secret or share it with others. Indeed, bribery and blackmail are based upon the fact that someone has access to information that they know someone else wishes either to find out or to remain hidden, respectively. Some managers adopt a policy where they inform employees purely on a 'need to know' basis. In other words, they only tell them what they need to know to do their job. The problem here is that staff also have access to vital information (e.g. that a piece of production equipment is about to malfunction) and they may retaliate by withholding this from management who adopt this approach. Research consistently shows that employees value managers who share as much information with them as they can (Hargie *et al.*, 2004). If information is power, then this power should be used benignly within organisations. Information can be powerful in another way. If I want you to stop smoking, I could give you some material to read that clearly documents the dangers of this practice. This may then persuade you to change your attitude towards smoking. Where the information is perceived to be objective and accurate and includes statistical details (e.g. the percentage of smokers compared to nonsmokers who contract serious illnesses) its potency is heightened (Allen *et al.*, 2000). Furthermore, the amount of information used in persuasive messages is important, and here more is better. As shown by Tormala and Petty (2007: 17), the 'numerosity effect, whereby presenting more persuasive information leads to more persuasion, is quite pervasive'.

Referent power

This relates to the power of the reference group. Our behaviour is shaped to a considerable extent by our wish to belong to and be accepted by certain groups of people (Haslam and Reicher, 2008). As summarised by Dillard *et al.* (2007b: 467): 'It is well established that individuals often look to others to determine how to behave and what opinions to hold.' Thus, we are likely to adopt the response patterns of those we identify with, like, and to whose group we aspire. The widely used marketing technique of product endorsement by well-known and popular personalities is a good example of the use of referent power as a tool of influence. In many cases the celebrity has no real knowledge of or insight into the product being endorsed, but this does not negatively impact upon the power of the message. Sorenson *et al.* (2001) used the term *misplaced authority* to refer to the use of celebrities to endorse specialised products in this way. One example is when an actor who plays the role of a doctor in a television series is used to advertise and recommend a medical product. The actor has no actual medical expertise or authority but there is an implicit or inferred link planted in the target's mind.

In similar vein, hotels and restaurants often have signed photographs of great and good clients prominently displayed. The implication is that to be in such an establishment is to be with the 'in crowd'. Salespeople use another form of reference power termed *ubiquity technique* when they tell a target that lots of relevant and significant others are now using a particular item. Research has shown that this process of using *social proof* to validate the acceptability of a product or behaviour by dint of the fact that it is used by significant others is a highly effective compliance-gaining technique (Cialdini, 2007). Thus, sports stars are paid fortunes just to wear or use a certain product, as the producers know this will trigger enormous referent group sales from those who wish to emulate their hero. This became known as the *wannabe phenomenon*, after the thousands of teenage girls who wanted to be like the pop star Madonna (Hargie *et al.*, 2004).

Among teenagers, referent power in the form of peer pressure is particularly potent. As mentioned in Chapter 9, at this age the need to be accepted by peers is at its strongest and so certain types of fashion simply must be followed. When this is compounded by the fact that the attachment to referent media symbols (music, sports and film stars) is at a high level, the potential for manipulation is huge. Managers of male pop music stars have long realised the value of this human phenomenon. A few planted female fans beginning to scream at a concert sets the example for the rest so that a cacophony of screaming soon ensues. As expressed by Cialdini (2007: 116): 'One means we use to determine what is correct is to find out what other people think is correct . . . We view a behaviour as more correct in a given situation to the degree that we see others performing it.' Interestingly, this means that the young females then have a high level of involvement in the occasion and so do not evaluate it critically through the central route (e.g. they do not study the extent to which the singers are singing in tune). Peripheral processing is dominant as they enjoy their heightened emotionality and rate the concert to be a great success. All of this in turn leads to increased merchandising sales (CDs, tee-shirts, posters, etc.).

Referent power is most potent under two conditions. First, if we are *uncertain* about how to behave in a situation we follow the 'herd instinct' by looking to members of our reference group for guidance, and copying what they do. This is summed up in the well-known aphorism 'Monkey see, monkey do'. Second, we are more likely to be influenced by *similar* others. For example, if a female teenager goes to a party where all the females are dancing in a group while the males are sitting round a table, she is more likely to join the dancing group. This is part of the wider process of *conformity* in groups, given that: 'Social influence implies a pressure towards conformity with individual or group beliefs and behaviors' (Vishwanath, 2006: 325). While this will be discussed in more depth in Chapter 14, it is worth noting here that when we are in the presence of others, there is strong overt or covert pressure to agree with the views of the majority, and follow group norms. As noted by Ho and McLeod, (2008: 193) in relation to *spiral of silence theory*: 'Individuals, driven largely by the fear of isolation, scrutinize their environment to evaluate the climate of opinion.' Two needs guide our behaviour in such circumstances – the need to be accepted and the need to know what is the right thing to do (Aronson *et al.*, 2007). These are powerful determinants in shaping our attitudes and behaviour.

In a classic study in this field, Sherif (1936) used the *autokinetic phenomenon* (where a tiny bulb in a pitch black room appears to move if stared at for a few minutes) to study conformity. The bulb does not actually move, since this is an illusion caused by neural processes and unconscious eye movements. Sherif asked subjects to estimate the distance the bulb had moved. Interestingly, two things happened. First, after some discussion, groups eventually reached agreement about the movement distance. Second, different groups differed widely in their estimates. Furthermore, once an estimate had been agreed upon it became internalised and resistant to change. Consequently, when a member from a group with a previously 'socially anchored' score was placed in a new group, they persisted with the estimate they had developed in their initial group. In this way, the reference group score was internalised and influenced future behaviour. The fact that the subjects had participated in formulating the norm meant that they were more committed to the decision. A fascinating real-life variant of Sherif's experiment occurred in the Republic of Ireland when people became convinced that statues outside churches were moving. This 'movement' was caused by the *autokinetic phenomenon*, but huge crowds gathered each evening and the massed throng convinced one another that a miracle was being witnessed.

In a second famous study on conformity, Asch (1952) developed a system wherein subjects were required to publicly choose which one of three lines matched a fourth 'target' line in length. The task was very simple, so that when it was completed individually, few subjects made any errors of judgement. However, by placing a naive subject next to last in a line of confederates who all concurred on an incorrect choice of line, the pressure to conform could be measured. Asch found that only 25 per cent of subjects did not conform at all to the incorrect majority, while 33 per cent conformed on more than half of the trials. Some 5 per cent conformed on all the blatantly incorrect decisions. When interviewed later, those who conformed admitted that they disagreed with the others but felt under pressure to concur. As aptly described by Asch (1940: 455), what occurred represented 'a change in the object of judgment, rather than in the judgment of the object'. In other words, the decision was not internalised, and so subjects demonstrated public compliance but not private acceptance. This was confirmed in a neat reversal of the study procedures, in which Asch ran experiments where there was only one confederate who made the clearly incorrect decision on each trial. In these instances, the group of naive subjects strongly affirmed the correctness of their decision and treated the single deviating confederate with bemusement and scorn.

Expert power

We live in the age of 'the expert'. In courtrooms, on television screens and in newspapers, expert sources are used to give a definitive perspective on issues. This is because people who are perceived to be experts, in that they have specialised knowledge or technical skill, have high persuasive power. Here the basis of the power is the extent to which the agent is seen as *an authority*. As shown in Box 12.3, this type of power is conveyed by what are known as the 'Three Ts' – titles, threads and trappings.

The acid test of expert power is credibility. In his review of research in this field, Pratkanis (2007: 31) concluded: 'The advice "be credible" should be heeded by all who seek to persuade.' Indeed, Clampitt (2010: 136) noted that 'every message has a

---

Box 12.3 The three Ts of expert power

1 ***Titles*** are ubiquitous across all societies (e.g. king, chief, president, emperor). Powerful people use them to set themselves apart from others. The power of titles is illustrated by the way they are sought and used. Schoolchildren are introduced to them from an early age ('principal', 'vice principal', etc.) and they acquire importance thereafter. In the UK, the Honours system dispenses a huge range of titles every year (Lord, Lady, Sir, Member of the British Empire, etc.). These carry no monetary value but the social caché attached means that there is no shortage of people eager to accept them. Similarly, employees often work much longer hours for little or no more money just by being given a designated title such as 'unit coordinator'. In organisations, titles often reflect both the job level and expertise of the individual (e.g. 'chief technician'). Because we are so accustomed to the role of titles we give respect to those who hold important ones. Thus, a 'Professor of Nuclear Physics' is perceived as having a high level of expertise in this field, and so will be more influential when speaking on this topic.

2 ***Threads*** refer to the specialised clothes worn by experts to set them apart from others. Examples abound – from the fire officer's uniform, to the vicar's black robes and white dog collar, to the 'power' suits worn by business people. While some of these clothes may be functional, for the most part their purpose is that of clearly setting the expert apart from the general populace.

3 ***Trappings*** are all the paraphernalia used to convey specialised knowledge or know-how. This encompasses framed certificates on the wall, specialist books on shelves, or sophisticated pieces of equipment. For example, for the layperson a visit to the dentist entails an encounter with a baffling array of all kinds of strange apparatus, including a special chair, unusual lights and various implements for probing, drilling, filling and extracting. All of these combine to convey the impression of a high level of expertness.

---

credibility tag attached to it that determines, to a large extent, how that message will be treated'. If the source of the message is regarded as lacking in credibility, then it will have little persuasive power. Thus, Schutz (1998) showed how attacks upon the credibility of a source who has negatively evaluated someone can serve to weaken the force of the criticism. Gass and Seiter (2009) identified three important features of credibility. First, it is a *perceptual phenomenon* – it is the target who decides whether a particular source is credible or not; the same person may be regarded as credible by one target and not credible by another. Second, it is *situational*, in that a person may be regarded as credible in one context but not in another. Third, it is *dynamic* in that perceptions of credibility can change over time; someone we once perceived to be highly credible may eventually seem less so.

Judgements of credibility are based upon two factors, competence and trust-worthiness. We judge competence based upon the extent to which people 'know their stuff'. If we go to a store to buy a hi-fi system and the assistant keeps admitting insufficient knowledge of the technical details of the equipment and continually seeks advice from someone in the office, we will not see that person as being an expert, and so their advice will carry little power. Part of this is to do with confidence, in two senses. First, we need to be confident in the person's expertise. Second, the agent must behave in a confident manner. We would never be taken in by a 'no-confidence trick-ster'. The counterbalance to competence is trust. If someone is perceived to be highly competent but untrustworthy, their credibility rating drops dramatically. Trust has been shown to be central to successful outcomes in interpersonal encounters involving persuasion attempts, such as buyer–seller dyads (Andersen and Kumar, 2006). Trust may be based on our previous experience of the source, upon what others have told us about them, or upon perceived neutrality. In relation to the latter, we will place more trust in a colleague who tells us that their new *Nevercrash* computer is superb than in a highly competent salesperson in the *Nevercrash* store who gives us the same story. The former has no personal stake in selling the message and so is more credible.

Thus, in terms of expert power we give less credence to those whom we regard as honest if they are incompetent, and tend to have lower trust in those with a vested interest regardless of their level of expertise. One highly influential event is when people argue against their own interest. For example, in the following statements we are more likely to be influenced by A than B.

A: I'm a meat eater myself, but I have read the research and it does show that a vegetarian diet is better for your health.

B: As a committed vegetarian I have read the research and it shows that a vegetarian diet is better for your health.

Staying with the vegetarian theme, on one occasion I was at a conference and went to the local dining area for an evening meal. Looking for vegetarian food, I tried a few restaurants without much luck. I then visited an Italian restaurant, where upon explaining my requirements the owner said she could certainly cater for me but she would recommend the Spanish restaurant in the same complex. I explained that I had been there but the waitress I had spoken to had told me they did not really do much in the way of vegetarian food. The owner said that was untrue as she knew the range of food and would commend it. Her demeanour was most helpful and she was knowledgeable about vegetarian cuisine, but she was also arguing against her own interest in terms of losing my business. The result was that I ended up staying in her restaurant for the meal. My trust in her had increased as a result of her perceived lack of bias.

A meta-analytic review has shown that what is known as 'testimonial evidence' is an effective influencing technique (Reinhard, 1998). This refers to the use of factual statements and opinions of experts that support the speaker's message. A good example is the fact that in this book scholarly sources have been regularly cited to back up arguments. For this effect to be impactful, the supporting source must have high credibility and the evidence cited has to be believable. Interestingly, Reinhard also found that when people are in the middle of a discussion, the introduction of testimonial evidence serves to make the impact of this technique even more powerful. Thus, it is useful to have relevant sources to hand to quote during discussions.

The relationship

We are much more likely to be influenced by those with whom we have developed a close relationship. In fact, the link between relationships and the persuasion process is the focus of one of the best selling popular self-help books in this field (having sold over 16 million copies): *How to Win Friends and Influence People* by Dale Carnegie. It has long been known that the more similar people are, the greater will be their liking for one another – this is termed the *law of attraction* (Byrne, 1971). Indeed, the phenomenon of *homophily* has been found to be of central importance in the communication process (Wolvin and Coakley, 1996). Homophily refers to the extent to which people share significant similarity in terms of aspects such as age, dress, appearance, cultural background, religion, political outlook, educational level, social status, habits, interests, beliefs, values, attitudes, etc. Just as birds of a feather flock together, so people who perceive themselves to share significant commonalities tend to more readily form bonds. In highlighting the potency of similarity as a potential influencing weapon, Cialdini (2001: 150–151) noted: 'Those who want us to like them so that we will comply with them can accomplish that purpose by appearing similar to us in a wide variety of ways.' Part of this involves communication accommodation, whereby in order to enhance relational development we adapt our behaviours to converge with, or become similar to, those of the other person (Hajek *et al.*, 2007). The opposite is *heterophily*, where individuals have major differences across these dimensions. In essence, the greater the heterophily, the more difficult the influence process becomes.

In a meta-analysis of studies in the field, Miller *et al.* (2001) found that perceived similarity to another was associated with strong feelings of sympathy or empathy for them if they were in a difficult situation. However, this was moderated by whether or not the person was thought to be responsible for their predicament. Thus, if an individual's need for help (e.g. money) is regarded as being due to external causes (e.g. being burgled), levels of sympathy and empathy are significantly higher than if the cause seems to be personal (e.g. spending too much on drink or drugs). In addition to similarity, relational liking is improved by six other main factors:

1   ***Increased contact under positive circumstances.*** As we get to know people our liking for them tends to increase, providing this takes place within a conducive context. Even a few minutes of initial relational communication with a stranger prior to making a persuasion attempt can significantly increase the success rate (Burger, 2007).

2   ***Physical attractiveness.*** Beautiful people tend to be better liked than unattractive ones. This is discussed further below.

3   ***Association with success.*** Successful people act as a form of social magnet that attracts others. It is as if we are drawn to them in the hope that some of their glitter will rub off on us. We might be able to share in their success or be seen to be successful just by being with them. So powerful is this drive that people visit wax museums to look at and be photographed beside waxwork models of famous people.

4   ***Praise.*** We tend to like people who give us valued social rewards (see Chapter 4).

5   ***Use of less formal name.*** There is a whole psychology to the use of names, whether titles (Professor), formal address (Mr, Mrs), first name, pet name or nickname. As relationships deepen, forms of address become less formal. Spouses rarely address one another by title and more often use pet names (e.g. honey, sweetheart). Salespeople are usually trained to get on first-name terms with clients as soon as possible to deepen the relationship. At the other end of the continuum, there is the process of *dehumanisation*. When individuals are not to be treated as humans the labels attributed to them reflect this. Thus, terrorists use derogatory terms such as 'legitimate target', 'collaborator' or 'traitor' for those they plan to kill.

6   ***Eating together.*** As discussed by Hargie *et al.* (2004), food and drink are essential for human survival and we have an innate drive to seek and protect our sources of sustenance. Although food and drink are plentiful in the western world, the instinct remains. This means that we usually choose to eat, 'have a cuppa' or go for a drink with people who we like and trust. The ubiquitous business breakfasts and lunches therefore serve a very useful function as part of the process of influence. They help to cement the bonds between people and thereby lubricate the flow of commerce.

As Hargie *et al.* (2000) found, the existence of a good relationship allows for the expression of negative emotions from professional to client (e.g. anxiety, frustration). For example, a patient who is trying to move away from drug abuse, and who perceives the health professional as someone who genuinely cares, is more likely to accept statements such as 'Look, what you are doing to yourself and your family is just awful. You are harming yourself and causing a great deal of grief to everyone who cares about you.' Indeed, when expressed in the context of a positive relationship, such statements of negative affect have been shown to be related to greater adherence to the advice and direction offered. This is because the communication of genuine concern is likely to be reciprocated by the wish of the target person to sustain the balance of the relationship, and so comply. The forceful delivery of negative messages from a liked and respected agent also serves to heighten the person's awareness of the gravity of the behaviour.

Attractiveness

There is now an abundance of research to show that good-looking people are well regarded (Swami and Furnham, 2007a). From as early as four years of age, children have learned the norms of attractiveness (Swami and Furnham, 2007b) and show a preference for physically attractive others. We are bombarded every day with images of attractiveness in newspapers, magazines and on cinema and television screens. The media industry is well aware that beauty is popular and so sells well. Ugly film or pop stars are very much an exception. Furthermore, judgements of beauty are becoming more universally consistent. In their review of research in this field, Little and Perrett (2002: 28) concluded: 'Across many studies it has been found that there is a high degree of agreement from individuals within a particular culture, and high agreement between individuals from different cultures.' Hargie (2006b) illustrated how those rated high in attractiveness are seen as friendlier, more intelligent, popular and interesting, receive higher academic grades, are more likely to be approached for help by strangers, have more dates, better employment prospects and higher earning potential, and are less likely to be found guilty in court. The only downsides are that they are more likely to be viewed as vain, materialistic and prone to have extramarital affairs. Of particular interest here is that they are also rated as more persuasive – they have greater credibility and are perceived to be higher in expertise, trustworthiness and likeability.

It is small wonder then that the sale of anything which enhances our attractiveness is a huge business. People buy all manner of items, including make-up, wigs and cosmetic surgery, in order to appear more beautiful. However, as discussed in Chapter 10, another reason for the above bonanza of benefits is that from an early age people react positively to physically attractive individuals who, as a result, develop better interpersonal skills, self-esteem, confidence and optimism. As expressed by Johnston (1994: 155): 'It is not only the beauty, but also the social skills of attractive people that enhance their persuasiveness.' But one thing the research clearly shows is that for individuals to optimise their persuasiveness they should maximise their attractiveness (Reinhard *et al.*, 2006). It is also the case that initial judgements of physical attractiveness are moderated by psychological, sociological, relational and contextual influences (Duck, 1995). Features such as sense of humour, similarity to the other person, dress, scent, attentiveness, competence and sensitivity all affect overall ratings of attractiveness. These aspects can be employed by an influencing agent to make full use of the power of attraction.

Humour

Meyer (2000: 328) pointed out that the 'use of humor clearly enhances one's leadership and persuasive influence because of the nearly universal admiration of this skill (in moderation – overuse of humor can lower credibility)'. Of course, the humour has to be affiliative and prosocial, since humour that is used to demean others is dysfunctional for relational development (Wanzer *et al.*, 2010). Furthermore, sarcastic wits are regarded as influential but not popular, while clowning wits are seen as popular but not influential (Foot, 1997). Appropriate humour has been found to be a key

---

Box 12.4 Advantages of humour in persuasion

Humour can facilitate persuasion by:

- building rapport and making the target more favourably disposed towards the agent – we like people who make us laugh and are therefore more likely to be influenced by them
- encouraging the target to attend more closely to the message – humour is engaging and increases our attentiveness
- producing in the target a feeling of relaxation and related increased receptivity to the message
- increasing retention by making the message more memorable
- filling cognitive space – if we are laughing we are not thinking of counterarguments
- encouraging peripheral rather than central processing of the message. The feel-good factor inculcated by humour is in itself persuasive.

---

determinant of interpersonal attraction (Cann *et al.*, 1997). For instance, one study of dating behaviour in college students found that a good sense of humour was rated by both males and females as the most important feature of a member of the opposite sex (Buss, 1988). Humour facilitates persuasion in a number of ways (Foot and McCreaddie, 2006; Skalski *et al.*, 2009), and these are summarised in Box 12.4. A meta-analysis of research in the field of advertising revealed that humour significantly enhances attention, positive emotions and recall (Eisend, 2009). Likewise, the use of humour by professionals has been found to be effective across a wide range of settings including health care, education, sales and management (Campbell *et al.*, 2001; Bergeron and Vachon, 2008; Hughes and Avey, 2009; Wanzer *et al.*, 2010).

Logical proofs

Appeals to reason and logic are potent persuasive devices. Carefully constructed and forcefully delivered arguments, with clear premises leading to logical conclusions, are very persuasive. This section examines the six logical proofs that can be used to convince others of the rationality of one's position: message delivery; counter-attitudinal advocacy; case study; sidedness; request size; and reciprocation.

Message delivery

In terms of delivery of arguments, these are more persuasive when there is a *powerful* speech style, wherein the person speaks in a firm, authoritative tone and uses intensifiers – words or phrases that magnify the potency of what is being communicated (e.g. 'definitely', 'absolutely', 'I can say without a shadow of doubt'). By contrast, a *powerless* style is characterised by five main features:

1   *hesitations* ('Um . . . ah . . .')
2   *hedges or qualifiers* ('I sort of think . . .', 'It might possibly be . . .')
3   *disclaimers* ('I don't have any real knowledge of this area, however . . .', 'I might be wrong, but . . .')
4   *tag questions* ('. . . don't you think?', '. . . isn't it?'), and statements made with a questioning intonation
5   *lower voice volume*.

In a review of the area, Durik *et al.* (2008) concluded 'that messages with hedges led to less persuasion, more negative perceptions of the source, and weaker evaluations of the argument'. In their meta-analytic review of research in this area, Burrell and Koper (1998) found that a powerful speech pattern was perceived to be more credible and persuasive. Likewise, in their analysis of this field, Holtgraves and Lasky (1999: 196) concluded: 'A speaker who uses powerless language will be perceived as less assertive, competent, credible, authoritative, and in general evaluated less favorably than a speaker who uses powerful language.' If uncertainty has to be expressed, a powerful style should employ *authoritative doubt*, which underlines that the dubiety is from a vantage point of expertise (e.g. 'I know the literature very well and the evidence is just not clear on that . . .'). A powerless style accepts the blame for the uncertainty ('I'm not very well experienced in this . . .'). However, Holtgraves and Lasky also noted that speech power forms a continuum from low to high, so that degree of powerlessness may be important in determining impact. In other words, the occasional hesitation, hedge, tag question or lowered voice may have no impact on persuasiveness but a high number of each will.

While early work in this field suggested that there was a gender difference in that males used a more powerful speech style, whereas females tended to employ powerless speech, later studies refuted this (McFadyen, 1996). What seems to be the case is that females may *choose* to use powerless speech more often if they see this as being in line with the cultural norm or feminine style they wish to portray (Hargie, 2006b).

A related element of language intensity is the extent to which the message contains emotionality and specificity. In terms of the former it can be delivered along a continuum from mild (e.g. 'I am annoyed.') to high emotional intensity (e.g. 'I am furious.'). With regard to the latter, this again forms a continuum from low ('A few of them came and they stayed for a little while.') to high specificity ('Nine of them came and they stayed for 45 minutes.'). Hamilton and Hunter (1998a) in a review of research into this aspect found that stress was a moderating variable on the effects of emotional intensity. Relaxed targets are more persuadable as a result of the increased stress/arousal from high intensity messages, whereas with highly stressed receivers the added stress from the emotionality causes a boomerang effect. One other finding was that high emotional intensity had an impact upon discrepant messages delivered by credible agents. Presumably the emotionality underlines the importance of what is a discordant message from a believable source.

Another aspect of message delivery, as highlighted by Bull (2001b, 2003) in his analysis of the importance of rhetoric in political persuasion, is use of three-part lists ('we must fight, fight and fight again') and contrasts ('the dark night we have lived through with this government will be transformed into a bright new dawn'). In political speeches these have been shown to attract audience applause – a good indicator of approval and acceptance. The former tactic is part of the *repetition strategy*, whereby the speaker 'stays on message' to ensure that it gets through and people remember it. The power of repetition was recognised by Lewis Carroll (1898/1998) in *The Hunting of the Snark*, when he has the Bellman say:

> . . . I have said it thrice:
> What I tell you three times is true.

Repetition of arguments has been shown to be effective in increasing their persuasive power (Moons *et al.*, 2009). Statements heard more than once tend to be rated as more valid than those heard for the first time – an effect known as the *illusion of truth*. As shown by Song and Schwarz (2010: 111) in their review of research: 'The mere repetition of a statement facilitates its perception as true.' One reason for this is that, having heard the statement in the past, when we hear it again we experience a 'feeling of familiarity' with it, which in turn serves to increase its perceived validity. Indeed, the Nazi propaganda minister Joseph Goebbels demonstrated the potency of repetition when he argued that if you told a lie often enough people would believe it to be the truth. He claimed that: 'It would not be impossible to prove with sufficient repetition and psychological understanding of the people concerned that a square is in fact a circle' (cited in Baillargeon, 2007: 19). This is related to the *mere exposure effect*, wherein the more frequently we encounter an unfamiliar stimulus the more favourably we begin to evaluate it (Gass and Seiter, 2009). One hypothesised reason for this effect is *perceptual fluency*, which purports that positive feelings are generated by repetition of a message due to the fact that the more we are exposed to a stimulus the easier it becomes for us to process it. Thus, it is common to hear people say that they did not like something at first but after a while 'it grew on them'.

The use of metaphor is also important in message delivery. This term is derived from the Greek words for over (meta) and carry (pherein), and so the term indicates that an example from one area is carried over to another. For instance, a salesperson may say that the product being sold is 'like gold dust', to indicate that it has a range of positive properties such as being rare, very valuable and highly sought after. Sopory and Dillard (2002) carried out a meta-analytic review of research into the use of metaphors (this subsumed analogies, similes and personification), as compared to literal language, in persuasion. Their conclusion was that: 'Theorists since Aristotle have proposed that metaphor could be fruitfully used for persuasion. The meta-analytic summary of existing empirical studies affirms this supposition regarding metaphor's suasory effectiveness over literal counterparts' (p. 413). They found that the persuasive power of metaphors was greatest when they were novel, easily understood by the target, used early in the message, single and not extended,

However, a word of caution is required here. Metaphors must be used skilfully and care needs to be exercised if using them in a negative fashion. One linguistic form that is widely employed by public speakers is that of *rebuttal analogy*. This occurs when a speaker uses an analogy as part of an attack on the position of an opponent. For example, an opposition politician might attack the government's policy on health by saying, 'They have done too little too late. *What they are doing is the equivalent of giving a patient an aspirin to treat stomach cancer.*' The part in italics is an example of rebuttal analogy. Its purpose is to rebut the other side's arguments by showing them

377

to be ridiculous or absurd. But research has found that this form of message delivery needs to be used with caution, as it often causes a boomerang effect (Whaley and Wagner, 2000). Those who use it are rated as more impolite and less likeable. Furthermore, when compared to non-analogy equivalents, it prompts the target person to formulate more counter-arguments to the message and to remember fewer of the arguments put forward by the speaker. With partisan listeners, such as at a party political conference, rebuttal analogy, especially when humorous, can be acceptable to the audience. But even here the analogy should not be too insidious, especially if it likely to be reported by the media to neutral observers (to whom it may seem like a 'smart-ass' comment). Overall, the research findings advise against the use of this tactic. It would be better for our hypothetical politician to reword the above example as follows: 'They have done too little too late. *They have failed so many seriously ill people in our society, who need and deserve to receive the best possible treatment. Their record is truly shameful.*'

Another question is whether a speaker should have a clear and explicit conclusion at the end of an argument or leave this implicit and allow the audience to draw it out for themselves (see also Chapter 10 for more information on closure skills). The evidence here is clear: 'Messages with explicit conclusions are more persuasive than those with implicit conclusions' (O'Keefe, 2006: 334). In a meta-analysis of research in this field, Cruz (1998: 228) explained why this is the case:

> The more explicit the conclusions to a persuasive message, the better the conclusion is comprehended. Greater conclusion comprehension produces perceptions that the source of the message advocates a more extreme position. Finally, perceptions that the source holds a more extreme position produces more attitude change.

Counter-attitudinal advocacy

It has been found that the act of having to argue for a position that is contrary to one's own point of view can result in modifications to one's original perspective and a shift towards the other viewpoint. This occurs for two reasons. First, as will be discussed in more depth later, individuals have a desire to portray a consistent sense of self. Consequently, when they publicly espouse an opinion that runs counter to their beliefs, their attitudes tend to move in the direction of the public utterances. This phenomenon is part of what is known as the *saying is believing effect* (Holtgraves and Kashima, 2008). Second, the cognitive processes involved in counter-attitudinal advocacy can lead to a positive reappraisal of the arguments involved (Hamilton and Hunter, 1998b). In their review of research in this field, Preiss and Allen (1998) found that when participation in such a task is voluntary, attitude change is highest when a small incentive is offered; if involvement is mandatory, there is more change when the incentive is large. They argued that this is likely to be because those who are strongly opposed to the contradictory position will be less likely to volunteer to participate, and so those who do agree to take part may not be so diametrically opposed and hence more willing to change. When participation is compulsory, those who are paid well for completion of the task may feel under an obligation to reciprocate this high reward by working hard at the formulation of arguments for the case they are being employed to advocate. The processes involved in processing and presenting these arguments are then more likely to impact upon personal beliefs and opinions.

Case study

What is known as *the power of exemplary narrative*, or to put it more simply the power of purposive storytelling, has been shown to be effective in persuasive communication (Pinnington, 2001). From childhood we are nurtured on a diet of 'Once upon a time . . .' stories, and as adults the inner child in us responds reflexively and positively to case studies about actual people and events. One reason for the success of this tactic is that 'the vividness and psychological closeness of a single case study is often more relevant to an individual than are scientific data' (Ohme, 2001: 314). While, as mentioned earlier, statistics can heighten the power of evidence, they may appear to be cold and detached and we can get lost in the detail. Moreover, the oft-quoted remark by Mark Twain that 'There are lies, damned lies and statistics' means that we are often suspicious of statistics. The fact that academics often engage in the intellectual equivalent of arm wrestling over the validity of one another's statistical methods does not help.

On the other hand, we can readily identify with and indeed enjoy human-interest stories. The agent can use such tales to persuade the audience about the importance of the message being delivered. In terms of effectiveness, it does not seem to matter whether the narrative is fictional or true. This technique has a long history. For example, the early Christian church found that 'the medieval exemplum' (a brief story used to illustrate a particular moral point) was a much more effective tactic for conversion than subtle and learned sermons about doctrine (Scanlon, 1994). As discussed by Pinnington (2001), preachers were therefore encouraged to use relevant examples in order to persuade more easily. This is also shown in the Bible, where Christ made forceful use of 'the parable', which was a case study in the form of a moral tale. A key feature of the potency of persuasive narrative is the extent to which the target becomes engaged with the story. Thus, the phenomenon of *absorption* (also known as *transportation*) is important, wherein the 'message recipient is cognitively and affectively invested in a narrative' (Slater and Rouner, 2002: 179). This means that the story should be well told and of interest to the listeners. In terms of cognitive processing, successful narratives tend to be assimilated through the peripheral as opposed to the central route. Those who are engrossed in a story are less likely to employ counter-arguments and be more affected by the emotional part of the message. In this way, narrative messages have been shown to be more effective than statistical ones (Weber *et al.*, 2006; DeWit *et al.*, 2008).

Given its effectiveness it is not surprising that the case study tactic can be found in the practice of a wide a spectrum of persuaders (Hoeken and Hustinx, 2007), such as advertisers, politicians and insurance salespeople. Of course it is not an either/or decision with regard to statistics and case studies. Indeed, in a major study involving 1270 participants and 15 different messages, Allen *et al.* (2000) found that a combination of statistics and narrative produced the most potent influencing message. Likewise in their review of the area, Gass and Seiter (2009: 160) concluded: 'The best advice we can offer is to combine the two.'

Sidedness

An important decision is whether to use one-sided or two-sided arguments. In other words, should the disadvantages of what is being recommended also be recognised? Research findings show that one-sided messages are best with those who already support the view being expressed. Accordingly, at party political conferences the leader should present a partisan perspective designed to boost the faithful. Equally, it would be unusual for a clergyman to stand up in church and express doubts about the existence of God. When preaching to the converted it is necessary to target the message in a single direction. One-sided messages are also better with those of a lower IQ, who may become confused if presented with seemingly contradictory arguments. What is known as *attribute framing*, where certain aspects are emphasised, is important in accentuating advantages. For example, consumers are more likely to buy beef that is labelled as 75 per cent lean as opposed to beef labelled as 25 per cent fat (Pratkanis, 2007).

Two-sided arguments are more appropriate with those with a higher IQ. Thus, in a study of college students, Feng and Burleson (2008) found that arguments were rated as more effective when they not only presented the efficacy and feasibility of the advised action, but also addressed its potential limitations. Since intelligent people are well capable of formulating counter-arguments, it is best to openly recognise that there are two sides to an argument, rather than attempt to 'insult their intelligence'. It is also better to present the disadvantages as well as advantages to those who are initially opposed to the message, who have heard an opposing perspective earlier, or who will hear one later. In all these instances, of course, while the opposing perspective should be recognised, it should also be countered. The evidence here is quite clear (Allen, 1998; O'Keefe, 2006). The most effective approach is a refutational two-sided presentation, where there is recognition of the opposing point of view but a clear refutation of it. This is much more effective than either not mentioning the opposing arguments at all or, even worse, using a non-refutational two-sided presentation where the counter-perspective is highlighted but not undermined.

Request size

Two alternatives exist in relation to the scale of request made in persuasion attempts. The first is *foot-in-the-door* (FITD), where a very small first request is made, and if acceded to this is followed by a slightly larger request, and so on. To take a simple example, if I want to borrow €20 from a colleague, I could use the FITD approach to say that I had forgotten my wallet and initially ask for €10 to get me through the day. If the person agrees to this, when I meet them later I could then say how really kind it was of them to help but that I have remembered that I had to do some shopping and ask if they could possibly increase the loan to €20. In fact, the technique of asking for a very small amount has been found to be effective. Thus, a famous study by Cialdini and Schroeder (1976) illustrated how donations to charities increase when the agent adds the term 'even a penny will help' when making the request. More recent research has confirmed the utility of this 'legitimisation of paltry favours' effect when making requests for donations (Shearman and Yoo, 2007; Takada and Levine, 2007). However, two mediating factors seem important here (Andrews *et al.*, 2008). First, the request must be made face to face. Second, the request is more successful if it is for an immediate monetary donation, as opposed to a pledge from the target to donate.

The second is *door-in-the-face* (DITF), where a very large initial (and usually unacceptable) request is made, and once rejected a much more reasonable one follows. To continue the example of borrowing €20 from a colleague, using DITF I would say how I had forgotten my wallet and ask for a loan of €100, knowing it would probably be refused. I then ask if they could spare €50 or even just €20. Now my target amount seems much more reasonable – and in fact I have made two concessions from the first request.

Both FITD and DITF, which are termed *sequencing requests*, have been shown to be successful tactics when used skilfully (Guéguen and Pascual, 2005). Their effectiveness depends upon circumstances. For example, a cult is unlikely to be successful if it has a DITF strategy of stopping passers-by in the street and asking them to join their group, explaining that this will involve giving all of their money to the cult, breaking all contacts with family and friends, wearing strange clothes, accepting new and seemingly weird beliefs, living a frugal existence and having to recruit strangers. Rather, a FITD strategy is more usual. In their text on cults, Tourish and Wohlforth (2000) termed this tactic the *spiral of escalating commitment*. Here, potential recruits are initially invited to attend an evening meeting to hear more about the group. This is then followed by an increased level of request, such as participation in a weekend conference. In this way, the potential member is slowly 'sucked in' and the level of request gradually escalates, until the person has become a fully-fledged cult participant.

One explanation for the success of FITD is *self-perception theory* (Johnston, 1994). This purports that we make inferences about our attitudes, values and beliefs based upon how we behave. When we carry out an action we infer that we did so because we are the type of person who would perform such an act. In other words, our overt behaviour is seen as reflecting our inner 'self'. Then, when asked to perform a slightly larger action in the same vein, we wish to portray a consistent self and so we also accede to this request. Meta-analytic reviews of FITD have shown it to be effective (Dillard *et al.*, 1984; Fern *et al.*, 1986) provided that the conditions listed in Box 12.5 are met.

DITF is also known as *reciprocation of concessions*. The rationale here is that the target feels bad about having made the initial refusal. Furthermore, the agent has now made a concession in request size and so the target is under pressure to reciprocate. Compliance with the later request serves both to reciprocate the agent's concession and to personally make the target feel better. DITF also seems to benefit from *perceptual contrast*, wherein the second request is judged in the context of the initial one, and in comparison is perceived to be smaller than it really is. Many stores use the DITF tactic in this way by placing very expensive items at the entrance, so that when customers then encounter comparatively cheaper ones further into the shop these appear to be more reasonably priced than if they had been viewed without the contrast effect. Successive research reviews have confirmed the effectiveness of DITF (Fern *et al.*, 1986; O'Keefe and Hale, 1998, 2001; Turner *et al.*, 2007). However, they also show that for DITF to be successful the conditions listed in Box 12.6 must be met.

Box 12.5 Foot-in-the-door (FITD) conditions

For the FITD tactic to be successful, the following conditions must be met:

- ***The cause should be prosocial.*** If the request is made for purely selfish reasons it can be much more easily resisted; if it is in some way antisocial then it can be rejected with impunity.
- ***No incentive should be given for carrying out the initial request.*** If a reward is given, this may change the interpreted reason for the action (e.g. 'I did it purely for the money.'). This, in turn, can make refusal easier for subsequent requests, especially if there is no concomitant increase in the scale of the reward.
- ***The follow-up requests should be related to the initial one.*** A later request is more easily rejected by the target without any fear of appearing to be inconsistent if it is unrelated to the issue or theme of the first one.
- ***There should not be a huge discrepancy between each subsequent request.*** If the disparity is too large the request may be more easily rejected as being 'unreasonable'.

Box 12.6 Door-in-the-face (DITF) conditions

For the DITF tactic to be successful the following conditions must be met:

- ***The same agent must make both requests.*** If a different person makes the second request, the effect disappears. For example, a student approaches the class professor and asks for a large donation to the students' end of term party. This is refused. Later, another student approaches and asks for a smaller sum. Here, no real concession has been made, as it has become a different interaction with new rules. Furthermore, how many more such requests are liable to be made? The effect has been at best compromised and at worst destroyed.
- ***The beneficiary should be the same for both requests.*** If the recipient is different in the second request the effect is lost. For example, if the agent requests a large sum from the target for one charity initially, and then follows this up by asking for a smaller sum for a different charity, again the concession 'rules' have changed.
- ***The requests need to be delivered face to face.*** When the request is made by telephone the likelihood of success is much weaker. One reason for this is that research has shown that it is easier to refuse requests when they are mediated as opposed to when made in person (Hargie *et al.*, 2004).
- ***There is no time delay between the requests.*** If there is a delay the power of the effect diminishes. There is truth in the maxim that 'Time changes everything'. When making the second request at a later time, the initial scenario has to be reconstructed and may be difficult to recreate, and the pressure to reciprocate has eased for the target.
- ***The requests should be prosocial.*** As with FITD, purely selfish or antisocial requests can be readily rejected.

One final tactic here is known as *foot-in-the-mouth* (FITM; Howard, 1990). This occurs when before making a request of the target, the agent asks the HAY ('How are you?') question. The purpose here it to get the reply 'Good'. Having given this reply, the target then feels under internal pressure to stay consistent with this expressed mood. In the case of a request to help a charity, they also then feel a sense of obligation to try to help less fortunate others who are not feeling so good. For both reasons, they are more likely to accede to the request. However, Dolinski *et al.* (2001) carried out experiments to show that it is the establishment of initial dialogue with the target prior to making the request that may be crucial during influence attempts. They argue that in relation to FITM it may well be the effect of having an interaction with the agent that is the important element of this technique.

Reciprocation

In our interactions with others there seems to be a need for balance between what we give and what we receive. For example, Chapter 9 highlighted how in social situations when one person discloses to another, the recipient then feels under pressure to make a reciprocal disclosure. Cialdini (2001: 50), in noting that 'one of the most widespread and basic norms of human cultures is embodied in the rule for reciprocation', identified three main characteristics of this phenomenon:

1   The expectation of reciprocity is such a potent facet of the human condition that it often supersedes other factors that may influence compliance.
2   The rule applies even to uninvited first favours. Hence, companies often offer customers free samples or free trials, so that the recipient then feels under an obligation to return the favour.
3   To relieve ourselves of any lingering feeling of indebtedness we may actually return more to the giver than we received from them.

Reciprocity can be used in two ways, First, by *pre-giving* and so placing the target in the position of indebtness. Then, when a favour is sought in return it is more likely that the target will comply. If not, debt reminders can be invoked such as 'I did that for you . . . You owe me.' Favours also increase liking and gratitude, which in turn can influence compliance (Goei and Boster, 2005). A favour has been shown to be most effective when it is used with a stranger. The target attributes it to benevolent intentions rather than an ulterior motive on the part of the agent; the target feels that a high level of benefit has been received; the agent is perceived to have made a significant sacrifice in making it; and the subsequent persuasion attempt is regarded as prosocial rather than antisocial (Goei *et al.*, 2007). Second, a *promise* can be made that if the target performs a certain action, this will be rewarded by a reciprocal event at a later time. Colloquially this is known as 'You scratch my back and I'll scratch yours'. For example, a manager may say to a member of staff, 'If you complete this task I will recommend you for a performance bonus.'

Promises work best when there is a close and trusting relationship between people. There is then less danger of what is known as the *low-ball technique*, where someone gets another to do something by making a promise with no intention of keeping it. For example, in a classic study in Iowa, USA, Pallak *et al.* (1980) investigated methods to persuade natural gas consumers to conserve their usage. They began by just asking a sample of domestic users to be fuel conscious. This had absolutely no effect when usage figures were measured. They then contacted a new sample but this time informed them that those who agreed to take part would later be named in newspaper articles as model citizens. The effect was immediate. Within a month participants had made significant reductions in gas consumption. Then the researchers contacted them to say that it was not going to be possible to publicise their names after all. What happened to energy usage now? Well interestingly it continued to drop even more. Although they had been low-balled into the initial behaviour, once established the new response became resistant to change. There are clear ethical problems about using the low-ball technique, but as this study illustrated it certainly can be effective.

Emotional proofs

Emotions have been shown to be a very powerful force in driving and shaping human thoughts and behaviour. Appeals to the heart are as successful in effecting influence as appeals to the head (Andersen and Kumar, 2006; Timmers and van der Wijst, 2007). In their review of research in this field, Dillard and Peck (2001: 38) concluded: 'There is a great deal of evidence that affect plays a significant role in the process of opinion change.' There are literally thousands of terms to describe affective states (Hargie, 2006b). However, as discussed in Chapter 3, there are six main categories of emotion – sadness, happiness, surprise, disgust, anger and fear. Each contains a large number of subcategories (e.g. sadness subsumes, inter alia, embarrassment, chagrin, guilt, shame, distress and depression). Given the power and ubiquity of emotions in our lives, they are potent persuasion tools.

The *dual-systems approach* argues that emotions fall into one of two categories. Energetic arousal is seen as positive affect and experienced as exuberance, vigour, etc. Tense arousal is viewed as negative affect, experienced as anxiety, nervousness, etc. These are in turn linked to two underlying physiological behaviour-guiding systems:

1   The *behaviour approach system* (BAS) is triggered by cues of reward and escape from punishment. The activation of the BAS leads to the experience of positive affect.

2   The *behaviour inhibition system* (BIS) is triggered by cues of punishment and non-reward. The activation of the BIS leads to the experience of negative affect.

The discrete-emotions approach purports that negative emotions arise from a situation where the environment is hindering the achievement of the individual's goals, while positive emotions arise from a situation where the environment facilitates the individual's goals. As discussed earlier, this in turn impacts upon the way in which persuasion attempts are processed (see Box 12.2). It is therefore important to examine how both negative and positive emotions can be invoked to 'move' people to act in certain ways.

Threat/fear

As a core emotion, threatening messages that heighten our sense of fear can be very effective in changing attitudes and behaviour (Joffe, 2008). The *protection motivation model* has shown that there are four main prerequisites for fear to be successful as a weapon of influence (Sutton, 1982):

1   The likelihood and consequences of the threatened outcome must be severe enough to *really frighten* the target. The threat appraisal must be high so that it is perceived as noxious and real and the target must feel vulnerable (deHoog *et al.*, 2005). This can be difficult to achieve, since the psychological phenomenon of *unrealistic optimism* means that most people believe they are less likely than the average to suffer from negative experiences in life and more likely to experience the positive aspects (Chambers, 2008). For example, others are seen as being more likely to get heart disease or cancer than oneself. Young people in particular are often immune to health messages – they believe that it is old people who get sick. For health educators this sense of invulnerability is difficult to overcome in terms of fear induction. Another phenomenon that is relevant here is the *third-person effect*, whereby people believe that media messages have the greatest effect not on them (first person), or people like them (second person) but on 'others' (third person) (Sun *et al.*, 2008). A consequence of this is that if people believe they are less likely to be influenced by media messages they may become more passive, less critical, consumers, and so more susceptible to persuasion attempts (Chapin, 2008).

   While a sense of vulnerability is essential to the effectiveness of fear appeals, more generally it makes targets susceptible to persuasive messages. Contrary to popular beliefs, research on cults has shown that while about one-third of the people who join these bodies are psychologically disturbed, the remaining two-thirds are normal (Tourish and Wohlforth, 2000). However, the latter are more vulnerable to recruitment when they have just undergone a personal trauma such as bereavement, divorce, job loss or serious illness. Vulnerability is also high when the individual is experiencing a major change of circumstance. For example, young adults who have left home to go to college are often unsettled and confused. Their social anchors have been drawn up and they find they are afloat in a new world having to fend for themselves, often for the first time. Their support network is not at hand and levels of uncertainty and insecurity can be high. As a result, many cults, religions and various other bodies (sporting, political, etc.) specifically target the college fresher population, seeing this as fertile fishing ground. Furthermore, as intelligent (and often energetic, attractive and articulate) individuals, once such students join a group they can be great emissaries to further its cause.

2   In relation to fear appeals, the second prerequisite is that there must be *specific recommendations* about how to prevent or remove the danger. The steps needed to remove the threat must be clear and unambiguous.

3   The perceived *response efficacy* has to be high. In other words, the target must believe that what is being recommended will be *effective* in circumventing or overcoming the threat. The remedial actions should be shown to work.

4   The target needs to be *willing to take action* to remove the threat. There should be a high level of *coping appraisal and self-efficacy* so that the target is confident about being able to implement the recommended behaviours. Thus, Rimal (2002) showed that a crucial determining factor in the success of fear appeals was how highly individuals rated their own ability to carry out the recommended actions. If the target feels able to implement and maintain these, then fear messages are more likely to be successful.

If all four factors are operative, then threat/fear is a potent tool for persuasion. If one or more is absent then the power of the message is reduced accordingly. For example, someone may accept that being a very heavy drinker is detrimental to health and carries a much higher risk of illness and earlier mortality. They may agree that if they drank less or stopped drinking altogether they would have a drastically reduced rate of risk. However, they may also believe that they need to drink and just could not give it up. Here the power of the threat/fear message begins to dissipate. The target may then either respond with feelings of hopelessness ('I'm going to die anyway so I might as well enjoy my drink.') or reject the threat ('There is no real evidence to show any causal link between alcohol intake and ill health.').

Much of the early work on threat and fear appeals was carried out in the field of health, and indeed the *health belief model* emphasised the above four points, as well as a fifth aspect of *cue to action* (Rutter and Quine, 2002). Here, a specific event triggers the entire process. For example, a friend who smoked heavily dies of cancer and this then makes you think seriously about the dangers of smoking. The *parallel response model* (Leventhal, 1970) illustrated how people cope with fear messages by responding at one of two levels:

1   ***Fear control.*** This is concerned with controlling or reducing internal feelings of fear. Here the person avoids the negative messages that arouse fear. The heavy drinker responding at this level would avoid newspaper articles or television programmes that highlight the risks of heavy alcohol intake. They may also make a distinction between *general beliefs* ('heavy drinking is harmful to health'), and *personal beliefs* that either minimise the degree of risk ('I don't really drink that much.') or emphasise personal immunity ('Drinking never causes me any problems. I'm built for it.'). They may also engage in rationalisations such as generalising from the particular ('I know a man who drank heavily all his life and he lived to be over 80 years old.') or accentuating the positive ('Taking a drink actually improves my well-being, by helping me to relax.').

2   ***Danger control.*** Here the person responds in such a way as to reduce the danger that causes the fear. Thus, the person would cut down or eliminate alcohol. In other words, the fear message is accepted and acted upon.

In a meta-analysis of research into fear arousal and persuasion, Mongeau (1998: 65) concluded: 'Overall, increasing the amount of fear-arousing content in a persuasive message is likely to generate greater attitude and behavior change.' However, he also found that the use of this tactic was not always successful. Fear is more effective with older subjects (i.e. with adults as opposed to schoolchildren) and with low anxiety individuals. With highly anxious people it may backfire, so that the heightened anxiety induced by an intense fear scenario can inhibit attention and increase distraction. This in turn reduces comprehension, or results in the message either being ignored completely or rejected. Thus, if people already have very high levels of fear about a subject, attempting to increase this even further has been shown to be counterproductive (Muthusamy *et al.*, 2009). For example, Job (1988) illustrated how some health promotion campaigns that use fear appeals (e.g. anti-smoking) may actually boomerang because they raise the stress levels in an already anxious individual, who then responds by actually performing the targeted behaviour (i.e. reaching for a cigarette) to reduce this increased anxiety. The reactions of the target therefore need to be carefully and constantly monitored. The objective is to encourage change, not instil panic and an accompanying 'flight' reaction (where the target just wants to escape from the threatening message).

One interesting extension is the effect of what is known as *fear-then-relief* (FTR) upon compliance. A series of studies has shown that when fear is instilled in people and then suddenly removed, compliance with requests increases (Dolinski, 2007). In one study, while a jaywalker was crossing a road, a police whistle was blown. The jaywalker then turned round and was relieved to discover there was in fact no police officer present. These subjects were asked to complete a questionnaire, as were jaywalkers who did not hear a whistle and a control group of pedestrians who were not jaywalkers. The results showed that the FTR group more frequently acceded to the questionnaire completion request. This technique seems to work for two reasons (Perloff, 2008). First, the relief experienced upon removal of the threat is reinforcing. This enhanced positive emotional mood is then associated with the subsequent request, thereby increasing the likelihood of acquiescence. Second, the sudden relief from anxiety means that the target is in a cognitive state of temporary mindlessness, being still distracted by the danger that was nearly experienced. This means that they are less attentive to the request (and less likely to engage in central route processing of it) and so more susceptible.

Moral appeals

Part of the socialisation process in all societies is that individuals are taught the difference between what is right and what is wrong. Behaviour that is upright, ethical, honest, etc. is viewed positively by others and encouraged, while that which is underhand, immoral, deceitful, etc. is disapproved of and discouraged. These societal norms play a powerful role in the development of a personal moral code that in turn shapes our responses. Most people are susceptible to appeals to conscience, in the form of reminders that we have a duty to 'do the right thing', and that if we do not fulfil our moral obligations we will feel bad about ourselves. Thus, inducing 'anticipated guilt', where the person is persuaded that by pursuing a course of action later feelings of guilt will be experienced, can move the individual to act in such a way as to prevent the guilt occurring (Lindsey, 2005). Few people like to be left feeling guilty, regretful or ashamed, or to be the subject of opprobrium from significant others, and so messages that target the moral domain can be persuasive.

An important aspect here, as summarised by Dillard and Peck (2001: 42), is that 'Guilt may prompt efforts to redress the failure, but only if the transgression can be remedied.' In other words, inducing a sense of guilt is useful in moving someone to act, only if they can do so in such a way as to right the wrong. If the misdemeanour is irreversible or not salvageable, then all that a moral appeal will do at best is to make the target feel very bad. Furthermore, induced guilt does not always produce the desired result. In his review of the area, O'Keefe (2006) noted that guilt may backfire in that it may cause the target not to change their behaviour in line with previous attitudes and beliefs, but instead to change those attitudes and beliefs to be consistent with the new behaviour. O'Keefe also illustrated that while more explicit guilt appeals do induce greater guilt, less explicit guilt appeals are actually more effective in changing behaviour. The reason for this seems to be that more explicit guilt appeals induce greater resentment or anger in the target, and this tempers the success of the appeal.

Moral appeals take a number of forms, as shown in Box 12.7. Although these

---

Box 12.7 Types of moral appeal

- **Duty calls.** These remind people that they have a moral obligation, or responsibility, to carry out certain actions. For example, a parent may be told that it is their duty to provide for their child. In fact, insurance companies use this technique to sell life policies. The person who dies obviously will not benefit financially from the policy, but it is argued that they have a duty to their family to provide for them in the event of their death.

- **Altruism exhortations.** These are direct attempts to trigger a caring or altruistic response in the target person, who has no obligation to help and will receive no tangible benefit from giving assistance. Many charities operate at this level, when they appeal to the population to help others less fortunate than themselves. Likewise, beggars may ask you to give them money 'out of the kindness of your heart'.

- **Social esteem precepts.** Here, social norms are invoked to underline the probability that the reaction of others to a response will be either negative ('You will be shunned if you do that.') or positive ('You will be well thought of if you do this.'). Most of us care about the reactions of others, and so the danger of being ostracised on the one hand, or the likelihood of recognition and social approval on the other, are powerful forces.

- **Self-feeling injunctions.** The concept of self-regard is an important force in driving behaviour. For example, people who donate anonymously to charities do not receive social esteem, but they do have a reward in the form of positive self-feeling. This means that individuals can be influenced by appeals at this level, cast either in a negative manner ('You will find it very difficult to live with yourself if you do not do this.') or in a positive frame ('You will feel good if you do this.').

- **Altercasting appeals.** This involves encouraging others to 'step outside themselves' and examine their behaviour objectively. The individual is then asked to consider the view either that only a bad, uncaring person would continue with the present behaviour, or that a good and caring person would carry out the recommended action. For example, a heavy gambler whose family was suffering and in severe debt could be asked: 'Wouldn't you agree that anyone who cared anything for their family would try to stop this?'

can be effective tactics, there are also drawbacks to their use and so this strategy needs to be treated with some caution (Hargie *et al.*, 2004). Since we do not like to be made to feel guilty, we tend to dislike the person who has caused this to occur, and we are then more likely to avoid them in future. This is especially true when what we have done cannot be easily remedied. Another finding is that an accusation of being uncaring results in the target being more likely to accede to a second moral appeal, providing the follow-up one is made by a different person. This is because the target then wishes to show that he or she is not uncaring and so the accusation was unfounded. For example, you pass a charity collector shaking a tin in the street without donating and the person calls after you, 'I can see that you really care about those a lot less fortunate than yourself. I wouldn't like to have to rely on you for help.' A few streets later you encounter another charity collector waving a tin. There is now an increased probability that you will donate.

Scarcity value

While this aspect of persuasion is sometimes included within logical proofs (e.g. Hargie *et al.*, 2004), there is also a strong element of emotionality involved and so it can also be incorporated within emotional proofs. The scarcity principle operates on the basis that once the availability of something is restricted it becomes more valuable and desirable. Items that are hard to get tend to have more value and appeal. There is a perfectly good rationale here – our experience tells us that the best things in life are often in scarce supply. The phenomenon of an increased desire for what is scarce is part of what is known as *reactance theory* (Brehm, 1966), which explains how, when access to something is denied, or when restrictions are placed upon an item or activity, our freedom of choice is threatened. This results in the phenomenon of reactance, which refers to the reaction we have to the imposition of restrictions on our freedom. Such reaction involves a combination of anger and negative cognitions, such as counter-arguing and source derogation (Rains and Turner, 2007).

Reactance can be reduced by various strategies. What is known as the *but you are free to accept or to refuse* technique has been shown to increase the success of a request (Guéguen and Pascual, 2005). Here, the agent makes a request but adds the caveat that the person has the freedom to refuse. Having been given this 'increased' freedom, people feel more in control and less under duress, with the result that they become more acquiescent. Likewise, *acknowledging resistance* increases compliance. By simply saying 'I know you might not want to, but . . .' before making the request the agent can increase the number of people who comply. It seems that the act of openly acknowledging and accepting the target's feelings of resistance serves to reduce this resistance. For example, in one study the number of subjects who gave to an experimenter requesting money for a parking meter increased from 58 per cent to 91 per cent by including the 'I know you might not want to, but . . .' preface (Knowles and Riner, 2007). Similarly, what is known as *the power of 'Yes'* helps to reduce reactance. Here, the agent avoids saying 'No' but rather says 'Yes' and then adds a caveat. For instance, if a 17-year-old girl asks her mother if she can have a party in the house, rather than replying 'No, you cannot!' it is better for the mother to say something like, 'Yes you can, if you buy all of the food and drink, your father and

I act as security, and you cover the costs for a professional cleaning company to come in the next day.'

When we are threatened by something being denied to us, we react to this threat by experiencing an increased desire for the restricted item. Indeed, the more restricted an item, the greater tends to be its appeal. This process first occurs in children at around the age of two years, when temper tantrums are often the order of the day if a much wanted toy, snack or activity is not immediately forthcoming. One early study showed that when children at this age were offered access to toys of parallel attractiveness, if one was unavailable (behind a Plexiglas barrier) this was the one upon which most attention was focused (Brehm and Weintraub, 1977). Likewise, if teenagers are told by parents not to date a certain person, their desire to be with the forbidden individual is often heightened. Although the best things in life may be free, we only fully appreciate them if they become less available. In fact, we expect to pay more for the better things in life. We know that the best house, suit or computer costs more. Shops that sell 'rare artefacts' or 'precious gems' do not 'stack 'em high and sell 'em cheap'. A key implication of this is that we can persuade others to do something by convincing them that there is scarcity value attached to it. For example, people pay exorbitant fees to join clubs that market themselves as 'exclusive'.

There are three important factors attached to scarcity value:

1   Resources attain an even greater value when they are seen to be *newly scarce*. This holds both for items that were once plentiful but have now become rare, and for recently discovered or invented items that are not yet widely available. Salespeople are able to sell more easily things that are brand new but still hard to get hold of (Hargie *et al.*, 2004). Indeed, the price of an item usually remains high so long as it is scarce but tends to drop as availability increases.

2   If we have to *compete* for the scarce resource it attains even greater attraction in our eyes. It is for this reason that auctioneers are delighted when two or more people begin to bid seriously for the same object. The winner is then likely to pay well above the odds to secure it.

3   *Losses are more influential than gains.* Gain and loss appeals take the form of a 2×2 matrix, where the outcome is described as either desirable or undesirable and the likelihood of attaining it is portrayed as either more likely or less likely (O'Keefe and Jensen, 2009). Scarcity value is increased where the outcome is seen as highly desirable but the likelihood of achieving it is less likely. Research shows that messages are more effective when scarcity benefits can be presented not as gains but as preventable losses (Pratkanis, 2007). What is known as *prospect theory* (Tversky and Kahneman, 1981) shows that people are more concerned with minimising losses than maximising gains. There has been shown to be truth in the maxim that 'a penny lost is valued more highly than a penny earned' (Rasmussen and Newland, 2008: 157). Thus, the prospect of something becoming scarce as a result of losing it motivates us more than the thought of gaining something of equal value. For example, smokers are influenced more when told by a physician how many years of life they are likely to lose if they do not quit, as opposed to how many years they will gain if they give up (Cialdini, 2001), and that if they do not stop smoking their lungs

will not heal than if they stop their lungs will heal (Ohme, 2001). Similarly, antidrug ads targeted at adolescents have been shown to be more effective when the message is framed in terms of loss rather than gain language (Cho and Boster, 2008).

Interestingly, in a study into the effects of advertising in Poland, Pietras (2001) showed how the technique of scarcity value that relied upon 'limited supply' or 'limited time offer' tactics were less effective as consumer goods became more widely available. She suggested that in affluent societies the deeper psychological principles underlying the scarcity principle (e.g. the uniqueness of the item, competition with others) are more effective and concluded that 'different compliance-gaining tactics may be best suited to different groups ... their efficacy strongly depends on the demographic and psychological characteristics of consumers' (p. 93).

Consistency and commitment

A powerful human drive is the desire to be regarded as *consistent*. We have a need to show others that we mean what we say and will do what we promise. This means that once we have made a public declaration of *commitment* to a course of action we are more likely to rate it highly and continue with it. A ubiquitous strategy in many organisations and institutions is to get people to make such a declaration. Its potency is reinforced if the person also makes the declaration in writing. Examples of the successful use of this tactic include 'I am an alcoholic ...' declarations made at Alcoholics Anonymous gatherings, personal testimonies or confessions by members of religious denominations, and statements of devotion to one another made by couples during the marriage ceremony. At another level, performers know that if they can get the audience actively involved (e.g. by clapping, laughing, cheering, chanting or singing along) their level of perceived enjoyment will increase accordingly. This tactic has been aptly termed the *clap trap* (Huczynski, 1996). Involvement increases enjoyment and so reduces the likelihood of central processing. Such a strategy is used at mass rallies (witness the 'Sieg Heil' roars and Nazi salutes during Hitler's speeches), in religious services, the armed forces and in the best classrooms. Involvement in synchronised group activities such as marching, chanting and singing has been shown to enhance group bonding and loyalty (Wiltermuth and Heath, 2009).

Thus, the twin pillars of consistency and commitment can be used to shape and direct the behaviour of others. The principle of *retrospective rationality* means that once people perform a certain behaviour or publicly state a point of view they are then more likely to infer in retrospect that they really believe in what they said or did (Iyengar and Brockner, 2001). In reviewing this area Cialdini (2001: 96) concluded: 'Commitments are most effective when they are active, public, effortful, and viewed as internally motivated (uncoerced).' They are also more impactful when the decision taken is final. It is useful to examine the commitment aspects of persuasion in further depth, including: public declaration; implementation intentions; level of initial commitment; voluntary act; finality.

Public declaration

When the behaviour is enacted publicly rather than privately, the commitment to it is greater. The presence of others has a significant impact – we like to be seen as true to our word. Those who change their mind or renege on what they said are generally perceived as fickle, weak or untrustworthy. Consequently, oaths of allegiance made in public are a key element in the initiation ceremonies of many bodies. Once you have publicly sworn undying allegiance to a cause it becomes more difficult to retract. For example, Islamic suicide bombers usually make a videotaped statement before they go on their mission. This is a very public declaration, as the tape may be seen by millions of people. Having made such a declaration, it then becomes extremely difficult to recant. In fact, members of terrorist organisations who become disillusioned about their organisation may turn informer rather than face the opprobrium of being seen to go back on their sworn oath. More generally, the media love to expose public figures who have broken promises or shown inconsistency, and relish stories involving crooked cops, unfrocked vicars or corrupt politicians. Where someone is inconsistent, the use of *induced hypocrisy* is a powerful force. As noted by Stone *et al.* (1997), this occurs when an individual is:

* reminded of having publicly espoused a personal position
* confronted with evidence of having failed to live up to this position.

When both of these events occur, the effect of the induced hypocrisy is powerful. The individual experiences cognitive dissonance and is motivated to be more consistent in future. Having been shown to have broken our word, and as such to be hypocritical, we then have a renewed determination to 'put this right'.

Implementation intentions

An important distinction has been made between *goal intentions*, where the individual makes a simple commitment to a particular action ('I intend to do X.') and *implementation intentions*, which involve detailed planning about when, where and exactly how X will be carried out (Gollwitzer, 1999). Research across a wide range of fields has shown that individuals who plan at the implementation level are much more likely to carry out the stated behaviour (Rutter and Quine, 2002).

Level of initial commitment

The more actively involved the person is in the public declaration process, the more binding their commitment becomes. One way of ensuring that people stay committed to the message they have recently been persuaded to adopt is to get them to proselytise about it. This tactic is used by many religions and cults. On the high street of most major cities one meets individuals selling a message either on an individual basis or, as with 'manic street preachers', to all and sundry. Having to 'sell' the message means that it becomes cognitively embedded and resistant to change. It is more difficult later to reject that which you have publicly and vehemently espoused. If individuals have to make sacrifices as part of their commitment they are more likely to 'bond' with the behaviour. Thus, many bodies have initiation ceremonies or 'rites of passage' where the initiate may have to endure humiliations before becoming a fully fledged member. Likewise, terrorist leaders recognise the importance of getting volunteers involved in an early 'mission', especially one where targets are killed. The volunteer is then literally 'blooded' and more likely to aver the worth of the cause. People also rate the strength and depth of their belief or attitude based upon the extent of effort they have shown to it in the past. Thus, if you decided to become a vegetarian six months ago but since then have lapsed and eaten flesh at least once a week, you are likely to rate your commitment to vegetarianism lower than if you had never eaten flesh since.

Voluntary act

If the behaviour has been freely chosen, the individual is more committed to it. There is now a huge volume of research to show that freedom of choice is a central factor in the influence equation. In reviewing this area, Iyengar and Brockner (2001: 16) concluded: 'The provision of choice seems inherently linked with intrinsic motivation, perceived control and personal commitment.' If we can argue that a public commitment was made as a result of threat or duress, then we do not feel the need to stick to it. For example, some American prisoners of war (POWs) held by communists in the Korean and Vietnam conflicts made public statements in favour of their captors and against US policy. Interestingly, some stayed committed to what they had said and remained there after the war, while others argued they had been forced by physical or psychological torture to say what they had, and never personally believed in what they were told to say. The reaction of others is similarly mediated by the extent to which they perceive the declaration to be coerced.

Snyder and Omoto (2001) identified five key motivations for the phenomenon of *volunteerism*, where individuals volunteer to give of their time in the service of others. Such volunteerism is crucial for the survival of many organisations (Haski-Leventhal and Bargal, 2008). As shown in Box 12.8, the first two motivations are other-centred and the last three self-focused. Those who want to encourage others to volunteer need to take cognisance of these different motivations. For example, if producing a publicity video aimed at recruitment, as many of these motivations as possible should be targeted. As expressed by Snyder and Omoto (2001: 295): 'Rather than adopt a *one size fits all* approach to volunteer recruitment and training, organizations may be better served by creating advertisements and recruitment materials that differentially speak to the different motivations.'

Finality

We are heavily influenced by commitments that are irrevocable. If there is a possibility that we can change our minds, the alternatives may linger and eventually influence our behaviour. However, if the deed is final, we are more likely to become convinced of its worth. For example, once you have signed the legal contract to sell your house you

Box 12.8 Motivations for volunteerism

1 *A general personal system of values and beliefs* that includes a felt humanitarian obligation to help others. Self-centred, materialistic, egotists who believe that 'it's a jungle out there' and that only the fittest will survive, are less likely to become volunteers.

2 *Specific concern for or interest in the target group* to whom the voluntary work is directed. For example, a committed Christian in the developed world may be motivated to go and give practical help to other fellow Christians in the third world.

3 *A desire to develop a greater understanding of the field* in which one will be working. This is the rationale behind work placement programmes. The person can spend some time in the type of environment that they feel they wish to work in, and gain firsthand insight into what is involved.

4 *As part of personal development.* This may include the motivation to feel a sense of challenge, e.g. volunteering to become a member of the crew of a lifeboat. It may also be a wish to enlarge one's social network – by meeting other volunteers who are of the same age and likely to hold similar attitudes and beliefs.

5 *A need to enhance one's self-esteem and feel better about oneself.* Thus, someone who earns a high salary in a very competitive but not socially satisfying job may stay in the job to earn money but at the same time become involved in charity activities in their spare time.

are more likely to believe that you have made the correct decision. Likewise, some in society argue that because divorce is possible it encourages less of a commitment to marriage.

Commitment to a cause is particularly strong amongst vociferous minority groups, who maintain their attitudes by using three techniques (Wojciszke, 2001):

1 *Increasing their belief in the subjective validity of their own attitudes and the invalidity of opposing perspectives.* This serves to increase the difference between ingroup and outgroup. The minority believes that their views represent the only rational or logical possibility. Those who hold an opposing view are not thinking straight, do not know the full facts and so must be put right, or are just biased against the minority.

2 *Overestimating the amount of social support for one's position.* Thus, the minority group convinces itself that it has huge support for its views. This is part of what is known as the *false consensus effect*, where we believe (erroneously) that our beliefs or behaviours are more prevalent than is actually the case.

3 *Belief in the moral superiority of one's position.* Not only does the minority group see its perspective as valid, but members also believe that they hold the high moral ground. A good example of this is those militant minority groups who claim to have God on their side, and so are fighting for a 'just cause' or 'holy war'.

These three perspectives are part of the phenomenon of groupthink (see Chapter 14).

Self-prophecy

The self-prophecy effect occurs when we are requested to predict our future performance. Having made a public prediction, we then feel under pressure to live up to this. There is considerable evidence to support the potency of self-prophecy in guiding future behaviour. In their review of research in this field, Spangenberg and Greenwald (2001: 52) concluded:

> Several researchers have shown in multiple contexts that predicting one's own behavior can induce subsequent action consistent with the prediction, yet different than would otherwise have been observed ... its robustness – regarding both the magnitude of the effect size and the variety of contexts in which it has been observed – is compelling.

In well over three decades of experience in higher education, I have become very aware of how asking final year students to predict their degree classification or dissertation grade produces remarkably accurate results. In fact, during supervision of their dissertations, students, without overtly realising its effect, return to their initial self-prophecy by asking questions such as 'Is the literature review at first class standard?', 'What do I need to do to make sure this is upper second?' One problem with self-prophecy, of course, is that it can be negative as well as positive. Those involved in the therapeutic professions have to deal with clients with poor self-esteem and low expectations of self-efficacy. They too are likely to match their projected level of negative performance. As part of the process of goal setting, therapists must therefore encourage clients to be as positive as possible in their prophecies, while staying within realistic parameters.

A related perspective here is the *theory of planned behaviour*. As mentioned in Chapter 2, this purports that a person's responses can be predicted from their behavioural intentions since 'the best predictor of behaviour is the person's intention to perform the behaviour' (Rutter and Quine, 2002: 11). Thus, if a self-prophecy is framed in terms of behavioural intentions, the likelihood of the prophecy being realised is strengthened. The theory of planned behaviour further argues that intentions are determined by two main factors:

1   *Attitude to the behaviour.* This is based upon one's beliefs about the consequences (e.g. 'Taking drugs would adversely affect my health.') and related evaluations thereof (e.g. 'It would be wrong to risk my health.').

2   *Subjective norms* – in the form of perceived social pressure to carry out the behaviour (e.g. 'My parents do not want me to take drugs.'), moderated by the individual's desire to comply with this pressure (e.g. 'I respect my parents and do not want to let them down.').

Klinger and Bierbraver (2001) highlighted how three key aspects of the theory of planned behaviour are important. They illustrated these in relation to the processes a Turkish immigrant in Germany may go through in making a decision about whether to attempt to assimilate:

1   *Behavioural evaluation.* The Turkish person has to decide whether it would be good to become a German – would doing so result in positive or negative outcomes?
2   *Normative evaluation.* This involves a consideration of prevailing social norms and pressures in the person's ingroup. What would the attitudes and reactions of one's family and friends be?
3   *Competence evaluation.* This relates to perceived ability to perform the necessary behaviours. For example, has the Turkish person a strong belief in their ability to learn to speak fluent German?

These three evaluations are also likely to be influential in the formation of a final self-prophecy. To return to the above example, a student may believe that a first class degree would be very beneficial (behavioural evaluation), and positively acclaimed by family and friends (normative evaluation), but that it is just beyond their ability level or requires more work than they are prepared to expend (competence evaluation). The student will therefore predict the more achievable, yet still personally and socially laudable, upper second and gear their work schedule accordingly.

OVERVIEW

From the review of research presented in this chapter it is clear that persuasion is a multifaceted and complex area. Success or failure in persuading others is determined by a range of often interlocking elements. As noted by Meyers-Levy and Malaviya (1999: 45): 'The complex process of persuasion is intricately dependent on a myriad of contextual, situational, and individual difference factors.' For example, Rogers (1983) demonstrated how different people respond in differing ways to innovation. Some people want to be first to have a new gizmo and warmly embrace all novel developments, whether in technology, procedures or processes. Their motto tends to be 'off with the old and on with the new'. Such individuals have been termed *innovators*. At the other end of the scale are those who are extremely reluctant to change their ways at all, and do not want to adopt new approaches or even adapt to them. Their mantra is 'I like things just as they are.' This group of people are called *laggards*. In between the two ends of the continuum, some will react more swiftly than others to change and as such are more amenable to persuasion.

There is therefore no set of fixed guidelines or magic formula with regard to persuasion. Rather, it is necessary to consider the target, the situation in which the interaction is taking place and the way in which the persuasion attempt is made. Like all communication, this is a two-way process and so the target makes an evaluation of the agent in considering how to respond. This chapter has followed Aristotle's template for analysing persuasion in terms of ethos (personal proofs), logos (logical proofs) and pathos (emotional proofs). A knowledge of each of the subelements of these areas, as summarised in Box 12.9, provides detailed insight into the fascinating world of persuasion.

Box 12.9 Summary of main persuasion tactics

Personal proofs
✔ Muster all the *power* you have to good effect.
✔ Develop a good *relationship* with the target.
✔ Make yourself as *attractive* as possible.
✔ Use appropriate *humour*.

Logical proofs
✔ Deliver the message in a *confident and authoritative* manner.
✔ Try to get the target to *argue against their own position*.
✔ Back up your arguments with *case studies* as well as *hard evidence*.
✔ Give *two-sided arguments with intelligent people*, but refute the counterarguments.
✔ Have a *consistent sliding scale of sequential request*, either low gradating to high or vice versa.
✔ Invoke the norm of *reciprocation*.

Emotional proofs
✔ Employ *threat/fear*, especially with older and less anxious subjects.
✔ Introduce *moral appeals* to make the person feel guilty.
✔ Emphasise the *scarcity value* of the item.
✔ Get a public declaration of *commitment*, to which the target will then want to be *consistent*.
✔ Ask the target to make a *self-prophecy* about their performance, as this will then tend to guide their behaviour.

Chapter 13

Working things out together: the skill of negotiating

INTRODUCTION

ONE OF THE GREATEST challenges of social life is dealing with difference (Kirkpatrick *et al.*, 2006). Diversity in race, religion, gender or generation leads to people adopting contrasting cultural practices, beliefs, values and ways of doing things. These differences, in turn, can cause problems when people from disparate backgrounds have to attempt to sort out areas of disagreement (Hackley *et al.*, 2006). Of such is the stuff of wars, communal conflicts and industrial disputes. But even at a more mundane level, amongst families and friends, there is a frequent lack of concordance when deciding what to do or where to go. Negotiation is one way of overcoming such difference. As Lewicki *et al.* (2007: v) pointed out: 'Negotiation is not only common, it is also essential to living an effective and satisfying life. We all need things – resources, information, cooperation and support from others. Others have those needs as well, sometimes compatible with ours sometimes not.' This means we inevitably have to enter into regular exchanges of give and take with other people. While many think of it primarily in the context of resolving international disagreements, employer–trade union wage disagreements or hostage situations, in fact we all have to negotiate on a day-to-day basis. It may take place in the context of, for example, agreeing where to eat, what movie to see, what time the children should be home by, where to go on holiday, or more formally the sale and purchase of houses and cars. In this sense, negotiation is pervasive in our lives.

Professionals, of course, have added responsibilities for negotiating with colleagues, managers, clients and so on as part of their work role.

All jobs necessitate a capacity to negotiate and bargain effectively with a range of others. For some, such as real estate agents or car salespeople, negotiation is of paramount importance. Yet, despite the huge volume of recent literature on the topic (see Roloff and Li, 2010), many practitioners receive little or no instruction or training in this dimension of practice (Gates, 2006). Furthermore, this is a skill that has to be learned and can be taught (Taylor *et al.*, 2008). From a developmental perspective, research findings show that as children mature their capacity for complex negotiation routines becomes more refined and developed (Green and Rechis, 2006). Very young children are totally egocentric. They want what they want and they want it NOW. Learning that others also have needs and wants is an important part of the maturation process and essential for negotiation. Thus, research has shown that most children at the age of three to four years behave in a very selfish fashion, but by the age of seven to eight years have learned the importance of egalitarianism when dealing with others (Fehr *et al.*, 2008).

A main reason why negotiation is a ubiquitous aspect of our everyday experience is that conflict is a pervasive feature of personal and social existence. Finnegan and Hackley (2008: 7) pointed out: 'Negotiation and nonviolent action are arguably the two best methods humanity has developed for engaging constructively with conflict. Both have played central roles in helping manage or resolve seemingly intractable conflicts.' Were there no clashes of interests or thwarting of objectives (actual or apparent) in a setting where each party is to some extent reliant on the other to do what it wants, there would be no need to negotiate. Van Kleef *et al.* (2008: 14) noted: 'Social conflict may be said to occur when two or more parties have (or perceive) a divergence of interests ... Conflicts may vary tremendously in terms of the stakes, the likelihood and possible consequences of stalemate, and the relationship between the parties.' Conflict is without doubt endemic in many walks of life. However, it is not always negative and – at least in moderation – may actually be productive.

An element of competition can start the flow of creative juices, increase the motivation of all parties and produce improved end results. As summarised by Paramasivam (2007: 92): 'Well-managed disagreement boosts productivity, reduces stress, sparks creativity, enhances working relationships and benefits workplace diversity.' The secret is to deal with it at optimal levels to ensure that it has positive effects. When conflict remains unresolved the results may be very damaging. Failure to ameliorate disputes can have a range of dysfunctional consequences, including unresolved resentment, relationship breakdown, industrial strikes, lengthy litigation, financial loss, the death of hostages and civil strife. Mishandled, through avoidance, overly aggressive arguments or even recourse to violence or the threat of violence, and the destructive potential can be far-reaching. Negotiating is a more positive alternative that has a very important contribution to make to conflict management (Thompson, 2005). But what exactly does negotiation entail and how can we perform this process more effectively? This chapter attempts to answer these questions by charting the core features of negotiation and delineating the key skills and strategies required for successful outcomes.

DEFINITION OF NEGOTIATION

Negotiation has been conceptualised in many ways (see Morley, 2006) as, for example:

- a *game* in which both sides carry out strategic moves (such as making offers)
- an *economic forum* in which resources are exchanged
- a *cognitive information processing exercise* in which individuals have to use a range of intra- and inter-personal processes to make decisions
- a *form of reflexive social action* in which people are concerned with the inter-pretation of messages and meanings in particular social and historical contexts.

In general terms, for negotiation to occur there has to be some incompatibility of interest, both sides must be interested in seeking a settlement, and the process often involves exchanging concessions in order to reach agreement. The term 'negotiation' has been defined in a variety of ways. Some definitions emphasise the importance of communicating with and eventually influencing the other side. In this sense, 'negotiation is a highly interdependent process in which each party continuously incorporates information from the other party to develop responses that might lead to resolution of the conflict at hand' (Weingart *et al.*, 1999: 387). The notion of exchange was underscored by Robbins and Hunsaker (2009: 349) who defined negotiation as 'a process in which two or more parties exchange goods or services and attempt to agree upon the exchange rate for them'.

As well as emphasising the relationship element and the search for mutual benefit, negotiation has been viewed as 'an attempt by two parties to change the terms and conditions of their relationship in a situation in which it is to their mutual benefit to do so or in which it is impossible to quit the relationship' (Whitney, 1990: 77). This definition highlights the fact that on occasion people simply must negotiate with one another. Parents and their young children negotiate (often passionately) about many issues, but neither can just walk away from the relationship. Similarly, it is difficult for professionals not to negotiate with one another, or with clients, if they are to effectively execute their duties. In large organisations, subdivisions have to negotiate regularly if the firm is to thrive. For example, the sales, production and delivery departments must all coordinate their actions and agree a joint schedule. There is no point in salespeople winning sales that production cannot meet, or agreeing deadlines that delivery cannot make.

The issue of truth-telling was raised by Morley (1981: 86) who defined negoti-ation as 'an exercise in which parties struggle to exploit asymmetries of interest and power, each knowing that the other may disguise or misrepresent their real position'. Here, there is a recognition that since there are differences in interests and resources, both sides know that the other is likely to be economical with the truth by concealing or distorting their real situation. The reason for this is that: 'There are very few negotiating situations where you can afford to be completely open and honest without risking being exploited by the other side' (Mills, 1991: 2). Continuing with this theme, Morley (1981) viewed negotiation as a type of 'incomplete antagonism' or 'precarious partnership' that allows each participant the opportunity to manipulate perceptions of common interest while endeavouring to achieve private goals. In an attempt to move away from such confrontational encounters, many large corporations, such as Ford, Xerox, Whirlpool and Chrysler, drastically reduced their number of potential suppliers. The driving rationale here was to develop supply lines based upon mutual trust and positive relationships rather that on cut-throat price battles (Jeffries and Reed, 2000).

Although the terms 'negotiating' and 'bargaining' are often used synonymously, distinctions have been made between them. While parties may enter negotiation with no intention of reaching a settlement (e.g. it may be in their interests to prolong a dispute so as to achieve a better final outcome), when they bargain it is their firm intention to make a deal. In this sense, when we bargain we negotiate for agreement. Thus, bargaining has been defined as 'an operative desire to clarify, ameliorate, adjust or settle the dispute or situation' (Lall, 1966: 31), in a process which involves 'making the other side sufficiently content with an agreement to want to live up to it' (Fisher and Ury, 1981: 75).

In reviewing definitional issues, Thompson (1990) identified five defining features of negotiation:

1   There is a conflict of interest on at least one issue.
2   The parties are involved in a voluntary relationship, where communication is emphasised and no one is coerced into being at the negotiation.
3   The interaction is concerned with the division or exchange of resources and intermediate solutions or compromises are possible.
4   Discussion centres upon the sequential presentation of offers, evaluation of these, and subsequent concessions and counter-offers.
5   Offers and proposals do not determine outcomes until agreed upon by both parties.

However, this process does not always run smoothly and indeed Mnookin *et al.* (1996) noted three core tensions:

1   maximising one's own personal profit while at the same time attempting to ensure equity and a fair deal for both sides
2   standing up for one's own position, yet showing concern for the interests and needs of the other side
3   personal interests versus clients' interests. For example, a social worker has to negotiate on behalf of clients and get the best deal possible for them, but is also a government employee who needs to show to line managers an ability to stay within budgetary limits.

In relation to the latter point, Susskind and Mnookin (1999) argued that many people negotiate on behalf of others and not just for personal gain. For example, when you buy a car the salesperson is acting on behalf of the garage owner and the motor company, while you may be representing your entire family who will use the vehicle. Indeed, many professionals have jobs in which negotiating on behalf others is central to their work (agents, lawyers, politicians, union officials, etc.).

FUNCTIONS OF NEGOTIATION

Negotiation serves a number of very important purposes (see Box 13.1). In essence, this involves engaging in a structured and reasonably formal process during which each side should be given the opportunity to put forward their arguments, and also show a willingness to listen to the views of the other parties involved. The eventual

---

Box 13.1 Purposes of negotiation

To enable people to engage in a process in which parties:

1 present a sequence of arguments to support their case
2 state their preferences
3 recognise and acknowledge what the other side sees as important
4 try to achieve an in-depth understanding of all the issues
5 ascertain areas of agreement and disagreement
6 enter into a series of offers and bids relating to personal targets
7 seek out options to overcome areas of disagreement
8 engage in a process of mutual concession-making
9 formally agree and ratify a final deal that is acceptable to both sides, and that can be successfully implemented.

---

goal is to attempt to reach a mutually beneficial compromise position that will be acceptable to all those involved.

NEGOTIATING STRATEGIES

The main decisions to be made during a negotiation encounter can be interpreted in terms of a 'negotiation decision tree' (Figure 13.1). The first decision is whether or not to enter into negotiation at all. Malhotra and Bazerman (2007: 282) advised that a decision not to negotiate should occur:

> when the costs of negotiation exceed the amount you stand to gain ... when negotiation would send the wrong signal to the other party, when the potential harm to the relationship exceeds the expected value from the negotiation, when negotiating is culturally inappropriate, or when your BATNA beats the other side's best possible offer.

If a decision is taken not to negotiate, then the latter Best Alternative To Negotiated Agreement (BATNA) should already have been formulated. Ury (2007: 58) describes a BATNA, or what he also refers to as a Plan B, as the best course of action to protect your interests in the event that you cannot reach agreement with the other side. Thompson (2005) pointed out that a BATNA is a fact of life rather than something that a negotiator wishes for. This is because negotiations can and do fail, and when this occurs a party with no BATNA may find itself in serious difficulties. The BATNA comes into operation at various stages (see Figure 13.1).

Two aspects of the BATNA are important. First, the opposing side may attempt to moderate your perceptions of your BATNA in a negative fashion. In other words, they may attempt to persuade you that in fact your BATNA is actually worse than you had thought. It is therefore important to work out your BATNA carefully and object-ively, and not to deviate from your belief in this whatever the counter-arguments. Second, you should attempt to ascertain what the other side's BATNA is, and be aware that they may not tell the truth about this. However, in one interesting study, Paese and

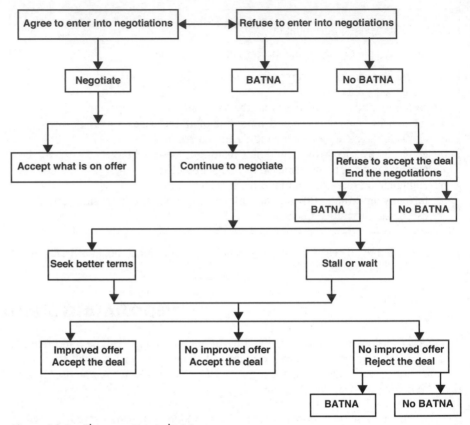

Figure 13.1 The negotiation decision tree

Gilin (2000) found that when one side disclosed their BATNA early in the negotiations, this actually reduced the demands and increased the truthfulness of the other. It would seem that in this instance the act of one party stating what their position was if the negotiations failed provided the impetus for the other side to try to reach an acceptable settlement.

If negotiation begins, it may be either a short or long process, depending upon how things progress. Indeed, 'time-outs' are often an important part of the scenario, where both sides leave to consult privately with relevant colleagues. These time-outs can be very useful to provide each side with the time, space and distance to take a 'helicopter view' of what is happening. To adapt a well-known analogy, during time-outs the solidity of the wood on offer can be separated from the shape of the trees surrounding the deal.

Another possibility is that of stalling, during which one side may engage in *avoidance negotiation*, which is defined as 'an effort to defeat negotiation by mimicking its purpose' (Wallihan, 1998: 267). This may be part of what is an overall avoidance strategy, where one side withdraws from any active engagement in negotiation (Taylor, 2002). However, it can also take the form of *demand avoidance* where one side prefers the status quo but is under pressure to be 'seen' to be negotiating.

It may also be part of *opportunistic avoidance* where eventual agreement is not ruled out, but one side knows that a delay in reaching settlement is to their benefit. For example, a strike may be costing a factory owner dearly, and so by holding up negotiations the union could get a better eventual deal for its members. Wallihan illustrated how nations, before they declare war on their neighbours, need to be seen to have 'tried to reason' with them, and so negotiate for a time before declaring them to be 'intransigent', 'aggressive' or 'insulting'.

In essence, there are four main strategies that can be employed during negotiations (Hargie *et al.*, 2004):

1 **Unilateral concession.** Using this strategy, one side simply yields to the demands of the other. Bingham (2007: 113) aptly summarised the advantage and disadvantages of just giving in: 'This strategy makes sense if you may be wrong, if you are in a weak position, if you want something in the future, and if you want to preserve the relationship. However, it may be a mistake if you believe you are right, the issue is important, and the other is unethical.' In general, however, it is not a viable long-term strategy and where it happens the loser can feel rather aggrieved and resentful at the outcome. Weitzman and Weitzman (2000) speculated that suppressed anger held on to after such experiences of poorly resolved conflict could even increase morbidity over the long term.

2 **Individual gain.** Here, one party is interested only in how best to maximise its share, with no thought whatsoever for the other side. There is no concern as to whether others do well or badly, just an all-encompassing focus upon self. In one-off negotiations this may work, but the other side will feel alienated, and if further negotiations are required then this approach may well backfire.

3 **Competition.** This usually occurs in what is known as *distributive bargaining* where both parties attempt to obtain a higher share of the distribution of benefits than the other. Competition is also more likely in *zero-sum* payoff situations, so called because the total sum involved in the negotiation equals zero and a gain to one person is a direct loss to the other. For example, if I offer to sell you my watch for €80 and you will only give me €60 then if I accept, you have benefited by €20 and I have lost by the same amount. As a result, this is also referred to as *win–lose* negotiation. It is, of course, possible to reach a compromise by finding some common ground between the initial offers through distributive bargaining – for example in agreeing to split the difference at a price of €70 for the watch. A danger with competition is that the whole negotiation edifice may collapse if neither side is willing to concede what they perceive to be defeat (or surrender), and so it becomes *lose–lose* negotiation. As Lax and Sebenius (2006: 8) concluded: 'The aggressive win-lose negotiator gets a better deal some of the time. But he or she may damage relationships in the process, may overlook more creative agreements, and may even precipitate a deadlock, thereby causing promising discussions to break down.'

4 **Cooperation.** In this strategy, negotiation is viewed as a form of problem-solving exercise, with the goal of achieving the best possible deal for both sides. Here the emphasis is upon *integrative bargaining*, in the context of a *variable-sum* payoff in which both sides can benefit from the deal. This transforms the negotiation into a *win–win* encounter, or what is known as a *mutual gains*

approach (Movius *et al.*, 2006). Unlike distributive bargaining where the focus is upon how to 'cut up the cake' with each intent upon getting the bigger share (or even the whole lot), the possibility of both producing a bigger cake is acknowledged when cooperation is countenanced. Gatchalian (1998) discussed how this approach can be used constructively in labour relations disputes. There is also evidence that females prefer a cooperative strategy and may do less well than males when negotiating in competitive or distributive encounters (Solnick, 2001; Niederle and Vesterlund, 2008). Conditions favouring a win–win approach are outlined in Box 13.2. A word of caution is warranted, however, since someone who is very cooperative may experience internal pressures to compromise and so may be vulnerable to manipulation by a competitive and deceptive opponent (Murray, 1990). Also, effective negotiators are able to employ cooperative and competitive behaviours at different points within a negotiation. This is important since negotiators have both to 'cooperate to ensure that the supply of resources available for exchange is as large as possible and to compete to ensure that they are able to claim an acceptable share of these resources for themselves' (Neale and Fragale, 2006: 32).

Four possible outcomes can emanate from these negotiating strategies.

1   There may simply be *no agreement* and negotiation breaks down.
2   There may be a *victory for one side over the other*. In negotiation parlance, *Pareto superior* agreements occur when the outcome offers benefits to one party without incurring losses for the other. *Pareto inferior* agreements occur when one side ends up worse off while the other does not gain any benefit (Jeffries and Reed, 2000).
3   A *compromise solution* connecting the two offers may be agreed.
4   An *integrative agreement* can occur in which both sides achieve higher joint benefits than in the compromise. Such *Pareto optimal* agreements occur where

---

Box 13.2 The seven rules for win–win negotiations

1   Have a main goal of achieving an outcome that maximises the outcome *for both sides*.
2   Do not view negotiation as simply getting the best for oneself. Likewise, do not see it as a contest in which you have to beat the other side. These strategies are likely to result in conflict and lessen the benefits for everyone.
3   Remain flexible and do not adopt an entrenched position. Remember there are many routes to Success City in negotiations.
4   Develop a good relationship with the other party, founded on mutual trust.
5   Foster the capacity to distinguish the people from the problem – overcoming the latter should be seen as a joint venture.
6   Investigate the needs that may be driving demands – often demands can be adapted in ways that still satisfy the underlying needs.
7   Approach the task on the basis of logic and reason, rather than being swept along on a tide of emotion.

both sides achieve the best possible gains and the benefits to one side cannot be improved without reducing the gains to the other.

A widely used, if somewhat contrived, example that illustrates the difference between these approaches is that of two sisters arguing over who should have an orange. If negotiation breaks down, neither gets the orange. In unilateral concession, one sister would just give the orange to the other, and in the individual gain approach, one sister would try to get the entire orange. In the competitive strategy, a compromise could be reached whereby they agree to divide it in half and distribute the halves equally. However, using the cooperative mode, following discussion they discover that one sister wants the orange to squeeze for juice, while the other just wants the peel for a cake she is baking. As a result, they reach an integrative agreement where one sister gets all of the peel and the other gets all of the juice. Both benefit more than in any of the other styles. A more realistic example would be where a salesperson offers a retail buyer a new product on trial at €50 per unit for 100 units. The buyer in return initially offers €40 per unit. In relation to the above four strategies:

1   Negotiation may break down and no sale is made.
2   The seller agrees to sell for €40, or the buyer agrees to pay the €50.
3   They split the difference at a price of €45.
4   They work out a new deal wherein the retail chain agrees to take not just 100 but 10,000 units of the new product over a set period, if a price of €40 is accepted. In other words, both sides benefit.

Pruitt (1990) highlighted three main reasons why integrative agreements are the most effective negotiating outcome.

1   They are likely to be more stable, whereas compromises are often unsatisfactory to one or both parties, leading to issues not being fully resolved and thus resurfacing in the future.
2   Since they are mutually beneficial, they help to develop the relationship between the two parties. This, in turn, facilitates communication and problem solving in later encounters. An important feature in negotiation is what is known as the *response-in-kind* (Weingart *et al.*, 1999). This refers to the norm of reciprocity, whereby if we receive something positive from another person we feel obliged to reciprocate by giving something positive back (see Chapter 12 for more information on reciprocation). Alternatively, if we receive negative feedback from others we are likely to return it in kind. Integrative behaviour is likely to beget integrative responses from the other side. As Watkins (2006: 11) cautioned: 'Driving deals that are too favourable for you can leave counterparts bitter, disinclined to energetically implement agreements, and looking for payback next time.'
3   Where aspirations are high and both sides are loath to concede, compromise may simply not be possible and an integrative approach, which allows both sides to gain, will be the best solution.

STAGES IN THE NEGOTIATION PROCESS

Negotiations have been conceptualised as typically progressing through and characterised by a series of sequential stages. The five key sequential negotiation stages are as follows:

1   pre-negotiation
2   opening
3   exploration
4   bargaining
5   settlement.

Each of these will now be explored in turn.

The pre-negotiation stage

Before people meet face to face, time and effort should be devoted to preparing for the encounter. Time devoted to planning is time very well spent, so negotiators should never short-change themselves on making ready. Indeed, preparation is often regarded as the most important part of negotiation (Simons and Tripp, 2007). Thus, Cairns (1996: 64), citing the maxim 'Failing to prepare is preparing to fail', cautioned negotiators to 'ignore it at their cost'. In fact, where the negotiation is particularly important it can be useful to have a simulation or rehearsal of the entire process, where some members play the role of the opposition. Rackham (2007) investigated differences in the planning strategies of skilled and average negotiators. As well as interviewing negotiators about their planning techniques, real planning sessions were observed and recorded. There were actually no differences in amount of planning time per se. Rather, it was what they did with the time that mattered. Skilled negotiators considered a much wider range of possible outcomes and options – 5.1 per issue as opposed to 2.6 for average negotiators – and gave over three times as much attention to areas of common ground.

The main aspects of the planning stage have been shown to be goals, the key issues involved in goal achievement and ways of surmounting any obstacles (Roloff and Jordan, 1992). The key dimensions of the pre-negotiation stage are now examined in more detail.

Formulating realistic goals

To adapt an old maxim: 'If you don't know where you are going, how will you know what direction to take and whether you have arrived?' Before entering into negotiations it is essential to be fully aware in advance as to what exactly your goals are. Indeed, as shown in Figure 13.1, the first decision to be made is whether or not to enter into negotiations at all. For example, the other side may be seen to be completely inflexible and impossible to deal with, your demands may simply not be negotiable, or the goals may be achievable in some other way. If negotiation seems the best option, the next issue to be decided is with which party it is most appropriate to deal. Once this has been worked out, then the serious business of planning really begins. This encompasses making decisions about three main aspects of the process:

1   Formulate your *resistance point*. This is the bottom line beyond which you decide that a deal will not be done. It has also been termed the *reservation price* (Carnevale and Pruitt, 1992) and the *minimum necessary share* (Morley, 2006). It is also sometimes called the 'walk-away' point, for obvious reasons.

2   Decide upon your *target point* or *target range*. This is also known as the *aspiration level* (Whitney, 1990). It is the ideal point that you hope to achieve. Here, the goal of negotiation may be viewed in terms of achieving an exact amount (target point), or as settling somewhere between an upper and lower limit (target range). Rackham (2007) found that skilled negotiators were significantly more likely to plan in terms of a *settlement range* (e.g. 'I'd like €30 per item but would settle for €26 minimum.'), whereas average negotiators planned around a fixed *point* (e.g. 'I want to get €28 per item.'). It has also been shown that negotiators obtain better results if they focus their efforts upon achieving their target point rather than concentrating upon not going below their resistance point (Galinsky *et al.*, 2002). Some research has found that males tend to set higher target points than females, and so achieve higher gains. One suggested reason for this is that women may moderate material benefits to ensure positive relational outcomes (Kray and Babcock, 2006). There is also some evidence that norms and expectations of gender behaviour may make negotiation more difficult for females – women who negotiate assertively can be negatively labelled by males (e.g. as 'ball breakers') (Babcock and Laschever, 2008). Similarly, females who make higher demands tend to be evaluated more negatively than males who negotiate at the same level (Bowles *et al.*, 2007).

3   Work out precisely what your *BATNA* is. As explained earlier, this is the Best Alternative to a Negotiated Agreement. Formulating a BATNA can help to clarify what your resistance point should actually be. If a settlement is not reached at or above this point, is no agreement then definitely the best option? What exactly are the ramifications of this?

It is important to remember that the other party has target and resistance points. Deals will be struck somewhere between the two sets of resistance points, and so this is known as the settlement range. It is also referred to as the Zone of Possible Agreement (ZOPA; Lax and Sebenius, 2006). If there is no ZOPA, in that these resistance points are hopelessly far apart, then negotiations will break down. In the example given in Figure 13.2, the buyer would ideally wish to purchase at a target price of €550, whereas the seller's ideal price is €650. The respective resistance points, which represent the worst deals for each side, are €600 for the buyer and €500 for the seller, and so this is the ZOPA within which any eventual settlement will occur. One of the first things an experienced negotiator attempts to do is to ascertain the target and resistance points of the other side, so a deal can be made that is closer to the opponent's resistance point.

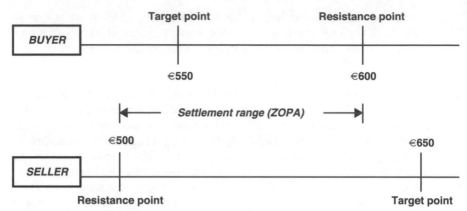

Figure 13.2 Example of target and resistance points in negotiation

Identifying key issues

When examining issues, a guiding principle is to be as flexible and open as possible. Try not to conceptualise the process as a single issue debate. Think laterally to identify everything that might be important. Negotiators have been shown to differ in their degree of self-monitoring. High self-monitors are more occupied with situational norms, the impression they create and how they are being reacted to by others. They then adjust their performance accordingly. Low self-monitors are guided in their behaviour to a greater extent by internal states. Jordan and Roloff (1997), in an analysis of written pre-negotiation plans, discovered that those of high self-monitors were not only more elaborate than low self-monitors, but also that this type of negotiator subsequently achieved a higher percentage of their initial profit goals.

Issues vary widely depending upon the context. For example, in an industrial purchasing negotiation they may include aspects such as unit costs, quality of product, guarantees, payment terms and related financing, delivery dates and costs, insurance, installation costs, buy-back agreements and penalty clauses for missed deadlines. Once the main issues have been identified, they should then be prioritised. Which are absolutely essential and which are more peripheral? How, in what ways and to what extent are issues linked? In essence, as much information as possible should be gathered about all aspects of the negotiation. For each issue identified, the target, resistance and satisfaction points should also be located. This serves to guide later behaviour as negotiations get under way. While plans may be altered somewhat during the course of negotiations, generally speaking good preparation leads to better outcomes. As Hargie *et al.* (2004: 189) put it: 'It is impossible to be too well informed approaching a negotiation.'

Gathering information

Forewarned is definitely forearmed when negotiating. Indeed, large corporations go to great lengths to protect key information from competitors, while some have also been known to use various forms of espionage to ascertain such information from others. It is vital that all members are fully apprised of their own team's perspectives on all of the key issues. The arguments in favour, and likely counter-arguments and how these can be overcome, should all be worked out in advance. Metaplanning is also important, in that Party A should try to see the planning world through the eyes of Party B. It is useful to consider realistically how much they know about your position. Do they have an accurate picture of your true BATNA? Similarly, as much information as possible should be gleaned about the other side's likely position on each issue. As advised by Davies (1998: 128): 'You need to know as much as you can about your opposite number: who they are, what they want, how they are likely to act and react.' For example, what is their BATNA and what are the ramifications thereof for both parties? In addition to the issues per se, it is also useful to know something about the interactive style of the other party. Do they tend to play hardball or are they likely to be more cooperative?

This process of information gathering allows areas of potential agreement and conflict to be formulated. Staking out common ground shared by both sides is always important. This enables the negotiation to be built upon a solid foundation of early joint agreement. However, likely areas of disagreement should also be identified, together with possible proposals for overcoming them. This includes an analysis of what and how much you can concede, and what concessions you may realistically seek from the other side in return.

Deciding upon the type of negotiation to pursue

The next phase of the pre-negotiation considerations is the decision about how to 'play' the negotiation. As mentioned in relation to strategies to pursue, one option is to view the other side as the enemy, to be engaged in a win–lose macho battle of might in which the purpose is to defeat them in the war of attrition that is negotiation. An alternative is to perceive the activity as a collaborative win–win venture in which the goal is to cooperate so as to achieve the optimum outcome for both sides. The latter strategy has been widely recommended for most negotiating situations (Thompson, 2005). It does not benefit either side to become embroiled in a battle of wits and wills, during which they may at best lose potential gains and at worst be damaged or destroyed (Lax and Sebenius, 2006). That said, Shapiro (2000), in recommending the more constructive approach, also highlighted the often short-sighted and unnecessary predilection towards 'hard' bargaining in many sections of society. Conditions that promote collaborative negotiations include being involved with the other side in a long-term negotiating relationship and trusting them not to take advantage of one's willingness to cooperate.

Cultural background is also a factor here, since it can affect how negotiators conceptualise the process and behave during actual negotiations (Gelfand and Brett, 2004; Morrison and Conaway, 2006; Alon and Brett, 2007). Salacuse (1998), in an investigation involving 310 negotiators from North America, Latin America and Europe, across professions such as law, engineering, accounting, the military, teaching and marketing, identified a range of factors that are affected by culture (see Box 13.3).

Box 13.3 Variations in negotiations across cultures

Factor	Cultural response range	
Communication style	Indirect	Direct
Aspirations	Individualist	Collectivist
Protocol	Informal	Formal
Goal	Task	Relationship
Negotiator selection	Experience/ability	Status/position
Attitude to negotiation	Win–win	Win–lose
Persuasion preference	Logic/reason	Affective/emotional
Attitude to time	High/clock-driven	Low/events-driven
Team structure	Consensus	Leader dominated
Risk taking	High/risk tolerant	Low/risk averse
Nature of agreements	Explicit	Implicit

Some studies have found that the Japanese are much more amenable to win–win encounters than are the Russians (LePoole, 1991), and more likely to adapt tactics in line with the other party when involved in intercultural integrative negotiations (Adair *et al.*, 2001). However, Salacuse (1998) also found that professional and occupational culture was as important in determining negotiation behaviour as was national culture. Similarly, Metcalf *et al.* (2007), in a study of 1000 business people across four countries (Finland, Turkey, USA, Mexico), found considerable similarities in negotiation styles across countries, and also differences in approach between negotiators from the same country. They concluded that rather than depending upon pre-set cultural stereotypes, negotiators should take cognisance of the individual attitudes of the other party. A similar conclusion was reached by Movius *et al.* (2006: 390) in their detailed investigation of cultural differences in negotiation:

> It is a mistake to assume that all individuals from a culture have the same personality or background . . . and it is also a mistake to ascribe difficulties or uncertainties that emerge during negotiations to 'the unique culture' of a given country.

Formulating an agenda

Following on from the above considerations, a proposed agenda for the negotiation can be drawn up to include the items that you wish to discuss and the preferred order. Of course, the other side will have its own ideas about what should be discussed and when. Indeed, agreeing an agenda may form the first part of negotiations – what is sometimes referred to as 'talks about talks'. Where possible, the idea is to collaborate on and jointly agree the agenda, as this sets the tone for the substantive business to follow (Mattock and Ehrenborg, 1996). As part of this, general rules about the process should also be clarified. An important element here may be the actual location for the negotiations. In some settings this may not be a problem – for example, in sales negotiations the salesperson usually visits the buyer. There is an advantage to negoti-ating on your own 'home ground' where you will tend to feel more relaxed and the opposition may be less settled (Mills, 1991). However, there can also be benefits in visiting the other person's patch to gain some insight into where they are coming from (e.g their status in the organisation and the nature of the operation per se). Negotiations may, of course, take place at a neutral location so that neither side feels disadvantaged. This is often the case in political negotiations, where much of the dispute is about territory.

Flexibility is important in relation to how issues are to be addressed. Rackham (2007) found that average negotiators tended to use sequence planning where each issue had to be dealt with in turn (i.e. Issue 1 → Issue 2 → Issue 3 → Issue 4). The problem is that the other side may wish to discuss Issue 4 first. More successful negotiators therefore simply planned in terms of issues, which they would then be willing to discuss in any order. The term *monochronicity* refers to the tendency to deal with information one issue at a time, while *polychronicity* relates to the capacity to deal with many different issues simultaneously (Turner and Reinsch, 2007). Brett *et al.* (1998) found that negotiators high in polychronicity were more effective. In their study of simulated negotiation encounters they discovered that joint gains (win–win encounters) were influenced by three key factors: 'a value for information sharing, an ability to deal with multiple issues simultaneously, and the motivation to keep on improving the option on the table' (p. 78).

Planning for settlement

Settlement details can often be forgotten about during the heat of negotiations. The pressure to reach a deal may lead to an unrealistic agreement – one that cannot be implemented – being finalised. There is no point in reaching an unworkable settle-ment, and so part of the preparatory phase should include an analysis of the extent to which a desired deal will actually work in practice. As part of this phase, thought should be given to how the settlement will be documented, ratified and implemented. For example, who has the authority to sign the agreement, and do they also have the power to make it stick? Who are the real key players who must be persuaded that the deal is beneficial for them?

Having said all of the above about the importance of preparation, flexibility must be the key as things do not always go according to plan. Indeed, Wilson *et al.* (2001: 305) described the negotiation as 'a complex planning environment'. It may sometimes be necessary to formulate multiple goals in circumstances where there are only fuzzy criteria for ordering priorities. Again, while pre-planning is essential, initial decisions typically have to be revisited and revised when the negotiation gets under way.

The opening stage

Here the parties meet face to face. As discussed in Chapter 10, the opening phase of any interaction is of key importance, and negotiation is no exception. During the initial meeting, decisions are made about how cooperative or competitive the other party is likely to be, and whether the social relationship will be conducive to the task in hand. As the ideal is the development of a win–win framework, the general advice here is to be cooperative and courteous, but also well organised (Scott, 1988). A significant finding is that negotiators often reciprocate each other's use of strategies and tactics (Brett *et al.*, 1998). This process, where the approach adopted by one side causes the other to reciprocate, is known as *entrainment*, and it has been shown to be a valuable negotiating tactic (Taylor, 2002). Thus, if one party seems frosty and adopts a rather belligerent opening stance, it is likely that the other will follow suit; threats will provoke counter-threats, demands counter-demands and so on. On the other hand, a more integrative, cooperative and amenable approach is also likely to be responded to in kind (Weingart *et al.*, 1999).

The first main substantive step is usually that of agreeing an agenda. This sets the tone for what is to follow, and so should be enacted in a non-confrontational manner and in a spirit of partnership. This can be facilitated by the use of 'We' language to indicate joint responsibility for the process (e.g. 'We seem to agree that our main joint concerns are . . .'). Ideally the negotiation environment should be warm, comfortable and free from distractions. The location should allow for both formal and informal encounters between parties, and space should be set aside for participants to mingle over coffee and biscuits. Berry (1996) identified a number of factors as being central to the establishment of a good negotiating rapport:

- paying attention to and allowing time for opening rituals such as personal introductions
- verbally and nonverbally displaying signs of receptivity and enthusiasm
- ascertaining what issues the other side regards as important and giving recognition to these
- portraying any identified difficulties as problems to be solved jointly
- avoiding point scoring or cheap one-upmanship ploys to gain an early advantage; these can backfire and cause problems for the entire relationship.

The final act of the opening phase is usually the ratification of an agreed agenda, endorsed by all those present. At this point the negotiation can proceed into the exploration phase.

The exploration stage

Here, parties begin to examine one another's positions. This allows each side to become familiar with the main proposals being put forward by the other. If these are in complete symmetry and harmony, then an agreement may be possible without further negotiation. If there are areas of disagreement, then these should be fully identified and clarified. Party A can only hope to satisfy the demands of Party B, and vice versa, if they know exactly what these are. As mentioned earlier, the opposition may not be completely truthful about their position, and cognisance should be taken of this in evaluating their proposals. For example, if they say they need 100 units of X, it may be the case that their true target point is closer to 90 units.

An important aspect at this stage is probing in depth beyond the expressed surface level demands to explore the needs that may underpin these. What each say they *want* is not always what they really *need* and following concerted discussion and sharing of perspectives this often becomes clear. In addition, the needs may be capable of being met in ways other than expressed in the initial demands. But this realisation usually takes some time and so the exploration stage should not be rushed. Indeed, later breakdowns in the negotiation process can often be traced back to a lack of time devoted to initial exploration and clarification of demands, needs and wants.

The goal here is to achieve a panoramic view of the other side and chart the full topography of their needs terrain. The contours of the peaceful valleys where areas of agreement lie, and of the rugged hills of dispute that will have to be climbed, should then be carefully drawn. In addition, ways in which both sides can help one another to climb these hills should also be identified. It is important to remember that the purpose is not to begin bargaining at this juncture. The main goal relates to the exploration and clarification of core areas of each other's position. It has been shown that an in-depth understanding of the precise nature of the outcome gains that can be made by the other side, rather than just an awareness of their interests, leads to more effective negotiation (Moran and Ritov, 2007). Central to all of this is the skill of listening (Finnegan and Hackley, 2008). As explained in Chapter 7, this involves paying attention to the other person's verbal and nonverbal messages, to the slant or emphasis they put on what they say, as well as listening to what is not being said. In her analysis of hostage situations, Dunne (2001: 15) pointed out: 'The best negotiators are good listeners who handle stress well and are able to argue logically and calmly.' If the auguries are good following exploration, then the parties can move on to the next stage, that of bargaining.

The bargaining stage

Once a decision has been made to move from initial explorations to more substantive bargaining, two main processes come into play: making proposals and concession making.

Making proposals

The opening proposals must be clearly stated. Both parties should fully understand precisely what the other is proposing. The generally accepted rule here is that the initial proposal should be high (if you are selling) or low (if buying), but realistically so. For instance, if you apply for a job where the salary is negotiable and you learn that the average executive in a similar post earns €120,000, it would be inappropriate to ask for a starting salary of €400,000. Initial bids should not be so high or low that they appear to be lacking in credibility, are seen as nonsensical, or the person making them is regarded as highly avaricious. Outrageous opening proposals can quickly lead to a 'take it or leave it' position and negotiation breakdown (Gatchalian, 2000). The first offer should also be stated in a confident manner. If a high/low bid is made in an apologetic fashion it is immediately undermined. It is important to avoid 'one-down' statements such as 'I think this is probably far too much to ask for, but . . .'. Realistically high/low opening gambits presented in an assertive fashion serve a number of important functions:

- They influence the opposition's estimate of your target and resistance points and can in turn move their target point more favourably in your direction.
- They provide information about the other side's goals. Careful scrutiny of their reaction allows insight into their target and resistance points (do they seem stunned at one end of the reaction scale or completely unsurprised at the other?).
- They allow 'generous' concessions to be made if necessary.
- They make the eventual settlement, with your concessions, appear more appealing to the other side.

There can be benefits in linking proposals to other conditions. For example, 'We are prepared to accept your offer of €120 per unit if you agree to take at least 10,000 units.' Such proposals are typical in integrative bargaining encounters.

Another decision here is whether or not to make the first proposal. Is it better to get in first or to play a waiting game so that your bid can take advantage of the knowledge gleaned from the other side's opening shot? It seems that there are advantages and disadvantages in both strategies, so a decision about this issue needs to be based on the specific nature of the negotiation. The advantages are that the side that goes first:

- is proactive, and the second party then becomes reactive and may be more on the defensive
- sets the initial rate – there is evidence from distributive negotiation that if the seller makes the initial offer, the settlement price is higher than if the buyer makes the initial offer (Magee *et al.*, 2007)
- can make the other side revise their target point in the light of the initial demand – studies show that the other side may 'anchor' around the level of the opening offer and fail to moderate their counterproposal back towards their own target; the eventual settlement is then more favourable for the party making the first proposal (Carnevale and De Dreu, 2006).

Some of the disadvantages, on the other hand, are that the side that opens may:

- not bid at a sufficiently high (or low) level and so be at an immediate disadvantage
- be put on the defensive by the other party if they begin to probe the initial offer
- have to make the first concession after the other party has made a counterproposal.

Concession making

When both sides have made their opening pitches, the process moves on to one of trying to formulate mutually acceptable compromises in which each party moves towards the other's position. Positional bargaining has been described by Fisher and Ury (1981) as happening when each side adopts its own position and argues for this, but also makes concessions in order to secure a compromise. A concession is a change in the level of demand made by Party A in the direction of Party B's interests that reduces the level of benefit for A (Hargie *et al.*, 2004). Concessions lead to *position loss*, which can be interpreted as a willingness to compromise and be cooperative. However, if too many are conceded too quickly this can result in *image loss* where the person is viewed as someone weak and easily manipulated. Interestingly, Morris *et al.* (1999) discovered that negotiators often attribute the bargaining behaviour of the other party to personality and personal predispositions (e.g. disagreeableness, truculence) rather than to the circumstances of the negotiation with which they are confronted. Such misperception can evoke a more hostile response, if a lack of willingness to compromise is attributed to the other party being seen as an obstinate or greedy individual, as opposed to being interpreted as due to the fact that the organisation to which the person belongs has given strict guidelines about what can and cannot be negotiated.

A core dimension of negotiation is the ability to persuade the opposition to make concessions. Pruitt (1981) identified four main tactics in this regard:

1   ***Promote a friendly atmosphere.*** The goal here is to develop a friendly relationship between bargainers that is conducive to 'give and take'. Friends will not want the negotiation to spoil or destroy their relationship and so are willing to forgo economic benefits so as to reduce conflict and possible negative relational outcomes (McGinn, 2006). For example, Halpern (1994) found that buyers offered higher opening amounts and sellers made lower initial demands when dealing with friends as opposed to strangers. Interestingly, this bias to cooperate can have a downside. Friends can actually lose out on a better deal for both sides, owing to the fact that they wish to avoid the appearance of being awkward. A relational bias towards affiliation means they are liable to settle for the first mutually acceptable solution to emerge, when more debate and discussion about all the alternatives might have produced a higher, Pareto optimal result (Jeffries and Reed, 2000).

2   ***Impose time pressures.*** This is a common tactic used in attempts to influence others. For example, companies offer bargain discount rates – but only for a set time period; time-share salespeople offer a 'special price' which will be withdrawn if the prospective buyer leaves without signing a contract; and in hostage negotiation, threats may be made to execute hostages at a set time if demands are not met.

3   ***Increase the impression of firmness.*** This may involve making small concessions but few of them as a way of seeking reciprocal concessions from the other side. Firmness can be enhanced through emphasising that there are specific reasons for the concessions such as:

- *emphasising that this is a one-off event* ('Just this once and just for you – do not tell anyone else I gave you it at this price.')
- *stating that the concession is based on special circumstances* ('There is a new model coming in next month so I want to sell off this one.')
- *seeking a reciprocal concession* ('I'll increase my offer for the house if you include the carpets in the price.'). This latter tactic may involve *logrolling* – that is, trading off pairs of issues that differ in importance to both parties. For example, a car dealer may agree to install a sound system (at small personal cost) rather than reduce the price of the car, while the customer values this service and sees it as adequate compensation for no price reduction. Experienced negotiators have been shown to use logrolling more often and more effectively than novice negotiators (Loewenstein and Thompson, 2006).

4   ***Reduce the opponent's resistance*** to making concessions by using a range of techniques including:

- *face-saving devices* that make it easier for the other side to concede without appearing to lose or be weak. This can involve some of the techniques discussed in (3) above in relation to perceptions of firmness (e.g. explaining that you understand the concession will only be 'one-off'). This is important since 'Sensitivity to the other side's face does more than head off resistance: it lays the groundwork for trust' (Kolb and Williams, 2007: 211).
- *being optimistic.* In a series of experiments, Bottom and Paese (1999) found that when bargainers were optimistic going into a negotiation and believed that their counterpart had considerable latitude for concession, they tended to come out with a more profitable deal compared to those who had actually a more accurate view of the situation.
- *logical arguments* (see Chapter 12 for a full review of how such arguments can be persuasive).
- *a promise of beneficial outcomes* (e.g. a head of a university department may argue that if more staff were allocated to the department the research profile would improve, in turn bringing in more money and greater prestige for the university). Kennedy (1998) termed this tactic 'sell cheap, get famous', a title derived from the entertainment industry where actors reputedly may be persuaded to lower their fee on the promise that the film will make them famous and open the door to untold fame and fortune.
- *highlighting the disadvantages* that would befall the other party were the deal to fall through.
- *reference to objective criteria* (e.g. a trade union may refer to the average percentage pay rise for comparable workers that year).
- *'salami slicing'.* This is so called on the basis that if you request a whole salami from someone they may well refuse. However, if you ask for just one slice you are more likely to succeed. If you keep getting more small slices you end up with most of the salami.
- *'good person/bad person'.* This is obviously a variant of the soft cop/hard cop routine. Here, one negotiator plays the role of the tough cookie while

the other is much more amenable and affiliative. The 'good' negotiator may argue openly with the 'bad' one to give the other side a break. When used skilfully this can encourage the other party to seek to cut a deal with the 'good' person. Sometimes the 'bad person' is a difficult third party outwith the immediate encounter ('My boss would sack me if I accepted this offer.').

- *indicating the need to refer to a higher authority*. The other party will sometimes concede when confronted with a situation in which a negotiator claims not to have the authority to accept the present offer, but were it to be changed ever so slightly the deal could be agreed then and there.

- *use of threats*. These, however, are not usually recommended since they are invariably viewed as hostile and are dysfunctional for the relationship between the two parties (Putnam and Roloff, 1992). The threatened side is likely to counter with threats of equal force; will not be committed to any settlement achieved; and will feel resentful, attempting to seek revenge where possible. Research findings clearly show that threats are associated with less successful outcomes (Olekalns and Smith, 2001). As Fisher (2001: 77) put it: 'Making threats is a particularly expensive and dangerous way of trying to exert influence.' For example, in 1997 the then chief executive of British Airways (BA) sent a letter to cabin crews involved in an industrial dispute with the company. In it he threatened that anyone who went on strike risked being sacked. As a result some 2000 staff simply called in sick instead, disrupting the airline's schedule at a huge financial cost to BA. If threats are used these should be portrayed as emanating from a third party ('There is no way my union members would accept that. If I go back and put it to them I know they will want to go on strike.').

- *fait accompli*. Under certain conditions a pre-emptive strike may force the other side's hand. Terrorists may set off a large bomb explosion so that they are then seen to be negotiating from a position of strength (with the threat potential of further such bombs also ever-present). A spouse may buy a new dining-room suite and have it delivered arguing that it can be sent back within ten days if the partner so desires.

- *use of power*. People who control resources have been found to have a definite advantage in negotiations (Cai *et al.*, 2001; Magee *et al.*, 2007). This is because 'powerful negotiators tend to end up with the larger share of the pie' (Van Kleef *et al.*, 2006: 559). An extreme example is that a shop-owner is unlikely to cede to a polite request to give all the money in the cash register to a stranger, whereas if the stranger is wielding a handgun then the request is likely to be granted. In this case the gun represents greater power. Imbalances of power have a marked influence upon negotiating encounters in that those who have power will tend to use it and so be less open to making concessions or listening to counter-arguments. Thus, Kipnis and Schmidt (1990: 49) found: 'The more one-sided the power relationship at work, the more likely managers are to demand, get angry and insist with people who work for them, and the more likely they are to act humble and flatter when they are persuading their bosses.' However, it is hardly surprising that people are happier with the outcomes of bargaining encounters when both sides have equal power (Mastenbroek, 1989). People tend to be unhappy if they feel they have been 'forced' to reach a settlement. As pointed out by Korobkin (2007: 255): 'Before attempting to employ bargaining power, the negotiator must carefully compare the gains that might be achieved to the increased risk of impasse today and the costs of angering, alienating, or reducing trust among potential future trading partners.'

Garko (1992) carried out an investigation into the influencing strategies employed by physician executives (those carrying out managerial roles) when attempting to gain compliance from superiors. They found that with superiors who interacted in an attractive fashion (were attentive, friendly, relaxed), reason was used most frequently. On the other hand, with superiors who interacted in an unattractive style, assertiveness, bargaining, coalition formation with others and reference to higher authority were more likely to be used. Thus, it would seem that with people of higher power or status, the negotiating tactics of subordinates are influenced by the interactive approach of the former.

Concessions are an integral part of negotiations. Where differences exist, without concessions there can be no mutual agreement. It is important though that concession making is guided by the pointers shown in Box 13.4.

The settlement stage

Catching the settlement moment is a key aspect of negotiation. There comes a time when the other side is receptive and a deal can be struck. If this is missed, problems

---

Box 13.4 Pointers for making concessions

Bargainers should:

- not concede too readily
- make concessions as small as possible
- monitor the number and rate of concession making
- link concessions to an image of firmness.

Bargainers should not:

- concede too soon in the negotiations
- make the first main concession
- make unilateral concessions
- make large initial concessions – this is likely to give an impression of weakness
- concede without due consideration of the positive and negative consequences *for both parties*
- always engage in reciprocal concessions. A concession by the other side may be justified in its own right – it may bring their bid down to what is a reasonable level.

---

can arise. When a settlement attempt is made too early the other party can feel pressurised and resentful. Conversely, if the opportunity is missed, further issues may then be raised and more concessions sought by the opposition. The closing stage is important in all interactions (see Chapter 10), including negotiation. A number of central elements have been identified as being crucial to agreeing a settlement (e.g. Cairns, 1996; Kennedy, 1998) and these will now be considered.

Trial closure

Here, one side behaves as if a deal has been agreed and so is moving beyond this to the fine-grained implementation issues. It includes what are known as 'assumptive questions' where the assumption of a deal is inferred in the question (see Chapter 5). An example would be: 'Do you intend to pay by cheque or credit transfer?' Linked to this is what is termed 'summary closure'. This involves providing a summary of what the other side has gained in the way of concessions, what the benefits are for them of the deal as it stands, and outlining the potential dangers of failing to agree this deal.

Looking for settlement signals

Positive closure signals include the following:

- *implementation questions*: 'You could definitely deliver at that price?'
- *confirmatory statements*: 'That seems like a good deal.'
- *physical actions*: tidying up papers, bringing out a contract
- *nonverbal responses*: smiling, looking relaxed or excited, clasping the hands enthusiastically
- *overt settlement verbalisations*: 'Okay. Can we agree on this?', 'Right, let's get the paperwork sorted.'

The end of the line

At some stage there comes a point beyond which it is not possible to concede any further. The secret is to convince the opposition that in all honesty this point has been reached and any deal must be struck at this limit. In some cases negotiators may hold back a small concession to be conceded as a final inducement to settlement. One potential shortfall of this strategy, however, is that a reputation can be gained of always having something else to concede if the other side bargains long and hard enough.

Split the difference

This is quite common in sales negotiations as a way of cutting a deal. You offer €600, I ask for €550 and we finally settle for €575. It is fine in a basic one-off negotiation for a single item, but where issues are more complex it is not always applicable. In addition, if one side has already conceded a considerable amount and the other has conceded little, then the 'difference' is not just what is left.

Celebrate success

Both sides need to feel that the agreement has been a good one from their point of view. This cements the relationship and facilitates future encounters. It also helps to ensure that the deal will not unravel, but will actually be implemented. Celebrations may include smiles, handshakes and hugs, breaking open the bubbly or having a meal out together.

Document the agreement

Formal agreements are typically enshrined in a written legal contract although the actual drafting and signing may take place at a later date (Guirdham, 2002). Settlements that cannot be enforced are of little value. Likewise, pursuing disputes through the courts is an expensive and messy business. It is important, therefore, that all parties are agreed on the exact terms of the settlement. Time spent jointly reviewing and agreeing the precise nature of what has been negotiated can avoid substantial difficulties at a later date. For example, the ongoing confusions and uncertainties amongst political parties that plagued subsequent development in Northern Ireland in the aftermath of the Belfast Agreement can be traced back to areas of the settlement that were left (deliberately) vague. Thus, one party to this Agreement later used the interesting semantic argument that while what was negotiated was an (interim) *agreement* it was not a (final) *settlement* (of the political dispute). Paying attention to detail and ensuring that this is contained in the written documentation can pay dividends when it comes to implementing the resolution.

Implementation considerations

To negotiate an agreement that will later hit the buffers is merely to construct a future disagreement. But in more complex bargaining contexts, the devil is in the detail. For this reason, it is worth spending time discussing how, and in what ways the deal will actually be implemented in practice. Who will do what, when will it be done and how is it to be carried out? Also, what are the ramifications if what has been agreed is not implemented? What penalties and costs will be incurred by either side, and how are these to be included in the contract?

NEGOTIATING SKILLS

There is general agreement that negotiation is a higher-order skill involving a range of other subskills (Taylor, 2002; Kesting and Smolinski, 2007). As expressed by Lewicki (1997: 265): 'Effective negotiation is not a single skill; rather it is a complex collection of elements that entail aspects of strategizing, advocacy, communication, persuasion, and cognitive packaging and repackaging of information.' Similarly, McRae (1998: 2) likened negotiation to 'a symphony orchestra of skills. Each instrument (subskill) must be used together with all the others in a harmonious and congruent manner. If one instrument (subskill) is off, the whole orchestra will be off'.

While there is consensus in most texts about what good negotiators should do, and a host of laboratory studies have been conducted in this area, there is not a great deal of empirical research into the behaviour of negotiators in real encounters. The main reason for this is that conducting such research necessitates obtaining the agreement of both parties to the negotiation, and this is obviously difficult to arrange – especially given the delicate nature of such encounters. One major empirical study was carried out by Rackham and his co-workers (2007) in which they studied 48 successful negotiators over a total of 102 separate negotiating sessions, and compared their behaviour with that of a similar number of average negotiators. They used three criteria to select the effective negotiators, namely: they should be regarded as successful by both sides; they should have a consistent record of significant success over time; and they should have a low incidence of implementation failures – they should reach agreements that stick. They found that skilled negotiators showed significant differences to average negotiators on a range of behaviours. These and other key negotiating behaviours will now be reviewed.

Leadership

One feature of many professional negotiation encounters is that it is a group phenomenon. More than two people are involved. Indeed, even if only two individuals engage face to face, they will be reporting to and liaising with a range of members, colleagues and/or superiors in their organisation. This means that the skilled negotiator must have the capacity to organise and coordinate a group of individuals. Each group in a negotiation is rarely a homogeneous entity. Many groups suffer from divisions and disagreements between members. A minority may not concur with the majority view as to the way ahead. Intra-group disharmony has to be dealt with in such a way that it does not jeopardise the negotiation effort and outcomes. This means that care and attention need to be devoted to decisions about who is to be part of the overall team, and exactly who should be involved at the negotiating table (Wood, 2001). There should be a designated leader – someone who is a recognised content expert in the field within which the negotiation is taking place, and who also has successful experience of bargaining. This individual, who should have skills in consensus building, will then coordinate and direct the team effort in preparing for, conducting and evaluating the effectiveness of the bargaining encounters (see Chapter 14 for more information on leadership skills).

Empathising and problem solving

It is clear that the ability to be empathic is a characteristic of effective negotiators (Lax and Sebenius, 2006; Martinovski et al., 2007). The capacity to empathise by seeing the world through the eyes of the other person is very important. People are unlikely to readily accept your view of their situation, but rather need to be reassured that you appreciate their perspective. Thus, efforts should be made to understand where the other side is coming from, and to communicate this understanding overtly. It is said that in negotiation the cheapest (and often most warmly received) concession that you can make is to show that you are paying attention to what the other side is saying. You need to ascertain what their concerns are and why they have these. Why might they accept or reject your proposals? Linked to this, when presenting a proposal, skilled negotiators frame this as a problem to be solved. The golden rule is to 'present your proposals as solutions to problems. State the problem before you give your answer' (Morley, 2006: 413). Bald proposals are often seen as selfish moves and as the other side listens they formulate counter-arguments as a way of obstructing these. When cast as a joint problem with a suggested solution, the listening perspective changes and the encounter becomes more cooperative.

Controlling emotionality

While negotiation is often regarded as a logical process, emotions are an important part of the process (Carnevale and De Dreu, 2006; Martinovski, 2010). The most effective negotiators are those who, as well as being able to think logically, can also understand and control their emotions (Fisher and Shapiro, 2006). As shown by Adler *et al.* (1998), the two most intense emotions in negotiation are fear and anger. The former may be caused by anxieties such as the deal falling through, being told untruths, losing out unnecessarily or not achieving all that one should. The development of a good trusting relationship helps to reduce such fear-arousing thoughts. High levels of anger have been shown to be destructive to the negotiation process (Taylor, 2002), and so must be controlled. The expression of anger can be directed towards the offer (e.g. 'That offer is ridiculous.'), or can be targeted directly at the other person (e.g. 'You are being ridiculous.'). Where the anger is focused upon the offer, the other side is more likely to make larger concessions, but when it is directed at the person, the other side tends to concede less (Van Kleef *et al.*, 2008). Those who display anger also suffer a loss of image, in that the other person forms very negative impressions of them, expresses lower levels of satisfaction with the negotiation, and is loath to interact with them in the future (Van Kleef *et al.*, 2006). Anger can be caused by one side:

- being found to have given misleading or untrue information
- insisting on discussing unimportant details
- not listening to what the other has to say
- making unreasonable or excessive demands
- being rude or overtly aggressive
- querying the other person's ability or authority to negotiate
- overstepping their authority
- going over the other person's head to deal with their superior.

While expressing concern for the feelings of the other party is important in all negotiations, in crisis situations, where this dimension has been shown to be of particular import, 'detecting and controlling emotional arousal is one of the primary concerns of negotiators' (Rogan and Hammer, 1995: 554). As a result, in these contexts (e.g. suicide attempts, criminal barricades, hostage taking or prison revolts) the tactics used include:

- communicating empathy and concern for the other
- using an encouraging and agreeing style to calm the other person
- making appeals to the person ('Please, please do not hurt anyone.')
- giving frequent reassurance
- protecting and saving the perpetrator's face
- slowing the pace of negotiation
- emphasising that the interaction is one of problem solving (as opposed to crisis).

In third party dispute resolution work, emotion is also of importance, in the sense that the negotiator has to carefully manage the often strong feelings of participants. By the time a dispute reaches the stage of arbitration or mediation, the emotions of both sides are frequently already highly charged (Barry *et al.*, 2006). An important role of the negotiator in such disputes is to separate the substantive or cognitive issues of fact that separate the parties from the related affective issues that are the result of a damaged or dysfunctional relationship. For the mediator, an ability to empathise with the feelings of participants has been found to be related both to successful dispute resolution and to participant satisfaction (Zubek *et al.* 1992).

Rackham (2007) identified two negative emotional facets of negotiation that can be dysfunctional for the process, and so need to be curbed:

1 *Irritators.* As the name suggests, irritators are words or phrases used by one side that irritate, annoy or offend the other. Examples include:

   - 'unreasonable demand' (this is doubly irritating – the proposal may have been put forward as being perfectly reasonable, and the term 'demand' suggests aggression)
   - 'very fair offer' (again this is annoying as it is up to the other side to decide what is fair and what is not)
   - 'you are being unhelpful' (such an accusation is likely to cause problems for the relationship as it is an attack on the other party's interactive style).

   Rackham (2007) found that less skilled negotiators used about five times as many irritators as skilled ones. Often these irritators are used without too much conscious thought. When caught up in the emotional heat of the occasion, they can slip out. Thus, negotiators need to take care with their forms of expression. There is little point in describing an offer as a 'good deal' if the other side does not think it is.

2 *Defend/attack spirals.* This occurs when one side accuses or attacks the other and this is responded to in kind, leading to a spiral of retaliation with the result that emotions become heated and the entire relationship begins

425

to disintegrate. As summarised by Lytle *et al.* (1999: 32): 'The reality is that negotiations, especially in the dispute context, often become ugly and difficult . . . parties may find themselves drawn to respond to threats with counter-threats, escalating the negotiations to a standoff from which it is difficult or embarrassing to retreat.' For example:

A: You don't seem to want to resolve this, as you keep raising objections to every reasonable proposal we make. We may have to pull out of these talks.

B: On the contrary, you have done everything to prevent an agreement and we are the ones who have had to deal with your ridiculous demands. So don't try to threaten us, as we may be ahead of you out of the door.

A: You think that *we're* the problem? I don't believe I'm hearing this.

B: That's exactly been the problem. You just don't listen.

Given the potential relationship damage that can emanate from such encounters, not surprisingly Rackham (2007) found that skilled negotiators were significantly less likely to get entangled in emotional defend/attack spirals.

Building trust

Trust is at the heart of relationships, and negotiation is no exception. We rarely develop or maintain positive relationships with people of whom we are suspicious or wary. As shown by Alon and Brett (2007), the outcome of a negotiation is highly dependent on a relationship of trust. Trust has been defined as 'the extent to which a person is confident in, and willing to act on the basis of, the words, actions, and decisions of another' (McAllister, 1995: 25). It can be divided into three separate components (Jeffries and Reed, 2000):

- *Cognitive trust* refers to the extent to which we believe someone has sound technical know-how or a solid knowledge base.
- *Affective trust* is rooted in the degree of emotional feeling of attachment, and of mutual care and concern for one another's well-being, that exists.
- *Organisational trust* encompasses both intra-organisational (the extent to which staff trust others in their own organisation) and inter-organisational (the degree to which staff in two corporations trust one another) dimensions.

Where all three types of trust are present at high levels, negotiations are enhanced. The skill of self-disclosure is central to such relationship development and trust (see Chapter 9). Rackham (2007) termed this 'giving internal information'. His results showed that effective negotiators used this skill more than average negotiators, especially in relation to their feelings about the way the negotiation was progressing. He pointed out: 'This revelation may or may not be genuine, but it gives the other party a feeling of security because such things as motives appear to be explicit and aboveboard' (p. 180). As a result, the use of self-disclosure is likely to contribute to the establishment of trust in the negotiator. This technique can also serve as an alternative to disagreeing, for example:

- 'I'm very worried that we seem to be so far apart on this.'
- 'I'm uncertain how to react to what you've just said. I like most of it, but I feel some doubts.'

Providing focus

A key aspect of negotiation is the ability to keep the discussion focused on the main issues at hand. Two subskills are important here: questioning and behaviour labelling.

Questioning

Given the fundamental importance of this skill in social encounters (see Chapter 5), it is not surprising that questioning is central to effective negotiation. Rackham (2007) found that skilled negotiators asked over twice as many questions as average negotiators. Questions serve several important functions in negotiations. A primary purpose is to gather detailed information about the other side and their aspirations and concerns. They also allow the questioner to control the focus and flow of the interaction since the opposition has to answer the questions and in so doing has less space for contemplation. This, in turn, gives one's own side a breathing space to reflect on the current state of affairs. Finally, questions can act as an alternative to an overt statement of disagreement. Compare the following:

A: No. Our members would never accept that proposal.
B: You know our members fairly well. How do you think they would react to this proposal?

The approach used in B is much less abrasive and more likely to produce a receptive response.

Behaviour labelling

Skilled negotiators have been shown to more often signal in advance the behaviour they are about to use by labelling it (Rackham, 2007). For example, rather than asking a question outright (e.g. 'How many can it produce per day?') they are more likely to announce it in advance (e.g. by saying 'Can I *ask you a question*? How many can it produce per day?'). Other examples of behaviour labelling include:

- 'I would like to *make a proposal*.'
- 'It would be useful for me to *listen* to your views.'
- 'Could I *suggest a compromise* here.'
- 'If I could just *explain* to you why we see this as so important.'

Rackham found that skilled negotiators used five times as many instances of behaviour labelling as their average counterparts. This process of labelling is beneficial in that it reflects a formal and rational approach to bargaining, and subtly puts pressure on opponents to reciprocate in a logical fashion (Morley, 2006). Since it flags the behaviour that is about to follow, it provides focus, reduces ambiguity and clarifies the purpose of the next comment. It also helps to ensure that the negotiation is conducted at a moderate pace. Part of this labelling process also involves the acknowledgement of *joint progress* (e.g. 'We are getting on really well here.'). Effective negotiators are twice as likely to make statements labelling joint progress as their less effective counterparts (McRae, 1998).

However, one behaviour which average negotiators were more likely to label was that of expressing disagreement (e.g. 'I disagree with that because . . .'). By comparison, the skilled negotiators gave reasons which in themselves were expressions of disagreement, but tried to avoid overt statement of dissent. Rackham argued that the order in which our thought processes occur involves deciding that an argument is unacceptable and then assembling the reasons to show why. He posited that average negotiators follow this tendency overtly, whereas those who are more skilled are able to stifle this initial impulse. When one side has put forward an argument it is likely that a blunt statement of disagreement will increase their antagonism and aggression and make them less likely to give in. Indeed, Dunne (2001: 15) illustrated how in hostage contexts the general advice is that 'the negotiator should never reply "no" to any question posed by the kidnapper'. The calm presentation of counter-arguments, without a public statement of negation, encourages logical debate such that the eventual acceptance of alternative proposals then involves much less loss of face. It is therefore a useful general rule to always give reasons before (or as an alternative to) expressing disagreement. Furthermore, what has been termed *process labelling* has been shown to be effective in resolving disagreements (Lytle *et al.*, 1999). This involves openly stating and recognising that both sides simply cannot agree about an issue, and that it may be more productive to move on to discuss other aspects first and return to the contentious issue later.

Testing understanding and summarising

As discussed earlier in the chapter, it is crucial for both parties in a negotiation to be fully cognisant with what has been discussed and agreed. It is not unusual for a negotiation to end with each side holding differing views about what has been agreed. A primary concern among less skilled negotiators is to achieve agreement, and so they tend to ignore rather than confront areas of potential ambiguity or misunderstanding. Rackham (2007) found that to circumvent such confusion, skilled negotiators checked for agreement on all of the issues to ensure that the deal could be fully ratified and implemented. Thus, they used *summaries* at the end of key points in the negotiation, to check that both sides were in full agreement about precisely what had been decided. A linked skill here was that of *reflection*, and indeed this skill has been shown to have a number of advantages in encounters where clarification of communication is important (see Chapter 6). Examples of reflections in negotiating include:

- 'So delivery times are absolutely vital.'

- 'In essence you are saying that if we can move on volume you could move on price.'
- 'You are clearly concerned about this.'

This type of reflective statement helps to portray concern for the other side.

Reasoned argument

As explained in Chapter 12, the use of logic can be very persuasive. In negotiations, the image of rationality is desirable. Rackham (2007) identified two aspects that should be avoided to ensure that arguments are used to maximum effect: retaliatory counterproposals and argument dilution

Retaliatory counterproposals

A mistake made by inexperienced negotiators is to respond to a proposal with an immediate counterproposal, for example:

A: We will offer you this at a price of €10 per unit providing we are your sole supplier for the next 12 months.
B: Well what we want is for you to pay all delivery costs and guarantee delivery times.

Here, while delivery and guarantees may be important to B, these could have been addressed after responding to A's initial proposal. Rackham (2007) found that skilled negotiators used about 50 per cent fewer counterproposals than average negotiators. Counterproposals are not recommended in negotiation for three reasons:

- *They muddy the waters.* One side has put forward a proposal and suddenly a different one is introduced by the opposition. Which should be discussed? One at a time? Both together? In some instances the first side retaliates to the counterproposal by introducing a third proposal and this immediately throws the entire process completely out of kilter.
- *They are annoying.* One side has made what they regard as a valid proposal and they want this to be fully considered. A counterproposal completely ignores their bid, and so they in turn are less likely to treat this with respect or consideration.
- *They are regarded as blocking tactics* rather than serious proposals per se, and so counterproposals tend to get lost in the negotiation mists that follow. Arguments then begin to become emotional rather than logical.

Argument dilution

Less skilled negotiators tend to give more reasons to justify their bids. This is not good practice since the more reasons that are proffered, the better chance the opposition has of finding and highlighting a weakness in at least one of them. This then puts the first party on the back foot. Rackham (2007) argued that this is because weaker arguments tend to dilute stronger ones. Interestingly, Rackham also found that an unexpectedly high proportion of skilled negotiators had little formal higher education and suggested that graduates, having been steeped in a culture of devising numerous reasons to defend and justify a case, then suffer from the dilution effect in negotiation encounters. Skilled negotiators tended to put forward one reason at a time and would only introduce another reason if they were in danger of losing ground.

OVERVIEW

This review of negotiation has examined the nature of the activity and charted its defining features. The relationship between negotiating and bargaining has been explained. There is a burgeoning literature in this field and this has identified a range of strategies and skills central to effectiveness. The alternative strategies of negotiation were charted and the likely outcomes of each discussed. The typical process of negotiation was outlined and the role of concession making therein highlighted, and tactics for producing concessions from the other party itemised. Finally, the key skills employed by effective negotiators were discussed in concert with the behaviours that they tend not to employ.

In the mind of the layperson, negotiation is often perceived as a game of hardball played by tough-minded, hard-boiled, aggressive individuals. Here, the objective is seen as winning at all costs and if the other party is singed in the process, well then they should avoid the heat of the negotiating kitchen in future. But this win–lose perspective is both short-sighted and mistaken. The focus in negotiation should not be on how to divide up the spoils but rather on how to improve the spoils for both parties. The objective is not victory for one side, but for both. To achieve such win–win outcomes, the following points need to be borne in mind:

- view negotiation in a cooperative frame
- try to develop a good relationship and a sense of mutual trust
- identify all of the issues at the outset
- these issues should be reinterpreted as necessary
- be flexible as to how your goals are to be achieved
- identify and highlight areas of agreement and common interest
- begin with these to establish initial rapport
- show a concern for partnership through the use of 'We' language
- always listen carefully to and empathise with the other side
- use questions to understand their perspective and slow the pace
- overtly recognise and acknowledge what they see as important
- never lose sight of the total picture when single issues are being discussed.

- Think laterally about new options that might be introduced to overcome disagreements.
- Treat differences as challenges to be overcome.
- Stay rational and avoid emotionality.
- Separate the people from the problem – be kind to the former and work hard on the latter.
- Use gentle persuasion techniques rather than threats or coercion.
- Formally review, agree and ratify the final settlement.

Chapter 14

Working with others: skills of participating in and leading small groups

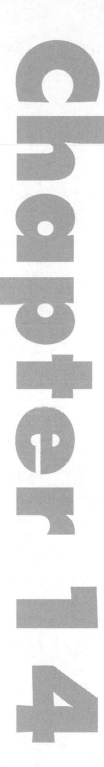

INTRODUCTION

T HE RATIONALE FOR THIS chapter was aptly summarised by
Levine and Moreland (2006: 1): 'Why study groups? The answer is
simple – it is impossible to understand human behavior without considering the role that groups play in people's lives.' Groups are an integral part of the human experience. Baron and Kerr (2003: 1) argued that
this is because: 'Groups play a crucial role in human affairs. They shape
our perceptions and attitudes, provide support in times of distress and
affect our performance and decision-making.' Not only do they make it
easier for us to complete a wide array of tasks, but they also provide a
sense of identity (Postmes and Jetten, 2006). If someone is asked to write
about or explain who they are, it is not long before they begin to anchor
a sense of self in some particularly salient group membership/s. We
are born into a social group (the family) and, as we grow, come to play a
more active part in an increasing number and range of other groups.
Growing out from the family, children find themselves in playgroups,
school classes, sports teams, youth groups and so on. In later life these
are replaced by a host of other groups, such as student societies, work
teams, drama groups, choirs, golf clubs, leisure classes, trade union
committees, parent–teacher associations and political party executives,
to mention but a very few of the myriad possibilities.

Increasingly, the contemporary workplace is structured to optimise the dynamic potential of small groups, especially when moulded
into teams (Hargie and Tourish, 2009). Such teams require skilled
leadership. As shown by Tourish *et al.* (2007: 5): 'Effective leadership is
increasingly recognised as an important factor in determining the

ability of organisations to achieve their aims and objectives. Many organisations are therefore investing a great deal of time and money on various forms of leadership development.' Indeed McCallum and O'Connell (2009) pointed out that in the USA some $50 billion is spent annually on leadership development, most of which is devoted to developing the skills of individual leaders. Focusing upon health care delivery, Northouse and Northouse (1998) made the point that many functions which were previously performed by an individual both in community and acute care settings are now team based. This is perhaps particularly true of mental health care where Yalom and Leszcz (2005) identified a wide diversity of group involvement.

Shifting the setting from the workplace to the community, again groups play a prominent role. They may include volunteer, civic or church groups that meet the needs of different sections of the community, and in different ways. The phenomenal rise in popularity of various forms of self-help group can be included here. In this regard, Napier and Gershenfeld (2004: 62) referred to 'an explosion of self-help groups: groups organized to help members deal with grieving, illness, divorce, low self-esteem, being a woman, being a man, and numerous other concerns'. They estimated some half a million variants in the USA alone, with a collective membership of approximately six million people.

Different attempts have been made to impose order on the wide variety of groups that exist by developing a typology of categories (e.g. Lickel *et al.*, 2006; Spencer-Rodgers *et al.*, 2007). Much of this work relates to the functional significance of groups for the individual. Johnson *et al.* (2006) identified three main motivational drivers for group membership. First, is the desire for *affiliation* – the need to belong and feel a sense of connectedness with others. These needs are met through membership of small, intimate groups such as family or friends. A second drive is the need for *achievement*, in terms of feeling a sense of competence, success and mastery. Such needs are met through, for example, membership of sports teams or established business corporations. The third type of motivation relates to *identity* needs, in terms of maintaining and enhancing one's sense of self-identity. Individuals can meet these needs through, for example, membership of political parties, church congregations or supporters' clubs. Of course, these needs are not mutually exclusive, so membership of particular groups can help to satisfy more than one type of need.

Perhaps the most common distinction here is that between *task* and *process* alternatives. These have also been referred to as the *task* and *social* (Fujishin, 2007) or *task* and *relationship* (Northouse, 2009) dimensions of groups. This distinction is also portrayed as a continuum of communication with *content* messages at one extreme and *process* messages at the other. The former are primarily concerned with substantive issues, quality of decisions reached, amount of output, etc. In task groups such as committees or boards of directors' meetings, most of the interaction is at this level. Process messages, by contrast, address relational matters, the internal workings of the group and the well-being of its members. Process groups rely strongly upon such contact: examples include those delivering a therapeutic service. However, most groups share elements of both; it is the relative proportion that serves to locate them at some point on a task/process continuum. *Midrange groups* are those where content and process exchanges are roughly balanced. A more differentiated list of group types can be found in Box 14.1.

> *Box 14.1* Common types of small group
>
> 1 *Family* – this is our first group.
> 2 *Friendship/leisure* – meet needs for affiliation, emotional expression and relaxation.
> 3 *Work* – facilitate productivity.
> 4 *Self-help/action* – mobilise individual and community support for courses of action.
> 5 *Training/therapy groups* – promote personal awareness and growth.
> 6 *Spiritual* – meet transcendent needs.
> 7 *Laboratory/focus* – short-term groups whose purpose is to provide research data.

While many of the communication skills that form part of dyadic interaction can also be used when people get together in groups, there are added complexities associated with the latter. These are not just a matter of scale. As Rosengren (2000: 87) pointed out:

> As the number of communicating units (n) in a communicative system grows, the number of potential direct relations (R) between the units of the system also grows … In parallel with this increasing complexity of group structure (this *quantitative change*), the communicative system of the group undergoes some qualitative change. Individual communication rapidly turns into group communication.

It is with such factors that this chapter is concerned. The starting point is a consideration of what exactly is meant by 'a group', and a number of basic features associated with the concept. This will be developed further by concentrating upon the characteristics and skills associated with a rather special and particularly important position within the group – that of leader.

DEFINING FEATURES OF A GROUP

Devising a formal definition of 'group' is more difficult than it might initially appear. It is fairly self-evident that a group necessarily involves a plurality of individuals – but how many? While four or five people would probably be acceptable, would 40 or 50 – and what about four or five thousand? Is a group the same as a gathering, a crowd or a mob? What about an audience, is it necessarily a group? Can a group be thought of as any social category – e.g. all Portuguese women over two metres tall? Have groups special characteristics and qualities that set them apart from other social aggregates? Indeed, does the word 'group' refer to a specific entity at all? For example, in an early treatise on the subject, Cartwright and Zander (1968) concluded that it merely marks an area of study whose boundaries are altogether blurred and uncertain.

One common distinction is that between small groups and larger collectives. This chapter is concerned with the former. Describing a group in this way suggests that a quite precise numeric specification should be possible. However, while figures can be found suggesting membership of from two to five at the lower end, to 15 to 20 at the upper, there is little agreement on precise numbers, leading many to abandon attempts to define small groups purely in terms of size per se. Size alone does not seem to be what really counts. Rather, the telling factor is its ability to facilitate or inhibit other interactive processes. As summarised by Gamble and Gamble (2008: 310): 'What is the optimal size for a group? In task-oriented groups it is the smallest number of people capable of handling the assigned task.' A number of more significant features of what exactly constitutes a small group have been teased out by, for example, Johnson and Johnson (2009) and Levine and Hogg (2008) and these will now be considered.

Interaction

To belong to a group, members must be able to interact with others who are also part of the collective. Until relatively recently the importance of face-to-face interaction was stressed. This requirement was conspicuous in an early definition by one of the early authorities in this field, George Homans (1950: 1), who defined a group as 'a number of people who communicate with one another often over a span of time, and who are few enough so that each person is able to communicate with all the others, not at secondhand, through other people, but face-to-face'. Face-to-face communication is, of course, more media rich than alternative forms. This characteristic also forms the basis of the distinction between *primary* and *secondary* groups, first drawn by Cooley (1929). Primary groups are typified by the potential for close and frequent face-to-face association. But do people have to be in each other's presence for 'groupness' to occur? What about those who regularly keep in contact via the internet? It is now accepted that virtual groups, which make use of technologically mediated interaction, should not be denied group status on that count alone. However, in this text the focus is upon face-to-face communication.

Influence

Extending the previous point, not only should members interact but they should also be subjected to mutual influence in the process. Each must be able, to some extent, to make a difference to the way that others think, feel and behave and be influenced in return. Indeed, this is one of the most important stipulations of 'groupness'. In this way, as noted by Wheelan (2005: 121): 'Group members and the group create a mutual influence system.'

Shared goal/s or common interest/s

The fact that groups are typically formed for some identifiable purpose and that those who belong share at least one common goal has long been regarded as an essential characteristic (Hare, 1976). Furthermore, having a common goal, vision and sense of mission have been shown to be very important sources of influence in focusing the group's energies and shaping its processes and procedures (Hare and O'Neill, 2000). Indeed, Larson (2010b) illustrated how effective groups produce 'synergy', which refers to the gains in performance outputs that accrue when individuals work as a cohesive group as compared to the same number of individuals working on their own. In the case of a formal group, its goal is often reflected in the name (e.g. Eastham Branch of the Animal Rights Movement; Eastham Photographic Society; Eastham Miners' Welfare). Interestingly, when a group's goal has been attained (or rendered obsolete), members may channel their energies in other directions, thereby ensuring the continued existence of the group. Eastham Miners' Welfare may still meet to have a drink and play snooker even though the Eastham coal pit has long since closed and the miners have found alternative employment. New goals can come to dominate group activities. In other cases the achievement of the group goal or goals results in the group's demise. Apart from acting to maintain the group and direct its activities, goals also influence the development of particular structures and procedures within it. Such considerations will be dealt with more fully in a later section of the chapter.

Interdependence

In addition to interacting with and influencing each other, the interdependence of group members has been highlighted as a core defining feature of a small group (Stangor, 2004). Members share a *common fate*. If the group fails to achieve the set goal no member is successful. Thus, events that affect one person will have a bearing on the rest of the group and group outcomes will affect each individual member.

Shared group identity

Another important feature is the requirement that members see themselves as belonging to a group: that they share a sense of group identity. This type of more subjective criterion involves the concept of people's self-categorisations. As such, a group exists to the extent that two or more individuals consider themselves as belonging to the same social category. The corresponding perceptions of non-group members are also important. Members must be seen by outsiders to belong to this collective. As expressed by Hogg (2004: 203): 'Groups exist by virtue of there being outgroups. For a collection of people to be a group, there must, logically, be other people who are not in the group.' The concept of *entitativity* is of importance in this regard. Entitativity refers to the perception that a collection of individuals actually constitutes a separate entity or group. There is a continnum here, in that groups may be more or less entitativite. Thus, intimacy groups such as a family will be perceived as being very high in entitativity, while loose associations such as individuals standing on a railway platform will be seen as very low in entitativity (Rydell and McConnell, 2005).

437

Shared social structures

When individuals join a group they begin to function in terms of a system of expectations that shapes what they do as members and their contribution to the collective. They begin to take on a *role* and abide by a set of *norms* that specify appropriate conduct. They will also slot into a particular *status* structure, according to which prestige and a sense of value are bestowed. These pivotal elements of group structure will be returned to shortly.

Various definitions combine sets of these key characteristics. For example, Johnson and Johnson (2009: 8) defined a small group as 'two or more individuals in face-to-face interaction who are aware of their positive interdependence as they strive to achieve mutual goals, aware of their membership in the group, and aware of the others who belong to the group'. Along similar lines, Beebe and Masterson (2000: 2) delineated small group communication as 'interaction among a small group of people who share a common purpose or goal, who feel a sense of belonging to the group, and who exert influence on one another'.

WHY DO PEOPLE JOIN GROUPS?

Why are groups so common? What factors can account for this predilection to gravitate towards and associate with others within such social units? One common explanation is that individuals rely upon group membership in order to achieve goals and satisfy certain felt needs that would be either more difficult or impossible to satisfy alone. McGrath *et al.* (2000) argued that all groups exist to fulfil two main functions – to complete tasks and to satisfy member needs. As mentioned earlier, groups meet human needs for affiliation, achievement and identity. Another delineation of needs is material, interpersonal or informational, and again groups play a role in their fulfilment.

Material needs

It may be to the benefit of all for a number of individuals to pool their various resources in order to complete a task and gain some tangible goal. Each will differ in the knowledge, skills and physical attributes as well as possible tools and equipment to be contributed. Indeed the gregarious nature of Homo sapiens is thought to stem from the advantages of hunting in groups and sharing the kill. Trade union and cooperative movements are among the examples of aggregates being formed to further the material well-being of members. The group may directly provide advantages or be indirectly instrumental in bringing them about. For instance, a person may join the local golf club to avail of the related business contacts that come with membership. We may therefore become attracted to a group on account of the sorts of things that participants do and the outcomes they achieve. This attraction is strongest when those outcomes coincide with what we want for ourselves and when membership is believed to enhance our opportunities for success.

Interpersonal needs

By their very nature, to be successfully met these require some form of group contact. Individuals on their own cannot satisfy them. Such needs, according to Schutz (1955) in a seminal work, may be for varying degrees of:

- *inclusion* – to want to belong or feel part of a social entity
- *control* – to dominate or be controlled
- *affection* – at the extremes, to love (and be loved) or hate.

Argyle (1995) also proposed that much of interpersonal behaviour is in response to social drives for affiliation, dominance, dependency, ego-identity or aggression. But, of course, being able to dominate depends upon one or more others who are prepared to be submissive. Likewise, it is impossible to be dependent if there is no one to depend upon. The sense of identity that membership affords has already been mentioned and is among the advantages of being part of a collective. In sum, we gravitate towards groups whose members we find attractive, and where we feel that we will fit in and be well received.

Information needs

While we may not have to join a group in order to gain knowledge of aspects of our physical environment, it is only through association with others that we come to an understanding of the social world that we inhabit and, indeed, of ourselves. As discussed in Chapter 9, social comparison is an important phenomenon. According to *social comparison theory* (Festinger, 1954; Guimond, 2006), individuals make judgements about the quality of their abilities, or accuracy and justifiability of beliefs and opinions, by watching others perform similar tasks, or listening to what they have to say on relevant topics. By so doing you gradually create an impression of yourself, including your strengths and weaknesses. For example, it is only possible to decide if you are a good, average or poor student by comparing your marks with others on your course. Darley (2001) outlined the implications for self-esteem of such comparative processes. Feelings of self-worth are heightened when the individual compares favourably with others on tasks valued by other members (and diminished when the opposite is the case).

Social comparison processes can have pronounced effects for the group as well. A common finding is that collectives often take more extreme decisions than individuals on their own. This refers to the process whereby, after discussion, members of a group are likely to decide upon a more extreme decision than if they had acted alone. One explanation for this *risky shift* or *group polarisation* effect makes use of social comparison (Levine and Moreland, 2006). This is because members obtain insights into the stances taken by others in the group in relation to the issue as it is discussed. Being seen to be 'middle of the road' or 'sitting on the fence' tends to be unattractive, so initial positions are shifted to be more extreme in the direction of the prevailing pole. Another aspect here is that the riskier decision is not the responsibility of any one individual – there is collective accountability. As a result, the group as a whole decides upon a riskier or more polarised position than would members acting as individuals, and so with sole responsibility for the outcome. To conclude this line of thought, to be a loner is not only to be denied potential material benefit and fellowship, but also an understanding of ourselves and our social worlds. Little wonder that small groups are so prevalent.

HOW ARE GROUPS ORDERED AND REGULATED?

Given that groups are made up of individuals, each with particular and perhaps contrasting personalities, opinions and preferences, it seems reasonable to ask how they manage to become sufficiently organised and coordinated for goals to be pursued efficiently and effectively. Order within the group is made possible through the creation of structure in respect of *norms*, *roles* and *status*, and the related processes of *conformity* and *cohesion*.

Norms

The emergence of norms is of crucial importance in regulating the activities of members. As groups evolve, regularities of operation begin to emerge reflecting the creation of expectations on the part of members. The most common of these are *performance norms*, whereby new members are give explicit or implicit messages about what the group regards as acceptable standards of behaviour in terms of work levels, outputs, attitude to punctuality, dress code and so on (Robbins and Judge, 2010). Norms can be defined as:

> behaviours, attitudes, and perceptions that are approved of by the group and expected – and, in fact, often demanded – of its members. Such socially established and shared beliefs regarding what is normal, correct, true, moral and good generally have powerful effects on the thoughts and actions of group members.
>
> (Baron and Kerr, 2003: 6)

Thus, it is not only overt performance that is subject to a normative influence, but also the characteristic perceptions, thoughts and feelings that members entertain. Napier and Gershenfeld (2004) teased out four main types of norm, differing in levels of formality and explicitness:

1   ***Documented.*** These sets of prescriptions are explicit and written down in a formal code of conduct. They are typically communicated directly to those in the group, together with the consequences of violation. Examples would include giving a newcomer the members' handbook of rules and regulations governing club activities, or a new student a list of the terms and conditions of residence in the university's halls of accommodation.

2   ***Explicit.*** Here the norm is drawn to the attention of members, but the expectations would not typically be codified or documented. As such they are slightly

less formal, but certainly not to be disregarded. Thus, if a CEO addressing new employees at an induction session states, 'We like our male executives to present the right image for the company, wearing a smart suit, collar and tie', although this may not be written into the contract of employment, the newcomers are very likely to take cognisance of this advice.

3   ***Implicit.*** Requirements are not stated directly but have to be assimilated more discreetly by, for instance, watching what established members do and following their example. It is often only when a violation occurs that one becomes conscious of the existence of the norm. For example, some years ago a friend of mine was undertaking a teacher training course. On his first day of teaching practice at a very formal school he did not realise that in the staffroom it was the norm that everyone sat in a particular chair. He broke this implicit norm by sitting in an available seat, but was quickly told by another member of staff, 'Mr Davies usually sits there.'

4   ***Invisible.*** Here the norms are so tightly woven into the fabric of group life that they can no longer be identified as separate threads: they have become virtually invisible. No one is aware of them but everyone simply and automatically acts in accordance. These 'rules' sometimes have to do with standards of politeness or decorum, such as acknowledging the presence of another.

Not all aspects of group life are governed to the same extent by norms. Those most stringently subjected to this type of influence include activities:

- directly concerned with the achievement of group goals and the satisfaction of members' needs, especially the needs of the most powerful in the group
- commonly associated with group membership by those both within and outside the group
- amenable to public scrutiny – thus, strict norms govern the physical examination of a patient, but not the colour of underwear the doctor should wear while conducting it!

On the other hand, behaviours that have a strong physiological basis and those that can only be performed at considerable personal cost to the individual are less likely to come under strong normative control.

Apart from facilitating goal achievement, norms serve to increase regularity and predictability in the operation of the group (Hogg and Reid, 2006). Members can determine, with reasonable accuracy, what is likely to happen in most situations. This sets down guidelines as to the nature and extent of their own involvement (Hornsey *et al.*, 2007). For the individual they also provide a clear picture of social reality together with a firm sense of belonging (Oyserman *et al.*, 2006). Personal needs for status and esteem can also be satisfied through the operation of norms. Thus, many of the tacit rules of everyday conversation are intended to avoid causing offence or embarrassment in public. A further advantage of having certain actions norm governed is that it obviates the necessity of frequently having to rely upon personal influence. It can be pointed out, for example, that new recruits to the military are expected to behave in a deferential manner to all commanding officers: it is not just me – it is the system, the way things are done around here.

Regardless of how they are communicated, whether in writing or by a disapproving look, norms as discussed here are decidedly *prescriptive*. They stipulate what should and should not be done. Members, to a greater or lesser extent, are required to comply. Furthermore, the fact that certain norms have to do with the maintenance and integrity of the group must not be overlooked. There is a *proscriptive* element involving evaluation, in that those who contravene norms can be labelled 'bad' or morally flawed and deserving of punishment by the rest of the members – and may even take the form of exclusion from the group. This is reflected in the disapprobation associated with terms such as traitor, deserter, scab, etc., often levelled at those who violate the norms.

Roles

Norms apply to all group members, although not necessarily to the same extent. In any group, however, it would be highly undesirable for everyone to act in exactly the same way. A committee where everyone acted as secretary would get little done (although anything that was done would be well documented!). Against a backdrop of shared norms, it is important that individuals take on different tasks if the group is to make the most of its resources and maximise productivity. A differentiation of functions is required. Specific sets of expectations concerning the behaviour of those in particular positions in the group are referred to as *roles*. Bormann (1990: 161) put it as follows: 'Role, in the small group, is defined as that set of perceptions and expectations shared by the members about the behaviour of an individual in both the task and social dimension of group interaction.'

Particular roles that evolve are a function of a number of determinants, including the nature of the specific group and its tasks. Nevertheless, it would seem that there are certain roles which typify small group interaction (Forsyth, 2010). Some of these were identified and labelled in an important piece of early work by Benne and Sheats (1948), and confirmed by Mudrack and Farrell (1995). This encompassed three categories of role:

1 **Task roles** (e.g. information giver, information seeker, opinion giver, opinion seeker, evaluator-critic or energiser). These contribute to the ability of the group to successfully accomplish its objective.
2 **Relationship-building and maintenance roles** (e.g. encourager, harmoniser, compromiser, follower or gatekeeper). Here the focus is upon promoting good internal relations, a strong sense of solidarity and a congenial social atmosphere.
3 **Individual roles** (e.g. aggressor, blocker, recognition seeker, playboy or dominator). Unlike the previous two categories, these tend to be self-serving and dysfunctional to the smooth and successful operation of the group.

Additionally, some groups have a member who tends to be much more reticent than the rest, who interacts minimally with others and fails to participate fully in group activities. This individual is commonly labelled an *isolate*, and indeed in larger groups may for the most part go unnoticed. The fact that such individuals do not become fully involved does not mean that they have nothing to offer, as tactful handling by an adroit leader can often demonstrate. Again, when a group is dogged by setback and failure it is not uncommon for some member to be singled out as the cause and accused of not 'pulling their weight' or 'letting the group down'. This poor unfortunate becomes the *scapegoat*. By 'identifying' the source of failure, members can have their flagging beliefs in the worth of the group reaffirmed and redouble their efforts to achieve the goal. The projection of unacceptable personal feelings or tendencies upon the scapegoat can also mitigate feelings of guilt among others.

In many respects a role can only be properly appreciated as it fits in with that of others in a system or network. For example, to fully grasp what a teacher does requires some understanding of pupils, classroom assistants, school principals, etc. Likewise, nurses operate in a context of patients, doctors, consultants, etc. To add a further level of complication, we all take on a number of roles to be played out, although not necessarily in the same situation. A teacher may also be a mother, daughter, wife, captain of the local ladies' hockey team, joker of the evening art class, etc. This can on occasion lead to *role conflict* when the demands of one are incompatible with those of another. Given that members do not invariably slip smoothly into well-moulded roles in the first place, it is small wonder that problems often arise to disrupt group life. Some of these, it has been suggested (Shaw, 1981; Burton and Dimbleby, 2006), stem from differences between the:

- ***perceived role*** – what the recipient understands is required
- ***expected role*** – what others in the group expect
- ***enacted role*** – what the person actually does.

When a member is no longer sure what the demands are, that person is said to be in a state of *role confusion*.

Status

Roles in part reflect status differences that exist between various positions in the group. Status refers to the evaluation of a position in terms of the importance or prestige associated with it, and represents a further structuring of the group. Most groups are hierarchically organised in this respect, with high-status positions affording greater opportunities to exercise social power and influence. Although status and power are usually closely associated, this need not necessarily be the case. Thus, members of the British monarchy are often portrayed as having very high status but relatively little power. As shall be seen in the following section, one facet of intra-group communication has to do with the acknowledgement and confirmation of status differences. This frequently operates at a covert level; for example, the chairperson *directs* the secretary while the secretary *advises* the chairperson.

Conformity

Despite what has just been said about norms, roles and status, none would make much contribution to ordering and structuring group existence if members disregarded them. They must conform: there must be pressures to fit in. The origins of these influences may be internal. From an informational point of view, it can be personally comforting for members to be able to enjoy a sense of surety derived from accepted group norms; from being able to buy into a shared sense of social reality. In addition, feelings of shame or guilt welling up from within may be sufficient to force miscreants to mend their ways. However, as explained by *social identity theory*, a group can also provide members with a social identity – it becomes tied up in their sense of who they are: its ways are their ways (Hornsey, 2008). Members then comply because they have accepted a particular group-based self-categorisation.

On the other hand, external pressures in the form of positive and negative group sanctions may be brought to bear to force compliance (Wit, 2006). Tourish *et al.* (2009) charted the types of pressures employed by many companies to effect the conformity of employees to corporate norms and practices. New entrants are given mentors to shape appropriate behaviour. Praise and other forms of reward are bestowed for behaving appropriately; criticism or ridicule for failing to do so. Rewards are often allocated to teams rather than individuals, and so peer pressure to behave in such a way as to achieve set goals is intensified. Extreme cases of recalcitrance may result in boycott or indeed expulsion.

But conformity to the commonly held views and practices of the majority can also have advantages for the group. It tends to increase efficiency, facilitate group maintenance, reduce uncertainty and confusion among members and project a strong group image to others. Factors that promote conformity (Napier and Gershenfeld, 2004) include the following:

- an extreme norm
- strong pressure to conform
- member self-doubt
- large group
- reinforcement of appropriate behaviour
- members' need to self-ingratiate
- a strong sense of group identity.

Under circumstances where a number of these factors apply, the forces generated to conform to the ways of the group should never be underestimated. They can lead to young people dressing in strange ways and sporting peculiar haircuts. More seriously, drug abuse and antisocial behaviour may be promoted. In the extreme, examples of soldiers, paramilitary groups and street gangs behaving with unbelievable brutality towards victims have been attributed to group pressures to abide by the ways of the group. Destructiveness can also be turned in on the group itself. This is common in cults, where pressures for conformity can be enormous (Lalich, 2004). For example, in 1978 more than 900 members of the Peoples Temple cult died in Guyana (after relocating from the USA) by drinking poisoned punch in an act of apparent mass suicide. Similarly, in March 1997, 39 men and women belonging to the Heaven's Gate cult committed group suicide in the belief that they would make contact with a spacecraft flying in the tail of a passing comet. The spacecraft was believed to be their passport to paradise.

Cohesion

Cohesiveness has been thought of as the bonding agent that holds the group together. It refers to the degree of attraction among those who belong to the group and to each other as members. Cohesion also tends to further concentrate the influences to conform. Some groups are tight-knit, cohesive teams while others tend to be rather loosely made up of individuals many of whom may have only a weak sense of affiliation to fellow members or the work of the group. A number of advantages of belonging to a cohesive group have been identified (Johnson and Johnson, 2009). The main ones are listed in Box 14.2. A key distinction here is between task cohesion – commitment to the goals, tasks and activities of the group, and social cohesion – attraction towards and liking amongst group members. Both are necessary for success. As shown by Sullivan and Feltz (2005), a sports team that is high on social cohesion will enjoy their get-togethers, but if they are low on task cohesion in terms of how they operate as a functional unit, then they will not win many games.

One common problem in groups is *social loafing*. This refers to the phenomenon whereby individuals reduce their effort when working as part of a group. As shown by van Dick *et al.* (2009: 233): 'An enormous number of empirical studies have been carried out for over more than three decades which repeatedly demonstrated that, when working in groups, individuals typically fall short of their usual performance shown when working alone.' Part of the problem here is that of *freeriding*, where individuals think they can reduce their personal effort as this will be compensated for by the group as a whole. This is most likely to occur where the group member believes the reduced effort is unlikely to be detected. Hargie *et al.* (2004) identified a range of measure to reduce loafing and freeriding. These include incorporating individual contributions as part of the overall team task, encouraging maximum involvement and participation by all members, ensuring that the task and the group are as interesting as possible, and fostering a strong sense of group identity and loyalty.

However, pressures against dissent within a group can result in less desirable outcomes through flawed decision making. One of these tendencies is *groupthink* (Janis, 1982, 1997), which is brought about by an internal dynamic to prematurely

---

Box 14.2 Advantages of group cohesion

Cohesive groups are typified by the following:

1 ease of goal setting
2 commitment to goal attainment
3 heightened productivity
4 reduced absenteeism
5 willingness of members to endure greater hardships and difficulties
6 increased morale and satisfaction
7 resolute defence against external criticism or attack
8 participants listening to and accommodating other members
9 less anger and tension
10 more support.

---

conform to the suggested group position. Groupthink is a beguiling seductress – but the consequences can be grave for those falling under her spell. Groupthink is exemplified by a mad dash to reach consensus and void potential differences of opinion and internal conflict. The group actively discourages any opposing views and there is no real critical scrutiny of alternative options, or of the possible negatives of the consensus view. Several reviews of groupthink and studies investigating conditions under which it flourishes have been carried out (e.g. Esser, 1998; Henningsen *et al.*, 2006). It tends to be fostered under conditions where:

- levels of cohesiveness are high
- there are time pressures to reach a decision
- the group is in crisis
- minority dissent is stifled
- the group is under external threat
- there is a sense of group infallibility or moral superiority
- the group is insulated from outside influence
- there is a very dominant leader who vigorously champions a specific option to the denigration of others.

The Bay of Pigs incident and the Watergate scandal are two often-cited examples of faulty political decision making attributed to groupthink (Raven, 1998). In the case of the former, during the Kennedy presidency in the USA, an elite governmental advisory group backed an abortive attempt by Cuban exiles to invade Cuba and wrestle political control from President Castro. It was, in reality, an ill-conceived piece of adventurism doomed to fail from the start. At the time of planning though there was no significant dissenting voice capable of bringing a meaningful dimension of realism to the deliberations. The Watergate scandal centred on the use of illicit surveillance of political opponents and led to the eventual resignation of President Nixon. Again it seems that the internal dynamics of the group taking the decision to sanction the operation and subsequent cover-up militated against the raising of objections.

In the modern business world, many organisations operate on the basis of largely discrete self-functioning teams comprising four to 12 individuals. The team is tasked to work on a specific time-framed project. These self-directed groups have a leader with a strong sense of focus, operate independently of the larger corporation, usually generate considerable commitment from members, and are under time pressure to complete their task. All of this increases the possibility of groupthink among members (Kassin *et al.*, 2008). Hargie *et al.* (2004) recommended steps that can be taken to help organisations avoid such groupthink (see Box 14.3).

In sum, through the establishment and operation of norms, status and roles, together with pressures to act accordingly, regular and predictable patterns of activity come to characterise much of group life. For many, this process evolves through identifiable stages as the group changes from being little more than a gathering of relative strangers, at initial meetings, to eventually becoming a properly functioning unit. This raises the question as to how groups develop over time.

Box 14.3 Avoiding groupthink

Groupthink is less likely to beset group decision making when the following conditions pertain:

1 tasks are established that involve everyone
2 clear performance goals are set for the group
3 individual contributions are capable of being identified, evaluated and rewarded
4 the expression of minority opinion and the dissenting voice is cherished, not punished or ignored
5 the leader avoids adopting a particular stance in relation to the issue, especially at an early stage in the discussion
6 the expression of a range of viewpoints is promoted
7 each member is given responsibility for critically examining views put forward
8 three questions are posed of any major decision – What's wrong with it? How can it be improved? What other possibilities have not been considered?
9 subgroups are assigned the task of independently developing solutions
10 independent parties are brought in from outside the group from time to time to review its deliberations
11 one member is given the role of 'devil's advocate'
12 after arriving at a decision, a 'second chance' meeting is held during which all members, including the leader, express residual concerns and uncertainties
13 members are made aware of the insidious dangers of groupthink.

GROUP FORMATION

A wide variety of models of group formation has been formulated (Arrow *et al.*, 2004). The most popular model presenting a picture of groups evolving through fixed stages following a progressive and predictable path is that proposed by Tuckman (1965). He identified four such stages, later extended to become five (Tuckman and Jensen, 1977), based upon reviews of over 50 investigations of mostly short-term therapy and training groups. These stages have become known as *forming, storming, norming, performing* and *adjourning*.

1 **Forming.** Initially group life is characterised by a good deal of uncertainty and confusion. Individuals are essentially strangers and there is a need to get to know each other both at a social level but also in terms of who does what. A clear picture of group goals and how they can best be achieved may also be missing. This tends to increase the dependence of members on a leader where one is present. Despite this uncertainty, there may be a good deal of optimism in the group and in this 'honeymoon' period little explicit conflict.
2 **Storming.** This second stage is typified by a great deal of negative emotion

stemming from conflict and intense disagreement. Initial individual uncertainty over what to do and how to do it now gives way to individuals' attempts to impose their interpretations on the group. Cliques and temporary subgroups can form as those with shared views or agendas come together. Since there is a poorly formed role structure individuals disagree vehemently over who should be doing what. One member may feel aggrieved that someone else has suddenly begun to do the tasks that they had taken on. Lacking a recognised status structure, there can also be considerable resentment and hostility over what are seen as illegitimate attempts by some to impose authority on others. It is therefore not surprising that a recurring theme in the literature is the importance for the group of dealing with emotional issues (Kelly, 2001).

3   *Norming.* Assuming that the group makes it through to the calmer waters of this next stage, we now find conflict ebbing as a growing consensus, unity of purpose and shared sense of identity begin to take hold (Wheelan, 2004). Group structures become established, differentiating member roles, norms and status. Members now begin to form a clearer vision of the group, what it is about and where they, as well as others, fit in. While conflict may not be banished for good, at least the group is better prepared to handle it.

4   *Performing.* Now members are in a position to begin working smoothly, efficiently and productively to achieve goals. They synchronise efforts and harmonise contributions, cooperating with one other to meet challenges, solve problems, reach decisions and implement agreed strategies.

5   *Adjourning.* Most groups reach the adjourning phase when specific goals are achieved and there is nothing left to do. In other instances a set lifespan may have been envisaged when the group was created and that time has now arrived. Alternatively, the end may come when members leave through lack of continued commitment or for other reasons (Smith and Mackie, 2007). Once more, there may be a marked emotional dimension to what takes place during this valedictory phase. If strong social cohesion has been created members may have become close friends. As shown in Chapter 10, closure is difficult, and so a deep sense of loss, loneliness and grief can develop at the prospect of social bonds being broken as participants go their separate ways. This is sometimes partly mitigated by vows to remain in contact, plans for reunions, etc. Additionally, much talk at this time is usually devoted to *grave dressing* – reflecting on how good the group was and what it accomplished.

But do all groups go through these same stages? If so, do they invariably follow the same sequence? Is progress always as ordered as suggested by the above model? For many who have reflected upon group development, the answer to these questions is 'No'. Doubt has been cast on the traditional, single fixed-sequence view of group development (Chidambaram and Bostrom, 1997). Although Wheelan (2004) proposed phases not unlike those identified by Tuckman and Jensen, she argued that a group can become 'stuck' at a stage and fail to progress further. Regression to an earlier phase is another possibility. Worchel (1994) purported that a group moves through re-emerging cycles during its existence. He identified six stages:

1   Discontent – the individual has minimal engagement with the group.

2   A precipitating event brings members together.
3   Group identification is created and forces to conform established.
4   The group agrees goals and strategies to enhance productivity.
5   Individuation – the achievement of goals is associated with a growing focus by members upon personal needs.
6   Disintegration – as members' contributions become more self-serving, conflict and division increase leading to decay and group disintegration. Disintegration produces discontent – and another cycle commences.

For others, group life is typified by efforts to cope with recurring themes or issues. From a psychodynamic stance, these centre on unconscious assumptions that create an emotional climate and influence members to satisfy unconscious needs and control anxiety (Bion, 1961; Morgan and Thomas, 1996). Three basic assumptions concern:

- *dependency* – the search for someone to take control of, protect and deliver the group
- *fight/flight* – a united effort to repel or evade attack from within or outside the group and thereby control anxiety
- *pairing* – bringing pairs of members together, unconsciously motivated by the desire to create a solution to the difficulties of the group.

TEAMS

Teams are a special type of group that have become extremely popular where people come together to complete tasks, such as in the workplace. Many organisations have responded to ever-present pressures to increase quality production in a more efficient way by turning to teams as core operational units charged with delivering success (Levi, 2007). This strategic move has often been associated with a flattening of the organisational structure, reducing status differentials and devolving power to lower levels. There is good evidence that more is achieved by having staff pool their efforts in well-managed, self-directed and committed units of this type rather than either striving on their own or being at odds with others (Chaudhry-Lawton *et al.*, 1992; O'Hair *et al.*, 2007). Hewlett-Packard discovered that efficiency improved by some 50 per cent when the company restructured around quality teams. Declines in absenteeism reported by Xerox headquarters and by the Nissan UK plant in Sunderland were attributed in part to structural changes that placed greater emphasis on teamwork, increased autonomy and responsibility.

But what sets teams apart from the types of small group that have already been explored? When embedded in an organisational setting, Drucker (2007) pointed to issues such as task interdependence amongst members, a shared sense of being an intact social entity and being seen to be so by others as being crucial. For Kinlaw (1991), teams are cohesive, develop their own ways of doing things and are largely self-managing. Katzenbach and Smith (1993) highlighted the tendency for teams to achieve more than would have been expected from considering the contributions of members as individuals. Extending some of these ideas, Wilson (2004) concluded that the key features of a team are that it interacts about a shared problem or interdependent goal, provides leadership from within, and the members apply mutual influence in the completion of tasks. More particularly, Guirdham (2002) and Hargie *et al.* (2004) characterised effective teams as outlined in Box 14.4.

INTRA-GROUP COMMUNICATION

Cattell (1951: 163) coined the term 'group syntality', which he argued 'defines for the group precisely what personality does for the individual'. The syntality or 'personality' of the group is shaped by the context in which the group operates, the nature of the individual members and by the interplay between them. Effective intra-group communication has been shown to be a critical element in group functioning (Silberstang and London, 2009). Regardless of how groups develop and the stages through which this occurs, communication amongst members is the growth hormone that makes it happen. It is a prerequisite for the emergence and perpetuation of norms and roles, conformity and coherence, and for the achievement of outcomes. Frey (1999) pointed to both the constitutive and functional nature of the phenomenon: groups emerge through communication and it is in this way that they achieve their objectives. At the same time, the communication process is heavily influenced in turn by the internal structures that are created, as will be seen in the next section.

The importance of communication in the group cannot therefore be overestimated. Nowhere is this more so than with teams, where it is paramount (Galanes *et al.*, 2006). Communication makes it possible for those belonging to the group to organise themselves, pool resources and through cooperative action solve common difficulties

---

Box 14.4 How to spot an effective team

Effective teams have the following characteristics:

- highly specific task objectives that are clearly understood and accepted by all members
- a high level of ownership of and commitment to group tasks
- a great deal of mutual trust and respect for members
- a culture of inclusivity
- strong support within the unit
- a firm sense of collective accountability
- quality communication that is honest and open with participants feeling listened to and understood
- self-control, self-motivation and self-direction
- interaction and socialising outside the strict work setting
- conflicts are accepted and worked through
- an emphasis upon positive, constructive feedback to members
- collective success or failure and a reliance upon all members to create and maintain an acceptable image
- members whose skills, knowledge and abilities complement each other and enhance the group.

---

or reach a desired goal. But in addition the resolution of interpersonal and indeed personal difficulties within the group and the creation and maintenance of harmonious relationships rely upon effective communication. These two types of communication were discussed earlier in the chapter. In relation to groups, they have been referred to as *content* and *process* dimensions, or alternatively, as *task* and *socio-emotional* (also referred to as *person-focused* or *relational*) communication. Task communication, as the name suggests, concerns substantive group activities and typically operates in accordance with reason and logic. On the other hand, 'person-focused behaviors are those that facilitate the behavioral interactions, cognitive structures, and attitudes that must be developed before members can work effectively as a team' (Burke *et al.*, 2006: 291). This does not necessarily mean that each communicative act must be either task or relational in function. It is not a question or 'either or'. While ostensibly discussing how to solve a task issue, members may contemporaneously be forming impressions of where they stand in relation to the others in terms of status, positive regard and so on.

Interaction processes

In early but still pertinent work, Bales (1950, 1970) teased out task and socio-emotional (roughly comparable to relational communication) aspects of group communication using a system that he developed, known as *interaction process analysis*. He found that specific contributions of participants to small group interaction could be analysed and pigeon-holed in one of 12 distinct categories. They are briefly presented in Box 14.5. Six of these are concerned with task functions. Of these, three involve, first, giving suggestions and directions; second, opinions and points of view; and third,

---

Box 14.5 Interaction process analysis categories

Socio-emotional: positive

1 Shows solidarity, supports, rewards.
2 Shows tension release, jokes, laughs, defuses.
3 Agrees, shows passive acceptance, concurs, complies.

Task: neutral

4 Gives suggestions, directions, implying autonomy for the other.
5 Gives opinion, evaluation, analysis, expresses wishes and feelings.
6 Gives orientation, information, clarification, confirmation.
7 Asks for orientation, information, clarification, confirmation.
8 Asks for opinion, evaluation, analysis, expresses wishes and feelings.
9 Asks for suggestions, directions, implying autonomy for the other.

Socio-emotional: negative

10 Disagrees, shows passive rejection, acts formally, withholds help.
11 Shows tension, asks for help, withdraws.
12 Shows antagonism, undermines other's status, defends or asserts self.

---

orientation and clarification. These are mirrored in three further task functions, this time with a focus upon asking for (rather than giving) suggestions, opinions or orientation. The remaining six categories relate to socio-emotional reactions with a neat symmetry between the positive and negative. The three positives are: showing solidarity, helping or rewarding; showing tension release (e.g. joking, laughing) or satisfaction; and showing agreement, acceptance or understanding. The final three categories, also in the socio-emotional area but negative in character are: showing antagonism; showing tension, withdrawing, or asking for help; and disagreeing or rejecting.

By analysing the communication between members in this way, interesting insights can be gained into the type of group and how it operates. It can be established, for example, whether most of what takes place is concerned with task or relational issues, and, if the latter, the type of relationships that seem to predominate in the group. Different sorts of difficulty are detectable. As explained by Poole (1999), a group sometimes struggles to achieve a compromise between task and socio-emotional concerns. If it devotes all of its energies to completing the task, disagreements and friction may be experienced amongst members. This places a demand upon the group to pay greater heed to relational needs or risk becoming dysfunctional or even fragmented. However, if the balance tips too much towards relational matters, the task may not get done, hence a need for readjustment. At the level of the individual, the extent and nature of the contribution of members, reflecting the roles taken up, can also be profiled through observation systems such as interpersonal process analysis.

A common finding to emerge from this sort of detailed observation and analysis is that some members participate markedly more than others in discussion. This seems to be a function of several factors, including the following:

1   *Position and status in the group* – high-status members, particularly group leaders, tend to contribute extensively.
2   *Knowledge* – those with relevant information are frequently vociferous and indeed may be encouraged to be so by other group members.
3   *Personality* – extraverts, almost by definition, are more communicative than their introverted colleagues. There is some evidence to suggest that individuals have their characteristic levels of participation across groups, although these are not immutable.
4   *Physical location* – those centrally located in the group frequently take a more active part.
5   *Group size* – it has been found that differences between members in the amount of contribution to group interaction increase in relation to increases in overall group size. In addition, the potential for dissensus becomes greater as the group size increases beyond ten members (Klimek *et al.*, 2008). One reason for this is that the complexity of interrelationships increases in line with group size. Rosengren (2000) identified the following formula to chart the number of dyadic relationships (R) in a group, as a factor of the number of members (n):

$$R = \frac{n\,(n-1)}{2}$$

Thus, a group of six people would have $6 \times 5 \div 2 = 15$ separate potential two-way relationships between members. However, as the group size grows, the number of potential relationships increases dramatically, such that a group of 12 people will involve 66 possible two-way relationships.

As well as quantitative differences existing between high and low participants, contrasts in the typical form of their communications have also been identified. While high participators tend to provide information, give opinions and make suggestions, low participators, when they do contribute, are more likely to ask questions or express agreement. Again the target of such communication is frequently different. Low contributors, for the most part, direct contributions to individual members, but high contributors are more inclined to address their remarks to the group. This is frequently associated with attempts to exert influence and exercise power. Those who contribute most are also likely to be the recipients of frequent messages from others.

Communication networks

As participants interact with one another, regularities begin to emerge in the form of identifiable patterns of communication. Restrictions on member access that may develop as group structures emerge, help shape such networks (Brown, 2000). Researchers have investigated the effects of these patterns, or communication networks, on a number of variables, including group efficiency and member satisfaction. In early experiments carried out by Bavelas (1950), five subjects were each given a number of cards, each containing several symbols. Their task was to identify the symbol common to each member's card. Since the subjects were located in separate booths, channels of communication between them could be carefully controlled by the experimenter, creating the four networks outlined in Figure 14.1

In each of the four diagrams in Figure 14.1, the circles represent particular group members and the adjoining lines are available channels of communication. Thus, in the Circle arrangement (a) and (b) could communicate, but not (a) and (e) – at least not directly. Beyond the rather special circumstances of the experiments conducted by Bavelas, it should be appreciated that members in other group situations do not necessarily have to bear the particular spatial relationship to each other depicted in the diagrams in Figure 14.1 for that specific network to pertain. It is rather the pattern of communication channels in each case that is the telling feature. In other words, people may be physically sitting in a circle but typify a wheel communication network as they direct their contributions for the most part to one member who in turn reciprocates. This person becomes the hub in the wheel through which communication is channelled to the rest of the group.

Networks differ in two important respects:

- **connectivity** – the number of channels available to members in the network
- **centrality** – the extent to which a member is tied or connected to other members; this is a function of the number of channels from a given position to each other position.

The Circle in Figure 14.1 contains five channels and is therefore a more highly connected structure than any of the others. It is also the least centralised structure,

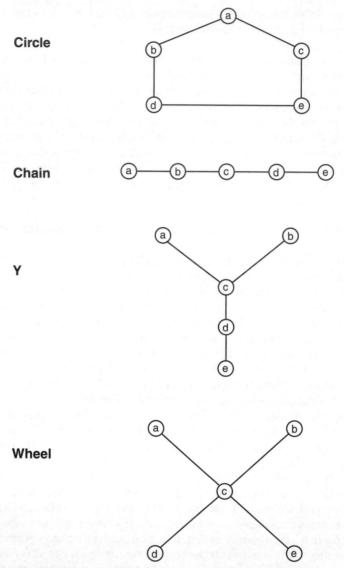

Figure 14.1 Communication networks

followed by the Chain, Y and Wheel, in order. With the Wheel it can be seen that one person (c) can communicate directly with a total of four others.

Results from a number of research studies suggest that these networks have a significant impact on group efficiency and member satisfaction (Wilke and Wit, 2001). Group productivity (in terms of the number of tasks completed) and efficiency (measured by time taken to complete each and the number of messages needed) were found to increase with increases in group centrality. The Wheel was therefore more productive and efficient followed by the Y, the Chain and the Circle. The likelihood of emerging as group leader was also found to be directly related to the centrality of the person's position in the arrangement. The increased productivity and efficiency of more centralised structures is likely due to organisational and informational factors – it is easier to control what takes place without at the same time overwhelming the key person with information. As tasks become more complex though, this may not be so. Highly centralised networks may be less rather than more effective due to the unreasonable data-processing demands placed upon the individual at 'the hub'. Most everyday tasks that groups face are much less straightforward than those set in the laboratory by researchers such as Bavelas (Hartley, 1997).

While more centrally organised groups tend to be more productive and efficient (especially when dealing with simple problems), members frequently manifest low morale and express little satisfaction with group activities. Subjects operating in the Circle typically express much greater satisfaction with their involvement in the group than those in the Wheel, in spite of the fact that they may not collectively achieve as much. This is most likely a result of the greater independence of action enjoyed by members in the former.

As well as more elaborate tasks being tackled in naturally operating groups, the communication channels between members are not limited in the contrived fashion described by Bavelas, nor are they unchanging. Networks are typically completely connected, in principle, with each individual free to communicate with every other. In practice, however, those patterns that actually emerge frequently resemble one of the more restricted configurations already examined. A range of factors, including the roles being played by different individuals, may serve to reduce the number and sequence of channels typically used. Physical arrangements determining visual accessibility of certain members to others may also play a part (Johnson and Johnson, 2009). The likelihood of initiation of conversation, for instance, depends upon those individuals being able to engage in eye contact.

What the group is essentially about will also dictate the most accommodating network for the task. As pointed out by Northouse and Northouse (1998), a completely connected pattern typified by openness and high connectivity would best suit a therapy group. The Wheel, by contrast, would better serve the purposes of one where the intention is for one member to disseminate information to the others in a limited space of time.

Having considered the defining characteristics of groups, some of the reasons for their existence, the mechanisms by which they become ordered and regulated, and the types and patterns of communication between members, the next step is to examine a particularly influential position within the group – that of leader – and the characteristics and skills associated with leadership.

LEADERS AND LEADERSHIP

The related topics of *leader* and *leadership* are amongst the most widely explored in the fields of group structure and dynamics and indeed of larger social aggregates. However, there is considerable debate on a range of issues to do with why certain members become leader: the exceptional qualities (if any) that set them apart, their early experiences of playing leadership roles, the special nature of their contribution to collective life, even the defining features of leadership itself (Amit *et al.*, 2009; Haslam *et al.*, 2010). One thing is agreed, however, and that is that all of these matters are centrally important in shaping groups, their functioning and effectiveness. Providing neatly manicured definitions of leader and leadership is not an easy task. Alternatives abound for each. Furthermore, while the terms are related, they should not be confused. The former pre-dates the latter. From the dawn of history, scholars have been fascinated by the powers bestowed upon certain individuals to govern the lives of others. In the Chinese book of wisdom *Tao Te Ching*, dating from 600 BC, it was written that most leaders are despised, some leaders are feared, few leaders are praised and the very good leader is never noticed.

A *leader* refers to a person who occupies a certain high-status position and fulfils an associated role in the group. That person, according to Galanes *et al.* (2006), may be leader by dint of the fact that she or he:

- exerts a positive influence on the group to achieve the group goal

and/or

- has been placed in a position to lead (e.g. chairperson, supervisor, coordinator)

and/or

- is perceived by the other members as the leader.

In some situations a *designated* leader may be formally appointed to organise the group, perhaps by an outside person or body. While carrying the title of leader confers legitimate power, the respect and acceptance of the membership may still have to be earned to tap other sources, such as referent power, and function effectively. When accepted in this way, having a designated leader can be a tremendously facilitative resource, acting as a catalyst to organise and regulate activities, siphon off internal tensions, assuage potential power struggles and maximise productivity. But not all leaders are put in place in this formal way. Others emerge from within the group to take on a leadership role. It is often they (the 'power behind the throne'), rather that the titular head, who wield the real power and to whom the rest look for guidance and support. One big advantage that *emergent* leaders have is that they are known to members, have risen to the top through association with them and are regarded as 'one of us'. Issues of acceptance, allegiance and respect are therefore less likely to surface.

Not all leaders provide leadership. Neither does the fact that a group lacks a conspicuous leader mean that leadership is lacking. All who are part of the collective can make a contribution in this direction and in effective groups members are prepared to share responsibility for leadership skills. For this reason, the study of 'followership', which emphasises the process of reciprocal influence between leaders and followers, has attracted growing interest (Hollander, 2009). So what exactly is leadership? Concurring with Baker (2001: 475), most would agree that 'we all know what leadership is until someone asks us to define it specifically'. The word 'leadership' did not appear in the English language until about 1800 and as such is much more recent than 'leader'. Since then, there have almost been as many definitional variants as there are contributors who have proffered a meaning for the term. Northouse (2007: 3) defined leadership as 'a process whereby an individual influences a group of individuals to achieve a common goal', and drawing upon a classificatory scheme proposed by Bass (1990), he further identified several foci amongst available sets of definitions:

1   ***Leadership as group process.*** The emphasis here is upon the leader at the centre of group operations and as catalyst for change. The mechanisms through which influence comes to be channelled in this way and the relationship between leader and follower, has also been a topic of enquiry. After all, leaders can only adopt and continue to fulfil their role with the consent of followers. From this point of view, leadership can be thought of as the process of being accepted by group members as the leader (Lord and Brown, 2004).

2   ***Leadership as personality.*** Here the focus is upon the unique complement of personality traits and personal qualities that enable one member to attain a dominant position and exercise influence over the rest. This issue will be returned to shortly.

3   ***Leadership as power.*** Those who have taken this line accentuate the issue of power at the heart of leadership and how it is handled in the relationship with followers. Is it concentrated in the personification of an authoritarian tyrant or distributed in a more egalitarian fashion? In the world of the modern organisation, Bennis and Townsend (2005) argued that traditional practices of top-down leadership are not only outdated but also quite dysfunctional. Simply ordering others to do one's will is no longer effective. Rather, it must be recognised that the workforce is the fulcrum for change in creative partnership with the person 'at the top'. Issues of power can be further extended by introducing political and ideological dimensions into thinking about leadership. Thus, Gemmill and Oakley (1992: 114) argued that what leadership ultimately provides is a 'social defense whose central aim is to repress uncomfortable needs, emotions and wishes that emerge when people attempt to work together'.

4   ***Leadership as goal achievement.*** This perpective is reflected in the definition of Andriessen and Drenth (1998: 323): 'Leadership is that part of the role of a (appointed or elected) leader that is directly linked to influencing the behaviour of the group ... through the direction and coordination of activities that are important in connection with the tasks of the group.' Earlier in the chapter the importance of goals to the formation and functioning of groups was recognised. This sentiment has found its way into attempts to distil the essence of leadership. After all, if goals figure prominently in group life, if success is measured in terms of goal output, and if leadership is to have any real significance as a group-based concept, then it must in some way serve to facilitate goal achievement. Thus, De Souza and Klein (1996) found that those individuals to emerge as group leaders in an experimental task-completion setting were more committed to the group goal and had higher task ability.

THEORIES OF LEADERSHIP

Fascination with the role of leader has not merely been confined to the investigations of social scientists. Although not studied extensively and scientifically until the second half of the last century, leadership has intrigued philosophers and historians for much longer. But even restricted to the social sciences, a range of theories and perspectives has been advanced to account for why or how leaders emerge and with what effects. As expressed by Gessner *et al.* (1999: xiii): 'Leadership theories are like fingerprints: everyone has them and no two are alike.' A comprehensive review of alternatives is well beyond the reach of this chapter, but it is useful to examine several of the better known.

Trait approach

What is proposed here is that leaders possess certain personality traits and capacities that set them apart from the rest and make it possible for them to lead. Without this unique advantage, any attempt to fill this role is doomed to failure. In its earliest form, it was furthermore believed that these crucial predispositions were innate – that leaders were born, not made. Proponents of this *Great Person* (invariably *Man*) *Theory* pointed to colossal heroic figures as 'proof' of their views. Alexander the Great was an even greater leader than his father Philip II. From biblical times there is a long tradition of chosen ones having the hand of God placed upon them and a divine right to rule conferred. Indeed, Machiavelli in the early sixteenth century provoked the wrath of the Church by audaciously proposing a set of principles by which a commoner could *learn* to exert the influence of leadership.

The belief that leadership is inborn would receive little contemporary support from serious social scientists. This still leaves open the possibility that predisposing attributes can be acquired, perhaps early in life. Considerable research effort has been put into their identification and isolation. At best a handful of weak associations have emerged with leaders tending to be taller, more attractive, healthy, intelligent, confident, extraverted and having a greater desire for dominance (Hogg and Vaughn, 2008). However, an extensive and frequently cited review by Stogdill (1974) failed to unearth a distinct set of general qualities or abilities of leadership. Indeed, while Alexander the Great, Mahatma Gandhi, Winston Churchill and Nelson Mandela all share the accolade of being towering global figures, it is probably their differences that impress rather than their similarities. If given a battery of personality tests, would a common leadership factor emerge? That said, however, Kirkpatrick and Locke (1991) listed six basic traits that distinguish leaders from non-leaders in management:

- drive
- desire to lead
- honesty/integrity
- self-confidence
- cognitive ability
- knowledge of the business.

It is readily acknowledged, however, that these operate at the level of pre-conditions and are not in themselves sufficient for success (Van Yperen and Van de Vliert, 2001). Yet interest in this line of research keeps being rekindled. In the mid-1970s, House (1976) reintroduced the notion of the charismatic leader, originally mooted by Weber (1947). Charismatic leaders are those who 'by force of their personality are capable of having a profound and extraordinary effect on followers' (Schermerhorn *et al.*, 1995: 171). Several alternative versions of this theory now exist. While inconsistencies and ambiguities persist (Yukl, 2010), their major impact has been in addressing the behavioural manifestations of charismatic leadership rather than weeding out under-lying personality factors per se. Again the fact that leaders can lose charisma poses questions for a strict personality-based explanation.

For others the quest to isolate a leader personality type or elements thereof has become transmogrified into a search for behavioural skills and competencies that seem crucial, at least in some situations.

Situation approach

If we cannot explain why certain people come to prominence through concentrating upon those individuals and dissecting their personalities, then perhaps we can do so by shifting the direction of enquiry to the circumstances of their rise to power. In its most extreme form, the situational approach attributes leadership not to the person but to the particular demands of the situation. Here there are no universally important traits of leadership, nor does it follow that a person who becomes leader in one situation will do so in another, as trait theory would predict. Winston Churchill scarcely covered himself in glory during his military service during World War I, but the perilous situation that Britain faced when he became Prime Minister during the later world conflict made him an ideal person to lead the nation on that occasion. Once circumstances changed with the advent of peace, however, he lost power at the next general election. But should the individual not be factored into the equation in some way? His or her unique contribution, in whatever form that may take, is still important. Churchill coming to power when he did was a feature of the situation faced and the special qualities that he could bring to tackling it.

Contingency approach

Theories that can be listed here have in common the assumption that effective leader-ship is a function of situational variables including task demands and the approach adopted by the leader in tackling them. Perhaps the best known is that proposed by Fiedler (1967, 1986). Using a variety of group situations, ranging from sports groups through to military and industrial settings, Fiedler's starting point was that some leaders were more committed to the nature or structure of the task and reaching a goal. Others were more oriented to achieving good personal relationships within the group. He concluded that it was unusual to find individuals who were equally orientated to both group socio-emotional needs and task completion.

Turning attention to the situational context, three factors seemed important:

1   the relationship between leader and members
2   the degree to which the task was clearly structured
3   the amount of power enjoyed by the leader to reward and punish members.

Fiedler found evidence that the type of leader required in order for group performance to be enhanced was contingent upon the nature of the situation defined in terms of these three factors. For instance, task-oriented leaders appear to be most effective when they are on very good terms with group members, the task is clearly structured and they are in a powerful position within the group. Such leaders are also effective when on poor terms with group members, the task is ambiguous and they have limited power. However, it would appear that when moderate relationships exist between leader and group members, when the task is reasonably clear and when the leader has an intermediate position of influence, the leader who emphasises good relationships within the group is the most effective at achieving member participation and productivity. Effectiveness therefore depends upon a proper match between elements of the situation and the type of leadership provided.

While much research has been produced in broad support of Fiedler's findings, criticisms have also been levelled. One source stems from the fact that the theory provides little explanation for the patterns of relationship between personal and situational variables (Northouse, 2007). Another major criticism is that group performance is measured in terms of task or goal completion. But output is only one measure of a group's value. Group members' satisfaction may be equally important yet not contribute to the achievement of the extrinsic goal. It will be recalled from earlier in the chapter that the most satisfied members do not necessarily belong to the most productive groups. Furthermore, the validity of the instrument used to measure leadership orientation (task vs. relation) has been brought into question (Fiedler, 1993).

Transformational approach

As part of a more recent way of thinking about the topic, 'transformational leadership' can be traced back to the work of Burns (1978). He focused upon the relationship between leaders and followers and distinguished between its *transactional* and *transformational* characterisations:

- *Transactional leadership* concentrates upon the exchange nature of the leader–follower relationship. Each makes a contribution in return for some reciprocating input from the other party. Leaders provide expertise and direction, followers contribute effort and compliance. Leaders dispense rewards, followers meet their production targets. This attitude has typified much traditional thinking.
- *Transformational leadership* focuses on the process by which the leader engages with members in such a way as to raise to new heights the levels of motivation, aspiration and commitment of the whole group. As part of this transmogrification, a new way of thinking and feeling is brought about such that the greater good of the collective takes precedence over the separate needs of individuals, creating a different set of moral values that they all share.

Mahatma Gandhi is a good example of this type of leader, who did much more than merely offer political direction to the Indian people in exchange for, let's say, their recognition and patronage. He offered them a new vision of independence to which they could aspire together with a sense of hope, belief and commitment to its achievement.

This early contribution by Burns (1978) has since been extended most noticeably by Bass and his co-workers (Bass, 1985, 1996; Bass and Riggio, 2005; Conger and Riggio, 2007). Leaders who provide this sort of influence are thought to raise members to new levels of accomplishment by:

- heightening their conscientiousness about actual and potential goals
- having them promote the greater interests of the group over narrow personal agendas
- bringing attention to bear upon higher order needs.

Transformational leadership is therefore provided when the leader induces members to see beyond their own limited personal interests, recognising and embracing the mission of the group. Followers, in turn, tend to respond with a sense of trust, loyalty and mutual respect towards the leader and are sufficiently motivated to accomplish more than they would have initially thought possible. As a corollary, they experience conditions conducive to the maximisation of their full potential. According to Bass (1985), four factors lie behind this effect:

1   *Charisma or idealised influence.* As noted by Amernic *et al.* (2007: 1841): 'Charisma is assumed to be an important component of transformational leadership.' However, Bass (1995) proposed that charisma was a necessary but not sufficient condition of transformational leadership – a leader could be charismatic but not necessarily transformational. For him, it was important that the transformational leader be someone that the rest can look up to and wish to emulate, capable of commanding confidence, allegiance, unwavering loyalty, and encapsulating a vision to be shared by all. On the other hand, it has been noted that there are key differences between these two concepts (Yukl, 2010). Thus, it is argued, a leader can be transformational but not charismatic. In this way, whereas transformational leaders exist in most organisations, charismatic leaders are the exception.

2   *Inspirational motivation.* This factor is about instilling a strong sense of will to achieve for the good of the group. It is created through developing ownership of a collective vision of the group and what it is going to achieve, together with an appreciation of the part that the individual member has to play in bringing this to fruition. Team spirit and collaboration for the good of the organisation are important. Emotion, dynamism and symbolism are often tools at the disposal of the transformational leader in this regard.

3   *Intellectual stimulation.* It should not be thought, however, that transformational leadership is merely a more sophisticated way of brainwashing followers to do the bidding of the leader – but now with a smile. When truly implemented, this approach stimulates followers to challenge their established ways

of thinking, evaluating and reacting, as well as those of the leader and the organisation. Members should be both encouraged and facilitated to consider innovative approaches for tackling problems and bringing these to the attention of the group.

4   *Individualised consideration.* Transformational leaders should also be capable of dealing with members on an individual basis, listening to their concerns, acknowledging their needs and taking an interest in their personal development.

The transformational approach to explaining leadership can rightly claim a number of advantages. It offers a broader perspective than some of the alternatives and emphasises not only the relationship between leader and follower, but also introduces a moral dimension to the process. In addition to a certain intuitive appeal, a considerable body of supportive empirical research for this form of leadership has now been generated, particularly in organisations, showing that it is associated with 'higher performance and perceived effectiveness of leaders ... lower turnover rates, higher productivity, lower employee stress and burnout, and higher satisfaction' (Robbins and Judge, 2009: 455).

However, concerns have also been mooted about this approach (Northouse, 2007; Tourish *et al.*, 2010; Yukl, 2010). There is a tendency to assume that certain traits and personal qualities set transformational leaders apart, but we know little about what precisely these are. It is unclear why some leaders employ a transformational approach while others do not. Similarly, we have little understanding of the underlying psychological processes employed by transformational leaders to influence followers to achieve higher levels of performance (Avolio *et al.*, 2009). Concomitantly, there has been a lack of research into the contextual determinants of effective transformational leadership. For example, this approach has been shown to be particularly difficult to implement within public sector organisations, where policymakers rather than leaders transform the context, and the extent of leadership discretion is constricted by central government (Currie and Lockett, 2007). Furthermore, the primary level of analysis tends to be pitched at the dyad between the leader and individual followers rather than at the organisation. Tourish and Pinnington (2002) also drew attention to the inordinate levels of power necessitated by transformational leadership, the lack of associated checks and balances, and the misconception and mishandling of dissent amongst followers, as problematic areas. They argued that in the context of corporate management, this form of leadership may mean that 'the leader may be able to impose his or her vision on recalcitrant followers, however erroneous it is. The edge of a cliff might seem the starting point of an adventurous new journey' (p. 152).

Behavioural approach

The final approach to be considered here shifts the focus from the traits and aptitudes that may set leaders apart and places it upon how leaders actually conduct themselves when providing leadership in different situations. What do effective leaders do that their ineffective counterparts fail to, and vice versa? Here, performance can be analysed at different levels from the broad examination of styles of leadership to the fine-grained identification of skills and actions that express them.

Leadership styles

Style generally can be thought of 'as *how* what is done is done, with the characteristic manner in which someone handles an interactive episode' (Dickson, 2006: 167). Leadership style has been defined as '*the combination of traits, skills, and behaviors leaders use as they interact with followers*' (Lussier and Achua, 2010: 70). Differences have been reported in this respect between leaders of more and less successful teams (Kayes *et al.*, 2005). Leadership style has been linked to levels of member job satisfaction, organisational commitment and evaluation of leader competence (Skogstad and Einarsen, 1999; Dubrin, 2010), enjoyment (Fox *et al.*, 2000), creativity (Sosik *et al.*, 2000) and even mental health (Gardiner and Tiggemann, 1999). It has already been shown that leaders can be mainly task oriented or relation oriented. But perhaps the best-known variants of style are those introduced by Lewin *et al.* (1939). In what is now considered a classical study involving groups of juvenile boys in a recreational youth centre, they distinguished three types:

1   *Autocratic* – the leader was instructed to be totally authoritarian, directing, giving orders and making all decisions.
2   *Democratic* – the leader encouraged participation, helped group members to interact, and consulted them when taking decisions.
3   *Laissez-faire* – the leader more or less left the boys to get on with it.

The results revealed that members were more dependent on the leader and lacking in cooperation with their peers when led by an autocratic leader. When the leaders adopted a democratic approach, the same boys showed more initiative and responsibility for the progress of the group and were friendlier towards each other, even when the leader left the room. In the laissez-faire or leaderless group, the boys lacked interest in their tasks and failed to complete successfully any that had been set. Aggressive acts were more frequent under autocratic and laissez-faire leaders. Finally, it was found that the democratic leader was the most liked, the autocratic leader the least so. Transferred to a 'real-life' working environment, Packard and Kauppi (1999) found that those who recorded their immediate supervisor's style as democratic, rather than autocratic or laissez-faire, also reported that they enjoyed greater support, less work pressure and more job satisfaction, while Skogstad *et al.* (2007) showed that the laissez-faire style was correlated with increased conflict between workers and greater role ambiguity.

Muczyk and Reimann (1987) suggested that such styles actually involve two separate dimensions.

1   *Autocratic–democratic* – charts the extent to which leaders allow members to become actively involved in the decision-making process.
2   *Permissive–directive* – determines the degree to which leaders tell members what to do.

463

When these two dimensions are put together, four possibilities exist:

- *Directive autocrat* – members are permitted little autonomy in organising their work and the leader makes all significant decisions.
- *Permissive autocrat* – members have considerable autonomy in organising their work, but the leader makes all significant decisions.
- *Directive democrat* – members are permitted little autonomy in organising their work but are actively involved in the decision-making process.
- *Permissive democrat* – members have considerable autonomy in organising their work and are actively involved in the decision-making process.

Related to these four options, *directive* and *participative* styles (House and Mitchell, 1974; Larson *et al.*, 1998; Somech, 2005) are two further contrasting possibilities commonly referred to that derive from the same underlying issues of the management of power and members' involvement:

1 *Participative leaders* – share power with members, actively involve them in decision making, and seek their views and suggestions, taking these into account rather than trying to impose personal opinions.
2 *Directive leaders* – give instructions, clarify regulations, make their preferences known and seek to influence others to their way of thinking when reaching decisions. Two subcomponents were proposed by Peterson (1997):

- *outcome directiveness* has to do with advancing a solution favoured by the leader
- *process directiveness* concerns the degree to which steps taken to reach an outcome (but not the outcome itself) are shaped by the leader. In the study undertaken by Peterson this element emerged as a significant predictor of the quality of both decisions reached by groups and the processes they used.

A much more elaborate system for identifying leadership styles and one of the most popular was first introduced in the 1960s by Blake and Mouton. Since then it has undergone several revisions (Blake and Mouton, 1985; Blake and McCanse, 1991). According to this model a range of leadership patterns can be plotted on a managerial grid formed from the intersection of two basic dimensions:

1 *Concern for people* relates to the leader's commitment to members, their levels of satisfaction, working conditions, sense of being valued, loyalty to the organisation, etc. This type of person is epitomised by what is termed the 'servant-leader', who has a high desire to serve others, by showing empathy and concern for their welfare, putting the needs of workers to the fore and building a sense of community (Andersen, 2009; Avolio *et al.*, 2009).
2 *Concern for production* has to do with the leader's dedication to the task in terms of achieving organisational goals, maximising quality output and getting results.

Each of these dimensions can be plotted on an axis and scored from low to high on a nine-point scale. Various styles can be identified in the resulting matrix, characterised by a combination of a certain level of concern for people on the one hand, and for production on the other. Five principal styles to emerge are as follows:

1 *Impoverished management* – low on concern for people and production. This person simply goes through the motions but provides no meaningful influence (similar to the laissez-faire leader already mentioned).

2 *Country club management* – high concern for people but low for production. Here leaders concentrate narrowly on relationships within the workforce and the needs of its members, to the neglect of output.

3 *Middle-of-the-road management* – medium concern for people and for production. In this case, a balance is struck between relational and task matters.

4 *Produce or perish* – low concern for people but high concern for production. This is also referred to as the authority compliance style, where members' concerns only count to the extent that they may hamper output. Achievement and the processes that promote it are all important.

5 *Team leadership* – high on people and high on production. This style integrates the importance of both factors. Members are treated as important, their ideas and contributions valued and their active involvement encouraged. A team environment is created, based on respect and trust. This boosts morale and satisfaction, and so promotes high level production.

While the 'team leader' would appear to win the best style award hands down, there is some concern that this potent combination of high production coupled with high care for people may not be pertinent to all situations (Quinn and McGrath, 1982). The maturity of the group (i.e. whether newly formed or existing) can have a major influence on optimal leadership style. The best style for a newly formed group, for instance, may be one where task issues are promoted over those of group members. While leaders are thought to have a preferred style and a fallback alternative when this customary approach fails, *opportunism* describes a person who makes use of any combination of these five styles as circumstances require.

It is not only in relation to the work of Blake and Mouton and their leadership grid that questions are raised as to which style is best. While democratic, participative options have much to commend them and fit neatly into a broader western political ideology, the answer is that no one style is 'right' or 'best'. Indeed, Müller and Turner (2007) showed that the effectiveness of leadership styles is dependent on the type of work project involved. Napier and Gershenfeld (2004: 207) contended that 'it is the ability of leaders to first identify the most appropriate behavioral response called for in a particular situation and then to actually use it as needed that separates those who are successful from the rest'.

Groups under directive leadership have been criticised for being prone to flawed decision making. Larson *et al.* (1998), however, found that where such leaders possess information favouring the best choice alternative, they can actually outperform their participative counterparts. In a study by Kahai *et al.* (1997), the degree of structure of the task also played a part. With moderately structured tasks, participative leadership was conducive to proposing solutions but this advantage was lost as the level of structure increased. Likewise, gender has been found to be related to ideal leadership style, with females preferring a more relational and democratic approach (Vecchio and Boatwright, 2002; Trinidad and Normore, 2005). Interestingly, Gardiner and Tiggemann (1999) discovered that it was only in female-dominated industries that females were more interpersonally oriented than males. The cultural background of participants should also be taken into account. Different cultures have contrasting perspectives on leadership and what it means. Thus, Torres (2000) found that Brazilians had a general preference for less participative styles of leadership than did Americans. On the other hand, Den Hartog *et al.* (1999) produced evidence that aspects of charismatic/transformational leadership are strongly endorsed across a broad range of cultures and have some claim to universality. In sum, Hargie *et al.* (2004) listed a set of fourfold considerations that are central to decisions about which leadership style may be most effective, namely:

1   the task faced by the group
2   the nature, abilities and characteristics of the members
3   the past history of the group and its members
4   the pressures and demands of the external environment.

Leadership skills

Gentry *et al.* (2009) carried out a major study involving almost 15,000 managers in which they compared changes in the perceived importance of key managerial skills over the past 15 years. Two of the most dramatic changes were that the significance of 'relationship' and 'time management' skills in management were regarded as much more important today. This is not surprising. Leaders are much more accessible now as a result of mobile technology and so there is a greater need to manage their time efficiently. But remote communications also carry the risk of reduced opportunities for face-to-face interaction, and so concerted efforts need to be made to ensure relationships are fostered. Leaders are required to fulfil a range of functions thereby making considerable demands on the complement of skills, competencies and tactics which they must have at their disposal. Being a potent agent of influence, building teams, making effective presentations, negotiating and bargaining, selecting and appraising are just some of the sets of skills identified by Hargie *et al.* (2004) in a management context.

Indeed, the number of diverse and varied actions demanded of a leader when trying to accomplish goals and maintain good internal relations under contrasting sets of circumstances makes the task of defining specific skills a daunting one. Perhaps this is one reason behind the observation by Morley and Hosking (1986) that the literature on leadership was not well informed by actual research into the nature of effective leadership skills. More recent empirical investigations into leadership skills and competencies have, however, been carried out (e.g. Deschamps, 2005; Marta *et al.*, 2005; Mumford *et al.*, 2007; Gentry *et al.*, 2009; McCallum and O'Connell, 2009). Still, it is true to say that the majority of contributions to this literature are based upon conceptual analysis and experiential insights rather than systematic research.

Providing inclusive leadership is undoubtedly a multifaceted process (Hollander,

2009). In the workplace, meetings are typically valued by members of staff, especially when they provide an opportunity for face-to-face contact with immediate and senior management (Hargie, 2007). For the workforce, they offer an important avenue into the decision-making process. People in turn are more likely to comply with decisions reached under circumstances affording some level of ownership (Deetz and Brown, 2004). One of the common functions expected of leaders by most groups, therefore, involves taking charge of discussions (Adams and Galanes, 2008). This service is particularly significant to the sort of small group interaction focused upon in this chapter.

Several publications (e.g. Hanna and Wilson, 1998; Hargie *et al.* 2004; Wilson, 2004; Adams and Galanes, 2008; Johnson and Johnson, 2009) have teased out taxonomies of skills and tactics involved in this activity. These sources will be drawn upon in the following outline of the major requirements demanded of those leading group discussions. Additionally, most of the skills already covered in this book have a role when applied to this particular enterprise.

Preparation

The work of leading a productive discussion doubtlessly begins in advance of members coming together. Tasks to be taken on board by (or on behalf of) the leader include:

- researching the issue/s fully, if knowledge is lacking
- identifying the purpose of the meeting and formulating an agenda, if appropriate; in formal meetings, this may be distributed in advance for agreement by members
- selecting a suitable location and making all necessary physical arrangements, including seating, equipment, materials, refreshments, etc.
- choosing when it is best to hold the meeting and how long it should last
- deciding who should be present, including particular people not part of the group who may be usefully invited on account of their relevant expertise.

Getting started

Much of relevance here has already been covered in relation to set induction in Chapter 10. Many of the ways of effecting perceptual, social, cognitive and motivational sets discussed there can be tailored to this particular situation and will not be repeated. Briefly, the leader should carry out the following tasks:

1 *Introduce all present.* If members are meeting for the first time, it is particularly important that time be taken to ensure that each is known to the rest and that all begin to feel at ease with the company. Icebreaking chit-chat can help people relax and assuage primary tension before moving on to meaningful discussion of more substantive issues.

2 *Identify roles.* Where people have been brought along for a particular reason, this should be made known. Alternatively, the leader may invite a participant to take on a special role, e.g. secretary, observer, devil's advocate, etc.

3   *Establish the agreed aim of the meeting and what it is designed to accomplish.*

4   *Agree procedures to follow.* Where an agenda has been drawn up, the leader may want to agree the order in which items are taken. Additionally, the ground rules to be followed as well as strategic steps to achieving the goal may need to be dealt with. If the task in hand is essentially to solve a problem, it may be prudent to suggest:

- spending some time analysing the problem and its causes
- agreeing the criteria that an acceptable solution would have to meet
- brainstorming possible solutions
- critically evaluating suggestions
- selecting an agreed option
- considering implementation issues.

5   *Direct a clear question at the group.* This is a way of getting the discussion going and focusing the group's attention on the first of the issues to be tackled.

Structuring and guiding discussion

Once the discussion has been initiated, the leader has a role in keeping it on target. Here a judicious balance has to be struck between on the one hand allowing the discussion to run amok, and on the other perpetrating a slow strangulation by forcing it into a straightjacket of the leader's choosing. The style of leadership selected (e.g. directive vs. participative) will influence how this delicate task is carried out. Structuring and guiding the discussion can be achieved in different ways:

- *Be alert to digression.* When members raise a peripheral issue, point out that this may be an interesting debate for another occasion, but right now it would divert the group from its goal in the limited time set aside to achieve it.
- *Clarify.* It is essential that participants fully appreciate what is happening. Where it is felt that a point has not been fully grasped or been misunderstood, the leader may clarify (see Chapter 8 for further discussion on this aspect of explaining) or invite the person who made it to do so.
- *Elaborate.* Certain contributions may be thought more worthy of having greater attention paid to them than others. Here the leader can elaborate directly by offering further information or encourage extended discussion by using techniques such as probing questions (see Chapter 5) and paraphrases (see Chapter 6).
- *Summarise.* In addition, it is useful for the leader to provide transitional summaries at the end of each phase of the meeting or discussion before introducing the next issue. These act as signposts, reminding members where they have been, where they are now and where they are going. This can be a very effective way of guiding the discourse.

Managing conflict

Conflict during discussion is sometimes mistakenly regarded as invariably destructive and to be avoided at all costs. While it may heighten tension in the group and challenge the skill of the leader in dealing with it, having members express different views and opinions can be to the advantage of the group outcome. This form of 'good conflict' (Cragan *et al.*, 2009) can help to circumvent the perils of groupthink as described earlier in the chapter. It is controlling conflict that counts. Tactics to consider include the following:

- *Focus on issues not on personalities.* When conflict becomes personalised it tends to shift from being potentially productive to invariably counterproductive. In this form, internal group relations will suffer.
- *Make all contributors feel that their suggestions have at least some merit.* The leader should avoid creating a situation of 'winners' and 'losers', or having some stakeholders feel sidelined or humiliated. Ways of giving face to those whose line of argument is ultimately not taken up should be found. Likewise, all should feel that they have received a 'fair hearing'.
- *Highlight broader areas of agreement.* If discussion reaches loggerheads, taking the group back to a point where all were in agreement on some broader matter can ease tension.
- *Emphasise 'we' and 'us'.* It is an oft-quoted mantra that 'There is no "I" in team.' Constantly re-establishing a sense of group unity prevents factionalism and damaged morale. Another well-known expression is that TEAM stands for Together Everyone Achieves More. Even in a situation where views of one member or faction prevail over those of another, the contribution of all to the quality of the decision reached by the group should be stressed.

Regulating participation

The following set of tactics addresses the task of conducting the discussion so that everyone has an opportunity to contribute, thereby ensuring an orderly meeting:

- *Encourage contributions.* Here some of the techniques of reinforcement discussed in Chapter 4 can be employed. Members who feel rewarded for their contributions, or who see others being rewarded, are more likely to contribute further. In particular, the leader should pay special attention to the more reticent member who may have an important input to make but may only be prepared to do so if directly invited in a tactful way. It is a mistake, though, to assume that the leader must comment on each contribution received. Frequently a more useful response is simply silence, or inviting the group or individual members to respond, if none is immediately forthcoming.
- *Discourage contributions.* On the other hand, the garrulous member has to be prevented from monopolising the proceedings. Decisions as to how much one person is permitted to hog the floor will be taken based upon the value of their input, amongst other considerations. It may be necessary to thank

diplomatically some for their commitment to the discussion while reminding them that they have already spoken twice on the issue while others still have not been heard, and that if there is time remaining at the end they will be returned to.

- ***Prevent overtalk.*** While all members should be encouraged to contribute to the discussion, if they all insist in doing so at the same time then the effect will be lost. Regulating contributions by bringing individuals in and out of the conversation at particular times is something that effective chairpersons are particularly skilled at doing. Much of this can be conducted nonverbally (see Chapter 3).

Closing

A good deal of what was said in Chapter 10 on closure is directly applicable here. In drawing the discussion to a close, the leader should do the following:

- Ensure that there is general agreement on the decision/s taken and that no remaining doubt or confusion exists.
- Identify any outstanding business still to be finalised.
- Establish how the outcome of the meeting is to be taken forward. If certain members have been tasked with doing certain things, this should be re-established. It is always advisable to have this committed to paper, in the form of a minute, as quickly as possible.
- Deal with any residual tension that may exist, perhaps from an earlier dis-agreement. It may be sufficient to mention the contribution of a member still 'smarting', without of course appearing to patronise that person. Taking time to personally have a few informal words before leaving may also be appreciated.
- Thank all for their efforts in achieving the aims of the discussion.

OVERVIEW

This chapter has been concerned with small groups, how they operate and the manner in which leaders emerge and leadership is exercised within them. Groups, in this sense, can be thought of as involving a plurality of individuals who influence each other in the course of interaction and share a relationship of interdependence in pursuit of some common goal or goals. Members also characteristically develop a sense of belonging to this particular social entity. People come together to form groups to satisfy needs which may be interpersonal, informational or material. In so doing they become part of an ordered and regulated system which evolves through the establishment of norms, or commonly expected and accepted ways of perceiving, thinking, feeling and acting; the enactment of roles including that of leader; and the creation of identifiable forms and patterns of communication between members.

Additionally, leadership has been highlighted as virtually synonymous with the act of influencing others in a range of group contexts. However, it is important to bear in mind the distinction between leadership and leader. While specific individuals may occupy the position of leader, acts of leadership can be manifested by any group member. Theories of leadership offer contrasting explanations about the emergence of leaders and their functioning. Focusing on the actual performance of leaders, their behaviour can be examined on two levels: leadership styles at the macro level and leadership skills and tactics at the micro level. While different styles have been suggested, the three most commonly mentioned are autocratic, democratic and laissez-faire.

Underlying dimensions for these and other stylistic variants have to do with the extent to which the leader takes all important decisions single-handedly; directs what subordinates should do and denies them autonomy; and concentrates on group task or relational issues. Finally, it was emphasised that the skills involved in leading group discussions are crucial to effective leadership. The core skills involved were analysed within the categories of getting started, structuring and guiding discussion, managing conflict, regulating participation, and closing.

Chapter 15

Conclusion

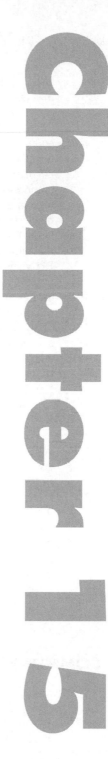

Humans seem to have an innate predisposition to commune with one another. Our ability to develop sophisticated methods for communicating both within and between generations is the core dimension that separates us from all other species. The research reviewed in Chapter 1 showed that the better able we are to communicate, the more successful we will be in all walks of life. As noted by Egan (2007: 97): 'Interpersonal communication competence is crucial for . . . just about everything we do.' An increased knowledge and comprehension of communication enables us to understand and adapt our own behaviour to situational demands, as well as providing us with deeper insights into the responses of others.

This book has been concerned with an examination of the central components of interpersonal communication, namely the skills that individuals employ in order to achieve their goals in social encounters. The theory behind the skills approach to the study of interpersonal behaviour, as outlined in Chapters 1 and 2, has provided a key conceptual framework that has been successfully applied across numerous settings and in a wide range of research studies.

Thus, there is a solid theoretical base underpinning the skills perspective. In his historical overview of this field, Argyle (1994: 142) noted: 'One of the implications of looking at social behaviour as a social skill was the likelihood that it could be trained.' This proved to be the case, and there has been an enormous explosion of interest in communication skills training. When individuals receive systematic skills tuition, their social performance has been shown to improve (Hargie, 2006b). Not surprisingly, there has been a concomitant and exponential growth in publications pertaining to interpersonal skills within a variety of social and professional contexts. As evidenced by the references in this text, research in this field has been voluminous.

This book has not offered a cookbook approach to the study of interpersonal interaction. Interpersonal communication is a complex and often strange phenomenon, which on occasion can become dysfunctional and cause immense difficulties in terms of human relationships (Spitzberg and Cupach, 2007; Vangelisti and Hampel, 2010). There are no 'right' or 'wrong' ways to communicate with others. One aspect emphasised throughout the book is that most skills have a 'happy medium' in terms of usage. For example, someone who bombards us with questions, continually self-discloses, or reinforces every single thing we say or do, would not be regarded as skilled. In this sense, a measured combination of skills is preferable.

Indeed, two important elements of goals were highlighted by Shah and Kruglanski (2000). The first is that of *multifinality* wherein any one means of achieving a goal may serve more than one purpose. For example, a negotiator who demonstrates an interest in and pays attention to the other side may achieve the twin goals of (a) building a good relationship and (b) making the chances of a successful negotiation more likely. The second is *equifinality*, whereby the same goal can be attained in a variety of equally effective ways. Thus, there are alternative approaches that can be employed in any particular interactive episode to achieve a desired outcome, and it is up to the individual to select what is deemed to be the most appropriate mix. Such selection, however, demands an extensive knowledge of the range of alternatives available and their likely effects in any given context. It is at this level that the present book has been geared.

The model of the interpersonal process outlined in Chapter 2 provides a conceptual framework, which can be used as a basis for making such strategic decisions. Awareness of the skills covered and of their behavioural determinants, as presented in the remaining chapters, will contribute to the increased understanding of the process of interpersonal communication. These furnish the reader with a language with which to study and interpret this process more fully. Fiske (2000: 77) pointed out that for the most part 'people do not know how they coordinate, plan, construct their action, or interpret each other's action'. While for much of the time we operate at this subconscious level, it is also necessary to have insight into and understanding of the skills and strategies that underpin human intercourse. Such knowledge enables us to operate swiftly and effectively without always having to think consciously about what we should do. When problems arise it also allows us to analyse possible underlying reasons and make alternative responses.

COMMUNICATION ETHICS

Before ending this book, it is important to consider the importance of communication ethics. There is a growing literature in the field of 'interpersonal justice' that refers to 'the degree to which people are treated with politeness, dignity and respect' (Colquitt *et al.*, 2001: 427). We expect to be treated with fairness in interactions and react negatively if we perceive this not to be the case (Skarlicki *et al.*, 2004). When people have information, they can use it for good or ill. It is the same with interpersonal skills. It is possible to use the information contained in this book in ethical or unethical ways. For example, the influencing techniques reviewed in Chapter 12 could be used in a manipulative and Machiavellian manner to get others to do what we want. Alternatively, they can be employed for the greater good of everyone. In the business world there have long been criticisms of the lack of communication ethics (Hargie *et al.*, 2004). The ethical manager is seen as being something akin to the yeti. Several people claim to have seen one in the distance, there is some circumstantial though not very convincing evidence that one exists, but no one has actually encountered the beast face to face, and we would be rather taken aback if we saw it in all its glory. But it is clear that in the end an unethical style of operating will be costly for both relational and more material goals (Clampitt, 2010). A code for communication professionals, put forward by Montgomery *et al.* (2001), included the following guidelines:

1   ***Tell the truth.*** As discussed in Chapter 9, harmless white lies (like telling someone their new suit is lovely when you really don't like it) can sometimes be conducive to relationships, but as deceit increases, the potential for dysfunctional outcomes escalates.

2   ***Do not harm others.*** The autonomy of others should be recognised and their independent decisions encouraged. Using interpersonal skills in a devious fashion (e.g. persuading people to act against their best interests) is not good practice. Selling others something they don't need at an inflated price is an example of a breach of this moral code. Spreading false and malicious rumours is another.

3   ***Treat others justly.*** Being aggressive, bullying or demeaning is not part of any decent moral code. Other people should be treated honourably and with respect. As discussed in Chapter 11, a 'soft' form of assertiveness is the best policy. Here the rights of both sides are protected equally and there is concern for the relationship.

4   ***Act professionally at all times.*** Respect information given in private and treat it confidentially. Behave in such a way as to inspire confidence. For example, listen carefully, respond in a manner that is apposite to the other person's emotional needs, and do not use inappropriate humour. Recognise that communication must be worked at. Attend professional development courses to update and sharpen your interpersonal skills.

5   ***Treat others as equals.*** In most professional–client encounters there is asymmetry, in that the former often has knowledge and status that the latter does not possess. This can cause *dysfunctional discordance* in the relationship (Morrow and Hargie, 2001). The concept of *concordance* is therefore important as a way of trying to achieve greater balance, whereby professional interactions are conceived as a meeting between equals. It is possible to behave in a power-crazed fashion by, for example, asking all the questions and only rewarding responses that suit your intentions for the other person. This is not good practice. Rather, it is better to empower others to participate as fully as possible. Explain to them what your goals are throughout the interaction and check these for agreement. Concordance necessitates adopting a more reflective than directive style.

OVERVIEW

Success in most walks of life is predicated on communicative ability. As shown in this book, we now know a great deal about the key constituents of effective social performance. The areas selected for inclusion were: nonverbal communication, reinforcement, questioning, reflecting, listening, explanation, self-disclosure, set induction, closure, assertiveness, influencing, negotiating and group interaction. It is recognised that this selection is not exhaustive, since other specialised skills may be employed in particular settings. Nevertheless, these represent core behavioural elements of skilled interpersonal communication. For this reason, the practising professional needs to have a sound working knowledge of them.

However, in the final analysis improvements in performance necessitate practical action. In other words, it is only by converting knowledge of skills into actual behaviour that increments in social competence can occur. This may necessitate changes in existing behavioural repertoire, and this is not always easily achieved. The most difficult part of learning new responses is often the unlearning of old ones. Thus, it is essential to experiment with various social techniques in order to develop, refine, maintain or extend one's existing repertoire of skills. Once a wide repertoire has been developed, the individual thereby becomes a more effective communicator with the ability to adjust and adapt to varying social situations. For most professionals, this is a prerequisite to effective functioning.

Bibliography

Achinstein, P. (1983) *The Nature of Explanation*. Oxford: Oxford University Press.

Adair, W., Okumura, T. and Brett, J. (2001) Negotiation behaviour when cultures collide: the United States and Japan, *Journal of Applied Psychology*, 86, 371–385.

Adams, N., Bell, J., Saunders, C. and Whittington, D. (1994) *Communication Skills in Physiotherapist–Patient Interactions*. Jordanstown: University of Ulster Monograph.

Adams, K. and Galanes, G. (2008) *Communicating in Groups: Applications and Skills*, 7th edn. Boston, MA: McGraw-Hill.

Adams, R. and Kleck, R. (2003) Perceived gaze direction and the processing of facial displays of emotion, *Psychological Science*, 14, 644–647.

Adler, R. and Elmhorst, J. (2008) *Communicating at Work*, 9th edn. Boston, MA: McGraw-Hill.

Adler, R. and Rodman, G. (2006) *Understanding Human Communication*, 9th edn. New York: Oxford University Press.

Adler, R., Rosen, B. and Silverstein, E. (1998) Emotions in negotiation: how to manage fear and anger, *Negotiation Journal*, 14, 161–179.

Adler, R., Rosenfeld, L. and Proctor, R. (2006) *Interplay: The Process of Interpersonal Communication*, 10th edn. New York: Oxford University Press.

Adler, T. (1993) Congressional staffers witness miracle of touch, *APA Monitor*, Feb, 12–13.

Afifi, T. and Steuber, K. (2009) The revelation risk model (RRM):

factors that predict the revelation of secrets and the strategies used to reveal them, *Communication Monographs*, 76, 144–176.

Afifi, T., Caughlin, J. and Afifi, W. (2007) The dark side (and light side) of avoidance and secrets, in B. Sitzberg and W. Cupach (eds) *The Dark Side of Interpersonal Communication*. Mahwah, NJ: Lawrence Erlbaum Associates, Inc.

Afifi, W. (2006) Nonverbal communication, in B. Whaley and W. Samter (eds) *Explaining Communication: Contemporary Theories and Exemplars*. Mahwah, NJ: Lawrence Erlbaum Associates, Inc.

Afifi, W. (2010) Uncertainty and information management in interpersonal contexts, in S. Smith and S. Wilson (eds) *New Directions in Interpersonal Communication Research*. Thousand Oaks, CA: Sage.

Afifi, W. and Caughlin, J. (2006) A close look at revealing secrets and some consequences that follow, *Communication Research*, 33, 467–488.

Afifi, W. and Guerrero, L. (2000) Motivations underlying topic avoidance in close relationships, in S. Petronio (ed.) *Balancing the Secrets of Private Disclosures*. Mahwah, NJ: Lawrence Erlbaum Associates, Inc.

Afifi, W. and Johnson, M. (2005) The nature and function of tie-signs, in V. Manusov (ed.) *The Sourcebook of Nonverbal Measures: Going Beyond Words*. Mahwah, NJ: Lawrence Erlbaum Associates, Inc.

Ajzen, I. (1991) The theory of planned behaviour, *Organizational Behavior and Human Decision Processes*, 50, 179–211.

Akande, A. (1997) Determinants of personal space among South African students, *Journal of Psychology*, 131, 569–571.

Alavosius, M., Adams, A., Ahern, D. and Follick, M. (2000) Behavioural approaches to organisational safety, in J. Austin and J. Carr (eds) *Handbook of Applied Behaviour Analysis*. Reno, CA: Context Press.

Albarracin, D., Johnson, B. and Zanna, M. (2005) *The Handbook of Attitudes*. London: Routledge.

Albert, S. and Kessler, S. (1976) Processes for ending social encounters, *Journal of the Theory of Social Behaviour*, 6, 147–170.

Alberti, R. and Emmons, M. (2008) *Your Perfect Right: Assertiveness and Equality in Your Life and Relationships*, 9th edn. Atascadero, CA: Impact.

Alberts, J.K. (1992) An inferential/strategic explanation for the social organisation of teases, *Journal of Language and Social Psychology*, 11, 153–178.

Algoe, S., Buswell, B. and DeLamater, J. (2000) Gender and job status as contextual cues for the interpretation of facial expression of emotion, *Sex Roles*, 42, 183–208.

Ali, M. and Levine, T. (2008) The language of truthful and deceptive denials and confessions, *Communication Reports*, 21, 82–91.

Allday, R. and Pakurar, K. (2007) Effects of teacher greetings on student on-task behaviour, *Journal of Applied Behavior Analysis*, 40, 317–320.

Allen, J., Waitzkin, H. and Stoeckle, J. (1979) Physicians' stereotypes about female health illness: a study of patients' sex and the information process during medical interviews, *Women and Health*, 4, 135–146.

Allen, K. and Stokes, T. (1987) Use of escape and reward in the management of young children during dental treatment, *Journal of Applied Behavior Analysis*, 20, 381–89.

Allen, M. (1998) Comparing the effectiveness of one- and two-sided messages, in

M. Allen and R. Preiss (eds) *Persuasion: Advances Through Meta-analysis*. Cresskill, NJ: Hampton Press.

Allen, M. and Stiff, J. (1998) An analysis of the sleeper effect, in M. Allen and R. Preiss (eds) *Persuasion: Advances Through Meta-analysis*. Cresskill, NJ: Hampton Press.

Allen, M., Bruflat, R., Fucilla, R., Kramer, M., McKellips, S., Ryan, D., *et al.* (2000) Testing the persuasiveness of evidence: combining narrative and statistical forms, *Communication Research Reports*, 17, 331–336.

Allen, M., Timmerman, L., Ksobiech, K., Valde, K., Gallagher, E., Hookham, L., *et al.* (2008) Persons living with HIV: disclosure to sexual partners, *Communication Research Reports*, 25, 192–199.

Allwinn, S. (1991) Seeking information: contextual influences on question formulation, *Journal of Language and Social Interaction*, 10, 169–184.

Alon, I. and Brett, J. (2007) Perceptions of time and their impact on negotiations in the Arabic-speaking Islamic world, *Negotiation Journal*, 23, 55–73.

Altman, I. (1977) The communication of interpersonal attitudes: an ecological approach, in T. Houston (ed.) *Foundations of Interpersonal Attraction*. London: Academic Press.

Altman, I. and Taylor, D. (1973) *Social Penetration: The Development of Interpersonal Relationships*. New York: Holt, Rinehart & Winston.

Alvesson, M. and Sveningsson, S. (2003) Managers doing leadership: the extra-ordinarization of the mundane, *Human Relations*, 56, 1435–1459.

Ambady, N. and Skowronski, J. (eds) (2008) *First Impressions*. New York: Guilford Press.

Amernic, J., Craig, R. and Tourish, D. (2007) The transformational leader as *pedagogue, physician, architect, commander*, and *saint*: five root metaphors in Jack Welch's letters to stockholders of General Electric, *Human Relations*, 60, 1839–1872.

Amiot, C., Blanchard, C. and Gaudreau, P. (2007) The self in change: a longitudinal investigation of coping and self-determination processes, *Self and Identity*, 7, 204–224.

Amit, K., Popper, M., Gal, R. and Mamane-Levy, T. (2009) Leadership-shaping experiences: a comparative study of leaders and non-leaders, *Leadership and Organization Development Journal*, 30, 302–318.

Andersen, J. (2009) When a servant-leader comes knocking . . ., *Leadership and Organization Development Journal*, 30, 4–15.

Andersen, P. (2005) The touch avoidance measure, in V. Manusov (ed.) *The Sourcebook of Nonverbal Measures: Going Beyond Words*. Mahwah, NJ: Lawrence Erlbaum Associates, Inc.

Andersen, P. (2006) The evolution of biological sex differences in communication, in K. Dindia and D. Canary (eds) *Sex Differences and Similarities in Communication*, 2nd edn. New York: Lawrence Erlbaum Associates, Inc.

Andersen, P. (2008) *Nonverbal Communication: Forms and Functions*. Long Grove, IL: Waveland Press.

Andersen, P. and Andersen, J. (2005) Measurements of perceived nonverbal immediacy, in V. Manusov (ed.) *The Sourcebook of Nonverbal Measures: Going Beyond Words*. Mahwah, NJ: Lawrence Erlbaum Associates, Inc.

Andersen, P. and Kumar, R. (2006) Emotions, trust and relationship development in business relationships: a conceptual model for buyer-seller dyads, *Industrial Marketing Management*, 35, 522–535.

Andersen, P., Guerrero, L., Buller, D. and Jorgensen, P. (1998) An empirical comparison of three theories of nonverbal immediacy exchange, *Human Communication Research*, 24, 501–535.

Andersen, P., Guerrero, L. and Jones, S. (2006) Nonverbal behaviour in intimate interactions and intimate relationships, in V. Manusov and M. Patterson (eds) *The Sage Handbook of Nonverbal Communication*. Thousand Oaks, CA: Sage.

Anderson, D., Ansfield, M. and DePaulo, B. (1999) Love's best habit: deception in the context of relationships, in P. Philippot, R. Feldman and E. Coats (eds) *The Social Context of Nonverbal Behaviour*. Cambridge: Cambridge University Press.

Anderson, R. (1997) Anxiety or ignorance: the determinants of interpersonal skill display, *Dissertation Abstracts International: The Sciences and Engineering*, 57 (9-B): 5959.

Andrews, K., Carpenter, C., Shaw, A. and Boster, F. (2008) The legitimization of paltry favors effect: a review and meta-analysis, *Communication Reports*, 21, 59–69.

Andriessen, E. and Drenth, P. (1998) Leadership: theories and models, in P. Drenth, H. Thierry and C. de Wolff (eds) *A Handbook of Work and Organizational Psychology, Volume 4: Organizational Psychology*. Hove, UK: Psychology Press.

Anonymous (1998) To reveal or not to reveal: a theoretical model of anonymous communication, *Communication Theory*, 8, 381–407.

Ansfield, M. (2007) Smiling when distressed: when a smile is a frown turned upside down, *Personality and Social Psychology Bulletin*, 33, 763–775.

Anthony, A. (2008) Baby P stepfather rape case raises questions over impact on child witnesses. *The Observer*, 3 May. http://www.guardian.co.uk/society/2009/may/03/child-witnesses-baby-p-stepfather (accessed 2 December 2009).

Antos, G., Ventola, E. and Weber, T. (eds) (2008) *Handbook of Interpersonal Communication*. Berlin: Mouton de Gruyter.

Archer, J., Kilpatrick, G. and Bramwell, G. (1995) Comparison of two aggression inventories, *Aggressive Behavior*, 21, 371–380.

Archer, R. (1979) Role of personality and the social situation, in G. Chelune (ed.) *Self-disclosure*. San Francisco: Jossey-Bass.

Argyle, M. (1983) *The Psychology of Interpersonal Behaviour*, 4th edn. Harmondsworth: Penguin.

Argyle, M. (1988) *Bodily Communication*, 2nd edn. New York: Methuen.

Argyle, M. (1994) *The Psychology of Interpersonal Behaviour*, 5th edn. London: Penguin.

Argyle, M. (1995) Social skills, in N. Mackintosh and A. Colman (eds) *Learning and Skills*. London: Longman.

Argyle, M. and Cook, M. (1976) *Gaze and Mutual Gaze*. Cambridge: Cambridge University Press.

Argyle, M., Furnham, A. and Graham, J. (1981) *Social Situations*. Cambridge: Cambridge University Press.

Arnes, D. (2008) Assertiveness expectancies: how hard people push depends on the consequences they predict, *Journal of Personality and Social Psychology*, 95, 1541–1557.

Arnold, E. and Boggs, K. (2006) *Interpersonal Relationships: Professional Communication Skills for Nurses*, 5th edn. Los Angeles, CA: W. B. Saunders.

Aron, A., Mashek, D. and Aron, E. (2004) Closeness as including other in the self, in D. Mashek and A. Aron (eds) *Handbook of Closeness and Intimacy*. Mahwah, NJ: Lawrence Erlbaum Associates, Inc.

Aron, A., Mashek, D., McLaughlin-Volpe, T., Wright, S., Lewandowski, G. and Aron, E. (2006) Including close others in the cognitive structure of the self, in M. Baldwin (ed.) *Interpersonal Cognition*. New York: Guilford Press.

Aronson, E. (2007) The evolution of cognitive dissonance theory: a personal appraisal, in A. Pratkanis (ed.) *The Science of Social Influence: Advances and Future Progress*. New York: Psychology Press.

Aronson, E. (2008) *The Social Animal*, 10th edn. New York: W.H. Freeman.

Aronson, E., Wilson, T. and Akert, R. (2007) *Social Psychology*, 6th edn. Upper Saddle River, NJ: Pearson.

Arrow, H., Poole, M., Henry, K., Wheelan, S. and Moreland, R. (2004) Time, change, and development: the temporal perspective on groups, *Small Group Research*, 35, 73–105.

Asai, A. and Barnlund, D. (1998) Boundaries of the unconscious private and public self in Japanese and Americans: a cross-cultural comparison, *International Journal of Intercultural Relations*, 22, 431–452.

Asante, M., Miike, Y. and Yin, J. (2007) *The Global Intercultural Communication Reader*. London: Routledge.

Asch, S. (1940) Studies in the principles of judgments and attitudes: II. Determination of judgments by group and by ego standards, *Journal of Social Psychology*, 12, 433–465.

Asch, S. (1952) *Social Psychology*. Englewood Cliffs, NJ: Prentice-Hall.

Ashmore, R. and Banks, D. (2001) Patterns of self-disclosure among mental health nursing students, *Nurse Education Today*, 21, 48–57.

Astrom, J. (1994) Introductory greeting behaviour: a laboratory investigation of approaching and closing salutation phases, *Perceptual and Motor Skills*, 79, 863–897.

Astrom, J. and Thorell, L. (1996) Greeting behaviour and psychogenic need: interviews on experiences of therapists, clergymen and car salesmen, *Perceptual and Motor Skills*, 83, 939–956.

Audit Commission (1993) *What Seems To Be the Matter? Communication Between Hospitals and Patients*. London: HMSO.

Auerswald, M. (1974) Differential reinforcing power of restatement and interpretation on client production of affect, *Journal of Counseling Psychology*, 21, 9–14.

Augoustinos, M. and Walker, I. (1995) *Social Cognition*. London: Sage.

Auslander, B., Perfect, M., Succop, P. and Rosenthal, S. (2007) Perceptions of sexual assertiveness among adolescent girls: initiation, refusal, and use of protective behaviors, *Journal of Pediatric and Adolescent Gynecology*, 20, 157–162.

Austin, J. and Carr, J. (eds) (2000) *Handbook of Applied Behavior Analysis*. Reno, NV: Context Press.

Austin, J. and Vancouver, J. (1996) Goal constructs in psychology: structure, process and content, *Psychological Bulletin*, 120, 338–375.

Avolio, B., Walumbwa, F. and Weber, T. (2009) Leadership: current theories, research, and future directions, *Annual Review of Psychology*, 60, 421–449.

Avtgis T., Rancer, A., Kanjeva, P. and Chory, R. (2008) Argumentative and aggressive communication in Bulgaria: testing for conceptual and methodological equivalence, *Journal of Intercultural Communication Research*, 37, 17–24.

Axtell, R. (1991) *Gestures: The Do's and Taboos of Body Language around the World*. New York: Wiley.

Axtell, R. (1999) Initiating interaction: greetings and beckonings across the world, in L. Guerrero, J. DeVito and M. Hecht (eds) *The Nonverbal Communication Reader: Classic and Contemporary Readings Disclosures*, 2nd edn. Prospect Heights, IL: Waveland Press.

Babcock, L. and Laschever, S. (2008) *Why Women Don't Ask: The High Cost of Avoiding Negotiation – and Positive Strategies for Change*. London: Paitkus.

Back, K. and Back, K. (2005) *Assertiveness at Work: A Practical Guide to Handling Awkward Situations*, 3rd edn. London: McGraw-Hill.

Baddeley, A., Eysenck, M. and Anderson, M. (2009) *Memory*. Hove, UK: Psychology Press.

Baillargeon, N. (2007) *A Short Course in Intellectual Self-defense: Find Your Inner Chomsky*. New York: Seven Stories Press.

Baker, H., Crockett, R., Uus, K., Bamford, J. and Marteau, T. (2007) Why don't health professionals check patient understanding? A questionnaire-based study, *Psychology, Health and Medicine*, 12, 380–385.

Baker, R. (2001) The nature of leadership, *Human Relations*, 54, 469–494.

Baker, W. (1994) *Networking Smart: How to Build Relationships for Personal and Organizational Success*. New York: McGraw-Hill.

Balachandra, L., Bordone, R., Menkel-Meadow, C., Ringstrom, P. and Sarath E. (2005) Improvisation and negotiation: expecting the unexpected, *Negotiation Journal*, 21, 415–423.

Balcetis, E. (2008) Where the motivation resides and self-deception hides: how motivated cognition accomplishes self-deception, *Social and Personality Psychology Compass*, 2, 361–381.

Baldwin, M. (ed.) (2000) *The Use of Self in Therapy*, 2nd edn. New York: Haworth Press.

Bales, R. (1950) *Interaction Process Analysis: A Method for the Study Of Small Groups*. Cambridge, MA: Addison-Wesley.

Bales, R. (1970) *Personality and Interpersonal Behavior*. New York: Holt, Rinehart and Winston.

Balzer Riley, J. (2008) *Communication in Nursing*, 6th edn. St Louis, MO: Mosby.

Bambacas, M. and Patrickson, M. (2008) Interpersonal communication skills that enhance organisational commitment, *Journal of Communication Management*, 12, 51–72.

Bandura, A. (1986) *Social Foundations of Thought and Action: A Social Cognitive Theory*. Englewood Cliffs, NJ: Prentice-Hall.

Bandura, A. (1989) Self-regulation of motivation and action through internal standards and goal systems, in L. Pervin (ed.) *Goal Concepts in Personality and Social Psychology*. Hillsdale, NJ: Lawrence Erlbaum Associates, Inc.

Bandura, A. (1997) *Self-efficacy: The Exercise of Control*. New York: W.H. Freeman.

Bandura, A. (2006) *Psychological Modeling: Conflicting Theories*. Piscataway, NJ: Aldine Transaction.

Bangerter, A. (2000) Self-presentation: conversational implications of self-presentational goals in research interviews, *Journal of Language and Social Psychology*, 19, 436–462.

Bangerter, A., Clark, H. and Katz, A. (2004) Navigating joint projects in telephone conversations, *Discourse Processes*, 37, 1–23.

Banks, D. (1972) A comparative study of the reinforcing potential of verbal and non-verbal cues in a verbal conditioning paradigm. Unpublished doctoral dissertation, University of Massachusetts.

Banse, R. and Scherer, K. R. (1996) Acoustic profiles in vocal emotion expression, *Journal of Personality and Social Psychology*, 70, 614–636.

Bardine, B. (1999) Students' perceptions of written teacher comments: what do they say about how we respond to them, *High School Journal*, 82, 239–247.

Bargh, J. (2005) Bypassing the will: towards demystifying behavioral priming effects, in R. Hassin, J. Uleman and J. Bargh (eds) *The New Unconscious*. Oxford: Oxford University Press.

Bargiela-Chiappini, F. and Harris, S. (1996) Interruptive strategies in British and Italian management meetings, *Text*, 16, 269–297.

Barnabei, F., Cormier, W. H. and Nye, L. S. (1974) Determining the effects of three counselor verbal responses on client verbal behavior, *Journal of Counseling Psychology*, 21, 355–359.

Baron, R. and Byrne, D. (2000) *Social Psychology*, 9th edn. Boston: Allyn and Bacon.

Baron, R. and Kerr, N. (2003) *Group Process, Group Decision, Group Action*, 2nd edn. Buckingham: Open University Press.

Baron, R. and Markman, G. (2000) Beyond social capital: how social skills can enhance entrepreneurs' success, *Academy of Management Executive*, 14, 106–116.

Baron, R., Cowan, G., Ganz, R. and McDonald, M. (1974) Interaction of locus of control and type of reinforcement feedback: considerations of external validity, *Journal of Personality and Social Psychology*, 30, 285–292.

Barry, B., Fulmer, I. and Goates, N. (2006) Bargaining with feeling: emotionality in and around negotiation, in L. Thompson (ed.) *Negotiation Theory and Research*. New York: Taylor and Francis.

Barwise, P. and Meehan, S. (2008) So you think you're a good listener, *Harvard Business Review*, 88, 22.

Bass, B. (1985) *Leadership and Performance Beyond Expectations*. New York: Free Press.

Bass, B. (1990) *Bass and Stogdill's Handbook of Leadership: A Survey of Theory and Research*. New York: Free Press.

Bass, B. (1996) *A New Paradigm of Leadership: An Inquiry into Transformational Leadership*. Alexandria, VA: US Army Research Institute for the Behavioral and Social Sciences.

Bass, B. and Riggio, R. (2005) *Transformational Leadership*. New York: Psychology Press.

Bassnett, S. (2007) Well, it's a matter of, um, plain speaking, *The Times Higher Education*, 21/28 December, p. 20.

Baum, J., Frese, M. and Baron, R. (eds) (2006) *The Psychology of Entrepreneurship*. Mahwah, NJ: Lawrence Erlbaum Associates, Inc.

Bavelas, A. (1950) Communication patterns in task-oriented groups, *Journal of the Acoustical Society of America*, 22, 725–730.

Bavelas, J. and Chovil, N. (2006) Nonverbal and verbal communication: hand gestures and facial displays as part of language use in face-to-face dialogue, in V. Manusov and M. Patterson (eds) *The Sage Handbook of Nonverbal Communication*. Thousand Oaks, CA: Sage.

Baxter, J., Boon, J. and Marley, C. (2006) Interrogative pressure and responses to minimally leading questions, *Personality and Individual Differences*, 40, 87–98.

Baxter, L. and Sahlstein, E. (2000) Some possible directions for future research, in S. Petronio (ed.) *Balancing the Secrets of Private Disclosures*. Mahwah, NJ: Lawrence Erlbaum Associates, Inc.

Beagrie, S. (2007) How to . . . speak in public, *Occupational Health*, 59, 26.

Beall, M., Gill-Rosier, J., Tate, J. and Matten, A. (2008) State of the context: listening in education, *International Journal of Listening*, 22, 123–132.

Beattie, G. (2004) *Visible Thought: The New Psychology of Body Language*. London: Routledge.

Beaulieu, C. (2004) Intercultural study of personal space: a case study, *Journal of Applied Social Psychology*, 34, 794–805.

Beaumeister, R. (1999) The nature and structure of the self, in R. Beaumeister (ed.) *The Self in Social Psychology*. Philadelphia, PA: Psychology Press.

Beaver, D. (2007) With visual aids, more is less, *ABA Banking Journal*, 99, 61.

Beaver, H. (2005) Nobody knows you're nervous: how to conquer those public speaking jitters, *ABA Banking Journal*, 96, 60.

Beaver, H. (2006) They don't like my accent, *ABA Banking Journal*, 98, 49.

Beck, C. (1999) *Managerial Communication: Bridging Theory and Practice*. Upper Saddle River, NJ: Prentice-Hall.

Beebe, S. and Masterson, J. (2000) *Communication in Small Groups: Principles and Practice*, 6th edn. New York: Longman.

Beezer, R. (1956) *Research on Methods of Interviewing Foreign Informants*, Alexandria, VA: George Washington University, Human Resource Office.

Beharry, E. (1976) The effect of interviewing style upon self-disclosure in a dyadic interaction, *Dissertation Abstracts International*, 36, 4677B.

Beier, E. and Young, D. (1998) *The Silent Language of Psychotherapy*. New York: Aldine De Gruyter.

Bell, C. (1806) *Essays on the Anatomy of Expression in Painting*. London: J. Murray.

Bell, R. and Healey, J. (1992) Idiomatic communication and interpersonal solidarity in friends' relational cultures, *Human Communication Research*, 18, 307–335.

Beneson, J., Aikins-Ford, S. and Apostoleris, N. (1998) Girls' assertion in the presence of boys, *Small Group Research* 29, 198–211.

Benjamin, A. (2001) *The Helping Interview with Case Illustrations*, 4th edn. Boston, MA: Houghton Mifflin.

Benn, A., Jones, G. and Rosenfield, S. (2008) Analysis of instructional consultants' questions and alternatives to questions during the problem identification interview, *Journal of Educational and Psychological Consultation*, 18, 54–80.

Benne, K. and Sheats, P. (1948) Functional roles of group members, *Journal of Social Issues*, 4, 41–49.

Bennis, W. and Townsend, R. (2005) *Reinventing Leadership: Strategies to Empower the Organization*. New York: HarperCollins.

Benoit, W. (1998) Forewarning and persuasion, in M. Allen and R. Preiss (eds) *Persuasion: Advances Through Meta-analysis*. Cresskill, NJ: Hampton Press.

Benoit, W. and Benoit, P. (2008) *Persuasive Messages: The Process of Influence*. Malden, MA: Blackwell.

Bente, G., Donaghy, W. and Suwelack, D. (1998) Sex differences in body movement and visual attention: an integrated analysis of movement and gaze in mixed-sex dyads, *Journal of Nonverbal Behavior*, 22, 31–58.

Berger, C. (1994) Power, dominance and social interaction, in M. Knapp and G. Miller (eds) *Handbook of interpersonal communication*, 2nd edn. Beverly Hills, CA: Sage.

Berger, C. (1995) A plan-based approach to strategic communication, in D. Hewes (ed.) *The Cognitive Basis of Interpersonal Communication*, Hillsdale, NJ: Lawrence Erlbaum Associates, Inc.

Berger, C. (2000) Goal detection and efficiency: neglected aspects of message production, *Communication Theory*, 10, 135–138.

Berger, C. (2002) Goals and knowledge structures in social interaction, in M. Knapp and J. Daly (eds) *Handbook of Interpersonal Communication*, 3rd edn. Thousand Oaks, CA: Sage.

Berger, C., Roloff, M. and Roskos-Ewoldsen D. (eds) (2010) *The Handbook of Communication Science*. Thousand Oaks, CA: Sage.

Berger, J. (2005) Ignorance is bliss? Ethical considerations in therapeutic nondisclosure, *Cancer Investigation*, 1, 94–98.

Bergeron, J. and Vachon, M. (2008) The effects of humour usage by financial advisors in sales encounters, *International Journal of Bank Marketing*, 26, 376–398.

Berlew, D. (1990) How to increase your influence, in I. Asherman and S. Asherman (eds) *The Negotiating Sourcebook*. Amherst, MA: Human Resource Development Press.

Bernard, H. (2006) *Research Methods in Anthropology: Qualitative and Quantitative Approaches*. Lanham, MD: AltaMira Press.

Bernieri, F. (2005) The expression of rapport, in V. Manusov (ed.) *The Sourcebook of Nonverbal Measures: Going Beyond Words*. Mahwah, NJ: Lawrence Erlbaum Associates, Inc.

Berry, W. (1996) *Negotiating in the Age of Integrity: A Complete Guide to Negotiating Win/Win in Business*. London: Nicolas Brealey.

Beukeboom, C. (2009) When words feel right: how affective expressions of listeners change a speaker's language use, *European Journal of Social Psychology*, 39, 747–756.

Bhattacharya, J. and Isen, A. (2008) On inferring demand for health care in the presence of anchoring, acquiescence, and selection biases, NBER Working Paper no. W13865. http://ssrn.com/abstract=1106591 (accessed 2 December 2009).

Billing, M. (2001) Arguing, in W. Robinson and H. Giles (eds) *The Handbook Of Language and Social Psychology*. Chichester: Wiley.

Bingham, L. (2007) Avoiding negotiation: strategy and practice, in A. Schneider and

C. Honeyman (eds) *The Negotiator's Fieldbook: The Desk Reference for the Experienced Negotiator*. Chicago, IL: American Bar Association.

Bion, W. (1961) *Experiences in Groups and Other Papers*. London: Tavistock.

Birdwhistell, R. (1970) *Kinesics and Context*. Philadelphia, PA: University of Pennsylvania Press.

Blairy, S., Herrera, P. and Hess, U. (1999) Mimicry and the judgment of emotional facial expressions, *Journal of Nonverbal Behavior*, 23, 5–41.

Blake, B. and McCanse, A. (1991) *Leadership Dilemmas – Grid Solutions*. Houston, TX: Gulf Publishing.

Blake, B. and Mouton, J. (1985) *The Managerial Grid III*, Houston, TX: Gulf Publishing.

Blakemore, J., Berenbaum, S. and Liben, L. (2008) *Gender Development*. Hove, UK: Psychology Press.

Blankenship, K. and Craig, T. (2006) Rhetorical question use and resistance to persuasion: an attitude strength analysis, *Language and Social Psychology*, 25, 111–128.

Bless, H. (2001) The consequences of mood on the processing of social information, in A. Tesser and N. Schwarz (eds) *Blackwell Handbook of Social Psychology: Intraindividual Processes*. Malden, MA: Blackwell.

Bless, H., Bohner, G., Hild, T. and Schwarz, N. (1992) Asking difficult questions: task complexity increases the impact of response, *European Journal of Social Psychology*, 22, 309–312.

Bloch, C. (1996) Emotions and discourse, *Text*, 16, 323–341.

Blonna, R. and Water, D. (2005) *Health Counseling: A Microskills Approach*. Sudbury, MA: Jones and Bartlett.

Bloom, A. (2009) Beware the carrot: rewards don't work, *Times Education Supplement*, 13 November. http://www.tes.co.uk/article.aspx?storycode=6027535 (accessed 2 December 2009).

Blundel, R. (1998) *Effective Business Communication: Principles and Practice for the Information Age*. London: Prentice-Hall.

Bochner, D. (2000) *The Therapist's Use of Self in Family Therapy*. Northvale, NJ: Jason Aronson.

Boddy, J., Carvier, A. and Rowley, K. (1986) Effects of positive and negative verbal reinforcement on performance as a function of extroversion-introversion: some tests of Gray's theory, *Personality and Individual Differences*, 7, 81–88.

Bodie, G. (2010) A racing heart, rattling knees, and ruminative thoughts: defining, explaining, and treating public speaking anxiety, *Communication Education*, 59, 70–105.

Bodie, G., Worthington, D., Imhof, M. and Cooper, L. (2008) What would a unified field of listening look like? A proposal linking past perspectives and future endeavors, *International Journal of Listening*, 22, 103–122.

Bolden, G. (2008) Reopening Russian conversations: the discourse particle *-to* and the negotiation of interpersonal accountability in closings, *Human Communication Research*, 34, 99–136.

Bolden, G. (2009) Beyond answering: repeat-prefaced responses in conversation, *Communication Monographs*, 76, 121–143.

Bolton, R. (1986) *People Skills: How to Assert Yourself, Listen to Others, and Resolve Conflicts*. Sydney: Simon and Schuster.

Boore, J. (1979) *Prescription for Recovery*. London: RCN.

Boothe, J. and Borrego, J. (2004) Parent's acceptance of behavioral interventions for children with behavior and communication problems, *Child and Family Behavior Therapy*, 26, 1–15.

Borisoff, D. and Merrill, L. (1991) Gender issues and listening, in D. Borisoff and M. Purdy (eds) *Listening in Everyday Life*. Lanham, MD: University Press of America.

Borisoff, D. and Purdy, M. (1991a) What is listening?, in D. Borisoff and M. Purdy (eds) *Listening in Everyday Life*. Lanham, MD: University Press of America.

Borisoff, D. and Purdy, M. (eds) (1991b) *Listening in Everyday Life*. Lanham, MD: University Press of America.

Bormann, E. (1990) *Small Group Communication: Theory and Practice*. New York: Harper and Row.

Borrego, J. and Urquiza, A. (1998) Importance of therapist use of social reinforcement with parents as a model for parent–child relationships: an example with parent–child interaction therapy, *Child and Family Behavior Therapy*, 20, 27–54.

Bostrom, R. (1990) *Listening Behavior: Measurement and Applications*. New York: Guilford Press.

Bostrom, R. (1996) Memory, cognitive processing and the process of 'listening': a reply to Thomas and Levine, *Human Communication Research*, 23, 298–305.

Bostrom, R. (2006) The process of listening, in O. Hargie (ed.) *The Handbook of Communication Skills*, 3rd edn. London: Routledge.

Bottom, W. and Paese, P. (1999) Judgment accuracy and the asymmetric cost of errors in distributive bargaining, *Group Decision and Negotiation*, 8, 349–364.

Boudreau, J., Cassell, E. and Fuks, A. (2009) Preparing medical students to become attentive listeners, *Medical Teacher*, 31, 22–29.

Bousfield, D. (2008) *Impoliteness in Interaction*. Amsterdam: John Benjamins.

Bowe, H. and Martin, K. (2007) *Communication Across Cultures: Mutual Understanding in a Global World*. Cambridge: Cambridge University Press.

Bowles, H., Babcock, L. and Lai, L. (2007) Social incentives for gender differences in the propensity to initiate negotiations: sometimes it does hurt to ask, *Organizational Behavior and Human Decision Processes*, 103, 84–103.

Bowman, B., Punyanunt-Carter, N., Cheah, T., Watson, W. and Rubin, R. (2007) Does listening to Mozart affect listening ability?, *International Journal of Listening*, 21, 124–139.

Bracken, C. and Lombard (2004) Social presence and children: praise, intrinsic motivation, and learning with computers, *Journal of Communication*, 54, 22–37.

Bradbury, A. (2006) *Successful Presentation Skills*. London: Kogan Page.

Brammer, L. and MacDonald, G. (2003) *The Helping Relationship: Process and Skills*, 8th edn. Boston, MA: Pearson Education.

Brammer, L., Shostrom, E. and Abrego, P. (1989) *Therapeutic Psychology: Fundamentals of Counselling and Psychotherapy*. Englewood Cliffs, NJ: Prentice-Hall.

Brashers, D., Goldsmith, D. and Hsieh, E. (2002) Information seeking and avoiding in health contexts, *Human Communication Research*, 28, 258–271.

Brataas, H., Thorsnes, S. and Hargie, O. (2010) Themes and goals in cancer outpatient – cancer nurse consultations, *European Journal of Cancer Care*, 19, 184–191.

Braun, M. and Bryan, A. (2006) Female waist-to-hip and male waist-to-shoulder ratios as determinants of romantic partner desirability, *Journal of Social and Personal Relationships*, 23, 805–819.

Braverman, J. (2008) Testimonials versus informational persuasive messages: the moderating effect of delivery mode and personal involvement, *Communication Research*, 35, 666–694.

Breakwell, G., Hammond, S., Fife-Schaw, C. and Smith, J. (eds) (2006) *Research Methods in Psychology*, 3rd edn. London: Sage.

Brehm, J. (1966) *A Theory of Psychological Reactance*. New York: Academic Press.

Brehm, J. and Weintraub, M. (1977) Physical barriers and psychological reactance: two-year-olds' responses to threats to freedom, *Journal of Personality and Social Psychology*, 35, 830–836.

Brehm, S., Miller, R., Perlman, D. and Campbell, S. (2006) *Intimate Relationships*, 3rd edn. New York: McGraw-Hill.

Brennan, T. (2009) Gossip – tales of the human condition, *The Psychologist*, 22, 24–26.

Brett, J., Adair, W., Lempereur, A., Okumura, T., Shikhirev, P., Tinsley, C., *et al.* (1998) Culture and joint gains in negotiation, *Negotiation Journal*, 14, 61–86.

Brett, J., Shapiro, L. and Lytle, A. (1998) Breaking the bonds of reciprocity in negotiation, *Academy of Management Journal*, 41, 410–424.

Brewer, N., Chapman, G., Schwartz, J. and Bergus, G. (2007) The influence of irrelevant anchors on the judgments and choices of doctors and patients, *Medical Decision Making*, 27, 203–211.

Brodsky, S., Hooper, N., Tipper, D. and Yates, S. (1999) Attorney invasion of witness space, *Law and Psychology Review*, 23, 49–68.

Bronson, P. and Merryman, A. (2009) *NurtureShock: New Thinking about Children*. New York: Twelve.

Brooks, W. and Heath, R. (1993) *Speech Communication*. Dubuque, IA: W. C. Brown.

Brophy, J. (1981) Teacher praise: a functional analysis, *Review of Educational Research*, 51, 5–32.

Brown, C. and Sulzerazaroff, B. (1994) An assessment of the relationship between customer satisfaction and service friendliness, *Journal of Organizational Behavior Management*, 14, 55–75.

Brown, D. (2007) *Tricks of the Mind*. London: Transworld.

Brown, E. (1997) Self-disclosure, social anxiety, and symptomatology in rape victim-survivors: the effects of cognitive and emotional processing, *Dissertation Abstracts International: The Sciences and Engineering*, 57(10-B), 6559.

Brown, G. (2006) Explaining, in O. Hargie (ed.) *The Handbook of Communication Skills*, 3rd edn. London: Routledge.

Brown, G. and Armstrong, S. (1989) Explaining and explanations, in E. Wragg (ed.) *Classroom Teaching Skills*, 2nd edn. London: Croom Helm.

Brown, G. and Bakhtar, M. (1988) Styles of lecturing: a study and its implications, *Research Papers in Education*, 3, 131–153.

Brown, G. and Edmunds, S. (2009) Lectures, in J. Dent and R. Harden (eds) *A Practical Guide for Medical Tecahers*. Amsterdam: Elsevier.

Brown, H. (1996) Themes in experimental research on groups from the 1930s to the 1990s, in M. Wetherell (ed.) *Identities Groups and Social Issues*. London: Sage in association with the Open University.

Brown, J., Stewart, M. and Ryan, B. (2003) Outcomes of patient-provider interaction, in T. Thompson, A. Dorsey, K. Miller and R. Parrott (eds) *Handbook of Health Communication*. Mahwah, NJ: Lawrence Erlbaum Associates, Inc.

Brown, P. and Levinson, S. (1978) Universals in language usage: politeness phenomena, in E. Goody (ed.) *Questions and Politeness: Strategies in Social Interaction*. Oxford: Blackwell.

Brown, R. (2000) *Group Processes*, 2nd edn. Oxford: Blackwell.

Brownell, J. (1995) Responding to messages, in J. Stewart (ed.) *Bridges not Walls: A Book about Interpersonal Communication*, 6th edn. New York: McGraw-Hill.

Brownell, J. (2005) *Listening: Attitudes, Principles, and Skills*, 3rd edn. Boston, MA: Allyn & Bacon.

Bruner, J., Goodnow, J. and Austin, G. (1956) *A Study of Thinking*. New York: Wiley.

Bryan, A. and Gallois, C. (1992) Rules about assertion in the workplace: effects of status and message type, *Australian Journal of Psychology*, 44, 51–59.

Bryon, K., Terranova, S. and Nowicki, S. (2007) Nonverbal emotion recognition and salespersons: linking ability to perceive and actual success, *Journal of Applied Social Psychology*, 37, 2600–2619.

Buck, R. (1994) Facial and emotional functions in facial expression and communication: the readout hypothesis, *Biological Psychology*, 38, 95–115.

Buckmann, W. (1997) Adherence: a matter of self-efficacy and power, *Journal of Advanced Nursing*, 26, 132–137.

Buckwalter, A. (1983) *Interviews and Interrogations*. Stoneham: Butterworth.

Bugelova, T. (2000) Comparative analysis of communication skills of university students and median level executives in relation to career orientation, *Studia Psychologica*, 42, 273–277.

Bull, P. (2001a) Nonverbal communication, *The Psychologist*, 14, 644–647.

Bull, P. (2001b) Massaging the message, *The Psychologist*, 14, 342–343.

Bull, P. (2002) *Communication under the Microscope: The Theory and Practice of Microanalysis*. London: Routledge.

Bull, P. (2003) *The Microanalysis of Political Communication: Claptrap and Ambiguity*. London: Routledge.

Bull, P. (2006) What is skilled interpersonal communication?, in M. B. Hinner (ed.) *Freiberger Beitraege zur interkulturellen und Wirtschaftskommunikation: A Forum for General and Intercultural Business*. Frankfurt: Peter Lang.

Bull, P. and Frederikson, L. (1995) Nonverbal communication, in M. Argyle and A. Colman (eds) *Social Psychology*. London: Longman.

Buller, D. (2005) Methods for measuring speech rate, in V. Manusov (ed.) *The Sourcebook of Nonverbal Measures: Going Beyond Words*. Mahwah, NJ: Lawrence Erlbaum Associates, Inc.

Buller, D. and Burgoon, J. (1996) Interpersonal deception theory, *Communication Theory*, 6, 203–242.

Buller, D. and Burgoon, J. (1998) Emotional expression in the deception process, in P. Anderson and L. Guerrero (eds) *Handbook of Communication and Emotion: Research, Theory, Applications, and Contexts*. San Diego, CA: Academic Press.

Buller, D. and Hall, J. (1998) The effects of distraction during persuasion, in M. Allen and R. Preiss (eds) *Persuasion: Advances Through Meta-analysis*. Cresskill, NJ: Hampton Press.

Burden, P. and Byrd, D. (2009) *Methods for Effective Teaching: Meeting the Needs of All Students*, 5th edn. Boston, MA: Allyn & Bacon.

Burger, J. (2007) Fleeting attraction and compliance with requests, in A. Pratkanis (ed.) *The Science of Social Influence: Advances and Future Progress*. New York: Psychology Press.

Burgoon, J. (1980) Nonverbal communication in the 1970s: an overview, in D. Nimmo (ed.) *Communication Yearbook 4*. New Brunswick, NJ: Transaction Publishers.

Burgoon, J. (1995) Cross-cultural and intercultural applications of expectancy violation theory, in R. L. Wiseman (ed.) *Intercultural Communication Theory*. Thousand Oak, CA: Sage.

Burgoon, J. (2005) Measuring nonverbal indicators of deceit, in V. Manusov (ed.) *The Sourcebook of Nonverbal Measures: Going Beyond Words*. Mahwah, NJ: Lawrence Erlbaum Associates, Inc.

Burgoon, J. and Bacue, A. (2003) Nonverbal communication skills, in J. Greene and B. Burleson (eds) *Handbook of Communication and Social Interaction Skills*, Mahwah, NJ: Lawrence Erlbaum Associates, Inc.

Burgoon, J. and Dunbar, N. (2006) Nonverbal expressions of dominance and power in human relationships, in V. Manusov and M. Patterson (eds) *The Sage Handbook of Nonverbal Communication*. Thousand Oaks, CA: Sage.

Burgoon, J. and Langer, E. (1995) Language, fallacies, and mindlessness–mindfulness in social interaction, in B. Burleson (ed.) *Communication Yearbook, 18*. Thousand Oaks, CA: Sage.

Burgoon, J. and Levine, T. (2010) Advances in deception detection, in S. Smith and S. Wilson (eds) *New Directions in Interpersonal Communication Research*. Thousand Oaks, CA: Sage.

Burgoon, J., Birk, T. and Pfau, M. (1990) Nonverbal behaviors, persuasion, and credibility, *Human Communication Research*, 17, 140–169.

Burgoon, J., Walther, J. and Baesler, E. (1992) Interpretations, evaluations, and consequences of interpersonal touch, *Human Communication Research*, 19, 237–263.

Burgoon, J., Buller, D. and Woodall, W. (1996) *Nonverbal Communication: The Unspoken Dialogue*. New York: McGraw-Hill.

Burgoon, J., Guerrero, L. and Floyd, K. (2010) *Nonverbal Communication*. Boston, MA: Allyn & Bacon.

Burkard A., Knox, S., Groen, M., Perez, M. and Hess, S. (2006) European American therapist self-disclosure in cross-cultural counselling, *Journal of Counseling Psychology*, 50, 324–332.

Burke, C., Stagl, K., Klein, C., Goodwin, G., Salas, E. and Halpin, S. (2006) What type of leadership behaviors are functional in teams? A meta-analysis, *Leadership Quarterly*, 17, 288–307.

Burleson, B. (2003) Emotional support skill, in J. Greene and B. Burleson (eds) *Handbook of Communication and Interaction Skills*. Mahwah, NJ: Lawrence Erlbaum Associates, Inc.

Burleson, B. (2007) Constructivism: a general theory of communication skill, in B. Whaley and W. Samter (eds) *Explaining Communication: Contemporary Theories and Exemplars*. Mahwah, NJ: Lawrence Erlbaum Associates, Inc.

Burleson, B. (2008) What counts as effective emotional support? Explorations of individual and situational differences, in M. Motley (ed.) *Studies in Applied Interpersonal Communication*. Thousand Oaks, CA: Sage.

Burleson, B. (2010a) The nature of interpersonal communication: a message centered approach, in C. Berger, M. Roloff and D. Roskos-Ewoldsen (eds) *The Handbook of Communication Science*. Thousand Oaks, CA: Sage.

Burleson, B. (2010b) Explaining recipient responses to supportive messages: development and tests of a dual-process theory, in S. Smith and S. Wilson (eds) *New Directions in Interpersonal Communication Research*. Thousand Oaks, CA: Sage.

Burley-Allen, M. (1995) *Listening: The Forgotten Skill*. New York: Wiley.

Burnham, T. and Phelan, J. (2000) *Mean Genes: From Sex to Money to Food: Taming Our Primal Instincts*. Cambridge, MA: Perseus.

Burns, J. (1978) *Leadership*. New York: Harper & Row.

Burrell, N. and Koper, R. (1998) The efficacy of powerful/powerless language on attitudes and source credibility, in M. Allen and R. Preiss (eds) *Persuasion: Advances Through Meta-Analysis*. Cresskill, NJ: Hampton Press.

Burton, G. and Dimbleby, R. (2006) *Between Ourselves: An Introduction to Interpersonal Communication*. London: Hodder.

Buslig, A. and Burgoon, J. (2000) Aggressiveness in privacy-seeking behavior, in S. Petronio (ed.) *Balancing the Secrets of Private Disclosures*. Mahwah, NJ: Lawrence Erlbaum Associates, Inc.

Buss, A. (1983) Social rewards and personality, *Journal of Personality and Social Psychology*, 44, 553–563.

Buss, A. and Perry, M. (1992) The aggression questionnaire, *Journal of Personality and Social Psychology*, 63, 452–459.

Buss, D. (1988) The evolution of human intersexual competition: tactics of mate attraction, *Journal of Personality and Social Psychology*, 54, 616–628.

Butler, J., Pryor, B. and Grieder, M. (1998) Impression formation as a function of male baldness, *Perceptual and Motor Skills*, 86, 347–350.

Buttny, R. and Morris, G. (2001) Accounting, in W. Robinson and H. Giles (eds) *The New Handbook of Language and Social Psychology*. Chichester: Wiley.

Byrne, D. (1971) *The Attraction Paradigm*. New York: Academic Press.

Byrne, P. and Long, B. (1976) *Doctors Talking to Patients*. London: HMSO.

Byrne, S. and Hart, P. (2009) The boomerang effect: a synthesis of findings and a preliminary theoretical framework, in C. Beck (ed.) *Communication Yearbook 33*. New York: Routledge.

Cai, D., Wilson, S. and Drake, L. (2001) Culture in the context of intercultural negotiation: individualism-collectivism and paths to integrative agreements, *Human Communication Research*, 26, 591–617.

Cairns, L. (1996) *Negotiating Skills in the Workplace: A Practical Handbook*. London: Pluto Press.

Cairns, L. (2006) Reinforcement, in O. Hargie (ed.) *The Handbook of Communication Skills*, 3rd edn. London: Routledge.

Calderhead, J. (1996) Teachers: beliefs and knowledge, in D. Berliner (ed.) *The Handbook of Educational Psychology*. New York: Macmillan.

Caliendo, T. (2004) A proposed solution to jury confusion in patent infringement cases involving means-plus-function claims, *Brigham Young University Law Review*, 1, 209–234.

Callan, M., Powell, N. and Ellard, J. (2007) The consequences of victim physical attractiveness on reactions to injustice: the role of observers' belief in a just world, *Social Justice Research*, 20, 433–456.

Cameron, D. (1994) Verbal hygiene for women: linguistics misapplied? *Applied Linguistics*, 15, 382–398.

Cameron, D. (2000) *Good to Talk? Living and Working in a Communication Culture*. London: Sage.

Cameron, D. (2009) A language in common. *The Psychologist*, 22, 578–580.

Cameron, G., Schleuder, J. and Thorson, E. (1991) The role of news teasers in processing TV news and commercials, *Communication Research*, 18, 667–684.

Cameron, J. and Pierce, W. (1994) Reinforcement, reward and intrinsic motivation: a meta-analysis, *Review of Educational Research*, 64, 363–423.

Cameron, J. and Pierce, W. (1996) The debate about rewards and intrinsic motivation: protests and accusations do not alter the results, *Review of Educational Research*, 66, 39–51.

Campbell, K., Martin, M. and Wanzer, M. (2001) Employee perceptions of manager humor orientation, and assertiveness, responsiveness, approach/avoidance strategies, and satisfaction, *Communication Research Reports*, 18, 67–74.

Campbell, R., Benson, P., Wallace, S., Doesbergh, S. and Coleman, M. (1999) More about brows: how poses that change brow position affect perceptions of gender, *Perception*, 28, 489–504.

Cann, A., Calhoun, L. and Banks, J. (1997) On the role of humour appreciation in interpersonal attraction: it's no joking matter, *Text*, 10, 77–89.

Cannell, C. F., Oksenberg, L. and Converse, J. M. (1977) Striving for response accuracy: experiments in new interviewing techniques, *Journal of Marketing Research*, 14, 306–321.

Cappella, J. and Schreiber, D. (2006) The interaction management function of nonverbal cues: theory and research about mutual behavioural influence in face-to-face settings, in V. Manusov and M. Patterson (eds) *The Sage Handbook of Nonverbal Communication*. Thousand Oaks, CA: Sage.

Capstick, J. (2005) Pupil and staff perceptions of rewards at a pupil referral unit, *Emotional and Behavioural Difficulties*, 10, 95–117.

Caris-Verhallen, W., Kerkstra, A. and Bensing, J. (1999) Nonverbal behaviour in nurse–elderly patient communication, *Journal of Advanced Nursing*, 29, 808–818.

Carlson, L., Feldman-Stewart, D., Tishelman, C. and Brundage M. (2005) Patient–professional communication research in cancer: an integrative review of research methods in the context of a conceptual framework, *Psycho-Oncology*, 14, 812–828.

Carmeli, A. and Schaubroeck, J. (2007) The influence of leaders' and other referents' normative expectations on individual involvement in creative work, *Leadership Quarterly*, 18, 35–48.

Carmichael, C., Tsai, F., Smith, S., Caprariello, P. and Reis, H. (2007) The self and intimate relationships, in C. Sedikides and S. Spencer (eds) *The Self*. New York: Psychology Press.

Carnevale, P. and De Dreu, C. (2006) Motive: the negotiator's raison d'être, in L. Thompson (ed.) *Negotiation Theory and Research*. New York: Taylor and Francis.

Carnevale, P. and Pruitt, D. (1992) Negotiation and mediation, *Annual Review of Psychology*, 43, 531–582.

Carpiac-Claver, M. and Levy-Storms, L. (2007) In a manner of speaking: communication between nurse aides and older adults in long-term care settings, *Health Communication*, 22, 59–67.

Carroll, L. (1866/2003) *Alice's Adventures in Wonderland*. London: Penguin.

Carroll, L. (1898/1998) *The Hunting of the Snark*. London: Penguin.

Carter, K. (1990) Teacher's knowledge and learning to teach, in W. Houston (ed.) *Handbook of Research on Teacher Education*. New York: Macmillan.

Carter, S. and Sanna, L. (2006) Are we as good as we think? Observers' perceptions of indirect self-presentation as a social influence tactic, *Social Influence*, 1, 185–207.

Cartwright, D. and Zander, A. (1968) *Group Dynamics*, 3rd edn. New York: Harper and Row.

Carver, C. and Scheier, M. (1999) Themes and issues in the self-regulation of behavior, in R. Wyer (ed.) *Advances in Social Cognition*. Mahwah, NJ: Lawrence Erlbaum Associates, Inc.

Carver, C. and Scheier, M. (2000) On the structure of behavioral self-regulation, in M. Boekaerts, P. Pintrich and M. Zeidner (eds) *Handbook of Self-Regulation*. San Diego, CA: Academic Press.

Case, A. and Paxson, C. (2008) Stature and status: height, ability, and labor market outcomes, *Journal of Political Economy*, 116, 499–532.

Case, A., Paxson, C. and Islam, M. (2009) Making sense of the labour market height premium: evidence from the British Household Panel Survey, *Economics Letters*, 102, 174–176.

Castonquay, L. and Beutler, L. (eds) (2005) *Principles of Therapeutic Change that Work*. New York: Oxford University Press.

Catanzaro, S. and Mearns, J. (1999) Mood-related expectancy, emotional experience, and coping behavior, in I. Kirsch (ed.) *How Expectations Shape Experience*. Washington, DC: American Psychological Association.

Cattell, R. (1951) New concepts for measuring leadership, in terms of group syntality, *Human Relations*, 4, 161–184.

Caughlin, J. and Scott, A. (2010) Toward a communication theory of the demand/withdraw pattern of interaction in interpersonal relationships, in S. Smith and S. Wilson (eds) *New Directions in Interpersonal Communication Research*. Thousand Oaks, CA: Sage.

Cavell, T. and Malcolm, K. (eds) (2006) *Anger, Aggression, and Interventions for Interpersonal Violence*. Mahwah, NJ: Lawrence Erlbaum Associates, Inc.

Cayanus, J. and Martin, M. (2008) Teacher self-disclosure: amount, relevance, and negativity, *Communication Quarterly*, 56, 325–341.

Cayanus, J., Martin, M. and Goodboy, A. (2009) The relation between teacher self-disclosure and student motives to communicate, *Communication Research Reports*, 26, 105–111.

CBI (2008) *Taking Stock: CBI Education and Skills Survey 2008*. London: Confederation of British Industry.

Cervone, D., Caldwell, T. and Orom, H. (2008) Beyond person and situation effects: intraindividual personality architecture and its implications for the study of personality and social behaviour, in F. Rhodewalt (ed.) *Personality and Social Behavior*. New York: Taylor & Francis.

Chaikin, A. and Derlega, V. (1976) Self-disclosure, in J. Thibaut, J. Spence and R. Carson (eds) *Contemporary Topics in Social Psychology*. Morristown, NJ: General Learning Press.

Chakrabarti, B. and Baron-Cohen, S. (2008) The biology of mind-reading, in N. Ambady and J. Skowronski (eds) *First Impressions*. New York: Guilford Press.

Chambers, J. (2008) Explaining false uniqueness: why we are both better and worse than others, *Social and Personality Psychology Compass*, 2, 878–894.

Chamorro-Premuzic, T. (2007) *Personality and Individual Differences*. Malden, MA: Blackwell.

Chandler, P. and Sweller, J. (1992) The split-attention effect as a factor in the design of instruction, *British Journal of Educational Psychology*, 62, 233–246.

Channa, R. and Siddiqi, M. (2008) What do patients want from their psychiatrist? A cross-sectional questionnaire based exploratory study from Karachi, *BMC Psychiatry*, 8, 14. http://www.pubmedcentral.nih.gov/picrender.fcgi? artid=2275251&blobtype=pdf (accessed 2 December 2009).

Chapin, J. (2008) Third-person perception and racism, *International Journal of Communication*, 2, 100–107.

Chaplin, W., Phillips, J., Brown, J., Clanton, N. and Stein, J. (2000) Handshaking, gender, personality, and first impressions, *Journal of Personality and Social Psychology*. 79, 110–117.

Charrow, R. and Charrow (1979) Making legal language understandable: a psycholinguistic study of jury instructions, *Columbia Law Review*, 79, 1306.

Chaudhry-Lawton, R., Lawton, R., Murphy, K. and Terry, A. (1992) *Quality: Change through Teamwork*. London: Century Business.

Chelune, G. (1976) The self-disclosure situations survey: a new approach to measuring self-disclosure, *JCSAS Catalog of Selected Documents in Psychology*, 6, (ms. no. 1367), 111–112.

Chen, S., Fitzsimons, G. and Andersen, S. (2007) Automaticity in close relationships, in J. Bargh (ed.) *Social Psychology and the Unconscious: The Automaticity of Higher Mental Processes*. New York: Psychology Press.

Cheng, C. and Chun, W. (2008) Cultural differences and similarities in request rejection: a situational approach, *Journal of Cross-Cultural Psychology*, 39, 745–764.

Chesebro, J. and McCroskey, J. (2001) The relationship of teacher clarity and immediacy with student state receiver apprehension, affect, and cognitive learning, *Communication Education*, 50, 59–68.

Chesner, S. and Beaumeister, R. (1985) Effects of therapist's disclosure of religious beliefs on the intimacy of client self-disclosure, *Journal of Social and Clinical Psychology*, 3, 97–105.

Chidambaram, L. and Bostrom, R. (1997) Group development (I): a review and synthesis of development models, *Group Decision and Negotiation*, 6, 159–187.

Chirumbolo, A. and Leone, L. (2008) Individual differences in need for closure and voting behaviour, *Personality and Individual Differences*, 44, 1279–1288.

Cho, H. and Boster, F. (2008) Effects of gain versus loss frame antidrug ads on adolescents, *Journal of Communication*, 58, 428–446.

Chovil, N. (1997) Facing others: a social communicative perspective on facial displays, in J. Russell and J. Fernandez-Dols (eds) *The Psychology of Facial Expression.* Cambridge: Cambridge University Press.

Christenfeld, N. (1995) Does it hurt to say um?, *Journal of Nonverbal Behavior*, 19, 171–186.

Church, R., Kelly, S. and Lynch, K. (1999) Immediate memory for mismatched speech and representational gesture across development, *Journal of Nonverbal Behavior*, 24, 151–174.

Cialdini, R. (2001) *Influence: Science and Practice.* Boston: Allyn and Bacon.

Cialdini, R. (2007) *Influence: The Psychology of Persuasion.* New York: HarperCollins.

Cialdini, R. and Schroeder, D. (1976) Increasing compliance by legitimizing paltry contributions: when even a penny helps, *Journal of Personality and Social Psychology*, 34, 599–604.

Cialdini, R., Wosinska, W., Barrett, D., Butner, J. and Gornik-Durose, M. (2001) The differential impact of two social influence principles on individualists and collectivists in Poland and the United States, in W. Wosinska, R. Cialdini, D. Barrett and J. Reykowski (eds) *The Practice of Social Influence in Multiple Cultures.* Mahwah, NJ: Lawrence Erlbaum Associates, Inc.

Cianni-Surridge, M. and Horan, J. (1983) On the wisdom of assertive jobseeking behavior, *Journal of Counseling Psychology*, 30, 209–214.

Cipani, E. and Schock, K. (2007) *Functional Behavioral Assessment, Diagnosis, and Treatment: A Complete System for Education and Mental Health Settings.* New York: Springer.

Citkowitz, R. (1975) The effects of three interview techniques – paraphrasing, modelling, and cues – in facilitating self-referent affect statements in chronic schizophrenics, *Dissertation Abstracts International*, 36, 2462B.

Clampitt, P. (2010) *Communicating for Managerial Effectiveness: Problems, Strategies, Solutions*, 4th edn. Thousand Oaks, CA: Sage.

Cline, V., Mejia, J., Coles, J., Klein, N. and Cline, R. (1984) The relationship between therapist behaviors and outcome for middle and lower class couples in marital therapy, *Journal of Clinical Psychology*, 40, 691–704.

Clore, G. and Byrne, D. (1974) A reinforcement-affect model of attraction, in T. Huston (ed.) *Perspectives on Interpersonal Attraction.* New York: Academic Press.

Cody, M. and McLaughlin, M. (1988) Accounts on trial: oral arguments in traffic court, in C. Antakis (ed.) *Analysing Everyday Explanations: A Casebook of Methods.* London: Sage.

Cody, M. and Seiter, J. (2001) Compliance principles in retail sales in the United States, in W. Wosinska, R. Cialdini, D. Barrett and J. Reykowski (eds) *The Practice of Social Influence in Multiple Cultures.* Mahwah, NJ: Lawrence Erlbaum Associates, Inc.

Cohen-Cole, S. (1991) *The Medical Interview: The Three-function Approach.* St. Louis, MO: Mosby-Yearbook.

Cohen-Cole, S. and Bird, J. (1991) Function 1: gathering data to understand the patient, in S. Cohen-Cole (ed.) *The Medical Interview: The Three-function Approach.* St. Louis, MO: Mosby-Yearbook.

Coleman, E., Brown, A. and Rivkin, I. (1997) The effects of instructional explanations on learning from scientific texts, *Journal of the Learning Sciences*, 6, 347–365.

Collett, P. (2003) *Book of Tells: How to Read People's Minds from their Actions*. London: Transworld Publishers.

Collins L., Powell, J. and Oliver, P. (2000) Those who hesitate lose: the relationship between assertiveness and response latency, *Perceptual and Motor Skills*, 90, 931–943.

Colquitt, J., Conlon, D., Wesson, M., Porter, C. and Ng, K. (2001) Justice in the millennium: a meta-analytic review of 25 years of organizational justice research, *Journal of Applied Psychology*, 86, 425–445.

Comadena, M., Hunt, S. and Simonds, C. (2007) The effects of teacher clarity, non-verbal immediacy, and caring on student motivation, affective and cognitive learning, *Communication Research Reports*, 24, 241–248.

Conan Doyle, A. (2001) *A Study in Scarlet*. London: Penguin (first published 1887, Ward Lock & Co).

Conger, J. and Riggio, R. (eds) (2007) *The Practice of Leadership: Developing the Next Generation of Leaders*. San Francisco, CA: Jossey Bass.

Connor, A. and Howett, M. (2009) A conceptual model of intentional comfort touch, *Journal of Holistic Nursing*, 27, 127–135.

Conway, A., Jarrold, C., Kane, M., Miyake, A. and Towse, J. (2007) *Variation in Working Memory*. New York: Oxford University Press.

Conway, L. and Schaller, M. (2007) How communication shapes culture, in K. Fiedler (ed.) *Social Communication*. New York: Psychology Press.

Cook, E. (2009) *Ask Your Father: The Questions Children Ask and How to Answer Them*. London: Short Books.

Cook, M. (1970) Experiments on orientation and proxemics, *Human Relations*, 23, 61–76.

Cooks, L. (2000) Family secrets and the lie of identity, in S. Petronio (ed.) *Balancing the Secrets of Private Disclosures*. Mahwah, NJ: Lawrence Erlbaum Associates, Inc.

Cooley, C. (1929) *Social Organization*. New York: Scribner.

Cooper, J. (2007) *Cognitive Dissonance: Fifty Years of a Classic Theory*. Thousand Oaks, CA: Sage.

Cooren, F. and Fairhurst, G. (2004) Speech timing and spacing: the phenomenon of organizational closure, *Organization*, 11, 793–824.

Coover, G. and Murphy, S. (2000) The communicated self: exploring the interaction between self and social context, *Human Communication Research*, 26, 125–147.

Corey, G. (2005) *Theory and Practice of Counselling and Psychotherapy*, 7th edn. Belmont, CA: Brooks/Cole–Thomson Learning.

Corey, S. (1940) The teachers out-talk the pupils, *School Review*, 48, 745–752.

Cormier, S., Nurius, P. and Osborn, C. (2008) *Interviewing and Change Strategies for Helpers: Fundamental Skills and Cognitive Behavioral Interventions*, 6th edn. Pacific Grove, CA: Brooks/Cole.

Corpus, J. and Lepper, M. (2007) The effects of person versus performance praise on children's motivation: gender and age as moderating factors, *Educational Psychology*, 27, 1–22.

Corts, D. and Pollio, H. (1999) Spontaneous production of figurative language and gesture in college lecturers, *Metaphor and Symbolic Activity*, 14, 81–100.

Coupland, J., Coupland, N. and Grainger, K. (1991) Integrational discourse: contextual variations of age and elderliness, *Ageing and Society*, 11, 189–208.

Coupland, J., Coupland, N. and Robinson, J. (1992) How are you? Negotiating phatic communion, *Language in Society*, 21, 207–230.

Cowan, N., Morey, C. and Chen, Z. (2007) The legend of the magical number seven, in S. Della Sala (ed.) *Tall Tales about the Brain: Separating Fact from Fiction*. Oxford: Oxford University Press.

Cragan, J., Wright, D. and Kasch, C. (2009) *Communication in Small Groups: Theory, Process, Skills*, 7th edn. Boston, MA: Wadsworth Cengage Learning.

Craig, K., Hyde, S., and Patrick, C. (1997) Genuine, suppressed, and fake facial behaviour during exacerbation of chronic low back pain, in P. Ekman and E. Rosenberg (eds) *What the Face Reveals: Basic and Applied Studies of Spontaneous Expression Using the Facial Action Coding System (FACS)*. Oxford: Oxford University Press.

Craig, O. (2009) It's possible to ask any question if you do so nicely, *The Sunday Telegraph*, 23 August, p. 16.

Craighead, L., Wilcoxon, L., Heather, N., Craighead, W. and DeRosa, R. (1996) Effect of feedback on learning rate and cognitive distortions among women with bulimia, *Behavior Therapy*, 27, 551–563.

Crano, W. and Prislin, R. (eds) (2008) *Attitudes and Attitude Change*. Hove, UK: Psychology Press.

Crawford, M. (1995) Gender, age and the social evaluation of assertion, *Behavior Modification*, 12, 549–564.

Creswell, D., Lam, S., Stanton, A., Taylor, S., Bower, J. and Sherman, D. (2007) Does self-affirmation, cognitive processing, or discovery of meaning explain cancer-related health benefits of expressive writing?, *Personality and Social Psychology Bulletin*, 33, 238–250.

Criminal Justice System (2007) *Achieving Best Evidence in Criminal Proceedings: Guidance on Interviewing Victims and Witnesses and Using Special Measures*. http://www.cps.gov.uk/publications/docs/Achieving_Best_Evidence_FINAL.pdf (accessed 2 December 2009).

Crusco, A. and Wetzel, C. (1984) The Midas touch: effects of interpersonal touch on restaurant tipping, *Personality and Social Psychology Bulletin*, 10, 512–517.

Cruz, M. (1998) Explicit and implicit conclusions in persuasive messages, in M. Allen and R. Preiss (eds) *Persuasion: Advances Through Meta-analysis*. Cresskill, NJ: Hampton Press.

Crystal, D. (1997) *The Cambridge Encyclopaedia of Language*, 2nd edn. New York: Cambridge University Press.

Cupach, W. and Canary, D. (1997) *Competence in Interpersonal Conflict*. New York: McGraw-Hill.

Cupach, W. and Metts, S. (1990) Remedial processes in embarrassing predicaments, in J. Anderson (ed.) *Communication Yearbook Vol. 13*. Newbury Park, CA: Sage.

Curhan, J. and Pentland, A. (2007) Thin slices of negotiation: predicting outcomes from conversational dynamics within the first five minutes, *Journal of Applied Psychology*, 92, 802–811.

Currie, G. and Lockett, A. (2007) A critique of transformational leadership: moral, professional and contingent dimensions of leadership within public services organizations, *Human Relations*, 60, 341–370.

D'Augelli, A., Hershberger, S. and Pilkington, N. (1998) Lesian, gay and bisexual youth and their families: disclosure of sexual orientation and its consequences, *American Journal of Orthopsychiatry*, 68, 361–371.

Dabbs, J. (1985) Temporal patterns of speech and gaze in social and intellectual conversation, in H. Giles and R. St Clair (eds) *Recent Advances in Language, Communication and Social Psychology*. Hove, UK: Lawrence Erlbaum Associates, Inc.

Dabbs, J. (1997) Testosterone, smiling, and facial appearance, *Journal of Nonverbal Behavior*, 21, 45–55.

Dabbs, J., Bernieri, F., Strong, R., Campo, R. and Milun, R. (2001) Going on stage: testosterone in greetings and meetings, *Journal of Research in Personality*, 35, 27–40.

Daly, J., Kreiser, P. and Roghaar, L. (1994) Question-asking comfort: explorations of the demography of communication in the eighth grade classroom, *Communication Education*, 43, 27–41.

Daly, J., McCroskey, J., Ayres, J., Hopf, T. and Ayres, D. (eds) (1997) *Avoiding Communication: Shyness, Reticence and Communication Aprehension*, 2nd edn. Cresskill, NJ: Hampton Press.

Danish, S. and Hauer, A. L. (1973) *Helping Skills: A Basic Training Program*. New York: Behavioral Publications.

Darley, J. (2001) Social comparison motives in ongoing groups, in M. Hogg and S. Tindale (eds) *Blackwell Handbook of Social Psychology*. Malden, MA: Blackwell.

Darwin, C. (1872/1955) *The Expression of Emotions in Man and Animals*. London: John Murray.

Davidhizar, R. and Giger, J. (1997) When touch is not the best approach, *Journal of Clinical Nursing*, 6, 203–206.

Davies, J. (1998) The art of negotiating, *Management Today*, November, 126–128.

Davis, J., Thompson, C., Foley, A., Bond, C. and DeWitt, J. (2008a) An examination of listening concepts in the healthcare context: differences among nurses, physicians, and administrators, *International Journal of Listening*, 22, 152–167.

Davis, J. Foley, A., Crigger, N. and Brannigan, M. (2008b) Healthcare and listening: a relationship for caring, *International Journal of Listening*, 22, 168–175.

Davitz, J. R. (1964) *The Communication of Emotional Meaning*. New York: McGraw-Hill.

DeCarolis, D. and Saparito, P. (2006) Social capital, cognition, and entrepreneurial opportunities: a theoretical framework, *Entrepreneurship Theory and Practice*, 30, 41–56.

Deci, E. and Ryan, R. (1985) *Intrinsic Motivation and Self-determination in Human Behavior*. New York: Plenum Pess.

Deci, E., Koestner, R. and Ryan, M. (1999) A meta-analytic review of experiments examining the effects of extrinsic rewards on intrinsic motivation, *Psychological Bulletin*, 125, 627–668.

Deetz, S. and Brown, D. (2004) Conceptualizing involvement, participation and workplace decision processes, in D. Tourish and O. Hargie (eds) *Key Issues in Organizational Communication*. London: Routledge.

DeGrada, E., Kruglanski, A., Mannetti, L. and Pierro, A. (1999) Motivated cognition and group interaction: need for closure affects the contents and processes of collective negotiations, *Journal of Experimental Social Psychology*, 35, 346–365.

deHoog, N., Stroebe, W. and de Wit, J. (2005) The impact of fear appeals on processing and acceptance of action recommendations, *Personality and Social Psychology Bulletin*, 31, 24–33.

Del Greco, L. (1983) The Del Greco assertive behavior inventory, *Journal of Behavioral Assessment*, 5, 49–63.

Demarais, A. and White, V. (2005) *First Impressions: What You Don't Know About How Others See You*. New York: Bantam.

deMayo, R. (1997) How to present at case conference, *Clinical Supervisor*, 16, 181–189.

Demetriou, H. and Wilson, E. (2008) A return to the use of emotion and reflection, *The Psychologist*, 21, 938–940.

Den Hartog, D. N., House, R. J., Hanges, P. J., *et al.* (1999) Culture specific and cross-culturally generalizable implicit leadership theories: are attributes of charismatic/transformational leadership universally endorsed?, *Leadership Quarterly*, 10, 219–256.

DePaulo, B., Kashy, D., Kirkendol, S. and Wyer, M. (1996) Lying in everyday life, *Journal of Personality and Social Psychology*, 70, 779–795.

DePaulo, B., Lindsay, J., Malone, B., *et al.* (2003a) Cues to deception, *Psychological Bulletin*, 129, 74–118.

DePaulo, B., Wetzel, C., Sternglanz, R. and Walker Wilson, J. (2003b) Verbal and nonverbal dynamics of privacy, secrecy, and deceit, *Journal of Social Issues*, 59, 391–410.

Derevensky, J. and Leckerman, R. (1997) Teachers' differential use of praise and reinforcement practices, *Canadian Journal of School Psychology*, 13, 15–27.

Derlega, V. and Chaikin, A. (1975) *Sharing Intimacy: What We Reveal to Others and Why*. Englewood Cliffs, NJ: Prentice-Hall.

Derlega, V., Metts, S., Petronio, S. and Margulis, S. (1993) *Self-disclosure*. Newbury Park, CA: Sage.

Derlega, V., Winstead, B. and Folk-Barron, L. (2000) Reasons for and against disclosing HIV-seropositive test results to an intimate partner: a functional perspective, in S. Petronio (ed.) *Balancing the Secrets of Private Disclosures*. Mahwah, NJ: Lawrence Erlbaum Associates, Inc.

Derlega, V., Winstead, B., Mathews, A. and Braitman, A. (2008) Why does someone reveal highly personal information? Attributions for and against self-disclosure in close relationships, *Communication Research Reports*, 25, 115–130.

Deschamps, J. (2005) Different leadership skills for different innovation strategies, *Strategy and Leadership*, 33, 31–38.

De Souza, G. and Klein, H. (1996) Emergent leadership in the group goal-setting process, *Small Group Research*, 26, 475–496.

DeVito, J. (1993) *Essentials of Human Communication*. New York: HarperCollins.

DeVito, J. (2005) *Essentials of Human Communication*, 5th edn. Boston, MA: Pearson Education.

DeVito, J. (2008a) *Human Communication: The Basic Course*, 11th edn. Boston, MA: Pearson Education.

DeVito, J. (2008b) *The Interpersonal Communication Book*, 12th edn. Boston, MA: Pearson Education.

de Vries, R., Bakker-Pieper, A., Siberg, R., Gameren, K. and Vlug, M. (2009) The content and dimensionality of communication styles, *Communication Research*, 36, 178–206.

DeWit, J., Das, E. and Vet, R. (2008) What works best: objective statistics or a personal testimonial? An assessment of the persuasive effects of different types of message evidence on risk perception, *Health Psychology*, 27, 110–115.

DiBiase, R. and Gunnoe, J. (2004) Gender and culture differences in touching behavior, *Journal of Social Psychology*, 144, 49–62.

Di Blasi, Z., Harkness, E., Ernst, E., Georgiou, A. and Kleijnen, J. (2001) Influence of context effects on health outcomes: a systematic review, *Lancet*, 357, 757–762.

Dickson, D. (1981) Microcounselling: an evaluative study of a programme. Unpublished PhD thesis, Ulster Polytechnic.

Dickson, D. (1999) Barriers to communication, in A. Long (ed.) *Interaction for Practice in Community Nursing*. Basingstoke: Macmillan.

Dickson, D. (2006) Reflecting, in O. Hargie (ed.) *The Handbook of Communication Skills*, 3rd edn. London: Routledge.

Dickson, D. and Hargie, O. (2006) Questioning, in O. Hargie (ed.) *The Handbook of Communication Skills*, 3rd edn. London: Routledge.

Dickson, D. and McCartan, P. (2005) Communication, skill and health care delivery, in D. Sines, F. Appleby and M. Frost (eds) *Community Health Care Nursing*, 3rd edn. Oxford: Blackwell.

Dickson, D., Saunders, C. and Stringer, M. (1993) *Rewarding People: The Skill of Responding Positively*. London: Routledge.

Dickson, D., Hargie, O. and Morrow, N. (1997) *Communication Skills Training for Health Professionals*, 2nd edn. London: Chapman and Hall.

Dickson, D., Hargie, O. and Rainey, S. (2000) Communication and relational development between Catholic and Protestant students in Northern Ireland, *Australian Journal of Communication*, 27, 67–82

Dickson, D., Hargie, O., O'Donnell, A. and McMullan, C. (2009) Adapting to difference: organisational socialisation in the Northern Ireland workplace, *Shared Space*, 7, 33–52.

Dieckmann, L. (2000) Private secrets and public disclosures: the case of battered women, in S. Petronio (ed.) *Balancing the Secrets of Private Disclosures*. Mahwah, NJ: Lawrence Erlbaum Associates, Inc.

Dijksterhuis, A., Chartrand, T. and Aarts, H. (2007) Effects of priming and perception on social behaviour and goal pursuit, in J. Bargh (ed.) *Social Psychology and the Unconscious: The Automaticity of Higher Mental Processes*, New York: Psychology Press.

Dillard, J. (1990) The nature and substance of goals in tactical communication, in M. Cody and M. McLaughlin (eds) *The Psychology of Tactical Communication*. Clevedon: Multilingual Matters.

Dillard, J. (1997) Explicating the goal construct: tools for theorists, in J. O. Greene (ed.) *Message Production: Advances in Communication Theory*. Mahwah, NJ: Lawrence Erlbaum Associates, Inc.

Dillard, J. (1998) The role of affect in communication, biology, and social relationships, in P. Andersen and L. Guerrero (eds) *Handbook of Communication and Emotion: Research, Theory, Applications, and Contexts*. San Diego, CA: Academic Press.

Dillard, J. (2008) Goals-plans-action theory of message production, in L. Baxter and D. Braithwaite (eds) *Engaging Theories in Interpersonal Communication: Multiple Perspectives*. Thousand Oaks, CA: Sage.

Dillard, J. (2010) Persuasion, in C. Berger, M. Roloff and D. Roskos-Ewoldsen (eds) *The Handbook of Communication Science*. Thousand Oaks, CA: Sage.

Dillard, J. and Peck, E. (2001) Persuasion and the structure of affect: dual systems and discrete emotions as complementary models, *Human Communication Research*, 27, 38–68.

Dillard, J., Hunter, J. and Burgoon, M. (1984) Sequential-request strategies: meta-analysis of foot-in-the-door and door-in-the-face, *Human Communication Research*, 10, 461–488.

Dillard, J., Weber, K. and Vail, R. (2007a) The relationship between the perceived and actual effectiveness of persuasive messages: a meta-analysis with implications for formative campaign research, *Journal of Communication*, 57, 613–631.

Dillard, J., Shen, L. and Vail, R. (2007b) Does perceived message effectiveness cause persuasion or vice versa? 17 consistent answers, *Human Communication Research*, 33, 467–488.

Dillon, J. (1982) The multidisciplinary study of questioning, *Journal of Educational Psychology*, 74, 147–165.

Dillon, J. (1988) The remedial status of student questioning, *Journal of Curriculum Studies*, 20, 197–210.

Dillon, J. (1990) *The Practice of Questioning*. London: Routledge.

Dillon, J. (1997) Questioning, in O. Hargie (ed.) *The Handbook of Communication Skills*, 2nd edn. London: Routledge.

Dillow, M., Dunleavy, K. and Weber, K. (2009) The impact of relational characteristics and reasons for topic avoidance on relational closeness, *Communication Quarterly*, 57, 205–223.

Dimberg, U., Thunberg, M. and Elmehed, K. (2000) Unconscious facial reactions to emotional facial expressions, *Psychological Science*, 11, 86–89.

Dimbleby, R. and Burton, G. (1998) *More than Words: An Introduction to Communication*. London: Routledge.

Dindia, K. (2000a) Self-disclosure, identity, and relationship development, in K. Dindia and S. Duck (eds) *Communication and Personal Relationships*. Chichester: Wiley.

Dindia, K. (2000b) Sex differences in self-disclosure, reciprocity of self-disclosure, and self-disclosure and liking: three meta-analyses reviewed, in S. Petronio (ed.) *Balancing the Secrets of Private Disclosures*. Mahwah, NJ: Lawrence Erlbaum Associates, Inc.

Dindia, K. and Canary, D. (eds) (2006) *Sex Differences and Similarities in Communication*, 2nd edn. Mahwah, NJ: Lawrence Erlbaum Associates, Inc.

Ding, D. (2006) An indirect style in business communication, *Journal of Business and Technical Communication*, 20, 87–100.

Dinsbach, A., Feij, J., and de Vries, R. (2007) The role of communication content in an ethnically diverse organization, *International Journal of Intercultural Relations*, 31, 725–745.

Dittmar, H. (1992) Perceived material wealth and first impressions, *British Journal of Social Psychology*, 31, 379–392.

Dixon, J. and Durrheim, K. (2004) Dislocating identity: desegregation and the transformation of place, *Journal of Environmental Psychology*, 24, 455–473.

Dohrenwend, B. (1965) Some effects of open and closed questions on respondents' answers, *Human Organization*, 24, 175–184.

Dolgin, K. (1996) Parents' disclosure of their own concerns to their adolescent children, *Personal Relationships*, 3, 159–169.

Dolgin, K. and Berndt, N. (1997) Adolescents' perceptions of their parents' disclosure to them, *Journal of Adolescence*, 20, 431–441.

Dolgin, K. and Lindsay, K. (1999) Disclosure between college students and their siblings, *Journal of Family Psychology*, 13, 393–400.

Dolinski, D. (2007) Emotional see-saw, in A. Pratkanis (ed.) *The Science of Social Influence: Advances and Future Progress*. New York: Psychology Press.

Dolinski, D. and Kofta, M. (2001) Stay tuned: the role of the break in the message on attribution of culpability, in W. Wosinska, R. Cialdini, D. Barrett and J. Reykowski (eds) *The Practice of Social Influence in Multiple Cultures*. Mahwah, NJ: Lawrence Erlbaum Associates, Inc.

Dolinski, D., Nawrat, M. and Rudak, I. (2001) Dialogue involvement as a social influence technique, *Personality and Social Psychology Bulletin*, 27, 1395–1406.

Dovidio, J., Ellyson, S., Keating, C., Heltman, K. and Brown, C. (1988) The relationship of social power to visual displays of dominance between men and women, *Journal of Personality and Social Psychology*, 54, 233–242.

Dow, B. and Wood, J. (eds) (2006) *The Sage Handbook of Gender and Communication*. Thousand Oaks, CA: Sage.

Dowd, E. and Milne, C. (1986) Paradoxical interventions in counseling psychology, *The Counseling Psychologist*, 14, 237–282.

Downing, J. and Garmon, C. (2002) A guide to implementing PowerPoint and overhead LCD projectors in communication classes, *American Journal of Communication*, 5. http://www.acjournal.org/holdings/vol5/iss2/articles/guide.pdf (accessed 2 December 2009).

Drahota, A., Costall, A., and Reddy, V. (2008) The vocal communication of different kinds of smile, *Speech Communication*, 50, 278–287.

Draper, P. (2005) Patronizing speech to older patients: a literature review, *Reviews in Clinical Gerontology*, 15, 273–279.

Drucker, P. (2007) *Management: Tasks, Responsibilities, Practices*. Edison, NJ: Transaction.

Dryden, W. and Constantinou, D. (2004) *Assertiveness Step by Step*. London: Sheldon Press.

Dubrin, A. (1994) Sex differences in the use and effectiveness of tactics of impression management, *Psychological Reports*, 74, 531–544.

Dubrin, A. (2010) *Leadership: Research Findings, Practice, and Skills*, 6th edn. Mason, OH: Cengage Learning.

Duck, S. (1995) Repelling the study of attraction, *The Psychologist*, 8, 60–63.

Duck, S. (1999) Expressing meaning to others, in J. Stewart (ed.) *Bridges Not Walls*, 7th edn. Boston, MA: McGraw-Hill.

Duck, S. and McMahan, D. (2009) *The Basics of Communication: A Relational Perspective*. Thousand Oaks, CA: Sage.

Duck, S. and Wood, J. (2005) What goes up may come down: sex and gendered patterns in relational dissolution, in M. Fine and J. Harvey (eds) *Handbook of Divorce and Relationship Dissolution*, Mahwah, NJ: Lawrence Erlbaum Associates, Inc.

Duggan, A. and Bradshaw, Y. (2008) Mutual influence processes in physician–patient communication: an interaction adaptation perspective, *Communication Research Reports*, 25, 211–226.

Duggan, A. and Parrott, R. (2001) Physicians' nonverbal rapport building and patients' talk about the subjective component of illness, *Human Communication Research*, 27, 299–311.

Dulany, D. (1968) Awareness, rules and propositional control: a confrontation with S-R behavior theory, in T. Dixon and D. Horton (eds) *Verbal Behavior and General Behavior Theory*. Englewood Cliffs, NJ: Prentice-Hall.

Dunbar, N. and Burgoon, J. (2005) Measuring nonverbal dominance, in V. Manusov (ed.) *The Sourcebook of Nonverbal Measures: Going Beyond Words*. Mahwah, NJ: Lawrence Erlbaum Associates, Inc.

Duncan, S. and Fiske, D.W. (1977) *Face-to-face Interaction: Research, Methods and Theory*. Hillsdale, NJ: Lawrence Erlbaum Associates, Inc.

Dunne, H. (2001) One wrong word and we lose him, *Daily Telegraph*, 29 October, p. 15.

Durik, M., Britt, A., Reynolds, R. and Storey, J. (2008) The effects of hedges in persuasive arguments: a nuanced analysis of language, *Journal of Language and Social Psychology*, 27, 217–234.

Dweck, C. (2000) *Self-theories: Their Role in Motivation, Personality and Development*. Philadelphia, PA: Psychology Press.

Dweck, C. (2007) The perils and promises of praise, *Educational Leadership*, 65, 34–39.

Ebesu-Hubbard, A., Tsuji, A., Williams, C. and Seatriz, V. (2003) Effects of touch on gratuities in same-sex and cross-gender interaction, *Journal of Applied Social Psychology*, 33, 2427–2438.

Edwards, A., Elwyn, G. and Mulley, A. (2002) Explaining risks: turning numerical data into meaningful pictures, *British Medical Journal*, 324, 827–830.

Edwards, R. and Bello, R. (2001) Interpretation of messages: the influence of equivocation, face concerns, and ego involvement, *Human Communication Research*, 27, 597–631.

Egan, G. (2007) *The Skilled Helper: A Problem-Management and Opportunity Development Approach*, 8th edn. Belmont, CA: Brooks/Cole.

Eggen, P. and Kauchak, D. (1999) *Educational Psychology: Windows on Classrooms*. Upper Saddle River, NJ: Prentice-Hall.

Egodigwe, L. (2003) Here comes the suits: raising the style standard in the office, *Black Enterprise*, 33, 59.

Ehrlich, R., D'Augelli, A. and Danish, S. (1979) Comparative effectiveness of six counselor verbal responses, *Journal of Counselling Psychology*, 26, 390–398.

Eisend, M. (2009) A meta-analysis of humor in advertising, *Journal of the Academy of Marketing Science*, 37, 191–203.

Eisler, R., Hersen, M., Miller, P. and Blanchard, D. (1975) Situational determinants of assertive behavior, *Journal of Consulting and Clinical Psychology*, 43, 330–340.

Ekman, P. (1985) *Telling Lies*. New York: Norton.

Ekman, P. and Friesen, W. (1969) The repertoire of non-verbal behaviour: categories, origins, usage and coding, *Semiotica*, 1, 49–98.

Ekman, P. and Friesen, W. (2003) *Unmasking the Face*. Cambridge, MA: Malor Books.

Ekman, P. and Keltner, D. (1997) Universal facial expressions of emotion, in U. Segerstrale and P. Molnar (eds) *Nonverbal Communication: Where Nature Meets Culture*. Mahwah, NJ: Lawrence Erlbaum Associates, Inc.

Ekman, P. and O'Sullivan, M. (1991) Facial expression: methods, means and mouses, in R. Feldman and B. Rime (eds) *Fundamentals of Nonverbal Behaviour*. Cambridge: Cambridge University Press.

Ekman, P. and Rosenberg, E. (eds) (2005) *What the Face Reveals*. New York: Oxford University Press.

Ekman, P., O'Sullivan, M., Friesen, W. and Scherer, K. (1991) Invited article: face, voice and body in detecting deceit, *Journal of Nonverbal Behavior*, 15, 125–135.

Elliot, A. and Niesta, D. (2008) Romantic red: red enhances men's attraction to women, *Journal of Personality and Social Psychology*, 95, 1150–1164.

Ellis, A. and Beattie, G. (1986) *The Psychology of Language and Communication*. London: Weidenfeld and Nicholson.

Ellis, K. (2000) Perceived teacher confirmation: the development and validation of an instrument and two studies of the relationship to cognitive and affective learning, *Human Communication Research*, 26, 264–292.

Ellison, C. and Firestone, I. (1974) Development of interpersonal trust as a function of self-esteem, target status and target style, *Journal of Personality and Social Psychology*, 29, 655–663.

Elwell, W. and Tiberio, J. (1994) Teacher praise: what students want, *Journal of Instructional Psychology*, 21, 32–28.

Emmons, R. (1989) The personal striving approach to personality, in L. Pervin (ed.) *Goal Concepts in Personality and Social Psychology*. Hillsdale, NJ: Lawrence Erlbaum Associates, Inc.

Endres, J., Poggenpohl, C. and Erben, C. (1999) Repetitions, warnings and video: cognitive and motivational components in preschool children's susceptibility, *Journal of Legal and Criminological Psychology*, 4, 129–149.

Engleberg, I. (2002) Presentations in everyday life: linking audience interest and speaker eloquence, *American Journal of Communication*, 5. http://www. acjournal.org/holdings/vol5/iss2/special/engleberg.htm (accessed 2 December 2009).

Engleberg, I. and Daly, J. (2004) *Presentations in Everyday Life: Strategies for Effective Speaking*. Boston, MA: Houghton Mifflin Harcourt.

Ennis, E., Vrij, A. and Chance, C. (2008) Individual differences and lying in everyday life, *Journal of Social and Personal Relationships*, 25, 105–118.

Epstein, J., Griffin, K. and Botvin, G. (2000) Role of general and specific competence skills in protecting inner-city adolescents from alcohol use, *Journal of Studies on Alcohol*, 61, 379–386.

Erb, H. and Bohner, G. (2007) Social influence and persuasion: recent theoretical developments and integrative agreements, in K. Fiedler (ed.) *Social Communication*. New York: Psychology Press.

Erceau, D. and Guéguen, N. (2007) Tactile contact and evaluation of the toucher, *Journal of Social Psychology*, 147, 441–444.

Erickson, M. and Rossi, E. (1975) Varieties of double bind, *American Journal of Clinical Hypnosis*, 17, 143–147.

Erickson, T. and Mattson, M. (1981) From words to meaning: a semantic illusion, *Journal of Verbal Learning and Verbal Behavior*, 20, 540–551.

Erwin, P. (1993) *Friendship and Peer Relations*. Chichester: Wiley.

Esser, J. (1998) Alive and well after 25 years: a review of groupthink, *Organizational Behavior and Human Decision Processes*, 73, 116–141.

Esteves, F. (1999) Attentional bias to emotional facial expressions, *European Review of Applied Psychology*, 49, 91–97.

Eysenck, M. (1998) Perception and attention, in M. Eysenck (ed.) *Psychology: An Integrated Approach*. Harlow: Addison Wesley Longman.

Faraone, S. and Hurtig, R. (1985) An examination of social skill, verbal productivity, and Gottman's model of interaction using observational methods and sequential analyses, *Behavioral Assessment*, 7, 349–366.

Farber, B. (2003) Patient self-disclosure: a review of the research, *Journal of Clinical Psychology*, 59, 589–600.

Farber, B. (2006) *Self-disclosure in Psychotherapy*. New York: Guilford Press.

Farley, S. (2008) Attaining status at the expense of likeability: pilfering power through conversational interruption, *Journal of Nonverbal Behavior*, 32, 241–260.

Feeney, J., Noller, P., Sheehan, G. and Peterson, C. (1999) Conflict issues and conflict strategies as contexts for nonverbal behaviour in close relationships, in P. Philippot, R. Feldman and E. Coats (eds) *The Social Context of Nonverbal Behavior*. Cambridge: Cambridge University Press.

Fehr, E., Bernhard, H. and Rockenbach, B. (2008) Egalitarianism in young children, *Nature*, 454, 1079–1083.

Feigenbaum, W. (1977) Reciprocity in self-disclosure within the psychological interview, *Psychological Reports*, 40, 15–26.

Feldman, R. (1985) *Social Psychology: Theories, Research and Applications*. New York: McGraw-Hill.

Feldman, R. and Tyler, J. (2006) Factoring in age: nonverbal communication across the age span, in V. Manusov and M. Patterson (eds) *The Sage Handbook of Nonverbal Communication*. Thousand Oaks, CA: Sage.

Feldman, R., Philippot, P. and Custrini, R. (1991) Social skills, psychopathology, and nonverbal behavior, in R. Feldman and B. Rime (eds) *Fundamentals of Nonverbal Behaviour*. Cambridge: Cambridge University Press.

Feng, B. and Burleson, B. (2008) The effects of argument explicitness on responses to advice in supportive interactions, *Communication Research*, 35, 849–874.

Fern, E., Monroe, K. and Avila, R. (1986) Effectiveness of multiple request strategies: a synthesis of research results, *Journal of Marketing Research*, 23, 144–152.

Fernandez-Dols, J.-M. (1999) Facial expression and emotion: a situationist view, in P. Philippot, R. Feldman and E. Coats (eds) *The Social Context of Nonverbal Behaviour*. Cambridge: Cambridge University Press.

Ferraro, F. and Garella, A. (1997) Termination as a psychoanalytic event, *International Journal of Psycho-Analysis*, 78, 27–41.

Festinger, L. (1954) A theory of social comparison processes, *Human Relation*, 7, 117–40.

Festinger, L. (1957) *A Theory of Cognitive Dissonance*. Stanford, CA: Stanford University Press.

Feyereisen, P. and Havard, I. (1999) Mental imagery and the production of hand gestures while speaking in younger and older adults, *Journal of Nonverbal Behavior*, 23, 153–171.

Fiedler, F. (1967) *A Theory of Leadership Effectiveness*. New York: McGraw-Hill.

Fiedler, F. (1986) The contribution of cognitive resources and leader behaviour to organizational performance, *Journal of Applied Social Psychology*, 16, 532–548.

Fiedler, F. (1993) The leadership situation and the black box in contingency theories, in M. Chemers and R. Ayman (ed.) *Leadership, Theory and Research: Perspectives and Directions*. New York: Academic Press.

Fiedler, K. (1993) Constructive processes in person cognition, *British Journal of Social Psychology*, 32, 349–364.

Fiedler, K. (2007) Frontiers of research on social communication: introduction and overview, in K. Fiedler (ed.) *Social Communication*. New York: Psychology Press.

Fiedler, K. and Bless, H. (2001) Social cognition, in M. Hewstone and W. Stroebe (eds) *Introduction to Social Psychology*, 3rd edn. Oxford: Blackwell.

Figley, C. (ed.) (2002) *Treating Compassion Fatigue*. New York: Brunner/Mazel.

Fine, M. and Harvey, J. (eds) (2005) *Handbook of Divorce and Relationship Dissolution*. Mahwah, NJ: Lawrence Erlbaum Associates, Inc.

Finkenauer, C. and Hazam, H. (2000) Disclosure and secrecy in marriage: do both contribute to marital satisfaction?, *Journal of Social and Personal Relationships*, 17, 245–263.

Finkenauer, C., Frijns, T., Engels, R. and Kerkhof, P. (2005) Perceiving concealment in relationships between parents and adolescents: links with parental behavior, *Personal Relationships*, 12, 387–406.

Finnegan, A. and Hackley, S. (2008) Negotiation and nonviolent action: interacting in the world of conflict, *Negotiation Journal*, 24, 7–24.

First, E. (1994) The leaving game, or I'll play you and you play me: the emergence of dramatic role play in 2-year-olds, in A. Slade and D. Wolf (eds) *Children at Play: Clinical and Developmental Approaches to Meaning and Representation*. New York: Oxford University Press.

Fisch, H., Frey, S. and Hirsbrunner, H. (1983) Analysing nonverbal behavior in depression, *Journal of Abnormal Psychology*, 92, 307–318.

Fishbach, A. and Ferguson, M. (2007) The goal construct in social psychology, in A. Kruglanski and E. Higgins (eds) *Social Psychology: Handbook of Basic Principles*, 2nd edn. New York: Guilford Press.

Fisher, C., Corrigan, O. and Henman, M. (1991) A study of community pharmacy practice, *Journal of Social and Administrative Pharmacy*, 8, 15–23.

Fisher, D. (1984) A conceptual analysis of self-disclosure, *Journal for the Theory of Social Behavior*, 14, 277–296.

Fisher, R. (2001) Negotiating power: getting and using influence, in I. Asherman and S. Asherman (eds) *The Negotiating Sourcebook*, 2nd edn. Amherst, MA: Human Resource Development Press.

Fisher, R. and Shapiro, D. (2006) *Beyond Reason: Using Emotions as You Negotiate*. London: Random House.

Fisher, R. and Ury, W. (1981) *Getting to Yes: Negotiating an Agreement Without Giving In*. London: Hutchinson.

Fisher, S. and Groce, S. (1990) Accounting practices in medical interviews, *Language in Society*, 19, 225–250.

Fiske, A. (2000) Complementarity theory: why human social capacities evolved to require cultural complements, *Personality and Social Psychology Review*, 4, 76–94.

Fiske, J. (1990) *Introduction to Communication Studies*, 2nd edn. London: Routledge.

Fiske, S. and Berdahl, J. (2007) Social power, in A. Kruglanski and E. Higgins (eds)

Social Psychology: Handbook of Basic Principles, 2nd edn. New York: Guilford Press.

Fiske, S. and Taylor, S. (2008) *Social Cognition: From Brains to Culture*. New York: McGraw-Hill.

Fiske, S., Cuddy, S. and Glick, P. (2007) Universal dimensions of social cognition: warmth and competence, *Trends in Cognitive Sciences*, 11, 77–83.

Fitness, J. (2001) Betrayal, rejection, revenge, and forgiveness: an interpersonal script approach, in M. Leary (ed.) *Interpersonal Rejection*. Oxford: Oxford University Press.

Flack, W., Laird, J. and Cavallaro, L. (1999) Separate and combined effects of facial expressions and bodily postures on emotional feelings, *European Journal of Social Psychology*, 29, 203–217.

Fleeson, W. and Noftle, E. (2008) The end of the person–situation debate: an emerging synthesis in the answer to the consistency question, *Social and Personality Compass*, 2, 1667–1684.

Flemmer, D., Sobelman, S., Flemmer, M. and Astrom, J. (1996) Attitudes and observations about nonverbal communication in the psychotherapeutic greeting situation, *Psychological Reports*, 78, 407–418.

Flintoff, J. (2001) Sayonara to ceremony, *Financial Times Weekend*, 5–6 May, p. 1.

Floyd, K. (2006) An evolutionary approach to understanding nonverbal communication, in V. Manusov and M. Patterson (eds) *The Sage Handbook of Nonverbal Communication*. Thousand Oaks, CA: Sage.

Flynn, J., Valikoski, T. and Grau, J. (2008) Listening in the business context: reviewing the state of research, *International Journal of Listening*, 22, 141–151.

Foley, M. and Duck, S. (2006) Relational communication, in O. Hargie (ed.) *The Handbook of Communication Skills*, 3rd edn. London: Routledge.

Foot, H. (1997) Humour and laughter, in O. Hargie (ed.) *The Handbook of Communication Skills*, 2nd edn. London: Routledge.

Foot, H. and McCreaddie, M. (2006) Humour and laughter, in O. Hargie (ed.) *The Handbook of Communication Skills*, 3rd edn. London: Routledge.

Ford, E. (2006) Lie detection: historical, neuropsychiatric and legal dimensions, *International Journal of Law and Psychiatry*, 29, 159–177.

Ford, S. and Hall, A. (2004) Communication behaviours of skilled and less skilled oncologists: a validation study of the Medical Interaction Process System (MIPS), *Patient Education and Counseling*, 54, 275–282.

Forgas, J. P. (1994) Sad and guilty? Affective influences on the explanation of conflict in close relationships, *Journal of Personality and Social Psychology*, 66, 56–68.

Forgas, J. and Williams, K. (2001) Social influence: introduction and overview, in J. Forgas and K. Williams (eds) *Social Influence: Direct and Indirect Processes*. Philadelphia, PA: Psychology Press.

Forrester, D., Kershaw, S., Moss, H. and Hughes, L. (2008) Communication skills in child protection: how do social workers talk to parents?, *Child and Family Social Work*, 13, 41–51.

Forsyth, D. (2010) *Group Dynamics*, 5th edn. Belmont, CA: Wadsworth Cengage Learning.

Forsythe, S. (1990) Effect of applicant's clothing on interviewer's decision to hire, *Journal of Applied Social Psychology*, 20, 1579–1595.

Fosshage, J. (1998) On aggression: its forms and functions, *Psychoanalytic Inquiry*, 18, 45–54.

Fowler, F. and Mangione, T. (1990) *Standardised Survey Interviewing: Minimizing Interviewer-related Error*. Newbury Park, CA: Sage.

Fox, E., Lester, V., Russo, R., Bowles, R., Pichler, A. and Dutton, K. (2000) Facial expressions of emotion: are angry faces detected more efficiently?, *Cognition and Emotion*, 14, 61–92.

Fox, L., Rejeski, W. and Gauvin, L. (2000) Effects of leadership style and group dynamics on enjoyment of physical activity, *American Journal of Health Promotion*, 14, 277–283.

Freeman, P., Rees, T. and Hardy, L. (2009) An intervention to increase social support and improve performance, *Journal of Applied Sport Psychology*, 21, 186–200.

French, J. and Raven, B. (1959) The bases of social power, in D. Cartwright (ed.) *Studies in Social Power*. Ann Arbor, MI: Institute for Social Research.

French, P. (1994) *Social Skills for Nursing Practice*, 2nd edn. London: Chapman and Hall.

Freshwater, D. (2003) *Counselling Skills for Nurses, Midwives and Health Visitors*. Maidenhead: Open University Press.

Frey, L. (1999) Introduction, in L. Frey, D. Gouran and M. S. Poole (eds) *The Handbook of Group Communication Theory and Research*. Thousand Oaks, CA: Sage.

Frick, R. (1992) Interestingness, *British Journal of Psychology*, 83, 113–128.

Fridlund, A. and Russell, J. (2006) The function of facial expressions: what's in a face?, in V. Manusov and M. L. Patterson (eds) *The Sage Handbook of Nonverbal Communication*. Thousand Oaks, CA: Sage.

Friedman, H. (1979) The concept of skill in nonverbal communication: implications for understanding social interaction, in R. Rosenthal (ed.) *Skill in Nonverbal Communication: Individual Differences*. Cambridge, MA: Oelgeschlager, Gunn and Hain.

Friesen, W. (1972) Cultural differences in facial expression: an experimental test of the concept of display rules. PhD thesis, University of California, San Francisco.

Friesen, W., Ekman, P. and Wallblatt, H. (1980) Measuring hand movements, *Journal of Nonverbal Behavior*, 4, 97–113.

Frijda, N. (2006) *The Laws of Emotion*. London: Routledge.

Fry, L. (1983) Women in society, in S. Spence and G. Shepherd (eds) *Developments in Social Skills Training*. London: Academic Press.

Fujishin, R. (2007) *Creating Effective Groups: The Art of Small Group Communication*, 2nd edn. Lanham, MD: Rowman and Littlefield.

Furnham, A., Lavancy, M. and McClelland, A. (2001) Waist-to-hip ratio and facial attractiveness: a pilot study, *Personality and Individual Differences*, 30, 491–502.

Furst, D. and Criste, A. (1997) Students as consumers: using 'satisfaction surveys' in the classroom, *Reaching Today's Youth: The Community Circle of Caring Journal*, 2, 11–13.

Fussell, S. and Kreuz, R. (1998) Social and cognitive approaches to interpersonal communication: introduction and overview, in S. Fussell and P. Kreuz (eds) *Social and Cognitive Approaches to Interpersonal Communication*. Mahwah, NJ: Lawrence Erlbaum Associates, Inc.

Gable, J. (2007) *Counselling Skills for Dieticians*, 2nd edn. Oxford: Blackwell.

Gable, S. and Shean, G. (2000) Perceived social competence and depression, *Journal of Social and Personal Relationships*, 17, 139–150.

Gage, N., Belgard, M., Dell, D., Hiller, J., Rosenshine, B. and Unruh, W. (1968) *Explorations of the Teachers' Effectiveness in Explaining*. Stanford, CA: Stanford University Centre for Research and Development in Teaching. http://www.eric.ed.gov/ERICDocs/data/ericdocs2sql/content_storage_01/0000019b/80/37/dc/58.pdf (accessed 3 December 2009).

Galanes, G., Adams, K. and Brilhart, J. (2006) *Effective Group Discussion: Theory and Practice*, 12th edn. Boston, MA: McGraw-Hill.

Galinsky, A., Mussweiler, T. and Medvec, V. (2002) Disconnecting outcomes and evaluations: the role of negotiator focus, *Journal of Personality and Social Psychology*, 81, 1131–1140.

Gall, M. (1970) The use of questions in teaching, *Review of Educational Research*, 40, 709–721.

Gallagher, M. (1987) The microskills approach to counsellor training: a study of counsellor personality, attitudes and skills. Unpublished DPhil thesis, University of Ulster, Jordanstown.

Gallagher, M. and Hargie, O. (1992) The relationship between counsellor interpersonal skills and core conditions of client-centred counselling, *Counselling Psychology Quarterly*, 5, 3–16.

Gamble, T. and Gamble, M. (2008) *Communication Works*, 9th edn. New York: McGraw-Hill.

Gardiner, M. and Tiggemann, M. (1999) Gender differences in leadership style, job stress and mental health in male- and female-dominated industries, *Journal of Occupational and Organizational Psychology*, 72, 301–315.

Garko, M. (1992) Physician executives' use of influence strategies: gaining compliance from superiors who communicate in attractive and unattractive styles, *Health Communication*, 4, 137–154.

Garrison, M. and Bly, M. (1997) *Human Relations: Productive Approaches for the Workplace*. Boston, MA: Allyn and Bacon.

Garven, S., Wood, J., Malpass, R. and Shaw, J. (1998) More than suggestion: consequences of the interview techniques from the McMartin Preschool Case. Paper presented at the American Psychology and Law Association Biennial Conference, Redondo Beach.

Gaskell, G., Wright, D. and O'Muircheartaigh, C. (1993) Reliability of surveys, *The Psychologist*, 11, 500–503.

Gass, R. and Seiter, J. (2009) Persuasion and compliance gaining, in W. Eadie (ed.) *21st Century Communication: A Reference Handbook*. Thousand Oaks, CA: Sage.

Gatchalian, J. (2000) Principled negotiations – a key to successful collective bargaining, *Management Decision*, 36, 222–225.

Gates, S. (2006) Time to take negotiation seriously, *Industrial and Commercial Training*, 38, 238–241.

Gathercole, S. (2008) Working memory in the classroom, *The Psychologist*, 21, 382–385.

Gathercole, S., Pickering, S., Knight, C. and Stegmann, Z. (2004) Working memory skills and educational attainment: evidence from national curriculum assessments at 7 and 14 years of age, *Applied Cognitive Psychology*, 18, 1–16.

Gaume, J., Gmel, G. and Daeppen, J (2008) Brief alcohol interventions: do counsellors' and patients' communication characteristics predict change?, *Alcohol and Alcoholism*, 43, 62–69.

Gayle, B., Preiss, R. and Allen, M. (1998) Another look at the use of rhetorical questions, in M. Allen and R. Preiss (eds) *Persuasion: Advances Through Meta-analysis*. Cresskill, NJ: Hampton Press.

Gayle, B., Preiss, R. and Allen, M. (2006) How effective are teacher-initiated classroom questions in enhancing student learning?, in B. Gayle, R. Preiss, N. Burrell and M. Allen (eds) *Classroom Communication and Instructional Processes: Advances through Meta-analysis*. Mahwah, NJ: Lawrence Erlbaum Associates, Inc.

Gee, S., Gregory, M. and Pipe, M. (1999) What colour is your pet dinosaur? The impact of pre-interview training and question type on children's answers, *Journal of Legal and Criminological Psychology*, 4, 111–128.

Geen, R. (1990) *Human Aggression*. Milton Keynes: Open University Press.

Geen, R. (2001) *Human Aggression*, 2nd edn. Buckingham: Open University Press.

Geers, A. and Lassiter, G. (1999) Affective expectations and information gain: evidence for assimilation and contrast effects in affective experience, *Journal of Experimental Social Psychology*, 35, 394–413.

Gelfand, M. and Brett, J. (2004) (eds) *Handbook of Negotiation and Culture*. Palo Alto, CA: Stanford University Press.

Gellatly, A. (1986) How can memory skills be improved?, in A. Gellatly (ed.) *The Skilful Mind: An Introduction to Cognitive Psychology*. Milton Keynes: Open University Press.

Gemmill, G. and Oakley, J. (1992) Leadership: an alienating social myth?, *Human Relations*, 45, 113–129.

Gentry, W., Harris, L., Baker, B. and Leslie J. (2009) Managerial skills: what has changed since the late 1980s, *Leadership and Organization Development Journal*, 29, 167–181.

Georgesen, J. and Harris, M. (1998) Why's my boss always holding me down? A meta-analysis of power effects on performance evaluations, *Personality and Social Psychology Review*, 2, 184–195.

Gervasio, A. H. (1987) Assertiveness techniques as speech acts, *Clinical Psychology Review*, 7, 105–119.

Gerwing, J. and Bavelas, J. (2004) Linguistic influences on gesture's form, *Gesture*, 4, 157–195.

Gessner, M., Arnold, V. and Mobley, W. (1999) Introduction, in W. Mobley, M. Gessner and V. Arnold (eds) *Advances in Global Leadership, Volume 1*. Greenwich, CN: JAI Press.

Ghetti, S. and Goodman, G. (2001) Resisting distortion, *The Psychologist*, 14, 592–595.

Giacolone, R. and Rosenfeld, P. (1987) Impression management concerns and reinforcement interventions, *Group and Organizational Studies*, 12, 445–453.

Gibbs, J., Ellison, N. and Heino, R. (2006) Self-presentation in online personals: the role of anticipated future interaction, self-disclosure, and perceived success in internet dating, *Communication Research*, 33, 152–177.

Gibbs, R. and Bryant, G. (2008) Striving for optimal relevance when answering questions, *Cognition*, 106, 345–369.

Gilbert, J., Boulter, C., Rutherford, M. (1998) Models of explanations, Part 2: Whose voice? Whose ears?, *International Journal of Science Education*, 20, 187–203.

Giles, H. and Le Poire, B. A. (2006) Introduction: the ubiquity and social meaningfulness of nonverbal communication, in V. Manusov and M. Patterson (eds) *The Sage Handbook of Nonverbal Communication*. Thousand Oaks, CA: Sage.

Giles, H. and Ogay, T. (2007) Communication accommodation theory, in B. Whaley and W. Samter (eds) *Explaining Communication: Contemporary Theories and Exemplars*. Mahwah, NJ: Lawrence Erlbaum Associates, Inc.

Giles, H. and Street, R. (1994) Communicator characteristics and behaviour, in M. Knapp and G. Miller (eds) *Handbook of Interpersonal Communication*, 2nd edn. Thousand Oaks, CA: Sage.

Giordano, J. (2000) Effective communication and counseling with older adults, *International Journal of Aging and Human Development*, 51, 315–324.

Gleason, J. and Perlmann, R. (1985) Acquiring social variation in speech, in H. Giles and R. St Clair (eds) *Recent Advances in Language, Communication and Social Psychology*. Hove, UK: Lawrence Erlbaum Associates, Inc.

Glenberg, A., Schroeder, J. and Robertson, D. (1998) Averting the gaze disengages the environment and facilitates remembering, *Memory and Cognition*, 26, 651–658.

Glueckauf, R. and Quittner, A. (1992) Assertiveness training for disabled adults in wheelchairs: self-report, role-play, and activity pattern outcomes, *Journal of Consulting and Clinical Psychology*, 60, 419–425.

Glynn, C. and Huge, M. (2008) Opinions as norms: applying a return potential model to the study of communication behaviors, *Communication Research*, 34, 548–568.

Goby, V. and Lewis, J. (2000) The key role of listening in business: a study of the Singapore insurance industry, *Business Communication Quarterly*, 63, 41–51.

Goei, R. and Boster, F. (2005) The roles of obligation and gratitude in explaining the effectiveness of favors on compliance, *Communication Monographs*, 72, 284–300.

Goei, R., Roberto, A., Meyer, G. and Carlyle, K. (2007) The effects of favor and apology on compliance, *Communication Research*, 34, 575–595.

Goffman, E. (1959) *The Presentation of Self in Everyday Life*. Garden City, NY: Doubleday.

Goffman, E. (1972) *Relations in Public: Micro-studies of the Public Order*. Harmondsworth: Penguin.

Golden, N. (1986) *Dress Right for Business*. New York: McGraw-Hill.

Goldin-Meadow, S. (1997) When gestures and words speak differently, *Current Directions in Psychological Science*, 6, 138–143.

Goldin-Meadow, S. and Wagner, S. (2005) How our hands help us learn, *Trends in Cognitive Science*, 9, 234–241.

Goldman, M. (1980) Effect of eye-contact and distance on the verbal reinforcement of attitude, *Journal of Social Psychology*, 111, 73–78.

Goldstein, M., Bornstein, M., Schwade, J., Baldwin, F. and Brandstadter, R. (2007) Five-month-old infants have learned the value of babbling. Poster presented at the biennial meeting of the Society for Research in Child Development, March. http://babylab.psych.cornell.edu/wp-content/uploads/2009/04/srcd07_still_face_handout.pdf (accessed 2 December 2009).

Gollwitzer, P. (1999) Implementation intentions: strong effects of simple plans, *American Psychologist*, 54, 493–503.

Gómez, A., Morales, J., Huici, C., Gaviria, E. and Jiménez, J. (2007) When the world understands me ... and my alignment with the group: from self-verification to verification of one's group identity, *International Journal of Psychology and Psychological Therapy*, 7, 213–236.

Gonzales, A., Hancock, J. and Pennebaker, J. (2010) Language style matching as a predictor of social dynamics in small groups, *Communication Research*, 37, 3–19.

Good, T. and Brophy, J. (2008) *Looking in Classrooms*, 10th edn. New York: Allyn and Bacon.

Gordon, R., Druckman, D., Rozelle, R. and Baxter, J. (2006) Non-verbal behaviour as communication: approaches, issues and research, in O. Hargie (ed.) *The Handbook of Communication Skills*, 3rd edn. London: Routledge.

Gormally, J. (1982) Evaluation of assertiveness: effects of gender, rater involvement and level of assertiveness, *Behavior Therapy*, 13, 219–225.

Gosling, S., Craik, K., Martin, N. and Prior, M. (2005a) Material attributes of personal living spaces, *Home Cultures*, 2, 51–88.

Gosling, S., Craik, K., Martin, N. and Prior, M. (2005b) The Personal Living Space Cue Inventory: an analysis and evaluation, *Environment and Behavior*, 37, 683–705.

Gosling, S., Gaddis, S. and Vadzire, S. (2008) First impressions based on the environments we create and inhabit, in N. Ambady and J. Skowronski (eds) *First Impressions*. New York: Guilford Press.

Gouran, D. (1990) Introduction: speech communication after seventy-five years, issues and prospects, in G. Phillips and J. Wood (eds) *Speech Communication: Essays to Commemorate the 75th Anniversary of the Speech Communication Association*, Carbondale and Edwardsville, IL: Southern Illinois University Press.

Graff, M. (2007) Rise of the cyber-cheat, *The Psychologist*, 20, 678–679.

Graham, S., Huang, J., Clark, M. and Helgeson, V. (2008) The positives of negative emotions: willingness to express negative emotions promotes relationships, *Personality and Social Psychology Bulletin*, 34, 394–406.

Granhag, P. and Vrij, A. (2007) Deception detection, in N. Brewer, and K. Williams (eds) *Psychology and Law: An Empirical Perspective*. New York: Guilford Press.

Gray, B. (2003) Negotiating with your nemesis, *Negotiation Journal*, 19, 299–310.

Gray, H. (2008) To what extent, and under what conditions, are first impressions valid?, in N. Ambady and J. Skowronski (eds) *First Impressions*. New York: Guilford Press.

Gray, H. and Ambady, N. (2006) Methods for the study of nonverbal communication, in V. Manusov and M. Patterson (eds) *The Sage Handbook of Nonverbal Communication*. Thousand Oaks, CA: Sage.

Graziano, P., Reavis, R., Keane, S. and Calkins, S. (2007) The role of emotion regulation in children's early academic success, *Journal of School Psychology*, 45, 3–19.

Green, V. and Rechis, R. (2006) Children's cooperative and competitive interactions in limited resource situations: a literature review, *Applied Developmental Psychology*, 27, 42–59.

Greenbaum, P. and Rosenfeld, H. (1980) Varieties of touching in greetings: sequential structure and sex-related differences, *Journal of Nonverbal Behavior*, 5, 13–25.

Greenberg, M. A. and Stone, A. A. (1992) Emotional disclosure about traumas and its relation to health: effects of previous disclosure and trauma severity, *Journal of Personality and Social Psychology*, 63, 75–84.

Greene, J. (1995) An action-assembly perspective on verbal and nonverbal message production: a dancer's message unveiled, in D. Hewes (ed.) *The Cognitive Basis of Interpersonal Communication*. Hillsdale, NJ: Lawrence Erlbaum Associates, Inc.

Greene, J. (2000) Evanescent mentation: an ameliorative conceptual foundation for research and theory on message production, *Communication Theory*, 10, 139–155.

Greene, K., Derlega, V. and Mathews, A. (2006) Self-disclosure in personal relationships, in A. Vangelista and D. Perlman (eds) *The Cambridge Handbook of Personal Relationships*. New York: Cambridge University Press.

Greenleaf, C. (1998) *Attention to Detail: A Gentleman's Guide to Professional Appearance and Conduct*. New York: Mass Market Press.

Greenspoon, J. (1955) The reinforcing effect of two spoken sounds on the frequency of two responses, *American Journal of Psychology*, 68, 409–416.

Gregg, A. (2007) When vying reveals lying: the timed antagonistic response alethiometer, *Applied Cognitive Psychology*, 21, 621–647.

Gregg, V. (1986) *Introduction to Human Memory*. London: Routledge and Kegan Paul.

Gress, J. and Heft, H. (1998) Do territorial actions attenuate the effects of high density? A field study, in J. Sanford and B. Connell (eds) *People, Places, And Public Policy*. Edmond, OK: Environmental Design Research Association.

Griffin, E. (2008) *A First Look at Communication Theory*, 7th edn. New York: McGraw-Hill.

Grigsby, J. and Weatherley, D. (1983) Gender and sex-role differences in intimacy of self-disclosure, *Psychological Reports*, 53, 891–897.

Groogan, S. (1999) Setting the scene, in A. Long (ed.) *Interaction for Practice in Community Nursing*. Basingstoke: Macmillan.

Guadagno, R. and Cialdini, R. (2007) Gender differences in impression management in organizations: a qualitative review, *Sex Roles*, 56, 483–494.

Gudjonsson, G. (1999) Police interviewing and disputed confessions, in A. Memon and R. Bull (eds) *Handbook of the Psychology of Interviewing*. Chichester: Wiley.

Gudjonsson, G. (2001) False confession, *The Psychologist*, 14, 588–591.

Gudleski, G. and Shean, G. (2000) Depressed and nondepressed students: differences in interpersonal perceptions, *Journal of Psychology*, 134, 56–62.

Gudykunst, W. (1991) *Bridging Differences: Effective Intergroup Communication*. Newbury Park, CA: Sage.

Gudykunst, W. and Matsumoto, Y. (1996) Cross-cultural variability of communication in personal relationships, in W. Gudykunst, S. Ting-Toomey and T. Nishida (eds) *Communication in Personal Relationships Across Cultures*. Thousand Oaks, CA: Sage.

Gudykunst, W. and Ting-Toomey, S. (1996) Communication in personal relationships across cultures: an introduction, in W. Gudykunst, S. Ting-Toomey and T. Nishida (eds) *Communication in Personal Relationships Across Cultures*. Thousand Oaks, CA: Sage.

Gudykunst, W., Ting-Toomey, S. and Nishida, T. (eds) (1996) *Communication in Personal Relationships Across Cultures*. Thousand Oaks, CA: Sage.

Guéguen, N. and Fisher-Lokou, J. (2003) Another evaluation of touch and helping behavior, *Psychological Reports*, 90, 267–269.

Guéguen, N. and Pascual, A. (2005) Improving the response rate to a street survey: an evaluation of the 'but you are free to accept or to refuse' technique, *Psychological Record*, 55, 297–303.

Guerrero, L. (2005) Observer ratings of nonverbal involvement and immediacy, in V. Manusov (ed.) *The Sourcebook of Nonverbal Measures: Going Beyond Words*. Mahwah, NJ: Lawrence Erlbaum Associates, Inc.

Guerrero, L. and Floyd, K. (2006) *Nonverbal Communication in Close Relationships*. Mahwah, NJ: Lawrence Erlbaum Associates, Inc.

Guerrero, L., Andersen, P. and Afifi, W. (2007) *Close Encounters: Communication in Relationships*. Thousand Oaks, CA: Sage.

Guimond, S. (ed.) (2006) *Social Comparison and Social Psychology: Understanding Cognition, Intergroup Relations, and Culture*. Cambridge: Cambridge University Press.

Guirdham, M. (2002) *Interactive Behaviour at Work*, 3rd edn. Harlow: Pearson.

Gupta, S. and Shukla, A. (1989) Verbal operant conditioning as a function of extraversion and reinforcement, *British Journal of Psychology*, 80, 39–44.

Gupton, T. and Le Bow, M. (1971) Behavior management in a large industrial firm, *Behavioral Therapy*, 2, 78–82.

Haase, R. F. and Di Mattia, D. (1976) Spatial environment and verbal conditioning in a quasi-counseling interview, *Journal of Counseling Psychology*, 23, 414–421.

Hackley, S., Waters, N. and Woodside, S. (2006) How creating 'communities of learning' and 'common cultures' fosters collaboration: the e-Parliament, the Israeli Settlements Project, and the Mexican Negotiation Skills Training Workshop, *International Negotiation*, 11, 37–64.

Haddock, G. and Maio, G. (2008) Attitudes: content, structure and functions, in M. Hewstone, W. Stroebe and K. Jonas (eds) *Introduction to Social Psychology: A European Perspective*, 4th edn. Malden, MA: Blackwell.

Hagihara, A., Tarumi, K. and Nobutomo, K. (2006a) Physicians' and patients' recognition of the level of the physician's explanation in medical encounters, *Health Communication*, 20, 101–104.

Hagihara, A., Odamaki, M., Nobutomo, K. and Tarumi, K. (2006b) Physician and patient perceptions of the physician explanations in medical encounters, *Journal of Health Psychology*, 11, 91–105.

Hajek, C., Villagran, M. and Wittenberg-Lyles, E. (2007) The relationships among perceived physician accommodation, perceived outgroup typicality, and patient inclinations toward compliance, *Communication Research Reports*, 24, 293–302.

Hall, E. (1966) *The Hidden Dimension*. Garden City, NY: Doubleday.

Hall, J. (1984) *Nonverbal Sex Differences: Communication Accuracy and Expressive Style*. Baltimore, MD: Johns Hopkins University Press.

Hall, J. (1996) Touch, status, and gender at professional meetings, *Journal of Nonverbal Psychology*, 20, 23–44.

Hall, J. (2006) Women's and men's nonverbal communication: similarities, differences, stereotypes, and origins, in V. Manusov and M. Patterson (eds) *The Sage Handbook of Nonverbal Communication*. Thousand Oaks, CA: Sage.

Hall, J. and Andrzejewski, S. (2008) Who draws accurate first impressions? Personal correlates of sensitivity to nonverbal cues, in N. Ambady and J. Skowronski (eds) *First Impressions*. New York: Guilford Press.

Halone, K. and Pecchioni, L. (2001) Relational listening: a grounded theoretical model, *Communication Reports*, 14, 59–71.

Halpern, D. F. (2000) *Sex Differences in Cognitive Abilities*, 3rd edn. Mahwah, NJ: Lawrence Erlbaum Associates, Inc.

Halpern, J. (1994) The effect of friendship on personal business transactions, *Journal of Conflict Resolution*, 38, 647–664.

Hamilton, C. (2008) *Communicating for Results*, 8th edn. Belmont, CA: Wadsworth.

Hamilton, D. (2005) *Social Cognition: Key Readings*. New York: Psychology Press.

Hamilton, M. and Hunter, J. (1998a) The effect of language intensity on receiver evaluations of message, in M. Allen and R. Preiss (eds) *Persuasion: Advances Through Meta-analysis*. Cresskill, NJ: Hampton Press.

Hamilton, M. and Hunter, J. (1998b) A framework for understanding meta analyses of persuasion, in M. Allen and R. Preiss (eds) *Persuasion: Advances Through Meta-analysis*. Cresskill, NJ: Hampton Press.

Hamilton, W., Round, A. and Sharp, D. (1999) Effects on hospital attendance rates of giving patients a copy of their referral letter: randomised control trial, *British Medical Journal*, 318, 1392–1395.

Hammen, C. (1997) *Depression*. Hove, UK: Psychology Press.

Hancock, D. (2000) Impact of verbal praise on college students' time spent on homework, *Journal of Educational Research*, 93, 384–389.

Hanna, M. and Wilson, G. (1998) *Communicating in Business and Professional Settings*, 4th edn. New York: McGraw-Hill.

Hanzal, A., Segrin, C. and Dorros, S. (2008) The role of marital status and age on men's and women's reactions to touch from a relational partner, *Journal of Nonverbal Behavior*, 32, 21–35.

Hardy, C. and van Leeuwen, S. (2004) Interviewing young children: effects of probe structures and focus of rapport-building talk on the qualities of young children's eyewitness statements, *Canadian Journal of Behavioural Science*, 36, 155–165.

Hare, A. P. (1976) *Handbook of Small Group Research*. New York: Free Press.

Hare, L. and O'Neill, K. (2000) Effectiveness and efficiency in small group academic peer groups: a case study, *Small Group Research*, 31, 24–53.

Hargie, O. (1983) The importance of teacher questions in the classroom, in M. Stubbs and H. Hiller (eds) *Readings on Language, Schools and Classrooms*. London: Methuen.

Hargie, O. (2006a) Skill in theory: communication as skilled performance, in O. Hargie (ed.) *The Handbook of Communication Skills*, 3rd edn. London: Routledge.

Hargie, O. (2006b) Training in communication skills: research, theory and practice, in O. Hargie (ed.) *The Handbook of Communication Skills*, 3rd edn. London: Routledge.

Hargie, O. (2006c) Skill in practice: an operational model of communicative skilled performance, in O. Hargie (ed.) *The Handbook of Communication Skills*, 3rd edn. London: Routledge.

Hargie, O. (2007) Managing your communications: a key determinant of organizational success, in R. Karlsdottir (ed.) *Læring, Kommunikasjon og Ledesle i Organisasjoner*. Trondheim: Tapir Akademisk Forlag.

Hargie, O. (2009) Listening, in H. Reis and S. Sprecher (eds) *Encyclopedia of Human Relationships*. Thousand Oaks, CA: Sage.

Hargie, O. and Tourish, D. (1999) The psychology of interpersonal skill, in A. Memon and R. Bull (eds) *Handbook of the Psychology of Interviewing*. Chichester: Wiley.

Hargie, O. and Tourish, D. (eds) (2009) *Auditing Organizational Communication: A Handbook of Research, Theory and Practice*. London: Routledge.

Hargie, O., Morrow, N. and Woodman, C. (2000) Pharmacists' evaluation of key communication skills in practice, *Patient Education and Counseling*, 39, 61–70.

Hargie, O., Dickson, D. and Tourish, D. (2004) *Communication Skills for Effective Management*. Basingstoke: Palgrave Macmillan.

Hargie, O., Dickson, D., Mallett, J. and Stringer, M. (2008) Communicating social identity: a study of Catholics and Protestants in Northern Ireland, *Communication Research*, 35, 792–821.

Hargie, O., Brataas, H. and Thorsnes, S. (2009) Cancer patients' sensemaking of conversations with cancer nurses in outpatient clinics, *Australian Journal of Advanced Nursing*, 26, 70–78.

Harper, J. (2004) Presentation skills, *Industrial and Commercial Training*, 36, 125–127.

Harper, M. and Welsh, D. (2007) Keeping quiet: self-silencing and its association with relational and individual functioning among adolescent romantic couples, *Journal of Social and Personal Relationships*, 24, 99–116.

Harper, V. and Harper, E. (2006) Understanding student self-disclosure typology through blogging, *The Qualitative Report*, 11, 251–261.

Harrigan, J. (2005) Proxemics, kinesics and gaze, in J. Harrigan, R. Rosenthal and K. Scherer (eds) *The New Handbook of Methods in Nonverbal Behavioral Research*. Oxford: Oxford University Press.

Harris, J. (1973) Answering questions containing marked and unmarked adjectives and adverbs, *Journal of Experimental Psychology*, 97, 399–401.

Harris, M. and Garris, C. (2008) You never get a second chance to make a first impression: behavioral consequences of first impressions, in N. Ambady and J. Skowronski (eds) *First Impressions*. New York: Guilford Press.

Harris, P. and Brown, B. (1998) The home and identity display: interpreting resident territoriality from home exteriors, *Journal of Environmental Psychology*, 16, 187–203.

Harris, S., Dersch, C. and Mittal, M. (1999) Look who's talking: measuring self-disclosure in MFT, *Contemporary Family Therapy*, 21, 405–415.

Hartley, P. (1997) *Group Communication*. London: Routledge.

Hartley, P. (1999) *Interpersonal Communication*, 2nd edn. London: Routledge.

Harwood, J., Ryan, E., Giles, H. and Tysoski, S. (1997) Evaluations of patronizing speech and three response styles in a non-service-providing context, *Journal of Applied Communication*, 25, 170–195.

Haski-Leventhal, D. and Bargal, D. (2008) The volunteer stages and transitions model: organizational socialization of volunteers, *Human Relations*, 61, 67–102.

Haslam, S. and Reicher, S. (2008) Questioning the banality of evil, *The Psychologist*, 21, 16–19.

Haslam, S., Reicher, S. and Platow, M. (2010) *The New Psychology of Leadership*. Hove, UK: Psychology Press.

Hastings, S. (2000a) Asian Indian 'self-suppression' and self-disclosure: enactment and adaptation of cultural identity, *Journal of Language and Social Psychology*, 19, 85–109.

Hastings, S. (2000b) 'Egocasting' in the avoidance of dialogue: an intercultural perspective, in S. Petronio (ed.) *Balancing the Secrets of Private Disclosures*, Mahwah, NJ: Lawrence Erlbaum Associates, Inc.

Hatfield, E., Cacioppo, J. and Rapson, R. (1994) *Emotional Contagion*. Cambridge: Cambridge University Press.

Hattie, J. and Timperley, H. (2007) The power of feedback, *Review of Educational Research*, 77, 81–112.

Haugtvedt, C. and Petty, R. (1992) Personality and attitude change: need for cognition moderates the persistence and resistance of persuasion, *Journal of Personality and Social Psychology*, 63, 308–319.

Hawkes, K., Edelman, H. and Dodd, D. (1996) Language style and evaluation of a female speaker, *Perceptual and Motor Skills*, 83, 80–82.

Hawkins, K. and Power, C. (1999) Gender differences in questions asked during small decision-making group discussions, *Small Group Research*, 30, 235–256.

Hawley, P., Johnson, S., Mize, J. and McNamara, K. (2007) Physical attractiveness in preschoolers: relationships with power, status, aggression and social skills, *Journal of School Psychology*, 5, 499–521

Hayashi, M. (2009) Marking a 'noticing of departure' in talk: eh-prefaced turns in Japanese conversation, *Journal of Pragmatics*, 41, 2100–2129.

Hayes, J. (2002) *Interpersonal Skills at Work*, 2nd edn. London: Routledge.

Heath, C. (1984) Talk and recipiency: sequential organization in speech and body movement, in J. M. Atkinson and J. Heritage (eds) *Structures of Social Actions*. Cambridge: Cambridge University Press.

Heath, R. and Bryant, J. (2000) *Human Communication Theory and Research: Concepts, Contexts, and Challenges*. Mahwah, NJ: Lawrence Erlbaum Associates, Inc.

Heatherton, T., Krendl, A., Macrae, C. and Kelley, W. (2007) A social brain sciences approach to understanding self, in C. Sedikides and S. Spencer (eds) *The Self*. New York: Psychology Press.

Hebl, M. and Mannix, L. (2003) The weight of obesity in evaluating others: a mere proximity effect, *Personality and Social Psychology Bulletin*, 29, 28–38.

Hecht, M. and LaFrance, M. (1998) License or obligation to smile: the effect of power and sex on the amount and type of smiling, *Personality and Social Psychology Bulletin*, 24, 1332–1342.

Heller, K. (2006) The cognitive psychology of circumstantial evidence, *Michigan Law Review*, 105. http://ssrn.com/abstract=891695 (accessed 2 December 2009).

Heller, M. (1997) Posture as an interface between biology and culture, in U. Segerstrale and P. Molnar (eds) *Nonverbal Communication: Where Nature Meets Culture*. Mahwah, NJ: Lawrence Erlbaum Associates, Inc.

Henningsen, D., Henningsen, M., Eden, J. and Cruz, M. (2006) Examining the symptoms of groupthink and retrospective sensemaking, *Small Group Research*, 37, 36–64.

Henry, J. (2009) School pupils praised too much, says research, *Daily Telegraph*, 19 September. http://www.telegraph.co.uk/education/primaryeducation/6209938/School-pupils-praised-too-much-says-research.html (accessed 2 December 2009).

Henry, S., Medway, F. and Scarbo, H. (1979) Sex and locus of control as determinants of children's responses to peer versus adult, *Journal of Educational Psychology*, 71, 604–612.

Hensley, W. and Cooper, R. (1987) Height and occupational success: a review and critique, *Psychological Reports*, 60, 843–849.

Henss, R. (1996) Waist-to-hip ratio and attractiveness: replication and extension, *Personality and Individual Differences*, 19, 479–488.

Heritage, J. (1998) Oh-prefaced responses to inquiry, *Language in Society*, 27, 291–334.

Heritage J. and Robinson J. (2006) The structure of patients' presenting concerns: physicians' opening questions, *Health Communication*, 19, 89–102.

Heritage J., Robinson J., Elliott, M., Beckett, M. and Wilkes, M. (2007) Reducing patients' unmet concerns in primary care: the difference one word can make, *Journal of General Internal Medicine*, 22, 1429–1433.

Herndon, L., Brunner, T. and Rollins, J. (2006) The Glaucoma Research Foundation patient survey: patient understanding of glaucoma and its treatment, *American Journal of Opthamology*, 141, S22–28.

Heslin, R. and Alper, T. (1983) Touch: a bonding gesture, in J. Wiemann and R. Harrison (eds) *Nonverbal Interaction*. London: Sage.

Hess, U., Philippot, P. and Blairy, S. (1999) Mimicry: facts and fiction, in P. Philippot, R. Feldman and E. Coats (eds) *The Social Context of Nonverbal Behavior*. Cambridge: Cambridge University Press.

Hess, U., Adams, R. and Kleck, R. (2008) The role of facial expression in person perception, in N. Ambady and J. Skowronski (eds) *First Impressions*. New York: Guilford Press.

Hetsroni, A. (2007) Open or closed – this is the question: the influence of question format on the cultivation effect, *Communication Methods and Measures*, 1, 215–226.

Hettema, J., Steele, J. and Miller, W. (2005) Motivational interviewing, *Annual Review of Clinical Psychology*, 1, 91–111.

Hewes, D. (1995) Cognitive interpersonal communication research: some thoughts on criteria, in B. Burleson (ed.) *Communication Yearbook, 18*. Thousand Oaks, CA: Sage.

Hewes, D. and Planalp, S. (1987) The individual's place in communication science, in C. Berger and S. Chaffee (eds) *Handbook of Communication Science*. Newbury Park, CA: Sage.

Highlen, P. and Baccus, G. (1977) Effects of reflection of feeling and probe on client self-referenced affect, *Journal of Counseling Psychology*, 24, 440–443.

Highlen, P. and Nicholas, R. (1978) Effects of locus of control, instructions, and verbal conditioning on self-referenced affect in a counseling interview, *Journal of Counseling Psychology* 25, 177–183.

Hill, C. (1989) *Therapist Techniques and Client Outcomes*. Newbury Park, CA: Sage.

Hill, C. (1992) Research on therapist techniques in brief individual therapy: implications for practitioners, *The Counseling Psychologist*, 20, 689–711.

Hill, C. (2004) *Helping Skills: Facilitating Exploration, Insight and Action*, 2nd edn. Washington, DC: American Psychological Association.

Hill, C. and Gormally, J. (1977) Effects of reflection, restatement, probe and nonverbal behaviors on client affect, *Journal of Counseling Psychology*, 24, 92–97.

Hill, C., Helms, J., Tichenor, V., Spiegel, S., O'Grady, K. and Perry, E. (1988) Effects of therapist response modes in brief psychotherapy, *Journal of Counseling Psychology*, 35, 222–233.

Hiller, J., Fisher, G. and Kaess, W. (1969) A computer investigation of verbal character-istics of effective classroom lecturing, *American Educational Research Journal*, 6, 661–675.

Hind, C. (1997) *Communication Skills in Medicine*. London: BMJ Publishing Group.

Hinton, P. (1993) *The Psychology of Interpersonal Perception*. London: Routledge.

Hirsh, J. (2009) Choosing the right tools to find the right people, *The Psychologist*, 22, 752–755.

Hirt, E., Lynn, S., Payne, D., Krackow, E. and McCrea, S. (1999) Expectations and memory: inferring the past from what must have been, in I. Kirsch (ed.) *How Expectations Shape Experience*. Washington, DC: American Psychological Association.

HMSO (1995) *Health Services Commissioner for England, for Scotland and for Wales, Annual Report for 1994–5*. London: HMSO.

Ho, S. and McLeod, D. (2008) Social-psychological influences on opinion expression in face-to-face and computer-mediated communication, *Communication Research*, 35, 190–207.

Hobson, R. and Lee, A. (1996) Hello and goodbye: a study of social engagement in autism, *Journal of Autism and Developmental Disorders*, 28, 117–127.

Hoeken, H. and Hustinx, L. (2007) The impact of exemplars on responsibility stereo-types in fund-raising letters, *Communication Research*, 34, 596–617.

Hoffman, R. (1995) Disclosure needs and motives after a near-death experience, *Journal of Near-Death Studies*, 13, 237–266.

Hoffnung, R. (1969) Conditioning and transfer of affective self-references in a role-played counseling interview, *Journal of Consulting and Clinical Psychology*, 33, 527–531.

Hofstede, G. (1980) *Culture's Consequences: International Differences in Work-related Values*. Beverly Hills, CA: Sage.

Hogan, K. and Speakman, J. (2006) *Covert Persuasion: Psychological Tactics and Tricks to Win the Game*. New York: Wiley.

Hogg, M. (2001) Social categorisation, depersonalization, and group behavior, in M. Hogg and S. Tindale (eds) *Blackwell Handbook of Social Psychology: Group Processes*. Malden, MA: Blackwell.

Hogg, M. (2004) Social categorisation, depersonalization, and group behavior, in M. Brewer and M. Hewstone (eds) *Self and Social Identity*. Malden, MA: Blackwell.

Hogg, M. and Reid, S. (2006) Social identity, self-categorization, and the communica-tion of group norms, *Communication Theory*, 16, 7–30.

Hogg, M. and Vaughn, G. M. (2008) *Social Psychology*, 5th edn. Harlow: Pearson.

Hollander, E. (2009) *Inclusive Leadership: The Essential Leader-Follower Relationship*. New York: Taylor & Francis.

Holli, B., Calabrese, R. and Maillet, J. (2003) *Communication and Education Skills for Dietetics Professionals*, 4th edn. Baltimore, MD: Lippincott Williams and Wilkins.

Holli, B., O'Sullivan Maillet, J., Beto, J. and Calabrese, R. (2008) *Communication and Education Skills for Dietetics Professionals*, 5th edn. Baltimore, MD: Lippincott Williams and Wilkins.

Holliday, A., Hyde, M. and Kullman, J. (2004) *Intercultural Communication*. London: Routledge.

Holliday, R. and Albon, A. (2004) Minimising misinformation effects in young children with cognitive interview mnemonics, *Applied Cognitive Psychology*, 18, 263–281.

Hollinger, L. and Buschmann, M. (1993) Factors influencing the perception of touch by elderly nursing home residents and their health caregivers, *International Journal of Nursing Studies*, 30, 445–461.

Holman, D. (2000) A dialogical approach to skill and skilled activity, *Human Relations*, 53, 957–980.

Holtgraves, T. and Kashima, Y. (2008) Language, meaning, and social cognition, *Personality and Social Psychology Review*, 12, 73–94.

Holtgraves, T. and Lasky, B. (1999) Linguistic power and persuasion, *Journal of Language and Social Psychology*, 18, 196–206.

Homans, G. (1950) *The Human Group*. New York: Harcourt, Brace.

Honess, T. and Charman, E. (2002) Members of the jury – guilty of incompetence?, *The Psychologist*, 15, 72–75.

Hooper, C. (1995) A behavioral analysis of clinical performance discriminating novice from expert nurses, *Dissertation Abstracts International Section A: Humanities and Social Sciences*, 56 (6-A), 2098.

Hopper, R., Bosma, J. and Ward, J. (1992) Dialogic teaching of medical terminology at the Cancer Information Service, *Journal of Language and Social Psychology*, 11, 63–74.

Hornsey, M. (2008) Social identity theory and self-categorization theory: a historical review, *Social and Personality Psychology Compass*, 2, 204–222.

Hornsey, M., Dwyer, L. and Oei, T. (2007) Beyond cohesiveness: reconceptualizing the link between group processes and outcomes in group psychotherapy, *Small Group Research*, 38, 567–592.

Horwitz, B. (2001) *Communication Apprehension: Origins and Management*. Albany, NY: Delmar.

Hosek, A. and Thompson, J. (2009) Communication privacy management and college instruction: exploring the rules and boundaries that frame instructor private disclosures, *Communication Education*, 58, 327–349.

Hough, M. (2006) *Counselling Skills and Theory*, 2nd edn. London: Hodder Arnold.

House, J. (2005) Politeness in Germany: politeness in *Germany*?, in L. Hickey and M. Stewart (eds) *Politeness in Europe*. Clevedon: Multilingual Matters.

House, R. (1976) A 1976 theory of charismatic leadership, in J. Hunt and L. Larson (eds) *Leadership: The Cutting Edge*. Carbondale, IL: Southern Illinois University.

House, R. and Mitchell, R. (1974) Path-goal theory of leadership, *Journal of Contemporary Business*, 3, 81–97.

Houser, M. (2005) Are we violating their expectations? Instructor communication expectations of traditional and nontraditional students, *Communication Quarterly*, 53, 213–228.

Houston, V. and Bull, R. (1994) Do people avoid sitting next to someone who is facially disfigured?, *European Journal of Social Psychology*, 24, 279–284.

Howard, D. (1990) The influence of verbal responses to common greetings on compliance behavior: the foot-in-the-mouth effect, *Journal of Applied Social Psychology*, 20, 1185–1196.

Howe, N., Aquan-Assee, J., Bukowski, W., Rinaldi, C. and Lehoux, P. (2000) Sibling self-disclosure in early adolescence, *Merrill Palmer Quarterly*, 46, 653–671.

Hsiung, R. and Bagozzi, R. (2003) Validating the relationship qualities of influence and persuasion with the family social relations model, *Human Communication Research*, 29, 81–110.

Huang, L. (2000) Examining candidate information search processes: the impact of processing goals and sophistication, *Journal of Communication*, 50, 93–114.

Huczynski, A. (1996) *Influencing Within Organizations*. London: Prentice-Hall.

Hughes, L. and Avey, J. (2009) Transforming with levity: humor, leadership, and follower attitudes, *Leadership and Organizational Development Journal*, 30, 540–562.

Hutchby, I. and Wooffitt, R. (2008) *Conversation Analysis*. Malden, MA: Polity Press.

Huxley, A. (1954) *The Doors of Perception*. New York: Harper and Row.

Hybels, S. and Weaver, R. (2009) *Communicating Effectively*, 9th edn. New York: McGraw-Hill.

Imber, J. (2008) *Trusting Doctors: The Decline of Moral Authority in American Medicine*. Princeton, NJ: Princeton Press.

Imhof, M. (2010) Listening to voices and judging people, *International Journal of Listening*, 24, 19–33.

Inskipp, F. (2006) Generic skills, in C. Feltham and I. Horton (eds) *The Sage Handbook of Counselling and Psychotherapy*. London: Sage.

International Listening Association (2009) http://www.listen.org/ (accessed 2 December 2009).

International Medical Benefit/Risk Foundation (1993) *Improving Patient Information and Education on Medicines. Report from the Foundation's Committee on Patient Information*. Geneva: International Medical Benefit/Risk Foundation.

Irving, P. and Dickson, D. (2006) A re-conceptualization of Rogers' core conditions: implications for research, practice and training, *International Journal for the Advancement of Counselling*, 28, 183–194.

Irving, P. and Hazlett, D. (1999) Communicating with challenging clients, in A. Long (ed.) *Interaction for Practice in Community Nursing*. Basingstoke: Macmillan.

Ivanov, B., Pfau, M. and Parker, K. (2009a) The attitude base as a moderator of the effectiveness of inoculation strategy, *Communication Monographs*, 76, 47–72.

Ivanov, B., Pfau, M. and Parker, K. (2009b) Can inoculation withstand multiple attacks? An examination of the effectiveness of the inoculation strategy compared to the supportive and restoration strategies, *Communication Research*, 36, 655–676.

Ivey, A. and Ivey, M. (2007) *Intentional Interviewing and Counseling: Facilitating Client Development in a Multicultural Society*, 6th edn. Belmont, CA: Thomson Brooks/Cole.

Ivey, A., Ivey, M. and Simek-Downing, L. (1987) *Counseling and Psychotherapy: Integrating Skills, Theory, and Practice*, 2nd edn. Englewood Cliffs, NJ: Prentice-Hall.

Ivey, A., Ivey, M. and Zalaquett, C. (2010) *Intentional Interviewing and Counseling: Facilitating Client Development in a Multicultural Society*, 7th edn. Belmont, CA: Thomson Brooks/Cole.

Iyengar, S. and Brockner, J. (2001) Cultural differences in self and the impact of personal and social influences, in W. Wosinska, R. Cialdini, D. Barrett and J. Reykowski (eds) *The Practice of Social Influence in Multiple Cultures*. Mahwah, NJ: Lawrence Erlbaum Associates, Inc.

Izard, C. (1997) Emotions and facial expressions: a perspective from differential emotions theory, in J. Russell and J. Fernandez-Dols (eds) *The Psychology of Facial Expression*. Cambridge: Cambridge University Press.

Jacobs, C. and Coghlan, D. (2005) Sound from silence: on listening in organizational learning, *Human Relations*, 58, 115–138.

Jacobson, R. (1999) Personal space within two interaction conditions as a function of confederate age and gender differences, *Dissertation Abstracts International: Section B: the Sciences and Engineering*, 59(7-B), 3743.

Jalongo, M. (2010) Listening in early childhood: an interdisciplinary review of the literature, *International Journal of Listening*, 24, 1–18.

James, W. (1890) *Principles of Psychology*. Chicago, IL: Encyclopaedia Britannica.

James, W. (1892) *Psychology: The Briefer Course*. New York: Henry Holt.

Janis, I. (1982) *Groupthink*, 2nd edn. Boston, MA: Houghton-Mifflin.

Janis, I. (1997) Groupthink, in R. Vecchio *et al.* (eds) *Leadership: Understanding the Dynamics of Power and Influence in Organizations*. Notre Dame, IN: University of Notre Dame Press.

Janse, E. (2004) Word perception in fast speech: artificially time-compressed vs. naturally produced fast speech, *Speech Communication*, 42, 155–173.

Janusik, L. (2007) Building listening theory: the validation of the conversational listening span, *Communication Studies*, 58, 139–156.

Jarrett, C. (2008) Mind wide open, *The Psychologist*, 21, 294–297.

Jeffries, K. and Reed, R. (2000) Trust and adaptation in relational contracting, *Academy of Management Review*, 25, 873–882.

Jensen, K. (1996) The effects of selected classical music on writing and talking about significant life events, *Dissertation Abstracts International: Humanities and Social Sciences*, 56(12-A), 4602.

Job, R. (1988) Effective and ineffective use of fear in health promotion campaigns, *American Journal of Public Health*, 78, 163–167.

Joffe, H. (2008) The power of visual material: persuasion, emotion and identification, *Diogenes*, 217, 84–93.

John, O., Robins, R. and Pervin, L. (2008) *Handbook of Personality: Theory and Research*, 3rd edn. New York: Guilford Press.

Johnson, A., Crawford, M., Sherman, S., Rutchick, A., Hamilton, D., Ferreira, M., *et al.* (2006) A functional perspective on group memberships: differential need fulfillment in a group typology, *Journal of Experimental Social Psychology*, 42, 707–719.

Johnson, A., Becker, J., Wigley, S., Haigh, M. and Craig, E. (2007) Reported argumentativeness and verbal aggressiveness levels: the influence of type of argument, *Communication Studies*, 58, 189–205.

Johnson, C. and Dabbs, J. (1976) Self-disclosure in dyads as a function of distance and the subject-experimenter relationship, *Sociometry*, 39, 257–263.

Johnson, D. and Johnson, F. (2009) *Joining Together: Group Theory and Group Skills*, 10th edn. Upper Saddle River, NJ: Pearson Education.

Johnson, S. (2008) I second that emotion: effects of emotional contagion and affect at work on leader and follower outcomes, *Leadership Quarterly*, 19, 1–19.

Johnson, S. and Bechler, C. (1998) Examining the relationship between listening effectiveness and leadership emergence: perceptions, behaviors and recall, *Small Group Research*, 29, 452–471.

Johnston, D. (1994) *The Art and Science of Persuasion*. Boston, MA: McGraw-Hill.

Joinson, A. (2001) Self-disclosure in computer-mediated communication: the role of self-awareness and visual anonymity, *European Journal of Social Psychology*, 31, 177–192.

Jones, S. (1999) Communicating with touch, in L. Guerrero, J. DeVito and M. Hecht (eds) *The Nonverbal Communication Reader: Classic and Contemporary Readings*. Prospect Heights, IL: Waveland Press.

Jones, S. (2005) The Touch Log Record: a behavioral communication measure, in V. Manusov (ed.) *The Sourcebook of Nonverbal Measures: Going Beyond Words*. Mahwah, NJ: Lawrence Erlbaum Associates, Inc.

Jones, S. (2008) Nature and nurture in the development of social smiling, *Philosophical Psychology*, 21, 349–357.

Jones, S. and LeBaron, C. D. (2002) Research on the relationship between verbal and nonverbal communication: emerging integrations, *Journal of Communication*, 52, 499–521.

Jones, S. and Yarbrough, A. (1985) A naturalistic study of the meanings of touch, *Communication Monographs*, 52, 19–56.

Jones, S., Collins, K. and Hong, H. (1991) An audience effect on smile production in 10 month old infants, *Psychological Science*, 2, 45–49.

Jones, W., Hobbs, S. and Hockenbury, D. (1982) Loneliness and social skill deficits, *Journal of Personality and Social Psychology*, 42, 682–689.

Jordan, J. (1998) Executive cognitive control in communication: extending plan-based theory, *Human Communication Research*, 25, 5–38.

Jordan, J. and Roloff, M. (1997) Planning skills and negotiator accomplishment: the relationship between self monitoring and plan generation, plan enhancement, and plan consequences, *Communication Research*, 24, 31–63.

Jourard, S. (1961) Religious denomination and self-disclosure, *Psychological Bulletin*, 8, 446.

Jourard, S. (1964) *The Transparent Self*. New York: Van Nostrand Reinhold.

Jourard, S. (1966) An exploratory study of bodily accessibility, *British Journal of Social and Clinical Psychology*, 26, 235–242.

Jourard, S. (1971) *Self-disclosure*. New York: Wiley.

Jucks, R., Bromme, R. and Runde, A. (2007) Explaining with nonshared illustrations: how they constrain explanations, *Learning and Instruction*, 17, 204–218.

Judge, T. and Cable, D. (2004) The effect of physical height on workplace success and income: preliminary test of a theoretical model, *Journal of Applied Psychology*, 89, 428–441.

Justine, A. and Howe, B. (1998) Player ability, coach feedback, and female adolescent athletes' perceived competence and satisfaction, *Journal of Sport and Exercise Psychology*, 20, 280–299.

Kadunc, T. (1991) Teacher's nonverbal skills and communication research, *The Global Educator*, 11, 2–4.

Kagan, C. (2007) Interpersonal skills and reflection in regeneration practice, *Public Money and Management*, 27, 169–174.

Kagan, C. and Evans, J. (1995) *Professional Interpersonal Skills for Nurses*. London: Chapman and Hall.

Kahai, S., Sosik, J. and Avolio, J. (1997) Effects of leadership style and problem structure on work group process and outcome in an electronic meeting system environment, *Personnel Psychology*, 50, 121–136.

Kahn, M. (2008) Etiquette-based medicine, *New England Journal of Medicine*, 358, 1988–1999.

Kahn, R. and Cannell, C. (1957) *The Dynamics of Interviewing*. New York: Wiley.

Kahn, S. (1981) Issues in the assessment and training of assertiveness with women, in J. Wine and M. Smye (eds) *Social Competence*. New York: Guilford Press.

Kaiser, S. (1999) Women's appearance and clothing within organizations, in L. Guerrero, J. DeVito and M. Hecht (eds) *The Nonverbal Communication Reader: Classic and Contemporary Readings*, Prospect Heights, IL: Waveland Press.

Kalma, A. (1992) Gazing in triads: a powerful signal in floor apportionment, *British Journal of Social Psychology*, 31, 21–39.

Kang, Y. (1998) Classroom context, teacher feedback and student self-effiacy, *Dissertation Abstracts International Section A: Humanities and Social Sciences*, 59(2-A), 0419.

Kappas, A., Hess, U. and Scherer, K. (1991) Voice and emotion, in R. Feldman and B. Rime (eds) *Fundamentals of Nonverbal Behaviour*, Cambridge: Cambridge University Press.

Karagözoglu, S., Kahve, E., Koç Ö. and Adamişoglu, D. (2007) Self esteem and assertiveness of final year Turkish university students, *Nurse Education Today*, 28, 641–649.

Karremans, J. and Verwijmeren, T. (2008) Mimicking attractive opposite-sex others: the role of romantic relationship status, *Personality and Social Psychology Bulletin*, 34, 939–950.

Karremans, J., Stroebe, W. and Claus, J. (2006) Beyond Vicary's fantasies: the impact of subliminal priming and brand choice, *Journal of Experimental Social Psychology*, 42, 792–798.

Kassin, S. and Gudjonsson, G. (2004) The psychology of confessions: a review of the literature and issues, *Psychological Science in the Public Interest*, 5, 33–67.

Kassin, S., Fein, S. and Markus, H. (2008) *Social Psychology*, 7th edn. Boston, MA: Houghton Mifflin.

Katz, D. and Stotland, E. (1959) A preliminary statement of a theory of attitude theory and change, in S. Koch (ed.) *Psychology: A Study of a Science, Vol. 3*. New York: McGraw-Hill.

Katz, M., Jacobson, T., Veledar, E. and Kripalani, S. (2007) Patient literacy and question-asking behavior during the medical encounter: a mixed-methods analysis, *Journal of General Internal Medicine*, 22, 782–786.

Katzenbach, J. and Smith, D. (1993) *The Wisdom of Teams: Creating the High-Performance Organization*. Boston, MA: Harvard Business School Press.

Kaya, N. and Erkip, F. (1999) Invasion of personal space under the condition of short-term crowding: a case study on an automatic teller machine, *Journal of Environmental Psychology*, 19, 183–189.

Kayes, A., Kayes, D. and Kolb, D. (2005) Experiential learning in teams, *Simulation and Gaming*, 36, 330–354.

Kazdin, A. (2008) *Behavior Modification in Applied Settings*, 6th edn. Long Grove, IL: Waveland Press.

Keats, D. (2000) *Interviewing: A Practical Guide for Students and Professionals*, Buckingham: Open University Press.

Kellermann, K. (1992) Communication: inherently strategic and primarily automatic, *Communication Monographs*, 59, 288–300.

Kellerman K., Reynolds, R. and Chen, J. (1991) Strategies of conversational retreat: when parting is not sweet sorrow, *Communication Monographs*, 58, 362–383.

Kelley, H. (1950) The warm–cold variable in first impressions of persons, *Journal of Personality*, 18, 431–439.

Kelley, H. and Thibaut, J. (1978) *Interpersonal Relations: A Theory of Interdependence*. New York: Wiley

Kelly, A. and McKillop, K. (1996) Consequences of revealing personal secrets, *Psychological Bulletin*, 120, 450–465.

Kelly, F. and Daniels, J. (1997) The effects of praise versus encouragement on children's perceptions of teachers, *Individual Psychology*, 53, 331–341.

Kelly, J. (1982) *Social Skills Training: A Practical Guide for Interventions*. New York: Springer.

Kelly, J. (2001) Mood and emotion in groups, in M. Hogg and S. Tindale (eds) *Blackwell Handbook of Social Psychology: Group Processes*, Malden, MA: Blackwell.

Keltner, D. (1997) Signs of appeasement: evidence for the distinct displays of embarrassment, amusement, and shame, in P. Ekman and E. Rosenberg (eds) *What the Face Reveals: Basic and Applied Studies of Spontaneous Expression Using the Facial Action Coding System (FACS)*. Oxford: Oxford University Press.

Kendon, A. (1967) Some functions of gaze direction in social interaction, *Acta Psychologica*, 26, 22–63.

Kendon, A. (1984) Some use of gestures, in D. Tannen and M. Saville-Troike (eds) *Perspectives on Silence*. Norwood, NJ: Ablex.

Kendon, A. and Ferber, A. (1973) A description of some human greetings, in R. Michael and J. Crook (eds) *Comparative Ecology and Behaviour of Primates*. London: Academic Press.

Kenman, L. (2007) Tone and style: developing a neglected segment of business communication, *Business Communication Quarterly*, 70, 3005–3008.

Kennedy, G. (1998) *Kennedy on Negotiation*. Aldershot: Gower.

Kennedy, J. and Zimmer, J. (1968) Reinforcing value of five stimulus conditions in a quasi-counseling situation, *Journal of Counseling Psychology*, 15, 357–362.

Kennedy, S., Hodgson M., Edgett, L., Lamb, N. and Rempel, R. (2006) Subjective assessment of listening environments in university classrooms: perceptions of students, *Journal of the Acoustical Society of America*, 119, 299–309.

Kennedy, T., Timmons, E. and Noblin, C. (1971) Nonverbal maintenance of conditioned verbal behavior following interpretations, reflections and social reinforcers, *Journal of Personality and Social Psychology*, 20, 112–117.

Kennelly, K.J. and Mount, S.A. (1985) Perceived contingency of reinforcements, helplessness, locus of control and academic performance, *Psychology in the Schools*, 22, 465–469.

Kenny, D. and West, T. (2008) Zero acquaintance: definitions, staitistical model findings and process, in N. Ambady and J. Skowronski (eds) *First Impressions*. New York: Guilford Press.

Kern, J. (1982) Predicting the impact of assertive, empathic-assertive and non-assertive behavior: the assertiveness of the assertee, *Behavior Therapy*, 13, 486–498.

Kesting, P. and Smolinski, R. (2007) When negotiations become routine: not reinventing the wheel while thinking outside the box, *Negotiation Journal*, 23, 419–438.

Kestler, J. (1982) *Questioning Techniques and Tactics*. Denver, CO: McGraw-Hill.

Kidwell, M. (2009) What happened? An epistemics of before and after in 'at-the-scene' police questioning, *Research on Language and Social Interaction*, 42, 20–41.

Kim, H. and Ko, D. (2007) Culture and self-expression, in C. Sedikides and S. Spencer (eds) *The Self*. New York: Psychology Press.

Kimmel, M. (2004) *The Gendered Society*, 2nd edn. New York: Oxford University Press.

King, A. (1992) Comparison of self-questioning, summarizing and notetaking-review as strategies for learning from lectures, *American Educational Research Journal*, 29, 303–323.

Kinlaw, D. (1991) *Developing Supervised Work Teams: Building Quality and the Competitive Edge*. Lexington, MA: Lexington Books.

Kinzler, K., Dupoux, E. and Spelke, E. (2007) The native language of social cognition, *Proceedings of the National Academy of Sciences*, 104, 12577–12580.

Kipling, R. (1902) The elephant child, in R. Kipling *Just-so Stories*. London: Macmillan.

Kipnis, D. and Schmidt, S. (1990) The language of persuasion, in I. Asherman and S. Asherman (eds) *The Negotiating Sourcebook*. Amherst, MA: Human Resource Development Press.

Kircanski, K., Craske, M. and Bjork, R. (2008) Thought suppression enhances memory bias for threat material, *Behaviour Research and Therapy*, 46, 462–476.

Kirkpatrick, D., Duck, S. and Foley, M. (2006) *Relating Difficulty*. London: Routledge.

Kirkpatrick, S. and Locke, E. (1991) Leadership: Do traits matter?, *Academy of Management Executive*, 5, 48–60.

Kirouac, G. and and Hess, U. (1999) Group membership and the decoding of nonverbal behaviour, in P. Philippot, R. Feldman and E. Coats (eds) *The Social Context of Nonverbal Behaviour*. Cambridge: Cambridge University Press.

Kirsch, I. (1999) Response expectancy: an introduction, in I. Kirsch (ed.) *How Expectations Shape Experience*. Washington, DC: American Psychological Association.

Klakovich, M. and dela Cruz, F. (2006) Validating the Interpersonal Communication Assessment Scale, *Journal of Professional Nursing*, 22, 60–67.

Klaver, J., Lee, Z. and Rose, G. (2008) Effects of personality, interrogation techniques and plausibility in an experimental false confession paradigm, *Legal and Criminological Psychology*, 13, 71–88.

Kleck, R. and Strenta, A. (1985) Physical deviance and the perception of social outcomes, in J. A. Graham and A. M. Kligman (eds) *The Psychology of Cosmetic Treatments*. New York: Praeger.

Klein, R. and Knäuper, B. (2008) Predicting attention and avoidance: when do avoiders attend?, *Psychology and Health*, 23, 1–19.

Kleinke, C. (1977) Compliance to requests made by gaze and touching experimenters in field settings, *Journal of Experimental Social Psychology*, 13, 218–223.

Kleinke, C. (1986) *Meeting and Understanding People*. New York: W.H. Freeman.

Klimek, P., Hanel, R. and Stefan Thurner, S. (2008) To how many politicians should government be left?, *Physics and Society*. http://arxiv.org/PS_cache/arxiv/pdf/0804/0804.2202v1.pdf (accessed 2 December 2009).

Klinger, E. and Bierbraver, G. (2001) Acculturation and conflict regulation of Turkish immigrants in Germany: a social influence perspective, in W. Wosinska, R. Cialdini, D. Barrett and J. Reykowski (eds) *The Practice of Social Influence in Multiple Cultures*. Mahwah, NJ: Lawrence Erlbaum Associates, Inc.

Klinger, E., Barta, S. and Maxeiner, M. (1981) Current concerns: assessing therapeutically relevant motivation, in P. Kendall and S. Hollon (eds) *Assessment Strategies for Cognitive Behavioral Interventions*. New York: Academic Press.

Knapp, M. (2006) An historical overview of nonverbal research, in V. Manusov and M. Patterson (eds) *The Sage Handbook of Nonverbal Communication*. Thousand Oaks, CA: Sage.

Knapp, M. and Hall, J. (2010) *Nonverbal Communication in Human Interaction*, 7th edn. Boston, MA: Wadsworth Cengage Learning.

Knapp, M. and Vangelisti, A. (2009) *Interpersonal Communication and Human Relationships*, 6th edn. Boston, MA: Allyn and Bacon.

Knapp, M., Hart, R., Friedrich, G. and Schulman, G. (1973) The rhetoric of goodbye: verbal and nonverbal correlates of human leave-taking, *Speech Monographs*, 40, 182–198.

Knobloch, L. (2010) Relational uncertainty and interpersonal communication, in S. Smith and S. Wilson (eds) *New Directions in Interpersonal Communication Research*. Thousand Oaks, CA: Sage.

Knowles, E. and Linn, J. (2004) Approach-avoidance model of persuasion: alpha and omega strategies for change, in E. Knowles and J. Linn (eds) *Resistance and Persuasion*. Mahwah, NJ: Lawrence Erlbaum Associates, Inc.

Knowles, E. and Riner, D. (2007) Omega approaches to persuasion: overcoming resistance, in A. Pratkanis (ed.) *The Science of Social Influence: Advances and Future Progress*. New York: Psychology Press.

Knowles, E., Butler, S. and Linn, J. (2001) Increasing compliance by reducing resistance, in J. Forgas and K. Williams (eds) *Social Influence: Direct and Indirect Processes*. Philadelphia, PA: Psychology Press.

Knowlton, S. and Berger, C. (1997) Message planning, communication failure and cognitive load: further explorations of the Hierarchy Principle, *Human Communication Research*, 24, 4–30.

Knox, S. and Hill, C. (2003) Therapist self-disclosure: research-based suggestions for practitioners, *Journal of Clinical Psychology*, 59, 529–539.

Knox, S., Hess, S., Petersen, D. and Hill, C. (1997) A qualitative analysis of client perceptions of the effects of helpful therapist self-disclosure in long-term therapy, *Journal of Counseling Psychology*, 44, 274–283.

Ko, S., Judd, C. and Blair, I. (2006) What the voice reveals: within- and between-category stereotyping on the basis of voice, *Personality and Social Psychology Bulletin*, 32, 806–819.

Koehler, N., Rhodes, G., and Simmons, L. (2002) Are human female preferences for symmetrical male faces enhanced when conception is likely? *Animal Behaviour*, 64, 233–238.

Koermer, C. and Kilbane, M. (2008) Physician sociality communication and its effect on patient satisfaction, *Communication Quarterly*, 56, 69–86.

Koermer, C. and McCroskey, L. (2006) Sociality communication: its influence on customer loyalty with the service provider and service organization, *Communication Quarterly*, 54, 53–65.

Kolb, D. and Williams, J. (2007) Breakthrough bargaining, in R. Lewicki, B. Barry and D. Saunders (eds) *Negotiation: Readings, Exercise and Cases*, 5th edn. New York: McGraw-Hill.

Kolotkin, R., Wielkiewicz, R., Judd, B. and Weisler, S. (1983) Behavioral components of assertion: comparison of univariate and multivariate assessment strategies, *Behavioral Assessment*, 6, 61–78.

Komaki, J. (1982) Managerial effectiveness: potential contributions of the behavioral approach, *Journal of Organizational Behavior Management*, 3, 71–83.

Korda, M. (1975) *Power! How to Get It, How to Use It*. New York: Random House.

Kormanik, M. and Rocco, T. (2009) Internal versus external control of reinforcement: a review of the locus of control construct, *Human Resource Development Review*, 8, 463–483.

Korobkin, R. (2007) On bargaining power, in A. Schneider and C. Honeyman (eds) *The Negotiator's Fieldbook: The Desk Reference for the Experienced Negotiator*. Chicago, IL: American Bar Association.

Kortt, M. and Leigh, A. (2010) Does size matter in Australia? *Economic Record*. http://econrsss.anu.edu.au/~aleigh/pdf/BodySize.pdf (accessed 2 December 2009).

Kowalski, R. (1996) Complaints and complaining: functions, antecedents, and consequences, *Psychological Bulletin*, 119, 179–196.

Kowalski, R. (1999) Speaking the unspeakable: self-disclosure and mental health, in R. Kowalski and M. Leary (eds) *The Social Psychology of Emotional and Behavioral Problems*. Washington, DC: American Psychological Association.

Kozak, M., Sternglanz, R., Viswanathan, U. and Wegner, D. (2007) The role of thought suppression in building mental blocks, *Consciousness and Cognition*, 17, 1123–1130.

Krähenbühl, S. and Blades, M. (2006) The effect of interviewing techniques on young children's responses to questions, *Child: Care, Health and Development*, 32, 321–331.

Kramer, M. (2001) *Business Communication in Context*. Upper Saddle River, NJ: Prentice-Hall.

Kramer, R. (1998) Revisiting the Bay of Pigs and Vietnam decisions 25 years later: how well does the groupthink hypothesis stand the test of time?, *Organizational Behavior and Human Decision Processes*, 73, 236–271.

Krasner, L. (1958) Studies of the conditioning of verbal behaviour, *Psychological Bulletin*, 55, 148–170.

Krause, R., Steimer, E., Sanger-Alt, C. and Wagner, G. (1989) Facial expression of schizophrenic patients and their interaction partners, *Psychiatry*, 52, 1–12.

Kray, L. and Babcock, L. (2006) Gender in negotiations: a motivated social cognitive analysis, in L. Thompson (ed.) *Negotiation Theory and Research*. New York: Taylor & Francis.

Kreps, G. (1988) The pervasive role of information in health and health care: implications for health care policy, in J. Anderson (ed.) *Communication Yearbook 11*, Beverly Hills, CA: Sage.

Kreps, G. and Thornton, B. (1992) *Health Communication: Theory and Practice*. Prospect Heights, IL: Waveland Press.

Kruglanski, A. (2004) *The Psychology of Closed Mindedness: Essays in Social Psychology*. New York: Psychology Press.

Kunda, Z. and Fong, G. (1993) Directional questions direct self-conceptions, *Journal of Experimental Social Psychology*, 29, 63–86.

Kupperbusch, C., Matsumoto, D., Kooken, K., Loewinger, S., Uchida, H., Wilson-Cohn, C. and Yrizarry, N. (1999) Cultural influences on nonverbal expressions of emotion, in P. Philippot, R. Feldman and E. Coats (eds) *The Social Context of Nonverbal Behavior*. Cambridge: Cambridge University Press.

Kurtz, S., Silverman, J. and Draper, J. (1998) *Teaching and Learning Communication Skills in Medicine*. Abingdon: Radcliffe Medical Press.

LaFrance, M. and Harris, J. (2004) Gender and verbal and nonverbal communication, in M. Paludi (ed.) *Praeger Guide to the Psychology of Gender*. Westport, CT: Greenwood Press.

LaFrance, M. and Hecht, M. (1999) Option or obligation to smile: the effects of power and gender on facial expression, in P. Philippot, R. Feldman and E. Coats (eds) *The Social Context of Nonverbal Behavior*. Cambridge: Cambridge University Press.

Lakin, J. (2006) Automatic cognitive processes and nonverbal communication, in V. Manusov and M. Patterson (eds) *The SAGE Handbook of Nonverbal Communication*. Thousand Oaks, CA: Sage.

Lalich, J. (2004) *Bounded Choice: True Believers and Charismatic Cults*. Berkeley, CA: University of California Press.

Lall, A. (1966) *Modern International Negotiation: Principles and Practice*. New York: Columbia University Press.

Lamb, M., Sternberg, K., Orbach, Y., Hershkowitz, I. and Esplin, P. (1999) Forensic interviews of children, in A. Memon and R. Bull (eds) *Handbook of the Psychology of Interviewing*. Chichester: Wiley.

Lamb, R. (1988) Greetings and partings, in P. Marsh (ed.) *Eye to Eye: Your Relationships and How They Work*. London: Sidgwick and Jackson.

Land, M. (1984) Combined effect of two teacher clarity variables on student achievement, *Journal of Experimental Education*, 50, 14–17.

Lang, G. and van der Molen, H. (1990) *Personal Conversations: Roles and Skills for Counsellors*. London: Routledge.

Lange, A. and Jakubowski, P. (1976) *Responsible Assertive Behavior*. Champaign, IL: Research Press.

Langer, E., Blank, A. and Chanowitz, B. (1978) The mindlessness of ostensibly thoughtful action, *Journal of Personality and Social Psychology*, 36, 635–642.

Langlois, J., Kalakanis, L., Rubenstein, A., Larson, A., Hallam, M. and Smoot, M. (2000) Maxims and myths of beauty: a meta-analytic and theoretical review, *Psychological Bulletin*, 126, 390–423.

Larson, C. (2010a) *Persuasion: Reception and Responsibility*, 12th edn. Boston, MA: Wadsworth.

Larson, J. (2010b) *In Search of Synergy in Small Group Performance*. New York: Psychology Press.

Larson, J., Foster-Fishman, P. and Franz, T. (1998) Leadership style and the discussion of shared and unshared information in decision-making groups, *Personality and Social Psychology Bulletin*, 25, 482–495.

Lausberg, H., Zaidel, H., Cruz, R. and Ptito, A. (2007) Speech-independent production of communication gestures: evidence from patients with complete callosal disconnection, *Neuropsychologia*, 45, 3092–3104.

Laver, J. and Hutcheson, S. (eds) (1972) *Communication in Face-to-face Interaction*, Harmondsworth: Penguin.

Lawler, E. (1983) Reward systems in organisations, in J. Lorsch (ed.) *Handbook of Organizational Behavior*. Englewood Cliffs, NJ: Prentice-Hall.

Lawler, J. (1991) *Behind the Screens*. Melbourne: Churchill Livingstone.

Lawrence, J. (2001) Does academic praise communicate stereotypic expectancies to black students?, *Dissertation Abstracts International: Section B: the Sciences and Engineering*, 61(10-B), 5622.

Lawyer, J. and Katz, N. (1985) *Communication and Conflict Management Skills*. Dubuque, IO: Kendall/Hunt.

Lax, D. and Sebenius, J. (2006) *3-D Negotiation: Powerful Tools to Change the Game in Your Most Important Deals*. Boston, MA: Harvard Business School Press.

Lazarus, A. (1971) *Behavior Therapy and Beyond*. New York: McGraw-Hill.

Lazowski, L. and Andersen, S. (1991) Self-disclosure and social perception: the impact of private, negative and extreme communications, in M. Booth-Butterfield (ed.) *Communication, Cognition and Anxiety*. Newbury Park, CA: Sage.

Leakey, R. (1994) *The Origin of Mankind*. London: Weidenfeld and Nicolson.

Leaper, C. (2000) Gender, affiliation, assertion, and the interactive content of parent–child play, *Developmental Psychology*, 36, 381–393.

Leaper, C. and Ayres, M. (2007) A meta-analytic review of gender variations in adults' language use: talkativeness, affiliative speech, and assertive speech, *Personality and Social Psychology Review*, 11, 328–363.

Leaper, C. and Smith, T. (2004) A meta-analytic review of gender variations in children's language use: talkativeness, affiliative speech, and assertive speech, *Developmental Psychology*, 40, 993–1027.

Leaper, C. and Valin, D. (1996) Predictors of Mexican-American mothers' and fathers' attitudes towards gender equality, *Hispanic Journal of Behavioral Sciences*, 18, 343–355.

Leary, M. (1996) *Self-presentation: Impression Management and Interpersonal Behavior*. Boulder, CO: Westview Press.

Leary, M. (2001) Towards a conceptualisation of interpersonal rejection, in M. Leary (ed.) *Interpersonal Rejection*, Oxford: Oxford University Press.

Leathers, D. (1979) The impact of multichannel message inconsistency on verbal and nonverbal decoding behavior, *Communication Monographs*, 46, 88–100.

Lecheler, S., de Vreese, C. and Slothuus, R. (2009) Issue importance as a moderator of framing effects, *Communication Research*, 36, 400–425.

Leodoro, G. and Lynn, M. (2007) The effect of server posture on the tips of whites and blacks, *Journal of Applied Social Psychology*, 37, 201–209.

LePoire, B., Hallett, J., and Erlandson, K. (2000) An initial test of inconsistent nurturing as control theory: how partners of drug abusers assist their partners' sobriety, *Human Communication Research*, 26, 432–457.

LePoole, S. (1991) *Never Take No for an Answer: A Guide to Successful Negotiating*. London: Kogan Page.

Lepper, M., Greene, D. and Nisbett, R. (1973) Undermining children's intrinsic interest with extrinsic rewards: a test of the 'overjustification' hypothesis, *Journal of Personality and Social Psychology*, 28, 129–137.

Lepper, M., Keavney, M. and Drake, M. (1996) Intrinsic motivation and extrinsic reward: a commentary on Cameron and Pierce's meta-analysis, *Review of Educational Research*, 66, 5–33.

Leslie, J. and O'Reilly, M. (1999) *Behavior Analysis: Foundations and Applications to Psychology*. Amsterdam: Harwood.

Lester, M. (2008) *McGraw-Hill's Essential ESL Grammar: A Handbook for Intermediate and Advanced ESL Students*. New York: McGraw-Hill.

Leventhal, H. (1970) Findings and theory in the study of fear communications, in L. Berkowitz (ed.) *Advances in Experimental Social Psychology Volume 5*. New York: Academic Press.

Levi, D. (2007) *Group Dynamics for Teams*, 2nd edn. Thousand Oaks, CA: Sage.

Levine, J. and Hogg, A (eds) (2008) *Encyclopedia of Group Processes and Intergroup Relations*. Thousand Oaks, CA: Sage.

Levine, J. and Moreland, R. (eds) (2006) *Small Groups*. New York: Psychology Press.

Levine, R. (2006) *The Power of Persuasion: How We're Bought and Sold*. Oxford: Oneworld Publications.

Levine, T. and McCornack, S. (2001) Behavioral adaptation, confidence, and heuristic-based explanations of the probing effect, *Human Communication Research*, 27, 471–502.

Levinson, S. (2006) Cognition at the heart of human interaction, *Discourse Studies*, 8, 85–93.

Levy, D. (1999) The last taboo, *Time*, 28 June, p. 77.

Lewicki, R. (1997) Teaching negotiation and dispute resolution in Colleges of Business: the state of the practice, *Negotiation Journal*, 13, 253–269.

Lewicki, R., Saunders, D., Minton J. and Barry, B. (2007) Preface, in R. Lewicki, B. Barry and D. Saunders (eds) *Negotiation: Readings, Exercise and Cases*, 5th edn. New York: McGraw-Hill.

Lewin, K., Lippitt, R. and White, R. K. (1939) Patterns of aggressive behaviour in experimentally created social climates, *Journal of Social Psychology*, 10, 271–299.

Lewis, P. and Gallois, C. (1984) Disagreements, refusals, or negative feelings: perception of negatively assertive messages from friends and strangers, *Behavior Therapy*, 15, 353–368.

Ley, P. (1988) *Communicating with Patients*. London: Chapman and Hall.

Leydon, G., Boulton, M., Moynihan, C., Jones, A., Mossman, J., Boudioni, M. and McPherson, K. (2000) Cancer patients' information needs and information seeking behaviour: in depth interview study, *British Medical Journal*, 320, 909–913.

Li, S. and Li, Y. (2007) How far is far enough? A measure of information privacy in terms of interpersonal distance, *Environment and Behavior*, 39, 317–331.

Liaw, S. (2004) Considerations for developing constructivist web-based learning, *International Journal of Instructional Media*, 31, 309–321.

Libby, L. and Eibach, R. (2007) How the self affects and reflects the content and subjective experience of autobiographical memory, in C. Sedikides and S. Spencer (eds) *The Self*. New York: Psychology Press.

Lickel, B., Rutchick, A., Hamilton, D. and Sherman, S. (2006) Intuitive theories of group types and relational principles, *Journal of Experimental Social Psychology*, 42, 28–39.

Lieberman, D. (2000) *Learning: Behaviour and Cognition*, 3rd edn. Belmont, CA: Wadsworth.

Lieberman, P. (1998) *Eve Spoke: Human Language and Human Evolution*. London: Picador.

Lietaer, G. (2004) Carl Rogers' verbal responses in 'On Anger and Hurt': content analysis and clinical reflections, in R. Moodley, C. Lago and A. Talahite (eds) *Carl Rogers Counsels a Black Client: Race and Culture in Person-Centred Counselling*. Ross-on-Wye: PCCS Books.

Lightsey, O. R. and Barnes, P. W. (2007) Discrimination, attributional tendencies, generalized self-efficacy, and assertiveness as predictors of psychological distress among African Americans, *Journal of Black Psychology*, 33, 27–50.

Lin, M., Harwood, J. and Hummert, M. (2008) Young adults' intergenerational communication schemas in Taiwan and the USA, *Journal of Language and Social Psychology*, 27, 28–50.

Lin, W. and Pfau, M. (2007) Can inoculation work against the spiral of silence? A study of public opinion on the future of Taiwan, *International Journal of Public Opinion Research*, 19, 155–172.

Lindon, J. and Lindon, L. (2007) *Mastering Counselling Skills*, 2nd edn. Basingstoke: Palgrave Macmillan.

Lindsey, L. (2005) Anticipated guilt as behavioural motivation: an examination of appeals to help unknown others through bone marrow donation, *Human Communication Research*, 31, 453–481.

Linehan, M. and Egan, K. (1979) Assertion training for women, in A. Bellack and M. Hersen (eds) *Research and Practice in Social Skills Training*. New York: Plenum Press.

Lipkin, M. (1996) Physician–patient interaction in reproductive counseling, *Obstetrics and Gynecology*, 88, S31–S40.

Lishner, D., Cooter, A. and Zald, D. (2008) Rapid emotional contagion and expressive congruence under strong test conditions, *Journal of Nonverbal Behavior*, 32, 225–239.

Little, A. and Perett, D. (2002) Putting beauty back in the eye of the beholder, *The Psychologist*, 15, 28–32.

Livingstone, J., Testa, M. and VanZile-Tamsen, C. (2007) The reciprocal relationship between sexual victimization and sexual assertiveness, *Violence Against Women*, 13, 298–313.

Locke, E. A. and Latham, G. P. (1990) *A Theory of Goal Setting and Task Performance*, Englewood Cliffs, NJ: Prentice-Hall.

Loewenstein, J. and Thompson, L. (2006) Learning to negotiate: novice and experienced negotiators, in L. Thompson (ed.) *Negotiation Theory and Research*. New York: Taylor & Francis.

Loftus, E. (1975) Leading questions and the eyewitness report, *Cognitive Psychology*, 7, 560–572.

Loftus, E. (1982) Interrogating eyewitnesses – good questions and bad, in R. Hogarth (ed.) *Question Framing and Response Consistency*. San Francisco, CA: Jossey-Bass.

Loftus, E. (2001) Imagining the past, *The Psychologist*, 14, 584–587.

Loftus, E. (2006) Memory distortion: problems solved and unsolved, in M. Garry and H. Hayne (eds) *Do Justice and Let the Sky Fall*. Mahwah, NJ: Lawrence Erlbaum Associates, Inc.

Loftus, E. and Palmer, J. (1974) Reconstruction of automobile destruction: an example of the interaction between language and memory, *Journal of Verbal Learning and Verbal Behavior*, 13, 585–589.

Loftus, E. and Zanni, G. (1975) Eyewitness testimony: the influence of the wording of a question, *Bulletin of the Psychonomic Society*, 5, 86–88.

Lõhmus, M., Sundström, L. and Björklund, M. (2009) Dress for success: human facial expressions are important signals of emotions, *Annales Zoologici Fennici*, 46, 75–80.

Long, K., Fortney, S. and Johnson, D. (2000) An observer measure of compulsive communication, *Communication Research Reports*, 17, 349–356.

Long, L. and Long, T. (1976) Influence of religious status and religious attire on interviewees, *Psychological Reports*, 39, 25–26.

Lord, R. and Brown, D. (2004) *Leadership Processes and Follower Self-identity*. Mahwah, NJ: Lawrence Erlbaum Associates, Inc.

Loukusa, S., Ryder, N. and Leinonen, E. (2008) Answering questions and explaining answers: a study of Finnish-speaking children, *Journal of Psycholinguist Research*, 37, 219–241.

Luft, J. (1970) *Group Processes: An Introduction to Group Dynamics*. Palo Alto, CA: National Press Books.

Lundgren, D. and Mitchell, M. (2000) Able but not motivated: the relative effects of happy and sad mood on persuasive message processing, *Communication Monographs*, 67, 215–226.

Lundsteen, S. (1971) *Listening: Its Impact on Reading and Other Language Acts*. New York: National Council of Teachers of English.

Lussier, R. and Achua, C. (2010) *Leadership: Theory, Application, and Skill Development*, 4th edn. Mason, OH: Cengage Learning.

Lytle, A., Brett, J. and Shapiro, D. (1999) The strategic use of interests, rights, and power to resolve disputes, *Negotiation Journal*, 15, 31–51.

Maag, J. (2003) *Behaviour Management: From Theoretical Implications to Practical Applications*, 2nd edn. Belmont, CA: Wadsworth.

McAllister, D. (1995) Affect- and cognition-based trust as foundations for interpersonal cooperation in organizations, *Academy of Management Journal*, 38, 24–59.

McBride, M. and Wahl, S. (2005) 'To say or not to say': management of privacy boundaries in the classroom, *Texas Speech Communication Journal*, 30, 8–22.

McCall, C., Blascovich, J., Young, A. and Persky, S. (2009) Proxemic behaviors as predictors of aggression towards black (but not white) males in an immersive virtual environment, *Social Influence*, 34, 138–154.

McCallum, S. and O'Connell, D. (2009) Social capital and leadership development: building stronger leadership through enhanced relational skills, *Leadership and Organization Development Journal*, 30, 152–166.

McCann, K. and McKenna, H. (1993) An examination of touch between nurses and elderly patients in a continuing care setting in Northern Ireland, *Journal of Advanced Nursing*, 18, 838–846.

McCartan, P. (2001) The identification and analysis of assertive behaviours in nurses. Unpublished PhD thesis, University of Ulster, Jordanstown.

McCartan, P. and Hargie, O. (2004a) Assertiveness and caring: are they compatible?, *Journal of Clinical Nursing*, 13, 707–713.

McCartan P. and Hargie O. (2004b) Effects of nurses' sex-role orientation on positive and negative assertion, *Nursing and Health Sciences*, 6, 45–49.

McCarthy, P. and Hatcher, C. (2002) *Presentation Skills: The Essential Guide for Students*. London: Sage.

McClave, E. (2000) Linguistic functions of head movements in the context of speech, *Journal of Pragmatics*, 32, 855–878.

McClelland, M., Acock, A. and Morrison, F. (2006) The impact of kindergarten learning-related skills on academic trajectories at the end of elementary school, *Early Childhood Research Quarterly*, 21, 471–490.

McConnell, A. and Strain, L. (2007) Content and structure of the self-concept, in C. Sedikides and S. Spencer (eds) *The Self*. New York: Psychology Press.

McCowan, R., Driscoll, M. and Roop, P. (1995) *Educational Psychology: A Learning-Centred Approach to Classroom Practice*. Needham Heights, MA: Allyn & Bacon.

McCroskey, J., Richmond, V. and McCroskey, L. (2006) Nonverbal communication in instructional contexts, in V. Manusov and M. Patterson (eds) *The Sage Handbook of Nonverbal Communication*. Thousand Oaks, CA: Sage.

McDaniel, R. (1994) *Scared Speechless: Public Speaking Step By Step*. Thousand Oaks: CA: Sage.

McDaniel, S., Beckman, H., Morse, D., Silberman, J., Seaburn, D. and Epstein R. (2007) Physician self-disclosure in primary care visits: enough about you, what about me?, *Archives of Internal Medicine*, 167, 1321–1326.

MacDonald, G. (2007) Self-esteem: a human elaboration of prehuman belongingness motivation, in C. Sedikides and S. Spencer (eds) *The Self*. New York: Psychology Press.

McEwan, H. (1992) Teaching and the interpretation of texts, *Educational Theory*, 42, 59–68.

McFadyen, R. (1996) Gender, status and 'powerless' speech: interactions of students and lecturers, *British Journal of Social Psychology*, 35, 353–367.

McFall, M., Winnett, R., Bordewick, M. and Bornstein, P. (1982) Nonverbal components in the communication of assertiveness, *Behavior Modification*, 6, 121–140.

McGaughey, I. (2004) Informed consent and knee arthroscopies: an evaluation of patient understanding and satisfaction, *The Knee*, 11, 237–242.

McGinn, K. (2006) Relationships and negotiations in context, in L. Thompson (ed.) *Negotiation Theory and Research*. New York: Taylor & Francis.

McGinniss, J. (1988) *The Selling of the President: The Classic Account of the Packaging of a Candidate*. New York: Penguin.

McGrath, J., Arrow, H. and Berdahl, J. (2000) The study of groups: past, present, and future, *Personality and Social Psychology*, 4, 95–105.

McGuire, W. J. (1981) Theoretical foundations of campaigns, in R. Rice and W. Paisley (eds) *Public Communication Campaigns*. Newbury Park, CA: Sage.

Machiavelli, N. (1514/1961) *The Prince*, trans. G. Bull. London: Penguin.

McInnes, A., Humphries, T., Hogg-Johnson, S. and Tannock, R. (2003) Listening comprehension and working memory are impaired in attention-deficit hyperactivity disorder irrespective of language impairment, *Journal of Abnormal Child Psychology*, 31, 427–443.

McKay, M., Davis, M. and Fanning, P. (2009) *Messages: The Communication Skills Book*. Oakland, CA: New Harbinger.

McKay, R., Langdon, R. and Coltheart, M. (2006) Need for closure, jumping to conclusions, and decisiveness in delusion-prone individuals, *Journal of Nervous and Mental Disease*, 194, 422–426.

McKenna, K. and Bargh, J. (2000) Plan 9 from cyberspace: the implications of the internet for personality and social psychology, *Personality and Social Psychology Review*, 4, 57–75.

McLaughlin, M., Cody, M. and Read, S. (eds) (1992) *Explaining One's Self to Others*. Mahwah, NJ: Lawrence Erlbaum Associates, Inc.

McLean, A. (2009) *Motivating Every Learner*. London: Sage.

MacLure, M. and Jones, L. (2009) *Becoming a Problem: How and Why Children Acquire a Reputation as 'Naughty' in the Earliest Years at School*. Economic and Social Research Council Report. http://www.esri.mmu.ac.uk/resprojects/reports/becomingaproblem.pdf (accessed 2 December 2009).

McNeil, D. (1992) *Hand and Mind: What Gestures Reveal About Thought*. Chicago, IL: University of Chicago Press.

McRae, B. (1998) *Negotiating and Influencing Skills*. Thousand Oaks, CA: Sage.

Mader, T. F. and Mader, D. C. (1990) *Understanding One Another: Communicating Interpersonally*, 2nd edn. Dubuque, IA: WCB Brown & Benchmark.

Maes, J., Weldy, T. and Icenogle, M. (1997) A managerial perspective: oral communication competency is most important for business students in the workplace, *Journal of Business Communication*, 34, 67–80.

Maes, S. and Gebhardt, W. (2000) Self-regulation and health behaviour: the health behaviour goal model, in M. Boekaerts, P. Pintrich and M. Zeidner (eds) *Handbook of Self-regulation*. San Diego, CA: Academic Press.

Magee, J., Galinsky, A. and Gruenfeld, D. (2007) Power, propensity to negotiate, and moving first in competitive interactions, *Personality and Social Psychology Bulletin*, 33, 200–212.

Maguire, P. (1985) Deficiencies in key interpersonal skills, in C. Kagan (ed.) *Interpersonal Skills in Nursing*. London: Croom Helm.

Maguire, P., Fairburn, S. and Fletcher, C. (1986) Consultation skills of young doctors, *British Medical Journal*, 292, 1573–1578.

Major, B. and Heslin, R. (1982) Perceptions of same-sex and cross-sex touching: it's better to give than to receive, *Journal of Personality and Social Psychology*, 6, 148–162.

Makoul, G., Zick, A. and Green, M. (2007) An evidence-based perspective on greetings in medical encounters, *Archives of Internal Medicine*, 167, 1172–1176.

Malhotra, D. and Bazerman, M. (2007) *Negotiation Genius: How to Overcome Obstacles and Achieve Brilliant Results at the Bargaining Table and Beyond*. New York: Bantam Dell.

Malloy, T., Albright, L. and Scarpati S. (2007) Awareness of peers' judgments of oneself: accuracy and process of metaperception, *International Journal of Behavioral Development*, 31, 603–610.

Malone, B. and De Paulo, B. (2001) Measuring sensitivity to deception, in J. Hall and

F. Bernieri (eds) *Interpersonal Sensitivity: Theory and Measurement*. Mahwah, NJ: Lawrence Erlbaum Associates, Inc.

Maltby, J., Day, L. and Macaskill, A. (2007) *Personality, Individual Differences and Intelligence*. Philadelphia, PA: Trans-Atlantic Publications.

Mandel, S. (1987) *Effective Presentation Skills: A Practical Guide for Better Speaking*. Los Altos, CA: Crisp Publications.

Mann, S. and Robinson, A. (2009) Boredom in the lecture theatre: an investigation into the contributors, moderators and outcomes of boredom amongst university students, *British Educational Research Journal*, 35, 243–258.

Mannetti L., Pierro, A., Kruglanski, A., Taris, T. and Bezinovic, P. (2002) A cross-cultural study of the Need for Cognitive Closure Scale: comparing its structure in Croatia, Italy, USA and the Netherlands, *British Journal of Social Psychology*, 41, 139–156.

Manthei, R. (1997) *Counselling: The Skills of Finding Solutions to Problems*. London: Routledge.

Manusov, V. and Patterson, M. (eds) (2006) *The Sage Handbook of Nonverbal Communication*. Thousand Oaks, CA: Sage.

Margo, A. (1997) Why Barbie is perceived as beautiful, *Perceptual and Motor Skills*, 85, 363–374.

Margutti P. (2006) 'Are you human beings?' Order and knowledge construction through questioning in primary classroom interaction, *Linguistics and Education*, 17, 313–346.

Marisi, D.Q. and Helmy, K. (1984) Intratask integration as a function of age and verbal praise, *Perceptual and Motor Skills*, 58, 936–939.

Markham, R. and Wang, L. (1996) Recognition of emotion by Chinese and Australian children, *Journal of Cross-Cultural Psychology*, 27, 616–643.

Marlowe, F. and Westman, A. (2001) Preferred waist-to-hip ratio and ecology, *Personality and Individual Differences*, 30, 481–489.

Marta, S., Leritz, L. and Mumford, M. (2005) Leadership skills and the group performance: situational demands, behavioral requirements, and planning, *Leadership Quarterly*, 16, 97–120.

Martin, C. and Ruble, D. (2004) Children's search for gender cues: cognitive perspectives on gender development, *Current Direction in Psychological Science*, 13, 67–70.

Martin, D. (1997) Slaughtering a sacred cow: the eyebrow flash is not a universal social greeting, *Dissertation Abstracts International: The Sciences and Engineering*, 58(5-B), 2751.

Martin, D. and Gayle, B. (2004) Humour works: communication style and humour functions in manager/subordinate relationships, *Southern Communication Journal*, 69, 206–222.

Martin, G. and Pear, J. (2007) *Behavior Modification: What It Is and How To Do It*, 8th edn. Upper Sadle River, NJ: Pearson.

Martin, G., Carlson, N. and Buskist, W. (2007) *Psychology*, 3rd edn. Harlow: Prentice-Hall.

Martin, J. (1970) *Explaining, Understanding and Teaching*. New York: McGraw-Hill.

Martinovski, B. (2010) Emotion in negotiation, in D. Kilgour and C. Eden (eds) *Handbook of Group Decision and Negotiation*. New York: Springer Verlag.

Martinovski, B., Traum, D. and Marcella, S. (2007) Rejection of empathy in negotiation, *Group Decision and Negotiation*, 16, 61–76.

Maslow, A. (1954) *Motivation and Personality*. New York: Harper and Row.

Mastenbroek, W. (1989) *Negotiate*. Oxford: Blackwell.

Masters, W. and Johnson, V. (1970) *Human Sexual Inadequacy*. Boston, MA: Little, Brown.

Matarazzo, J. D. and Wiens, A. N. (1972) *The Interview: Research on Its Anatomy and Structure*. Chicago, IL: Aldine-Atherton.

Mathews, A., Derlega, V. and Morrow, J. (2006) What is highly personal information and how is it related to self-disclosure decision-making?, The perspective of college students, *Communication Research Reports*, 23, 85–92.

Matlin, M. (2009) *Cognitive Psychology*, 7th edn. Hoboken, NJ: Wiley.

Matlin, M. and Stang, D. (1978) *The Pollyanna Principle: Selectivity in Language, Memory, and Thought*. Cambridge, MA: Schenkman.

Matsumoto, D. (2000) Culture and nonverbal behaviour, in V. Manusov and M. Patterson (eds) *The Sage Handbook of Nonverbal Communication*. Thousand Oaks, CA: Sage.

Matsumoto, D. and Willingham, B. (2009) Spontaneous facial expressions of emotion of congenitally and noncongenitally blind individuals, *Journal of Personality and Social Psychology*, 96, 1–10.

Matsushima, R., Shomi, K. and Kuhlman, D. (2000) Shyness in self-disclosure mediated by social skill, *Psychological Reports*, 86, 333–338.

Mattock, J. and Ehrenborg, J. (1996) *How to be a Better Negotiator*. London: Kogan Page.

Mayer, R. and Jackson, J. (2005) The case for coherence in scientific explanations: quantitative details can hurt qualitative learning, *Journal of Experimental Psychology*, 11, 13–18.

Mayer, R., Fennell, S., Farmer, L. and Campbell, J. (2004) A personalization effect in multimedia learning: students learn better when words are in conversational style rather than formal style, *Journal of Educational Psychology*, 96, 389–395.

Mehl, M., Vazire, S., Ramírez-Esparza, N., Slatcher, R. and Pennebaker, J. (2007) Are women really more talkative than men?, *Science*, 317(5834), 82.

Mehrabian, A. (1972) *Nonverbal Communication*. Chicago, IL: Aldine-Atherton.

Mehrabian, A. (2007) *Nonverbal Communication*. Piscataway, NJ: Aldine Transaction.

Mehrabian, A. and Blum, J. (1997) Physical appearance, attraction, and the mediating role of emotions, *Current Psychology: Developmental, Learning, Personality, Social*, 16, 20–42.

Melamed, J. and Bozionelos, N. (1992) Managerial promotion and height, *Psychological Reports*, 71, 587–593.

Memon, A. and Bull, R. (eds) (1999) *Handbook of the Psychology of Interviewing*. Chichester: Wiley.

Menzel, K. and Carrell, L. (1994) The relationship between preparation and performance in public speaking, *Communication Education*, 43, 17–26.

Merbaum, M. (1963) The conditioning of affective self-references by three classes of generalized reinforcers, *Journal of Personality*, 31, 179–191.

Meriac, J. and Villanova, P. (2006) Agreeableness and extraversion as moderators of the political influence compatibility–work–outcomes relationship, in

E. Vigoda-Gadot and A. Drory (eds) *Handbook of Organizational Politics*. Cheltenham: Edward Elgar Publishing.

Merrett, F. and Thorpe, S. (1996) How important is the praise element in the pause, prompt and praise tutoring procedures for older low-progress readers?, *Educational Psychology*, 16, 193–206.

Messer, D. (1995) *The Development of Communication: From Social Interaction to Language*. Chichester: Wiley.

Metcalf, L., Bird, A., Peterson, M., Shankarmahesh, M. and Lituchy, T. (2007) Cultural influences in negotiations: a four country comparative analysis, *International Journal of Cross Cultural Management*, 7, 147–168.

Metts, S. and Cupach, W. (2008) Face theory, in L. Baxter and D. Braithwaite (eds) *Engaging Theories in Interpersonal Communication: Multiple Perspectives*. Thousand Oaks, CA: Sage.

Metts, S. and Mikucki, S. (2008) The emotional landscape of romantic relationship initiation, in S. Sprecher, A. Wenzel and J. Harvey (eds) *Handbook of Relationship Initiation*. New York: Psychology Press.

Metts, S. and Planalp, S. (2002) Emotional communication, in M. Knapp and J. Daly (eds) *Handbook of Interpersonal Communication*, 3rd edn. Thousand Oaks, CA: Sage.

Meyer, J. (1997) Cognitive influences on the ability to address interaction goals, in J. O. Greene (ed.) *Message Production: Advances in Communication Theory*. Mahwah, NJ: Lawrence Erlbaum Associates, Inc.

Meyer, J. (2000) Humor as a double-edged sword: four functions of humor in communication, *Communication Theory*, 10, 310–331.

Meyer, W. V., Miggag, W. and Engler, U. (1986) Some effects of praise and blame on perceived ability and affect, *Social Cognition*, 4, 293–308.

Meyers-Levy, J. and Malaviya, P. (1999) Consumers' processing of persuasive advertisements: an integrative framework of persuasion theories, *Journal of Marketing*, 63, 45–60.

Michalak, J., Troje, N., Fischer, J., Vollmar, P., Heidenreich, T. and Schulte, D. (2009) Embodiment of sadness and depression – gait patterns associated with dysphoric mood, *Psychosomatic Medicine*, 71, 580–587.

Miczo, N., Segrin, C. and Allspach, L. (2001) Relationship between nonverbal sensitivity, encoding, and relational satisfaction, *Communication Reports*, 14, 39–48.

Migge, B. (2005) Greeting and social change, in S. Muhleisen and B. Migge (eds) *Politeness and Face in Caribbean Creoles*. Amsterdam: John Benjamins.

Milakovich, J. (1999) Differences between therapists who touch and those who do not, in E. Smith, P. Clance and S. Imes (eds) *Touch in Psychotherapy: Theory, Research, and Practice*. New York: Guilford Press.

Milburn, T. (1998) Psychology, negotiation and peace, *Applied Psychology and Preventive Psychology*, 7, 109–119.

Millar, R. and Gallagher, M. (2000) The interview approach, in O. Hargie and D. Tourish (eds) *Handbook of Communication Audits for Organisations*. London: Routledge.

Millar, R. and Tracey, A. (2006) The employment interview, in O. Hargie (ed.) *The Handbook of Communication Skills*, 3rd edn. London: Routledge.

Millar, R., Crute, V. and Hargie, O. (1992) *Professional Interviewing*. London: Routledge.

Miller, A. and Hom, H. (1997) Conceptions of ability and the interpretation of praise, blame and material rewards, *Journal of Experimental Education*, 65, 163–177.

Miller, G. (1956) The magic number seven, plus or minus two, *Psychological Review*, 63, 81–96.

Miller, J. and Eller, B. F. (1985) An examination of the effect of tangible and social reinforcers on intelligence test performance of middle school students, *Social Behaviour and Personality*, 13, 147–157.

Miller, K., Cooke, L., Tsang, J. and Morgan, F. (1992) Nature and impact of positive and boastful disclosures for women and men, *Human Communication Research*, 18, 364–369.

Miller, L. and Kenny, D. (1986) Reciprocity of self-disclosure at the individual and dyadic levels: a social relations analysis, *Journal of Personality and Social Psychology*, 50, 713–719.

Miller, L., Berg, J. and Archer, R. (1983) Openers: individuals who elicit intimate self-disclosure, *Journal of Personality and Social Psychology*, 44, 1234–1244.

Miller, L., Cody, M. and McLaughlin, M. (1994) Situations and goals as fundamental constructs in interpersonal communication research, in M. Knapp and G. Miller (eds) *Handbook of Interpersonal Communication Skills*, 2nd edn. Thousand Oaks, CA: Sage.

Miller, P. (2000) *Nonverbal Communication in the Classroom*. New York: Miller and Associates.

Miller, P., Kozu, J. and Davis, A. (2001) Social influence, empathy, and prosocial behavior in cross-cultural perspective, in W. Wosinska, R. Cialdini, D. Barrett and J. Reykowski (eds) *The Practice of Social Influence in Multiple Cultures*. Mahwah, NJ: Lawrence Erlbaum Associates, Inc.

Miller, S., Brody, D. and Summerton, J. (1988) Styles of coping with threat: implications for health, *Journal of Personality and Social Psychology*, 54, 142–148.

Mills, H. (1991) *Negotiate: The Art of Winning*. Aldershot: Gower.

Mills, M. (1983) Adolescents' self-disclosure in individual and group theme-centred modelling, reflecting and probing interviews, *Psychological Reports*, 53, 691–701.

Milne, R. (1999) Interviewing children with learning disabilities, in A. Memon and R. Bull (eds) *Handbook of the Psychology of Interviewing*. Chichester: Wiley.

Milne, R. and Bull, R. (1999) *Investigative Interviewing: Psychology and Practice*. Chichester: Wiley.

Miltz, R. (1972) *Development and Evaluation of a Manual for Improving Teachers' Explanation, Technical Report 26*. Stanford, CA: Stanford University Centre for Research and Development in Teaching.

Mitchell, M. (2000) Able but not motivated: the relative effects of happy and sad mood on persuasive message processing, *Communication Monographs*, 67, 215–226.

Mittendorff, K., Geijsel, F., Hoeve, A., de Laat, M. and Nieuwenhuis, L. (2006) Communities of practice as stimulating forces for collective learning, *Journal of Workplace Learning*, 18, 298–312.

Mizes, J. (1985) The use of contingent reinforcement in the treatment of a conversion disorder: a multiple baseline study, *Journal of Behavior Therapy and Experimental Psychiatry*, 16, 341–345.

Mnookin, R., Peppet S. and Tulumello, A. (1996) The tension between empathy and assertiveness, *Negotiation Journal*, 12, 217–230.

Mogg, K., Millar, N. and Bradley, B. (2000) Biases in eye movements to threatening facial expressions in generalized anxiety disorder and depressive disorder, *Journal of Abnormal Psychology*, 109, 695–704.

Mojzisch, A., Schulz-Hardt, S., Kerschreiter, R. and Frey, D. (2008) Combined effects of knowledge about others' opinions and anticipation of group discussion on confirmatory information search, *Small Group Research*, 39, 203–223.

Mokros, H. and Aakhus, M. (2002) From information-seeking behavior to meaning engagement practice: implications for communication theory and research, *Human Communication Research*, 28, 298–312.

Molloy, J. (1975) *Dress for Success*. New York: Peter H. Wyden.

Monahan, J. (1998) I don't know it but I like you: the influence of nonconscious affect on person perception, *Human Communication Research*, 24, 480–500.

Monahan, J. and Lannutti, P. (2000) Alcohol as social lubricant: alcohol myopia theory, social self-esteem, and social interaction, *Human Communication Research*, 26, 175–202.

Monarth, H. and Kase, L. (2007) *The Confident Speaker: Beat Your Nerves and Communicate at Your Best in Any Situation*. New York: McGraw-Hill.

Mongeau, P. (1998) Another look at fear-arousing persuasive appeals, in M. Allen and R. Preiss (eds) *Persuasion: Advances Through Meta-analysis*. Cresskill, NJ: Hampton Press.

Montepare, J., Koff, E., Zaitchik, D. and Albert, M. (1999) The use of body movements and gestures as cues to emotions in younger and older adults, *Journal of Nonverbal Behavior*, 23, 133–152.

Montgomery, D., Wiesman, D. and DeCaro, P. (2001) Towards a code of ethics for organizational communication professional: a working proposal, *American Communication Journal*, 5(1). http://acjournal.org/holdings/vol5/iss1/special/montgomery.htm (accessed 2 December 2009).

Moody, J., Stewart, B. and Bolt-Lee, C. (2002) Showcasing the skilled business graduate: expanding the tool kit, *Business Communication Quarterly*, 65, 21–33.

Moon, Y. (2000) Intimate exchanges: using computers to elicit self-disclosure from consumers, *Journal of Consumer Research*, 26, 323–339.

Moons, W., Mackie, D. and Garcia-Marques, T. (2009) The impact of repetition-induced familiarity on agreement with weak and strong arguments, *Journal of Personality and Social Psychology*, 96, 32–44.

Moore, K. (2005) Become a better communicator by keeping your mouth shut. *Journal for Quality and Participation*, 28, 8–10.

Moors, A. and De Houwer, J. (2007) What is automaticity? An analysis of its component features and their interrelations, in J. Bargh (ed.) *Social Psychology and the Unconscious: The Automaticity of Higher Mental Processes*. New York: Psychology Press.

Moran, S. and Ritov, I. (2007) Experience in integrative negotiations: what needs to be learned?, *Journal of Experimental Social Psychology*, 43, 77–90.

Morgan, H. and Thomas, K. (1996) A psychodynamic perspective on group processes, in M. Wetherall (ed.) *Identities, Groups, and Social Issues*. London: Sage Publications and Open University Press.

Morgan, N. and Saxton, J. (2006) *Asking Better Questions*, 2nd edn. Markham, ON: Pembroke.

Morley, I. (1981) Negotiating and bargaining, in M. Argyle (ed.) *Social Skills and Work*. London: Methuen.

Morley, I. (2006) Negotiation and bargaining, in O. Hargie (ed.) *The Handbook of Communication Skills*, 3rd edn. London: Routledge.

Morley, I. and Hosking, D. (1986) The skills of leadership, in G. Debus, and H. Schrioff (eds) *The Psychology of Work and Organization*. North Holland: Elsevier.

Morokoff, P., Quina, K., Harlow, L., Whitmire, L., Grimley, D., Gibson, P., *et al.* (1997) Sexual Assertiveness Scale (SAS) for women: development and validation, *Journal of Personality and Social Psychology*, 73, 790–804.

Morris, M., Larrick, R. and Su, S. (1999) Misperceiving negotiation counterparts: when situationally determined bargaining behaviours are attributed to personality traits, *Journal of Personality and Social Psychology*, 77, 52–67.

Morris, M., Podolny, J. and Ariel, S. (2001) Culture, norms, and obligations: cross-national differences in patterns of interpersonal norms and felt obligations toward coworkers, in W. Wosinska, R. Cialdini, D. Barrett and J. Reykowski (eds) *The Practice of Social Influence in Multiple Cultures*, Mahwah, NJ: Lawrence Erlbaum Associates, Inc.

Morrison, J. (2008) *The First Interview*, 3rd edn. New York: Guilford Press.

Morrison, T. and Conaway, W. (2006) *Kiss, Bow, or Shake Hands: The Best-selling Guide to Doing Business in 60 Countries*, 2nd edn. Avon, MA: Adams Media.

Morrow, N. and Hargie, O. (2001) Effective communication, in K. Taylor and G. Harding (eds) *Pharmacy Practice*. London: Taylor & Francis.

Morrow, N., Hargie, O., Donnelly, H. and Woodman, C. (1993) Why do you ask? A study of questioning behaviour in community pharmacist–client consultations, *International Journal of Pharmacy Practice*, 2, 90–94.

Mortensen, K. (2008) *Persuasion I.Q.* New York: AMACOM.

Moskowitz, G. and Grant, H. (2009) *The Psychology of Goals*. New York: Guilford Press.

Motley, M. (1992) Mindfulness in solving communicators' dilemmas, *Communication Monographs*, 59, 306–313.

Movius, H., Matsuura, M., Yan, J. and Kim, D. (2006) Tailoring the mutual gains approach for negotiations with partners in Japan, China, and Korea, *Negotiation Journal*, 22, 389–435.

Moyers, T., Martin, T., Catley, D., Harris, K. and Ahluwalia, J. (2003) Assessing the integrity of motivational interviewing interventions: reliability of the Motivational Interviewing Skills Code, *Behavioural and Cognitive Psychotherapy*, 31, 177–184.

Muczyk, J. and Reimann, B. (1987) The case of directive leadership, *Academy of Management Executive*, 1, 301–311.

Mudrack, P. and Farrell, G. (1995) An examination of functional role behaviour and its consequences for individuals in group settings, *Small Group Research*, 26, 542–571.

Mulac, A. (2006) The gender-linked language effect: do language differences really make a difference?, in K. Dindia and D. Canary (eds) *Sex Differences and Similarities in Communication*, 2nd edn. Mahwah, NJ: Lawrence Erlbaum Associates, Inc.

Mulac, A., Bradac, J. and Gibbons, P. (2001) Empirical support for the gender-as-culture hypothesis: an intercultural analysis of male/female language differences, *Human Communication Research*, 27, 121–152.

Müller, R. and Turner, J. (2007) Matching the project manager's leadership style to project type, *International Journal of Project Management*, 25, 21–32.

Mumford, T., Campion, M. and Morgeson, F. (2007) The leadership skills strataplex: leadership skill requirements across organizational levels, *Leadership Quartlerly*, 18, 154–166.

Munro, I. and Randall, J. (2007) I don't know what I'm doing, how about you? Discourse and identity in practitioners dealing with the survivors of childhood sexual abuse, *Organization*, 14, 887–907.

Munter, M. (2000) *Guide to Managerial Communication*, 5th edn. Upper Saddle River, NJ: Prentice-Hall.

Murray, J. (1990) Understanding competing theories of negotiation, in I. Asherman and S. Asherman (eds) *The Negotiating Sourcebook*. Amherst, MA: Human Resource Development Press.

Muthusamy, N., Levine, T. and Weber, R. (2009) Scaring the already scared: some problems with HIV/Aids fear appeals in Namibia, *Journal of Communication*, 59, 317–344.

Myers, D. (2008) *Social Psychology*, 9th edn. Boston, MA: McGraw-Hill.

Myers, S. and Bryant, L. (2008) Emerging adult siblings' use of verbally aggressive messages as hurtful messages, *Communication Quarterly*, 56, 268–283.

Nagata, D., Nay, W. and Seidman, E. (1983) Nonverbal and verbal content behaviors in the prediction of interviewer effectiveness, *Journal of Counseling Psychology*, 30, 83–86.

Napier, R. and Gershenfeld, M. (2004) *Groups: Theory and Experience*, 7th edn. Boston, MA: Houghton Mifflin.

Neale, M. and Fragale, A. (2006) Social cognition, attribution, and perception in negotiation: the role of uncertainty in shaping negotiation processes and outcomes, in L. Thompson (ed.) *Negotiation Theory and Research*. New York: Taylor & Francis.

Nelson, T. (ed.) (2009) *Handbook of Prejudice, Stereotyping and Discimination*. Hove, UK: Psychology Press.

Nelson-Gray, R., Haas, J., Romand, B., Herbert, J. and Herbert, D. (1989) Effects of open ended versus close ended questions on interviewees' problem related statements, *Perceptual and Motor Skills*, 69, 903–911.

Nelson-Jones, R. (1996) *Effective Thinking Skills*. London: Cassell.

Nelson-Jones, R. (2005a) *Practical Counselling and Helping Skills*, 5th edn. London: Sage.

Nelson-Jones, R. (2005b) *Introduction to Counselling Skills*, 2nd edn. London: Sage.

Neuberg, S., Judice, T. and West, S. (1997) What the Need for Closure Scale measures and what it does not: toward differentiating among related epistemic motives, *Journal of Personality and Social Psychology*, 72, 1396–1412.

Newman, B. and Newman, P. (2007) *Theories of Human Development*. Mahwah, NJ: Lawrence Erlbaum Associates, Inc.

Newton, M. (2002) *Savage Girls and Wild Boys: A History of Feral Children*. London: Faber.

Nicholas, L. (2008) *Introduction to Psychology*, 2nd edn. Cape Town: Juta.

Nichols, R. (1947) Listening: questions and problems, *Quarterly Journal of Speech*, 33, 83–86.

Niederle, N. and Vesterlund, L. (2008) Gender differences in competition, *Negotiation Journal*, 24, 447–463.

Niikura, R. (1999a) The psychological processes underlying Japanese assertive behavior: comparison of Japanese with Americans, Malaysians and Filipinos, *International Journal of Intercultural Relations*, 23, 47–76.

Niikura, R. (1999b) Assertiveness among Japanese, Malaysian, Filipino, and U.S. white-collar workers, *Journal of Social Psychology*, 139, 690–699.

Nix, J., Lohr, J. and Mosesso, L. (1983) The relationship of sex-role characteristics to self-report and role-play measures of assertiveness in women, *Behavioral Assessment*, 6, 89–93.

Noar, S., Harrington, N. and Aldrich, R. (2009) The role of message tailoring in the development of persuasive health communication messages, in C. Beck (ed.) *Communication Yearbook 33*. New York: Routledge.

Noller, P. (1980) Gaze in married couples, *Journal of Nonverbal Behavior*, 5, 115–129.

Noller, P. (2005) Behavioral coding of visual affect behavior, in V. Manuslov (ed.) *The Sourcebook of Nonverbal Measures: Going Beyond Words*. London: Routledge.

Northouse, L. and Northouse, P. (1990) *Health Communication. Strategies for Health Professionals*, 3rd edn. New Jersey: Prentice-Hall.

Northouse, P. (2007) *Leadership: Theory and Practice*, 4th edn. Thousand Oaks, CA: Sage.

Northouse, P. (2009) *Introduction to Leadership: Concepts and Practice*. Thousand Oaks, CA: Sage.

Norton, R. W. (1983) *Communicator Style: Theory, Applications and Measures*. Beverly Hills, CA: Sage.

Nussbaum, J. and Coupland, J. (eds) (2004) *Handbook of Communication and Ageing Research*, 2nd edn. Mahwah, NJ: Lawrence Erlbaum Associates, Inc.

Nussbaum, J., Pitts, M., Huber, F., Krieger, J. and Ohs, J. (2005) Ageism and ageist language across the life span: intimate relationships and non-intimate inter-actions. *Journal of Social Issues*, 61, 287–305.

Oakes, P., Haslam, A. and Turner, J. (1994) *Stereotypes and Social Reality*. Oxford: Blackwell.

O'Brien, J. and Holborn, S. (1979) Verbal and nonverbal expressions as reinforcers in verbal conditioning of adult conversation, *Journal of Behaviour Psychiatry*, 10, 267–269.

O'Connor, E. and Simms, C. (1990) Self-revelation and manipulation: the effects of sex and Machiavellianism on self-disclosure, *Social Behaviour and Personality*, 18, 95–100.

Oettingen, G. and Gollwitzer, P. (2001) Goal setting and goal striving, in A. Tesser and N. Schwarz (eds) *Blackwell Handbook of Social Psychology: Intraindividual Processes*. Malden, MA: Blackwell.

Oettingen, G., Bulgarella, C., Henderson, M. and Gollwitzer, P. (2004) The self-regulation of goal pursuit, in R. Wright, J. Greenberg and S. Brehm (eds) *Motivational Analyses of Social Behavior*. Mahwah, NJ: Lawrence Erlbaum Associates, Inc.

Office Angels (2000) *Forget Kissing . . . Everyone's Busy Telling!* London: Office Angels.

Office of the Health Services Commissioner (2008) *Annual Report*. Victoria: Office of the Health Services Commissioner. http://www.health.vic.gov.au/hsc/downloads/annrep08.pdf (accessed 2 December 2009).

Oguchi, T. (1991) Goal-based analysis of willingness of self-disclosure, *Japanese Psychological Research*, 33, 180–187.

O'Hair, D., Friedrich, G. and Dixon, L. (2007) *Strategic Communication in Business and the Professions*, 6th edn. Boston, MA: Allyn & Bacon.

Ohata, K. (2005) Auditory short-term memory in L2 listening comprehension processes, *Journal of Language and Learning*, 5, 21–28.

Ohme, R. (2001) Social influence in media: culture and antismoking advertising, in W. Wosinska, R. Cialdini, D. Barrett and J. Reykowski (eds) *The Practice of Social Influence in Multiple Cultures*. Mahwah, NJ: Lawrence Erlbaum Associates, Inc.

Okanda, M. and Itakura, S. (2008) Children in Asian cultures say yes to yes–no questions: common and cultural differences between Vietnamese and Japanese children, *International Journal of Behavioral Development*, 32, 131–136.

O'Keefe, D. (2002) *Persuasion: Theory and Research*, 2nd edn. Thousand Oaks, CA: Sage.

O'Keefe, D. (2006) Persuasion, in O. Hargie (ed.) *The Handbook of Communication Skills*, 3rd edn. London: Routledge.

O'Keefe, D. and Hale, S. (1998) The door-in-the-face influence strategy: a random effects meta-analytic review, in M. Roloff (ed.) *Communication Yearbook 21*, Thousand Oaks, CA: Sage.

O'Keefe, D. and Hale, S. (2001) An odds-ratio-based meta-analysis of research on the door-in-the-face influence strategy, *Communication Reports*, 14, 31–38.

O'Keefe, D. and Jensen, J. (2009) The relative persuasiveness of gain-framed and loss-framed messages for encouraging disease detection behaviors: a meta-analytic review, *Journal of Communication*, 59, 296–316.

O'Leary, M. and Gallois, C. (1999) The last ten turns in conversations between strangers, in L. Guerrero, J. DeVito and M. Hecht (eds) *The Nonverbal Communication Reader: Classic and Contemporary Readings Disclosures*, 2nd edn. Prospect Heights, IL: Waveland Press.

Olekalns, M. and Smith, P. (2001) Understanding optimal outcomes: the role of strategy sequences in competitive negotiations, *Human Communication Research*, 26, 527–557.

Omarzu, J. (2000) Disclosure decision model: determining how and when individuals will self-disclose, *Personality and Social Psychology Review*, 4, 174–185.

Omata, K. (1996) Territoriality in the house and its relationship to the use of rooms and the psychological well-being of Japanese married women, *Journal of Environmental Psychology*, 15, 147–154.

Ong, L., de Haes, J., Hoos, A. and Lammes, F. (1995) Doctor–patient communication: a review of the literature, *Social Science and Medicine*, 40, 903–918.

Orbe, M. and Bruess, C. (2005) *Contemporary Issues in Interpersonal Communication*. Los Angeles, CA: Roxbury.

O'Reilly, C. and Puffer, S. (1989) The impact on rewards and punishments in a social context: a laboratory and field experiment, *Journal of Occupational Psychology*, 62, 41–53.

Orrego, V., Smith, S., Mitchell, M., Johnson, A., Yun, K. and Greenberg, B. (2000) Disclosure and privacy issues on television talk shows, in S. Petronio (ed.) *Balancing the Secrets of Private Disclosures*. Mahwah, NJ: Lawrence Erlbaum Associates, Inc.

Oskay-Özcelik, G., Lehmacher, W., Könsgen, D., Christ, H., *et al.* (2007) Breast cancer patients' expectations in respect of the physician–patient relationship and treatment management results of a survey of 617 patients, *Annals of Oncology*, 18, 479–484.

Oster, H., Hegley, D. and Nagel, L. (1992) Adult judgements and fine-grained analysis of infant facial expressions: testing the validity of a priori coding formulas, *Developmental Psychology*, 25, 954–962.

Ostrom, R., Serovich, J., Lim, J. and Mason, T. (2006) The role of stigma in reasons for HIV disclosure and non-disclosure to children, *AIDS Care*, 18, 60–65.

Owens, L., Slee, P. and Shute, R. (2000) It hurts a hell of a lot . . . The effects of indirect aggression on teenage girls, *School Psychology International*, 21, 359–376.

Oyserman, D., Brickman, D., Bybee, D. and Celious, A. (2006) Fitting in matters: markers of in-group belonging and academic outcomes, *Psychologiocal Science*, 17, 854–861.

Packard, S. and Kauppi, D. (1999) Rehabilitation agency leadership style: impact on subordinates' job satisfaction, *Rehabilitation Counselling Bulletin*, 43, 5–11.

Paese, P. and Gilin, D. (2000) When an adversary is caught telling the truth: reciprocal cooperation versus self-interest in distributive bargaining, *Personality and Social Psychology Bulletin*, 26, 79–90.

Paivio, A. (1971) *Imagery and Verbal Processes*. New York: Holt.

Pallak, M., Cook, D. and Sullivan, J. (1980) Commitment and energy conservation, *Applied Social Psychology Journal*, 1, 235–253.

Palomares, N. (2008) Toward a theory of goal detection in social interaction: effects of contextual ambiguity and tactical functionality on goal inferences and inference certainty, *Communication Research*, 35, 109–148.

Palomares, N. (2009a) Did you see it coming? Effects of the specificity and efficiency of goal pursuit on the accuracy and onset of goal detection in social interaction, *Communication Research*, 36, 538–560.

Palomares, N. (2009b) Women are sort of more tentative than men, aren't they? How men and women use tentative language differently, similarly, and counter-stereotypically as a function of gender salience, *Communication Research*, 36, 475–509.

Panayiotou, G., Brown, R. and Vrana, S. (2007) Emotional dimensions as determinants of self-focused attention, *Cognition and Emotion*, 21, 982–998.

Pansa, M. (1979) Verbal conditioning of affect responses of process and reactive schizophrenics in a clinical interview situation, *British Journal of Medical Psychology*, 52, 175–182.

Papini, D., Farmer, F., Clark, S., Micka, J. and Barnett, J. (1990) Early adolescent age and gender differences in patterns of emotional self-disclosure to parents and friends, *Adolescence*, 25, 959–976.

Papousek, H., Jürgens, U. and Papousek, M. (2008) *Nonverbal Vocal Communication: Comparative and Developmental Approaches*. Cambridge: Cambridge University Press.

Paramasivam, S. (2007) Managing disagreement while managing not to disagree: polite disagreement in negotiation discourse, *Journal of Intercultural Communication Research*, 36, 91–116.

Pardeck, J., Anderson, C., Gianino, E. and Miller, B. (1991) Assertiveness of social work students, *Psychological Reports*, 69, 589–590.

Park, B. and Kraus, S. (1992) Consensus in initial impressions as a function of verbal information, *Personality and Social Psychology Bulletin*, 182, 439–449.

Parks, M. (2006) *Personal Relationships and Personal Networks*. London: Routledge.

Parrott, R., Duncan, V. and Duggan, A. (2000) Promoting patients' full and honest disclosure during conversations with health caregivers, in S. Petronio (ed.) *Balancing the Secrets of Private Disclosures*. Mahwah, NJ: Lawrence Erlbaum Associates, Inc.

Parrott, R., Greene, K. and Parker, R. (1992) Negotiating child health care routines during paediatrician–parent conversations, *Journal of Language and Social Psychology*, 11, 35–46.

Paterson R. (2000) *The Assertiveness Workbook: How to Express Your Ideas and Stand Up for Yourself at Work and in Relationships*. Oakland, CA: New Harbinger.

Pathak, A. (2001) Teaching and assessing multimedia-based oral presentations, *Business Communication Quarterly*, 64, 63–71.

Patrick, H., Knee, C., Canevello, A. and Lonsbary, C. (2007) The role of need fulfillment in relationship functioning and well-being: a self-determination theory perspective, *Journal of Personality and Social Psychology*, 92, 434–457.

Patry, M. (2008) Attractive but guilty: deliberation and the physical attractiveness bias, *Psychological Reports*, 102, 727–733.

Paunonen, S., Ewan, K., Earthy, J., Lefave, S. and Goldberg, H. (1999) Facial features as personality cues, *Journal of Personality*, 67, 555–583.

Pavitt, C. (2000) Answering questions requesting scientific explanations for communication, *Communication Theory*, 10, 379–404.

Pavlov, I. (1927) *Conditioned Reflexes*. New York: Dover.

Peace, V., Miles, L. and Johnston, L. (2006) It doesn't matter what you wear: the impact of posed and genuine expression of happiness on product evaluation, *Social Cognition*, 24, 137–138.

Pearson, J. and Nelson, P. (2000) *An Introduction to Human Communication: Understanding and Sharing*, 5th edn. Boston, MA: McGraw-Hill.

Pearson, J. and Spitzberg, B. (1987) *Interpersonal Communication: Concepts, Components, and Contexts*, 2nd edn. Madison, WI: WCB Brown & Benchmark.

Pearson, J., Nelson, P., Totsworth, S. and Harter, L. (2006) *Human Communication*, 2nd edn. Boston, MA: McGraw-Hill.

Peau, M., Szabo, E., Anderson, J., Morrill, J., Zubric, J. and Wan, H. (2001) The role and impact of affect in the process of resistance to persuasion, *Human Communication Research*, 27, 216–252.

Peck, J. (1995) TV talk shows as therapeutic discourse: the ideological labor of the televised talking cure, *Communication Theory*, 5, 58–81.

Penman, R. (2000) *Reconstructing Communicating: Looking to a Future*. Mahwah, NJ: Lawrence Erlbaum Associates, Inc.

Pennebaker, J. and Francis, M. (1996) Cognitive, emotional, and language processes in disclosure, *Cognition and Emotion*, 10, 601–626.

Pentland, A. (2007) On the collective nature of human intelligence, *Adaptive Behavior*, 15, 189–198.

Penton-Voak, I. and Perrett, D. (2000) Female preference for male faces change cyclically: further evidence, *Evolution and Human Behavior*, 21, 39–48.

Perloff, R. (2008) *The Dynamics of Persuasion: Communication and Attitudes in the 21st Century*, 3rd edn. Mahwah, NJ: Lawrence Erlbaum Associates, Inc.

Perrett, D., Burt, D., Penton-Voak, I., Lee, K., Rowland, D. and Edwards, R. (1999) Symmetry and human facial attractiveness, *Evolution and Human Behavior*, 20, 295–307.

Perrott, E. (1982) *Effective Teaching*. London: Longman.

Pershing, J. (ed.) (2006) *Handbook of Human Performance Technology: Principles, Practice, Potential*. San Francisco, CA: Pfeiffer.

Pervin, L. (1978) Definitions, measurements and classifications of stimuli, situations and environments, *Human Ecology*, 6, 71–105.

Peterson, R. (1997) A directive leadership style in group decision making can be both virtue and vice: evidence from elite and experimental groups, *Journal of Personality and Social Psychology*, 72, 1107–1121.

Peterson, R. (2007) An exploratory study of listening practice relative to memory testing and lecture in business administration courses, *Business Communication Quarterly*, 70, 285–300.

Petrie, K., Booth, R., Pennebaker, J., Davison, K. and Thomas, M. (1995) Disclosure of trauma and immune response to a hepatitis B vaccination program, *Journal of Consulting and Clinical Psychology*, 63, 787–792.

Petronio, S. (2002) *Boundaries of Privacy: Dialectics of Disclosure*. Albany, NY: State University of New York Press.

Petronio, S. and Bantz, C. (1991) Controlling the ramifications of disclosure: 'don't tell anybody but . . .', *Journal of Language and Social Psychology*, 10, 263–270.

Petty, R. and Cacioppo, J. (1986) *Communication and Persuasion: Central and Peripheral Routes to Attitude Change*. New York: Springer Verlag.

Pezdek, K. and Banks, W. (eds) (1996) *The Recovered Memory/False Memory Debate*. San Diego, CA: Academic Press.

Pfau, M., Semmler, S., Deatrick, L., Mason, A., *et al.* (2009) Nuances about the role and impact of affect in inoculation, *Communication Monographs*, 76, 73–98.

Pfau, M., Szabo, E., Anderson, J., Morrill, J., Zubric, J. and Wan, H. (2001) The role and impact of affect in the process of resistance to persuasion, *Human Communication Research*, 27, 216–252.

Philippot, P. and Feldman, R. (2005) *The Regulation of Emotion*. London: Routledge.

Phillips, E. (1978) *The Social Skills Basis of Psychopathology*. New York: Grune and Stratton.

Phillips, K., Rothbard, N. and Dumas, T. (2009) To disclose or not to disclose? Status distance and self-disclosure in diverse environments, *Academy of Management Review*, 34, 710–732.

Phillips, M. (1998) *All Must Have Prizes*. London: Time Warner.

Piccinin, S., McCarrey, M., Fairweather, D., Vito, D. and Conrad, G. (1998) Impact of situational legitimacy and assertiveness-related anxiety/discomfort on motivation and ability to generate effective criticism responses, *Current Psychology: Developmental, Learning, Personality, Social*, 17, 75–92.

Pickering, M. (2006) The dance of dialogue, *The Psychologist*, 19, 734–737.

Picot, A., Reichwald, R. and Wigand, R. (2008) *Information, Organization and Management*. New York: Springer.

Pietras, M. (2001) Social influence principles in Polish advertising and consumer decision making, in W. Wosinska, R. Cialdini, D. Barrett and J. Reykowski (eds) *The Practice of Social Influence in Multiple Cultures*. Mahwah, NJ: Lawrence Erlbaum Associates, Inc.

Pilkington, C. and Smith, K. (2000) Self-evaluation maintenance in a larger social context, *British Journal of Social Psychology*, 39, 213–229.

Pinnington, A. (2001) Charles Handy: the exemplary guru, *Reason in Practice*, 1, 47–55.

Pipe, M., Lamb, M., Orbach, Y. and Cederborg, A. (eds) (2007) *Child Sexual Abuse: Disclosure, Delay, and Denial*. London: Routledge.

Pitts, M. and Roberts, M. (1997) *Fairweather Eden*. London: Century.

Placencia, M. (1997) Opening up closings – the Ecuadorian way, *Text*, 17, 53–81.

Planalp, S. (1998) Communicating emotion in everyday life: cues, channels and processes, in P. Andersen and L. Guerrero (eds) *Handbook of Communication and Emotion: Research, Theory, Applications, and Contexts*. San Diego, CA: Academic Press.

Plotnikoff, J. and Woolfson, R. (2009) *Measuring Up? Evaluating Implementation of Government Commitments to Young Witnesses in Criminal Proceedings*. Nuffield Foundation and NSPCC. http://www.nspcc.org.uk/Inform/research/Findings/measuring_up_report_wdf66579.pdf (accessed 2 December 2009).

Pollack, B. (1998) The impact of the sociophysical environment on interpersonal communication and feelings of belonging in work groups, in J. Sanford and B. Connell (eds) *People, Places, and Public Policy*. Edmond, OK: Environmental Design Research Association.

Poole, M. S. (1999) Group communication theory, in L. Frey, D. Gouran and M. S. Poole (eds) *The Handbook of Group Communication Theory and Research*. Thousand Oaks, CA: Sage.

Porter, R. and Samovar, L. (1998) Cultural influences on emotional expression: implications of intercultural communication, in P. Andersen and L. Guerrero (eds) *Handbook of Communication and Emotion: Research, Theory, Applications, and Contexts*. San Diego, CA: Academic Press.

Postmes, T. and Jetten, P. (eds) (2006) *Individuality and the Group: Advances in Social Identity*, London: Sage.

Postmes, T., Baray, G., Haslam, A., Morton, T. and Swab, R. (2006) The dynamics of social and personal identity formation, in T. Postmes and P. Jetten (eds) *Individuality and the Group: Advances in Social Identity*. London: Sage.

Powell, G. and Graves, L. (2006) Gender and leadership: perceptions and realities, in K. Dindia and D. Canary (eds) *Sex Differences and Similarities in Communication*, 2nd edn. Mahwah, NJ: Lawrence Erlbaum Associates, Inc.

Powell, M. and Snow, P. (2007) Guide to questioning children during the free-narrative phase of an investigative interview, *Australian Psychologist*, 42, 57–65.

Powell, M., Fisher, R. and Wright, R. (2007) Investigative interviewing, in N. Brewer and K. Williams (eds) *Psychology and Law: An Empirical Perspective*. New York: Guilford Press.

Powell, W. (1968) Differential effectiveness of interviewer interventions in an experimental interview, *Journal of Consulting and Clinical Psychology*, 32, 210–215.

Pratkanis, A. (2001) Propaganda and deliberative persuasion: the implications of Americanized mass media for established and emerging democracies, in W. Wosinska, R. Cialdini, D. Barrett and J. Reykowski (eds) *The Practice of Social Influence in Multiple Cultures.* Mahwah, NJ: Lawrence Erlbaum Associates, Inc.

Pratkanis, A. (2007) Social influence analysis: an index of tactics, in A. Pratkanis (ed.) *The Science of Social Influence: Advances and Future Progress.* New York: Psychology Press.

Preiss, R. and Allen, M. (1998) Performing counterattitudinal advocacy: the persuasive impact of incentives, in M. Allen and R. Preiss (eds) *Persuasion: Advances Through Meta-analysis.* Cresskill, NJ: Hampton Press.

Premack, D. (1965) Reinforcement theory, in D. Levine (ed.) *Nebraska Symposium on Motivation, Vol, 13.* Lincoln, NE: University of Nebraska Press.

Priest, P. and Dominick, J. (1994) Pulp pulpits: self-disclosure on 'Donohue', *Journal of Communication,* 44, 74–96.

Prkachin, K. (1997) The consistency of facial expressions of pain, in P. Ekman and E. Rosenberg (eds) *What the Face Reveals: Basic and Applied Studies of Spontaneous Expression Using the Facial Action Coding System (FACS).* Oxford: Oxford University Press.

Prochaska, J. and DiClemente, C. (1992) Stages of change in the modification of problem behaviors, in M. Hersen, R. Eisler and P. Miller (eds) *Progress in Behavior Modification.* Sycamore, IL: Sycamore Press.

Proctor, R. and Adler, R. (2007) *Looking Out, Looking In,* 12th edn. Belmont, CA: Wadsworth Press.

Proctor, R. and Dutta, A. (1995) *Skill Acquisition and Human Performance.* Thousand Oaks, CA: Sage.

Provine, R. (2000) *Laughter: A Scientific Investigation.* London: Penguin.

Prue, D. and Fairbank, J. (1981) Performance feedback in organizational behavior management: a review, *Journal of Organizational Behavior Management,* 3, 1–16.

Pruitt, D. (1981) *Negotiating Behavior.* New York: Academic Press.

Pruitt, D. (1990) Achieving integrative agreements, in I. Asherman and S. Asherman (eds) *The Negotiating Sourcebook.* Amherst, MA: Human Resource Development Press.

Pruitt, D. and Carnevale, P. (1993) *Negotiation in Social Conflict.* Buckingham: Open University Press.

Putnam, L. and Roloff, M. (1992) Communication perspectives on negotiation, in L. Putnam and M. Roloff (eds) *Communication and Negotiation.* Newbury Park, CA: Sage.

Quine, L., Rutter, D. and Arnold, L. (2002) Increasing cycle helmet use in school age cyclists: an intervention based on the theory of planned behaviour, in D. Rutter and L. Quine (eds) *Changing Health Behaviour.* Buckingham: Open University Press.

Quinlan, P. and Dyson, B. (2008) *Cognitive Psychology.* Harlow: Pearson Education.

Quinn, R. E. and McGrath, M. R. (1982) Moving behind the single solution perspective, *Journal of Applied Behavioral Science,* 18, 463–472.

Rabin, C. and Zelner, D. (1992) The role of assertiveness in clarifying roles and strengthening job satisfaction of social workers in multidisciplinary mental health settings, *British Journal of Social Work,* 22, 17–32.

Rackham, N. (1972) Controlled pace negotiation, *Industrial and Commercial Training,* 4, 266–275.

Rackham, N. (2007) The behavior of successful negotiators, in R. Lewicki, B. Barry and D. Saunders (eds) *Negotiation: Readings, Exercises, and Cases*, 5th edn. New York: McGraw-Hill/Irwin.

Rains, S. and Turner, M. (2007) Psychological reactance and persuasive health communication: a test and extension of the intertwined model, *Human Communication Research*, 33, 241–269.

Rakos, R. (1991) *Assertive Behavior: Theory, Research and Training*. London: Routledge.

Rakos, R. (2006) Asserting and confronting, in O. Hargie (ed.) *The Handbook of Communication Skills*, 3rd edn. London: Routledge.

Ransdell, S. and Gilroy, L. (2001) The effects of background music on word processed writing, *Computers in Human Behavior*, 17, 141–148.

Rasmussen, E. and Newland, M. (2008) Asymmetry of reinforcement and punishment in human choice, *Journal of the Experimental Analysis of Behavior*, 89, 157–167.

Rathvon, N. (2008) *Effective School Interventions*, 2nd edn. New York: Guilford Press.

Rautalinko, E. and Lisper, H. (2004) Effects of training reflective listening in a corporate setting, *Journal of Business and Psychology*, 18, 281–299.

Raven, B. (1992) A power/interaction model of interpersonal influence: French and Raven thirty years later, *Journal of Social Behavior and Personality*, 7, 217–244.

Raven, B. (1998) Groupthink, Bay of Pigs and Watergate reconsidered, *Organizational Behavior and Human Decision Processes*, 73, 352–361.

Raven, B. and Rubin, J. Z. (1983) *Social Psychology*, 2nd edn. New York: Wiley.

Raymond, G. (2003) Grammar and social organization: yes/no interrogatives and the structure of responding, *American Sociological Review*, 68, 939–967.

Rebellon, C. (2006) Do adolescents engage in delinquency to attract the social attention of peers? An extension and longitudinal test of the social reinforcement hypothesis, *Journal of Research in Crime and Delinquency*, 43, 387–411.

Rehling, D. (2008) Compassionate listening: a framework for listening to the seriously ill, *International Journal of Listening*, 22, 83–89.

Rehman, S., Nietert, P., Cope, D. and Kilpatrick, A. (2005) What to wear today? Effect of doctor's attire on the trust and confidence of patients, *American Journal of Medicine*, 118, 1279–1286.

Reid, D. and Parsons, M. (2000) Organisational behavioural management in human service settings, in J. Austin and J. Carr (eds) *Handbook of Applied Behaviour Analysis*. Reno, CA: Context Press.

Reid, L., Henneman, R. and Long, E. (1960) An experimental analysis of set: the effect of categorical instruction, *American Journal of Psychology*, 73, 568–572.

Reinhard, J. (1998) The persuasive effects of testimonial assertion evidence, in M. Allen and R. Preiss (eds) *Persuasion: Advances Through Meta-analysis*. Cresskill, NJ: Hampton Press.

Reinhard, M.-A., Messner, M. and Sporer, S. (2006) Explicit persuasive intent and its impact upon success at persuasion: the determining roles of attractiveness and likeability, *Journal of Consumer Psychology*, 16, 249–259.

Remland, M. (2006) Uses and consequences of nonverbal communication in the context of organizational life, in V. Manusov and M. Patterson (eds) *The Sage Handbook of Nonverbal Communication*. Thousand Oaks, CA: Sage.

Remland, M. (2009) *Nonverbal Communication in Everyday Life*, 3rd edn. Boston, MA: Allyn & Bacon.

Reno, R. and Kenny, D. (1992) Effects of self-consciousness and social anxiety on self-disclosure among unacquainted individuals: an application of the social relations model, *Journal of Personality*, 60, 79–95.

Resnick, L. (1972) Teacher behaviour in an informal British infant school, *School Review*, 81, 63–83.

Reykowski, J. (2001) Principles of social influence across cultures, in W. Wosinska, R. Cialdini, D. Barrett and J. Reykowski (eds) *The Practice of Social Influence in Multiple Cultures*. Mahwah, NJ: Lawrence Erlbaum Associates, Inc.

Reynolds, W. and Scott, B. (2000) Do nurses and other professional helpers normally display much empathy?, *Journal of Advanced Nursing*, 31, 226–234.

Richardson, D. and Green, L. (2006) Direct and indirect aggression: relationships as social context, *Journal of Applied Social Psychology*, 36, 2492–2508.

Richardson, D. and Hammock, G. (2007) Social context of human aggression: are we paying too much attention to gender?, *Aggression and Violent Behavior*, 12, 417–426.

Richins, M. (1983) An analysis of consumer interaction style in the marketplace, *Journal of Consumer Research*, 10, 73–82.

Richmond, V. and McCroskey, J. (2000) *Nonverbal Behavior in Interpersonal Relations*, 4th edn. Boston, MA: Allyn and Bacon.

Richter, L. and Kruglanski, A. (2004) Motivated closed mindedness and the emergence of culture, in M. Schaller and C. Crandall (eds) *The Psychological Foundations of Culture*. Mahwah, NJ: Lawrence Erlbaum Associates, Inc.

Rider, E. and Keefer, C. (2006) Communication skills competencies: definitions and a teaching toolbox, *Medical Education*, 40, 624–629.

Riggio, R. (1992) Social interaction skills and nonverbal behaviour, in R. Feldman (ed.) *Applications of Nonverbal Behavioral Theory and Research*. Hillsdale, NJ: Lawrence Erlbaum Associates, Inc.

Riggio, R. (2005) The Social Skills Inventory (SSI): measuring nonverbal and social skills, in V. Manusov (ed.) *The Sourcebook of Nonverbal Measures: Going Beyond Words*. Mahwah, NJ: Lawrence Erlbaum Associates, Inc.

Riggio, R. and Friedman, H. (1986) Impression formation: the role of expressive behavior, *Journal of Personality and Social Psychology*, 50, 421–427.

Rimal, R. (2002) Perceived risk and self-efficacy as motivators: understanding individuals' long-term use of health information, *Journal of Communication*, 51, 633–654.

Riseborough, M. (1981) Physiographic gestures as decoding facilitators: three experiments exploring a neglected facet of communication, *Journal of Nonverbal Behavior*, 5, 172–183.

Risjord, M. (2005) Reasons, causes, and action explanation, *Philosophy of the Social Sciences*, 35, 294–306.

Rittle-Johnson, B. (2006) Promoting transfer: effects of self-explanation and direct instruction, *Child Development*, 77, 1–15.

Roach, C. and Wyatt, N. (1999) Listening and the rhetorical process, in J. Stewart (ed.) *Bridges Not Walls*, 7th edn. Boston, MA: McGraw-Hill.

Robbins, S. and Hunsaker, P. (2009) *Training in Interpersonal Skills: TIPS for Managing People at Work*, 5th edn. Upper Saddle River, NJ: Pearson Education.

Robbins, S. and Judge, T. (2009) *Organizational Behavior*, 13th edn. Upper Saddle River, NJ: Pearson Education.

Robbins, S. and Judge, T. (2010) *Essentials of Organizational Behavior*, 10th edn. Upper Saddle River, NJ: Pearson Education.

Robinson, J. (1998) Getting down to business: talk, gaze, and body orientation during openings of doctor–patient consultations, *Human Communication Research*, 25, 97–123.

Robinson, J. (2006a) Nonverbal communication and physician–patient interaction: review and new directions, in V. Manusov and M. Patterson (eds) *The Sage Handbook of Nonverbal Communication*. Thousand Oaks, CA: Sage.

Robinson, J. (2006b) Soliciting patients' presenting concerns, in J. Heritage and D. Maynard (eds) *Communication in Medical Care: Interactions between Primary Care Physicians and Patients*. Cambridge: Cambridge University Press.

Robinson, J. and Heritage, J. (2006) Physicians' opening questions and patients' satisfaction, *Patient Education and Counseling*, 60, 279–285.

Robinson, J. and Stivers, T. (2001) Achieving activity transitions in physician–patients encounters: from history taking to physical examination, *Human Communication Research*, 27, 253–298.

Robinson, S., Sterling, C., Skinner, C. and Robinson, D. (1997) Effects of lecture rate on students' comprehension and ratings of topic importance, *Contemporary Educational Psychology*, 22, 260–267.

Roehling, M., Roehling, P. and Odland, L. (2008) Investigating the validity of stereotypes about overweight employees: the relationship between body weight and normal personality traits, *Group and Organization Management*, 33, 392–424.

Roese, N., Olson, J., Borenstein, M., Martin, A. and Shores, A. (1992) Same-sex touching behaviour: the moderating role of homophobic attitudes, *Journal of Nonverbal Behavior*, 16, 249–259.

Rogan, R. and Hammer, M.R. (1995) Assessing message affect in crisis negotiation: an exploratory study, *Human Communication Research*, 21, 553–574.

Rogers, C. (1951) *Client-centered therapy*. Boston, MA: Houghton Mifflin.

Rogers, C. (1980) *A Way of Being*. Boston, MA: Houghton Mifflin.

Rogers, C. (1991) *Client-centred Therapy*. London: Constable.

Rogers, E. (1983) *Diffusion of Innovations*. New York: Free Press.

Rogers, R. (2008) *Clinical Assessment of Malingering and Deception*, 3rd edn. New York: Guilford Press.

Rogers, W. (1978) The contribution of kinesic illustrators toward the comprehension of verbal behavior within utterances, *Human Communication Research*, 5, 54–62.

Roloff, M. and Jordan, J. (1992) Achieving negotiation goals: the 'fruits and foibles' of planning ahead, in L. Putnam and M. Roloff (eds) *Communication and Negotiation*. Newbury Park, CA: Sage.

Roloff, M. and Li, S. (2010) Bargaining and negotiation, in C. Berger, M. Roloff and D. Roskos-Ewoldsen (eds) *The Handbook of Communication Science*. Thousand Oaks, CA: Sage.

Rose, Y. and Tryon, W. (1979) Judgements of assertive behavior as a function of speech loudness, latency, content, gestures, inflection and sex, *Behavior Modification*, 3, 112–123.

Rosenbaum, B. (2001) Seven emerging sales competencies, *Business Horizons*, 44, 33–36.

Rosenblum, N., Wetzel, M., Platt, O., Daniels, S., Crawford, J. and Rosenthal, R. (1994) Predicting medical student success in a clinical clerkship by rating students' nonverbal behaviour, *Archives of Pediatric and Adolescent Medicine*, 148, 213–219.

Rosenfarb, I. (1992) A behaviour analytic interpretation of the therapeutic relationship, *The Psychological Record*, 42, 341–354.

Rosenfeld, H. (1987) Conversational control functions of nonverbal behavior, in A. Siegman and S. Feldstein (eds) *Nonverbal Behavior and Communication*. Hillsdale, NJ: Lawrence Erlbaum Associates, Inc.

Rosenfeld, H. and Hancks, M. (1980) The nonverbal context of verbal listener responses, in M. Kay (ed.) *The Relationship of Verbal and Nonverbal Communication*. The Hague: Mouton.

Rosenfeld, L. (2000) Overview of the ways privacy, secrecy, and disclosure are balanced in today's society, in S. Petronio (ed.) *Balancing the Secrets of Private Disclosures*. Mahwah, NJ: Lawrence Erlbaum Associates, Inc.

Rosenfeld, L., Kartus, S. and Ray, C. (1976) Body accessibility revisited, *Journal of Communication*, 26, 27–30.

Rosengren, K. (2000) *Communication: An Introduction*. London: Sage.

Rosenshine, B. (1968) *Objectively Measured Behavioural Predictors of Effectiveness in Explaining*. Stanford, CA: Stanford University Centre for Research and Development in Teaching.

Rosenshine, B. (1971) *Teaching Behaviour and Student Achievement*. Windsor: National Foundation for Educational Research in England and Wales.

Rosenthal, R. (2006) Applying psychological research on interpersonal expectations and covert communication in classrooms, corporations, and courtrooms, in S. Donaldson, D. Berger and K. Pezdek (eds) *Applied Psychology: New Frontiers and Rewarding Careers*. Mahwah, NJ: Lawrence Erlbaum Associates, Inc.

Rosenthal, R. and Jacobson, L. (1992) *Pygmalion in the Classroom*. New York: Irvington.

Roskos-Ewoldsen, D. and Monahan, J. (eds) (2007) *Communication and Social Cognition*. London: Routledge.

Roter, D. and Hall, J. (2006) *Doctors Talking With Patients/Patients Talking With Doctors: Improving Communication in Medical Visits*, 2nd edn. Westport, CT: Preager.

Roth, H. (1889) On salutations, *Journal of the Royal Anthropological Institute*, 19, 164–181.

Rotter, J. (1966) Generalized expectancies for internal versus external control of reinforcement, *Psychological Monographs*, *80*. (whole no. 609).

Rousseau, E. and Redfield, D. (1980) Teacher questioning, *Evaluation in Education*, 4, 51–52.

Routasalo, P. (1999) Physical touch in nursing studies: a literature review, *Journal of Advanced Nursing*, 30, 843–850.

Rowan, K. (2003) Informing and explaining skills: theory and research on informative communication, in J. Greene and B. Burleson (eds) *The Handbook of Communication and Social Interaction Skills*. Mahwah, NJ: Lawrence Erlbaum Associates, Inc.

Rowe, M. (1969) Science, silence and sanctions, *Science and Children*, 6, 11–13.

Rowe, M. (1974a) Pausing phenomena: influence on the quality of instruction, *Journal of Psycholinguistic Research*, 3, 203–233.

Rowe, M. (1974b) Wait-time and rewards as instructional variables, their influence on language, logic, and fate control. Part One – wait-time, *Journal of Research in Science Teaching*, 11, 81–94.

Rowell, P. and Ebbers, M. (2004) Constructing explanations of flight: a study of instructional discourse in primary science, *Language and Education*, 18, 264–281.

Rowland P., Coe, N., Burchard, K. and Pricolo, V. (2005) Factors affecting the professional image of physicians, *Current Surgery*, 62, 214–219.

Ruback, R. and Juieng, D. (1997) Territorial defence in parking lots: retaliation against waiting drivers, *Journal of Applied Social Psychology*, 27, 821–834.

Ruben, D. (1990) *Explaining Explanation*. London: Routledge.

Rubie-Davies, C. (2007) Classroom interactions: exploring the practices of high- and low-expectation teachers, *British Journal of Educational Psychology*, 77, 289–306.

Rubie-Davies, C., Hattie, J. and Hamilton, R. (2006) Expecting the best for students: teacher expectations and academic outcomes, *British Journal of Educational Psychology*, 76, 429–444.

Rubin, D., Yang, H. and Porte, M. (2000) A comparison of self-reported self-disclosure among Chinese and North Americans, in S. Petronio (ed.) *Balancing the Secrets of Private Disclosures*. Mahwah, NJ: Lawrence Erlbaum Associates, Inc.

Rudawsky, D. (2000) Speaking one's mind or biting one's tongue: when do angered persons express or withhold feedback in transactions with male and female peers?, *Social Psychology Quarterly*, 63, 253–263.

Rudman, L. and Glick, P. (2001) Prescriptive gender stereotypes and backlash toward agenic women, *Journal of Social Issues*, 57, 743–762.

Ruffner, M. and Burgoon, M. (1981) *Interpersonal Communication*. New York: Holt, Rinehart and Winston.

Russell, J. (1971) *Motivation*. Dubuque, IA: W.C. Brown,

Russell, J. (1997) Reading emotions from and into faces: resurrecting a dimensional-contextual perspective, in J. Russell and J. Fernandez-Dols (eds) *The Psychology of Facial Expression*. Cambridge: Cambridge University Press.

Russell, J. and Fernandez-Dols, J. (1997) What does a facial expression mean? in J. Russell and J. Fernandez-Dols (eds) *The Psychology of Facial Expression*. Cambridge: Cambridge University Press.

Rutter, D. and Quine, L. (2002) Social cognition models and changing health behaviours, in D. Rutter and L. Quine (eds) *Changing Health Behaviour*. Buckingham: Open University Press.

Ruusuvuori, J. (2001) Looking means listening: coordinating displays of engagement in doctor–patient interaction, *Social Science and Medicine*, 52, 1093–1108.

Ryan, E., Anas, A. and Friedman, D. (2006) Evaluations of older adult assertiveness in problematic clinical encounters, *Journal of Language and Social Psychology*, 25, 129–145.

Ryan, E., Anas, A. and Vuckovich, M. (2007) The effects of age, hearing loss, and communication difficulty on first, impressions, *Communication Research Reports*, 24, 13–19.

Ryan, R., Sheldon, K., Kasser, T. and Deci, E. (1996) All goals are not created equal: an organismic perspective on the nature of goals and their regulation, in

P. Gollwitzer and J. Bargh (eds) *The Psychology of Action: Linking Cognition and Motivation to Behavior*. New York: Guilford Press.

Rydell, R. and McConnell, A. (2005) Perceptions of entitativity and attitude change, *Personality and Social Psychology Bulletin*, 31, 99–110.

Ryff, C. and Singer, B. (2000) Interpersonal flourishing: a positive health agenda for the new millennium, *Personality and Social Psychology Review*, 4, 30–34.

Saigh, P. A. (1981) Effects of nonverbal examiner praise on selected WAIS subtest performance of Lebanese undergraduates, *Journal of Nonverbal Behavior*, 6, 84–88.

Salacuse, J. (1998) Ten ways that culture affects negotiating style: some survey results, *Negotiation Journal*, 14, 221–239.

Salter, A. (1949) *Conditioned Reflex Therapy*. New York: Capricorn Books.

Samp, J. and Solomon, D. (1998) Communicative responses to problematic events in close relationships I: the variety and facets of goals, *Communication Research*, 25, 66–95.

Sanchez, M. (2001) Effects of assertive communication between doctors and patients in public health outpatient surgeries in the city of Seville, *Social Behavior and Personality*, 29, 63–70.

Sanders, R. and Fitch, K. (2001) The actual practice of compliance seeking, *Communication Theory*, 11, 263–289.

Sandow, D. and Allen, A. M. (2005) The nature of social collaboration: how work really gets done, *Reflections*, 6, 1–14.

Sansone, C. and Harackiewicz, J. (eds) (2000) *Intrinsic and Extrinsic Motivation: The Search for Optimal Motivation and Performance*. San Diego, CA: Academic Press.

Santen, S., Rotter, T. and Hemphill, R. (2008) Patients do not know the level of training of their doctors because doctors do not tell them, *Journal of General Internal Medicine*, 23, 607–610.

Sarafino, E. (2004) *Behavior Modification: Principles of Behavior Change*, 2nd edn. Long Grove, IL: Waveland Press.

Sas, L. (2002) *The Interaction Between Children's Developmental Capabilities and the Courtroom Environment: The Impact on Testimonial Competency*. Research Report, Department of Justice, Canada. http://www.judcom.nsw.gov.au/publications/benchbks/sexual_assault/articles/Sas-Interaction_between_children_ and_ courtroom.pdf (accessed 2 December 2009).

Saunders, C. and Caves, R. (1986) An empirical approach to the identification of communication skills with reference to speech therapy, *Journal of Further and Higher Education*, 10, 29–44.

Saunders, C. and Saunders, E. (1993) Expert teachers' perceptions of university teaching: the identification of teaching skills, in R. Ellis (ed.) *Quality Assurance for University Teaching*. Buckingham: Open University Press.

Savin-Williams, R. and Dube, E. (1998) Parental reactions to their child's disclosure of a gay/lesbian identity, *Family Relations: Interdisciplinary Journal of Applied Family Studies*, 47, 7–13.

Saxton, T., DeBruine, L., Jones, B., Little, A. and Roberts, C. (2009) Face and voice attractiveness judgments change during adolescence, *Evolution and Human Behavior*. doi: 10.1016/j.evolhumbehav.2009.06.004.

Scanlon, L. (1994) *Narrative, Authority and Power: The Medieval Exemplum and the Chaucerian Tradition*. Cambridge: Cambridge University Press.

Schaller, M. (2008) Evolutionary bases of first impressions, in N. Ambady and J. Skowronski (eds) *First Impressions*. New York: Guilford Press.

Schatzman, L. and Strauss, A. (1956) Social class and modes of communications, *American Journal of Sociology*, 60, 329–338.

Scheflen, A. (1974) *How Behavior Means*. Garden City, NJ: Anchor.

Schegloff, E. (2000) Overlapping talk and the organization of turn-taking for conversation, *Language in Society*, 29, 1–63.

Schegloff, E. and Sacks, H. (1973) Opening-up closings, *Semiotica*, 8, 289–327.

Scherer, K. (1979) Acoustic concomitants of emotional dimensions: judging affect from synthesized tone sequences, in S. Weitz (ed.) *Nonverbal Communication: Readings with Commentary*, 2nd edn. New York: Oxford University Press.

Scherer, K. and Grandjean, D. (2007) Facial expressions allow inference of both emotions and their components, *Cognition and Emotion*, 22, 789–801.

Scherer, K., Johnstone, T. and Klasmeyer, G. (2003) Vocal expression of emotion, in R. Davidson, K. Scherer and H. Goldsmith (eds) *Handbook of Affective Sciences*. Oxford: Oxford University Press.

Schermerhorn, J., Hunt, J. and Osborn, R. (1995) *Basic Organizational Behavior*. New York: Wiley.

Schiavo, R., Kobashi, K., Quinn, C., Sefscik, A., *et al.* (1995) Territorial influences on the permeability of group spatial boundaries, *Journal of Social Psychology*, 135, 27–29.

Schirmer, J., Mauksch, L., Lang, F., Marvel, M., *et al.* (2005) Assessing communication competence: a review of current tools, *Family Medicine*, 37, 184–192.

Schlundt, D. and McFall, R. (1985) New directions in the assessment of social competence and social skills, in L. L'Abate and M. Milan (eds) *Handbook of Social Skills Training and Research*. New York: Wiley.

Schneider, D. (2005) *The Psychology of Stereotyping*. New York: Guilford Press.

Schneider, S. and Laurion, S. (1993) Do we know what we've learned from listening to the news?, *Memory and Cognition*, 21, 198–209.

Schofield, T., Parke, R., Castaneda, E. and Coltrane S. (2008) Patterns of gaze between parents and children in European American and Mexican American families, *Journal of Nonverbal Behavior*, 32, 171–186.

Schouten, A., Valkenburg, P. and Peter, J. (2007) Precursors and underlying processes of adolescents' online self-disclosure: developing and testing an 'Internet-Attribute-Perception' model, *Media Psychology*, 10, 292–315.

Schroth, M. (1992) The effect of delay of feedback on a delayed concept formation transfer task, *Contemporary Educational Psychology*, 17, 78–82.

Schubert, J. (2000) Give sorrow words: mourning at termination of psychoanalysis, *Scandinavian Psychoanalytic Review*, 23, 105–117.

Schullery, N. (1997) Communication behaviors of employed females: a survey focusing on argumentativeness and women's supervisory roles in organizations, *Dissertation Abstracts International: Humanities and Social Sciences*, 58(3-A), 0647.

Schutz, A. (1998) Assertive, offensive, protective, and defensive styles of self-presentation: a taxonomy, *Journal of Psychology*, 132, 611–628.

Schultz, C. B. and Shemman, R. H. (1976) Social class, development and differences in reinforcer effectiveness, *Review of Educational Research*, 46, 25–59.

Schutz, W. C. (1955) What makes groups productive?, *Human Relations*, 8, 429–465.

Schwab, S., Scalise, J., Ginter, E. and Whipple, G. (1998) Self-disclosure, loneliness and four interpersonal targets: friend, group of friends, stranger, and group of strangers, *Psychological Reports*, 82, 1264–1266.

Schwartz, B. (1989) *Psychology of Learning and Behaviour*. New York: Norton.

Science Daily (2007) Stereotype about female talkativeness unfounded, researchers report, 6 July. http://www.sciencedaily.com/releases/2007/07/070705152953.htm (accessed 2 December 2009).

Scofield, M. E. (1977) Verbal conditioning with a heterogeneous adolescent sample: the effects on two critical responses, *Psychology*, 14, 41–49.

Scott, B. (1988) *Negotiating: Constructive and Competitive Negotiation*. London: Paradigm Press.

Scott, M., McCroskey, J. and Sheahan, M. (1978) The development of a self-report measure of communication apprehension in organizational settings, *Journal of Communication*, 20, 104–111.

Sears, A. and Jacko, J. (eds) (2008) *The Human–Computer Interaction Handbook: Fundamentals, Evolving Technologies and Emerging Applications*, 2nd edn. New York: Lawrence Erlbaum Associates, Inc.

Seden, J. (2005) *Counselling Skills in Social Work Practice*. Maidenhead: Open University Press.

Sedikides, C. and Spencer, S. (eds) (2007) *The Self*. New York: Psychology Press.

Segerstrale, U. and Molnar, P. (1997) Nonverbal communication: crossing the boundary between culture and nature, in U. Segerstrale and P. Molnar (eds) *Nonverbal Communication: Where Nature Meets Culture*. Mahwah, NJ: Lawrence Erlbaum Associates, Inc.

Segrin, C. (1992) Specifying the nature of social skill deficits associated with depression, *Human Communication Research*, 19, 89–123.

Segrin, C. (2000) Interpersonal relationships and mental health problems, in K. Dindia and S. Duck (eds) *Communication and Personal Relationships*. Chichester: Wiley.

Segrin, C. and Taylor, M. (2007) Positive interpersonal relationships mediate the association between social skills and psychological well-being, *Personality and Individual Differences*, 43, 637–646.

Segrin, C., Hanzal, A., Donnerstein, C., Taylor, M. and Domschke, T. (2007) Social skills, psychological well-being, and the mediating role of perceived stress, *Anxiety, Stress and Coping*, 20, 321–329.

Seiter, J. and Dunn, D. (2001) Beauty and believability in sexual harassment cases: does physical attractiveness affect perceptions of veracity and the likelihood of being harrassed, *Communication Research Reports*, 17, 203–209.

Seppänen, J. (2006) *The Power of the Gaze: An Introduction to Visual Literacy*. New York: Peter Lang.

Serewicz, D. and Canary, M. (2008) Assessments of disclosure from the in-laws: links among disclosure topics, family privacy orientations, and relational quality, *Journal of Social and Personal Relationships*, 25, 333–357.

Serewicz, M., Hosmer, R., Ballard, R. and Griffin, R. (2008) Disclosure from in-laws and the quality of in-law and marital relationships, *Communication Quarterly*, 56, 427–444.

Sevilla, C. (1999) *Disorder in the Court: Great Fractured Moments in Courtroom History*. New York: Norton.

Shaffer, D., Pegalis, L. and Cornell, D. (1992) Gender and self-disclosure revisited: personal and contextual variations in self-disclosure to same-sex acquaintances, *Journal of Social Psychology*, 132, 307–315.

Shah, J. and Kruglanski, A. (2000) Aspects of goal networks: implications for self-regulation, in M. Boekaerts, P. Pintrich and M. Zeidner (eds) *Handbook of Self-regulation*, San Diego, CA: Academic Press.

Shannon, C. and Weaver, W. (1949) *The Mathematical Theory of Communication*. Champaign, IL: University of Illinois Press.

Shapiro, D. (2000) Supplemental joint brainstorming: navigating past the perils of traditional bargaining, *Negotiation Journal*, 16, 409–419.

Sharkey, W. (1997) Why would anyone want to intentionally embarrass me?, in R. Kowalski (ed.) *Aversive Interpersonal Behaviors*. New York: Plenum Press.

Sharpley, C., Jeffrey, A. and McMah, T. (2006) Counsellor facial expression and client-perceived rapport, *Counselling Psychology Quarterly*, 19, 343–356.

Shaw, M. (1981) *Group Dynamics: The Psychology of Small Group Behavior*. New York: McGraw-Hill.

Shearman, S. and Yoo, J. (2007) 'Even a penny will help!' Legitimization of paltry donation and social proof in soliciting donation to a charitable organization, *Communication Research Reports*, 24, 271–282.

Sherif, M. (1936) *The Psychology of Social Norms*. New York: Harper & Row.

Sherman, W. (1990) *Behavior Modification*. New York: Harper and Row.

Shotter, J. (2009) Listening in a way that recognizes/realizes the world of 'the other', *International Journal of Listening*, 23, 21–43.

Showalter, J. T. (1974) Counselor nonverbal behavior as operant reinforcers for client self-references and expression of feelings, *Dissertation Abstracts International*, 35, 3435A.

Sidanius, J. and Pratto, F. (1999) *Social Dominance: An Intergroup Theory of Social Hierarchy and Oppression*. Cambridge: Cambridge University Press.

Sidnell, J. (2006) Coordinating gestures, talk, and gaze in re-enactments, *Research on Language and Social Interaction*, 39, 377–409.

Siegel, J. (1980) Effects of objective evidence of expertness, nonverbal behavior and subject sex on client-perceived expertness, *Journal of Counseling Psychology*, 27, 117–121.

Sigler, K., Burnett, A. and Child, J. (2008) A regional analysis of aseertiveness, *Journal of Intercultural Communication Research*, 37, 89–104.

Silberstang, J. and London, M. (2009) How groups learn: the role of communication patterns, cue recognition, context facility, and cultural intelligence, *Human Resource Development Review*, 8, 327–349.

Silver, R. (1970) Effects of subject status and interviewer response program on subject self-disclosure in standardized interviews. Paper presented at American Psychological Association Convention, Miami Beach, Florida, 3–8 September. http://eric.ed.gov/ERICDocs/data/ericdocs2sql/content_storage_01/0000019b/80/36/31/e6.pdf (accessed 2 December 2009).

Simi, N. and Mahalik, J. (1997) Comparison of feminist versus psychoanalytic/dynamic and other therapists on self-disclosure *Psychology of Women Quarterly*, 21, 465–483.

Siminoff, L., Graham, G. and Gordon, N. (2006) Cancer communication patterns and the influence of patient characteristics: disparities in information-giving and affective behaviors, *Patient Education and Counseling*, 62, 355–360.

Simon, B. (1999) A place in the world: self and social categorization, in T. Tyler, R. Kramer and O. John (eds) *The Psychology of the Social Self*. Mahwah, NJ: Lawrence Erlbaum Associates, Inc.

Simons, T. and Tripp, T. (2007) The negotiation checklist, in R. Lewicki, B. Barry and D. Saunders (eds) *Negotiation: Readings, Exercise and Cases*, 5th edn. New York: McGraw-Hill.

Singh, D. (1993) Body shape and women's attractiveness: the critical role of waist-to-hip ratio, *Human Nature*, 4, 297–321.

Singh, D. and Young, R. (1996) Body weight, waist-to-hip ratio, breasts, and hips: role of judgements of female attractiveness and desirability for relationships, *Ethology and Sociobiology*, 16, 483–507.

Singh, R., Onglatco, M., Sriram, N. and Tay, A. (1997) The warm–cold variable in impression formation: evidence for the positive–negative asymmetry, *British Journal of Social Psychology*, 36, 457–478.

Sinha, S. and Mukherjee, N. (1996) The effect of perceived co-operation on personal space requirements, *Journal of Social Psychology*, 136, 655–657.

Sinha, S., Alka, R. and Parul, V. (1999) Selective attention under conditions of varied demands, personal space and social density, *Journal of the Indian Academy of Applied Psychology*, 24, 105–108.

Sinha, V. (1972) Age differences in self-disclosure, *Developmental Psychology*, 7, 257–258.

Siraj-Blatchford, I. and Manni, L. (2008) 'Would you like to tidy up now?' An analysis of adult questioning in the English Foundation Stage, *Early Years*, 28, 5–22.

Skalski, P., Tamborini, R., Glazer, E. and Smith, S. (2009) Effects of humor on presence and recall of persuasive messages, *Communication Quarterly*, 57, 136–153.

Skarlicki, D., Folger, R. and Gee, J. (2004) When social accounts backfire: the exacerbating effects of a polite message or an apology on reactions to an unfair outcome, *Journal of Applied Social Psychology*, 34, 322–341.

Skelton, J. and Hobbs, F. (1999) Concordancing: use of language-based research in medical communication, *The Lancet*, 353, 108–111.

Skinner, B. (1953) *Science and Human Behaviour*. London: Collier Macmillan.

Skinner, B. (1957) *Verbal Behavior*. New York: Appleton-Century-Crofts.

Skinner, B. (1971) How to teach animals, in R. Atkinson (ed.) *Contemporary Psychology*. San Francisco, CA: Freeman.

Skinner, B. (1974) *About Behaviorism*. New York: Vintage Books.

Skinner, B. (1977) The force of coincidence, in B. Etzel, J. Le Blanc and D. Baer (eds) *New Developments in Behavioral Research: Theory, Method and Applications*. Hillsdale, NJ: Lawrence Erlbaum Associates, Inc.

Skogstad, A. and Einarsen, S. (1999) The importance of a change-centred leadership style in four organizational cultures, *Scandinavian Journal of Management*, 15, 289–306.

Skogstad, A., Einarsen, S., Torsheim, T., Aasland, M. and Hetland, H. (2007) The destructiveness of laissez-faire leadership behaviour, *Journal of Occupational Health Psychology*, 12, 80–92.

Skowronski, J., Carlston, D. and Hartnett, J. (2008) Spontaneous impressions derived from observations of behaviour: what a long, strange trip it's been (and it's not over), in N. Ambady and J. Skowronski (eds) *First Impressions*. New York: Guilford Press.

Skubisz, C., Reimer, T. and Hoffrage, U. (2009) Communicating quantitative risk information, in C. Beck (ed.) *Communication Yearbook 33*. New York: Routledge.

Slater, M. and Rouner, D. (2002) Entertainment-education and elaboration likelihood: understanding the processing of narrative persuasion, *Communication Theory*, 12, 173–191.

Smetana, J. (2008) 'It's 10 o'clock: do you know where your children are?' Recent advances in understanding parental monitoring and adolescents' information management, *Child Development Perspectives*, 2, 19–25.

Smetana, J., Metzger, A., Gettman, D. and Campione-Barr, N. (2006) Disclosure and secrecy in adolescent–parent relationships, *Child Development*, 77, 201–217.

Smith, E. (1999) Traditions of touch in psychotherapy, in E. Smith, P. Clance and S. Imes (ed.) *Touch in Psychotherapy: Theory, Research, and Practice*. New York: Guilford Press.

Smith, E. and Mackie, D. (2007) *Social Psychology*, 3rd edn. Hove and New York: Psychology Press.

Smith, F., Hardman, F. and Higgins, S. (2006) The impact of interactive whiteboards on teacher–pupil interaction in the National Literacy and Numeracy Strategies, *British Educational Research Journal*, 32, 443–457.

Smith, R. and Boster, F. (2009) Understanding the influence of others on perceptions of a message's advocacy: testing a two-step model, *Communication Monographs*, 76, 333–350.

Smith, R. and Smoll, F. (2007) Social-cognitive approach to coaching behaviors, in S. Jowett and D. Lavallee (eds) *Social Psychology in Sport*. Champaign, IL: Human Kinetics.

Smith, S. and Wilson, S. (eds) (2010) *New Directions in Interpersonal Communication Research*. Thousand Oaks, CA: Sage.

Snavely, W. and McNeil, J. (2008) Communicator style and social style: testing a theoretical interface, *Journal of Leadership and Organizational Studies*, 14, 219–232.

Snyder, M. (1987) *Public Appearances, Private Realities*. New York: Freeman Press.

Snyder, M. and Omoto, A. (2001) Basic research and practical problems: volunteerism and the psychology of individual and collective action, in W. Wosinska, R. Cialdini, D. Barrett and J. Reykowski (eds) *The Practice of Social Influence in Multiple Cultures*. Mahwah, NJ: Lawrence Erlbaum Associates, Inc.

Snyder, M. and Stukas, A. (2007) Interpersonal processes in context: understanding the influence of settings and situations on social interaction, in K. Fiedler (ed.) *Social Communication*. New York: Psychology Press.

Soetens, B., Braet, C., Dejonckheere, P. and Roets, A. (2006) 'When suppression backfires': the ironic effects of suppressing eating-related thoughts, *Journal of Health Psychology*, 11, 655–668.

Solano, C. and Dunnam, M. (1985) Two's company: self-disclosure and reciprocity in triads versus dyads, *Social Psychology Quarterly*, 48, 183–187.

Solnick, S. (2001) Gender differences in the ultimate game, *Economic Inquiry*, 39, 189–200.

Somech, A. (2005) Directive versus participative leadership: two complementary approaches to managing school effectiveness, *Educational Administration Quarterly*, 41, 777–800.

Sommer, R. (1969) *Personal Space*. Englewood Cliffs, NJ: Prentice-Hall.

Song, H. and Schwarz, N. (2010) If it's easy to read, it's easy to do, pretty, good, and true, *The Psychologist*, 23, 108–111.

Sopory, P. and Dillard, J. (2002) The persuasive effects of metaphor, *Human Communication Research*, 28, 382–419.

Sorenson, R., De Bord, G. and Ramirez, I. (2001) *Business and Management Communication: A Guide Book*, 4th edn. Upper Saddle River, NJ: Prentice Hall.

Sosik, J., Kahai, S. and Avolio, B. (2000) Leadership style, anonymity and creativity in group decision support systems: the mediating roe of optimal flow, *Journal of Creative Behavior*, 33, 227–250.

Spangenberg, E. and Greenwald, A. (2001) Self- prophecy as a behavior modification technique in the United State, in W. Wosinska, R. Cialdini, D. Barrett and J. Reykowski (eds) *The Practice of Social Influence in Multiple Cultures*. Mahwah, NJ: Lawrence Erlbaum Associates, Inc.

Spencer-Rodgers, J., Hamilton, D. and Sherman, S. (2007) The central role of entitativity in stereotypes of social categories and task groups, *Journal of Personality and Social Psychology*, 92, 369–388.

Spitzberg, B. and Cupach, W. (2007) *The Dark Side of Interpersonal Communication*, 2nd edn. London: Routledge.

Spooner, S. (1976) An investigation of the maintenance of specific counseling skills over time, *Dissertation Abstracts International*, February, 5840A.

Stangor, C. (2004) *Social Groups in Action and Interaction*. New York: Psychology Press.

Stefanko, P. and Ferjencik, J. (2000) Identification of dimensions of opener ability, *Studia Psychologica*, 42, 279–282.

Steil, L. (1991) Listening training: the key to success in today's organizations, in D. Borisoff and M. Purdy (eds) *Listening in Everyday Life*. Lanham, MD: University of America Press.

Stein, T., Frankel, R. and Krupat, E. (2005) Enhancing clinician communication skills in a large healthcare organization: a longitudinal case study, *Patient Education and Counseling*, 58, 14–12.

Sternberg, R. (1988) *The Triangle of Love*. New York: Basic Books.

Steuten, U. (2000) Rituals among rockers and bikers, *Soziale Welt-zeitschrift fur Sozialwissenschaftliche Forschung und Praxis*, 51, 25.

Stevanoni, E. and Salmon, K. (2005) Giving memory a hand: instructing children to gesture enhances their event recall, *Journal of Nonverbal Behavior*, 28, 245–266.

Stevens-Long, J. and McClintock, C. (2008) Co-presence and group processes in online management education, in C. Wankel, and R. DeFillippi (eds) *University and Corporate Innovations in Lifelong Learning*. Charlotte, NC: Information Age Publishing.

Stewart, C. (2009) Message construction and editing, in W. Eadie (ed.) *21st Century Communication: A Reference Handbook*. Thousand Oaks, CA: Sage.

Stewart, C. and Cash, W. (2008) *Interviewing: Principles and Practice*, 12th edn. Boston, MA: McGraw-Hill.

Stewart, G., Dustin, S., Barrick, M. and Darnold, T. (2008) Exploring the handshake in employment interviews, *Journal of Applied Psychology*, 93, 1139–1146.

Stewart, J. and Logan, C. (1998) *Together: Communicating Interpersonally*, 5th edn. Boston, MA: McGraw-Hill.

Stewart, J., Zediker, K. and Witteborn, S. (2005) *Together: Communicating Interpersonally*, 6th edn. Los Angeles, CA: Roxbury.

Stilgoe, F. (2008) *The Talking Cure: Why Conversation is the Future of Healthcare*. London: Demos. http://www.demos.co.uk/files/Talking%20cure%20final-web.pdf (accessed 2 December 2009).

Stivers, T. (2001) Negotiating who presents the problem: next speaker selection in pediatric encounters, *Journal of Communication*, 51, 252–282.

Stivers, T. and Majid, A. (2007) Questioning children: interactional evidence of implicit bias in medical interviews, *Social Psychology Quarterly*, 70, 424–441.

Stogdill, R. (1974) *Handbook of Leadership: A Survey of Theory and Research*. New York: Free Press.

Stone, J., Wiegand, A., Cooper, J. and Aronson, E. (1997) When exemplification fails: hypocrisy and the motive for self-integrity, *Journal of Personality and Social Psychology*, 72, 54–65.

Strack, F. and Förster, J. (2009) *Social Cognition: The Basis of Human Interaction*. Hove, UK: Psychology Press.

Straub, D. and Karahanna, E. (1998) Knowledge worker communications and recipient availability: towards a task-closure explanation of media choice, *Organisational Science*, 9, 160–175.

Stricker, G. (1990) Self-disclosure and psychotherapy, in G. Stricker and M. Fisher (eds) *Self-disclosure in the Therapeutic Relationship*. New York: Plenum Press.

Stroebe, M., Schut, H. and Stroebe W. (2006) Who benefits from disclosure? Exploration of attachment style differences in the effects of expressing emotions, *Clinical Psychology Review*, 26, 66–85.

Stroebe, W. (2000) *Social Psychology and Health*. Buckingham: Open University Press.

Strömwall, L. and Granhag, P. (2007) Detecting deceit in pairs of children, *Journal of Applied Social Psychology*, 37, 1285–1304.

Strong, R. (2005) *Decisions and Dilemmas: Case Studies in Presidential Foreign Policy Making Since 1945*, 2nd edn. Armonk, NY: ME Sharpe.

Strong, S., Taylor, R., Branon, J. and Loper, R. (1971) Nonverbal behavior and perceived counselor characteristics, *Journal of Counseling Psychology*, 18, 554–561.

Strong, T. (2006) Reflections on reflecting as a dialogic accomplishment in counseling, *Qualitative Health Research*, 16, 998–1013.

Sue, D., Sue, D. and Ino, S. (1990) Assertiveness and social anxiety in Chinese–American women, *Journal of Psychology*, 124, 155–164.

Suganuma, M. (1997) Self-disclosure and self-esteem in old age, *Japanese Journal of Psychology*, 45, 12–21.

Sullivan, H. (1953) *The Interpersonal Theory of Psychiatry*. New York: Norton.

Sullivan, H. (1954) *The Psychiatric Interview*. New York: Norton.

Sullivan, P. and Feltz, D. (2005) Applying social psychology to sports teams, in F. Schneider, J. Gruman and L. Coutts (eds) *Applied Social Psychology: Under-*

standing and Addressing Social and Practical Problems. Thousand Oaks, CA: Sage.

Suls, J. M. and Wheeler, L. (eds) (2001) *Handbook of Social Comparison: Theory and Research.* New York: Plenum Press.

Sun, Y., Shen, L. and Pan, Z. (2008) On the behavioral component of the third-person effect, *Communication Research,* 35, 257–278.

Susskind, L. and Mnookin, R. (1999) Major themes and prescriptive implications, in R. Mnookin and L. Susskind (eds) *Negotiating on Behalf of Others.* Thousand Oaks, CA: Sage.

Sutherland, K. and Wehby, J. (2001) The effect of self-evaluation of teaching behaviour in classrooms for students with emotional and behavioural disorders, *Journal of Special Education,* 35, 161–171.

Sutherland, K., Wehby, J. and Copeland, S. (2000) Effect of varying rates of behaviour-specific praise on the on-task behavior of students with EBD, *Journal of Emotional and Behavioral Disorders,* 8, 2–8.

Sutton, S. (1982) Fear arousing communication: a critical examination of theory and research, in J. Eiser (ed.) *Social Psychology and Behavioral Medicine.* New York: Wiley.

Suzuki, E. and Sleyman, K. (2006) Assertiveness and anxiety among the patients with neurosis, *Japanese Journal of Human Sciences of Health-Social Services,* 13, 27–32.

Swami, V. and Furnham, A. (2007a) *The Psychology of Physical Attraction.* London: Routledge.

Swami, V. and Furnham, A. (eds) (2007b) *The Body Beautiful: Evolutionary and Socio-Cultural Perspectives.* Basingstoke: Palgrave Macmillan.

Swami, V. and Tovée, M. (2006) Does hunger influence judgments of female physical attractiveness?, *British Journal of Psychology,* 97, 353–363.

Swami, V., Caprario, C., Tovée, M. and Furnham, A. (2006) Female physical attractiveness in Britain and Japan: a cross-cultural study, *European Journal of Personality,* 20, 69–81.

Swami, V., Neto, F., Tovee, M. and Furnham, A. (2007a) Preferences for female body weight and shape in three European countries, *European Psychologist,* 12, 220–228.

Swami, V., Furnham, A., Georgiades, C. and Pang, L. (2007b) Evaluating self and partner physical attractiveness, *Body Image,* 4, 97–101.

Swann, W. (2009) Self-verification theory, in H. Reis and S. Sprecher (eds) *Encyclopedia of Human Relationships.* Thousand Oaks, CA: Sage.

Swann, W., Chang-Schneider, C. and Angulo, S. (2007) Self-verification in relationships as an adaptive process, in J. Wood, A. Tesser and J. Holmes (eds) *Self and Relationships.* New York: Psychology Press.

Swanson, S. (1999) Re-examination of assertiveness and aggressiveness as potential moderators of verbal intentions, *Psychological Reports,* 84, 1111–1114.

Swanson, S. and McIntyre, R. (1998) Assertiveness and aggressiveness as potential moderators of consumers' verbal behavior following a failure of service, *Psychological Reports,* 82, 1239–1247.

Swift, J., Gooding, T. and Swift, P. (1988) Questions and wait time, in J. Dillon (ed.) *Questioning and Discussion: A Multidisciplinary Study.* Norwood, NJ: Ablex.

Takada, J. and Levine, T. (2007) The effects of the even-a-few-minutes-would-help strategy, perspective taking, and empathic concern on the successful recruiting of volunteers on campus, *Communication Research Reports*, 24, 177–184.

Tallman, K., Janisse, T., Frankel, R., Sung, S., Krupat, E. and Hsu, J. (2007) Communication practices of physicians with high patient-satisfaction ratings, *The Permanente Journal*, 11, 19–29.

Tannen, D. (1995) Asymmetries: women and men talking at cross-purposes, in J. Stewart (ed.) *Bridges not Walls: A Book about Interpersonal Communication*. New York: McGraw-Hill.

Tannen, D., Kendall, S. and Gordon, C. (eds) (2007) *Family Talk: Discourse and Identity in Four American Families*. Oxford: Oxford University Press.

Tardy, C. (1988) Self-disclosure: objectives and methods of measurement, in C. Tardy (ed.) *A Handbook for the Study of Human Communication*. Norwood, NJ: Ablex.

Tardy, C. (2000) Self-disclosure and health: revisiting Sidney Jourard's hypothesis, in S. Petronio (ed.) *Balancing the Secrets of Private Disclosures*. Mahwah, NJ: Lawrence Erlbaum Associates, Inc.

Tardy, C. and Dindia, K. (2006) Self-disclosure: strategic revelation of information in personal and professional relationships, in O. Hargie (ed.) *The Handbook of Communication* Skills, 3rd edn. London: Routledge.

Taylor, D. and Altman, I. (1987) Communication in interpersonal relationships: social penetration processes, in M. Roloff and G. Miller (ed.) *Interpersonal Processes: New Directions in Communications Research*. Newbury Park, CA: Sage.

Taylor, K., Mesmer-Magnus, J. and Burns, T. (2008) Teaching the art of negotiation: improving students' negotiating confidence and perceptions of effectiveness, *Journal of Education for Business*, 83, 135–140.

Taylor, O. (1997) Student interpretations of teacher verbal praise in selected seventh- and eight-grade choral classes, *Journal of Research in Music Education*, 45, 536–546.

Taylor, P. (2002) A cylindrical model of communication behavior in crisis negotiations, *Human Communication Research*, 28, 7–48.

Taylor, S., Neter, E. and Wayment, H. (1995) Self-evaluation processes, *Personality and Social Psychology Bulletin*, 21, 1278–1287.

Teiford, J. (2007) *Social Perception: 21st Century Issues and Challenges*. New York: Nova Science Publishers.

Temple, L. and Loewen, K. (1993) Perception of power: first impressions of a woman wearing a jacket, *Perceptual and Motor Skills*, 76, 339–348.

Ternes, M. and Yuille, J. (2008) Eyewitness memory and eyewitness identification performance in adults with intellectual disabilities, *Journal of Applied Research in Intellectual Disabilities*, 21, 519–531.

Tesser, A. (1988) Toward a self-evaluation maintenance model of social behavior, in L. Berkowitz (ed.) *Advances in Experimental Social Psychology, Vol. 21*, New York: Academic Press.

Tesser, A. (2001) Self-esteem, in A. Tesser and N. Schwarz (eds) *Blackwell Handbook of Social Psychology: Intraindividual Processes*. Oxford: Blackwell.

Tessonneau, A. (2005) Learning respect in Guadeloupe, in S. Muhleisen and B. Migge (eds) *Politeness and Face in Caribbean Creoles*. Amsterdam: John Benjamins.

Teyber, E. (2006) *Interpersonal Process in Therapy: An Integrative Model*, 5th edn. Belmont, CA: Thomson Brooks/Cole.

Thibaut, J. and Kelley, H. (1959) *The Social Psychology of Groups*. New York: Wiley.

Thomas A. and Bull, P. (1981) The role of pre-speech posture change in dyadic interaction, *British Journal of Social Psychology*, 20, 105–111.

Thomas, K. (1976) Conflict and conflict management, in M. Dunnette (ed.) *Handbook of Industrial and Organizational Psychology*. Chicago, IL: Rand McNally.

Thomas, L. and Levine, T. (1994) Disentangling listening and verbal recall: related but separate constructs?, *Human Communication Research*, 21, 103–127.

Thomas, L. and Levine, T. (1996) Further thoughts on recall, memory, and the measurement of listening: a rejoinder to Bostrom, *Human Communication Research*, 23, 306–308.

Thompson, C. and Born, D. (1999) Increasing correct participation in an exercise class for adult day care clients, *Behavioral Interventions*, 14, 171–186.

Thompson, L. (1990) Negotiation behavior and outcomes: empirical evidence and theoretical issues, *Psychological Bulletin*, 108, 515–532.

Thompson, L. (2005) *The Mind and Heart of the Negotiator*, 3rd edn. Upper Saddle River, NJ: Pearson.

Thompson, T. (1998) The patient/health professional relationship, in L. Jackson and B. Duffy (eds) *Health Communication Research: A Guide To Developments and Directions*. Westport, CT: Greenwood Press.

Thorne, A. (2000) Personal memory telling and personality development, *Personality and Social Psychology Review*, 4, 45–56.

Thyne, J. (1963) *The Psychology of Learning and Techniques of Teaching*. London: University of London Press.

Tice, D. and Wallace, H. (2005) The reflected self: creating yourself as (you think) others see you, in M. Leary and J. Tangney (eds) *Handbook of Self and Identity*. New York: Guilford Press.

Tiedens, L. and Leach, C. (2004) *The Social Life of Emotions*. Cambridge: Cambridge University Press.

Tierney, E. (1996) *How to Make Effective Presentations*. Thousand Oaks, CA: Sage.

Tiersma, P. (2006) *Communicating with Juries: How to Draft More Understandable Jury Instructions*. Williamsburg, VA: National Center for State Courts. http://www.ncsconline.org/Juries/Communicating.pdf (accessed 2 December 2009).

Timberlake, W. and Allison, J. (1974) Response deprivation: an empirical approach to instrumental performance, *Psychological Review*, 81, 146–164.

Timmers, R. and van der Wijst, P. (2007) Images as anti-smoking fear appeals: the effect of emotion on the persuasion process, *Information Design Journal*, 15, 21–36.

Tizard, B., Hughes, M., Carmichael, H. and Pinkerton, G. (1983) Childrens' questions and adult answers, *Journal of Child Psychology and Psychiatry*, 24, 269–281.

Tobin, K. (1987) The role of wait time in higher cognitive learning, *Review of Educational Research*, 57, 69–95.

Togo, D. and Hood, J. (1992) Quantitative information presentation and gender: an interaction effect, *Journal of General Psychology*, 119, 161–167.

Tormala, Z. and Petty, R. (2007) Contextual contrast and perceived knowledge: exploring the implications for persuasion, *Journal of Experimental Social Psychology*, 43, 17–30.

Tormala, Z., Clarkson, J. and Petty, R. (2006) Resisting persuasion by the skin of one's teeth: the hidden success of resisted persuasive messages, *Journal of Personality and Social Psychology*, 91, 423–435.

Torrecillas, F., Martin, I., De la Fuente, E. and Godoy, J. (2000) Attributional style, self-control, and assertiveness as predictors of drug abuse, *Psicothema*, 12, 331–334.

Torres, C. (2000) Leadership style norms among Americans and Brazilians: assessing differences using Jackson's return potential model, *Dissertation Abstracts International: Section B: the Sciences and Engineering*, 60(8-B), 4284.

Tourish, D. (1999) Communicating beyond individual bias, in A. Long (ed.) *Interaction for Practice in Community Nursing*. Basingstoke: Macmillan.

Tourish, D. and Hargie, O. (2000) Communication and organisational success, in O. Hargie and D. Tourish (eds) *Handbook of Communication Audits for Organisations*. London: Routledge.

Tourish, D. and Hargie, O. (eds) (2004) *Key Issues in Organizational Communication*. London: Routledge.

Tourish, D. and Pinnington, A. (2002) Transformational leadership, corporate cultism and the spirituality paradigm: an unholy trinity in the workplace, *Human Relations*, 55, 147–172.

Tourish, D. and Wohlforth, T. (2000) *On the Edge: Political Cults Right and Left*. Armonk, NY: ME Sharpe.

Tourish, D., Pinnington, A. and Braithwaite-Anderson, S. (2007) *Evaluating Leadership Development in Scotland*. Aberdeen: Aberdeen Business School, Robert Gordon University.

Tourish, D., Collinson, D. and Barker, J. (2009) Manufacturing conformity: leadership through coercive persuasion in business organizations, *M@n@gement*, 12, 360–383.

Tourish, D., Craig, R. and Amernic, J. (2010) Transformational leadership education and agency perspectives in business school pedagogy: a marriage of inconvenience?, *British Journal of Management*, 21, S40–S59.

Townend, A. (2007) *Assertiveness and Diversity*. Basingstoke: Palgrave.

Tracy, K. and Coupland, N. (1990) Multiple goals in discourse: an overview of issues, *Journal of Language and Social Psychology*, 9, 1–13.

Tracy, R. and Robins, J. (2007) Self-conscious emotions: where self and emotion meet, in C. Sedikides and S. Spencer (eds) *The Self*. New York: Psychology Press.

Trenholm, S. and Jensen, A. (2007) *Interpersonal Communication*, 6th edn. New York: Oxford University Press.

Triesma, E. (1995) Dictionaries and death: do capital jurors understand mitigation?, *Utah Law Review*, 1, 20–69.

Trinidad, C. and Normore, A. (2005) Leadership and gender: a dangerous liaison?, *Leadership and Organization Development Journal*, 26, 574–590.

Tubbs, S. (1998) *A Systems Approach to Small Group Interaction*, 6th edn. Boston, MA: McGraw-Hill.

Tuckman, B. (1965) Developmental sequence in small groups, *Psychological Bulletin*, 63, 384–399.

Tuckman, B. and Jensen, M. (1977) Stages in small group development revisited, *Group and Organizational Studies*, 2, 419–427.

Turk, C. (1985) *Effective Speaking*. London: E. & F. N. Spon.

Turkat, I. and Alpher, V. (1984) Prediction versus reflection in therapist demonstrations of understanding: three analogue experiments, *British Journal of Medical Psychology*, 57, 235–240.

Turner, J. and Reinsch, L. (2007) The business communicator as presence allocator: multicommunicating, equivocality, and status at work, *Journal of Business Communication*, 44, 36–58.

Turner, M., Tamborini, R., Limon, M. and Zuckerman-Hyman, C. (2007) The moderators and mediators of door-in-the-face requests: is it a negotiation or a helping experience?, *Communication Monographs*, 74, 333–356.

Turney, C., Ellis, K., Hatton, N., Owens, L., Towler, J. and Wright, R. (1983) *Sydney Micro Skills Redeveloped: Series 1 and 2 Handbooks*, Sydney: Sydney University Press.

Turton, J. (1998) Importance of information following myocardial infarction: a study of the self-perceived needs of patients and their spouse/partner compared with the perceptions of nursing staff, *Journal of Advanced Nursing*, 27, 770–778.

Tusing, K. and Dillard, J. (2000) The sounds of dominance: vocal precursors of perceived dominance during interpersonal influence, *Human Communication Research*, 26, 148–171.

Tutton, E. (1991) An exploration of touch and its uses in nursing, in R. McMahon and A. Pearson (eds) *Nursing as Therapy*. London: Chapman and Hall.

Tversky, A. and Kahneman, D. (1981) The framing of decisions and the rationality of choice, *Science*, 211, 453–458.

Twenge, J. (1998) Assertiveness, sociability, and anxiety, *Dissertation Abstracts International: The Sciences and Engineering*, 59(2-B), 0905.

Twenge, J. (2006) *Generation Me: Why Today's Young Americans are More Confident, Assertive, Entitled – and More Miserable Than Ever Before*. New York: Simon & Schuster.

Uhlemann, M., Lea, G. and Stone, G. (1976) Effect of instructions and modeling on trainees low in interpersonal communication skills, *Journal of Counseling Psychology*, 23, 509–513.

Unzueta, M., Lowery, B. and Knowles, E. (2008) How believing in affirmative action quotas protects white men's self-esteem, *Organizational Behavior and Human Decision Processes*, 105, 1–13.

Ury, W. (2007) *The Power of a Positive No: How to Say No and Still Get to Yes*. New York: Bantam.

Uzell, D. and Horne, N. (2006) The influence of biological sex, sexuality and gender role on interpersonal distance, *British Journal of Social Psychology*, 45, 579–597.

van de Ridder, J., Stokking, K., McGaghie, W. and Cate, O. (2008) What is feedback in clinical education?, *Medical Education*, 42, 189–197.

Van Der Merwe, J. (1995) Physician–patient communication using ancestral spirits to achieve holistic healing, *American Journal of Obstetrics and Gynecology*, 1172, 1080–1087.

Van der Molen, H. and Gramsbergen-Hoogland, Y. (2005) *Communication in Organizations: Basic Skills and Conversation Models*. Hove, UK: Psychology Press.

van Dick, R., Tissington, P. and Hertel, G. (2009) Do many hands make light work? How to overcome social loafing and gain motivation in work teams, *European Business Review*, 21, 233–245.

Van Kleef, G., De Dreu, C., Pietroni, D. and Manstead, A. (2006) Power and emotion in negotiation: power moderates the interpersonal effects of anger and happiness on concession making, *European Journal of Social Psychology*, 36, 557–581.

Van Kleef, G., van Dijk, E., Steinel, W., Harinck, F. and Beest, I. (2008) Anger in social conflict: cross-situational comparisons and suggestions for the future, *Group Decision and Negotiation*, 17, 13–30.

Van Slyke, E. (1999) *Listening to Conflict: Finding Constructive Solutions to Workplace Disputes*. New York: AMACOM.

Van Yperen, N. and Van de Vliert, E. (2001) Social psychology in organizations, in M. Hewstone, and W. Stroebe (eds) *Introduction to Social Psychology*, 3rd edn. Oxford: Blackwell.

Vangelisti, A. and Caughlin, J. (1997) Revealing family secrets: the influence of topic, function, and relationships, *Journal of Social and Personal Relationships*, 14, 679–705.

Vangelisti, A. and Hampel, A. (2010) Hurtful communication: current research and future directions, in S. Smith and S. Wilson (eds) *New Directions in Interpersonal Communication Research*. Thousand Oaks, CA: Sage.

Vecchio, R. and Boatwright, K. (2002) Preferences for idealized styles of supervision, *Leadership Quarterly*, 13, 327–342.

Verner, C. and Dickinson, G. (1967) The lecture, an analysis and review of research, *Adult Education*, 17, 85–100.

Vishwanath, A. (2006) The effects of number of opinion seekers and leaders on technology attitudes and choices, *Human Communication Research*, 32, 322–350.

Vittengl, J. and Holt, C. (2000) Getting acquainted: the relationship of self-disclosure and social attraction to positive affect, *Journal of Social and Personal Relationships*, 17, 53–66.

Vondracek, F. (1969) The study of self-disclosure in experimental interviews, *Journal of Psychology*, 72, 55–59.

Vouloumanos, A. and Werker, J. (2007) Listening to language at birth: evidence for a bias for speech in neonates, *Developmental Science*, 10, 159–164.

Vrij, A. (2000) *Detecting Lies and Deceit: The Psychology of Lying and the Implications for Professional Practice*. Chichester: Wiley.

Vrij, A. (2001) Detecting the liars, *The Psychologist*, 14, 596–598.

Vrij, A. (2006) Nonverbal communication and deceit, in V. Manusov and M. Patterson (eds) *The Sage Handbook of Nonverbal Communication*. Thousand Oaks, CA: Sage.

Vrij, A. (2007) Deception: a social lubricant and a selfish act, in K. Fiedler (ed.) *Social Communication*. New York: Psychology Press.

Vrij, A., Edward, K., Roberts, K. and Bull, R. (2000) Detecting deceit via analysis of verbal and nonverbal behavior, *Journal of Nonverbal Behavior*, 24, 239–263.

Wagner, H. and Lee, V. (1999) Facial behavior alone and in the presence of others, in P. Philippot, R. Feldman and E. Coats (eds) *The Social Context of Nonverbal Behavior*. Cambridge: Cambridge University Press.

Waldo, C. and Kemp, J. (1997) Should I come out to my students? An empirical investigation, *Journal of Homosexuality*, 34, 79–94.

Waldron, V., Cegala, D., Sharkey, F. and Teboul, B. (1990) Cognitive and tactical dimensions of conversational goal management, *Journal of Language and Social Psychology*, 9, 101–118.

Walker, A. (1999) *Handbook on Questioning Children: A Linguistic Perspective.* Washington, DC: ABA Center on Children and the Law.

Walker, J. (2001) *Control and the Psychology of Health.* Buckingham: Open University Press.

Walker, K. (1997) Do you ever listen? Discovering the theoretical underpinnings of empathic listening, *International Journal of Listening*, 11, 127–137.

Walker, M. and Antony-Black, J. (eds) (1999) *Hidden Selves: An Exploration of Multiple Personality.* London: Routledge.

Walker, N. and Hunt, J. (1998) Interviewing child victim-witnesses: how you ask is what you get, in C. Thompson, D. Herrmann, J. Read, D. Bruce, D. Payne and M. Toglia (eds) *Eyewitness Memory: Theoretical and Applied Perspectives.* Mahwah, NJ: Lawrence Erlbaum Associates, Inc.

Wallach, J. (1986) *Looks That Work.* New York: Viking Penguin.

Wallihan, J. (1998) Negotiating to avoid agreement, *Negotiation Journal*, 14, 257–268.

Walma van der Molen, J. and van der Voort, T. (2000) The impact of television, print, and audio on children's recall of the news: a study of three alternative explanations for the dual-coding hypothesis, *Human Communication Research*, 26, 3–26.

Wang, J. (2006) Questions and the exercise of power, *Discourse Society*, 17, 529–548.

Wänke, M. (2007) What is said and what is meant: conversational implicatures in natural conversations, research settings, media, and advertising, in K. Fiedler (ed.) *Social Communication.* New York: Psychology Press.

Wanzer, M., Frymier, A. and Irwin, J. (2010) An explanation of the relationship between instructor humor and student learning: instructional humor processing theory, *Communication Education*, 59, 1–18.

Ward, M., Doherty, D. and Moran, R. (2007) *It's Good to Talk: Distress Disclosure and Psychological Wellbeing.* Dublin: Health Research Board.

Waring, E., Holden, R. and Wesley, S. (1998) Development of the marital self-disclosure questionnaire, *Journal of Clinical Psychology*, 54, 817–824.

Warner, L., Lumley, M., Casey, R., Pierantoni, W., Salazar, R., Zoratti, E., Enberg, R. and Simon, M. (2006) Health effects of written emotional disclosure in adolescents with asthma: a randomized, controlled trial, *Journal of Pediatric Psychology*, 31, 557–568.

Warren, L. and Hixenbaugh, P. (1998) Adherence and diabetes, in L. Myers and K. Midence (eds) *Adherence to Treatment in Medical Conditions.* Amsterdam: Harwood.

Waskow, I. (1962) Reinforcement in a therapy-like situation through selective responding to feelings or contect, *Journal of Consulting Psychology*, 26, 11–19.

Wasserman, E. and Neunaber, D. (1986) College students' responding to and rating of contingency relations: the role of temporal contiguity, *Journal of the Experimental Analysis of Behavior*, 46, 15–35.

Waterman, A., Blades, M. and Spencer, C. (2001) Is a jumper angrier than a tree?, *The Psychologist*, 14, 474–477.

Waterman, A., Blades, M. and Spencer, C. (2004) Indicating when you do not know the answer: the effect of question format and interviewer knowledge on children's 'don't know' responses, *British Journal of Developmental Psychology*, 22, 335–348.

Watkins, M. (2006) *The New Leader's Guide to Effective Negotiation*. Boston, MA: Harvard Business School Press.

Watson, K. and Barker, L. (1984) Listening behavior: definition and measurement, in R. Bostrom and B. Westley (eds) *Communication Yearbook 8*. Beverly Hills, CA: Sage.

Watzlawick, P., Beavin, J. and Jackson, D. (1967) *Pragmatics of Human Communication*. New York: Norton.

Wearden, J. (1988) Some neglected problems in the analysis of human operant behavior, in G. Davey and C. Cullen (eds) *Human Operant Conditioning and Behavior Modification*. New York: Wiley.

Webb, P. (1994) Teaching and learning about health and illness, in P. Webb (ed.) *Health Promotion and Patient Education*. London: Chapman and Hall.

Weber, K., Martin, M. and Corrigan, M. (2006) Creating persuasive messages advocating organ donation, *Communication Quarterly*, 54, 67–87.

Weber, M. (1947) *The Theory of Social and Economic Organizations*. New York: Free Press.

Webster, P. (1984) An ethnographic study of handshaking. Unpublished doctoral dissertation, Boston University.

Weger, H., Castle, G. and Emmett, M. (2010) Active listening in peer interviews: the influence of message paraphrasing on perceptions of listening skill, *International Journal of Listening*, 24, 34–49.

Wegner, D. (1994) Ironic processes of mental control, *Psychological Review*, 101, 34–52.

Weingart, L., Prietula, M., Hyder, B. and Genovese, R. (1999) Knowledge and the sequential processes of negotiation: a Markov chain analysis of response-in-kind, *Journal of Experimental Social Psychology*, 35, 366–393.

Weinstein, N. and Sandman, P. (2002) Reducing the risks of exposure to radon gas: an application of the Precaution Adoption Process Model, in D. Rutter and L. Quine (eds) *Changing Health Behaviour*. Buckingham: Open University Press.

Weirzbicka, A. (2004) The English expressions good boy and good girl and cultural models of child rearing, *Culture and Psychology*, 10, 251–278.

Weisbuch, M., Unkelbach, C. and Fiedler, K. (2008) Remnants of the recent past: influences of priming on first impressions, in N. Ambady and J. Skowronski (eds) *First Impressions*. New York: Guilford Press.

Weisbuch, M., Slepian, M., Clarke, A., Ambady, N. and Veenstra-VanderWeele, J. (2010) Behavioral stability across time and situations: nonverbal versus verbal consistency, *Journal of of Nonverbal Behavior*, 34, 43–56.

Weitlauf, J., Smith, R. and Cervone, D. (2000) Generalization effects of coping-skills training: influence of self-defense training on women's efficacy beliefs, *Journal of Applied Psychology*, 85, 625–633.

Weitzman, P. and Weitzman, E. (2000) Interpersonal negotiation strategies in a sample of older women, *Journal of Clinical Geropsychology*, 6, 41–51.

Wert, S. and Salovey, P. (2004) A social comparison account of gossip, *Review of General Psychology*, 8, 122–137.

West, C. (1983) Ask me no questions . . . an analysis of queries and replies in physician–patient dialogues, in S. Fisher and A. Todd (eds) *The Social Organization of Doctor–Patient Communication*. Washington, DC: Center for Applied Linguistics.

West, C. (2006) Coordinating closings in primary care visits: producing continuity of care, in J. Heritage and D. Maynard (eds) *Communication in Medical Care Interaction between Primary Care Physicians and Patients*. Cambridge: Cambridge University Press.

Westmyer, R. and Rubin, R. (1998) Appropriateness and effectiveness of communication channels in competent interpersonal communication, *Journal of Communication*, 48, 27–48.

Wetherell, M. (1996) Life histories/social histories, in M. Wetherell (ed.) *Identities, Groups and Social Issues*. London: Sage.

Whaley, B. and Wagner, L. (2000) Rebuttal analogy in persuasive messages: communicator likability and cognitive responses, *Journal of Language and Social Psychology*, 19, 66–84.

Wheelan, S. (2004) *Group Process: A Developmental Perspective*, 2nd edn. Boston, MA: Allyn and Bacon.

Wheelan, S. (2005) *The Handbook of Group Research and Practice*. Thousand Oaks, CA: Sage.

Wheeless, L., Erickson, K. and Behrens, J. (1986) Cultural differences in disclosiveness as a function of locus of control, *Communication Monographs*, 53, 36–46.

Wheldall, K. and Glynn, T. (1989) *Effective Classroom Learning: A Behavioural Interactionist Approach to Teaching*. Oxford: Blackwell.

Wheldall, K., Bevan, K. and Shortall, K. (1986) A touch of reinforcement: the effects of contingent teacher touch on the classroom behaviour of young children, *Educational Review*, 38, 207–216.

Whetzel, D. and McDaniel, M. (1999) The employment interview, in A. Memon and R. Bull (eds) *Handbook of the Psychology of Interviewing*. Chichester: Wiley.

White, B. and Saunders, S. (1986) The influence on patients' pain intensity ratings of antecedent reinforcement of pain talk or well talk, *Journal of Behaviour Therapy and Experimental Psychiatry*, 17, 155–159.

White, C. and Burgoon, J. (2001) Adaptation and communicative design patterns of interaction in truthful and deceptive conversations, *Human Communication Research*, 27, 9–37.

White, J., Rosson, C., Christensen, J., Hart, R. and Levinson, W. (1997) Wrapping things up: a qualitative analysis of the closing moments of the medical visit, *Patient Education and Counseling*, 30, 155–165.

Whitney, G. (1990) Before you negotiate: get your act together, in I. Asherman and S. Asherman (eds) *The Negotiating Sourcebook*, Amherst, MA: Human Resource Development Press.

Whitty, M. and Carr, A. (2006) *Cyberspace Romance: The Psychology of Online Relationships*. Basingstoke: Palgrave Macmillan.

Widener, C. (2005) Dos and don'ts at the podium, *Journal of Accountancy*, 200, 32.

Wigboldus, D., Spears, R. and Semin, G. (1999) Categorisation, content and the context of communicative behaviour, in N. Ellemers, R. Spears and B. Doosje (eds) *Social Identity*. Oxford: Blackwell.

Wiksell, W. (1946) The problem of listening, *Quarterly Journal of Speech*, 32, 505–508.

Wildermuth, S., Vogl-Bauer, S. and Rivera, J. (2007) Practically perfect in every way: communication strategies of ideal relational partners, *Communication Studies*, 57, 239–257.

Wilding, J., Cook, S. and Davis, J. (2000) Sound familiar, *The Psychologist*, 13, 558–562.

Wilke, H. and Wit, A. (2001) Group performance, in M. Hewstone, and W. Stroebe (eds) *Introduction to Social Psychology*, 3rd edn. Oxford: Blackwell.

Wilkins, P. (2003) *Person-centred Therapy in Focus*. London: Sage.

Willemyns, M., Gallois, C., Callan, V. and Pittam, J. (1997) Accent accommodation in the job interview: impact of interviewer accent and gender, *Journal of Language and Social Psychology*, 16, 3–22.

Williams, A. and Nussbaum, J. (2001) *Intergenerational Communication Across the Life Span*. Mahwah, NJ: Lawrence Erlbaum Associates, Inc.

Williams, C. (1997) A cross-cultural participant–observer description of intra-cultural communication behaviors: the greetings and partings of the Saramakan Bushnegroes, *Dissertation Abstracts International: Humanities and Social Sciences*, 58(3-A), 0648.

Williams, E. and Akridge, R. (1996) The Responsible Assertion Scale: development and evaluation of psychometric qualities, *Vocational Evaluation and Work Adjustment Bulletin*, 29, 19–23.

Williams, K. and Dolnik, L. (2001) Revealing the worst first: stealing thunder as a social influence strategy, in J. Forgas and K. Williams (eds) *Social Influence: Direct and Indirect Processes*. Philadelphia, PA: Psychology Press.

Williams, K. and Zadiro, L. (2001) Ostracism: on being ignored, excluded, and rejected, in M. Leary (ed.) *Interpersonal Rejection*. Oxford: Oxford University Press.

Williamson, T. (ed.) (2005) *Investigative Interviewing: Rights, Research, Regulation*. Uffculme: Willan.

Willis, F. and Dodds, R. (1998) Age, relationships and touch initiation, *Journal of Social Psychology*, 138, 115–124.

Willis, F. and Hamm, H. (1980) The use of interpersonal touch in securing compliance, *Journal of Nonverbal Behavior*, 5, 49–55.

Willis, J. and Todorov, A. (2006) First impressions: making up your mind after a 100-ms exposure to a face, *Psychological Science*, 17, 592–598.

Wilmot, W. (1995) The transactional nature of person perception, in J. Stewart (ed.) *Bridges not Walls: A Book About Interpersonal Communication*. New York: McGraw-Hill.

Wilson, G. (2004) *Groups in Context: Leadership and Participation in Small Groups*, 7th edn. Boston: McGraw-Hill.

Wilson, G. and Nias, D. (1999) Beauty can't be beat, in L. Guerrero and J. DeVito (eds) *The Nonverbal Communication Reader: Classic and Contemporary Readings*. Prospect Heights, IL: Waveland Press.

Wilson, J. (1990) *Politically Speaking: The Pragmatic Analysis of Political Language*. Oxford: Blackwell.

Wilson K. and Gallois C. (1993) *Assertion and Its Social Context*. Oxford: Pergamon Press.

Wilson, S. (2006) Communication theory and the concept of 'goal', in B. Whaley and W. Samter (eds) *Explaining Communication: Contemporary Theories and Exemplars*. Mahwah, NJ: Lawrence Erlbaum Associates, Inc.

Wilson, S. (2010) Seeking and resisting compliance, in C. Berger, M. Roloff and D. Roskos-Ewoldsen (eds) *The Handbook of Communication Science*. Thousand Oaks, CA: Sage.

Wilson, S., Greene, J. and Dillard, J. (2000) Introduction to the special issue on message production: progress, challenges and prospects, *Communication Theory*, 10, 135–138.

Wilson, S., Paulson, G. and Putnam, L. (2001) Negotiating, in W. Robinson and H. Giles (eds) *The Handbook of Language and Social Psychology*, Chichester: Wiley.

Wilson-Barnett, J. (1981) Communicating with patients in general wards, in W. Bridge and J. MacLeod Clark (eds) *Communication in Nursing Care*. London: Croom Helm.

Wiltermuth, S. and Heath, C. (2009) Synchrony and cooperation, *Psychological Science*, 20, 1–5.

Windschitl, M. (2001) Using simulations in the middle school: does assertiveness of dyad partners influence conceptual change?, *International Journal of Science Education*, 23, 17–32.

Wit, A. (2000) Interacting in groups, in O. Hargie (ed.) *The Handbook of Communication Skills*, 3rd edn. London: Routledge.

Wittebols, J. (2004) *The Soap Opera Paradigm: Television Programming and Corporate Priorities*. Lanham, MD: Rowman & Littlefield.

Wojciszke, B. (2001) The consequences of being an influential minority in the context of social controversies in the emerging Polish democracy, in W. Wosinska, R. Cialdini, D. Barrett and J. Reykowski (eds) *The Practice of Social Influence in Multiple Cultures*. Mahwah, NJ: Lawrence Erlbaum Associates, Inc.

Wolfe, C. (2007) Contingencies of worth, in R. Baumeister and K. Vohs (eds) *Encyclopedia of Social Psychology*. Thousand Oaks, CA: Sage.

Wolff, F., Marsnik, N., Taccy, W. and Nichols, R. (1983) *Perceptive Listening*. New York: Holt, Rinehart and Winston.

Wolff, K. (1950) *The Sociology of Georg Simmel*. New York: Free Press.

Wolpe, J. (1958) *Psychotherapy by Reciprocal Inhibition*. Stanford, CA: Stanford University Press.

Wolvin, A. (2009) Listening, understanding and misunderstanding, in W. Eadie (ed.) *21st Century Communication: A Reference Handbook*. Thousand Oaks, CA: Sage.

Wolvin, A. and Coakley, C. (1996) *Listening*, 5th edn. Boston, MA: McGraw-Hill.

Wood, J. (2004) *Interpersonal Communication: Everyday Encounters*, 4th edn. Belmont, CA: Wadsworth.

Wood, J. (2007) *Gendered Lives: Communication, Gender, and Culture*, 7th edn. Belmont, CA: Wadsworth.

Wood, J. (2009) Gender, in W. Eadie (ed.) *21st Century Communication: A Reference Handbook*. Thousand Oaks, CA: Sage.

Wood, R. and Williams, R. (2007) 'How much money do you spend on gambling?' The comparative validity of question wordings used to assess gambling expenditure, *International Journal of Social Research Methodology*, 10, 63–77.

Wood, T. (2001) Team negotiations require a team approach, *The American Salesman*, 46, 22–26.

Woodbury, H. (1984) The strategic use of questions in court, *Semiotica*, 48, 197–228.

Woodward, K. (2000) Questions of identity, in K. Woodward (ed.) *Questioning Identity: Gender, Class, Nation*. London: Routledge.

Woodworth, R. and Marquis, D. (1949) *Psychology: A Study of Mental Life*. London: Methuen.

Woolfolk, A. (1998) *Educational Psychology*, 7th edn. Needham Heights, MA: Allyn & Bacon.

Woolfolk, A. (2005) *Educational Psychology*, 9th edn. Harlow: Pearson.

Worchel, S. (1994) You can go home again: returning group research to the group context with an eye on developmental contexts, *Small Group Research*, 25, 205–223.

Worland, P. (1998) Proctor feedback in a modified PSI course format: the effects of praise, encouragement and group information, *Dissertation Abstracts International: Section B: The Sciences and Engineering*, 59(6-B), 3107.

Worley, D., Titsworth, S., Worley, D. W. and Cornett-DeVito, M. (2007) Instructional communication competence: lessons learned from award-winning teachers, *Communication Studies*, 58, 207–222.

Wragg, E. and Brown, G. (2001) *Explaining in the Secondary School*. London: RoutledgeFalmer.

Wright, C. and Nuthall, G. (1970) Relationships between teacher behaviors and pupil achievement in three experimental elementary science lessons, *American Educational Research Journal*, 7, 477–493.

Wright, D., Gaskell, G. and O'Muircheartaigh, C. (1997) How response alternatives affect different kinds of behavioural frequency questions, *British Journal of Social Psychology*, 36, 443–456.

Wright, P. (1980) Message-evoked thoughts: persuasion research using thought verbalizations, *Journal of Consumer Research*, 7, 151–175.

Wright, R. and Powell, M. (2006) Investigative interviewers' perceptions of their difficulty in adhering to open-ended questions with child witnesses, *International Journal of Police Science and Management*, 8, 316–325.

Wyatt, R., Katz, E. and Kim, J. (2000) Bridging the spheres: political and personal conversation in public and private spaces, *Journal of Communication*, 50, 71–92.

Wyer, R. and Gruenfeld, D. (1995) Information processing in interpersonal communication, in D. Hewes (ed.) *The Cognitive Basis of Interpersonal Communication*. Hillsdale, NJ: Lawrence Erlbaum Associates, Inc.

Wynn, R. (1996) Medical students, doctors – is there a difference?, *Text*, 16, 423–448.

Yager, G. and Beck, T. (1985) Beginning practicum: it only hurt until I laughed, *Counselor Education and Supervision*, 25, 149–156.

Yager, T. and Rotheram-Borus, M. (2000) Social expectations among African American, Hispanic, and European American adolescents, *Cross-Cultural Research*, 34, 283–305.

Yalom, I. (1995) *The Theory and Practice of Group Psychotherapy*, 4th edn. New York: Basic Books.

Yalom, I. and Leszcz, M. (2005) *The Theory and Practice of Group Psychotherapy*, 5th edn. New York: Basic Books.

Yanai, H., Schushan-Eisan, I., Neuman, S. and Novis, B. (2008) Patient satisfaction with endoscopy measurement and assessment, *Digestive Deseases*, 26, 75–79.

Yeates, D. and Wakefield, T. (2004) *Systems Analysis and Design*, 2nd edn. Harlow: Pearson Education.

Yeatts, D. and Hyten, C. (1998) *High Performing Self-managed Work Teams*. Thousand Oaks, CA: Sage.

Yeschke, C. (1987) *Interviewing: An Introduction to Interrogation.* Springfield, IL: CC Thomas.

Yik, M. and Russell, J. (1999) Interpretation of faces: a cross-cultural study of a prediction from Fridlund's theory, *Cognition and Emotion*, 13, 93–104.

Yoo, J. (2009) The power of sharing negative information in a dyadic context, *Communication Reports*, 22, 29–40.

Yoshioka, M. (2000) Substantive differences in the assertiveness of low-income African American, Hispanic, and Caucasian women, *Journal of Psychology*, 134, 243–259.

Young, T. and French, L. (1996) Height and perceived competence of U.S. presidents, *Perceptual and Motor Skills*, 82, 1002.

Yukl, G. (2010) *Leadership in Organizations*, 7th cdn. Upper Saddle River, NJ: Pearson Education.

Zahn, G. (1991) Face-to-face communication in an office setting: the effects of position, proximity and exposure, *Communication Research*, 18, 737–754.

Zajac, R., Gross, J. and Hayne, H. (2003) Asked and answered: questioning children in the courtroom, *Psychiatry, Psychology and Law*, 10, 199–209.

Zamboni, B., Crawford, I. and Williams, P. (2000) Examining communication and assertiveness as predictors of condom use: implications for HIV prevention, *AIDS Education and Prevention*, 12, 492–504.

Zaragoza, M., Belli, R. and Payment, K. (2006) Misinformation effects and the suggestibility of eyewitness memory, in M. Garry and H. Hayne (eds) *Do Justice and Let the Sky Fall.* Mahwah, NJ: Lawrence Erlbaum Associates, Inc.

Zebrowitz, L. and Montepare, J. (2008) First impressions from facial appearance cues, in N. Ambady and J. Skowronski (cds) *First Impressions.* New York: Guilford Press.

Zebrowski, J. (ed.) (2007) *New Research on Social Perception.* New York: Nova Science Publishers.

Zimmer, J. and Anderson, S. (1968) Dimensions of positive regard and empathy, *Journal of Counseling Psychology*, 15, 417–426.

Zimmerman, B. (2000) Attaining self-regulation: a social cognitive perspective, in M. Boekaerts, P. Pintrich and M. Zeidner (eds) *Handbook of Self-regulation.* San Diego, CA: Academic Press.

Zirploi, T. and Melloy, K. (2001) *Behavior Management: Applications for Teachers.* Upper Saddle River, NJ: Prentice-Hall.

Zubek, J., Pruitt, D., Peirce, R., McGillicuddy, N. and Syna, H. (1992) Disputant and mediator behaviors affecting short-term success in mediation, *Journal of Conflict Resolution*, 36, 546–572.

Zuker, E. (1983) *Mastering Assertiveness Skills.* New York: AMACOM.

Name index

Subject index

THE
OXFORD
Children's Book of
FAMOUS
PEOPLE

Oxford University Press, Great Clarendon Street, Oxford ox2 6DP

Oxford   New York   Athens   Auckland   Bangkok   Bogotá
Buenos Aires   Calcutta   Cape Town   Chennai   Dar es Salaam   Delhi
Florence   Hong Kong   Istanbul   Karachi   Kuala Lumpur   Madrid
Melbourne   Mexico City   Mumbai   Nairobi   Paris
São Paulo   Singapore   Taipei   Tokyo   Toronto   Warsaw
and associated companies in Berlin Ibadan

Oxford is a registered trade mark of Oxford University Press
© Oxford University Press 1994

First published 1994
First published in paperback 1996
This edition 1999

British Library Cataloguing in Publication Data
Data available

ISBN 0–19– 910599–5
1–3–5–7–9–10–8–6–4–2

Typesetting by Oxprint, Oxford
Printed in Spain

Consultants and Authors

Peter Aykroyd
Chris Baldick
George Bethell
Ephraim Borowski
Frederick Brogger
Malcolm Bull
Ian Chilvers
Mike Corbishley
Tony Drake
Canon John Fenton
Don Fowler
Gerald Haigh
Andrew Hawkey
Patrick Hickman-Robertson
Michael Hurd

Allan Jones
Paul Lewis
Bryan Loughrey
Howard Loxton
Deborah Manley
Peter Matthews
Colin McEvedy
Richard Milbank
Kenneth Morgan
Peggy Morgan
Daryl Moulton
Douglas Newton
Paul Noble
David Parkinson

R. B. Peberdy
Stephen Pople
Theo Rowland-Entwistle
Archie Roy
Steve Skidmore
Jennifer Speake
Louise Spilsbury
Richard Spilsbury
Richard Tames
Peter Teed
Nicholas Tucker
Trevor Williams
Elizabeth Williamson
Gillian Wolfe
Robert Youngson

THE
OXFORD
Children's Book of
FAMOUS
PEOPLE

Introduction

This book is about the great and the good – and a few of the not so good: people from ancient times to the present day, and from all over the world, who have made their mark on history.

Who to put in and who to leave out

If you and a friend made separate lists of the 10 most famous people who have ever lived, you would probably find that you only agreed on two or three names. Imagine the difficulty if your list were to include 1000 people!

We assembled a team of nearly 50 consultants, all of them experts in areas as diverse as popular music and ancient history, and asked for their informed opinions on who should be included. We also consulted Oxford University Press offices around the world so that we could draw on their expertise to give the book an international perspective.

A particular challenge we faced was to compare the achievements of people doing different things or living at different times. For example, is the former US president *Ronald Reagan* more famous – or more important – than the athlete *Carl Lewis*? And does the fact that *Carl Lewis* could run the 100 metres faster than *Jesse Owens* make him a 'better' athlete – even though *Owens* was the winner of four gold medals at the Berlin Olympics of 1936?

There are no right or wrong answers to such questions, and that is why you will find a wide variety of people from all periods of history within these pages. Politicians, writers, and scientists sit side by side with the stars of sport and film. Because the list is limited to 1000 entries, there are bound to be well-known men and women who do not appear; at the same time, there are plenty of people you may not have heard of. But that's part of the fun: on the same page you can learn all about *Picasso* and then find out about *Phidippides*, the man who ran the first marathon.

A–Z Section

The 1000 entries are arranged alphabetically for easy reference. Each one starts with a short headpiece giving, at a glance, the person's name, a brief description of why they are famous, and their birth and (where appropriate) death dates. The abbreviation c. (short for *circa*, a Latin word meaning 'about') before a date means that it is only approximate. The main article then tells you more about the person's life: their inspirations, their achievements, their failures, or their evil deeds.

The entries are lavishly illustrated with nearly 500 carefully selected pictures. These show not only what some of these famous people looked like but also some of their inventions, their paintings, their designs, and so on. Twenty maps showing former empires and famous journeys have been specially created.

At the end of many of the articles you will find a 'see also' panel listing one or more names. This guides you to other people in the book who are linked in some way to the entry you are reading.

Special Reference Section

After the main section of 1000 entries you will find the Thematic and Chronological Directories. The first of these directories lists the people in the book by their area of achievement, thus grouping together the artists, the musicians, the scientists, and so on; the second lists them by their date of birth, starting with those born over 3000 years ago. These directories may be useful for project work and offer an alternative way of getting information from the book.

Fascinating stories and fantastic achievements – turn the pages and discover some of the people who have *really* made the world go round!

Peter **Abelard**

French philosopher and scholar
Born 1079   Died 1142 aged 63

Born near Nantes, Peter Abelard's father wanted him to follow a military career but he chose to study instead. He taught theology (the study of religion) and founded a school which eventually became the University of Paris. In 1113 he tutored Heloise, the young niece of a church official. They fell in love, had a child, and married. Her uncle was outraged and had Abelard castrated. Abelard then became a monk and Heloise went into a nunnery. But they continued to write to each other, and these love letters have survived to tell their tragic story.

As a monk, and later a hermit, Abelard taught that people should defend the ideas of Christianity through logical thinking. He also wrote a book on ethics (the study of morals) and his autobiography, *The Story of My Misfortunes*. He was one of the leading philosophers, logicians, and theologians of medieval times. ◆

▼ *The tragic lovers were finally united in 1164 when Heloise died and was buried beside Abelard in Brittany.*

Abraham

Hebrew ancestor of both Jews and Muslims
Lived during the 20th century BC

According to the book of Genesis in the Bible, Abraham lived in the city of Ur in Mesopotamia (now mainly in Iraq). When he was about 75, God told him that he must leave his country and travel to Canaan, the promised land.

Abraham settled there, married, and had a son, Isaac. When Isaac had grown into a boy, God told Abraham to sacrifice him by placing him on an altar and killing him. Abraham and Isaac went into the mountains but before Isaac could be sacrificed, God told Abraham to stop. Abraham had proved that he would obey God and was even prepared to give him his own son. God blessed Abraham and his family and said that Isaac's children would be the founders of a great nation.

Abraham is important to Jews because he followed one God and because God led him to the promised land of Canaan or Israel, which the Jews have seen as their homeland ever since. He is important to Muslims because he was obedient to God. (According to Muslim tradition, Ishmael, the ancestor of the Arab peoples, was the son he nearly sacrificed.) And Abraham is important to Christians because he trusted in God's promises. ◆

Abu Bakr

First caliph of Islam
Born c.573   Died 634 aged about 61

In the year 610 near the Arabian town of Mecca, Muhammad began to receive messages from God. He soon began to preach the new religion of Islam, which means 'submitting to God'. Abu Bakr was one of the rich merchants who lived in the town of Mecca and was one of the first to believe in the new prophet. He became a close companion of Muhammad, who married Abu Bakr's daughter, Aisha. When the merchants of Mecca forced Muhammad to flee because they were worried that people would no longer come to Mecca to worship the pagan idols there, Abu Bakr went with him to Medina and became his chief adviser. When Muhammad died in 632, Abu Bakr was accepted as the 'successor of the Prophet of God', or Caliph of Islam. Abu Bakr extended the influence and rule of Islam by bringing the rest of Arabia under his control. He also began the Islamic conquests of Syria and Persia (modern Iran). ◆

👁 **see also**
Ali   Muhammad

Chinua **Achebe**

Nigerian novelist
Born 1930

B orn in eastern Nigeria, Chinua Achebe worked in broadcasting and the civil service before becoming a novelist. In his first and most famous novel, *Things Fall Apart* (1958), he describes the breakdown of African tribal life after the arrival of the British colonizers during the last century. In his memorable description of a traditional family, Achebe shows an understanding of the way the different cultures and rituals of Africa so often puzzle outsiders. Another novel, *A Man of the People* (1966), describes a dishonest African politician who wants to make as much money as he can while he has the chance. It is a funny-sad story, pointing out how difficult it can be for a country unused to political power to run itself properly during the first years of independence. Achebe has since written several children's books and has greatly helped younger African writers in their efforts to get their books published. ◆

John **Adams**

President of the United States of America from 1797 to 1801
Born 1735   Died 1826 aged 90

J ohn Adams, the son of a farmer from Massachusetts, trained to be a lawyer at Harvard University.

He became a strong supporter of American independence from Britain and wrote articles for the Boston newspapers arguing for American rights against what many considered to be unfair British colonial laws.

▲ *John Adams lived longer than any other president of America; he died a few months short of his 91st birthday. He died on the same day as Thomas Jefferson, the man who succeeded him as president.*

He was elected to the House of Representatives (America's law-making body) and earned himself a reputation for being outspoken, blunt, and decisive. He helped to write, and signed, the historic Declaration of Independence document of 1776 which renounced connections with Britain. Three years later he went to France to negotiate the treaties that ended the American Revolution (War of Independence). This was the revolt against British rule that resulted in the establishment of the United States of America.

Adams was the first American ambassador to Britain. Then, from 1789 to 1797, he acted as America's first vice-president, before becoming its second president in

1797. Before he died, he saw his son, John Quincy Adams, become America's sixth president. ◆

👁 **see also**
Jefferson   Washington

Aesop

Greek storyteller
Lived during the 6th century BC

A lthough Aesop is world-famous for his animal fables, we cannot be certain whether he actually wrote them or even if he was a real person! Tradition has it that Aesop was born in Thrace in Greece in the 6th century BC. He is said to have lived as a slave on the Greek island of Samos and on his release travelled extensively before being murdered at Delphi.

His fables, in which animals behave like humans, always end with a moral. Some of his moral catch-phrases, such as 'look before you leap', are still used today. His stories are short and entertaining and have been popular through the ages. Perhaps the most famous is *The Hare and The Tortoise.* ◆

▼ *An illustration from a 1912 edition of Aesop's* The Hare and the Tortoise.

Akbar

Emperor of the Mughal empire in northern India
Born 1542   Died 1605 aged 63

Akbar ruled the Mughal empire in India at the same time as Elizabeth I was queen of England. By the end of his reign, his lands covered an area as big as Europe, and he was more powerful than any European monarch.

Akbar was only 14 when he became emperor, and had to fight hard to build up his power. Sometimes he was ruthless. When he destroyed a rebel fort at Chitor, he built his enemies' heads into the walls of a tower. But Akbar preferred peace, and won most of his lands through treaties and marriages. The Mughal emperors were Muslims but the majority of Akbar's subjects were Hindus. To show that he respected their beliefs, he married a Hindu princess. He was much more tolerant about religion than European rulers living at the same time who forced their subjects to follow particular beliefs.

Akbar loved hunting with cheetahs, riding fierce camels and war elephants, and playing polo. He enjoyed painting, and also made tapestries and carpets. He had splendid palaces with beautiful gardens and he built the magnificent city of Fatehpur Sikri near Agra. It is still there today, almost unchanged, to remind us of Akbar's India. ◆

▼ *This map shows the extent of Akbar's Mughal empire in northern India.*

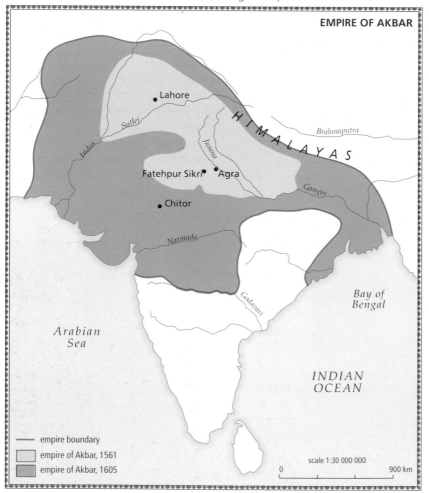

EMPIRE OF AKBAR

Lahore
HIMALAYAS
Sutlej
Indus
Jumna
Brahmaputra
Fatehpur Sikri • Agra
Ganges
• Chitor
Narmada
Godavari
Arabian Sea
Bay of Bengal
INDIAN OCEAN

— empire boundary
empire of Akbar, 1561
empire of Akbar, 1605

scale 1:30 000 000
0   900 km

Alaric

Leader of the Visigoths
Born 370   Died 410 aged 40

In the late 4th century, the western part of the Roman empire came under attack from various peoples, including the Visigoths. They swept down, in huge numbers, from western Russia across the River Danube into Roman territory.

In 394 Alaric, the Visigoth leader, fought for the Roman emperor Theodosius. But in the following year he led an uprising against the Romans. Still seeking new lands for his people, Alaric led his forces into Italy in 401 and besieged Rome, the capital of the western empire, from 408–410. In 410 he broke into the city and captured it. Although he was briefly in control of Rome, Alaric still could not negotiate for lands for his people. He marched south to invade southern Italy but died while waiting to invade the island of Sicily. ◆

Alcock and Brown

English pilot and navigator who made the first non-stop flight across the Atlantic Ocean
John Alcock
Born 1892   Died 1919 aged 27
Arthur Brown
Born 1886   Died 1948 aged 62

John Alcock was a motor mechanic but his interest switched from cars to aircraft. He learned to fly and became a flying instructor. In World War I he was awarded for his bravery as a pilot. After the war, Vickers Aircraft recruited him as a test pilot: they wanted someone to make an attempt to fly an aircraft across the Atlantic Ocean.

▲ *John Alcock and Arthur Brown sitting inside what is probably a Vickers Vimy, the aircraft in which they made their record-breaking flight.*

At 4.13 pm on 14 June 1919, Alcock took off from St Johns, Newfoundland in a specially adapted Vickers Vimy bomber with Arthur Brown as his navigator. They landed the next day in a bog in County Galway, Ireland. The flight lasted 16 hours 12 minutes and covered 3025 km at an average speed of 190 kmph. Alcock and Brown shared a £10,000 prize and both received knighthoods. Alcock died in a plane crash shortly afterwards but Brown, who was also a pilot, eventually became a manager in the Vickers Company. ◆

see also

Lindbergh

Louisa May **Alcott**

American author
Born 1832   Died 1888 aged 55

L ouisa May Alcott had a strict and frugal upbringing in Philadelphia. However, in spite of this, she was a strong young girl. She was quite hard on herself and listed her faults as 'idleness, impatience, selfishness, independence, activity, wilfulness, vanity, pride, and the love of cats'.

When she grew up she tried to earn money to support herself by writing romantic thrillers for magazines. Then, at 35, she wrote *Little Women*. This classic novel was about family life during the American Civil War and was an idealized version of her own difficult childhood with the heroine, Jo, modelled on herself.

The book was a huge success. The popularity of *Little Women*, and of the follow-up volumes which Alcott wrote, at last freed her family from money worries. But her health had been damaged when she spent a brief spell as a nurse during the Civil War, and this, together with long-established habits of hard work and self-denial and her shyness with strangers, made it difficult for her to enjoy her fame. ◆

Alexander the Great

Ancient Greek king and general who conquered the Persian empire
Born 356 BC   Died 323 BC aged 32

A lexander became King Alexander III of Macedonia (northern Greece) at the age of 20. He devoted his reign to making Macedonia more important and to conquering the huge Persian empire to the east. He achieved this in a few years in a succession of brilliant battles and sieges. He reached India, and sent an expedition by sea from the mouth of the Indus to Babylon. He would have gone further, but his army refused. He wanted both Greeks and Persians to be rulers so he appointed Persians as well as Macedonians to high positions. He angered his army by adopting customs from the Persians, some of which involved honouring him as if he were a god.

Alexander had a famous horse called Bucephalus which his father had given him when he was a boy. When the horse died Alexander built a city and named it after him. He also built many new cities called Alexandria and settled soldiers and other Greeks in them. The most famous is the one in Egypt which is still an important city today.

We do not know what Alexander intended to do with his empire, because he died of a fever in Babylon before he had a chance to organize it properly. When he died no one was able to keep the newly won empire together. After years of war among his generals it was split up into several smaller kingdoms, including Babylonia, Egypt, and Macedonia itself. ◆

▼ *This 2nd–1st century BC Roman mosaic shows Alexander the Great riding into battle against the Persian ruler Darius III.*

Alexander, Earl of Tunis

British general
Born 1891   Died 1969 aged 78

Harold Alexander was born into an aristocratic family. He originally wanted to be an artist but decided to make a career in the army and served as an officer in World War I. After the war he served in eastern Europe, Turkey, and India and showed a great talent for languages, learning to speak German, Russian, and Urdu. In 1937 he became the youngest major-general in the British army.

He distinguished himself in World War II, organizing the Allied retreats from France in 1940 and from Burma in 1942 (where he was nearly captured by the Japanese). He became General Eisenhower's deputy from 1943 and led the conquest of North Africa and the invasion of Italy. After the war he received many honours and served as a Governor-General of Canada and Minister of Defence. ◆

👁 **see also**
Eisenhower

Alfred

English King of Wessex from 871 to 899
Born 849   Died 899 aged 50

Among the early kings of England, Alfred is the most famous. He lived at a time when Britain was made up of many separate kingdoms. His kingdom of Wessex extended from present-day Devon to Hampshire. Like his brothers, Alfred was brought up to hunt and fight, but he was also interested in studying.

Danish invaders, who already occupied other parts of England,

▲ *The man shown holding two sceptres on this 9th-century ornament is believed to be Alfred, King of Wessex.*

tried many times to take Wessex. Alfred led battles against them and even tried to pay them off. With a new army he finally beat them back and established a proper 'English' kingdom in southern England.

Alfred, who became known as 'Alfred the Great', was as famous for his peacetime work as his wartime exploits. He founded the first English navy and a number of new towns called burhs. He issued a new code of laws and encouraged the country's religious life by re-founding monasteries that had been destroyed. He also encouraged the use of the Anglo-Saxon language, and during his reign the Anglo-Saxon Chronicles were begun. ◆

Ali

Arab ruler; the fourth Caliph of Islam from 656 to 661
Born c.600   Died 661 aged about 61

Ali Ibn Abi Talib was the cousin of the prophet of Islam, Muhammad. Ali became a Muslim as a boy and married Muhammad's daughter Fatima. Pious, wise, and brave, in 656 Ali was chosen as the fourth Caliph – the leader of the Muslims and ruler of the expanding Arab empire. Al-Najaf, near Kufa in Iraq, became his capital and a great centre of learning.

A revolt against Ali's rule was led by Muawiyah, the governor of Syria and a member of the powerful Umayyad family. In 661 Ali was assassinated and his power was passed to the Umayyads, who ruled from Damascus. A group of Muslims, known as the 'Shiat Ali' (party of Ali), refused to accept Umayyad rule as they thought only descendants of Ali should be Caliphs. They became known in Muslim history as Shiites. ◆

👁 **see also**
Muhammad

Muhammad Ali

American world champion boxer
Born 1942

After winning the amateur 'Golden Gloves' championship in 1959 and 1960, Cassius Clay from Louisville, Kentucky, became Olympic light heavyweight champion in 1960. He immediately became a professional and within four years was champion of the world.

Clay converted to the Islamic faith and changed his name to Muhammad Ali. Because of his beliefs, he refused to be called up into the American army to fight in

▲ *Muhammad Ali won a total of 56 boxing contests; 37 of these ended in knock-outs.*

the Vietnam War. His world title was taken away from him and he was banned from boxing from 1967 to 1970. He returned to the ring in the 1970s and, although he lost his title twice, he won in 1974 and 1978, thus becoming the first heavyweight boxer to win the world championship three times. ◆

see also
Louis, Joe

André-Marie **Ampère**

French physicist
Born *1775*   **Died** *1836 aged 61*

As a child André-Marie Ampère was gifted at mathematics; he even taught himself Latin in order to read old books on the subject. His

scientific interests were wide, but his greatest discoveries were in electricity.

In 1820 the Danish physicist Hans Christian Oersted discovered that an electric current in a wire would deflect (move) a nearby compass needle. Ampère worked out a mathematical law connecting the size of an electric current with the strength of the magnetic field it produced. This is now called Ampère's law. It is one of the most important laws in electromagnetism. Using it, Ampère was able to make instruments for measuring currents and voltages.

The unit of electric current, the ampere (sometimes shortened to 'amp') is named after him. ◆

see also
Oersted

Roald **Amundsen**

Norwegian explorer and the first man to reach the South Pole
Born *1872*   **Died** *1928 aged 55*

Roald Amundsen began a career studying medicine, but gave it up to go to sea. Soon he became excited by the idea of polar exploration. He set out on his first expedition in 1903 aboard a small vessel with a crew of six. It took just over three years for Amundsen to become the first person to sail north from the Atlantic to the Pacific through the Arctic Ocean, north of Canada.

Amundsen decided to try to reach the North Pole next, but on hearing that an American, Robert Peary, had already done this, he sailed for Antarctica instead. It was to be a race between Amundsen and a British expedition led by Robert Falcon Scott, which had set out earlier. Amundsen and four companions, using sledges hauled

by teams of dogs, reached the South Pole on 14 December 1911, almost a month before Scott's party. It was another first for Amundsen.

One of Amundsen's later adventures was in 1926 when he circled the North Pole twice in an airship. In 1928 Amundsen went to search for a friend who was missing on another airship flight over the North Pole. Amundsen set out to search for him, but his own plane was never seen again. ◆

see also
Peary   Scott

▼ *Roald Amundsen pictured during an expedition to the North Pole in 1925.*

11

▲ *An illustration from Hans Christian Andersen's tale* The Emperor's New Clothes *in which a pompous ruler is taught a lesson by a clever tailor.*

Hans Christian **Andersen**

Danish children's story writer
Born *1805*   **Died** *1875 aged 70*

Hans Christian Andersen was the only son of a poor shoemaker and of a mother who could hardly read. When he was 14 he walked all the way from his home in Odense to Copenhagen to try his luck in the big city. At the age of 17 he was put in a school with 12-year-olds. Because of this, and because he was so tall and clumsy, he was often mocked and bullied. Later in his life, when he began to write children's stories, he used this experience in the famous tale of *The Ugly Duckling*. He wrote his stories in simple language, just as he would have told them to a child. Even though such stories as *Thumbelina* and *The Little Mermaid* brought him fame throughout the world, Andersen remained a shy and lonely man. ◆

Elizabeth Garrett **Anderson**

Britain's first woman doctor
Born *1836*   **Died** *1917 aged 81*

At a time when all girls were expected to stay at home to be wives and mothers, the headmistress of Elizabeth Garrett Anderson's school encouraged her to seek a career.

When she was 22, Anderson decided that she wanted to be a doctor. (At this time, only men were allowed to be doctors.) She first trained as a nurse in London. Then, with the help of her professors, she studied in her spare time and was allowed to work as the first woman medical practitioner at the age of 29. But she was still not a fully-qualified doctor.

Anderson opened the St Mary's Dispensary for poor women and children, but she was still refused permission to study and become a doctor solely because she was a woman. So she went to Paris, studied there and passed her examinations, all in French and with six distinctions, and thus finally became a qualified doctor.

Elizabeth Garrett Anderson fought for the rights of women, especially women wanting to be doctors. Women in England were eventually accepted as medical students after the government passed the Medical Act of 1876. ◆

Saint **Andrew**

One of Christ's apostles and the patron saint of Scotland
Lived during the 1st century

Andrew was a fisherman who lived in Capernaum. He was a disciple of John the Baptist and then became an apostle of Jesus. Jesus had told both Andrew and his brother, Simon Peter (who later became Saint Peter), that they would be 'fishers of men', so Andrew went out into the world preaching the Gospel. The people of Patras in Greece claimed that he was crucified there.

A later legend said that in the 4th century, a native of Patras had a dream in which an angel told him to take some of Andrew's bones to a land in the north-west. He obeyed, and travelled until he reached Scotland. The angel then

told him to stop in Fife, where he built a church to hold the bones. The church was later called St Andrews. It became a centre for converting the Scottish people to Christianity. For this reason, Andrew was chosen to be the patron saint of Scotland. (He is also the patron saint of Greece and Russia.) His feast day is held on 30 November. ◆

👁 **see also**

Jesus   John the Baptist   St Peter

Maya **Angelou**

American writer and performer
Born 1928

Marguerite Annie Johnson was born in St Louis, Missouri. She suffered a traumatic childhood and did not speak for several years. After moving to California, she gave birth to a son when she was only 16.

Before becoming a writer, Angelou was a performer and singer. In the 1940s she toured Europe and Africa in the opera *Porgy and Bess* before returning to America to work as a nightclub singer.

Angelou tells the story of her early life in *I Know Why the Caged Bird Sings* (1970), the first part of her much acclaimed three-part autobiography. Her other writing includes plays, poetry, songs, articles, and fiction.

Angelou is now professor of American Studies at Wake Forest University in North Carolina. ◆

◀ *Many of Maya Angelou's autobiographical works tell of her struggles growing up as a black woman in the American South. In another book, All God's Children Need Traveling Shoes (1986), she recounts her return to the West African country of Ghana in search of her family's past.*

Susan Brownell **Anthony**

American defender of women's rights
Born 1820   Died 1906 aged 86

Susan Brownell Anthony came from a well-to-do Quaker family in Massachusetts who brought all their children up to be independent and to stand up for themselves.

Anthony was a clever child, and could read and write by the age of three. For most of her adult life she used her abilities in a battle for votes and rights for women and for black people.

She showed great courage in the face of hostile opponents and newspapers which printed dreadful stories about her. She was a single-minded, energetic woman, who some said was not easy to know or to like! She had the satisfaction of seeing equal voting rights for women introduced into four states of America in her lifetime. ◆

Mark **Antony**

Roman politician and soldier
Born 83 BC   Died 30 BC aged 53

Although we know him as Mark Antony, his proper Roman name was Marcus Antonius. Like other young men from distinguished families in Rome, Mark Antony held several posts in the army and served under the general Julius Caesar. After Caesar had been murdered, Antony delivered a speech to the people of Rome at the funeral, stirring them up against the murderers. He was well placed to succeed him but hostility rose between him and Octavius, Caesar's adopted son and heir (and who later became Emperor Augustus). They ruled

▲ *A marble sculpture of Mark Antony, made during his lifetime.*

together with Lepidus for a while before splitting up the Roman Empire, with Antony taking the eastern area.

At first he co-operated with Octavius and married his sister, Octavia. However, he soon came under the influence of the queen of Egypt, Cleopatra. Although Cleopatra was very powerful she cost him a lot of support in Rome. He eventually left Octavia to marry Cleopatra and broke with Octavius, deciding to establish his power independently in the East. In 34 BC he declared Caesarion (Cleopatra's son allegedly by Caesar) as Caesar's heir instead of Octavius and divided the eastern empire among his family. War with the rest of the Roman Empire followed. The turning point of the war was when Antony's troops were defeated by Octavius's at the great naval battle of Actium in 31 BC. Antony and Cleopatra retreated to Egypt, pursued by Octavius. Realizing that all was lost, Antony committed suicide, shortly followed by Cleopatra. ◆

👁 **see also**

Augustus   Caesar   Cleopatra

13

▲ St Thomas Aquinas depicted in a 16th-century stained glass window in Florence, Italy.

Saint Thomas **Aquinas**

Italian religious teacher and philosopher
Born c.1225   **Died** 1274 aged about 49

Thomas Aquinas was the seventh son of the Italian Count of Aquino. His brothers were army officers but Aquinas persuaded his mother to let him join the Dominican order of preaching friars. He studied in Paris where he formed a school at which he taught until the pope called him back to teach in Italy.

The most famous of Aquinas's many writings are the *Summa Philosophica* and the *Summa Theologiae*. These are accounts of the Christian faith treated both philosophically, with reasoned argument, and theologically, as unquestioning belief in God.

Aquinas was declared a saint in 1323. His teaching is today accepted as standard by the Roman Catholic Church. ◆

Yasser **Arafat**

Palestinian leader
Born 1929

Yasser Arafat has devoted his life to the struggle to create a homeland for the Palestinians who fled abroad when Israel fought for its independence from Britain in 1948. Arafat, the son of an Arab

▼ Yasser Arafat, leader of the Palestine Liberation Organization, seeks a Palestinian homeland free from Israeli rule.

merchant, was born in Jerusalem (which was then part of Palestine). In the 1950s he joined various guerrilla groups, including 'Fatah' (Victory) which organized raids against Israel. In 1969 he became leader of the Palestine Liberation Organization (PLO) which was recognized by Arab nations as the representative of all Palestinians.

After many years of attack and counter-attack, Arafat and the PLO reached an historic agreement with Israel in September 1993 in which the first steps were made towards a lasting settlement between both sides. ◆

Archimedes

Ancient Greek mathematician and engineer
Born c.287 BC
Died 212 BC aged about 75

Archimedes was born in the town of Syracuse in Sicily, at that time ruled by the Greeks. He was the son of an astronomer and spent his life studying geometry and using his ideas to develop new types of machines. One of the most famous is the Archimedean screw for pumping out water.

There are lots of stories about Archimedes and even if some of them are not completely true they still give us an idea of what this great man may have been like.

One famous story tells of how Archimedes tried to work out whether the king of Syracuse's crown was made of pure gold or not. Archimedes could not solve the problem until one day, in his bath, he realized that the water level rose higher the more of his body he immersed. He leapt out of the bath and ran naked through the streets shouting 'Eureka!' which means 'I've got it!' The experiment was done with the crown. He noted how high the water level rose when he put it in a bath. Next he took a piece of pure gold weighing the same as the crown and immersed it in the water. Did the water level rise to the same height? No, so the crown could not have been made of pure gold! ◆

Aristophanes

Ancient Greek writer of comedies
Born c.450 BC
Died c.385 BC aged about 65

Aristophanes wrote such funny comedies that they are still frequently revived today. The most famous of these are *Frogs*, making fun of the celebrated Greek dramatist Euripides; *Clouds*, which mocked the famous Greek philosopher Socrates; and *Lysistrata*. This last comedy attacks the idea that war is a glorious activity. It tells the story of some women who, fed up with being left behind on their own, tell their soldier-husbands they will have nothing more to do with them until they have stopped fighting. The wives win, and peace comes at last. It was typical of Aristophanes that he should attack a subject such as war that many others of his time took very seriously. ◆

see also

Socrates

Aristotle

Ancient Greek philosopher, teacher, and writer
Born 384 BC   **Died** 322 BC aged 62

At the age of 17 Aristotle joined Plato's Academy in Athens where he studied science and philosophy for 20 years. Shortly after Plato's death, Aristotle left the Academy and went to live on the Greek island of Lesbos, where he continued to study. In 343 BC he was appointed tutor to the young Alexander the Great. When Alexander succeeded to the throne, Aristotle returned to Athens and set up his own school, the Lyceum. He directed the Lyceum for 12 years, devoting himself to a wide range of teaching, writing, and research. His output was enormous and included collections of historical information as well as scientific and philosophical works.

In the Middle Ages Aristotle's work was rediscovered by Arab scholars (including Averroës) and translated into Latin. He was regarded as the supreme authority in science and philosophy and his ideas remained a key part of university education in Europe from the 13th to the 17th centuries. ◆

see also

Alexander the Great
Averroës Plato

Richard Arkwright

English inventor of textile manufacturing machines
Born 1732   **Died** 1792 aged 59

Richard Arkwright was the youngest of 13 children. He had no schooling and did not learn to read and write until he was middle-aged. At the age of ten he was sent to work in a barber's shop. While working there he discovered a method for dyeing hair that did not fade, and he became a rich and successful barber and wigmaker.

However, Arkwright's real claim to fame is his invention of the 'spinning frame', a machine for spinning cotton. He made it with the help of a skilled watchmaker, John Kay. Arkwright went on to invent and improve other machines used in textile manufacture. Many workers found their jobs were taken over by the new machines. They became very angry and tried to destroy the machines and even threatened Arkwright. But he was a determined man and his factories helped his home county of Lancashire become the centre of the world's cotton industry. ◆

▶ *Arkwright's spinning frame (1769) was driven by a water wheel.*

▲ *Louis Armstrong*

Louis **Armstrong**

American jazz trumpeter, entertainer, and singer
Born *1901*   **Died** *1971 aged 70*

L ouis Armstrong had a poor but happy childhood, even though his parents were separated. However, one day a silly prank (firing a pistol in the street) ended up with him being taken from his family to live in a children's home. It was there that he had his first music lessons and learned to play the cornet.

He left the home as a teenager and gradually started to earn a living as a musician. In the 1920s, he formed various small groups of his own, such as 'The Louis Armstrong Hot Five', and made some recordings that became famous among jazz fans worldwide.

In 1936 Armstrong appeared in his first film, *Pennies from Heaven.* From then on he gradually became a popular entertainer, famous for his cheerful, gravelly singing voice. His biggest popular song hits were 'Hello Dolly', recorded in 1964, and 'What a Wonderful World', recorded in 1968. ◆

Neil **Armstrong**

American astronaut; the first person to set foot on the Moon
Born *1930*

A s a young man, Neil Armstrong was always interested in flying. He earned his pilot's licence at the age of 16, even before he had learnt to drive a car. The following year he became a naval air cadet, and went on to fly in the Korean War.

In the 1950s Armstrong became a test pilot for NASA (National Aeronautics and Space Administration) before joining the US space programme in 1962. In 1969 he joined astronauts Aldrin and Collins on the *Apollo 11* mission, and on 20 July he became the first person to walk on the Moon. As he stepped off the lunar landing module, he said, 'That's one small step for man, one giant leap for mankind.' ◆

King **Arthur**

Legendary hero
Lived during the 6th century

T here are lots of tales about Arthur, in many different languages. The first written tales date from around 800, although Celtic people in Britain probably told stories about him before then. So who exactly was he? The simple answer is – we don't know. There was definitely no British king called Arthur. But there might have been a chieftain of that name who could have led an army against Anglo-Saxon invaders or against fellow Britons in a civil war. Some historians say his headquarters were in the West Country. Others believe that his base was in northern England, or even Scotland.

The Arthur of legend was a perfect Christian king who ruled Britain and conquered most of western Europe. He held court at Camelot with his queen, Guinevere. His 12 most trusted warriors were called the Knights of the Round

▼ *A tapestry showing the quest for the Holy Grail.*

Table. In many stories, these knights search for the Holy Grail, the cup which, according to Christian legend, was used by Jesus at the Last Supper. ◆

Aryabhata

Indian scientist
Born 476   Died c.550 aged about 74

Aryabhata was a pioneering mathematician and astronomer. At the age of 23, he summed up his knowledge in a poem of 121 verses, known as the 'Aryabhatiya'. It was written in Sanskrit, the ancient Indian language of learning. The poem explains how to work out many mathematical problems, including how to find the area of a triangle or a circle and the volume of a sphere or a pyramid. It also describes how to chart the paths of the Sun and the Moon, and predict their eclipses and explain why these eclipses happen. He was also able to calculate the length of the calendar year with great accuracy, and suggested that the Earth was a sphere, spinning on its own axis and revolving round the Sun. In India, scholars were still studying his works a thousand years after his death. In Europe, it took them the same length of time to discover for themselves his theory about the Earth's motion round the Sun. ◆

Asoka

Emperor of India from c.272 BC to 232 BC
Lived during the 3rd century BC

Asoka was the grandson of Chandragupta Maurya, the founder of the Maurya empire in ancient India. Asoka extended his empire to cover what is now Afghanistan, Pakistan, and most of India.

After coming to the throne Asoka waged many wars to extend his empire. However, he was deeply moved to see the suffering of wounded soldiers during one of his campaigns, and he was then converted to Buddhism. He declared that he would fight no more wars, and devoted the rest of his life to the spreading of Buddhism in India and abroad.

He governed according to the Buddhist principles of toleration and humanitarianism and believed in concern for human life and abstaining from harming animals. Asoka spread the teachings of Buddha throughout his empire by erecting pillars of stone with the main teachings of the Buddhist religion inscribed on them, and by sending missionaries to neighbouring countries. ◆

◉ **see also**
Chandragupta Maurya

Fred **Astaire**

American film actor and dancer
Born 1899   Died 1987 aged 88

Fred Austerlitz had a successful stage career dancing with his sister Adele from the age of seven. When Adele gave this up to get married, Fred looked for work in films. By 1933 he had changed his name to Fred Astaire and teamed up with Virginia ('Ginger') Rogers in *Flying Down to Rio*, the first of nine films they made together. Through films such as *Top Hat* (1935) and *Swing Time* (1936) they became cinema's most famous dancing couple.

Ginger Rogers also had a separate career as an actress in comedy films, winning an Oscar for *Kitty Foyle* in 1940. Astaire retired for a time in 1946, but returned to star in *Easter Parade* (1948) with Judy Garland. ◆

▶ *Fred Astaire and Ginger Rogers in Swing Time (1936).*

▲ At his execution, Atahualpa holds a cross in his hands to show his conversion to Christianity.

Atahualpa

Last ruler of the South American empire of the Incas
Born c.1502   **Died** 1533 aged about 31

Atahualpa and his brother Huascar were the sons and heirs of the great Inca emperor Huayna-Capac. After the emperor's death in 1525, civil war broke out with the two brothers on opposite sides. Huascar was captured and killed, and Atahualpa became emperor, the supreme Inca, based in modern Peru.

As emperor, he was thought to be a god descended from the Sun. People approached him with great respect. He used only the richest of objects, which were kept for him alone. He had complete power over his people, but he was expected to be fair and generous and to follow the ancient traditions of the Incas.

Atahualpa was captured by a small Spanish army in 1532. Even in captivity he continued to rule his people with strength and authority. But despite paying a ransom of gold and silver, he was executed the next year and the Spanish, led by Pizarro, conquered the Inca people. ◆

 see also
Pizarro

Kemal **Atatürk**

President of the new Republic of Turkey from 1923 to 1938
Born 1881   **Died** 1938 aged 57

Mustafa Kemal was born in Thessalonika, now part of Greece. At military college in Istanbul, then capital of the Ottoman empire, he was so good at mathematics that he was given the name Kemal which is Arabic for 'perfection'.

▶ Kemal Atatürk shown dressed in Turkish national costume.

As an officer, he fought in World War I when the Ottoman empire joined the German side. In 1918, Kemal joined other Turkish politicians in calling for Turkey to become an independent nation free of foreign control.

With his military skill, the Turks defeated the Greeks when Greece and Turkey went to war in 1921. Shortly after that, the Ottoman sultans were deposed and in 1923 a Turkish National Assembly was elected with Kemal as president of the new republic.

As president he ruled as a virtual dictator. His main policy was the modernization of Turkey. In 1934, he introduced the idea of surnames and took the surname Atatürk ('father of Turks'). ◆

Attila

Leader of the Huns against the Roman empire
Born 406   **Died** 453 aged 46

Attila was born into the tribe of the Huns, a race of warring nomads who had moved from the Asian steppes right up to the borders of the Roman empire in the West.

When he became king of the Huns in 434, he united his scattered people in a campaign against the Roman empire. For the next 20 years the Huns under Attila conquered and plundered almost the whole of Europe. Attila's greatest desire was to destroy Rome, and the pope was forced to pay him huge sums of money to save the city.

While his followers lived in luxury, Atilla ate only meat out of a wooden bowl. He was a short man, with deep-set eyes and a gaze which was hard and arrogant.

Although far from handsome, he was married many times; some say he had 300 wives.

When Attila died, the Huns cut their cheeks so that they could mourn their leader with tears of blood. ◆

Clement **Attlee**

Prime Minister of Britain from 1945 to 1951
Born 1883   Died 1967 aged 84

Clement Attlee was born into a middle-class family in London. In 1906 he qualified as a barrister, and then worked as a college tutor. When he taught at the London School of Economics, he lived amongst poor people in the East End and was disturbed to see the problems they faced.

This led to him joining and, in 1935, becoming leader of the Labour Party. When he replaced Churchill as prime minister in 1945 with an outstanding election victory, his government immediately began to carry out major changes in Britain. It increased state benefits and pensions and, in 1948, created the National Health Service. The railways and the coal, gas, and electricity industries were nationalized (taken over by the state). Attlee's government also granted independence to Britain's Asian colonies: India, Pakistan, Burma (Myanmar), and Ceylon (Sri Lanka). ◆

W. H. **Auden**

British poet
Born 1907   Died 1973 aged 66

Wystan Hugh Auden's life falls into two almost equal parts, divided by the year 1939 in which he emigrated to America. As a young man in England, Auden was angered by the society around him. The rise of Hitler's Nazi Party in Germany made him strongly anti-fascist. The books of poetry such as *Look Stranger!* (1936) that he published in the 1930s established him as leader among the young left-wing English poets. With his friend Christopher Isherwood, he wrote the verse plays *The Ascent of F6* (1936) and *On the Frontier* (1938).

In 1939 Auden went with Isherwood to America and later took American citizenship. Much of his later poetry was complex and intellectually demanding, reflecting his conversion to Christianity. He returned briefly to England from 1956 to 1961 as professor of poetry at Oxford University. ◆

Saint **Augustine of Canterbury**

Sent by Pope Gregory to convert the English to Christianity
Date of birth unknown
Died 604 or 605 age unknown

Augustine was the prior (deputy head) of St Andrew's monastery in Rome when Pope Gregory I sent him and 40 of his monks to convert the people in Britain to Christianity. There had been Christians in Britain while it was a Roman province, and there were some Christian communities worshipping in western Britain when Augustine arrived in 597. He landed in Kent and the king of Kent, Ethelbert, was persuaded by his wife to allow Augustine's mission to begin.

On Christmas Day 597 Augustine converted 10,000 people. The main place for worship was the capital of Kent, Canterbury. Augustine was made Archbishop of Canterbury and Primate (chief bishop) of Britain by Pope Gregory in 601. He founded the first monastery in Britain in Canterbury. ◆

▶ *This 13th-century chair in Canterbury Cathedral is named after Saint Augustine. It is the seat in which every archbishop is enthroned.*

Saint Augustine
of Hippo

Important early Christian writer
Born 354   Died 430 aged 75

Augustine grew up in a small town in North Africa, which was then part of the Roman empire. At the age of 16 he went to study law at Carthage University. By the time he was 22 he had a mistress and a son, but was able to support himself by teaching. Six years later he moved to Milan in Italy, where he taught the art of speech-making.

His beloved mother had been a Christian, but over the years Augustine felt he had grown away from God. Then suddenly one day, when he was looking again at an inspiring passage in the Bible, he decided to give up his career, leave his partner and son, and devote the rest of his life to God. His *Confessions* tells the story of his childhood, youth, and conversion.

When he wrote the *Confessions*, Augustine had just become Bishop of Hippo, a city near his home town in Africa where he remained until his death. He continued to write and in his most important work, *The City of God*, he urged Christians not to trust in Rome or in anything that it stood for, but to think of themselves instead as belonging to God's city in heaven. ◆

Emperor Augustus

First Roman emperor
Born 63 BC   Died AD 14 aged 76

Augustus started life as Gaius Octavius. His mother was the niece of Julius Caesar and, after his father died when Octavius was only four, Caesar adopted him and made him his heir.

When Caesar was killed, Octavius joined forces with Marcus Antonius (Mark Antony) against the murderers. Octavius ruled for a while with Mark Antony and

▼ *This map shows the full extent of the Roman empire under the rule of Augustus.*

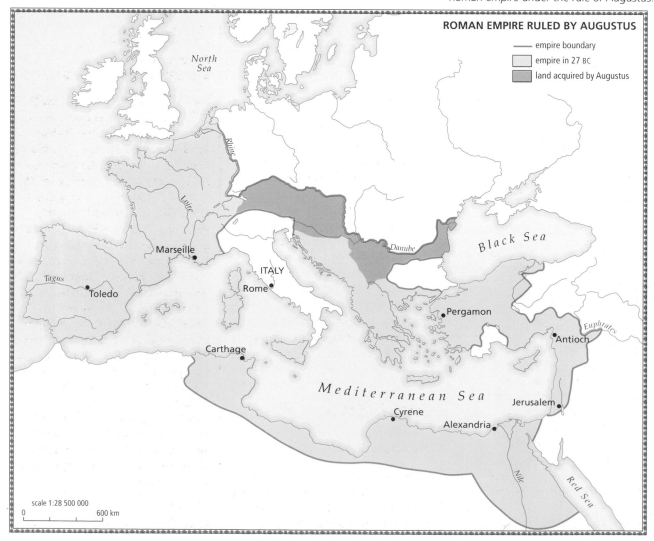

ROMAN EMPIRE RULED BY AUGUSTUS

— empire boundary
empire in 27 BC
land acquired by Augustus

North Sea

Rhine

Loire

Marseille

Tagus

Toledo

ITALY

Rome

Danube

Black Sea

Pergamon

Euphrates

Antioch

Carthage

Mediterranean Sea

Jerusalem

Cyrene

Alexandria

Nile

Red Sea

scale 1:28 500 000
0   600 km

Lepidus but before long civil war broke out in the Roman empire. Octavius defeated Antony (together with Cleopatra) and, in 29 BC, Octavius declared peace throughout the Roman world. He was now the most powerful man in Rome and took the name Augustus (meaning 'a person to be respected'). He established a new system of government: that of rule by one man, the emperor.

During his long reign he brought peace and enlarged the Roman empire. He also transformed the city of Rome. One writer said that Augustus 'could boast that he inherited it brick and left it marble'. On the deaths of his two grandsons he adopted Tiberius (his wife's son by a previous marriage) as his heir. ◆

see also

Mark Antony   Caesar   Cleopatra

Aung San Suu Kyi

Campaigner for human rights in Burma (Myanmar)
Born *1945*

Aung San Suu Kyi is the daughter of Aung San. He led Burma's struggle for independence, but was killed by a political rival. She studied in Burma and India, then at Oxford University. She married in England and had two children.

In 1988 Aung San Suu Kyi visited Burma. While she was there, a group of military leaders took power. She was appalled by their brutal rule, and helped form the National League for Democracy (NDL), who campaigned for a return to democracy. The NDL won elections held in 1990, but the government ignored the result and placed Aung San Suu Kyi under house arrest. In 1991 she was awarded the Nobel Peace Prize for her 'non-violent struggle for democracy and human rights'. ◆

Jane Austen

English novelist
Born *1775*   **Died** *1817 aged 41*

Jane Austen was the seventh child of a country clergyman. Her father and mother always encouraged their children's imaginative play, converting the rectory barn into a little theatre for plays put on by the family during summer holidays. By the age of 12 Austen was writing her own stories and reading them out loud to the rest of the household.

She never married but instead moved around with her family, living in several places, including Bath, the setting for many episodes in her books. The family moved to Winchester in May 1817 seeking medical attention for her ill-health but Austen died two months later. She is buried in Winchester Cathedral.

Her books are famous for their witty insight into human failings and for their humour. The best-known novels are *Sense and Sensibility* (1811), *Pride and Prejudice* (1813), *Mansfield Park* (1814), *Emma* (1816), and *Northanger Abbey* and *Persuasion*, both of which were published in 1818, the year after her death. ◆

Averroës

Arab scholar
Born *1126*   **Died** *1198 aged 72*

The Arabian scholar Ibn Rushd was known as Averroës among learned Christians in the Middle Ages. He was born in Cordoba, Spain and had such success as a doctor and a judge that he was appointed physician and adviser to the caliph (ruler) himself. However, Averroës is best known for his writings about the ideas of the Greek philosopher Aristotle. Averroës' thoughts about Aristotle were translated into Latin and it is through these translations that Christian scholars came to know about Aristotle. Averroës believed that faith and reason were separate ways of arriving at the truth, although this belief was not accepted by other Muslims. ◆

see also

Aristotle

Avicenna

Persian scholar
Born *979*   **Died** *1037 aged 58*

Avicenna is the name by which Ibn Sina was known among learned Christians in the Middle Ages. He was born near Bukhara in Persia (now modern Iran) and is said to have written more than 200 books on a wide range of subjects. His philosophical works owed a great deal to the ideas of Aristotle and to some of Plato's followers. His greatest work was a huge book called the *Canon of Medicine* which was used as a basic medical textbook by both Muslims and Christians for more than 500 years after his death. In it, Avicenna still used the basic ideas about how the human body works which had been put forward more than 1000 years earlier by Aristotle and Galen. However, he also included much more accurate information about anatomy as well as many sensible ideas based on his own experience as a doctor. ◆

see also

Aristotle   Galen   Plato

Charles **Babbage**

English mathematician
Born 1792   *Died* 1871 aged 78

Charles Babbage studied mathematics at Cambridge University. During his time there he calculated a correct table of logarithms which meant mathematical calculations could be done very accurately. However, most of his life was filled with his determination to build his own calculating machine.

He persuaded the British Government to invest £17,000 in the project (a very large sum of money in those days). He even invested £6000 of his own money. However, the project was never completed, mainly because the sort of machine that could be built at that time was too clumsy to do the work Babbage wanted it to do. Nevertheless, Babbage is often regarded as the 'grandfather of the modern computer' because of his original ideas. ◆

👁 **see also**

Pascal

J. S. **Bach**

German composer
Born 1685   *Died* 1750 aged 65

Johann Sebastian Bach was taught music by his father and then by his elder brother. Nobody seemed to teach him how to compose: he mainly taught himself by copying out the music of the composers he most admired. When he was 17 he took up his first important post as church organist in Arnstadt. He then worked as a court musician, first for the Duke of Weimar and then for Prince Leopold of Cöthen. His last and most important post was as organist and choirmaster of St Thomas's Church, Leipzig.

When working as a court musician, Bach wrote mainly chamber and orchestral works, including the six Brandenburg Concertos. When working for the church, he wrote organ music, cantatas, and great choral works, such as the *St Matthew Passion*.

Although he was very famous in his day (particularly as an organist), Bach's music was soon forgotten after his death. It was not until the 19th century that people began to realize how great it was.

He married twice and had 20 children. Two of them, Carl Philipp Emanuel (1714–1788) and Johann Christian (1735–1782), became, for a time, even more well known than their famous father. ◆

Francis **Bacon**

English politician and writer
Born 1561   *Died* 1626 aged 65

▲ *Although he was not a scientist himself, Bacon was central to the development of scientific methods and ideas.*

Francis Bacon was often ill as a child and spent a great deal of his time studying. He went to Cambridge University at the age of 12 and, after training to become a lawyer, spent most of his life working for the government.

Bacon is most famous for the 58 essays he wrote and published (1597–1625). People still enjoy reading what he had to say about human beings, their beliefs, and the world in which they live.

Bacon was knighted in 1603 and two years later published the *Advancement of Learning*, which gave his opinions on education at that time. In this and other books, he urged people to collect and classify facts about the world. He tried also to work out a method of using the facts collected to develop new scientific knowledge. In 1618 he became Lord Chancellor of England. ◆

Robert **Baden-Powell**

English founder of the worldwide Scouting movement
Born 1857   *Died* 1941 aged 83

Robert Baden-Powell was one of ten children. When he was 19 he joined the British army and was sent to southern Africa during the Boer War. One of his jobs there was to train some black African soldiers to scout out enemy country. He taught his scouts to notice details in the countryside, organizing them into small groups so that they could act more quickly.

When he returned to Britain he was surprised to learn that his *Aids to Scouting*, which he had written for his soldiers, was being taught in schools. He rewrote it as a book for boys and in 1908 founded the Boy

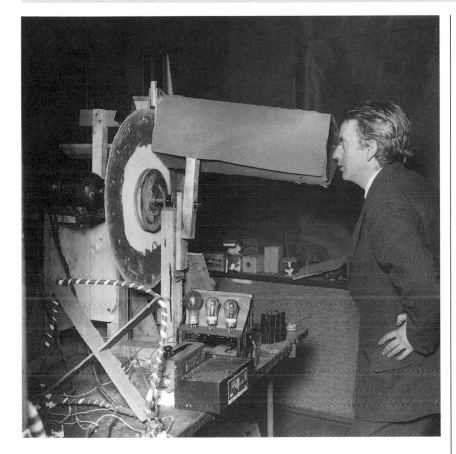

◄ *Baird looking at a picture on the screen of his first television set. The picture is being 'drawn' by spots of light from holes in the rotating disc.*

broadcast, using Baird's equipment. Baird was also responsible for the first sight and sound broadcast and the first outside broadcast (the Derby in 1931). A rival television system, which made use of cathode-ray tubes, took over from Baird's in 1933 and is still in use today. ◆

Vasco Núñez de **Balboa**

Spanish adventurer
Born c 1475   **Died** 1519 aged about 44

Vasco Núñez de Balboa was a member of a noble Spanish family. In 1501 he sailed across the Atlantic Ocean to make his fortune. After settling briefly on the island of Hispaniola (Haiti), he stowed away aboard a ship that was carrying an expedition to found a new settlement on the coast of Central America.

He proved to be a born leader. Within a year he had made the little settlement a success, and the king of Spain made him its Governor.

Balboa was told by locals that there was another ocean nearby, and great wealth for the taking. He decided he would find this other ocean. With a small party of Spaniards and several hundred American Indians, he hacked his way through the jungle until from a hilltop he could see the Pacific Ocean. He rushed down the hill into the water, crying out that the sea belonged to the king of Spain. He was rewarded with the title of Governor of the South Seas. ◆

Scout Movement. His sister, Agnes, helped found the Girl Guide Movement in 1910, and later his wife, Olave, became World Chief Guide. ◆

► *Baden-Powell seen wearing his soldier's uniform.*

John Logic **Baird**

Scottish inventor of the first television
Born 1888   **Died** 1946 aged 57

John Logie Baird's first jobs as an engineer were so miserable that when he was 26 he decided to become an inventor instead. His early ideas flopped and by the time he was 35 he was penniless. But in 1923 he started work on a machine that could transmit pictures, as well as sound, by radio. Soon he was able to send crude images by wireless transmitter to a receiver a few feet away.

Then, in January 1926, he gave the first public demonstration of television at the Royal Institution in London.

In 1929 the BBC made the first television

23

Honoré de **Balzac**

French novelist
Born *1799* ***Died*** *1850 aged 51*

Honoré de Balzac was an extremely hard-working novelist, sometimes working 16 hours at a stretch. His vast collection of novels deals with every aspect of French society, from private life in the town or country to stories with a political or military

◀ *The sculptor Rodin was commissioned to make this statue of Balzac in 1897.*

setting. Taken together, this long series of novels became known as *La Comédie Humaine* (The Human Comedy). But Balzac was not really a comic writer; instead, he described a whole society as he saw it, with characters from one novel reappearing in another. The total impression is of a world so real it is hard to remember it all came from one man's imagination. Balzac's extraordinary powers of observation and understanding make his characters as believable as the settings in which they appear, which he always describes very vividly. ◆

Joseph **Banks**

English explorer and botanist
Born *1744*   ***Died*** *1820 aged 77*

Joseph Banks, the son of a wealthy doctor, became interested in botany at school. After inheriting his father's fortune, he was able to explore the world looking for new plants and animals. His first expedition, in 1766, was to Labrador and Newfoundland.

In 1768 Banks set sail with Captain Cook on the *Endeavour* bound for Tahiti and the South Seas. During the three-year voyage, Banks took part in the first exploration of Australia. The beautiful Australian plants *Banksia* are named after him.

In 1788 he became President of the Royal Society, the most important British scientific society. He was a friend of King George III, and advised him on the enlargement of the gardens at Kew and on his merino sheep, which were later so important in Australia. He was a friendly and hospitable person, and his natural history

▲ *A portrait of the botanist Joseph Banks from 1773.*

collections and library were always available for other scientists to use. ◆

see also
Cook

Banting and **Best**

Canadian pioneers of the use of insulin
Frederick Banting
Born *1891*   ***Died*** *1941 aged 49*
Charles Best
Born *1899*   ***Died*** *1978 aged 79*

Frederick Banting graduated from the University of Toronto, Canada, and then served in World War I. He was awarded the Military Cross for his bravery.

After the war, whilst working as a doctor, he became interested in the disease diabetes. He managed to persuade Professor John MacLeod at Toronto to let him investigate the causes of this serious disease. Banting did not have much experience of research and so MacLeod appointed a young student, Charles Best, to help him.

Banting and Best carried out a

series of experiments on dogs. This proved that the hormone insulin, produced in the pancreas, can be used to treat diabetes. In 1922 a 14-year-old boy became the first person to be successfully treated using insulin.

Banting and MacLeod were awarded the Nobel Prize for Medicine in 1923. Banting was furious that Best had been left out and so generously shared his prize money with him. ◆

John **Bardeen**

American physicist
Born 1908   Died 1991 aged 83

Amplifiers, which make electrical signals stronger, and electronic switches were once big, expensive to operate, and broke easily. John Bardeen (with scientists William Shockley and Walter Brattain) made something better: the transistor.

Bardeen was born in Madison, Wisconsin, in America. He worked with Shockley and Brattain doing experiments on how electricity passed through materials called semiconductors. Just before Christmas 1947, one of the scientists spoke into a microphone and the world's first semiconductor transistor amplified the electrical signal to make the words sound louder. For this work, the team won the highest prize in science, the Nobel Prize, in 1956. The development of the transistor has made it possible to have such things as pocket calculators, digital watches, and portable computers.

Bardeen went on to study how some materials resist the flow of electricity whereas others, called superconductors, do not. By explaining how they worked, he won a share in a second Nobel Prize in 1972. ◆

Christiaan **Barnard**

South African surgeon who pioneered heart transplants
Born 1922

Christiaan Neethling Barnard graduated from the University of Cape Town in South Africa in 1946. He went on to become resident surgeon at the Groote Schuur Hospital and then took a scholarship to the University of Minnesota in America from 1956 to 1958. While there he learnt a lot about heart surgery. He returned to Groote Schuur to concentrate on open-heart surgery, and designed an artificial heart-valve for use in operations. He began doing experimental heart transplants on dogs. When he felt he was ready, he and his colleagues at Groote Schuur performed the world's first transplant on a human patient, Louis Washkansky. They gave him the heart of someone who had died in a car accident. Unfortunately, complications set in and the patient died 18 days later. However, Barnard's work proved that, given the right conditions, heart transplant operations could work. ◆

Thomas **Barnardo**

British founder of Dr Barnardo's children's homes
Born 1845   Died 1905 aged 60

Thomas Barnardo was a small, sickly child with poor eyesight, but he was always clever and high-spirited.

At 21 he moved to London to study medicine, but he abandoned his studies to preach and teach among the poor families of the East End. Appalled by the plight of the homeless children he saw in that area, Barnardo began to raise money to provide homes for them.

Barnardo had lots of energy, remarkable powers of organization, and a flair for fund-raising. In his lifetime nearly 60,000 needy and handicapped children were sheltered and schooled in Dr Barnardo's Homes. He believed that no child should be denied help. His influence led to the state taking greater responsibility for protecting children against neglect and abuse. ◆

▼ *Children and carers in one of the first homes set up by Thomas Barnardo.*

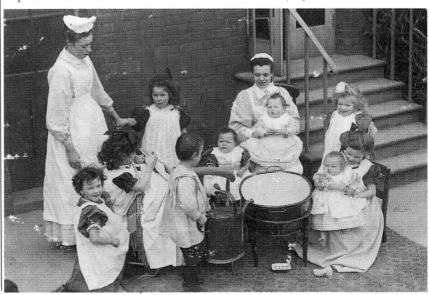

J. M. **Barrie**

Scottish author and playwright
Born *1860*   **Died** *1937 aged 77*

James Matthew Barrie was born to a fairly poor household, the son of a handloom weaver. When he was six years old, his mother became seriously ill. While she lay in bed Barrie spent many hours with her, reading books or listening to her stories. It was then that he decided to become a writer.

He went to university, and then settled in London. His first novels were about life in his home town of Kirriemuir, which he called 'Thrums'. Then he began writing plays, and these brought him wealth and fame.

His most famous play, *Peter Pan*, was first performed in 1904, and with its mixture of fairies and pirates, it was an immediate success. Although *Peter Pan* is still popular, many of his other plays and books are too sentimental for modern taste and are now neglected. ◆

Béla **Bartók**

Hungarian composer and pianist
Born *1881*   **Died** *1945 aged 64*

Béla Bartók was only five when his mother began to teach him the piano. After graduating from Budapest's Academy of Music, he

◀ *One of Béla Bartók's critics once said that listening to his music was worse than going to the dentist. Today he is considered one of the greatest 20th-century composers.*

became well-known as a concert pianist, often performing his own works. Bartók loved Hungary, and when he discovered its folk music he began to collect and study it intensively. This gradually changed the nature of his own music and helped to give it a particular style. Many people, however, found his music aggressive and difficult to listen to.

In 1940 he emigrated to America because the political situation in Hungary had become intolerable to him. Although he was unhappy in America, he wrote two of his most colourful and popular works there: the Concerto for Orchestra, and the Third Piano Concerto. Bartók's music includes many folk-song arrangements and piano pieces, and six splendid string quartets. His body was reburied in Budapest after the fall of Communism. ◆

▶ *A theatre poster to advertise Barrie's play* Peter Pan. *This play grew from stories Barrie had made up for the five sons of some friends (to whom he gave a home when their parents died).*

Matsuo **Basho**

Japanese poet
Born 1644   Died 1694 aged 50

Matsuo Basho was born near Kyoto, Japan, the fourth of seven children of a poor samurai (warrior). At the age of nine he became a companion to the eldest son of his warrior lord, and together they studied literature, especially poetry. In 1672 Basho moved to the capital city of Edo (now Tokyo), where he became well-known as a poet. In the last ten years of his life he went on several long journeys on foot around Japan. This was an unusual thing to do since the roads were very bad and bandits were very common, making travel very dangerous. Basho's accounts of his journeys include many of his best and most famous poems. He is regarded as the greatest master ever of the haiku, the 17 syllable poem. In 1694 Basho started off on another journey, but fell ill and died at the city of Osaka in October. ◆

> *On this Spring morning*
> *The moon shines pale through*
> *   the mist;*
> *It's a flower's face.* .
> > BASHO
> An example of his haiku poetry

Jean **Batten**

New Zealand solo aviator
Born 1909   Died 1982 aged 73

Born in Rotorua, New Zealand, Jean Batten had an early ambition to fly and came to Britain for training. By 1932 she was a skilful and daring pilot.

She obtained sponsors and soon made pioneering flights. In 1934 she set a record time for women flying solo from Britain to Australia.

◀ *Jean Batten and her plane,* Percival Gull.

Within the year, Batten became the first solo woman to make the return trip.

In 1935 Batten was the first woman to fly solo from Britain to Brazil, setting a speed record for both men and women pilots. In the next two years, she achieved two more absolute records – flying to New Zealand from Britain, and from Australia back to Britain.

Aviation historians rank Jean Batten as one of the top women solo pilots of the 1930s. She gave up flying when World War II began in 1939. ◆

🌐 **see also**
Earhart   Johnson

Charles **Baudelaire**

French poet
Born 1821   Died 1867 aged 46

Charles Baudelaire first showed his rebellious side by misbehaving at his senior school in Paris. Deciding to become a writer, he lived in the Latin Quarter of Paris along with other struggling writers and artists, and became addicted to the drug opium. In 1841 his family sent him to India in an attempt to give him a fresh start. But he soon returned to his former life and quickly ran up huge debts. Turning to poetry, Baudelaire wrote about the pleasures and miseries of the

life he was leading, but his 1857 collection of poems, *Flowers of Evil*, proved to be very controversial. However, the way Baudelaire expressed the longing for something good to live for, gave these poems enormous power. Modern poets still regard Baudelaire as the first 19th-century poet to explore the inner secrets of the soul with the same sort of openness we expect today. ◆

Franz **Beckenbauer**

German footballer and manager
Born 1945

Footballer Franz Beckenbauer played his first game for Bayern Munich at the age of 18, and after just 25 games he was picked for West Germany. In 1966 he was in the team that lost the World Cup Final to England. Beckenbauer gained his revenge by scoring one of the goals that knocked England out of the 1970 World Cup, and then went on to captain West Germany to World Cup victory in 1974. As captain of Bayern Munich, he lifted the European Cup three times (1974–1976) and earned the name 'Kaiser' (Emperor) because he was such a good leader on and off the field. After retiring as a player, he went on to further success as coach and manager of the German national team. ◆

Saint Thomas **Becket**

Archbishop of Canterbury from 1162 to 1170

Born 1118   *Died* 1170 aged 52

After training as a lawyer, a priest, and a knight, Thomas Becket entered the household of the Archbishop of Canterbury, where he soon attracted the attention of the new king, Henry II. At the age of 36, Becket became the king's chancellor, and in 1162 was made Archbishop of Canterbury.

To everyone's surprise, Becket resigned as chancellor and began to live like a holy man. Saying that his duty to God as archbishop now came before his duty to the king, Becket angered Henry by challenging his claims to power over the Church.

Six years of quarrelling followed and Becket excommunicated (cut off from membership of the Church) any bishops whom he felt did not support him. The king flew into a rage, saying 'Will no man rid me of this turbulent priest?' Four of his

▼ *Thomas Becket and Henry II depicted in a stained-glass window at Canterbury Cathedral.*

knights took him at his word, went to Canterbury and slaughtered the archbishop at his cathedral altar. This sensational event shocked the whole Christian world. People saw Becket as a martyr and even compared his death with Christ's crucifixion. In 1172 the pope declared Becket to be a saint. ◆

Henri **Becquerel**

French physicist who discovered radioactivity

Born 1852   *Died* 1908 aged 55

Henri Becquerel followed in the footsteps of his father and his grandfather who had both been well-known physicists. He was interested in crystals which glow (fluoresce) after absorbing sunlight. When Röntgen discovered X-rays in 1895, Becquerel was fascinated: he wanted to find out whether fluorescent minerals emit X-rays. He put some crystals of a uranium compound on top of a photographic plate wrapped in paper and then left them in sunlight for several hours. When he developed the plate he found, as expected, the outline of the crystals.

Becquerel left some of the crystals and a photographic plate in a drawer. When he developed the plate he was surprised to see an image of the crystals. He had accidentally found that the effect was not due to sunlight but that something was coming from the crystals themselves. In fact it was radiation coming from the uranium.

His enthusiasm influenced Pierre and Marie Curie and in 1903 the three friends were awarded the Nobel Prize for Physics for their research into radioactivity. ◆

 see also

Curie   Röntgen   Rutherford

Ludwig van **Beethoven**

German composer

Born 1770   *Died* 1827 aged 56

Ludwig van Beethoven's father and grandfather were both professional musicians, so it was quite natural for him to follow in their footsteps. It was not long before, as a young man, he decided to leave Germany and seek his fortune in Vienna, Austria.

He made influential friends and was soon in demand as a fashionable pianist and teacher. However, from about 1796 he began to go deaf and by the end of 1802 his deafness was serious. At first he was in despair, but he pulled himself together and began to concentrate more fiercely than ever on composition.

The music he now wrote, including the Third and Fifth Symphonies, was more powerful and dramatic than anything anyone had ever written before. It seemed to tell of a life and death struggle between tremendous forces, ending always in triumph. For example, the

▲ *Despite his own misery, partly caused by his deafness (his ear-trumpet is shown above), Beethoven wrote inspiring music.*

heroine of his opera *Fidelio* defends her husband against an evil tyrant; and the *Missa Solemnis* (Solemn Mass) includes a prayer for deliverance from the horrors of war.

Some of Beethoven's music was considered to be unplayable at the time, but it was later realized that they were masterpieces.

His influence on later composers was enormous – Brahms, Mendelssohn, and Wagner all greatly admired him. ◆

Menachem **Begin**

Polish-born prime minister of Israel from 1977 to 1983
Born 1913   Died 1992 aged 79

Menachem Begin was a freedom-fighter who became a peace-maker. He studied law and became active in the Zionist movement to found a Jewish state in Palestine. He escaped the Nazi invasion of Poland and enlisted in the Polish Army. He went with it to

Palestine and became a commander of a guerilla group which fought against the British army then occupying the country. A brilliant speaker, he became leader of the Herut (Freedom) party in 1948 and in 1970 became co-leader of the Likud (Unity) coalition. After 30 years in opposition he finally became prime minister in 1977.

Begin and the Egyptian president, Anwar Sadat, shared the Nobel Peace Prize in 1978 for their work in trying to bring peace to the troubled Middle East. ◆

see also
Sadat

Alexander Graham **Bell**

Scottish-born American inventor of the telephone
Born 1847   Died 1922 aged 75

Like other members of his family, Alexander Graham Bell trained to teach people to speak clearly. He went to America to continue this work and became convinced that he could teach totally deaf people to speak, even though they were unable to hear the sounds they were trying to imitate. He was also interested in other kinds of science, and was offered financial help towards his experiments from the parents of two deaf students whom he had taught to speak. One of his experiments led to his invention of the telephone, and he set up a company to develop and make telephones for sale.

In 1898 Bell became president of the National Geographic Society, and was so convinced that one of the best ways of teaching was through pictures that he started the *National Geographic* magazine, now world-famous for its superb colour pictures. ◆

▼ *This Bell telephone and terminal date from 1878. The Bell Telephone Company was the largest telephone company in the world for many years.*

Jocelyn **Bell**

Bristish astronomer
Born 1943

Jocelyn Bell studied at the universities of Glasgow and Cambridge. In 1967, while working in Cambridge with a group of fellow radio astronomers, she noticed a highly unusual radio signal. It consisted of very rapid, regular pulses. Her observation led the team of scientists to make the important discovery of pulsars.

Pulsars are incredibly dense, rapidly rotating remnants of stars that have previously exploded as supernovae. These stars emit a beam of radiation which can be received on Earth each time the star rotates. This can be as often as once every 0.03 seconds. The leaders of the research team, Antony Hewish and Martin Ryle, went on to win the Nobel Prize for Physics in 1974, although Bell is regarded as the discoverer of pulsars. In her subsequent scientific career Professor Bell has been awarded many prizes for her work. ◆

Giovanni **Bellini**

Italian artist
Born 1430   Died 1516 aged 86

Giovanni Bellini was born in Venice, Italy, into an artistic family. His father, Jacapo, was a painter and he established a family workshop. His brother, Gentile, became a painter of considerable importance and his brother-in-law, Mantegna, also became a very famous painter.

Giovanni was at first much influenced by his father's ideas and sketches (his father's two sketch-books still survive) but later Mantegna was to become his strongest influence.

▲ *Giovanni Bellini's* Madonna and Child with St Paul and St George.

Bellini developed a large workshop where many apprentices and assistants helped him carry out the numerous requests for religious paintings and portraits. As a teacher he influenced many who later became great artists themselves. He eventually became chief painter to the state and is considered to be the most important and inventive of the Venetian 'Madonna' artists. ◆

David **Ben-Gurion**

Israel's first prime minister
Born 1886   Died 1973 aged 87

David Ben-Gurion has been called 'the George Washington of Israel', because like Washington he fought for his country's independence and led it in its early years. His original name was Gruen, but he changed it to Ben-Gurion, 'son of a lion-cub', after he emigrated from Poland to Palestine in 1906.

Palestine was then part of the Turkish Ottoman empire, and Ben-Gurion was expelled as a trouble-maker by the Turks. He went to America and joined the Jewish Legion, which fought in the British army in Palestine in World War I.

After the war Palestine came under British rule. Ben-Gurion became general secretary of the Histadrut (the Confederation of Palestine Jewish Workers), and organized the defence of the Jewish settlers against hostile Arabs.

When European Jews wanted to enter Palestine and were not allowed to do so, Ben-Gurion began campaigning for an independent Jewish state. In 1947 the United Nations decided that Palestine should be divided between Jews and Arabs, and in 1948 Ben-Gurion proudly read out the proclamation which declared Israel independent and he became prime minister. He retired in 1953, but was recalled in 1955 to serve again as prime minister until 1963. ◆

👁 **see also**

Begin   Weizmann

30

Karl **Benz**

German builder of the first practical motor car
Born 1844   Died 1929 aged 85

Karl Benz was determined that he would produce the first road vehicle to use the internal combustion engine. In the 1880s the internal combustion engine existed, and even though several engineers had tried fitting one on to a horse carriage, they had not been very successful in producing a practical motor car.

Benz, however, realized that the engine and the carriage had to be designed together. He went on to build a three wheeled car which was patented in 1886. It was the first really successful automobile. He kept on improving his designs and by 1893 he was making four-wheeled cars that many people wanted to buy.

He teamed up with Gottlieb Daimler, his former rival, to start the great Daimler-Benz company. Benz's name still lives on in the Mercedes-Benz cars and lorries that are made today. ◆

see also
Daimler

Vitus **Bering**

Danish explorer
Born 1681   Died 1741 aged 60

Vitus Bering joined the Russian navy in 1703. He was a skilled navigator and in 1728 Tsar Peter the Great appointed him to lead an expedition to find out whether Asia and North America were connected by land. Bering sailed northwards along the coast of Asia and, when the coast turned westwards, he concluded that the two continents were separated by sea. In fact the distance between them, now known as the Bering Strait, is only about 80 kilometres. Five years later he headed the 600-man Great Northern Expedition along the Siberian coast. In 1741 he sailed west towards America and became the first European to sight Alaska, when he saw an Alaskan volcano. Foul weather and sickness forced him back. He was shipwrecked on a deserted island and died of scurvy with 19 of his crew. The survivors buried him on the island, which was later named Bering Island after him. ◆

▼ *Bering Island, Bering Sea, and the Bering Strait are all named after the Danish explorer Vitus Bering.*

Irving **Berlin**

Russian-born American songwriter
Born 1888   Died 1989 aged 101

Irving Berlin was born Israel Baline in Russia. When he was five his family left to go to New York. His father died when he was young and so, after only two years at school, he had to go to work. He worked as a newsboy, street singer, and singing waiter. Writing song lyrics got him a job with a music publisher and a printer's error gave him the idea for his professional name.

▲ *The 1948 film Easter Parade, starring two of Hollywood's greatest musical talents, Fred Astaire and Judy Garland, included many great Irving Berlin songs.*

Soon he started to write tunes too, although at the time he could not read music. In 1911 he hit the jackpot with 'Alexander's Ragtime Band', which sold 2 million copies by 1915. He wrote music and over 800 songs for shows and movies including *Top Hat* (1935), *Easter Parade* (1948), *White Christmas* (1954), and *There's No Business Like Show Business* (1954) which features stars such as Fred Astaire and Ginger Rogers, Judy Garland, Bing Crosby, Ethel Merman, and Marilyn Monroe. ◆

see also
Gershwin   Porter

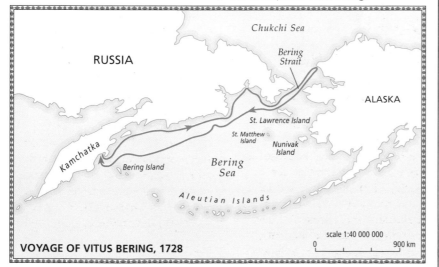

Chukchi Sea

RUSSIA

Bering Strait

ALASKA

St. Lawrence Island

St. Matthew Island

Nunivak Island

Kamchatka

Bering Island

Bering Sea

Aleutian Islands

scale 1:40 000 000
0   900 km

VOYAGE OF VITUS BERING, 1728

Hector **Berlioz**

French composer
Born *1803*   **Died** *1869 aged 65*

Hector Berlioz first trained to be a doctor like his father, but his love of music proved too strong and from 1826 he studied music at the Paris Conservatoire. In the following year he fell passionately in love with an Irish actress, Harriet Smithson. She rejected him and he recorded his feelings about her in the extraordinary *Symphonie fantastique*. This seems to have made her change her mind because they married in 1833, although they parted eight years later.

Berlioz made his living as a music critic and conductor while he wrote a series of remarkable works, such as the *Roméo et Juliette* symphony. However, he never quite recovered from the failure of his operatic masterpiece, *Les Troyens*, and died a disappointed man. ◆

St Bernadette

French girl who saw a vision of the Virgin Mary at Lourdes
Born *1844*   **Died** *1879 aged 35*

Marie-Bernarde Soubirous came from Lourdes, a French town close to the Spanish border. When she was 14 years old she announced that she had seen the Virgin Mary and that she had spoken to her. Neither her parents nor church officials believed her but she never changed her story.

Her claims aroused a great deal of public interest, so to avoid the publicity she was sent to a boarding-school. When she finally left school she went to live as a nun with the Sisters of Charity at Nevers. Here she was constantly plagued by sickness and suffered from asthma. Even when she was dying she

▲ *A souvenir postcard from Lourdes (1867) showing a vision of the Virgin Mary.*

JE SUIS L'IMMACULÉE CONCEPTION
U. L. FRAU VON LOURDES

showed considerable courage and good humour and won the admiration of her friends.

In 1933 Pope Pius XI canonized her as Saint Bernadette. Lourdes is now visited by thousands of pilgrims every year, particularly the sick. Many of them who are dipped in the water of a spring there claim to have been cured. ◆

Sarah **Bernhardt**

French actress
Born *1844*   **Died** *1923 aged 78*

When she was young, Sarah Bernhardt enrolled in acting school and got a place in the French national theatre company. She was sacked for slapping a senior actress and it was some years before she became a leading actress famed for her musical 'silvery' voice. She was worshipped by her fans as 'The Divine Sarah' and travelled the world with her own company. Her most famous roles included the title role in Racine's play *Phèdre*, and Marguerite Gautier in *The Lady of the Camellias*. She also played male roles including the lead in *Hamlet*.

She was the first great actress to appear in movies. During the making of the film *Tosca* she injured her knee while jumping from some battlements. In 1915, after years of pain, her leg had to be amputated – but she went on acting in parts that she could play mainly sitting down. ◆

◉ **see also**

Irving

▼ *This theatre poster advertises Sarah Bernhardt's role in* The Lady of the Camellias.

◀ *This statue,* The Ecstasy of St Theresa, *is one of Gianlorenzo Bernini's most famous. The facial expressions of his subjects and the way their costumes are draped suggest drama and movement. Bernini was also a skilled architect and a painter.*

Gianlorenzo
Bernini

Italian sculptor
Born 1598   Died 1680 aged 82

Gianlorenzo Bernini grew up in a sculpting family. He was influenced by classical Greek and Roman sculpture, by Michelangelo, and by painters of his time. He founded the 'Baroque' style of sculpture: straightforward natural subjects which have balance and harmony and therefore directly appeal to the viewer. His sculptures are meant to be seen from a front view rather than from all around. Bernini attempted to show the real spirit of the person he was sculpting through their facial expression. His technique was to make small terracotta clay models first and then, with the help of many assistants, to make the large pieces. He liked to use coloured marbles or bronze to add a painterly effect to his sculptures. ◆

Bernoulli family

Swiss family of mathematicians
Jakob Bernoulli
Born 1654   Died 1705 aged 50
Johann Bernoulli
Born 1667   Died 1748 aged 80
Daniel Bernoulli
Born 1700   Died 1782 aged 82

Jakob Bernoulli's father wanted him to be a clergyman but he followed his passion for mathematics instead. As a young man he travelled to meet other mathematicians, and at 33 he was made professor of mathematics at Basel University, Switzerland. His special interests were curves, infinite series, and calculus. One curve, the logarithmic spiral, so fascinated him that he had it carved on his gravestone.

Johann Bernoulli became a mathematician against his father's wishes, just as his older brother Jakob had done. The two brothers had similar mathematical interests and became rivals. Sometimes one would claim the other's discoveries as his own. While visiting France, Johann met the Marquis Guillaume de l'Hospial and agreed to supply him with his mathematical discoveries in return for a salary. The Marquis then passed the discoveries off as his own.

Daniel Bernoulli was Johann's son. Johann taught him mathematics, but was not happy when Daniel became very successful. Daniel also studied philosophy and medicine, and for a while taught anatomy and botany at Basel. He made important discoveries in calculus, probability, and vibrations, but is most famous for his work on the pressure of flowing liquids. ◆

Leonard
Bernstein

American composer and conductor
Born 1918   Died 1990 aged 72

When Leonard Bernstein was ten, his family acquired a piano. Bernstein liked it and began lessons, soon making quick progress. He went on to study music at Harvard University and at the Curtis Institute of Music, Philadelphia. When he was in his mid-twenties he became assistant conductor of a great symphony orchestra, the New York Philharmonic.

From the 1940s Bernstein became known as a composer of musical shows. The most famous and successful of these was *West Side Story*, which opened on Broadway, New York, in 1957 and was later made into a film. He wrote many kinds of orchestral and choral music as well as music for the stage, and was a highly respected conductor and pianist. ◆

Chuck **Berry**

American rock and roll singer
Born 1926

In the 1950s Charles 'Chuck' Berry invented the ringing guitar sound which inspired many 1960s pop groups, especially the Beatles and the Rolling Stones. Born in San Jose, California, Berry did a number of jobs while he tried to become a full-time musician. Once he got a recording contract, he had a string of hits with witty story-lines. These songs mixed country music with rhythm 'n' blues and an irresistible dance beat.

His songs, including 'Rock'n'Roll Music' (1957) and 'Sweet Little Sixteen' (1958), are world-famous and have been performed by hundreds of other musicians. John Lennon of the Beatles once said of him, 'If you tried to give rock'n'roll another name, you might call it Chuck Berry.' ◆

👁 **see also**

Lennon and
McCartney

◀ *One of Chuck Berry's songs was chosen as a sample of Earth music to go on board the* Voyager *space probe.*

Annie **Besant**

English campaigner for birth control, socialism, and the rights of women
Born 1847   Died 1933 aged 85

Annie Besant left her unhappy marriage when she was 26 and began working as a journalist. She cared deeply about poverty-stricken women who had to look after large families, and she began campaigning for birth control. When she published a book about it she was arrested and put on trial. Although she was released, her daughter was taken away from her.

The tragedy of losing her daughter pushed Besant into fighting for more reforms, especially for the London 'match girls'. These women worked long hours in unhealthy conditions making matches for four shillings (20 pence) a week. In 1888 they went on strike for better pay. Besant wrote about them in the newspapers and led a procession of match girls to the House of Commons. As a result, their strike was successful.

Besant then moved to India where she helped start the Central Hindu College at Varanasi (Benares). She believed strongly that India should be an independent country, free of British rule, and she started a newspaper to support this idea. She died before this dream became a reality. ◆

Henry **Bessemer**

English pioneer of steel manufacture
Born 1813   Died 1898 aged 85

Henry Bessemer's father was an engineer who fled from France during the Revolution. He established an engineering works in England and it was there that Henry Bessemer, after only a basic education, himself became an ingenious and skilled engineer. At 17 he founded a small business of his own in London, making a variety of products ranging from graphite for pencils to printing machinery. He flourished but his great success, in the 1850s, was a process for converting iron to steel by blowing air through it while molten. Steel was then scarce and expensive. By 1898, when Bessemer died, more than a million tonnes per year was being made in Britain alone by his process and it was also widely used abroad. Its only rival was the Siemens open-hearth process. Much of the steel produced by Bessemer's methods went into rails for the rapidly expanding railway system. ◆

👁 **see also**

Krupp   Siemens

◀ *Benazir Bhutto was inspired to go into politics by her father's death.*

Benazir **Bhutto**

Prime minister of Pakistan from 1988 to 1990 and from 1993 to 1996
Born *1953*

After studying in Pakistan, Benazir Bhutto completed her education in America and England. She returned to Pakistan but after her father, prime minister, Zulfikar Ali Bhutto, was executed, she spent a total of six years either in prison or under house arrest.

In 1986 she launched a campaign for open elections in Pakistan. The death of the president, General Zia-ul-Haq, in an air crash in 1988 did in fact lead to democratic elections. Benazir Bhutto's party won and she became prime minister at the age of 35. She was the first female leader of a Muslim state. In 1990, the opposition forced her out of office and charged her with corruption. She denied all charges and then campaigned to be re-elected as

prime minister. She won the vote in 1993 with a small majority. Her coalition government lasted until 1996. ◆

◉ **see also**
Bhutto, Zulfikar

Zulfikar Ali **Bhutto**

President and then prime minister of Pakistan from 1971 to 1977
Born *1928*   **Died** *1979 aged 51*

The Bhutto family have been important in the politics of India and Pakistan for many years. Zulfikar Ali Bhutto was educated at the universities of California and Oxford before becoming a lawyer. At the age of 30 he joined Ayub Khan's cabinet and within five years had become Foreign Minister of Pakistan. In 1967, he started his

own party, the Pakistan People's Party, which came to power in 1971. Bhutto was first president and later prime minister.

After the 1977 elections there were riots because some people thought Bhutto had rigged the vote. General Zia-ul-Haq staged a coup and overthrew Bhutto's government. Bhutto himself was arrested and charged with the murder of a political opponent. In spite of protests from around the world, he was hanged in April 1979. ◆

◉ **see also**
Bhutto, Benazir

Steve **Biko**

South African civil rights leader
Born *1946*   **Died** *1977 aged 30*

Stephen Biko went to the University of Natal in 1966 to study medicine. He soon became involved in student politics and in 1968 helped to found the South African Students' Organization. His main concern was for his own black people who suffered oppression under the apartheid system which deprived them of their basic rights. In 1972 Biko gave up his medical studies to help form the Black People's Convention, which worked to raise black people's awareness of oppression and to give them a sense of pride and hope for the future. His activities brought him into conflict with the government and he was often arrested and prevented from speaking in public. Then in 1977, after being arrested once again, he was so badly beaten in the police cells that he died before he could be brought to trial. Since his death he has become a symbol of the anti-apartheid movement. ◆

◉ **see also**
Mandela

Billy the Kid

American outlaw in the Wild West
Born 1859   Died 1881 aged 21

By the age of 12, William Bonney was already a gambler and card player, and had knifed a man for insulting his mother. In 1877, after more murderous exploits, he became involved in a war between two cattle-ranching families. As the leader of one of the gangs he was involved in one gun battle after another. He finally returned to cattle thieving and murdering when the war was over.

A sheriff called Pat Garrett was determined to catch Bonney, who was now known as Billy the Kid. He was captured in 1881 and sentenced to hang, but he managed to escape. Two months later, Garrett managed to corner him and shot him dead.

Billy the Kid murdered at least 21 people, but films have been made which show him as a popular hero. In reality, Bonney was a vicious murderer and a thief. ◆

Isabella **Bird**

British traveller and writer
Born 1832   Died 1904 aged 72

When she was 23 Isabella Bird visited Canada and America and carefully recorded much that she saw. Later she travelled to Australia, Japan, India, Tibet, Iran, Korea, and China and wrote successful books about her adventures. She married her family doctor and ceased her travels until his death five years later.

Isabella Bird often felt ill and depressed in England, but once abroad she rode great distances and lived under very hard conditions. She had 'the appetite of a tiger and the digestion of an ostrich'. At the age of 70, in pain from an injured spine, she rode a thousand miles through the Atlas Mountains in North Africa on a horse she mounted by stepladder. It was to be her last journey. ◆

Clarence **Birdseye**

American inventor and businessman
Born 1886   Died 1956 aged 70

Clarence Birdseye lived and died in New York but the idea for his most famous invention came to him when he was buying and selling furs in icy Labrador, Canada. During the severe winter, fresh food was hard to come by so the locals ate food that they had previously frozen. This fascinated Birdseye. When he returned home he began experimenting. He found that if he froze fish or vegetables very quickly between two metal plates, the flavour could be preserved.

In 1929 he became the first person to sell quick-frozen food in small packages. His idea was very successful and his food company grew and grew. Eventually he sold the company for a huge amount of money. Although he went on to invent many other things, he is best remembered for the packets of frozen food which still bear his famous name. ◆

Laszlo **Biro**

Hungarian-born inventor of the ball-point pen
Born 1900   Died 1985 aged 85

Laszlo Biro was born in Hungary, where he spent his early life as a journalist. With his brother Georg he worked on the idea of a pen with a tiny rolling ball at the tip instead of a pointed nib. This ball would allow a smooth flow of ink, although the problem was to get the ink right – not too runny, not too thick, and quick to dry.

In 1938 the brothers went to Argentina, away from the spreading Nazi influence in Europe. There they perfected and patented their ball-point pen – which has since become known simply as a biro.

At first biros were fashionable and expensive, but as time went by they became much cheaper. They were the most convenient everyday writing implements until the felt-tip pen was invented in the 1960s. ◆

▶ *Isabella Bird lived in this tent while travelling with a nomadic tribe in Persia (Iran).*

Otto von
Bismarck

*Prussian leader who helped create a
united Germany*
Born 1815   Died 1898 aged 83

Otto von Bismarck came from
a noble family in Prussia,
which was then only one amongst
many German-speaking states. After
serving in the army, he was elected
to the Prussian parliament and in
1851 represented Prussia in the
German Federal Diet, a parliament
of all German states. He dreamed
of uniting Germany under Prussian
leadership.

In 1862 King Wilhelm of Prussia
made Bismarck prime minister.
Bismarck then started to pursue
an aggressive policy against
neighbouring countries. After
capturing Danish territory with
Austrian help, Prussian armies
fought and defeated Austria in the
Seven Weeks War of 1866. More
success came in 1871 when Prussia
defeated France and expanded
Prussian borders.

These victories persuaded other
German states to join a German

▲ *Bismarck's Prussian army bombards
Strasbourg during the Franco-Prussian
War, 1870–1871.*

Reich (empire) with King Wilhelm
as Kaiser (emperor) and Bismarck
as chancellor. The Reich gained
colonies abroad and built up a fleet
to compete with the British Royal
Navy. In 1879 Bismarck made an
alliance with the Austro-Hungarian
empire. However, his career ended
after Wilhelm died. His successor,
Wilhelm II, was jealous of
Bismarck's power and dismissed
him in 1890. ◆

Georges **Bizet**

French composer
Born 1838   Died 1875 aged 36

Georges Bizet's parents were
both musical and gave him
his first lessons. He began to study
at the Paris Conservatoire when he
was only nine, and made a deep
impression both as a pianist and
composer. In 1857 he won the Prix
de Rome, which enabled him to
study in Italy for three years. On
returning to Paris he had a hard
struggle to make a living. Although
he wrote music of all kinds,
including a delightful Symphony
in C, which was not performed until
long after his death, opera was his
first love. Some of his operas, such
as *The Pearl Fishers* (1863) and *The
Fair Maiden of Perth* (1867), were
reasonably successful, but others
failed. Even his masterpiece,
Carmen (1875), shocked people by
its realism and was coolly received
at first. It is now one of the most
popular of all French operas. Like
all of Bizet's music, it is lively,
colourful, and full of the most
glorious melody. ◆

▼ *Maria Ewing plays the lead in the
English Royal Opera's production of
Bizet's* Carmen.

Tony **Blair**

Prime minister of the UK from 1997
Born *1953*

Tony Blair was educated at private schools in Durham and Edinburgh, then studied law at Oxford. He moved to London in 1976 to become a lawyer. He came from quite a rich family, but he wanted everyone to have a fair chance. So he went into politics as a member of the Labour Party and was elected to Parliament in 1983.

For the next 14 years Britain was governed by the Conservative Party. During that time, Blair played a large part in making the Labour Party more up-to-date, so that more people would vote for it.

In 1994 Blair became Labour Party leader. Then in 1997 a Labour government was voted into power, and Blair became prime minister. The following year he signed a peace settlement in Northern Ireland, after nearly 30 years of violence in the province. ◆

▼ *This is a page from William Blake's* Songs of Innocence and Experience.

William **Blake**

English poet, engraver, and artist
Born *1757* **Died** *1827 aged 69*

As a boy, William Blake loved poetry and art. When he was 10, he went to a drawing school, and at 14 he was apprenticed to an engraver, learning how to prepare illustrations for books. He was for a time a student at the Royal Academy in London, but he later returned to engraving.

As a young man, Blake began to write poetry and illustrate it with pictures of biblical visions he had experienced. He etched his poems on copper plates and coloured the printed pages. Much of his poetry is happy and full of tenderness. His later poems, though, show more anger and sadness.

In his lifetime, few people valued Blake's poetry, and a lot of it was thrown away. But he produced so much that today we still have a large quantity of his poetry to enjoy. ◆

Louis **Blériot**

French airman
Born *1872* **Died** *1936 aged 64*

Born in Cambrai, France, Louis Blériot first made a fortune making car headlamps. Then, when he was 30 he turned to aircraft design. In 1908 he created an aircraft control system not unlike that in use today – using elevators on the tail and later ailerons on the wings.

The first crossing of the English Channel by an aircraft was made by Blériot on 25 July 1909. He flew from Calais to Dover – a distance of some 34 kilometres. The flight took 37 minutes and won him a prize offered by the London paper, the *Daily Mail*. Blériot had designed this aircraft, his eleventh.

▲ *This illustration of Louis Blériot from the cover of a French magazine shows him flying over the cliffs at Dover after crossing the English Channel in his monoplane.*

It was a lightweight monoplane with a wooden frame and a fabric fuselage. ◆

Charles **Blondin**

French tightrope walker
Born *1824* **Died** *1897 aged 72*

Born into a circus family, Charles Blondin was an 'aerobat' at five years of age. He did various tricks, but the tightrope, or high wire, became his speciality.

In 1859 he achieved the feat for which he will always be known. He rigged a high wire above Niagara Falls and walked across, the first person ever to do so. Having made it look easy, he repeated the walk many times, and then devised various ways of adding to it. His most fearsome trick was to call for volunteers to be carried across either piggyback or in a wheelbarrow. ◆

Enid **Blyton**

English author of children's books
Born 1897   Died 1968 aged 71

Enid Blyton began her career as a teacher, but soon switched to journalism, and often wrote about education. She then began to write children's books.

Her first book was a collection of poems for children. In the late 1930s, just before World War II, she started publishing the *Noddy* stories, for very small children, and adventure stories such as the *Famous Five* and the *Secret Seven*, for older children.

It was not long before she was writing her school story series, like *Malory Towers* and *The Naughtiest Girl*.

Enid Blyton wanted to educate her readers, and to give them a clear idea of right and wrong behaviour. Her stories have been enjoyed by a great many children, although teachers and librarians have often said that the plots are too simple and the style of writing is flat and uninteresting. ◆

Humphrey **Bogart**

American film actor
Born 1899   Died 1957 aged 58

'Bogey' was the son of a New York surgeon. He suffered a lip wound in the US Navy during World War I which gave him

▶ *American actor Humphrey Bogart in the 1951 film Sirocco.*

a distinctive appearance and voice when he later became an actor. His first film appearances in the 1930s were usually in gangster movies, but he became famous as the detective Sam Spade in *The Maltese Falcon* (1941). Then came the romantic drama *Casablanca* (1942), with Ingrid Bergman, before he teamed up with his wife Lauren Bacall in films such as *To Have and Have Not* (1944) and *The Big Sleep* (1946). He won an Oscar for his role in *The African Queen* in 1951. ◆

Niels **Bohr**

Danish physicist who helped discover the structure of atoms
Born 1885   Died 1962 aged 77

Niels Bohr studied physics at Copenhagen University, before becoming a professor there.

He moved to England in 1912 and worked with the great physicist Ernest Rutherford, trying to discover what atoms really looked like. Bohr's work showed that atoms have a nucleus at the centre and that electrons are arranged in orbits a fixed distance away from the nucleus. In 1922 Bohr received the Nobel Prize for Physics for his work on atoms.

During World War II Bohr worked hard to help Jewish scientists find new jobs, away from the tortures that they faced under Hitler. He himself made a dramatic escape from Denmark and fled to America. In 1943 he worked on the atom bomb project. However, he was so horrified by the potential effects of such a bomb that he spent the rest of his life working on peaceful ways of using atomic energy. ◆

👁 **see also**
Rutherford

39

Simón **Bolívar**

Venezuelan general
Born *1783*   **Died** *1830 aged 47*

As a young man Simón Bolívar travelled twice to Europe. There he was inspired by new ideas which claimed that all people should be free and equal. Eager to free his own country, Venezuela, from Spanish rule, he joined a group of rebels there. In 1810 they captured Caracas, the capital city, but the Spaniards fought back. Bolívar became a military leader in 1811, recaptured Caracas in 1813 and was given the title 'Liberator'.

A year later, Bolívar was forced to flee South America. But by 1817 he had returned to fight again. In 1819 his forces defeated the Spaniards in Colombia. That same year he founded Gran Colombia (a group of South American states), and became president.

In 1822, Bolívar met José de San Martín, who freed Argentina and Chile from Spanish rule. Bolívar later helped defeat Spanish armies still in Ecuador, Venezuela and Peru, bringing Spanish power in South America to an end.

In upper Peru, the people decided to form a separate republic, called Bolivia, in honour of Bolívar.

▼ *In 1821 Bolívar's army liberated Venezuela.*

Although Bolívar was respected, few agreed with his idea of uniting the whole of South America. When he died in 1830, Bolívar was hated by many for his dictatorial ways, but is also admired as South America's greatest liberator. ◆

👁 **see also**
San Martin

George **Boole**

English mathematician
Born *1815*   **Died** *1864 aged 49*

George Boole's father worked as a cobbler but was interested in mathematics and making optical instruments. He passed these interests on to his son who, by the time he was 15, was well-grounded in mathematics and had taught himself Latin, Greek, French, and German. In 1849, although he had no university degree, he was appointed professor of mathematics in Queen's College, Cork, and in 1857 was elected Fellow of the prestigious Royal Society. At Cork he wrote 50 mathematical papers and four books and developed what is still known as Boolean algebra. In this, logical statements are represented by algebraic equations, and the numbers 0 and 1 are used to represent 'false' and 'true'. Boolean algebra is fundamental to the operation of today's modern computers. ◆

Daniel **Boone**

Hero of the American Frontier
Born *1734*   **Died** *1820 aged 85*

Daniel Boone never went to school. Instead he hunted with the Native Americans who visited his father's farm. He grew up almost as skilled as they were in tracking animals.

On his first attempt to lead settlers to the West, Boone's 16-year-old son was captured and tortured to death by Native Americans. Two years later he completed the journey and founded Fort Boonesborough in Kentucky. For 20 years he led the defence of this settlement against attack.

Perhaps because of his childhood experience, Boone seemed reasonably at ease among the Native Americans. He once said 'I wouldn't give a hoot in Hell for a man who isn't sometimes afraid.' From Kentucky he took his family further west to Missouri. He died there in his sleep. ◆

Catherine and William **Booth**

English founders of the Salvation Army
William Booth
Born *1829*   **Died** *1912 aged 83*
Catherine Booth
Born *1829*   **Died** *1890 aged 61*

As a young man William Booth knew poverty, because his father went bankrupt and died early. He joined the Methodist Church, but left because he wanted to preach his own ideas. In 1855

▲ *While many of William Booth's peers went abroad to do missionary work, he stayed at home to help deprived people in Britain's city slums.*

he married Catherine Mumford, a social worker. Together they started the Salvation Army, a Christian organization to fight sin and poverty. William became the Salvation Army's first General.

Catherine Booth believed that women had as much right to preach as men. She made sure that the Salvation Army gave equal rights to all its members. She died in 1890, but William Booth continued their work. His book, *In Darkest England*, gave many ideas on how to help people suffering from poverty, homelessness, and alcoholism. With the help of their son, Bramwell, and daughter, Evangeline, the Salvation Army grew worldwide, and today it is still active in helping poor and homeless people everywhere. ◆

Jorge Luis **Borges**

Argentinian writer
Born *1899*   **Died** *1986 aged 87*

Jorge Luis Borges experienced a wide variety of cultures in his youth. He was born in Buenos Aires, Argentina, and educated in Geneva, Switzerland. One of his grandmothers was English and from

an early age he read English literature. He also lived and wrote for a time in Spain. His great intellectual appetite was also fed by a wide reading of philosophy and theology from other cultures and ages.

He published many volumes of poetry, but he is most famous for his short stories; *Labyrinths* (1962) is an anthology of some of his best-known works. He used his great pool of knowledge to create unusual stories, some of which are often dream-like, cleverly blurring the boundaries between reality and fiction. ◆

Borgia family

Important Italian family in the late 15th and early 16th century
Alfonso Borgia
Born *1378*   **Died** *1458 aged 80*
Rodrigo Borgia
Born *1431*   **Died** *1503 aged 72*
Cesare Borgia
Born *1475*   **Died** *1507 aged 32*
Lucrezia Borgia
Born *1480*   **Died** *1519 aged 39*

The Borgias were an Italian family. The first Borgia to become famous was Alfonso. In 1455 he was elected Pope Calixtus III. He lived a simple life, but made his young nephew Rodrigo a cardinal and gave him great wealth.

Rodrigo Borgia worked in Rome for his uncle and for subsequent popes. Churchmen were forbidden to marry and have children. Rodrigo, however, had seven illegitimate children.

▶ *Rodrigo Borgia used corrupt means, blackmail, and bribery to be made Pope Alexander VI. He executed any who dared oppose his new position.*

In spite of this behaviour, he was elected as Pope Alexander VI in 1492. He then tried to make his children important and rich, especially his son, Cesare, and his daughter, Lucrezia.

Cesare wanted to conquer land in central Italy and make himself a prince. From 1499, with Pope Alexander's support, he attacked one city after another. But in 1503 Pope Alexander died. The new pope and his successor hated the Borgias. Cesare was arrested, and later taken to Spain and imprisoned. In 1506 he escaped, but died in 1507.

Lucrezia Borgia married three times, each time to a supporter of her father and brother. Her third husband was the duke of Ferrara. In Ferrara she encouraged leading painters and writers of the day. ◆

▲ *This is the centre panel of Hieronymus Bosch's triptych (painting on three panels) The Garden of Earthly Delights, his best-known work.*

Hieronymus Bosch

Flemish painter
Born *c.1450* ***Died*** *1516 aged about 65*

Bosch's real name was Jerome van Aken; 'Hieronymus' is simply the Latin form of Jerome, and 'Bosch' is a shortened version of the name of the town where he lived – Hertongenbosch. This was a prosperous place (in what is now the southern part of the Netherlands) and Bosch was the town's leading artist. We know little about his life, for few records have survived. However, his paintings clearly show that he had one of the most vivid imaginations in the history of art, for there has been nothing else quite like them before or since. He often painted weird demons and monstrous creatures – sometimes half-human and half-animal – to show the follies and sins of mankind. His pictures are not only bizarre and sometimes baffling, but also very beautiful, for he had a wonderful sense of colour. ◆

Sandro Botticelli

Italian painter
Born *c.1445* ***Died*** *1510 aged about 65*

Sandro Botticelli's real name was Alessandro Filipepi. 'Botticelli', meaning 'little barrel', was originally a nickname given to his chubby elder brother, but it stuck as a family name.

Botticelli lived almost all his life in Florence, which in the 15th century was a flourishing centre of art. The city was rich and proud, and Botticelli was one of its busiest artists, working for churches and noble families (who tried to outdo each other in splendour) as well as the civic authorities. At this time, most pictures were of religious subjects, but Botticelli's two most famous works are mythological scenes – *Primavera* (meaning 'Spring') and *The Birth of Venus*, both now in the Uffizi Gallery in Florence. They were painted for a member of the Medici family, who dominated political life in the city, and they were the first mythological paintings to be done on a large scale (each one is about three metres wide). They show the amazing gracefulness for which Botticelli is famous. In addition to painting, Botticelli was also commissioned to illustrate Dante's *Divine Comedy*. By the end of his career, however, his work had gone out of fashion. He was a sad and neglected figure when he died and his paintings did not become popular again until the 19th century. ◆

🔍 **see also**
Dante   Medici family

Boudica

Queen of the Iceni tribe
Date of birth unknown
Died AD *61 age unknown*

The Iceni tribe was one of the few tribes in Roman Britain that were allowed to govern themselves. However, when the king of the Iceni died in AD 59, the Romans decided to bring the area under full Roman rule. The Roman historian Tacitus wrote that the

▲ *This statue shows Boudica riding into battle. We do not know for certain if her chariot really did have sword blades attached to the axles. This could have been a myth spread among her terrified Roman victims, 70,000 of whom were said to have died during her rebellion.*

Romans plundered the kingdom, Boudica (the king's widow) was flogged, and her daughters were raped.

Tacitus described Boudica, whose name in her Celtic language meant 'Victory', as 'a very big woman, terrifying to look at, with a fierce look on her face'. She had a 'great mass of hair the colour of a lion's mane'. She gathered an army around her to fight the Romans. At first the rebellion went well as Boudica's army destroyed the towns of Colchester, Verulamium (now St Albans), and London. But then the Roman governor of Britain brought a great force from North Wales and destroyed the rebel army. Boudica poisoned herself to avoid capture by the Romans. ◆

David **Bowie**

English singer and songwriter
Born *1947*

David Robert Jones was born in Brixton, London. As David Bowie he became a songwriter and performer who remained a star by changing his looks and musical style to keep up with the times.

He was in many groups during the 1960s, but his first big hit was 'Space Oddity' in 1969. That led to a string of more than 40 hit records, including 'Let's Dance' (1983) which was No. 1 in both Britain and America at the same time.

When performing live, Bowie always liked to create a whole new personality for himself on stage, as he did in 1972 as 'Ziggy Stardust'. He also appeared in films and plays, but always returned to music. In 1983 he was paid 10.5 million US dollars for a concert in California, the highest sum ever paid to a rock star for a single show. ◆

Robert **Boyle**

Irish scientist
Born *1627*   **Died** *1691 aged 64*

Robert Boyle was a very clever boy and could speak Latin and Greek at the age of eight. In his twenties he took part in scientific experiments and discussions with a group who went on to found the Royal Society, a very prestigious association to this day.

Boyle did much to establish the method and ideas of modern chemistry. He wrote a famous book called the *Sceptical Chymist*. In this and other books he helped to explain ideas about atoms and elements. He insisted on the importance of doing experiments to test whether scientific ideas were really true. Boyle is best remembered for a law of physics: Boyle's law tells us mathematically how the volume of a gas will alter when the pressure is changed. ◆

Donald **Bradman**

Australian cricketer
Born *1908*

As a child, Donald Bradman practised cricket on his own by bouncing a golf ball against a wall and hitting it with a cricket stump. This practice paid off because he grew up to be the greatest run-scoring batsman of all time.

In his career he scored 28,067 runs at an average of 95 runs per innings. His highest-ever score was 452 not out, for New South Wales against Queensland, when he was 21. In his last Test innings as captain of Australia, he was bowled out for 0. Had it not been for that, he would have retired in 1948 with a Test average of over 100 runs per innings. ◆

William and Lawrence **Bragg**

English physicists
William Henry Bragg
Born *1862*   **Died** *1942 aged 79*
William Lawrence Bragg
Born *1890*   **Died** *1971 aged 81*

William and Lawrence Bragg shared the Nobel Prize for Physics in 1915 and were perhaps the most successful father and son team in the history of science.

In 1912 the German physicist Max von Laue showed that X-rays were waves and that they could be reflected from the layers of atoms inside crystals. William Bragg saw the importance of this and built the first spectrometer to measure the wavelengths of X-rays.

William and his son then worked together on the scattering of X-rays from different crystals. Lawrence worked out the formula that connects the wavelength of the X-rays to the spacing of atoms in the crystal structure. Scientists call this the Bragg law. ◆

see also
Becquerel   Röntgen

Tycho **Brahe**

Danish astronomer
Born *1546*   **Died** *1601 aged 54*

At university Tycho Brahe studied philosophy and other subjects. But on 21 August 1560 something happened which changed his life. It was predicted that on that day a small eclipse of the Sun would be seen in Copenhagen. Brahe was thrilled when the eclipse took place at the predicted time. He immediately turned his attention to astronomy and mathematics.

Brahe used various astronomical instruments for measuring the positions of stars and planets, but could only observe with the naked eye because Galileo's telescope was not yet invented. Before he died Brahe passed on his astronomical measurements to his assistant Johann Kepler, who later used them to produce the first accurate description of the movement of planets in our Solar System.

Brahe was a colourful figure who often courted trouble with other people. At the age of 19, during a midnight duel, his nose was cut off. From then on he had to wear a false metal nose. ◆

see also
Galileo   Kepler

▲ *Tycho Brahe pictured in the observatory he set up in Denmark.*

Johannes **Brahms**

German composer
Born *1833*   **Died** *1897 aged 63*

Johannes Brahms had his first music lessons from his father, who was a double-bass player. He began to study the piano when he was seven, and by the age of ten was performing in public concerts.

Although he was a fine pianist, Brahms really wanted to be a composer. His chance came when he met the composer Robert Schumann and his pianist wife, Clara. They treated him like a brother and did everything they could to encourage him. In 1863 he went to live in Vienna and his composing career really took off.

Brahms never married, though for a long time he was in love with Clara Schumann. What mattered to him most, however, was his music. He produced four great symphonies, chamber and piano music, songs, choral works such as the *German Requiem*, and also several fine concertos. ◆

see also
Beethoven   Schumann

Louis **Braille**

French inventor of a reading system for blind people
Born *1809*   **Died** *1852 aged 43*

Braille is a system of raised dots on paper that can be read by touch. It was invented by Louis Braille when he was only 15.

Born near Paris, Braille was blinded by an infection after an accident when he was three. He went to a special school where he excelled in music, becoming an organist and cellist. He decided to stay on at the school and became a teacher there.

Louis Braille spent most of his life improving and refining his reading system. It uses six dots in 63 combinations to provide letters, punctuation marks, numbers, and musical notation. Blind people can 'read' the dots by running their fingers lightly across the page. ◆

▲ *Constantin Brancusi's bronze sculpture* Mlle Pogany *(1913).*

Constantin **Brancusi**

Romanian sculptor
Born 1876   Died 1957 aged 81

Constantin Brancusi left home at the age of 11. He had no schooling until he attended art school in Bucharest. Later, when he was in Paris, he was fascinated by the work of the great sculptor Rodin, but refused to work with him because 'Nothing grows in the shade of big trees'.

Brancusi needed freedom to develop his ideas of completely streamlined shapes uncluttered by any fussy details. He was influenced by African art, Romanian folk art, and the exciting modern art of his time. His sculptures in polished metal, stone, and wood have grace, symmetry, and sleek lines.

Brancusi's masterpiece is a group of war memorial monuments including the 27-m high *Endless Column*. ◆

👁 **see also**
Rodin

Marlon **Brando**

American film actor
Born 1924

When Marlon Brando studied acting in New York, he learned how to identify completely with the character he was playing. He also developed a realistic style of speaking which was well-suited to the types of young people he was portraying. His early films often showed him as a rebel, as in *A Streetcar Named Desire* (1951) and *The Wild One* (1953). He won an Oscar for *On the Waterfront* (1954).

Later he played powerful, older men such as the Mafia leader Don Corleone in *The Godfather* (1972), which won him another Oscar. In *Superman* (1978) he was on screen as Superman's father for just nine minutes and was paid over 18 million US dollars. ◆

▼ *Marlon Brando as a member of a motorbike gang in* The Wild One *(1953).*

Willy **Brandt**

German chancellor and statesman
Born 1913   Died 1992 aged 78

Herbert Ernst Karl Frahm was a young man when the Nazis came to power in Germany. He opposed their policies and had to flee to Norway to escape the Gestapo. He changed his name to Willy Brandt and worked as a journalist in Norway and Sweden until Hitler and the Nazis were finally defeated in 1945.

Brandt returned to Germany and was elected to the Bundestag (parliament) in 1949 before becoming mayor of West Berlin in 1957. He led the city through the crisis of 1961 when the Berlin Wall was built by the Communists in the east of the city. This experience made him determined to improve relations with the Communist east. His chance came when he was elected chancellor of West Germany in 1969. He created policies of *Ostpolitik*, designed to reduce tension between east and west. For this he was awarded the Nobel Peace Prize in 1971. Just three years later Brandt was forced to resign when one of his assistants was found to be a spy. ◆

▲ A still life of a bottle, some fruit, and a napkin by Georges Braque. It is an example of the Cubist style he and Pablo Picasso developed.

Richard **Branson**

Chairman of the Virgin Group
Born 1950

Richard Branson is one of the UK's most successful businessmen. He says that he was successful by accident, going into businesses such as air travel because he was not happy with the existing service, rather than to make a fortune.

Branson left school early. He edited *Student* magazine, then set up the Student Advisory Centre (now called Help). In 1969 he started up Virgin, a successful record mail-order company. Soon afterwards he founded Virgin Records. The company expanded into publishing, recording, and selling other products, and changed its name to the Virgin Group.

Branson has continued to extend the Virgin brand into new areas, most notably Virgin Airways, Virgin Railways, Virgin Radio and Virgin Cola. In 1986 his boat won the coveted Blue Riband for the fastest crossing of the Atlantic by a boat. He was the first person to cross the Atlantic in a hot-air balloon in 1987, and has made several attempts to fly a balloon around the world. ◆

Georges **Braque**

French painter
Born 1882   Died 1963 aged 81

Georges Braque's father and grandfather were skilled painter-decorators. He was trained in this profession himself, but he took up art seriously when he was in his early 20s. At first he painted colourful landscapes, but in 1907 he met Pablo Picasso and this dramatically changed his outlook. Together, he and Picasso created the style known as Cubism, which was one of the great turning points in modern art. They specialized in still life pictures and painted objects as if we were seeing them from several angles at once. Their partnership come to an end during World War I. Braque was severely wounded during the war, but he recovered and later had a long and distinguished career as one of France's greatest painters. ◆

Art is meant to disturb, science reassures.

GEORGES BRAQUE

👁 **see also**

Picasso

Wernher von **Braun**

German rocket engineer
Born 1912   Died 1977 aged 65

Wernher von Braun was the son of a German baron. He became interested in rockets as a teenager after reading science fiction books.

It was during World War II that the real importance of rockets was recognized: unmanned rockets could carry bombs to enemy targets. Von Braun, a member of the German Nazi Party, headed a team that developed the first true missile. It was called the V-2 ('V' stood for *Vergeltung* which means 'vengeance'). This rocket was fuelled with alcohol and liquid oxygen and had an explosive warhead. It could travel a distance of about 300 km. Over a thousand V-2 rockets hit London during the war.

In 1945, when the war was over, von Braun surrendered to the Americans. They took him to America where he ran a rocket-building programme. This led to the building of the Saturn 5 rocket, used to launch America's manned missions to the Moon. ◆

Bertolt **Brecht**

German playwright and poet
Born *1898* **Died** *1956 aged 58*

Bertolt Brecht was a major influence on 20th century drama. He explored a new style of drama, using unusual staging and different styles of acting in order to achieve his aim of making audiences think about the moral and political implications of his plays.

Brecht was born in Augsburg, Germany, and studied medicine and philosophy at the universities of Munich and Berlin. After serving in World War I he achieved success with his play *Drums in the Night* (1924). Throughout the 1920s and early 1930s he wrote many more plays. In 1933 Brecht and his wife were forced to flee from Germany after Hitler came to power. Brecht eventually reached America where he was investigated for having Communist beliefs. He left America and returned to East Berlin in 1947 where he founded The Berliner Ensemble, a theatre company that became world famous.

Among Brecht's plays that have become classics are *Mother Courage and her Children*, *The Caucasian Chalk Circle*, and *The Resistable Rise of Arturo Ui*. ◆

Benjamin **Britten**

English composer
Born *1913* **Died** *1976 aged 63*

Benjamin Britten began writing music when he was only five. His Simple Symphony is made up of tunes he wrote as a child.

After studying at the Royal College of Music in London, Britten earned his living by writing music for documentary films and for concerts. He went to live in America at the beginning of World War II,

but could not forget England. When he returned, it was to write the work that made him world-famous: the opera *Peter Grimes* (1945).

Many of Britten's operas were written for the world's great opera houses. Others, such as *The Turn of the Screw* (1954) (a chilling ghost story), were designed for the festival he started in Aldeburgh, the Suffolk town he made his home.

But it was not just opera that made his name. Britten wrote splendid orchestral music, songs, and choral works, none more fine, perhaps, than his great *War Requiem* of 1962. ◆

Brontë sisters

English novel-writing sisters
Charlotte Brontë
Born *1816* **Died** *1855 aged 38*

Emily Brontë
Born *1818*
Died *1848*
aged 30

Anne Brontë
Born *1820*
Died *1849*
aged 29

Charlotte, Emily, and Anne were the daughters of a poor Irish clergyman. They lived in Haworth, a small town on the edge of the Yorkshire moors. Their mother died when Charlotte, the oldest child, was only five. After that, the sisters and their brother Branwell led their own lives mostly apart from their lonely father.

Later on, the sisters went to boarding school, and then became governesses. However, they hated being apart from each other, and eventually they all returned home where they started to write. In 1847 Charlotte wrote her masterpiece, *Jane Eyre*. This tells the story of a girl called Jane, who goes to a harsh school, and later becomes a governess. Jane falls in love with her employer, Mr Rochester. They are just about to marry when she discovers he has a wife already, a woman who is mad and locked up in a secret room in the same house.

Emily also wrote her only novel, *Wuthering Heights*, in the same year. Set in the bleak moors she knew so well, it tells the story of two very different boys, Edgar and Heathcliff, who both fall in love with the same girl, Catherine.

Anne had her novel *Agnes Grey* published in 1847. The sisters all wrote under pretend names, or 'pseudonyms'. Charlotte was 'Currer Bell', Emily was 'Ellis Bell', and Anne was 'Acton Bell': in those days it was easier to get published if you were a man!

Sadly, all three sisters died young. No other family of novelists has ever achieved so much as the shy and unworldly Brontës, whose books are still read very widely today. ◆

◀ *Laurence Olivier and Merle Oberon in the 1939 film adaptation of Emily Brontë's novel,* Wuthering Heights.

James **Brown**

American soul singer
Born 1928

James Brown had a hard childhood. When he was only 16 he was jailed for armed robbery. Turning to music kept him out of trouble, and in 1958 he had his first million-selling record, 'Try Me', a song in the gospel and rhythm 'n' blues styles. He gradually added hard, rhythmic guitars and frantic, punchy horns, creating a style which became known as funk.

His exciting live shows earned him the title Godfather of Soul. Hits like 'Papa's Got a Brand New Bag' (1965) and 'Living in America' (1986) confirmed his star status over a period of 20 years. ◆

John **Brown**

American anti-slavery campaigner
Born 1800   Died 1859 aged 59

'John Brown's body lies a-mouldering in the grave but his soul keeps marching on' goes a famous song. It celebrates the man who became a hero to Americans who were opposed to slavery.

John Brown was a white man with a large family. Seeking work, he settled down in a black township. He was angered by the way that the black slaves were treated. With five of his sons, he started illegally importing guns in to Kansas to help slaves fight for their freedom. One of their attacks on some slavery supporters ended in bloodshed. The attack, known as the 'Pottawatomie massacre', made him famous and much feared.

In 1859 he and 18 armed men captured a government armoury at Harpers Ferry in West Virginia, taking 60 hostages. They intended to arm the slaves and start a revolt. However, after two days marines stormed the armoury to free the hostages and capture Brown. He was tried and hanged shortly afterwards. ◆

📖 **see also**
Stowe   Tubman

◀ *A painting entitled* The Last Moments of John Brown.

▲ *The Pied Piper of Hamelin charms a group of rats.*

Robert **Browning**

English poet
Born 1812   Died 1889 aged 77

Robert Browning was the son of a bank clerk. Rather than go to school he stayed at home reading books from his father's large collection. He started writing poems from an early age and had his first published when he was only 21. He wrote his best-known poem, *The Pied Piper of Hamelin*, in 1842. It was based on an old German legend about a piper who charmed the rats out of the city with his music.

In 1846 Robert married Elizabeth Barrett, also a poet. Her father did not approve, so the couple had to run away to Italy to be together. They lived there happily, although sometimes Browning missed home. After they had been married for

15 years, Elizabeth died. Very saddened, Browning returned to England. There, he wrote what many people consider to be his masterpiece, *The Ring and the Book* (1869), based on an Italian murder story. ◆

Anton **Bruckner**

Austrian composer and organist
Born 1824   Died 1896, aged 72

Anton Bruckner was the son of a poor village schoolmaster who was also the local church organist. Bruckner soon learned everything his father could teach him, and in 1837 was accepted as a chorister at the great Augustinian monastery of St Florian. He was a very modest man and went on studying long after he had made a name for himself as a composer and virtuoso. From 1868 he worked in Vienna as a professor at the prestigious Conservatoire.

Bruckner was greatly admired for his improvisations and undertook important concert tours to Paris and London. He wrote 11 symphonies, but discarded the first two and left the finale of his last symphony (known as No. 9) unfinished. Fortunately it could be completed from his detailed sketches, and so joined the others as some of the most important symphonic works of the late 19th century. ◆

Pieter **Bruegel** (the Elder)

Flemish painter
Born c.1525   Died 1569 aged about 44

Pieter Bruegel was probably born in the village of Bruegel, near Breda in The Netherlands. There

is very little information about Bruegel's early life, but we do know that when he was in his twenties he travelled to Italy to see the great works of art there.

Although Bruegel was known for painting religious themes, he also painted people involved in ordinary village life. Some of his best-known paintings of such country folk are *Peasant Wedding* and *Peasant Dance*. Bruegel painted people honestly, with all their human failings, including drunkenness and greed. Some of his pictures carried strong messages about the good and bad, foolish and sensible things in life. His paintings are truly fascinating and need careful looking into to see all of the details.

His two sons, Pieter Bruegel the Younger and Jan Bruegel, are also well-known artists. ◆

Isambard Kingdom **Brunel**

British engineer
Born 1806   Died 1859 aged 53

As a boy, Brunel showed great skill at drawing and geometry. He trained with a maker of scientific instruments in France before returning to England to work.

In 1830 he entered a competition to design a bridge to span the Avon gorge in Bristol. He won, but his design for the Clifton Suspension Bridge was not actually completed until 1864, after his death.

The turning point of Brunel's career came in 1833 when he was made chief engineer of the Great Western Railway Company. His main task was to build a railway between London and Bristol. It was one of the finest engineering achievements of its day.

While working on the Great Western Railway, Brunel became interested in steamships. His plan was that passengers from London to Bristol would be able to travel on to New York. Brunel built the first steamship to cross the Atlantic, the *Great Western*, which was launched in 1838. It had paddle wheels and was built of wood. His second ship, the *Great Britain*, was a revolution in design. Launched in 1843, it had a screw-propeller and was built of iron. It was the largest ship of its time and the forerunner of modern ocean-going vessels. ◆

▼ *Brunel's steamship* Great Eastern *was used to lay the first transatlantic telegraph cable.*

Filippo **Brunelleschi**

Italian goldsmith and architect
Born 1377   *Died* 1446 aged 69

Filippo Brunelleschi grew up in Florence during the Renaissance – a time when scholars and artists were beginning to study the art and architecture of Ancient Rome and to encourage their use again. Brunelleschi, who trained as a goldsmith and did not turn to architecture until he was middle-aged, was the first architect to design buildings in this new spirit.

Brunelleschi took his ideas from the Florentine buildings he believed had been built by the Romans, but which had in fact been built hundreds of years after Roman times. His own buildings (churches, chapels, and a home for abandoned babies) have pleasing proportions which were quite new in Italian architecture. He also worked out the system for drawing in perspective that is still used today.

Brunelleschi was equally skilled as an engineer. He was given the job of providing Florence Cathedral with the largest dome to be built since Ancient Roman times and he invented a brilliant system for its construction. ◆

Sergey **Bubka**

Ukrainian record-breaking pole-vaulter
Born 1963

Sergey Bubka took up pole-vaulting at the age of 12 and showed exceptional speed and strength. When he was 19 he became world champion at the 1983 Helsinki championships.

Bubka could not attend the 1984 Los Angeles Olympic Games

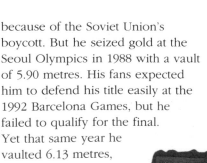

▲ *Since 1984 the pole-vaulter Sergey Bubka has broken the world record on 32 occasions.*

because of the Soviet Union's boycott. But he seized gold at the Seoul Olympics in 1988 with a vault of 5.90 metres. His fans expected him to defend his title easily at the 1992 Barcelona Games, but he failed to qualify for the final. Yet that same year he vaulted 6.13 metres, another world best.

Sergey Bubka has set the world record for the pole-vault over 30 times. ◆

Buddha (Siddhartha Gautama)

Indian religious teacher and founder of Buddhism
Born c.563 BC
Died c.483 BC aged about 80

Gautama was born at Lumbini (in modern Nepal). There is a story which says that a wise man predicted that Gautama would either be a great world ruler or a great religious teacher. His father, Suddhodhana, tried to turn his mind away from the religious life by keeping him within the gardens surrounding their home. Gautama married and he and his wife, Yasodhara, had a son called Rahula.

When Gautama was about 29 years old, he saw four signs, known to Buddhists as the 'heavenly messengers'. These changed his life.

▼ *A golden Buddha from the Wat Po temple in Bangkok, Thailand.*

They were an old man, a sick man, a corpse, and a wandering holy man who was seeking the truth. Their message of change, suffering, death, and the possibility of understanding the meaning of life led Gautama to leave his wife and child in the care of his family and go into the forest.

For six years he learnt from various religious teachers about meditation and strict disciplines of fasting and spiritual practice. At the end of that time he decided that depriving himself of sleep and extreme fasting weakened his body too much for deep reflection, so he broke his fast.

Gautama meditated for a whole night under a sacred tree, later called the Bodhi (enlightenment) tree. He made the breakthrough to understanding truth, which he called the Dharma. He discovered the causes of suffering, the nature of impermanence, and the need to purify the heart. His awakening to the truth is known as the Enlightenment.

After this, he was known as the Buddha (the Enlightened One) and spent the rest of his life teaching others the way to spiritual

understanding. His first sermon at Sarnath near Varanasi (Benares) outlined the Four Noble Truths and the Noble Eightfold Path which form the core of his teaching. For the next 45 years he travelled widely in northern India and taught many people. He ordained both monks and nuns, and instructed them to continue to teach others. ◆

Buffalo Bill

Scout for the US Cavalry, actor, and Wild West showman
Born *1846* **Died** *1917 aged 70*

Like many other people in the 'Wild West', William Cody (Buffalo Bill's real name) had little schooling and could just about write his name. At the age of 11 he was working to support his family. Later he fought in the American Civil War. After that he made his living supplying buffalo (bison) meat to railway workers. Cody's skill in shooting buffalo gave him his nickname.

▼ *A poster from 1899 advertising one of Buffalo Bill's popular Wild West shows.*

During the 1870s, Cody was a scout with the cavalry who were fighting the Indians. His hair-raising adventures made him famous, and he appeared on the stage in plays about himself. Cody became best known for his Wild West Show, an exhibition of horsemanship and mock battles which toured all over the world. ◆

 see also
Oakley

John **Bunyan**

English Puritan preacher and writer
Born *1628* **Died** *1688 aged 59*

John Bunyan's family had very little money but he managed to learn to read and write, which was fairly unusual for someone so poor.

Bunyan got married in 1649. His wife had two religious books which had a great influence on her husband. He became a strict Puritan, gave up having a good time, and devoted his life to preaching.

Soon after Charles II became king of Britain in 1660, strict laws were passed against Puritan preachers, and Bunyan went to prison several times. In Bedford town jail he began to write his most important book, *The Pilgrim's Progress*, which was published in 1678. This is the story of the journey through life of a man called Christian. It is an allegory, which means that the events in the story have a deeper, religious meaning. Christian faces many dangers and temptations, meets lots of people, and sees many different places before finally reaching God's Heavenly City. The story shows how Christian learns to choose between right and wrong, and gets nearer and nearer to God. ◆

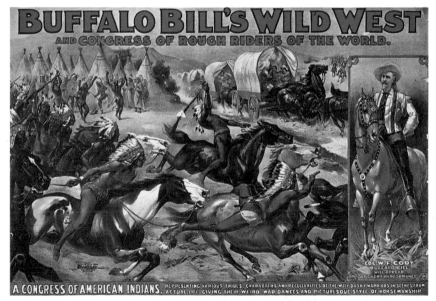

BUFFALO BILL'S WILD WEST
AND CONGRESS OF ROUGH RIDERS OF THE WORLD.

A CONGRESS OF AMERICAN INDIANS. REPRESENTING VARIOUS TRIBES, CHARACTERS AND PECULIARITIES OF THE WILY DUSKY WARRIORS IN SCENES FROM ACTUAL LIFE GIVING THEIR WEIRD WAR DANCES AND PICTURESQUE STYLE OF HORSEMANSHIP

Robert **Burns**

Scottish poet
Born *1759*   **Died** *1796 aged 37*

Robert Burns was one of seven children of a struggling farmer in Ayrshire, Scotland. Burns began writing poetry at school, and decided to make full use of the words, rhythms, and sounds of his own Scottish dialect.

Burns worked as a farmer but had little success, and he caused so much trouble through his many love affairs that he came close to leaving Scotland. But when some of his poems were published in 1786, he was recognized as a poet of genius, and he decided to remain in Scotland. In addition to his poetry, Burns wrote or adapted traditional Scottish songs, including 'Auld Lang Syne', 'A Red Red Rose', and 'Ye Banks and Braes o' Bonnie Doon'.

For most of his life Burns had to worry about money, especially after

▼ *Some of Burn's possessions and commemorative art works.*

marrying in 1788 and starting a family. At first he returned to farming. Then in 1791 he took a full-time job as an excise-man (tax collector) in Dumfries. His last major poem, 'Tam o' Shanter', was published that same year.

Burns has been translated into more languages than any British poet apart from Shakespeare, and his birthday on 25 January is celebrated annually by Scots all around the world. ◆

Richard **Burton**

English writer, translator, and explorer
Born *1821*   **Died** *1890 aged 69*

When Richard Burton went to Oxford University he could already speak six languages fluently. He later claimed he had learnt 29 more. Oriental languages were his particular interest. He translated 30 books, including *The Arabian Nights*, and he wrote 43 of his own, mostly about his explorations.

As a young man Burton joined the Indian Army and developed a taste for travelling. Carefully disguised as an Afghan Muslim, he crossed Arabia and entered cities forbidden to Europeans, such as Mecca. Later he went to Africa to search for the source of the Nile. On one expedition a native spear pierced his jaw severely wounding him. However, he was not easily deterred and returned to Africa several times. Together with John Speke, another English explorer, he discovered Lake Tanganyika.

Burton kept detailed records on the lives of the people he came across during his travels. He published many of them but after his death his wife destroyed most of his other papers, much to the regret of later scholars. ◆

▲ *Gatsha Buthelezi in traditional Zulu costume. He is the great-grandson of Cetshwayo, the former Zulu king.*

Gatsha **Buthelezi**

South African minister of home affairs
Born *1928*

Gatsha Mangosotho Buthelezi is leader of the Inkatha Freedom Party (IFP). Its supporters are mostly Zulu-speakers from the province of KwaZulu-Natal.

In the 1960s Buthelezi opposed white domination and apartheid. He was against the establishment of separate 'homelands' for blacks from different ethnic groups. But in 1972 he became chief minister of

KwaZulu, a 'Zulu' homeland. In 1975 he re-established Inkatha (first formed in the 1920s) as an organization to unite Zulus and restore the rights of the king.

In the 1980s members of the African National Congress (ANC) criticized Buthelezi for opposing its call for sanctions against apartheid and for collaborating with the ruling National Party (NP). Many young, urban Zulu-speakers sided with the ANC, but most older, rural-dwellers backed Inkatha. Many thousands from both sides have died in fighting between the two organizations.

In South Africa's first democratic elections, held in April 1994, Inkatha came third behind the ANC and the NP. Inkatha won the election in KwaZulu and Buthelezi became a minister in the national government. ◆

see also

Cetshwayo de Klerk Mandela

Josephine **Butler**

English campaigner for the rights of women
Born 1828 Died 1906 aged 78

Josephine Butler was a beautiful and educated woman. When she was quite young she saw that women were not allowed by law to be equal with men. She was happily married, but when her young daughter died, Butler decided to spend the rest of her life helping other women.

She began her work in Liverpool with prostitutes. At that time it was believed that prostitutes carried disease. Any woman suspected of being a prostitute could be arrested, examined by force, and imprisoned. Butler attacked this law and started what she called a 'Great Crusade' against it. Many people thought it

was wrong to defend prostitutes, and she was attacked several times. However, Butler knew that most women became prostitutes because they were poor. As a brave woman and a great speaker, she won the support of thousands of people and the laws were eventually changed. ◆

Richard **Byrd**

American polar explorer
Born 1888 Died 1957 aged 68

Richard Byrd started exploring when he was in command of American naval aircraft assisting an expedition to Greenland. Unlike many other polar explorers, Byrd believed in using aircraft and modern navigational aids rather than only dogs and sledges. In 1926 he made the first flight over the North Pole. (After Byrd's death, an old friend claimed that this was a hoax.)

Byrd mostly explored the Antarctic. He named a range of mountains 'Rockefeller' after the millionaire John D. Rockefeller who had financed one of his expeditions. On one occasion, whilst mapping the Antarctic, Byrd was trapped alone in a hut for five months and had to be rescued. ◆

see also

Rockefeller

Lord **Byron**

English poet
Born 1788 Died 1824 aged 36

George Gordon Byron was lame from birth, and rode on horseback whenever he could. When he was ten years old he inherited his great-uncle's estate, and became Lord Byron. As soon as

▲ Byron's poems, although condemned on moral grounds, exerted a great influence on poetry, music, the novel, opera, and painting in Britain and Europe. He was regarded by many as a hero figure.

he was old enough, he travelled through Europe on horseback. On his return to London he published a poem, *Childe Harold's Pilgrimage*, describing some of the wild landscapes he had seen. The poem was an immediate success.

Byron was a mixture of good and bad. He was described as 'mad, bad, and dangerous to know'. Many people were shocked by his numerous love affairs and he left England in bitterness. For a time he lived in Venice, where he wrote the long poem, *Don Juan*, which describes amazing adventures in extraordinary parts of the world.

In 1823 he went to Greece to help in the Greek struggle for independence from the Ottoman Turkish empire. However, before his soldiers could attack the Turkish fortifications, he caught a fever and died. ◆

'Tis strange – but true; for truth is always strange;
Stranger than fiction.

LORD BYRON
Don Juan

▲ *John Cabot departs from Bristol in 1497 in search of unknown lands.*

John **Cabot**

Italian discoverer of North America
Born c.1450
Died c.1498 aged about 48

John Cabot had an adventurous early life, during which he learned navigation. He settled in London in 1484. In 1496 King Henry VII of England heard of the expedition of Christopher Columbus to the West Indies and realized he was missing out on a chance of wealth and new colonies. So he instructed Cabot and his three sons Lewis, Sebastian, and Santius to sail in search of 'all heathen islands or countries hitherto unknown to Christians'.

The Cabots set off in 1497 in a tiny ship, the *Matthew*, with a crew of just 18 men. They reached the American coast after a voyage of 53 days, thus becoming the first Europeans to reach the North American mainland. However, Cabot thought that he was in north-east Asia!

On their return Cabot's report was so encouraging that the king sent him off on another expedition with a fleet of five ships. But Cabot found none of the gold or spices he was hoping for. ◆

 see also
Columbus

Gaius Julius **Caesar**

Roman general and dictator
Born c.100 BC
Died 44 BC aged about 57

Julius Caesar was born into an important Roman family and rose rapidly in his chosen career as a politician. He served his time in the army and then held various public offices. In 60 BC he was elected to the highest position in Rome, a consul. He was now in charge of the state's

▶ *A bust of Julius Caesar, the most famous of all Roman generals.*

administration and the armed forces, although he held power jointly with another consul. After his year of office he took on the governorship of provinces in northern Italy and Gaul (part of modern France). From here he conquered a vast new area in Gaul and Germany and invaded Britain twice, in 55 and 54 BC.

Caesar was now a very powerful leader with a huge army. He decided not to disband his troops, as he should have done by law, and marched into Italy in 49 BC. He crossed the River Rubicon which formed the boundary of Italy. From here there was no turning back. He had declared war on the Roman state. This meant civil war, and Pompey the Great fought against Caesar. The war lasted until 45 BC, and the next year Caesar declared himself 'dictator for life' – he was now the sole ruler. However, not everyone wanted to be ruled by

one man, and on 15 March in 44 BC Caesar was stabbed to death.

We know a great deal about Caesar and his times because people who were there wrote about him and also because he wrote his own accounts of his adventures and battles. From his writing we can see what an intelligent and powerful man he was. At one time in his career he was the lover of Queen Cleopatra of Egypt, although he was married to Calpurnia. Cleopatra bore him a son called Caesarion who was executed by the Emperor Augustus. ◆

🔊 **see also**

Mark Antony   Augustus   Cleopatra
Pompey

Calamity Jane

American heroine of the Wild West
Born about 1852   Died 1903 aged 51

Calamity Jane was born Martha Jane Burke in northern Missouri, America, but she grew up in western mining camps. She was a good horseback rider and an excellent shot with a rifle. In the rough life of the West she felt more comfortable dressed as a man.

She became attached to the 7th US Cavalry and some say she served as a scout to Colonel (later General) Custer. How she got her nickname is not clear. One story tells that she warned men that to offend her was to seek calamity.

By 1875 she was living in the gold-rush town of Deadwood in South Dakota. There she heroically helped the victims of a smallpox epidemic. She later married and moved to Texas, but returned to Deadwood and is buried there near the grave of Wild Bill Hickock. ◆

🔊 **see also**

Custer

▲ *Maria Callas pictured on the cover of a German magazine in 1959. She had the face and gift for dramatic expression and delighted audiences in such operas as* Madame Butterfly, Aïda, *and* Medea.

Maria **Callas**

American-born Greek soprano
Born 1923   Died 1977 aged 53

Maria Callas was born in New York. Her parents were Greek and her real name was Maria Kalogeropoulos. She trained in Athens and made her début there in 1941, but her international career began in 1947 when she sang Ponchielli's *La Gioconda* in Verona, Italy. Thereafter she appeared in all the major opera-houses, specializing in 19th-century Italian opera.

However, her stormy and self-critical temperament, and recurring vocal troubles, cast a shadow over her career. She was also the lover of the Greek shipping millionaire Aristotle Onassis, and for many years they made headline news. At her best, though, Callas was without equal as a dramatic soprano and spell-binding actress. She retired from the stage in 1965, but continued to make records. ◆

John **Calvin**

French-born Swiss Protestant Church reformer
Born 1509   Died 1564 aged 54

John Calvin was born and grew up in France and nearly became a priest in the Catholic Church. He studied law as well as religion. He was impressed by Martin Luther's teachings, and soon began to criticize the wealth and power of the pope and the Catholic Church.

It became too dangerous for him to stay in Catholic France, and he fled to the Protestant city of Basel in Switzerland. In 1536 he wrote a best-selling book, *The Institutes of the Christian Religion*. Calvin said Christians must use the Bible as their guide, not the pope or the Catholic Church. He taught that people could never be good enough to deserve to go to heaven, but God chose some people specially to be His 'elect'. He said that Christians might have a kind of vision which told them they were one of God's elect, but they should in any case live good and simple lives according to the teachings of Jesus.

In 1541 Calvin was asked to go to Geneva to lead the Protestants. There he organized schools and a university. There were all kinds of strict rules for everyday life; dancing, theatre-going, and card-playing were forbidden. Shopkeepers were punished if they charged too much. Unfaithful husbands and wives were executed, and a boy was beheaded for striking his parents. People had to wear plain clothes and avoid bright colours and women had to cover their hair. Calvin became the effective ruler of Geneva. By the time he died, his religious ideas were spreading across Europe. ◆

🔊 **see also**

Luther

Luis vaz de **Camoens**

Portuguese poet
Born *1524*   **Died** *1580 aged 56*

Luis vaz de Camoens' great poem, *The Lusiads*, is Portugal's national epic – in much the same way as Chaucer's *Canterbury Tales* is England's. It is the story of the spread of the Portuguese people around the world, and particularly of Vasco da Gama's voyage to the East.

Camoens studied for a life in the Church but did not become a priest. Instead he led a wayward and adventurous life. He was forbidden to marry the girl he loved and for whom he wrote his passionate poem, *Rimas*. He was banished for a time to Ceuta in North Africa, and there lost an eye. Back in Lisbon, his unruly behaviour got him banished again, this time to Goa in India rather than to jail.

In 1558 he was shipwrecked and lost almost everything except the manuscript of *The Lusiads*. Three years later it was published. The poem was a great success, but Camoens did not benefit much and died alone, in poverty. ◆

 see also

Gama

Albert **Camus**

French novelist
Born *1913*   **Died** *1960 aged 47*

Albert Camus was born in Algeria, of French and Spanish parentage. He grew up in North Africa where he had various jobs – he even played in goal for the Algiers football team!

When he moved to France he took up journalism and politics and fought heroically against the German occupation during World War II. After the war he decided to concentrate on writing. His most famous novels, *The Outsider* (1942) and *The Plague* (1947), express his idea of the 'absurd', the view that human life is meaningless and that happiness is only possible if we accept that life has no meaning other than what we give it.

Camus was awarded the Nobel Prize for Literature in 1957. He was killed tragically in a road accident only three years later. ◆

Giovanni **Canaletto**

Italian painter
Born *1697*   **Died** *1768 aged 70*

In the 18th century Venice was a great tourist attraction, just as it

▼ *One of Giovanni Canaletto's celebrated views of the Grand Canal in Venice.*

is today. However, 200 years ago the visitors were not people on package holidays, but aristocratic young gentlemen. They went to Italy to round off their cultural education, for no other country boasted such a wealth of art. Many of these young men took paintings and statues back to their own countries, and Giovanni Canaletto was the most famous of the artists who catered for this high-class 'tourist trade'. His views of Venice, packed with vivid detail, were like extremely large, very expensive postcards. Anyone who could afford one had a magnificent status-symbol souvenir. In the 1740s, war on the Continent made travel to Italy difficult and Giovanni Canaletto's business dried up. Most of his clients were British, so in 1746 he moved to England. He repeated his success there, staying for almost ten years painting views of London and of aristocrats' country houses. ◆

Canute

King of England, Denmark, and Norway in the early 11th century
Born c.994   *Died* 1035 aged about 41

Canute was the son of Swein I, King of Denmark. He came with his father on his invasion of England in 1013. Swein's Danish army had conquered the whole of England by the time he died, and Canute was declared king in February 1014. His reign in England nearly came to an end quickly, as the English king Ethelred (who had fled to Normandy when Swein invaded) returned. Canute went back to Denmark, but returned with an invasion force in 1015. By the end of the next year he really was the king of all England. He became king of Denmark in 1018 and king of Norway in 1030. ◆

◀ *This silver penny bears the head of King Canute.*

Al **Capone**

Italian-born American gangster
Born c.1899   *Died* 1947 aged about 48

Al Capone claimed that he was born in New York but it is more likely that he was born in Italy and emigrated with his family to America. Capone turned to crime very early, and was involved in New York street gangs when he was a teenager.

In 1920 the sale of alcoholic drinks was banned in America. This ban (called Prohibition) lasted for 13 years and many criminals, including Capone, made fortunes selling alcoholic drinks illegally. Capone operated in Chicago, becoming rich and influential through crime. He was very brutal, and was involved in the murder of seven members of a rival gang in the St Valentine's Day massacre. He was not arrested because he bribed many policemen and other officials.

Eventually, in 1932, Capone went to prison for not paying taxes. After only a few years he came out a sick man and died while still in his forties. ◆

▶ *This is a police mug shot of Al Capone taken in 1929. Capone was the crime king of Chicago during America's Prohibition years.*

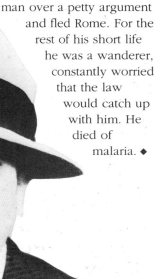

Michelangelo Merisi da **Caravaggio**

Italian painter
Born 1571   *Died* 1610 aged 38

In Michelangelo Merisi da Caravaggio's day, all ambitious young painters wanted to make their reputations in Rome – the 'artistic capital' of Europe. He arrived there when he was about 20 and for several years struggled to earn a living. However, his reputation grew and he started to win important commissions from the Church. His paintings were bold and exciting. The people in them looked real and solid because he used real Roman people as models for his saints and madonnas, a practice which caused great controversy. He had a highly original way of using light and shade, so that the most important parts of the picture stood out dramatically from the background. At the age of 35 he was famous all over Europe, and half the painters in Rome were trying to imitate him. His success story was ended by his violent temper. In 1606 he killed a man over a petty argument and fled Rome. For the rest of his short life he was a wanderer, constantly worried that the law would catch up with him. He died of malaria. ◆

Chester **Carlson**

*American inventor of modern
photocopying machines*
Born *1906*   **Died** *1968 aged 62*

Photocopying machines are now
so commonplace that it is
difficult to realize that they have
only been generally available for
about 30 years. At the touch of a
button photocopiers can produce
single or multiple copies of printed
pages, enlarged or reduced if
required, and some can reproduce
in colour.

The person responsible for this
revolution was a physicist called
Chester Carlson. As a young man he
worked with a firm in New York
who required many copies of
important documents. In 1938
Carlson produced his prototype
photocopier based on electrostatic
attraction of a black powder to
paper. He called this process
xerography (from the Greek word
for dry writing). His method was
not altogether successful and
needed adapting. It was not until
1959 that the first commercial
machine was put on the market,
by the now giant Rank Xerox
Corporation. Thanks to his skills,
ingenuity, and perseverence, Carlson
became a multi-millionaire. ◆

Andrew **Carnegie**

*Scottish-born American businessman
and benefactor*
Born *1835*   **Died** *1919 aged 83*

When he was 12, Andrew
Carnegie left Scotland for
America with his parents and
younger brother. They were very
poor, so instead of going to school
Carnegie went to work in a cotton
factory. Later, whatever job
Carnegie did, he tried to learn more
about it. He worked very long

hours, but read as much as he
could in his spare time. Soon he
was offered better jobs and he
saved his money carefully.

During the American Civil War,
railways were very important for
moving troops and ammunition.
Carnegie started a company in 1863
to make iron railway bridges instead
of wooden ones. Ten years later his
company began to produce steel
too. This made Carnegie very rich.
He was very generous with his
money: before he died, he had paid
for 2811 free public libraries around
the world. He also established
pension funds and gave financial
help to universities in Scotland and
in America. ◆

Lewis **Carroll**

English writer
Born *1832*   **Died** *1898 aged 65*

Lewis Carroll was the name used
by Charles Dodgson, a
mathematics teacher at Oxford
University, when he was writing
children's books and poems.
Charles Dodgson was the third child
in a family of 11, and he and his
brothers and sisters spent ages
playing literary games and drawing.

When he became a teacher at
Oxford, Carroll used to take the
daughters of his friend, Dean
Liddell, for boat-rides on the river.
On one of these river-trips he told
the story of *Alice in Wonderland* to
the young Alice Liddell. Later he
wrote the story down, and it was
published in 1865.

As well as *Alice in Wonderland*
and *Alice Through the Looking Glass*
(1872), he wrote poems and
another children's book, *Sylvie and
Bruno*. He was also a great letter
writer and he invented games and
puzzles. As an Oxford don, he also
published mathematical works.

Carroll's story books are sort of

▲ *Two of Lewis Carroll's most famous
creations, Alice and the Cheshire Cat.*

adventure stories, but they do not
unfold like ordinary stories.
Sometimes one thing will turn into
another, as if in a dream, while at
other times the people in the book
seem to be moving about in a
game, the rules of which are never
quite clear. ◆

Jacques **Cartier**

*French navigator and explorer who
claimed Canada for France*
Born *1491*   **Died** *1557 aged 66*

Jacques Cartier, an experienced
navigator, was 43 when he set
out with two ships and 61 men on
his first voyage to North America.
King Francis I of France had sent

him on the expedition to search for gold. He first explored the coast of Newfoundland, then sailed up the Gulf of St Lawrence to the Gaspé Peninsula, where he set up a cross and claimed the land for France.

The next year, 1535, Cartier was sent on a second expedition. On 10 August, the feast day of St Lawrence, he arrived at a river which he named after the saint. He sailed upstream as far as the place where Quebec now stands. The smallest of his ships sailed on as far as a village called Hochelaga, at the foot of a mountain which he named Mont Réal. The city of Montréal now stands there. A third voyage in 1541 in search of precious stones failed, and Cartier retired to France, honoured as a great explorer. ◆

👁 see also

Champlain

▼ In Jacques Cartier's first voyage to Canada he met a group of Iroquois Indians. Their chief let two of his sons sail back to France; they returned with Cartier on his second voyage.

Henri **Cartier-Bresson**

French photographer
Born 1908

Henri Cartier-Bresson is celebrated for capturing significant moments of events on film. He became interested in photography after training as a painter. Since 1933, when he held his first photographic exhibition, he has covered the world's great events for the media, and has published many books of camera studies. As a young man he worked with the great French film director Jean Renoir.

Cartier-Bresson uses mainly black and white film and a hand-held camera. He rarely resorts to the complex photographic equipment favoured by other photographers. He records 'the decisive moment' (also the title of one of his books), relying on his own skill and experience. ◆

▲ Henri Cartier-Bresson's style made an art form of news photography.

Pablo **Casals**

Spanish (Catalan) cellist and conductor
Born 1876   Died 1973 aged 96

Pablo Casals was already a capable pianist, organist, and violinist before he took up the cello at the age of 11. He studied in Barcelona, Madrid, and Brussels. His solo career began in 1898, and he was soon regarded as the world's greatest cellist. He was also famous as a chamber musician, teacher, and composer of instrumental and choral works. In 1936 he went into voluntary exile in Prades, in the French Pyrenees, in protest against General Franco's Fascist regime in Spain, and from 1946 to 1950 even refused to play in public. In 1950 he founded the Prades annual musical festival, and in 1956 he went to live in Puerto Rico where he also founded another important festival, the Casals Festival. ◆

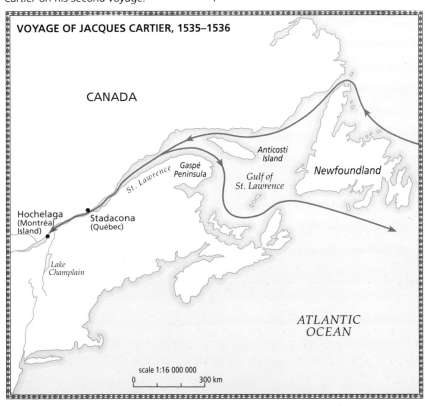

VOYAGE OF JACQUES CARTIER, 1535–1536

CANADA

Anticosti Island

Gaspé Peninsula

St. Lawrence

Gulf of St. Lawrence

Newfoundland

Hochelaga (Montréal Island)

Stadacona (Québec)

Lake Champlain

ATLANTIC OCEAN

scale 1:16 000 000
0   300 km

Giovanni **Casanova**

Italian adventurer
Born 1725   Died 1798 aged 73

Giovanni Casanova was a clever boy, and at first he studied to be a priest. However, he could not settle down to anything for very long, and he gambled, cheated, and lied his way through most of his life. He did not always keep out of trouble and he was in prison from 1755 to 1756, until he escaped and went to France. In his later years he settled down to be a librarian to the Count of Waldstein, in Bohemia.

What we know of Casanova comes from his very entertaining *Memoirs*. They are very boastful, especially about all his women friends, and it is not easy to know the truth. Even now, a man who boasts of many women friends may be called a 'Casanova'. ◆

Fidel **Castro**

Leader of the Communist revolution in Cuba
Born 1927

Under the harsh rule of General Batista, many poor Cubans lived in terrible conditions. Fidel Castro was amongst a group of people who decided to overthrow the government and for several years Castro led raids against government forces. He gathered more and more support until finally, in 1959, Batista fled the country.

Castro immediately began to change the Cuban way of life. He took over foreign-owned companies, but because many of these companies were American, the United States stopped all trade with Cuba. Castro then turned to Communist countries, such as the

▲ *A young Fidel Castro waves to his supporters.*

Soviet Union and China, for help.

In 1962, the Soviet Union tried to build nuclear missile bases in Cuba, with Castro's consent. The missiles were removed after the United States had blockaded Cuba and put pressure on the Russians.

Although Castro greatly improved conditions for the poor, many other Cubans wanted more freedom, and fled to America. ◆

Catherine the Great

Ruler of Russia from 1762 to 1796
Born 1729   Died 1796 aged 67

Born Princess Sophia Augusta, she came to Russia from Stettin, Prussia (now in Poland) at the age of 14 and was given the name Catherine when she was received into the Russian Orthodox Church. At 15 she married Peter the

Great's grandson, Peter III. After 17 years of marriage, Peter became tsar in 1762. Almost immediately he was replaced by Catherine and put to death by his guards.

Catherine at once set about reforming Russia and turning it into a strong power. She took a great interest in education, particularly for girls, and also did a lot to improve the care of the sick.

During her rule Russia expanded eastwards towards the Pacific Ocean, westwards to take over much of Poland, and southwards to the coast of the Crimea and the Black Sea. Her own skilful diplomacy made sure that these gains became permanent.

▲ *An enamel and copper portrait of Catherine the Great.*

While the landowning nobles lived well, most Russian people were serfs, little better than slaves, and badly treated. Catherine, who needed the support of the nobles, gave them even more powers over their serfs. This led to a serfs' revolt in 1773–1775 which was brutally put down. Later the French Revolution of 1789 increased Catherine's fear of revolt, and in her later years she ruled with a rod of iron. ◆

Edith **Cavell**

British nurse executed during World War I
Born 1865   Died 1915 aged 49

Edith Cavell was the daughter of a clergyman. When she was 25 she went to Belgium as a governess, and later trained as a nurse. In 1907 she became matron of Belgium's first training college for nurses.

In 1914 German troops marched into Brussels. Edith Cavell joined a group of people who helped British and French soldiers, trapped behind German lines, to escape to The Netherlands. During the next year hundreds of soldiers passed through the cellars of her clinic. Then, on 5 August 1915, Edith Cavell was arrested. She was condemned to death by a German military court and was shot on 12 October. She met her death calmly and bravely. ◆

▶ *Nurse Edith Cavell with a small boy outside Shoreditch Infirmary, England, where she was working in 1903.*

Patriotism is not enough. I must have no hatred or bitterness towards anyone.

EDITH CAVELL
on the eve of her execution

Henry **Cavendish**

English scientist
Born 1731   Died 1810 aged 78

Henry Cavendish's family had aristocratic connections, and he was well-educated. Nevertheless he lived very modestly, even after he inherited a fortune at 40.

His mother died when he was two years old and for 50 years he lived with his father, who was a scientist. Cavendish's first scientific work was helping with his father's experiments. Soon he was making discoveries of his own, particularly in chemistry and electricity.

Cavendish found that hydrogen (which he called 'inflammable air') was a component of water, and investigated many of the properties of hydrogen gas. He also calculated the mass and density of the Earth.

Many of his discoveries remained unknown in his lifetime because he seldom spoke to anyone. Even his servants hardly ever heard him speak; he would write notes for them instead. He allowed other scientists to use his large library – provided he didn't have to meet them or talk to them. ◆

Camillo **Cavour**

Italian politician
Born 1810   Died 1861 aged 51

When Camillo Cavour was born, the French ruled Italy. After the defeat of the French emperor, Napoleon, Italy was divided between Austria (in the north), the Pope, and smaller kingdoms and areas ruled by dukes in the south.

Cavour, who came from a noble family in Turin, became an officer in the army. In 1847 he entered politics and in the following year sat in the parliament in the Piedmont kingdom. Cavour wanted to see all of Italy united and freed from foreign rule. He became prime minister of Piedmont in 1852. By the time of his death in 1861 Italy was free of foreign rule and united under one king, Victor Emmanuel II. ◆

see also

Garibaldi   Victor Emmanuel II

61

William **Caxton**

English printer who set up the first printing press in England
Born c.1422 **Died** 1491 aged about 69

William Caxton liked to spend time writing, and in 1469 he started to translate into English a popular French romance called *The History of Troy*. Many people in England wanted a copy of this rather large book. Copies of books were once handwritten and so took a long time to complete. However, by this time books could be produced by the printing process introduced by Gutenberg in Germany some years earlier. Caxton learned how to do this, then set up his own press in Bruges, Belgium. Here he printed his English edition of *The History of Troy*, completing it by the end of 1473. In 1476, Caxton set up the first printing press in England, at Westminster in London.

During his lifetime, Caxton printed about 110 books. He also published Chaucer's *Canterbury Tales*, making this work available to many new readers. Before Caxton's printed editions, people spelt the same words in different ways. In his printing Caxton introduced a fixed spelling for words, a very important development in the standardization of English. ◆

◉ **see also**
Gutenberg

Benvenuto **Cellini**

Italian goldsmith, sculptor, and writer
Born 1500 **Died** 1571 aged 70

Benvenuto Cellini grew up in Florence in Italy and became the apprentice of a goldsmith. He was an excellent artist, but also a wild character. In 1516 he became involved in a fight and the city authorities sent him away. Throughout his life he was in trouble, and had to move from one city to another. But his work was so good that rich people were always asking him to make jewellery, medals, and sculptures.

In 1540 King Francis I invited Cellini to work for him at his court in France. He stayed for five years. During this time he made his famous gold salt-cellar for the king, topped with nude reclining figures. In 1545 he returned to Florence where he made the famous statue of Perseus and Medusa. When he was 58 Cellini began to write his *Autobiography*, in which he presented a lively picture of his life. ◆

Miguel **Cervantes**

Spanish writer
Born 1547 **Died** 1616 aged 68

The life of Miguel Cervantes reads like a tale of adventure. He spent his childhood travelling around Spain with his father, who supplied medicines for the poor. At the age of 21 he went to Italy and studied the work of the great Italian poets before enlisting as a soldier. He fought the Turks in the great sea battle of Lepanto in 1571 and was wounded three times. Later he was captured by pirates, and imprisoned for five years. He tried to escape, but had to be ransomed in the end.

Back in Spain his luck changed

▼ Cellini's gold salt-cellar on which there are sea-horses, fishes, and animals, representing the union of Earth and sea.

▲ *This illustration shows Cervantes' hero, Don Quixote, galloping to attack windmills which he has mistaken for giants waving their arms.*

when, in 1605, he published *Don Quixote*. It is a long book which is both funny and sad. It tells the tale of a poor hero who has many adventures, all caused by his own mistakes. The book was such a success that Cervantes could afford to spend the rest of his life writing. ◆

Cetshwayo

Last great Zulu king
Born c.1826   **Died** 1884 aged about 58

Cetshwayo was the nephew of Shaka the Zulu king. He fought as a warrior against white settlers at the age of 12, and in 1873 became king himself after the death of his father, Mpande. However, he could not claim his throne until six of his half-brothers had been killed and two more had fled. At first the British in South Africa supported Cetshwayo, but in 1878 they invaded Zululand. The Zulus won an early victory, wiping out a British regiment, but they were themselves defeated in 1879. Cetshwayo was captured and Zululand was divided

amongst 13 chiefs. Cetshwayo visited London to plead his case and the British restored him as ruler of central Zululand in 1883. However, he was soon expelled by his subjects and was forced to flee the country. ◆

 see also
Shaka

Paul **Cézanne**

French painter
Born 1839   **Died** 1906 aged 67

Paul Cézanne was born into an educated and wealthy family. He started studying law, but soon gave up in order to paint. His early pictures were not popular: people said they were hopelessly unskilled.

After studying art for a while in Paris, he settled in Pontoise, just north of Paris. After his father died, he returned to live in his birthplace, Aix-en-Provence, in southern France. As he had a lot of money he did not need to rely on selling his pictures to live. This gave him unusual freedom to develop his skills. He painted landscapes, still lifes, flowers, and portraits. By careful mixtures of colour and tone, he made his brush-strokes 'model' a hill or a figure without using an outline. His style of painting greatly influenced other artists. ◆

Marc **Chagall**

Russian painter
Born 1887   **Died** 1985 aged 97

Marc Chagall was brought up in the Jewish district of the small Russian town of Vitebsk. The people who surrounded him as a child, the stories they told, and the lively music they played, crop up again and again in his paintings.

As a young man he went to Paris at a time when there were a lot of changes going on in painting, writing, and music. Excited and influenced by these changes, Chagall went back to Russia, but his painting was not popular with the authorities, and he finally returned to Paris and settled there in 1923.

His work is highly imaginative, and blends reality with fantasy. Sometimes the figures in his paintings seem to be floating across the picture. He loved using clear, bright colours which shimmer on the canvas and glow in the stained-glass windows and tapestries which he designed in later life. ◆

▶ *Chagall's* Ecuyere aux colombes (Circus rider and doves).

Samuel de **Champlain**

French explorer and founder of Québec
Born 1567   Died 1635 aged 68

The first European settlers in Canada were the French. Because Samuel de Champlain was a fine navigator he was selected to go on an expedition to explore Canada's St Lawrence river. This was his first journey of exploration although he returned to North America many times.

In 1608 Champlain and 32 men founded the colony of Québec. Life was tough and death was commonplace on these expeditions. Only Champlain and eight others survived the first winter there. Champlain won the respect of the local American Indians by fighting in their wars, and he also traded with them for furs.

When the English attacked Québec in 1628, Champlain was in command of the colony. He was captured and sent to England. When England returned Canada to France in 1633, Champlain went back to Québec and died there. ◆

see also

Cartier

Chandragupta Maurya

Creator of the first empire in India
Lived during the 4th century BC

Chandragupta Maurya grew up in India over 2300 years ago. At that time there were many

▶ *In his time, Chandragupta Maurya ruled three-quarters of the Indian sub-continent. His empire lasted for another 100 years after his death.*

kingdoms in India. The most powerful was Magadha, in the north-east. Around 320 BC Chandragupta overthrew the king of Magadha and made himself king.

Chandragupta faced a crisis about 15 years later. The king of western Asia, Seleucus Nicator, and his army invaded north-west India. This threatened Chandragupta's lands. The armies of Seleucus and Chandragupta fought each other. Chandragupta's army won. In 303 BC the two kings made a treaty. It stated that Chandragupta would rule the Indus Valley (modern Pakistan) and adjoining lands. He thereby became the ruler of all of north India.

In 297 BC Chandragupta abdicated. The next two kings were his son Bindusara and his grandson Asoka. They extended the empire into central and south India. ◆

see also

Asoka

Charlie **Chaplin**

British-born film actor and director
Born 1889   Died 1977 aged 88

Charlie Chaplin's mother was a music-hall entertainer in London and from the age of five Chaplin took part in her act. When she became ill, the young Chaplin was sent to an orphanage. In 1910 he moved to America and four years later he began to appear in films. He became the best-loved comedian of the silent cinema, famous for his moustache, bowler hat, baggy trousers, and cane. Soon he was writing and directing his own films, and in 1919 he joined other stars and directors in founding their own United Artists film company.

In his most famous films, such as *The Kid* (1920) and *The Gold Rush* (1925), Chaplin played a sad little tramp who was bullied and confused by powerful people. Usually, though, he bounced back and was always on the side of

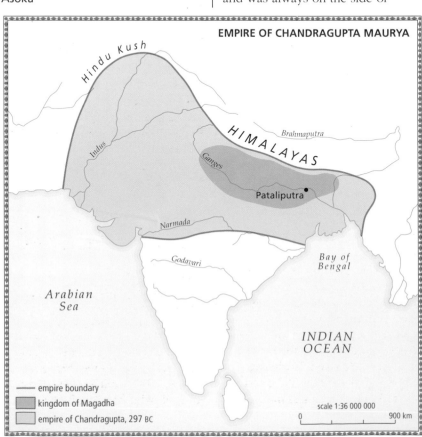

EMPIRE OF CHANDRAGUPTA MAURYA

Hindu Kush

Indus

HIMALAYAS

Brahmaputra

Ganges

Pataliputra

Narmada

Godavari

Bay of Bengal

Arabian Sea

INDIAN OCEAN

— empire boundary
■ kingdom of Magadha
■ empire of Chandragupta, 297 BC

scale 1:36 000 000

0   900 km

weaker or poorer people. He also made successful talking pictures such as *The Great Dictator* (1940), a fierce but amusing attack on Adolf Hitler and his Nazi followers.

Later Chaplin was excluded from America because he was suspected of supporting Communism. However, in 1972 he returned in triumph to be awarded a special Oscar 'for the incalculable effect he has had in making motion pictures the art form of this century'. ◆

Charlemagne

Holy Roman Emperor from 800 to 814
Born *742*   **Died** *814 aged 72*

As the eldest son of Pepin, king of the Franks, Charlemagne was born into a very powerful family. The Franks were barbarians who invaded part of the Roman empire and settled in what is now France and Germany during the 5th century. When King Pepin died in 768, he divided his kingdom between his two sons, Charles and Carloman. Three years later Carloman died, and Charles became the sole ruler.

In 771 Charles's aim as king was to enlarge the kingdom that he had inherited, but at the same time to spread Christianity among the people whom he had conquered. During his long reign of over 40 years he organized military campaigns, and extended the kingdom of the Franks into an empire which stretched across what is now northern Germany, and parts of Poland, the Czech and Slovak Republics, Hungary, Italy, Spain, and former Yugoslavia. His conquests earned him the name of 'Charlemagne' (Charles the Great).

Pope Leo III asked Charlemagne to take over territory in Italy, and crowned him Emperor of the Holy

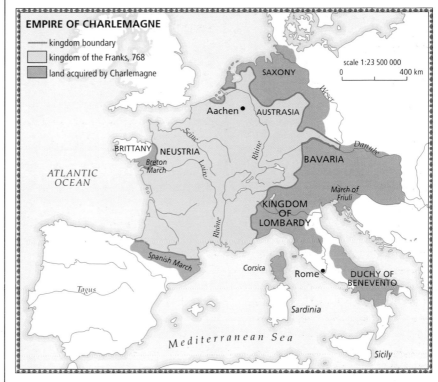

▲ *After Charlemagne's death, the great empire he had created fell apart.*

Roman Empire in Rome on Christmas Day in 800. Charlemagne wanted to show that the new emperor in the West could recreate some of the splendour and learning of the old Roman empire. He built some magnificent palaces, particularly at his capital city, Aachen, which became centres of learning and art, and famous musicians and scholars were invited to spend time at them. ◆

Charles Edward Stuart

Last serious Stuart contender for the British throne
Born *1720*   **Died** *1788 aged 67*

Charles Edward Stuart is usually known as Bonnie Prince Charlie. His grandfather was King James II, who was expelled when

the English people favoured the Protestant King William of Orange and his wife Queen Mary. But, like his grandfather, Charles was a Roman Catholic, and dreamed of going to Britain one day to claim the crown for himself.

Having lived in exile in Italy, Charles landed on the west coast of Scotland in 1745, in the reign of George II, with only 12 men. The Scottish Highlanders quickly rose to support the handsome prince, and four days later, with over 2000 supporters, Charles soundly beat an English army at Prestonpans, near Edinburgh. Charles and his army marched into England as far as Derby, but many of the Highlanders deserted on the march south so Charles retreated again to Scotland.

In 1746 his tattered army was beaten at Culloden Moor. For five months Charles was on the run, eventually escaping to France before finally settling in Italy. He turned to drink and did not do much with the rest of his life. ◆

Charles I

King of England and Scotland from 1625 to 1649

Born *1600*   **Died** *1649 aged 48*

Charles I was not born to be a king. He was backward and shy, and his brilliant elder brother, Henry, overshadowed him. But Henry died suddenly in 1612 and Charles became heir to the throne.

Charles was artistic, and his court was civilized and elegant. He was also very religious and wanted to make Church of England services more dignified and beautiful. However, Puritans and other critical people were afraid his strong-minded Catholic wife, Henrietta Maria, had too much influence and England would become Catholic again.

As king he ruled without parliament from 1629 until 1640, and tried to force his Scottish subjects to accept English church services. When this led to a war he could not afford, he promised to share some of his power with

▼ *A painting depicting the execution of Charles I (seen top left).*

parliament. But many people in parliament did not trust him and England slid into civil war.

Although he was defeated, Charles did not believe he should give up his power, and he broke promises to his enemies. He tried to start another war in alliance with the Scots, which eventually led to his trial and execution – the only English king to be publicly beheaded. ◆

Charles II

King of England, Scotland, and Ireland from 1660 to 1685

Born *1630*   **Died** *1685 aged 54*

Charles II was 18 and in exile when his father Charles I was executed. In 1651 he returned to England, and spent six weeks on the run after Cromwell defeated his attempt to win back his crown. He disguised himself as a servant, and finally escaped to face nine more years of poverty and insecurity in France and The Netherlands.

When Charles II regained his crown in 1660 after the collapse of

Cromwell's regime, he knew that he must rule with parliament and support the Church of England. So, although he was probably a Catholic, he kept quiet about it, and went along with parliament's laws which punished people for not attending Church of England services.

Charles's court was frivolous and worldly. He was easily bored by affairs of state and enjoyed the theatre, horse-racing, and gambling instead. He had many mistresses, including the actress Nell Gwynn. However, he was also a well-known patron of the arts and sciences, founding the Royal Society to encourage scientific research. ◆

◉ **see also**
Cromwell

Charles V

Habsburg emperor who ruled over vast territories

Born *1500*   **Died** *1558 aged 58*

Charles V, a devout Catholic, ruled over the largest

▲ *After retiring, Charles V spent much of his time worshipping God, listening to music, and dismantling and assembling mechanical clocks.*

collection of European lands since the time of Charlemagne. He inherited the throne of Spain through his mother in 1516, and three years later became ruler of Austria and The Netherlands and was elected Holy Roman Emperor. His Spanish subjects also conquered a vast new empire for him in Central and South America. His motto was *Plus ultra* (always further). His advisers wanted him to be 'God's standard-bearer', uniting all the Christian nations under his rule, waging war on the Muslim Ottoman Turks, and finally becoming 'Ruler of the World'.

Although Charles worked hard, he was not an inspiring leader of men; he always seemed to need more time, or money, to deal with the problems in his many scattered territories. By 1555 his long wars with France had led to no definite result, and he had failed to stop the Protestant ideas of Martin Luther from spreading in Germany,

although he did manage to blunt the continued Ottoman attack on Christian Europe.

He retired in 1556, giving up the Empire to his brother and all his other lands to his son Philip. ◆

Ray **Charles**
American singer and musician
Born 1930

Ray Charles Robinson had a tragic childhood: born in poverty, he lost his sight through illness at the age of seven, and both his parents had died by the time he was 15. He attended a Florida school for blind children where he learned to write musical arrangements in Braille. He became an accomplished pianist, and in time, one of the most inspirational musicians of the 20th century.

Recordings such as 'I Got A Woman' (1954) and 'What'd I Say' (1959) infuriated some churchgoers because they were basically rhythm 'n' blues songs with gospel-style vocals, although they were later recognized as being early examples of 'soul' music.

Other hits like 'Georgia On My Mind' (1960) and 'Crying Time' (1966) demonstrated his ability to play anything from jazz to country music, and earned Charles the widely-accepted nickname of 'The Genius'. ◆

Geoffrey **Chaucer**
English poet and writer
Born c.1340   Died 1400 aged about 60

When Geoffrey Chaucer was a small child, he was a page in the household of the Countess of Ulster, who was the wife of King

Edward III's son, Lionel. When he was older, Chaucer became one of the king's 'squires', making beds and serving at the royal table.

In the war between England and France (1337–1453) Chaucer was taken prisoner, but in 1360 the king paid a ransom for his release. Later he became a diplomat, travelling to France and Italy on missions for the king. While in Italy he read books by the Italian writers Boccaccio, Petrarch, and Dante, and later used some of their stories in his own writing.

By 1374 he was made Controller of Customs in the Port of London, but left in 1386, and began writing his best-known work, *The Canterbury Tales*. This is a cycle of linked tales told by a group of pilgrims who meet in London before going on a pilgrimage to Canterbury. By that time he had already written many other long poems, including *Troilus and Criseyde* (1385), a very sad love story.

Chaucer was one of the most learned men of his age. He died in 1400 and is buried in Poet's Corner in Westminster Abbey. ◆

👁 **see also**

Dante   Petrarch

▼ *An illustration from an early edition of Chaucer's* Canterbury Tales.

commander of the Nationalist armies after the death of Sun Yat-sen, who had been one of the original organizers of the Nationalist Party. Chiang Kai-shek used the armies to put down the warlords, and became ruler of China in 1928. He used his armies to try to crush the trade unionists and Communists but was not successful. Mao Zedong became leader of the remaining Communists.

When Japan invaded China in 1937, both Nationalists and Communists fought the Japanese occupiers. In 1945, when the Japanese had surrendered, the Communists started a civil war against the Nationalists. In 1949 Chiang Kai-shek had to flee to the island of Taiwan, which became known as the Republic of China (or Nationalist China). Chiang Kai-shek was its president until he died. ◆

Anton **Chekhov**

Russian dramatist
Born *1860* **Died** *1904 aged 44*

Although he was born into a poor family, Anton Chekhov became an eminent doctor, at one time working with prisoners in a remote settlement near Siberia. He soon began writing, starting with short stories which combined humour with a deep understanding of the sometimes comic, sometimes tragic way in which others live their lives. When he was 29 he wrote the first of many plays, where once again he mixed seriousness with the lightest of touches. On stage, his characters talk about their fantasies and failures with honesty and regret. Although they can usually see where they have gone wrong, they generally remain unable to do anything about their mistakes. These plays made Chekhov famous, but at the height of his powers he was struck down with tuberculosis.

▲ *Anton Chekhov (left) with another of Russia's most famous writers, Leo Tolstoy.*

His last play, *The Cherry Orchard*, is one of the greatest dramas ever written. ◆

◉ **see also**
Tolstoy

Chiang Kai-shek

Ruler of China from 1928 to 1949
Born *1887* **Died** *1975 aged 87*

Chiang Kai-shek trained as an army officer. In 1911 he helped in a rebellion to overthrow the dishonest rulers of the Chinese empire. China became a republic but was soon divided among warlords who kept power with their private armies.

Chiang Kai-shek joined the Nationalist Party, which believed in improving life for the peasants and poor workers. He became

◉ **see also**
Mao Zedong
Sun Yat-sen
Zhou Enlai

▶ *Chiang Kai-shek in 1930.*

▲ *A Chippendale mahogany bookcase.*

Thomas Chippendale

English 18th-century furniture maker
Born *c.1718* **Died** *1779 aged about 61*

Thomas Chippendale was born in Otley, Yorkshire, to a family of woodcarvers and cabinet-makers. We know nothing of his early life – even his date of birth is an estimate.

In 1727 the family moved to London, where there were many rich customers, and in 1749 Chippendale set up his own workshop to make furniture. At that time, wealthy people were looking for beautiful and fashionable things for their fine houses and they liked Chippendale's furniture very much.

Chippendale was especially good at making chairs, using his favourite dark mahogany wood. Many still exist today. They are beautifully designed and proportioned and although they look light and elegant, they are very strong and practical. He also made many dressers and chests of drawers, each one intricately decorated.

Thomas Chippendale had 11 children, and the family business carried on after his death. ◆

Chiyonofuji

Japanese sumo wrestler
Born *1955*

Chiyonofuji (the professional name of Mitsugu Akimoto) is probably the most successful ever sumo wrestler. He made his début in 1970 at the age of 15. Because he was very light, he was at a physical disadvantage when faced by much heavier wrestlers. So, he decided to embark on a rigorous weight-training programme and increased his muscle-size and weight.

He became a *yokozuna* in 1981, which is the highest sumo rank, and he is the only wrestler to achieve 1000 career wins. ◆

▼ *Sumo wrestler Chiyonofuji is famous for his speed and power.*

Frederick Chopin

Polish pianist and composer
Born *1810* **Died** *1849 aged 39*

It was always clear that Chopin would become a great pianist and composer of piano music. One of his compositions was published when he was seven, and he gave his first public concert a week before his eighth birthday.

Chopin loved Poland, but he realized that he would have to travel if his career was to prosper. Eventually he settled in Paris, but he never forgot his native land. The music he wrote – the brilliant polonaises and mazurkas, the powerful ballades – was Polish through and through. It was an inspiration to the Polish people in their struggle for independence from domination by Russia, Prussia, and Austria. Equally inspiring were his sparkling waltzes and romantic nocturnes. Chopin could make the piano talk. He could make it sing. ◆

Agatha Christie

English author of detective stories
Born *1890* **Died** *1976 aged 85*

As a child, Agatha Christie did not go to school at all. During World War I she worked in a hospital dispensary, where she learned some of the details of chemicals and poisons which proved so useful to her in her later career of detective-story writer.

She was married twice, once to Colonel Archibald Christie, from whom she was divorced in 1928, and then to the archaeologist Max Mallowan. His care with fragments of evidence and her detective skills combined well together when she helped him in his excavation of sites in Syria and Iraq.

Agatha Christie wrote several plays and over 70 detective novels. Her books are excellent stories which make the reader desperate to know what will happen next. Since her death, several of her books have been successfully turned into films and television series. Her two most famous detectives are Miss Marple and Hercule Poirot. ◆

▲ *An engraving of Queen Christina.*

Queen **Christina of Sweden**

Queen of Sweden from 1632 to 1654
Born *1626*   **Died** *1689 aged 62*

Christina was five when her father died. He was Gustavus Adolphus, King of Sweden. Christina immediately became Queen-elect, but did not rule until she was 18, in 1644. By then, the people of Sweden were tired of fighting wars. For 14 years Swedish soldiers had been fighting in Germany, in the 'Thirty Years' War'. In 1648 Christina helped to bring the war to an end.

Six years later, Christina suddenly gave up her throne and left Sweden. Everyone was shocked. She claimed that she was tired. In fact, she had secretly become a Roman Catholic. Sweden was a Protestant country and it was against the law of the country to become a Catholic. So, when Christina wanted to join the Roman Catholic Church, she had to go abroad.

Christina settled in Rome, where she became a friend of leading Catholic churchmen. She also supported musicians, writers, and painters, and made a large collection of paintings, medals, books, and manuscripts. ◆

👁 **see also**

Gustavus Adolphus

Winston **Churchill**

British statesman who led Britain during World War II
Born *1874*   **Died** *1965 aged 90*

Winston Leonard Spencer Churchill was the grandson of the seventh Duke of Marlborough. He did not do well at school, but joined the army and had many adventures in Cuba, India, and the Sudan. In 1899 Churchill left the army and went to South Africa as a newspaper reporter during the Boer War, where he was captured by the Boers but managed to escape.

In 1900 he was elected to parliament as a Conservative, but in 1904 fell out with his party and joined the Liberals. He held several government posts, including President of the Board of Trade (1908–1910), when he introduced labour exchanges (which were later called Job Centres), and Home Secretary (1910–1911). Before and during World War I he served as head of the Admiralty, and then resigned from government to command troops in France for a time. After serving again as a Liberal minister after the war he returned to the Conservative Party, and was Chancellor of the Exchequer from 1924 to 1929.

During the 1930s Churchill was not a government minister. He warned that there was a danger of another world war, but many people ignored him. However, when World War II came the prime minister, Neville Chamberlain, put Churchill in charge of the Admiralty again. When German armies were overrunning Europe in May 1940, King George VI asked him to be prime minister and

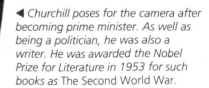

◀ *Churchill poses for the camera after becoming prime minister. As well as being a politician, he was also a writer. He was awarded the Nobel Prize for Literature in 1953 for such books as* The Second World War.

lead a coalition government of all parties. His courage and his speeches inspired the people to withstand air raids and military defeats, and carry on to victory. His speeches were a triumph over difficulties, for in his early years Churchill had a stutter, and he had to fight hard to cure it.

Churchill remained prime minister until the general election of 1945 brought Labour to power, just before the war ended. He became prime minister again from 1951 to 1955, and finally gave up politics in 1964. ◆

> *Never in the field of human conflict was so much owed by so many to so few.*
>
> WINSTON CHURCHILL, 1940
> (on the skill and courage of British airmen)

Marcus **Cicero**

Roman politician, writer, and philosopher
Born *106 BC*   **Died** *43 BC aged 63*

Marcus Cicero lived during the last decades of the Roman Republic. He was born at Arpinum, about 100 kilometres from Rome. His father sent him to study in Rome and Athens. Cicero then became a lawyer in Rome; he was a powerful speaker and quickly became a top barrister. Then he went into politics. In 63 BC he served as consul; that is, he was one of the two rulers of the Republic, who held office for one year. During the year another Roman, Catiline, and his followers plotted to overthrow the government. Their plans were discovered and Cicero had the leaders killed.

Cicero's later life was difficult. From 49 to 45 BC there was civil war between Julius Caesar and Pompey. Cicero supported Pompey, but Caesar won. This put Cicero in danger, but Caesar died in 44 BC. Caesar was succeeded by Octavius (later called Augustus). In 43 BC Cicero criticized Octavius and as a result, Cicero was murdered. ◆

see also

Augustus   Caesar   Pompey

Eric **Clapton**

English guitarist and singer
Born *1945*

Eric Patrick Clapton first became interested in American blues music as a teenager attending Kingston Art College. His understanding of this music style

▼ *Fellow musicians regard Clapton as one of the finest of all rock guitarists.*

was so in advance of his contemporaries that by the mid-1960s he was the most famous blues virtuoso in the country.

His early recordings with The Yardbirds, John Mayall, and the 'supergroup' Cream helped define the role of the 'guitar hero', and have inspired musicians ever since. In 1970 his band Derek and the Dominos recorded the song 'Layla', one of the greatest of all rock singles, and possibly Clapton's most inspired performance.

His award-winning CD *Unplugged* (1992) introduced a whole new generation of listeners to the blues. ◆

Georges **Clemenceau**

French premier during World War I
Born *1841*   **Died** *1929 aged 88*

As a young man Georges Clemenceau was a journalist, but his republican ideas were not welcome in the France ruled by Emperor Napoleon III. He went to live in America from 1865 to 1869, where he taught French and horse riding. On his return to France in 1870 Clemenceau helped create the new French Republic and worked for many years as a journalist and politician. He was a Deputy in the French parliament from 1876 to 1893 and again from 1902 until 1920.

After serving as premier from 1906 to 1909, he returned to lead his country in 1917. So strong was his leadership during World War I he earned the names 'the Tiger of France' and 'Father of Victory'. After the war he helped to draw up the Treaty of Versailles with other Allied leaders. He stood for election as president in 1920, but he lost and retired from active politics. ◆

◀ *This is believed to be a model of Cleopatra's head.*

Cleopatra

Queen of Egypt
Born *c.69 BC*
Died *30 BC aged about 39*

Cleopatra was the daughter of Ptolemy XII. It was the custom for brother and sister to marry and rule jointly. On her father's death, Cleopatra ruled Egypt with her younger brother Ptolemy XIII. However, Cleopatra's father had appointed Rome to be the guardians of his children. Egypt was no longer independent of the Roman empire.

Cleopatra was forced out of Egypt, but was restored to power by Julius Caesar, who allowed her to rule with another of her brothers. She lived with Caesar in Rome and bore him a son whom she called Caesarion. Caesar was assassinated in 44 BC, so Cleopatra then returned to Egypt and ruled jointly with her son.

A civil war soon followed in the Roman world, and Cleopatra became an ally and then mistress of Mark Antony. Antony permitted Cleopatra and Caesarion to be proclaimed joint rulers of Egypt and Cyprus. Cleopatra had three children by Antony, each of whom was proclaimed ruler of a part of the Roman empire.

In the civil war Antony and Cleopatra were defeated at the battle of Actium by Octavius (later the Emperor Augustus). They both committed suicide rather than be taken prisoner. Antony stabbed himself and Cleopatra let herself be bitten by a poisonous snake. ◆

🔵 **see also**

Mark Antony   Augustus   Caesar

Bill **Clinton**

President of the United States of America from 1993
Born *1946*

William J. Clinton grew up in Hot Springs, Arkansas, where he was inspired by his hero President Kennedy. From his early teens he too wanted to become a politician. After attending university at Washington, Oxford, and Yale, he became a professor of law. He married a lawyer, Hillary, in 1975 and began his political career as attorney general of Arkansas in 1976. Two years later he became the youngest U.S. Governor for 40 years. When he was defeated in 1980, it seemed that his political career was over. However, Clinton came back not only as Governor of Arkansas but also as the Democratic presidential candidate. He was elected president in 1992, and re-elected for a second term in 1996. ◆

Robert **Clive**

English founder of British rule in India
Born *1725*   ***Died*** *1774 aged 49*

Robert Clive was sent to India as a clerk in the East India Company but he hated his work and lost no time in joining the East India Company's army.

Clive distinguished himself in the fighting against the French and their

▼ *Robert Clive meeting with the nawab (ruler) of Bengal.*

Indian allies in south India. In 1756, he commanded the Company's army which defeated the Indian ruler of Bengal. Bengal was still a province of the Mughal empire and was one of India's richest areas. After this victory, the Mughal emperor granted the Company the right to collect the revenues of Bengal. In effect, the Company became the masters of Bengal and Clive had laid the foundations for British rule in India.

In later years, as the first governor of Bengal, Clive did much to cut out corruption and provide firm government, although he did accept large gifts himself. He was bitterly attacked for this when he came back to England and, although cleared by parliament, he became very depressed and finally killed himself. ◆

Christopher **Cockerell**

English engineer and inventor of the hovercraft
Born 1910

Christopher Cockerell trained as an engineer and in electronics. He was fascinated by the idea of a hovercraft, a machine travelling on a cushion of air. Other scientists had already shown that a machine like an upside-down tea tray would float on a cushion of air pumped down from above, but the air quickly escaped round the edges. Cockerell showed that a 'wall' of air was much better at trapping the air cushion. In his first experiments he fitted a cat food tin inside a coffee tin and blew air from a vacuum cleaner down between them.

His first hovercraft tests in 1959 created a great sensation. His experimental hovercraft travelled along England's south coast at 30 knots (55 km/h), and then climbed onto the beach.

Cockerell's invention is of greatest use in countries with poor road and rail systems because it can travel up rivers and across deserts. ◆

Jean **Cocteau**

French poet, dramatist, artist, and film-maker
Born 1889   Died 1963 aged 74

From boyhood, multi-talented Jean Cocteau was attracted to every kind of theatre from circus to classical drama. Friends organized a performance of his poems when he was only 16 and his first book of poems was published at 19. When he told the Russian impresario (showman), Diaghilev, that he wanted to create a ballet he was challenged 'Etonne-moi!' (Surprise me!). In collaboration with Picasso and composer Erik Satie he came

▼ *One of Cocteau's many talents was as an artist. He illustrated this poster for one of Diaghilev's Ballet Russe productions in Paris.*

up with the ballet *Parade* to music that incorporated typewriters and other unusual sounds. Novels, plays, movies, and distinctive drawings followed. Films such as *Beauty and the Beast* and *Orpheus* show his poetic use of cinematic effects. ◆

see also
Diaghilev   Picasso

Samuel **Coleridge**

English poet
Born 1772   Died 1834 aged 62

As a young man Samuel Coleridge enlisted in the army. He was quite unsuited for this life and was bought out by his brothers. He then moved to America where he planned to set up a community which could live and educate its children on better principles than the rest of society. The plan failed and Coleridge moved back to Cambridge where he had been a student.

He met the poet Wordsworth and moved to the Lake District to be near him. Coleridge had suffered from rheumatism all his life and the climate of the Lake District did not help. To relieve the pain he began taking the opium-based drug laudanum and he soon became addicted to opium itself.

Coleridge was one of the most important of the English poets. Together with Wordsworth he began what came to be known as the 'Romantic' movement in poetry. His most famous poems are *The Rime of the Ancient Mariner*, and *Kubla Khan*. ◆

see also
Wordsworth

Michael **Collins**

*Irish statesman who helped to win
independence for his country*
Born *1890* ***Died*** *1922 aged 31*

Michael Collins worked in an
accountant's office in London
from 1906 before returning to
Dublin to take part in the Easter
Rising of 1916. This was an armed
rebellion to force Britain to grant
Ireland independence, but it failed
and Collins was captured. After he
was released he became a Sinn Fein
MP, although Sinn Fein did not join
other British MPs in London. He
helped to free the republican
leader, Eámon De Valera, from
Lincoln Jail and led the Irish
Republican Army so successfully
that the British government put a
price of £10,000 on his head. When
a truce was declared in 1921,
Collins was one of the main Irish
negotiators. The treaty he signed,
which made most of Ireland
independent but which left
Northern Ireland under British
rule, was not accepted by all
republicans. In the civil war that
followed Collins led the Irish
government and its army, but

◀ *A Colt
revolver,
model 1873,
known as the
'Peacemaker'.*

was ambushed and killed by his
opponents in West Cork. ◆

👁 **see also**
De Valera

Samuel **Colt**

American gun maker
Born *1814* ***Died*** *1862 aged 47*

Samuel Colt was the inventor of
a handgun that could fire one
shot after another. The cylinder
containing the bullets moved round
as the gun was cocked for firing.
Colt's 'revolvers' and rifles did not
sell well at first and the company
manufacturing them had to close
down. But the US army liked them
and when the government ordered
1000 pistols for the Mexican War,
Colt was back in business. In 1855
he built the largest private armoury
in the world, based at Hartford in
Connecticut.

Colt's most famous gun was a
six-shooter called the
Peacemaker. First
sold in 1873, it
became the gun of the cowboy and
of the Wild West. ◆

Christopher **Columbus**

*Italian explorer who travelled to the
Americas*
Born *1451* ***Died*** *1506 aged 54*

Christopher Columbus, a skilled
sailor, was a man with a
dream. He knew that the Earth was
round, and thought the easiest way
to reach Japan was to sail west

▼ *On sailing west across the Atlantic
Ocean, Columbus came upon America,
a land which was unknown to Europeans
at that time.*

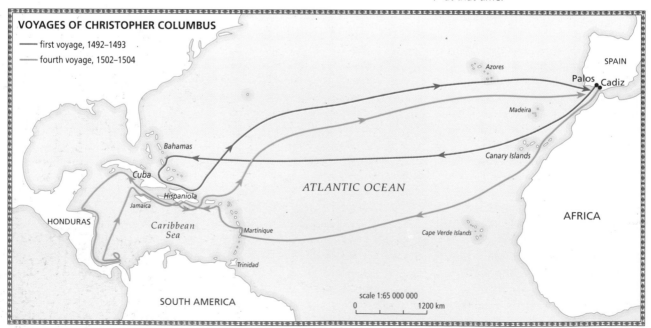

VOYAGES OF CHRISTOPHER COLUMBUS
— first voyage, 1492–1493
— fourth voyage, 1502–1504

SPAIN
Azores
Palos Cadiz
Madeira
Bahamas
Canary Islands
Cuba
Hispaniola
ATLANTIC OCEAN
Jamaica
HONDURAS Caribbean
Sea
Martinique
Cape Verde Islands
AFRICA
Trinidad
SOUTH AMERICA
scale 1:65 000 000
0   1200 km

around the globe. He looked for many years for a patron to finance such a voyage, and after many delays, he was eventually funded by Queen Isabella of Spain.

Columbus sailed with three small ships, *Santa Maria*, *Niña*, and *Pinta*, and about 90 men. After leaving the Canaries they sailed west until the morning of 12 October 1492 when a look-out sighted land. In fact it was one of the Bahama islands. Columbus was convinced it was the Indies and that he was very near Japan.

The *Santa Maria* was wrecked off the island Columbus named Hispaniola, so he decided to leave 40 men there to form a colony, and returned to Spain with the other two ships. He was hailed as a hero and was given the titles of Admiral of the Ocean Sea and Viceroy of the Indies. He set off again in 1493 with a fleet of 17 ships and 1200 men.

On his second arrival at Hispaniola Columbus found that all 40 of the men had been murdered. He founded another colony, and also visited Jamaica. Complaints were made about his harsh rule as viceroy, but in spite of this he was allowed to go on a third expedition in 1498. This time he reached the island of Trinidad and set foot on the mainland of South America.

However, Columbus was not a good governor and many more complaints about his rule reached Spain. A new governor, Francisco de Bobadilla, was sent to take over. He arrested Columbus and sent him back to Spain in chains.

Columbus was pardoned and in 1502 was allowed to make one more voyage. While exploring the coastline of Central America, he became convinced he was near the mouth of the Ganges in India. He returned to Spain and died shortly after, still believing he had reached the Orient. ◆

Nadia **Comaneci**

Romanian champion gymnast
Born 1961

Nadia Comaneci burst onto the gymnastics scene at the European championships of 1975 when, at the age of 13, she won four of the five gold medals. The following year she made Olympic history when she became the first gymnast ever to be awarded the perfect score (10·0) for her performance on the asymmetric bars. By the end of the competition, she had won gold medals for the asymmetric bars and the balance beam and was the overall Olympic champion, all at the age of 14. In 1989 she left Romania and settled in America. ◆

Confucius

Ancient Chinese teacher and writer
Born c.551 BC
Died 479 BC aged about 70

Confucius was the son of a poor nobleman. At the age of 15 he began work as an official in charge of public grain stores. When his mother died he followed the custom of returning home to mourn for three years. He gave up all pleasures and studied the ancient history and literature of the people of China. Afterwards he spent most of his life travelling as a teacher of young noblemen and officials.

Confucius's teachings were about what made an orderly society with contented people. He showed why the ancient books stressed the importance of polite behaviour and ceremonies. He said that noblemen and court officials should not plot to gain more power, but study music, poetry, and the history of their ancestors. Ceremonies should be a way of showing respect to ancestors, just as people should bow to their living rulers or to older people as a sign of obedience. Many of Confucius's sayings were written down in a collection called the *Analects*. The best known is 'Do not do to others what you would not have them do to you.' ◆

▼ *Confucius was a philosopher, rather than a religious leader. His teachings have become a widely held set of beliefs called Confucianism.*

Joseph **Conrad**

Polish-born English novelist
Born *1857* **Died** *1924 aged 66*

Joseph Conrad, the adopted name of Jozef Korzeniowski, was born in what was then Russian Poland. He arrived in England aged 20, and worked as a merchant seaman for the next 16 years. Learning English during this time, he used his seafaring experience to write some of his best novels, including *Lord Jim* (1900) and *The Shadow Line* (1917). However, Conrad was never interested in adventure for its own sake. In all his stories, individuals also battle against their own weaknesses as well as against natural dangers like storms, injury, or fire at sea. Conrad also had a fascination with human evil and despair, summed up unforgettably in his short novel, *Heart of Darkness* (1902). ◆

John **Constable**

English landscape painter
Born *1776* **Died** *1837 aged 60*

John Constable's father was a corn merchant who owned Flatford Mill in East Anglia. He expected his son to continue the successful family business, but John did not seem happy. So his father allowed him to train as an artist and at the age of 23 John began at the Royal Academy School in London.

Constable devoted himself almost entirely to landscape painting. Unlike a lot of earlier landscape artists, who painted pleasant but imaginary scenes, Constable chose

▶ *John Constable's painting of Flatford Mill, Suffolk. Constable is particularly admired for the way he created a sense of time of day with his atmospheric lighting effects.*

to show real places under differing conditions of light and weather. He caught the scudding movement of clouds, and the drama of storms, painting with vigorous strokes of the brush. Most of all he enjoyed painting the places he knew and loved best, particularly the Suffolk countryside. ◆

Constantine I ('the Great')

Roman emperor from 306 to 337
Born *c.274* **Died** *337 aged about 63*

By the time Flavius Valerius Constantinus, or Constantine, came to power in 306, the vast Roman Empire had been split into two parts: an eastern empire and a western empire.

Constantine, who was already a distinguished soldier, was with his father Constantius Chlorus, the emperor of the western empire, when he died in York in 306. The troops proclaimed the young Constantine as the new emperor of the west. For the next few years he fought many battles to defeat the emperor of the east and to win control over the whole empire and by 324 he had succeeded. He was then known throughout the huge empire as Constantine the Great.

He then set about building a new capital at Byzantium on the entrance to the Black Sea. He completed the task in 330 and called the city Constantinopolis, 'City of Constantine'.

Although he was not brought up as a Christian, he did not persecute Christians as earlier emperors had done. In 313 he issued an edict (order) allowing Christianity to be a recognized religion in the empire for the first time. He was baptized a Christian on his deathbed. ◆

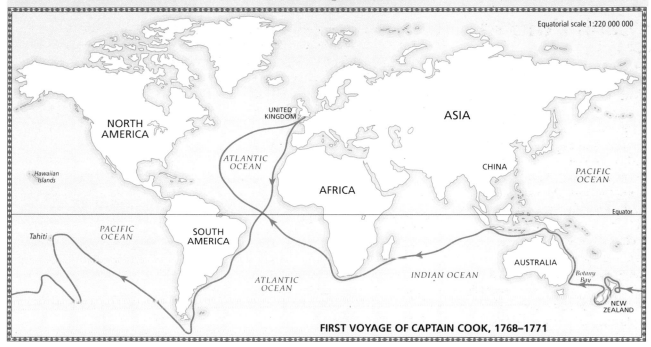

FIRST VOYAGE OF CAPTAIN COOK, 1768–1771

Equatorial scale 1:220 000 000

James **Cook**

English navigator and explorer
Born 1728   Died 1779 aged 50

James Cook went to sea when he was 18 as a ship's boy on a coal ship. In 1755 Cook volunteered for the Royal Navy as a seaman. He soon proved himself to be an outstanding navigator and was quickly promoted.

In 1768 the Royal Society organized a scientific voyage to Tahiti. Cook was given command of the ship *Endeavour*, taking on board some famous scientists. The voyage lasted three years. On the journey, Cook insisted that the sailors ate plenty of fresh fruit, and so became the first captain to save his crew from scurvy, a terrible disease caused by lack of vitamin C.

Cook became the first European to chart the coast of New Zealand, and the first to discover the eastern coast of Australia. He claimed these lands for the British Empire. He named one bay 'Botany Bay' because of its many fabulous plants. It later became a dreaded prison colony for British convicts.

▲ *James Cook circumnavigated the world on his first voyage.*

On his second voyage (1772–1775), Cook sailed south to Antarctica and then charted the Pacific and its many islands.

On his third voyage (1776–1779), the Admiralty ordered him to explore a possible sea route around North America from the Pacific. He discovered the Sandwich Islands (Hawaii), explored the Alaskan coast, then passed through the Bering Strait, before returning to Hawaii where he was killed by islanders in a scuffle on shore. ◆

👁 **see also**

Tasman

Nicolaus **Copernicus**

Polish astronomer
Born 1473   Died 1543 aged 70

Nicolaus Copernicus was very well educated and studied mathematics, law, and medicine, before becoming an astronomer.

At that time everyone believed that the Earth was at the centre of the universe. But Copernicus realized that this picture did not agree with his observations. He worked out that the Sun was at the centre, with all the planets moving round it. He also said that our Earth takes a year to travel round the Sun, and revolves on its own axis once every 24 hours.

Copernicus wrote his theory in a famous book, *De Revolutionibus* (1543), which was published just before he died. His ideas were considered very controversial. They challenged the views about the Solar System held since the time of the Ancient Greeks. They also challenged the Church's belief that God created the Earth at the centre of the universe.

In 1616 Copernicus's book was regarded as a source of evil ideas and put on the *Index*, a list of books that Roman Catholics were forbidden to read. It was not until 1835 that Copernicus's book was removed from the *Index*. ◆

77

Aaron **Copland**

American composer
Born 1900   **Died** 1990 aged 90

Although he was born in Brooklyn, Aaron Copland's parents were Russian emigrants whose surname was originally Kaplan. His sister gave him his first piano lessons, but he soon outstripped her and went on to advanced studies. In 1920 he felt that he needed the stimulus of the European musical scene. He therefore decided to go to Paris to experience all the latest developments in music. On returning to America in 1924 he supported himself by teaching and playing the piano. Gradually he became known as a composer – especially after 1938 when he produced three highly successful ballets on American subjects that made use of folk-songs and jazz rhythms: *Billy the Kid* (1938), *Rodeo* (1942), and *Appalachian Spring* (1944). He wrote music of all kinds but it was through his use of folk-songs and jazz that he became the first serious composer to develop a recognizably 'American' style. ◆

Hernán **Cortés**

Spanish conqueror of the Aztecs
Born 1485   **Died** 1547 aged 62

Hernán Cortés studied law in Spain, but decided to try to make his fortune in the West Indies. In 1511 he became a soldier and joined an expedition to Cuba. In 1519 Cortés's fleet of 11 ships sailed to Yucatán, on the Mexican coast, to explore the country.

Cortés then marched inland to Tenochtitlán (now Mexico City), the capital of the Aztec rulers of Mexico. He had about 600

▲ *Hernán Cortés*

Spaniards with him, and several thousand Native Americans who were enemies of the Aztecs. The Aztec ruler, Montezuma, at first gave the Spaniards a friendly welcome. But Montezuma was killed by his own people in a riot, and Cortés and his men had to escape.

The Spaniards returned and besieged the city, bringing with them guns, steel armour and weapons, and horses – all new to the Aztecs. Unknown to both sides, the Spaniards also had a powerful but invisible weapon: smallpox. This disease, along with the war, killed thousands of Aztecs. By 1521 Cortés had conquered the whole country, and the great Aztec civilization collapsed. For nine years he ruled Mexico as governor, before returning home to Spain. ◆

👁 **see also**

Montezuma

Margaret **Court**

Australian tennis champion
Born 1942

Margaret Court (born Margaret Smith) won 64 Grand Slam tennis titles between 1960 and 1973, more than any other woman. The Grand Slam tournaments are Wimbledon and the French, Australian, and US championships.

Court was the first Australian woman to win Wimbledon (1963), and the second to take all four Grand Slam championships (1970). She captured the Australian title a record 11 times and has won a record 13 titles at the French championships. She was also three-times winner of the Italian, German, and South African championships.

She was also an outstanding all-rounder. For example, she won five doubles and eight mixed doubles titles at the US championships as well as five singles titles. She played with great power and stamina, yet sometimes lost because of nerves. ◆

Jacques
Cousteau

French underwater explorer
Born 1910   Died 1997 aged 87

As a French naval officer, Jacques Cousteau was always keenly interested in exploring the oceans. In 1943 he helped invent the scuba or aqualung, a breathing device which allows divers to spend long periods under water. ('Scuba' stands for 'self-contained underwater breathing apparatus'.) He also developed the first underwater diving station and an observation vessel known as the diving saucer. Using his observation vessel and his scuba equipment, Cousteau made many amazing films and TV programmes about life in the world's oceans.

In 1960 Cousteau led a campaign to stop the planned dumping of

▼ *Jacques Cousteau is as famous for his environmental campaign work as for his films about ocean life.*

nuclear waste in the Mediterranean Sea. His fame helped swing public opinion behind him, and the plans were dropped. Since then he has continued to campaign for the conservation of the seabed, writing books and making more fascinating films about what goes on in the depths of the ocean. ◆

Thomas
Cranmer

Henry VIII's Archbishop of Canterbury
Born 1489   Died 1556 aged 66

Thomas Cranmer was a quiet Protestant scholar who kept his beliefs to himself. He was the only one of Henry VIII's close advisers who avoided the king's wrath. Henry was particularly pleased when Cranmer arranged his divorce from Catherine of Aragon. Cranmer served the young Edward VI loyally, and compiled the Book of Common Prayer. This was used in churches in Edward's reign, and is still sometimes used today.

Cranmer's Protestant faith strengthened as time went on. However, when Catholic Mary became queen, she put him in prison for heresy (not accepting Catholic teaching). Because he was lonely and old, he signed a statement giving up his beliefs. However, when he heard that he was going to be burnt at the stake anyway, he realized he was wrong to have made such a decision. As the fire was lit around him, he put the hand which had signed the statement into the flames first, saying 'This is the hand that wrote it, therefore it shall suffer first punishment'. ◆

👁 **see also**
Henry VIII   Mary I

Crazy Horse

Native American leader
Born c.1849   Died 1877 aged about 28

It is said that Tashunca-uitco was given the name of 'Crazy Horse' because a wild horse galloped through his parents' village at the moment of his birth.

He grew up to be a fighting leader. He and his followers fought against the American government's policy of making Native Americans stay in areas called 'reservations'. However, the US Army eventually proved to be too powerful for him, and he had to surrender at Camp Robinson in 1877. When Crazy Horse realized he was going to be locked up, he tried to fight his way out but was killed in the attempt. ◆

▶ *The Sioux Indian chief, Crazy Horse.*

Crick and Watson

British and American discoverers of the structure of DNA
Francis Crick **Born** *1916*
James Watson **Born** *1928*

During World War II, Crick was a physicist working on the development of radar. After the war his interest turned to a new science called molecular biology. Physicists and chemists were working together to try to unlock the secrets of chemicals found in the body. There was special interest in the chemicals we inherit from our parents that make us look like them. This information is contained in tiny structures called chromosomes which are found in all the cells of the body. These chromosomes are made of a complicated chemical called DNA.

You cannot see the detailed structure of DNA under a microscope. Several scientists including Maurice Wilkins and Rosalind Franklin in London investigated DNA by firing X-rays at it. The X-rays produced patterns as they passed through the DNA, but they were difficult to understand.

A young American man called James Watson came to Cambridge and joined Crick in the difficult task of sorting out what those X-ray patterns meant. With a sudden flash of inspiration, Watson realized that a so-called double helix (a spiral within a spiral) could describe the structure of DNA. This led to an understanding of how DNA can make copies of itself. It was the key to all kinds of research on what animals and plants inherit from their parents, and in 1962 Crick, Watson, and Wilkins shared a Nobel prize. ◆

◀ *Crick and Watson with a model of the double helix structure of DNA.*

Davy **Crockett**

North American folk hero
Born *1786*   **Died** *1836 aged 49*

Davy Crockett was the son of poor settlers, who lived in Greene County, Tennessee. Many tales are told of his adventures as a bear hunter. He was also famous for braving the unknown forests further

▲ *An illustration of the last stand at the Alamo, 6 March 1836, a battle in which Davy Crockett lost his life.*

west in what is now the United States of America. He married and settled in Tennessee, and became an army colonel and a lawman.

In 1827 he was elected to the Congress of the United States, where he defended the land rights of poor farmers in western Tennessee. When he was not re-elected in 1835, he set out for Texas, which was fighting for independence from Mexico. He died in the battle of the Alamo against the Mexicans. ◆

Samuel **Crompton**

British inventor of the spinning mule
Born *1753*   **Died** *1827 aged 73*

Samuel Crompton learned to spin cotton on a spinning jenny. This was a machine for spinning raw cotton into thread, invented by James Hargreaves. But the spinning jenny annoyed Crompton because the thread kept breaking and so he set out to design a better machine.

To pay for it, he played his home-made violin in local theatres.

The 'spinning mule', as his machine was called, was very successful. The thread was fine and very even. People wanted to know Crompton's secret, and he even thought of destroying the machine to stop them finding out. Instead, he showed some manufacturers how it worked, thinking that his invention would make him rich. However, once they knew the secret, they became more successful than Crompton, and paid him very little. He remained bitter, and poor, for the rest of his life. ◆

see also
Arkwright   Hargreaves

Oliver **Cromwell**

Lord Protector of Britain from 1653 to 1658
Born *1599* **Died** *1658 aged 59*

Oliver Cromwell was a boisterous schoolboy, but his stern schoolmaster had a great influence on him. Like many Puritans, he was brought up to believe that God had specially chosen him to do His will.

Cromwell's chance came when he was 41. He sat in the Long parliament of 1640, and was a strong supporter of parliament's powers. When civil war began, he trained his own cavalry. They joined parliament's victorious 'New Model Army', which Cromwell later commanded. He and his men never lost a battle.

After the war, Cromwell and other army leaders tried to make a deal with Charles I. But the king broke his promises.

Cromwell was clear about what to do, though many others were terrified. He put Charles on trial for bringing war to his people, and had him beheaded in 1649. After the collapse of parliamentary government, Cromwell declared that Britain was to be a republic ('the Commonwealth').

Cromwell fought several battles, crushing Irish resistance, and defeating the Scots in 1650 and 1651. His military victories made him the most powerful man in England. He was given the title Lord Protector (king in all but name) in 1653. He allowed more religious freedom than usual (except in Catholic Ireland), and gained a high reputation abroad as well. He tried to rule with parliament, though he also used his army to enforce what he thought was right.

▶ *An unfinished miniature of Oliver Cromwell.*

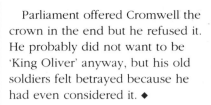

Parliament offered Cromwell the crown in the end but he refused it. He probably did not want to be 'King Oliver' anyway, but his old soldiers felt betrayed because he had even considered it. ◆

see also
Charles I   Charles II

Thomas **Cromwell**

Lord Great Chamberlain to Henry VIII
Born *c.1485* **Died** *1540 aged about 55*

Thomas Cromwell, the son of a blacksmith and innkeeper, rose to become one of the most powerful men in England. By 1513 he was making his living in England as a money lender and lawyer. Soon Cardinal Wolsey employed him as his legal and financial adviser. In 1523 Cromwell entered parliament and supported Wolsey's interests there.

When Wolsey died in 1530, Cromwell entered Henry VIII's service. He helped the king become Supreme Head of the Church of England and to divorce Catherine of Aragon. Cromwell promised to make Henry the richest king in England, and did so by organizing the closure of monasteries so that their wealth passed to the Crown.

Cromwell was a loyal servant of the king, and Henry showered him with honours. However, others hated him because of his ruthless use of power and he finally fell from favour. He was accused of treason and was beheaded. ◆

see also
Henry VIII   More   Wolsey

Tom **Cruise**

American film actor
Born *1962*

Tom Cruise had to work part-time in his high-school years to help support his divorced mother and three sisters. He began his acting career in a school production of the musical *Guys and Dolls*. As a teenager he acted in adverts and on TV. His first Hollywood film was *Endless Love* (1981).

Top Gun (1985) established Cruise as a major movie star. He continued to be a huge box-office attraction, with films like *Rain Man* (1988), in which he starred alongside his boyhood hero Dustin Hoffman, *A Few Good Men* (1993), *Mission Impossible* (1995), and *Jerry MacGuire* (1996). For the film *Interview With The Vampire* (1994) he was paid over $20 million, making him one of Hollywood's highest-earning stars. ◆

Marie **Curie**

French physicist and chemist
Born *1867*   **Died** *1934 aged 66*

Marie Curie was born Marya Sklodowska in Poland's capital, Warsaw. Women were not allowed to go to university in Poland at this time, so Marya worked hard as a governess and saved some money so that she could go to study at the Sorbonne University in Paris. When living in France, she changed her name to the French 'Marie'.

In 1894 Marie met a successful chemist called Pierre Curie, and in a year they were married. Working with her new husband, Marie Curie spent her whole life studying radioactive substances. She invented an instrument to measure radioactivity, and found that a

▲ *Marie Curie at work in her laboratory.*

substance called pitchblende (the ore from which uranium is extracted) was a thousand times more radioactive than uranium itself.

After several years' work, Marie and Pierre managed to separate out the material that made pitchblende so radioactive. They called it radium and received a Nobel prize for their work. After her husband's death in a road accident, Marie carried on with her work and received a second Nobel prize in 1911.

The dangers of radioactivity were not properly understood at that time, and Marie Curie suffered throughout her life from radiation burns on her skin. She eventually died from a form of blood cancer called leukaemia. ◆

👁 **see also**
Becquerel Röntgen Rutherford

General George A. **Custer**

American Civil War general
Born *1839*
Died *1876 aged 36*

George Armstrong Custer wanted to be an army officer, but was almost expelled

for misbehaviour from the US Military Academy at West Point. After his training, Custer fought in the American Civil War from 1861 to 1865. His commanding officer called him 'gallant' but 'reckless'. The newspapers called him the 'Boy General' because he was only 23 when he was promoted. His long, golden hair streaming, he raced his cavalry to victory after victory and became a legendary hero for his courage.

After the Civil War, Custer was sent to fight the Native Americans who still roamed the Great Plains. He often fought rashly and did not treat his men well, but the newspapers still praised him.

Then in 1876, Custer and all 266 of his troops were killed at Little Bighorn, South Dakota, by a larger force of over 3000 Sioux Indians led by Chief Sitting Bull. ◆

👁 **see also**
Sitting Bull

▼ *Custer's defeat at Little Bighorn became known as 'Custer's Last Stand'.*

Cyrus the Great

Founder of the Persian empire
Date of birth unknown
Died 529 BC age unknown

In about 550 BC Cyrus overthrew the King of the Medes and took possession of his capital. Within two years he had conquered the empire of Lydia, and taken the title of King of Persia. Then he added Babylonia, Syria, and Palestine to his empire and became master of all Asia from the Mediterranean to India. Soon he extended his rule from the Arabian desert to the Black Sea, the Caucasus, and the Caspian Sea.

Cyrus was a remarkable soldier who never executed or made slaves of the people he captured. Instead, he respected their religions and customs. He even allowed the Jews who were caught in Babylon to return to Jerusalem. ◆

see also

Darius

Louis Daguerre

French inventor of the first practical camera
Born 1789   Died 1851 aged 61

As a young man, Louis Daguerre worked as a tax collector and then became an artist. But what he really wanted to do was to produce an exact copy on paper of the world around him.

Daguerre was familiar with the camera obscura, where sunlight entered a dark box through a pin-hole and produced on a screen an image, or picture, of what was outside the box.

In the 1830s Daguerre designed a box in which the image fell on a flat metal plate; the plate was coated with a chemical called silver iodide, which turned black in sunlight. The bright part of the picture became dark and the darker parts of the picture were left lighter. Although it took a long time to produce a rather fuzzy picture, this was how the very first photographs were taken. ◆

see also

Fox Talbot   Niepce

Roald Dahl

British author
Born 1916   Died 1990 aged 74

Roald Dahl's early life was almost as adventurous as any of his novels. As a young businessman working for Shell Oil, he was sent to work in Africa. After some extraordinary adventures, some involving wild animals, Dahl volunteered for the Royal Air Force when Britain declared war on Germany in 1939. After flying in East Africa, he crashed his plane in flames in the middle of the Western Desert. Despite dreadful injuries Dahl was soon flying again in Greece and Syria, before transferring to the USA in 1943.

After World War II he started writing stories, at first for adults and later for children. His most popular children's books include *Charlie and the Chocolate Factory, The BFG, Revolting Rhymes,* and *The Witches.* During the 1980s he was the most popular children's author in the world. ◆

Gottlieb Daimler

German pioneer of the internal combustion engine
Born 1834   Died 1900 aged 66

Gottlieb Daimler started his career as an apprentice gunsmith. Later, he studied engineering and became interested in the internal combustion engine. He wanted to improve on the gas-driven internal combustion engines of the time.

Daimler studied the work of other engineers, and in 1883 he built an engine that ran on petrol. It was much more powerful than any other internal combustion engine of the time. In 1885 he used one to make what was probably the world's first motor bike. He went on to build cars that used his engines.

Daimler did not invent the petrol engine or the motor car. But, because he made better engines, he has an important place in the history of the motor car. ◆

▼ *A 1903 Daimler car.*

Dalai Lama

Spiritual and political leader of the Tibetan people
Born 1935

Tenzin Gyatso was born in a cow shed to a poor farming family who lived in north-east Tibet. When he was only two-and-a-half years old, a group of Buddhist leaders declared him to be the reincarnation of the previous Dalai Lama who had died in 1933. They installed him as their new leader, whom they believed was the Buddha of Compassion come down to Earth.

When he was four years old he went to a palace called Potala in Lhasa, the capital of Tibet. Thousands of people greeted him and wept with joy that their Dalai Lama had been found. Although he was so young, he seemed to know exactly what to do during the long ceremony of enthronement and spontaneously blessed many of his people. Life in the Potala was quite strict and lonely for the Dalai Lama. He had to study extremely hard and take many exams in Buddhist philosophy, which he passed with flying colours.

When he was 16 the Dalai Lama faced his greatest crisis. The Chinese invaded Tibet, killing many people and destroying the great Buddhist monasteries. For nine years he tried to coexist peacefully with the Chinese, but in 1959, when his life was threatened, he made a daring escape over the Himalayan mountain passes to India. The Dalai Lama now lives in a small Himalayan hamlet in India from where he takes care of the 120,000 Tibetan refugees who had followed him into exile, and tries to get the world to help his people in Tibet. He has become respected worldwide for his message of universal peace, and was awarded the Nobel Peace Prize in 1989. ◆

▶ One of Dali's quirky creations: the Lobster telephone.

Salvador **Dali**

Spanish painter
Born 1904   Died 1989 aged 85

Dali was a brilliant, very talented, and ambitious young man. He believed that his name, Salvador, meaning Saviour, meant that he was expected to save the true art of painting which he defined as 'an instant colour photograph that you can hold in your hand, of superfine images'.

Dali's paintings are very realistic; that is, objects look as real as he could make them. Yet what he painted, his subject matter, is bizarre. His interest in Freudian psychology led him to create extraordinary paintings which extend the boundaries of the imagination. For example, some of his paintings show strange and eerie dream worlds (sometimes nightmare worlds) inhabited by burning giraffes, tiny people, huge insects, and monstrous figures. People react very differently to his paintings: some people are horrified by what they see, while others are amused.

Dali is one of the most famous artists of the 20th century. He has influenced the film world, fashion, and particularly the world of advertising. ◆

John **Dalton**

English chemist and physicist
Born 1766   Died 1844 aged 77

When John Dalton was only ten he went to work for a man called Elihu who was very interested in science. Elihu realized that Dalton was very bright and started to teach him mathematics. Dalton did so well that when he was only 12 he became the head of a small country school, teaching children of all ages. He later became a lecturer at New College in Manchester and then went to London to lecture at the famous Royal Institution.

In his early twenties he began to keep a diary, which was mainly notes and theories about the weather. When he died there were 200,000 entries. He suggested, correctly, that auroras, of which there was a specially brilliant display in 1787, were electrical in origin. However, his most important work was the development of his atomic theory. The Greeks of the ancient world had some ideas about atoms but John Dalton was the first modern scientist to suggest that atoms of different elements had different weights. ◆

Dante Alighieri

Italian poet and writer
Born 1265 *Died* 1321 aged 56

Dante Alighieri grew up in Florence, Italy. When he was nine years old, he met a girl who was younger than himself, and she changed his life for ever. When he was older he wrote a lot of beautiful poetry about her. Dante called her Beatrice. We know very little about her except that she married another man and died quite young. Dante saw her occasionally when he was a young man, but only among groups of friends.

▼ *An illustration of part of Dante's* The Divine Comedy. *The poem is often seen as a metaphor for Dante's own spiritual development.*

In 1302 Dante quarrelled with the supporters of the Pope in Florence and spent the rest of his life in exile in other cities of northern Italy. His great poem, *The Divine Comedy*, describes his journey through Hell, Purgatory, and Paradise. Throughout, he feels that the love of Beatrice directs him, and at the end she herself guides him among the blessed souls in Paradise.

Dante was one of the first great poets to write in the ordinary language of the people, rather than in Latin. He used his local dialect to create one of the most beautiful poems that the world has ever known. ◆

Georges **Danton**

French revolutionary leader
Born 1759 *Died* 1794 aged 34

Georges Danton was a huge man, with striking features and a very powerful voice. Originally from a farming family, he trained to be a lawyer and worked in Paris. There he became much

▲ *Danton's powerful words and manner attracted thousands of people to his cause.*

admired by the working-class population for his rousing speeches against the king, Louis XVI, and the aristocracy. He helped to organize the uprising on 10 August 1792 that led to the overthrow of the monarchy, and then in 1793 voted for the king's execution. A few months later he became a member of the dictatorial Committee for Public Safety, which was set up to run France, and for three months he virtually led the country.

The Reign of Terror began during this period, during which at least 12,000 political prisoners, priests, and aristocrats were executed. Danton, however, disapproved of the Terror, and his growing moderation brought him into conflict with his enemies, including Robespierre, the merciless revolutionary leader. This conflict eventually led to Danton's arrest, trial, and execution by guillotine. ◆

◉ **see also**
Robespierre

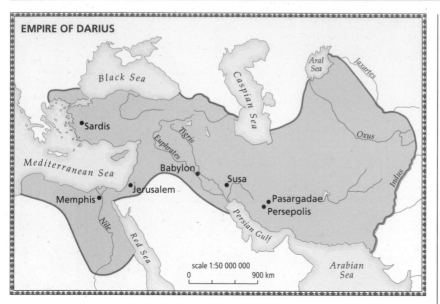

EMPIRE OF DARIUS

Black Sea · Caspian Sea · Aral Sea · Jaxartes · Sardis · Tigris · Euphrates · Oxus · Mediterranean Sea · Babylon · Jerusalem · Susa · Pasargadae · Persepolis · Memphis · Nile · Red Sea · Persian Gulf · Indus · Arabian Sea

scale 1:50 000 000
0   900 km

▲ The extent of the Persian empire in about 500 BC when it was ruled over by Darius I.

Darius I

Ruler of the ancient kingdom of Persia
Born c.558 BC
Died 486 BC aged about 72

Darius I took the throne of Persia in 521 BC. Persia was then a very large empire which controlled the countries along the eastern edge of the Mediterranean (now Turkey, Syria, Lebanon, Israel, Egypt, and Libya) and beyond to the east (now Iraq, Iran, Afghanistan, and Pakistan). As soon as Darius became king, he had to deal with revolts against him from all over the empire. He established peace by military force and then divided his empire into 20 provinces.

Darius went to war against Greece because they had helped Greek cities in Asia Minor (now Turkey) in their revolt against the Persians. The first fleet sent by Darius was destroyed in 492 BC off the north coast of Greece. In 490 BC Darius sent an army of perhaps 25,000 soldiers across to Greece. This ended in a disastrous defeat for the Persians. About 6400

Persian soldiers died compared to only 192 Greeks. Darius died a few years later and was succeeded by his son Xerxes. ◆

see also
Xerxes

Charles **Darwin**

English scientist, best known for his theory of evolution
Born 1809   **Died** 1882 aged 73

Charles Darwin's father was a doctor and he decided that Charles should also study medicine. But Charles found that he could not stand the sight of blood, and, after two years, he went to Cambridge University to study classics instead. However, he soon found that he was more interested in geology and botany.

He became the friend of the professor of botany, who suggested that Darwin would be a suitable person to go as the naturalist and companion to the captain of a naval survey ship, HMS *Beagle*. Darwin set sail on 27 December 1831 for what was to be a five-year journey.

The most important part of the

voyage for Darwin turned out to be the few weeks spent in the Galapagos Islands, which lie on the Equator, about 1000 km from the coast of South America. These islands have plants and animals that are found nowhere else. Darwin was surprised to discover that each island had its own particular sort of tortoise. Why, wondered Darwin, should this be?

When he got home, Darwin realized that some of the birds from the Galapagos Islands were also closely related to each other but different in the shapes of their beaks. Yet the birds from any one island were similar. They were all rather like some small birds that live on the South American mainland, and Darwin decided that some of these must have reached the Galapagos Islands accidentally, perhaps by being blown off course during a storm, and had evolved (changed) in their new home.

After investigating all the animals he could, Darwin developed his theory of natural selection. This theory proposed that although most young animals die, the ones that

▼ Darwin was the target of many humorously critical attacks, including this comment on 'Darwinism' from the English magazine Punch in 1881.

PUNCH'S ALMANACK FOR 1882.
MAN·IS·BVT·A·WORM·

86

survive are those best suited to their way of life. If, every now and again, an animal is born which has some feature that gives it an advantage, it will survive, and so will its offspring that are like it. In this way a process of natural selection enables a particular population to evolve.

Darwin hesitated to publish his ideas, possibly because he knew they would upset many people. But in 1859 his book called *The Origin of Species* came out. It caused an uproar, as it contradicted the ideas found in the Bible. But few people nowadays doubt the basic truth of Darwin's arguments. ◆

David

Second king of Israel
Lived during the 10th century BC

According to the story in the Bible, as a boy David watched over his father's sheep and killed the Philistine giant, Goliath, with a stone from his sling. He was invited to the court of King Saul of Judah to play his harp. Jonathan, the king's son, became his friend, and Saul's daughter Michal was his first wife.

After Saul and Jonathan were killed in a battle against the Philistines, David became king of Judah. In seven years of warfare he defeated the Philistines and other enemies, captured Jerusalem, and took the Ark of the Lord containing the Ten Commandments to the city. David became king over all the tribes of Israel as well as of Judah. He ruled for over 30 years, and was succeeded by his son Solomon. The Jews regarded David as the ideal king and hoped there would one day be another king, descended from him, called the Messiah. ◆

◉ **see also**

Solomon

Jacques-Louis David

French painter
Born 1748   Died 1825 aged 77

Jacques-Louis David began to study art at the age of 17 and at 26 he won a coveted prize (the Prix de Rome) which launched him on a highly successful career.

He became the most influential figure in the French art world. His early paintings were concerned with attention to detail, classic ideals, and 'republican' (i.e. anti-monarchy) ideas. During the French Revolution he voted for the execution of King Louis XVI and his portraits celebrated those who had died in the Revolution. His revolutionary activity led to a spell in prison.

Later, he passionately committed his painting to the cause of the Emperor Napoleon, but after Napoleon's defeat at Waterloo, David was forced to live abroad until he died. ◆

◉ **see also**

Louis XVI   Napoleon I

▲ *A detail from* The Blessing of Josephine, *one of the works Jacques-Louis David completed while employed as court painter to Napoleon I.*

Saint David

Christian monk and bishop
Lived during the 6th century

We know almost nothing about the life of this saint. His monastery was at 'Menevia', which is now called St Davids, in Dyfed, south-west Wales. Later writers nicknamed him 'the Waterdrinker' because he led a very simple life and refused to drink wine or beer. It is said that he founded ten monasteries, including the one at Glastonbury in England. The monks in these monastaries led lives of great hardship.

Since the 12th century St David has been the patron saint of Wales. His feast day is 1 March, when the Welsh wear leeks or daffodils in his honour. No one knows for sure how this ancient tradition started. ◆

▲ *Bette Davis in a still from the film Jezebel (1938). A formidable actress, she continued to make films until two years before her death.*

Bette **Davis**

American film actress
Born *1908* **Died** *1989 aged 81*

Ruth Elizabeth Davis came from Lowell, Massachusetts, and studied acting in New York. Film directors did not think she was beautiful enough for romantic roles, but in the 1930s she established herself as a powerful actress playing forceful women. She won Oscars for her roles in *Dangerous* (1935) and *Jezebel* (1938).

In films such as *The Little Foxes* (1941) and *All About Eve* (1950) she played cruel and selfish characters. In others, like *Now, Voyager* (1942), she played more likeable women, but her strong personality always shone through. In later life she scared audiences of *Whatever Happened to Baby Jane?* (1962) when she terrorized her crippled sister, played by Joan Crawford. ◆

Jefferson **Davis**

American statesman
Born *1808* **Died** *1889 aged 81*

Jefferson Davis was a soldier and cotton farmer in the southern US state of Mississippi. At that time all the work on the cotton plantations was done by black slaves. Davis treated his own slaves very well, and he did not consider that the whole system of slavery was a terrible evil.

In 1847 Davis became a national hero when he led Mississippian soldiers in a decisive stand against the Mexicans at Buena Vista. He then held important posts in the US government for some years. However, the rift between the northern states, which opposed slavery, and the southern states, which supported it, eventually led to him giving his complete support to the south.

During the Civil War that followed, Davis became president of the Confederate States of the south (1861–1865). He masterminded the Confederates' war effort against the much stronger northern states for four years until he was captured and imprisoned for treason. Although he was held in prison for two years, his case never came to court and he was released. ◆

Humphry **Davy**

English chemist, inventor of the miner's safety lamp
Born *1778* **Died** *1829 aged 51*

As a boy Humphry Davy had an extremely good memory and was quite a showman. He used to stand on a cart in the market place and tell Cornish folk-stories to crowds of children. He was later apprenticed to a surgeon, and while he worked making up medicines and pills he became interested in chemistry. When he was 21 he began to study a gas called nitrous oxide, which is sometimes called laughing gas. It was later used to put people to sleep while they had their teeth pulled out.

Scientists today remember Davy because he discovered so many new chemical elements. However, he is generally remembered for his invention of the miner's safety lamp. In 1813 a dreadful gas explosion occurred in a mine and more than 90 miners were killed. Davy was asked to help prevent such accidents in the future. The safety lamp he invented, which had a flame enclosed in glass so that it could not ignite undetected gases, must have saved thousands of lives. He made many scientific discoveries, but he always said that his greatest discovery was a young man who came to work for him: his name was Michael Faraday. ◆

👁 **see also**

Faraday

James **Dean**

American film actor
Born *1931* **Died** *1955 aged 24*

At school James Dean loved acting, and he went on to perform on stage and television before becoming a star at the age of 24 in *East of Eden* (1955). Within a few months he made two more films, *Rebel Without a Cause* (1955) and *Giant* (1956), but before they appeared in cinemas he crashed his sports car and died. Dean rapidly became a cult hero for teenagers who were angry at the way adults misunderstood them, just like the character he played in his second film, *Rebel Without a Cause*. ◆

Claude **Debussy**

French composer
Born 1862   *Died* 1918 aged 55

Claude Achille-Debussy began studying music at the Paris Conservatoire when he was ten. At first he hoped to become a great pianist, but he found that he was not quite good enough so he turned to composing instead.

As a composer he soon proved that he had genius. Such works as the *Prélude à l'après-midi d'un faune* (1892–1894) startled everyone. Instead of treating harmony according to the old rules, he used it freely, choosing chords for the sake of their effect, just as a painter chooses his colours.

Debussy's ideas set music free and opened up all sorts of possibilities for other composers to follow. He is therefore one of the most important composers of his day. Among his other works are the opera *Pelléas et Mélisande* (1892) and two important books of piano *Préludes* (1909–1910, 1911–1913). ◆

▲ *This illustration from Daniel Defoe's* Robinson Crusoe *(1719) shows the hero finding a footprint in the sand, proving that the island was inhabited.*

◀ *After the sudden and tragic end to his short film career, James Dean became a cult hero for young Americans in the 1950s.*

Daniel **Defoe**

English novelist
Born 1660   *Died* 1731 aged 71

Daniel Defoe, the son of a butcher, led an exciting and adventurous life. In 1685 he took part in the rebellion against King James II and was lucky to avoid execution. He was later put in prison for publishing opinions against the government, and even spent time as a secret agent.

Defoe is best known as the writer of *Robinson Crusoe*, which he published in 1719. Many people think of this as the first successful English novel. It tells how the hero survives after being shipwrecked on an island. Defoe also published his own newspaper, and wrote hundreds of pamphlets and articles on everything from politics to pirates. All his writing is vivid and realistic, like that of a good journalist. *A Journal of the Plague Year*, for example, tells exactly what it was like in London during the great plague of 1666. ◆

◀ Degas' Danseuses au Repos *(Dancers at Rest)*. In his paintings of ballet-dancers, Degas wanted to show the realities of the young dancers' hard work and exhaustion, not just the magic of the theatre as the curtain rises.

Edgar **Degas**

French painter
Born *1834* **Died** *1917 aged 83*

Edgar Degas was born into a wealthy Paris banking family. He wanted to be an artist from a young age, and his family had no objection to such an insecure life.

Degas was able to spend his time painting without worrying about money because his rich family supported him until he was well-known and established. Degas exhibited with the Impressionists, such as Monet and Renoir, but he was always an individualist rather than a member of a group. He realized that picture designs could break all the usual rules and that the artist need not place the main subject in the middle of the picture or show it complete. A picture showing just parts of people could look just as lifelike. He loved to paint scenes from unexpected angles, particularly ballet-dancers, because their bodies made exciting and unusual shapes. He was also a fine sculptor, making figures in wax which were then cast in bronze. His sculptures portrayed moving figures, mainly ballet-dancers. ◆

👁 **see also**

Monet Renoir

Charles **de Gaulle**

President of France from 1958 to 1969
Born *1890* **Died** *1970 aged 80*

As a child, Charles de Gaulle enjoyed playing war games. Later he went to St Cyr Military Academy. When he left in 1912 his reports said that he was 'average in everything except height'.

He was wounded and captured during World War I, and remained a soldier after the war. At the start of World War II he commanded a tank division. When France was invaded by the Germans in 1940, he escaped to England. From there he became the leader of all the French troops who had also escaped from occupied France. The Free French forces, with de Gaulle at their head, returned victorious to Paris in 1944 alongside the British and American troops.

De Gaulle was elected president of France in 1945, but resigned after only ten weeks. It was not until 1958 that he returned to power, when France was going through a political crisis. He survived a number of assassination attempts to become one of the most powerful presidents in French history. He insisted that France should be able to defend itself with its own nuclear weapons, and often argued with other leaders in Europe and the West. When he was defeated in a referendum (national vote) in 1969, he retired to his home village, where he died the following year. ◆

> *How can you govern a country which has 246 varieties of cheese?*
>
> Charles de Gaulle

F. W. **de Klerk**

President of South Africa from 1989 to 1994; deputy president from 1994
Born *1936*

Frederick Willem de Klerk became a lawyer after graduating from university. In 1972 he was elected to parliament for the National Party (NP). After 1978 de Klerk held a number of ministerial posts, including Internal Affairs and National Education. In 1989 he became president of South Africa.

Reacting to internal and international pressure, de Klerk surprised the world in 1990 by releasing political prisoners, including Nelson Mandela. De Klerk also legalized outlawed political parties such as Mandela's African National Congress (ANC). Negotiations between the ANC, NP, and other smaller parties led to the ending of apartheid. De Klerk and Mandela were awarded the Nobel Peace Prize in 1993 for their part in this achievement.

In 1994 the first election was held in which all adult South Africans could vote. It was won easily by the ANC; the NP came second. De Klerk became one of Mandela's two deputy presidents. ◆

👁 **see also**
Mandela

Eugène Delacroix

French painter
Born *1798*   **Died** *1863 aged 65*

Eugène Delacroix was born into an important French family, but as an artist he had to struggle for recognition. His new style of painting shocked those who felt that his work was not in the great tradition of French classical painting. To us, looking at his work from a 20th-century viewpoint, it does not seem at all outrageous. At the time, however, his use of bright colours and free handling of paint shocked the art world. His subject matter ranged from lively animal studies to scenes from African, Arab, and Jewish cultures, and to portraits and exciting stories from literary subjects. ◆

Cecil B. **De Mille**

American film director and producer
Born *1881*   **Died** *1959 aged 78*

Cecil B. De Mille started his career as an actor, but he soon became a director instead, and founded a film company which later formed part of Paramount Pictures. As a director he started making silent comedies, but he became more famous for *The Ten Commandments*, which he made twice, first as a silent film in 1923 and then again with sound and colour in 1956. This and his other 'epic' films based on stories from the Bible and from history were famous for their huge crowd scenes and their spectacular special effects, like the parting of the Red Sea in *The Ten Commandments*. ◆

▼ *Cecil B. De Mille (right) photographed during the filming of his 1956 film,* The Ten Commandments.

Deng Xiaoping

Chinese political leader
Born *1904*   **Died** *1997 aged 92*

Deng Xiaoping came from a rich family, but in 1920 he became a Communist and helped to bring about the revolution in China in 1949. By 1956 he was one of the leading people in the Communist government, but the next 20 years were difficult as he did not support Mao Zedong's extreme ideas. When Mao turned against those who disagreed with him, Deng lost all his power.

Mao died in 1976, and two years later Deng was the most powerful leader in China. He used his power to improve the standard of living. More food was grown, and factories began to produce goods such as clothing, sewing machines, bicycles, and television sets. Deng allowed small private businesses to develop, and ended the most severe government censorship of television and newspapers.

However, many people began to protest about the lack of democracy in China. Deng's Communist government felt threatened. In 1989 troops were ordered to put down a massive protest in Beijing and hundreds of demonstrators were killed. ◆

👁 **see also**
Mao Zedong

Robert **De Niro**

American film actor
Born *1943*

Robert De Niro lived as a child in a part of New York called Little Italy. After training as an actor, De Niro had his first major part in the film *Mean Streets* (1973) directed by Martin Scorsese. Scorsese had lived in the same part of New York as De Niro and this film was set in the streets they had both known.

De Niro is well-known for becoming totally involved in the characters he plays. For the 1979 film *Raging Bull*, he put on over 30 kg to play the part of a boxer. He even took part in three proper boxing contests. This dedication brought him an Oscar for Best Actor. He also won the award for Best Supporting Actor for his role in the 1974 film *The Godfather Part II*. ◆

▼ *In* The Deer Hunter *(1978) we see De Niro at work (as a steelworker), at play (deer-hunting), and as a volunteer in the Vietnam War.*

René **Descartes**

French philosopher and mathematician
Born *1596*   **Died** *1650 aged 54*

When René Descartes was 25, after studying, travelling, and serving in the army, he decided to devote his life to the study of philosophy and science. He settled in Holland, where he spent most of the rest of his life. He never married, although he had a daughter whose death at the age of five was said to be his greatest sorrow. He died of pneumonia in Stockholm, where he had gone to teach philosophy to Queen Christina of Sweden.

Descartes made a number of advances in mathematics, including the use of Cartesian coordinates in geometry. In philosophy he explored the certainty of knowledge. In his most famous philosophical book, *Discourse on Method* (1637), he argued that everything should at first be doubted because we can only be convinced of the truth after satisfying our doubts. This proved to him that he at least existed, because if he did not exist he could not think, much less doubt. And so he coined his most famous phrase: 'I think, therefore I am'. ◆

Eamon **De Valera**

Irish statesman
Born *1882*   **Died** *1975 aged 92*

The son of an Irish mother and a Spanish father, Eamon De Valera was born in America, but at the age of three he went to live in Ireland. When De Valera was older, he joined the Volunteers who rebelled in 1916 against British rule. The rebels had to surrender to the British, who shot most of their leaders.

De Valera was reprieved and later became leader of Sinn Féin (Ourselves Alone), which fought a guerrilla war against British rule from 1919 to 1921. Sinn Féin and the British then signed a treaty to set up an Irish Free State, but De Valera would not agree to it because Ireland was to be partitioned.

In 1926 he started a new party, Fianna Fáil (Warriors of Ireland). It won the 1932 general election, and Eamon De Valera was prime minister until 1948. He broke nearly all of Ireland's links with Britain, and in 1949 Ireland became a fully independent republic. For five years between 1951 and 1959 he was Taoiseach (prime minister) of the Republic, and between 1959 and 1973 he was president. ◆

Ninette **de Valois**

Irish-born ballet-dancer and founder of The Royal Ballet
Born *1898*

Ninette de Valois grew up in Ireland as Edris Stannus, but became famous as Ninette de Valois, dancing as a principal ballerina in England and Europe. By 1926 she was running her own ballet school, and in 1931 she formed the Vic-Wells Ballet. She was a brilliant organizer and teacher, and helped shape the careers of dancers such as Margot Fonteyn. Under her direction, the Vic-Wells Ballet became the Sadlers Wells Ballet, moved to Covent Garden, and was recognized in 1956 as The Royal Ballet.

Ninette de Valois created many famous ballets for her company. She worked hard so that Britain would have a great national ballet company and her achievement was recognized when she was made a Dame of the British Empire in 1951. ◆

🔎 **see also**

Fonteyn

▶ *De Valois as a young dancer. She retired as director of The Royal Ballet in 1961.*

▲ *Princess Diana was able to talk easily and naturally with all kinds of people, especially small children.*

Diana, Princess of Wales

Born 1961 Died 1997 aged 36

Diana Spencer became Lady Diana in 1975, when her father became the eighth Earl Spencer. She did not do particularly well at school; she then moved to London to work in a nursery school.

In 1981 Diana married Charles, Prince of Wales, the Queen's eldest son and the heir to the British throne. They had two sons, William and Harry, born in 1982 and 1984.

Diana's beauty, elegance and kindness won her many fans, and she became a great supporter of charities and good causes. Sadly, Diana and Charles separated in 1992 and later divorced. Diana withdrew from public life for a while, but later took up her charity work once more, notably for the Red Cross campaign to ban landmines in war zones.

On 31 August 1997 Diana was tragically killed in a car crash in Paris, France, at the age of only 36.

There was a tremendous outburst of grief among the people of Britain and throughout the world. ◆

Bartolomeu Dias

Portuguese navigator and explorer
Born c.1450 Died 1500 aged about 50

Nothing is known of the early life of Bartolomeu Dias except that he was an experienced sea captain, and a knight at the court of the Portuguese king, João II. In 1487 João sent him on an expedition to sail south along the west coast of Africa, looking for a sea route to India.

A storm blew Dias and the three little ships under his command out to sea, until his crews feared they would fall off the edge of the Earth. When the storm subsided Dias turned east, then north, and reached the African coast at Mossel Bay. After sailing as far as the Great Fish River on the south-east African coast, his men then insisted on going home. But Dias had seen that the coast of Africa turned northwards leaving the passage to India clear. Dias named the south-western point of Africa the 'Cape of Storms', but King João changed the name to 'Cape of Good Hope'. ◆

◀ This plate is illustrated with a scene from Dickens' Pickwick Papers.

Charles **Dickens**

English novelist
Born 1812   Died 1870 aged 58

Charles Dickens was born in Portsmouth. His father was a naval clerk who frequently got into debt. When this led to his imprisonment, the young Charles, then aged 12, was taken out of school and put to work in a factory pasting labels onto bottles of shoe polish.

Later, he went to school again, and left at 15 to become a reporter covering debates in the House of Commons. His genius for describing comical characters and his anger about social injustice were soon noticed. In 1836 he began *The Pickwick Papers*. The book was so popular that by the age of 24 Charles was famous in both Britain and America.

Dickens went on to write such powerful stories that Parliament sometimes passed laws to stop the various scandals he described so vividly. For example, after publishing his book *Nicholas Nickleby*, some of the cruel boarding-schools he described were forced to close down following such bad publicity.

Dickens also had a wonderful gift for creating larger-than-life characters in his novels: the villainous Fagin in *Oliver Twist*, the bitter Miss Havisham in *Great Expectations*, the drunken nurse Mrs Gamp in *Martin Chuzzlewit*, and the optimistic, unreliable Mr Micawber in *David Copperfield*, a character based on his own father. When Dickens died of a stroke, he was mourned all over the world, and his books have remained popular ever since. ◆

👁 see also

Thackeray

Emily **Dickinson**

American poet
Born 1830   Died 1886 aged 55

Emily Dickinson was born at Amherst, Massachusetts, and lived almost all her life there. After a visit to Washington and Philadelphia in her early twenties she lived in seclusion at the family home at Amherst. For the last 25 years of her life she scarcely ever left her own room, except at dusk when she would creep out into the garden if no one else was around.

Emily had a few close friends with whom she exchanged long letters. She may even have fallen in love with one of the men she wrote to, but she was so secretive that no one knows for certain who this man was. From the 1850s she channelled all her energy into her poetry, which she wrote down in beautiful little handmade books. Very few of her 1700 poems were published in her lifetime, so it was only after her death that she was fully recognized as a gifted poet. ◆

Denis **Diderot**

French philosopher and writer
Born 1713   Died 1784 aged 70

As a young man, Denis Diderot chose to study law. Soon his wide interests in mathematics, philosophy, and literature led him to become a teacher and translator.

In 1745 Diderot was put in charge of producing a French encyclopedia. Gathering a brilliant team of scholars around him, Diderot used this opportunity to support the use of reason rather than religion as the best way of understanding and improving society. In 1750 he was briefly sent to prison for these attacks upon religious beliefs.

The first volume of his encyclopedia appeared in 1751, and the last came out in 1772. The ideas developed within it did much to prepare its readers for the massive reaction against old ideas and practices that developed during the French Revolution, five years after his death. ◆

▶ Marlene Dietrich in a Hollywood publicity shot.

Joe **DiMaggio**

American baseball star
Born 1914

Joe DiMaggio, also known as 'Joltin' Joe' and 'the Yankee Clipper', played baseball for the New York Yankees from 1936 to 1951. He was a superb batter and was twice the top scorer for his team. In 1941, he set a new baseball record by making successful hits at least once in each of 56 consecutive games. He was also an excellent outfielder.

Even after he retired he remained in the public eye by marrying film star Marilyn Monroe in 1954. The marriage lasted only nine months. ◆

👁 **see also**

Monroe

▶ Baseball star Joe DiMaggio in 1951.

Rudolf **Diesel**

German inventor of the diesel engine
Born 1858   Died 1913 aged 55

Rudolf Diesel trained as an engineer in Munich, Germany. In the 1890s he began experiments on the internal combustion engine used to power cars. By 1897 he had perfected a simpler type of engine that did not need spark plugs and used a cheaper form of petrol, now called diesel. Diesel engines are widely used in lorries and are increasingly fitted into family cars. They are very economical to run, because they travel further per litre of fuel than ordinary cars with internal combustion engines.

Rodolf Diesel was not easy to work with and was often depressed. He died when he fell overboard crossing the English Channel. Some people think it may have been suicide. ◆

Marlene **Dietrich**

German-born American actress and singer
Born 1901   Died 1992 aged 91

Maria Magdalene Dietrich was born in Berlin, Germany. She first attracted attention for her appearances in the German and American versions of the film *The Blue Angel* (1930). She decided to stay in Hollywood, becoming a US citizen in 1937, and starred in such films as *Blonde Venus* (1932), *Destry Rides Again* (1937), and *Judgement at Nuremberg* (1961).

Not only was she an actress but she was also a singer, famous for her husky voice. She performed in cabarets for many years. She would often appear in trouser-suits, which was considered quite daring at the time. ◆

Diogenes

Ancient Greek philosopher
Born *c.400* BC
Died *c.325* BC *aged about 75*

Diogenes came to Athens with his father as an exile from his native city in the Black Sea region. Once in Athens, Diogenes studied philosophy. He developed his own ideas about how life should be conducted. He believed that people could become happy if they were content just to satisfy their own basic needs. He lived in extreme poverty himself. He taught that people should aim to become self-sufficient and train their bodies to need as little as possible and to have no shame. Diogenes was criticized by many people because of these views.

Diogenes and his followers were given the name 'Cynics', probably from the Greek word for dog, because dogs act without shame in public. ('The dog' was actually Diogenes' nickname.) ◆

Walt **Disney**

American cartoon film-maker
Born *1901*   **Died** *1966 aged 65*

Walter Disney grew up on a farm, and enjoyed sketching the animals. He established his own film company in Hollywood in 1923, creating Mickey Mouse in 1928 and Donald Duck in 1934. These quickly became the world's favourite cartoon characters. Then he made full-length animated films, including *Snow White and the Seven Dwarfs* (1937), *Pinocchio* (1940), and *Bambi* (1942). Sometimes he was criticized for changing famous stories to suit his cartoons.

His film company was the biggest producer of cartoons, but it also made children's films with real

© Disney

▲ *Some familiar characters from Walt Disney's cartoon adventure* Jungle Book, *made in 1967.*

actors, such as *Twenty Thousand Leagues under the Sea* (1954), and films like *Mary Poppins* (1964) which combined cartoon characters and real actors. In 1954 he opened Disneyland, the huge amusement park in California. He planned the even bigger Disneyworld in Florida, but this did not open until five years after his death. ◆

Benjamin **Disraeli**

Prime minister of Great Britain in 1868, and again from 1874 to 1880
Born *1804*   **Died** *1881 aged 76*

Benjamin Disraeli was Jewish by birth, and did not go to a well-known school. It was difficult for someone with his background to get to the top in Victorian Britain.

As a young man, he dressed in flashy clothes, and wore his black hair in long ringlets. He wrote some successful novels like *Coningsby* (1844) and *Sybil* (1846). However, although he became a Member of Parliament in 1837 and was chancellor of the exchequer several times, he did not have a long spell as prime minister until he was nearly 70!

He believed that the Conservative Party should improve the lives of ordinary people, especially when so many had the vote. In 1867, when he was chancellor of the exchequer, he introduced an important Reform Act which gave the vote to working men living in towns and cities. Between 1874 to 1880, when he was prime minister, he encouraged better housing for working people, and cleaner conditions in towns.

Disraeli wanted to see the British empire grow stronger than ever. He was supported in this by Queen Victoria, whom he charmed and flattered. In 1875 Britain took control of the newly-built Suez Canal. This canal formed the shortest route to India – an important part of the British Empire. ◆

see also

Gladstone   Victoria

Donato **Donatello**

Italian sculptor
Born *1386*   **Died** *1466 aged 71*

Donato Donatello trained as an apprentice in the workshop of Ghiberti, a goldsmith, painter, and sculptor. Donatello then worked for 30 years at the Cathedral in Florence where he developed his individual style. He was much influenced by, and extremely knowledgeable about the classical sculpture of ancient Greece and Rome. Nevertheless he was the first sculptor to explore the new ideas about perspective, a sort of mathematical system to show distance and to create the feel of three dimensions.

He sculpted, carved, and decorated in marble, bronze, and wood. Later on he learnt to deliberately distort figures to make their impact more powerful. For example, in his carved and painted figure of the aged *Mary Magdalene* he chose to make her very ugly in order to emphasize the dramatic appeal of his subject.

Until the time of Michelangelo, Donatello was the greatest and the most influential sculptor in Florence. ◆

see also

Michelangelo

▶ *Donato Donatello's sculpture,* Annunciation.

John **Donne**

English poet
Born *1572*   **Died** *1631 aged 59*

John Donne's first job was as an assistant to a senior government official. However, in 1601 his secret marriage to his employer's niece led to his dismissal. Already well-known as the author of some of the most passionate love poems ever written in Britain, he and his family led an uncertain existence until Donne decided to become a priest in 1615. His fame as a preacher grew quickly, and in 1621 he became dean of St Paul's Cathedral, a post he kept until his death. His poetry changed from its early interest in human emotion to the treatment of more religious themes. But even in this later work, Donne continued to write with immense feeling, in poems that were both complex and also very direct in their use of language. 'Death be not Proud' is the best-known of his Holy Sonnets. His sermons were

also famous and attracted large congregations, and many are still in print today. ◆

> *Death be not proud, though*
> *some have called thee*
> *Mighty and dreadful, for thou*
> *are not so.*
>
> JOHN DONNE
> Holy Sonnets no. 6, 1609

Fyodor **Dostoevsky**

Russian novelist
Born *1821*   **Died** *1881 aged 59*

Fyodor Dostoevsky first trained as a military engineer before becoming a writer. His early stories described the dreadful poverty then existing in Russia, and in 1849 he was arrested as a suspected political agitator. Condemned to death, he was pardoned while actually facing a firing squad. He then spent four years as a convict in Siberia. Returning to St Petersburg, Dostoevsky lived in poverty. In 1866 he wrote *Crime and Punishment*, one of the world's greatest novels. It describes a poor student who murders a mean old lady for her money. The student believes that he is justified in doing this because of what he sees as his superiority over his victim. But his conscience finally forces him to confess his crime. Further novels, such as *The Brothers Karamozov* (1880), concentrated on the human struggle to live a spiritual life faced by personality weaknesses and the general despair caused by the corruption in Russia in the 19th century. ◆

Frederick **Douglass**

American anti-slavery campaigner
Born *1817*   **Died** *1895 aged 78*

Frederick Augustus Washington Bailey was born as a slave and was separated from his mother as an infant. After one attempt in 1833, he finally managed to escape from slavery in 1838. He ended up in Massachusetts, where he used the name Douglass to avoid recapture. In 1841 he began to speak against slavery for the Anti-Slavery Society, telling people his own life story. He later wrote this down as *The Life and Times of Frederick Douglass*. From 1847 to 1860 he edited his own newspaper, *The North Star*, and during the Civil War he was a consultant to President Lincoln. He believed that ex-slaves should be armed, and enlisted his own sons in the Union army. After the war he became the first black man to hold high office in the American government when he became the American ambassador to Haiti. ◆

👁 **see also**
Stowe   Truth
Tubman

Arthur Conan **Doyle**

Scottish writer
Born *1859*   **Died** *1930 aged 71*

Arthur Conan Doyle trained as a doctor, but he was never very successful in this profession. Soon he found that he could earn more money by writing, so when he was 32 he gave up medicine and took up writing full time.

Doyle wrote all sorts of books, from historical romances to adventure stories. But it was his detective stories, with the brilliant Sherlock Holmes as their hero, which brought him money and fame. *A Study in Scarlet* (1887) was the first book which introduced the character of Sherlock Holmes. Doyle also wrote some very successful short stories in *The Adventures of Sherlock Holmes* (1891–1893).

Later, Doyle became tired of writing about Sherlock Holmes. He tried to kill him off in a deadly struggle with the arch-villain, Moriarty. However, Doyle's readers complained so much that he had to write another story, in which Holmes reappears and tells of his amazing escape. ◆

Francis **Drake**

English sea captain, and the first English person to sail round the world
Born *c.1540*   **Died** *1596 aged about 56*

At the time of Queen Elizabeth I, England and Spain were enemies (though they were not actually at war until the end of her reign). Elizabeth I allowed Francis Drake, an experienced sea captain, to plunder and steal from Spain's colonies, as long as he did it 'unofficially'. Drake went on several successful voyages, seizing treasure from Spanish colonies in South America and the West Indies. Drake was behaving little better than a pirate, but he was popular in England for his daring deeds.

Drake set out again in 1577 in his ship the *Pelican*, which was later renamed the *Golden Hind*. He plundered many South American settlements before sailing up the Californian coast. From there he crossed the Pacific Ocean, and returned home around the tip of Africa. For this remarkable

◀ *Anti-slavery campaigner Frederick Douglass.*

▲ *The English navy battles with the Spanish Armada in 1588.*

expedition, Elizabeth I honoured Drake by making him a knight.

In 1588 Spain planned to invade England with a great fleet of ships (or armada). When the Spanish Armada finally sailed towards England, Drake helped to defeat the fleet in the English Channel. ◆

see also

Elizabeth I

Alfred **Dreyfus**

French army officer, unjustly accused of spying for Germany
Born *about 1859*   **Died** *1935 aged 76*

Alfred Dreyfus, a Jewish French army officer, was arrested in 1894 and accused of spying for Germany. He was found guilty and sentenced to life imprisonment on Devil's Island, the French penal colony in South America.

His family and friends, including the novelist Emile Zola, challenged the sentence, but the authorities refused a new trial until 1899. Anti-Jewish feeling was so strong in the French army that his second trial was a mockery. It was known that he was innocent but the military establishment tried to conceal it. Dreyfus was sentenced to ten years imprisonment, but within days was pardoned by the French president.

In 1906 his case was reviewed and, at last, Dreyfus was declared innocent, and returned to the army. In World War I he commanded one of the forts defending Paris. ◆

see also

Zola

Alexandre **Dumas**

French writer
Born *1802*   **Died** *1870 aged 68*

Although Alexandre Dumas wrote many historical plays and stories, he is famous for creating the characters of d'Artagnan, Athos, Aramis, and Porthos in *The Three Musketeers* (1844–1845). Further adventures of the musketeers followed in *Twenty Years After* and *The Vicomte de Bragelone*. His other famous creation was *The Count of Monte Cristo* (1844–1845).

His successful writing career began in 1829 with the play, *Henri III*. Dozens of works followed this as Dumas kept up a hectic pace of writing and travelling. However, he almost never wrote a complete novel himself. He provided the plot and characters and often some of the important passages, and then left the main writing to a changing group of literary assistants. In this way he managed to produce many novels and stories. ◆

John **Dunlop**

Scottish inventor of the pneumatic tyre
Born *1840*   **Died** *1921 aged 81*

John Dunlop went to college to study to become a veterinary surgeon. He moved to Belfast, Ireland, when he was 27, and ran a successful vet's practice.

During the 1880s, bicycles were becoming very fashionable. They usually had solid rubber tyres, but Dunlop had the idea of a hollow tyre with air pressure inside it.

He patented his 'pneumatic' tyre in 1888. He never made a fortune out of it, though, for two reasons. One was that someone else, William Thompson, had patented an exactly similar idea in 1845, although it had not been made then because bicycles were much rarer. Another problem was that his pneumatic tyres were stuck to their wheels with glue, making it very difficult to mend punctures. It was not until other inventors came up with other methods of keeping pneumatic tyres fixed to wheels that they became really popular. ◆

▼ *A 1935 advert for the Dunlop Company, named after the inventor of the pneumatic tyre.*

Albrecht **Dürer**

German Renaissance artist
Born *1471*   **Died** *1528 aged 56*

Albrecht Dürer was one of 18 children; only three survived to adulthood. His artistic talent developed early. At the age of 13 he made a brilliant self-portrait, and at 15 he was apprenticed to a painter and book illustrator in Nürnberg, Germany. Four years later, when he had completed his apprenticeship, he went travelling to find out what other European artists were doing.

Although he produced many paintings, including water-colour landscapes, portraits, and studies of nature, his main achievement is in the difficult technique of print-making. He is one of the greatest-ever masters of engraving and making woodblock prints. The skill and beauty of his prints made him famous, and his work was often copied. He was a thoughtful, religious, and learned man, knowledgeable in many subjects. ◆

▼ *Dürer's woodblock print*
The Rhinoceros.

Antonín **Dvořák**

Czechoslovakian composer
Born *1841*   **Died** *1904 aged 62*

The Czechs are a very musical nation: therefore, it was quite natural for the young Antonín Dvořák to play the violin and join in the village music-making. When he was 12 he began to learn how to be a butcher, like his father and grandfather. However, he could not forget music, and eventually an uncle agreed to pay for him to have proper lessons.

When his studies were complete, Dvořák earned his living by playing the violin. He also wrote music, but it was not until he was nearly 40 that people began to recognize his importance as a composer.

Dvořák wrote many colourful operas, concertos, chamber music pieces, and nine symphonies, the ninth of which ('From the New World') was composed when he went to teach in America. His music is full of splendid, dance-like tunes that seem to have sprung out of the Czechoslovakian countryside. Dvořák made Czech music famous. ◆

Bob **Dylan**

American singer and songwriter
Born *1941*

Robert Zimmerman was a wild and reckless teenager who ran off to travel across America. He took the name Dylan from Welsh poet Dylan Thomas, and performed as a singer in New York's Greenwich Village coffee bars during the early 1960s. Two of his own songs, 'Blowin' in the Wind' (1962) and 'The Times they are a-Changin' (1963), became anthems for the Civil Rights movement in the USA. This started a new style, 'protest music', with songs about war, religion, politics, and racism.

Dylan's change from acoustic to electric instruments in the mid-1960s inspired a folk-rock craze, and he was called 'a spokesman for his generation'. His new writing technique, rich in strange images, bizarre characters, and hidden meanings, influenced many songwriters, including Lennon and McCartney of the Beatles.

For a time in the 1970s Dylan's music lost power, but in 1975 he recorded some of his best songs for *Blood on the Tracks*. He received a 'Grammy' award (similar to a film Oscar) in 1991 for lifetime achievement. ◆

 **see also**
Lennon and McCartney

Amelia **Earhart**

American pilot
Born *1898*   **Died** *1937 aged 40*

Amelia Earhart was always keen on aeroplanes, and as a young woman she took various odd jobs to pay for flying lessons. She was first noticed by the public when she flew across the Atlantic in

▲ *In 1932 Amelia Earhart became the first woman to fly across the Atlantic alone, completing the journey in 15 hours and 18 minutes.*

1928, even though she had really only been a passenger. However, she soon went on to make long-distance flights on her own and in 1932 she flew solo across the Atlantic. She became known as the 'Winged Legend'.

In 1937 she embarked on a trip around the world, with Fred Noonan as navigator. All the stops on the route were carefully planned, but one of them was at a small island in the Pacific Ocean. Her friends and advisers were worried about whether she and Noonan would be able to find it, even though they would be in radio contact. Their fears were justified. Although Earhart could be heard on the radio, she failed to find the island and the plane disappeared into the sea. ◆

see also

Batten   Johnson

George **Eastman**

American founder of the Kodak photographic company
Born 1854   Died 1932 aged 77

As a young man, George Eastman was a keen amateur photographer, but he felt photography was too complicated. Photographers had to put chemicals onto a photographic plate and load it into the camera before taking a picture. So in 1888, he developed and mass-produced a small, cheap box camera that was easy to use. He called it a Kodak camera, and inside was a roll of film long enough for 100 pictures. When the film was used up, the camera was returned to the Kodak factory. Kodak developed the pictures, and returned them with the camera loaded with a new roll of film.

> *You press the button, we do the rest.*
> QUOTE FROM A
> KODAK ADVERTISEMENT

Photography quickly caught on; Eastman made a lot of money and became known for his many generous charitable donations. ◆

see also

Daguerre   Fox Talbot   Niepce

Clint **Eastwood**

American film actor and director
Born 1930

Clinton Eastwood worked as a swimming instructor and lifeguard while taking occasional small parts in films, before he found a regular part in the TV series *Rawhide* from 1959. His first big film success was in *A Fistful of Dollars* (1964). It was called a 'spaghetti' western because it was filmed outside America by the Italian director Sergio Leone. This was followed by several more western films.

In the 1970s Eastwood began directing his own films, and also appeared as the detective Harry Callaghan in *Dirty Harry* and other violent films. His directing career developed in the 1980s and he was highly praised for his film *Bird* (1988) about the life of jazz saxophonist Charlie Parker. He won an Oscar for Best Director for his 1992 western, *Unforgiven*, in which he also starred. ◆

▶ *Clint Eastwood in a familiar western role.*

Arthur Stanley **Eddington**

English astronomer
Born 1882   Died 1944 aged 61

Arthur Eddington won a scholarship at 16 to Owens College, Manchester. After graduating in physics in 1902 he went to Cambridge University, where his distinguished career led to his appointment as chief assistant at the Royal Greenwich Observatory. From then on his life was devoted to astronomy. Appointed director of the Cambridge Observatory in 1914 and a Fellow of the Royal Society, he specialized in finding out how stars move and what they are made of, and in studying Einstein's general theory of relativity. He made important contributions to all three subjects. His famous book, *Fundamental Theory*, published after his death, was the result of 16 years of study. A quiet man, Eddington had the rare ability to write and lecture so clearly that even very difficult ideas could be understood by ordinary people. ◆

Mary Baker **Eddy**

American founder of the Christian Science Church
Born 1821   Died 1910 aged 89

A sickly child and a widow at 22, Mary Baker gave up her only son when he was six and became a semi-invalid. Her second marriage brought little comfort but in 1862 her life was transformed by healer-hypnotist Phineas Parkhurst Quimby, who believed that illness was an illusion with purely mental causes. (At first Mary lectured enthusiastically about Quimby but later denied his influence.) Although she was temporarily paralysed by a bad fall in 1866, she claimed to have cured herself with the inspiration of the Bible, thus founding 'Christian Science'. Her ideas were set out in her book, *Science and Health* (1875), through a newspaper, the *Christian Science Monitor*, and with the skilful help of her third husband, salesman Asa Eddy. Despite quarrels, lawsuits, and scandals her following grew and she died immensely rich. ◆

◀ *This picture of Edison is taken from the cover of a book called* World's Inventors. *It shows Edison with three of his inventions: the electric lamp; the phonograph; and a microphone to go inside a telephone receiver.*

Thomas **Edison**

American inventor of the phonograph and the electric lamp
Born 1847   Died 1931 aged 84

Thomas Edison's mother taught him at home and encouraged his interest in science. By the time he was ten he had made his own laboratory.

Edison set up his own company, which he called his 'invention factory'. One of his most important inventions was the world's first machine for recording sounds, the phonograph. The whole of our modern recording industry developed from this.

Edison also invented the electric lamp. It consisted of a wire inside a glass bulb from which all the air had been taken out to create a vacuum. When an electric current was passed through the wire, called a filament, it glowed white-hot and gave out light. While experimenting, Edison found that a current could also flow across the vacuum to a plate inside the bulb. He did not understand why, but we know today it is due to electrons escaping from the filament: it is known as the Edison effect. This discovery led to the invention of electronic valves and was the beginning of our modern electronics industry. ◆

Edward the Confessor

King of England from 1042 to 1066
Born c.1003   Died 1066 aged about 63

Edward grew up as a prince in exile in Normandy while Danish kings ruled England. When the last Danish king died, a powerful English lord, Earl Godwin, arranged for Edward to return and become king.

Edward married Edith, Earl Godwin's daughter. At first Edward tried to balance the influence of Earl Godwin by bringing friends of his own from Normandy, but gradually he left most of the running of the country to Godwin and the other English earls. Edward preferred to concentrate on religious and charitable works, such as building the first great church of Westminster Abbey in London. Edward and Edith had no children; this caused a dispute about who should be king of England after him and led to the Norman invasion and conquest of 1066.

Edward is called 'the Confessor' because his whole life bore witness to ('confessed') his Christian faith. In 1161 he was made a saint. ◆

Edward I

King of England from 1272 to 1307
Born 1239   Died 1307 aged 68

Edward was only 12 when he started to help his father, Henry III, rule the kingdom, and he was married by the time he was 16. He first showed his strength in battle by defeating a group of barons who were rebelling against his father, and then proved himself a courageous knight on crusade to the Holy Land.

After Edward became king in 1272, he was faced with rebellion by a powerful Welsh prince, Llywelyn. Edward invaded Wales and within five years Llywelyn was dead, and all Wales was under his control. Edward built a string of fortresses in Wales to demonstrate

▲ *Part of a French manuscript showing a scene from the battle of Crécy, 1346, won by Edward III's army.*

English strength. However, when he tried to conquer Scotland he was not so successful. ◆

👁 **see also**
Llywelyn

Edward III

King of England from 1327 to 1377
Born 1312   Died 1377 aged 64

Edward's parents, Queen Isabella and Edward II, quarrelled bitterly and his mother took him to

◀ *Kidwelly Castle, one of the Welsh fortresses built by Edward I.*

France. When Edward was 14, his mother and her lover, Roger Mortimer, murdered his father and crowned Edward king. Three years later, Edward had Mortimer killed.

Edward wanted to be a knight, fighting for fame and glory. In 1339 he invaded France, starting a war that was to continue for 100 years. Under Edward and his son, nicknamed the 'Black Prince', the English won many battles. The greatest was at Crécy in 1346. The English were so successful that Edward controlled almost as much territory in France as Henry II had done a century before.

By 1370, most of the fighting companions of Edward's youth were dead, as was his wife. And in France, a strong king was taking back the lands that Edward and his son had won. Edward lost his reputation as a true knight, and died a broken man. ◆

Gustave **Eiffel**

French engineer
Born *1832*   **Died** *1923 aged 91*

Gustave Eiffel was born in Dijon, France. He was interested in building with iron girders and he designed several large bridges and structures, including the framework for the Statue of Liberty, which stands in New York Harbor.

In 1889, there was a competition to design a monument for the anniversary of the French Revolution. Eiffel's winning design was an iron tower measuring over 300 m (984 ft) high. Although it was tall, it took only two years to build (1887–1889) and earned Eiffel the nickname 'magician of iron'. It was meant to last for 20 years but is still there today.

Eiffel also designed lock gates for the Panama Canal (1896). There was a scandal over the money for building it and Eiffel was one of those imprisoned. ◆

👁 **see also**

Lesseps

Albert **Einstein**

German-born physicist
Born *1879*   **Died** *1955 aged 76*

As a boy in Germany, Albert Einstein was very unhappy at school. His schoolmasters treated him badly because they thought he was not very clever. But, when he

▼ *The Eiffel Tower was built using 15,000 iron sections. Tourists can visit each of the four levels.*

▲ *Einstein and his wife Elsa visiting America in 1930.*

was 26, after moving to Zurich in Switzerland, he published several scientific papers that completely changed the way scientists think.

In 1914 he moved back to Berlin with his family. In 1921 he was awarded the top award in science, the Nobel prize, and modestly travelled third class to Stockholm to receive it.

It was not long before the Nazis started to gain military power in Germany. Although he was world-famous, Einstein suffered a lot of abuse because he was Jewish. Eventually he had had enough, and in 1933 he went to America where he lived for the rest of his life. He spent much of his time trying to persuade world leaders to abandon nuclear weapons.

Einstein's ideas in science were so new and strange that for many years ordinary people used to say that no one else could possibly understand them. But now his theories about time and space (relativity), about how very tiny particles like electrons and protons behave (quantum theory), and many others, are important parts of the courses that all physics students learn at university.

Not many people really deserve the title 'genius' but Einstein must be one of them. Nearly all branches of physics were changed by his theories, and without them lasers, television, computers, space travel, and many other things that are familiar today would never have been developed. ◆

Dwight **Eisenhower**

American president from 1953 to 1961
Born *1890*   **Died** *1969 aged 78*

From his childhood everybody called Dwight Eisenhower 'Ike', and his cheerful grin made him friends everywhere. He became a soldier during World War I and by World War II, although he had never been in action, he had risen to the rank of brigadier-general. His organizing skills led to his promotion to command American

▲ *A still from Eisenstein's film* Ivan the Terrible *(1944).*

forces in Europe in 1942.

Eisenhower held two more important army posts; he was chief of staff of the US Army, and in 1951 he was invited to be supreme commander of the NATO forces in Europe. In 1952 the Republican Party persuaded him to be its presidential candidate. He left the army, and his supporters swept him to power in the election with the slogan 'I like Ike'.

He served for two terms, winning a second election in 1956. During his presidency he brought the Korean War to an end and began the US space programme. ◆

Sergei **Eisenstein**

Russian film director
Born 1898   Died 1948 aged 50

Sergei Eisenstein's father wanted him to be an architect, but his real love was for the theatre. Surprisingly, his chance came when he had to leave his engineering training to serve in the army in the Russian Civil War of 1918. There

were theatre groups in the army, and Eisenstein was able to join in as a helper and director.

After the Civil War, and until his death, he was more interested in directing films. Eisenstein showed his genius for putting together scenes in an interesting and exciting way. He believed that a film director should create something more than just a series of pictures. He called this the art of 'montage', and directors ever since have been influenced by what he did. ◆

El Cid

Spanish soldier and national hero
Born c.1043   Died 1099 aged about 56

When El Cid (whose real name was Rodrigo Díaz de Vivar) lived, Spain was divided into many small kingdoms. Most of these were ruled by Muslim invaders from North Africa; a few were governed by Christian Spanish kings.

Rodrigo collected an army of brave and loyal men around him.

Sometimes they fought for a Christian lord, sometimes for a Muslim king. Although Rodrigo was bloodthirsty, he was such a successful leader that the Muslims nicknamed him El Cid (the lord).

Fifty years after his death, one of the greatest poems of Spain, the *Cantar de mío Cid*, was written. In the poem El Cid is described as the perfect knight, the bravest soldier, and (because he fought the Muslim invaders) the best of Christians. ◆

Eleanor of Aquitaine

Queen of France from 1137 to 1152 and of England from 1154 to 1189
Born c.1122   Died 1204 aged about 82

High-spirited and beautiful, Eleanor was heiress to the duchy of Aquitaine in south-west France. She married King Louis VII of France in 1137 but the marriage was not very happy and they divorced in 1152.

Eleanor then married Henry of Anjou, who shortly afterwards became King Henry II of England. This meant that Aquitaine passed into English control, which caused prolonged conflict between France and England.

Although they had eight children, Eleanor and Henry did not get on, and she lived mainly in Aquitaine. In 1173 Henry's sons rebelled against him, assisted by Eleanor. After that Henry kept Eleanor in prison, but when he died she gave a lot of support to her sons, first Richard (the Lionheart) and then John, when they each became king of England. ◆

see also

Richard I   John, King of England

Edward **Elgar**

English composer
Born *1857*   **Died** *1934 aged 76*

Edward Elgar's father ran a music shop in Worcester, so although Edward could never afford to study at a college, he was surrounded by music. He played the violin in local orchestras and was happy to write music for anyone who asked him.

He was a sensitive man and was easily discouraged. It was only when he married, in 1889, that he found someone who really believed in him. After this, his music blossomed, and in 1899 the *Enigma Variations* for orchestra proved that he was a musical genius. Oratorios, two great symphonies, concertos for violin and cello, and a symphonic poem, *Falstaff*, were further proof.

In 1920 his wife died. Elgar was broken-hearted, and for the rest of his life wrote almost nothing. ◆

El Greco

Spanish painter
Born *1541*   **Died** *1614 aged 73*

Even though Domenikos Theotcopulous was born on Crete, a Greek island, he lived in Toledo, Spain, from 1577 until he died. He became known by his nickname *El Greco*, which is Spanish for The Greek.

Little is known of his youth. He studied in Venice, under Titian, and in Rome, but it was in Toledo that he developed his own distinctive style. He mainly painted religious scenes, using distorted figures, which looked longer or shorter than in real life, and great contrasts of colour and light to express the great emotions of the spiritual events he portrayed. The strangeness of his art

inspired theories that he was mad, but his paintings do express the intense religious feeling of his adopted country, Spain. ◆

▲ *El Greco's paintings, like* The Adoration of the Shepherds *(above), seem more like 'modern' art than those of other artists of his time. His work greatly influenced later artists.*

George **Eliot**

English Victorian novelist
Born *1819*   **Died** *1880 aged 61*

George Eliot was the name adopted by Mary Ann Evans, the daughter of a Warwickshire estate manager. As an editor and journalist she worked with some of the most brilliant minds of the time. She finally started writing her own books under the name 'George Eliot' because she believed that male novelists were likely to be

treated more seriously by critics.

Her first novel, *Adam Bede*, was set in the countryside she remembered so well. It is rich both in detail and in her understanding of country people. She then wrote *The Mill on the Floss*, drawing on her own childhood for its descriptions of the growing tension between the heroine and her family. But her masterpiece, *Middlemarch*, was still to come. Written in 1871, it describes a small town society, from rich landowners and clergymen to shopkeepers and labourers. To read it is to feel part of a community that has long since disappeared. ◆

T. S. **Eliot**

American poet
Born *1888*   **Died** *1965 aged 76*

Although Thomas Stearns Eliot was born in the USA, he spent most of his life in England, first at Oxford University, then in London, where he worked as a bank clerk and as a publisher. His first important poem was *The Love Song of J. Alfred Prufrock*. Using language that is an intriguing mixture of the ordinary and the poetic, it describes the thoughts and feelings of a middle-aged man. In 1922 Eliot published an even more extraordinary poem, *The Waste Land*. This again combined everyday speech with highly unusual images in its description of what the poet saw as the worthless aspects of life in his own century. Traditional critics hated his modern approach, but younger ones saw it as an important breakthrough.

Later, Eliot became more religious and less daring. He turned to writing plays, including *Murder in the Cathedral* (about the death of Thomas Becket). In 1939 he wrote the jolly *Old Possum's Book of*

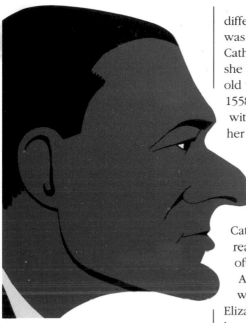

▲ *A newspaper caricature of T. S. Eliot.*

Practical Cats, which was the basis for the popular musical *Cats*, first performed in 1981. ◆

*Macavity, Macavity, there's no
  one like Macavity
There never was a Cat of such
  deceitfulness and suavity
He always has an alibi, and
  one or two to spare
At whatever time the deed took
  place – MACAVITY WASN'T
  THERE!*

T. S. ELIOT
Macavity: the Mystery Cat

Elizabeth I

Queen of England from 1558 to 1603
Born *1533* **Died** *1603 aged 69*

There was not much rejoicing when Elizabeth was born. Her father, Henry VIII, had wanted a son. When she was two, her mother, Anne Boleyn, was executed and Elizabeth then had four different stepmothers. Later, she was in great danger during her Catholic sister Mary's reign because she was a Protestant. The 25-year-old woman who became queen in 1558 was cautious, clever, quick-witted, and, unlike most girls of her time, very well educated.

Elizabeth could be very stubborn. She refused to change the Church of England set up in 1559, though at first neither Catholics nor Protestants were really satisfied. She would also often put off difficult decisions. Although Mary Queen of Scots was a great danger to her, Elizabeth took 17 years to agree to her execution. Even then Elizabeth tried to pretend she had allowed it by mistake.

Elizabeth did not like spending money either. She avoided an expensive war with Philip II of Spain for as long as possible, though she encouraged sailors like Drake to attack Spanish treasure ships, taking some of the treasure they captured. However, when the Spanish Armada set out to invade England, she became an inspiring war leader.

Queen Elizabeth I was a woman in a world of men. She cleverly controlled her powerful courtiers by being charming, witty, or angry. Everyone expected her to marry, and she promised parliament she would marry as soon as it was convenient – but it never seemed to be convenient. ◆

see also
Drake   Henry VIII
Mary, Queen of Scots   Raleigh

▼ *Elizabeth I, 'Good Queen Bess', was a popular queen. During her reign England became powerful and prosperous, and arts and literature flourished.*

Elizabeth II

Queen of the United Kingdom and Northern Ireland and Head of the Commonwealth from 1952
Born *1926*

Queen Elizabeth II is the 42nd ruler of England since William the Conqueror. Until she was ten years old she did not expect to be queen. It was only when her uncle, King Edward VIII, abdicated in 1936 that her father became King George VI and Elizabeth became heir to the throne. As a child she called herself 'Lilibet', a name that her family still use today. Her full names are Elizabeth Alexandra Mary.

Just before the outbreak of war in 1939, Elizabeth met a young sailor at a Royal Naval College. He was Prince Philip of Greece and was a distant relation. They married in Westminster Abbey when she was 21 and now have four children: Prince Charles, Princess Anne, Prince Andrew, and Prince Edward.

When her father King George VI died suddenly in 1952, Elizabeth was well-equipped to become queen. She had been taught much about the history of the United Kingdom and Commonwealth and had travelled all over Britain attending official duties. As queen, she undertakes more than 400 public engagements a year and has visited nearly every Commonwealth country at least once. In 1967 she introduced the 'walkabout' so that she could meet and talk with more of the general public. ◆

'Duke' **Ellington**

American jazz band leader, pianist, and composer
Born *1899*   **Died** *1974 aged 75*

Edward Kennedy Ellington's stylish clothes as a teenager

▶ When Duke Ellington wrote music for his jazz orchestra he took into account the particular skills of his players. His music differed from other jazz routines because it was completely composed, not improvised.

gained him the nickname Duke. He won a scholarship to art college, but was too busy learning jazz piano to attend.

In New York in 1927 he formed a ten-piece band, grandly calling it an orchestra, and became famous playing in Harlem's Cotton Club. Unlike most jazz musicians, he also wrote fully orchestrated works. Many hit records, including 'Don't Get Around Much Anymore' and 'It Don't Mean a Thing', spread his fame worldwide. Even the modern composer Igor Stravinsky counted Ellington as an influence.

He was the first black composer commissioned to write major film soundtracks and TV show themes. After 1965 he played many religious concerts in cathedrals, and continued working until his death. ◆

🕮 **see also**
Stravinsky

Ralph Waldo **Emerson**

American philosopher and poet
Born *1803*   **Died** *1882 aged 79*

Ralph Waldo Emerson was born in Boston, one of five sons of a church minister. His father died when he was eight, leaving his mother and aunt to look after the brothers on a meagre income. He studied theology at Harvard University and became a clergyman at 26. However, he resigned only three years later, shortly after the death of his first wife, because of his unorthodox religious views.

He travelled to Europe and in England made friends with several writers, including Thomas Carlyle with whom he corresponded for 38 years. On his return to America he settled in Concord, Massachusetts, and devoted his life to lecturing all over the country and to writing philosophical essays and poems. His belief that people should rely on their own powers of intuition and his great respect for nature were hugely influential in America. ◆

Empedocles

Ancient Greek philosopher
Born c.494 BC
Died c.434 BC aged about 60

Empedocles came from an aristocratic Sicilian family but spent much of his life in exile. Like other great scholars of his time he was knowledgeable in many subjects and tried to explain all the changes that take place in the world around us. He believed that the world consists of four elements – earth, air, fire, and water. This view persisted until the 17th century. He thought of the universe as two hemispheres, one bright (day) and one dark (night), revolving around the Earth. In human anatomy he believed the blood ebbed and flowed like the tides, a view which was accepted until 1628 when William Harvey showed that blood circulates continuously. He also believed that the world had once been populated by creatures now extinct because they could not survive, thus to some extent anticipating Charles Darwin's theory of evolution. ◆

👁 **see also**
Darwin   Harvey

Jacob **Epstein**

American-born English sculptor
Born 1880   *Died* 1959 aged 78

Jacob Epstein was born in New York, but he came to Europe as a young man and lived in England for most of his life, becoming a

▲ The Rock Drill, *one of Epstein's most individual and impressive pieces of work, was sculpted in bronze in 1913. This mechanical monster hints at the influence primitive art had on his early sculpture.*

British citizen in 1911. He was the most controversial sculptor of his time and his statues were often savagely attacked by journalists and critics. Some of them thought that Epstein's nude figures were obscene, and others thought that his work was clumsy and ugly. It was certainly unconventional, for he was more concerned with creating figures that were bold and full of life than with making them look detailed and realistic. However, he was much praised for his portrait busts (some of the most famous men and women of the 20th century were portrayed by him), and by the end of his career he was regarded by many as the 'Grand Old Man' of British sculpture. ◆

Desiderius **Erasmus**

Dutch scholar
Born c.1466   *Died* 1536 aged about 70

Desiderius Erasmus was an orphan, and grew up in a monastery which he loathed. He

was allowed to leave, and spent the rest of his life in the universities of Paris, Oxford, Cambridge, and Basel. He taught and studied, and wrote many books, including a collection of proverbs called *Adages* (1500).

Erasmus thought the wealthy Catholic Church of his day had forgotten the teachings of Jesus. He made a new, accurate Latin translation of the New Testament (1516). He also wrote a best-selling book poking fun at worldly, lazy monks, *The Praise of Folly* (1511). However, he never wanted to leave the Church, and disagreed strongly with the Protestant ideas of Martin Luther. ◆

In the country of the blind the one-eyed is king.

DESIDERIUS ERASMUS

👁 **see also**
Luther

▼ *Erasmus was one of the key figures in the Renaissance – a 'rebirth' of the arts which involved a return to classical principles.*

Eric the Red

Viking leader and explorer
Lived during the 10th century

The Vikings, skilled sailors and fierce fighters, travelled from Scandinavia to invade and settle in many European countries. It is from the *Sagas* – poetic stories of Viking heroes and adventures – that we know of one of the most famous of them, Eric the Red.

Eric came from a Viking settlement in Iceland. In the year 984 he led an expedition which discovered Greenland; he returned the following year to start a settlement there which survived until about 1400. The achievements of Eric and his followers are difficult to imagine. They sailed the coldest and roughest seas in the world in small wooden ships. They then

▼ *Vikings used longships like the one below for coastal raids. But for ocean voyages and cargo carrying, they used broader, sturdier boats called* knarrs.

settled down to scratch a living from the meagre soil of Greenland, far from home and surrounded by an unknown and hostile land.

Eric the Red is remembered as perhaps the first of the long line of European explorers (including his son Leif Ericsson) who set out to find and colonize new lands across the sea. ◆

 **see also**
Ericsson

Leif **Ericsson**

Viking explorer
Lived during the 11th century

The son of Eric the Red, Leif Ericsson lived in the Viking colony of Greenland. In about the year 1000, Ericsson bought a ship and set off westwards towards land which others had seen but had not yet visited – North America.

Ericsson named three parts of North America – Helluland, Markland, and Vinland (these were probably Baffin Island, Labrador, and Newfoundland or New England). He and his crew stayed for the winter in Vinland ('Wine-land') which had a mild climate, and he returned with samples of the timber which grew there.

Ericsson never returned to Vinland, but others did, and for a time there was a Viking colony there. Archaeologists and historians have searched for many years for the remains of this colony, but no definite sign of it has ever been found, and no one is quite sure of Vinland's exact position.

A splendid statue of Leif Ericsson, in the city of Reykjavik in Iceland, is a reminder that he discovered the North American continent 500 years before Columbus. ◆

see also
Eric the Red

M. C. **Escher**

Dutch graphic artist
Born *1898* ***Died*** *1972 aged 73*

Maurits Corneille Escher was one of the most brilliant engravers of the 20th century. He mastered several techniques of printmaking, especially woodcut and lithography. In woodcut the design is cut into a block of wood with metal tools, and in lithography it is drawn onto a specially prepared smooth stone. Escher was amazingly skilful at creating bewildering patterns and optical illusions. The most famous of his prints are the ones that represent 'impossible' buildings; they feature such visual tricks as staircases that seem to lead both up and down in the same direction, depending on

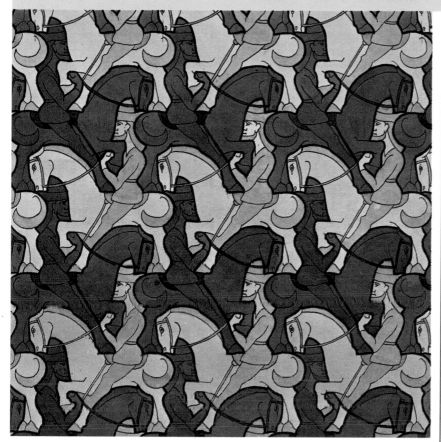

▲ Escher's *Symmetry Drawing E67.*

which way you look at them. Escher's prints are intriguing, and they have become very popular as posters. However, they have also provided serious food for thought for mathematicians and for psychologists interested in studying how the brain interprets what the eye sees. ◆

Euclid

Ancient Greek mathematician
Born *c.330* BC
Died *c.260* BC *aged about 70*

When Alexander the Great captured Egypt he set up a new city called Alexandria with a wonderful library and a university. It became the most important place in the world for people to go and study. Clever mathematicians such as Euclid moved from Greece to Alexandria to work.

Euclid was especially interested in geometry and wrote a textbook called *Elements of Geometry*. It has been described as 'the most studied book apart from the Bible'. For over 2000 years Euclid's textbook was the book all schoolchildren used as an introduction to geometry. Even the books used today are based on the way Euclid taught geometry. ◆

Leonhard **Euler**

Swiss mathematician
Born 1707   **Died** 1783 *aged 76*

In 1727 Leonhard Euler moved from his home in Switzerland to St Petersburg, Russia. There he published books on all aspects of mathematics including new theories on trigonometry and logarithms. He was a pioneer of pure mathematics and made major contributions to the fields of geometry, calculus, the theory of numbers, and to the practical application of mathematics. Perhaps as a result of his hard work he lost the sight in one eye.

In 1741 Frederick the Great invited Euler to join the Berlin Academy; he stayed there for 25 years. Frederick mockingly called him a 'mathematical cyclops' and Euler became increasingly unhappy. He returned to Russia, at the invitation of Catherine the Great, but soon after his arrival he lost the sight in his other eye. Blindness did not stop him, however, and he continued to apply his skills to the fields of mechanics, optics, acoustics, and astronomy. ◆

Fa Hsien

Chinese traveller and priest
Lived during the 5th century

Fa Hsien ('Splendour of Religious Law') was born in Shanxi province in China. He was a Buddhist priest who travelled from China to India so that he could visit the places where Buddha had lived and collect writings about the Buddha's teachings. He travelled to India in 402 and went on to Sri Lanka before returning home by sea. These long journeys involved crossing terrible deserts and freezing mountain passes, as well as being shipwrecked. He was still alive in 414 but other details of his life are uncertain. He wrote an account of his travels (*Record of Buddhist Kingdoms*) and also translated Buddhist teachings from Sanskrit into Chinese. ◆

◉ **see also**

Buddha

111

Peter **Fabergé**

Russian jewellery maker and designer
Born 1846   Died 1920 aged 74

Peter Fabergé inherited the family jewellery business in 1870. He soon became famous for making the kind of jewellery that the wealthy aristocracy of Europe liked – wonderful designs using gold, silver, jade, emeralds, and diamonds. His genius was such that these objects never looked vulgar. They were always beautiful and full of imaginative ideas.

He is particularly remembered for the jewelled Easter eggs which he made each year for the tsar of Russia to give to the tsarina.

▼ *The pictures at the top of this 1898 Fabergé egg are of Tsar Nicholas II and two of his daughters.*

In 1917 there was a revolution in Russia. The tsar was deposed and the new government of the people had no time for luxuries. Fabergé left Russia and lived out his remaining few years in Switzerland. ◆

Juan **Fangio**

Argentinian world champion motor racing driver
Born 1911   Died 1995 aged 81

Juan Fangio has been called the greatest racing driver of all time. He has won a record-breaking five world championships.

Born at Balcarce near Buenos Aires, Argentina, he became a travelling mechanic in 1928. He took up driving five years later and came to Europe in 1948 to try his luck. Before Fangio retired in 1958, he had won 24 Grand Prix races for manufacturers such as Mercedes-Benz and Ferrari.

Fangio's greatest race was the 1957 German Grand Prix, which he won after a pit stop had left him 48.5 seconds behind. He broke the lap record several times to catch and overtake his main rivals. ◆

Michael **Faraday**

English scientist
Born 1791   Died 1867 aged 75

As a young man Michael Faraday attended one of Sir Humphry Davy's lectures. He made careful lecture notes, bound them, and sent them to Davy, who was so impressed that he offered him a job. So, aged 22, Faraday became an assistant in the laboratories of the Royal Institution in London. In 1825 he succeeded Davy as director of the laboratory.

Faraday's most important work was to do with electricity and magnetism. Winding a coil of wire onto a piece of iron, he showed that when electricity was passed through the coil, the iron became a magnet. Then he wound another, separate coil onto the same piece of iron. When he switched on the current in the first coil he found that a current flowed in the second. He had, in fact, discovered the transformer. He then found that if he took a hollow coil and moved a magnet in and out, a current flowed in the coil. He had invented the dynamo. These were two very important discoveries which have helped shape the modern world.

Faraday also had the knack of explaining what he was doing in a simple way, so that ordinary people could understand. He started the famous Royal Institution Christmas Lectures in 1826. These science lectures for the general public have been held every year since, except for three years during World War I. ◆

👁 **see also**
Davy

Guy **Fawkes**

English conspirator who planned to blow up the Houses of Parliament in the Gunpowder Plot (1605)
Born 1570   Died 1606 aged 35

Guy Fawkes was brought up as a Protestant, but later became a Catholic. When James I became king in 1603, Guy Fawkes and other Catholics hoped for better treatment than they had received during Elizabeth I's reign. But James I allowed the persecution of Catholics to continue. In 1604, a small group of Catholics, led by Robert Catesby, plotted to kill the king. They invited Guy Fawkes to join them because of his ability to deal with explosives.

Concilivm Septem Nobilivm Angiorvm Conivrantivm in Necem Jacobi I.
Magnæ Britanniæ Regis, Totivsq Anglici Convocati Parliementi.
1.Bates - 2.Robert Winter - 3.Christopher Wright - 4.John Wright - 5.Thomas Percy - 6.Guido Fawkes - 7.Robert Catesby - 8.Thomas Winter.

▲ *This print shows the conspirators in the Gunpowder Plot. Guy (Guido) Fawkes is third from the right.*

The plan was to blow up the House of Lords when the king came to open Parliament on 5 November 1605. They hired a cellar and filled it with gunpowder. Guy Fawkes agreed to light the fuse. But the plot was discovered, and on 4 November Guy Fawkes was arrested. Although he was tortured, at first he bravely refused to name the other conspirators. Eventually he signed a confession, and was tried and executed.◆

👁 see also
James I

Federico **Fellini**

Italian film director
***Born** 1920   **Died** 1993 aged 73*

Federico Fellini grew up in Rimini, Italy, but at 18 he left for Florence and Rome. He worked as a cartoonist and journalist and scripted a radio serial before friendship with director Roberto Rossellini got him into movies as a writer and then director. The Oscar-winning *La Strada* (The Road)

(1954), made him internationally known. *La Dolce Vita* (The Sweet Life) (1960), a rather humorous look at fashionable society in Rome, was probably his greatest international success. However, it was less typical of his work than his films which mixed dream and reality, exploring personal memories and problems, such as $8\frac{1}{2}$, about a film director stuck in the middle of making a film and unsure how to go on. ◆

Ferdinand and **Isabella**

Rulers of Castile and Aragon in Spain
Ferdinand
***Born** 1452*
***Died** 1516   aged 63*
Isabella
***Born** 1451*
***Died** 1504*
aged 53

▶ *This 1496 dish bears the arms of Ferdinand and Isabella.*

When Ferdinand and Isabella were born, the Spanish peninsula contained five kingdoms. Three were small kingdoms: Portugal; Navarre (in the north-east); and Granada (in the south), which was inhabited by Muslims. The other two were Castile and Aragon. Isabella was the daughter of the king of Castile; Ferdinand was a son of the king of Aragon. In 1469 they married. As a result, they later became the joint rulers of the two kingdoms.

Ferdinand and Isabella acquired new income by several means, for example by forcing nobles to return land that had once belonged to previous rulers. They also demolished the castles of any nobles who opposed their rule. In 1492 they conquered Granada and expelled the Muslims. In 1503 they conquered the Kingdom of Naples in Italy, and in 1512 Ferdinand conquered Navarre.

Ferdinand and Isabella made Spain an important part of Europe. They supported Christopher Columbus, who discovered America for Spain. However, their reign also marked the start of the Spanish Inquisition, directed by Tomas da Torquemada. ◆

👁 see also
Columbus
Torquemada

Enrico **Fermi**

Italian-born American nuclear physicist
Born *1901*   **Died** *1954 aged 53*

Enrico Fermi was a physics professor at the University of Rome. In 1932 he heard about James Chadwick's discovery of the neutron, a particle in the centre of atoms. Fermi decided to do some experiments with neutrons himself. He set up a target made of uranium and bombarded it with neutrons, hoping to make a new substance. Although at the time he did not realize it, he had in fact discovered nuclear fission, the basis of nuclear power and atom bombs. For this work he was awarded the Nobel Prize for Physics in 1938. Later, Otto Hahn explained what was happening during nuclear fission.

During World War II, Fermi worked in America developing the first nuclear reactor. It was built in a squash court at the University of Chicago. This work led directly to the making of the atom bombs that were dropped on Hiroshima and Nagasaki in Japan in 1945 towards the end of World War II. ◆

👁 **see also**

Hahn

Ella **Fitzgerald**

American jazz singer
Born *1918*   **Died** *1996 aged 79*

Ella Fitzgerald was brought up in a New York orphanage. She became a singer because of a teenage dare. At 16 she was dared to sing in an amateur contest in Harlem, and won $25. Then, invited to sing with Chick Webb's band, she found success with hits like 'A-Tisket A-Tasket' (1938).

Fitzgerald brought jazz to new audiences as a star singer in the

▲ *Ella Fitzgerald is one of the most influential of popular jazz singers and her style is still much-copied even today.*

1950s. Her crystal-clear tones and perfect diction were unrivalled for singing popular songs. Indeed, Fitzgerald's finest achievement is her series of 'songbook' albums recorded in the late 1950s. Each contains the work of one popular writer, such as Cole Porter or George Gershwin. The albums are widely regarded as the best possible versions of the songs they contain, which include 'Manhattan' and 'Ev'ry Time We Say Goodbye'. ◆

👁 **see also**

Gershwin   Porter

F. Scott **Fitzgerald**

American novelist and short story writer
Born *1896*   **Died** *1940 aged 44*

Francis Scott Key Fitzgerald lived the same sort of life that he described in his novels, one of glamour, fame, and success. Born in Minnesota, he was educated at Princeton University and even as a youth he was determined to succeed in social, athletic, and literary fields.

He achieved instant fame with his first novel, *This Side of Paradise* (1920), and shortly after married the glamorous Zelda Sayre. Their pleasure-seeking lifestyle of party-going and big spending made them symbols of the high-living young generation of the 'Roaring Twenties'. Among Fitzgerald's most famous novels are *The Great Gatsby* (1925) and *Tender is the Night* (1934), which portray and analyse the mood of the times in which he lived.

Scott Fitzgerald died suddenly in Hollywood of a heart attack hastened by chronic alcoholism, leaving his final novel, *The Last Tycoon*, unfinished. ◆

Gustave **Flaubert**

French writer
Born *1821*   **Died** *1880 aged 58*

The son of a wealthy doctor, Gustave Flaubert first trained in law before withdrawing due to illness and turning to literature. His first published novel, *Madame Bovary* (1857), was also his greatest. Written over a period of five years, it describes the sad life of a romantic young village girl married to a dull, unsuccessful husband. In search of something better she has two love affairs, both of which end unhappily. She finally poisons herself, leaving her unsuspecting husband heart-broken. Flaubert records this whole story in great detail, as if it were something that had happened in real life. This made *Madame Bovary* the most realistic novel of its time, setting a pattern for future novelists all over the world. ◆

▲ *This stained glass window in St James's Church, London, depicts Alexander Fleming at work in his laboratory.*

Alexander **Fleming**

English discoverer of penicillin
Born 1881   **Died** 1955 aged 73

A lexander Fleming trained as a doctor at St Mary's Medical School, London, and then spent his entire working life there. He became interested in the infections caused by bacteria that resulted in so much disease. He joined researchers looking for vaccines that would kill such bacteria.

One day in 1928 when Fleming was working in his laboratory, he noticed that a mould had formed on one of his experimental dishes containing live bacteria. The bacteria next to the mould were dying. Fleming realized that the mould was producing a substance which killed the bacteria. The mould was called *Penicillium notatum*.

Fleming showed that penicillin could kill many dangerous bacteria, but he was slow to see that it could be used as a medical treatment and,

in any case, he found it very hard to produce, except in very small quantities. So there was little interest in penicillin until 1941, when Howard Florey, an Australian pathologist, Ernst Chain, a German-born biochemist, and other scientists at Oxford University found a way of making enough penicillin to begin treating patients with serious infections. The results were spectacularly successful. In 1945 Fleming, Florey, and Chain shared a Nobel prize for their work. ◆

Margot **Fonteyn**

English classical ballet dancer
Born 1919   **Died** 1991 aged 72

M argot Fonteyn, the adopted name of Peggy Hookham, grew up in Hong Kong where she studied dance. When she came back to England she quickly became very successful, dancing from 1934 onwards with Sadler's

Wells Ballet, later to become the Royal Ballet. While still in her teens, she took on some of the great classic roles, including Odette-Odile in *Swan Lake*. For nearly 30 years, Fonteyn was the company's leading ballerina. Her remarkable technique and warm personality made her very popular.

Fonteyn had two great partnerships. One was with the choreographer Frederick Ashton, who created many outstanding roles for her. The second, from 1962, was with the brilliant Russian dancer Rudolf Nureyev.

Fonteyn continued to dance, create new roles, and teach until she was well into her fifties. ◆

👁 **see also**

Nureyev

▼ *Margot Fonteyn was one of the world's greatest classical ballerinas. In 1979 she gave new insights into the world of dance by writing and presenting a television series.*

▼ In this picture Henry Ford is seen standing next to the ten-millionth Model T, produced in June 1924, and the very first Model T, built in 1908.

Henry **Ford**

American manufacturer of early cars
Born 1863   **Died** 1947 aged 83

Henry Ford was born on his family's farm in Michigan, America, but he did not like farming. At 15 he became an apprentice in a machine shop, and in 1893 he built his first car. He drove it for about 1500 kilometres, then sold it and built two bigger cars. Then, in 1903, he started the Ford Motor Company.

Using light, strong steel, he built cheap cars for everyone to buy. In 1908, he built the first Ford 'Model T', the 'Tin Lizzie', which sold for $825. He was soon selling a hundred cars a day. By 1927, 15 million Model Ts had been made, and the Ford Motor Company was worth 700 million dollars.

The cars were made on an assembly line: as they slowly moved the 300 metres through the factory, workers completed simple single tasks on them. It was boring work, but Ford paid the highest wages in the industry.

Early Fords were simple, cheap, and reliable: 'Anyone can drive a Ford' was one slogan. But keeping things simple sometimes meant less choice. 'You can have any colour you like,' said Henry Ford of his Tin Lizzie, 'so long as it's black'. ◆

John **Ford**

American film director
Born 1895   **Died** 1973 aged 82

John Ford, the adopted name of Sean O'Feeney, got his first job in movies as a props man before beginning to direct films. He developed his skills on dozens of short films and westerns, with a lot of emphasis on action. *The Iron Horse* (1924), a big-scale silent movie set around the building of the Union-Pacific intercontinental railway, was his first huge success. Human dramas such as *The Grapes of Wrath* (1940), *How Green Was My Valley* (1941), and *The Quiet Man* (1952) also gained acclaim (and Academy Awards). Ford is best remembered, though, for directing classic westerns such as *Stagecoach* (1939). ◆

see also

Griffith   Wayne

Jean **Foucault**

French scientist
Born 1819   **Died** 1868 aged 49

The son of a poor bookseller, Jean Foucault's original ambition was to become a reporter for a newspaper, recounting the latest scientific news. He acquired a reputation for the clarity of his writing and in 1855 was appointed physicist at the Paris Observatory. This gave him the opportunity to try out some ideas and he is famous for two important experiments. First, in

▼ Foucault demonstrates his pendulum at the Panthéon in Paris.

1850, he demonstrated the rotation of the Earth by using a very long pendulum. This was set swinging along a line marked on the floor but as the Earth slowly turned, the direction of the swing of the pendulum deviated more and more from the line. His second great experiment was to measure the speed of light over a distance of 20 metres, by means of apparatus involving rotating mirrors. Previously, the speed of light could be deduced only from astronomical observations. Foucault's value was 298,000 kilometres per second: the precise value is 299,792 kilometres per second, so Foucault's rather basic experiment in fact produced a very accurate result. ◆

see also
Galileo Huygens

George **Fox**

English founder of the Society of Friends (the Quakers)
Born 1624 Died 1691 aged 66

George Fox grew up as a strong Christian. However, he became confused about the best way to worship God, believing that there was an 'inner light' in everyone which helped them to understand Christ's teachings. He thought that people should meet together to worship God quietly as equal friends, without priests and ceremonies. He began to win followers, who became the 'Society of Friends'.

Fox travelled around preaching. He ignored the manners of the time, speaking as an equal to upper-class people, and never taking his hat off to show respect. This soon got him into trouble. Once,

◀ *George Fox, seen here in a painting from 1654, believed in looking for the good in everyone.*

when on trial, Fox told the magistrate that he should quake before the Lord: in response the magistrate called him and his followers 'Quakers'.

He was imprisoned eight times, but he kept the Friends together in spite of persecution. His teachings have lived on in the Quaker movement today. ◆

William **Fox Talbot**

English scientist remembered for his work on photography
Born 1800 Died 1877 aged 77

William Fox Talbot was a bright boy, who was especially interested in science. While he was at school he caused so many explosions with chemicals that his housemaster forbade him to do further experiments. Instead, Fox Talbot found a friendly blacksmith who, in the housemaster's words, 'lets him explode as much as he pleases!'.

When Fox Talbot was 33 and on holiday in Italy, he was looking at a camera obscura (rather like a pin-hole camera) and thought how wonderful it would be if the pictures could be recorded on paper. Six years later he had invented the photographic process in which a negative is made first and then a print is made from the negative. We still use the same idea today.

In 1851 Fox Talbot had the idea of breaking up a picture into tiny dots so that photographs could be produced on a printing machine. If you look through a magnifying glass at any of the photographs in this book you will see they are made up of tiny dots. ◆

see also
Daguerre Niepce

▲ This painting by Giotto is entitled St Francis Preaching to the Birds.

Saint **Francis of Assisi**

Italian founder of the Franciscan order of friars
Born *1182*   **Died** *1226 aged about 44*

Francis had all the makings of a successful man of the world. Then, when he was 22, he suffered a serious illness and began to feel that helping the poor was more important than making money. The new Francis worked for no money, let robbers beat him up, and kissed lepers. He was still searching for a pattern to follow in his life. He found it in the instructions given by Christ to his disciples: 'Go to the lost sheep… Heal the sick… Cleanse lepers… Provide no gold, silver or copper to fill your purse, no pack for the road, no second coat, no shoes, no stick: the worker earns his keep.'

Francis became a travelling preacher, owning nothing but his coat and living on the food that people gave him. Francis inspired others to live like him, and in 1210, with the permission of the Pope, he set up a new order of 'friars' (brothers), called the Franciscans. At this point there were just 12 of them. Within nine years there were Franciscans all over Europe, but Francis himself was not interested in running such a large organization and refused to be their leader. He travelled to Egypt in 1219 to preach to the Muslims and made other missionary journeys. But for most of his life he stayed near his home town of Assisi with a small group of followers, praying and preaching until his death in 1226. ◆

Francisco **Franco**

Spanish dictator from 1939 to 1975
Born *1892*   **Died** *1975 aged 82*

Francisco Franco was born into a navy family, but he decided to be a soldier. He became an officer at 18 and was gradually promoted until he was one of Spain's top generals. Then, in 1931, King Alfonso XIII left the country and Spain became a republic. Franco often criticized this republican government for the disorder in Spain.

In 1936 there was a military uprising against the republican government. Franco joined the rebels and soon became their leader. Civil war began between the two sides, and Franco was given military aid by Mussolini and Hitler. One million people died before Franco won the war in 1939.

Franco then became *caudillo* (dictator) and ruled Spain, without allowing any opposition or criticism, for 36 years. Before he died, he named Juan Carlos, grandson of Alfonso XIII, to be king after his death. ◆

Anne **Frank**

Jewish girl who wrote a diary when in hiding during World War II
Born *1929*   **Died** *1945 aged 15*

After the rise of Hitler and the Nazis in Germany, Anne Frank's father, Otto, moved his family to Amsterdam in The

▼ Since Anne Frank's diary was first published in 1947 it has been translated into over 30 languages.

Netherlands. When the Germans invaded and the family heard of the plans to put all Jews into concentration camps, they went into hiding. They concealed themselves in a hidden room in Otto Frank's former warehouse with four other Jews. Dutch friends smuggled them tiny rations of food.

Anne kept a lively diary, noting down daily events in these cramped quarters. She always seemed to remain cheerful. In spite of everything, she wrote 'I still believe that people are really good at heart.'

Two years later, on 4 August 1944, the secret room was broken into and the families sent to concentration camps. Anne, her mother, and her sister all died. Otto survived and published Anne's diary in 1947. The Franks' hiding place in Amsterdam has been converted into a museum. ◆

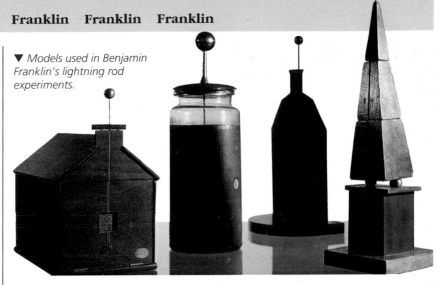

▼ Models used in Benjamin Franklin's lightning rod experiments.

Aretha **Franklin**

American singer
Born 1942

Aretha Louise Franklin was the daughter of a baptist minister. She began her career in his Detroit church, and was a gospel-singing prodigy at the age of 12.

Columbia Records made her sing jazz when they signed her in 1960, but she eventually found her feet at Atlantic Records seven years later when she was restyled as 'The Queen of Soul'. A string of hits such as 'Respect', 'Chain of Fools' (both 1967), and 'Think' (1968), established her as possibly the finest female vocalist of her generation.

In recent years she has enjoyed chart success duetting with famous admirers such as the Eurythmics, George Michael, and Whitney Houston. ◆

Benjamin **Franklin**

American statesman and scientist
Born 1706   Died 1790 aged 84

As a young man Benjamin Franklin tried a number of jobs in America and in England. In America he set up his own publishing business, and by the age of 23 was printing all the money for Pennsylvania. In 1753 he became the postmaster for that colony.

He was always interested in science, and proved that lightning was just a giant electrical spark. He took the risk of flying a kite up into a thundercloud and showed that an electrical spark would jump from a key tied to the wet string. This famous experiment resulted in the development of the lightning conductor or rod.

In 1757 he was appointed to be the representative of Pennsylvania in London. He spoke in Parliament against the British government's tax policies towards the American colonies. Then, after helping Thomas Jefferson write the Declaration of Independence in 1776, he served in Paris. Here he managed to persuade France to support the American colonists in their fight for independence against the British during the American Revolution (War of Independence). ◆

👁 **see also**
Jefferson

John **Franklin**

British arctic explorer
Born 1786   Died 1847 aged 61

In the early 19th century, it was thought that a way could be found to the Pacific round the north of Canada – the so-called 'North-West Passage'.

In 1845, the experienced explorer Sir John Franklin sailed for the North-West Passage with two ships, *Erebus* and *Terror*. They were never seen again.

Many search parties looked for Franklin. In 1857, after official efforts stopped, Lady Franklin paid for a further search. This party found the remains of some of the expedition on King William Island. A note explained that Franklin had died in 1847.

The exact cause of the deaths of the Franklin party is a mystery. A modern theory says that they were poisoned by the lead in the food cans they took with them, but nobody is really sure. ◆

Dawn **Fraser**

Australian Olympic swimming champion
Born *1937*

Dawn Fraser is the only swimmer to win the same event, the 100 metres freestyle, at three successive Olympic Games – Melbourne (1956), Rome (1960), and Tokyo (1964).

The youngest of a Sydney family of eight children, Fraser began competitive swimming when she was aged 11. She trained hard and estimates she swam 10,000 kilometres in ten years. She was the first woman to swim 100 metres in under one minute. She also broke the 100 metres world record nine times.

Fraser was a very popular figure but her high spirits annoyed Australian swimming officials. In 1965 she was suspended from competition for three years over a prank carried out at the Tokyo Olympic Games. She never swam as well again. ◆

Frederick I
('Barbarossa')

Holy Roman Emperor from 1155 to 1190
Born *c. 1123*
Died *1190 aged about 67*

In the Middle Ages Germany and northern Italy formed an empire – the Holy Roman Empire. In Germany the princes were very important because they elected the king of Germany and the king was then crowned emperor by the pope. Frederick was the son of the Duke of Swabia in south-west Germany, and nephew of Emperor Conrad III. When Conrad died in 1152, the German princes elected Frederick to be king. He was crowned emperor in Rome by Pope

Adrian IV. The Italians called him 'Barbarossa' meaning 'red beard'.

Frederick made many attempts to increase his power in Italy but he was eventually forced to give in to Pope Alexander III, who did not approve of him, in 1177 after a long, humiliating struggle. However, Frederick still managed to assert his power in Germany. Once this was assured he left the empire in the hands of his son and went to fight in the Crusades in the Holy Land. He won two victories against the Muslims but was later drowned while crossing a river. ◆

▼ *This bronze and gold head of Frederick I dates from 1160.*

Frederick II
('the Great')

King of Prussia from 1740 to 1786
Born *1712*   **Died** *1786 aged 74*

Born in Berlin, Frederick II was son and heir to Frederick William I, the king of Prussia. Prussia's lands were in various places. They included territories around Berlin and further to the east. Frederick was an unhappy child. His father spent much of his time with the army. Frederick, however, hated army life; he preferred books and music.

When Frederick became king he conquered Silesia, a rich territory, south-east of Berlin, which was ruled by Austria. Austria twice tried to take it back, but failed. In 1772 Prussia joined Russia and Austria in seizing parts of Poland. Frederick thereby obtained the land between the two main parts of Prussia, which was now much larger and richer: Frederick had made it a leading power in Europe. ◆

> *My people and I have come to an agreement which satisfies us both. They are to say what they please, and I am to do what I please.*   FREDERICK II

Sigmund **Freud**

Austrian psychologist
Born *1856*   **Died** *1939 aged 83*

As a doctor Sigmund Freud worked with patients who were very depressed or who often had strange ways of behaving that made other people think them extremely odd. The usual sort of treatment for mental illness at that time was lots of rest in the hope that things would gradually get better on their own. Freud decided instead to talk to such people at great length. He believed strange behaviour was often linked to past worries, worries which often reappeared in dreams and nightmares.

Although patients could not at first remember what it was that had once made them so unhappy, Freud found that, given time, troubled memories often came back. After talking to Freud openly about such things, many patients felt much better, at last able to shed problems that had been poisoning their lives without their knowing it.

By the time of Freud's death many other doctors were treating patients in similar ways, listening carefully to all they had to say and so helping them to get better. ◆

see also

Jung

Robert **Frost**

American poet
Born 1874   Died 1963 aged 88

Robert Frost was 11 when his father died and his family moved across America from San Francisco to New England. The people and landscapes of New England were to provide an inspiration for Frost's rhythmical, rural verse that made him one of America's most popular poets.

The turning point in Frost's career came in 1912 when he sold his farm and moved to England in order to concentrate on his writing. He met up with several poets and in 1913 published his first volume of poetry, *A Boy's Will*. This was followed a year later by *North of Boston*. He returned to America to great public acclaim and became a professor at Amherst College, Massachusetts. He

published several more volumes of poetry and won many literary prizes, including the Pulitzer Prize four times. He became professor of poetry at Harvard between 1939 and 1943 before returning to Amherst where he remained until his death in 1963.◆

Elizabeth **Fry**

English prison reformer
Born 1780   Died 1845 aged 65

Elizabeth Gurney was the daughter of a wealthy Quaker banker. In 1800 she married Joseph Fry, a London merchant. Although she had a large family, she still found time to work amongst the poor. She became particularly concerned about prison conditions, believing firmly that prisoners should always be helped to become better citizens.

At that time prisons were often very violent places and full of disease, but Fry insisted on visiting some of the worst in Britain and Europe. She was responsible for ensuring that women prisoners were always looked after by women staff. She also managed to get prisons to start educating or training some of their prisoners, so that it was sometimes possible for them to get jobs when they were released. Near her own home, Fry opened a free school and began the first proper training course for nurses. When she died she was mourned by thousands. ◆

▼ *Prison reformer Elizabeth Fry visiting women inmates at Newgate prison.*

Athol **Fugard**

South African playwright
Born 1932

Athol Fugard studied at Cape Town University. It was while he was in Cape Town that he first became involved in the theatre and acting world. In 1958 he moved to Johannesburg with his wife who was herself an actress.

Fugard's many plays explore the former South African policy of racial discrimination known as apartheid. They include *The Blood Knot* (1961) about the troubled relationship between two black brothers, *Boesman and Lena* (1968) about the lives of a homeless black couple, and *Master Harold and the Boys* (1982) which portrays the relationship between a white teenager and two of his family's black servants. ◆

Yukichi **Fukuzawa**

Japanese writer who introduced Western ideas to 19th-century Japan
Born 1835   Died 1901 aged 66

Fukuzawa came from a poor samurai (warrior) family. He was one of the first Japanese to visit America and Europe, and in 1866 published the first volume of his best-selling book, *Conditions in the West,* in which he described everyday life in Western countries.

In 1868 a new government came to power, keen to learn more about the West and spread new ideas. For the rest of the 19th century Fukuzawa was the most influential commentator on Western ideas. His school, which he founded in 1868 (and which later became a famous university), trained many of Japan's leaders, and his books and other writings were read by thousands of Japanese. He is known as one of the founders of modern Japan. ◆

Robert **Fulton**

American steamboat pioneer
Born 1765   Died 1815 aged 49

When he was 17, Robert Fulton left his home town to go to Philadelphia. A few years later he set sail for England where he became involved in designing and building machinery, locks, and aqueducts for the rapidly expanding canal system.

In 1797 he went to France and spent several years there. He experimented with a steamboat on the Seine and designed a submarine, *Nautilus*, a periscope, and torpedoes which would have been used against British ships. He then returned to America and in 1806 designed the *Clermont*, a steam-powered boat, 40 metres long, propelled by 4.5-metre wide paddle wheels. It sailed 240 kilometres up the Hudson river from New York to Albany and back in less than three days. This proved that steam propulsion could be used commercially, and before long Fulton had built many steamboats. This new development marked the beginning of the end of the era of sailing ships. ◆

👁 **see also**
Brunel

▶ *In this self-portrait, Fulton is seen demonstrating his submarine periscope.*

▲ *Clark Gable in his famous role as Rhett Butler in* Gone with the Wind *(1939).*

Clark **Gable**

American film actor
Born 1901   Died 1960 aged 59

Clark Gable was a factory worker and oil-driller before he started acting. At first he appeared in films as a villain, but in 1934 he found success with the romantic comedy *It Happened One Night*, for which he won an Oscar. During the 1930s he was the most popular 'leading man' in Hollywood films, famous for his muscular good looks.

His greatest role was as the handsome Rhett Butler in the American Civil War drama *Gone*

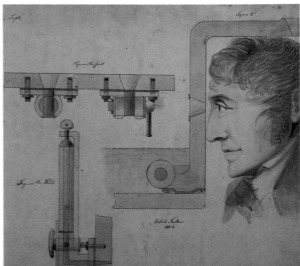

with the Wind (1939). He was still acting in films at the time of his death. His last film, *The Misfits*, with Marilyn Monroe, came out the year after he died. ◆

Yuri **Gagarin**

Soviet cosmonaut; the first man in space
Born 1934 Died 1968 aged 34

Yuri Gagarin was born into a poor farmer's family in a village, now renamed Gagarin, near Smolensk in Russia. While at college, he joined an air club near Moscow and learned to fly. Soon after college he joined the air force and began to fly fighter planes.

Because Gagarin was daring and skilled, he was singled out for space training. Being small also helped, as the first spacecraft did not have enough room inside for tall people.

His spaceship, *Vostok*, was launched from the Baykonur site in the Kazakh desert on 12 April 1961. Although his flight around the Earth took only 1 hour 48 minutes, it was the first human journey into space.

Only seven years later Gagarin was killed while testing a new plane. He was buried with honours alongside the Kremlin wall in Moscow's Red Square. ◆

Thomas **Gainsborough**

English painter
Born 1727 Died 1788 aged 61

Thomas Gainsborough was born in Sudbury, Suffolk, and he loved the local East Anglian countryside. Landscape painting was his greatest joy, but he could make more money by painting portraits, so he reluctantly

> *Painting and punctuality mix like oil and vinegar.*
> THOMAS GAINSBOROUGH, 1772

devoted most of his time to that. He worked in Ipswich and Bath, and in London where he settled in 1774. His only real rival as the leading British portrait painter of his time was Sir Joshua Reynolds. They were completely different in temperament (Gainsborough was easygoing and often unpunctual in his work; Reynolds was sober-minded and the complete professional), but they had great mutual respect. Gainsborough painted some of the most graceful and dignified portraits (particularly of beautiful women) in the history

▼ *A typical portrait by Thomas Gainsborough, entitled* Giovanna Baccelli.

of art, and although landscape remained a 'sideline' for him, he was an inspiration to his great East Anglian successor, John Constable. ◆

👁 **see also**
Constable

Galen

Greek medical doctor
Born c.130 Died c.200 aged about 70

Claudius Galenus (Galen) was a famous doctor of the Ancient World. He was born in the Greek town of Pergamum, where he studied to be a doctor and tended the wounds of a troop of gladiators. This taught him a lot about the human body and how to try to heal it. He noticed that when nerves are cut, muscles may not work. He also found that arteries carried blood, not air as many people believed. However, he was not always right. For instance, he believed that our bodies have four liquids: phlegm, black bile, yellow bile, and blood and that when we have the right balance between them we are healthy.

Galen became doctor to the Roman emperors and was very famous. However, he was quarrelsome and was not always very popular. ◆

👁 **see also**
Hippocrates

Galileo **Galilei**

Italian astronomer; the first person to use a telescope to look at the Sun, Moon, and planets
Born 1564   Died 1642 aged 77

Galileo Galilei is nearly always referred to just by his first name. He was the eldest of seven children, whose father was a musician and scholar from one of the noble families of Florence. Galileo himself became a good organist and enjoyed playing the lute, but it was his contributions to science that made him famous. His father sent him to the University of Pisa to study medicine, but he was much more interested in mathematics and physics. In 1589 he became a professor of mathematics.

In 1609 Galileo made a small telescope, having heard about this new invention in The Netherlands.

▼ *Galileo's sketches of the phases of the Moon. He saw that instead of having a smooth surface it was covered in craters and mountains.*

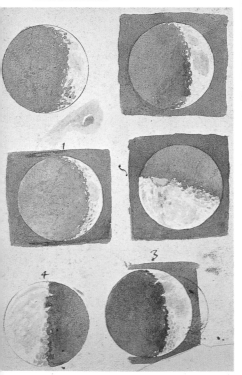

Through his observations of the planets, he discovered four moons circling the planet Jupiter, craters on the Moon, spots on the Sun, and rings around Saturn. He also observed that the planet Venus has phases like the Moon's. This could only mean that Venus travelled around the Sun. Galileo became convinced that the Earth and all the other planets orbit the Sun.

At that time the Christian Church thought any idea that the Earth was not the centre of the Universe went against the Scriptures. The book published by the astronomer Copernicus in 1543, setting out such a theory, had been officially banned by the Church.

Galileo's views on the subject and the books he wrote were to get him into serious trouble with the Church. As the Church was very powerful in those days Galileo was forced to say publicly that he did not agree with Copernicus in order to avoid torture or even execution. Although he made this declaration, he never changed his real belief. ◆

👁 **see also**

Copernicus

Luigi **Galvani**

Italian doctor and physicist
Born 1737   Died 1798 aged 61

Luigi Galvani was born in Bologna, Italy, where he trained to be a doctor. He began to do experiments to test what electricity would do to muscles. In those days there were no batteries like the ones we have today. Instead, Galvani used a machine to generate electricity. He sent electricity through frogs' legs and noticed that the legs jumped. He then discovered he could do the same thing without the electrical machine. He touched the legs with a copper hook hanging from an iron rail and the legs twitched. He thought he had discovered 'animal electricity' but really he had found the starting point for making a simple battery. However, he was right to say that our muscles work using electricity. ◆

👁 **see also**

Volta

Vasco da **Gama**

Portuguese explorer, the first European to complete the sea route to India
Born c.1469   Died 1524 aged about 55

Vasco da Gama had already distinguished himself as a brave soldier in the service of the King of Portugal when he was chosen to lead a voyage to India around the Cape of Good Hope in southern Africa. Since Christopher Columbus had failed to find a westward sea route to India, the Portuguese were determined to find the eastward route.

Da Gama sailed in 1497 with four small ships and 170 men. Unlike earlier navigators he did not hug the African coast, but sailed boldly into the Atlantic before turning east to round the Cape. The little fleet ran into a storm, and many men mutinied, but da Gama had the ringleaders arrested.

The fleet reached the coast north of the Cape of Good Hope after three months without seeing land. They cruised along the coast, stopping at various places. To their astonishment, they found flourishing Arab towns with stone houses on the coast of what is now Mozambique. Da Gama found a friend in the Sultan of Malindi, who supplied two Arab pilots to guide him to India.

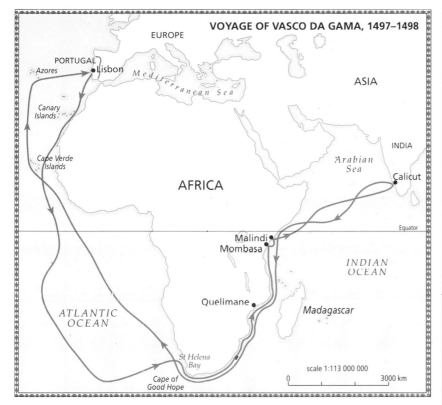

VOYAGE OF VASCO DA GAMA, 1497–1498

▲ Vasco da Gama's voyage round the coast of Africa to India (1497–1498) opened up an important new trade route by sea between Europe and Asia.

With their aid he made a peaceful voyage across the Indian Ocean to south-west India. Da Gama set up a trade agreement with the local people and returned to Portugal with a rich cargo of spices, two years after he set out. He had lost two-thirds of his men and half his ships, but he had done what he set out to do.

Da Gama made two more voyages to India. In 1502 he took 19 ships to help the Portuguese settlers in Goa. Then in 1524, after 20 years in retirement, he went as viceroy (local ruler) to Goa, where the Portuguese colonial government was having difficulties. However, he died of fever only two months after he arrived. ◆

👁 see also

Columbus   Dias

Indira **Gandhi**

Prime minister of India from 1966 to 1977 and from 1980 to 1984
***Born** 1917 **Died** 1984 aged 66*

Indira Priyadarshani was the only child of Jawaharlal Nehru, India's first prime minister. After her mother died she became a close companion to her father. She married a journalist, Feroze Gandhi, with whom she had two sons: Rajiv and Sanjay. Sanjay died in a plane crash when he was only 33.

Indira Gandhi followed her father's interest in politics and was elected president of the Indian National Congress, the country's main political party, in 1959. During these early political years, she worked as her father's aide while he was prime minister. She became Minister for Information and Broadcasting in 1964 and two years later she became prime minister.

For several years she was quite successful and popular. However opponents in the Congress party thought she had too much power. In 1975, faced with the growing opposition threat, she declared a state of emergency. Opponents of her policies were even sent to prison. This made her very unpopular and she lost the general election of 1977.

She came back to power with a large majority in 1980. Soon after this she was faced with unrest in the Punjab where some Sikhs were demanding their own state. A group of armed Sikhs occupied the Golden Temple, the holiest Sikh shrine, in Amritsar. In June 1984 Mrs Gandhi ordered her troops to storm the Golden Temple and a large number of people were killed. A few months later, Mrs Gandhi was shot dead by one of her Sikh bodyguards in revenge for the attack in Amritsar. She was succeeded by her son Rajiv ◆

👁 see also
Nehru

▼ Prime minister Indira Gandhi during one of the happier moments of her two often troubled periods of rule.

Mahatma **Gandhi**

Indian leader in the struggle for independence from British rule
Born *1869* **Died** *1948 aged 78*

Mohandas Karamchand Gandhi was a shy, nervous boy, but when he was 18 he travelled alone to study in London. He returned to India in 1890 and struggled to make a living as a lawyer.

In 1893 Gandhi accepted an offer to represent a firm of Indian merchants in a court case in South Africa. Soon after his arrival, he realized how many problems blacks, Asians, and other non-whites faced, and he decided to stay on to help his fellow countrymen. Gandhi represented them in court and became quite wealthy. But he soon rejected his wealth and lived more simply.

During this time, Gandhi developed his strategy of non-violence. The idea was to oppose unjust laws by non-violent protest. He was sent to prison three times, but by imposing hardship upon himself and also showing no sign of anger or hatred, Gandhi believed that he could persuade his opponents that his cause was just.

When he first returned to India in 1915, Gandhi was not opposed to British rule. But after a massacre in 1919, when soldiers opened fire on a crowd of unarmed Indians, killing nearly 400 people and wounding over 1000, Gandhi changed his mind. Over the next 20 years, Gandhi led the Indian National Congress party in three major campaigns against British rule, but on each occasion he was arrested and sent to prison.

During these years Gandhi campaigned to improve the status of the untouchables, the lowest group in the Hindu social order. He also believed that people and nations should be self-sufficient. He set an example by devoting part of each day to spinning home-made cloth. In his eyes, industrialization, as in Europe and North America, usually led to exploitation, greed, and squalor.

Gandhi struggled in vain to overcome the growing gap between the Hindu and Muslim populations, which led in 1947 to the creation of the separate Muslim state of Pakistan. When India and Pakistan became independent from Britain in 1947, there was an explosion of violence between the different communities. Gandhi appealed for peace. He was assassinated by a Hindu extremist in January 1948.

Although his real name was Mohandas Gandhi, he was known by millions of people as Mahatma, meaning Great Soul. ◆

👁 **see also**
Jinnah Nehru

◀ *Gandhi pictured on the step of 10 Downing Street, London in 1931 before meeting Prime Minister Ramsay MacDonald.*

Greta **Garbo**

Swedish-born American film actress
Born *1905* **Died** *1990 aged 85*

Greta Gustafsson grew up in Stockholm, Sweden, and worked as a model before she started acting in films. She travelled to Hollywood and became a star in romantic silent films such as *The Torrent* (1926). When talking pictures came in, her Swedish accent meant that she was given roles as distinguished European ladies, such as the great Swedish queen in *Queen Christina* (1933) and the tragic heroine of *Anna Karenina* (1935). She was famous for her beauty and for her serious expression, but she was also very private and disliked publicity. She made her last film in 1941. ◆

▼ *Famed for her serious expression, it was headline news when Garbo smiled for the first time on screen (in* Ninotchka, *1939).*

Gabriel **Garcia Marquez**

Latin-American writer
Born 1928

Born in a poor town in Colombia, Garcia Marquez still managed to study law and journalism at university. He soon began writing short stories which mixed close attention to detail with dream-like descriptions of magical events. His most famous novel is *One Hundred Years of Solitude* (1967). This describes the adventures of a family settled in a new town in the middle of a South American jungle. Myth and legend combine with ordinary human affairs in an unforgettable way. This magical-realism style has since encouraged many other novelists to experiment with fantasy in their own books. Garcia Marquez is not always popular with his government for criticizing the huge gaps between rich and poor in South America. He was awarded the Nobel Prize for Literature in 1982. ◆

Giuseppe **Garibaldi**

Italian guerrilla fighter who helped to unite Italy
Born 1807   Died 1882 aged 74

As a young man, Garibaldi worked as a sailor, becoming a sea captain in 1832. After taking part in an unsuccessful mutiny in 1834, he escaped to France and then to South America. There he led an adventurous life, driving cattle and fighting in rebel armies.

Well known now as a brave but sometimes reckless fighter, Garibaldi led a group of Italians back to northern Italy in 1848, to

▲ *A wall-painting showing Garibaldi and Victor Emmanuel II meeting in 1860.*

help in the war against Austria. The next year he helped to defend Rome against the French, before being forced into exile in 1849. He returned to Italy in 1854, and retired to the island of Caprera.

> *I can offer you neither honours nor wages; I offer you hunger, thirst, forced marches, battles, and death. Anyone who loves his country, follow me.*
>
> GIUSEPPE GARIBALDI

He came out of retirement to fight for Victor Emmanuel II, the King of Piedmont. In 1860 he led 'the Thousand' (*i Mille*) guerrilla volunteers in red shirts in a successful revolt in Sicily, and then defeated the army of the King of Naples. Southern Italy became united under Victor Emmanuel. Garibaldi's name is still famous in Italy. Almost every town has a square or street named after him. ◆

👁 **see also**

Cavour   Victor Emmanuel II

Marcus **Garvey**

Jamaican campaigner for the rights of black people
Born 1887   Died 1940 aged 52

As a young man, Marcus Garvey worked as a printer, but no one would employ him after he had led a strike. He then took jobs in Central America and was shocked to see the discrimination against West Indians.

In 1914 Garvey started the Universal Negro Improvement Association (UNIA) in Jamaica. He said the black peoples' struggle for fair treatment was like the African countries' fight against European rule. In 1917 he started branches of the UNIA in America. It printed newspapers, ran a shipping line, and opened community centres called Liberty Halls.

Garvey's movement soon had branches all over the world. Then the UNIA was banned in African countries and Garvey was accused of fraud and deported from America to Jamaica. He died in poverty in London. However, his ideas inspired many others to work to win equality for black people. ◆

Bill **Gates**

American founder of Microsoft and major figure in the computer world
Born *1955*

Bill Gates began writing computer programs at 13. He went to Harvard University, and while he was there he developed BASIC, a simple and easy-to-use computer programming language. He believed that personal computers (PCs) would eventually spread to every home and office. So in 1975 Gates and his school friend Paul Allen founded the company Microsoft to develop software (computer programs) for PCs. Microsoft expanded, and in 1981 produced MS-DOS, the operating system used on most PCs. 1983 saw the creation of Windows, a program in which the user points at icons (small pictures) with a hand-held pointer (a mouse) and clicks on them to open files and programs.

By 1993 Microsoft had become the world's largest computer-industry company, and Gates was massively rich: by mid-1997 his personal fortune was estimated at $42 billion, making him the richest person in the world. In recent years, Microsoft has been accused of trying to monopolise the industry, particularly access to the Internet. ◆

Antoni **Gaudí**

Spanish architect and designer
Born *1852*   **Died** *1926 aged 74*

Antoni Gaudí was proud of his family of coppersmiths. From them he learned to appreciate craftsmanship and to use it in all his buildings. He also passionately loved his native country (the part of Spain called Catalonia) and was inspired by its Gothic and Arab-influenced architecture.

◀ A Gaudí mosaic 'dragon' in a Barcelona park.

Gaudí's church of the Holy Family (the Sagrada Familia) in Barcelona is one of the most extraordinary buildings in Europe. Gaudí worked on it for 43 years – over half his lifetime – but the huge church is still unfinished. A forest of tall openwork towers soars above walls encrusted with plants and animals (mostly carved by Gaudí himself) and with colourful pottery mosaics – a Gaudí trademark. ◆

Paul **Gauguin**

French artist
Born *1848*   **Died** *1903 aged 54*

Although he was born in Paris, Paul Gauguin's mother was Peruvian and he spent his childhood in Lima. Later he joined the merchant navy and eventually settled in France where he became a successful businessman. However, when he was 35 years old, he decided to give up his job and devote all of his time to his hobby: painting.

Gauguin became convinced that European artists had forgotten how to express true feelings in simple, direct ways. At first he studied peasant art in Brittany, but finally he left Europe altogether to find his own way of painting.

He went to Tahiti, an island in the South Pacific Ocean. There he painted the local people going about their daily tasks and he developed a strong personal style of his own. When his paintings were shown in Paris, he was proud that many people were shocked by what they saw.

At the age of 54 Gauguin died in the Marquesas Islands in the Pacific, after years of ill health, disappointment, and poverty. ◆

▼ A typical painting by Paul Gauguin. He usually painted the Tahitians and their island in these bright, strong colours.

Karl **Gauss**

German mathematician, astronomer, and physicist
Born *1777*   **Died** *1855 aged 77*

Karl Gauss's father was a poor labourer who could not afford to pay for his son to go to school. Fortunately for Gauss, his great mathematical talent was noticed and the Duke of Brunswick offered to pay for his education.

When he was only 30, Gauss was appointed director of the observatory at Göttingen in west Germany, and he remained there for the next 47 years. His breadth of interest was enormous, embracing arithmetic, algebra, and geometry; probability and statistics; astronomy and physics; mechanics and optics; surveying and telegraphy. His scientific results were recorded in several hundred publications. Through these, and by correspondence and personal contact, Gauss influenced scientific and mathematical thought throughout Europe. He also profoundly influenced later generations and Einstein could scarcely have formulated his theory of gravity without knowledge of Gauss's work. ◆

see also

Boole   Einstein   Euler   Pascal

Joseph **Gay-Lussac**

French physicist and chemist
Born *1778*   **Died** *1850 aged 71*

After studying in Paris, Joseph Gay-Lussac joined a team of young scientists and started to investigate gases, with the help and guidance of an older scientist. After various experiments, Gay-Lussac found that equal volumes of gas expand by equal amounts when their temperatures are raised – unlike solids and liquids. Later he discovered that gases combine in simple volume ratios. For example, two volumes of hydrogen combine with one volume of oxygen to form water. This is now called Gay-Lussac's law.

Ever curious, Gay-Lussac wanted to know whether the Earth's magnetic field altered at high altitudes. In 1804 he tried to find out by going up in a hydrogen balloon. Even at a height of 7 km he discovered that the magnetic field was the same as at ground level. No one had ever been so high in a balloon before. ◆

Genghis Khan

Mongol emperor
Born *1162*   **Died** *1227 aged 65*

Genghis Khan was first called Temujin. He was married when he was nine, as was the custom in his tribe. But in the same year his father was poisoned by his Tartar enemies. Temujin was not old enough to lead his father's men, and they deserted him.

As soon as he could, Temujin begged 20,000 soldiers from a friendly chief and set about making himself leader of all the Mongol tribes. His methods were brutally efficient: to make sure there was no rebellion from defeated tribes, he killed everyone taller than a cart axle – all the adult warriors – while everyone shorter had to swear loyalty to him.

By 1206 Temujin was recognized as lord of all the Mongols, having united eastern and western Mongolia. He took the title 'Genghis Khan', which means 'Ruler of All'. Now he led his armies against the Chinese empire.

By the time of his death his empire extended from the shores of the Pacific to the northern shores of the Black Sea. This empire had been won through brilliant leadership, iron discipline, and unimaginable cruelty, particularly against conquered peoples. His grandson, Kublai Khan, carried on his empire and finally completed the conquest of China. ◆

see also

Kublai Khan

▼ *Before his death, Genghis Khan and his followers created the Mongol empire, the largest empire in history.*

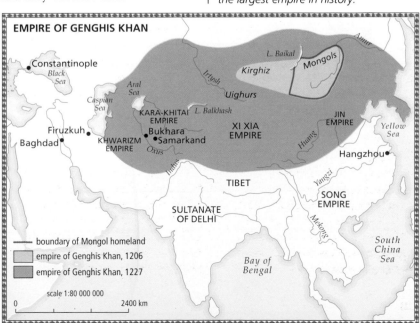

EMPIRE OF GENGHIS KHAN

— boundary of Mongol homeland
☐ empire of Genghis Khan, 1206
☐ empire of Genghis Khan, 1227

scale 1:80 000 000
0   2400 km

Saint **George**

Christian martyr who became the patron saint of several countries
Lived during the 3rd century

We know very little for sure about this saint and martyr. George was probably a soldier, who was killed in Palestine for his Christian faith by the Romans. However, centuries later, a famous story grew up about him.

It told of a dragon which was terrorizing a whole country. The dragon demanded first sheep and then a human being to keep it satisfied. The first victim was to be the king's own daughter, but George attacked the dragon, and led it away. Then he told the people that if they became Christians, he would rid them of

▲ *A 15th-century carving showing St George and the dragon.*

the monster. Fifteen thousand men agreed to be baptized, and George killed the dragon.

Venice, Genoa, Portugal, and Catalonia, as well as England, took George as their patron saint. His feast day is on 23 April. ◆

George I

King of Great Britain from 1714 to 1727
Born 1660   Died 1727 aged 67

When Queen Anne died in 1714 she had no children, so the crown was passed to the German George of Hanover. He was the great-grandson of James I of England, and as a German prince

had fought with the British against the French. Once in Britain George became rather shy and lazy. He had never learned to speak English, and so was forced to talk to his ministers in French. Although he was disliked, his reign provided stability in Britain. He was happy to leave all important decisions to Parliament and his ministers, especially Robert Walpole. He missed Germany, however, and on one of his visits to Hanover he died there of a stroke. ◆

👁 **see also**

James I   Walpole

George III

King of Great Britain from 1760 to 1820
Born 1738   Died 1820 aged 81

George was known as one of the most expert botanists in Europe. Unfortunately, when he succeeded his grandfather George II, he was not such a success as king. This was partly because he interfered rather awkwardly in the country's politics and lost many friends.

When the American colonies objected to the taxes the British made them pay, George was firmly against giving in to them. This led to the American Revolution in 1775, and George became even more unpopular when the British were driven out of America in 1781 after a long and bitter conflict.

In his own family George was a loving but very jealous father. When his sons broke away from him he was so upset he suffered periods of mental illness. Doctors now suspect he was really suffering from porphyria, a disease which produces some of the symptoms of madness. From 1811 until his death, his son ruled as Prince Regent in his place. ◆

Geronimo

Apache Indian chief
Born 1829   Died 1909 aged 80

Geronimo's name comes from the Spanish for Jerome; his Apache name, Goyaale, means 'the clever one'.

Geronimo grew up in Mexico. In about 1877 the American government, wanting land for settlers, moved the Apaches onto a reservation in Arizona. Geronimo escaped and fought against the troops. He was returned to the reservation, but fled to Mexico with a band of men. From concealed mountain camps they made raids on both sides of the border. Soon he was recaptured, but he fled again briefly in 1885, before finally surrendering. He ended his days in Oklahoma, where he became a farmer and dictated his life story. ◆

George Gershwin

American composer
Born 1898   Died 1937 aged 38

George Gershwin was the son of Jewish parents who had emigrated from Russia to New York. He did badly at school, and showed no interest in music until one day when he was ten he heard another schoolboy playing the violin. He started having piano lessons and made very quick progress.

As a young man he started writing songs for shows. During the 1920s and 1930s he turned out a stream of music, much of which is still sung and played: songs such as 'Somebody Loves Me', 'Fascinating Rhythm', and 'A Foggy Day'. Many of the words of his songs were written by his elder brother Ira.

▲ *Gershwin's opera* Porgy and Bess *shows the influence black American jazz and blues music had on his own compositions.*

Gershwin always wanted to be a more serious composer, and he wrote orchestral and piano music, and an opera, *Porgy and Bess* (1934–1935). Sadly, he died of a brain tumour when he was only 38. ◆

see also

Porter   Rodgers

J. Paul **Getty**

American multi-millionaire oilman
Born 1892   Died 1976 aged 83

Jean Paul Getty went to university in southern California and in Oxford before joining his father's oil company. By the age of 24 he was a millionaire, and in 1930, when his father died, he took over the company. Before long he had taken over other companies to form a business empire of more than 100 companies, headed by his own Getty Oil Company.

Outside of business his main interest was in art, and he used his considerable fortune to buy many paintings and sculptures. In 1953 he founded the J. Paul Getty Museum, in Malibu, California, to house his art collection. ◆

Alberto Giacometti

Swiss sculptor
Born 1901   Died 1966 aged 64

Alberto Giacometti was the son of a painter, so art was in his blood. For most of his life he lived and worked in Paris, the centre of the art world at the time. However, it was an exhibition of his work in New York in 1948 that made him internationally famous. At this exhibition he showed sculpture in a new style he had created. His figures were tall and extremely thin, with a gaunt, wasted look. World War II had only recently ended and many people thought that Giacometti's strange, tragic figures captured the spirit of the time in a moving way. This sudden success did not go to Giacometti's head, because he lived only for his art and did not care about fame or riches. ◆

◀ *Giacometti's* Trois Hommes Qui Marchent *(Three Men Walking) (1948) is typical of his post-World War II sculpture.*

André **Gide**

French novelist
Born *1869*   **Died** *1951 aged 82*

André Paul Guillaume Gide was born in Paris in 1869. His father, who died when he was only 11, was professor of law at the Sorbonne, the University of Paris. Gide was an only child and had a lonely youth. He was educated at home and then in a Protestant secondary school.

Gide loved all kinds of literature and wrote poetry, biography, fiction, drama, travel journals, and literary criticism. He rejected his strict Protestant upbringing in his life and work, and for young French people in the years after the end of World War I, he symbolized their rebellion against conventional attitudes.

His work is almost entirely autobiographical and includes *The Immoralist* (1902), *Strait is the Gate* (1909), *The Counterfeiters* (1926), and an almost lifelong *Journal* published in four volumes (1947–1951). He was awarded the Nobel Prize for Literature in 1947. ◆

Gilbert and **Sullivan**

English playwright and composer who wrote operettas together

William Gilbert
Born *1836*   **Died** *1911 aged 74*

Arthur Sullivan
Born *1842*   **Died** *1900 aged 58*

Before William Gilbert and Arthur Sullivan worked closely together writing their 14 operettas, they had independent careers. Gilbert trained as a barrister, but soon became known for his plays and comic verse, such as the *Bab Ballads*. Sullivan published his first

▲ *A scene from Gilbert and Sullivan's operetta* HMS Pinafore.

anthem in 1855 when he was still a chorister of the Chapel Royal. He then studied in London and Leipzig, and made his name with some music written for a performance of Shakespeare's *The Tempest* in 1862.

Gilbert and Sullivan's operettas, which include *HMS Pinafore* (1878), *The Pirates of Penzance* (1879), and *The Mikado* (1885), were so successful that the theatre manager and producer Richard D'Oyly Carte built the Savoy Theatre especially for their works. But things did not always run smoothly: Gilbert had a quick temper, and Sullivan suffered greatly from ill health. Their partnership ended in 1896. ◆

Giotto di Bondone

Italian painter
Born *c.1267*   **Died** *1337 aged about 70*

Giotto di Bondone lived in Florence with his wife and their eight children, and painted frescos (wall paintings on plaster) of religious subjects. Perhaps the most splendid are those in the Arena Chapel in Padua which tell stories from the lives of Jesus Christ and the Virgin Mary. There is a famous series of frescos in Assisi which show scenes from the life of St Francis, but it is not certain whether Giotto actually painted these.

Giotto developed a style that was unique at that time. He used paint to give the impression that people are solid objects, and not merely flat shapes. For the first time, figures looked like real people, showing human emotions.

Because of his fame and success, Giotto was given the job of designing a bell-tower for Florence Cathedral, but the building was not completed until after his death. ◆

William **Gladstone**

English prime minister four times between 1868 and 1894
Born *1809*   **Died** *1898 aged 88*

William Ewart Gladstone's father was a rich Scottish businessman who educated his son at Eton and Christ Church, Oxford. Gladstone was clever and deeply religious. He was also very energetic, working a 16-hour day even when he was an old man.

Gladstone was 23 when he first became a Member of Parliament, and was prime minister for the last time aged 84. He began as a Conservative but later created the

▲ *A cartoon caricature of William Gladstone from 1869.*

Liberal Party. He believed that people should have the chance to help themselves. In 1870, when he was prime minister, school education was provided for every child under ten. In 1884 ordinary men – but not women – in the countryside got the vote.

Unlike his great rival Benjamin Disraeli, Gladstone did not have an easy relationship with Queen Victoria. She was never comfortable in his presence and disapproved of his policies, which she considered to be revolutionary.

Gladstone wanted above all to bring peace to Ireland. He fought hard to give Home Rule (the right to run their own home affairs) to the Irish. Many people in the British Parliament and in Ulster bitterly opposed him. In 1894 poor health forced him to resign as prime minister, and he died four years later. ◆

see also
Disraeli   Victoria

John **Glenn**

American astronaut who was the first American in space
Born 1921

John Glenn was working as an American air force pilot, and had more than 2000 hours of flight time, when he was picked for the NASA astronaut training programme along with six other former pilots. The programme to put a man into space was accelerated after the Russian cosmonaut Yuri Gagarin made a successful flight in 1961. John Glenn was chosen to be the first American to be launched into space. His flight was postponed ten times because of bad weather and computer failures, but eventually he took off on 20 February 1962 for a flight that took him three times round the Earth.

After retiring from NASA, Glenn entered politics as a senator from Ohio and in 1984 tried unsuccessfully to become the Democratic presidential candidate. ◆

Owain **Glyndwr**

Leader of the last Welsh revolt against English rule
Born c.1354
Died c.1416 aged about 62

Owain Glyndwr was a northern Welsh landowner who was angered by the way his countrymen were being crippled by English taxes. In 1400 a local quarrel between Glyndwr and an English lord flared up into a national uprising. Glyndwr proclaimed himself Prince of Wales and summoned his first independent Welsh parliament at Machynlleth in 1404.

Henry IV, the king of England, could do little to stop the revolt. Worse still, Glyndwr was a natural ally for English lords plotting against the king, and in 1403 Glyndwr lent his support to the rebellion led by the Percy family in the north of England.

In 1405 the tide turned against Glyndwr, especially after Prince Henry, later to become Henry V, took over the English campaign. Within three years Glyndwr had lost his main strongholds. But even when his supporters abandoned him, he still fought on as an outlaw. Centuries after his death, he remained an inspiring legend for many Welsh people. ◆

see also
Henry V   Llywelyn the Great

◀ *John Glenn was the first American to orbit the Earth. He did so in the spacecraft* Friendship 7, *in a flight lasting five hours.*

Gobind Singh

Tenth and last Sikh Guru
Born 1666   Died 1708 aged 41

Gobind Singh was born in Bihar, India, the son of the ninth Guru, whose name was Tegh Bahadur. Guru Gobind Singh was very well educated, a good horseman, and trained to fight in self-defence. He also had a very generous and kind nature and Sikhs consider him an ideal human being.

In 1699 when the Sikhs came together for the festival of Baisakhi at Anandpur, Guru Gobind Singh asked for five Sikhs who were prepared to give their lives for their faith. These five went through a new form of initiation into the order of the Khalsa (the order of Sikhs dedicated to following the Guru in all respects). Many more followed them. All the men added Singh (lion) to their names and the women added Kaur (princess), to show their equality and unity, like brothers and sisters.

Guru Gobind Singh was killed by a mystery assassin. As he lay dying, he said that the Sikh holy book was to succeed him in guiding the community rather than another human being. The book became known as the *Guru Granth Sahib*. ◆

see also
Nanak

Joseph Goebbels

German Nazi leader
Born 1897   Died 1945 aged 47

Paul Joseph Goebbels, the son of a factory foreman, attended eight universities and became a doctor of philosophy at Heidelberg

▶ *Joseph Goebbels*

University in 1921. Rejected by the army because of a club foot, he joined the newly formed Nazi party in 1924. At first he edited the party newspaper and later was put in charge of Nazi propaganda. He organized party rallies and demonstrations and when Hitler came to power in 1933 Goebbels became minister of propaganda. This meant that he was in control of the press, broadcasting, education, and culture throughout Germany. This enabled him to spread hatred against Jews and any other people who did not fit the Nazi idea of a perfect German. He remained at the centre of the Nazi government throughout World War II. When the Nazis finally faced defeat, Goebbels committed suicide in Berlin with Hitler, first killing his wife and six children. ◆

see also
Hitler

Hermann Goering

German Nazi leader
Born 1893   Died 1946 aged 53

Hermann Wilhelm Goering flew in World War I with the famous Richthofen squadron. Later he went to university but gave up his studies to join the Nazi movement in 1922, and became one of Adolf Hitler's close advisers. In 1928 he was elected to the German Reichstag (parliament) and became its president in 1932.

He was made commander of the German air force in 1934 after Hitler had come to power, and began secretly to build up the Luftwaffe (air force). He later helped form the Gestapo (secret police) and Germany's first concentration camps.

At the start of World War II Hitler made him a Reichsmarshal, but Goering fell out of favour when the Luftwaffe lost the Battle of Britain in 1940. He was dismissed from the Nazi Party in 1945 after his unauthorized attempts to make peace with the Allies. He was sentenced to death for war crimes at the Nuremberg trials, but swallowed poison to avoid execution. ◆

see also
Hitler

Johann von Goethe

German poet
Born 1749   Died 1832 aged 82

Johann Wolfgang von Goethe is considered the founder of modern German literature and in his old age people would make pilgrimages to his Weimar home to visit him. His writings show that he was influenced by many people, such as great philosophers, Shakespeare, Byron, folk singers, and, not least, by the many women he fell in love with.

Goethe was amazingly versatile: he made important discoveries in

▲ *This illustration shows and scene from Goethe's* drama Faust. *Faust is guided by the devil who takes the form of Mephistopheles (seen right).*

science; he was a good actor, and also a theatre director. But he is best remembered for his great plays, his novel *The Sorrows of Werther* (1774), his many songs, and above all the poetic drama *Faust* (1808) in which the hero sells his soul to the devil in exchange for enjoying all that the world can offer him. ◆

William **Golding**

English novelist
Born 1911   Died 1993 aged 82

Born in Cornwall, William Golding studied at Oxford University before becoming a schoolteacher. After many initial rejections from publishers, his first novel, *Lord of the Flies* (1954), quickly became a classic. In it Golding describes a group of junior schoolboys stranded alone on an island. Although they manage to agree among themselves over some matters, quarrels between them soon lead to disaster. Other novels by Golding also explore the best and worst in human nature, including *The Inheritors* (1955) and *Pincher Martin* (1956). In 1983 he was awarded the Nobel Prize for Literature and he was knighted five years later. ◆

Samuel **Goldwyn**

American pioneer film producer
Born 1882   Died 1974 aged 81

Samuel Goldfish was a Polish orphan who emigrated first to London, then America. He worked in a glove factory and as a salesman before he and his brother-in-law set up as film-makers. Taking the name Goldwyn, he became a top producer and an influential star-maker. When his own company became part of M.G.M. (Metro-Goldwyn-Mayer) in 1924 he left to become an independent producer. Films such as *Wuthering Heights* (1939), which made Laurence Olivier a star, and *The Little Foxes* (1941) were typical of his use of famous writers and adaptations of their work. He insisted on only making films suitable for the whole family to see. Some of his amusingly illogical remarks, such as 'Include me out' (known as 'goldwynisms'), have become as famous as his pictures ◆

A verbal contract isn't worth the paper it is written on.
SAMUEL GOLDWYN

▼ *A camera man and a sound man attempting to film a lion (who is supposed to be roaring!) to make the logo that appears before all M.G.M. movies.*

Mikhail
Gorbachev

Leader of the USSR from 1985 to 1991
Born 1931

Mikhail Gorbachev was born on a farm in the Stavropol region of Russia. He studied hard at school and gained a place at Moscow University to study law. A bright and popular student, he joined the Communist Party in his second year. At the early age of 39 he became Party leader of the Stavropol region. In 1985, at the age of 54, he became General Secretary of the Communist Party and in doing so took over the leadership of the whole of the USSR.

For the first time in 60 years, the USSR had a relatively young and reforming leader. He launched three new policies: *perestroika*, meaning 'restructuring', to make the economy more efficient; *glasnost*, to make the country more open and honest; and *demokratizatsiya*, to give people initiative. His policies

▲ *Mikhail Gorbachev with the American president Ronald Reagan at the Geneva Summit in 1985. Their interpreters can be seen behind them.*

were popular abroad: he withdrew Soviet troops from Afghanistan so ending a long war there, and he signed an agreement with America to reduce the number of short-range nuclear missiles.

But problems grew at home. The economy was in trouble. The nationalities (Latvians, Ukrainians, Moldavians, and others) began to demand more independence. His reforms displeased the Party's conservatives and they tried to overthrow him in 1991. Even though he survived that coup, his power was much weakened. When Russia and the other states of the union formed a new Commonwealth of Independent States, Gorbachev resigned. He had introduced sweeping reforms but could not hold the Soviet Union together. ◆

 see also
Yeltsin

Nadine
Gordimer

South African writer
Born 1923

The prize-winning writer Nadine Gordimer was born in Springs, Natal and educated at a convent school and at the University of Witersrand, Johannesburg. Her first book was *Face to Face*, a collection of short stories published in 1949. This was followed by another collection, *The Soft Voice of the Serpent*, in 1952.

She is renowned for her many novels set in South Africa. As an opponent of apartheid (the former policy of racial segregation), she explores the life of the white middle classes and how political racism and bigotry affect them. Her novels include *The Lying Days* (1953), *A Guest of Honour* (1970), the Booker Prize winning *The Conservationist* (1974), and *My Son's Story* (1990). She was awarded the Nobel Prize for Literature in 1991. ◆

Francisco de
Goya

Spanish painter
Born 1746   Died 1828 aged 82

Francisco de Goya spent most of his career in the Spanish capital, Madrid. There he worked mainly for the court, and in 1799 he was appointed King Charles IV's principal painter. He painted many portraits of the royal family and courtiers, designed tapestries for the royal palaces, and also produced religious pictures for churches.

His most original works, however, are of a much more unusual kind. When he was 46 he suffered a mysterious illness that temporarily paralysed him and left him stone-deaf for the rest of his life. This traumatic experience made him think deeply about human suffering and inspired him to paint imaginative scenes, often involving terror or the supernatural.

After Spain was invaded by the French armies of Napoleon in 1808, Goya also produced a number of anti-war paintings and prints. ◆

▲ *Although he is perhaps best-remembered for the horrific images he painted, Goya was also a great portrait painter, as this study shows.*

W. G. **Grace**

English cricket hero
Born 1848   Died 1915 aged 67

William Gilbert Grace was born near Bristol, and was taught to play cricket, along with his two brothers, by his mother. Mrs Grace must have been a very good coach, because all three Grace brothers

▲ *This illustration of cricketer W. G. Grace, England's best all-rounder in his day, is from an 1896 calendar.*

ended up playing first-class cricket for Gloucestershire.

'W. G.', as he was known, made his début at the age of 16. Although he later qualified as a doctor, he carried on playing cricket until the age of 60. He completely changed the way cricket was played and was so popular with spectators that notices were sometimes displayed outside grounds, saying: 'Admission sixpence; if Dr Grace plays, one shilling.' During his career, which lasted nearly 45 years, Grace scored 54,896 runs (including 126 centuries), took 2876 wickets, and held 877 catches. ◆

Steffi **Graf**

German tennis player
Born 1969

Steffi Graf became a professional tennis player at 13, and within three years had become one of the top 10 tennis players in the world. From August 1987 to March 1991

she reigned as the world's top female player, winning a record number of international tennis tournaments.

In 1988 Graf completed an unequalled 'Golden Grand Slam', winning the four most important individual tournaments (the US Open, the French Open, Wimbledon, and the Australian Open), plus the Olympic gold medal. She helped Germany win the Federation Cup, one of the three major team tournaments. She has earned her place in history as one of the world's greatest sportswomen. ◆

Martha **Graham**

American modern dancer and choreographer
Born 1894   Died 1991 aged 97

Even as a very small child Martha Graham loved dancing, and as soon as she had completed her formal schooling she devoted her life to dance. She studied dance in Los Angeles and when she was 25 she became a professional dancer. At first she toured America with a dance company, but eventually appeared in New York dancing on her own.

Graham developed her own style of ballet, dancing to classical and modern music. She also made up her own very unusual, imaginative dances. When she was 35 she formed her own dance company, employing modern artists and composers to design colourful sets, costumes, and music for her ballets. Her dances were based on many unusual themes, including ancient Greek legends and the lives of Native American Indians. She stopped performing when she was 75, but continued to teach and to make up ballets. ◆

Kenneth **Grahame**

Scottish writer
Born *1859* **Died** *1932 aged 73*

Kenneth Grahame's mother died when he was five and he and his brothers and sisters went to live with his grandmother. Grahame did well at school but instead of going to university he got a job with the Bank of England. He eventually rose to be its Secretary – the person whose signature you see on currency notes.

When he was in his twenties he began to write essays in his spare time. Later came stories about a family of orphans, collected in *The Golden Age* (1895) and *Dream Days* (1898). However, he is best known for *The Wind in the Willows* (1908). Its hero, Toad, and his riverside friends, Ratty, Mole, and Badger, first appeared in bedtime stories and letters to Grahame's son, Alastair. ◆

▼ *A scene from* Toad of Toad Hall, *a popular play based on Grahame's* Wind in the Willows.

Cary **Grant**

British-born American film actor
Born *1904* **Died** *1986 aged 82*

Archibald Leach (Cary Grant's real name) was born in Bristol, England. He always wanted to be an entertainer and in 1920 he went to America to try his luck. At first he worked as a singer and an actor in stage musicals before becoming famous as an actor in Hollywood films. A lot of his success was due to his good looks and his witty and charming personality. He rose to fame alongside Marlene Dietrich in *Blonde Venus* (1932). His best-remembered films include comedies such as *Bringing up Baby* (1938) and *Father Goose* (1964), and suspense dramas such as *To Catch a Thief* (1955) and *North by Northwest* (1959), in which he was directed by Alfred Hitchcock. He received an Academy Award ('Oscar') in 1970 for his contribution to the film world. ◆

👁 **see also**

Dietrich

Ulysses S. **Grant**

Commander of the Union armies in the American Civil War; American president from 1869 to 1877
Born *1822* **Died** *1885 aged 63*

After 11 years in the army Ulysses Simpson Grant resigned and tried farming. He failed, and so took a job in his father's leather goods business. When the American Civil War broke out in 1861 he volunteered for the Union Army of the northern states. Within four months his expertise and skill as a commander had earned him promotion to brigadier-general. A series of victories, including Vicksburg and Gettysburg in 1863, led President Abraham Lincoln to appoint Grant commander-in-chief of all the Union armies. Grant's drive and ruthlessness forced the Confederates of the southern states to surrender in April 1865.

Three years later, in 1868, Grant won the American presidential election for the Republicans with the slogan 'Let us have peace'. Even though scandals and bribes rocked

▲ *Published in 1885, this series of pictures traces Ulysses S. Grant's military career.*

his government, he managed to win re-election in 1872.

Grant refused to run for a third term, and retired in 1877. He invested his considerable savings in a firm which went bankrupt in 1884, leaving him with heavy debts. To make money he wrote his memoirs. It was a race against time, for he knew he was dying of cancer. Almost as soon as he finished the work he died, but the book earned his family $450,000. ◆

see also

Lee   Lincoln

Graham **Greene**

English writer
Born 1904   Died 1991 aged 87

Graham Greene was the son of a headmaster and he attended his father's school as a pupil. From early on he was very aware of the difficult position this put him in; he owed loyalty both to his fellow pupils and also to his father. This may be why in novels like *Our Man in Havana* (1958) or *The Honorary Consul* (1973) Greene often describes characters who are also split between conflicting duties.

Finally he ran away from school, later becoming a journalist, then an author and playwright. Some of his novels can be read like detective stories. Others, like *Brighton Rock* (1938) or *The Power and the Glory* (1940), take on important issues like belief in God or how far the poor and oppressed should rebel against their own, often corrupt, political leaders. ◆

Gregory I

Italian religious leader, and the first monk to become pope
Born c.540   Died 604 aged about 64

Gregory came from a rich and noble Christian family. His great-great-grandfather had been pope, three of his aunts lived as nuns, and his father was an official in the government in Rome. Gregory himself was made chief magistrate of Rome. However, in 574 he gave up everything in order to become a monk. He lived in the family house, which he turned into a monastery.

This peaceful life was frequently interrupted by official duties for the pope. Then, in 590, Gregory himself was chosen by the people of Rome to become pope. Although he was sad to leave the quiet of his monastery, he was very active in his papal duties. He sent his monks out to preach all over Italy and also to Britain. He reformed the way in which the Church carried out its business and how its services were presented and sung. Through his writings and by the way he lived his own life, he changed the way Church leaders behaved. Gregory showed how it was possible to combine a monk's existence of reading and prayer with a pope's life of action and power. ◆

Wayne **Gretzky**

Canadian ice-hockey star
Born 1961

Wayne Gretzky was born in Brantford, Ontario. He began skating before he was three and was playing organized ice hockey by eight. In 1979, when he was 18, he joined the Edmonton Oilers and became the youngest player to score 50 goals and more than 100 points in a season.

In the 1981–1982 season Gretzky scored a record 92 goals. In 1985–1986 he achieved another record by scoring 215 points. He became the National Hockey League's most valuable player of the season for a record ninth time in 1989. He has also broken the NHL's all-time scoring record of 1850 points. ◆

▼ *Wayne Gretzky in action for the Los Angeles Kings in 1993.*

Edvard **Grieg**

Norwegian composer and pianist
Born *1843*   **Died** *1907 aged 64*

Edvard Grieg's family originally came from Scotland. His mother taught him to play the piano when he was six years old. When he was 15 the great Norwegian violinist Ole Bull advised him to study at the famous Leipzig Conservatoire, for in those days German music and German methods dominated the whole of Europe. After an unhappy time in Leipzig, Grieg lived for a while in Copenhagen, supporting himself by giving piano recitals and gradually adding to his own compositions. In 1867 he married his cousin, Nina Hagerup, who had a fine soprano voice. He wrote many songs for her, and together they toured Europe giving recitals. Grieg loved Norwegian folk music, and his own compositions soon took on a distinctive Norwegian flavour themselves. His many songs and piano works brought him fame and popularity, in particular his Piano Concerto in A minor and the incidental music he wrote for Henrik Ibsen's play *Peer Gynt*. ◆

see also
Ibsen

Walter Burley **Griffin**

American architect and city planner
Born *1876*   **Died** *1937 aged 61*

Walter Burley Griffin, one of Australia's best-known architects, was really an American. He was born in Chicago, and was working there in 1912 for Frank Lloyd Wright when he won the competition for planning a new capital city for Australia – Canberra.

The Australians did not really want a new capital city and they certainly did not like the idea of an American designing it. Despite this, Griffin managed to lay out most of the roads of the new city before he gave up and moved to Sydney. Canberra today has the shape that Griffin intended, thanks to his persistence. Griffin made the most of the mountainous countryside of New South Wales and created a magnificent chain of lakes which runs right through the city centre. The centre is very grand, with broad, straight avenues focused on the headquarters of the Australian government – the Capitol. ◆

see also
Wright, Frank Lloyd

D. W. **Griffith**

American film pioneer and director
Born *1875*   **Died** *1948 aged 73*

David Wark Griffith left school early to work as a lift-boy to help support his family before becoming a touring actor. He tried

▼ *D. W. Griffith (in the white hat) directs a close-up shot on one of his early film sets.*

to write plays and in 1908 he sold some story ideas to early film-makers and this brought him the chance to direct a movie. He made over 400 silent films (usually lasting only 12 minutes) in which he and cameraman 'Billy' Blitzer developed the use of many basic cinema techniques: close-ups, long-shots, fades, and cutting between shots. Then came two great epics of the silent cinema: the hugely profitable three-hour *The Birth of a Nation* (1915) and the even more ambitious but financially unsuccessful *Intolerance* (1916). Griffith made more movies, some with sound, but in the 1930s he found it impossible to raise backing for the kind of films he wanted to make. ◆

Grimm brothers

German brothers who recorded and published fairy tales
Jakob Grimm
Born *1785*   **Died** *1863 aged 78*
Wilhelm Grimm
Born *1786*   **Died** *1859 aged 73*

Sons of a German lawyer, Jakob and Wilhelm Grimm both went to university with the intention of

▲ *An illustration from* Sleeping Beauty, *one of the fairy tales the Grimm brothers recorded.*

becoming civil servants. But once there they became more interested in folk tales, spending their time listening to and studying the stories, songs, and poems that people had told and sung long before the invention of printing. Between 1812 and 1815 they published around 200 of the best stories; these included *Snow White, Sleeping Beauty, Hansel and Gretel, Cinderella,* and *Little Red Riding-hood.*

At the time the brothers said that they wrote down the tales exactly as they heard them. But in reality it is believed that they rewrote most of the stories in order to make them longer and more satisfying to readers. Even so, the Grimm brothers were very important in the effort to keep fairy tales alive, so that people can still read them today long after the older, spoken versions have been forgotten.

Together they also compiled a huge German dictionary. They saw the study of language and the collecting of fairy tales as equally important tasks in their quest to hold on to the heritage of the German language. ◆

Walter **Gropius**

German architect
Born *1883*   **Died** *1969 aged 86*

Walter Gropius was the son of an architect. From early on he designed buildings that used only modern materials. In 1914 he built some factories constructed purely from glass and steel. He also borrowed ideas from modern art, sometimes making his buildings look like abstract paintings. In 1919 he founded the 'Bauhaus' in Germany, a school of design that used the most outstanding artists, sculptors, and architects of the day. Students there were taught how to use smooth surfaces, bright colours, and three-dimensional design in their buildings.

In 1933 the Bauhaus was closed down by the Nazis. Gropius, who had left the Bauhaus five years before that, moved to England in 1934 because of the growing power of the Nazi government. After designing more striking modern buildings in Britain he finally settled in America. There he worked closely with other designers in his search for truly modern architecture fitting for life in the 20th century. ◆

Che **Guevara**

Latin American revolutionary
Born *1928*   **Died** *1967 aged 39*

Ernesto Guevara de la Serna was born in Rosario, Argentina. He led a comfortable early life, and trained to be a doctor. However, after going on a long journey through Latin America, the poverty he saw convinced him that there had to be a revolution to improve life for the poor. So in 1956 he joined Fidel Castro's campaign to overthrow the Cuban dictator Batista. Guevara fought as a guerrilla leader and then, when Castro won, he became a diplomat and a minister in the Cuban government.

But Guevara was not happy doing routine work; he wanted to spread the revolution to other poor countries. He travelled secretly in Africa and South America before he surfaced in Bolivia where he was captured and executed by the army. After his death Che Guevara became a romantic symbol of revolution and his face appeared on millions of posters throughout the world. ◆

see also

Castro

▼ *A poster of Che Guevara, hero of revolutionaries all over the world.*

▲ *King Gustavus Adolphus, who strived to make Sweden the most important power in northern Europe.*

Gustavus Adolphus

King of Sweden from 1611 to 1632
Born *1594*   **Died** *1632 aged 37*

Gustavus Adolphus was only 16 when he succeeded his father as king of Sweden. At that time Sweden was in danger: it was fighting with Denmark, Poland, and Russia. To save his kingdom, Gustavus II made a treaty with Denmark (1613) and stopped fighting Poland. But he continued the war against Russia, to stop Russia from taking Sweden's land to the east of the Baltic Sea. Russia finally made peace in 1617.

During the rest of his reign, Gustavus strived to make Sweden even more powerful. He founded schools and encouraged industry, especially mining. He improved the army and equipped it with the latest weapons.

In 1618 war began in Germany between Protestant rulers in the north and Catholic rulers in the south. During the 1620s the Catholics conquered northern lands and reached the Baltic Sea, which meant that they could stop Sweden's trade with Germany. Gustavus, who was a Protestant, resolved to fight back. Between 1630 and 1632 Swedish forces fought their way to south Germany, but, during the ensuing Battle of Lützen, Gustavus was killed. ◆

👁 **see also**
Christina

Johann Gutenberg

German inventor of printing in Europe
Born *c.1400*
Died *c.1468 aged about 68*

Before Johann Gutenberg's invention, most books were handwritten, with a few produced using carved wooden blocks. Both methods were slow, so few books were available and these were very expensive. Only monasteries, universities, and the very wealthy could afford them.

Gutenberg was skilled at working with metals, and invented a mould with which he was able to cast a lot of identical copies of each letter of the alphabet on metal stamps. The stamps could be put together to form words, and arranged to make whole pages. After ink had been applied to the metal stamps, any number of copies could be made on paper, using a specially constructed press.

Gutenberg's best-known work is called the *42-line Bible* or *Gutenberg Bible*. He began to print pages of this Bible in 1452 and it took him until 1456 to finish the whole work and print only 300 copies. He gave up printing altogether in 1460. He had made little money out of it, and died a poor man. ◆

Fritz Haber

German chemist
Born *1868*   **Died** *1934 aged 65*

At the end of the 19th century many people felt that the world faced starvation if new forms of nitrogenous fertilizers were not found to increase food production. Ten years later Fritz Haber devised a process for 'fixing' the abundant

▼ *The chemist Fritz Haber was also the inventor of the gas mask, worn here by German anti-aircraft crew in World War I.*

nitrogen in the air by combining it with hydrogen derived from water. Haber's method is still one of the most important of all industrial chemical processes. In 1918 this was recognized by the award of the Nobel Prize for Chemistry.

After Germany's defeat in World War I Haber tried to restore his country's fortunes by using his chemical expertise in other ways. However, his brilliant career came to a sudden end in 1933 when the Nazis forced him to leave the country because he was Jewish. He died soon afterwards having settled in Switzerland. ◆

Hadrian

Emperor of Rome from AD 117 to AD 138
Born c. AD 76   **Died** AD 138
aged about 62

Hadrian's full name was Publius Aelius Hadrianus and he was born in Spain, then part of the Roman empire. He held important posts in the Roman government and was adopted by Emperor Trajan as his son and heir after his own parents died. Hadrian worked hard for his adopted father, serving both in the army and as governor of several provinces before becoming emperor on Trajan's death.

Hadrian travelled throughout his lands, more than any other Roman emperor (he visited Britain in AD 121). He made many improvements to the armies and governments of the Roman colonies he visited. He loved culture and was particularly fond of Athens where he paid for many new buildings. He also built a splendid country house for himself on the outskirts of Rome at a place now called Tivoli.

He was also responsible for one of the most impressive monuments to survive from the Roman world – the great stone wall known as

▲ *Hadrian's Wall ran 117 km from the mouth of the River Tyne in Northumberland to the Solway Firth. It formed a strong defensive barrier between what was then Britain and Caledonia.*

Hadrian's Wall. It was built to protect the northern boundary of the Roman province of Britain from attacks by the Scots. ◆

👁 **see also**

Trajan

Otto **Hahn**

German chemist
Born 1879   **Died** 1968 aged 89

Otto Hahn's parents wanted him to be an architect, but he was drawn instead to chemistry. During the 1930s he began to investigate uranium. This has the heaviest atoms of any natural element. He discovered that bombarding uranium atoms with neutrons (extremely small particles) breaks the atoms into smaller, lighter ones. This process is called nuclear fission. As the atoms break up, they release enormous amounts of energy. This meant that nuclear fission could be used as a new power source, or as a new type of weapon. During World War II, many scientists worked on atomic weapons, but Hahn worked on other projects. After the war he

became an opponent of further research on atomic weapons.

He received the Nobel Prize for Chemistry in 1944 and the Enrico Fermi Award in 1966. ◆

👁 **see also**

Fermi   Oppenheimer   Rutherford

Haile Selassie

Emperor of Ethiopia
Born 1892   **Died** 1975 aged 83

Haile Selassie became king of Ethiopia in 1928 and emperor in 1930. Before that he was known as Prince Ras Tafari.

In 1935 Italy invaded Ethiopia. Haile Selassie asked the League of Nations for its help but none was given. He was forced to seek exile in Britain, where he remained until the British helped him drive the Italians out in 1941. Once he was restored to the throne, he initiated a slow programme of economic and social reforms in an effort to modernize Ethiopia. However, he seemed to lose touch with the problems of the country and his extravagent lifestyle made him unpopular. In 1974 he was overthrown by an army revolt and died – possibly murdered – the next year. Nonetheless, he is revered by followers of the Rastafarian religion in the Caribbean who regard him as a messenger of God. ◆

Edmond **Halley**

English astronomer remembered for his work on Halley's comet
Born 1656   Died 1742 aged 85

While studying at Oxford University Edmond Halley became a good astronomer and mathematician. He was so keen on astronomy that he left Oxford before getting his degree to spend two years on the island of St Helena in the South Atlantic, making charts of the southern sky.

Halley also made studies of the Earth's magnetism, tides, and weather. From 1696 to 1698 he was deputy controller of the mint (where coins are made) at Chester, and after that he commanded a Royal Navy ship for two years. In 1703 he became a professor at Oxford, and in 1720 was made Astronomer Royal.

Halley worked out that a bright comet seen in 1682 was the same one that had appeared in 1531 and 1607. He correctly predicted that it would be seen again in 1758, although he did not live to see it. It is now called Halley's Comet. ◆

Frans **Hals**

Dutch portrait painter
Born c.1581   Died 1666 aged about 85

In the 16th century Holland was ruled by Spain, but after a long struggle it won independence in 1609. The Dutch developed a great feeling of national pride, and Frans Hals was the artist who best represented his countrymen's new optimism and self-confidence. His most famous works were group pictures of civic guards – volunteer part-time soldiers who were ready to defend their country against any further threat from Spain.

Hals had a great gift for depicting

▲ *Frans Hals's picture of* The Laughing Cavalier *(1624) shows his remarkable ability to capture a sense of fleeting movement and expression.*

lively expressions and a sense of movement, and he made most earlier group portraits look like stiffly-posed school photographs. In spite of his popularity, Hals was constantly in trouble because he lacked money (he was twice married and had ten children to support) and he died in poverty. ◆

Hammurabi

King of Babylon from 1792 BC to 1750 BC and creator of the first Babylonian empire
Lived during the 18th century BC

Hammurabi lived almost 4000 years ago in Mesopotamia. Mesopotamia was an area in the Middle East between the rivers Tigris and Euphrates. (Most of Mesopotamia is now in modern Iraq.) In 1792 BC Hammurabi became King of Babylon, which was one of about 30 cities in southern Mesopotamia. Each city was independent and ruled by its own king.

Hammurabi was a cunning man. One by one, he attacked and conquered other cities in southern Mesopotamia, until he had brought them all within an empire ruled from Babylon. The empire – known as the Babylonian empire – was almost 800 kilometres long and

▼ *Through carefully planned attacks, Hammurabi extended the lands he inherited until he ruled over the Babylonian empire.*

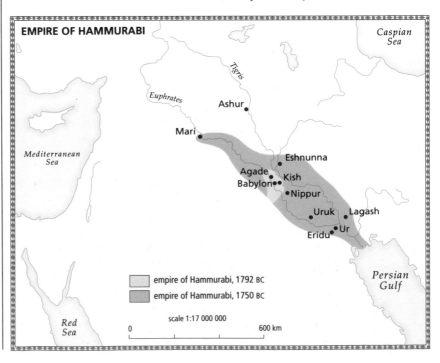

EMPIRE OF HAMMURABI

Caspian Sea

Tigris

Euphrates

Ashur

Mari

Mediterranean Sea

Eshnunna

Agade
Babylon   Kish
•Nippur
Uruk   Lagash
Eridu•   •Ur

Red Sea

Persian Gulf

☐ empire of Hammurabi, 1792 BC
▨ empire of Hammurabi, 1750 BC

scale 1:17 000 000
0   600 km

about 250 kilometres wide. It stretched from Mari, north-west of Babylon, down to the Persian Gulf to the south-east. Hammurabi issued laws and governed the empire through officers to whom he sent orders. He was regarded as a careful planner and an efficient ruler. He was also much more than a warrior; he encouraged agriculture, literature, and intellectual pursuits and his reign become known as 'the golden age of Babylon'. ◆

George Frideric Handel

German composer
Born *1685* **Died** *1759 aged 74*

George Handel's father wanted him to become a lawyer and he was very unhappy when the boy insisted on studying music instead. When he was 18 Handel went to Hamburg to work as an orchestral player and learn all he could about opera. He wrote two operas. One of

▼ *A portrait of Handel from the house where he was born in Halle.*

them, *Almira*, was a great success and he was invited to Italy, the home of opera in the 18th century.

He stayed in Italy for nearly three years and wrote many successful works. However, he was still restless. In 1710 he visited London and was so happy there that he decided to make it his home, even though he had already accepted an appointment in Hanover. Fortunately, the Elector of Hanover became King George I of England in 1714 and he forgave the composer, so Handel was able to continue working in England.

Handel wrote orchestral works, such as the *Music for the Royal Fireworks* and the *Water Music* suite, and many fine concertos. However, he is probably best known for his oratorios (a kind of opera without scenery or costumes), including the famous *Messiah* (1742). ◆

Tom **Hanks**

American film actor
Born *1956*

Tom Hanks spent much of his childhood on the move, because his father was a travelling cook. While at school in Oakland, California, he took up acting, and he continued to act throughout school and college.

After college Hanks went first to New York, then to Los Angeles looking for work. He acted in his first film in 1979, but it was his role in *Splash* (1984) that brought him to international attention. He had mixed success for the next few years, but *Big* (1988) and *Sleepless in Seattle* (1993) were huge box-office successes. Hanks became one of the most successful film actors of the 1990s. In 1995 he became only the second person ever to win the Oscar for Best Actor two years

running. He won it in 1994 for his role as an Aids victim in *Philadelphia*, then in 1995 for his role as the slow-witted hero of *Forrest Gump*. ◆

Hannibal

Carthaginian general
Born *247 BC* **Died** *183 BC aged 64*

Carthage, a colony founded by the Phoenicians in North Africa, became a powerful and wealthy trading nation. In 264 BC it clashed with the other great power at the time, Rome. Hannibal's father, Hamilcar, was the general in charge of Carthaginian forces in this first war. The Romans defeated Carthage and made it pay huge fines.

At the age of nine, Hannibal was taken to Spain by his father on a campaign. His father made him swear to be a lifelong enemy of Rome and the Roman empire.

In 221 BC, at the age of 25, Hannibal took over the command of the Carthaginian forces in Spain. He attacked the town of Saguntum in northern Spain, and war broke out again. Although the Romans sent an army against him, Hannibal outwitted them by marching right across the Alps into Italy. He started with about 40,000 soldiers and 37 elephants (mainly to frighten the Roman troops) but, after the crossing, only 26,000 men and 12 elephants were left.

Hannibal raised a new army and defeated the Romans in several major battles. The Romans were in despair of ever defeating Hannibal, until they appointed a new general, Cornelius Scipio. He finally defeated Hannibal's army at Zama in North Africa in 202 BC. Hannibal returned to Carthage, but eventually committed suicide to avoid being captured by the Romans. ◆

James Keir **Hardie**

Scottish politician and first leader of the modern British Labour Party
Born *1856* **Died** *1915 aged 59*

James Keir Hardie was born in a one-roomed house, and by the age of ten he was working in a coal mine. Here he saw miners risking appalling injuries and even death in return for very low wages. Hardie thought trades unions could improve conditions for working people, and by 1886 he was a full-time union organizer in Ayrshire. Later he realized a new political party was needed to speak up for working people in Parliament. In 1892 he stood for Parliament in West Ham, Essex, and became the first independent Labour Member of Parliament. He wore a soft tweed cap, which angered the other, smartly dressed MPs, but 'the man in the cloth cap' became a working-class hero.

Hardie spoke out in Parliament against unemployment and poverty, and demanded votes for women. At first his was a lone voice, but by 1906 the number of Labour MPs had grown to 29, and Hardie became the new party's first leader. Hardie was a pacifist, and when World War I broke out in 1914 he hoped that an international strike would stop it. He was bitterly disillusioned when most of his Labour and socialist colleagues supported the war, and died a disappointed man. ◆

Thomas **Hardy**

English novelist and poet
Born *1840* **Died** *1928 aged 87*

The son of a stonemason, Thomas Hardy was born – and spent much of his life – in Dorset. He even set many of his novels there and in the surrounding counties (calling the area 'Wessex').

Hardy first worked as an architect and church-restorer in London, but he also began writing novels and poetry. After the success of his fourth novel, *Far From the Madding Crowd* (1874), he returned to his beloved Dorset.

▲ *A drawing of Thomas Hardy from an 1892 edition of the magazine* Vanity Fair. *At that time he was a very popular and successful novelist.*

This novel was one of many describing the ups and downs of country life in the West Country. However, the good humour running through his early work began to disappear in favour of a sadder approach to life. He increasingly saw his characters as victims of a cruel and uncaring world. For example, in *Tess of the D'Urbervilles* (1891), he describes an innocent girl destroyed by a villainous lover and a series of unlucky mishaps.

In 1874 Hardy married, but the relationship was never easy. He described the type of difficulties he and his wife had in his novel *Jude the Obscure* (1895). However, readers were not ready for this sort of honesty about marriage, and the outcry against him caused Hardy to abandon novels and concentrate on poetry. Hardy experimented with different rhymes and verse forms; his *Collected Poems*, published two years after his death, contains over 900 poems.

The death of his wife in 1912 led to some beautiful poems in which Hardy expresses his regrets about their past unhappiness together. In 1914 he married again and lived quietly until his death. ◆

James **Hargreaves**

English inventor of the spinning 'jenny'
Born *c.1720* **Died** *1778 aged about 58*

Spinning wheels have been used for thousands of years to twist the wool fibres from sheep into the long threads or 'yarns' used for weaving. In about 1764 an uneducated weaver from Lancashire called James Hargreaves invented a machine which one person could use to spin several threads at the same time. He called this machine a 'jenny' after his young daughter.

Other spinners thought that Hargreaves' machine would put them out of work because it was so much faster than the old methods. They broke into his house and destroyed his jennies and his weaving loom. This scared him and so he moved his family to Nottingham. He and a partner set up a small mill to spin yarn and he worked there for the rest of his life.

In 1770 Hargreaves received a patent for his invention but he never became rich even though there were thousands of jennies in use by the time he died. ◆

◉ **see also**

Arkwright   Crompton   Jacquard

Harun al-Rashid

Arabian ruler from 786 to 809
Born c.764   Died 809 aged about 45

Harun al-Rashid was brought up in the Islamic religion. He fought against the Christians in Constantinople and earned the title 'al-Rashid' (the one following the right path). After being governor of Tunisia, Egypt, Syria, Armenia, and Azerbaijan he became Caliph (ruler) of the entire Arab empire in 786. The empire stretched from the Mediterranean Sea to India.

Harun al-Rashid's palace in

▼ *Though believed to be a cruel and extravagent ruler, Harun al-Rashid is the hero in many of the stories in* The Arabian Nights.

▲ *William Harvey (right) demonstrates his theory of the circulation of the blood to King Charles I, who employed Harvey as his doctor.*

Baghdad became famous for its riches and jewels, and its food, wine, women, poetry, and song. The empire was also rich and produced textiles, metal goods, and paper (at this time paper was unheard of in Europe). Harun al-Rashid's fabulous wealth and his many wives passed into legend in the stories of *The Arabian Nights*. ◆

William **Harvey**

English physician who discovered how blood travels round the body
Born 1578   Died 1657 aged 79

William Harvey was the eldest of seven sons of a wealthy farming family. His brothers all did well as merchants in London, but he went off to study medicine. He was a very successful doctor, and became court physician to King James I and then to King Charles I.

Harvey made a careful study of the heart and blood vessels (veins and arteries) in the dozens of different animals which he cut up. For more than 1500 years doctors had followed the writings of the ancient Greek physician Galen, who taught that blood moves backwards and forwards in the vessels that carry it. But Harvey found that valves in the blood vessels allow the blood to move in only one direction.

Harvey showed that blood is pumped from the heart all the way round the body and back to the heart, where it begins its journey again. He was the first person to describe the circulation of the blood accurately. ◆

◉ **see also**

Galen

Vaclav **Havel**

*President of Czechoslovakia from 1989
and then president of the new Czech
Republic from 1992*
***Born** 1936*

Vaclav Havel's family was anti-
Communist, even though they
lived in Communist Czechoslovakia.
Havel worked in a theatre as a
stage-hand and later became a
playwright. His plays became very
popular but when the Russians
invaded Czechoslovakia in 1968,
Havel, who was known for his
views on human rights, found
that his plays were banned. He
managed, however, to continue
to write and to publish abroad.

From 1979 to 1983 he was
imprisoned for helping to create
Charter 77, a declaration for human
rights, and in 1989 he was jailed
again for inciting a rebellion against
the government. After his release
he helped form Civic Forum, an
organization which led mass
protests to demand freedom and
democracy. After a general strike
was threatened, the Communist

▼ *Vaclav Havel, the most famous
campaigner for democracy in former
Czechoslovakia.*

government resigned. Havel was
elected president by a landslide
victory. He tried to preserve a
united Czechoslovakia, but the
federation broke up in 1992 and
was split into the Czech and Slovak
Republics; Havel became president
of the Czech Republic. ◆

👁 **see also**
Masaryk

Robert **Hawke**

*Prime minister of Australia from 1983
to 1991*
***Born** 1929*

Robert (Bob) Hawke was born
in South Australia. After
graduating from the University of
West Australia he went to England
to study at Oxford University. On
his return to Australia he worked as
a lawyer for the Australian Council
of Trade Unions. Later he became
its president and from 1970 until
1980 he was a skilful negotiator on
behalf of trade unionists. In 1980 he
was elected to parliament and three
years later became leader of the
Labour Party. Within a month he
was prime minister as the Labour
Party swept to victory in the
election. In all he won four general
elections between 1983 and 1990
before being replaced as leader of
the party and as prime minister by
Paul Keating. He retired from
politics in 1992. ◆

Stephen **Hawking**

English physicist
***Born** 1942*

Stephen Hawking, one of the
most brilliant thinkers of
modern times, has been Lucasian
Professor of Mathematics at

▲ *In his* A Brief History of Time, *Hawking
argues that our universe and an infinite
number of universes like it, are all part of
one great 'super-universe'.*

Cambridge University since 1979,
the same position Isaac Newton
once occupied. He is a worthy
successor to that great scientist
because his research into the
nature of black holes, relativity,
gravitation, and cosmology has
been outstandingly important,
influencing in a profound way the
work of many other scientists.

Hawking has travelled and
lectured widely. Apart from his
technical papers and books, he
has also written highly successful
publications for the general reader:
his *A Brief History of Time* (1988)
was a huge best-seller. His lengthy
list of fellowships, prizes, medals,
and honorary degrees awarded by
the most prestigious institutions in
the world is an acknowledgement
of his intellectual service to
humankind. To achieve all this he
has triumphed over a crippling
neurological handicap which has
confined him to a wheelchair for
much of his career. ◆

Nathaniel **Hawthorne**

American writer
Born 1804   Died 1864 aged 59

Nathaniel Hawthorne was born in Massachusetts. His father was a sea captain who died when his son was four. After living a sheltered life with his mother, Hawthorne decided to become a writer. One of his ancestors had been a judge in 1692 when some innocent people were executed in Salem for the supposed crime of witchcraft. Troubled by this cruel story, Hawthorne wrote about the harsh attitudes of the early American settlers in *Twice-told Tales* (1837). His most famous novel, *The Scarlet Letter* (1850), tells the story of one of the early settlers in America named Hester Prynne, condemned to wear a large scarlet 'A' for life because she had once committed adultery. She eventually finds happiness, helping others in distress and so setting an example to those who once condemned her.

Hawthorne later became the American consul in Liverpool, England, from where he visited Italy, the inspiration for his last completed novel, *The Marble Faun*, published in 1860. ◆

Franz Joseph **Haydn**

Austrian composer
Born 1732   Died 1809 aged 77

Franz Joseph Haydn's father was poor and could do little to help a son who wanted to become a musician. Fortunately a relative agreed to pay for Haydn's education, and in 1740 the organist of Vienna's great cathedral, St Stephen's, took him into the choir, where he remained until he was 17.

Although he did not receive any formal lessons, he learned all he could, and taught himself to compose by studying the music he most admired. In 1759 he obtained his first official appointment, as musician to Count Morzin, and in 1761 he went to work for Prince Esterházy, at the prince's splendid palace at Eisenstadt. Haydn served the Esterházy family for 30 years. He wrote operas for their private opera-house, and church music for their private chapel. He also wrote symphonies and quartets, concertos, songs, and piano music for their day-to-day entertainment.

His fame spread far beyond the walls of the Eisenstadt palace. When the time came for him to retire, his music was known and loved throughout Europe. Haydn's music is ingenious and inventive. Without him, the symphony, of which he wrote 104, and the string quartet might never have become such important musical forms. ◆

▼ The luxurious Neptune pool in the grounds of newspaper tycoon William Hearst's grand Californian castle.

William Randolph **Hearst**

American newspaper tycoon
Born 1863   Died 1951 aged 88

William Randolph Hearst left university early to take control of the *Examiner* newspaper in San Francisco, which was owned by his father. After making it very successful, Hearst then bought the *New York World* newspaper. He increased its circulation by printing sensational and often exaggerated stories that people liked to read. Using the money he made, he bought other papers and by 1927 he owned a total of 25 newspapers and magazines.

Hearst became very rich and powerful. He built a huge and extravagant castle for himself at San Simeon in California and invited lots of Hollywood stars to stay there. In 1941 the film-maker Orson Welles made and starred in *Citizen Kane*, a film about a newspaper tycoon which many people believe is really about Hearst. ◆

see also
Welles

Georg **Hegel**

German philosopher
Born *1770*   **Died** *1831 aged 61*

Georg Hegel was born in Stuttgart and spent much of his life teaching in various German colleges. At first he studied theology (religion), although even at that time he was writing and editing pieces on philosophy. He also worked as a newspaper editor and was even a headmaster of a school for a while. Then, in 1818, he became professor of philosophy at Berlin University. He remained there until he died during a cholera epidemic in 1831.

Hegel's philosophy, found in such works as *The Phenomenology of Mind* (1807) and the later *Encyclopedia of the Philosophical Sciences* (1817), is notoriously difficult. This is partly because he tried to bring all knowledge and systems of thought into just one all-embracing reality through his idea of the 'dialectic'. In his dialectic, Hegel stated that the truth to any given question could only be found by combining the two opposite answers to that question. This, and his ideas on society, religion, history, and art influenced many later thinkers. ◆

Henry **Heinz**

American businessman
Born *1844*   **Died** *1919 aged 73*

Even when he was a child, Henry Heinz was interested in selling food. By his 16th birthday he already had employees working for him, growing food for the market in the city of Pittsburgh.

Heinz's first company was set up to sell horseradish. In 1876 he reorganized it and began building it into a major national company.

▲ *An early poster advertising Heinz spaghetti. Henry Heinz kept an eye on every stage of the production of his foods, from the farming to the advertising.*

By 1905 it was the largest producer of pickles, vinegar, and ketchup in America and Heinz had acquired the nickname 'Pickle King'. He especially enjoyed being involved in the marketing of his products and the '57 varieties' slogan was chosen in 1896 because he liked the sound of it. He was a thoughtful man who cared about the welfare of his staff, and supported 'Pure Food' laws at a time when most of his competitors opposed them.

The Heinz family controlled the company until 1969 and they are still the largest shareholders. ◆

Werner Karl **Heisenberg**

German physicist
Born *1901*   **Died** *1976 aged 74*

Werner Karl Heisenberg studied at the German universities of Munich and Göttingen. Then, from 1924 to 1926, he went to work in Denmark with Neils Bohr. At that time the world's physicists were struggling with the problem of wave-particle duality – the fact that the electron sometimes behaves like a particle and sometimes like a wave. Heisenberg said that it was wrong to think of the electron in this way and suggested that we can only know about it by observing the light that it emits. Using this idea he put together a mathematical method of predicting the behaviour of atomic particles. He was awarded the 1932 Nobel Prize for Physics for this work.

Heisenberg went on to show that we cannot measure an atomic particle's speed and position at the same instant. Each can be measured separately, but measuring one of them alters the other – so we cannot know both exactly. This is known as Heisenberg's Uncertainty Principle. During World War II Heisenberg was made director of Hitler's atomic bomb programme, but Germany was defeated before the work could be completed. ◆

◉ **see also**

Bohr

Ernest **Hemingway**

American writer
Born 1899   Died 1961 aged 62

Much of Ernest Hemingway's writing is based on his own adventurous life. He drove an ambulance in World War I and was a war correspondent in World War II and the Spanish Civil War. He was a big-game hunter, a deep-sea fisherman, and loved bullfighting. He was considered a hard drinker, a fighter, and was married four times.

His books reflect his life and interests. His first major success, *A Farewell to Arms* (1929), dealt with his experiences in Italy in World War I; *Death in the Afternoon* (1932) was a study of bullfighting; *For Whom the Bell Tolls* (1940) was set in the Spanish Civil War; and *The Old Man and the Sea* is about an aged fisherman trying to catch a huge marlin. His writing skills were rewarded with the Pulitzer Prize in 1953 and the Nobel Prize for Literature in 1954.

Despite his success, Hemingway became depressed by his failing health and shot himself in 1961. ◆

Jimi **Hendrix**

American rock singer and musician
Born 1942   Died 1970 aged 27

James Marshall Hendrix was one of the most exciting, unusual, and imaginative rock guitarists ever. He began his career in his Seattle home by imitating records of blues guitarists. He then played the guitar with many top soul groups. He started his own band in New York, but moved to London in 1966 to form the trio The Jimi Hendrix Experience. He immediately found success with 'Hey Joe' (1967) and, despite the strangeness of his sound, followed it with five more hit singles and three albums before his death in 1970. Many later guitarists have imitated Hendrix, but none have managed to play quite like him. ◆

▼ *Jimi Hendrix's group, The Jimi Hendrix Experience, disbanded in 1969, but he continued to record and perform until his death a year later.*

◀ *Sonja Henie brought artistic as well as athletic skills to the sport of ice-skating.*

Sonja **Henie**

Norwegian ice-skater and film actress
Born 1912   Died 1969 aged 57

When she was just 11 years old, and already a champion in her own country, Sonja Henie caused a sensation by performing in the 1924 Olympic Games. She went on to win gold medals in the Olympic Games of 1928, 1932, and 1936. She also won a record ten world titles and was European champion six times.

When Henie retired from competitive skating she started a new acting career. She starred in 11 popular Hollywood films, earning more money than any sportsperson had done before. She became an American citizen in 1941. ◆

▲ *This is a detail from the Monument to Discoveries in Lisbon, Portugal. Henry the Navigator is on the right.*

Henry the Navigator

Portuguese prince who organized and paid for Portuguese exploration in the 15th century
Born 1394   Died 1460 aged 66

Henry was the son of King John I of Portugal. After a time as governor of a town in Morocco, he became governor of the Algarve province in Portugal.

Although he did not go on any voyages, Henry devoted his life to exploration. He provided ships and finance for the Portuguese captains who were pushing further and further down the coast of Africa and into the Atlantic. As a result, Portugal become a powerful sea-trading nation, seeking new countries to trade with and new products to bring back to Europe.

By the time Henry died, Portuguese ships had explored the African coast as far as what is now Sierra Leone, and had sailed up the Gambia river. Contacts made with the African people eventually gave rise to the Portuguese slave trade. ◆

Henry IV

King of France from 1589 to 1610
Born 1553   Died 1610 aged 56

Henry was born into a French noble family in the mid-16th century. At this time the people of France were bitterly divided. In the Middle Ages all French people had been Catholic Christians. But from the 1530s many had become Protestant Christians, or 'Huguenots'. From the 1560s Catholics and Huguenots fought each other.

Henry was brought up as a Huguenot and later fought in wars against the Catholics, who were led by the King of France. In 1584, however, the king's brother died and Henry became heir to the throne. Then in 1589 the king died and Henry was crowned king. Catholics, however, would not accept this because Henry was a Huguenot. Another war broke out and Huguenots again fought Catholics, but could not defeat them.

Wanting peace for France, Henry became a Catholic in 1593 and the fighting finally stopped in 1598. At the same time Henry established political rights and some religious freedom for the Huguenots, and before too long France began to prosper again. Henry died in 1610 when a Catholic fanatic stabbed him to death. ◆

Henry V

King of England from 1413 to 1422
Born 1387   Died 1422 aged 35

Henry's father, Henry Bolingbroke, was at one time a trusted adviser to King Richard II. But when Richard banished Bolingbroke, the young Henry was left in the king's care. The next year (1399) Henry's father came back, seized the English throne from Richard, ruled as Henry IV, and declared young Henry to be heir to the kingdom of England.

Henry V became king on his father's death in 1413. King Charles VI of France did not take the new English king seriously, and Henry vowed to make him regret this. He

▼ *The battle of Agincourt, 1415, at which Henry V defeated the French army.*

made careful preparations for war and invaded France in 1415. Within two months Henry had destroyed the French army at Agincourt. Henry kept up the military pressure for the next five years, until the French king had to agree to let Henry marry his daughter, and so become heir to the French throne.

Henry was now the most powerful ruler in Europe, and he even started making plans to go on crusade to the Holy Land. But seven years of fighting had exhausted him. During another long French siege he caught fever and died, leaving a nine-month-old baby as his successor. ◆

Henry VIII

King of England and Wales from 1509 to 1547

Born 1491   Died 1547 aged 55

When Henry VIII came to the throne in 1509 he seemed to have everything. He was tall, handsome, and good at hunting and

jousting. He was religious, well educated, and musical. He was devoted to his new wife Catherine of Aragon, and he soon found an energetic and loyal minister in Thomas Wolsey, whom he made Lord Chancellor.

But Henry wanted a son to succeed him, and was prepared to stop at nothing to get his own way. He grew tired of Catherine, who had given him a daughter, Mary. He wanted to marry a woman of the court, Anne Boleyn. Wolsey failed to persuade the pope to give the king a divorce, and so he was dismissed from the post of minister.

Henry, with his new minister, Thomas Cromwell, and the Archbishop of Canterbury, Thomas Cranmer, found a more ruthless solution. Henry broke with the pope and the Catholic Church. He married Anne Boleyn (and divorced Catherine afterwards), became Supreme Head of the English Church, and destroyed the monasteries because he wanted their wealth. Henry dealt ruthlessly with those who opposed him. Few people close to him, especially his wives, escaped trouble.

The old Henry was a terrifying figure. He had a painful ulcer on his leg, and was so overweight that a machine had to haul him upstairs. But to many of his people he was a great king. When he died his councillors did not dare announce the news for three days.

Henry VIII married six times and his wives suffered various fates. They were: Catherine of Aragon (divorced), Anne Boleyn (beheaded), Jane Seymour (died), Anne of Cleves (divorced), Catherine Howard (beheaded), and Catherine Parr (survived). He had three children: Mary I (daughter of Catherine of Aragon), Elizabeth I (daughter of Anne Boleyn), and Edward VI (son of Jane Seymour). ◆

▲ *A famous portrait of Henry VIII by Hans Holbein.*

◉ **see also**

Cranmer   Elizabeth I   Mary I
More   Wolsey

Katherine Hepburn

American film actress
Born 1909

Katherine Hepburn's first film, *Bill of Divorcement*, made her a star in 1932. She was then identified with witty comedies, such as *Bringing Up Baby* (1938) and a series of movies with Spencer Tracy (her partner in private life). She also triumphed in mature roles, in *The African Queen* (1951), *The Lion in Winter* (1968), and as the elderly mother in *On Golden Pond* (1981), for which she was awarded one of her four Academy Awards (Oscars). This was despite a trembling caused by Parkinson's disease and an eye ailment, the result of dunkings in a Venice canal for scenes in *Summer Madness* (1955). ◆

153

Barbara Hepworth

English abstract sculptor
Born 1903   Died 1975 aged 72

Like her friend, the sculptor Henry Moore, Barbara Hepworth went to Leeds School of Art and then to the Royal College of Art in London. A scholarship took her to Italy, where she learnt to carve marble. Her work progressed from basic carving of stone or wood to using bronze, sometimes curving metal into shapes joined by thin metal rods resembling strings of musical instruments. Much of her work is abstract, not intended to represent anything. It focuses on shape, texture, size, and surface. After World War II she gained an international reputation as one of the greatest modern sculptors, and carried out many commissions for public places. She died in a fire at her studio in St Ives, Cornwall. ◆

👁 **see also**
Moore

▼ *Barbara Hepworth's sculpture in wood entitled* Single Form.

Hereward the Wake

English Anglo-Saxon leader
Dates of birth and death unknown

Very little is known about Hereward the Wake's life. He was a tenant of the abbey of Peterborough in Lincolnshire. In 1070 a Norman abbot, Turold, got control of that abbey, and Hereward, with other Anglo-Saxon tenants and some Danish pirates, decided to rebel against him. They burnt and plundered the abbey, and made off with its treasure to the Isle of Ely, a marshy area that Hereward could easily defend.

Anglo-Saxons from other parts of the country, who were resisting the Normans, came to Ely to join Hereward. In 1071 King William I (William the Conqueror) decided to take action, and attacked the rebel stronghold. Hereward managed to escape but what happened to him then is not really known. Hereward has lived on in many people's imaginations as an outlaw hero who defied the power of the Normans. ◆

👁 **see also**
William I

Hero of Alexandria

Ancient Greek inventor
Lived during the 1st century AD

We know very little about Hero of Alexandria's life. However, we do know about his marvellous inventions because copies of the books he wrote have been passed down through the centuries. His books contain descriptions of mechanical toys and playthings he invented. The most famous was a small ball which whizzed round by the force of steam. This was the first use of a steam-engine, but it was to be another 1700 years before anyone thought of using steam to drive machines other than toys. He also produced several toys using water; they have been given such names as 'Hero's magic fountain' and 'Hero's magic jug'.

Apart from toys, Hero also invented useful devices, such as his 'dioptra'. This could measure the distance between far-off points and also their height. It was similar to the theodolite used by surveyors today, when examining land before plans can be made for building houses or roads. ◆

Herod

King of the Jews at the time when Jesus was born
Born c.74 BC   Died 4 BC aged about 69

Herod was appointed king of the Jews in 40 BC. Although he was given the province of Judaea (now modern Israel) by the Romans, he had to fight to make it his kingdom. This Herod (there were several) was called 'the Great' because of the forceful way he ruled. But the Jewish population would probably not have agreed with this title, since he ruthlessly put down rebellions.

Herod's first job was to besiege Jerusalem, and eventually he took control there. When he found out about the birth of Jesus, whom people were calling the future king of the Jews, he ordered all children under the age of two in Bethlehem to be put to death. Jesus and his family escaped to Egypt, and Herod died the same year.

Throughout his life Herod was a suspicious man, always thinking that there were plots against him.

▲ *This illustration depicts Herod's massacre of innocent children and Jesus' escape to Egypt.*

For this reason he executed his own son and those of his sister, Salome, and he also executed his wife, her mother, and the High Priest. ◆

Herodotus

Ancient Greek historian
Born *c.484 BC*   ***Died*** *c.424 BC*

Herodotus came from the Greek town of Halicarnassus (now on the coast of Turkey) but spent years travelling throughout Greece, Asia, and Africa. In 444 BC he sailed to southern Italy as one of the founders of a new Greek colony called Thurii. Once there Herodotus devoted his time to writing a nine-volume history of Greece. He particularly wanted to record the struggles between the Greeks and the Persians. Herodotus is thought to be an important historian today because he did not just accept what other writers had said before but collected evidence for himself. ◆

William and Caroline Herschel

German-born British astronomers
William Herschel
Born *1738*   ***Died*** *1822 aged 83*
Caroline Herschel
Born *1750*   ***Died*** *1848 aged 97*

William Herschel started his working life following in his father's footsteps as an oboist in a German military band. In 1757 he came to England and worked as a musician, eventually settling in Bath. His sister Caroline joined him there in 1772. Gradually his interest in astronomy grew and he started to build his own telescopes.

In 1781 he discovered the planet Uranus, the first planet to be found with the help of a telescope. This discovery changed his life. King George III supported Herschel financially so he could devote himself completely to astronomy.

Herschel directed his tremendous energy towards making many observations of a much higher quality than anyone had done before. He made catalogues of nebulas and double stars, and discovered moons around Uranus and Saturn.

Caroline Herschel soon became his devoted assistant and an expert herself. She went on to do research of her own, discovering new comets and nebulas. She was awarded the Gold Medal of the Royal Astronomical Society for making a huge catalogue of her brother's observations. ◆

▼ *This huge mirror telescope was built and used by William Herschel.*

Heinrich **Hertz**

German physicist
***Born** 1857   **Died** 1894 aged 36*

Heinrich Hertz was born into a rich and well-educated family. He studied hard and in 1878 went to the University of Berlin.

Earlier, in 1865, the physicist James Clerk Maxwell had written down the laws of electromagnetism. These predicted the existence of electromagnetic waves which could travel through a vacuum. Hertz was encouraged to try to find them.

In 1888 he set up his most famous experiment. He used an electrical circuit to make sparks jump across a gap between two metal rods. He noticed that this caused pulses of electricity in a similar circuit some distance away. He had become the first person to broadcast and receive radio waves.

Unfortunately Hertz was not a very healthy man. He died at the age of 36 just before Marconi demonstrated that radio waves could be used to send messages over long distances.

The unit of frequency is called the *hertz* in his honour. ◆

see also
Marconi   Maxwell

Thor **Heyerdahl**

Norwegian explorer
***Born** 1914*

Thor Heyerdahl always had his own definite ideas about how human civilization might have spread during the world's early history. He was convinced that early progress was spread by those from advanced communities travelling to other parts of the world.

To prove that this might have been so, he and five companions

▶ *In their papyrus reed craft Ra, Thor Heyerdahl and a crew of six set off from the port of Safi in Morocco in 1969 to cross the Atlantic.*

built a simple balsa-wood raft called the *Kon-Tiki*. In 1947 they sailed it from Peru to Eastern Polynesia to prove that Indians from South America could once have made this journey. Their journey involved great danger but to everyone's delight the *Kon-Tiki* expedition landed safely.

Heyerdahl's next project was to cross the Atlantic from Morocco to the Caribbean, this time in *Ra*, a reproduction of an ancient Egyptian boat made of papyrus. His idea was to suggest that South America could once have been influenced by ideas from Egyptian civilization. Heyerdahl wrote popular books about both of these expeditions.

While many scholars are still not convinced by his theories, they all admire Heyerdahl's bravery and skill. ◆

Rowland **Hill**

English reformer of the postal system
***Born** 1795   **Died** 1879 aged 83*

When he was 12, Rowland Hill began to teach mathematics at his father's school. Their school became famous because the pupils made their own rules and enforced them without corporal punishment.

Hill was very interested in the

▼ *The Penny Black and the Two Pence Blue, two of the first adhesive stamps, are now valuable collectors' items.*

postal system in England at the time. In 1837 he published a pamphlet suggesting that instead of making very expensive charges, all letters weighing up to half an ounce (14 grams) should be delivered anywhere in the country for one penny. He also recommended the use of 'a bit of paper just large enough to bear the stamp and covered at the back with a glutinous wash' – in other words, an adhesive postage stamp.

Post Office officials opposed it, but most people thought it was an excellent idea, and the 'Penny Post' came into use in 1840. Later Hill was knighted by Queen Victoria for giving Britain the world's first proper postal service. ◆

Edmund **Hillary**

New Zealand mountaineer who was one of the first men to climb Everest
Born 1919

Edmund Hillary worked as a bee-keeper before taking up mountain-climbing. After climbing in the New Zealand Alps and the Himalayas, he became a member of the British Everest expedition in 1953. When almost at the summit, it was left to Hillary and Tenzing Norgay, a Sherpa tribesman from Nepal, to make the final climb. This they did on 29 May. News of their success reached Britain on the day of Queen Elizabeth's coronation. Hillary was knighted by the new queen in July 1953.

Since then he has made other trips to Everest, becoming a good friend to the local Sherpa people. With them he has worked on schemes for building new schools and hospitals. ◆

👁 **see also**
Tenzing Norgay

Hipparchus

Greek astronomer and mathematician
Lived during the 2nd century BC

Although his dates of birth and death are unknown, and few of his writings survive, Hipparchus was probably the greatest astronomer of ancient times.

He carried out much of his work on the Greek island of Rhodes, for many years carefully observing the Sun, Moon, planets, and stars, using astronomical instruments of his own invention. Lenses had not been invented yet, so he made all his observations with the naked eye. He was the first person to make a scientific link between the movement of the Sun, stars, and planets and the Earth's seasons. His calculations were amazingly accurate. He compiled the earliest-known star catalogue of the 'positions' of 850 stars, and measured their brightness on a scale of 'magnitudes' where the brightest stars are of first magnitude, the faintest being of sixth magnitude. This method is still the basis of modern astronomical brightness scales. He was also the inventor of trigonometry, in which the angles of triangles and the lengths of their sides can be calculated. ◆

Hippocrates of Cos

Greek physician, sometimes called the 'father of medicine'
Born c.460 BC
Died c.370 BC aged about 90

Unfortunately we do not know much about Hippocrates, but the little we do know shows him to have been a kind and sensible doctor. He was born and worked

▲ *Two sides of a coin minted in Hippocrates' honour in 50 BC.*

on the Greek island of Cos where there was a medical school. In his time most people believed that illnesses were caused by evil spirits or bad magic, but Hippocrates taught that disease was often caused by not eating good food or by living in a dirty place. He is reported to have written 70 books about medical treatment. Apart from Galen, no other doctor had more influence on Western medicine than Hippocrates.

Hippocrates kept careful records of people's illnesses and how they responded to treatment. He was a good surgeon and could set broken bones straight. He taught his methods to other doctors, including his own two sons. ◆

👁 **see also**
Galen

Emperor **Hirohito**

Emperor of Japan from 1926 to 1989
Born *1901*   **Died** *1989 aged 87*

Hirohito was the eldest son of Crown Prince Yoshihito of Japan. Hirohito visited Europe in 1921, the first crown prince of Japan to travel abroad. When he returned, his father retired because of mental illness and Hirohito became prince regent, ruling in his place.

He became emperor in 1926 and although his reign was foreseen as being one of *Showa* ('bright peace'), Japan soon became involved in war. First Japan invaded China and then joined World War II on the side of Germany and Italy.

Hirohito did not want war against America, but he could not stop his military leaders from attacking Pearl Harbor, an American naval base in Hawaii. Only at the end of the war did Hirohito overrule his generals. Speaking on the radio for the first time, he announced Japan's surrender in 1945.

After the war he stayed on as emperor, but real power was given to the people and their elected politicians. Japan became friendly with its old enemies in the West, but even after his death many could not forgive Hirohito for the things his armies had done during World War II. ◆

Alfred **Hitchcock**

English film director
Born *1899*   **Died** *1980 aged 81*

Alfred Hitchcock was the son of a London poultry dealer. He was good at drawing and got a job writing and designing captions for silent films. He soon worked his way up to become a film director.

▲ *In Alfred Hitchcock's thriller* The Man Who Knew Too Much *(1956), James Stewart and Doris Day play a couple whose son is kidnapped by spies.*

In 1926 *The Lodger* began his long series of suspense thrillers, in which he makes a very brief appearance each time. His film *Blackmail* (1928) was the first British talking picture. He directed *The Thirty-Nine Steps* (1935) and several other films in England, but then moved to Hollywood and became even more famous as a director of frightening thrillers such as *Rebecca* (1940), *Psycho* (1960), and *The Birds* (1963). ◆

Adolf **Hitler**

Austrian-born dictator of Nazi Germany
Born *1889*   **Died** *1945 aged 56*

Adolf Hitler's father died when his son was 14. As a young man Hitler frittered away his inheritance so he then had to earn his own living. He painted postcards and advertisements in Vienna, Austria, until World War I when he fought in the German army and was awarded the Iron Cross for bravery.

When Germany lost the war, Hitler was so angry about the terms of the peace treaty that he turned to politics. He joined the National Socialist (Nazi) Party and soon became its leader. Many joined the

▼ *Adolf Hitler pictured at a rally in 1934, the year in which he succeeded Hindenburg as head of state.*

Nazi Party, and in 1923 they tried to seize power in Munich. This attempt failed and Hitler went to prison.

> *The broad mass of a nation . . . will more easily fall victim to a big lie than to a small one.*
>
> ADOLF HITLER
> *Mein Kampf,* 1923

There he wrote *Mein Kampf* (My Struggle) (1923) which set out his ideas: he believed Germany's problems were caused by Jews and Communists and that Germany needed a strong Führer (leader) to be great again. Times were hard and his ideas caught on. Although he got only 37 per cent of the votes in the presidential election, Hitler was invited by President Hindenburg to become chancellor (chief minister) in 1933.

When Hindenburg died in 1934, Hitler became president, chancellor, and supreme commander of the armed forces. All opposition to his rule was crushed. Millions of people were sent to concentration camps, and Jews gradually lost all their rights. Hitler became an ally of Fascist Italy and began to push Germany's boundaries outwards. In 1938 he invaded Austria and in 1939 occupied Czechoslovakia and finally attacked Poland too.

This started World War II. Hitler took personal command of Germany's war plans, including a disastrous invasion of the USSR. However, after almost six years, and having ordered the deaths of millions of Jews and others in extermination camps, he was defeated by the Allied powers. He shot himself in his underground shelter in Berlin. ◆

👁 **see also**

Goebbels   Goering
Mussolini   Rommel

Thomas **Hobbes**

English philosopher
Born *1588*   **Died** *1679 aged 91*

Thomas Hobbes's early life was mainly spent as tutor to the Duke of Devonshire's family. When the English Civil War broke out, Hobbes fled to France for 11 years, believing that his theories about the state put him in danger. These theories, set out in his treatise *Leviathan* (1651), say that all power comes from the people; they hand it over to a monarch, who protects them in return for their absolute obedience.

Hobbes's opinion that religion too should be subject to the state led to accusations of atheism. However, he was protected by King Charles II, so he was able to continue defending his controversial views on almost everything right up until his death. ◆

Ho Chi Minh

Founder of the Vietnamese Communist Party and president of North Vietnam
Born *1890*   **Died** *1969 aged 79*

Ho Chi Minh (meaning 'He who shines') was born Nguyen Tat Thanh in Vietnam when it was part of Indo-China, a colony ruled by France. While working in London and Paris he met French Communists who believed it was wrong for France to rule over colonies. They helped him travel to the Soviet Union, where he trained as a Communist organizer. He went to live just outside Vietnam so he could organize a Communist Party inside Indo-China without being arrested, founding the Indo-China Communist Party in 1930.

In 1941, during World War II, Japan entered Indo-China and Ho set up an underground movement,

▲ *When the city of Saigon was captured by the North Vietnamese in 1975, it was renamed Ho Chi Minh City in Ho's honour.*

the Vietminh (supported and funded by the Allies), to fight them. He hoped to take over when the Japanese left in 1945, but the French returned. In 1946 Ho declared war on the French: his forces finally won in 1954.

Vietnam was then divided at the Geneva Conference and Ho became President of North Vietnam. Non-Communist South Vietnam was supported by America, but Ho was determined to reunite the two. He backed the South Vietnam Communists, called the Vietcong, who were fighting their government and the Americans.

In 1965 the United States began to bomb North Vietnam. Its people spent much of their lives in shelters, but the bombing made them even more loyal to Ho. Six years after his death, the two Vietnams were united under the rule of the Communist Party. ◆

Dorothy **Hodgkin**

English chemist
Born 1910   *Died* 1994 aged 84

Dorothy Hodgkin was born in Cairo but most of her life has been spent in her chemistry laboratory in Oxford.

If a chemist wants to make a new drug or copy a chemical that occurs naturally, it is necessary to know what sort of atoms it contains and how they fit together. In other words a plan or design is needed, just as you would need one to build a house. Professor Hodgkin is the world's leading expert in solving this kind of problem.

In 1964 she became only the third woman ever to be awarded the Nobel Prize for Chemistry (the other two were Marie Curie and Irène Joliot-Curie). She received it for finding out how the atoms are arranged in penicillin and vitamin B12. The following year she became only the second woman to be awarded the very special Order of Merit (Florence Nightingale was the other). ◆

William **Hogarth**

English painter and engraver
Born 1697   *Died* 1764 aged 66

William Hogarth was the most important British artist of his period. For generations, foreign artists (such as Van Dyck) had dominated British painting, but Hogarth showed that he could be just as good and just as original as the competition from across the Channel. He was a superb portrait painter, but because he refused to flatter the people he portrayed, he was not able to earn his living this way. Instead he invented a new type of picture – or rather series of pictures. In a series of six or eight scenes he represented successive incidents from a story that illustrated the reward of goodness and the punishment of wickedness. He not only attacked cruelty and injustice, but also poked fun at pompous people, and his pictures had tremendous impact. Engravings of them sold in large numbers and pirate publishers made their own

▼ *The artist William Hogarth specialized in scenes from London life, such as this one,* The Election – Canvassing for Votes.

copies. Hogarth was a strong character and he successfully campaigned to have a Copyright Act passed by Parliament to prevent people cashing in on his work. ◆

Katsushika **Hokusai**

Japanese painter and printmaker
Born 1760   *Died* 1849 aged 89

Katsushika Hokusai is the most famous Japanese artist and one of the greatest of any country or time. Completely dedicated to his art and a master of every subject he chose to depict, he produced a huge number of paintings, prints, and drawings – about 30,000 works in all. Like most Japanese artists of his time, he made his living mainly through coloured prints made from engraved woodblocks; his most famous work is the set of prints *Thirty-six Views of Mount Fuji* (1826–1833), showing Japan's

▲ *Katsushika Hokusai was an expert at creating scenes with just a few simple lines in his woodblock prints. In the Well of the Great Wave of Kanagawa (above) is one of the most famous of his prints.*

sacred mountain in a marvellous variety of views and weather conditions. In the 1850s his prints became well-known in Europe; they influenced the Impressionist artists with their freshness, vigour, and love of life. ◆

Hans **Holbein** the Younger

German painter
Born 1497   Died 1543 aged 46

Hans Holbein was born in Augsburg in the south of Germany, where his father and uncle were painters. Holbein decided to become a painter as well. He worked with his father and then travelled around Germany to learn from other painters. He

eventually settled in Basel (in modern Switzerland), where he became a friend of the churchman and scholar Erasmus. In Basel he produced portraits and prints, including three portraits of Erasmus, and he illustrated a Bible.

In 1526 Holbein went to England, where he met friends of Erasmus and painted their portraits too. One of the people he met, and later painted, was the politician and author Thomas More. Holbein's paintings were so lifelike and colourful that they attracted the interest of Henry VIII. Holbein was appointed court painter. He painted over 100 pictures of Henry, his family, and English nobles. ◆

◉ **see also**
Erasmus   Henry VIII

Billie **Holiday**

American jazz singer
Born 1915   Died 1959 aged 44

Billie Holiday's father played banjo and guitar in a jazz band, and at 15 she was in New York singing in jazz clubs. Her distinctive voice and emotional appeal brought her rapid success. All through the 1940s and 1950s she toured and recorded, making two trips to Europe, in 1954 and 1958. Her best-known records are probably 'Strange Fruit', 'Fine and Mellow', 'Lover Man', and 'Violets for my Furs'.

At the time when Holiday was touring, there was still a great deal of prejudice against blacks in the American South, and as a black singer, Holiday came across a lot of racism.

Her personal life was also filled with problems, particularly her addiction to drugs. This eventually brought about her tragic early

death, at a time when she should have been reaching the peak of her artistic abilities. ◆

Buddy **Holly**

American singer and songwriter
Born 1936   Died 1959 aged 22

Like many early rock'n'roll musicians, Texas-born Charles Hardin Holley began by playing country music but, as leader of Buddy Holly and the Crickets, he went on to become one of rock'n'roll's greatest songwriters. He was also, in 1936, the first musician to use two guitars, bass, and drums, which became the standard line-up for pop groups in the 1960s. His hits, including 'That'll be the Day' (1957), 'Rave On' (1958), and 'It Doesn't Matter Any More' (1959), have been recorded by many artists and still sound fresh today.

Tragically, Holly died in a plane crash at the peak of his success, when he was only 22. ◆

▼ *Buddy Holly had an instantly recognizable 'hiccuping' singing style. The music he wrote influenced many later pop musicians.*

Gustav **Holst**

English composer
Born *1874*   **Died** *1934 aged 59*

Gustav Holst's family originally came from Sweden. His parents were both pianists and wanted him to be a concert pianist but a crippled arm made this impossible. However, from the age of 18 Holst made his living through music as a choir director, a trombonist in a dance band and an orchestra, and finally as director of music at St Paul's Girls' School and at Morley College in London.

The inspiration for Holst's composition came from several varied sources – English folk music, Hindu scriptures, and from the poems of John Keats, Walt Whitman, and Thomas Hardy. His most famous work is *The Planets* orchestral suite, composed between 1914 and 1916.

He lectured at the Royal College of Music in London, where he had been a student, and at universities in Britain and America, and he has had a long-lasting influence on musical education in schools. His experience as a teacher developed his interest in works for small choirs and orchestras, such as his *St Paul's Suite* (1913) which was written for amateur string-players. ◆

Homer

Greek poet
Lived during the 8th century BC

Homer is believed to be the author of two very long poems about the gods and heroes of ancient Greece. These are the *Iliad*, about the capture of the city of Troy (Ilium), and the *Odyssey*, an account of the adventures of the hero Odysseus during his long journey home to Greece from Troy.

We know almost nothing about Homer. Later Greek and Roman writers thought that he was a blind, wandering poet. It is also thought that he came from one of the cities in Asia Minor (now Turkey). Some people think he may not have existed at all, and his poems were just collections of verses which were recited in royal courts by travelling storytellers. However, most experts of this early Greek period and its literature now believe that there was a man called Homer who composed these long, epic poems. They think that Homer did not write the poems down but took famous stories and put them all together, before reciting them from memory. His poems were probably not actually written down for another 100 years. ◆

▼ *In Homer's* Odyssey, *the hero Odysseus survives many trials such as storms, fierce monsters, and strange temptations such as the 'Sirens' depicted on this vase from c.480* BC.

Soichiro **Honda**

Japanese car and motor cycle manufacturer
Born *1906*   **Died** *1991 aged 85*

Soichiro Honda was always interested in cars and machinery. In 1948 he started a business making motor cycles using ex-army tools and parts. At that time, machinery and vehicles were scarce in Japan because many resources had been used up in World War II. However, Honda still managed to build up what became the largest motor cycle firm in the world. In the 1960s Honda started making cars as well, and these were just as successful.

Honda was always more interested in making things than in having business meetings, and it was his instinct for knowing what motor cyclists and motorists wanted that made him successful. He was one of a group of business leaders who made Japan into a leading industrial nation. ◆

Robert **Hooke**

English physicist, chemist, and inventor of the compound microscope
Born 1635 Died 1703 aged 67

As a child, Robert Hooke was very bright, and was said to have mastered a geometry course and learned to play the organ in one week. Unfortunately he grew up to be very bad-tempered and was always having rows with other scientists. He was so worried these scientists might steal his discoveries that he sometimes left proof of his experiments in code. The result of his secrecy and grumpiness was that he did not get the credit for all his discoveries.

Hooke studied the way metals behave when they are stretched and described it in a way that we still call 'Hooke's Law'. He also developed a new version of the microscope. A Dutch scientist called Leeuwenhoek had shown how useful microscopes could be in many branches of science, but he only had a microscope with one lens. Hooke invented a much more powerful one with several lenses, called the compound microscope. He described his invention and many other pieces of apparatus in his book *Micrographia*. ◆

see also
Leeuwenhoek

William **Hoover**

American businessman
Born 1849 Died 1932 aged 83

People often talk of 'hoovering' the carpet when they mean cleaning it with a vacuum cleaner. William Hoover never liked his name to be used in this way. He may have been embarrassed because he knew that it was

▲ *An early advertisement for the 'Hoover', now a household name.*

actually J. Murray Spangler who invented the first upright household vacuum cleaner. (Perhaps we should talk of 'spanglering' our carpets!) Spangler was caretaker at a department store in Ohio when Hoover met him. Spangler's original invention looked very similar to some of today's 'Hoovers', with its dust-bag on the outside of the upright handle. Hoover talked Spangler into selling him the rights to his invention and then set up the Hoover Suction Sweeper Company to manufacture it. In 1908 the company produced its first cleaner which proved to be a great success. ◆

Harry **Houdini**

Hungarian-born American magician and entertainer
Born 1874 Died 1926 aged 52

Harry Houdini was the stage name of Erich Weiss. His family had emigrated to America from Hungary when he was a child. He began his career as a trapeze artist, but it was as a magician who

could perform amazing escapes that he became famous.

Houdini taught himself how to escape from all kinds of chains and bindings. He toured America and Europe, attracting publicity for his show by performing stunts, such as escaping from a strait-jacket or prison cell. He even escaped from an airtight tank full of water, but his most famous trick was the 'Chinese torture cell' into which he was locked, hanging upside down, with his ankles held by stocks.

All Houdini's acts were tricks which depended on his physical strength, skill, and fitness. He was annoyed whenever it was suggested that he had special powers, and he would expose others who claimed that they had supernatural powers, such as fraudulent mind-readers, by performing their tricks himself. ◆

▼ *During his career, Houdini invented many new acts, including making an elephant disappear and walking through a brick wall.*

Edwin **Hubble**

American astronomer
Born *1889*   **Died** *1953 aged 63*

Edwin Hubble trained as a lawyer but in 1913 began astronomical research at Yerkes Observatory, Wisconsin. This was to be the beginning of a distinguished career during which his observations and brilliant deductions showed that many so-called nebulae (gas and dust clouds) were in fact galaxies far outside our own Milky Way galaxy. By ingenious methods Hubble managed to measure their distances and speeds. Many of Hubble's pioneering discoveries were made in California with the Mount Wilson Observatory's 2.5 m wide telescope which came into operation about the time (1919) Hubble joined its staff. He discovered that the universe is expanding and that the speeds at which galaxies are moving away from us are proportional to their distances from us. Known as Hubble's Law, this theory is the basis for modern cosmology's concept of the Big Bang, the explosion that began our universe. Hubble also introduced a useful classification of types of galaxies according to shape, which is still in use today.

Older astronomers who worked at Mount Wilson many years ago still remember Hubble, pipe in mouth, standing in the cold, darkened dome of the observatory, guiding the enormous telescope with which he mapped the universe. ◆

Henry **Hudson**

English explorer and navigator
Born *c.1565*   **Died** *1611 aged about 46*

The first part of Henry Hudson's life is a mystery. The earliest report of him is that on 1 May 1607 he sailed from London as captain of

▲ *English explorer Henry Hudson and his crew coming ashore and meeting Native American Indians in 1610.*

the tiny ship, *Hopewell*. He was looking for a sea route to China to the north of Europe and Asia. This and a second voyage proved to be unsuccessful.

Hudson then took a job with the Dutch East India Company, and in a slightly larger ship, the *Half Moon*, he explored the east coast of North America, and in particular the Hudson River, which was later named after him.

In 1610 Hudson set sail on board the ship *Discoverie*, with a small crew and a boy, his own son John. He was hoping to reach China by way of the North Pole. He discovered what became known as Hudson Bay, where he had to spend the winter. Next summer the crew mutinied and set Hudson, his son, and some of the others adrift in a small boat. They were never seen again. ◆

Howard **Hughes**

American businessman and film producer
Born *1905*   **Died** *1976 aged 70*

Howard Hughes took over the successful Hughes Tool Company, which made and sold oil-drilling equipment, when his father died in 1924. He used some of his inherited wealth to produce Hollywood films, the most famous of which include *Hell's Angels* (1930), *Scarface* (1932), and *The Outlaw* (1944). He was also interested in flying and set up the Hughes Aircraft Corporation. In 1935 he set a new record speed of 563 km per hour in a plane he designed himself. All in all, he broke the world speed record three times. Less successful was his design for a giant flying boat to carry 750 passengers; the *Spruce Goose*, built in 1947, flew just 1.5 km. For the last 25 years of his life Hughes was a recluse, living a secret life out of public view. He died while being flown to Houston for medical treatment. ◆

Langston **Hughes**

American writer
Born *1902*   **Died** *1967 aged 65*

James Mercer Langston Hughes was born in Joplin, Missouri and educated at Lincoln University. He rose to prominence in the 1920s as part of the Harlem Renaissance, an influential black American literary movement.

Hughes's first major poem, 'The Negro Speaks of Rivers', was published in 1921. This was followed by the experimental and influential volumes of poetry, *The Weary Blues* (1926) and *The Dream Keeper and Other Poems* (1932). In these collections Hughes showed his knowledge of folk culture through his use of lyrical verse, jazz, and blues.

Hughes continued to express the life of black Americans in his writing which included his two-volume autobiography, *The Big Sea* (1940) and *I Wonder as I Wander* (1956), and the *Simple* stories ◆

Victor **Hugo**

French poet, novelist, and dramatist
Born 1802   Died 1885 aged 83

Victor-Marie Hugo was the son of an officer in Napoleon's army and he spent a lot of his boyhood travelling around Europe. By the time he was in his early teens he was writing poetry and plays. When he was just 17 he was already busy founding a literary magazine and had won three prizes for his poetry. He was also involved in politics and in the 1840s his anti-monarchy opinions led to him being banished from France by the emperor, Napoleon III. He lived in exile from 1851 until 1870, mainly in the Channel Islands.

Hugo produced a great number of novels, poems, and plays but is perhaps best known for the novels *The Hunchback of Notre Dame* (1831), about a deformed bell-ringer and the beautiful woman he falls in love with, and *Les Misérables* (1862), about an innocent man condemned to life imprisonment. ◆

Baron von **Humboldt**

German scientist and explorer
Born 1769   Died 1859 aged 89

Friedrich Heinrich Alexander von Humboldt was a member of a noble German family, and a man of many talents. He studied biology, geology, metallurgy, mining, and politics at university. From 1799 to 1804 he and a companion explored the rainforests surrounding the Amazon and Orinoco rivers in

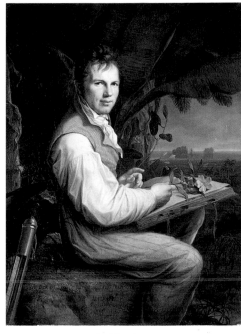

▲ *Baron von Humboldt spent over 20 years writing up an account of his travels in South America.*

South America, travelling nearly 10,000 km. He studied the Peru Current, sometimes called the Humboldt Current, a flow of cool water along the coast of Peru, and reported that guano (the excrement of sea birds) would make good fertilizer. He also identified the cause of mountain sickness and gathered over 60,000 plant specimens.

For over 20 years Humboldt lived in Paris, working on scientific experiments and writing up the results of his explorations, before returning to his birthplace, Berlin. In 1829 he spent six months in Siberia, investigating the geography of that region and studying its weather and geology. He then organized the setting up of a chain of weather stations around the world. For a time he was sent on diplomatic missions by the government of Prussia. Humboldt spent the rest of his long life writing a five-volume book about the universe, entitled *Cosmos*. ◆

▼ *A poster for the richly entertaining 1939 film version of Victor Hugo's* The Hunchback of Notre Dame.

▲ *A wall painting in a town in Iraq portrays Saddam Hussein as a mighty military leader.*

David **Hume**

Scottish philosopher and historian
Born 1711   Died 1776 aged 65

Although he was born and died in Edinburgh, David Hume spent several years in France, where he wrote his major philosophical work, the *Treatise of Human Nature* (1739–1740). Doubting the existence of God, Hume directed his investigations towards providing natural and, if possible, scientific explanations for the way in which human beings think and experience the world. In particular, he was interested in cause and effect: we can see that something may follow after something else, but how can we be really certain that it is caused by it?

A leader in Scottish intellectual life, Hume extended his reputation beyond philosophy with his best-selling historical works, *Political Discourses* (1751) and *History of England* (1754–1762). ◆

Saddam **Hussein**

President of Iraq from 1979
Born 1937

Saddam Hussein came from a poor peasant family. When he was 22 he took part in a plot to kill the prime minister of Iraq. Hussein was shot but escaped, cutting the bullet out of his leg with his penknife. After living in exile in Egypt and being imprisoned, he helped overthrow the government of Iraq in 1968. Although he had never been in the army, he appointed himself general and has been president since 1979, giving top jobs to his relatives and friends.

Hussein's war against Iran (1980–1988) ended in stalemate and his invasion of Kuwait (1990–1991) ended in defeat. These wars cost a million lives. Despite this, Hussein has remained firmly in power, although many Kurdish tribes-people have fought against Hussein's troops to try to gain self-government in the northern areas of the country. He is feared by his people but also admired for standing up to Western powers such as America and its allies. ◆

Christiaan **Huygens**

Dutch mathematician who developed the pendulum clock
Born 1629   Died 1695 aged 66

Christiaan Huygens's parents realized he was a brilliant mathematician when he was very young. His father was an official in the Dutch government and Huygens had a good education.

▼ *Christiaan Huygens built the first pendulum clock, thereby heralding the beginning of truly accurate time measurement.*

Huygens was not only a great mathematician but he was also good at making things. He made a lot of improvements to the telescope (invented by Galileo in 1609), which made it possible to observe the rings around Saturn for the first time. Huygens also built the first pendulum clock, which was more accurate than other clocks at that time.

He also studied light, and concluded that it moves in waves that spread out, just as the ripples on a pond travel outwards when a stone is dropped into the water. But many scientists preferred Newton's idea that light is a stream of tiny particles. Huygens's 'wave theory' was ignored for 150 years until Thomas Young was able to prove that light really does behave like a wave. ◆

see also

Galileo   Newton   Young

Ibn Batuta

Moroccan traveller and writer
Born 1304   Died 1368 aged 64

When he was a boy, Ibn Batuta studied the Koran very thoroughly. By the age of 21 he was an expert in Muslim theology and law, and he set out on a pilgrimage to Mecca. At first he was homesick, but he was to go on to travel more than 120,000 kilometres over the next 28 years.

Ibn Batuta journeyed to Damascus and joined a pilgrimage there. At Mecca he joined other pilgrims returning to Persia (now Iran). He continued to travel in Asia Minor (now Turkey), observing and keeping records, relating tales and

▼ *Ibn Batuta was one of the greatest Muslim travellers. This map shows some of his journeys around India between 1332 and 1344. He recorded his travels around the world in his book* Rihla *(Journey), which is valued by historians because of the information it gives about the time in which he lived.*

wonders. He then travelled north to Kazan on the River Volga, and on to Constantinople.

Ibn Batuta crossed the Hindu Kush mountains and remained in the service of the Sultan of northern India for eight years. He was sent to accompany a returning Chinese embassy, but a storm destroyed the fleet of junks before they could leave. He was left with only his prayer mat and ten pieces of gold. He eventually reached China in 1344, before finally returning home. Later he travelled throughout Spain and crossed the Sahara to Timbuktu before dictating a fascinating account of his travels. ◆

Ibn Khaldun

Arab historian
Born 1332   Died 1406 aged 74

Ibn Khaldun was the first person to try to write about why events happened in history and not just to record what happened. He was born in Tunis, North Africa and lived at a time of many changes, when wars, plagues, famines, and trade could make some kingdoms suddenly poor and others suddenly rich. He travelled widely throughout the Arab world, serving as a high official, a general, a professor, and a judge. He was also robbed, imprisoned, and shipwrecked. When the world-conqueror Tamerlane conquered the city of Damascus and took captives, he was so interested to meet Ibn Khaldun that he set him free afterwards. These adventures gave Ibn Khaldun plenty of knowledge of life in different countries and helped him write a great history of the world as he knew it. ◆

see also

Tamerlane

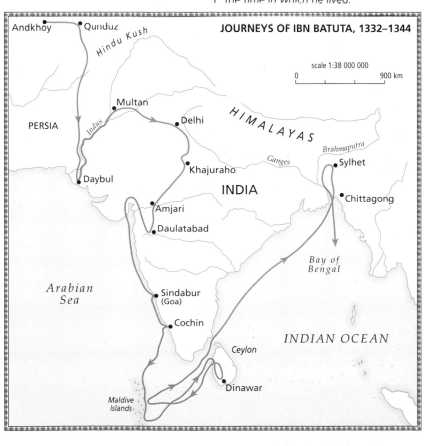

JOURNEYS OF IBN BATUTA, 1332–1344

scale 1:38 000 000

0   900 km

Andkhoy   Qunduz   Hindu Kush

Multan

PERSIA   Indus   Delhi

HIMALAYAS

Brahmaputra

Ganges   Sylhet

Daybul   Khajuraho

INDIA   Chittagong

Amjari

Daulatabad

Arabian Sea   Bay of Bengal

Sindabur (Goa)

Cochin

INDIAN OCEAN

Ceylon

Dinawar

Maldive Islands

Henrik **Ibsen**

Norwegian playwright
Born 1828   Died 1906 aged 78

Henrik Ibsen became a chemist's assistant when he was 15. He planned to go to university but failed the entrance exam. He turned to journalism instead and also began writing poetry and plays. Then, in 1851, he was given a job as stage director and resident playwright at the Norwegian Theatre. Here he began to formulate his ideas about drama and the psychological development of characters.

He married in 1858 and in 1864 moved to Italy and then to Germany. During the next few years, Ibsen wrote several plays which established him as the founder of modern drama and one of the world's greatest playwrights. These include: *A Doll's House* (1879), *Ghosts* (1881), and *Hedda Gabler* (1890). He returned to Norway in 1891 but was forced to abandon writing after suffering a stroke in 1900. ◆

Muhammad **Iqbal**

Indian poet and political leader
Born 1877   Died 1938 aged 61

Muhammad Iqbal studied in Lahore, Cambridge, London, and Munich. He earned his living as a university teacher and a lawyer but his fame came through his poetry. He wrote about the past glory of Islam and the need for Muslims to revive it.

In his role as a political leader, Iqbal at first supported the struggle to free India from British rule. However, later he became convinced that Indian Muslims needed a separate country of their own. In 1930 he spoke to the annual meeting of the Muslim League at Allahabad and called upon his fellow Muslims to set up such a state. The League finally decided to do this in 1940, two years after his death. The new country – Pakistan – came into being in 1947.

Iqbal had written his poetry in Persian and in Urdu, and Urdu became the national language of Pakistan. Pakistanis regard Muhammad Iqbal as the father of their country and Iqbal Day is celebrated in his honour every year. ◆

👁 **see also**
Jinnah

Henry **Irving**

English actor-manager
Born 1838   Died 1905 aged 67

John Henry Brodribb worked as a merchant's clerk but was fascinated by the theatre. An inheritance provided him with enough money for the costumes, swords, and wigs he needed to equip himself as an actor. He also bought his way into the lead role in an amateur production of Shakespeare's *Romeo and Juliet* at a London theatre. Success as Romeo encouraged him to turn professional under the stage name Henry Irving. He spent many years working in touring companies before gaining his place as a leading actor, playing a conscience-stricken murderer in the melodrama *The Bells* in 1871. From 1878 he took over the management of the Lyceum Theatre in London. Here, for over 20 years, he presented plays by Shakespeare and romantic dramas. In 1895 he became the first actor to be knighted, bringing a new respectability to the acting profession. ◆

👁 **see also**
Garrick   Kean

◀ *Henry Irving dressed for playing the role of Cardinal Wolsey. His successful managerial partnership of the Lyceum Theatre with the actress Ellen Terry lasted 24 years.*

Isaiah

Hebrew prophet
Lived during the 8th century BC

Isaiah was an important Hebrew teacher whose writings are found in the section of the Bible known as the Prophets. In the Bible, a prophet is someone who speaks for God rather than foretells future events. There are 15 such men in the Prophets, and Isaiah, Jeremiah, and Ezekiel are renowned as the major ones. Many of Isaiah's teachings appear in the book of the Bible which has been given his name. His name actually means 'salvation of God'. He looked forward to the time when the God of Israel would appear on Earth to be worshipped by everyone. He thus urged his people 'Prepare ye the way of the Lord', warning that the unfaithful could be punished. Many Christians believe that Isaiah was probably referring to the coming of Jesus Christ. ◆

Ito Hirobumi

Japanese statesman who served four times as prime minister
Born *1841*   **Died** *1909 aged 68*

Ito Hirobumi was the son of a peasant. He became an attendant in a samurai (warrior) family and at the age of 14 was adopted by the family. In 1862, together with four other young samurai, he secretly boarded a British cargo ship, and went to London. When he returned he took part in the revolution which overthrew the rule of the Tokugawa shogun (warlord) in favour of the emperor. He spent the rest of his life working for the newly formed government, which wanted to reform the country and take on some western ideas. Ito helped to organize a new tax system and

▲ *Ito Hirobumi was an influential figure in the modernization of Japan.*

travelled abroad again in order to study European constitutional models before writing the Japanese constitution which set up a Diet (parliament). He served four times as prime minister, the first time in 1885 and the last in 1900.

In 1904–1905 Japan defeated Russia in a war over which country should control Korea. Ito was sent to govern Korea for the Japanese. He wanted to work with the Koreans rather than ruling by force but he was assassinated by a Korean nationalist. ◆

👁 **see also**
Tokugawa Ieyasu

Ivan the Terrible

Tsar of Russia from 1547 to 1584
Born *1530*   **Died** *1584 aged 53*

Ivan became Grand Prince of Moscow when he was only three years old. At 16 he had himself crowned 'tsar and grand prince of all Russia'. (Tsar is Russian for 'Caesar', meaning emperor.) His rule marked a turning point for Russia in foreign affairs. In 1552 he defeated the Mongol-Tartars at Kazan, so ending their 300 years of domination. The eastern road across Siberia to the Pacific was now open. Russia also tried to expand its borders westwards towards the Baltic Sea, but, even after 20 years of war, Ivan failed to keep the land he had gained.

Ivan lived up to his name 'the Terrible': in an orgy of terror in 1581 he killed not only his enemies but also his friends, and even his own son. After his son's death he became quite insane and his mad howls could be heard ringing through the Kremlin. He died in a sudden fit in 1584. ◆

▼ *By the age of 16 Ivan the Terrible was ruler of Russia.*

Andrew **Jackson**

President of the United States of America from 1829 to 1837

Born *1767*   **Died** *1845 aged 78*

Andrew Jackson was born two months after his father died. A slave on his uncle's plantation remembered him as 'the most mischievous of youngsters thereabouts'. Jackson avoided school and loved fighting and racing horses. As a 14-year-old soldier in the American Revolution (War of Independence), he was captured by the British. In prison he caught smallpox, and while he was ill his mother died. Jackson survived, and gambled away the money he had been left by his father. Later he apprenticed himself to a lawyer, but his wild ways won him few clients. He moved west, and caused a scandal by marrying his landlady's daughter before her divorce was final. Even so, his new family helped him to become a politician, a judge, and a major-general.

In 1812 America declared war on Britain because Britain was opposed to the westward expansion of the United States and was also trying to limit American trade with Europe. Jackson also fought against the Creek Indians, who had joined the British, and was nicknamed 'Old Hickory' because of his toughness. In 1815 he slaughtered British troops who were attacking New Orleans, an act that made him a hero to the American people.

Jackson was elected as the seventh president of America in 1828, and again in 1832. He was the first president to represent the pioneers of the West. These people wanted to farm the hunting grounds of the Native American Indians. President Jackson tried to move all Native American Indians to the west of the Mississippi River, a policy that caused great suffering to them. ◆

Michael **Jackson**

American singer and songwriter

Born *1958*

Michael Jackson was hailed as a singing and dancing genius from the age of six. He began his show-business career in 1970 when he and his brothers formed a group called The Jackson Five. In 1971 he began his solo career.

While filming *The Wiz*, a 1978 remake of *The Wizard of Oz* with a black cast, Jackson met producer and composer Quincey Jones. They worked closely together, and Jackson's first album with Jones was *Off the Wall* (1979), which sold 19 million copies. This was followed by *Thriller* (1982), which sold 38 million and became the biggest selling album ever, and by *Bad* (1987). ◆

Joseph-Marie **Jacquard**

French inventor of the automatic loom

Born *1752*   **Died** *1834 aged 82*

Weaving plain cloth on a loom is easy because the cross-thread (weft) passes over one long thread (warp) then under the next, then over the next, and so on. Making patterned cloth is complicated because the weft passes under a different set of threads each time it crosses the loom. If the operator makes a mistake then the pattern is ruined.

In 1805 Joseph-Marie Jacquard invented an automatic loom. This used a chain of cards punched with holes to control needles and hooks attached to the warp threads. Where a card had a hole the needle went through and the hook was lifted up. This lifted the correct set of warp threads. By using a different set of cards a different pattern could be woven.

Local weavers thought that Jacquard's loom would put them out of work. They burnt his machines and tried to drown him in the river Rhône. He survived and the French government paid him for his invention. Jacquard's design was so successful that it quickly spread throughout the world and is still used today. ◆

see also

Arkwright   Compton

Hargreaves

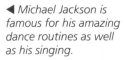

◀ *Michael Jackson is famous for his amazing dance routines as well as his singing.*

▲ *Mick Jagger is renowned for his famous pout and energetic live performances.*

Mick **Jagger**

English singer and songwriter
Born 1943

Michael Philip Jagger's father was a P.E. instructor who stressed the importance of physical fitness. Jagger heeded his father's advice and became one of the most athletic of all musical performers, the unforgettable frontman of the rock group the Rolling Stones.

The group emerged from London's thriving rhythm and blues scene in the early 1960s, and at first they were content to copy the blues songs which had inspired them. By 1963, however, Jagger was writing songs with guitarist Keith Richards, and together they produced such rock classics as 'Satisfaction' (1965), 'Jumpin' Jack Flash' (1968), and 'Brown Sugar' (1971).

Jagger has also occasionally acted, and made solo records, and in 1985 he duetted with David Bowie on a chart-topping single, 'Dancing in the Street', which raised a lot of money for famine relief in Africa. ◆

see also
Bowie

James I

James VI of Scotland from 1567 to 1625;
James I of England from 1603 to 1625
Born 1566   Died 1625 aged 58

James did not have a very happy childhood. His father, Lord Darnley, was murdered, and his mother, Mary, Queen of Scots, was executed. James became king of Scotland when he was only a baby, and was brought up strictly by Scottish nobles.

James was a highly intelligent man. He loved peace, and, unlike many others, did not want to

▼ *Like many kings at that time, James I believed his power came from God.*

persecute people for their religion. But he was lazy, extravagant, and rather undignified. He was criticized for having favourites and for giving them too much power.

When James became the first Stuart King of England he hoped for an easier life. But in 1605 a group of Catholics nearly blew him and his Parliament up in the Gunpowder Plot. The Puritans were also dissatisfied, as he did not change the Church of England as they demanded. However, in his reign a fine new English translation of the Bible was made, now called the 'King James Bible', or the 'Authorized Version'. ◆

see also
Fawkes   Mary, Queen of Scots

Henry **James**

American writer
Born 1843   Died 1916 aged 72

Henry James was born into a wealthy New York family. Determined to be a writer, he believed that Europe would provide him with more ideas for his books. In 1876 he went to Britain, and he stayed there for the rest of his life.

Altogether he wrote 20 novels and over 100 short stories. In his writing he aimed to create characters so lifelike that readers would eventually feel that they knew them as people. Such very detailed descriptions take time, and James's novels are often very long. In his shorter stories he sometimes described supernatural events, most famously in *The Turn of the Screw* (1898).

James's fiction had a large influence upon future writers who also tried to achieve the same degree of characterization and realism in their novels. ◆

Jesse **James**

American outlaw
Born 1847   Died 1882 aged 34

At the age of 15, Jesse James joined a group of southern guerrillas and fought against the Unionists in the American Civil War.

When the war ended in 1865, Jesse and his brother Frank formed a gang of outlaws. During the next ten years they carried out many daring robberies and hold-ups. Then, in 1876, one bank robbery went wrong. Most of the gang were killed or captured, but Jesse and Frank escaped and formed a new gang. There was now a price on their heads, and in 1882 a gang member shot Jesse and claimed the reward.

Legend has turned Jesse James into a hero, but he was really the leader of a ruthless gang who murdered at least ten people. ◆

▶ *A wanted man: Jesse James.*

Thomas **Jefferson**

President of the United States of America from 1801 to 1809; author of the American Declaration of Independence
Born 1743   Died 1826 aged 83

Thomas Jefferson was born in Virginia, a colony still ruled by Britain. He later inherited a large plantation there, worked by slaves. He became a successful lawyer before going in to politics and being elected to the local government. He joined in many debates on the Colonies' independence from Britain and he was so respected that he virtually wrote the Declaration of Independence himself. (It later became the basis for the American Constitution.) This declaration resulted in the American War of Independence (1776–1783).

Jefferson was elected governor of Virginia (1779–1781), and then rose up the political ladder, eventually becoming the third president of America in 1801. Perhaps his greatest achievement then was the purchase from Napoleon of the territory of Louisiana, which was soon explored by Merriweather Lewis and William Clark. However, Jefferson was probably most proud of his last great achievement, the foundation of the University of Virginia in 1819. ◆

see also
Lewis and Clark
Washington

Edward **Jenner**

English discoverer of the smallpox vaccination
Born 1749   Died 1823 aged 73

In Edward Jenner's time there were regular outbreaks of a deadly disease called smallpox and it claimed tens of thousands of lives in England alone. Jenner heard stories of milkmaids claiming that they could get protection from smallpox if they caught cowpox, a mild disease which affected cows, and he decided to investigate.

In 1796 Jenner took the contents of a blistering pimple from the arm of a milkmaid suffering from cowpox and injected it into an eight-year-old boy. The boy became ill with cowpox but soon recovered from this mild infection. Jenner then injected him with smallpox. The boy did not become ill; the cowpox had made him immune to smallpox.

In 1798 Jenner published the results of his work, and within three years people as far away as America and India were receiving the new protection from smallpox. Jenner's discovery made him rich; he was rewarded by parliament with sums totalling £30,000, an enormous amount of money in those days. ◆

see also
Pasteur

REWARD!
– DEAD OR ALIVE –

$5,000.00 will be paid for the capture of the men who robbed the bank at
NORTHFIELD, MINN.

They are believed to be Jesse James and his Band, or the Youngers.

All officers are warned to use precaution in making arrest. These are the most desperate men in America.

Take no chances! Shoot to kill!!

J. H. McDonald,
SHERIFF

Jesus

Jewish prophet and teacher who became the founder of Christianity

Born c.4 BC*
Crucified C.AD 28 or 29 aged about 32 or 33

There are four written accounts of the life of Jesus, called the gospels of Matthew, Mark, Luke, and John. They are found in the New Testament section of the Bible. The gospels gather together many stories about Jesus. According to these stories, Jesus' mother was Mary but his father was God, instead of Mary's husband, Joseph. Apart from the story of his birth in a stable in Bethlehem, not much is known about Jesus' childhood.

At about the age of 30, Jesus was baptized by his cousin, John the Baptist. After this, Jesus began to preach and large crowds gathered to listen to him. Jesus taught them to love God and their neighbours, particularly those in need. He explained that God cares more about what goes on in our hearts than about just keeping rules. He called people to be sorry for their sins, in preparation for the 'kingdom' of God. He told them that God is a father who looks after us and forgives us, and he taught them the Lord's Prayer.

Jesus' followers came to believe that he was the Messiah or Christ (a king whom the Jewish people were waiting for, to come and save them). Jesus chose 12 men from among his followers to help preach his message of love, humility, and trust in God. They were called Apostles, 'those who are sent out'.

Jesus was very popular and the Jewish religious leaders felt that he was a threat to them. Realizing that his life might be in danger, Jesus made a special occasion of his last meal with his apostles (known as the Last Supper). He took bread and

gave it to them to eat, saying 'This is my body', and gave them wine to drink, saying 'This is my blood'.

Later that night, Jesus was arrested, after Judas, one of the Apostles, had shown the Jewish religious authorities where to find him. He was put on trial before the Roman governor, Pontius Pilate, and sentenced to death by crucifixion (being nailed to a wooden cross). This day is now marked as Good Friday.

On the third day after Jesus' death, news spread that he had risen from the dead. Easter Sunday is the day when Jesus' resurrection from the dead is celebrated. Jesus' followers became known as Christians. Soon there were many non-Jewish as well as Jewish Christians, thanks to early preachers like Paul, who travelled widely through the Roman empire.

▲ *Part of a stained glass window showing Jesus blessing little children.*

Muslims also think Jesus was a prophet, but they do not believe, as Christians do, that he was God himself, who had become a human being to save the world from sin and death. ◆

*At the time when Jesus was born, the Romans dated years from the legendary foundation of Rome. About 500 years after the lifetime of Jesus, Christian scholars worked out a new system, counting from what they thought was the year of his birth. Historians now know that he was born a few years earlier than this, in about 4 BC.
BC stands for Before Christ.
AD stands for Anno Domini, 'in the year of our Lord'.

👁 **see also**

John the Baptist Mary
St Paul St Peter

► *Jinnah's portrait on a banknote from Pakistan. He is shown wearing Western clothing which was quite unusual for a Muslim leader at that time.*

Mohammed Ali Jinnah

Founding father of the state of Pakistan
Born *1876* **Died** *1948 aged 71*

While he was working as a lawyer in India, Mohammed Ali Jinnah became involved in politics. He joined the Indian National Congress, an organization which wanted India to become an independent country, free from British rule. Jinnah believed that unity between Hindus and Muslims was the best way to make this happen. However, he became concerned that the Congress was interested only in the Hindu population of India. He left and joined the Muslim League, which represented Muslim interests.

Under his leadership, the Muslim League grew in importance. During the independence negotiations with the British, Jinnah and the Muslim League fought hard for a new separate state for Muslims. Despite bitter fighting between Hindus and Muslims, this new state – Pakistan – was formed in 1947. Jinnah became governor-general of Pakistan, but he only lived for another 13 months.

In Pakistan, he is known as Qaid-i-Azam, 'the great leader'. ◆

 see also

Gandhi, Mahatma   Iqbal

Joan of Arc

French peasant girl who led the French against the English
Born *1412*   **Died** *1431 aged 18*

Joan, the daughter of a peasant, grew up in north-east France. She was a devout and intelligent child and, unlike many children then, she could also read and write.

As Joan later remembered: 'I was in my thirteenth year when God sent voices to guide me. At first I was very frightened.' The voices kept returning and she stopped being afraid. She recognized them as St Michael, St Catherine, and St Margaret, the patron saints of France. They spoke about the sufferings of France since the English had invaded, under Henry V. The true heir to the French throne, Charles the Dauphin, had not yet been crowned king. The saints told Joan to put on men's clothes to lead the fight against the English.

Joan managed to persuade Charles of her mission. He sent her with troops to Orléans, the last city in northern France still resisting the English. Within a week of her arrival in May 1429, the siege of Orléans ended. Two months later, the English had been defeated and Charles was crowned king of France in Reims Cathedral.

Known as 'the maid of Orléans', Joan carried on the fight. However, after a year she was captured by the duke of Burgundy, an ally of the

▼ *A portrait of Joan of Arc from 1420.*

English. King Charles of France made no attempt to rescue her.

The English put Joan on trial as a witch and a heretic (a person who disagrees with the Church's teaching). They insisted that the Devil inspired her to wear men's clothes and to claim such power. Joan was found guilty and was burnt at the stake in Rouen in May 1431. Twenty-five years later, the French king proclaimed her innocent, and nearly 500 years after her death the pope declared her a saint. ◆

👁 **see also**
Henry V

Sir Elton **John**

English singer and songwriter
Born 1947

Reginald Dwight went to Pinner Grammar School, then to the Royal Academy of Music in London. After college he played piano in a hotel, then later joined a local group. In 1967 he changed his name to Elton John. He went to America to appear in a concert in 1970, and became an 'overnight success'. His first international hit was 'Your Song' (1971), followed by a string of hit records and sell-out concerts. His involvement with good causes brought him into close contact with Diana, Princess of Wales, and at her funeral in Westminster Abbey he sang a specially written version of his song 'Candle in the Wind' in tribute to her. ◆

👁 **see also**
Diana, Princess of Wales

▶ *The head of a statue of King John in Worcester Cathedral.*

King **John**

King of England from 1199 to 1216
***Born** 1167   **Died** 1216 aged 48*

John was the youngest son of Henry II and Eleanor of Aquitaine. From an early age he was nicknamed 'Lackland' because, while his older brothers were all given some of Henry's lands to look after, he had nothing.

When he was king, John went too far in attacking his enemies, and he did not respect his friends enough. His supporters began to lose trust in him, and let the French king invade Normandy. In the fight to win the land back, John used every means he could to raise money in England. Finally his subjects refused to pay any more because the king was acting illegally. In 1215 they made a great list of their rights called Magna Carta (the Great Charter), and John had to agree to respect it. He died the next year, a humiliated king. ◆

👁 **see also**
Eleanor of Aquitaine   Richard I

Pope **John XXIII**

Italian Pope from 1958 to 1963
***Born** 1881   **Died** 1963 aged 81*

Angelo Roncalli came from a large farming family. They were so poor he sometimes had to carry his shoes to school to save the leather. At the age of 12 he went to the seminary (school for priests) in Bergamo and from there to Rome. In World War I he was a hospital chaplain. After the war the pope sent him to various European countries as his ambassador, and then in 1953 he became bishop of Venice.

He was unexpectedly elected pope in 1958, at the age of 76. He visited children in hospital and prisoners in jail, and was especially concerned with helping the poor and with movements for international peace. He was on good terms with the Protestant and Orthodox churches and with Jews, and this helped to change the image of the pope. He also asked the Catholic bishops from across the world to help him solve the problems of the Roman Catholic Church. More than 2000 bishops met in Rome between 1962 and 1965 at the Second Vatican Council. Unfortunately, 'good Pope John' died before the council ended. ◆

John the Baptist

Jewish prophet who lived at the same time as Jesus

Born *c.4* BC
Died *c.AD 28 aged about 32*

According to the Bible, John was the son of a priest, Zacharias, and his wife Elizabeth, who was the cousin of Mary, the mother of Jesus. In about AD 27 John began preaching on the banks of the River Jordan. He asked people to be sorry for the wrong they had done and to lead a new life. To show that they had repented and that their sins were washed away, John immersed them in the River Jordan. This sign of cleansing is called baptism and gives John his title. Jesus himself was baptized by John.

John criticized the Jewish ruler, Herod Antipas, for marrying his brother's wife, Herodias. So Herodias had John arrested and put in prison. At a banquet, Herodias persuaded her daughter Salome to dance for the king and his guests and to ask for the head of John the Baptist as her reward. Herod did not want John killed, but he had promised Salome that she could have whatever she wished, so John was beheaded. The severed head was carried in on a dish and presented to Salome, who gave it to her mother. ◆

👁 **see also**

Jesus **Mary**

Pope **John Paul II**

Polish-born Pope from 1978
Born *1920*

Before becoming pope, John Paul II was called Karol Wojtyla (pronounced Voy-ti-wa).

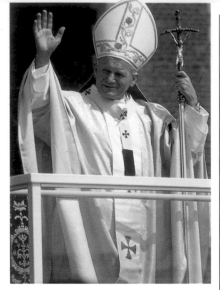

▲ *John Paul II has travelled more widely and been seen by more people than any other pope in history.*

His father was a soldier and his mother, who died when he was nine, was a teacher. 'Lolek' (as he was known) was good at studies and sports, especially football and skiing.

By the time his father died in 1941, Poland had been occupied by Nazi Germany and the Soviet Union. During World War II, Karol was forced to work in a stone quarry. His first ambition was to be an actor, and six of his plays were later published. But he thought the Polish people needed priests more urgently, so in 1946 he became a priest and went to study in Rome. In 1964 he was made Archbishop of Kraków and three years later he became a cardinal.

His election as pope in 1978 was a complete surprise. The pope before him, John Paul I, had died after only 33 days in office. Wojtyla was chosen because he was only 58, which was young by papal standards. As pope he is very strict on sexual morality, wants priests to stay out of politics, and is opposed to women priests. ◆

Amy **Johnson**

English pilot
Born *1903*   **Died** *1941 aged 37*

As a young woman, Amy Johnson became interested in flying and joined the London Aeroplane

▼ *Amy Johnson photographed in 1930 standing by her aeroplane* Jason I, *a De Havilland Gipsy Moth. This was the plane in which she made her record flight to Australia.*

Club. As well as learning to fly, she wanted to know about engines, and she became the first Englishwoman to be a qualified ground engineer for servicing planes.

In 1930 she became the first woman to fly to Australia. She was disappointed, though, because she had just failed to beat the existing record for the journey, made by another pilot, Jim Mollison. Shortly afterwards she and Mollison were married.

In the early 1930s she made a number of long-distance flights including trips to Japan, Capetown, and America. Some of these were made with Jim Mollison, and some of them alone. In 1941 her aircraft plunged into the sea and was lost in mysterious circumstances. ◆

Lyndon B. Johnson

President of the United States of America from 1963 to 1969
Born *1908*   **Died** *1973 aged 64*

Lyndon Baines Johnson was born in Texas, where he later worked as a teacher. He entered politics in 1931 as a Democrat and was elected to the House of Representatives in 1937 and to the Senate in 1949. He became vice-president when J. F. Kennedy was elected president in 1960. This meant that when Kennedy was assassinated in Dallas three years later, Johnson automatically became president himself.

America was badly shaken by the assassination and Johnson helped to restore calm by acting firmly and with dignity. This earned him a great deal of public respect. When presidential elections were held the following year, he won by a massive majority of 15 million votes.

During his time as president, Johnson improved health care for the elderly and civil rights for black Americans. However, he lost a lot of popular support when he increased American involvement in the Vietnam War, and he refused to stand for re-election. ◆

Samuel Johnson

English poet, critic, and lexicographer
Born *1709*   **Died** *1784 aged 75*

Samuel Johnson was born in Staffordshire, where he later opened a private school with his wife. When this proved to be unsuccessful he went to London with his pupil David Garrick and began a career as a writer. Although he did not make much of a living at first, he soon became well known among people in the book trade.

He was then asked to write a dictionary. This took nearly eight years to complete. The dictionary was published in 1755 and made him very famous and remained in constant use for over a century.

> *Lexicographer. A writer of dictionaries, a harmless drudge.*
>
> SAMUEL JOHNSON
> A Dictionary of the English Language (1755)

In 1764 Johnson founded the 'Literary Club' for writers and artists. One member was James Boswell who wrote a biography of Johnson, *Life of Samuel Johnson* (1791). Among other things, this book recorded many of Johnson's witty sayings since he was renowned for his conversation and wit as well as being regarded as the leading critic and literary scholar of his day. ◆

Michael Jordan

American basketball player
Born *1963*

Born in Brooklyn, Michael Jordan was a leading college basketball player at the University of North Carolina. He then began an outstanding career with the Chicago Bulls, becoming the National Basketball Association's most valuable player in 1988.

Jordan is renowned in professional American basketball for his high scoring. By 1992 he had achieved a record average of 32.3 points in 589 games for the Bulls. He is known as 'Air' Jordan because of the height he can leap.

He competed in the Barcelona Olympics in 1992 with the 'Dream Team'. This US team consisted of top millionaire professional players instead of the usual college amateurs. Not surprisingly, the team easily won the Olympic gold medal. ◆

▼ *Michael Jordan announced his retirement from professional basketball in 1998.*

Joseph

Hebrew adviser to the Pharaoh of Egypt
Lived during the 18th century BC

According to a story in the Bible, Joseph was the son of Jacob and Rachel. Jacob gave Joseph a coat of many colours and Joseph dreamed that he would be a great man. His jealous half-brothers sold him to merchants travelling to Egypt and told their father that his favourite son was dead.

Joseph was sold as a slave in Egypt and was sent to prison for offending his master's wife. In prison he told people the meaning of their dreams. When Pharaoh, the ruler of Egypt, had some strange dreams, Joseph was sent for. He said that the dreams foretold a famine. Pharaoh ordered Joseph to oversee the building of granaries to store corn before the famine came.

When Joseph's brothers travelled to Egypt to buy corn, they did not recognize him. But he knew who they were. His younger brother and father joined him to live in Egypt.

The stories of Joseph are found in the Book of Genesis in the Bible. There is a chapter named after him in the Muslim scriptures, the Koran, too. ◆

▼ *An illustration from the story of Joseph.*

James **Joule**

English scientist who experimented with heat
Born *1818* **Died** *1889 aged 70*

James Joule's father was a wealthy brewer. In his twenties, Joule helped run the brewery, but he always managed to find time for doing experiments. He had no

▲ *Joule used this electromagnet in some of his experiments.*

proper education, but taught himself whatever he needed to know.

Joule was fascinated by heat: he measured the amount of heat produced by all kinds of processes. He noticed that doing work always produces heat. The 'work' could be as different as boring a hole in a piece of metal with a drill, or pushing a wheel round with water. He found that a certain amount of work always produced a certain amount of heat.

Joule wrote about something we call 'energy', and explained that energy is never destroyed; it is just changed into different forms. When you jump up and down you use lots of energy; when you stop jumping where has the energy gone? The ground you were jumping on will have got hot, and so will you. Your jumping energy has become heat energy. This is a very important rule in science and became known as the 'law of the conservation of energy'. ◆

James **Joyce**

Irish novelist
Born *1882* **Died** *1941 aged 58*

The eldest of ten children from a poverty-stricken family, James Joyce still managed to go to university. Deciding early on to become an author, he then moved to Paris, surviving by writing and teaching. His popular book *Dubliners* (1914) contains some of the best short stories ever written. Two years later he wrote an autobiographical novel, *A Portrait of the Artist as a Young Man*. This also proved popular, although it seemed shocking to some people. But this public unease was nothing compared with the scandal following Joyce's masterpiece *Ulysses* (1922). This extraordinary novel deals with one day in the life of an unsuccessful Irish businessman. It deals equally with all sides of life and also constantly expériments with different uses of language. With its publication, Joyce became one of the most famous 20th-century novelists. ◆

> 'All moanday, tearsday, wailsday, thumpsday, frightday, shatterday.'
> JAMES JOYCE
> Ulysses

Carl **Jung**

Swiss psychologist
Born *1875*   **Died** *1961 aged 85*

Carl Jung believed, as Sigmund Freud did, that people with mental troubles could be helped by talking about them with a doctor. But unlike Freud, Jung believed that we are all born with certain problems which have to do with what sort of people we are.

Some people, for example, will always feel better in company; Jung called these 'extroverts'. Others are happier on their own; in Jung's terms, 'introverts'. Jung believed it was important for us to feel at home with both types of behaviour,

otherwise we can sometimes become rather unbalanced.

Jung discovered that his patients' dreams could sometimes give them a good idea about where they were going wrong in their lives. For example, if someone always dreamt about fierce, wild animals, Jung might suggest this was because they were refusing to face up to their own angry feelings. He would suggest that they try to turn all this energy into something creative like painting or writing.

This interest led Jung to study art and myths from all over the world. The strong similarities he found within them proved to him that all human beings are much the same at heart. ◆

◉ **see also**
Freud

Justinian

Emperor of the Byzantine Empire from 527 to 565
Born *483*   **Died** *565 aged 82*

Justinian was born in the countryside, about 180 kilometres north-west of Constantinople (modern Istanbul), which was then the capital of the Roman Empire. In Constantinople Justinian had an uncle, who was made emperor in 518. The new emperor, however, lacked a son to succeed him, so he made Justinian his heir. In 523 Justinian married Theodora, a beautiful and strong-minded woman who had once been a child actress. She became very influential and played an important part in the government of the empire.

The empire had once included all the lands round the Mediterranean, but before Justinian's birth Germanic tribesmen had conquered western Europe and north-west Africa. When Justinian became emperor, in 527, he was determined to reconquer the lost lands. His armies won back north-west Africa, Italy, and south-east Spain.

Justinian also strengthened his government. His officers compiled three collections of laws, so that people could know which laws were in use. He also encouraged the Church. In Constantinople alone he paid for 30 new churches, including Hagia Sophia, one of the largest and most magnificent churches ever built. ◆

▼ *6th-century mosaics from Ravenna, Italy, showing Justinian and Theodora.*

Franz **Kafka**

Czechoslovakian writer
Born *1883*   **Died** *1924 aged 40*

Franz Kafka was born in Prague and lived most of his life there, but he wrote in German, which was then Czechoslovakia's official language (it was still part of the Austrian empire). He lived quite an uneventful life, working for an insurance company until illness – tuberculosis – forced him to retire. In his lifetime he published only a few stories, and he left instructions for his unpublished works to be destroyed. However, the person in charge of his will, Max Brod, disregarded these instructions. Two of Kafka's novels, *The Trial* (1925) and *The Castle* (1926), published after his death, gained him a reputation as one of the most powerful and original writers of the 20th century. They are written in a beautifully clear style, but they portray a nightmarish world in which individuals are frightened and bewildered by sinister and oppressive forces of authority. ◆

Kalidasa

Indian writer
Lived during the 5th century

Kalidasa was probably the greatest Indian writer of all time. He wrote in Sanskrit, the Indian classical language of learning and religion, and is known to have been the author of at least three dramas and three long poems. He was a Hindu, possibly a Brahmin priest, and took his stories from Hindu mythology. His name means 'servant of Kali', Kali being the wife of the god Siva. Kalidasa was expert at describing the pains of love and the beauty of nature. His most famous play, *Sakuntala*, tells the story of King Dusyanta who falls in love with the beautiful forest nymph, Sakuntala. Their love is placed under a curse by the sage Durrasas, but they are eventually reunited. Their son, Bharata, became the legendary founder of India (which is officially called 'Bharat' in Hindi). ◆

▼ *An illustration from Kalidasa's* Sakuntala. *King Dusyanta and Sakuntala meet by a river bank in the forest.*

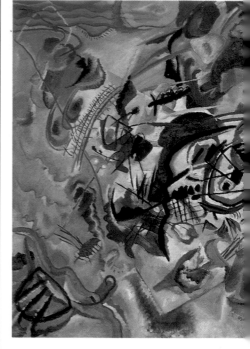

Wassily **Kandinsky**

Russian artist
Born *1866*   **Died** *1944 aged 77*

At the age of 30 Wassily Kandinsky gave up a promising career teaching law and went to art school in Munich. Since childhood he had been fascinated by colour and later on by science and music. Once he became an experienced artist he began to make experimental pictures in which colour was all important.

Kandinsky is famous as the first artist to paint pictures that did not look like anything recognizable: he was the first 'abstract' artist. He decided that painting recognizable objects harmed his pictures. Instead he wanted to make his pictures seem somehow like music: they did not mean anything in particular but they had a deep effect on the viewer. Just as musical sounds affect people deeply, Kandinsky believed colours and forms could also express and inspire emotions. These

▲ *Before Kandinsky, no one had dreamt that a work of art might not easily be recognizable as something real. His pictures, such as this one, Composition No.7 (1919), are more to do with what goes on in the mind.*

'colour music' pictures astonished the world.

Although Kandinsky was always strongly influenced by his Russian background, he travelled widely around Europe, becoming first a German and later a French citizen. His thoughts, teachings, writings, and artwork caused an artistic revolution. ◆

Immanuel **Kant**

German philosopher
Born 1724   Died 1804 aged 79

Immanuel Kant was born in the town of Königsberg (renamed Kaliningrad in 1945), then part of the German state of Prussia. He taught in its university for 42 years.

He is regarded by many as the greatest Western philosopher since Socrates. His *Critique of Pure Reason* (1781) looked at the basic philosophical question of how we know or experience something: is it because of the qualities of the object itself or because there are some ideas within ourselves that enable us to make sense of that object? Kant decided that, in addition to 'things in themselves', there exist inborn ideas, which he called 'categories'. Kant also wrote other works, including two other *Critiques* on what it means to act morally and on issues such as what we really mean when we say something is beautiful. ◆

Gary **Kasparov**

Soviet chess champion
Born 1963

Gary Kasparov was born Harry Weinstein in Azerbaijan. He was Soviet junior chess champion at 12, and an international Grand Master five years later. In 1981 he won the USSR national title,

▼ *Gary Kasparov was only 22 when he became world chess champion in 1985.*

replacing his fellow countryman Anatoly Karpov at the top of the world rankings. He challenged Karpov for the world title in 1984, but the match was postponed because both players were ill. Then, in 1985, Kasparov beat Karpov to take the title, thus becoming the youngest-ever world champion. He is now considered the greatest chess player of all time.

Kasparov favours playing planned, attacking chess. He has defended his title successfully against Karpov three times   in 1986, 1987, and 1990. In 1993 he brushed aside a challenge by Nigel Short of Great Britain in a match played in London. ◆

Kenneth **Kaunda**

President of Zambia from 1964 to 1991
Born 1924

Kenneth David Kaunda was born in Lubwe, Northern Rhodesia (now Zambia), the son of a teacher. He worked as a teacher and headmaster in Lubwe from 1943 to 1948. In 1950 he joined the African National Congress (ANC), which was seeking independence for Zambia (and other central African countries) from Britain. He worked for the ANC for many years, facing arrest and imprisonment for his activities. Then in 1958 he broke away from the ANC to form the Zambia African National Congress (ZANC). A year later Kaunda was arrested again. On his release he became president of the United National Independence Party (UNIP). In 1964 UNIP won the national elections and Kaunda became the first president of an independent and newly-named Zambia. He remained in power for 27 years until he was defeated in elections in 1991. ◆

Yasunari **Kawabata**

Japanese novelist
Born 1899   *Died* 1972 aged 72

Yasunari Kawabata became an orphan early on in his life and had a lonely childhood. After leaving Tokyo University he wrote *The Izu Dancer* (1924). This autobiographical novel contains a lot of powerful descriptions, as if Kawabata were determined to make his readers experience what he was writing about as vividly as possible.

Kawabata was very influenced by ancient Japanese poetry, and his most famous novel *Snow Country* (1956) has the atmosphere of a long poem, with one event running into another as if in a dream. In his work Kawabata often conveys an image of beauty but there is also a feeling of loneliness and a constant interest in death. He was awarded the Nobel Prize for Literature in 1968 but only four years later he committed suicide after the death of an old friend. ◆

Edmund **Kean**

English actor
Born 1789   *Died* 1833 aged 44

Edmund Kean was a child singer, dancer, and acrobat. However, he was not very happy at home and ran away to live with his uncle. At 15 he was working as an actor wandering from town to town looking for work, but it was ten years before he got his big chance – to act at the famous Drury Lane theatre in London.

With his flashing eyes and expressive style of acting, Kean soon became noted for playing wicked and villainous characters. He was considered one of the greatest tragic actors but was less successful in romantic roles. Scandals in his private life damaged his career and drink ruined his health. He collapsed while acting in Shakespeare's play *Othello* at the Covent Garden theatre in London, and died nine weeks later. ◆

Buster **Keaton**

American star of silent films
Born 1895   *Died* 1966 aged 70

Joseph Keaton's parents were comedians. They trained him when he was very young to perform in their stage act. He was given his name 'Buster' when he fell down the stairs and survived unhurt. When he was 21 he joined the comedian Roscoe 'Fatty' Arbuckle in making short films.

From 1919 he started making his own films, such as *Our Hospitality* (1923) and *The Navigator* (1924), in which he escaped from one disaster after another with hardly a single change of expression. He was nicknamed 'Great Stone Face' because of this. In his greatest film, *The General* (1927), he played an engine-driver caught up in the American Civil War. Sadly, his career ended with the arrival of the 'talkies' (talking pictures). ◆

👁 **see also**
Chaplin

John **Keats**

English poet
Born 1795   *Died* 1821 aged 25

John Keats's father died in a riding accident when John was only eight years old. Six years later his mother died of tuberculosis. When he was 16 he started to train as a doctor and later studied medicine at Guy's Hospital, London. But by this time he was determined to be a poet, and in 1817 he published his first book of poems.

While Keats never doubted his own talents, bad reviews meant that he could never earn enough money from writing alone. Even so, he went on to write some of the best-known poems in the English

▼ *Buster Keaton, seen here in a still from the 1925 film* Go West, *was one of the greatest comedians of the silent screen.*

language, including 'Ode to a Nightingale', 'The Eve of St Agnes', and the mysterious 'La Belle Dame Sans Merci'.

Keats became seriously ill after a walking tour in Scotland and later died in Rome of tuberculosis. ◆

Fast-fading violets covered up
   in leaves;
And mid-May's eldest child,
The coming musk-rose, full of
   dewy wine,
The murmurous haunt of flies
   on summer eves.

              JOHN KEATS
       'Ode to a Nightingale' (1820)

Helen **Keller**

American writer who achieved success despite being deaf and blind
Born 1880   Died 1968 aged 87

Helen Keller had a severe illness when she was a baby, which left her deaf and blind. As a result she could not make any recognizable sounds. Desperate to help her, Keller's parents employed 20-year-old Anne Sullivan, once blind herself, as her teacher. Patiently, Sullivan taught Keller the names of objects by pressing letters into her hand. She taught her to speak by letting her feel the vibrations in her own throat. Keller soon showed that she was an intelligent student. She learned to read and write fluently in Braille, and eventually studied for a university degree.

Keller tried to help as many people like herself as she could. Her own amazing success was a great inspiration, and she toured the world giving lectures. She wrote many books, including *The Story of My Life*, published in 1902. ◆

▲ An early advertisement for Kellogg's cornflakes. Today Kellogg's is a thriving multi-million pound business.

William **Kellogg**

American businessman and founder of the Kellogg Company
Born 1860   Died 1951 aged 91

William Kellogg worked with his brother John at a hospital in Battle Creek, Michigan. Because his brother was the director of the hospital, Will Kellogg was able to try out all sorts of cereal foods in an attempt to improve patients' diets. Toasted cornflakes proved to be so popular that Kellogg started to sell them to the general public, first of all by mail order. Although cornflakes were not entirely new, they had never before been sold as a breakfast food. The Kellogg Company was set up in 1906 to manufacture them and Kellogg advertised them energetically: they were a big success. Cornflakes dramatically changed American breakfast-eating habits and made Kellogg a fortune. In 1930 he started the W. K. Kellogg Foundation, a charity which gave large sums of money for social improvements. It particularly supported work to help children. ◆

Ned **Kelly**

Australian outlaw
Born 1855   Died 1880 aged 25

Ned Kelly's father was transported as a criminal from Ireland to Australia. From the age of 15 Kelly was also constantly in trouble. Between 1878 and 1880 he operated in the Kelly Gang with his brother and two others. They were famous for holding up and killing three policemen in 1878, and had a price of up to £2000 on each of their heads.

The police seemed powerless against them. Many were outraged by their crimes, but to others Ned Kelly became a hero. He claimed to be fighting for justice for the poor against the rich and powerful.

The final shoot-out with police came after an attempted train ambush. Kelly tried to escape in a suit of armour, but was shot in the legs. He was tried for murder and hanged in Melbourne jail. ◆

◀ The home-made suit of armour worn by Ned Kelly.

William **Kelvin**

British physicist
Born 1824   Died 1907 aged 83

William Thomson Kelvin was born in Ireland but when he was six his family moved to Scotland. His father taught him and William proved to be a brilliant student. He went to Glasgow University at the age of ten and was writing important scientific papers when he was just 16. In 1892, after making many contributions to science and industry, he was made Baron Kelvin of Largs. (Largs is a Scottish town.)

Kelvin was a pioneer in the study of electromagnetism. He and Michael Faraday put forward the idea of an electromagnetic 'field'. Later James Clerk Maxwell used this suggestion in his famous theory on electromagnetism.

Kelvin was very practical and he invented several devices concerned with sending messages through wires. In 1866 Queen Victoria knighted him for designing a transatlantic telegraph cable.

Kelvin also did important work in the field of thermodynamics. Most importantly, he put forward the idea of absolute zero – the temperature at which all molecules and atoms stop moving. The scientific unit of temperature is named after him. ◆

👁 **see also**

Faraday Joule Maxwell

John Fitzgerald **Kennedy**

President of the United States of America from 1961 to 1963
Born 1917   Died 1963 aged 46

John Kennedy was one of nine children. His elder brother Joe

▲ *J. F. Kennedy was the youngest man to be elected as the president of America. He was also the youngest to die while in office.*

was killed in 1944. Kennedy's father had decided Joe would be president one day; John now took Joe's place.

The whole family helped Kennedy win his first election as a Democratic member of the House of Representatives in 1946. One opponent said, 'It's that family of his. They're all over the state.' He received the same support in 1952 when he became a senator from Massachusetts.

In 1960 he was elected president of America. Handsome and inspiring, in his first speech he said, 'My fellow Americans, ask not what your country can do for you, but what you can do for your country'.

Although he was energetic and intelligent, Kennedy soon faced problems. He gave American help to Cuban refugees trying to invade Communist Cuba. They failed, making America look foolish. Nevertheless, Kennedy did stop the USSR from building nuclear missile bases on Cuba in 1962. He also sent military advisers and troops to Vietnam, which led, after his death, to American involvement in the Vietnam War. At home, he proposed laws to give black Americans equal rights, but Congress did not pass these laws in his lifetime.

> *Mankind must put an end to war or war will put an end to mankind.*
>
> JOHN KENNEDY, 1961

In November 1963 Kennedy travelled to Dallas, Texas, to gather support in the American South. He was shot and killed by a sniper while travelling in an open car. The world mourned Kennedy not only for what he did, but for the good he could have done had he lived. ◆

see also
Khrushchev

Jomo **Kenyatta**

President of Kenya from 1964 to 1978
Born *c.1894*   **Died** *1978 aged about 84*

Kamau wa Ngengi was born into the Kikuyu tribe in Kenya. He was baptized Johnstone Kamau and educated by Scottish missionaries before getting a job in Nairobi. Jomo Kenyatta, as he became known, joined the Kikuyu Central Association and visited London on their behalf. He lived in Britain during the 1930s and studied anthropology.

Back in Kenya, Kenyatta became president of the Kenya African

▼ *Jomo Kenyatta, first president of the independent Republic of Kenya.*

Union in 1947. At this time many Kikuyu formed a secret group called 'Mau Mau' which used violence to drive white farmers from Kikuyu lands. Although he denied it, Kenyatta was suspected by the British rulers of Kenya of leading Mau Mau. In 1953 he was sentenced to seven years' hard labour. Although released from prison in 1959 he was kept under close watch until 1961. Then, when Kenya became independent of Britain in 1963, Kenyatta became the first prime minister. In the following year he was made the first president of the Republic of Kenya. His years in power brought some stability and prosperity to the country. ◆

Johannes **Kepler**

German astronomer
Born *1571*   **Died** *1630 aged 58*

Johannes Kepler was the son of a soldier. His early intention was to be a Lutheran Church minister and he studied theology at university. But it turned out that he had a flair for mathematics, and his interest in astronomy grew.

In 1594 he became a professor of mathematics at Graz, where he settled and married. Four years later the family was forced to flee because of religious persecution and he went to work for the Danish astronomer Tycho Brahe. When Brahe died in 1601, Kepler got his job. He also inherited a huge number of Brahe's astronomical observations.

Using Brahe's observations of Mars, Kepler proved that the planet's orbit around the Sun is an oval shape and not a circle. Later he worked out two more important laws about the orbits of the planets.

Kepler's whole life was afflicted by war, religious persecution, bad

▲ *Johannes Kepler discovered three important laws of planetary motion.*

luck, and ill health. Yet he is remembered as one of the greatest astronomers of his age. ◆

John Maynard **Keynes**

English economist
Born *1883*   **Died** *1946 aged 63*

John Maynard Keynes was a successful pupil at Eton school and at Cambridge University, where he went on to become a lecturer. During World Wars I and II (1914–1918 and 1939–1945) he was an adviser on economics to the government.

Economics is the science which studies trade, industry, employment, finance, and banking. Keynes believed in an economy planned by the government. He proposed that financial crises and unemployment could be prevented if the government intervened and took control of interest rates and public spending. Politicians and economists have argued about Keynesian economics ever since. Some say his ideas do not work; others say that they have never been properly tried. ◆

Imran **Khan**

Pakistani cricket captain
Born *1952*

Imran Khan perfected his cricket at school in Lahore, Pakistan, and in Worcester, England, before going to Oxford University where he captained the cricket team in 1974. He then took up county cricket, playing for Worcestershire and for Sussex.

He made his test début for Pakistan in 1971 and became captain in 1982. He has played for his country 75 times and is only the third player to score over 3000 test runs and take 300 test wickets. In 1983 he became the second player to score a century and take ten wickets in a test match. In first class cricket he has scored over 16,000 runs and taken over 1200 wickets.

Javed Miandad and Imran Khan were the only players to appear in all of the first five World Cup tournaments. Khan has also taken a record 34 wickets in World Cup matches. ◆

▲ *Ayatollah Khomeini (second from left) ruled Iran under strict and traditional Islamic religious principles.*

▶ *Imran Khan captained Pakistan to victory in the World Cup in 1992.*

Jahangir **Khan**

Pakistani squash champion
Born *1963*

The name 'Jahangir' means 'conqueror of the world', and that is exactly what Jahangir Khan became in the world of squash. He came from a family of squash players and at 15 won the World Amateur championship of 1979.

In 1981 he lost to the Australian Geoff Hunt in the final of the British Open championship. Astonishingly he did not lose another game until 1986, when he was beaten by Ross Norman of New Zealand in the world championship final. In the course of that remarkable run of victories, Khan become world squash champion five times in a row (1981–1985). He won the world championship again in 1988. ◆

Ayatollah Ruhollah **Khomeini**

Iranian religious leader
Born *1900*   **Died** *1989 aged 89*

Ayatollah Ruhollah Khomeini was born in Khomein, central Iran. He spent most of his life studying the Islamic faith and teaching at the holy city of Qum, where he was recognized as an 'Ayatollah' (guide sent from God). It was not until he was in his sixties that he became directly involved in the world of politics.

In the 1960s he spoke out against the shah (king) of Iran who was using Iran's oil-wealth to change the country's old way of life. Khomeini was against giving more freedom to women and taking land and education out of the hands of religious leaders. In 1964 he was forced to live abroad because of his opposition to the shah. However, the rapid changes in Iran made the shah so unpopular that in 1979 he fled abroad and Khomeini returned.

For the next ten years Khomeini was the most important person in Iran. He did not actually govern but little could be done without his approval. In the name of Islam, opponents of his rule were imprisoned, tortured, and executed.

Anybody wanting to banish theft from the world must cut off the thief's hands.

AYATOLLAH RUHOLLAH KHOMEINI

Iran was feared by neighbouring countries and the West as a supporter of terrorists. A war with Iraq was fought from 1980 to 1988 with great loss of life on both sides. When Khomeini died in 1989 there were scenes of wild grief in Iran. ◆

Nikita Khrushchev

Soviet leader who denounced Stalin
Born 1894   Died 1971 aged 77

Nikita Sergeyevich Khrushchev was a metal worker who joined the Communist Party in 1918. He became a party worker in Kiev and Moscow, where he became First Secretary in 1935. He became Secretary of the Ukraine region in 1938, but resigned during World War II to organize resistance in the Ukraine against German forces. When Stalin died in 1953 there was a power struggle amongst the Communist leaders. Khrushchev emerged as First Secretary of the Communist Party. In an historic speech at the Party Congress in 1956 he took the bold step of denouncing Stalin. People finally realized the bad things Stalin had done, and Khrushchev's power grew. In 1958 he became prime minister. Although he wanted peace with America he almost went to war with them over the Cuban missile crisis in 1962. Two years later he was replaced by Brezhnev and Kosygin who initially shared power. ◆

👁 **see also**
Kennedy
Stalin

Khufu

Egyptian pharaoh; builder of the Great Pyramid
Lived during the 26th century BC

Khufu is best known as the builder of the Great Pyramid at Giza on the banks of the River Nile. The pyramid, together with others nearby, was one of the seven wonders of the ancient world.

The ancient Egyptians made elaborate preparations for the journey after death to the next world. The Great Pyramid was made mainly of locally quarried limestone. About 2,300,000 blocks weighing about two-and-a-half tons each were used to build the structure, which was originally 146 metres high. Building such a pyramid required great skill – the construction had to be carefully measured and the stones cut to fit accurately. Each of the pyramid's four sides was built at an angle of exactly 52 degrees. Today the Great Pyramid still dominates the skyline even though many of its outside blocks of stone have been rubbed away over time. ◆

▼ *The Great Pyramid, built on the order of the Egyptian king Khufu.*

◀ *Jean-Claude Killy in action.*

Jean-Claude Killy

French champion skier
Born 1943

Jean-Claude Killy had very strong legs which helped him to become an excellent ski racer. He was world champion in 1966 and was awarded the 'National Order of Merit' by France's President de Gaulle. In 1967 he won the World Alpine Skiing Cup, having won every downhill event he entered.

Probably his finest moment came at the Grenoble Winter Olympics of 1968 where he won the three gold medals for the downhill, slalom, and giant slalom races; he was also world champion again that year. He then decided to become a professional skier and to try to make a living from acting in films and television commercials. ◆

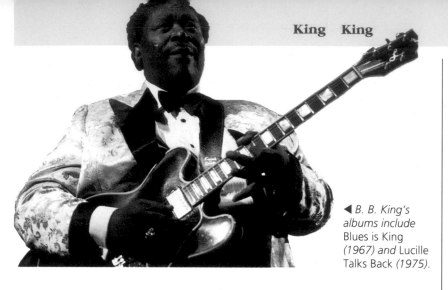

◀ B. B. King's albums include Blues is King (1967) and Lucille Talks Back (1975).

B. B. **King**

American blues guitarist and singer
Born 1925

R iley King was born to sing the blues: he grew up during the Great Depression, a poor black farm boy in the tough southern state of Mississippi. He was always musical, singing in church when he was four, and learning guitar as a teenager. He became known as 'Blues Boy', a nickname he later shortened to 'B. B.' King.

He started recording in 1949, and his distinctive guitar playing on such early classics as '3 O' Clock Blues', 'Please Love Me', and 'You Upset Me Baby' immediately revealed him to be a master musician. King has remained both popular and influential over the years, and together with his faithful guitar 'Lucille' he is one of the most familiar figures in blues music. ◆

Martin Luther **King** Jr

American civil rights leader
Born 1929   **Died** 1968 aged 39

A t the age of 15 Martin Luther King Jr went to college on a special programme for gifted students. After gaining his degree in divinity in 1948, he trained to be a Baptist minister as his father and grandfather had been before him.

He became a pastor in Montgomery, Alabama, two years later, and joined the struggle for black people's rights straight away. He led a boycott of the buses in Montgomery because they had separate seats for blacks and whites. The blacks shared cars or walked until the bus company gave in and allowed all passengers to sit anywhere they chose.

This victory convinced King that the best way for black people to win their rights was to break laws in a non-violent way. In Atlanta and Birmingham, he led 'sit-ins' by blacks in 'whites only' eating places. In spite of being attacked, arrested, and imprisoned, King and his followers kept up their campaign. In August 1963, 200,000 people joined their march on Washington. At the end of this march, he gave his famous 'I have a dream' speech, which inspired millions of people throughout the world to campaign for civil rights. Here is an extract:

'I have a dream that one day this nation will rise up and live out the true meaning of its creed: "We hold these truths to be self-evident; that all men are created equal." I have a dream that one day on the red hills of Georgia the sons of former slaves and the sons of former slave-owners will be able to sit down together at the table of brotherhood. I have a dream that my four little children will one day live in a nation where they will not be judged by the colour of their skin but by the content of their character.'

▼ *Martin Luther King Jr waves to the crowd during the civil rights march in Washington in 1963.*

The next year the Civil Rights Bill was made law and King was given the Nobel Peace Prize. However, other black leaders opposed him because they believed that blacks should fight violence with violence.

In 1968 he was killed by a sniper in Memphis, Tennessee. Only the night before his death, King said: 'I may not get to the promised land with you, but I want you to know tonight that we as a people will.' ◆

👁 **see also**

Malcolm X

William Lyon Mackenzie **King**

Prime minister of Canada from 1921 to 1930 and from 1935 to 1948
***Born** 1874   **Died** 1950 aged 75*

William Lyon Mackenzie King was named after his grandfather, William Lyon Mackenzie, who had been the first mayor of Toronto. He had led a rebellion in 1837 demanding a better deal for the hard-working pioneer farmers. King wanted to help ordinary people too.

He began his career in politics in 1900, and as minister of labour drafted a law to help people settle strikes. He became leader of the Liberal Party in 1919 and was elected prime minister in 1921. King's government introduced Canada's first old-age pension and developed a foreign policy independent of Great Britain.

The problems caused by the world economic crisis in 1929 led to King's government losing the 1930 election to the Conservatives. However, he returned to power in 1935 and led his nation through the war years 1939–1945. After the war his government provided free training for returning soldiers. It also introduced family allowances and unemployment insurance to protect people from hardship. ◆

Mary **Kingsley**

English explorer and traveller in Africa
***Born** 1862   **Died** 1900 aged 37*

Mary Kingsley's father was a doctor who spent most of his time travelling abroad. Her mother was constantly ill and Mary looked after her and her little brother. She was never given any schooling, but she learned to read and taught herself Latin, physics, chemistry, mathematics, and engineering from her father's library. From his letters and books she learned about warm countries beyond England with strange plants and animals.

Her parents died when she was 30 and she was left poor and alone. However, she was determined to visit the places she had read about.

During 1893 and 1894 she travelled in West Africa to collect specimens of fish for the Natural History Museum in London, and to gather information about African religions. She explored the forests north of the River Zaïre (Congo) on foot and by paddling in a dug-out canoe. She became very interested in the lives of the African people.

She wrote two successful books and became a popular lecturer. In 1900 she went to South Africa to nurse the soldiers in the Boer War. She died there of fever. ◆

▶ *Mary Kingsley was one of the most famous travellers in Africa during the 19th century. Through her journeys and her encounters with the local population, she challenged the accepted view of the 'primitive' native.*

▲ An illustration by Kipling for one of his Just So Stories, *'How the Elephant Got His Trunk'.*

Rudyard **Kipling**

Indian-born English author
Born *1865*   **Died** *1936 aged 70*

When Rudyard Kipling was only six years old he was sent by his British parents from their home in India back to England. There he spent five miserable years staying with a foster-mother he hated. However, he became much happier when he went to boarding school, and was quickly noticed as a budding young writer.

At 16 he returned to India and began writing short stories and poems describing the lives of the British and Indian people. In 1894 he wrote *The Jungle Book*, which includes stories about an Indian child, Mowgli, brought up by a family of wolves.

Kipling next wrote the *Just So Stories*: a series of fables describing how the leopard got its spots, the camel its hump, and many others. His finest novel, *Kim*, about an orphan boy of the same name, appeared in 1901. Kipling was the first English writer to win the Nobel Prize for Literature (in 1907). ◆

Horatio **Kitchener**

British soldier
Born *1850*   **Died** *1916 aged 65*

Horatio Kitchener was born in south-west Ireland. He decided to become a soldier and joined the British army in 1871. Before long he was promoted to senior posts. From 1892 to 1899 he was commander-in-chief in Egypt, and defeated Sudanese Muslims at the famous battle of Omdurman (1898). From 1900 to 1902 he led the British army in the Boer War, and defeated the Afrikaner people of South Africa. He served in India as commander-in-chief (1902–1909) and in Egypt (1911–1914).

In 1914 war broke out in Europe. Germany and Austria-Hungary stood on one side; France, Russia, and Britain on the other. Britain's prime minister, Herbert Asquith, made Kitchener secretary of state for war. Kitchener feared that the war would be long and gruelling and Britain would need a bigger army. He modernized the British forces and soon recruited a million men. In summer 1916 he sailed for Russia, but his ship hit a mine and sank. Kitchener drowned. ◆

▲ Kitchener calls for volunteers on a World War I army recruiting poster.

Paul **Klee**

Swiss painter
Born *1879*   **Died** *1940 aged 60*

Paul Klee is one of the best-loved artists of the 20th century. He produced a huge amount of work (oils, water-colours, drawings, prints), but he had an astonishingly vivid imagination and never repeated himself. Some of his paintings are purely abstract, but most of them are based on the things that he saw around him. They are full of radiant colours and a joyous love of life.

Klee spent most of his career in Germany, where he was much admired as a teacher of art as well as for his work as a painter. When

Hitler came to power in 1933, however, he opposed all modern art and Klee was forced to give up his teaching post in Dusseldorf and return to Switzerland. In the last five years of his life he suffered from a painful illness and was depressed by political events as Europe headed for war. He continued to paint superb pictures, but in them a grim humour often replaced the playful wit of his earlier work. ◆

John **Knox**

Scottish religious reformer who set up the Protestant Church of Scotland
Born *1505*   **Died** *1572 aged 67*

John Knox was a devout Protestant as a young man when Scotland was still a Catholic country, ruled with French help. He went to England, and became a chaplain to Edward VI, but when Catholic Mary I came to the throne he and many other Protestants had to escape. He spent most of his exile in Geneva, Switzerland, where he was influenced by John Calvin.

In 1559 he returned to Scotland, determined to set up a Protestant Kirk (Church) like Calvin's at Geneva. His fiery preaching helped to begin a rebellion, which forced out the Catholics. He drew up the 'Scottish Confession', a statement of Protestant beliefs. No one was supposed to go to Catholic services, nor obey the pope.

Although the Catholic Mary Queen of Scots arrived in Scotland in 1561, the Protestant Kirk grew stronger. Knox made things very

The First Blast of the Trumpet Against the Monstrous Regiment of Women.

JOHN KNOX
Title of one of his pamphlets

difficult for Mary and she lost her throne in 1567, partly because of him. His preaching and writing played an important part in the formation of the Protestant Church in Scotland. Protestants there who followed him were afterwards called Presbyterians. ◆

see also
Calvin   Mary I   Mary, Queen of Scots

Robert **Koch**

German bacteriologist
Born *1843*   **Died** *1910 aged 66*

Robert Koch studied medicine at the University of Göttingen in Germany. His teacher there believed that diseases were caused by microscopic organisms. Koch spent his life identifying these organisms and applying his knowledge to the world's most deadly diseases. He and his assistants devised a method of growing bacteria outside the

body so that the bacteria can then be studied.

Koch started work on the animal disease, anthrax. He studied the life cycle of the tiny bacteria that cause anthrax and also found the tiny spores which infect the land where animals graze.

Koch then studied tuberculosis (TB). Today TB can be prevented by inoculation but it used to be a deadly killer causing thousands of deaths each year. The bacteria responsible are extremely small but Koch used his superb practical skills to identify and grow them. This work enabled others to develop a vaccine against the disease.

Koch spent the rest of his life studying other diseases such as cholera, bubonic plague, and malaria. He was awarded the Nobel Prize for Medicine in 1905. ◆

see also
Jenner   Pasteur

▼ *Koch was also a teacher, and many of his students became great scientists.*

Helmut **Kohl**

German chancellor from 1982 to 1998
Born 1930

Helmut Kohl became an active member of the German Christian Democratic Union (CDU Party) in 1947, and in 1959 he was elected to the local parliament in West Germany. In 1973 he became the CDU Party's national chairman, and in 1982 chancellor (prime minister) of West Germany.

Kohl is a passionate believer in international co-operation. He made strong links with the USA, and strengthened the ties between West Germany and the rest of the European Community (now the European Union, or EU). After World War II Germany was split into two parts, and Berlin was divided by a huge wall. When the Berlin Wall fell in 1989, Kohl was instrumental in bringing East and West Germany together. When they merged in 1990 to become the Federal Republic of Germany, Kohl became chancellor. He was re-elected for the last time in 1994. ◆

Paul **Kruger**

President of the first South African Republic from 1883 to 1904
Born 1825   Died 1904 aged 78

Paul Kruger's parents were Boer farmers in southern Africa. The Boers were the descendants of Dutch settlers who did not like the power that the British had in southern Africa. In 1835 Kruger's family, along with many other Boers, travelled north to form their own independent country. They settled in territory they called the Transvaal.

In 1877 Britain decided that the Transvaal should also come under its rule. Kruger, by this time a respected politician, led the opposition to this and became a general in a rebel army against British troops. In 1883 the Transvaal regained its independence from Britain and Kruger was elected as its first president. He was re-elected three times.

However, more trouble was to come. When gold was first discovered, prospectors from all over the world rushed out to South Africa. The new settlers were not

▲ *A sketch of Paul Kruger from a 1900 edition of the magazine* Vanity Fair.

popular with the Boers, and Kruger did his best to exclude them from the Transvaal, banning them from full citizenship until they had been in the country for at least seven years. The British government objected to this, and the second Boer War followed. After the Boers were defeated, Kruger went to Europe and eventually died in Switzerland. ◆

Alfred **Krupp**

German industrialist
Born 1812   Died 1887 aged 75

As a young man Alfred Krupp inherited a share in a nearly bankrupt steel works in Essen from his father Friedrich. Gradually he restored the business, bought out his co-heirs, and founded one of the world's great industrial dynasties. His steel was in huge demand for railways, steamships, and later for armaments.

In 1862 he introduced the Bessemer steel-making process from Britain and secured control of German coal and Spanish iron-ore supplies. He was a stern employer but noted for his concern for his employees. He was succeeded by his son Friedrich (1854–1902) and later his daughter Bertha (1886–1957). In World Wars I and II the Krupp firm supplied vast quantities of arms to the German government. Krupp's grandson Alfred was imprisoned by the Allies for war crimes, but soon released: once again the House of Krupp flourished, but this time as a public corporation. ◆

👁 see also
Bessemer

Kublai Khan

Mongolian general and ruler
Born 1215   Died 1294 aged 79

Kublai Khan was a grandson of Genghis Khan, one of the most terrifying soldiers in history, who had begun life as an obscure chief of a wandering tribe and ended it as ruler of a huge empire in central Asia. When Kublai was ten years old, he fought on horseback in his grandfather's last campaign.

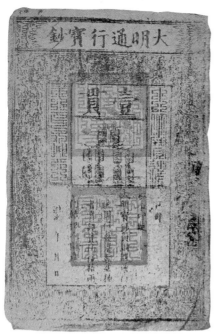

▲ *One of the first banknotes issued by the Mongolian ruler Kublai Khan.*

When Kublai grew up and became leader (Great Khan) of the Mongols he completed his grandfather's conquest of China and established his capital at Khanbalik (now Beijing). Kublai added Korea and Burma to his Yuan (Mongol) empire, which now stretched from the Black Sea to the China Sea. His rule was reported to be harsh and he enforced obedience. He appointed many foreigners, including the Venetian explorer Marco Polo, to work for him. It is through Polo's praise of the wonderful riches that he found in the East that the name of Kublai Khan became known in Europe. ◆

👁 see also

Genghis Khan   Marco Polo

▶ *A character from Kurosawa's 1954 western-style masterpiece, Seven Samurai.*

Akira **Kurosawa**

Japanese film director
Born *1910*   **Died** *1998*

After the tragedy of the great Kanto earthquake of 1923, Japanese audiences were ready for light entertainment, and Akira Kurosawa remembered the imported films that he saw in the following year. They helped shape the style of his films when he became a director.

Sanshiro Sugata, his first film, was criticized by the army in 1943 for being too foreign. After the war, *They Who Tread on the Tiger's Tail* was banned by the American authorities because it was thought to be 'anti-democratic'. Many of his films tell dramatic stories from violent periods in Japanese history; some of them have been called 'eastern westerns'. Kurosawa was awarded a special Oscar in March 1990 for his unique contribution to cinema. ◆

Marquis de **Lafayette**

French soldier, revolutionary, and politician
Born *1757*   **Died** *1834 aged 77*

The Marquis de Lafayette was as famous in America as he was in his native France. He became a popular American hero when he joined the French, who were fighting alongside American colonists against the British in the American Revolution (War of Independence). He was at the battle of Brandywine and at the final conflict at Yorktown in 1781. Several American towns were even named after him, including ones in Louisiana, in Alabama, and in Indiana.

During the French Revolution, which began on 14 July 1789, the people formed a National Assembly to rule the country. Their slogan was 'liberty, equality, fraternity'. Lafayette became the vice-president of the National Assembly and introduced a declaration of citizens' rights similar to the American Declaration of Independence.

Hated by king and court, Lafayette was forced to flee his country in 1792. He returned later and played a leading part in the revolution of 1830. ◆

Lao Tzu

Chinese thinker
Lived during the
6th century BC

▲ *The Chinese philosopher Lao Tzu is commonly regarded as the founder of Taoism.*

Chinese scholars traditionally held Lao Tzu to be the author of *Tao Te Ching* (The Book of Changes), which sets out the basic ideas of the Taoist religion. However, it is now thought that *Tao Te Ching* dates from the 3rd century BC, while western scholars believe Lao Tzu may have lived in the 6th century BC and that the book was written by several authors. At least 350 other books have tried to explain its teachings.

Taoists believe that all things are connected and the aim of life is peace and harmony. Taoism tells people to trust their senses and instincts rather than reason and official laws as Confucius taught. Under the T'ang dynasty (618–907)

> *A journey of a thousand miles must begin with a single step.*
>
> LAO TZU

Lao Tzu was worshipped as an ancestor of the emperors. Even after Taoism lost official favour it remained popular with ordinary people and was a great influence on Chinese art. There are still 2000 Taoist temples in Taiwan. ◆

see also
Confucius

Pierre Laplace

French mathematician and astronomer
Born *1749*
Died *1827 aged 77*

Pierre Simon Laplace came from a poor farming family but showed such intelligence that neighbours paid for his school education. By the age of 18 he had been appointed professor of mathematics at the Paris Military School. His success led to him becoming a Count of the Napoleonic Empire and a Marquis.

His work as an astronomer is reckoned by scientists to be second only to Isaac Newton's. Laplace proved the stability of the Solar System (showing that no two planets could collide), studied the orbit of the Moon, and worked on the shape and rotation of Saturn's rings. He also introduced the nebular hypothesis of the origin of the Solar System: the theory that the Solar System originated from a cloud of gas. He wrote a

number of very important and influential books yet, at the end of his long life, he said 'What we know is minute; what we are ignorant of is vast'. ◆

see also
Newton

René La Salle

French explorer
Born *1643*   **Died** *1687 aged 44*

René La Salle was born into a wealthy family in Rouen, France. As a young man he went to 'New France' – the French colonies in Canada. There he began to explore, with a view to seeking new land for the French settlers.

His biggest achievement was to travel the length of the Ohio and Mississippi rivers to the Gulf of Mexico, claiming the lower valley of the Mississippi for France in 1682 and calling it 'Louisiana' after the French king, Louis XIV.

La Salle's last expedition was by sea, with a fleet of ships, to the Gulf of Mexico. He wanted to see if a

colony could be set up at the mouth of the Mississippi. However, the fleet got lost, and after two years searching for the Mississippi delta, La Salle's men mutinied and killed him. ◆

Laurel and Hardy

English and American comic actors
Stanley Laurel
Born *1890* **Died** *1965 aged 75*
Oliver Hardy
Born *1892* **Died** *1957 aged 65*

Stanley Laurel, whose real name was Arthur Stanley Jefferson, was an English comedian who played in pantomimes before travelling to America. He started appearing in films there in 1917. Oliver Norvell Hardy came from Georgia, America, where he first appeared on stage at the age of eight. He started acting in films in

▼ *Laurel and Hardy, one of the most successful comedy partnerships.*

1914. Both appeared in dozens of silent films before they began their successful partnership in the 1927 silent comedy *Putting Pants on Philip.*

In the next 30 years they made over 100 silent and talking pictures, and achieved great success with films such as *Sons of the Desert* (1934), *Way Out West* (1937), and *Blockheads* (1938). Their humour came from the contrast between the small, thin, confused Laurel and the big, fat, irritable Hardy. ◆

Rod Laver

Australian tennis player
Born *1938*

At 13, Rod Laver was selected for a tennis coaching course by a Brisbane newspaper. As a left-handed player, called 'the Rockhampton rocket' after his home town, he became good enough to win the Australian Amateur championship in 1960. Two years later he did the 'Grand Slam', winning the Australian, French, US, and Wimbledon championships in the same year.

He then turned professional, and was barred from these championships until they became 'open championships' (for both amateur and professional players) in the late 1960s. In 1969 Laver won the Grand Slam once again. ◆

Antoine Lavoisier

French chemist who became known as the 'father of modern chemistry'
Born *1743* **Died** *1794 aged 50*

As a young man Antoine Lavoisier became interested in improving street lighting and studied how different fuels burnt in

▲ *This is the apparatus used by Lavoisier to investigate burning. The substances to be burned were placed in the furnace (left). The change in water level in the bell jar (right) showed how much air was used up during the burning.*

lamps. Burning became a subject that interested him and his careful experiments of burning substances in air, and those of the English chemist Joseph Priestley, made Lavoisier realize that air contains two gases; he called one 'oxygen' and the other 'azote', which we now know as nitrogen. He proved that when a substance is burnt it combines with oxygen in the air. This really moved chemistry into the modern age. Lavoisier went on to give chemicals many of the names we now use and arranged them into family groups.

Lavoisier came from a wealthy family and invested his money in a business called tax-farming. The tax-farmers were paid by the government to collect all the taxes. Their profits provided Lavoisier, and other investors, with a great deal of money. But many of the people were poor and hated tax-farmers. During the French Revolution they rebelled, and by 1794 France was ruled by people who hated the king, the aristocracy, and tax-farmers. Lavoisier was found guilty of being a tax-farmer and was executed by the guillotine. ◆

👁 **see also**

Priestley

D. H. **Lawrence**

English novelist
Born *1885*   **Died** *1930 aged 44*

David Herbert Lawrence was the son of a coal-miner and a schoolteacher. He went to Nottingham University and trained as a teacher. By this time he had started writing, and in 1913 produced his greatest novel, *Sons and Lovers*. This describes his childhood and the strong relationships he had both with his mother and with friends. In other novels, such as *The Rainbow* (1915), Lawrence describes his characters' most secret feelings.

Later on, Lawrence felt that British industrial society was too cut off from nature and genuine feelings. With his wife, Frieda, he travelled extensively in search of the ideal surroundings for his restless spirit. His poor health gradually got worse, and he finally died in France of tuberculosis. ◆

T. E. **Lawrence**

English hero who helped in the Arabs' struggle for independence; also known as Lawrence of Arabia
Born *1888*   **Died** *1935 aged 46*

As a young man, Thomas Edward Lawrence enjoyed exploring castles and following the routes of the crusaders in Palestine. He learnt Arabic and travelled around North Africa.

In 1914 Lawrence went to Cairo as a British intelligence officer to help Arab troops to free their country from Turkish rule. Lawrence led dashing camel-back raids to dynamite railway lines. The Turks offered a high price to anyone who could capture 'al-Urans, destroyer of engines'. In 1917 he was captured and tortured. After the Turks were defeated, Lawrence became a hero. But he refused all honours and retired to write *The Seven Pillars of Wisdom*, which describes his experiences in the Arabs' struggle. Lawrence was bitterly disappointed when Britain and France did not give the Arabs complete independence.

Lawrence died in 1935 when he swerved on his motorbike to avoid two boys on a country road. ◆

▼ *T. E. Lawrence photographed in the traditional Arab clothing that he often wore.*

Leakey family

British archaeologists who discovered fossil humans in East Africa
Louis Leakey   **Born** *1903*
Died *1972 aged 69*
Mary Leakey   **Born** *1913*
Died *1996 aged 83*
Richard Leakey   **Born** *1944*

Louis Leakey is best remembered for his archaeological work in East Africa, where he made his first discoveries between 1925 and 1936.

Louis and his wife Mary concentrated their explorations for fossils in the Olduvai Gorge in Tanzania. In 1959 Mary discovered a skull of a large 'southern ape', *Zinjanthropus* (later called *Australopithecus*) *boisei*, which dated back about 1.7 million years. The Leakeys also discovered the remains of *Homo habilis*, at that time the earliest human known, and *Homo erectus*, the maker of many beautiful implements found throughout Africa.

After Louis' death, Mary continued at Olduvai Gorge, uncovering living places and implements of East Africa's earliest inhabitants. Then, at Laetoli, in Tanzania, she discovered the footprints of our ape-like ancestors who lived more than 3.5 million years ago.

Their son Richard Leakey has made important discoveries of human fossils at many places in East Africa and Ethiopia. In 1984 he discovered an almost complete *Homo erectus* skeleton at Lake Turkana in Kenya. His first love, though, is wildlife, and he is now in charge of Kenya's game parks. ◆

Edward **Lear**

English poet who wrote limerick verse
Born *1812*   **Died** *1888 aged 75*

Edward Lear was the 20th child
of a wealthy stockbroker and
his wife. But when he was 13 his
father lost all his money and went
to prison, and the children had to
find work.

At 19, Edward produced a book
of drawings of the parrots at
London Zoo, and the Earl of Derby
invited him to his estate to draw his
animals too. While he was there,
Edward made up limericks and
illustrated them for the earl's
grandchildren. He published them
in *A Book of Nonsense* in 1846, and
they were an immediate success.

He spent most of his life
travelling, painting, and writing
'nonsense' verse. In these verses
nutcrackers, chairs, birds, and
creatures like the Dong with the
Luminous Nose, the Pobble, and the
Jumblies were given human feelings
and characters. Lear invented words
such as the 'runcible' spoon and the
'scroobious' bird. ◆

Le Corbusier

European architect
Born *1887*   **Died** *1965 aged 77*

Le Corbusier – the name adopted
by Charles-Edouard Jeanneret –
was born in Switzerland. He
became famous for his campaign to
construct new types of buildings.
He thought that houses should be
on columns, to free the ground
underneath, with flat roofs for
terraces and gardens. In flats with
limited space, Le Corbusier mixed
large, open-plan, sometimes split-
level rooms, with much smaller
rooms for sleeping.

Le Corbusier believed that

modern towns could offer decent
living conditions to large
populations. In 1925 he designed a
workers' city of 40 houses in
France. However, local people were
suspicious of his designs, and he
had more success planning
individual houses. Then in 1947 he
was given another opportunity and
designed a large housing complex
for 1800 people in Marseille. The
plan for this *Unité d'Habitation*
included a school, a hotel and, on
the roof, a nursery, open-air theatre,
and gymnasium.

Although he had many fresh
modern ideas for housing, some
people still preferred more
traditional ideas – an argument that
continues to this day. ◆

Robert E. **Lee**

*Commander of the Confederate troops
during the American Civil War*
Born *1807*   **Died** *1870 aged 63*

Robert Edward Lee studied at
the US Military Academy at
West Point, before becoming an

▲ *This picture shows the Battle of
Winchester (September 1864) during the
American Civil War of 1861–1865. After
winning several battles between 1862
and 1863, Lee's Confederate army of the
South finally surrendered in 1865.*

army officer. In the war between
America and Mexico (1846–1848),
his bravery made him famous.

Many years later, when the Civil
War broke out, Lee decided to
return to Virginia where he was
born. In April 1861 he resigned from
the US army and trained the
Confederate army of the South. They
won several major victories but were
poorly equipped; they did not have
enough guns and had little food.

At the battle of Gettysburg in
1863 Lee's forces were
outnumbered and defeated. For
the next year and a half he was
forced back on the defensive until
his ragged and hungry army
surrendered at Appomattox
Courthouse in April 1865.

Lee spent the last five years of
his life as president of Washington
College in Virginia. ◆

 see also

Grant   Lincoln

Lee Kuan Yew

Prime minister of Singapore from 1959 to 1990
***Born** 1923*

After studying law at Cambridge University, England, Lee Kuan Yew founded the People's Action Party in Singapore in 1954. He became the first prime minister of independent Singapore in 1959 and helped to make the country one of the most prosperous in Asia, with excellent public housing, transport, health, and education services. He insisted on discipline and order, imposing strict laws against litter, long hair, and chewing-gum. Impatient of criticism, he was quite prepared to lock up awkward journalists, strikers, and political opponents and to ban satellite television because, unlike the local news media, he could not control it. Lee gave up office in 1990 but remained powerful behind the scenes. ◆

Anton van Leeuwenhoek

Dutch pioneer of the microscope
***Born** 1632   **Died** 1723 aged 90*

Anton van Leeuwenhoek worked in a fabric shop in Amsterdam. When he was 22 he went home to Delft, opened his own shop, and stayed there for 70 years.

He was always interested in scientific things and made a simple microscope with just one lens. Until that time, people had treated the microscope more like a toy than a useful scientific instrument. Leeuwenhoek used his microscope to study the fibres of the fabrics he worked with and then began to look at leaves and flowers, and

▲ A portrait of Anton van Leeuwenhoek from 1695.

small creatures such as bees and lice. He also studied blood, skin, and hair. He was the first person to describe blood cells and to see that blood flowed in tiny veins known as capillaries. ◆

👁 **see also**
Hooke

Gottfried Leibniz

German philosopher, mathematician, and physicist
***Born** 1646   **Died** 1716 aged 70*

Leibniz was one of the greatest thinkers of the 17th century. He tackled philosophical questions and was devoted to the cause of world peace. He was a scientist, too, and met Huygens and Boyle among others, and suggested new ideas about force, time, and energy.

> *Two things are identical if one can be substituted for the other without affecting the truth.*
> GOTTFRIED LEIBNIZ, 1704

His greatest achievement was the discovery of a new mathematical method called calculus. Scientists use this to deal with quantities that are constantly varying. Newton had developed a similar method for his work on gravity and so there was a bitter row about who had been first. Newton had started work on it in 1665 but Leibniz published his results in 1684, three years before Newton. In fact, they probably discovered the method simultaneously. ◆

👁 **see also**
Boyle   Huygens   Newton

George Lemaitre

Belgian astronomer
***Born** 1894   **Died** 1966 aged 72*

George Lemaitre was born in Charleroi, Belgium and studied to be an engineer. After being a soldier in World War I his interest changed to science.

During the 1920s, astronomers noticed that the universe seemed to be spreading out in all directions and this puzzled them. Lemaitre suggested that everything in the universe was once squashed together like a snowball. This exploded, blowing everything apart, like bits flying away from a snowball when it hits a wall. Although this happened a long time ago, the parts of the universe – the galaxies and stars we see today – are still moving apart, long after the 'big bang'. Today, many astronomers agree with Lemaitre's 'big bang' theory of the universe. ◆

👁 **see also**
Hubble

Vladimir **Lenin**

Communist ruler of the new USSR from 1917 to 1924
***Born** 1870   **Died** 1924 aged 53*

When Lenin was 17, his elder brother was hanged for trying to kill the Russian tsar. This opened Lenin's eyes to the problems of his country: a weak tsar, a corrupt Church and nobility, and millions of poor and angry peasants and factory workers. Like many people, Lenin saw revolution and the Communist ideas of Karl Marx as the only solution.

Within a few months of going to university in 1887 to study law, he was expelled for taking part in a student protest meeting. After getting his degree in 1891, he continued his political activity, and was sent first to prison and then into exile in Siberia. While he was in Siberia he took the name 'Lenin', from the River Lena.

In 1898 the Russian Social-Democratic Workers' Party was formed. In an effort to gain power, Lenin helped to split the party in 1903, leading the Bolsheviks ('Majority') against the Mensheviks ('Minority'). The Bolsheviks later became known as the Russian Communist Party.

From 1905 until 1917, Lenin lived in exile. He returned to Russia when the tsar was overthrown and a new government began to rule. Lenin called for a revolution to put a Bolshevik government into power and this revolution led to him becoming the real ruler of Russia. In 1922 the old Russian empire was transformed into the Union of Soviet Socialist Republics (USSR). It lasted until 1991. Lenin's embalmed body is kept in a mausoleum in Red Square, Moscow. ◆

see also

Gorbachev Marx Stalin Yeltsin

Suzanne **Lenglen**

French champion lawn tennis player
***Born** 1899   **Died** 1938 aged 39*

Suzanne Lenglen came from a poor family, but her parents backed her ambition to succeed as a tennis player. She won her first big championship aged 15 and her first Wimbledon title in 1919.

▲ *On the 100th anniversary of his birth, a third of the people of the world were living in countries run by Communist governments inspired by Lenin's first successful Communist revolution.*

After that, she lost only one match until 1926. In seven years, Lenglen captured six Wimbledon singles and doubles titles as well as the Olympic championship in 1921. She became a professional player in 1926, which meant she could no longer compete in amateur tennis tournaments such as Wimbledon and the Olympics.

Most all-time rankings of women tennis players place Suzanne Lenglen first. Her success made women's tennis a popular and important sport. ◆

◀ *Suzanne Lenglen in action during the 1922 Wimbledon championships.*

Lennon and McCartney

English songwriters and musicians
John Lennon
Born *1940*   **Died** *1980 aged 40*
Paul McCartney
Born *1942*

When they met in 1957, John Winston Lennon and James Paul McCartney were just two Liverpool teenagers with a passion for rock 'n' roll. Lennon was wild and rebellious while McCartney was more studious, but this unlikely partnership was to revolutionize popular music in the 1960s.

They were the principal songwriters in the Beatles, and the incredible success of their songs kept the group at the top of the charts for seven years. These songs ranged from catchy pop to psychedelic rock, and included such all-time favourites as 'She Loves You' (1963), 'Yesterday' (1965), 'Yellow Submarine' (1966), and the classic album *Sgt. Pepper's Lonely Hearts Club Band* (1967).

Lennon and McCartney started recording separately in 1970 when the Beatles split up. Neither was as consistent on his own, although McCartney in particular has enjoyed some enormous solo hits. Lennon's peace anthem 'Imagine' (1971) has become a much-loved classic and was widely played at the time of his murder in 1980. ◆

▼ *McCartney and Lennon singing together in the incredibly successful group, the Beatles.*

▲ *The mysterious half-smile of Leonardo da Vinci's* Mona Lisa *still fascinates visitors at the Louvre Museum, Paris.*

Leonardo da Vinci

Italian artist, scientist, and inventor
Born *1452*   **Died** *1519 aged 67*

The young Leonardo da Vinci was described as handsome, strong, and charming, a talented musician and an excellent conversationalist. At 15 he was apprenticed to a leading Italian artist who taught him painting, sculpture, metal casting, mosaics, jewellery, and costume design. At 20 he was a master painter but considered himself to be as much an engineer as an artist.

He began many grand paintings but actually finished very few. Although his artistic output was small he brilliantly solved the problem of how to make faces and people look three-dimensional on a flat surface by shading light into dark. His painting *Mona Lisa* is probably the most famous portrait in the world. Another of his great masterpieces is a wall painting of *The Last Supper*.

Leonardo wanted to understand and know about everything he saw. He was one of the first to dissect human bodies and understand how muscles and bones work, and how a baby grows in the womb.

He examined all of nature: how plants and trees grow, how rocks are formed, and what laws govern the wind and oceans. He even suggested that the Sun stood still, and did not move around the Earth as most people believed. He also planned buildings, and worked out how to divert a river and how to construct canals. He invented weapons and acted as military adviser to the Duke of Milan. His skills also included arranging festivals and grand theatricals and inventing amusing mechanical toys.

Although Leonardo was both greatly admired and highly respected he was not really understood. His scientific work was far ahead of that of his contemporaries, including a flying machine nearly 400 years before the first powered aircraft, and most of his ideas remained in his notebooks undeveloped. It is amazing that one man could have created so much. ◆

Ferdinand de **Lesseps**

French engineer and diplomat
Born *1805*   **Died** *1894 aged 89*

Between the ages of 21 and 44, Ferdinand de Lesseps worked as a diplomat in several countries. During his late twenties he worked in Egypt. While working there, he had the idea for the Suez Canal. It would connect the Mediterranean Sea to the Red Sea through Egypt. At that time, ships sailing between Europe and Asia had to pass round Africa – a very long route.

Work began in 1860, thanks to Lesseps's enthusiasm and planning (and despite British opposition at first). Progress was expensive and slow, but in 1869 the canal was opened. Lesseps became a national hero in France, and was honoured in Britain.

His next project was the Panama Canal, begun in 1881, linking the Pacific and Atlantic oceans. It was dogged by technical and financial problems, and in 1893 Lesseps was found guilty of bribery. By then, however, he was very ill, and he died shortly afterwards. ◆

see also

Eiffel

Carl **Lewis**

American athlete
Born *1961*

Carl Lewis comes from a sporting family. His father is a sports teacher, his mother and sister are international athletes, and his brother is a soccer player. Lewis's own career is one of the most successful ever in athletics history. Not only has he had the longest run of long jump victories ever, but he has also been the world's best sprinter.

In 1983 he had three wins at the Helsinki world championships. Then, at the 1984 Olympics, he equalled Jesse Owens's record of four gold medals, triumphing in the 100 m, 200 m, long jump, and 4 × 100 m relay. He retained his gold medals for 100 m and the long jump at the 1988 Seoul Olympics. ◆

C. S. **Lewis**

English author
Born *1898*   **Died** *1963 aged 64*

After a lonely childhood, partly spent playing imaginative games with his older brother, Clive Staples Lewis became an outstanding scholar who taught at both Oxford and Cambridge universities. He wrote academic books and science fiction for adults and then decided to write books and stories for children too.

The Lion, the Witch and the Wardrobe was the first of a series of seven stories which describe the activities of a family of children who stray into the fairyland world of Narnia. In each story they are faced by a choice between good and evil. The adventures are so exciting that many young readers miss the fact that Lewis is using the stories as an allegory to preach a Christian message. His great hero, Aslan the lion, is a symbol for Jesus Christ. ◆

◀ *Olympic gold-medal winner Carl Lewis.*

◀ *A painting of Lewis and Clark on the Columbia River during their expedition to the Louisiana Purchase territory (1804–1806).*

Lewis and **Clark**

Leaders of the first expedition to cross the American continent
Meriwether Lewis
Born *1774* **Died** *1809 aged 35*
William Clark
Born *1770* **Died** *1838 aged 68*

In 1803 the US government bought from France a large piece of land in North America called 'The Louisiana Purchase'. President Thomas Jefferson decided to send an expedition to explore it and to cross the Rockies to reach the Pacific Ocean.

Jefferson chose Meriwether Lewis to lead the expedition, and he then chose William Clark, an expert on Native American Indians, to go with him. With about 40 other men, mostly soldiers, they started out in 1804 from St Louis, in boats and canoes up the Missouri river.

Eventually, they left the river and climbed a pass through the Rocky Mountains. They had many adventures, including close encounters with grizzly bears, which no white man had seen in America before. In November 1805 they reached the Pacific Ocean. After the winter they returned by roughly the same route.

The explorers brought back a lot of information about the land, the Native American Indian population, and the plants and animals. The expedition's many journals and maps were studied for years afterwards. ◆

◉ **see also**
Jefferson

Abraham **Lincoln**

American president from 1861 to 1865
Born *1809*   **Died** *1865 aged 56*

As a child, Abraham Lincoln hardly ever went to school, but he loved reading. Books were scarce and expensive then; he read the Bible and *Aesop's Fables* over and over again.

Lincoln tried various jobs before becoming a lawyer, a politician, and eventually a candidate for the presidency of the United States. During his campaign to be elected president, one of his main concerns was the split between Americans who thought slavery was wrong, and those who thought it was right. In a speech in 1858, he said 'I believe this government cannot endure permanently half slave and half free.' Two years later he was elected president.

After the American Civil War began in 1861, Lincoln was criticized at first because the North did not win quickly. Then, on 1 January 1863, he introduced the Emancipation Proclamation, freeing all US slaves. (Southerners, of course, did not free their slaves until they had lost the war.)

In 1863, Lincoln made a speech after the terrible battle of Gettysburg, saying that the soldiers had died so 'that government of the

▼ *The statue of Abraham Lincoln at the Lincoln Memorial in Washington, DC. It stands 5.8 m tall.*

people, by the people, for the people, shall not perish from the earth'. Later, Americans realized that Lincoln had summed up the spirit of democracy.

Lincoln had plans for healing the wounds caused by the war, but was killed before he could carry them out. He was shot by a fanatical supporter of the southern states. ◆

see also
Grant   Lee

Charles Lindbergh
American aviation pioneer
Born 1902   Died 1974 aged 72

Charles Lindbergh always had an ambition to fly aeroplanes. He went to college in 1920, but soon left so that he could learn to fly. After a time in the Army Air Service he had a regular job flying mail across America.

In 1926 a prize was put up for the first non-stop flight from New York to Paris. Several famous airmen decided to attempt this. Some were killed in the attempt. On 20 May 1927 Lindbergh took off in a specially built aeroplane called the *Spirit of St Louis*. He landed at Le Bourget Airport, Paris, $33\frac{1}{2}$ hours later, having flown 5800 km.

Lindbergh became a hero on both sides of the Atlantic, and went on to be an important adviser during the growth of long-distance air travel. Towards the end of his life he became interested in conservation, and opposed the development of supersonic aeroplanes as he believed they would have a bad effect on the Earth's atmosphere. ◆

▶ *Lindbergh described his journey across the Atlantic in a book,* Spirit of St Louis, *which won him a Pulitzer Prize.*

Carolus **Linnaeus**
Swedish botanist
Born 1707   Died 1778 aged 70

Carolus Linnaeus was fascinated by plants from an early age and was lucky enough to live at a time when many new plants and animals were being discovered.

When he was older, Linnaeus worked out a method of giving two-part names to every different species. In this way each kind of plant and animal had a name which was not used for any other. It was said at the time that 'God created; Linnaeus set in order', for his system made it possible for each new discovery to be slotted into an arrangement of similar species.

Linnaeus was made professor of medicine and then of botany at Uppsala University, Sweden, where he had been a student. In 1753 he became a Knight of the Polar Star in recognition of his work, and later he was made a count.

Wherever he went he collected

plants and made notes on all that he saw. He published over 180 works, the most important of which is *Systema Naturae*, which is still used today by scientists who classify the living world.

Linnaeus was born Carl Linné but became known as Carolus Linnaeus as all his works were in Latin. ◆

Joseph **Lister**
British surgeon who introduced sterilization in operating theatres
Born 1827   Died 1912 aged 84

Joseph Lister trained to be a doctor and attended one of the first operations to be performed under anaesthetic. He was appalled at the huge number of people who died after surgery. Surgeons, working in their ordinary clothes, and with unwashed hands, boasted that they could cut off a leg in 25 seconds. Not surprisingly, many of the patients died.

Lister tried moving the patients' beds further apart to prevent infection, but things were no better. Then he read Louis Pasteur's findings about bacteria in the air, and began to look for something that would keep operating theatres perfectly clean.

Lister suggested that as carbolic acid was used to purify sewage, perhaps it would kill bacteria in surgery too. Carbolic acid was sprayed into the air during operations, and heat was used to kill bacteria on the knives and instruments that were used. At first no one believed Lister's success, but by 1879, most of the London hospitals were using his methods, and many patients lived who would have died without them. ◆

see also
Pasteur

Franz **Liszt**

Hungarian composer and piano virtuoso
Born *1811*   ***Died*** *1886 aged 74*

Music came naturally to Franz Liszt. He began to play the piano when he was only five, and gave his first public concert when he was nine. A group of Hungarian noblemen were so impressed they gave him money to study in Vienna and Paris. By the time he was 12 he was being compared with the greatest adult pianists of the day.

◀ *Liszt was a handsome young man whose piano recitals made him as popular and wealthy in his own time as the pop stars of today.*

Liszt was more than just a great pianist: he was also a fine composer. His music was technically brilliant and very adventurous, and pointed the way to new musical developments. One of his inventions was the symphonic poem, an orchestral work that told a story in terms of music. *Les Préludes*, *Mazeppa*, and *Hamlet* are examples, but he also wrote vast quantities of music of all kinds. ◆

David **Livingstone**

Scottish missionary and explorer
Born *1813*   ***Died*** *1873 aged 60*

Although his family was poor, David Livingstone worked very hard and saved enough money to train as a doctor. In 1841 he sailed for southern Africa to join a Christian mission station in what is now Botswana.

In 1853 Livingstone began his first great expedition to search for new trade routes through Africa. He walked from the middle of Africa to the Atlantic coast, then headed east until he reached the Indian Ocean. He was the first European to see the Victoria Falls. When Livingstone returned to Britain in 1856 he was hailed as a hero because he was the first European to cross Africa from west to east.

Livingstone's second expedition, up the Zambezi River by steamboat, was a disastrous failure. His wife died of fever and many other lives were lost before the expedition collapsed in 1864.

Livingstone's third expedition, to find the source of the River Nile, began in 1866. He vanished and some people thought he had died. But in 1871 the American journalist Henry Morton Stanley found Livingstone on the shore of Lake Tanganyika. 'Dr Livingstone, I presume,' were Stanley's famous words when they met.

Livingstone died in 1873. His body was shipped to England and buried in Westminster Abbey. ◆

◀ *An elephant trumpets a greeting as Livingstone's boat, the Ma Roberts, passes by on a voyage along the Shire River in Malawi, Africa.*

David **Lloyd George**

British prime minister from 1916 to 1922
Born 1863 Died 1945 aged 82

As a young Liberal Member of Parliament, David Lloyd George began to fight for a better life for poorer people. By 1908 he was appointed Chancellor of the Exchequer, and in 1911 he introduced new legislation making richer people pay more in taxes to help the sick and unemployed.

When World War I broke out in 1914, Britain was poorly prepared and at first did not do very well. Two years later the prime minister, Asquith, was pushed out and Lloyd George took his place. He set about winning the war, and struggled to make people, especially the army generals, change their old-fashioned ways. In 1918 victory came, and Lloyd George easily won the general election that followed. He began the task of helping to rebuild Europe, and helped set up the League of Nations to keep the peace. In 1922 he was forced to resign by his opponents, but he remained an important figure in British politics until the 1940s. ◆

Llywelyn the Great

Mediéval Welsh ruler
Born c.1172 Died 1240 aged about 67

Although he was heir to the kingdom of Gwynedd (Snowdonia) in north Wales, Llywelyn·spent his childhood in exile. When he was older he fought back, and by 1194 he had deposed his uncle David. By 1200 he had become master of most of northern Wales. Five years later he married the illegitimate daughter of King John of England, and began to threaten English lands in the south. This was too much for King John, who invaded Wales in 1211.

Fortunately for Llywelyn, John's troubles in England meant that he had little time to deal with the Welsh. Seizing his chance, Llywelyn forced Welsh rulers to recognize his leadership. Two years after John's death, the English acknowledged that Llywelyn was ruler of most of Wales. Shortly before his death, he became a monk, after a lifetime spent encouraging the Welsh to think of themselves as a united people. ◆

see also
King John

John **Locke**

English philosopher .
Born 1632 Died 1704 aged 72

John Locke was one of the most learned men of his time, educated in the sciences, politics, religion, and philosophy. But he was a practical as well as an academic man. He would advise young people, whose company he greatly enjoyed, not to waste their free time on playing games, but to find pleasure in doing useful things like gardening or carpentry.

He published a number of books which have greatly influenced political and philosophical thought. His most famous, *Essay Concerning Human Understanding*, explores the idea that experience is the only source of knowledge. He was also a firm believer in the rights of the individual, and wrote that no one, whether priest or ruler, has the right to force another person to take on his/her beliefs. ◆

Henry Wadsworth **Longfellow**

American poet
Born 1807 Died 1882 aged 75

The son of a lawyer, Henry Wadsworth Longfellow was a university teacher before deciding to concentrate on writing. He soon became the most famous American poet of his time. His works include 'Paul Revere's Ride', 'The Wreck of the Hesperus', and 'Excelsior'. These have strong rhythms and tell their exciting

▲ *Hiawatha, the hero of Longfellow's epic poem, sails into the sunset in this 1910 edition of* The Song of Hiawatha.

stories in vivid language. Longfellow's most famous poem is the longer *The Song of Hiawatha*. This describes the life of Hiawatha, an Indian brave who was brought up by the daughter of the Moon. He becomes leader of his tribe before hard times lead to the death of his lovely wife, Minnehaha. Before his own death Hiawatha warns about the coming of the white man. The whole poem is told in a catchy, almost sing-song rhythm. ◆

Louis XIV

King of France from 1643 to 1715
Born *1638*   **Died** *1715 aged 76*

Louis XIV became King of France at the age of four on the death of his father. His mother, Anne of Austria, at first ruled for him, helped by her powerful chief adviser, Cardinal Mazarin.

After Mazarin died, Louis was determined to rule alone. As he said himself, 'L'état, c'est moi' ('I am the state'). He became known as the Sun King because he chose the Sun as his royal badge.

Although he brought some improvements to France, there were darker sides to his reign. He fought expensive and unsuccessful wars and at home he was cruel to the Huguenots (Protestants), telling them that they had to become Roman Catholics. Two hundred thousand of them refused and left the country.

Louis had a magnificent palace built in Versailles. However, the life of luxury that he and his court enjoyed angered those who were struggling to survive. After ruling for 72 years, he died a lonely figure, no longer respected by his people. ◆

Louis XVI

King of France from 1774 to 1792
Born *1754*   **Died** *1793 aged 38*

Louis XVI came to the throne at the age of 19. A weak man, he often relied on the advice of his strong-minded wife, the beautiful Marie Antoinette of Austria, even though she was unpopular because of her high spending. Eventually the French nobles began to oppose much that Louis tried to do.

In 1788 he summoned the estates-general (a sort of parliament) to

▲ *This plate commemorates the execution of King Louis XVI in 1793.*

help him get his way against these nobles. However, it only added to his troubles by demanding reforms on behalf of the people. When the French Revolution started in 1789, Louis and his family were taken away and kept under guard.

Instead of trying to come to an agreement with the new forces in France, Louis and his family fled from Paris in a horse and carriage in 1791, but he was recognized and brought back. In 1792 he was found guilty of treason for having dealings with enemies of the Revolution, and in 1793 he was beheaded by guillotine. Nine months later Marie Antoinette met a similar fate. ◆

see also
**Danton   Marie Antionette
Robespierre**

Joe **Louis**

American world-champion boxer
Born *1914*   **Died** *1981 aged 67*

Joseph Louis Barrow was born in Lafayette, Alabama. He became a professional boxer in 1934 and world heavyweight champion in 1937 when he knocked out the reigning champion James Braddock. He was the first black man to be allowed to fight in the world championship for 22 years.

Nicknamed the 'Brown Bomber', Joe Louis successfully defended his title a record 25 times over a period of almost 12 years. Out of 66 professional fights, he won 63; 49 were by knockouts.

He retired in 1949, but made two unsuccessful comebacks. His last important fight was in 1951 when he lost to Rocky Marciano. ◆

Ignatius **Loyola**

Spanish founder of the Society of Jesus (also known as the Jesuits)
Born 1491   Died 1556 aged 65

Born in Spain, Ignatius Loyola became a knight and fought in battles. In 1521, however, he was hit in the legs by a cannon-ball. He was badly wounded and underwent two operations. While recovering, he read books about Jesus and the saints which affected him deeply.

▲ *A portrait of Saint Ignatius Loyola by Rubens.*

After this spiritual transformation Loyola lived in a cave for a year, thinking and praying. After visiting Jerusalem in the Holy Land, he returned to Spain to study to be a priest. He also studied in Paris, where he met a group of like-minded companions.

When in Rome shortly afterwards, Loyola and his companions decided to create a new 'order' of religious men. Called the Society of Jesus, its members ('Jesuits') aimed to spread the ideas of Christianity. In 1540 Pope Paul III gave his approval for the Society. Loyola became leader, and wrote the Society's rules. He also completed his famous book of prayers, *The Spiritual Exercises*. By the time of Loyola's death there were over 1000 Jesuits, working in many countries. ◆

Lumière brothers

French inventors of the first films
Auguste Lumière
Born 1862   Died 1954 aged 91
Louis Lumière
Born 1864   Died 1948 aged 83

Auguste and Louis Lumière's father, Antoine, was an artist and photographer. The boys were extremely clever and when Louis was only 18 they started a factory for making photographic plates.

In 1894 Antoine visited Paris where he saw Thomas Edison's 'kinetoscope', a machine where you looked through a hole at a series of pictures inside a spinning drum. He was amazed by the appearance of movement this created. When he told his sons about it, they immediately set about solving the problem of projecting moving pictures on to a screen. Louis, inspired by watching the action of a sewing machine, designed a mechanism for holding each 'frame' in front of the light beam for a split second before moving the next one into position.

In 1895 the Lumière brothers demonstrated their *cinematographe* in Paris. Even though their first film only showed workers leaving the Lumière factory, the audience was wildly enthusiastic and the cinema industry was born. ◆

👁 **see also**

Edison

▼ *Auguste and Louis Lumière opened the world's first cinema in Paris to show their films.*

▲ *A page from Martin Luther's German translation of the Bible (c.1530).*

Martin **Luther**

German religious reformer
Born *1483*   **Died** *1546 aged 62*

As a young monk, Martin Luther was worried that the Catholic Church had become too wealthy and powerful and that many churchmen had forgotten the teachings of Jesus.

Luther became a priest in 1507 and a teacher of theology (religion) at the University of Wittenberg in Saxony. However, it was not long before an argument began between Luther and other churchmen. He said that people must study the Bible for themselves, and did not need to say a certain number of prayers, or go to special church services. This implied that priests, and the whole organization of the Catholic Church, were not really so important.

Soon Luther was in trouble. In 1520 he was expelled from the Catholic Church by the pope. In the following year, the Holy Roman Emperor, Charles V, ordered Luther to appear before a special meeting of all the princes in Germany. Luther still refused to give up his beliefs, even though the emperor condemned him, and he was in danger of being put to death.

Fortunately for Luther, the ruler of Saxony protected him and some other German princes supported him too. He was able to spend the rest of his life teaching and writing. He also got married and raised a large family.

By the time Luther died, his followers (called 'Lutherans') had formed a new Protestant Church which was quite separate from the Catholic Church. ◆

see also

Calvin

Albert **Luthuli**

Zulu leader who campaigned peacefully against apartheid
Born *1898*   **Died** *1967 aged 69*

Albert Luthuli was born into a Christian Zulu family in Southern Rhodesia (now Zimbabwe). His father was a Christian missionary. After teaching for 15 years Luthuli was elected tribal chief in his family home at Groutville, Natal.

After World War II he joined the African National Congress (ANC) which was working for black people to be given full political rights in South Africa. Luthuli did not believe in violence; instead he led campaigns of peaceful disobedience against the apartheid laws that kept people of different races apart.

When he was elected president of the ANC in 1952, the government responded by taking away his chieftainship. Later he was arrested, and in 1959 he was banned from leaving his home district for five years. The following year the ANC itself was banned. Despite the ban, Luthuli was allowed to go to Oslo in 1961 when the Swedish government awarded him the Nobel Peace Prize for all that he had done in opposing discrimination against black people in South Africa. ◆

see also

Buthelezi   Mandela

Douglas **MacArthur**

Commander of the United States army during World War II
Born *1880*   **Died** *1964 aged 84*

Following in his father's footsteps, Douglas MacArthur joined the US army. He was an outstanding soldier. In 1930 he was appointed

▼ *General Douglas MacArthur photographed in the Philippines in 1944.*

◄ A scene from a production of Shakespeare's Macbeth in which Macbeth, holding the bloodied weapons he has used to kill Duncan, discusses the terrible deed with his wife.

Chief of Staff, and from 1935 he organized American defences in the Philippines (a US territory).

In December 1941, more than two years after the beginning of World War II, Japanese armies landed in parts of south-east Asia, including the Philippines. MacArthur and his forces resisted the invasion at first but were eventually forced out. MacArthur was transferred to Australia and for two years commanded Allied attacks against the Japanese. Finally, in the spring of 1945, American troops recaptured the Philippines.

MacArthur, who was now the commander of all US army forces in the Pacific, received the Japanese surrender in September 1945. He was then placed in command of the Allied occupation of Japan and took an active role in many reforms.

Five years later, North Korea invaded South Korea. The United Nations agreed to support the South and MacArthur was ordered to oppose the invasion. His forces pushed the North Koreans back, but were forced to retreat from an invading Chinese army. He eventually repelled the Chinese but then had ideas about attacking China itself. President Truman would not agree to this plan and MacArthur was dismissed. ◆

Macbeth

King of Scotland from 1050 to 1057
Born *c.1005*
Died *c.1057 aged about 52*

Macbeth was a king of Scotland who became the subject of the play *Macbeth* written by William Shakespeare in 1606. Shakespeare based some of his play on facts he found in *Chronicles of England, Scotland, and Ireland* (1577) by Raphael Holinshed, the 16th-century historian. Macbeth was commander of the forces of Duncan I, king of Scotland. He seized the Scottish throne after he had defeated and killed Duncan in battle in 1040. In Shakespeare's play, Macbeth murders Duncan after a prophecy spoken by three witches, and with encouragement from his wife, Lady Macbeth.

Macbeth's reign was prosperous until he himself was defeated in 1054 by Malcolm III, son of Duncan, and Siward, Earl of Northumberland. However, Macbeth remained king until he was killed by Malcolm in 1057. Lulach, Macbeth's stepson, then reigned for a few months before Malcolm succeeded him. ◆

👁 **see also**

Shakespeare

John A. Macdonald

First prime minister of Canada, from 1867 to 1873 and from 1878 to 1891
Born *1815* **Died** *1891 aged 76*

John Alexander Macdonald emigrated with his family from Scotland to Kingston, Upper Canada (now Ontario) when he was five years old. When he was ten he was sent to a boarding school. At the age of 15 he began to work in a law office and before he turned 21 he opened his own office and became a successful lawyer. Macdonald's personal life was not always happy. His first son, John Alexander, died when just a baby. His first wife, Isabel, spent most of her life sick in bed. A daughter from his second marriage was an invalid.

Macdonald was first elected to government in 1844. In 1865 he and a former rival, George Brown, began persuading others to unite Britain's six North American colonies to form a single country – or 'confederation'. He chaired the London conference of 1866 to create the Dominion of Canada and he was chosen to be Canada's first prime minister the following year.

During his years as prime minister, Canada expanded territorially with the new provinces of Manitoba, British Columbia, and Prince Edward Island, and also experienced growth in its economy. Macdonald encouraged the building of a railway across the country and the development of industry. ◆

Ramsay **MacDonald**

Prime minister of Britain in 1924 and from 1929 to 1935
Born 1866   Died 1937 aged 71

Ramsay MacDonald, the son of a Scottish maid, became a Labour Member of Parliament in 1906. He became leader of the Labour Party in 1911, but resigned at the start of World War I because of his unpopular belief in negotiation, not war, with Germany. He was re-elected as party leader in 1922 and in 1924 became the first Labour prime minister, serving from January until November. He won a second term in 1929. However, unemployment was very high and in 1931 MacDonald recommended a cut in unemployment benefits to help solve the financial crisis. His cabinet rejected this idea but MacDonald was able to continue as leader by forming a national coalition government with the support of Conservatives and Liberals. The Labour Party called him a traitor and expelled him. Nevertheless he remained in office until failing health forced his resignation in 1935. ◆

Niccolò **Machiavelli**

Italian political writer
Born 1469   Died 1527 aged 58

Niccolò Machiavelli was born near Florence in Italy. Little is known about his life until 1498, when he was appointed to an important post in the government of Florence. For most of the 15th century, Florence had been dominated by the Medici family. However, in 1494 the Medicis had been driven out. Machiavelli worked for the new government. Between 1500 and 1508 he visited the courts of many foreign rulers, including that of Cesare Borgia, a ruthless prince in central Italy.

In 1512 the Medici family returned to Florence and expelled their enemies, including Machiavelli. He went home to the family farm, but he really wanted to return to work. He wrote several books about politics to try to please the Medici family. In 1520 they gave him a minor post, but in 1527 they were again driven out of Florence. Machiavelli also lost his job and died soon afterwards.

Machiavelli is famous for his writings, notably his book *The Prince* (1513). This book tells rulers how to increase their power, often through the cruel manipulation of other people. ◆

see also

Borgia family   Medici family

Charles Rennie **Mackintosh**

Scottish architect, designer, and painter
Born 1868   Died 1928 aged 60

Charles Rennie Mackintosh was the son of a police superintendent. As a child in Glasgow he had only one aim – to be an architect. He studied in Glasgow where he became friendly with some painters and designers of stained glass, jewellery, furniture, and embroidery. They became known as the 'Glasgow Group' and Mackintosh became the group's leading light. He and his friends wanted to combine the best of Scottish art with the New Art (Art Nouveau) from Europe. In his most famous building, the Glasgow

▲ *The library of the Glasgow School of Art is typical of Mackintosh's clear, bold design style.*

School of Art, we can recognize the cragginess of Scottish castles combined with the flowing plant forms of Art Nouveau. Glaswegians flocked to the tearooms that Mackintosh designed for the city. Each one had different and unusual decoration and furniture. They have now mainly been destroyed.

Mackintosh did not find much success in his lifetime and he gave up architecture when he was only 41 to spend the rest of his life painting. However, he is now regarded by many as a pioneer of modern design. ◆

James **Madison**

President of the United States of America from 1809 to 1817
Born 1751   Died 1836 aged 85

James Madison was born in Port Conway in the state of Virginia. In 1776 Virginia and 12 other states broke away from British rule to form the United States. In 1787 Madison represented Virginia at a conference to plan the organization of the government of the new country. He favoured a strong central system with upper and lower houses of elected members, and helped to draft the American Constitution (the basic principles of government). Two years later, he was elected to the House of Representatives. There he planned the Bill of Rights, which made the Constitution fairer in operation.

Madison was secretary of state in Thomas Jefferson's government (1801–1809) before becoming president himself in 1809. As president he took the United States into the war of 1812 with Britain. This ended after three years with the signing of the Treaty of Ghent, which restored all territories conquered in the war to their original owners. ◆

 see also

Jefferson

Madonna

American singer
Born 1958

Madonna Louise Ciccone was the most successful female singer of the 1980s. Born in Michigan, America, she studied dancing, and then combined her dancing skills with pop singing after moving to New York. Some of her outrageous clothes attracted as much attention as her singing. Her hits, including 'Into the Groove' (1985), 'Like a Virgin' (1986), 'Like a Prayer' (1989), and 'Vogue' (1990), had simple dance tunes, but unusual words and images. Her album *True Blue* (1986) was the No. 1 album in 28 countries.

Madonna has also acted in several films, including *Desperately Seeking Susan* (1985), *Dick Tracy* (1990), and *A League of Their Own* (1992). ◆

Ferdinand Magellan

Portuguese navigator and explorer
Born c.1480   Died 1521 aged about 41

Ferdinand Magellan was the son of a noble Portuguese family. He was a page at the Portuguese court before serving in the army, and then sailing with merchants to Indonesia.

Magellan thought there must be a way around the Americas to the East Indies. The king of Portugal rejected his plan for a voyage of discovery, so he offered his services to King Carlos of Spain.

Magellan set sail in 1519 with five small ships. When the fleet anchored for the winter in San Julián Bay, in Argentina, his Spanish captains mutinied. Magellan hanged one of the ringleaders.

When the fleet finally continued on its journey, one ship was wrecked in a storm, and another turned back to Spain. Magellan battled against the bad weather conditions through the straight between Tierra del Fuego and the mainland of South America. (The strait is now called the Magellan Strait after him.) He emerged into calm sea, which he named the Pacific (peaceful) Ocean.

The ships still sailed on and eventually reached the Philippines. Magellan had at last succeeded in reaching the East Indies by sailing westwards. However, before he could sail for home he was killed in a skirmish there. ◆

▼ *After Magellan's death, one of his ships, the* Vittoria, *carried on to Spain. It thus became the first vessel to circumnavigate the world.*

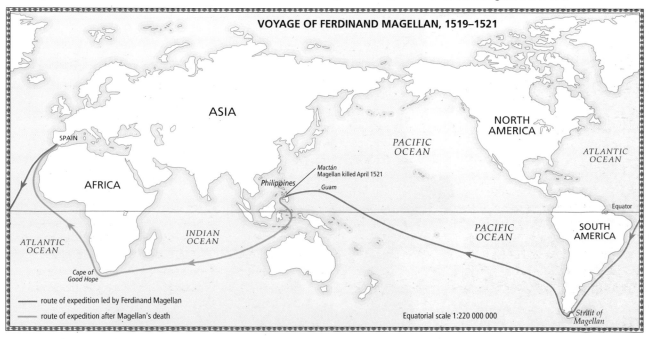

VOYAGE OF FERDINAND MAGELLAN, 1519–1521

ASIA

NORTH AMERICA

PACIFIC OCEAN

ATLANTIC OCEAN

SPAIN

Mactán
Magellan killed April 1521

Philippines

Guam

Equator

AFRICA

ATLANTIC OCEAN

INDIAN OCEAN

PACIFIC OCEAN

SOUTH AMERICA

Cape of Good Hope

—— route of expedition led by Ferdinand Magellan
—— route of expedition after Magellan's death

Equatorial scale 1:220 000 000

Strait of Magellan

René **Magritte**

Belgian painter
Born *1898*   ***Died*** *1967 aged 68*

René Magritte was one of the most famous of the Surrealist painters. The Surrealists were a group of artists and writers who wanted to explore the power of their subconscious minds; Surrealist paintings often look more like what we might see in dreams than representations of the real world. Once the novelty of this style had worn off, many such paintings looked repetitive and contrived. Magritte, however, seemed to have limitless imagination, and he kept freshness and wit in his work throughout his career. His paintings are full of bizarre images including enormous rocks that float in the air and fishes with human legs, all presented with a delightful kind of deadpan humour, but also a sense of mystery. ◆

▼ *Magritte delighted in placing everyday things in unfamiliar situations, as in Golconda (1953), where men wearing bowler hats fall like rain from the sky.*

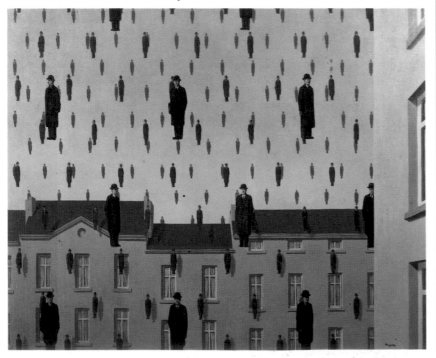

Mahavira

Indian religious leader
Born *c.599 BC*
Died *c.527 BC aged about 72*

Mahavira ('Great Hero') is often called the founder of the religion known as Jainism but he probably only reformed a religion which already existed. He is said to have lived around the same time as Buddha. Both lived in the Ganges valley, left their families when they were 30, and lived lives of extreme poverty and deep thinking. When they felt sure that they understood the meaning of human life and how it should be lived, they spent the rest of their lives teaching their beliefs to others. Mahavira is said to have starved himself to death when he was 72: the highest goal for a Jain monk or nun is to die of starvation, although this does not happen very often.

Both Jains and Buddhists believe that all living things are reborn many times and that the true aim of life is to escape rebirth by living

▲ *An illustration from a 15th-century version of the Kalpasutra, the Jain Holy Scriptures.*

correctly. Both believe that this involves not harming any other living thing. Jains go even further than Buddhists in this respect. They are such strict vegetarians that they take great care not to hurt even the tiniest of insects. Jain nuns and monks even carry brooms to sweep all surfaces to avoid crushing insects accidentally.

Buddhism spread through much of Asia but Jainism, which now has about 3 million followers, is found mainly in India. ◆

👁 **see also**
Buddha

Gustav **Mahler**

Austrian composer and conductor
Born *1860*   ***Died*** *1911 aged 50*

Gustav Mahler was one of 12 children born to a poor inn-keeper and his wife. He is said to have begun composing at around the age of four and was sent to study music in the Czech capital,

Prague, when he was only ten. As a student at the Vienna Conservatory of Music, he had to give music lessons to support himself. Later he made his fortune as a brilliant conductor, working with great orchestras in Budapest, Hamburg, Vienna, and New York.

Mahler loved writing long, complicated works for large orchestras. These include nine completed symphonies. Some are unusual because they combine solo singers or choirs with the orchestra. This is also true of one of his most famous compositions, *Das Lied von der Erde* (Song of the Earth) (1909), where an alto, a tenor, and an orchestra perform songs based on ancient Chinese poems.

Mahler's music was mostly ignored for 50 years after his death but he is now praised as a pioneer of modern classical music and an important influence on composers such as Schoenberg, Shostakovich, and Britten. ◆

see also

Britten   Schoenberg   Shostakovich

Margaret **Mahy**

New Zealand children's writer
Born 1936

Margaret Mahy was a school librarian in Christchurch, New Zealand, when she began writing children's stories. The very first to be published, *A Lion in the Meadow* (1969), won a medal from the New Zealand Library Association. *The Haunting* (1982), a tale of a boy who is possessed by a ghost, won the Carnegie Medal, which is awarded in Britain to the outstanding children's writer of the year. Her lively and imaginative books have pictures by top illustrators such as Helen Oxenbury. They often play on the interaction

of fantasy and reality in stories such as *Mrs Discombobulous*, who gets sucked into her washing-machine and comes out into another world, and *The Dragon of an Ordinary Family*, about a pet dragon. ◆

see also

Blyton   Dahl

Malcolm X

American civil rights leader
Born 1925   Died 1965 aged 39

As a boy, Malcolm Little, son of a Baptist minister, saw his home burned down by the Ku Klux Klan (a group dedicated to terrorizing black people). He later moved to Boston where he was imprisoned for seven years for burglary. Here he became a follower of Elijah Muhammad, founder of the Black Muslims. Working for the Black Muslims, Malcolm toured and lectured, campaigning for black Americans to seek self-government, not equality with whites. He told them that they had to be prepared to use violence as a means of self-defence. It was during this time that

▼ *Malcolm X awaiting his turn to speak at a Black Muslim rally in Washington DC in 1961.*

he changed his name to Malcolm X.

After quarrelling with Muhammad, Malcolm X left the Black Muslims and gradually modified his views on separatism. In 1964 he formed the Organization of Afro-American Unity to promote links between black people in Africa and America. Hostility continued between his followers and the Black Muslims and he was shot and killed at a rally in New York City. *The Autobiography of Malcolm X* (1965) remains a best-seller and a film about his life was released in 1993. ◆

Thomas **Malory**

English writer
Lived during the 15th century

No one knows for sure who Thomas Malory was, but many believe him to have been a knight who was imprisoned in London for unknown crimes for 20 years. It was possibly during this time that Malory finished his great book about King Arthur's knights of the Round Table and their quest for the Holy Grail. Much of this work was translated from French sources, but Malory added his own touches while keeping the original French title, *Le Morte d'Arthur* (The Death of Arthur). In 1485 the whole work was published by William Caxton, the first British printer. The stories about King Arthur, his bride Guinevere, the magician Merlin, and the gallant Sir Lancelot, soon proved popular with readers. Malory's beautiful use of language also has a magic of its own. Many future writers went on to write their own versions of these stories, including the poet Alfred Tennyson in his *Idylls of the King*. ◆

see also

Arthur   Caxton   Tennyson

Thomas **Malthus**

English economist and philosopher
Born *1766* **Died** *1834 aged 68*

Thomas Malthus was a clergyman who looked for the underlying causes of the misery of poor people in the England of his time. He believed that population growth was the problem, and that the production of food and other resources would not be enough to supply the expanding population. He felt that unless the birth-rate was controlled, starvation, war, and disease would prevent many people from advancing beyond the most basic standard of living.

When his short *Essay on Population*, setting out these views, was first published in 1798, it caused furious controversy. Malthus revised and enlarged the *Essay* in 1803, and his later views were rather more optimistic about the future of humankind ◆

Nelson **Mandela**

President of South Africa from 1994
Born *1918*

Nelson Mandela is related to the Xhosa royal family, but spent much of his childhood herding cattle. After going to university, he qualified as a lawyer.

Mandela helped form the Youth League of the African National Congress (ANC) in 1943. The Youth League stressed the need for the ANC to identify with the hardships and struggles of ordinary black people against racial discrimination.

The ANC led peaceful mass protests against apartheid ('separate development'), the policy introduced by the National Party (NP) in 1948 to justify and strengthen white domination.

▲ *Nelson Mandela (left) and F. W. de Klerk were awarded the Nobel Peace Prize in 1993 for their efforts to end apartheid in South Africa.*

Many protesters were imprisoned or killed. In 1960 the ANC was outlawed. In reply, Mandela and others established 'Umkhonto we Sizwe' (Spear of the Nation), a guerrilla army, in 1961.

In 1964, after months in hiding, Mandela was arrested and imprisoned for life. Offered a conditional release by the government, he refused to compromise over the issue of apartheid. Eventually, as a result of internal and international pressure, Mandela was released in 1990 by President de Klerk. He led the ANC in negotiations, and these resulted in the first democratic elections to be held in South Africa. The ANC won easily, and Mandela became president. In his new role, Mandela has promoted reconciliation among all South Africans. ◆

👁 **see also**
Buthelezi   de Klerk   Tutu

Benoit **Mandelbrot**

Polish-born American mathematician
Born *1924*

Benoit Mandelbrot was born in Warsaw, Poland, and moved to Paris with his family in 1936. There he met an uncle who was an important mathematician. His uncle advised him to avoid geometry, but Mandelbrot liked geometry best of all branches of mathematics and continued to study it.

After World War II Mandelbrot

▼ *A fractal image generated by a computer. The patterns of such fractal images repeat endlessly.*

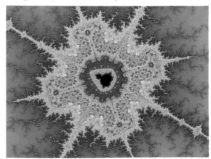

moved to America and worked on various projects. He soon became interested in what he called 'fractal geometry' – a term used to describe shapes that are repeated indefinitely, each time smaller. Fractals can be generated on a computer screen and often resemble natural shapes. Because of this similarity, fractals can be used to create models of natural changes, for example how a coastline may change through erosion, or how tree roots branch out. Fractals can also create amazing computer art. ◆

Edouard **Manet**

French painter
Born *1832*   **Died** *1883 aged 51*

Edouard Manet came from a wealthy family, and no one looked less like a 'bohemian' artistic rebel than he did. He was every inch a gentleman. However, he had unconventional ideas about art. Most painters of his time followed tradition, but Manet liked to look at

▼ *Manet's paintings were mainly of everyday life, such as this one of a couple at a Parisian café,* Chez le Père Lathuille's *(1879).*

everything freshly. He chose subjects from everyday life that no one had thought of painting before, and he painted with broad, sketchy brushstrokes, rather than with fine detail as was the current trend. Many art critics were outraged. However, a group of up-and-coming young artists – known as the Impressionists – loved his work and he became associated with them. By the end of his career the critics had come to appreciate the sparkling beauty of his paintings. Two years before his death Manet was made a member of France's Legion of Honour – a great distinction. ◆

see also

Monet   Pissarro   Renoir

Mao Zedong

One of the founders of the People's Republic of China in 1949
Born *1893*   **Died** *1976 aged 82*

Mao Zedong was one of the first to join the new Chinese Communist Party in 1921. They worked alongside the Guomindang (Nationalist Party), led by Chiang Kai-shek, until 1927, when the Nationalists had many Communists

killed. Mao helped the remaining Communists to survive by setting up a 'soviet' (elected council). At first the Communists fought off the Nationalists, but in 1934 the attacks became too strong. Mao then led the Communists on the 'Long March', nearly 10,000 km over mountains and deserts to a new base. Thousands died on the way.

In 1937 the Japanese invaded China. Chiang Kai-shek retreated to the mountains, but Mao sent the 'people's liberation army' to help people in occupied villages. When the Japanese finally left, Mao received great support from the people in the civil war against Chiang Kai-shek.

By 1949 Mao's forces had captured Beijing and set up a People's Republic, making Mao leader of a quarter of the world's people. He encouraged peasants to overthrow their landlords and work together on collective farms.

In 1957 he ordered the peasants to join their collective farms into large 'communes'. Some peasants worked in 'brigades' on the fields, while others were told to open factories or furnaces to make iron. This was all part of Mao's plan for a 'great leap forward' in industry. However, many of the schemes did not succeed because not enough money was being spent on new technology or education.

In 1959 Mao retired from the post of chairman of the Republic but re-emerged in 1966 to start the 'Cultural Revolution'. This new movement was intended to keep Chinese Communism free from outside influence and to ensure that Mao and his ideas remained at the forefront of life in China. The Cultural Revolution finally ended when Mao died. ◆

see also

Chiang Kai-shek   Deng Xiaoping

Diego **Maradona**

Argentinian footballer
Born 1960

Diego Maradona was born in Buenos Aires and quickly showed the skills that made him an Argentinian league footballer by the age of 15. He was voted South American Footballer of the Year in 1979 and 1980. After leading Argentina's youth team to World Cup success in 1979, he joined the full national squad in their unsuccessful attempt to keep the World Cup in 1982.

In 1986, as Argentina's captain, he lifted up the World Cup after brilliant performances throughout the tournament. He led Argentina once again in the 1990 World Cup final, although they were beaten 1–0 by West Germany. ◆

Guglielmo **Marconi**

Italian pioneer of radio
Born 1874   Died 1937 aged 63

Guglielmo Marconi began his experiments on sending radio signals in Italy before deciding to move to England.

He realized that if signals were to travel long distances he needed to have a very high aerial, so he began to use balloons and kites. In 1897 he sent a signal just over 14 km across the Bristol Channel. In 1899 he set up his apparatus in two American ships and was able to report on the America's Cup yacht race. This caused great excitement and Marconi became famous. But some scientists still did not believe that you could send signals very far. They thought the waves would go straight up and get lost in space.

In 1901 Marconi finally convinced everyone by sending a signal all the way from Cornwall to Newfoundland. It was later proved that the waves bounced back off special layers in the atmosphere, and that was how they were able to travel round the world. ◆

Maria Theresa

Empress of Austria-Hungary from 1740 to 1780
Born 1717   Died 1780 aged 63

Maria Theresa was the eldest daughter of Charles VI, who was the head of the Habsburg family and ruled Austria, Hungary, and other lands. Normally only a male could become ruler of the Habsburg lands, but Charles's only son died. Charles declared that Maria Theresa should inherit the family lands.

When Charles died in 1740, foreign rulers would not accept Maria Theresa as ruler, and tried to invade some of her territories. Frederick II of Prussia seized an area of her land called Silesia. Between 1757 and 1763 her forces fought the Prussians, but failed to recapture their land.

▶ *A portrait of Empress Maria Theresa.*

Maria Theresa was a well-loved ruler. She introduced many reforms to help the poorer people and built up agriculture and industry, so increasing the wealth of the empire. ◆

Marie Antoinette

French queen who was beheaded after the French Revolution
Born 1755   Died 1793 aged 37

Marie Antoinette was the 11th daughter of the Holy Roman Emperor Francis I of Austria and Maria Theresa. In 1770 she married Louis, who later became King Louis XVI of France. Marie Antoinette kept to her own small circle of friends, and her extravagance helped to create enormous debts for Louis. At the same time discontent in France led to the Revolution of 1789. Marie Antoinette tried to

persuade Louis to seek refuge with his army away from Paris, but he refused. Later they and their children were held prisoner in Paris, and in 1792 the palace was stormed and the monarchy was overthrown. Marie Antoinette was accused of betraying France to the Austrians and was guillotined in October 1793. ◆

see also

Louis XVI   Maria Theresa

Duke of **Marlborough**

English general and statesman
Born 1650   *Died* 1722 aged 72

John Churchill, the first Duke of Marlborough, became powerful during the reign of James II. But he was an Anglican and disliked James's attempt to turn the country back to Catholicism. In 1688 Churchill deserted James for William of Orange (William III) and became a general in William's army, but he was not trusted and William dismissed him. However, at the end of his life, William saw that Marlborough was the man to lead the fight against Louis XIV's France and appointed him Commander-in-Chief of the English army.

In the early years of Queen Anne's reign, Marlborough was the most famous Englishman in Europe: he was the statesman who held together the Grand Alliance against Louis, and the general who led their armies to a string of dazzling victories. He lived until 1722, dying in Blenheim Palace, Oxfordshire. The palace was the grateful nation's gift for his victories although it was only partly completed before he died. ◆

see also

Louis XIV   William III

Bob **Marley**

Jamaican reggae singer and songwriter
Born 1945   *Died* 1981 aged 36

Bob Marley was born to a black mother, and a white father who left home before Bob was born. He lived with his mother in Trenchtown, in Kingston, Jamaica, where living conditions were harsh. When he joined the group the 'Wailin' Wailers' he wrote many songs about life in Trenchtown.

By 1965 the Wailers' reggae music was attracting listeners far beyond Jamaica. A recording contract in the United Kingdom brought world fame in the 1970s. Unfortunately, in 1977 he contracted cancer in the foot. It spread throughout his body and he died just a few years later. ◆

Marx Brothers

American actors and entertainers
Groucho (Julius) Marx
Born 1890   *Died* 1977 aged 87
Chico (Leonard) Marx
Born 1891   *Died* 1961 aged 70
Harpo (Adolph, later Arthur) Marx
Born 1893   *Died* 1964 aged 71
Zeppo (Herbert) Marx
Born 1901   *Died* 1979 aged 78

The Marx brothers were trained by their mother to be a singing and dancing group. They later switched successfully to comedy. Each of them had a distinctive character. Zeppo played straight, romantic roles. Groucho, with his moustache, cigar, and funny walk, was always cracking jokes. Harpo, whose name came from his beautiful harp playing, never spoke. He communicated by strange noises, gestures, and funny faces. Chico spoke with an Italian accent and was often seen playing the piano. Most of their films concentrate on the three most famous and comical of the brothers: Chico, Harpo, and Groucho. ◆

> *I never forget a face, but in your case I'll be glad to make an exception.*
>
> GROUCHO MARX

◀ *Harpo, Chico, and Groucho Marx playing the fools for a Hollywood publicity photograph.*

◄ *Karl Marx in a poster from about 1920. In the years before he died, Marx suffered ill-health. Had it not been for the money that Engels gave him, he would not have been able to support his family or continue his work.*

Karl **Marx**

German philosopher
***Born** 1818   **Died** 1883 aged 64*

Karl Marx studied at the University of Bonn and then moved to Berlin in 1836. Here Marx developed ideas that were to change his life.

In 1843 Marx, now a journalist, began a journey round Europe. He moved to Brussels where he met Friedrich Engels. Together they worked for the Communist League, and in 1848 wrote *The Communist Manifesto*, which ended with the words: 'The workers have nothing to lose but their chains. They have a world to win. Workers of all countries, unite!'

Ideas like these led to Marx being expelled from Brussels and then from France and Germany. In 1849 he fled with his family to London. There, with the help of Engels, he developed his Communist ideas.

Marx wrote that 'Communism (is) the positive abolition of private property'. Under Communism, people would own all things in common and share them fairly. Marx believed this would happen, but only if working people organized themselves. That is why he became one of the leaders of the International Working Men's Association (the 'First International'). By 1869 it had 800,000 members and Marx had published Volume I of *Das Kapital* (Capital), the most important work of his life. After Marx's death, Engels published Volumes II and III. ◆

👁 **see also**

Lenin   Stalin   Trotsky

Mary

Mother of Jesus
Dates of birth and death unknown

The significant events in the life of Mary are recorded in the Gospels. According to Luke, Mary was visited by the angel Gabriel, who told her that she would give birth to Jesus. When she was pregnant Mary travelled to Bethlehem with her husband Joseph to take part in a population census. The familiar nativity stories are told by Matthew and Luke.

According to Matthew, Joseph and Mary fled to Egypt while Jesus was still young to escape Herod. They returned to Nazareth and Jesus was taken to the temple in Jerusalem as a boy. At His crucifixion, Jesus spoke to His mother from the Cross and entrusted her to His disciple John.

Over the centuries, different Christians have held a variety of beliefs about the religious significance of Mary. She is regarded by many as the Mother of God who listens to prayers. She is also thought by many believers to be responsible for miracles of healing. She is respected by Muslims and is mentioned in the Koran. ◆

Mary I

Queen of England and Wales from 1553 to 1558
***Born** 1516   **Died** 1558 aged 42*

Mary was the daughter of Henry VIII and the Catholic Catherine of Aragon. Soon after she became queen, on the death of her half-brother, Edward VI, she married Philip II of Spain. She hoped he would help her make England Catholic again, as she was determined to stamp out Protestant belief. During her short reign over 300 Protestants, including Archbishop Cranmer, were burnt at the stake because the queen considered them heretics (for not accepting Catholic teaching).

Mary was a sick woman, and she died after a reign of only five years. She was succeeded to the throne by Elizabeth I. ◆

👁 **see also**

Cranmer   Elizabeth I   Henry VIII
Philip II of Spain

Mary, Queen of Scots

Queen of Scotland from 1542 to 1567
***Born** 1542   **Died** 1587 aged 44*

Mary was the daughter of King James V of Scotland. He died a week after her birth, so she became queen of Scotland when she

▲ *Mary's beauty, the drama of her life, and the bravery of her death have ensured a lasting fascination in her.*

was only a few days old. She was born at a time of conflict between Scotland and England, and was brought up in the French court for safety. In 1558 the English throne passed to Elizabeth I, a Protestant, but many Catholics viewed Elizabeth as illegitimate and thought Mary had a better claim to the throne. She returned to Scotland in 1561, but her ambitions lay in England.

At first Mary managed to remain a Catholic queen without offending the powerful Scottish Protestants. However, she was accused of being involved in several scandals, including a plot to murder her second husband, the Earl of Darnley, and in 1567 she was forced to abdicate (give up the throne). She sought safety in England, but Elizabeth feared her and kept her in captivity for 19 years. Eventually Mary was found guilty of involvement in a Catholic plot to kill Elizabeth, and she was beheaded in 1587. ◆

see also

Elizabeth I

Thomas **Masaryk**

Czechoslovak politician and philosopher
Born 1850   *Died* 1937 aged 87

Thomas Masaryk was born in Moravia (now Slovakia), which was then part of the Austro-Hungarian empire. The empire's inhabitants included Germans, Hungarians, Czechs, Slovaks, and other peoples. Masaryk became a philosopher, and in 1882 he was appointed a professor in the Czech University of Prague.

In Prague, Masaryk became interested in politics. When World War I broke out in 1914, he saw that the Austro-Hungarian empire would be defeated. Masaryk thought that the Czechs and Slovaks should have their own independent country, and he went to the enemy countries – Britain, Russia, and the USA – to win support for the idea. When the war ended in 1918, the victorious Allies created the independent country of Czechoslovakia. Its people elected Masaryk as their first president. ◆

see also

Havel

Henri **Matisse**

French artist
Born 1869   *Died* 1954 aged 84

Henri Matisse began a career in law and took drawing classes only as a hobby. He proved to be exceptionally talented. He developed a colourful free style, often considered shocking. He made a famous portrait of his wife, nicknamed 'Green Stripe' because he boldly painted green shadows on her face!

The human figure dominated Matisse's drawings, prints, book illustrations, paintings, and sculpture. Later he used North African patterns and shapes in his pictures, and later still cut and pasted paper to create coloured pictures of simplified shapes.

Matisse said that for more than 50 years he had not stopped working for an instant. He even worked from his wheelchair in old age. ◆

▼ *A colourful Matisse cut-out picture entitled* The Sadness of the King.

▲ In 1956 Stanley Matthews became the first European Footballer of the Year.

Stanley **Matthews**

English football player
Born 1915

As a boy, Stanley Matthews kicked a small rubber ball around everywhere he went. Practising like this earned him the name 'the Wizard of the Dribble' because of his skilful ball control.

Matthews played his first football league match in 1931 and his first for England in 1934. He won an FA Cup winners' medal while playing for Blackpool Football Club in 1953. He helped to set up three goals in this amazing match after Blackpool were losing 3–1 to Bolton with only minutes to go. This extraordinary game is now known as the 'Matthews final'.

Matthews was still playing first division football when he retired at the aged of 50. ◆

Guy de **Maupassant**

French writer
Born 1850   *Died* 1893 aged 42

Guy de Maupassant was the son of a Normandy aristocrat. He served in the army and worked as a government clerk before being encouraged to become a writer by the novelist Gustave Flaubert. Flaubert encouraged him to aim for the highest standards and never to be content until he had found exactly the right word.

Maupassant wrote six novels and about 300 short stories which were immensely popular in his lifetime and remain much admired today. These stories, considered by some critics to be the greatest of the short-story genre, are written in a direct and free-flowing style, realistically describing the details of the characters' lives. ◆

👁 **see also**

Flaubert

▼ Guy de Maupassant endured mental illness for much of his adult life, and was insane when he died.

James Clerk **Maxwell**

Scottish physicist
Born 1831   *Died* 1879 aged 47

At 14 James Clerk Maxwell was asked to speak to scientists of the Royal Society of Edinburgh about his work in geometry, and when he was only 24 he became professor at Aberdeen University. He retired ten years later to write about his theories on electricity and magnetism. Then, at the age of 40, he was invited to become the first professor of experimental physics at Cambridge and, while he was there, the famous Cavendish Laboratory was built.

Some years before, the scientist Michael Faraday had talked about magnets and electric currents having 'lines of force' and made pictures of them. Maxwell heard about this and developed a mathematical theory that explained it. He suggested that if the magnet moved back and forth it would make waves run along the lines of force Faraday had discussed.

Maxwell then made the amazing suggestion that light is in fact incredibly rapid waves on the lines of force. The waves are called 'electromagnetic waves'. He was able to prove that this is true. His mathematics also suggested that there ought to be other kinds of electromagnetic waves with shorter and longer wavelengths than light. Sadly he died before any of the others could be discovered, but we now know that radio, infra-red, ultraviolet rays, X-rays, and gamma rays all belong to Maxwell's electromagnetic wave family. ◆

👁 **see also**

Faraday

John **McAdam**

Scottish engineer
Born 1756   Died 1836 aged 80

John McAdam was nearly 60 when he took the job which was to make him famous. He had been a merchant for most of his life but when he was in his middle forties he became interested in roads. He spent years travelling thousands of miles at his own expense to study the appalling state of Britain's muddy roads.

In 1815 he was made General Surveyor of the Bristol roads. McAdam believed that most of the roads should be dug up and remade by laying 25 cm of small broken stones, each no bigger than 2.5 cm, on a flat well-drained bed. The wheels of the carriages using the road would then compact the stones until the surface was smooth, hard, and easy to maintain.

McAdam's system worked so well in Bristol that soon it was known all over the country, and a new word for it, 'macadamizing', had entered the language. Even today the word 'tar-macadam', or 'tarmac' for short, preserves his name. ◆

▲ *The secret account books of Lorenzo and Cosimo de Medici alongside two Italian gold florins, Europe's most stable currency at the time of the Medicis.*

Joseph **McCarthy**

American politician who campaigned against suspected Communists
Born 1908   Died 1957 aged 48

Joseph McCarthy, a farmer's son from Wisconsin in the American mid-West, first studied to become a lawyer. Then, after World War II, he was elected a Republican senator. He found fame in 1950 by making a speech in which he said he knew the names of 205 Communists in the US State Department. Although he provided no proof he attracted a lot of support, and many people in public life were accused of 'un-American activities'. Many books and films were censored because they were suspected of encouraging revolts against the government. Then in 1954 McCarthy accused US army officers of being Communist sympathizers. The hearings were shown on television and McCarthy appeared to the American public as a bully and a liar. In December that year he was publicly criticized by the senate and the 'McCarthyism' era was effectively over. ◆

Medici family

Italian aristocratic family who dominated the city of Florence from the 15th to the 18th century

In the Middle Ages Florence was a rich and important city. Among its leading families was the powerful Medici family, whose members were bankers and traders. In theory Florence was a republic, governed by leading inhabitants rather than a monarch or a nobleman. But during the 15th century, the supporters of the Medici family dominated the city government. The Medici decided on policies for the city in private, which their supporters then implemented. The first Medici to rule in this way was Cosimo the Elder (1389–1464, ruled from 1434), regarded as the model for Niccolò Machiavelli's book *The Prince*. He was followed by Piero the Gouty (1414–1469, ruled from 1464), and Lorenzo the Magnificent (1449–1492, ruled from 1469).

The Medici family always had enemies in Florence. At various times these enemies drove them out of the city, but they were always restored to power again eventually. Members of the Medici family – Piero di Lorenzo, Alexandro, Cosimo, and their descendants – ruled Florence on and off until the middle of the 18th century.

The Medici family wanted to make Florence the most beautiful city in the world. They are famous for their generous support of Florence's numerous artists and sculptors, including Brunelleschi, Botticelli, and Michelangelo. ◆

◉ **see also**

Borgia family   Brunelleschi
Botticelli   Machiavelli
Michelangelo

Mehemet Ali

Egyptian ruler
Born *1769* **Died** *1849 aged 80*

An Albanian by birth, Mehemet Ali entered the service of the sultan (king) of the Ottoman empire. In 1798 he was sent to Egypt to fight off French invaders, and in 1805 he used the strength of his troops to make himself 'Pasha' (ruler) of Egypt. With French help he set up a modern European-style army and navy and improved agriculture and education. Between 1820 and 1822 he conquered the Sudan and in 1823 founded Khartoum as its capital. Although his troops fought on the Ottoman side during the Greek War of Independence, this did not stop him trying to take Syria from the Ottomans in the 1830s. He was too ill to rule in person during the last two years of his life, but members of his family continued to rule Egypt until 1952. Mehemet Ali is regarded by many as the founder of modern Egypt. ◆

Golda **Meir**

Prime minister of Israel from 1969 to 1974
Born *1898* **Died** *1978 aged 80*

Golda Mabovitch was born in the Ukraine, the daughter of a carpenter. She was brought up in Milwaukee, America, and trained to become a schoolteacher. In 1917 she married, and emigrated to Palestine four years later.

She became an active member in the Zionist movement, which fought for a homeland for Jews in Palestine. On the eve of Israel's independence in 1948 she was sent to America to raise funds for defence, returning with $50 million.

She held various government posts before being appointed foreign minister in 1956 – a position she held for nine years. Now a widow, she changed her name to Meir, the Hebrew form of her married name, Myerson.

In 1969 the prime minister died suddenly, and Meir was asked to take over until elections. She was such a success that after the elections she was asked to carry on. She took a tough line with Israel's Arab enemies, while trying to reach a lasting peace. In 1973 the Yom Kippur War, the fourth conflict between Israel and the Arab

▼ *Golda Meir, prime minister of Israel from 1969 to 1974, was one of the world's first women prime ministers.*

countries, broke out. Although peace was soon negotiated, her government was severely criticized because of early defeats, and she resigned. ◆

🔍 **see also**
Ben-Gurion   Weizmann

Lise **Meitner**

Austrian-born Swedish physicist
Born *1878* **Died** *1968 aged 89*

Lise Meitner was born in Austria and studied at Vienna University. Afterwards she moved to Berlin to study theoretical physics. Sexual prejudice at that time meant that she was not allowed to use the same laboratories as the men and so she had to work in an old carpentry shop. In spite of this, she and her colleague Otto Hahn did important work on radioactivity. In 1918 she and Hahn announced the discovery of a new radioactive element – protactinium.

After World War I Meitner returned to Berlin but when Hitler came to power she was forced to flee Germany because of her Jewish origins. She took refuge in Sweden where she eventually became a citizen. She continued working and in 1939 published a paper explaining how uranium nuclei could split after being bombarded with neutrons. For this explanation of nuclear fission she was awarded a share in the 1966 Enrico Fermi Prize for Atomic Physics. She was horrified when this discovery was used to make bombs and refused to work on the atom bomb. ◆

🔍 **see also**
Fermi   Hahn

▲ *Australia's Nellie Melba was the leading singer of her generation.*

Nellie **Melba**

Australian soprano
Born 1861   **Died** 1931 aged 69

Nellie Melba derived her stage name from Melbourne, the city of her birth. Her real name was Helen Porter Mitchell. In October 1887 she made her operatic début, in Brussels, as Gilda in Verdi's *Rigoletto*. Triumphant appearances in London and Paris soon followed, and by 1892 the operatic world was at her feet. She even had two famous foods, Peach Melba and Melba toast, named in her honour!

London's Covent Garden Opera House remained especially dear to her, and she made her last appearance there, in her favourite role of Mimi in Puccini's *La Bohème*, on 8 June 1926. She made many recordings between 1904 and 1926 which preserved the quality and natural agility of her exceptional voice. Her singing partnership with the tenor Enrico Caruso was particularly memorable. ◆

see also
Sutherland   Te Kanawa

Herman **Melville**

American writer
Born 1819   **Died** 1891 aged 72

Herman Melville had to leave his New York school early because his father became bankrupt, and then died, when Herman was only 12. In 1839 he took a job as cabin boy on a ship bound for England, and then worked on a whaling ship. Life at sea was hard and he escaped to a South Sea island. After a difficult and adventurous journey home to America, he published two novels based on his experiences, *Typee* (1846) and *Omoo* (1847).

Several more of Melville's books were also inspired by his own adventures at sea. The most famous is *Moby-Dick*. Published in 1851, it tells the story of Ahab, the captain of a whaling ship, and his obsession with the huge whale (Moby Dick) who had bitten off his leg in a previous encounter.

Melville also published several volumes of verse and completed another novel, *Billy Budd*, just before he died. ◆

▼ *A poster for the 1956 film version of Herman Melville's* Moby-Dick.

Mencius

Chinese philosopher
Born c.371 BC
Died c.289 BC aged about 82

Mencius was the most influential follower of the great Chinese thinker Confucius. He was born in Shantung, taught by the grandson of Confucius, and himself became a teacher. What he really wanted, however, was to be trusted adviser to a powerful and well-meaning king. He spent much of his life travelling from court to court looking for such a ruler but never found one. Instead he spread his ideas through his writings, which were studied in China over the following 2000 years. Mencius believed that people were naturally good – but that their goodness needed to be encouraged by a wise ruler. If the ruler was fair and kind, his subjects would want to obey him willingly, but if he was cruel or wicked Mencius declared that it would be right for them to rebel against him. ◆

see also
Confucius

Gregor **Mendel**

*Austrian monk who developed the
theory of genetic inheritance*
Born 1822   *Died* 1884 aged 61

As a young man Gregor Mendel joined a monastery and became a monk. The monastery supplied schools with teachers, and Mendel was sent to university to train as a science teacher. He spent his life teaching science in a local school and living a quiet religious life in the monastery.

Mendel had his own little garden in the monastery where he grew edible peas, and also sweet peas with pretty coloured flowers. He became interested in how the different characteristics, such as size and colour, were passed down from parent plants. He kept careful records of what all the parent plants looked like and what sort of young plants their seeds produced. He grew many generations of pea plants and finally worked out a set of rules to explain how the different characteristics were passed down (the subject we now call genetics).

He published his work in a local magazine for botanists, but at the time it went unrecognized. Then, 16 years after Mendel's death, the Dutch botanist Hugo de Vries discovered Mendel's paper, and Mendel's Laws of Heredity became the basis of all studies of heredity. ◆

Dimitri **Mendeléev**

*Russian chemist who first arranged the
'periodic table' of chemical elements*
Born 1834   *Died* 1907 aged 72

Dimitri Mendeléev studied science in France and in Germany and then became a professor of chemistry in the Russian university of St Petersburg. He was interested in the atomic weights of different elements and made a list of all 63 of the chemical elements known at that time, putting them in order of increasing

▼ *Dimitri Mendeléev, the youngest of 15
children, had a troubled youth. His father
was blind and his mother ran a factory to
support a large family. Both his parents
died before he was 20.*

atomic weight. He then rearranged the list into a continuous pattern of rows and columns and found that all the elements in the same column were similar to each other. This arrangement of chemical elements is called the 'periodic table'.

When Mendeléev worked out this table he found there were gaps, and he predicted that new elements would be discovered to fill these gaps. He looked at the sort of elements in the same column as the gap and was able to say what the new element would be like.

At first scientists were rather suspicious of Mendeléev's predictions, but within a few years some of these new elements were discovered and Mendeléev became a world-famous scientist. ◆

Felix **Mendelssohn**

German composer and conductor
Born 1809   *Died* 1847 aged 38

Felix Mendelssohn was handsome, intelligent, highly educated, and born into a very wealthy family. He gave his first public concert when he was nine. By the time he was 16, and had completed his String Octet, it was clear to everyone that he was also a musical genius.

Good fortune followed him through the rest of his life. He became one of the most popular composers of the day in England as well as in Germany. His music, such as the 'Italian' Symphony, *The Hebrides* overture, the music for *A Midsummer Night's Dream*, the Violin Concerto, and the oratorio *Elijah*, pleased everyone. However, he took his duties seriously and worked so hard as a teacher and conductor that he undermined his

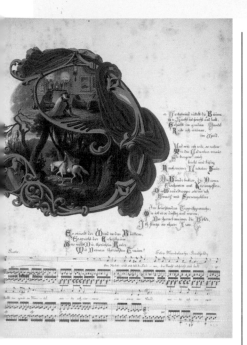

▲ *Felix Mendelssohn composed this music to accompany the words of a song written by Heinrich Heine.*

health. When his beloved sister, Fanny, died, Mendelssohn seemed to lose the will to live and died only a few months later. ◆

Yehudi **Menuhin**

American-born British violinist
Born 1916

Yehudi Menuhin was the eldest of a family of remarkable musicians. He began violin lessons when he was four years old, and made his first public professional appearance (in San Francisco) in 1924. A sensational Paris début in February 1927, followed by an even greater success in New York in November, launched him on an international career. Concert tours followed throughout the world, and he began recording in 1927.

In 1959 Menuhin made his home in London (eventually taking British citizenship in 1985). He has directed important festivals and appeared frequently as a conductor. In 1963

he founded a specialist school for exceptionally talented young musicians. He was knighted in 1965 and made a Peer in 1993. ◆

Robert **Menzies**

Australian statesman and prime minister from 1939 to 1941 and 1949 to 1966
Born 1894   Died 1978 aged 83

Robert Gordon Menzies was born in Jeparit, Victoria, and studied at Melbourne University. After working as a lawyer he started a career in politics, first in Victoria and then with the United Australia Party. Within a few years he was a member of the Federal Government and in 1939 became prime minister of Australia. He was forced to resign two years later when colleagues were dissatisfied with his leadership of Australia's war effort during World War II but returned to the premiership in 1949. The United Australia Party had by now become the Liberal Party and Menzies remained its leader for 17 years. During his time in office Australia changed considerably. Its industry became more advanced, people moved to the country from all over Europe and Asia, and Menzies created closer ties with America.

Menzies was knighted for his services to Australia in 1963, three years before his retirement. ◆

Gerardus **Mercator**

German map-maker
Born 1512   Died 1594 aged 82

Born in Germany, Gerhard Kremer was later known by the Latin version of his name – Gerardus Mercator. He was a skilled engraver, instrument-maker, and surveyor, which were all excellent qualifications for a map-maker.

At that time, European explorers were setting off to distant and unknown places. Mercator was the best of the map-makers who were putting the explorations and discoveries on paper and trying to make a sensible map of the world. He produced a beautifully drawn world map in 1569 which today shows how much of the world had been discovered and how much was still unknown.

Mercator started work on a book of 100 maps; when he died his son completed it. It was the first map collection to be called an 'Atlas'. Mercator's name is now given to a 'projection' of the Earth's surface on a flat sheet of paper. Although this projection is commonly used, it does give a distorted idea of the true areas of some countries. ◆

▼ *This map of the world is from Gerardus Mercator's* Atlas. *It shows his method of portraying the roughly spherical Earth on a flat piece of paper.*

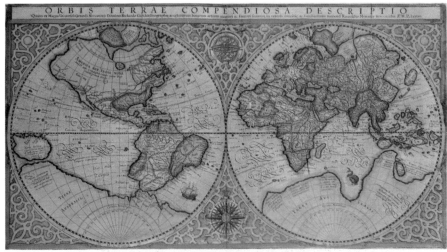

Eddy **Merckx**

Belgian champion cyclist
Born *1945*

Eddy Merckx was born just outside Brussels, the Belgian capital. He was a very good student at school and enjoyed playing soccer and basketball. Then, at the age of 14, he discovered cycling and made such rapid progress that he was world amateur champion when he was only 18.

The following year he became a professional, and an amazing run of success ensued. Between 1966 and 1978, when he retired, he triumphed five times in the Giro d'Italia (Tour of Italy) as well as winning the Tour de France five times. However, he was always the first to admit that he owed much of his success to the loyal team of riders who supported him. ◆

Klemens **Metternich**

Austrian chancellor and foreign minister
Born *1773*   **Died** *1859 aged 86*

In the 19th century Europe was made up of a number of large empires (such as the Austrian Empire) or confederations of smaller states (such as the German Confederation).

Although Klemens Metternich was born in Germany, his father was an Austrian diplomat. Metternich studied at Strasbourg University and followed in his father's footsteps. In 1794 he was sent as a diplomat to England. Later he held various government posts and became Austria's foreign minister in 1809. The Austrian emperor made Metternich a prince in 1813. His skill in negotiating put Austria in a strong position after the defeat of the French emperor, Napoleon. Although Metternich continued to rise in the government of Austria (he was made chancellor in 1821), a revolution in 1848 forced him to resign. He lived in exile in England for many years but returned to Vienna in 1851, where he died eight years later. ◆

Michelangelo Buonarroti

Italian sculptor, painter, poet, and architect
Born *1475*   **Died** *1564 aged 88*

At the age of 13, against his family's wishes, Michelangelo

▼ *This part of Michelangelo's Sistine Chapel fresco tells the story of Adam and Eve's expulsion from Paradise.*

became apprenticed to a painter, and a year later he went to study at a school for sculptors.

He longed to understand exactly how the human body worked. He dissected corpses at a hospital, and the things he learned from his dissections made him able to paint, draw, or sculpt figures with an accuracy that astounded everyone.

For all his gifts, Michelangelo was a difficult personality. He quarrelled easily and was often depressed, imagining enemies everywhere. He was furious when Pope Julius II asked him in 1508 to paint the ceiling of his chapel. He thought it was a plot by his enemies to keep him away from sculpting. But the painting which he did on the ceiling of the Sistine Chapel turned out to be one of the most astonishing creations in the history of art. It took four years to complete.

Michelangelo then worked for some years at the great church of St Peter in Rome and is mainly responsible for its magnificent dome. Later in his life his work changed in feeling, and his final painting in the Sistine Chapel, completed in 1541, is sombre and heavy. In his later sculpture his forms merge into each other and are very emotional compared to the serenity of his earlier work, such as the huge statue of David made between 1501 and 1504. ◆

Arthur **Miller**

American dramatist
Born 1915

Arthur Miller's father was a small New York manufacturer who lost his money in America's economic slump in the 1930s. After working in a warehouse, Miller saved up to go to university and he soon began writing plays. *Death of a Salesman* (1949) is considered to

be his masterpiece. It describes a pleasant but weak hero who instead of facing reality lives a false life of public cheerfulness and optimism. When the gap between this fantasy life and his own failures becomes too great, he finally kills himself.

Miller's other great play, *The Crucible* (1962), describes the hysteria that accompanied witch-hunting in 17th-century America. Miller makes a direct contrast here between this fanatical behaviour and the persecution of American Communists in his own time.

In 1956 Miller married the actress Marilyn Monroe. They divorced in 1961, and his play *After the Fall* (1964) describes some of the difficulties of their relationship. ◆

see also
Monroe, M

Glenn **Miller**

American bandleader and trombonist
Born 1904   Died 1944 aged 40

Glenn Miller went to university before becoming a professional trombonist. He was in demand as an instrumentalist but had less success at forming his own band until he started the Glenn Miller Orchestra in 1937. With his 'new sound', made by increasing the number of saxophones, this 'big band' soon became popular, with compositions such as 'Moonlight Serenade', 'Pennsylvania 65000', and 'Little Brown Jug'. The band even appeared in two Hollywood movies: *Sun Valley Serenade* (1941) and *Orchestra Wives* (1942).

Miller was given a commission in the US army during World War II and led the air force band playing in Europe. Returning to London from performances in Paris, his plane disappeared and no trace of it has ever been found. ◆

▲ Glenn Miller's composition 'Moonlight Serenade' became famous as his band's signature tune.

A. A. **Milne**

English writer
Born 1882   Died 1956 aged 74

Some writers are less famous than the characters they create. This is certainly true of Alexander Alan Milne, the creator of Winnie the Pooh and Christopher Robin. In real life, Christopher Robin was Milne's son (also called Christopher) and the stories that Milne wrote about Christopher's teddy bear (Pooh) and other toys have become classics.

Winnie the Pooh was published in 1926 and *The House at Pooh Corner* followed two years later. The books were illustrated by Ernest Shepherd.

Milne also wrote two books of verse for children: *When We Were Very Young* (1924) and *Now We Are Six* (1927).

Although Milne wrote magazine articles, essays, plays, and a detective novel, he will always be remembered for creating Pooh, Piglet, Eeyore, and the rest of the characters who lived in the Hundred Acre Wood. ◆

John **Milton**

English 17th century poet
Born *1608*   **Died** *1674 aged 65*

At Cambridge University John Milton first thought of becoming a clergyman, but decided instead to put his great gifts into poetry. One of his first major poems was *Lycidas*, written in memory of a friend who had drowned. Like other poets he was greatly influenced by Latin and Greek literature, but Milton also brought to this poem his own strongly Christian vision of life. He created a new form of poetry, one which was both passionate and scholarly at the same time.

When the English Civil War began in 1642, Milton sided with Parliament against King Charles I. He wrote many articles and pamphlets attacking the monarchy and defending people's freedom to choose their own leaders as well as to publish and read what they liked.

Milton's work led to serious eye-strain, and in 1652 he went blind. When Charles II was restored to the throne in 1660, Milton was arrested, but eventually pardoned. At about this time he wrote one of the greatest poems in existence, *Paradise Lost*. This is a very long poem re-telling the Bible story of how Satan tempted Adam and Eve into disobeying God. Composed entirely in Milton's head and dictated to members of his family, *Paradise Lost* uses poetic language to create an effect that is both magnificent and moving. ◆

Minamoto Yoritomo

Japanese shogun
Born *1147*   **Died** *1199 aged 52*

Minamoto Yoritomo was the first samurai (warrior) to rule Japan as 'shogun' (supreme commander) in the name of the emperor.

When he was a young man his family, the Minamoto, led a rebellion against the Taira family, who held almost all the power in government. In 1185 forces led by his half-brother Yoshitsune defeated the Taira on land and sea, and Yoritomo ensured every last one of the Taira was hunted down. Then he became jealous of Yoshitsune's success. Yoshitsune raised a revolt which failed, so he fled north, but was eventually killed. This left Yoritomo as master of the whole country. Rather than make himself emperor – which might have made him new enemies – he forced the child-emperor of the time to say he was ruling in his name. Yoritomo decided to make the eastern coastal city of Kamakura, near present-day Tokyo, his military headquarters, and this effectively became the central government of Japan. This shogunate was to last until 1333. ◆

see also

Tokugawa

Joan **Miró**

Spanish painter
Born *1893*   **Died** *1983 aged 90*

Apart from Picasso, Joan Miró was the greatest Spanish

▼ Animal Composition *by Joan Miró. His style includes simple forms, bright colours, and a sense of fun.*

painter of the 20th century. His most famous pictures are dream-like fantasies featuring strange insect-like creatures with human expressions. They are colourful, bizarre, and amusing. Miró said they were inspired by hallucinations brought on by hunger when he was a poor young artist. He also worked with many other art forms including stained glass and pottery.

Miró was extremely versatile and hard-working. He was still learning new techniques when he was in his eighties and worked up to the day of his death. From 1919 to 1940 he lived mainly in Paris, and after that on the island of Majorca, but he always kept strong links with his birthplace, Barcelona. ◆

👁 **see also**
Picasso

Joni **Mitchell**

Canadian singer and songwriter
Born 1943

Roberta Joan Anderson displayed a talent for painting in high school, but she abandoned plans for a career in art when she learnt to play the guitar and became interested in folk music. Her skill as a songwriter was soon noticed, and her songs were sung by others before she recorded them herself under the name Joni Mitchell.

Her early albums *Clouds* (1969) and *Ladies of the Canyon* (1970) contained many of her best-loved songs: 'Both Sides Now', 'Chelsea Morning', 'Big Yellow Taxi', and 'Woodstock', which became one of the definitive statements about the 'hippie' generation. Her later jazz-influenced recordings have proved less commercial, but her reputation as one of pop's premier songwriters remains undiminished. ◆

▲ *Joni Mitchell abandoned her art studies and plans to become a commercial artist. Instead she became a successful singer and songwriter.*

François **Mitterand**

President of France from 1981 to 1995
Born 1916   Died 1996 aged 79

François Mitterand studied law and politics, and graduated from the University of Paris in 1938. A year later his country was at war with Germany and Mitterand joined the army. He was wounded and captured by the Germans. He managed to escape at his third attempt and joined the French resistance, fighting against the German occupation of France. After the war he entered politics and was elected to the National Assembly. During the 1950s he served as a government minister in a number of posts and then in 1971 became leader of the Socialist Party. He stood unsuccessfully for the post of President of France on two occasions before finally being elected in 1981. Although he encountered many problems during his first seven years of office, he was re-elected in 1988. ◆

Molière

French playwright and actor
Born 1622   Died 1673 aged 51

Molière was the son of a successful upholsterer. His real name was Jean-Baptiste Poquelin. He first studied law at university, then left home to become an actor, adopting the stage name Molière. He toured France with a group of friends and began to write plays for this new company.

In 1658, after about 12 years of touring, the group was given a permanent theatre in Paris by King Louis XIV. From that time on, Molière wrote many more delightful plays. Although most of these were comedies, they often had a serious side too, attacking human failings such as snobbishness, hypocrisy, and meanness. One of his funniest plays is called *Le Malade Imaginaire* (The Imaginary Invalid). It is about someone who always thinks he is more ill than he really is. Tragically, one night Molière, who was acting the main part, collapsed and then died only a few hours later. ◆

▼ *A 17th-century portrait of Molière, one of France's greatest playwrights.*

Piet **Mondrian**

Dutch painter
Born *1872*   **Died** *1944 aged 71*

Piet Mondrian was one of the most important painters in the creation of abstract art – art that does not represent anything, but exists purely for the sake of its shapes and colours. He was rather an odd character, and was obsessively tidy and self-disciplined.

Until he was about 50 he had little financial success, for his kind of painting was slow to win admirers. He used only right-angled shapes and the most basic colours – blue, red, and yellow, and black and white. Gradually, however, people realized that his pictures had a beauty and elegance of their own, and many other artists imitated him. He lived in Paris for most of his career, but left in 1938 because of fears about impending war; he spent two years in London, then settled in New York in 1940. ◆

Claude **Monet**

French painter
Born *1840*   **Died** *1926 aged 86*

As a child in Paris, Claude Monet hated school and spent his time making cartoon-style pictures of his teachers. He became so clever at it that at the age of 16 he was earning pocket money making quick portraits.

When he first became an artist, Monet struggled for many years in poverty while his art was ignored, laughed at, and considered the work of a lunatic. He insisted on working outdoors to make on-the-spot pictures, but because the weather continually changed he had to work quickly, energetically applying pure, bold colour straight onto the canvas. His colourful

▲ *Monet designed and planned every aspect of his garden at Giverney himself. His paintings of the garden became increasingly abstract towards the end of his life.*

pictures did not attempt to copy a scene; they gave an impression of it (hence the term Impressionism), concentrating on the effects of light and atmosphere.

From his mid-fifties, Monet was regarded as the famous grand old man of Impressionism. His output of paintings was enormous. He particularly liked to paint the same subject many times in different weather conditions and seasons. He painted the Thames in London in different lights, and at home in his garden he made a series of wonderful pictures of water-lilies. In fact, his garden at Giverny, 65 km northwest of Paris, provided the greatest single inspiration for Monet's artistic work for over 40 years. ◆

👁 **see also**
Manet   Pissarro

Mongkut

King of Siam from 1851 to 1868
Born *1804*   **Died** *1868 aged 64*

As a young man Mongkut became a Buddhist monk and a learned scholar. Unusually for a member of the royal family he was able to travel freely around Siam (now called Thailand). Meetings with American and French missionaries made him intensely interested in western languages and science. After becoming king in 1851 (when he became known as Rama IV) he encouraged trade between Siam and western countries. Although he was unable to make many changes to Siam's traditional way of life, he ensured that his sons learned as much as possible about western culture so that they could begin to introduce great reforms. The life of the royal family's English governess, Anna Leonowens, was later made into a musical play, *The King and I.* ◆

James **Monroe**

President of the United States of America from 1817 to 1825
Born 1758   Died 1831 aged 73

James Monroe was born in Virginia, North America, when Virginia was still a British colony. In 1775, while Monroe was at college, the American Revolution (War of Independence) broke out between Britain and its American colonies. The following year, Monroe joined the American army. He fought in several battles, in which he showed great courage. In 1779, after three years away, he returned to Virginia. Two years later, the British forces surrendered.

Having helped the 'United States' to win independence, Monroe entered politics. Between 1782 and 1816 he served in the Virginia legislature and the national Congress; was governor of Virginia; was an American diplomat in Europe; and was secretary of state. In 1816, he was elected president.

At this time, much of Central and South America consisted of Spanish colonies. From 1818 onwards the Spanish colonists overthrew their foreign rulers and founded new countries (such as Argentina and Mexico). To help preserve the independence of these countries, Monroe declared in 1823 that European countries should not interfere in American countries. (In return, the United States would not interfere in Europe.) This policy was followed for almost a century. It was called 'The Monroe Doctrine'. ◆

Marilyn **Monroe**

American screen idol
Born 1926   Died 1962 aged 36

Marilyn Monroe was born Norma Jean Mortenson. She had a miserable childhood in Los

▲ *Marilyn Monroe in one of her classic Hollywood publicity poses.*

Angeles foster homes because her mother was mentally ill.

After working as a model and in minor film roles, Monroe starred in her first big role in *Niagara* in 1953. Two of her best-known films, *Gentlemen Prefer Blondes* (1953) and *Some Like it Hot* (1959), show she was a fine comic actress. However, she also took serious, dramatic roles in films like *The Misfits* (1961), her last film.

She was married three times, including to baseball star Joe DiMaggio and playwright Arthur Miller, who wrote *The Misfits* for her. She died from a drug overdose in 1962. Even now, many years after her death, she is remembered as one of the most beautiful stars of cinema history. ◆

👁 **see also**

DiMaggio   Miller, Arthur

Joe **Montana**

American football quarterback
Born 1956

From the age of eight it was obvious that Joe Montana had great football ability. He played brilliantly for Notre Dame, the college renowned for football, and was signed up by the San Francisco 49ers in 1979. He suffered a serious back injury in 1986 which put his future as a player in doubt but amazingly he recovered.

His exploits with the 49ers have made him possibly the best attacking quarterback ever to play American football. Despite many injuries, he led his team to victory in four Superbowl matches, winning the Most Valuable Player award three times.

In 1992 he joined the Kansas City Chiefs on a three year contract. ◆

▼ *Joe Montana seen here playing for the Kansas City Chiefs.*

▲ *Maria Montessori with children being taught by the methods she devised.*

Maria
Montessori

Italian developer of a new system of educating young children
Born *1870*   **Died** *1952 aged 81*

Maria Montessori was the only child of a civil servant. In 1890 she became Italy's first woman medical student and graduated with distinction.

As a doctor Montessori publicized the plight of disturbed children who were kept in asylums meant for insane adults. In 1900 she became director of Rome's first special school for 'degenerates', as children with severe learning difficulties were then called. She taught these children by new methods, and they did as well in the state examinations as 'normal children'.

In 1906 she opened a school for three- to six-year-olds on a poor estate. She began to notice that the children's urge to master their surroundings was so strong that they could be left to organize their own learning when given the right equipment and materials. Visitors from abroad were astonished to find the children calm, tidy, courteous, and absorbed in what they were doing. They learned to read and write without difficulty.

From 1912 until her death she travelled and lectured on her methods and worked hard to keep up the standards of the many Montessori schools that opened all over the world. ◆

Claudio
Monteverdi

Italian composer
Born *1567*   **Died** *1643 aged 76*

Claudio Monteverdi studied with the organist of Cremona Cathedral and made such good progress that he published a collection of short choral compositions when he was only 16. Several collections of madrigals (songs for voices, usually without instruments) soon followed. In 1592 he entered the service of the Duke of Mantua, whose court was one of the most musical in Italy. There he worked as a singer, instrumentalist, and composer. Apart from madrigals, which were often very colourful and dramatic, Monteverdi wrote operas. His *Orfeo* (1607) is regarded as the first great masterpiece of the operatic form that had only just been invented.

In 1612 he became Master of Music at St Mark's Cathedral, Venice. This gave him the chance to write magnificent music for the services, but when the first public opera-house was opened in Venice (1637) he turned again to opera. Like *Orfeo*, Monteverdi's last operas, *The Return of Ulysses* (1641), and *The Coronation of Poppea* (1642), are regarded as masterpieces. ◆

Montezuma II

Emperor of the Aztecs for 18 years
Born *c.1480*   **Died** *1520 aged about 40*

The Aztecs controlled most of Mexico and parts of Central America for over 100 years before they were conquered by the Spanish. Aztec emperors were elected by government, army, and religious leaders. They ruled with the help of a group of nobles to advise them. They had every

▼ *This mask represents one of the most important Aztec gods, Tezcatlipoca.*

possible luxury, but they and the people who served them were restricted by many rituals and customs. Emperors were remote, mysterious figures, rarely showing themselves to the common people.

Montezuma II became emperor in 1502. He was greatly feared. Unlike the previous emperor, he gave greater power to his own family and the nobility, and took it away from other people such as members of the merchant class. During his reign, his army conquered many cities, and he brought lands ruled by the Aztecs more firmly under his control.

Then, in 1519 the Spanish, led by Hernán Cortés, entered the Aztec capital of Tenochtitlán. Montezuma was killed during one of the battles. ◆

see also

Cortés

▲ A 19th-century plate commemorating the Montgolfier brothers' great ballooning achievements.

Montgolfier brothers

French designers of the hot-air balloon
Joseph Montgolfier
Born *1740*   **Died** *1810 aged 69*
Jacques Montgolfier
Born *1745*   **Died** *1799 aged 54*

The Montgolfier brothers worked as paper-makers and they owned a factory at Annonay, near Lyon. At that time nobody believed that people would ever fly, but that did not stop the Montgolfiers experimenting. They discovered that a smoke-filled bag would rise above a fire made of straw and wool, and thought they had discovered a new gas, which they called 'electric smoke'. In fact this was only hot air, as they realized later.

On 5 June 1783 they flew a silk balloon, lined with paper, and filled with hot air from a burning brazier. It travelled over a kilometre in its ten-minute flight. The brothers were determined to make the first balloon to carry passengers.

On 15 October, François Pilâtre de Rozier went up in the brothers' tethered balloon. All was then ready for the first free-flight attempt to take place. The intrepid Pilâtre de Rozier, and his friend the Marquis d'Arlandes, took off in Paris in the Montgolfiers' balloon on 21 November 1783. They travelled 9 km in 25 minutes, until the brazier they carried burnt a hole in the balloon. ◆

Field Marshal Montgomery

English commander of Allied forces during World War II
Born *1887*   **Died** *1976 aged 89*

Bernard Law Montgomery trained at the military academy at Sandhurst and fought in World War I. He stayed in the army after the war and by the time of the outbreak of war in Europe again in 1939, he commanded the 3rd Division of the British Army. He took part in the invasion force to France and its evacuation from Dunkirk. In 1942 he took command of the 8th Army and it was under his leadership that the British won one of the most important battles of the war in the Middle East, at El Alamein. Montgomery continued the offensive against the German army (led by Rommel) in North Africa. Then, in February 1943 Montgomery's forces came under the command of the American General, Dwight Eisenhower. They took part in the invasion of France in June 1944 and Montgomery received the German surrender at his headquarters on 3 May 1945. In the following year he was created Viscount Montgomery of Alamein, taking the title from his most famous victory. ◆

L. M. **Montgomery**

Canadian author of children's novels
Born *1874*   **Died** *1942 aged 67*

Lucy Maud Montgomery was just two years old when her mother died and she was sent to live with her grandparents on Prince Edward Island. When she grew up she became a teacher, but she left this job to take care of her grandmother after her grandfather died.

She had kept a diary for many years, and eventually she began writing stories and poems, which were published in one of the local newspapers. Her first novel, *Anne of Green Gables*, was published in 1908. It was an instant best-seller. In the book, an elderly brother and sister ask for a boy from an orphanage to help on their farm. They are sent a girl, Anne, by mistake, and they come to love her very much. Montgomery continued to write a great deal and produced seven sequels to *Anne*, other novels for children and adults, an autobiography, and many poems and short stories. ◆

Henry **Moore**

English sculptor
Born *1898*   **Died** *1986 aged 88*

By the time he was 11, Henry Moore had decided to become a sculptor. After fighting in World War I he returned to Yorkshire, where he had been born. He started teaching but disliked it so much that he enrolled at Leeds School of Art. After a scholarship to study at the Royal College of Art in London, he travelled to Italy in order to widen his understanding of sculpture.

Henry Moore's work was always based on nature: rock formations, stones and bones, landscape itself, and the human figure. He never tried to copy precisely the source of his ideas, but rather to suggest a likeness.

He was 50 before he was internationally recognized. He had exceptional energy, finally completing about 800 sculptures in wood, stone and bronze, 4000 drawings and 500 prints. ◆

see also
Hepworth

◀ *Sculptures such as this* Family Group *(1948–1949) are among Henry Moore's most famous works. They simplify the human form using smooth, gently curving lines.*

Thomas **More**

English scholar executed by Henry VIII
Born *c.1477*   **Died** *1535 aged about 58*

Thomas More was a devout Catholic, who, as a young man, nearly became a monk. Henry VIII enjoyed More's company, but More was not deceived by the king's favour. He once said, 'If my head could win him a castle in France, it would not fail to go.' More was also a successful lawyer and scholar, and wrote a popular book called *Utopia* about an imaginary perfect world.

▲ *Portrait of Thomas More from 1527.*

After Cardinal Wolsey had failed to grant Henry VIII his divorce from Catherine of Aragon, the king made Thomas More his chancellor. But More believed the king was wrong to divorce his wife, and to break with the Catholic Church to get his way. He refused to swear an oath accepting Henry's actions, even after being imprisoned in the Tower of London for 17 months. He was beheaded, saying on the scaffold: 'I die the king's good servant, but God's servant first.' ◆

see also
Henry VIII   Wolsey

▲ *William Morris created many colourful designs like this for fabric and wallpapers.*

William **Morris**

English artist, poet, and socialist politician
Born *1834* **Died** *1896 aged 62*

After getting a degree from Exeter College, Oxford, William Morris started work as an architect, but he soon gave up architecture to become a painter like his friends Edward Burne-Jones and Dante Gabriel Rossetti. Later he helped to set up his own firm of fine art craftworkers who designed furniture and wallpaper. He was also an accomplished poet, basing many of his poems and stories on ancient sagas of Icelandic origin.

In 1883 he joined a socialist political party, the Social Democratic Federation, and travelled the country to speak at meetings and lead marches. When he quarrelled with the leaders of the Social Democratic Federation, he helped to start another party, the Socialist League.

Five years before he died he began yet another venture, setting up the Kelmscott Press which published beautifully bound and illustrated books. ◆

see also
Rossetti

Samuel **Morse**

American inventor of Morse code
Born *1791* **Died** *1872 aged 80*

Samuel Morse studied painting in London and worked as a successful portrait painter in America for many years.

But Morse was also a scientist. On a return voyage to America, a fellow passenger demonstrated some electromagnetic devices. Morse realized he could adapt them to make an electric current put dots and dashes on paper, and he invented a dot-and-dash code for each letter of the alphabet. He used it to send coded messages along a wire to an electrical receiver, which printed the dots and dashes. It was the quickest way to communicate over long distances, and more successful than rival telegraph systems in Europe.

In 1843 Morse constructed a 65-kilometre telegraph between Baltimore and Washington for the American government. Soon other towns and cities were linked by Morse's telegraph system, and he became rich and famous. ◆

Moses

Leader and prophet of the Hebrews
Probably lived in the 13th century BC

According to the Bible, Moses was born while the Hebrews were slaves in Egypt. Pharaoh, the ruler of Egypt, had ordered that all Hebrew baby boys must be killed. So Moses' mother hid him in a basket in the bulrushes (reeds) on the banks of the River Nile. Pharaoh's daughter found him and he grew up in the palace.

Moses had to run away to Arabia after attacking an Egyptian who was ill-treating a Hebrew slave. In Arabia he felt the presence of God when he saw a burning bush, and he knew that he had to return to his people.

Back in Egypt he and his brother Aaron asked Pharaoh to release the Hebrew slaves. Pharaoh refused so God sent ten plagues to Egypt. Pharaoh agreed to let the people go and Moses led them in the 'Exodus' (departure) across the Red Sea.

They wandered in the wilderness for 40 years. During this time Moses received the Ten Commandments on two tablets of stone at Mount Sinai and bound the people to God in a covenant (agreement) that they would keep His laws. Moses died before the people reached the 'promised land' of Canaan. ◆

see also
Joseph

▲ *To many musicians, Mozart is, quite simply, the greatest of all composers.*

Wolfgang Amadeus **Mozart**

Austrian composer
Born *1756*   **Died** *1791 aged 35*

When the Salzburg violinist Leopold Mozart realized that his children, Maria Anna and Wolfgang Amadeus, were exceptionally musical, he set about teaching them all he could. But even he must have been surprised when he discovered just how talented his son was. By the time Wolfgang was five he was able to compose quite good pieces of music, and as a performer of the harpsichord and violin he could outshine much older musicians.

In 1762 Leopold took his children on tour to Munich and then Vienna. In the following year they travelled around Germany, France, and England. In 1770 they toured Italy. Everywhere they went, young Mozart impressed all the leading musicians he met.

When eventually the touring had to stop, Mozart joined his father as one of the Archbishop of Salzburg's court musicians. However, he hated being treated like a servant. In 1781 he went to Vienna, determined to earn a living as best he could.

He taught and gave concerts. He composed music of all kinds and, for a while, was successful. However, things began to go wrong, and his last few years were spent in comparative poverty. He was given the cheapest of funerals and his grave was soon forgotten.

Mozart wrote 41 symphonies and 27 piano concertos, besides much chamber and solo piano music. The complete list of his works contains over 600 titles. Finest of all, perhaps, are his operas: *The Marriage of Figaro*, *Così fan tutte*, *Don Giovanni*, and *The Magic Flute*. ◆

Robert **Mugabe**

First prime minister of independent Zimbabwe
Born *1924*

Robert Mugabe was born at a Catholic mission north of Salisbury, the capital of Southern Rhodesia (now Zimbabwe). His mother hoped he would become a priest, but he trained to be a teacher instead.

Rhodesia was then a colony ruled by Britain. Robert Mugabe travelled to other countries in Africa in the 1950s and saw people fighting for independence from British rule. With others, he founded the Zimbabwe African National Union (ZANU) to fight for majority rule by black people in his own country. ZANU was banned and Mugabe was sent to prison; he had gained six university degrees by the time he was released.

He then joined the ZANU guerrilla fighters who were attacking Rhodesian forces from Mozambique. A cease-fire was declared and free elections took place in 1980. Robert Mugabe was elected prime minister by an overwhelming majority, and Rhodesia was renamed Zimbabwe. ◆

Muhammad

Islamic prophet
Born *c.570*   **Died** *632 aged about 62*

Muhammad's father, Abdullah, died before he was born, and his mother, Aminah, died when he was only six. Therefore, he was brought up under the protection of his grandfather, Abdul Muttalib, and his uncle, Abu Talib. They came from the powerful Quraish tribe who looked after the Kaaba, the central religious shrine in the city of Mecca in Arabia.

As he grew up Muhammad worked as a shepherd, and later with the trading caravans that travelled all over the Arabian peninsula. He was known as *al-amin*, the trustworthy one. He worked for a widow, Khadija, who later asked him to marry her when she was 40 and he was 25.

Muhammad used to pray alone in a cave on Mount Hira outside Mecca, and there he received his first revelations from God. Muhammad believed that he had to preach to the people of Mecca that there is only one God, Allah, and that they were wrong to worship idols (images). The people laughed at him and insulted him. Khadija and a few others believed in his message and encouraged him to continue to preach.

In 619 Khadija and Abu Talib, the powerful uncle who had protected him, died. With the loss of these two important supporters, some of the Meccans plotted to kill Muhammad. In 622 he emigrated from Mecca to Medina with his followers. This move is called the *hijra* (migration) and marks the beginning of the Muslim calendar.

In Medina Muhammad acted as a leader when the people needed help with disputes. He taught them about religion and he organized armed resistance to anyone, including the Meccans, who was hostile to the new Muslim community. He led various campaigns and defeated the Meccans. In 630 Muhammad entered Mecca peacefully. The people there became Muslims and destroyed the idols. By the time of Muhammad's death most of the tribes in the Arabian peninsula had acknowledged his authority. He was buried in Medina.

For all Muslims, Muhammad is the example of a person whose life was rightly guided by God. He is their model husband, parent, statesman, soldier, honest trader, and man of God.

The revelations Muhammad received during the last 23 years of his life were later written down and are called the Koran. ◆

👁 **see also**

Ali

◀ *The Dome of the Rock mosque in Jerusalem, built 691–692, covers the sacred spot from which Muslims believe Muhammad ascended to Heaven.*

▲ The Dance of Life *by Munch.*

Edvard **Munch**

Norwegian painter
Born 1863   **Died** 1944 aged 80

Edvard Munch had a miserable childhood. His mother died when he was five, his sister died when he was 11, and his father became almost insane with grief. The one compensation was that Edvard was looked after by a kind aunt, who encouraged his gift for art.

The sufferings he had seen affected his paintings. He depicted people, showing their fears and anxieties, in a way that no other artist had done before. At first, people could not understand his strange pictures, but gradually he was recognized as a genius. At the age of 44 he had a mental breakdown – he had been working too hard, drinking too much, and was unhappy in love. When he recovered, he had a much more cheerful outlook. He gave up his scenes of death and sickness in favour of subjects such as landscapes. However, his 'madness' was part of his genius, and he never quite recaptured the magic of his early work. ◆

Rupert **Murdoch**

Australian media magnate
Born *1931*

Keith Rupert Murdoch's father was an Australian newspaper publisher. After graduating from Oxford University, Murdoch worked on British newspapers until his father died in 1952. He then returned to Australia to run the family newspapers. Immediately he changed their style, introducing more gossip and sport, so that they sold more copies. His newspaper empire grew and in the 1970s and 1980s he bought control of British newspapers, including *The Sun* and *The Times*. Many workers lost their jobs when he introduced new print technology and there were angry scenes at his News International company. In 1985 he became an American citizen and bought the film company 20th Century Fox, and in 1989 he launched the satellite TV station which became BSkyB. ◆

Benito **Mussolini**

Dictator of Italy from 1926 to 1943
Born *1883*   **Died** *1945 aged 61*

Benito Mussolini was involved in politics from an early age and was often arrested for his activities. He began to believe that the only way to change society was through the use of violence.

After World War I, many people were scared that there would be a revolution in Italy, as there had been in the Soviet Union. In 1919 they gave Mussolini funds to set up the Fascist Party to oppose the Socialists and Communists. His Fascists attacked trade unionists, broke up strikes, and then 'marched' on Rome in 1922.

The king asked Mussolini to be prime minister and Mussolini gradually took more power for himself. By 1926, *il Duce* ('the Leader'), as he was now known, had become a dictator.

In 1935, to increase Italy's power and his own glory, Mussolini invaded and conquered Ethiopia. His great friend in Europe was Hitler. They formed an alliance, which took Italy into World War II on Germany's side in 1940. However, Mussolini's armies suffered many defeats. By 1943 Mussolini had been overthrown and placed under arrest. German paratroops rescued him and put him back in power in northern Italy. The end, though, was not far away. When Italy was finally defeated, Mussolini was shot by his Italian enemies and his body was hung upside-down in the Piazza Loreto in Milan. ◆

◉ **see also**
Hitler

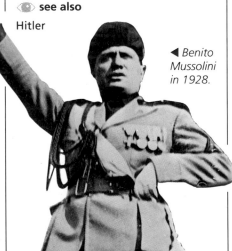

◄ *Benito Mussolini in 1928.*

Modest **Mussorgsky**

Russian composer
Born *1839*   **Died** *1881 aged 42*

Although Modest Mussorgsky was taught the piano by his mother, and played a concerto when he was nine, music was not thought to be a proper career for the son of a wealthy landowner. He therefore entered the St Petersburg Cadet School and in due course took a commission in the army. However, he continued to play the piano and compose short pieces, and in 1858 he left the army in order to become a full-time composer.

Despite some success, life became a struggle and he began to drink heavily. The result was that he left many compositions unfinished, or in a very muddled state. His music, however, showed great power and originality, such as his historical operas *Boris Godunov* and *Khovanshchina*, the symphonic poem *St John's Night on the Bare Mountain*, and the piano suite *Pictures at an Exhibition*. After his death his works were 'polished', but not always improved, by such composers as Rimsky-Korsakov. ◆

◉ **see also**
Rimsky-Korsakov

Eadweard **Muybridge**

English photographer
Born *1830*   **Died** *1904 aged 74*

When Edward James Muybridge emigrated to America at the age of 22 he changed his name to Eadweard to sound more 'Anglo-Saxon'. He became a professional landscape photographer in

▲ *Eadweard Muybridge's famous photographs showing a horse running at full gallop.*

California, but when asked to photograph a horse at full gallop he became fascinated with the idea of photographing movement. In 1877 and 1878 he succeeded, using 24 cameras and a system of trip wires stretched across a track. As a horse ran past, its hooves broke the wires and triggered the shutters. This was the first time anyone had shown that a galloping horse lifts all its feet off the ground at the same time. Muybridge went on to photograph many animals, publishing his famous book *Human and Animal Locomotion* in 1887. ◆

Vladimir **Nabokov**

Russian-born American writer
Born 1899   Died 1977 aged 78

Vladimir Nabokov was well educated and spoke Russian, English, and French at a very young

age. As a teenager he published two volumes of poetry before his family was forced to flee Russia following the Communist Revolution of 1919.

Nabokov studied at Cambridge University before living in Berlin and Paris. During this time he wrote poems, short stories, and plays as well as nine novels including *Despair* and *Invitation to a Beheading*. These were published under the false name V. Sirin. In 1940, Nabokov and his family moved to America and he became an American citizen. He taught at Stanford, Wellesley, and Cornell universities while continuing to write. Known for his imaginative writing, Nabokov received public and financial success with his novel *Lolita* (1955). ◆

Guru **Nanak**

First leader of the Sikhs
Born 1469   Died 1539 aged 70

Nanak was born a Hindu, but when he grew up he worked for a Muslim and learned about the Muslim religion too. When he was older he became a religious teacher, preaching a new faith using ideas from both Hinduism and Islam. This new religion, called Sikhism, was based on one God and on the equality of all human beings.

Nanak believed that he had seen God and wrote about his experience in one of his early songs. This song can be found in the Sikh holy book, the Guru Granth Sahib. To reach unity with God he said people should meditate, pray, sing hymns, and follow the advice of a spiritual guide ('guru').

Nanak travelled a great deal to teach people about God's path. Eventually he settled in the village of Kartarpur and lived as the teacher of ordinary men and women. They listened to Nanak's teachings and followed his advice and example. Nanak became known as Guru Nanak. Before he died, Nanak appointed his most trusted follower, Lehna, as his successor. Lehna was given the name Guru Angad. ◆

▼ *Amritsar, a city in the Punjab region of India, is the holy city of Sikhism. The Golden Temple (below) is the holiest of all Sikh temples.*

Fridtjof **Nansen**

Norwegian explorer and scientist
Born *1861*   **Died** *1930 aged 68*

Fridtjof Nansen began his varied career as a zoologist. On a whaling voyage he saw Greenland, and decided to lead an expedition to cross it. With five other men he made the first crossing of the island in 1888–1889.

Later Nansen led a more daring expedition. He left his specially designed ship, the *Fram*, drifting slowly across the frozen Arctic Ocean whilst he tried to reach the North Pole on foot. Eventually he had to turn back, but had got nearer to the Pole than anyone before him.

Nansen then worked as a scientist, becoming first a professor of zoology, and then a professor of oceanography, the study of oceans. In 1921 he was appointed League of Nations High Commissioner for refugees, and was awarded the Nobel Peace Prize in 1923 for his work in this field. ◆

Napoleon I

Emperor of France from 1804 to 1814 and again in 1815
Born *1769*   **Died** *1821 aged 51*

Napoleon Bonaparte was only ten when he entered military school. After graduating, he was rapidly promoted and soon commanded an entire army and conquered northern Italy for France. Next he invaded Egypt in 1798, but his fleet was defeated by Nelson at the battle of the Nile. By this time, the French Revolution had been going on for ten years. However, the Directory, who were in charge, were in a mess so Napoleon returned to Paris because he believed France needed firm government. In November 1799, after a coup d'état (overthrow of a government), he became the new leader of France. Over the next five years, Napoleon worked hard and made many changes to improve ordinary people's lives. At the same time, his armies were successful abroad. In 1804 he became emperor, and by 1807 his was the largest empire in Europe since the days of Rome.

But then things began to go wrong. The Spanish, with British help, drove the French out of Spain. Then, in 1812, Napoleon made his worst mistake by invading Russia. The Russians steadily retreated, drawing Napoleon's army deeper into Russia and further from its supplies. Napoleon reached Moscow, but still the Russians refused to make peace, and Napoleon realized that he had to retreat. His army was now caught by the bitter Russian winter, and his frozen, starving men died in their thousands.

By now many French people were disillusioned with Napoleon's rule. After his defeat at the battle of Leipzig and the invasion of France in 1814, Napoleon was banished to the Mediterranean island of Elba.

In 1815 he escaped and landed in France. The soldiers who were sent

▼ Napoleon Crossing the Alps *by Jacques Louis David.*

to stop him welcomed him as emperor instead and he returned to Paris. But after his defeat at the battle of Waterloo, Napoleon was again exiled, this time to the island of St Helena in the south Atlantic. He died six years later. ◆

see also
Napoleon III   Nelson   Wellington

Napoleon III

Emperor of France from 1852 to 1870
Born 1808   Died 1873 aged 64

After Napoleon Bonaparte was banished from France with the rest of his family, the French king, Louis Philippe, was put back on the throne. Louis Napoleon, Bonaparte's nephew, dreamed of returning to France as a great ruler himself. In 1836 and 1840, he tried to start rebellions in France against the king. Both these failed and he was first exiled to America, and then later spent six years in prison before escaping to England.

In 1848, Louis Philippe was expelled from France. Louis Napoleon returned, this time to be elected president, and then became Emperor Napoleon III in 1852. His style of rule was undemocratic but he brought industrial development to France. His foreign policy was less successful, because he was always interfering in other countries' affairs.

From 1856 he suffered ill health, and eventually allowed his ministers to assume more power. In 1870 France declared war on Prussia but was heavily defeated. Louis Napoleon was again thrown out of France, and died just three years later in England. ◆

see also
Napoleon I

Gamal Abdel Nasser

President of Egypt from 1956 to 1970
Born 1918   Died 1970 aged 52

As a boy Gamal Abdel Nasser joined demonstrations against the British, who ruled Egypt with the help of the Egyptian king. Then, when he was in the army, he joined a secret group who managed to overthrow King Farouk in 1952 and get rid of the remaining British troops. Two years later Nasser became prime minister and then, in 1956, president.

In that year Egypt was invaded by Britain, France, and Israel after Nasser took over the Suez Canal from its foreign owners. Their action was criticized by many nations and they soon withdrew, leaving Nasser with even more power in Egypt.

He tried to use this power to unite Arab countries, but their divisions proved too deep. In 1967 Egypt was defeated in the Six Day War by Israel. Nasser died of a heart attack three years later. ◆

▼ *Nasser addressing a huge crowd in Cairo in 1961. When he died in 1970, he was greatly mourned. He had helped to turn Egypt into a politically powerful country.*

◀ *Martina Navratilova*

Martina Navratilova

Czech-born American tennis champion
Born 1956

Martina Navratilova was born in Czechoslovakia, but moved to America in 1975 when she started to become a successful tennis player. In 1981 she became a US citizen and the following year was the first woman professional tennis player to earn more than one million dollars in a season.

Her favourite championship has always been Wimbledon, where she has won nine singles finals (1978–1979, 1982–1987, and 1990), beating the record set by fellow American, Helen Wills Moody. She was the most outstanding woman tennis player of the 1980s. ◆

Nebuchadnezzar

King of Babylon from 605 BC to 562 BC
Born *c.630 BC*
Died *c.562 BC aged about 68*

Nebuchadnezzar II was the last great ruler of the ancient city of Babylon, which stood by the river Euphrates in the territory of modern Iraq. Nebuchadnezzar extended Babylonian power over a huge area by successful military campaigns in Syria, Palestine, and Egypt. Two of his campaigns, in 597 and 587 BC, were against the city of Jerusalem. The Bible reports how he destroyed Jerusalem and took its inhabitants, including the young Jewish prophet Daniel, as captives to Babylon.

Nebuchadnezzar built massive defensive walls around Babylon and enlarged and adorned its temples and palaces. He also built the Hanging Gardens, an artificial hill with terraces and trees, for his wife, a foreign princess who was homesick for her own country. These hanging gardens were one of the seven wonders of the ancient world. ◆

▼ *Part of the Ishtar Gate, which was the main entrance to the city of Babylon.*

Pandit Jawaharlal Nehru

First prime minister of independent India, from 1947 to 1964
Born *1889*   **Died** *1964 aged 74*

At the age of 15, Pandit Nehru was sent away from home to study in England. He studied science at Cambridge University and later studied law in London. He returned to India in 1912 and joined his father's law practice.

Nehru supported Mahatma Gandhi and became one of the most prominent leaders of the Indian nationalist movement. In 1920 he started working for the Indian National Congress, an organization that led India's struggle to gain freedom from British rule. He served as its president in 1929 and again from 1936 to 1937. However, he was frequently sent to prison for his opposition to British rule.

In 1946 he was again elected president of the Indian National Congress. He led the team that negotiated with the British government the terms and timetable for India's independence. He became the first prime minister of independent India in 1947, and remained prime minister until he died 17 years later.

Nehru strongly believed in parliamentary democracy and brought rapid economic development to his country. His government concentrated on establishing large-scale industrial units and new hydroelectric projects to generate power to meet India's needs.

Nehru's reputation at home and abroad suffered a severe blow when China invaded India in 1962. Many Indians blamed Nehru and his policies for the unprepared state of the Indian army at the time of the invasion. He died two years later after a stroke. ◆

The light has gone out of our lives and there is darkness everywhere.

NEHRU, JANUARY 1948
Speech following
Gandhi's assassination.

 **see also**

Gandhi, Indira   Gandhi, Mahatma

Horatio Nelson

Britain's greatest admiral
Born *1758*   **Died** *1805 aged 47*

Although he was never a strong child, Horatio Nelson was always determined to go to sea. At the age of 12 he accompanied his sailor uncle to the Falkland Islands. At 15 Nelson joined the navy, and six years later was given command of his own ship.

Despite frequent illnesses, Nelson made a name for himself as a skilled and popular commander. His success began during Britain's war against the French in 1793. Despite being blinded in his right eye

▲ This illustration shows Nelson explaining the plan of attack to his officers prior to the battle of Trafalgar.

during a battle, Nelson was soon made an admiral. More injuries followed, including the loss of his right arm from below the elbow. But still he pursued the French, destroying their navy in 1798 at the battle of the Nile.

▼ The uniform Nelson was wearing when he was shot.

Nelson is most famous for the battle of Trafalgar in 1805. His 27 ships encountered 33 French and Spanish vessels. Nelson signalled to his fleet, 'England expects that every man will do his duty' and once again the French navy was beaten. However, during the fighting Nelson was shot by a French sniper and died on the deck of his ship, the *Victory*. ◆

 see also
Napoleon I

Nero

Emperor of Rome
Born AD 37   **Died** AD 68 aged 30

Nero was adopted by his mother's uncle, the Emperor Claudius, in AD 50. He married Claudius' daughter Octavia and so became part of the ruling household. Nero's mother Agrippina made sure that her son became emperor after Claudius by poisoning the true heir, Britannicus.

Nero was said to be a cruel man, even arranging for his own mother and

wife to be murdered. We do not know that he actually started the Great Fire of Rome in AD 64, as some historians suggest, but he used the opportunity to rebuild large parts of the city and to build an enormous palace for himself, called the Golden House. He blamed the Christians for the fire and used it as an excuse to persecute and massacre them.

In AD 68 there were uprisings against him starting in southern Gaul (now France). He committed suicide when he realized that everyone, including his own bodyguard, had deserted him. ◆

Thomas Newcomen

British inventor of an early steam-engine
Born 1663   **Died** 1729 aged 66

Thomas Newcomen was a blacksmith. In 1698 he used his skill in working with metal to build a steam-engine. Seven years earlier a military engineer called Thomas Savery had built the first steam-engine. It could be used to pump water out of a mine or well, but it was very dangerous to use because it required enormous steam pressure which could easily burst the pipes. Newcomen developed a much safer engine, but it was rather slow and could not do a lot of work. About 60 years later James Watt found a way of making Newcomen's engine work much better, and this new type of engine was used to drive machines in many different industries. The steam-engine was one of the important developments that led to the Industrial Revolution. ◆

see also
Watt

◀ Isaac Newton was knighted for his contributions to the world of science in 1702 and elected president of the Royal Society in 1703. This is his original manuscript for his book on the theory of light and colour.

Isaac **Newton**

English scientist
Born *1642* **Died** *1727 aged 84*

Isaac Newton went to Cambridge University when he was 19, and was already doing important research in his second year. But then, because of the great plague, he had to go home to Lincolnshire for two years until the danger of catching the disease was past.

Many people have heard the story of Newton watching an apple fall from a tree. He was only 23 but was already thinking about the movement of the Earth, the Moon, and the planets. He realized that, just as the force of gravity pulled the apple to Earth, gravity keeps the Moon in its orbit. It is rather like a piece of string tied to a stone that you whirl around your head; if the string breaks, the stone is flung away. Without gravity the Moon would fly off into space.

Newton tried to make a telescope to study the stars, but found that if he used lenses the bright images had coloured edges. In trying to find out why this happened, he invented the mirror telescope. This does not give coloured edges, and many of our present-day telescopes are based on Newton's design. He was so persistent in asking questions about the coloured edges that he was the first person to discover that white light is a mixture of all the different colours. Raindrops make a rainbow and a prism makes a spectrum by splitting up the white light. Before Newton, people thought that the raindrops or the prism added the colour.

Newton's greatest book, written in Latin and usually called *The Principia* (1686–1687), has had an enormous effect on the way scientists, and especially physicists, have thought ever since. ◆

👁 **see also**

Huygens Leibniz Young

Nicholas II

Tsar of Russia from 1894 to 1917
Born *1868* **Died** *1918 aged 50*

The tragedy of Russia's last tsar (emperor) was that he was a weak man who tried too hard to be a strong one. At first Nicholas II made all the big decisions about running the country himself, without a representative government. But this proved to be a disaster because he lived a completely different life from his people and was ignorant of the country's real problems.

Russia's disastrous defeat by Japan in 1904–1905 was one of the main causes of the revolution that took place in Russia in 1905. Nicholas was forced to allow a

◀ This picture of Tsar Nicholas II and his family was taken not long before they were all murdered in 1918.

Duma (parliament) to be elected. A period of relative prosperity followed and Nicholas won popular support for the war against Germany (1914). However, he then unwisely took personal command of the armies, leaving the government to the tsarina Alexandra and the priest Rasputin. (Rasputin was a rogue who seemed to have enormous influence over Alexandra after he had helped to treat the crown prince who suffered from a rare blood disease.) Mismanagement of Russia's part in World War I and government chaos resulted in Nicholas giving up the throne in February 1917. He was imprisoned with his family until they were murdered in July 1918 near Ekaterinburg by the Communist revolutionaries. ◆

see also

Rasputin

Jack **Nicklaus**

American champion golfer
Born 1940

Although he only started to play the game at the age of ten, Jack Nicklaus showed his golfing potential by playing a round of only 69 shots over a 6.49-km course when he was 13. While still at Ohio State University, he became US amateur champion. Then, when he turned professional in 1961, he began his run of tournament successes by winning the US Open championship in 1962.

Since then the 'Golden Bear', as he is known to his fans, has won more major tournaments than anyone else in golfing history, including four US Opens and five US Masters championships. ◆

see also

Palmer

Joseph **Niepce**

French pioneer of photography
Born 1765   Died 1833 aged 68

Like his brother Claude, Joseph Niepce began life as an army officer but both retired around 1800 to live on the family country estate near Chalons-sur-Saône.

The two brothers were familiar with an early steamship – the *Pyroscaphe* – which had undergone trials on the Saône river. In 1807 they designed and patented a kind of internal combustion engine, the pyréolophore, which they hoped – vainly as it happened – might be used for ship propulsion. In 1816 Claude went to England to promote the pyréolophore and Joseph turned his hand to the reproduction of pictures by the then popular technique of lithography. This led him to study possible methods of making permanent photographs (he called them heliographs) on a pewter plate, and later on paper. In order to develop his invention Niepce went into partnership with another French photographic pioneer, Louis Daguerre, in 1826, but ultimately contributed little more. ◆

see also

Daguerre   Eastman   Fox Talbot

Friedrich **Nietzsche**

German philosopher
Born 1844   Died 1900 aged 55

Born into a strict Protestant family in Saxony, Germany, Friedrich Nietzsche broke with Christianity in his twenties and devoted himself to classical literature and philosophy. The composer Richard Wagner

▲ *Nietzsche suffered from ill-health in his thirties and in 1889 had a permanent breakdown brought on by overwork and loneliness.*

influenced him greatly at first, but Nietzsche later rejected him and most German culture of the time.

In books such as *Thus Spoke Zarathustra* (1883–1892), Nietzsche challenged cultural values passed down through many centuries from classical, Jewish, and Christian traditions. He held that notions of 'the good', 'the true', and 'the beautiful' are illusions; what matters is 'the will to power' – man's quest for a higher form of existence. (Nietzsche discounted women except as mothers of future 'supermen'.) He was isolated from mainstream philosophy by his extreme views, and suffered ill-health for the last decade of his life.

His philosophy is notorious because the Nazis misused it as justification for their racist policies, even though his ideas and theirs were not really compatible. ◆

see also

Wagner

▲ *Florence Nightingale, the 'lady with the lamp', pictured doing her nightly rounds during the Crimean War.*

Florence **Nightingale**

English founder of modern nursing
Born *1820*   **Died** *1910 aged 90*

Florence Nightingale decided she wanted to be a nurse, but this caused bitter arguments with her family, who thought that nursing was not a job for respectable women. It was not until 1851 that Nightingale got her own way and started work in a small London hospital. She was so successful that the Secretary of State for War asked her to go to the Crimean War to take charge of the nursing of wounded British soldiers.

She set sail in 1854 with 38 nurses. Within a month they had 1000 men to look after. Nightingale worked 20 hours a day to improve the nursing of ordinary soldiers. Every night she visited the wards, and the soldiers loved her as 'the lady with the lamp'. Her story was published in newspapers back home and she became a national heroine. The public donated £45,000 for her to spend as she saw fit. In 1860 she spent it on the development of the Nightingale training school for nurses at St Thomas's Hospital, London.

In 1907 she became the first woman ever to be awarded the Order of Merit. ◆

🔊 **see also**
Seacole

Vaslav **Nijinsky**

Russian ballet-dancer
Born *1890*   **Died** *1950 aged 60*

Vaslav Nijinsky's parents were dancers, and both he and his sister followed in their footsteps. When he was ten he was enrolled in the Imperial Ballet School in St Petersburg, Russia. By the time he was 20 he was touring the world. The great ballet producer,

◀ *Nijinsky in a scene from the ballet Scheherazade.*

Diaghilev, made him the star of many of his ballets. Nijinsky was always looking for new techniques and styles, and he often offended classical ballet fans. Much of what he did, though, was later recognized and used in modern ballet.

Nijinsky's later life was tragic. By the time he was in his 30s he was showing signs of mental illness. This became progressively worse and he spent much time in hospital. He died, after much sadness and suffering, in London in 1950. He was reburied in Paris in 1953. ◆

🔊 **see also**
Diaghilev   Nureyev

Richard **Nixon**

President of the United States of America from 1969 to 1974
Born *1913*   **Died** *1994 aged 81*

Richard Nixon began his career as a lawyer, and served as an aviation ground officer in World War II. In 1946 he was elected to the House of Representatives, and after four years he became a senator. When Eisenhower became president in 1953, Nixon was his vice-president. Nixon himself failed to win the election for president in 1960, but won in 1968.

At the time US troops were involved in the Vietnam War. Nixon realized that the Communists could not be defeated, and so from 1971 he began to withdraw the soldiers. Afterwards he improved relations with Communist China and the Soviet Union.

Nixon was easily re-elected in 1972, but his second term of office was rocked by scandals. During the 1972 election campaign, some of Nixon's supporters burgled the Watergate Hotel, the headquarters of the opposing Democratic Party. Nixon denied all knowledge of the break-in, but eventually he had to admit he had helped to cover up the facts. He resigned in 1974. ◆

Kwame **Nkrumah**

Leader of Ghana from 1957 to 1966
Born 1909   Died 1972 aged 62

O riginally a teacher, Kwame Nkrumah later studied in America and in England. In both countries he met people who were working for the rights of black people and they inspired him. He decided to return to the Gold Coast to fight for his country's independence from Britain.

He founded the Convention People's Party in 1949 and called for 'positive action'. This led to his imprisonment in 1950. While in prison, he won an election so easily that not only was he released, he was also made 'Leader of Government Business'. In 1954 he became prime minister. The Gold Coast gained independence in 1957 and was renamed Ghana. Nkrumah became its president in 1960.

There followed many problems for Nkrumah's government and it became increasingly unpopular. While he was on a trip to China in 1966, he was deposed. He died in exile in Guinea in 1972. ◆

Alfred **Nobel**

Swedish inventor of dynamite who left a fund for the Nobel prizes
Born 1833   Died 1896 aged 63

A lfred Nobel's father invented a submarine mine, and went on to manufacture explosives.

Alfred became obsessed with what his father was doing. During his own experiments, Alfred's factory blew up, killing his brother. But he continued experimenting and invented a much safer explosive which he called 'dynamite'. This was used for blasting through rock. He also invented another explosive which was used for shooting bullets out of guns.

Nobel died a wealthy but sad man because people thought of him as someone who manufactured destruction. He had hoped that terrible weapons would prevent war because no one would dare use them. He was wrong. In his will he left a fund of over $9 million to give prizes (Nobel prizes) in five fields: literature, physics, chemistry, physiology and medicine, and peace. (In 1969 a sixth prize – for economics – was added.) They have become the highest award anyone can be given. ◆

Sidney **Nolan**

Australian painter
Born 1917   Died 1992 aged 75

S idney Nolan was the most internationally famous of all Australian painters. He worked at various odd jobs before becoming a full-time artist when he was 21. He is best-known for his paintings of landscapes and scenes from Australian history. His most famous paintings are those representing Ned Kelly, the 19th-century outlaw who became an Australian folk-hero. Nolan painted in a highly original way, showing the dramatic mood of his subjects without treating them realistically. He travelled all over the world and found inspiration in the strange beauty of Antarctica and New Guinea as well as in his own country. ◆

▼ *Sidney Nolan's* Dog and Duck Hotel.

Michael **Nostradamus**

French physician and astrologer
Born 1503   Died 1566 aged 63

Was a man living in the 16th century able to predict the Great Fire of London of 1666, the French Revolution, World War II, the rise of both Napoleon and Adolf Hitler and that Man would walk on the moon? The answer is 'yes', only if we are to believe the claims of the supporters of the French astrologer, Nostradamus.

Michael Nostradamus (the Latinized form of his real name, Michel de Notredame) was a well-known doctor when he wrote a series of over 900 predictions about the future of the world in two books called *The Centuries* (1555–1558). The problem with these predictions is that they are very vague and could be made to mean almost anything. They are written in several languages, contain anagrams and riddles and are not placed in chronological order.

We should hope that Nostradamus was not always accurate in his predictions. He even claimed that the world will end in 1999:

Like the great king Angolmois
The year 1999, seventh month,
The great king of terror will
    descend from the sky,
At this time, Mars will reign for the
    good cause.

This verse supposedly predicts the end of the world, although some people claim that it predicts an invasion from outer space! ◆

Rudolf **Nureyev**

Russian ballet-dancer and choreographer
Born 1938   Died 1993 aged 55

When Rudolf Nureyev was a child he was a member of a children's dance group which travelled about performing traditional folk dances. Later he joined his local ballet company. In 1955 he went to the Kirov ballet school in Leningrad (now St Petersburg), one of the top ballet schools in Russia. From there he joined the Kirov Ballet and became a principal dancer.

In 1961 Nureyev went to Paris with the Kirov. While he was there he decided not to go back to the Soviet Union. He asked for 'political asylum' (protection and refuge from a country) and stayed on in the West. He became famous throughout the world, dancing all the great ballet roles. He was admired for his powerful personality as well as the strength which showed in his dancing. ◆

👁 **see also**
Fonteyn   Nijinsky

Julius **Nyerere**

President of Tanzania from 1964 to 1985
Born 1922

Julius Nyerere was born the son of a chieftain at a village on Lake Victoria, Tanganyika (now Tanzania). After going to university and working as a teacher, he helped to form the Tanganyika African National Union (TANU), which did very well in Tanganyika's first elections of 1958. Tanganyika became independent in 1961 as a result of TANU's success. Nyerere was elected prime minister. He resigned after a short time, but became President of the Republic of Tanganyika in 1962.

◄ *This is the first official portrait of Julius Nyerere, made in 1963.*

In 1964 Tanganyika and Zanzibar decided to merge to form 'the United Republic of Tanzania. Nyerere became its first president. He was regularly re-elected at five-yearly intervals, and became one of the longest serving leaders in Africa until he retired in 1985. His views are listened to throughout the world and Tanzania has remained one of the most politically stable countries in Africa. ◆

Annie **Oakley**

American star of Wild West shows
Born *1860*   **Died** *1926 aged 66*

Phoebe Anne Moses learned to shoot when she was very young. When she was a child she hunted game which she sold for money to pay off the mortgage on the family farm. She married a marksman whom she met in a shooting competition. They started their own trick-shooting act, and together they toured variety shows and circuses.

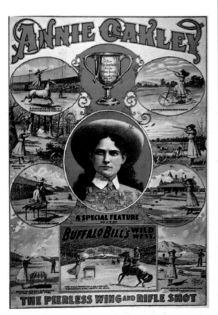

▲ *A 1901 poster for Buffalo Bill's Wild West Show featuring Annie Oakley.*

When Annie Oakley (her stage name) was 25 she and her husband joined the famous 'Buffalo Bill' Cody's Wild West Show. For 17 years, she amazed audiences with her rifle-shooting skills. She was such a good shot that she could split a playing card held edge-on from 30 paces away. She could also hit a coin thrown in the air, and even shoot cigarettes held in her husband's lips. ◆

👁 **see also**
Buffalo Bill

Daniel **O'Connell**

Irish political campaigner
Born *1775*   **Died** *1847 aged 71*

Daniel O'Connell was a lawyer who had a great gift for speaking in public. He was one of the main campaigners for rights which the Catholic Irish people had lost when their country was joined to Britain in 1801 and their parliament in Dublin was closed.

His first campaign was to change the law forbidding Catholics to hold positions of power. He set up a Catholic Association, which even the poorest peasants were invited to join. In 1828 he won an election even though it was illegal for him, as a Catholic, to be a candidate. The British parliament gave in and passed a law for Catholic freedom in 1829 and he became an MP.

In the 1840s O'Connell led his second campaign to undo the 1801 Union of Britain and Ireland. His work was only the start of a struggle which went on until 1921. He is remembered for his efforts to unite all classes of Irish people, and because he always stood for political campaigns, not violence, to win what he thought was right. ◆

Hans Christian **Oersted**

Danish physicist who discovered electromagnetism
Born *1777*   **Died** *1851 aged 73*

Hans Oersted was the son of a chemist and so started life surrounded by scientific apparatus. He studied at the university of Copenhagen and, to complete his education, travelled to meet Europe's leading scientists. He learnt a lot and in 1806 was given a job at his old university.

He also gave public lectures which became very popular. At one of these, in April 1820, Oersted tried an experiment he had never done before. He put a compass underneath a wire and then switched on an electric current: the magnetized compass needle moved!

Oersted realized the importance of what he had seen. Up to that time, scientists believed that electricity and magnetism were different forces. He had proved that they were connected.

Other scientists took up the study of this 'electromagnetism'. Their work produced new scientific theories and many important inventions such as the dynamo and the electric motor. ◆

👁 **see also**
Ampere   Faraday

▼ *The equipment used in Oersted's famous compass experiment.*

Georg **Ohm**

German physicist
Born *1787*   **Died** *1854 aged 67*

After leaving university, Georg Ohm held a series of teaching jobs. In 1817 he started teaching mathematics and physics at a Jesuit school in Cologne, Germany. Here he did some original research into electricity. In 1827 he published *The Galvanic Circuit Treated Mathematically*. This book contains an explanation of his famous law which shows that the current flowing in an electric circuit is proportional to the voltage (i.e. the current increases when the voltage increases). This became known as Ohm's law. Resistance to the current in an electrical circuit is measured in units called ohms.

Ohm's law makes the relationship between voltage and current very simple to understand but at first scientists in Germany did not take the idea seriously. Finally, in 1841, the Royal Society of London acknowledged the importance of Ohm's work by awarding him its prestigious Copley medal. His fame then spread in Germany where he was eventually made a professor of physics at Munich University. ◆

▲ *Georgia O'Keeffe's* Yellow Walnut Tree Leaves with Daisy *looks abstract because it shows such enlarged, though precise, details of the subject.*

matter, usually based on plant-life and landscapes. Her paintings are very expressive, and include huge flower paintings which seem to magnify the structure of petals and stamens, gently revealing the most intimate parts of the plant, thus making us look at something familiar in a new way. ◆

Georgia **O'Keeffe**

American painter
Born *1887*   **Died** *1986 aged 99*

Georgia O'Keeffe was born into a prosperous dairy-farming family in Wisconsin, America. She hated school and by the age of 12 decided that she would be an artist.

Much of her work was influenced by the landscapes of New Mexico and south-west America. She was considered very 'avant-garde' (innovative) because she adopted an abstract style for her subject

Laurence **Olivier**

English actor
Born *1907*   **Died** *1989 aged 82*

Even when he was still a child people noticed how good Laurence Olivier was at acting, so when he left school he went to study at the Central School of Speech and Drama in London.

The first 'hit' that he acted in was *Private Lives* by Noel Coward, but he became really well known in 1935 when he played Romeo in Shakespeare's play *Romeo and Juliet*. A year later he was the

leading actor at the Old Vic, an important London theatre, and took several major parts in Shakespeare plays. He then became an international star when he appeared in films such as *Wuthering Heights* (1939) and *Henry V* (1944). He was knighted in 1947.

As well as being an actor, Olivier directed many plays and in 1962 he was made the first Artistic Director of the National Theatre company. He was made a life peer, becoming Lord Olivier, in 1970. ◆

Omar **Khayyam**

Persian poet and scientist
Born *1048*   **Died** *1123 aged 75*

Omar Khayyam was born in Nishapur, Persia (now Iran); his surname may mean that he was the son of a tent-maker. He proved to be a brilliant scholar, excelling in history, law, medicine, and, above all, astronomy and mathematics. He wrote a famous textbook on algebra which was known in Europe as well as in the East. He was put in charge of reforming the calendar to make it more accurate and also set up an observatory and school of astronomical research in Isfahan.

Omar Khayyam is also world-famous as a poet – thanks to an English poet, Edward Fitzgerald, who lived over 700 years after Omar's death. His four-line poems (rubaiyat) praise the pleasures of life but also show that he thought deeply about religion. At least 250 of them survive. Fitzgerald had the idea of putting them together and translating them as though they were one long poem. Since he published his version in 1859 – *The Rubaiyat of Omar Khayyam* – they have been translated into many other languages. ◆

▲ *An illustration from* The Rubaiyat of Omar Khayyam.

J. Robert **Oppenheimer**

American nuclear physicist
Born 1904   Died 1967 aged 62

Julius Robert Oppenheimer was a student at Harvard University before going to study in Europe, where he met the world's leading physicists. He then returned to America to conduct research into sub-atomic particles.

During World War II, Albert Einstein and others warned that if Nazi Germany developed a nuclear weapon then the rest of the world would be in great danger. In response the American government gathered together a group of scientists to build their own atomic bomb. Oppenheimer set up a laboratory at Los Alamos, New Mexico, and led the project. On 16 July 1945, Oppenheimer's team successfully tested the first atomic bomb. Three weeks later 'A-bombs' were used to destroy the Japanese cities of Hiroshima and Nagasaki, killing thousands of people.

In 1963 the American president, Lyndon Johnson, presented Oppenheimer with the Enrico Fermi Award for Atomic Physics. ◆

〰 **see also**
Einstein   Fermi

George **Orwell**

English novelist
Born 1903   Died 1950 aged 46

George Orwell, the pen-name of Eric Blair, was born in India and educated in England. He served for five years in the Burmese police force and also spent some time living as a tramp, earning a bit of money by washing dishes. These experiences were later used in some of his novels, as were memories of his time spent fighting for the Republicans in the Spanish Civil War.

Orwell was a great journalist, but he only became famous as a novelist in the last few years of his life. In 1945 he wrote *Animal Farm*, an allegory describing how some farm animals first get rid of their harsh master, Mr Jones, only to suffer even worse cruelties from their own ruthless pig-rulers. In fact, Orwell was really attacking the way that the Russian Revolution of 1917 was betrayed by the tyrant Stalin, who ended up behaving even more badly than the former tsar (emperor).

Four years later Orwell wrote *Nineteen Eighty-Four*, a novel set in what was then the future. It described a bleak world where workers must exercise every day in front of a 'tele-screen' which also spies on them. Anyone showing any signs of independence is caught and executed. It is a powerful novel describing the horrors of total dictatorship. ◆

▼ *George Orwell working as a radio journalist in 1945. From 1947 he suffered from tuberculosis and he was in and out of hospital until his death in 1950.*

Nikolaus **Otto**

German inventor and industrialist,
Born *1832* ***Died*** *1891 aged 59*

The son of a farmer, Nikolaus Otto left school at 16 to work for a local merchant. He soon left to seek his fortune in Cologne and there became interested in a new kind of engine which had been developed by a French engineer, Jean Lenoir. Like the steam-engine, it depended on a piston working in a cylinder but the power was provided by the explosion of a mixture of gas and air instead of by steam. This was the ancestor of the internal combustion engine which – using petrol or oil as a fuel – was destined to revolutionize transport on land, sea, and in the air.

▲ *Otto's four-stroke engine was a great success. It was reliable, efficient, and relatively quiet.*

Otto's engine used a four-stroke firing sequence, which was different from Lenoir's two-stroke version, and he was granted a patent in 1876. During the next ten years he sold 30,000 of his engines – the 'silent Otto' – but then his patent was declared invalid. Unknown to Otto the principle of his engine had already been patented, but not developed, in 1862 by another Frenchman, Alphonse Beau de Rochas. ◆

👁 **see also**

Benz Diesel

▲ *Jesse Owens winning one of four gold medals – for the 100 yards, 220 yards, 4 × 100 yards relay, and long jump – at the 1936 Olympic Games in Berlin.*

Wilfred **Owen**

English poet during World War I
Born *1893* ***Died*** *1918 aged 25*

Wilfred Owen was already a poet when World War I began. After he enlisted in the army in 1915, the atmosphere in his poems soon changed from romance to bitter anger against the slaughter then going on in the trenches. As he puts it himself in his poem 'Anthem for Doomed Youth':

> What passing-bells for these
>   who die as cattle?
> Only the monstrous anger of
>   the guns.

In 1917 he returned to England with injuries, but went back to France the following year. He was shot dead one week before the end of the war. His poems, published after his death, did much to change the notion that war was still a brave and noble thing. Instead, he painted an unforgettable picture of the pointless waste, stupidity, and cruelty that had led to the deaths of so many young men on both sides in the trenches. ◆

Jesse **Owens**

American champion athlete
Born *1913* ***Died*** *1980 aged 67*

James Cleveland (J. C., thus 'Jesse') Owens from Alabama was 22 when he took part in an athletics meeting in Michigan. Within 45 minutes he had equalled the world record for the 100 yards, and broken the records for the 220 yards, the 220 yards hurdles and the long jump. His long jump world record lasted for 25 years.

The next year, 1936, was Olympic year. Adolf Hitler, the leader of Nazi Germany, wanted the Berlin Games to show the world that what he called 'the Aryan race' of white Europeans was superior to any other. After Jesse Owens had demolished that myth by winning four gold medals, Hitler refused even to shake hands with the black American athlete. ◆

Niccolò **Paganini**

Italian violinist and composer
Born 1782   Died 1840 aged 57

Although he began, at the age of five, to learn to play the mandolin, Niccolò Paganini soon turned to the violin. Urged on by an ambitious father, he made such good progress that he performed in public when he was only 12. In the following year the great violinist Alessandro Rolla declared that Paganini had nothing left to learn, but recommended that he study composition with Ferdinand Paer.

In 1801 Paganini broke away from his tyrannical father and worked as an orchestral player until 1809. He then began the career of a virtuoso soloist, travelling all over Italy and mesmerizing his audiences with his fabulous technique and strong sense of showmanship. Having conquered Italy, he then proceeded to conquer the rest of Europe, amassing great wealth in the process. Such was his technical wizardry that many people believed the rumour that he had been taught by the devil himself. ◆

Thomas **Paine**

British political thinker
Born 1737   Died 1809 aged 72

Thomas Paine devoted his life to speaking out for freedom, which meant he was loved and admired by many people, but hated and feared by others. In 1774 he emigrated to America, where he wrote a pamphlet called *Common Sense* (1776), a rousing call for independence from Britain. He also wrote against slavery and in favour of women's rights. In 1787 he returned to England where he wrote *The Rights of Man* (1791–1792), in which he supported the French Revolution and called for an end to illiteracy, poverty, unemployment, and war. Fearing arrest for treason, he fled to France in 1792 and was warmly welcomed. However, he was imprisoned when he opposed the execution of Louis XVI. He returned to America in 1802, but his last great book, *The Age of Reason* (1794–1795), had made him unpopular there; its plea for religious tolerance was considered anti-Christian. ◆

Palladio

Italian architect and writer
Born 1508   Died 1580 aged 72

Andrea di Pietro da Gondola, who became known as Palladio, was one of the greatest of all Italian architects. He began as a humble stone carver and at the age of thirteen was apprenticed to a carver in Padua. However, before long he ran away to Vicenza, a rich city near Venice. When he was 27 he was befriended by a group of gentlemen and scholars and, through them, began to learn about the architecture of Ancient Rome.

Palladio was particularly interested in the measurements and proportions that Ancient Roman architects had used and in the kinds of buildings they had designed. The houses (villas) that he designed in the countryside outside Venice are based on Roman country houses and farms. Like all his buildings, these houses had to be useful as well as beautiful.

Palladio wrote four books and illustrated them with examples of classical Roman architecture and his own buildings. These books have influenced architects ever since, particularly British architects of the eighteenth century who, following Palladio's example, invented a 'Palladian' style. ◆

▼ *Palladio used Ancient Roman principles of balance, proportion, and symmetry to design a range of fine buildings with elegant rooms, such as this one in the Villa Barbaro in Italy.*

Arnold **Palmer**

American champion golfer
Born 1929

Professional golf in America and Britain has achieved such wide popularity today thanks to the attacking style of Arnold Palmer in the 1950s and 1960s.

Pennsylvanian-born Palmer won the American amateur title in 1954. In his first major professional championship, the 1958 US Masters, he snatched a dramatic victory on the last two holes. Palmer went on to win all of the world major professional trophies except the US PGA championships, at a time when golf was becoming popular with television viewers. He was a strong and exciting player and attracted large crowds of fans wherever he competed.

After his best playing days were over, Palmer became a designer of golf courses around the world. ◆

👁 **see also**

Nicklaus

Emmeline and Christabel **Pankhurst**

Leaders of the suffragette campaign to win votes for women in Britain
Emmeline Pankhurst
Born 1858   Died 1928 aged 69
Christabel Pankhurst
Born 1880   Died 1958 aged 77

Emmeline Goulden married a lawyer, Richard Pankhurst, who believed that women should have the same rights as men. In 1903, after her husband had died, she and her forceful eldest daughter Christabel founded the Women's Social and Political Union, the 'suffragettes'. They and their supporters interrupted political meetings, smashed shop windows, and did all they could to win women the right to vote. When they were arrested they went on hunger strike. Christabel escaped to Paris in 1912 so that she was free to organize the campaign. They became quite ruthless, and even broke with Emmeline's younger daughter, Sylvia, because she worked independently from them with poor women in London's East End. When war came in 1914, Emmeline and Christabel urged women to work for their country.

Eventually, in 1918, women over the age of 30 in Britain were given the vote and in 1928, a month after Emmeline Pankhurst's death, all women in Britain were given the same voting rights as men. ◆

> *We are here to claim our rights as women, not only to be free, but to fight for freedom. That is our right as well as our duty.*
> CHRISTABEL PANKHURST, 1911

▼ *Emmeline and Christabel Pankhurst posing in prison uniform to rouse sympathy and admiration for the suffragette campaign.*

▶ *This Land League poster from 1881–1882 urged tenant farmers to refuse to pay rent while Charles Parnell and others were imprisoned for the cause. The campaign worked and they were released.*

Mungo **Park**

Scottish explorer who located the River Niger in West Africa
Born 1771   Died 1806 aged 34

Having first studied medicine, Mungo Park went to London where a group of gentlemen interested in African exploration chose him to search for the River Niger in West Africa.

In 1795 he set out on horseback from the mouth of the River Gambia. He travelled inland from one African kingdom to the next before being captured by Muslim nomads, who made him beg for his food and drink from a cattle trough. Park escaped and on 21 July 1796 had his first sight of the River Niger near Ségou. He followed it to Sansanding, where the onset of the rainy season forced him to return.

In England his book *Travels in the Interior Districts of Africa* was very successful, and in 1805 he was asked to lead a military expedition to follow the Niger to the sea. He set out with 42 British volunteers, but the rains came and many of the men died. At Sansanding he built a boat but by the time he launched it, only four men remained alive. Ill and in fear of the Muslim tribesmen, they travelled down river firing into the bush. They were attacked at Bussa and Park was last seen jumping overboard. ◆

▶ *Mungo Park led one of the first European expeditions to investigate the course of the River Niger. He played an important part in early European exploration of Africa.*

THE LAND WAR!

NO RENT!

O LANDLORDS GRASSLAND

nant Farmers, now is the time. Now is the hour.
u prayed false to the first call made upon you.
REDEEM YOUR CHARACTER NOW.

NO RENT

UNTIL THE SUSPECTS ARE RELEASED.

e man who pays Rent (whether an abatement
offered or not) while PARNELL, DILLON &c.,
e in Jail, will be looked upon as a Traitor to his
untry and a disgrace to his class.

o RENT, No Compromise, No Landlords' Grassland,
Under any circumstances.

void the Police, and listen not to spying and delu-
g Bailiffs.

NO RENT! LET THE LANDTHIEVES DO THEIR WORST!

HE LAND FOR THE PEOPLE!

Charles **Parnell**

Irish political leader
Born 1846   Died 1891 aged 45

Charles Parnell was a Protestant landowner in Ireland. However, he sympathized with the poverty of Catholic farmers and believed that the Irish should have their own government instead of being ruled from London as part of the United Kingdom.

He became an MP in the British Parliament in 1875, and was soon noted for his long speeches. In 1880 he became leader of the Home Rule Party. He was also president of the Land League which backed farmers who refused to pay rents for the land. The government imprisoned Parnell for this, but with so much support in Ireland they had to release him and help farmers to pay their debts and buy their own land.

By 1885 the demand for Home Rule had become so popular in Ireland that Parnell's party had 86 MPs and the British prime minister, William Gladstone, needed his help to stay in power. Gladstone decided to give Home Rule to Ireland but it did not come for another 35 years, because some MPs voted against the Bill. Parnell led more campaigns for Home Rule up to 1890 but then became involved in a divorce case. The Home Rule Party voted against him as their leader; he died the following year. ◆

see also
Gladstone

Blaise **Pascal**

French mathematician
Born 1623   Died 1662 aged 39

Blaise Pascal was a mathematical genius. By the age of 12 he had worked out the first 32 theorems of the Ancient Greek mathematician Euclid. At 16 he published a geometry book about parts of cones called conic sections. The French philosopher and mathematician René Descartes hardly believed that a 16-year-old could produce such advanced mathematics.

By the time he was 19 Pascal had invented a calculating machine for adding and subtracting numbers. Unfortunately it was too expensive to make and was never used.

Pascal was also very interested in Evangilista Torricelli's work with barometers. Pascal proved that the atmosphere really does have weight by sending his brother in law up a mountain with a barometer. The level of mercury in the tube dropped the higher he went.

Ten years before his death Pascal became a devout Catholic, abandoned his scientific and mathematical work and instead devoted his time to writing about religion and philosophy. ◆

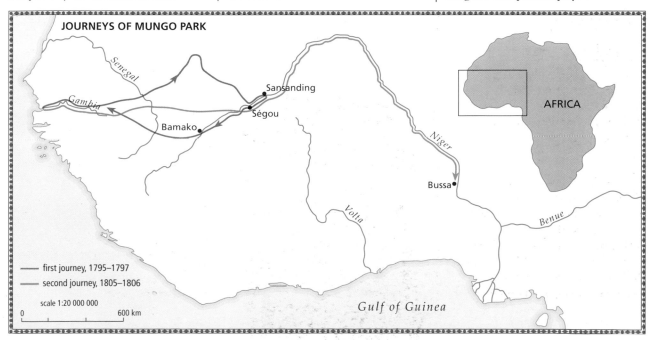

JOURNEYS OF MUNGO PARK

Senegal

Gambia

Sansanding

Ségou

Bamako

Niger

AFRICA

Bussa

Volta

Benue

Gulf of Guinea

—— first journey, 1795–1797
—— second journey, 1805–1806

scale 1:20 000 000
0   600 km

Louis **Pasteur**

French scientist who discovered that bacteria cause disease
Born *1822*   **Died** *1895 aged 72*

L ouis Pasteur was not a very
clever boy at school and was
mainly interested in painting. But
his life changed when he began
to study chemistry. He became
fascinated by the subject, worked
very hard, and in his twenties had
already become famous for his
experiments.

In 1856 Pasteur was asked to
help the French wine industry
because much of the wine was
going sour. He showed that this
was caused by a tiny living
organism, a yeast, which could
be killed by heat. This heating
process was named 'pasteurization'
and is used today to make milk
safe to drink.

Pasteur's most important work,
however, was his study of what
causes disease. He showed that
microscopic living organisms,
'germs' (bacteria), carried disease

▼ *Pasteur's scientific achievements
included a life-saving vaccine against
rabies.*

from one person to another. He
made a special study of a disease
called anthrax which kills cattle and
sheep. He isolated the anthrax
bacteria and prepared a weak form
which he injected into sheep; this
gave them immunity to the disease.
A similar method had been used
by Edward Jenner for preventing
smallpox in people.

Louis Pasteur then made a life-
saving vaccine for treating and
preventing the deadly disease called
rabies. He spent his whole life
dedicated to his work, and died a
respected and well-loved man. ◆

👁 **see also**
Jenner   Koch

Saint **Patrick**

The patron saint of Ireland
Born *c.390*   **Died** *c.460 aged about 70*

P atrick was born into a family of
Christians in Roman Britain. At
the age of 16 he was captured by
Irish pirates. He spent the next six
years as a slave in Ireland, where
there was no practised religion,

before escaping back to Britain.
According to his own later writings,
he was now a much changed
person. He trained to become
a priest, and in about 435 he
returned to Ireland. From then on
he devoted his life to converting
the Irish people to Christianity.
He worked mainly in the north,
where he had his own bishopric
at Armagh.

He is still the most popular saint
in Ireland, although no one is sure
where he died and was buried.
His feast day is 17 March, and in
pictures he is often shown treading
on snakes because, among many
other legends, St Patrick is
supposed to have driven all the
snakes out of Ireland. ◆

Saint **Paul**

Christian saint and apostle
Born *c.3*   **Died** *c.65 aged about 62*

T his Christian saint was originally
named Saul, after the first king
of Israel. He was Jewish by birth
and was also a Roman citizen. He
was so gifted that he was sent to
Jerusalem to train as a rabbi (a
Jewish religious teacher). In the
years after the crucifixion of Jesus
he joined others in persecuting
Jesus's followers.

The story of Saul's conversion
to Christianity tells how he was
travelling to Damascus one day
when he saw a light and heard the
voice of Jesus asking, 'Saul, Saul,
why do you persecute me?'. Blinded
for a while by the great light, he
was led to Damascus and there
he was baptized as a Christian.

He spent three years quietly
praying and thinking, and then
joined other Christians in Jerusalem.
This was the beginning of a life of
missionary journeys, teaching
people about Jesus. Paul, as he was

▲ *This 15th-century fresco shows St Paul (right) visiting St Peter, another Christian saint, in jail.*

now called, taught and wrote letters to the Christian congregations to help them to understand their new religion and follow its teachings.

Paul's life was very difficult. He was shipwrecked, beaten for his beliefs, and often criticized by those who had been followers of Jesus right from the beginning. Roman soldiers arrested him in Jerusalem after a mob of people attacked him because they thought he had ignored Jewish laws. He used his right as a Roman citizen to 'appeal to Caesar', which meant going to Rome to be tried. In Rome he was imprisoned for two years. He was probably killed in the reign of the Emperor Nero. ◆

👁 **see also**

Jesus

Linus **Pauling**

American chemist
Born 1901   **Died** 1994 aged 93

Linus Pauling was awarded the 1954 Nobel Prize for Chemistry for his work on the structure of molecules. He used information from X-ray diffraction and other techniques to find the lengths of the bonds holding the atoms together and the angles between them. He then used quantum mechanics to explain how the bonds were formed. His ideas explained the shape of simple molecules and helped scientists to understand some very complicated molecules such as proteins.

Pauling was a pacifist and campaigned for many years against the testing of nuclear weapons. He published his views in a book called *No More War!* and also took a petition, signed by over 11,000 scientists, to the United Nations calling for a ban on weapons testing. He was awarded the 1962 Nobel Peace Prize for his efforts, thus making Pauling one of the few people to receive two different Nobel Prizes. ◆

Luciano **Pavarotti**

Italian tenor
Born 1935

In 1961, after a period of study, Luciano Pavarotti won an international singing competition and made his début as Rodolfo in Puccini's *La Bohème*. He was first heard outside Italy in 1963 when he went to Holland and London, and in the following year he toured Australia with Joan Sutherland. He made his American début in 1968, since which time he has appeared in all the world's great opera houses and is widely regarded as one of the greatest tenors of the day.

Pavarotti is a great favourite with the general public, partly because of his larger-than-life personality and remarkable physical appearance. He has been closely associated in friendly rivalry with the tenors Placido Domingo and José Carerras. ◆

👁 **see also**   **Sutherland**

▼ *Luciano Pavarotti singing in his usual flamboyant manner.*

Ivan **Pavlov**

Russian physiologist whose experiments led to the study of behaviour in animals
Born 1849   Died 1936 aged 86

Ivan Pavlov's father was a priest and Pavlov himself started to prepare for the priesthood. However, he soon became more interested in science and decided to study science and medicine at university.

He became intrigued by the way we digest food and did lots of experiments with dogs. He knew that when a hungry dog is shown food it will immediately start to dribble saliva. This is called a reflex action. Pavlov cut open the cheeks of his dogs to reveal their salivary glands, so that he could observe the dribbling more clearly. He then rang a bell every time food was brought to the hungry dogs. After a while, ringing the bell alone was enough to make the dogs dribble. The dogs had learnt to expect food when the bell rang. Dribbling had become a reflex response to the bell ringing as well as to food.

Pavlov's experiments made scientists think more about why animals behave the way they do and how they learn different types of behaviour. ◆

Anna **Pavlova**

Russian-born ballerina
Born 1881   Died 1931 aged 49

Anna Pavlova's unusual talent for dancing was spotted while she was still at school. She was enrolled at the St Petersburg Imperial Ballet School and in 1906 the Imperial Russian Ballet gave her the title of prima ballerina. A year later she danced *The Dying Swan*, a ballet specially created for her.

By 1913 Pavlova had decided to leave Russia to set up her own company. Her aim was to bring ballet not only to the great European and American cities, but to places such as India, Africa, and South America where it had hardly ever been seen.

Over a period of 20 years she covered thousands of miles and gave nearly 5000 performances, amazing audiences with her lightness and grace. From 1912 she was based in London, where she was an inspiration to many younger English dancers. ◆

🕮 **see also**

Fonteyn

▼ *Anna Pavlova holding the final pose in a performance of* The Dying Swan, *her most famous role.*

Lester Bowles **Pearson**

Canadian politician who played an important role in international affairs
Born 1897   Died 1972 aged 75

As a young man, Lester Bowles Pearson worked as a stretcher-bearer in Greece with the Canadian army during World War I. He joined another regiment in 1917 and went to England. On his return home he completed a degree at the University of Toronto and tried careers in law, business, and teaching before he joined the Department of External Affairs.

Eventually he became a diplomat, working in London and also in Washington. He represented Canada when the United Nations was set up in 1945, and was president of the UN General Assembly in 1952. When there were problems between Israel and Egypt he suggested sending in a UN peacekeeping force. The idea worked well, and Pearson won the Nobel Peace Prize in 1957.

Pearson became leader of the Canadian Liberal Party in 1958. His party was in opposition at first, but in 1963 it won the election and Pearson became prime minister. Before he retired in 1968 his government had introduced welfare programmes, including a pension plan and a scheme to provide medical care for everyone. ◆

Robert **Peary**

American Arctic explorer
Born 1856   Died 1920 aged 63

On 6 April 1909, accompanied by four Inuits (Eskimos) and a black American friend, Matthew Henson, Robert Peary reached the North Pole after a long and very exhausting sledge journey. At least that is what everyone thought at the time. But during the 1980s, when Peary's record books were re-examined and his calculations checked, it seems that he got it wrong and probably missed the North Pole by about 80 kilòmetres. Nevertheless Peary can claim fame for the many journeys that he made across the Arctic ice-cap.

Robert Peary spent all of his working life in the United States navy and led many expeditions to little-known areas of the frozen north. Over a period of 20 years he studied Greenland and its isolated inhabitants. The native people befriended him and assisted him on his expeditions. Peary was the first person to prove beyond doubt that Greenland is an island. ◆

Robert **Peel**

British prime minister from 1834 to 1835 and from 1841 to 1846; he also founded the first police force
Born 1788   Died 1850 aged 62

Robert Peel was a tall, handsome man who became a brilliant scholar at Oxford University. Thanks to his father's money and influence, he became a Member of Parliament when he was only 21, supporting the Tory (Conservative) Party. He held a number of government posts in Britain and Ireland before becoming home secretary, where he was in charge of law and order. He started the London Metropolitan Police force, and policemen were called 'bobbies' and 'peelers' after him.

Peel became a baronet in 1830 when his father died, and was briefly prime minister from 1834 to 1835. Then, as leader of the Conservative Party, he became prime minister again in 1841, staying in power until 1846. To

▲ *Robert Peel is best remembered for starting the police force in London. The arrival of 'peelers' helped to stop a lot of petty crime, particularly amongst young boys.*

help poorer people he reduced the taxes on goods, especially food, and brought back income tax instead. His party split, though, when he repealed the Corn Laws (which had kept the price of bread high by putting taxes on imported grain), and he resigned as prime minister. He was afterwards thought of as the founder of modern conservatism. ◆

I. M. **Pei**

Chinese-born American architect
Born 1917

Ieoh Ming Pei was born in Canton in southern China. When he was 18 he went to America to study architecture and has worked there ever since. He became an American citizen in 1948 and is considered one of the country's most successful architects. Most of his buildings have bold and simple forms, like gigantic pieces of sculpture. Some of them (for instance, his extension to the National Gallery of Art in Washington D.C.) look from the outside like huge blocks of stone or concrete. Others (like the tall and slender John Hancock Tower in Boston) are made of steel and glass, which reflect the sky and the Sun. Pei is most famous in Europe for the pyramids of steel and glass in the courtyard of the Louvre in Paris. They look like sculpture, but they are there to let light into a great underground hall – Pei's new entrance to all the museums in the Louvre. ◆

▼ *Pei's elegant glass pyramids act as the roof for the Louvre's new subterranean service area and make it feel light and airy.*

▲ Pelé, who wore the number 10 team shirt, is thought by many to be the greatest football player of all time.

Pelé

Brazilian football player
Born *1940*

Edson Arantes do Nascimento was given the nickname 'Pelé' by the friends he played football with as a boy. He showed so much promise for his first club, Noroeste, that he was signed by the top club Santos and was picked to play for the national Brazilian team when he was only 16. A year later, in 1958, he scored two goals to help Brazil win the World Cup final.

In a career that lasted until 1977, Pelé showed that he was the complete footballer, combining speed and ball-control with fierce and accurate shooting. Before leaving Santos to play for the New York Cosmos in 1971, he had scored 1216 goals in 1254 games. He also played 110 games for Brazil, winning World Cup winners' medals in 1958 and 1970. ◆

William **Penn**

English Quaker who founded the colony of Pennsylvania
Born *1644*   **Died** *1718 aged 73*

William Penn was very religious from an early age and eventually converted to the Quaker faith. Quakers believe that each person must look for true religion in their own heart and in their own way. The Anglican Church (Church of England) at the time found this hard to accept, preferring instead that everyone should worship in the same style. Penn was expelled from Oxford University for refusing to go to compulsory Church of England services and was later imprisoned for preaching his own faith.

On his release Penn met other Quakers who were all looking for a place where they could follow their own beliefs in freedom. In 1680 Penn asked King Charles II for a gift of land in the Americas in return for a large debt the king owed Penn's father. The gift came, made up of land on the east coast between Maryland and New York. It was called Pennsylvania ('Penn's woods'). Penn sailed out there with other Quakers. Once established, he was so honest and just in his dealings with the local Native Americans that there was very little trouble between them and the Quakers, although he did have some difficulties with his own often unruly followers. ◆

👁 **see also**

Fox

Samuel **Pepys**

English diarist
Born *1633*   **Died** *1703 aged 70*

On 1 January 1660, Samuel Pepys (pronounced 'peeps') started writing a diary. He wrote in code, probably because he did not want his wife to read it. His diary shows that although he was fond of her, he also enjoyed flirting and

▼ The Fire of London in 1666 was recorded by Pepys in his diary.

having affairs with other women.

Pepys had a good job organizing supplies for the navy. He travelled in the ship which brought Charles II back to England in 1660, and also attended his coronation. Pepys's boss was the king's brother, the Duke of York (later James II).

Pepys lived through the terrible plague of 1665, and the Fire of London the following year, and recorded these events in his diary. He kept his diary for nine years. When you read it, you can almost step straight back into the London of Charles II. ◆

see also

Charles II

Pericles

Ancient Greek statesman
Born c.495 BC
Died c.429 BC aged about 66

Pericles dominated the city of Athens' affairs from 461 BC. He helped to make Athens a great city

and developed the way it was organized, so that all the male adult citizens could meet in a large assembly and make decisions about peace and war and new laws. These decisions were inscribed on stone and publicly displayed. This was the first recorded democracy.

Pericles also made Athens strong by extending the city's walls and by making sure the navy was capable of controlling the seas around Greece. Athens was then able to build an empire from the cities and islands that looked to it for protection. Pericles also arranged for beautiful buildings to be built on the hill of the Acropolis. The most famous of these is the Parthenon, a large temple to the city's goddess Athene.

Pericles had enemies, and not everyone thought that democracy was the best way of running the city. Many of the comic plays written at the time made cruel fun of him. However, Pericles was such a good speaker in the assemblies that he remained in control for many years. He was elected 'general' (a political office as well as a military one) fifteen times.

Pericles wanted Athens to be at peace but he could not avoid a war with Sparta, a city in southern Greece. War broke out in 431 BC and Athens was eventually defeated. Pericles died in a great plague that hit Athens soon after the beginning of the war. ◆

Eva **Perón**

Argentinian political leader
Born 1919   **Died** 1952 aged 33

Maria Eva Duarte was born near Buenos Aires, Argentina. Her family was poor so she went to Buenos Aires at the age of 15 to become an actress. She met Juan

▲ *Eva Perón (Evita) became immensely popular with the Argentinian public because she devoted herself to helping the poor, and improving education and women's rights.*

Perón there in 1944 when she was a successful radio actress and married him the following year.

Juan Perón had held various government posts since 1943. When he became president of Argentina in 1946, Eva (or 'Evita' as she was known) virtually ran the ministeries of Labour and of Health. By 1947 she owned or controlled almost every radio station in Argentina, and had closed or banned over 100 newspapers and magazines.

She was a gifted speaker and campaigned hard for women's rights. However, her bid to become vice-president was blocked by military leaders who feared she might one day become president and be in charge of them. Her death from cancer shortly afterwards contributed to the decline of her husband's regime. ◆

Henri Philippe Pétain

French general and head of state from 1940 to 1944

Born *1856* **Died** *1951 aged 95*

Henri Philippe Omer Pétain was a soldier who became an instructor at army school, before being made a general in 1914. In World War I he became a national hero for organizing the halting of the German advance at Verdun in 1916, and in 1917 he was made French commander-in-chief.

He served in a number of posts before retiring from the army in 1931 to enter politics. As minister for war from 1934 he was responsible for preparations for World War II. In 1940 he became prime minister and signed a truce with Germany which surrendered three-fifths of France to German control. From 1940 to 1942 Pétain was head of a French government

▼ *In this poster, Henri Pétain, the hero of World War I, tries to reassure the French people that, as prime minister, he will help them through the difficult times – namely World War II.*

set up in the town of Vichy. This government had no real power, and had even less when German forces completed their occupation of France.

At the end of World War II Pétain was arrested by the Allies and tried for treason because he had worked closely with the Germans. He was sentenced to death but this was altered to life imprisonment. ◆

Peter the Great

Tsar of Russia from 1682 to 1725

Born *1672* **Died** *1725 aged 52*

Peter came to the throne as joint tsar with his half-brother Ivan at the age of ten, but spent his childhood playing and being educated in the countryside outside Moscow. His stepsister, Sophia, ruled in his place until she tried to take power for herself. In 1689 Peter took charge and sent Sophia to a nunnery.

After Ivan's death in 1696, Peter became sole ruler. He spent two years in western Europe studying various industries, and brought back

▲ *This painting portrays Peter the Great as a ship's carpenter. Carpentry was a hobby at which he became highly skilled.*

to Russia teachers of all the arts and crafts which his country most needed. The reforms he introduced with the help of foreign statesmen and craftsmen turned Russia into a more modern country, with an army and navy, schools and universities, and its first public newspaper.

Peter was also a soldier tsar and spent much of his life at war. His greatest victory was against the Swedes at Poltava in 1709 during the 21-year 'Northern War'. His victories in this war enabled him to build a new capital city for Russia, St Petersburg, on the Baltic coast.

Peter had a son, Alexei, by his first wife Eudoxia, but Alexei plotted against Peter and was put to death in 1718. As he had no other heir, Peter's second wife, Catherine, became Catherine I, Empress of Russia, when he died in 1725. ◆

Saint Peter

Leader of the 12 apostles, the first followers of Jesus

Lived during the 1st century

Peter (originally called Simon) and his brother, Andrew, were

J'AI ÉTÉ AVEC VOUS DANS LES JOURS GLORIEUX

JE RESTE AVEC VOUS DANS LES JOURS SOMBRES...

SERVIR

·1918· 1940

fishermen who lived near the Sea of Galilee. One day when they were out fishing, Jesus called to them to follow him and become 'fishers of men'. From then on Peter and Andrew were especially close to Jesus until his death.

Jesus gave Simon the name Cephas, which means a stone. Peter comes from the Greek equivalent, *petra*. Peter seems to have been the first person to say that Jesus was the Messiah (the Jewish leader prophesied in the Old Testament of the Bible). In Matthew's gospel Jesus says that Peter and his faith are the rock on which the Church will be built.

There are many stories about Peter in the gospels. He seems to have been a person who made mistakes as well as showing great faith. When Jesus was arrested in Jerusalem and taken away to be tried, Peter, in a state of panic, denied three times that he knew him. Afterwards he wept bitterly at his betrayal.

After the crucifixion of Jesus, Peter preached that Jesus was alive. He was imprisoned twice, but escaped and travelled round the Mediterranean telling people about Jesus and his teaching.

There is a tradition that Peter spent the last years of his life, before being crucified for his beliefs, as the first bishop of Rome. ◆

see also

Jesus

Francesco Petrarch

Italian poet and scholar
Born 1304   Died 1374 aged 70

Francesco Petrarch (Petrarca in Italian) was the son of an Italian exile. He spent his childhood

▲ Riders prepare to form a procession on this frieze from the Parthenon which is now in the British Museum, London. Phidias directed all of the sculpture for the Parthenon.

in Italy and France, before attending university in Bologna in 1320 to study the classics. He returned to Avignon, where he had spent some time as a child, on the death of his father in 1326. A year later he saw and fell in love with a woman whom he called Laura. Her true identity is still a mystery but she was the inspiration behind the love lyrics of Petrarch's *Canzoniere* (1342), a book of sonnets, songs, and madrigals.

Petrarch's association with the wealthy Colonnas and Visconti families allowed him to travel extensively in Europe and he became known for his genius and great learning. His writing includes the epic poem *Africa* (1338–1341), *The Life of Solitude* (1344), and several volumes of letters. ◆

Phidias

Ancient Greek sculptor
Born c.490 BC
Died c.430 BC aged about 60

Phidias was the most famous artist of ancient Greece. Sadly, all of his sculptures have long been

destroyed, so we have to rely mainly on the writings of ancient Greek and Roman authors to get an idea of his genius. He was renowned for the grandeur of his work and no one else portrayed so nobly the majesty of the gods and goddesses. His statue of Zeus, the king of the gods, in his huge temple at Olympia, was one of the seven wonders of the ancient world. It was made of gold and ivory, as was his statue of Athena in her temple – the Parthenon – at Athens.

Phidias was the director of all the decorative sculpture of the Parthenon, and fortunately much of it survives (most of it is in the British Museum). He probably did not carve any of it himself, but he must have approved it and it gives some idea of how beautiful his own work must have been. One other direct link with him survives; in the 1950s archaeologists excavated his workshop at Olympia and found a cup with the inscription 'I belong to Phidias' – the ancient equivalent of his tea-mug. ◆

Phidippides

Greek soldier who ran the first 'marathon'
Lived during the 5th century BC

In 490 BC Persian invaders landed on Greek shores at Marathon. Legend has it that Phidippides, one of the Greek soldiers, ran to seek help from the Spartans. To do this he covered a distance of about 240 km. Some say that he then ran back to take part in the battle. Eventually, the Greeks managed to beat off the Persian attack, losing only about 190 men while the Persians lost over 6000.

According to the legend, the Greek general, Miltiades, sent Phidippides to carry the news of the victory to Athens. He raced the 40 km to Athens, announced the victory, and dropped down dead.

The long-distance race which we call the marathon derives its name from Phidippides's run. The length of the race varied for a while but eventually settled at 26 miles (42 km – similar in length to Phidippides's legendary run). An extra 385 yards was added at the 1908 Olympics held in London so that the race could finish in front of the Royal Box; 26 miles and 385 yards (42.2 km) has remained the official length of the marathon ever since. ◆

Philip II of Spain

King of Spain from 1556 to 1598
Born 1527   Died 1598 aged 71

Philip II of Spain was the richest, mightiest ruler in Christian Europe. His empire included parts of Italy, the Netherlands, and vast stretches of South and Central America, as well as Spain and Portugal. From 1559 he never left these last two kingdoms. As his reign went on he spent more and more time in his monastery-cum-palace, the Escorial, several miles from Spain's capital, Madrid.

Philip was a very serious Roman Catholic, at a time when wars to do with religion were ravaging Europe. He involved his peoples in many of these wars, but he rarely let his religious aims get in the way of more worldly ones. For example, when he sent the Spanish Armada to attack England in 1588, it was for military and not religious reasons. His reign was part of the so-called 'Golden Age' of Spain. However, Philip spent so much of Spain's wealth on his wars that the Spanish era of power and prosperity was almost over by the time he died.

Philip's second wife was Mary I of England. ◆

◗ **see also**

Mary I

▼ *A detail from a Dutch stained-glass window showing Philip II of Spain and his wife, Mary, Queen of England.*

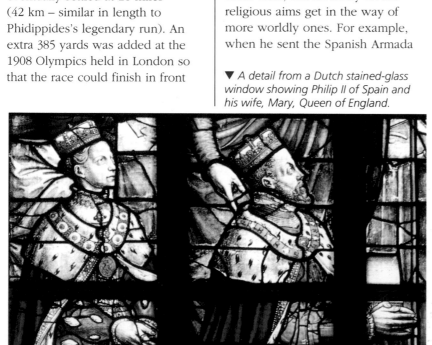

Pablo Picasso

Spanish painter and sculptor
Born 1881   Died 1973 aged 91

Pablo Picasso showed a truly exceptional talent for art when very young. By the age of 11, he was writing and illustrating art magazines as a hobby. He hated school and never learned to write well. He loved painting and worked at nothing else.

He often helped his father, a painter, with his work. One evening his father left Picasso to finish a picture of pigeons. On his return, he saw an astonishingly lifelike painting. He gave his son his own palette and brushes and never painted again. Picasso was just 13.

Many people realized that Picasso was a genius, but he wanted to do things in his own way, even if he disappointed those who expected him to become a traditional painter. At first he suffered years of poverty, but he was both courageous and self-disciplined, with an enormous appetite for hard work.

As his extraordinary talents developed, he was constantly breaking the rules of artistic tradition; he shocked the public with his strange and powerful pictures. He intentionally avoided 'copying' real life in his paintings,

◀ *Many of Picasso's figure paintings shocked audiences with their distorted views of their subjects, like this one, Portrait of Dora Maar.*

> *I paint objects as I think them, not as I see them.*
> PABLO PICASSO, 1959

but designed new forms to give fresh ways of seeing things in the world around us.

Picasso made drawings, paintings, collages, prints, theatre sets, sculptures, pottery, and ceramics. His style changed many times, but he is probably best known for his 'Cubist' pictures, which used simple geometric shapes and only a few colours. His life's work entirely changed our ideas about art. ◆

see also
Braque

Auguste **Piccard**

Swiss engineer and scientific explorer
Born 1884   **Died** 1962 aged 78

With his twin brother Jean, Auguste Piccard qualified as an engineer in Zurich. Together they developed a keen interest in ballooning – ultimately to investigate what happens high in the Earth's atmosphere – and in 1913 made a 16-hour ascent. During World War I they both joined the balloon section of the Swiss army. After the war, Jean emigrated to America to follow a university career, but Auguste continued his ballooning while professor of physics at Brussels University.

▼ *Auguste Piccard with a sketch of his 'mesoscaphe' – an under-sea 'helicopter'. This was a diving boat with a rotor propellor which would allow it to descend and ascend vertically to depths of 1800 m.*

In 1931 he attracted worldwide publicity with an ascent of nearly 16,000 m, using the first balloon to be equipped with a pressurized gondola. Two years later he reached over 16,200 m. But his dream had always been 'to plunge into the sea deeper than any man before', to explore the ocean depths. This he achieved, with his son Jacques, in a self-propelled diving machine called a bathyscaphe. Together they descended to over 3000 m in 1953; Jacques – in a later vessel, the *Trieste* – went down to almost 11,000 m in 1960. ◆

see also
Gay-Lussac   Montgolfier brothers

Mary **Pickford**

American film star
Born 1893   **Died** 1979 aged 86

Mary Pickford was the stage name of Canadian-born Gladys Smith. She was acting when she was only five years old and at 15 was already appearing on stage in New York, earning a living for her family.

She began working in movies as an extra for D. W. Griffith's Biograph Company and became the first star of the silent screen. From 1913, as Mary Pickford, a succession of sweet and innocent roles, such as *Rebecca of Sunnybrook Farm* (1917) and *Pollyanna* (1920), made her 'America's sweetheart' – and also one of America's richest women. In 1919 she formed United Artists with Charlie Chaplin, Douglas Fairbanks (her husband) and Griffith, to ensure film profits went to them rather than the studio bosses. ◆

see also
Chaplin   Goldwyn

Piero della Francesca

Italian painter
Born *c.1415*   **Died** *1492 aged about 75*

Piero della Francesca was one of the most important painters in one of the greatest periods of Italian art. He was a mathematician as well as an artist and his paintings have an almost geometric harmony.

They are mainly on religious subjects, although he also did a few portraits. Sometimes they can look a little stiff at first sight, but they have a solemn dignity and a subtle beauty of colouring which other painters could not match. Piero was born and died in the

little town of Sansepolcro, about 40 miles from Florence, and most of his best paintings are in places that until recently were not much visited by travellers. Because of this, they were virtually ignored for four centuries after his death. It was not until the early 20th century that he was 'rediscovered' by art historians and took his deserved place among the great masters. ◆

▼ *One of Piero della Francesca's most famous paintings, entitled* The Baptism of Christ.

Lester **Piggott**

English champion jockey
Born *1935*

Lester Piggott rode his first winner in 1948 at the age of 12, and soon established a winning habit as a flat-race jockey. He had his first Derby winner in 1954 and, by 1983, had ridden a record nine winners in that classic race.

Between 1964 and 1971 he was champion jockey each season. He retired from the saddle in 1985 to become a trainer, by which time he had ridden over 4000 winners. Because he did not pay as much income tax as he should have done, he was sent to prison for tax evasion in 1987. Piggott returned to racing in 1990. ◆

Camille **Pissarro**

French painter
Born *1830*   **Died** *1903 aged 73*

Camille Pissarro was one of the leading Impressionists – the artists who revolutionized painting with their bright colours and sketchy brushwork. He was the oldest of the group, and the others tended to regard him as a kindly father figure. Like the other Impressionists, he endured great poverty early in his career, and it was only in the last ten years of his life that he achieved any financial success. By this time his eyesight was failing and he had to give up painting landscapes out of doors: many of his late pictures were views of Paris that he painted while looking out of windows. Eventually he became completely blind. ◆

see also
Manet   Monet

William **Pitt** (the younger)

Prime minister of Britain from 1783 to 1801 and from 1804 to 1806
Born 1759   Died 1806 aged 46

William Pitt, the younger son of the Earl of Chatham, who was also named William Pitt, became a member of Parliament in 1781 at the age of 22. In 1783, at the age of 24, he became the youngest person to hold the office of prime minister.

For the next ten years his government worked hard to ensure Britain's economic recovery after the American War of Independence. During this time he raised taxes to pay off Britain's debts, and reduced widespread smuggling.

When France declared war on Britain in 1793 after the French Revolution, Pitt fought back hard, forming an alliance with Russia, Sweden, and Austria. He censored the newspapers and sometimes imprisoned without trial those who wanted a revolution in Britain too. Nearer to home, he secured the Union of Great Britain and Ireland in 1800 after the Irish uprising two years earlier. However, the strain of so many wars eventually seemed to be too much for him, and he died only two years into his second term as prime minister. ◆

Francisco **Pizarro**

Spanish conqueror of the Inca empire
Born c.1474   Died 1541 aged about 67

As a young man, Francisco Pizarro looked after a herd of pigs. He then decided to go to Hispaniola in the Caribbean to try his fortunes there and to take part in several exploring expeditions.

In 1522 he was scratching a living as a landowner in Panama when he heard rumours of the Inca empire in Peru and its fabulous wealth. Having made an expedition to check that it really existed, he returned to Spain in 1528 and asked permission from the king, Emperor Charles V, to conquer the land.

▲ *Once Francisco Pizarro had conquered the Inca empire, it was not long before the Spaniards had conquered the whole country of Peru.*

In 1532 Pizarro arrived in Peru to find the country split by civil war. He seized the emperor, Atahualpa, and demanded a huge ransom of gold and silver. After the money was paid, Pizarro had Atahualpa executed on the grounds that he was plotting against the Spaniards. Spain now ruled the Incas – Pizarro had conquered the Inca empire of several million people with an initial force of just 180 men. But he did not enjoy his victory for very long. In 1541 he was killed by rival Spaniards. ◆

see also
Atahualpa   Charles V   Cortés

Max **Planck**

German physicist
Born 1858   Died 1947 aged 89

Max Planck was appointed professor of physics at Kiel and then Berlin universities. He spent much of his early research on thermodynamics – the branch of physics that deals with the transformation of heat into other forms of energy. In 1900 he solved a problem that had troubled scientists for a long time: hot objects radiate heat energy but the energy stops suddenly instead of tapering away gradually as scientists expected. Planck explained this by saying that energy is always transferred in fixed amounts, rather like money. Just as in money there is a smallest-value coin, and a donation of money cannot be less than this, so energy has a smallest value. It is called a quantum of energy. Different currencies have different smallest coins. Similarly, different energy exchanges have different-sized quanta – though they are always extremely small. Planck's 'quantum theory' was developed further by other scientists, and was one of the most important discoveries of the 20th century. Planck was awarded the Nobel Prize for Physics in 1918. ◆

see also
Fermi   Heisenberg   Schrödinger

Sylvia **Plath**

American novelist and poet
Born *1932*   **Died** *1963 aged 30*

Since Sylvia Plath's death by suicide, she has been one of the most discussed women writers of the 20th century. She has become a feminist heroine, seen as both a rebel and a victim. In 1956 she married the English poet Ted Hughes, but they separated in 1962 and she lived alone in London.

Shortly before her death, her only novel, *The Bell Jar* (1963), was published; it tells of a woman student's emotional breakdown. Plath also published two volumes of poetry in her lifetime, but it was the collection published after her death, *Ariel* (1965), that made her reputation. Her best-known poems deal hauntingly with personal pain and tragedy, but she wrote tender and witty poems as well. ◆

Plato

Ancient Greek philosopher
Born *429 BC*   **Died** *347 BC aged 82*

Plato was born into an important Athenian family. He was well educated and at the age of 20 became a pupil of Socrates. The teachings of Socrates had an enormous influence on Plato's thinking and on what he wrote.

When Socrates was put to death in 399 BC, Plato went to live for a time in Megara, west of Athens. He also travelled for the next 12 years throughout Greece and to Egypt, Italy, and Sicily. In 387 BC he returned to Athens and started a school of philosophy. Most schools were held in the open air, in shady walks or under the colonnaded verandas of public buildings. His school was established in a park and gymnasium (sports ground)

about 2 km outside the city walls. This park was sacred to Academus, and so Plato's school became known as the Academy (a word still used for some types of school). The Academy of Plato lasted until 529.

Plato believed, like Socrates, that the right way to teach was to ask questions and then let the pupils discover the truth for themselves. A great deal of this teaching was published in his *Dialogues,* which were discussions between various people. Probably Plato's most famous work was *The Republic,* in which he discusses the ideal state or society. Plato describes the last hours and thoughts of Socrates in a book called *Phaedon.* ◆

👁 **see also**

Avicenna   Socrates

▼ *A detail of* Aristotle and Plato *(right) from Raphael's painting* School of Athens.

Plutarch

Ancient Greek historian
Born *C.AD 46*
Died *c.120 aged about 74*

The son of a philosopher, Plutarch studied philosophy himself in Athens and later lectured on this subject in Rome. In his travels through Egypt, Greece, and Italy, he set about collecting as much information as possible about the Greek and Roman heroes he later described in his greatest book, *Plutarch's Lives.* This was written in order to encourage respect between Greeks and Romans by describing the lives of the most noble citizens from both countries. Plutarch's short biographies did not stop simply at details of his subject's childhood, achievements, and death. He also added interesting stories about them, aiming to please as well as educate his readers. Translated

into English in 1579, *Plutarch's Lives* greatly influenced William Shakespeare. In plays like *Julius Caesar, Coriolanus*, and *Antony and Cleopatra*, Shakespeare often quotes whole passages taken from Plutarch with little alteration. Plutarch also wrote about philosophy and religion. ◆

see also
Shakespeare

Pocahontas

Native American girl who befriended some English settlers in America
Born *1595*   **Died** *1617 aged 22*

▲ *This portrait of Pocahontas, painted by an unknown artist in 1616, shows her dressed like an English lady.*

Pocahontas (her name means 'the little playful one') was the favourite daughter of Powhatan, chief of the area where the first English settlement was established at Jamestown, Virginia in 1607. She was about 12 when one of the settlers, Captain John Smith, was dragged before her father to be clubbed to death. Pocahontas pleaded successfully for his life to be spared.

Some years later, Pocahontas was taken hostage by the English in Jamestown who wanted her father to return his English prisoners. During her time in Jamestown she converted to Christianity and, to cement Anglo-Native American relations, she married a tobacco planter, John Rolfe. He took her and their baby son to London and they lived there for a year. However, she became homesick and decided to return home. She joined a ship that was sailing for Virginia, but died of smallpox before it had left England. ◆

Edgar Allan **Poe**

American poet and writer
Born *1809*   **Died** *1849 aged 40*

Edgar Allan Poe's mother died when he was only three and he was adopted by a wealthy merchant who took him to England. After going to school in London, Poe returned to America to study at the University of Virginia. He then joined the army, but managed to get himself discharged for neglect of duty in 1831.

By this time, Poe had already published two volumes of poems and he decided to make his living by writing. He edited newspapers and magazines, and wrote stories, verse, and critical essays. Although he was admired as a poet – *The Raven and Other Poems* was

published in 1845 – he is most famous for his horror stories, such as *The Fall of the House of Usher* (1839), which tells the tale of a madman who buries his sister alive. Many of his stories have inspired horror movies.

Poe failed to earn much of a living by writing, and became an alcoholic. After his wife's death in 1847 he became more depressed and wrote less and less. ◆

Jackson **Pollock**

American painter
Born *1912*   **Died** *1956 aged 44*

Jackson Pollock was the most famous representative of a style of painting known as Abstract Expressionism. In this, the artist virtually attacks the canvas with paint to express emotions directly and powerfully. Pollock also often laid his canvases on the floor and dripped paint on to them, a form which became known as 'Action Painting'.

Abstract Expressionism is now recognized as one of America's most original contributions to art, but Pollock endured poverty and mockery before he achieved success – one magazine article even dubbed him 'Jack the Dripper'. ◆

▼ *Jackson Pollock's* Mural *(1943) is typical of his work.*
University of Iowa Museum of Art, Oil on canvas.
Gift of Peggy Guggenheim.

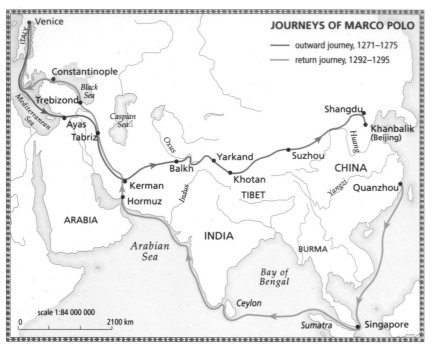

JOURNEYS OF MARCO POLO
— outward journey, 1271–1275
— return journey, 1292–1295

scale 1:84 000 000
0   2100 km

Marco **Polo**

Italian merchant and traveller
Born c.1254 **Died** 1324 aged about 70

In the 13th century, Cathay, as people then called China, was a romantic, unknown land to most Europeans. When Marco Polo was 18 he was invited by his father and uncle, Niccolò and Maffeo, to go with them to the court of the emperor Kublai Khan at Khanbalik (Beijing). Niccolò and Maffeo had already visited Kublai Khan, the first Europeans to do so.

The three merchants set out from their home in Venice in 1271. They went by ship to the Mediterranean coast of Turkey, and the rest of the way overland. They took the southern branch of the Silk Road, along which merchants from China regularly brought silk to Europe. The road runs north of the Himalayas, and across the Gobi Desert. The whole journey took nearly four years.

Kublai Khan received them warmly at court. Marco, who had a gift for languages, became a civil

▲ *The book Marco Polo wrote on his return from the Chinese empire contained descriptions of Kublai Khan's court and of the countries he visited.*

servant and travelling diplomat for Kublai. He was sent on many missions, visiting India, Myanmar (Burma), and Sri Lanka.

After 17 years the Polos decided it was time to return home. They went by sea, by way of Singapore, Sri Lanka, and the Persian Gulf. They arrived back in Venice in 1295 with a fortune in jewels, having been away 24 years.

Marco spent the last 30 years of his life as a Venetian merchant. At one time he was captured by the Genoese and became a prisoner of war in Genoa. While there he dictated the story of his travels. This is not a story of his personal adventures but a description of the almost unknown Mongol Empire. Many readers thought he was making things up, and Venetians called him *Il Milione*, meaning 'he of the million lies'. Later, though, people realized his account was mostly true. It influenced

Christopher Columbus's decision to look for a westward route to China and Japan. ◆

👁 **see also**
Columbus   Kublai Khan

Pol Pot

Prime minister of Cambodia from 1975 to 1979, and leader of the Khmer Rouge
Born 1928 **Died** 1998 aged 73

Pol Pot grew up in Cambodia, when Cambodia was part of Indo-China – a French territory. Having trained as a Buddhist monk and been educated at a French university, he joined the anti-French resistance under Ho Chi Minh. Cambodia achieved independence from France in 1953.

In 1960 Communists in Cambodia founded their own Communist Party, which was later called the Khmer Rouge. Pol Pot, who had risen to a high position within the Party, organized country people to

▼ *Visible evidence of the many people who died in Cambodia at the hands of Pol Pot's Khmer Rouge.*

270

fight the government. In 1975 they won control and Pol Pot became prime minister.

Between 1975 and 1979, his government forced the inhabitants of the capital city, Phnom Penh, to move into the countryside. He ordered that enemies of the Khmer Rouge should be killed; over 2 million people may have died. Something had to be done to stop the killing: in December 1979, the Vietnamese army invaded Cambodia and Pol Pot fled into Thailand. In his absence, he was sentenced to death for some of the worst crimes in history. ◆

see also
Ho Chi Minh

Pompey

Roman general and politician
Born *106* BC   **Died** *48* BC *aged 58*

In 510 BC the inhabitants of Rome drove out their king. Thereafter, they elected two consuls each year to rule the city for a year. The system worked well until the 1st century BC, when wars broke out between rivals for power. Between 88 and 81 BC there were wars between Sulla and Marius (who died in 86 BC), then between Sulla and Marius's followers.

Pompey raised an army to support Sulla, and thereby became one of Rome's most important politicians. Between 83 and 81 BC he destroyed Sulla's enemies, and then put down other revolts against the Roman government. Pompey's success gave him great prestige: he was elected consul in 80 BC, and for the next 20 years he held important government posts.

The other leading Roman at this time was Julius Caesar. Pompey and Caesar worked closely together at

first, but in 49 BC they quarrelled and began a civil war. Pompey and his supporters fled to Greece, where Caesar defeated them at Pharsalus (48 BC). Pompey fled to Egypt, but was murdered later the same year. ◆

see also
Caesar

Alexander **Pope**

English poet
Born *1688*   **Died** *1744 aged 56*

Alexander Pope educated himself at home with the help of his father. He was unable to go to school because of a crippling spinal disease and later was banned from studying at university because of his Roman Catholic background.

Pope started writing poetry when he was very young, soon showing mastery of the rhyming couplets which were so popular then. When only 23 he wrote *An Essay in Criticism,* a witty poem which includes the now famous line, 'To err is human, to forgive, divine'. Three years later he wrote his mock epic poem, *The Rape of the Lock.* He also translated Homer's *Odyssey* and *Iliad,* edited an edition of Shakespeare's works, and wrote many poems which were sharply critical of the writers and politicians of his time. His brilliant poetry gave much pleasure to others, except, of course, to those he was attacking. ◆

see also
Homer

Ferdinand **Porsche**

German car designer
Born *1875*   **Died** *1951 aged 76*

As a young man Ferdinand Porsche was an engineer with the Daimler-Benz company before becoming a designer for the Auto-Union racing team in 1930.

In 1934 he designed a revolutionary new type of car, to be produced cheaply, with the engine, unusually, at the rear. This idea was taken up enthusiastically by the Nazi government. In 1936 they promised to produce the Volkswagen (German for 'people's car') in large numbers for the civilian (non-military) market. This car became known as the Beetle, and proved to be immensely popular worldwide. By the late 1980s over 20 million had been sold.

Ferdinand Porsche also designed the Porsche sports car, first built in 1948. His son formed the Porsche Company in the same year. ◆

▼ *Two of Ferdinand Porsche's most famous car designs: a 1947 version of his VW Beetle (bottom), and a 1951 soft-top version of his up-market Porsche (top).*

Cole **Porter**

American songwriter
Born *1891*   **Died** *1964 aged 73*

Cole Porter started to play the violin when he was six and the piano when he was eight. He had even written an operetta and had a waltz published by the time he was eleven. The son of wealthy parents, he went to both Yale and Harvard universities, studying law and music. After World War I Porter took classes with composer Vincent d'Indy in Paris.

> *In olden days a glimpse of*
> *   stocking*
> *Was looked on as something*
> *   shocking*
> *Now, heaven knows,*
> *Anything goes.*
>
> COLE PORTER
> 'Anything Goes', 1934

See America First (1916) was his first musical on Broadway but his most successful shows were *Anything Goes* (1934), *Kiss Me Kate* (1948), *Can Can* (1953) and *Silk Stockings* (1955). A horse-riding accident in 1937 left him confined to a wheelchair and in great pain. However, this did not stop the flow of songs with their cleverly rhymed lyrics and sparkling tunes. ◆

🕮 **see also**
Berlin Gershwin Rodgers

Beatrix **Potter**

English writer and illustrator of children's stories
Born *1866*   **Died** *1943 aged 77*

Beatrix Potter enjoyed sending letters to her friends' children; when she ran out of news, she filled the pages with her own pictures and a story about a rabbit

◀ *An illustration from Potter's* The Tale of Peter Rabbit.

called Peter. The children loved them so much that she sent *The Tale of Peter Rabbit* to six publishers, but none of them would publish it. Instead, she had the book printed with her own money, and gave copies of it to children. It became so popular that in 1902 a publisher named Frederick Warne agreed to reprint *Peter Rabbit* for her. Thousands of copies were sold.

With the royalties from *Peter Rabbit*, and other tales such as *Squirrel Nutkin* and *The Tailor of Gloucester*, Potter bought a small farm in the Lake District. During the next ten years she wrote *The Tale of Tom Kitten*, *The Tale of Jeremy Fisher*, and many more, using the landscape and the animals around her for inspiration. She stopped writing after her marriage in 1913. ◆

Nicolas **Poussin**

French painter
Born *1594*   **Died** *1665 aged 71*

Nicolas Poussin grew up in Normandy, northern France.

When he was about 17, a painter came to the nearby town to paint pictures for the church. The painter aroused Poussin's interest in art and he made up his mind to become a painter. He went to Rouen and Paris to study.

In 1624 Poussin decided to go to Rome, which was then an important artistic centre. Many artists in Rome painted pictures that showed a lot of action and excitement. Poussin tried to paint in the same way but his paintings seemed dull. Instead he developed his own way of composing pictures, often showing small groups of people enjoying the countryside. Poussin's works attracted much interest and he soon became famous. In 1640 Poussin returned to Paris, becoming the court painter to King Louis XIII until 1643. He then went back to Rome.

The careful composition of his paintings, and their special atmosphere, influenced other painters and made Poussin one of France's foremost landscape painters in the 17th century. ◆

Elvis **Presley**

American rock and roll singer
Born 1935   Died 1977 aged 42

Elvis Presley was born into a poor family in Mississippi. As a teenager he spent much of his time with black musicians, learning a lot about blues and gospel music. In 1953 he paid to make a record for his mother's birthday at Sun Records in Memphis. The owner liked his unusual mixture of styles, and offered him professional recording work.

His first local hit was 'That's All Right' in 1954, and he created a sensation on television by swivelling his hips while singing. Adults were outraged, but teenagers loved it. By 1956 he was a national

▼ *For many years Elvis Presley was the most popular singer in the world.*

star, making huge hits like 'Hound Dog', 'Blue Suede Shoes', and 'Jailhouse Rock'. Known as the 'King of Rock 'n' Roll', Presley eventually recorded 94 gold singles and over 40 gold albums. He also starred in 27 films.

He continued touring and recording during the 1960s. During the 1970s he spent more and more time at Graceland, his huge house in Memphis. He died there of heart failure in 1977. Many thousands of his fans still visit Graceland every year. ◆

Joseph **Priestley**

English chemist who discovered oxygen
Born 1733   Died 1804 aged 70

Joseph Priestley was a minister in the Unitarian Church and also very interested in politics. Although he had no scientific education, he also became very keen on doing experiments.

Priestley's real claim to fame is his outstanding work studying gases, and particularly his identification of oxygen, which he called 'dephlogisticated air'. The importance of oxygen in burning was shown by the great French chemist Antoine Lavoisier.

Priestley's political opinions got him into a great deal of trouble. He fled to London with his family when a mob burned down his home because of his support for the ordinary French people during the French Revolution. Before long it was not safe for him to remain in England and he quickly left for the United States of America. He was warmly welcomed and spent the rest of his life working mainly for the Unitarian Church. ◆

👁 **see also**

Lavoisier

▲ *Sergei Prokofiev composed seven symphonies, including the popular First Symphony (1917).*

Sergei **Prokofiev**

Russian composer
Born 1891   Died 1953 aged 61

Sergei Prokofiev had his first music lessons from his mother, who was an excellent pianist. He began composing when he was five, could play Beethoven sonatas when he was nine, and by the age of 11 had written two operas. When he was 13 he went to study at the St Petersburg Conservatory of Music.

His first important compositions, two piano concertos, caused a great scandal. People thought them far too noisy. But later works, such as the popular First Symphony (the 'Classical'), helped them to change their minds. Other compositions by Prokofiev include operas, piano and violin concertos, and ballets such as *Romeo and Juliet* (1935).

After the 1917 Russian Revolution, and the founding of the USSR, Prokofiev spent many years in America and France. But he could not stay away and returned home in 1927 and again in 1934. One of the first pieces he wrote on his return was the delightful children's tale *Peter and the Wolf* (1936). ◆

▲ *Alain Prost driving for Ferrari in 1990.*

Alain **Prost**

French champion motor-racing driver
Born *1955*

Although Alain Prost was very talented at football he chose to be a motor racing driver instead. In 1980 he drove in his first Formula One Grand Prix. He has since driven for the McLaren, Ferrari, and Williams manufacturing teams.

Prost has roared home first in more than 50 Grand Prix races. He has also scored the most points in Grand Prix racing – over 700 – and has won the world championship four times. The last time was in 1993, the year he retired.

Prost is also well known for the studious way he plans and tackles each race. This is why he has the nickname 'The Professor'. ◆

Marcel **Proust**

French author
Born *1871*   **Died** *1922 aged 51*

Marcel Proust suffered from asthma throughout his life, and his growing ill health led him gradually to withdraw from people into his own company. But by this time he had wide knowledge of the ways of rich French society, which he used in the writing of his seven-part novel *Remembrance of Things Past*.

Proust's work is not easy, and was originally refused by so many publishers he eventually had to pay for its publication himself. But over the years *Remembrance of Things Past* has come to be seen as one of the great classics of literature, full of revealing ideas about human thoughts, feelings, and relationships. ◆

Claudius **Ptolemy**

Egyptian astronomer and geographer
Lived during the 2nd century

Ptolemy lived and worked in Alexandria from 127 to 151. His great book *The Almagest* was published in about 140. It was an encyclopedia of all that was known in astronomy in Ptolemy's day and was accepted as the truth about the Solar System for about 15 centuries. It taught that the Earth was the centre of the universe with the Sun, Moon, planets, and stars all revolving about our planet. Ptolemy also published an important book on the principles of geography in which he dealt with the problems of constructing accurate maps using mathematics. The book contained a map of the known world.

Ptolemy's books were preserved and much later were translated and studied by Arabian astronomers who found that they had to modify his theories to fit their more accurate observations. Ultimately Ptolemy's Earth-centred theory of the universe was replaced by Copernicus's Sun-centred theory. ◆

◉ **see also**

Copernicus

Giacomo **Puccini**

Italian composer
Born *1858*   **Died** *1924 aged 65*

Giacomo Puccini was the last and greatest of a long line of composer-musicians who lived and worked in Lucca, Italy. At first it seemed that he would become a church organist like his father, but he was increasingly drawn to opera.

▲ *Puccini's opera* La Bohème *is famous for its dramatic effect and realism.*

After studying at the Milan Conservatory, Puccini entered a competition for a one-act opera. He failed to win a prize, but so impressed the great music publisher Giulio Ricordi that he was offered a contract to compose a full-length work. Although this first project was not successful, Ricordi still had faith in Puccini, and was rewarded by a series of wonderfully melodious and theatrically effective operas that are among the most popular ever written. The most famous are *Manon Lescaut* (1893), *La Bohème* (1896), *Tosca* (1900), *Madame Butterfly* (1904), and *Turandot* (produced posthumously in 1926). ◆

Henry **Purcell**

English composer and organist
Born 1659   Died 1695 aged 36

Henry Purcell became a chorister of the Chapel Royal – the musicians and clergy employed by the English monarch for religious services. In 1674 he was appointed tuner of the Westminster Abbey organ, and in 1677 succeeded Matthew Locke as 'composer to the King's violins'. Two years later he became organist of Westminster Abbey.

Purcell wrote many fine choral works for royal occasions, as well as anthems and chamber music. He also wrote incidental music for many plays, and a series of 'semi-operas' (plays with much music), such as *King Arthur* (1691) and *The Fairy Queen* (1692). His only real opera, *Dido and Aeneas* (1689), was very dramatic and emotional and is considered to be his masterpiece. Purcell is universally regarded as one of the greatest of all English composers. ◆

Alexander **Pushkin**

Russian poet, playwright, and novelist
Born 1799   Died 1837 aged 37

Alexander Pushkin was born into a wealthy family in Moscow and educated in St Petersburg, where his talent for poetry was noticed. After leaving school he worked for the government, but continued to write poetry. His political poems angered the government and he was banished to southern Russia. Here he started one of his greatest works, the novel *Eugene Onegin*, which portrayed current trends in Russian life.

The public read his poems eagerly and his fame grew. The tsar, recognizing his popularity, summoned him to Moscow and gave him a personal pardon. But his writing continued to be censored, and he was spied on. In 1836 he was wounded in a duel with a French baron who admired his wife and died two days later. ◆

▼ *The famous Russian writer Alexander Pushkin in a portrait from 1827.*

Pythagoras

Ancient Greek mathematician
Born c.582 BC
Died c.497 BC aged about 85

At the age of about 40 Pythagoras set up a strange religious community in southern Italy. It was called the Pythagorean Brotherhood and its members lived according to rules made by Pythagoras. The Pythagoreans lived a very strict, simple life and spent much of their time doing mathematics. Pythagoras believed that mathematics held the key to all the secrets of the universe, and he believed some numbers were magical.

He is best remembered for 'Pythagoras's theorem', a simple rule in geometry linking the lengths of the sides of right-angled triangles. But Pythagoras also did some of the very first scientific experiments by listening to the sounds of stretched strings of different lengths and working out the mathematics of octaves and harmony. Pythagoras's mathematical ideas became important to the philosopher Plato, and through him influenced other scientists such as Galileo, Kepler, and Newton. ◆

 see also
Galileo Kepler Newton Plato

275

Mu'ammar al-**Qaddafi**

Libyan leader from 1969
Born 1942

Mu'ammar al-Qaddafi's father was a Bedouin (nomadic Arab) farmer. Qaddafi was educated at the University of Libya and at the Military Academy. He came to power in Libya in 1969 as the leader of an army revolt which overthrew the country's king, Idris, and made himself president in 1977. He used Libya's oil-wealth to improve living conditions in his otherwise very poor country, and also to buy modern planes and weapons for the armed forces.

Qaddafi's government has been involved in a number of incidents with neighbouring countries, including Chad, Sudan, and Uganda. He has also been unpopular with some Western countries because of his support for terrorist and revolutionary groups. In 1986 the American president, Ronald Reagan, authorized the bombing of the Libyan capital, Tripoli, in retaliation for alleged acts of terrorism against American nationals. Some of Qaddafi's own children were killed and injured in the raid.

Qaddafi is a strict Muslim and in 1973 he outlawed alcohol and gambling in Libya. Many of his theories, based on the ideas of Mao Zedong, are kept in his *Green Book*. ◆

👁 **see also**
Mao Zedong   Reagan

François **Rabelais**

French writer
Born c.1494   **Died** 1553 aged about 59

The son of a rich landowner, François Rabelais became a Franciscan monk before qualifying as a doctor. However, he is more famous for his work as a writer. In 1532 he published his comic masterpiece *Pantagruel*, followed two years later by *Gargantua*. Both books describe the adventures of a giant father and son, both of whom have huge appetites. They are aided by a trouble-making monk called Frère Jean, whose behaviour is so un-Christian that both books were eventually banned by the Church authorities in Paris.

Although Rabelais constantly makes his readers laugh, his books also attack the worst political, educational, and religious abuses of his time. Although for some years his books could only be read outside France, he had a large

▼ *An illustration from François Rabelais' humorously critical novel about the giant Gargantua.*

influence on future French writers, as well as upon British authors such as Jonathan Swift. ◆

👁 **see also**
Swift

Yitzhak **Rabin**

Prime Minister of Israel from 1974 to 1977 and from 1992 to 1995
Born 1922   **Died** 1995 aged 73

After graduating from agricultural college, Yitzhak Rabin joined the Jewish Defence Force during World War II. He later played an important part in Israel's victory over the Arab troops in the Six-Day War (June 1967). In 1973 Rabin became a Labour member of parliament, and a few months later prime minister. From 1984 to 1986 he was defence minister in a coalition government, then became prime minister again in 1992.

Rabin believed that Israel should withdraw from the Arab territories it had occupied since the Six-Day War. He began negotiations with Yasser Arafat, head of the Palestine Liberation Organization. This outraged many Jewish people, and there were demonstrations and violent clashes between Jews and Palestinians. Tragically Rabin was assassinated in October 1995, by a Jew determined to end the peace process. ◆

Jean **Racine**

French playwright and poet
Born 1639   **Died** 1699 aged 59

Jean Baptiste Racine was brought up by his Catholic grandmother who sent him to a strict religious school. Later, however, he moved away from a possible career in the Church and left for Paris where he started to write poetry. He found favour at the court of King Louis XIV and began to write plays. His earliest were *The Thebiad* (1664) and *Alexander the Great* (1665). These were followed by many others, including his masterpiece, *Phèdre* (1677). The subjects for his plays often came from Greek mythology. The plots were simple, but his characters expressed a whole range of complex emotions.

In 1677 Racine retired from dramatic writing, married, and settled down in domestic happiness until his death in 1699. ◆

Sergey **Rakhmaninov**

Russian composer and pianist
Born 1873   **Died** 1943 aged 69

Sergey Rakhmaninov studied music first at the St Petersburg Conservatory and then (1888) at the Moscow Conservatory. His first opera, *Aleko* (1893), was a success, but his First Symphony failed completely. He became very depressed, and even lost faith in his ability to compose. Fortunately, he was helped to recover by a course of hypnosis.

The success of his second piano concerto (1901) finally restored his confidence. As a pianist he began touring in 1899, visiting America for the first time in 1909. He left Russia after the 1917 Revolution and settled in America, where he pursued the hectic career of a popular concert pianist. Although this greatly reduced the time he could devote to composition, he wrote many fine songs and piano pieces, as well as four piano concertos, *Rhapsody on a Theme of Paganini* for piano and orchestra, and three symphonies. ◆

▲ *This drawing of Sergey Rakhmaninov was made when he was 43. His dramatic and emotional style of music thrilled concert audiences.*

Walter **Raleigh**

English courtier and explorer
Born c 1552   **Died** 1618 aged about 66

Walter Raleigh supposedly first pleased Elizabeth I when he laid his fine velvet cloak over a puddle so the queen's shoes would not get muddy. He was certainly a great favourite of her's after he came to court in 1581. However, he did not always please her, especially when he married Elizabeth Throgmorton, a lady-in-waiting. He was sent to the Tower of London, and then banished from court for a time.

Raleigh was an accomplished soldier who had fought in France and Ireland, and helped to prepare England's defences against the Spanish Armada. He was also fascinated by the riches of America. He never went there himself, but his expeditions probably brought potatoes to Britain for the first time, and whether he brought tobacco from America or not, Raleigh made pipe-smoking fashionable at court. In 1595 he went to South America

and searched unsuccessfully for El Dorado, a mythical land said to be full of gold.

James I, who became king in 1603, distrusted Raleigh, and imprisoned him in the Tower of London for over 12 years. Raleigh wrote a *History of the World*, and did many scientific experiments while he was there.

In 1616 James allowed Raleigh to go back to South America to search for gold. However, his expedition found no gold and got into a fight with the Spanish instead. Raleigh returned home a sick man, and, in 1618, James finally ordered his execution. ◆

I have a long journey to take, and must bid the company farewell.

WALTER RALEIGH, 1618 (his last words before being executed)

▼ *Although Queen Elizabeth I enjoyed Walter Raleigh's company, she did not think he was reliable, and never gave him any real power.*

Ramakrishna

Indian holy man and religious teacher
Born *1836* **Died** *1886 aged 50*

Gadadhar Chatterji was the son of a poor family. His only language was Bengali; he spoke no English or Sanskrit. From a very early age his only real interest was his religious spiritual quest. His eldest brother, Ramkumar, offered to pay for his education, but he declined, saying he wanted no 'mere bread-winning education'. Instead he devoted himself to prayer. First he worshipped the Hindu goddess Kali. Then he became a sannyasin (monk) and took the name Ramakrishna. Later he learned about Islam and Christianity, and came to the conclusion that all religions were equal paths to the same goal.

Thousands came to listen to him speak and his followers began to collect his sayings so that they could be written down and published throughout the world. These followers kept his memory alive long after his death. His wife, Sarada-devi, whom he married when she was five, became a saint and was known as Divine Mother to Ramakrishna's disciples. ◆

▲ *Rameses II was pharaoh for 66 years, probably the longest time an Egyptian king ever ruled.*

Rameses II

King of Egypt from 1304 BC to 1237 BC
Lived during the 13th century BC

In ancient times, the kingdom of Egypt was one of the richest places in the world. Rameses became king (pharaoh) of Egypt in about 1304 BC. He wanted to increase Egypt's land and power. For 16 years he and his army fought against Egypt's main enemy, the Hittites, who ruled a powerful empire in an area which is now modern Turkey. Eventually the two sides made peace and Rameses married a Hittite princess.

During Rameses' long reign, Egypt prospered and there was a substantial programme of building. He founded a new capital city in the flat delta of the Nile and called it 'Pi-Riamses', the 'Land of Rameses'. Throughout Egypt he built numerous temples. One of these, at Abu Simbel in south Egypt, is very famous because the front consists of four enormous statues of Rameses himself. ◆

Raphael

Italian painter
Born *1483* **Died** *1520 aged 37*

Raffaello Sanzio (Raphael's real name) was apprenticed at the age of seven to his father, an artist. He began by learning to mix up colours for his father's pictures.

▶ *One of the things people like about Raphael's paintings is the naturalness of his figures, like the rounded characters in this fresco,* Galatea *(1513).*

He was already a master painter by 17 and worked in Florence and then in Rome. He was employed by the pope to work on the Vatican and the Sistine Chapel, for which he designed tapestries.

His great interest was in painting the human figure, especially the Madonna and Child (Mary and Jesus). By showing tender glances and reaching-out gestures, he made them look loving, unlike the cool and formal pictures people were

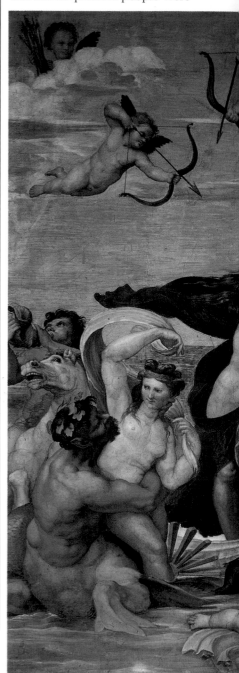

used to. He had amazing skill at taking ideas from others and, by varying and changing them, making something quite new of his own. His work shows exquisite beauty and harmony; he painted nothing ugly, horrible, or shocking.

He crammed an astonishing amount of artistic achievement into his short life, and received many honours for his wall paintings, portraits, huge figure compositions, engravings, and tapestry designs.

He died on his 37th birthday, and left behind an idea of 'perfection' in painting. For centuries he was regarded as the greatest painter of all time. ◆

> *Raffaello was quite right to be jealous of me, for all he knew of art he learned from me.*
>
> MICHELANGELO
> talking about Raphael

Rasputin

Favourite of the Russian royal family
Born 1871   *Died* 1916 aged around 45

Rasputin was the son of Russian peasants. He presented himself as a holy man who could heal people. In 1905 in St Petersburg – the capital of Russia at the time – he met the Russian empress (tsarina), Alexandra, and the emperor (tsar), Nicholas II. Their son, Alexei, suffered from haemophilia. This meant that if he cut himself, the bleeding would not stop. Because Rasputin was able to make Alexei feel calm, he became popular with Alexandra.

In 1914 Russia went to war with Germany. The following year, the tsar left the court and took command of the Russian army. While he was away, Alexandra, under Rasputin's influence, dismissed government ministers, and replaced many of them with incompetent men. Rasputin and Alexandra were largely responsible for the tsar's failure to respond to the ever rising tide of discontent amongst the Russian people, which eventually led to the Russian Revolution (1917). A group of noblemen tried to kill Rasputin, to remove his evil influence. They

▲ *The famous Russian priest, Rasputin.*

poisoned him, shot him, and then threw him in the River Neva where he drowned. ◆

see also

Nicholas II

Maurice **Ravel**

French composer
Born 1875   *Died* 1937 aged 62

Joseph Maurice Ravel first became well-known as a pianist and a conductor and he made a number of concert tours. However, apart from these excursions, he led a quiet and retiring life devoted to composing music.

Ravel had studied music at the Paris Conservatoire, under the direction of the composer Gabriel Fauré among others. Ravel turned to many different composers for inspiration, but developed his own uniquely personal style. He often drew on unusual sources, such as fairy tales or magic, for his themes.

His main works are songs and piano pieces, but he also wrote orchestral pieces such as the famous *Boléro* (1928), two piano concertos, ballets, and two short operas. One of his most famous piano works, *Gaspard de la Nuit*, is one of the most difficult to play that has ever been written. ◆

Satyajit **Ray**

Indian film director
Born 1921   Died 1992 aged 71

With a musician mother, writer father, and writer and painter grandfathers, Satyajit Ray was brought up in artistic circles. He, however, originally planned a career in science but changed his plans while studying with the poet Rabindranath Tagore (a family friend) and became interested in book illustration instead.

Working on the story of Apu, a Brahmin boy growing up in poverty in a Bengal village, made Ray want to film this book. Helping French director Jean Renoir to film *The River* on location in India increased his interest in cinema.

▲ *Satyajit Ray (left) directing one of his films. He liked spontaneity and preferred to use the first filming of a scene rather than a retake.*

Over the next five years, using amateur actors and filming mainly at weekends, he made *Pather Panchali* (completed 1955). It won a major prize at the Cannes Film Festival and was followed by two other films continuing Apu's story called *Unvanquished* (1956) and *World of Apu* (1959). Among the best of his other films are *The Music Room* (1958) and *The Chess Players* (1977). ◆

👁 **see also**

Tagore

Ronald **Reagan**

President of the United States of America from 1981 to 1989
Born 1911

Ronald Reagan came from a poor family in Illinois. After working his way through college, he became a radio sports announcer. His good looks and voice helped him get a Hollywood contract in 1937, and he made his first film that year. In total he made around 50 films.

His acting career was interrupted when he joined the air force in World War II. (He did not see active service but made training films instead.) Witty and energetic, for several years after the war he was president of the Screen Actors Guild. He also worked in television. He was so good at making speeches that many people told him he should be a politician.

Reagan joined the Republican Party in 1962 and was elected governor of California in 1966. He believed that government had become too big and powerful and it also cost too much, and was hindering instead of helping most Americans. Having lost the Republican presidential nomination in 1968 and 1976, he won it in 1980 and defeated Jimmy Carter to become president. He was re-elected for another term in 1984. He was not only the oldest, but also one of the most popular and conservative American presidents. During his presidency, military expenditure increased enormously while less money was spent on welfare benefits for the poor. In 1987 a treaty was signed with Mikhail Gorbachev of the Soviet Union to eliminate all ground-based, intermediate-range nuclear missiles. ◆

👁 **see also**

Gorbachev

Rembrandt van Rijn

Dutch painter
Born 1606   Died 1669 aged 63

Rembrandt went to university when he was only 14. A year later he left to develop his artistic talent. He used his family as models, and mastered the skill of painting facial expressions. He particularly loved to paint portraits. Indeed he painted himself 60 times, leaving a record of how he looked from a young man to old age.

Rembrandt's sufferings began with the death of three of his children, then of his mother and of his wife, Saskia, leaving him with one son, Titus. His pictures became less popular, and debts made him practically bankrupt, although he still worked on.

As he grew older, Rembrandt became extra-sensitive to the real person behind the face he was painting. He no longer bothered with people's clothes or with backgrounds, but concentrated on the true personality. Truth became more important than beauty.

After the death of Titus and of Rembrandt's mistress, the only close relation left was their daughter, Cornelia. Though she was devoted to him, Rembrandt was often lonely. This is reflected in his sombre last paintings. ◆

Pierre Auguste **Renoir**

French painter
Born 1841   Died 1919 aged 78

Pierre Auguste Renoir was the son of a tailor, and grew up knowing that good craftsmanship was essential in the making of

▲ The Luncheon of the Boating Party *by the French artist Pierre Auguste Renoir shows his use of bright colours and interest in lively scenes.*

quality work. At the age of 13 he was apprenticed to a porcelain manufacturer to produce hand-painted designs. He later moved over to painting fans and then to decorating blinds.

However, Renoir became dissatisfied with this work, and began to study figure drawing and anatomy at evening classes. He worked in a famous studio where he met other young artists who were interested in capturing the dappled effects of light and shadow in their paintings. With them he founded the group of painters known as the Impressionists, who held their first exhibition in 1874. Renoir's early work suffered ridicule, but he soon became successful as a portrait painter. He also enjoyed painting busy scenes of ordinary people in bright colours, using bold brushstrokes without fussy detail. He continued to work up until his death and produced over 6000 paintings. ◆

👁 **see also**
Manet Monet Pissarro

Paul **Revere**

American patriot during the American Revolution
Born *1735* **Died** *1818 aged 83*

At the age of 13 Paul Revere was apprenticed to his father, a Boston silversmith. Later he set up his own workshop and became an ardent patriot who wanted his country to be free of British rule. Along with others, and disguised in war-paint and feathers, he threw crates of tea into the sea at the so-called 'Boston Tea Party' to protest against British taxation.

On 16 April 1775 a single lantern in the North Church steeple in Boston signalled that the British troops were marching inland to capture a munitions store and two patriots, Hancock and Adams, who were hiding at Lexington. Paul Revere rode through the night to warn the country people and to urge them to resist. At Lexington the British soldiers were fired on by armed farmers, and they were made to retreat by a larger force. This was the beginning of the American Revolution (War of Independence). Revere took an active role and in 1776 was put in command of Castle William, defending Boston Harbour.

After the war Revere established the first copper-rolling mill in the United States. He eventually died a wealthy and successful merchant and manufacturer. ◆

▼ *A print showing the 'Boston Tea Party' protest against British taxation on 16 December 1773.*

▲ *The giant statue of a sun god on the island of Rhodes, the Colossus of Rhodes, was one of the seven wonders of the ancient world. This cartoon, 'The Rhodes Colossus', from the British magazine* Punch, *gives an idea of how important Cecil Rhodes was in Africa by 1895.*

Cecil **Rhodes**

British colonist in southern Africa
Born *1853*   **Died** *1902 aged 48*

As a boy Cecil Rhodes suffered from weak lungs, so he went to southern Africa where the climate would be better for him. He worked on a cotton farm but later moved to Kimberley to mine for diamonds.

Between 1873 and 1881, Rhodes spent time at Oxford University studying for a degree. During these years he decided that the British should extend their rule throughout Africa. He began to make the money to fulfil his dream in the mines at Kimberley. By 1891 his company, De Beers, owned 90 per cent of the world's diamond mines.

Rhodes had entered parliament in the Cape Colony in 1881, and he became prime minister in 1890. Against opposition from Paul Kruger and the Boers of the Transvaal, he pushed British rule northwards, creating a new colony which was called Rhodesia (now Zimbabwe) after him.

In 1895 Rhodes supported the 'Jameson raid', which attempted to overthrow Kruger's government in the Transvaal. It failed, and Rhodes had to resign as prime minister. When he died he left £3 million in his will to pay for overseas students to go to Oxford University. ◆

👁 **see also**
Kruger

Richard I

King of England from 1189 to 1199
Born *1157*   **Died** *1199 aged 41*

Richard was the third son of Henry II and Eleanor of Aquitaine. In 1173 his mother persuaded him to rebel, with two of his brothers, against Henry. The revolt failed, but 16 years later Richard forced his ageing father to

▲ *Richard I, portrayed here at rest on his tomb, was known as Richard the Lionheart because of his bravery in battle.*

make Richard heir to all his lands in England and France, leaving nothing for John, Richard's younger brother.

Once in power, Richard went on the Third Crusade to the Holy Land with the other kings and nobles of Europe. They failed to capture Jerusalem, but Richard defeated Saladin, the Muslim leader, at Arsuf. On the way back to England, Richard was taken prisoner by one of his enemies, the Duke of Austria. His government in England had to pay a huge ransom for his release.

Although he was king for ten years, Richard spent a total of only five months of his reign in England; the last five years of his reign were devoted to fighting the King of France. He died of blood poisoning, caused by an arrow in his shoulder, while besieging a town in the French kingdom of Aquitaine. ◆

👁 **see also**
Eleanor of Aquitaine   Saladin

Richard III

King of England from 1483 to 1485
Born *1452*   **Died** *1485 aged 32*

The son of the Duke of York, Richard lived in the shadow of his elder brother, who became King Edward IV in 1461, while Richard was created Duke of Gloucester. In the continuing feud for the English throne between the house of York and the house of Lancaster, Richard helped his brother defeat Lancastrian challenges. This struggle, which lasted for 30 years, became known as the War of the Roses because of the red rose badge worn by the Lancastrians and the white rose badge worn by the Yorkists.

When Edward died in 1483, Richard did away with the nobles

the French monarchy, given order and unity to the country, and won for France a leading position in European affairs. However, his excessive taxation, his refusal to operate any form of democratic government, and his crushing of the power of the French nobility meant that he created many enemies for himself, and there were several attacks on his life. ◆

Nikolay **Rimsky-Korsakov**

Russian composer and teacher
Born *1844*   **Died** *1908 aged 64*

Nikolay Rimsky-Korsakov's first ambition was to be a sailor, and in 1856 he became a naval cadet. However, he was also inspired by the new spirit in Russian music and at the age of 15 began to write a symphony. Apart from a few piano lessons, he was entirely self-taught and almost completely ignorant of musical theory. He made strenuous efforts to catch up on his musical knowledge and, though still a naval officer, eventually became a professor at the St Petersburg Music Conservatory in 1871. He proved to be a fine teacher (Stravinsky was one of his pupils). He was also a great admirer of Russian music and produced his own versions of Borodin's incomplete opera *Prince Igor*, and Mussorgsky's opera *Boris Godunov*. His own finest compositions are distinguished by their brilliant orchestration. They include such operas as *The Legend of Tsar Sultan* (1900) and *The Golden Cockerel* (1907), and the symphonic suite *Sheherazade* (1888). ◆

👁 **see also**

Stravinsky

▲ Triple Portrait of the Head of Richelieu. *During the reign of King Louis XIII (1601–1643), Armand Jean Richelieu was the most powerful man in France*

who might become his enemies, imprisoned his brother's two sons (the rightful heirs to the throne) in the Tower of London, and had himself proclaimed king – all within three months. Until then he had been a popular and trusted man, but now he began to lose support. When England was invaded by Henry Tudor, a Lancastrian bethrothed to the Yorkist heiress, Elizabeth of York, Richard was deserted by many of his followers. He was killed on the battlefield at Bosworth and his crown was found on a thorn-bush. ◆

Armand Jean **Richelieu**

French cardinal and politician
Born *1585*   **Died** *1642 aged 57*

Armand Jean Richelieu became a bishop when he was only 22. He later came to the notice of Marie de Medici, then acting as regent for her son, Louis XIII. Through her influence Richelieu won a place at the French court and in 1622 was made a cardinal.

When he was 39 Richelieu became chief (prime) minister and together with Louis XIII, who was now king, he virtually ruled the country. One of his major aims was to restore the monarchy to its former absolute power. To do this he tried to curb the politically strong and ambitious nobles, who enjoyed virtual independence from royal authority. Richelieu's foreign policy was directed at restoring French influence and power in Europe, especially against Austria and Spain which were controlled by the Habsburg dynasty.

By the time of his death in 1642, Richelieu had restored the power of

Diego **Rivera**

Mexican painter
Born *1886* **Died** *1957 aged 70*

Diego Rivera studied art and politics in Europe from 1907 to 1921. At that time he was much influenced by Pablo Picasso, the famous Spanish master of modern art. But when Rivera went home to Mexico, he deliberately turned his back on fashionable European styles of painting. He said he was more interested in 'art for the people'. He revived older methods of painting such as fresco (using water-colours on wet plaster) and encaustic painting (using heat to fuse wax colours onto a surface).

Rivera loved to paint scenes from Mexican life and history, particularly the history of ordinary people. He also much admired the American Indians, and painted huge murals (paintings that decorate walls and ceilings) in vivid colours, showing how the Aztecs were destroyed by the Spaniards. His sympathy for Communism, though, sometimes got him into trouble. His huge mural for the American Rockefeller Center in New York was removed

▲ *Many of Diego Rivera's paintings, like this one,* The Market at Tenochtitlan, *portray the culture and history of Mexico.*

because it contained a picture of Lenin, the first leader of the Communist Soviet Union. ◆

◉ **see also**

Picasso

José **Rizal**

Filipino nationalist
Born *1861* **Died** *1896 aged 35*

José Rizal is known as the father of Filipino independence – though he himself had never really campaigned for it.

The son of a wealthy landowner, Rizal proved himself to be a brilliant medical student in Spain and Germany. While abroad he became leader of a group of students who wanted reforms in the Philippines, which were then a Spanish colony. Rizal wrote two novels which called for an end to the wealth and power of Spanish friars in his country. He also wanted equal rights for all Filipinos and Spaniards although

he did not call for complete independence from Spain. Returning home, he founded a school and hospital but was falsely accused of plotting revolution and was executed. This convinced Filipinos that Spanish rule must come to an end. ◆

Robert I

King of Scotland from 1306 to 1329
Born *1274* **Died** *1329 aged 54*

Robert 'the Bruce' came from an aristocratic Scottish family. He was very ambitious, and grew up wanting to become king of Scotland. To gain the Scottish throne, Bruce stabbed his main rival in a quarrel, and a month later he was crowned King Robert I.

At first things went badly for the new king. England was at war with Scotland, and wanted to have control over its neighbour. Many of

▼ *Robert I pictured with his second wife in 1306. As king of Scotland, he won independence for his country from England.*

Robert's family and supporters were captured and savagely treated by the English king, Edward I. Robert was forced to go into hiding and almost lost heart. There is a story that while he was sheltering in a cave, he saw a spider struggling again and again to climb up to her web and not giving up. The spider's example inspired him to keep on fighting against the English. Finally, in 1314, he overwhelmed Edward II's army in the fierce battle of Bannockburn.

King Robert's victory did not end the fighting with England, but at least Scotland was once again an independent kingdom. He died of leprosy in 1329, a great hero. ◆

see also
Edward I

Tom **Roberts**

Australian painter
Born *1856* **Died** *1931 aged 75*

Tom Roberts was born in England and emigrated to Australia when he was 13. In 1881 he went to Europe to study art, mainly in London. When he returned to Melbourne in 1885 he painted in a new style based on the work of French Impressionists such as Monet and Renoir. At first his work was too unusual for Australian taste (one critic called it 'a pain to the eye'), but Roberts gradually won acclaim as the leading Australian painter of his time. He painted traditional subjects such as portraits and also scenes of Australian rural life, full of local colour. Many Australian painters were influenced by his work and he is regarded as a father figure of Australian art. ◆

see also
Monet   Renoir

Paul **Robeson**

American classical actor and singer
Born *1898* **Died** *1976 aged 77*

Paul Robeson studied law at university, but in the 1920s, when he qualified, it was difficult for black people to get work as lawyers. So instead he became an actor and a singer. He played the title role in Shakespeare's *Othello* in London and New York. He also starred in films, including *Sanders of the River* (1935), and *Show Boat* (1936).

Robeson had a wonderful, natural bass voice which captured listeners' attention. The song 'Ol' Man River' from *Show Boat* is always associated with him, as are such songs as 'Water Boy' and 'Ma Curly Headed Babby'.

After visiting the Soviet Union in the 1930s, Robeson became interested in Communism. In 1950 the American government took away his passport because he would not deny being a Communist. This caused him great grief and bitterness and seriously affected his career. He eventually left America and stayed away until 1963, when he returned for health reasons. ◆

Maximilien **Robespierre**

Famous leader in the French Revolution
Born *1758* **Died** *1794 aged 36*

After studying in Paris, Maximilien Robespierre returned to his home town, Arras, where he worked as a lawyer until he was 30. In 1789 he was elected as a deputy to represent his province in the Estates-General (parliament). Unlike many other deputies, Robespierre saw himself as representing the poor as well as the rich.

▲ *Robespierre is mostly remembered for the thousands of people he sent to the guillotine before he himself was executed, rather than for his ideas.*

The French Revolution started in 1789 and Robespierre made a name for himself through the power of his speeches. He pressed for the ideas of the Revolution – liberty for all, equality for all, and fraternity (brotherhood) of all.

By 1793 there was civil war in the west, an invasion in the north-east, and people were starving. Robespierre and his supporters, the Jacobins, decided that ruthless action was needed to feed the people, to raise a citizen army, and to get rid of the Revolution's enemies. He joined the Committee of Public Safety, which organized these activities.

This was the time of 'the Terror', when anyone might be accused of treason, quickly tried, and executed. Robespierre thought this was necessary, but as thousands were killed, many saw it as brutal tyranny. By the summer of 1794, people were sick of the Terror. Robespierre's revolutionary colleagues rose against him and he was sent to the guillotine. ◆

see also
Danton

285

John D. **Rockefeller**

American industrialist and multimillionaire
Born *1839*   **Died** *1937 aged 97*

John Davison Rockefeller was a businessman when the first oil well was drilled in America in 1859. Four years later he started an oil refinery in Ohio. By 1870 his company, the Standard Oil Company, began to buy up many other oil companies.

By 1882 Standard Oil had 95 per cent of all the refining business in America. This monopoly made him into a multimillionaire. Once he had made his fortune Rockefeller began to look for good and useful ways to spend his money. In 1891 he paid for the University of Chicago to be established, and he later set up the Rockefeller Institute for Medical Research (which became Rockefeller University) in New York City. In 1913, after retiring from the oil business, he began the Rockefeller Foundation to finance charitable activities. ◆

Richard **Rodgers**

American composer of musicals
Born *1902*   **Died** *1979 aged 77*

As a schoolboy, Richard Rodgers wrote songs for amateur shows and was determined to become a composer. Then, when he was 16, he met 23-year-old lyric writer Lorenz Hart. 'Fly With Me' (1919), written for Columbia University amateurs, began a 25-year writing partnership. Their Broadway hits include 'On Your Toes' (1936) and 'Pal Joey' (1940). In 1943, the year Hart died, Rodgers found a new lyricist in Oscar Hammerstein II – a friend since

▲ *The screen version of Rodgers and Hammerstein's stage musical* South Pacific *was filmed in 1958.*

1914 with whom he had worked occasionally. Among the shows they wrote together are *Oklahoma!* (1943), *Carousel* (1945), *South Pacific* (1949), *The King and I* (1951), and *The Sound of Music* (1959), all filmed by Hollywood. Although Rodgers always composed to reflect the character and situation of the storylines, the result was a succession of hit songs. ◆

◉ **see also**
Gershwin   Porter

Auguste **Rodin**

French sculptor
Born *1840*   **Died** *1917 aged 77*

Auguste Rodin was sent to boarding school for a short time to improve his poor studies, but his only interest was drawing. When he was older he began work as a stonemason, carrying out the designs of others for decorations on buildings. His techniques became highly skilled and he began to study the works of famous sculptors in museums.

He was powerfully influenced by the statues of Michelangelo and visited Italy to see more of them. His own figures eventually became famous for their unusually life-like quality and sense of movement. They were so realistic that he was even accused of taking a cast from a live model.

Like other artists at the time, Rodin discovered that sculpture need not look entirely finished to be effective or powerful. However, his work caused endless quarrels amongst his critics. Many changes were usually requested before his figures could be placed in public places. One of his most famous, 'The Thinker', was attacked and damaged by a vandal. ◆

Erwin **Rommel**

German field commander in North Africa in World War II
Born *1891*   **Died** *1944 aged 52*

Erwin Rommel joined the German army in 1910 and won medals for gallantry in World War I. Remaining in the army after the war, he also wrote books about military tactics. At the start of World War II he was in charge of the guards at Hitler's headquarters, but in 1940 he moved to a Panzer tank division and headed the invasion of France in May. Then, when Italian forces collapsed in North Africa, Rommel was sent out as head of the Afrika Korps. He fought a successful campaign until he was defeated at El Alamein in October 1942. Rommel then served in France as Inspector of Coastal Defences.

He had become unhappy with Hitler's leadership and gave his support to a plot to assassinate the Nazi dictator. In July 1944 the plot

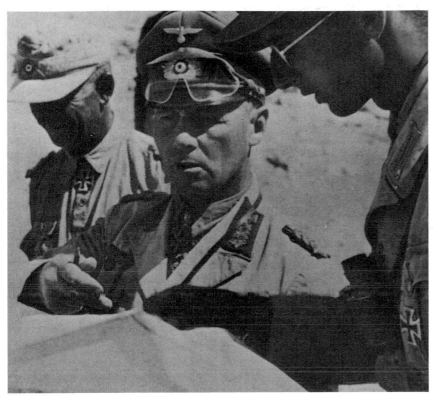

▲ *General Erwin Rommel leading German troops in North Africa in 1941.*

failed and Rommel's involvement was discovered. Already badly injured by an Allied air attack on his car, he took poison to save his family from trial and execution. ◆

👁 **see also**

Hitler

Wilhelm **Röntgen**

German scientist who discovered X-rays
Born 1845   **Died** 1923 aged 77

In 1895 Wilhelm Röntgen was doing experiments in which he applied a strong electric current to metal plates inside a glass tube from which most of the air had been removed. His tube was covered with black cardboard and the room was dark. To his amazement, he noticed that a chemical on the bench across the room was glowing. After many further experiments he decided that the tube was giving out rays that went through both the glass and the cardboard. He called these mysterious rays X-rays. (The letter X is often used to mean unknown.) Today, X-rays are commonly used in hospitals or at the dentist to see inside the human body. For his work on X-rays, Röntgen was awarded the Nobel Prize for Physics in 1901. ◆

▼ *This cartoon from 1900, five years after X-rays were discovered, imagines what a beach scene might look to their discoverer, the physicist Wilhelm Röntgen.*

Eleanor **Roosevelt**

American humanitarian and First Lady
Born 1884   **Died** 1962 aged 78

Eleanor Roosevelt was orphaned when she was ten and brought up by her strict grandmother. She was taught at home, until at 15 she went to school in England. When she was 17 her uncle, Theodore Roosevelt, became president of the United States of America.

Eleanor married a distant cousin, Franklin Delano Roosevelt, and supported him when he became a politician. Then he caught polio. To save his career, Eleanor became 'the legs and eyes of a crippled husband'. On his behalf, she visited mines, slums, hospitals – all places he could not go to himself.

Eleanor Roosevelt always spoke up for the poor, Black people, and women. Many thought she should keep quiet when her husband became president in 1932, but others admired her honesty.

After her husband's death in 1945, Eleanor Roosevelt continued to make speeches and write for newspapers. She was also a US delegate to the United Nations and in 1946 became the chairwoman of the United Nations Human Rights Commission. ◆

👁 **see also**

Roosevelt, Franklin D.
Roosevelt, Theodore

election in 1944, but only six months later, and with war victory in sight, he suddenly died. ◆

👁 **see also**
Churchill   Roosevelt, Eleanor
Roosevelt, Theodore   Stalin

Franklin D.
Roosevelt

President of the United States of America four times, from 1933 to 1945
Born 1882   Died 1945 aged 63

Franklin Delano Roosevelt, a cousin of the former American president, 'Teddy' Roosevelt, had to fight hard to overcome a physical handicap. He developed polio at the age of 40, and his legs were almost paralysed.

By this time however, Roosevelt, a Democrat, had already served in the New York State senate, and as Assistant Secretary for the Navy. Although he was badly crippled he soon returned to politics. In 1928 he was elected governor of New York State, and four years later became president of America.

At this time, America was in a terrible state. One worker in four was out of work, many families were too poor even to buy food, and 5000 banks had failed. Roosevelt promised a 'New Deal', and launched a programme which

▲ *The 'New Deal' programme of social and economic reform launched by Franklin D. Roosevelt (seen here, right, in 1932) made him popular with working people.*

enabled banks to reopen and created jobs for the unemployed. He also began radio broadcasts to the nation, known as his 'Fireside Chats'. The success of these and later measures ensured his election as president again in 1936.

> *The only thing we have to fear is fear itself.*
> FRANKLIN D. ROOSEVELT
> First speech as president, 1933

In 1940, with World War II raging in Europe, Roosevelt was elected for a third term, the first and last president to be so. In December 1941, after the Japanese had bombed Pearl Harbor, America entered the war. Roosevelt guided the country through its darkest days, working closely with the leaders of Britain and the Soviet Union, Winston Churchill and Joseph Stalin. He won a fourth

Theodore
Roosevelt

President of the United States of America from 1901 to 1908
Born 1858   Died 1919 aged 60

Theodore Roosevelt was born into a wealthy family. He was a weak child who suffered from asthma and he had to build up his health and strength. He was always known as 'Teddy', and cartoonists likened him to a bear. Toy makers began making stuffed animals that they called 'teddy bears'.

Roosevelt entered politics at the age of 23, but the death of his wife and his mother on the same day in 1884 shattered him, and he became a cattle-rancher in Dakota instead.

In 1898 Roosevelt led a cavalry regiment, the Rough Riders, in Cuba during the Spanish American War. Then he became vice-president of America in 1901. Six months later, when President McKinley was assassinated, Roosevelt became president.

As president, Roosevelt broke up trusts (big business monopolies), settled a damaging coal strike, and bought a strip of land to build the Panama Canal. Through his efforts, Panama became independent from Colombia.

After he was elected president in his own right in 1904, he helped to bring peace in a war between Russia and Japan and was awarded the Nobel Peace Prize in 1906.

When he retired, Roosevelt

hunted big game in Africa and led an expedition to explore the River of Doubt in Brazil, now called the Roosevelt or Teodoro River. ◆

👁 see also
Roosevelt, Eleanor
Roosevelt, Franklin D.

Diana **Ross**

American singer
Born 1944

Detroit singer Diana Ross had 18 hits with the 1960s all girl group the Supremes on the Tamla Motown record label before she went solo in 1970, notching up over 40 more hits. Her voice is thin but radiates star quality. In a cleverly planned career, guided by Motown boss Berry Gordy Jr, she conveniently changed style from soul to pop, jazz, or disco to suit the times. She also appeared in several musical films, including *Lady Sings the Blues* (1972) and *The Wiz* (1978). Eventually she became a part-owner of Motown. ◆

Dante Gabriel **Rossetti**

British painter and poet
Born 1828   Died 1882 aged 53

Dante Gabriel Rossetti's father was an Italian political refugee who fled to England. He named his son after the great Italian poet Dante, but he was known by his other name, Gabriel. His sister Christina became a well-known poet, and although Gabriel was also a talented writer, he was more interested in painting. In 1848 he and some friends founded the Pre-Raphaelite Brotherhood, aiming to revive the sincerity and freshness of early Italian paintings (before the time of Raphael, whom they disliked).

In 1862 Rossetti's wife died and he was so devastated he buried the only manuscript of his poems with her; seven years later friends persuaded him to have the poems dug up and published. After his wife's death Rossetti became obsessed with another strikingly beautiful woman, Jane Morris, who was married to his business partner, the great designer William Morris.

▼ *Rossetti's* The Blessed Damozel. *He also wrote a poem with the same title.*

He painted her many times and his love for her broke up his friendship with her husband. At the end of his life Rossetti became an eccentric recluse (he kept a wide variety of unusual animals, including a wombat) and had become dependent on drugs and alcohol. ◆

👁 see also
Dante   Morris   Raphael

Gioachino **Rossini**

Italian composer
Born 1792   Died 1868 aged 76

Both of Gioachino Rossini's parents were professional musicians and they gave him his first lessons. From 1806 he studied at the Liceo Musicale in Bologna. His career in operatic composition began in 1810, and he found great success with his 1816 opera, *The Barber of Seville*. By 1829, when his greatest serious opera *William Tell* was produced in Paris, he had written no fewer than 39 operas – sometimes three or four a year. And then, quite suddenly, he stopped. For the rest of his life he wrote only songs, piano pieces, and a little church music, including the *Stabat Mater* and the *Petite Messe solennelle*. The reason for his early retirement seems to have been a mixture of ill-health, depression, and sheer exhaustion, plus a belief that his style of music had become rather out of date. Thus he produced no more of the brilliant comic operas, and powerful serious operas, that had delighted audiences throughout Europe. ◆

Mayer Amschel **Rothschild**

German founder of the Rothschild banking empire
Born 1744   **Died** 1812 aged 68

Mayer Amschel Rothschild had to give up being a student when his parents died and went to work in a bank instead. Gradually he built up his own banking business in Frankfurt and, with the help of his five sons, he started branches all over Europe. His eldest son, Anselm, worked with him in Frankfurt. Another son, Nathan, started the London branch in 1804. Then Jakob, the youngest son, set up the Paris branch in 1811. In the 1820s, after their father's death, Salomon Mayer and Karl Mayer opened new branches in Vienna and Naples. The brothers always carried out their business activities together as one family.

The family fortune was made during the wars against Napoleon I, when they lent money to the warring countries. Later during the Industrial Revolution they made money buying and selling the stocks and shares of the new companies in Europe. All five sons were rewarded by becoming barons of the Austrian empire.

In London, Nathan Mayer Rothschild was followed by his son Lionel Rothschild (1808–1879), who became the first Jewish Member of Parliament in 1858. Later he lent £4 million to prime minister Benjamin Disraeli for Britain to become the main owner of the Suez Canal. ◆

👁 **see also**
Disraeli

▶ *Henri Rousseau's jungle paintings depict brightly coloured worlds filled with apes and other wild animals lurking amongst the striking assortment of flowers and trees.*

Henri **Rousseau**

French painter
Born 1844   **Died** 1910 aged 66

Henri Rousseau worked for the Paris Customs Office and was given the nickname 'Le Douanier' (the customs officer). When he was 49 he took early retirement so he could devote himself full-time to his hobby of art. He painted all sorts of subjects, often being inspired by pictures he saw in books or by visits to the zoo. Pablo Picasso was one of his admirers, but many other people mocked his work.

Rousseau was the most famous of all 'naive' painters (or 'primitive' painters, as they are sometimes known). This title was given to artists who did not have any professional training and painted in a style that was in some ways childlike. Sometimes this can look clumsy, but painters with the imagination of Rousseau compensated with the charm and freshness of their work. Rousseau died a pauper, but soon after his death he was hailed as an artistic genius. ◆

👁 **see also**
Picasso

Jean-Jacques **Rousseau**

Swiss philosopher
Born 1712   **Died** 1778 aged 66

Jean-Jacques Rousseau's early life was a series of scandals and adventures, all later narrated with gusto in his *Confessions*, which were published after his death. After 1741 he settled in Paris and began making his reputation as a writer. His essay *Discourse on the Arts and Sciences* (1750), in which he praised the natural state of humankind, as opposed to the highly artificial society of 18th-century France, brought him fame and financial security.

In 1762 Rousseau published *Emile*, a novel about a young man's education, and *On the Social Contract*. The latter, with its revolutionary views on civil society, which Rousseau believed should be governed by 'the general will', attracted the hostility of the authorities. Rousseau fled to Switzerland and England for some years. He is remembered as a republican whose political ideas helped to fuel the French Revolution. ◆

▲ *Ruben's painting* The Kidnapping of Ganymede *is full of movement and colour.*

Peter **Rubens**

Flemish painter and ambassador
Born *1577*   **Died** *1640 aged 62*

When he was 14 Peter Rubens became an apprentice painter in Antwerp; seven years later he became a master painter. When he was 23 he travelled to Italy to learn about art and to develop his own extraordinary talents.

He had a charming personality, and made friends easily. He became adviser as well as court painter to the Spanish rulers of Flanders, and they sent him to Spain and England. He spoke several languages well and combined the two careers of painter and diplomat.

When the demand for his paintings became too great, he set up a studio with several first-class assistants. They kept up a huge output of paintings which Rubens planned and finished off himself.

His paintings (usually on biblical or mythological subjects) are crowded with figures, but seem spacious and light. His work is bold, energetic, full of colour, splendour, and optimism.

At the age of 53, four years after the death of his first wife, he married his second wife, a 16-year-old girl, Hélène Fourment. His interest in his new young family can be seen in the more domestic painting of his last ten years. ◆

Arthur **Rubinstein**

Polish-born American pianist
Born *1887*   **Died** *1982 aged 95*

Arthur Rubinstein was already a capable pianist when he was just three years old, and after a period of study in Berlin from the ages of 10 to 13, he began his international career. He made his first American tour in 1906. By this time he had given up studying, and this sometimes showed in some of his performances. Then in 1932 he withdrew from the concert platform for a period of intensive study and reassessment. Rigorous discipline was now added to a brilliant technique, and the success of his 1937 American tour swept away any doubts the critics may have had. He became an American citizen in 1941 and made concert appearances well into his 90s, specializing in the music of Mozart, Chopin, and Debussy. ◆

Bertrand **Russell**

British philosopher, pacifist, and campaigner
Born *18/2*   **Died** *1970 aged 97*

Bertrand Russell came from an aristocratic family and had a privileged childhood – even though both his parents died before he was two years old.

He studied mathematics and philosophy at Cambridge University and this led to his most important philosophical work. He tried to show that all mathematics was derived from a few simple laws of logic. Later he extended these ideas to show that knowledge was based, via logic, on simple observations. Neither project was completely successful, but his ideas greatly influenced mathematics and philosophy. He was an excellent writer, and won the Nobel Prize for Literature in 1950. To the public, though, he was best known for his political and social views, and for his many broadcasts. He was a lifelong pacifist, and in 1958 helped to start the Campaign for Nuclear Disarmament (CND). ◆

Babe **Ruth**

American baseball player
Born *1895*   **Died** *1948 aged 53*

George Herman Ruth went to a school for poor children in Baltimore, which is where he began his baseball career as a pitcher with the Baltimore Orioles. Then, known to all the fans as 'Babe Ruth', he became a member of the Boston Red Sox and hit 29 home runs in 1919. The next year, playing for the New York Yankees, he hit 54 home runs and became so popular that by 1925 he was earning more money than the president of America. In 1927 he raised his record to 60 home runs in a season, and by the time he retired in 1935 he had scored a career total of 714. He is considered by some to be the greatest baseball player of all time. ◆

see also

DiMaggio

Ernest **Rutherford**

New Zealand scientist who revealed the structure of atoms
Born *1871*   **Died** *1937 aged 66*

Ernest Rutherford came from a family of eleven children and grew up on his family's small farm in New Zealand. He was very clever and studied at university in New Zealand before going to Cambridge University.

At Cambridge he began work on the exciting new subject of radioactivity. He discovered that radioactive substances produce three different types of radiation. At this time, scientists were only just beginning to study the inside of atoms. For more than 2000 years atoms had been thought of as like

▲ *Ernest Rutherford was awarded the Nobel Prize for Physics in 1908 for his work on radioactivity.*

tiny marbles, but Rutherford's experiments showed that in the centre of an atom there is a tiny, heavy blob, the nucleus, and that most of the atom consists of empty space.

Rutherford gathered other brilliant scientists in his laboratory in Cambridge. These included James Chadwick (who discovered the neutron) and John Cockcroft (who built an atom-smashing proton accelerator). The work of these and others, like Marie and Pierre Curie, Enrico Fermi and Niels Bohr, began a new age of physics: the 'nuclear age'. It has produced radiation for treating cancer, nuclear power-stations which generate electricity, and also nuclear weapons. ◆

see also

Bohr   Curie
Fermi

Mohammed Anwar el **Sadat**

President of Egypt from 1970 to 1981
Born *1918*   **Died** *1981 aged 63*

As a young officer in the Egyptian army, Mohammed Anwar el Sadat joined the revolt which overthrew King Farouk in 1952. In 1964 he became vice-president of Egypt to President Abdel Nasser, and when Nasser died in 1970, Sadat became president.

During the 1973 war between Israel and its Arab neighbours, the Egyptian army broke through Israel's defences. This proved that the Israelis were not unbeatable. After the fighting Sadat felt that Egypt was strong enough to make a separate peace deal with Israel, even though many other Arab nations did not agree with this. But Sadat knew that Egypt, a poor country, was just

▼ *President Sadat was much admired for his peace-making efforts.*

made poorer by constant fighting. In 1977 he flew to Jerusalem to talk with the Israeli prime minister, Menachem Begin. They were awarded the Nobel Peace Prize the following year for their efforts to bring peace in the troubled Middle East. A peace treaty was finally signed in 1979 in Washington following the so-called Camp David negotiations.

In 1981 Sadat was assassinated by an extreme Muslim group. ◆

see also
Begin   Nasser

Camille **Saint-Saëns**

French composer, pianist, and organist
Born 1835   Died 1921 aged 86

Camille Saint-Saëns composed his first piece of music when he was three, and made his concert début at the age of 10, playing concertos by Beethoven and Mozart. He studied at the Paris Conservatoire, impressing everyone with his dazzling gifts as pianist, organist, and composer. There seemed to be nothing he could not do. And so it continued throughout his long, enormously prolific life. His compositions include 13 operas, of which *Samson et Dalila* (1877) is the most famous, 10 concertos (five of which are for piano), three symphonies, sacred and secular choral works, and a great many songs and piano pieces. He was also a great supporter of other composers' works, including those of Liszt and Schumann, and did much to revive an interest in Bach, Gluck, Mozart, and Rameau. ◆

see also
Bach   Liszt   Mozart   Schumann

▲ *Saladin was an heroic Muslim leader and warrior during the 12th century. His name literally means 'the Welfare of the Faith'.*

Saladin

Muslim soldier who fought against the Christian crusaders
Born 1137   Died 1193 aged 55

Throughout his childhood, Saladin was taught how to fight and how to honour his God. In the years to come he was to do both, by waging *jihad* (holy war), the Muslim equivalent to the Christian crusade.

When he was 14, Saladin became a soldier and fought against other Muslims in Egypt. Before he could attack the Christian crusaders, he had to unite the different Muslim kingdoms. This took him 15 years to achieve. In 1187 he lead the Muslims against the Christians in the Holy Land. Saladin destroyed the Christian army at Hattin,

recaptured Jerusalem, and resisted the new Christian attack led by Richard the Lionheart (Richard I of England).

Although he was a great soldier, Saladin could also be kind and gentle. He built schools, mosques, and canals, and encouraged scholars and theologians. His people saw him as a hero who revived memories of the first Muslim conquests under Muhammad. ◆

see also
Muhammad   Richard I

Abdus **Salam**

Pakistani physicist
Born 1926   Died 1996 aged 70

Abdus Salam was educated at Government College, Lahore, and then went to England to study physics and mathematics at Cambridge University.

In 1957 he became professor of theoretical physics at Imperial College, London. While he was there he investigated the forces between the extremely small particles that make up the parts of an atom. These fundamental particles are sometimes called 'the building blocks of matter'.

Salam became the first Pakistani to win a Nobel Prize when he shared the 1979 Physics Prize with two other physicists, Steven Weinberg and Sheldon Glashow. Their theories about the interactions between fundamental particles have since been tested by experiments and their predictions confirmed.

Salam became the first Director of the International Centre for Theoretical Studies in 1964. The Centre was set up in order to help and encourage physicists from developing countries. ◆

UNE CURIEUSE CEREMONIE A BOULOGNE-SUR-MER
Les Grenadiers Argentins devant le monument du général San-Martin

José de **San Martin**

Argentinian soldier and statesman
Born *1778*   **Died** *1850 aged 72*

Although he was born in Argentina, José de San Martin lived in Spain from the age of six and was an officer in the Spanish army for 20 years. Then, in 1812, he was persuaded to switch sides and join the South American rebels who were fighting for independence from Spain. He raised an army in northern Argentina and then led them over the Andes to defeat the Spanish at Santiago, thus assuring the independence of Chile. He then landed his troops on the Peruvian coast and took control of the capital, Lima. He was given the title of Protector of Peru in 1821. In the following year he met with Simon Bolívar and, after some initial disagreement, he left the liberation of the rest of Peru to Bolívar. San Martin sailed to Europe where he lived for the rest of his life. ◆

see also
Bolívar

◀ *Agentinian soldiers salute a monument to José de San Martin, the general who played a vital part in the liberation of their country.*

Jean-Paul **Sartre**

French philosopher, playwright, and novelist
Born *1905*   **Died** *1980 aged 75*

Jean-Paul Sartre, who worked first as a teacher, gained attention as a philosopher with his book *Being and Nothingness* (1943). This is the most important French statement of existentialist philosophy, the philosophy which believes there is no such thing as inherited character and that to go from 'nothingness' into 'being', people must choose who they want to be and what they want to do. In short, human beings have to 'make' themselves by making conscious decisions.

Sartre joined the French Resistance against the invading German forces during World War II. His long novel *The Roads to Freedom* (1945–1949) draws on his experience of the French defeat at the beginning of the war. His existentialism continued to find expression in concerns over human relationships in plays such as *In Camera* (1944). In his later literary and political projects, Sartre usually worked with his long-time lover Simone de Beauvoir. ◆

Friedrich **Schiller**

German writer
Born *1759*   **Died** *1805 aged 45*

Apart from his friend Johann Goethe, Friedrich Schiller was the greatest German writer of his period. He is best known as a dramatist and poet, but he also wrote historical and philosophical works and translated plays by Racine and Shakespeare.

Schiller's first important work was the play *The Robbers* (1781); it is an attack on political tyranny and shows a passionate concern for freedom, the central theme of Schiller's work. In 1782 Schiller moved from Stuttgart to Mannheim, where he became resident playwright for the city's famous theatre. In 1794 he met Goethe in Weimar, and on his personal recommendation Schiller became professor of history at the nearby University of Jena.

Many of his plays were used as the basis for operas; his most popular play, *William Tell* (1804), was made into an opera by Rossini. His most famous poem is 'Ode to Joy' (1785), part of which Beethoven set to music in his *Ninth Symphony*. ◆

see also
Goethe   Rossini

Heinrich **Schliemann**

German-born American archaeologist
Born *1822*   **Died** *1890 aged 68*

By the age of 26 Heinrich Schliemann had already been a cabin-boy, a grocer, and a bookkeeper. His tremendous energy and determination enabled him to learn more than eight languages in ten years. He went on to make a fortune as a merchant in Russia. Then, in 1863, he retired from work, became an American citizen, and put all his energy and money into archaeology. It had long been an ambition of his to find an historical basis for the stories of the siege of Troy, as described in Homer's tale, the *Iliad*.

▲ *This stunning gold crown was one of the treasures Heinrich Schliemann discovered in his excavation of the ancient site of Mycenae in Greece.*

During an archaeological dig in Hissarlik, Turkey, which had begun in 1871, Schliemann discovered the fortifications of a city and some golden jewellery. He had found what many believed to be the city of Troy, as described by Homer. He carried out three more excavations at Hissarlik and later discovered the remains of a prehistoric civilization in Turkey. He also discovered the remains of the Mycenaean civilization in Greece between 1874 and 1876. ◆

👁 **see also**

Homer

Arnold
Schoenberg

Austrian composer
Born 1874   Died 1951 aged 76

A rnold Schoenberg was a mainly self-taught composer. His highly romantic orchestral work, *Transfigured Night* (1900), brought him a lot of attention. However, before long he found that his music

no longer followed the rules that had served composers for nearly 300 years. He looked for an explanation and found it in the development of his own new scale system, where no note was considered more important than any other. He also believed that the notes should always appear in a strict sequence. His ideas appalled ordinary music lovers, but began to influence other composers.

▼ *Arnold Schoenberg would often give talks before perfomances of his challenging musical works to explain what they meant.*

Because his music met with opposition, Schoenberg was obliged to teach in order to earn a living. When he was forced to leave his teaching post in Berlin in 1933 by the Nazis (because he was Jewish), he settled in Paris and then in America, where he taught at the University of California. He is now regarded by many as one of the most revolutionary and influential composers of the 20th century. ◆

Erwin
Schrödinger

Austrian physicist
Born 1887   Died 1961 aged 73

A fter studying science in Vienna and serving in World War I, Erwin Schrödinger moved to Zurich, Switzerland. When he was 39 he developed a theory which described sub-atomic particles as waves. He applied his 'wave mechanics' to the hydrogen atom and got an equation which predicted results that other scientists had found but had not explained. He shared the 1933 Nobel Prize for Physics with Paul Dirac for this work.

Schrödinger tried hard to attach physical meaning to the symbols used in his equations but was never completely successful. Other scientists were happy to interpret wave equations as descriptions of the probable behaviour of particles, but Schrödinger himself never accepted this view.

In 1933 he fled in disgust from Hitler's Nazis: he was one of the few non-Jewish scientists to do so. He eventually found refuge in Ireland where he became senior professor at the Dublin Institute for Advanced Studies in 1940. ◆

👁 **see also**

Bohr

295

▲ *This 19th-century painting shows Schubert playing his music to an admiring audience.*

Franz **Schubert**

Austrian composer
Born 1797   *Died* 1828 aged 31

As a child, Franz Schubert showed a remarkable talent for music. His father taught him to play the violin, and his elder brother taught him the piano. When he was nine he began to study harmony and counterpoint (the art of adding melody as an accompaniment).

In 1808 he became a chorister of the imperial court chapel. He founded a students' orchestra in which he played and also sometimes conducted. By this time he was also writing music, including quartets for his family to play. When he left college, he became a schoolmaster like his father, although he soon gave it up to concentrate on composing.

In his short life Schubert wrote an amazing amount of music, including nine symphonies, several operas, much fine chamber music, and over 600 songs. He seldom had any money but he lived happily and had many friends who admired his music and encouraged him. ◆

Robert **Schumann**

German composer
Born 1810   *Died* 1856 aged 46

Robert Schumann was an outstanding pianist and wrote many of his finest works for that instrument. He started studying law, but soon turned to music full-time. In 1832 he injured his right hand in an attempt to improve his playing technique and had to abandon all hopes of a concert career. After this set-back he concentrated on his work as a composer, but he also became known as an enthusiastic champion of German music.

His marriage to Clara Wieck (1840) proved to be very happy and resulted in a great outpouring of songs and piano music. She was a brilliant pianist herself and often performed his works, including the popular A minor Piano Concerto. Sadly, in 1854 Schumann's mental health gave way and he spent the rest of his life in an asylum. ◆

◉ **see also**
Brahms

Albert **Schweitzer**

German mission doctor, theologian, and musician
Born 1875   *Died* 1965 aged 90

As a young man, Albert Schweitzer was brilliantly successful. He became a doctor three times over, first of philosophy, then of theology, and finally of medicine. He also studied music and gained an international reputation as an organist.

Schweitzer was a man of strong convictions and was passionate in his belief that all life was precious. Because of this, he left the concert halls and universities of Europe behind him and went to Lambarene in West Africa to work as a mission doctor. He started work in 1913 and

▼ *Albert Schweitzer passionately believed in what he called 'reverence for life'. His work as a missionary inspired many to follow his example.*

stayed there for the rest of his life. In 1963 the hospital at Lambarene treated 500 patients, although its methods were getting out of date.

Schweitzer received the Nobel Peace Prize in 1952 for 'efforts on behalf of the Brotherhood of Nations'. ◆

Robert **Scott**

English Antarctic explorer
Born *1868* **Died** *1912 aged 43*

Robert Falcon Scott, a British naval officer, was placed in command of a British Antarctic Expedition, and in 1901 sailed south in the ship *Discovery*. His party returned two years later, having reached further south than anyone else at that time.

In 1910 Scott, by then a captain, again travelled to the Antarctic, this time in an attempt to be first to the South Pole. The expedition was dogged by bad planning and bad luck. Within 200 miles of the Pole, Captain Scott set out on the final stretch with four colleagues: Oates, Wilson, Bowers, and Evans. They reached the South Pole on 18 January only to find that the Norwegian explorer Amundsen had beaten them by a month. Bitterly disappointed, they turned back, but were overtaken by blizzards, and died from starvation and exposure.

> *Great God! this is an awful place.*
>
> ROBERT SCOTT
> Comment on the South Pole
> in his diary.

The bodies of Scott and his colleagues were recovered eight months later. Their notebooks, letters, and diaries described the brave but grim events. The gallant manner of Scott's failure was much admired by the British people, and he became a national hero. ◆

see also
Amundsen

▲ *These are some of the items of clothing worn by Robert Scott on his first Antarctic expedition.*

Walter **Scott**

Scottish writer and poet
Born *1771* **Died** *1832 aged 61*

Walter Scott became one of the most famous writers in Europe. He was so popular that a railway station (Waverley) and a football team (Heart of Midlothian) were named after his novels. Although Scott was lame, he became a great walker and grew to love the Scottish Border countryside with its many legends.

After training in Edinburgh as a lawyer, he married and returned to the Borders. He enjoyed collecting the old Border ballads, and wrote poems of his own, such as 'Marmion' and 'The Lady of the Lake'. Their mixture of romance, history, and action was very popular.

His first novel, *Waverley*, mixed real people such as Bonnie Prince Charlie with characters that Scott had invented. It brought history to life in a way that no other writer had ever managed. *Waverley* was an instant success, and so were his other novels such as *Old Mortality*, *The Heart of Midlothian*, *Ivanhoe*, and *Rob Roy*.

Streams of people visited his home and tourists began visiting Scotland after reading his books. But in 1826 his publishing company collapsed, leaving huge debts. Scott managed to clear the debts by writing but died after six years of hard work. ♥

Mary **Seacole**

Jamaican nurse who helped in the Crimean War
Born *1805* **Died** *1881 aged 76*

Mary Seacole's mother was black and her father was a Scottish officer with the British army in Jamaica. Her mother taught her African cures for tropical illnesses, and Mary became known as a 'doctress' in Jamaica.

In 1854 the British army was sent to fight Russia in the Crimean War. Seacole went to England to join the nurses whom Florence Nightingale had taken to the Crimea. She was turned down because she was black, so she went out to the Crimea at her own expense and opened a store and eating-place near the front lines.

Seacole showed great bravery, going among the men with medicine and supplies of food. When the fighting was fierce she bandaged the wounded and comforted the dying. Her work was remembered by many soldiers who, when the war had finished, gave money to save her from poverty. ◆

Sequoya

Native American Indian who created the Cherokee alphabet

Born 1760   Died 1843 aged 83

Sequoya was probably the son of a British trader but he was brought up by his Cherokee mother. He was an artist and a warrior who fought for the US Army in the Creek War of 1813–1814.

Having served in the army, he felt it was important that the Cherokee people had their own writing system to keep them independent of white Americans. Adapting letters from English, Greek, and Hebrew, he came up with an alphabet of 86 symbols in 1821. He taught it to young people and it was soon in use in schools, books, and newspapers. His work helped thousands of Native Americans to read and write. Sequoya went on to negotiate on their behalf with the US government over resettlement of their lands.

In tribute to his contribution to American culture, his name was given to the giant redwood tree and to the Sequoia National Park in California. ◆

Georges **Seurat**

French painter

Born 1859   Died 1891 aged 31

Georges Seurat came from a wealthy family. Unlike many famous artists, he never had to worry about earning a living and could work how and when he pleased. He loved the colourful paintings of the Impressionists, such as Monet and Renoir, but he thought that he could take their ideas further. Working slowly and patiently, he devised a method of completely covering the canvas with tiny dots of pure, bright paint. From close up they looked like abstract

▼ *Seurat's greatest work,* Sunday Afternoon on the Isle of the Grande Jatte *(1884–1886), is considered by many to be one of the landmarks of modern art.*

patterns, but when viewed from the right distance the patterns blended together perfectly to create a scene that sparkled with light and colour. This technique was called 'Pointillism', from the French word 'point', meaning 'dot'. Seurat was being hailed as the brightest new star in French painting when he died very suddenly; the official cause was meningitis, but a friend said that he had killed himself with overwork. He loved painting so much that he usually had time for little else. ◆

👁 **see also**

Monet   Renoir

7th Earl of **Shaftesbury**

English aristocrat who helped the poor

Born 1801   Died 1885 aged 84

Anthony Ashley Cooper was an unhappy child. His father

▲ *Shah Jahan's magnificent Taj Mahal. Many people from all over the world travel to see and marvel at it.*

was cold and distant, and his mother was selfish. Only his nurse, Maria Millis, loved him; she taught him his Christian faith and this inspired everything he did.

He entered parliament in 1826 and was determined to devote his life to helping the poor. He campaigned to bring in laws which helped many people in Britain's industrial cities. These laws ensured that children were no longer employed in textile mills; women and children did not work in coal-mines; and boys did not climb dangerous sooty chimneys to sweep them. He also helped to reduce the working day for adults in factories to ten hours.

He helped to start 'ragged schools' for very poor children, and the 'Arethusa Training Ship' to train boys for the merchant navy. He ran soup kitchens for the hungry, and improved conditions for the mentally handicapped. Though his family was rich (he became the 7th Earl of Shaftesbury when his father died in 1851), he was often quite short of money because he gave so much away. ◆

Shah Jahan

Indian Mogul leader
Born 1592   Died 1666 aged 74

In the 16th century, India was largely made up of independent states, each with its own ruler. One of the most important was the Mogul empire. Shah Jahan became ruler of this empire in 1627. During his reign, Mogul power extended and the capital at Delhi was rebuilt. In fact, Shah Jahan was always interested in architecture and many great buildings were erected during his time as emperor, the most famous being the Taj Mahal. This was built at Agra as a tomb when his favourite wife, Mumtaz Mahal, died after 17 years together.

Twenty thousand men worked on the Taj Mahal, producing a beautiful, white marble domed building, which gleamed in the sunlight and was reflected in the waters of a pool.

Shah Jahan became ill in 1657, and this caused a war between his four sons. Eventually Aurangzeb, the third son, killed his rivals, imprisoned his father, and seized the throne. When Shah Jahan died he was buried at the Taj Mahal with his wife. ◆

Shaka the Zulu

First great chief of the Zulu nation in southern Africa
Born c.1787   Died 1828 aged about 41

Shaka was born the son of Senzangakona, a chieftain of the Zulu nation in southern Africa. His mother, Nandi, was an orphaned princess of the Langeni tribe. When he was a child, Shaka and his mother were banished from the Zulu villages by Senzangakona and had to go back to the Langeni. There they were treated very badly and were eventually banished by the Langeni too.

They found shelter with the Mtetwa tribe, and there Shaka became a warrior. After Senzangakona's death, Shaka returned to the Zulu as chieftain. He reorganized the Zulu army into regiments known as the *impi*, giving them more deadly *assegais* (stabbing spears), changing their battle tactics, and training them to march up to 80 km a day. This training made the Zulu the strongest nation in southern Africa.

When Shaka became chief, there were fewer than 1500 Zulu; by 1824 he ruled over 50,000 people because he incorporated defeated clans into the Zulu nation. He could, however, be a very cruel leader: when his mother died in 1827, he had 7000 Zulu put to death as a sign of his grief. Shaka was murdered in 1828 by his own half-brothers. ◆

🔘 **see also**

Buthelezi   Cetshwayo

William **Shakespeare**

English playwright and poet
Born *1564*   **Died** *1616 aged 52*

William Shakespeare was the eldest child of the bailiff (mayor) of Stratford-upon-Avon. In 1582 Shakespeare married Anne Hathaway. Their first child, Susannah, was born the following year and twins, Hamnet and Judith, followed in 1585. Hamnet died when he was 11.

▲ *This miniature portrait of William Shakespeare was painted in 1588. Shakespeare died on 23 April (traditionally thought to be his birthday) in 1616, and was buried in Holy Trinity Church in his home town of Stratford.*

Nobody knows what Shakespeare was doing for a living in his early twenties, but by 1592 he was earning money as an actor and playwright in London while his wife and family remained in Stratford. He soon became a leading member of a theatrical company called the Lord Chamberlain's Men. In 1603, when James I succeeded Queen Elizabeth I on the throne, the company changed its name to the King's Men.

> *What are these,*
> *So withered, and so wild in their attire,*
> *That look not like th'*
> *inhabitants o' the earth*
> *And yet are on 't?*
>
> WILLIAM SHAKESPEARE
> *Macbeth*
> (description of the three witches)

Between 1599 and 1613 their main base was the Globe Theatre on the south bank of the River Thames, and in 1609 they acquired the Blackfriars Theatre in the City of London.

Shakespeare seems to have taken little or no interest in the printing or publication of his work, and one or two of his plays may have been lost. A complete collection was not published until seven years after his death. This so-called *First Folio* included all his plays except for *Pericles*. The number of plays which are wholly or mostly written by Shakespeare is generally agreed to be 37. He also wrote 154 sonnets.

Shakespeare's most famous plays are probably the four great tragedies, *Hamlet*, *Macbeth*, *Othello*, and *King Lear*. He also wrote popular comedies, such as *A Midsummer Night's Dream* and *Twelfth Night*, and many history plays. The best-known of these are *Julius Caesar* and *Antony and Cleopatra*, which deal with Roman history, and a long cycle of eight plays dealing with English history from the reign of *Richard II* to the reign of *Richard III*. Other favourites in the theatre are *The Merchant of Venice*, *Romeo and Juliet*, and *The Tempest*.

By 1597 Shakespeare was so successful that he was able to buy one of the finest houses in Stratford, New Place, and it was here that he retired with his family for the last few years of his life. ◆

Uday **Shankar**

Indian dancer and choreographer
Born *1900*   **Died** *1977 aged 77*

Uday Shankar undertook formal art training in Bombay and at the Royal College of Art in London in the 1920s. In London he met the famous ballerina Anna Pavlova and created two dances for her dance company.

He returned to India in 1929 and formed his own dance company which appeared regularly in Europe and the United States. With his brother, the sitarist Ravi Shankar, he explored ways of using folk dance as dance drama. Shankar used Western theatrical techniques to spread the popularity of traditional Hindu dance to Europe and America. Some fans of traditional dance disapproved of his experimental work, but many important and influential Indians supported what he was trying to do. ◆

see also
Pavlova

George Bernard **Shaw**

Irish playwright
Born *1856*   **Died** *1950 aged 94*

George Bernard Shaw moved from Ireland to London at the age of 20 and had a go at writing novels. These were not very successful, but people did begin to take an interest in his magazine articles. Many of these were about politics, as the young Shaw was a keen supporter of the Fabian Society, a group of Socialists.

Shaw's first successful play was *Widowers' Houses*, performed in 1892. The play, which attacked

▲ *A poster for* My Fair Lady, *the 1964 musical film adaptation of George Bernard Shaw's play* Pygmalion.

slum landlords, upset those people who did not like to see themselves criticized on stage. Shaw went on to write many famous plays. *Saint Joan* is about Joan of Arc, who led the French army against the English in the Middle Ages. Many people know the story of his play *Pygmalion* because of the musical version, *My Fair Lady.*

However, Shaw's plays are more than just stories. They contain powerful arguments against things and ideas that Shaw considered unfair, dangerous, or silly. Shaw explained these ideas in prefaces or introductions to his published plays. He was awarded the Nobel Prize for Literature in 1925. ◆

Mary **Shelley**

English writer
Born *1797* **Died** *1851 aged 54*

Mary Shelley was the daughter of Mary Wollstonecraft, a writer and feminist, and William Godwin, a novelist and writer on politics. At 16, Mary ran away with the poet Percy Bysshe Shelley. She married Shelley after his first wife's suicide in 1816.

Her novel, *Frankenstein,* a pioneering science-fiction story, was published when Mary was only 19. It tells how Frankenstein, a student, creates a living creature out of parts taken from dead bodies.

Mary also wrote short stories, biographies, and travel literature, including an entertaining account of the continental tour she and Percy undertook when they eloped, entitled *History of a Six Weeks' Tour* (1817). Mary continued to write after Percy was drowned in 1822. ◆

see also

Shelley, Percy

Percy **Shelley**

English poet
Born *1792* **Died** *1822 aged 29*

A lot of Percy Bysshe Shelley's work reflected his radical beliefs. He was expelled from Oxford University in 1811 for distributing a pamphlet, attacking religious belief, which he had written with a student friend. And no one would publish his long poem, *Queen Mab*, for fear of prosecution over its celebration of free love, republicanism, and vegetarianism, so he published it himself in 1813.

Shelley married 16-year-old Harriet Westbrook in 1811, but left her when he fell in love with another 16-year-old. This was Mary, daughter of William Godwin, the man whose writing had shaped Shelley's own ideas. They married after Harriet's suicide and spent the summer of 1816 on Lake Geneva with Lord Byron. In 1818 they left England to travel in Europe. They eventually settled in Italy, and it was here that Shelley wrote some of his greatest works, including *Prometheus Unbound* (1820), 'To a Skylark' (1820), and 'Adonais' (1821), written on the death of Keats. Shelley was drowned just a year later when his sailing boat, *Ariel*, overturned in a storm off the Italian coast. ◆

see also

Byron   Keats   Shelley, Mary

▼ *This artistic impression of Percy Bysshe Shelley's funeral was painted in 1889, many years after Shelley's tragic early death.*

Shi Huangdi

First emperor of all China
Born *259* BC   **Died** *210* BC *aged 49*

Shi Huangdi's aim was to found an empire that would last 10,000 generations. In fact it collapsed four years after his death.

At 13 Shi Huangdi became ruler of Quin (Chin), the most powerful of the half-dozen states into which China was then divided. He conquered all the others and had created a single Chinese empire by 221 BC. He then united it by building roads and canals and making everyone obey the same laws and use the same weights and measures. All important officials were appointed directly by the emperor. Monuments and temples were built in his honour and frontier defences were improved to make a single Great Wall. When he died he was buried in a huge, elaborate tomb guarded by 10,000 warriors made of terracotta. ◆

▼ *Shi Huangdi's Great Wall is the only man-made structure that is visible from the Moon.*

Bill Shoemaker

American champion jockey
Born *1931*

Bill Shoemaker was the world's most successful jockey. When he retired in 1989, he had achieved 8833 wins from 40,350 mounts.

He was born prematurely weighing just 1.35 kg. However, his grandmother saved his life by putting him in a shoebox inside an open oven door for his first 24 hours. He grew to be only 1.5 m (4 ft 11 in) tall.

He began working with horses as a teenager and became a jockey in 1949. He was America's champion jockey ten times and also leading money winner ten times. He has won top races such as the Kentucky Derby and Belmont Stakes several times.

In 1991 Shoemaker was injured in a car crash and has since been confined to a wheelchair, although he still manages to train horses. ◆

👁 **see also**
Piggott

▲ *An early Sholes typewriter.*

Christopher Sholes

American inventor who developed the typewriter
Born *1819*   **Died** *1890 aged 71*

Christopher Sholes worked as a printer and as a newspaper editor but his main interest was inventing. He was so attracted by the idea of producing a letter-printing machine that he spent the rest of his life developing and improving the typewriter.

Sholes was granted a patent for a

typewriter in 1868 but he could not raise enough money to develop the idea. Eventually he sold his design to the Remington Arms Company. The first Remington typewriters went on sale in 1874. They only wrote in capital letters but they had many of the features we recognize today: levers struck an inked ribbon to print the letters and the paper moved along to space out the characters. Sholes also arranged the keys in almost exactly the same 'QWERTY' pattern found on modern typewriters and computer keyboards. ◆

Dmitry **Shostakovich**

Russian composer
Born *1906*   **Died** *1975 aged 68*

Dmitry Shostakovich's mother was a professional pianist and gave him his first lessons. From 1919 he studied at the Petrograd Conservatoire, but as his family was poor he helped out by playing the piano in a cinema. Success came early. Although his First Symphony was written in 1926 as a graduation exercise, it was hailed as a masterpiece. His career continued to prosper until 1936, when the newspaper *Pravda* suddenly attacked his opera *The Lady Macbeth of the Mtsensk District* for being a disgrace to the Soviet way of life and for a while he found himself out of favour. He was greatly admired during the war years – his Seventh Symphony was composed in Leningrad (now St Petersburg) while the city was under siege by the Nazis in 1941. Besides operas, ballets, choral, and instrumental works of every kind, Shostakovich wrote 15 symphonies and 15 string quartets

which are now considered to be among the most important of the 20th century. ◆

Jean **Sibelius**

Finnish composer
Born *1865*   **Died** *1957 aged 91*

Jean Sibelius wrote his first piece of music when he was ten, and began to study the violin in earnest four years later. In 1885 he enrolled at the University of Helsinki as a law student, but turned to music in the following year. His first ambition was to become a concert violinist, but he then turned to composing. Success came in 1892 with the symphonic poems *En Saga* and *Kullervo*. Both were based on Finnish legends. This delighted the Finns, who were struggling against Russian domination and were anxious to keep their culture alive. Sibelius completed the first of his seven symphonies in 1899. These, together with his violin concerto and symphonic poems, brought him international fame. But gradually he became disillusioned with the latest developments in music, and after completing the symphonic poem *Tapiola* in 1926 he gave up composing altogether. ◆

Siemens family

German family of engineers and industrialists
Werner von Siemens
Born *1816*   **Died** *1892 aged 75*
(Charles) William Siemens
Born *1823*   **Died** *1883 aged 60*
Frederick Siemens
Born *1826*   **Died** *1904 aged 77*

When Werner von Siemens was 24 his father died leaving him with nine brothers and sisters to look after. He took this

responsibility seriously and helped to build Europe's most important family of engineers.

Werner served in the army but his main interest was science and, in particular, electricity. In 1848 he set up the business that built Germany's first telegraph line.

Werner's younger brother (Charles) William also trained as a scientist and then went to England. Another brother, Frederick, joined William and the two of them worked on improving the furnaces used in industry. In 1856 they developed a 'regenerative' furnace that used hot, waste gases to heat the air being pumped into the furnace. This made glass-making much more efficient and replaced old-fashioned ways of making steel.

Frederick went back to Germany in 1867 to take over a large glassworks which another brother, Hans, had set up. William stayed in England and in 1883 was knighted by Queen Victoria in recognition of his contributions to science and industry. ◆

◗ **see also**

Bessemer

▼ *A cartoon of (Charles) William Siemens from* Punch *magazine, 1883.*

PUNCH'S FANCY PORTRAITS.—No. 146.

SIR C. W. SIEMENS, D.C.L., F.R.S., &c.

THE ELECTRIC KNIGHT-LIGHT.

▲ *Igor Sikorsky seen at the controls of the first flight of his invention, the Sikorsky VS-300, on 14 September 1939.*

Igor **Sikorsky**

Russian-born American aeronautical engineer
***Born** 1889   **Died** 1972 aged 83*

As a boy in Russia, Igor Sikorsky built a model helicopter which flew, powered by a rubber band. Forty years later, in 1939, he built what was to be the world's first commercially successful helicopter. This was built in large numbers, mainly for military purposes, and was the forerunner of all modern helicopters.

In the years between, Sikorsky had trained as an engineer in Russia and in 1908, after meeting the aeroplane pioneer Wilbur Wright in Paris, he returned home to give serious attention to fixed-wing aircraft. In 1913 he built the first four-engined passenger aeroplane. In 1919 he emigrated to America. There he produced successful 'flying boats', which, in the 1930s, were used for passenger services across the Atlantic and the Pacific oceans. However, he still pursued his dream of a vertical take-off aircraft and this was realized with his VS-300 model in 1939. By 1957, when he retired, Sikorsky had seen the helicopter develop in power, size, and versatility. ◆

👁 **see also**
Wright brothers

Paul **Simon**

American singer and songwriter
***Born** 1942*

New York's folk-rock duo, Simon and Garfunkel, had many hit records during the 1960s and 1970s. The best known was probably 'Bridge over Troubled Waters' (1970). They split up after this record and Art Garfunkel turned mainly to film acting while Paul Simon pursued a solo career as a singer and songwriter. Although he was often dismissed in the early stages of his career as an imitator of Bob Dylan, Simon's work on albums like *There Goes Rhymin' Simon* (1973) and *Still Crazy After All These Years* (1975) showed him to be a sensitive and intelligent songwriter.

Simon and Garfunkel have played several concerts together since they originally split up. The most memorable was probably their concert in Central Park, New York, in 1981.

In 1986 Simon recorded the album *Graceland* with many top African musicians. Many people consider this celebration of African and American music to be his finest album to date. ◆

Frank **Sinatra**

American singer and film star
***Born** 1915   **Died** 1998 aged 82*

Francis Sinatra was born in a tough neighbourhood in New Jersey, where he may have made the first underworld (organized crime) contacts for which he has often been criticized. He started as a singer when he was about 20

▼ *Frank Sinatra was particularly linked with the song 'My Way', which spent a record 122 weeks in the British pop charts from 1969 to 1971.*

and in 1939 was 'discovered' by bandleader Harry James. His style of singing romantic ballads with emotive and characteristic phrasing delighted his teenage fans, but he could also sing witty and moody numbers.

He began acting in films in the 1940s but was not taken seriously as an actor until the non-singing role of an American soldier in *From Here to Eternity* (1953), which won him an Oscar. He went on to star in many more films, both musicals and dramas. He continued to sing in live concerts even when he was in his seventies. ◆

Sitting Bull

Sioux Indian chief
Born *c.1834* **Died** *1890 aged about 56*

Sitting Bull was a Sioux Indian chief whose Indian name was Tatanka Iyotake. He is most famous for his part in the defeat of General Custer and his cavalrymen at the battle of Little Bighorn in 1876. This battle came about because the Americans broke the Sioux resettlement treaty, which Sitting Bull had agreed to in 1868.

After this battle, Sitting Bull and his followers were relentlessly pursued by the American army and were forced to escape to Canada. They returned to America in 1881 and Sitting Bull became famous once again, this time for his appearances in Buffalo Bill's Wild West shows. He finally settled on a reservation in South Dakota where he continued to lead the Sioux in their refusal to sell their lands to white settlers. He was killed shortly after while 'resisting arrest' during an uprising there. ◆

◉ **see also**
Buffalo Bill   Custer

▲ *Sioux Indian Chief Sitting Bull was also a 'medicine man', and was believed to possess magical powers.*

Adam **Smith**

Scottish philosopher and economist
Born *1723* **Died** *1790 aged 67*

Adam Smith was educated at Glasgow and then Oxford University. In 1751 he returned to Glasgow as a professor of logic and moral philosophy and published his first major work, *The Theory of Moral Sentiments,* in 1759. He left Glasgow in 1764 to travel for two years as tutor to the Duke of Buccleuch. Upon his return he settled down to write his most famous book, *The Wealth of Nations.* This has become one of the most important books on economics. In it Smith explained the development of capitalism and how it made people better off. He also introduced his most famous idea, 'the invisible hand' of competition, which ensures that economic activity can produce prosperity for all even though individuals act only in their own self-interest. These ideas remain powerful today and have influenced many governments. After completing this major work, Smith became commissioner of customs in Scotland and moved to Edinburgh, where he died two years later. ◆

> *There is no art which one government sooner learns of another than that of draining money from the pockets of the people.*
>
> ADAM SMITH, 1776

Charles Kingsford **Smith**

Australian pilot
Born *1897* **Died** *1935 aged 62*

Charles Kingsford Smith was educated in Australia and trained as an engineer. When World War I broke out he joined the Royal Flying Corps. After being wounded, he was made a flying instructor.

In 1924 he returned to Australia and became chief pilot for Western Australian Airways. Two years later he started his own airline. From then until his death, he made many record-breaking flights. He and co-pilot Charles Ulm flew round Australia in less than 11 days in 1927, and in 1928 they flew across the Pacific Ocean from California to Australia, the first people to do so. In 1930 they flew to England from Australia in just under 13 days, and in 1934 Smith and another co-pilot, Gordon Taylor, made the first west-to-east crossing of the Pacific.

In those days, long flights were frightening adventures and were full of risks. Smith's luck eventually ran out. One day in 1935, while flying from India to Singapore with co-pilot Thomas Pethybridge, his plane disappeared over the Indian Ocean. ◆

Jan **Smuts**

*Prime minister of South Africa from 1919
to 1924 and from 1939 to 1948*
Born *1870*   **Died** *1950 aged 80*

After going to school in southern
Africa, Jan Christiaan Smuts
went to Cambridge University
where he was a brilliant student. In
1895 he went to Cape Town and
began work as a lawyer.

In 1899 a war started between the
British, who ruled the colonies of
southern Africa, and the Boers
(Afrikaners), who were white
settlers of Dutch descent. Smuts
fought against the British, and at the
end of the war in 1902 he began to
work for the colonies to become
self-governing instead of being
ruled by Britain.

The Transvaal area got its own
government in 1907,
and all the
colonies were
united into one
country, the Union
of South Africa, in
1910. The new
Union remained
part of the
British
empire.

◀ *This photograph was
taken in 1914 when Jan
Smuts was about to
become an ally of Britain
in World War I.*

During World War I, Smuts
became a member of the War
Cabinet in London. After the war,
he became prime minister of South
Africa from 1919 until 1924.

He became prime minister again
in 1939, when South Africa allied
itself to Britain in World War II.
This time Smuts stayed in power
until 1948, when he was defeated in
the elections by Daniel Malan, who
put forward 'apartheid' policies to
keep the different races apart in
South Africa. ◆

Garry **Sobers**

West Indian cricketer
Born *1936*

As a boy in Barbados, Garfield
Sobers was good at all sports,
but eventually he decided to devote
himself to cricket. He was an
excellent batsman, scoring a Test
match record at the time of 365 not

out for the West Indies against
Pakistan in 1958. He held this
record until 1994 when Brian Lara
scored 375 runs for the West Indies
against England. Sobers could also
bowl left-handed in two different
styles: fast-medium and slow spin.

When he retired in 1974, his Test
match record was 8032 runs, 235
wickets, and 109 catches, making
him one of the best all-round
cricketers in the world. He was also
the first player to score six sixes in
one over. ◆

Socrates

Ancient Greek philosopher
Born *c.469 BC*
Died *399 BC aged about 70*

At first Socrates followed his
father's profession as a
sculptor. Like most men at that time
in Athens he also served in the army.

Turning later to philosophy,
Socrates did not open a school or
give public lectures as some
philosophers did. He simply felt he
had a mission to correct people's
ignorance. His method was to
engage people in 'question and
answer' sessions. He was the first to
use a set of rules, or logic, to
discuss important matters. He
questioned the way people thought
and acted. We know about his ideas
and teaching methods from his
follower, Plato. Plato wrote down
Socrates' ideas and published them.

Socrates upset some people in
government and important positions
in Athens. In 399 BC he was accused
of corrupting young men by making
them ask awkward questions about
the society in which they lived.
He was found guilty and the
judges condemned him to death by
drinking some poisonous hemlock. ◆

◉ **see also**
Plato

King **Solomon**

King of Israel during the 10th century BC
Born *c.980* BC
Died *c.922* BC *aged about 58*

Solomon succeeded his father, David, to the throne of Israel when he was about 20 years old. He strengthened the fortifications of Jerusalem and other cities and enlarged his army by adding horsemen and chariots. He made alliances with the rulers of Egypt and other nations, and planned a large programme of trade, industry, and construction. The first Jewish temple in Jerusalem was built during his reign and many foreign rulers came to visit his court.

Solomon had a reputation for being wise, but this wisdom was not shown in the way he ruled his land. He was extravagant and used heavy taxation and forced labour for his building programme. This caused hardship and unrest among the people. There was rebellion during his lifetime, and after he died Israel was divided again. The northern kingdom kept the name Israel while the southern part was called Judah. ◆

🔘 see also

David

▼ *Solomon shown dictating the Bible's Book of Proverbs. It was once believed that he wrote three proverbs.*

Solon

Ancient Greek statesman
Born *c.630* BC
Died *c.560* BC *aged about 70*

Solon was born into a noble family in Athens but had little money. As a young man he worked as a merchant. He also took part enthusiastically in the political life of Athens, especially in its arguments and wars with other Greek states. In 594 BC he was appointed chief archon of Athens (nine archons, who were like magistrates, governed the city each year). Solon was told to create reforms to help the city out of its economic depression. His particular job was to calm the arguments which broke out among the rich nobles and the poorer people. The nobles not only controlled the running of the state but owned nearly all the land. The poor had to borrow from the rich, becoming slaves when they could not repay the debt. Solon made great changes immediately. He cancelled the debts and made laws to forbid slavery because of debt. He also made some important changes to the constitution so that all citizens could have some share in the government of their city-state. With these reforms, Solon helped to establish the first democracy. ◆

▲ *Solzhenitsyn's book* The Gulag Archipelago *(1973) is about the Soviet labour-camp network.*

Alexander **Solzhenitsyn**

Russian writer
Born 1918

In 1945 Alexander Solzhenitsyn was arrested for criticizing Stalin, the ruthless Russian leader. He spent eight years in labour camps and three more in exile before being released in 1956. In 1962 he caused a sensation with his book *One Day in the Life of Ivan Denisovich*, which described the effort it took to survive just one day in the appalling conditions of the labour camps. Some of his later writings, critical of the authorities, were banned in the Soviet Union. They were published in other countries, however, and in 1970 Solzhenitsyn was awared the Nobel Prize for Literature.

He was deported from the Soviet Union in 1974 and went to Germany before settling in America. He made an emotional return to Russia in 1994. ◆

Sophocles

Ancient Greek playwright
Born c. 496 BC
Died 406 BC aged about 90

In the 5th century BC, the Greek city of Athens was a very rich and lively place. Its inhabitants were especially keen on the arts and they encouraged artists and writers of all kinds. Every spring, Athens held a competition for new plays. In 468 BC, the winning plays were written by Sophocles.

Born near Athens, Sophocles studied music, poetry, and drama, and then started to write his own plays. During his long life he wrote 123 plays, and won the Athens drama competition 24 times. Seven of his plays have survived. They tell the sad stories of important people in Greek legends. They are so powerful and gripping that they are still performed today. ◆

Spartacus

Leader of a slave revolt against the Romans 74–71 BC
Date of birth unknown
Died 71 BC age unknown

Spartacus was a bandit who was captured in the province of Thracia (now north-eastern Greece and Turkey) and forced to be a slave. He was sold to be trained as a gladiator in Capua, Italy. In the gladiatorial school there he led an uprising of fellow gladiators against the cruelty of the owner. They escaped and were soon joined by other runaway slaves.

Spartacus' men easily defeated the first army of 3000 Roman soldiers sent against them. The army of slaves grew to about 90,000 men and for two years they defeated the Roman forces. Eventually, however, the rebellious slaves were defeated in a battle in which Spartacus was killed. Six thousand of his slave companions were captured and crucified. ◆

Steven **Spielberg**

American film director, writer and producer
Born 1947

As a boy, Steven Spielberg began using his father's cine-camera to film toy trains. At school he made several amateur science fiction films.

His big impact on the cinema came in 1975 with the tense thriller *Jaws*, which quickly made more money than any other film. After making *Close Encounters of the Third Kind* in 1977, he broke box-office records again with the success of *Raiders of the Lost Ark* (1981) and *E.T.* (1982), which made more than 700 million US dollars. His film *Jurassic Park* (1993), with its amazing dinosaur special effects, again broke all box-office records. In 1994 Spielberg was awarded his first Oscar for Best Director for his film *Schindler's List*. This black and white film about the Holocaust also won six other Oscars, including one for Best Film. ◆

Mark **Spitz**

American swimming champion
Born 1950

Mark Spitz began swimming at the age of two, and his father began to coach him seriously when he was eight. In 1968, when he was at Indiana University, Spitz predicted that he would win six gold medals at the Mexico Olympics. In fact, he won only two, both in the relay races. Embarrassed by this failure, he trained hard for the 1972 Munich Olympics. There he broke all records by winning seven gold medals in seven events, and in each of these events he set a new world record. ◆

Joseph **Stalin**

Dictator of the Soviet Union from the 1920s to 1953
Born 1879   **Died** 1953 aged 73

Joseph Vissarionovich Dzhugashvili's parents wanted him to be a priest, but he was expelled from his Christian

▼ *Steven Spielberg comes face to face with the star from one of his most famous films, E.T.*

college for his 'disloyal ideas'. Later he joined the Russian Social-Democratic Workers' Party and became a full-time revolutionary. He proved himself to be tough, brave, and dedicated, and was invited by Lenin to join the Bolshevik Party leadership in 1912. It was then that he took the name 'Stalin' (man of steel).

In 1917, Stalin was a loyal supporter of Lenin's seizure of power during the Revolution, and in 1922 he became secretary of the Communist Party (as the Bolsheviks were now known). However, as Lenin lay dying, he asked his comrades to remove Stalin from this important post because 'he is too rude and uncomradely'. But Lenin died in 1924 before any action could be taken.

In the years that followed, Stalin helped to build a strong nation through a series of Five-Year Plans intended to industrialize and modernize the Soviet Union. His greatest achievement was to lead his country, as 'Generalissimo', to victory over the Nazis in World War II. After this, Communist influence spread through much of Europe.

But all this was done at great human cost. Stalin arranged for all his rivals to be killed until he became dictator. Soviet people lived

◀ It was the plight of poor families like this, forced to live in their car, that inspired Steinbeck's novels.

in fear of arrest, torture, and execution by the notorious secret police (later called the KGB). Millions of people were sent to labour camps for opposing Stalin's wishes, and in the countryside millions more died of starvation during the 1920s and 1930s.

It was only after his death in 1953 that people felt free to criticize Stalin. The leaders of the Communist Party denounced him in 1956, and in 1961 his body was removed from its place of honour in the Lenin Mausoleum in Red Square. ◆

👁 **see also**

Lenin Trotsky

John **Steinbeck**

American writer
Born 1902   Died 1968 aged 66

Most of John Steinbeck's writing explores America's agricultural society and the relationship between people and the land. This is hardly surprising considering that Steinbeck grew up in a farming region in California.

By 1935 Steinbeck had written several books and stories, but it was his novel *Tortilla Flat* that gave him his first popular success. This was followed by *Of Mice and Men*, a touching story of two very different farm workers. In 1939, Steinbeck's greatest work was published. *The Grapes of Wrath* is the story of a poor fruit-picking family migrating from America's dust bowl to California. His detailed and sympathetic portrayal helped bring the problems suffered by homeless farmers to the public's attention.

Steinbeck's later writing included novels, short stories, screenplays and also non-fiction. He was awarded the Nobel Prize for Literature in 1962. ◆

▼ A cartoon depicting Stalin as the captain of his country.

КАПИТАН СТРАНЫ СОВЕТОВ
ВЕДЕТ НАС ОТ ПОБЕДЫ
К ПОБЕДЕ!

Gloria **Steinem**

American women's rights campaigner
Born 1934

Gloria Steinem was born in Toledo, Ohio. During the 1960s she was involved in campaigns against racism and American involvement in the Vietnam war. In 1971 she helped to establish the National Women's Political Caucus, which encourages women to become politicians.

Steinem has been a leading campaigner for women's rights, determined to gain women more freedom in situations such as work, politics, and everyday life. She helped to found the Women's Actions Alliance to fight inequality, and in 1972 she launched *Ms.* magazine, which reports on issues affecting women. ◆

Ingemar **Stenmark**

Swedish world champion skier
Born 1956

Ingemar Stenmark learnt to ski at the age of five in his home village just outside the Arctic Circle. He won his first national championship at the age of eight and at 13 he was selected to train for the Swedish junior team. He went on to become the best skier in the world. He won three successive overall World Cup titles (1976–1978), and in 1980 won two gold medals at the Winter Olympics even though he had a metal plate in his ankle after breaking it the previous year. He retired in 1989, having won 15 World Cup championships for the slalom and giant slalom skiing competitions. His 86 wins made him the most successful skier of all time. ◆

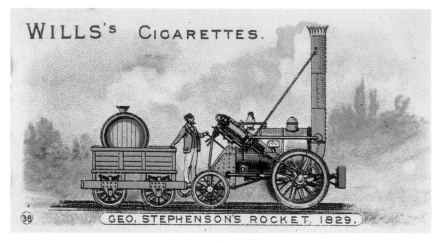

WILL'S CIGARETTES.

GEO. STEPHENSON'S ROCKET, 1829.

George **Stephenson**

English engineer and builder of the world's first public railway
Born 1781   Died 1848 aged 67

As a teenager George Stephenson had various jobs working with mining engines. He had never been to school, but he taught himself to read by attending night-classes. He became a colliery engineer, and in 1812 was appointed to be an engine-builder at Killingworth colliery, near Newcastle.

Stephenson spent the rest of his working life designing and building railways and railway locomotives. Between 1814 and 1826 he built railway engines for pulling coal. In 1823 he was put in charge of building a railway from Stockton to Darlington that would carry people. When it opened in 1825, Stephenson himself drove the engine which pulled the world's first steam-hauled passenger train. Stephenson's successes led to the building of railways throughout Britain. He also won a competition with his design for an efficient locomotive, called 'The Rocket', which was built by his son Robert. He used the money he had made from his inventions to set up

▲ *Stephenson's locomotive 'The Rocket' earned him £500 when it won a competition in 1829.*

schools for miners' children and night-schools for the miners so they could get an education. ◆

Robert Louis **Stevenson**

Scottish writer
Born 1850   Died 1894 aged 44

Robert Louis Stevenson was brought up in Edinburgh.

▼ *A fictional map of Treasure Island, from Robert Louis Stevenson's book of the same name.*

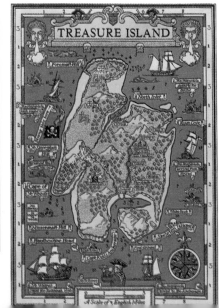

TREASURE ISLAND

When he left university he travelled abroad to escape the cold and wet Scottish climate. Stevenson's first books described his tours in Belgium and France, and his journey to California to marry an American, Fanny Osbourne.

Stevenson's exciting adventure story *Treasure Island* was published in 1883. This thrilling book about pirates and treasure was an instant success. Three years later his fame soared when the novel *The Strange Case of Dr Jekyll and Mr Hyde*, a fascinating horror story, was published.

In 1889 Stevenson and his family settled on the Polynesian island of Samoa. He continued to write, and the islanders called him 'Tusitala', meaning 'Storyteller'. ◆

Marie **Stopes**

Scottish founder of the first birth control clinic in London
Born 1880   Died 1958 aged 77

Marie Stopes was born in Edinburgh. She studied science in England and Germany and later also studied philosophy. She married when she was 31, but her marriage was unhappy and she and her husband soon separated.

At the time many people thought it was wrong to talk about sex and birth control. As a result they were ignorant when they got married, and this often caused problems. Because of her own unhappy marriage, Marie Stopes decided to do something about this. She wrote two books: *Married Love* and *Wise Parenthood*. The books explained sex, birth control, and family planning clearly. Some people were shocked by the books, but others were pleased and many wrote to Marie Stopes thanking her and asking for more information. In

1918 she married again. With her second husband she opened the first family planning clinic in 1921 in London. ◆

Harriet Beecher **Stowe**

American anti-slavery author
Born 1811   Died 1896 aged 85

Harriet Stowe was born in Connecticut, America, the seventh of nine children. In 1832 the family moved to Cincinnati, where she and her older sister Catherine set up one of the first colleges for women.

Stowe married a professor, and for the next 18 years she lived through one of the most dramatic periods in North American history. In the Southern states slave-owning was legal, but many of the Northern states had abolished slavery. Slaves from the South would often try to escape to the North and into Canada where they could be free. Only the Ohio River separated Stowe from a slave-holding community, and runaway slaves were sometimes sheltered on their way north by Stowe and her friends.

Her book *Uncle Tom's Cabin* describes in

vivid, moving language the hardships and tragedy of a slave's life. It was read by more people than any other novel of its time, and influenced the decision to abolish slavery for good. ◆

◉ **see also**
Tubman

Antonio **Stradivari**

Italian maker of violins
Born 1644
Died 1737 aged 93

Antonio Stradivari began work as a pupil of Niccolo Amati, a violin maker, but he was soon putting his own label on the violins he made. Over the years he developed new shapes for his violins and a new kind of varnish, whose secret was never discovered. Soon a Stradivarius violin became a prized possession for musicians all over the world because of its powerful and penetrating tone. In his life, Stradivari made more than 1100 instruments, including lutes, guitars, and mandolins as well as violins. ◆

◀ *Because the sound of a Stradivarius violin is said to be the finest in the world, they are now among the most expensive violins to buy.*

Johann **Strauss I and II**

Two important members of a musical Austrian family
Johann I
Born *1804*   **Died** *1849 aged 45*
Johann II
Born *1825*   **Died** *1899 aged 73*

Johann Strauss I began his musical career as a violinist. Shortly after the birth of his son (Johann II) he formed his own orchestra and played in the inns and dance-halls of Vienna. Soon everyone was dancing to the waltzes and lively dance tunes he composed. His fame rapidly spread throughout Europe and he undertook many successful tours.

Johann II began writing music when he was six years old. However, his father did not want him to take up a musical career and he had to study in secret. It soon became clear that he was very talented. When it came to waltzes, no one could rival Johann II. He was the 'Waltz King' of Vienna. *The Blue Danube* and *Tales from the Vienna Woods* delighted everyone, as did his polkas, quadrilles, and marches. His operettas, such as *Die Fledermaus* (The Bat) (1874), were equally successful.

Johann I had other musical sons, Josef (1827–1870) and Eduard (1835–1916), who also wrote splendid dance tunes, but neither of them could rival their famous elder brother. ◆

Richard **Strauss**

German composer and conductor
Born *1864*   **Died** *1949 aged 85*

Richard Strauss was a classical composer who became well-known for dramatic music which

▲ *Richard Strauss's opera* Salome *(1905) was based on an Oscar Wilde play.*

interpreted stories from literature or history. He was still composing when he was well into his eighties.

Born in Munich, Strauss was the talented son of a horn player. He started his musical training early and his first symphony was performed when he was 20. He then developed his own distinctive and bold personal style. He went on to compose many pieces which he called tone poems. His first great success in this style was *Don Juan* (1889). Later, he turned to opera and wrote the startling *Salome* (1905) and *Elektra* (1909). His most popular opera was probably *Der Rosenkavalier* (1911) which was in a more traditional style with tuneful waltzes. Strauss also wrote many songs and was a distinguished conductor. ◆

Igor **Stravinsky**

Russian composer and conductor
Born *1882*   **Died** *1971 aged 88*

Although Igor Stravinsky showed an early talent for music, it was some time before he found his feet as a composer. His first great

success came with the ballets he wrote between 1910 and 1913 – *The Firebird, Petrushka*, and *The Rite of Spring* made him the most talked-about composer in Europe. However, many people were outraged by *The Rite of Spring* and thought it was simply a horrible noise.

Because of World War I and the Russian Revolution, Stravinsky decided to leave Russia. He lived first in Switzerland and then in America. His music also took a new turn. It still used interesting harmonies and exciting rhythms, but it was no longer as savage as it had been. As a conductor, he conducted *The Firebird*, which he turned into a concert suite, about a thousand times.

Even at the end of his life Stravinsky was still experimenting with new ways of writing music. When he died, the world lost one of the most adventurous musical explorers of all time. ◆

Achmad **Sukarno**

Indonesian president from 1945 to 1967
Born *1901*   **Died** *1970 aged 69*

Achmad Sukarno originally trained as an engineer. He was also brilliant at making speeches and could talk in half-a-dozen different languages. He was a founder-member of the movement for Indonesian independence from Holland. While the Dutch ruled, he spent 13 years in prison or in exile abroad. During the Japanese occupation of Indonesia during World War II, he confirmed his position as the country's leading nationalist. After the Japanese surrender, Sukarno claimed the title of President of Indonesia in 1945. He then led the fight against a Dutch re-conquest. Firmly in power from 1950, he began to act like a world-leader overseas and a dictator at home, while Indonesia suffered increasing economic difficulties. He eventually lost power to the army in 1966 and General Suharto became president in 1967. ◆

Suleiman I

Muslim ruler of the Ottoman empire from 1520 to 1566
Born c.1494   Died 1566 aged about 71

Suleiman was the only son of Sultan Selim I. While his father was sultan (king), he became governor of Manisa in Asia Minor. There he learnt the skills that he needed when he became sultan of the Ottoman empire in 1520.

▼ *This map shows Suleiman's empire at its greatest extent. The Ottomans were a mighty sea power at this time and were feared throughout the area of the Mediterranean Sea.*

Under Suleiman's rule, the Ottoman empire prospered and expanded to its greatest extent. His first military success came when he conquered Belgrade in 1521. The following year he conquered the Mediterranean island of Rhodes, and then in 1526 he defeated the Hungarian armies in a battle at Mohács. In all, he made conquests in the Balkans, the Mediterranean, Persia (now Iran), and North Africa.

Suleiman gathered around himself many statesmen, lawyers, architects, and poets. Because he tried to modernize their laws, the Ottomans gave Suleiman the name *Kanuni*, which means 'lawgiver'. In Europe, though, his opponents called him 'Suleiman the Magnificent'.

In his later life, Suleiman's reign was troubled by arguments between his three sons. Suleiman himself was still actively involved in military matters when he died during a siege in Hungary in 1566. ◆

Sultan of Brunei

Head of the state of Brunei from 1967
Born 1946

His Majesty Sultan Sir Muda Hassanal Bolkiah Mu'izuddin Waddaulah succeeded his father as Sultan of Brunei in 1967, when he was only 21. Up until that time he had been preparing for his future role of ruler of his country.

At the time of his succession to the throne, Brunei had been under British control for nearly 80 years. It became independent in 1984, and the Sultan became prime minister as well as ruler of the state. Brunei is an Islamic country, and the Sultan is regarded as the leader of the large Muslim community.

Brunei is a country which has become wealthy because of its petroleum industry. It has a high level of employment and well-developed systems of health care and education. ◆

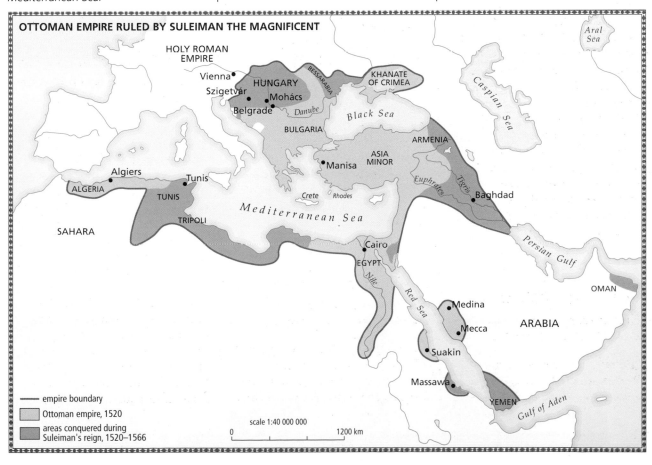

OTTOMAN EMPIRE RULED BY SULEIMAN THE MAGNIFICENT

— empire boundary
Ottoman empire, 1520
areas conquered during Suleiman's reign, 1520–1566

scale 1:40 000 000
0   1200 km

Sun Yat-sen

Founder of the Nationalist Party which ruled China before the Communists
Born *1866* **Died** *1925 aged 58*

While studying as a doctor in Hong Kong, Sun Yat-sen joined a group of revolutionaries who were intent on overthrowing the corrupt Manchu dynasty which ruled China. He made several journeys to China with a secret army but all attempts at revolution failed. From 1896, Sun Yat-sen lived in exile. Then, in 1911, there was a successful revolution against the rulers, and Sun Yat-sen returned to China and was proclaimed president.

The new republic of China was broken into districts which were ruled by warlords' armies. Because of the power of the warlords, Sun Yat-sen was president in a part of south China only. He founded the People's National Party to carry out his 'Three Principles of the People'. His first principle was a united China. The second was democracy or people's rights. The third was to create a nation where industry was modernized and peasants had enough land to feed their families. He began to build an army to march against the warlords, but died before it set out. ◆

◀ *Sun Yat-sen pictured with his wife.*

Joan Sutherland

Australian soprano
Born *1926*

Joan Sutherland was taught to sing first by her mother, and then professionally in Sydney and at London's Royal College of Music. She made her début in London's Covent Garden in 1952 in Mozart's *The Magic Flute*. In 1959 her performance in the Covent Garden production of Donizetti's *Lucia di Lammermoor* established her as an outstanding soprano. Sutherland and her husband, who is a pianist and conductor, have toured the world's opera houses, specializing in 19th-century French and Italian opera, and have made many outstanding recordings. She retired in 1990. ◆

Shin'ichi Suzuki

Japanese violinist and founder of the Suzuki Method
Born *1898* **Died** *1997 aged 99*

After studying the violin in Japan, and later in Berlin, Shin'ichi Suzuki and three of his brothers formed a string quartet. Later he founded the Tokyo String Orchestra.

Suzuki felt that everyone should learn to play an instrument. It occurred to him that if children could learn to speak by repeating simple words and phrases and gradually moving on to more complicated sentences, they might also be able to learn to play an instrument in the same way. So, he devised a method whereby young children could learn to play in easy stages, starting with simple tunes and repeating them day after day until playing became second nature.

The Suzuki Method spread all over the world. It is used to teach many kinds of instruments. ◆

▲ An illustrated scene from Gulliver's Travels. Although Swift mocked humankind in this and many of his other books, he showed great affection for many individual people.

Jonathan **Swift**

Irish-English author
Born 1667   Died 1745 aged 77

Jonathan Swift was born in Ireland of English parents. For 30 years he was Dean of St Patrick's Cathedral in Dublin, but was more famous as a writer of satire – fiction that is sometimes comic, sometimes serious, but always critical of people and their society.

His best-known satire is *Gulliver's Travels*, which describes the journeys of a ship's doctor, Lemuel Gulliver. He visits Lilliput, where everyone is tiny, then Brobdingnag, a land of giants. After more journeying, Gulliver arrives at a country ruled by gentle talking horses. These behave so much better towards each other than humans do that Gulliver longs to stay with them, dreading the return to his own world of back-biting, poverty and war. ◆

Irena **Szewinska**

Polish athletic champion
Born 1946

Irena Kirszenstein began her athletics career as an 18-year-old at the 1964 Tokyo Olympics, where she won silver medals in the long jump and 200 m, and gold in the 4 × 100 m relay. The following year she broke the world record for the 200 m, the event for which she won another gold at the 1968 Mexico Olympics. By now she had married her coach, Janusz Szewinski.

As Irena Szewinska she carried on breaking the 200 m world record regularly into the 1970s, before winning a third Olympic gold medal in the 400 m at Montreal in 1976. By the time she retired she had become one of the best athletes ever, with ten European championship medals, seven Olympic medals, and four World Cup medals to her name. ◆

Sir Rabindranath **Tagore**

Indian poet, philosopher, and musician
Born 1861   Died 1941 aged 80

Rabindranath Tagore was born into a rich Bengali family and was sent to England to study law. He started writing poems at a very young age, and published his first poems when he was 17 years old. He also wrote a number of plays and novels. In his writing he tried to blend together the best traditions of Indian and European literature.

Tagore won the Nobel Prize for Literature in 1913, and was given a knighthood by the British government in 1915. He renounced this title in 1919 in protest against the Jallianwala Bagh incident in India, when a British general ordered troops to fire on an unarmed crowd, killing about 400 people. A song written and composed by Tagore was adopted as the national anthem of India in 1950. ◆

Tamerlane

Central Asian conqueror
Born c.1336   Died 1405 aged about 69

Timur, later known as 'Tamerlane' or 'Tamburlaine' in the West, was the great-grandson of a minister of Genghis Khan. His ambition was to rebuild the empire of that great conqueror.

When he was about 20, Timur began to claim power over the other tribes in the area around Samarkand (now in Uzbekistan). By 1369, he had brutally defeated all his rivals. He now moved further afield. For the next 35 years he raided and conquered the regions from the Black Sea to the Indus. In 1404 he staged an immense celebration of his victories, displaying his captured treasures. His next great expedition was to be against China. He set out in 1405, but died on the way of a fever. He was buried in Samarkand.

Timur was lame in his right leg, and so the Persians called him 'Timur lenk', meaning 'Timur the lame', which became 'Tamerlane'. ◆

◉ **see also**

Genghis Khan

▶ Tamerlane's burial place.

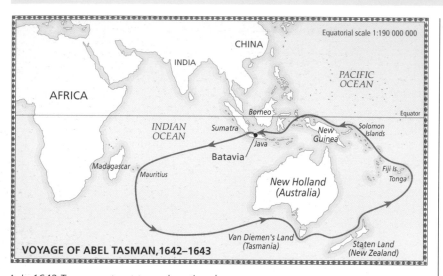

VOYAGE OF ABEL TASMAN, 1642–1643

▲ In 1642 Tasman set out to explore the South Pacific from Batavia in Java. He became the first European to reach the island now called Tasmania and to see New Zealand, Tonga, and Fiji.

Abel **Tasman**

Dutch explorer
Born c.1603
Died c.1659 aged about 56

Abel Tasman was a sailor who worked for a trading company called the Dutch East India Company. He was based in Java, then a Dutch colony and now part of Indonesia. In 1642 Anthony Van Diemen, the governor of the Dutch East Indies, sent Tasman to explore the seas further south in the hope of finding a route across the Pacific Ocean to Chile.

Tasman sailed west across the Indian Ocean, then turned south-east. Eventually he came to a forested coast, and named the territory 'Van Diemen's Land' (now called Tasmania). He then carried on east and found more land, which he named 'Staten Land' (now known as New Zealand). Heading back to Java, Tasman lost his way. He sighted Tonga and then Fiji before reaching home. He had also sailed right round Australia without knowing it! ◆

Elizabeth **Taylor**

British-born American film actress
Born 1932

Elizabeth Taylor was born in London, but grew up in Hollywood as a child actress. She appeared in films from the age of 10 and enjoyed great success in *National Velvet* in 1944.

She became one of the most glamorous stars of the 1950s and 1960s, and also attracted much attention because of her several

▼ Elizabeth Taylor in a Hollywood publicity shot. She started her career as a child actress in films such as Lassie Come Home.

short-lived marriages. She was married twice to the great Welsh actor Richard Burton, with whom she acted in *Cleopatra* (1963). She played the title role in this film and had to make 65 costume changes.

Her most memorable performances are of strong-minded women. She won Oscars for playing such women in *Butterfield 8* (1960) and *Who's Afraid of Virginia Woolf?* (1966). ◆

Pyotr Ilyich **Tchaikovsky**

Russian composer
Born 1840   **Died** 1893 aged 53

If you like ballet or like listening to music, you will probably know and love Tchaikovsky. Songs and symphonies, operas and ballets, concertos and serenades all poured from his pen.

Pyotr (Peter) Tchaikovsky was born into a wealthy Russian family and grew up in the town of Votkinsk, near the Ural Mountains. He was sent to boarding school in St Petersburg when he was eight, and eventually became a law student. It was not until he was 23 that he decided to devote his life to music. He enrolled in Russia's first Conservatory of Music in St Petersburg, run by the brilliant pianist Anton Rubinstein.

When he was 26 he wrote his first symphony, and followed it with some piano pieces, the 'Children's Album', written for his nieces and nephews. He also wrote difficult piano works, like the piano concertos, which even Rubinstein and other top pianists could hardly play at the time. But it is his fairytale ballets that many people know: *Swan Lake*, *Sleeping Beauty*, and *The Nutcracker*.

Despite his great success and fame, Tchaikovsky was often unhappy, and he suffered seriously from depression. Nine days after conducting his moving Sixth Symphony, the *Pathétique*, he died. Some mystery surrounds the cause of his death; one theory is that he committed suicide after revelations of a scandalous affair. ◆

see also

Rubinstein

Kiri **Te Kanawa**

New Zealand soprano
Born 1944

Five weeks after Kiri was born into a poor Maori family, she was adopted by Tom and Nell Te Kanawa, who named her Kiri, the Maori word for bell.

After winning many singing prizes in New Zealand and Australia, Te Kanawa studied at the London Opera Centre and then joined the Royal Opera Company. She made her Covent Garden début in 1970, her first major role being that of the Countess in Mozart's *The Marriage of Figaro*. She has specialized in the music of Mozart and Richard Strauss and made many outstanding recordings of opera and also of American musicals, such as Bernstein's *West Side Story*. ◆

see also

Bernstein   Mozart   Strauss

Thomas **Telford**

Scottish civil engineer
Born 1757   Died 1834 aged 77

Thomas Telford started his working life as an apprentice stonemason. But because of his

▲ *Telford engineered the Menai suspension bridge which connects the Welsh mainland to Anglesey.*

skills, hard work, and constant thirst for knowledge, Telford became one of Europe's leading civil engineers. His canals, bridges, harbours, and roads can be found all over Britain, still in use today.

In 1793 Telford was given his first big project: to build the Ellesmere Canal, linking the rivers Severn and Mersey. This canal made his reputation, and soon he was in great demand. He was an outstanding road builder too, and his road from London to the Welsh port of Holyhead was one of the most important routes in the country. His famous Menai suspension bridge still carries this road to the island of Anglesey.

In 1820 the Institution of Civil Engineers invited Telford to be its first president. He held this post until his death, and his influence greatly helped civil engineering become a respected profession. In 1963 the town of Telford in Shropshire was named after him. ◆

see also

Brunel

Shirley **Temple**

American child film actress
Born 1928

Shirley Temple started acting in short films at the age of four, and was given a special Oscar when she was only five for her success in the film *Stand up and Cheer* (1934). Over the next few years she was America's favourite child star, usually playing the part of a little orphan who got her way with adults by smiling sweetly and dancing or singing.

Unfortunately, she did not succeed in becoming an adult actress and made her last film, *Fort Apache* (1948), at the age of 20. Under her married name, Shirley Temple Black, she has taken on various diplomatic roles. She became US representative to the United Nations in 1969 and then ambassador to Ghana in 1974, and to Czechoslovakia in 1989. ◆

Alfred, Lord Tennyson

English poet
Born *1809*   **Died** *1892 aged 83*

Alfred, Lord Tennyson, was born in Somersby, Lincolnshire, and educated at Trinity College, Cambridge.

By 1833 he had published two sets of poems which received bad reviews. This was followed by the death of his close friend, Arthur Hallam, and caused Tennyson to suffer a great depression. In the following nine years, Tennyson wrote and rewrote many poems but published hardly any.

This changed in 1842 with the successful publication of *Poems*. His elegy for Hallam, *In Memoriam*, was published in 1850 and he succeeded William Wordsworth as Poet Laureate in the same year.

Tennyson continued to enjoy great popularity with works such as *The Charge of the Light Brigade* and *Idylls of the King*, a retelling of the Arthurian legends. He was made a Baron in 1884. ◆

see also
Wordsworth

Tenzing Norgay

One of the first two men to reach the summit of Mount Everest
Born *1914*   **Died** *1986 aged 71*

Tenzing Norgay was a Sherpa, one of the Himalayan people who have the reputation of being hardy mountaineers. Tenzing made his first trip as a porter (load carrier) on the British expedition to Mount Everest in 1935. Over the next 15 years he made 17 more expeditions to the Himalayas and became an experienced mountaineer and sirdar, a Sherpa leader.

In 1953 he was invited to lead the Sherpas on another British expedition to Everest. This was his nineteenth Himalayan climb. By now Tenzing was a major climber in his own right and he was selected to be in one of the assault parties to attempt the final climb to the summit. On 29 May, Tenzing and Edmund Hillary of New Zealand stood on the top of Everest, the first people to do so. ◆

see also
Hillary

▶ *Tenzing Norgay and Edmund Hillary on their way to conquering Mount Everest in 1953.*

Mother Teresa

Christian missionary in India
Born *1910*   **Died** *1997 aged 87*

Agnes Gonxha Bojaxhiu grew up in a loving home in Albania. Like her brother and sister, she went to the local school, but by the time she was 12 she became a nun, taking the name Teresa.

In 1928 she was sent to India to teach at St Mary's High School convent in Calcutta. One day she felt that God needed her to be among the poorest, forgotten people of the city. So, in 1948 she left the convent, setting aside her nun's habit and putting on an Indian sari.

She moved into the slums of Calcutta, where she gathered together destitute children and sheltered them. In 1950 the Roman Catholic Church allowed her to start a new sisterhood, the Congregation of the Missionaries of Charity. She opened a Home for the Dying in Calcutta in 1952, as well as a leper colony called Shanti Nagar ('Town of Peace'). After that, Mother Teresa opened over 60 more schools, orphanages, and homes

▲ *Mother Teresa, also known as the 'saint of the gutter'.*

for the dying worldwide. In 1979 she received the Nobel Peace Prize, which she accepted on behalf of the poor and destitute everywhere. In 1990, after an illness, she retired from her most active work. ◆

Saint **Teresa of Avila**

Spanish nun
Born *1515*   **Died** *1582 aged 67*

Teresa came from a devoutly Christian family. As a child she read about the lives of the saints and wanted to follow their example. When she was a teenager, she became ill with fever. Believing she might die, she remembered her childhood dreams of heaven, and decided to become a nun. When she was better, she ran away from home and joined a Carmelite convent just outside the town.

The Carmelite order of nuns had been founded 400 years before. But standards of obedience to the rules had slipped, and Teresa was greatly disappointed by the nuns' behaviour. In 1562 Teresa began her mission to reform the Carmelite order. She insisted, for example, that the nuns slept on straw, wore

rope sandals, and ate no meat. Teresa spent the last 16 years of her life travelling around Spain, restoring Carmelite houses to their original purity. ◆

see also
Augustine of Hippo

Valentina **Tereshkova**

Russian cosmonaut; the first woman to go into space
Born *1937*

Valentina Tereshkova spent her childhood on a farm. When she was older she worked in a tyre factory and then in a textile mill. But she had an adventurous spirit, and in her spare time she made as many as 163 parachute jumps.

Because of her lack of fear and her dedication, she was picked for space training in 1962. It was only a year later that she piloted a spacecraft, *Vostok 6*, in a group flight that lasted three days. Her spaceship made 48 orbits of the Earth.

Although she was a colonel in the Soviet air force, Tereshkova devoted herself to helping others in many spheres – as a figure in politics, as a diplomat on trips round the world, and as a campaigner for peace and women's rights. ◆

William Makepeace **Thackeray**

English writer
Born *1811*   **Died** *1863 aged 52*

The two most important novelists of Victorian times were probably Charles Dickens and William Makepeace Thackeray.

Thackeray was born in Calcutta, India, educated at public school and Cambridge University in England, and had an inheritance that enabled him to travel widely on the continent. In 1836 this money finally ran out and Thackeray began writing for newspapers and periodicals using false names such as Michael Angelo Titmarsh and George Savage Fitzboodle!

Thackeray wrote humorously about the English upper-middle classes, pointing out their faults and bad behaviour. His greatest work, *Vanity Fair*, was published in monthly instalments between 1847–1848. Other works of his include *The Book of Snobs*, *The Luck of Barry Lyndon*, *The Newcomes*, and *Henry Esmond*.

In contrast to his comic writing, Thackeray suffered tragedy in his private life. His second child died early and his wife suffered a permanent mental breakdown. Thackeray himself died suddenly one Christmas Eve. ◆

see also
Dickens

▼ *A portrait of Thackeray from 1867.*

Margaret **Thatcher**

British prime minister from 1979 to 1990
Born *1925*

Margaret Thatcher was born Margaret Roberts. She studied chemistry at Oxford University and later became a barrister. Having been elected to Parliament in 1959, she gained her first cabinet post as Minister of Education in 1970. She replaced Edward Heath as Conservative Party leader in 1975.

In 1979 the Conservatives won the General Election, and Margaret Thatcher became the first woman prime minister of Britain. She at once set about lowering taxes and reducing government control of businesses. Later, many state-owned businesses like British Telecom were sold to private owners.

In 1982 Thatcher reacted quickly when Argentina invaded the British colony of the Falkland Islands. A British task force recaptured the

◀ *Thatcher was renowned for her tough style; she tolerated little disagreement, either from the opposition or from within her own party.*

islands, but many British and Argentinian soldiers died.

In 1983 she led the Conservatives to another election victory, and in 1987 she became the first prime minister in the 20th century to be elected to a third consecutive term of office.

Margaret Thatcher's toughness in foreign affairs led to her being called 'the Iron Lady' and she earned respect from many people throughout the world. By the end of 1990, though, her popularity had declined. She came under attack from colleagues in the cabinet who thought that her style of government was too autocratic, or domineering. There were also disagreements about Britain's role in Europe. She resigned after a contest for the leadership of the Conservative Party. ◆

Themistocles

Ancient Greek statesman and soldier
Born *c.528 BC*
Died *c.462 BC aged about 66*

As leader of Athens and creator of its navy, Themistocles, an ambitious and daring man, saved Greece from being conquered by the Persians.

Not much is known about his early life. In 490 BC, he became an Athenian politician after the Greeks had defeated the Persians at the battle of Marathon. He favoured building a navy because he believed that the Persians would attack again, and that the war would be decided at sea. Aristides, the then leader of Athens, opposed this plan. He was banished in 482 BC and Themistocles took his place.

In 480 BC, a small force from Sparta fought the Persians to the death at Thermopylae. Then the new Athenian navy under Themistocles destroyed the Persian fleet at the battle of Salamis. In the following year, Athens and Sparta combined to overwhelm their common enemy.

In 470 BC, Themistocles was accused of conspiracy against Athens. He was exiled and fled to live in Persia. ◆

Dylan **Thomas**

Welsh poet
Born *1914*   **Died** *1953 aged 39*

Dylan Thomas was born in Swansea, Wales, and his strong feeling for the Welsh countryside and people runs through his best writing.

Thomas published his first book of poems and moved to London around the age of 20. While in London he met most of the famous writers of the time, and also

▼ *This portrait of a young Dylan Thomas is by the English painter Augustus John.*

developed a habit of long drinking sessions with his friends.

In 1949 he returned to Wales and wrote the radio play *Under Milk Wood*. The play celebrates, with affection and gentle humour, the characters of a small Welsh seaside town. Thomas, now famous for his poetry readings, was invited to America for a reading tour. However, the effects of alcoholism caught up with him and he collapsed and died while in New York. ◆

Daley **Thompson**

English decathlon champion
Born 1958

The decathlon involves ten different running, jumping, and throwing events in two days, so it takes a very good all-round athlete to win this competition. Daley Thompson is undoubtedly Britain's greatest ever decathlete.

After showing promise as a junior decathlete, Thompson became Commonwealth champion in 1978. He went on to win two Olympic gold medals (1980 and 1984), two European championships (1982 and 1986), and one world championship (1983). During this time he set four world record scores. He was the

▲ *Daley Thompson taking part in the 1988 Olympic Games in Seoul, Korea.*

first athlete ever to hold the World, Olympic, European, and Commonwealth titles all at the same time. ◆

Joseph **Thomson**

English physicist who discovered the electron
Born 1856   Died 1940 aged 83

In 1876, Joseph Thomson went to Trinity College, Cambridge. He stayed for the rest of his life becoming one of the university's most famous professors.

Thomson investigated the cathode rays given out when hot metals are placed in strong electric fields. (These are the rays used in television tubes.) He was trying to prove that these rays were streams of particles and not waves, as German physicists believed.

To solve the problem, Thomson built a 'vacuum' tube in which he could bend a beam of rays using magnetic and electric fields. He then calculated the mass and charge of the particles in the beam. In 1897 he announced his remarkable results. At that time scientists believed that the hydrogen atom was the smallest piece of matter:

Thomson's 'corpuscles' were about 1000 times lighter! He had found the first sub-atomic particle – the electron. He was awarded the Nobel Prize for Physics in 1906. ◆

see also
Bohr   Rutherford

Jim **Thorpe**

American all-round athlete
Born 1887   Died 1953 aged 66

Jim Thorpe was an outstanding athlete at college. Later, at the 1912 Olympic Games in Stockholm, he became the first man to win gold medals in both the pentathlon and decathlon. Afterwards, Olympic officials took away his medals because he had previously played professional baseball for money. At that time, only amateurs (who did not get paid) could compete in the Games.

Thorpe then turned fully professional. He played major-league baseball from 1913 to 1919 and was also an outstanding American football player from 1917 to 1929.

It was not until after his death that Thorpe's victories at the Stockholm Games were officially recognized and his gold medal status was restored. ◆

Jacopo **Tintoretto**

Italian painter
Born *1518* **Died** *1594 aged 75*

Jacopo Tintoretto's real name was Jacopo Robusti; his nickname comes from his father, who was a cloth dyer ('tintore' in Italian). He lived almost all his life in Venice, where he was the most successful painter of his time. Part of his success came from his crafty business methods. Once, when several artists were asked to submit sketches in competition for a ceiling painting, Tintoretto instead did a full-size painting and had it secretly raised in position the day before the competition was to be judged. This initiative won him the commission, but not surprisingly it made him unpopular with his fellow artists.

Tintoretto was a man of great energy who painted a huge amount of work for churches and public buildings in Venice. He worked there for more than 20 years on marvellously dramatic scenes from the life of Christ and the Virgin Mary. His style was very dynamic and energetic, but also full of tender human feelings. ◆

Titian

Italian painter
Born *c.1488* **Died** *1576 aged about 88*

Tiziano Vecellio (Titian's Italian name) was born in a village north of Venice. His family was not rich but was well respected because his father was a local official.

Titian trained to be a painter in the workshop of Giovanni Bellini, the most famous Venetian painter of his time. When Bellini died in 1516, Titian took over his post as the city's official painter. He worked on

322

paintings for the great churches and families of Venice, and he became so successful and famous that kings and nobles from other parts of Europe also commissioned work from him.

Titian's wonderful skill in composing a painting enabled him to break all the traditional rules of how pictures should be arranged. He deeply impressed other artists in Venice by his modern, bold style. No other painter had placed the Madonna and Child in the corner of a picture and not in the centre, as Titian did. He used oil paint with sumptuous, glowing colours which suited the splendour and richness of the Venice of his time. In many of his later works, Titian often used

▼ Salome with the Head of John the Baptist *(1515) by the great Venetian artist Titian.*

his fingers instead of a brush to make finishing touches or highlights. ◆

👁 **see also**
Bellini

Josip **Tito**

President of Yugoslavia from 1953 to 1980
Born *1892* **Died** *1980 aged 87*

Josip Broz was the son of a blacksmith in Croatia, which was then part of the Austrian empire. He was called up to fight for Austria against Russia in World War I. After the war he stayed in Russia to help the Communists, who had just come to power.

When he came home in 1920,

Croatia was part of a new kingdom which soon took the name 'Yugoslavia'. As well as the Croats it included people of five other national groups, and was virtually ruled as a dictatorship.

In 1921 Tito founded the Yugoslav Communist Party. The government declared it illegal, so in the 1920s and 1930s he was either in prison for his beliefs or working for Communist causes in other countries, which is where he first used the undercover name 'Tito'.

In 1941, during World War II, the Germans invaded and occupied Yugoslavia. Tito built up a resistance force, the Partisans, and after many struggles they finally chased the Germans out and set up a new Communist state with Tito as leader. The homelands of all six national groups became equal republics in the state. At first Tito ran the government as the Soviet Union ordered, but in 1948 he broke away. His Partisan comrades stood by him and he kept Yugoslavia free from Soviet control. Although the government was still Communist, it gave the people more freedom and let workers and farmers manage their own factories and farms. Tito was eventually made president for life in 1974. ◆

Tokugawa Ieyasu

Japanese ruler
Born 1542   Died 1616 aged 74

Tokugawa Ieyasu was born at a time of endless civil wars in Japan. Growing up surrounded by spies, he learned to be tough and cunning. As a young warrior he supported the shogun (warlord) Oda Nobunaga in bringing large areas of Japan under his control. After Nobunaga's assassination Ieyasu married the sister of

▲ *The original jacket design for the first edition of Tolkein's* The Hobbit *(1937).*

Hideyoshi, who was very powerful and controlled a lot of land. Ieyasu promised that if Hideyoshi died he would help his baby son, Hideyori, inherit Hideyoshi's lands. However, Ieyasu broke his word and smashed Hideyori's supporters at the great battle of Sekijahara in 1600. He then took over his opponents' lands and was appointed shogun in 1603. He abdicated two years later but still controlled affairs. Ieyasu founded Edo (now Tokyo), which became Japan's biggest city. His family ruled for over 250 years, bringing economic strength and improved educational standards. After his death a fabulous shrine was built to honour him at Nikko. ◆

Think of being uncomfortable as normal and you will never be bothered by it.
TOKUGAWA IEYASU

J. R. R. **Tolkien**

South African-born English novelist
Born 1892   Died 1973 aged 81

When John Ronald Reuel Tolkien was three years old he and his younger brother returned from South Africa with their mother to live in the countryside around Birmingham, England. His father died before he could join them, and when Tolkien was 12 his mother died too. She left the boys in the care of a priest, Father Francis Morgan, who saw to it that they had a good education.

Tolkien became very interested in old languages and they remained a fascination for him for the rest of his life. He read Classics at Oxford University, and, after serving in the army during World War I, he returned to become a professor there from 1925 to 1959. However, he became most famous for the stories he made up to amuse his children. He invented creatures, like elves and hobbits, with their own languages, and gave them adventures. His first fantasy novel, *The Hobbit*, appeared in 1937, but it took him another 12 years to complete the three volumes of *The Lord of the Rings*. Since then, his books have sold millions of copies and have been read by people all over the world. ◆

Leo **Tolstoy**

Russian novelist
Born *1828*   **Died** *1910 aged 82*

Leo Tolstoy was born into one of Russia's most famous noble families. His mother died when he was two and his father when he was eight, so he was brought up by his aunt. He did not go to school but was educated at home by a governess. He later studied at Kazan University, but left before finishing his course.

At the age of 23 he became an artillery officer in the Caucasus and took part in the Crimean War. He wrote his first stories during the war, drawing on his own early life. *Childhood* was published in 1852, followed by *Boyhood and Youth*. After taking part in the defence of Sevastopol, he wrote his famous *Sevastopol Sketches*.

During the 1860s and 1870s he spent much of his time and energy on studying education. He also published a magazine and wrote stories for children. It was during this period, 1863 to 1869, that he wrote *War and Peace*, considered by many to be the greatest novel in the world. It gives a picture of Russia just before and during the war against Napoleon in 1812. Next he worked on *Anna Karenina*, about a married woman's tragic love affair with a soldier. By the time the book was finished, Tolstoy was facing a crisis in his life. He was an aristocrat, but he was beginning to reject his life of luxury for the simple life of a peasant. In spite of his marriage and his writing, he felt he was living selfishly. He developed a new religious philosophy based on peace, love, and a humble life.

Finally, one night he felt that he must get away. He left his home secretly, but died of pneumonia at a railway station just ten days later. ◆

Tomás de **Torquemada**

Head of the Spanish Inquisition from 1483 to 1498
Born *1420*   **Died** *1498 aged 78*

Tomás de Torquemada was born in Valladolid in northern Spain, where he later went to university. He then became a Dominican friar. When aged about 32 he was appointed head of the Dominican friars in Segovia. In Segovia he later met Princess Isabella and came to know her well.

▲ *During the Spanish Inquisition, Torquemada became famous for his severity and the harshness of his judgements.*

In 1474 Princess Isabella became Queen of Castile, the largest kingdom in Spain. Isabella was a Catholic Christian, but her subjects included Jews, Muslims, and Christians who had converted from the other religions. Isabella feared these groups. In 1478 an 'Inquisition' was established – a system of law courts which would examine Christians suspected of not being true Christians. At first the inquisition worked badly, so in 1483 Isabella placed Torquemada in charge.

Torquemada reorganized the inquisition, giving it new rules by which to operate. Its trials were often conducted in secret, under torture. Before Torquemada's death the inquisition tried about 100,000 cases and executed over 2000 people. Torquemada also persuaded Isabella to order Jews to become Christians or leave the country: about 50,000 eventually departed. ◆

🕮 **see also**

Ferdinand and Isabella

Henri de **Toulouse-Lautrec**

French painter
Born *1864*   **Died** *1901 aged 36*

Henri de Toulouse-Lautrec was the son of an aristocrat and as a boy loved sports and horse-riding. However, he had two childhood accidents that damaged the bones in his legs and this left him stunted. (He is sometimes described as a midget, but in fact he grew to be about 1.5 m (5 feet) tall). His large head made him look a grotesque figure, but he accepted his misfortune without bitterness, and never mentioned it except to make a joke about it. His father and uncle were amateur artists, and when he was 21 he was given money to set up his own studio in Paris. He became famous for his pictures of life in dance-halls, theatres, cafés, circuses, and brothels. He was also a brilliant poster designer for many of the stage stars of his time.

▲ *Toulouse-Lautrec made many paintings and drawings of life in the famous Parisian nightclub 'The Moulin Rouge', including this one of the singer Yvette Guilbert.*

Alcohol and venereal disease ruined his health, however. He suffered a breakdown in 1899 and died just two years later. ◆

Toussaint l'Ouverture

Caribbean anti-slavery leader
Born c.1743   Died 1803 aged about 60

Pierre Dominique Toussaint's father is said to have been an African chief who was taken as a slave to a sugar plantation in the French colony of St Domingue in the Caribbean. Toussaint was born there. He was clever, and his father helped him to learn to read French and Latin and study mathematics. He was freed from slavery in 1777.

In 1791 the other slaves on the island rebelled against their masters and Toussaint eventually became their commander, turning the rebels into a strong fighting force. By 1798 both the French colonists and the British invaders had been beaten. Toussaint's followers gave him the name 'l'Ouverture', meaning the opener of the way to freedom.

In 1802 the French emperor, Napoleon, sent in his army to recapture Toussaint's country. Toussaint agreed to make peace with the French commander, who promised to do him no harm. The promise was false and Toussaint was sent to prison in France, where he died. His soldiers rose up and defeated the French and renamed their free country Haiti. ◆

Trajan

Roman emperor
Born AD 53   Died 117 aged 64

Trajan was born in Spain and served with his father in the army before holding various posts in the running of the provinces of the empire. The Emperor Nerva adopted Trajan as his heir; he became emperor in AD 97 when Nerva died.

The Emperor Trajan then spent most of his reign at war, against the Dacians, Armenians, and Parthians. To mark his victory over the Dacians, Trajan built a huge public square (called a forum) in Rome and the column which is 38 metres high. From top to bottom it is carved with scenes from his military campaigns. Trajan's Column gives us a unique picture of military life, and death, in the Roman Empire, as its carvings show soldiers making camp, marching, and fighting.

Many public works were undertaken during Trajan's reign. He was a popular and respected emperor who commanded the loyalty of his subjects. ◆

🕮 **see also**

Hadrian

▼ *This carved detail from Trajan's Column shows Trajan making a sacrifice before the departure of his troops to fight the Dacians in the war of 101–106.*

Anthony **Trollope**

English writer
Born 1815 *Died* 1882 aged 67

Anthony Trollope was a very busy Victorian writer. He wrote 47 novels, and many plays, short stories, and biographies and still had the time to pursue a career as a civil servant in the Post Office! In fact, it was Trollope who helped to introduce pillar boxes for letters in Great Britain. Trollope managed to combine his two jobs by writing a set amount of words every day before going to work.

As a writer, Trollope is best remembered for the *Barsetshire Chronicles*, a series of five novels about church life set in the fictional county of Barset; and *The Pallisers*, a series which explored political life. Trollope's interest in politics was lifelong and he stood unsuccessfully for Parliament in 1867. ◆

▼ *Anthony Trollope worked on his many books in his spare time.*

▲ *Leon Trotsky was one of the most important figures of the Russian Revolution.*

Leon **Trotsky**

One of the leaders of the Russian Revolution
Born 1879 *Died* 1940 aged 60

Lev Davidovich Bronstein was born of Jewish parents on a farm in the Ukraine, part of the Russian empire. He was expelled from university for political activities and was then banished to Siberia when he opposed the tsar's rule. He escaped from there and fled the country under his new name, Trotsky, which he took from one of his prison guards.

Trotsky returned to Russia in 1917 when the tsar had been overthrown. He joined Lenin's Bolshevik Party (later to become known as the Communist Party). He was one of the main organizers of the October Revolution when the Bolsheviks seized power. He then took charge of foreign affairs and defence, and built a new army, the Red Army, which won the bitter Russian civil war of 1918–1921.

Trotsky was a brilliant linguist, writer and speaker, but his impatience and bitter tongue made him many enemies in the Communist Party. After Lenin's death, he was deprived of power by Stalin. In 1927 he was expelled from the party, and two years later was driven out of the USSR. He was murdered with an ice-pick in Mexico on Stalin's orders. ◆

👁 **see also**
Lenin Stalin

Pierre **Trudeau**

Prime minister of Canada from 1968 to 1984
Born 1919

Pierre Trudeau became involved in politics when he supported the workers during a miners' strike at Asbestos, Québec, in 1950. In 1965 he was elected to parliament and he became prime minister in 1968. He insisted on the use of both French and English as the two official languages of Canada.

In 1982 he negotiated a new law which meant that Britain no longer had to give formal approval for amendments to the Canadian constitution. The same law also gave Canadians a Charter of Rights and Freedoms, which made sure that all people, including those from minority groups, would be treated fairly. He retired as prime minister in 1984. ◆

Harry S. **Truman**

President of the United States of America from 1945 to 1953
Born 1884 *Died* 1972 aged 88

Harry S. Truman became vice-president of the United

States of America in 1945. However, President Roosevelt died only 83 days later, and Truman suddenly found himself leader of the world's most powerful nation. At this time America was involved in World War II, and Truman took the decision to drop atomic bombs on Hiroshima and Nagasaki in Japan. This killed almost a million people but ended the war with Japan. After that he turned to Europe and provided Marshall Aid to help rebuild countries ravaged by war.

His main aim was to contain the power of the Communists in Europe and Asia. During his two terms of office, Truman helped to create the North Atlantic Treaty Organization (NATO) and led America into the Korean War in 1950. In 1951 he survived an assassination attempt by Puerto Rican nationalists. ◆

see also

Roosevelt

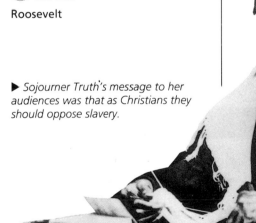

▶ *Sojourner Truth's message to her audiences was that as Christians they should oppose slavery.*

Sojourner **Truth**

American anti-slavery campaigner
Born c.1797
Died 1883 aged about 86

Sojourner Truth was born into slavery and was originally called Isabella. She was abused as a young woman and between 1810 and 1827 she had at least five children. Then in 1827 she was freed under a New York law that banned slavery. Isabella took the name Van Wagener from her last owner. One of her first acts as a free woman was to fight a court battle for the return of her youngest son, who had been sold illegally as a slave in the South.

She came to believe that God wanted her to preach His message of love, so in 1843 she changed her name to Sojourner ('traveller') Truth and became an evangelist. She began to travel through the states of the North, where she often attracted very large crowds. As well as preaching Christianity she also spoke against slavery and, from the 1850s, in favour of votes for women. Although she could not read or write, she supported herself and her family by selling *The Narrative of Sojourner Truth*, which she had dictated herself. ◆

see also

Douglass   Stowe   Tubman

Ts'ai Lun

Chinese inventor of paper
Born c.50   **Died** 118 aged about 68

Ts'ai Lun is remembered as the man who discovered how to make one of the simplest and most revolutionary of all inventions – paper. He was an important court officer who must have spent much of his working day dealing with the laws, letters, and tax returns which running the government of a country involves. According to the official history of his times, Ts'ai Lun made his discovery in the year 105. The raw materials he used to make the first paper included tree-bark, hemp, rags, and old fishing-nets. Paper made an excellent, smooth surface for elegant Chinese brush-writing and was much cheaper than the other materials that were usually used, such as vellum (soft, scraped leather), silk, or bamboo. The Chinese soon realized that this new invention had many possible uses – such as for writing on, for wrapping things, and for making lanterns and screens. ◆

Harriet **Tubman**

American anti-slavery worker
Born *c.1820*   **Died** *1913 aged about 93*

Harriet Tubman was born into slavery and as a child and young woman she worked under terrible conditions on the slave plantations in the southern states of America. Finally, however, she managed to escape. She made her way north on the 'Underground Railroad' – not a real railway but a famous escape system for runaway slaves. These slaves were taken to Canada or the northern states of America, where slavery was illegal. Escaping slaves were called passengers. The homes they hid in were called stations, and the escape organizers were called conductors.

Harriet Tubman became the most famous 'conductor' of all. Over a period of ten years she helped more than 300 slaves to escape, including her aged parents. She became known as the 'Moses of her people' because, like Moses, she led so many slaves into freedom. She opened schools for ex-slaves, and eventually settled in New York where she opened the Harriet Tubman Home for Aged Negroes. ◆

◈ **see also**
Douglass   Stowe   Truth

Jethro **Tull**

English agricultural engineer
Born *1674*   **Died** *1741 aged 66*

Jethro Tull studied at Oxford University and in 1699 qualified as a lawyer. However, the work did not really suit him and he turned to farming instead. To gain experience he travelled widely throughout Europe before settling down to farm on an estate in England.

At that time it was the custom for farmers to sow seed by hand, scattering handfuls as they walked up and down the fields. The crop then had to be weeded by hand. Tull invented a horse-drawn seed drill which sowed the seed in parallel rows. When the weeds appeared they could be removed by a horse-drawn hoe. He described his method in a famous book called *Horse-Hoeing Husbandry* (1731). However, mechanized agriculture was slow to be adopted in England, where labour was then plentiful and cheap, although it quickly became popular in North America where labour was scarce and expensive. ◆

J. M. W. **Turner**

English landscape painter
Born *1775*   **Died** *1851 aged 76*

Joseph Mallord William Turner, the son of a London barber, was an exceptionally talented child. At the age of 14 he became a student at the Royal Academy schools, and at 16 his work was first exhibited to the public.

After a sketching tour in Italy Turner became particularly interested in colour and light. His subject, nearly always landscape, seems to be a fantastic magical world of lighting effects, threatening weather conditions, and mysterious shadows. A friend described his way of working: 'He began by pouring wet paint onto the paper until it was saturated. He poured, he scratched, he scrabbled at it in a kind of frenzy, and the whole thing was chaos – but gradually as if by magic the lovely ship, with all its exquisite detail came into being. By lunch-time it was finished.'

Turner's energy was astonishing. He produced about 500 oil paintings and over 20,000 watercolours and drawings. In his will, he left the

▼ The Fighting Temeraire, *one of Turner's many dramatic works set at sea.*

majority of his paintings and his drawings to the British people; most are in the Tate Gallery, London. ◆

Marie **Tussaud**

French wax modeller
Born *1760* **Died** *1850 aged 89*

Marie Grosholtz was just six years old when she was taught how to work in wax. Her portraits became so famous that by the time she was 20 she was living in the Palace of Versailles and working as the art teacher to Louis XIV's sister. In 1789 the French Revolution broke out, and during those terrible days Marie was called upon to make models of the severed heads of aristocrats, many of them her friends, after they had been killed by the revolutionaries.

Marie married a French engineer, François Tussaud, and in 1802 she received permission from Napoleon to take her waxwork collection to England. She began making models of important English men and women, as well as of notorious criminals who had been executed. In 1835 she set up a permanent exhibition in London, which still exists today. ◆

Tutankhamun

Ancient Egyptian boy-king
Born *c.1370 BC*
Died *1352 BC aged about 18*

The modern world discovered Tutankhamun, the Egyptian boy-king, in 1922, when the English archaeologist Howard Carter

uncovered his secret tomb. We call Tutankhamun the boy-king because he died young, after reigning for only nine years. He became the pharaoh (god-king) when he was only about ten years old through his marriage to the princess Ankhesenpaaten, who was the daughter of the pharaoh, Akhenaten, and his queen, Nefertiti. We are not sure who his parents were. ◆

Desmond **Tutu**

Archbishop of Cape Town from 1986
Born *1931*

Desmond Mpilo (meaning 'life') Tutu was the son of a primary school headmaster and a domestic servant. He soon discovered what it was like to be black and poor in South Africa. He trained to be a teacher, but in the 1950s the South African government decided that black children should only be given a basic education. Tutu could not accept this decision, so he left teaching to become a priest in the Anglican Church.

In the 1960s and 1970s he and his family spent some time in Britain. They were amazed at the civilized way they were treated compared to their experiences in South Africa. This made him speak out against *apartheid* (the policy of racial separateness and discrimination)

▲ *Desmond Tutu, one of the leading figures in the struggle against apartheid in South Africa.*

when he returned to his own country. In 1975 he became Dean of Johannesburg and could have lived in an area reserved for whites. Instead he chose to live in Soweto, a crowded township of a million black people. In 1984 he was awarded the Nobel Peace Prize for his 'non-violent struggle against apartheid'. ◆

◉ **see also**

de Klerk   Mandela

▶ *The contents of Tutankhamun's tomb contained many works of art, like this solid-gold coffin, which are now displayed in a museum in Cairo, Egypt.*

Mark **Twain**

American writer
Born 1835   Died 1910 aged 74

Mark Twain's real name was Samuel Langhorne Clemens. When he was four, his family moved to the small town of Hannibal on the Mississippi River, where his father opened a grocery store. He spent his childhood watching the giant lumber rafts and the steamboats on the river. When he was 11 his father died, and Sam left school to do odd jobs to earn money for his family.

At 13 he was apprenticed to a printer, and later began writing for local newspapers. Then, for almost four years, he worked as a pilot on the local steamboats; later he remembered those years as the most carefree of his life. After trying his luck next as a gold-miner he became a full-time writer, using the pen-name 'Mark Twain', a phrase from his steamboat days meaning 'two fathoms deep'.

He was a great storyteller and wrote in a brilliantly funny way about the Southern way of life. In *Tom Sawyer* (1876) and *The Adventures of Huckleberry Finn* (1884) he painted a wonderful picture of life on and around the Mississippi, describing it exactly as the boys in the story would see it. He wrote many other novels and also a book about his travels. ◆

▼ *A publisher's advert for Mark Twain's story* Huckleberry Finn *(1884), with an illustration of the novel's leading character.*

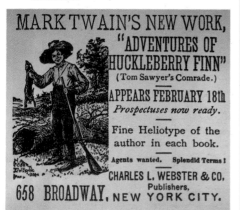

Pope **Urban II**

French pope who launched the First Crusade
Born c.1042   Died 1099 aged about 57

Born in north-east France, Urban's original name was Odo de Lagery. He became a monk of the famous monastery at Cluny in France. In 1079 the Abbot of Cluny sent Odo to Rome. The pope, Gregory VII, was impressed by Odo, and made him a cardinal. In 1088 he was elected pope, and took the name Urban II.

A few years before, Muslim Turks from Asia had invaded the Holy Land, and had stopped European pilgrims from visiting the Holy Places known to Jesus. Many Europeans were angry about this, and wanted to do something. In 1095, at Clermont in France, Urban proclaimed a crusade (a word derived from the Spanish 'cruzada', meaning 'marked by the cross'). He appealed for fighting men from Europe to go and reconquer the occupied lands. Several armies set off. Jerusalem was captured from the Muslims on 15 July 1099. Urban died just a few days later. ◆

Rudolph **Valentino**

Italian-born American film actor
Born 1895   Died 1926 aged 31

Rudolph Valentino was born in Castellaneta, Italy. At 18 he travelled to America, where he

▲ *Rudolph Valentino in a publicity shot for* Son of the Sheik *(1926). His many female fans were devastated by his early death, which was caused by a perforated ulcer.*

worked as a dancer and a film 'extra'. He became a star during the 1920s, acting in films such as *The Sheik* (1921), *Blood and Sand* (1922), and *Son of the Sheik* (1926). He was adored by film fans for his handsome appearance in such romantic roles. His early death attracted thousands of fans to his funeral to mourn the most glamorous leading man of the silent film era. ◆

Cornelius **Vanderbilt**

American businessman
Born 1794   Died 1877 aged 83

Cornelius Vanderbilt was the son of a poor farmer and boatman in Port Richmond, New York. He left school at 11 and when he was 16 he borrowed money to buy a ferry boat. It was the first of a long series of business operations which would make him one of the richest men in the world.

Eventually Vanderbilt ran a very profitable steamship company. By 1846 he was a millionaire. Then, at the age of 70, he started to buy railroad companies, and made even more money. When he died he had amassed a fortune of 100 million dollars.

Vanderbilt is remembered as an example of the American dream. Americans have always proudly believed that people in their country can start from nothing and, by working hard, become rich and prosperous. Cornelius Vanderbilt was one of the first people to demonstrate this. ◆

Anthony **van Dyck**

Flemish painter
Born *1599*   **Died** *1641 aged 42*

Anthony van Dyck was a boy genius. He painted brilliant portraits while he was still in his mid-teens and by the time he was 20 he was the best painter in Flanders, apart from the great Rubens. He worked as Rubens' assistant for two years, and then branched out, travelling to England and then Italy, where he lived from 1621 to 1628.

After a four-year stay in Antwerp, his home town, he settled in England in 1632 as court painter to King Charles I, who knighted him. Charles was a great art lover and van Dyck painted many portraits of him and his family and also of his courtiers. These paintings were so elegant, poised, and dashing that they set a standard for 'society' portraiture for generations; Gainsborough was deeply influenced by them more than a century later. Van Dyck also painted religious scenes and landscapes, but it is as a portraitist that he ranks among the greatest painters of all time. ◆

see also
Gainsborough   Rubens

Jan **van Eyck**

Flemish painter
Born *c. 1390*
Died *1441 aged about 50*

Jan van Eyck was one of the greatest European painters of his time. He spent most of his career in Bruges in Belgium, where he worked for Philip the Good, Duke of Burgundy. Philip employed him on secret diplomatic missions as well as for his artistic skills. For centuries van Eyck was regarded as the inventor of oil painting. We know that it was in fact used before his time, but he was certainly one of the first to master the technique. His craftsmanship was superb and he created effects of glowing colour and exquisite detail that are still amazing to see. Because he showed the potential of oil paint so brilliantly, van Eyck is considered to be one of the most important figures in European art. ◆

▼ *Jan van Eyck's The Arnolfini Marriage (1434), a fine example of his skill in handling oil paint.*

Vincent **Van Gogh**

Dutch painter
Born *1853*   **Died** *1890 aged 37*

The son of a pastor (minister of a Protestant church), Vincent Van Gogh was taught that a meaningful life meant devoting oneself to others. He became deeply religious, and trained to be a missionary. However, his moody personality prevented him from being successful in the Church or in other jobs that he tried.

Van Gogh then taught himself to draw and paint. His dark and sombre early paintings show the miserable lives of the working poor. Later he went to France, where he experimented with clear, bright colours. His technique of excited, bold brushstrokes shows deep emotion and a sort of frenzy even when the subject itself is peaceful. His pictures are of the ordinary things in life: his bedroom, a chair, a bunch of sunflowers. He rarely painted any grand subjects.

Van Gogh spent the last two years of his life in southern France. He was very busy but often depressed and suffered periods of insanity; he cut off one of his own ears during one such crisis. After only ten years of painting, he committed suicide. He died poverty-stricken, having sold only one painting during his lifetime. ◆

▼ *Van Gogh's painting of* The Church at Auvers-sur-Oise *(1890).*

Ralph **Vaughan Williams**

English composer
Born *1872*   **Died** *1958 aged 85*

Ralph Vaughan Williams's family was wealthy and able to support him through an unusually long period of study at the Royal College of Music, Cambridge University, Berlin, and Paris. Although he started to compose when he was six, he developed very slowly. It was only in 1903, when he began to collect and study British folk-song, that his music began to find its own special voice. His music includes opera, choral works, concertos, chamber music, songs, and a series of nine important symphonies. He also wrote music for films, one of which, *Scott of the Antarctic*, became the basis for his Seventh Symphony (*Sinfonia Antarctica*). ◆

Diego **Velázquez**

Spanish painter
Born *1599*   **Died** *1660 aged 61*

Diego Velázquez, born in Seville, Spain, had one of the most continuously successful careers in the history of art. He produced masterpieces when he was still in his teens. When he was 24 he painted a portrait of King Philip IV of Spain. Philip was so impressed that he declared that from then on no other artist would be allowed to paint him.

Philip honoured Velázquez with various court posts in Madrid. These jobs only left Velázquez time to paint about three pictures a year. However, these include some of the finest portraits in the world. He depicted his subjects with great sympathy, whether he was portraying king or commoner. Even the wretched court fools kept to amuse the king were given a sense of dignity in Velázquez's portraits. ◆

Giuseppe **Verdi**

Italian composer
Born *1813*   **Died** *1901 aged 87*

The wonderful thing about Giuseppe Verdi is that the older he grew, the greater his music became. He wrote his last operas, *Otello* and *Falstaff*, considered to be his masterpieces, between the ages of 74 and 80, when most people have long been retired.

Verdi's parents were poor and his musical education was paid for by a neighbour, a wealthy merchant. Even so, he failed to gain entry to the Milan Conservatory of Music and had to study privately. His first opera, *Oberto*, was quite successful and he was asked to write more. But tragedy struck: his wife and two young children died within two months of each other. Verdi was heartbroken and vowed never to write another note.

▼ *A caricature of the famous Italian composer Giuseppe Verdi.*

Fortunately, he was tempted to write a new opera, *Nabucco*, and its success launched his career as Italy's most famous composer. His most popular operas include *Rigoletto* (1851), *La Traviata* (1853), and *Aida* (1871). They are loved for their bold tunes and the wonderful way he can make his characters come alive. Verdi also wrote a String Quartet (1873) and a famous Requiem (1874). ◆

Jan **Vermeer**

Dutch painter
Born *1632*   **Died** *1675 aged 43*

Not very much is known about Jan Vermeer's life. His father kept an inn, and Jan Vermeer may have worked there. He married at 21 and had 11 children. He became head of the Painters' Guild twice, and was well respected. But he ran up debts, particularly to his baker, to whom he gave two paintings in return for credit. After his death, his wife tried to buy back the paintings, but she also became bankrupt.

Vermeer did not become famous until 200 years after his death, when his paintings were recognized as masterpieces. He worked extremely slowly and produced only about 40 paintings. He painted Dutch people doing ordinary domestic jobs, but he handled light and colour so cleverly that his figures are solid and strong, yet serene and gentle. ◆

Jules **Verne**

French novelist
Born *1828*   **Died** *1905 aged 77*

Jules Verne used his knowledge of geography and science to give his exciting and imaginative

▲ *Jules Verne worked for a time writing the words for operas before turning to science fiction novels such as* Twenty Thousand Leagues Under the Sea, *from which this illustration is taken.*

stories a backdrop of realistic detail. What makes his novels even more intriguing is that in them he actually anticipated future scientific developments; he forecast the invention of aeroplanes, submarines, television, guided missiles, and even space satellites!

His first book, *Five Weeks in a Balloon* (1863), started life as a non-fiction essay about an exploration of Africa in a balloon but he rewrote it as an imaginative story at the suggestion of his publisher. Its instant success inspired Verne to write more 'science fiction' and adventure novels. Among the most famous are *Journey to the Centre of the Earth* (1864), *Twenty Thousand Leagues Under the Sea* (1869), and *Around the World in Eighty Days* (1873), which recounts the travels of Phileas Fogg. ◆

Paolo **Veronese**

Italian painter
Born *1528*   **Died** *1588 aged 60*

Paolo Veronese's real surname
was Caliari. He was born in
Verona (from which he gets his
nickname), but he spent almost all
his working life in Venice. There
he ranked with Tintoretto as the
leading painter at the end of the
16th century. This was a golden
period in Venice's history, when the
city grew rich as one of the world's
most important trading centres.

Veronese's paintings are
wonderfully colourful and
decorative, reflecting Venice's
success and material splendour. He
tended to treat every subject like a
glorious pageant and this got him
into trouble with the religious
authorities. They objected to what
they considered irrelevant 'vulgar'
figures in a painting he had done
of *The Last Supper.* Veronese

cleverly got round the problem by
simply changing the title to *The
Feast in the House of Levi* – the title
of a less solemn dining scene from
the Bible. ◆

👁 **see also**

Tintoretto

Hendrik **Verwoerd**

*Prime minister of South Africa from
1958 to 1966*
Born *1901*   **Died** *1966 aged 65*

Hendrik Verwoerd was the man
who developed the apartheid
(separation by race) system which
enslaved South Africa's black
population. Under apartheid black
people were forced to live
separately from whites and could
only get low-paid jobs. Marriage
between blacks and whites was
forbidden.

Verwoerd was a university
teacher and taught in Germany for
a while. During World War II he
edited a newspaper and was on
the side of the Nazis. In 1950 he
became South Africa's minister of
native affairs, and it was then that
he organized the apartheid policy.
He became prime minister in 1958.
When the other Commonwealth
countries objected to apartheid he
took South Africa out of the
Commonwealth in 1961. He also
introduced harsh measures to
silence black opposition, including
the banning of the African National
Congress. In 1966 he was
assassinated in parliament. ◆

👁 **see also**

De Klerk   Luthuli   Mandela

Andreas **Vesalius**

Belgian doctor, surgeon, and author
Born *1514*   **Died** *1564 aged 49*

Andreas Vesalius was a professor
at Padua University, Italy,
where he lectured in surgery. He
had to teach anatomy and this was
done using textbooks written by
Galen, a Greek doctor who had
lived over 1000 years earlier.
Vesalius dissected many dead
human bodies and realized that
Galen's books were inaccurate. He
thought they were probably based
on animals rather than humans.
Vesalius abandoned Galen's books
and taught anatomy from his own
knowledge of dissection.

In 1543 he published *On the
Structure of the Human Body*, a
remarkable set of anatomy
textbooks, with drawings by a pupil
of the painter Titian. Vesalius
became famous, and was appointed
court doctor to the Holy Roman
Emperor, Charles V, and his son,
Philip II of Spain. However, he was

▼ *In spite of his problems
with Church authorities,
Veronese, who painted
this religious scene,
was a devout
Catholic.*

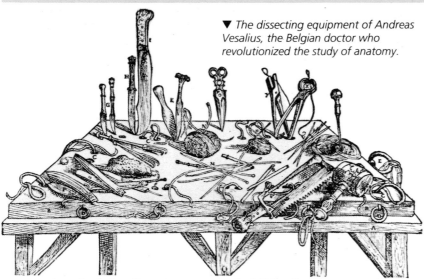

▼ *The dissecting equipment of Andreas Vesalius, the Belgian doctor who revolutionized the study of anatomy.*

sentenced to death for dissecting human bodies (which was then illegal). The sentence was lifted, provided he made a pilgrimage to Jerusalem. He made the journey but unfortunately died while on the way home. ◆

see also

Galen

Amerigo **Vespucci**

Italian explorer
Born *1451*   **Died** *1512 aged 61*

Amerigo Vespucci was an Italian merchant who settled in Spain as an agent for the Medici Bank. He was the contractor who organized the supplies for Christopher Columbus for his voyages to the west. In due course, Vespucci became chief navigator for the Medici Bank, making maps of the lands discovered by Columbus and other explorers.

As a navigator, Vespucci sailed across the Atlantic Ocean from Europe, and in 1501–1502 he explored the South American coast as far south as the Río de la Plata. It was then that he realized he was looking at another continent, not at parts of Asia as Columbus had believed.

In 1507 a German mapmaker, Martin Waldseemüller, published a map in which the newly discovered lands to the west were given a name. That name, he said, should be America, because he believed Amerigo had discovered it. In fact, Vespucci did not discover America, but he was one of the first people to realize it might be a separate continent and not part of Asia. ◆

see also

Columbus

Victor Emmanuel II

The first king of Italy from 1861 to 1878
Born *1820*   **Died** *1878 aged 58*

Victor Emmanuel II succeeded his father as king of the state of Sardinia-Piedmont in 1849. At that time Italy was divided into several small separate states. Through the middle years of the 19th century, politicians worked to create a united Italy from these states.

Victor Emmanuel had the imagination to see that the future for Italy lay with more democratic forms of government than there

were at the time. He appointed Camillo Cavour as prime minister of Piedmont in 1852. They were both central figures in the period of political unrest that followed. Their vision of a united and liberated Italy, free from foreign rule and intervention, resulted in many battles. They enlisted the help of Giuseppe Garibaldi to help defeat the Austrians in northern Italy (with Napoleon III's France as their ally). Several years later, Garibaldi's forces also captured Sicily and Naples, and handed over the whole of southern Italy to Victor Emmanuel. A vote was taken to accept him as king and in 1861 Victor Emmanuel became the first king of a united Italy. Only the Vatican, a small state ruled by the pope, stayed independent, and remains so to this day. In 1870 Victor Emmanuel II made Rome his capital. ◆

see also

Cavour   Garibaldi

▼ *A cartoon caricature of Victor Emmanuel II from the English magazine* Vanity Fair *in 1870.*

Victoria

*Queen of the United Kingdom from
1837 to 1901*
Born 1819   Died 1901 aged 81

As a child, Victoria was lively and strong-willed. She could be moody, and had firm likes and dislikes, but she was sensible too. She was very interested in new inventions: she enjoyed travelling on some of the early railways, and photography fascinated her. She was musical and could draw well.

In spite of the fact that she was only 18 when she became queen, Victoria clearly had a clever understanding of the British political system. Although the real ruling was done by parliament, she succeeded in exerting some influence. At 21 she married her German cousin, Prince Albert. The queen was devoted to her 'dearest Albert', and they had nine children together. When Albert died suddenly of typhoid in 1861, Victoria was desperately unhappy. She refused to appear in public for some years, and wore black for the rest of her life. It was the prime minister, Benjamin Disraeli, whose tactful, flattering ways she liked, who finally managed to coax her into public life again.

During Victoria's 63-year reign, the longest in British history, the British Empire grew to a vast size, making Britain the richest country in the world. Her popularity now at its height, her Golden and Diamond Jubilees (marking 50 and 60 years on the throne respectively) were causes for huge celebrations. ◆

👁 **see also**

Disraeli   Gladstone

◄ *During the Victorian age, as the 19th century is often known, Britain was one of the most powerful nations in the world. Its queen, Victoria, was a strong figurehead for the country's success. She was also Empress of India.*

Pancho **Villa**

Mexican bandit and freedom fighter
Born 1877   Died 1923 aged 46

Imagine a gang of Mexican bandits galloping across a dusty plain – guns slung across their backs, bullets in cross-belts on their chests, sombreros hanging behind by their straps. That was Pancho Villa and his band.

Even Villa's early life is like a film script. It is said that as a young man he killed his boss's son because he assaulted his sister, and had to escape into the mountains.

Revolutions and governments came and went in Mexico at the turn of the century. Villa sometimes sided with the revolutionaries and sometimes fell out with them. Miraculously he stayed alive, even when he killed a number of Americans and President Wilson sent an army after him.

Eventually he made peace with the Mexican Government, and he was allowed to settle down as a farmer. Unfortunately, after a few years his luck ran out and he was assassinated by one of his old enemies. ◆

Virgil

Ancient Roman poet
Born 70 BC   Died 19 BC aged 50

Virgil was born near Mantua in Italy. Although his parents were not rich, he had a good education in Cremona, Milan, and Rome. He then returned to his family farm to write. Among his important poems are the series of poems called the *Eclogues* which are about the countryside and its people, and the series called the *Georgics* which are about farming.

Virgil's most important work is the epic poem (poem-story) called the *Aeneid* written at the request of the Emperor Augustus. It tells of the mythical hero Aeneas and his escape from the burning city of Troy, his adventures on his journey across the sea to Carthage and then to Italy, and his foundation of the city of Lavinium, south of Rome.

Although Virgil devoted the last 11 years of his life to writing the *Aeneid*, he did not finish it and ordered that the manuscript should be burnt after his death. However, the Emperor Augustus ordered it to be published. ◆

see also

Augustus

Vitruvius

Roman architect and writer on architecture
Lived during the 1st century BC

Marcus Vitruvius Pollio, an official architect (at one time in the service of Julius Caesar), was not well-known in his own lifetime. He became famous because of the ten books on architecture that he wrote in his old age and dedicated to Caesar Augustus. These books contain the only accounts of the rules that had guided Greek and Roman architects and builders. They describe the kind of skills that an architect in public service was then expected to have, including construction, water-engineering, and the control of public health.

His descriptions, particularly of measurement and ornament, were important to Italian architects of the 15th and 16th centuries (like Palladio), who wished to revive the architecture of Ancient Rome. ◆

see also

Palladio

Antonio **Vivaldi**

Italian composer
Born 1678   Died 1741 aged 63

Little is known of Antonio Vivaldi's early life, except that he was born in Venice and taught to play the violin by his father. He then trained as a priest and was ordained in 1703. In the same year he began to teach music at the Conservatorio della Pietà in Venice. The Conservatorio was an orphanage for girls which had a famous choir and orchestra. Vivaldi helped train the girls and wrote music for them to play. As his fame spread throughout Italy, he spent more and more time away from the Conservatorio and finally left there in 1738.

Vivaldi composed all kinds of music, including over 40 operas, but he is most famous for his concertos; he wrote over 500, nearly half for solo violin. He also wrote concertos for flute, oboe, bassoon, recorder, and mandolin. Some have descriptive titles, such as *The Four Seasons* and *The Hunt*, and their music cleverly conjures up the appropriate atmosphere. ◆

▼ *This painting from 1723, by Francois Morellon La Cave, is the only known portrait of the composer Antonio Vivaldi.*

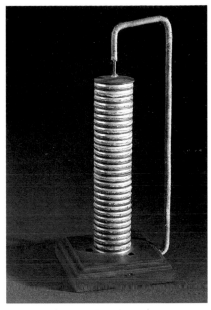

▲ *The voltaic pile (the first electric cell) invented by Italian physicist Alessandro Volta. The volt (unit of electromotive force) is named after him.*

Alessandro **Volta**

Italian inventor of the first battery
Born 1745   Died 1827 aged 82

A friend of Alessandro Volta's, a scientist called Luigi Galvani, wrote telling him about a puzzling experiment that he had done: he had hung a piece of frog muscle on a brass hook, and when the muscle came in contact with some iron wire it twitched. Some people thought that the muscle must be producing its own 'animal electricity', but Volta proved that it was the contact of the brass and the iron that produced the electricity and made the muscle twitch. Volta did many experiments with different metals. He made a pile of coins of two different metals, separated the coins with card soaked in salt solution and produced an electric current. This was the first battery. ◆

see also

Galvani

Voltaire

French writer and philosopher
Born *1694* **Died** *1778 aged 83*

The son of a wealthy lawyer, Voltaire was born Francois-Marie Arouet. In 1718 he adopted the pen-name Voltaire, and started to write plays and witty, hard-hitting articles. He was imprisoned for a year for criticizing the power of the French monarchy and the Church. In 1726 he was exiled to England, and after returning, he unfavourably compared British freedom with the censorship of France and he was finally chased out of Paris in 1734. In 1754 he went to Switzerland, where he spent the rest of his life. He wrote his famous novel *Candide* there in 1758. This describes the adventures of an innocent young man who believes that life is always for the best. With everything around him getting steadily worse, he finally decides that it is, after all, quite a dangerous world. ◆

Richard **Wagner**

German composer
Born *1813* **Died** *1883 aged 69*

Richard Wagner was brought up in a theatrical family and until the age of 15 he seemed more likely to become a playwright than a composer. In the end he did both, by writing the words and music for his own operas.

Wagner studied music at Leipzig University, but he really began to learn his trade when he worked in various German opera-houses. His own first attempts at opera failed. Then *Rienzi* and *The Flying Dutchman* were successful and his luck changed.

Wagner was not content with ordinary opera. He wanted something better, something that would combine all the arts into a music drama. In 1853 he began to write *The Ring of the Nibelungs*, a cycle (series) of four music dramas based on German legends.

He completed it in 1874. This magnificent production confirmed Wagner as one of the greatest musical geniuses the world has ever known. Wagner was as passionately interested in theatre as he was in music. In 1876 he opened his own opera house in Bayreuth, Germany, and it was here that the first performance of *The Ring of the Nibelings* took place. ◆

◀ *Derek Walcott collecting his Nobel Prize in December 1992.*

◀ *Voltaire was persecuted for his belief that people had a right to think what they liked.*

Derek **Walcott**

West Indian poet
Born *1930*

Derek Walcott was born in St Lucia and later went to the University of the West Indies. He then lived in Trinidad, founding a theatre workshop and writing plays which often combined singing with storytelling and dancing. He also wrote poetry which experimented with different types of English, including local dialect. Walcott was always fascinated by the ancient Greek writer Homer, finding many similarities between his descriptions of the Greek islands and the different islands of the Caribbean today. This influence found its way into Walcott's poem 'Omeros' (1989) and his own version of Homer's *The Odyssey*, both of which won him much fame. In 1992 Walcott was awarded the Nobel Prize for Literature – the greatest honour any writer can receive. ♦

👁 see also
Homer

Lech **Walesa**

Polish trade union leader, and president of Poland from 1991 to 1995
Born *1943*

Lech Walesa started work as an electrician in the shipyards in Gdansk, Poland, in 1966. He soon became involved in protests against the Communist government's treatment of workers, and in 1976 he was sacked for his activities. In 1980 workers went on strike for higher wages and Walesa joined those who were occupying the yards. In the same year they created a new, independent trade union called Solidarity and 10 million workers throughout Poland registered to join.

The Communist government was alarmed at what was happening. Solidarity was banned and Walesa detained for nearly a year. He continued to fight for workers' rights and in 1983 was awarded the Nobel Peace Prize. Eventually the government gave way and Solidarity became legal again in 1989. The trade union became a political party and Walesa, as its leader, won a landslide victory against the Communists in the free presidential elections of 1990. ♦

Robert **Walpole**

First prime minister of Britain
Born *1676*   **Died** *1745 aged 68*

Robert Walpole became a member of parliament in 1701. Although he was briefly imprisoned in the Tower of London in 1712 for taking bribes, his hard work and attention to detail, and the support he received from King George I, enabled him to rise to a position of great influence. In 1721 he became first lord of the treasury and chancellor of the exchequer and so was the king's chief minister.

His policy of avoiding foreign wars and so keeping taxes down helped him keep power; so did his tactic of giving well-paid jobs as rewards to his own supporters. But his enemies attacked him for this type of corruption, and he became less popular. Finally in 1742 he was forced to resign.

The job of prime minister did not exist before Walpole. He helped create it by taking on the major responsibility for getting things done in the House of Commons. From Walpole's time onwards, the practice of having one chief (prime) minister continued, just as it does today. ♦

Andy **Warhol**

American artist
Born *1928*   **Died** *1987 aged 59*

Andy Warhol was the son of Czech immigrants to America; his original name was Andrew Warhola. In the 1950s he was a highly successful commercial artist, winning prizes for his shoe advertisements and earning huge sums. Then, in 1962, he became an overnight sensation when he exhibited pictures of Campbell's Soup cans and was hailed as a leader of Pop Art, which took its subjects from the worlds of advertising, packaging, and television. He produced his pictures by the commercial process of silk-screen printing, which meant they could be duplicated as many times as he wanted, with variations of colour if required. His fame grew rapidly with brightly coloured portraits of Marilyn Monroe and other celebrities. He also made films, often with a strong documentary feel like *Chelsea Girls* (1966) and wrote books, including *Popism* (1980). When he died he left a colossal fortune, but opinions on him are divided. To some he was a genius, to others merely a brilliant con-man. ♦

▼ *Andy Warhol first made his name with paintings of commercial products such as Campbell's Soup cans.*

Booker T. **Washington**

Founder of Tuskegee Institute, a famous college for black Americans
Born 1856   Died 1915 aged 59

When Booker Taliaferro Washington was nine years old, slavery in America was abolished. He had been a house servant, but he could read and wanted to teach. When he was 16 he travelled 500 miles with almost no money to a school for black teachers. To pay for their studies, all the students worked. Washington cleaned the school. Later, he started a college for black students at Tuskegee, Alabama. The students themselves built most of it and Washington persuaded some rich White Americans to give donations.

In a speech in 1895, Washington said that blacks and whites could be separate like fingers, but that they could work together like a hand. Some black leaders disagreed, but at that time Washington thought black people needed education and jobs more than civil rights. ◆

George **Washington**

The first president of the United States of America
Born 1732   Died 1799 aged 67

George Washington did not have much schooling, but he was always very practical. At 14 he helped to survey some frontier land. A year later he had his own surveying business, and in 1752 he inherited his brother's land.

Britain and France were then rivals, both owning colonies and both trying to control North America. As a soldier in the British army, Washington fought against the French for five years, and his exploits made him well known in Virginia, the British colony where he was born.

After the war, Washington settled down to be a farmer on his Mount Vernon plantation. However, he gradually came to believe that the American colonists had to fight for freedom from Britain. In 1775 he was made commander-in-chief of the colonists' army, and they began to fight what became known as the American Revolution (War of Independence).

Washington's perseverance and grit kept the rebels going. Often his troops were famished and sometimes they went barefoot in the snow. In 1783, after the war had been won, Washington went back to Mount Vernon. Although he was a national hero, he did not want public office.

Nevertheless, in 1789 he was unanimously elected the first president of the United States. He accepted the job, and his re-election in 1792, but he refused a third term. America's capital city was named in his honour. ◆

▼ *This painting shows George Washington (standing, left) and his troops crossing the River Delaware as they flee from the British after the battle of Whiteplains in 1776 during the American Revolution.*

Robert **Watson-Watt**

Scottish inventor of radar
Born 1892   Died 1973 aged 81

During World War I Robert Watson-Watt worked as a weather forecaster. He noticed that when there were thunderstorms about you could hear crackles on the radio. He wondered whether it might be possible to use these crackles to find out where the thunderstorms were.

In the years just before World War II, the British government asked Watson-Watt to find out whether it would be possible to use a beam of radio waves to heat up an enemy aeroplane so much that its bombs would explode in the air (rather as we now use microwaves to heat things in microwave ovens). He quickly proved that it would be impossible, but while doing the necessary sums he realized that a narrow beam of radio waves would bounce off an aeroplane. Thinking back to the crackles on the radio he devised a way of using the reflected waves from an aeroplane to find out how far away and in which direction that aeroplane was. Thus began the development of radar (radio detection and ranging). ◆

James **Watt**

Scottish designer of a new steam-engine
Born 1736   Died 1819 aged 83

Having trained as a mathematical instrument-maker, James Watt was given a model of Thomas Newcomen's steam-engine to repair. He studied the model carefully. It was clearly a clever idea to use steam pressure to drive an engine, but Newcomen's design did not work well; it was very inefficient and wasted a lot of fuel. Watt began to make improvements, which, over the next ten years, made the steam-engine much more effective. Then in 1775 he went into partnership with Matthew Boulton, a businessman, and began manufacturing steam-engines.

▲ *A model of James Watt's design for a steam-engine.*

Watt's steam-engines began to transform British industry. Iron manufacturers used them to drive the great hammers which crushed the iron. The textile industry used the engine to power the new machinery invented by Richard Arkwright. In coal-mining, men and women no longer had to carry the coal to the surface in sacks as it could be lifted up by winding-gear powered by the Watt engine.

▲ *Jean-Antoine Watteau's* The Shepherd, *which is typical of the paintings that made him famous.*

So although Watt did not invent the steam-engine it was because of his improvements that it became so effective. ◆

🜨 **see also**
Arkwright   Newcomen   Stephenson

Jean-Antoine **Watteau**

French painter
Born 1684   Died 1721 aged 36

Jean-Antoine Watteau was the most important French painter of the early 18th century. He specialized in scenes called *fêtes galantes* (which can be translated as 'scenes of gallantry' or 'courtship parties'). They showed beautifully dressed young people idling away their time in dreamy, romantic settings. His style was exquisitely graceful and charming; it set the tone for the light-hearted approach followed by many 18th-century French artists. However, Watteau was not simply a frivolous painter. His pictures have an underlying feeling of sadness, for the people in them seem to realize that all earthly pleasure is short-lived. Watteau himself was cruelly aware that life is short, for he died young of tuberculosis. ◆

John **Wayne**

American film actor
Born 1907   Died 1979 aged 72

Marion Morrison worked behind the scenes in film studios before taking small acting parts, first under the name of 'Duke' Morrison and then from 1930 as John Wayne. His first leading role came in the western film *Stagecoach* (1939), and he went on to become the most famous star of westerns.

He also starred in war films like *Sands of Iwo Jima* (1950), and directed two films in the 1960s. His tough patriotic roles made him a national hero for many American film fans. In total, he made more than 175 films. He finally achieved Oscar success for his leading role in *True Grit* (1969). ◆

Josiah **Wedgwood**

English founder of the Wedgwood pottery factory
Born *1730*   **Died** *1795 aged 64*

The Wedgwood pottery firm founded by Josiah Wedgwood in 1759 still makes plates, bowls, cups, and saucers today. It is especially famous for its blue pottery ornaments, with delicate white patterns and scenes laid on the top.

▲ *Josiah Wedgwood developed the style of pottery using white figures in relief on a blue background, known as 'Jaspar ware', which is now world-famous.*

Josiah Wedgwood was born into a family who owned a pottery factory, and at the age of nine he began his career as a potter. He became an expert at the job and invented better materials and methods for producing top-class pottery. In 1759 he set up his own factory and became famous for a cream-coloured table service, called Queen's ware, that he made for King George III's wife, Queen Charlotte.

Josiah Wedgwood's grandson was the famous scientist Charles Darwin. ◆

👁 **see also**

Darwin

Chaim **Weizmann**

Russian-born first president of Israel
Born *1874*   **Died** *1952 aged 77*

At school in Russia, Chaim Weizmann became interested in science. He was extremely able but laws against Jews made entry into university difficult so he left Russia to finish his education. Manchester University offered him a job and he settled in England. During World War I he worked in a laboratory producing vital chemicals for explosives.

Weizmann believed passionately in Zion, an independent homeland for Jews in Palestine. Britain announced backing for the idea (the Balfour Declaration, 1917) and Weizmann travelled the world seeking the support of other nations. He became leader of a political group known as the Zionists.

After World War II the British governed Palestine and some Jews began a campaign of terror against them. Weizmann condemned this, and the Zionists dismissed him as their leader. But in the end Weizmann was needed to persuade the Americans to support a Jewish nation. In 1948 the nation was born and called Israel. Weizmann was elected its first president. ◆

Orson **Welles**

American film actor and director
Born *1915*   **Died** *1985 aged 70*

As a young actor Orson Welles became famous in 1938 for presenting a radio play about invaders from Mars as if it were a real newsflash. People listening to *The War of the Worlds* were terrified and thousands of them fled in panic. Welles had to apologize.

A few years later, Welles went to Hollywood to make his masterpiece of film direction, *Citizen Kane* (1941), in which he also starred as a selfish millionaire newspaper-owner. The new techniques he used for combining sound and pictures in this and other films, including *The Magnificent Ambersons* (1942), *Macbeth* (1948), and *Touch of Evil* (1958), inspired many other film directors. ◆

▼ Citizen Kane, *directed by and starring Orson Welles, is regarded by many as his greatest film.*

Duke of **Wellington**

One of England's greatest generals, and prime minister from 1828 to 1830
Born 1769   Died 1852 aged 83

Arthur Wellesley was born in Dublin, Ireland. He joined the army at the age of 18 and served in India for eight years, where he won a number of battles and became a major-general.

But it was in Spain and Portugal that he won his great reputation (for which he was made Duke of Wellington), during the Peninsular War against Napoleon's French armies. In 1812 and in 1813 the English attacked, with support from the Portuguese and Spanish troops, driving the French out of Spain and back into France.

When Napoleon escaped from Elba, Wellington lead the allied armies against him. At the battle of Waterloo in 1815, Wellington's troops defeated the French again.

After Waterloo Wellington continued to serve his country, holding many positions in government, including that of prime minister from 1828 to 1830. For a time he was unpopular because he did not want to give the vote to more people, fearing that it might lead to revolution as in France. But by the end of his long life most people had come to admire him. ◆

see also

Napoleon I

H. G. **Wells**

English novelist
Born 1866   Died 1946 aged 79

Herbert George Wells left school at 14 in order to train as a shopkeeper before deciding to go to university and become a teacher.

▲ *John Wesley holding a service during a storm while travelling to America.*

Then, after much hard work and continuing poverty, he became well-known as a novelist of science fiction. In his books he described air and submarine travel long before anyone believed such journeys were remotely possible. Always restlessly energetic, Wells also wrote his massive *An Outline of History* (1920) as well as popular works about science and politics. One of the best-known people of his time, Wells interviewed famous political leaders and was always ready with an opinion on world events. But it is as a novelist he is best remembered. *The Time Machine* (1895) and *The Invisible Man* (1897) have remained very popular and have also proved to be particular favourites with many film-makers. ◆

see also

Verne

John **Wesley**

English Christian evangelist who founded the Methodist Church
Born 1703   Died 1791 aged 88

John Wesley was the son and grandson of clergymen. Not surprisingly, he too chose to enter the Church and was ordained as a priest in 1728. With his brother, Charles, he formed a group of men who tried to lead methodical lives, praying and reading the Bible together, and going to church regularly. They were nicknamed 'methodists'.

In 1738 Wesley had an experience that changed his life. At a gospel meeting he felt his heart 'strangely warmed' and he knew that he was 'saved' by Jesus. From then on he committed himself to changing the lives of ordinary people through God's love. For 50 years he travelled all over England, holding services and preaching. Sometimes his meetings were held in churches, but often in fields and market-places. He organized 'methodist' societies and used ordinary people as preachers.

Although Wesley originally wanted to remain loyal to the Church of England, a split came in 1784 when Wesley broke Church rules by ordaining a group of Methodist preachers. Reluctantly Wesley watched his movement grow into a separate Church. ◆

Walt **Whitman**

American poet
Born *1819* **Died** *1892 aged 72*

Walt Whitman was born on Long Island, New York. He was the third of eight children and was five years old when his family moved to Brooklyn.

Between 1838 and 1850, Whitman took up a series of jobs including teaching journalism and newspaper editing. In 1855 he published *Leaves of Grass*, a book of 12 poems. During the next five years Whitman revised this and wrote further poems. By the third edition of *Leaves of Grass,* there were over 130 poems in the book. This is now regarded as one of the most important books in American literary history and Whitman is known as the greatest American poet of the 19th century.

During the American Civil War, Whitman worked as a volunteer nurse in Washington. His wartime experiences formed the basis of his poems printed in *Drum Taps* and *Sequel to Drum Taps*.

In 1873 Whitman suffered a stroke that paralysed him. He moved to Camden, New Jersey, where he lived by printing, writing, and through donations from admirers. ◆

Frank **Whittle**

English inventor of the jet engine
Born *1907* **Died** *1996 aged 89*

In 1927, as a 20-year-old flight cadet studying at the Royal Air Force College, Frank Whittle wrote a paper on 'Future Developments in Aircraft Design'. He suggested that aeroplanes would soon be flying at more than 800 km/h (the fastest then was 300 km/h), at great heights, and with jet engines rather than propellers.

▲ *Frank Whittle's jet engine (above) proved to be a great success when it was tested in the aeroplane Gloster E28/39 (top) in 1941.*

In 1929, Whittle tried to persuade the Air Ministry that jet propulsion was possible. His engine would burn cheap fuel oil; the gases produced would turn turbine blades as they rushed out, and the force of the gases would drive the plane forward. However, the Air Ministry was not interested, so Whittle went back to flying.

Later, Whittle started a company called Power Jets Ltd. The RAF let him work full-time on his engine, and it was tried, on the ground, on 12 April 1937. A special aeroplane, the Gloster E28/39, was designed to take the engine, and on 15 May 1941 it flew for the first time, perfectly.

As Whittle had predicted, the jet engine was more efficient at high speeds and great altitudes, and by 1944 Power Jets Ltd. was producing the first jet fighter. Whittle's jet engine went on to power most modern aeroplanes. ◆

William **Wilberforce**

English leader of the campaign to end slavery in the British empire
Born *1759* **Died** *1833 aged 73*

William Wilberforce was member of parliament for Hull from the age of 21. His life's work began when he met John Newton, the captain of a slave ship, who had realized how wrong it was to buy and sell human beings as slaves. From 1785, Wilberforce campaigned to stop the slave trade. Finally, in 1807, parliament passed a law to abolish it. But employers in the West Indies still wanted slaves, and the trade continued secretly. So Wilberforce and his supporters decided there must be a law stopping people from owning slaves at all. After another long campaign, a law to abolish slavery

▼ *These brutal-looking chains are remnants from the cruel slave trade which politician William Wilberforce spent years struggling to abolish.*

in the British empire eventually went through Parliament in 1833. By this time, however, Wilberforce's health was failing and he died shortly after. ◆

Oscar **Wilde**

Irish dramatist
Born *1854*   **Died** *1900 aged 46*

The son of a wealthy surgeon and of a poet, Oscar Wilde came from Dublin to Britain at the age of 20. Soon known as the wittiest man in London, he was also renowned for the attention he paid to his clothes. Dressed in a velvet jacket, knee breeches, and black silk stockings, he and his stories and journalism soon became famous in America as well as in Britain. In the 1890s he wrote a number of brilliant comedies which were both wonderfully amusing and also sharply critical of the times in which they were written. The best of these, *The Importance of being Earnest* (1895), mixes farce with social criticism so successfully it has never been rivalled since. Sadly Wilde was convicted in the same year of homosexual activities, at that time still illegal. The two hard years he spent in Reading Jail broke his spirit, and he died only three years after his release. ◆

I can resist everything except temptation.

OSCAR WILDE
Lady Windermere's Fan (1892)

William I

King of England from 1066 to 1087
Born *c.1027*   **Died** *1087 aged about 60*

William was born in Falaise, France. When he was about eight years old, his father died, leaving no other children. The young William was chosen to take his father's title and thus became the Duke of Normandy.

William grew up to be tough, efficient, determined, and a brave fighter. After a difficult struggle, first against rebellious lords and then against the French, he gained control of Normandy. Meanwhile the King of England, Edward the Confessor, had promised the English crown to William, his cousin. But Harold of Wessex, the strongest of the Anglo-Saxon nobles, also wanted to be king.

When King Edward died in 1066, Harold proclaimed himself king. William immediately built a great invasion fleet and crossed the English Channel. The Saxon and Norman armies met at the battle of Hastings, where Harold was killed. William ruthlessly went on to conquer the rest of England and became known as William the Conqueror. He gave land to his barons and erected royal castles. The barons also built castles and took control of lands, but William made sure they stayed loyal to him. In 1086 he organized the greatest land survey that had ever been made; this culminated in the Domesday Book. ◆

▼ *The Bayeux Tapestry in France tells the story of the Norman Conquest of England and the events that led up to it.*

William III

*King of Britain, Scotland, and Ireland
from 1689 to 1702*
Born 1650   Died 1702 aged 51

William of Orange was born in The Netherlands and was the Protestant ruler of the Dutch people. He was married to Mary, the eldest daughter of the Catholic king of England, James II.

William had one great aim: to stop the powerful Louis XIV of France from swallowing up more land in Europe. When, in 1688, William was invited by some leading English politicians to save England from the Catholic James II, he agreed, thinking that if he became the king of England he would be helped in his fight against the French. The plan met with virtually no resistance and in 1689 Parliament jointly offered him and Mary the crown of England, Scotland, and Ireland.

William was never a popular king, and the Catholic Irish people still supported James. William finally defeated James in Ireland at the battle of the Boyne in 1690. Many Irish Protestants today still call themselves 'Orangemen' because of William's victory. ◆

William of Sens

*French mason and architect
Lived in the 12th century*

William of Sens worked as a stonemason and architect in the days when the Christian Church was extremely powerful in Europe. Talented workmen travelled from country to country in the service of the Church. William came to Canterbury from Sens, a French city where a cathedral in the new Gothic style had just been finished. He had won a competition to

▲ *A view of the Choir at Canterbury Cathedral, much of which was built by William of Sens after the original had been destroyed by fire in 1180.*

design Canterbury's new cathedral in the most up-to-date French style. Three years later he had a tragic accident when he fell from the scaffolding. Although he was disabled, he was still able to continue the cathedral choir with the help of another architect, William the Englishman. After six years in England, William of Sens returned home where he died. ◆

William the Silent

Founder of the Republic of Holland
Born 1533   Died 1584 aged 51

William owned an immense amount of land and held the title of Prince of Orange. The Spanish king, Philip II, who ruled

The Netherlands at the time, appointed William the governor of Holland, Zeeland, and Utrecht in 1555. But from about 1561 William, with other great lords, began to openly oppose Spanish rule. Although the opposition was first about foreign control, it soon became a question of religion. The Spanish were Catholics but in The Netherlands the Protestant Christian religion was more dominant. By 1566 there was open rebellion against Spanish rule. Eventually William became the national leader against the Spaniards, and tried to unite the country. Although this did not last, William continued his fight against the Spaniards, who offered a reward for his assassination. In 1584 William was shot by a fanatical Catholic thought to be a Spanish agent.

William was known as 'the Silent' because he could be relied upon to keep secrets. ◆

◀ **see also**

Philip II

▼ *A portrait of William the Silent painted when he was 46.*

▲ *Many of Tennessee Williams's plays have been turned into films, including* A Streetcar Named Desire *which is set in a New Orleans slum.*

Tennessee **Williams**

American writer
Born 1911   Died 1983 aged 71

Tennessee Williams, the adopted name of Thomas Lanier Williams, was born in Columbus, Mississippi, an area that provided the inspiration for many of his plays. After going to university, Williams supported his writing by taking various jobs before winning a grant from the Rockefeller Foundation for his play *The Battle of Angels* in 1940. This was followed by the award-winning play, *The Glass Menagerie* (1945).

Williams continued to confirm his status as an important playwright with *A Streetcar Named Desire* (1947) and *Cat on a Hot Tin Roof* (1955) which both won Pulitzer Prizes. They are notable for their brilliant dialogue and for scenes of high emotional tension.

Williams's early works are regarded as his best; in his later years he was often in ill health as he struggled with an addiction to alcohol and sleeping pills. ◆

Woodrow **Wilson**

President of the United States from 1913 to 1921
Born 1856   Died 1924 aged 67

Woodrow Wilson began his career as a lawyer, but soon turned to teaching. By 1890 he was a professor at Princeton University, and in 1902 he was elected its president. Then, in 1910, he was elected as the Democratic Governor of New Jersey.

Only two years later Wilson was elected president of America. When World War I broke out in Europe in 1914, Wilson kept America out of it, and was very popular at home for this. But in 1917 German submarines began sinking American merchant ships, so America declared war on Germany.

Just before the end of the war,

Wilson outlined 'Fourteen Points' for a peace settlement. He persuaded other countries to agree to most of these points, including the setting up of the 'League of Nations' (an earlier form of the United Nations). However, the American Congress refused to let America join the League. Despite this, Wilson, now a sick man, was awarded the 1920 Nobel Peace Prize for helping to found the League. ◆

Thomas **Wolsey**

English cardinal and chief minister to Henry VIII
Born c.1474   Died 1530 aged about 56

Thomas Wolsey started his career as a priest. In Tudor England an ambitious boy from an ordinary family could still get to the top by being a priest, and Wolsey finally got a job at court. The young Henry VIII realized that Wolsey would serve him loyally and well. In 1515 the king made him chancellor. Wolsey also became Archbishop of York, and later a cardinal (a very senior priest in the Roman Catholic Church). He soon became richer than the nobles at Henry's court, and built wonderful palaces, including the huge Hampton Court.

In 1529 the king wanted the pope to give him a divorce from Catherine of Aragon. Wolsey tried his best to get it, but the pope refused. Henry seldom forgave failure. Wolsey was sent away to York, but would not stop meddling in politics. Henry summoned the elderly cardinal to London to accuse him of treason but Wolsey was sick and he died at Leicester Abbey on the way. ◆

👁 **see also**

Henry VIII

▲ *Stevie Wonder had his biggest hit in 1984 with 'I Just Called to Say I Love You'.*

Stevie **Wonder**

American pop musician and singer
Born 1950

Steveland Morris of Saginaw, Michigan, was renamed Little Stevie Wonder at the age of ten by Berry Gordy Jr, the owner of Tamla Motown Records. Stevie was blind, but played harmonica, piano, organ, and drums superbly. He had his first No. 1 hit, 'Fingertips' when he was only 13 years old. Twenty hits later, in the 1970s, he struck out in a new direction, adding funky electronic keyboards to his sound and singing about the problems faced by black Americans. It was Stevie Wonder who led the campaign to turn Martin Luther King's birthday into a national holiday in America. He became even more successful in the 1980s with several hit records, including 'Ebony and Ivory' (1982), a duet with Paul McCartney. ◆

◉ **see also**

McCartney

Virginia **Woolf**

British novelist
Born 1882   **Died** 1941 aged 59

Virginia Woolf had a restless, brilliant intelligence which was revealed in her essays and stories. An early believer in Women's Liberation, she was also fascinated by the act of writing itself.

In her novels, she breaks away from normal story-telling techniques in favour of a style closer to how we all actually think from moment to moment. In their thoughts, her characters often pass from the present to the past as one memory piles on another. Her characters also react to experience in a very personal way, describing events or sights immediately as they seem at that particular moment. This does not always make Woolf's writing easy to read, but she is always interesting and original.

Although she was a successful author and was part of a group of leading writers of the day, Woolf was not always happy. She finally committed suicide when she felt she was slipping once again into the deep depression which had tormented her for much of her life. ◆

◀ *Among Woolf's novels are* Mrs Dalloway *(1925),* To the Lighthouse *(1927), and* Orlando *(1928).*

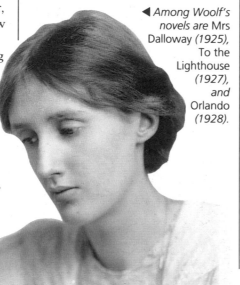

Frank **Woolworth**

American founder of the Woolworth chain of stores
Born 1852   **Died** 1919 aged 67

▲ *The Woolworth Building in New York, built in 1913. At 241.4 m tall, it was the world's tallest building at the time.*

Early in his working life, Frank Woolworth had the idea for a new kind of shop. With help from his boss, W. H. Moore, he set up a 'five and ten cent' store in 1879 with a wide range of goods for sale at low prices. Customers flocked to his shop. His idea was also taken up by his brother, his cousin, and a few close friends, including W. H. Moore, who all opened similar businesses. In 1912 all these stores merged to form the F. W. Woolworth chain. The following year the company built the Woolworth Building in New York, which was for many years the world's largest skyscraper. By the time Woolworth died, there were more than 10,000 stores in the chain, including many in Canada, Britain, and Germany. ◆

William **Wordsworth**

English nature poet
Born *1770*   **Died** *1850 aged 80*

After studying at Cambridge University, William Wordsworth spent some time in France, where he fell in love with Annette Vallon, the daughter of a surgeon. But although they had a child, Wordsworth left her before they could marry. His money ran out and he had to return to England.

In 1798 he published his first collection of poems, *Lyrical Ballads*, in partnership with his great friend, the poet Samuel Taylor Coleridge. Wordsworth's poems caused a sensation because he wrote about ordinary events in plain language. One of his most famous poems, 'To Daffodils' starts:

I wandered lonely as a cloud
That floats on high o'er vales and
   hills,
When all at once I saw a crowd,
A host, of golden daffodils.

This new simplicity was a great contrast to the more showy types of poetry that were popular at the time.

Because both of his parents had died when he was a child, he was always close to his sister, Dorothy. In 1799 he moved to the Lake District and lived with Dorothy and also with his wife Mary, whom he married in 1802. The Lake District was an area he loved and its scenery inspired much of his writing. ◆

see also
Tennyson

Christopher **Wren**

English mathematician, astronomer, and architect of St Paul's Cathedral
Born *1632*   **Died** *1723 aged 90*

It did not take people long to realize that Christopher Wren was very clever. After studying at Oxford University, he soon became a teacher there. He was particularly good at mathematics and physics. While still a young man, he was made a professor of astronomy at Oxford in 1661.

In London, in 1662, he helped to found a club of men keen to explore the world through science. King Charles II was very interested in it, and it was called 'The Royal Society'. Many outstanding men were members, including Robert Boyle and Isaac Newton. This society still exists today.

▶ *St Paul's Cathedral, which dominates the skyline in the City of London, is considered by many to be the finest building Wren designed.*

Wren began to design buildings, and proved to be brilliant at that as well. The chapel at Pembroke College in Cambridge and the Sheldonian Theatre in Oxford were among his earliest buildings. Then, in 1666, the Great Fire destroyed most of London. Wren drew up a plan for rebuilding the entire city. Sadly his plan was never used. However, St Paul's Cathedral needed to be rebuilt, and Wren was chosen to design it. The construction of his magnificent plan was completed in 1710.

Wren worked very hard: he rebuilt 52 London churches destroyed by the fire, and the list of other buildings he designed seems endless. He was knighted in 1672, and became President of the Royal Society in 1680. ◆

see also
Boyle   Newton

Wright Brothers

American flying pioneers who built and flew the first aeroplane

Wilbur Wright
Born *1867* **Died** *1912 aged 45*
Orville Wright
Born *1871* **Died** *1948 aged 76*

Orville Wright was a champion cyclist, and so the two brothers set up a shop where they made and sold bicycles. Neither of the brothers had a proper education, but they had tremendous mechanical skills. They both enjoyed the new sport of gliding, and decided to try and build a bicycle with wings and a petrol engine to drive a propeller round.

By 1903 the Wright brothers had built *The Flyer*. It was a biplane (with two sets of wings) and the pilot lay flat across the lower wing. A series of bicycle chains and gears connected the engine to two propellers which rotated at about 450 times a minute. On 17 December 1903, at Kitty Hawk in North Carolina, Orville Wright made a 12-second flight over a distance of 36 m. This was the first aeroplane flight in history. Later that morning Wilbur flew for nearly a minute. They carried on building better aeroplanes and in 1905 Wilbur flew 38 km in a half-hour flight.

The brothers were the sons of a minister, Bishop Milton Wright. They never smoked or drank

▲ *In 1903 the Wright brothers made the first-ever powered flight in their hand-built aeroplane,* The Flyer.

alcohol, and neither of them married. Wilbur died of typhoid fever in 1912, and his brother Orville gave up building planes a couple of years later. ◆

Frank Lloyd Wright

American architect
Born *1867*   **Died** *1959 aged 91*

Frank Lloyd Wright was the most prolific and versatile of the great architects of the 20th century. His career lasted almost 70 years (he worked almost to the day of his death) and he designed about 1000 buildings, of which about 400 were erected. He worked in a variety of styles and was highly inventive in his use of materials and architectural forms. Wright also wrote many books and articles (including an autobiography), through which he promoted his ideas. His ideal was 'organic architecture', in which buildings harmonize with their environment and their users.

Wright had achieved a considerable reputation by the time he was in his thirties. However, until he was about 60, most of his commissions were fairly small. From the late 1930s, though, he designed many large public buildings in America, including the Guggenheim Museum in New York. He was a forceful personality – one of the central figures of modern American cultural life. ◆

▶ *Wright said his inspiration for the Guggenheim Museum in New York was a child's spinning top.*

John **Wycliffe**

Medieval scholar who challenged the
power of the Roman Catholic Church
Born c.1330   Died 1384 aged about 54

Nothing is known about Wycliffe until the 1360s. By then he was about 30 years old, studying and teaching theology at Oxford University.

In 1374 Edward III sent him to Flanders to negotiate with ambassadors from the Pope about the taxes that the King had to pay to Rome. Wycliffe questioned the Pope's right to collect money, and went on to challenge the wealth and power of the Catholic Church in general.

Over the next ten years his views became more and more extreme. Wycliffe attacked the authority of the Church, and encouraged people to pray directly to God. He issued the first translation of the Bible from Latin into English so that people could read the Bible for themselves. This was considered very shocking. He was condemned as a dangerous heretic (for not accepting Catholic teaching), and his writings were publicly burnt.

Wycliffe's ideas helped to inspire the 'Lollards', people who protested against the power of the Catholic Church. They in turn inspired the Protestants in the 16th century. ◆

see also

Edward III

Xerxes

King of Persia from 485 BC to 465 BC
Born c.519 BC
Died 465 BC aged about 54

Xerxes came to the throne of the huge Persian empire on the death of his father Darius I. Darius had invaded the Greek mainland, but his army had been thoroughly defeated by the Greeks at the battle of Marathon.

It was now important for Xerxes to show Persia's strength. He made preparations for the largest invasion the Greeks had ever seen. The army crossed into Greece by building a bridge of boats across the narrow straits, called the Hellespont (now the Dardanelles), which divided Greece from Asia Minor (now Turkey).

The two armies first clashed in 480 BC, at a narrow mountain pass called Thermopylae. Here a small Greek force held the pass against the Persians. However, the Persians managed to find a mountain track which led them round to the rear. They killed all but two of the 300 defenders. The way to Athens was now open to the Persians, and Xerxes' army captured the city.

The only hope for the Greeks was to defeat the Persians at sea. They did this at the famous sea battle of Salamis in 480 BC, and the Persian navy was destroyed. King Xerxes returned home, but his army stayed and was defeated in Plataea the next year. Persia was no longer a threat to Greece. ◆

see also

Darius I

▲ *Persepolis was the capital of the Persian empire until it was burnt down after its capture in 331BC by Alexander the Great. Parts of it still remain intact (above).*

W. B. **Yeats**

Irish poet and dramatist
Born 1865   Died 1939 aged 73

William Butler Yeats went to school in London, but for his holidays he was sent to his grandparents in Sligo on the west coast of Ireland. He loved to listen to the Sligo people talk of fairies and ghosts, and of the time when great kings, queens, and warriors inhabited Ireland.

When he was older he collected the folklore and myths of Ireland, and helped to found a national theatre in Dublin. He met and fell in love with a woman called Maude Gonne, who inspired much of his greatest poetry but refused to marry him. In his later years, his poetry increased in power, drawing on the ancient myths and his personal emotions. Many of his best-known poems appeared in *The Tower* (1928), and *The Winding Stair* (1929). He won the Nobel Prize for Literature in 1923. ◆

Boris **Yeltsin**

Russian president who led his country to democracy
Born 1931

Boris Nikolayevich Yeltsin was born in Sverdlovsk in the Urals. He began work as a builder and joined the Communist Party in 1961. By 1968 he was a full-time party worker, and in 1976 was appointed First Secretary of the Sverdlovsk District Central Committee. Life in the Soviet Union changed in the 1980s when Mikhail Gorbachev became General Secretary of the Soviet Communist Party. The many changes he introduced were welcomed by Yeltsin, who became First Secretary of the Moscow City Party Committee in 1985. However, Yeltsin soon clashed with Gorbachev, who tried to stop him running for President of Russia in 1990. Yeltsin, no longer a member of the Communist Party, stood for election anyway and won easily. This gave him the authority to become a world figure. When there was an attempt to overthrow Gorbachev in 1991, Yeltsin bravely led the opposition to the coup. With the break-up of the Soviet Union into individual country states, Yeltsin continued to lead Russia to democracy. But economic problems

◀ The Russian president Boris Yeltsin pictured at the Helsinki Summit in 1992. Faced with severe economic problems and unrest among his people, he consistently called for international aid.

caused a lot of discontent and Yeltsin made the decision to dissolve the Russian parliament in 1993 in order to push through his economic reforms. His Communist opponents led an armed uprising against him but Yeltsin was able to put this down with the help of his loyal troops. ◆

see also
Gorbachev

Yoshida Shigeru

Japanese prime minister
Born 1878   Died 1967 aged 89

Born the son of a politician, Yoshida Shigeru studied politics at Tokyo University, and then made his career as a statesman and politician. He served as Japan's ambassador to Scandinavia, Italy, and Britain. However, the military in Japan did not trust his international outlook and he did not serve in office during World War II. He was imprisoned in June 1945 for recommending that Japan should surrender in the closing stages of

the war, and then released three months later with the arrival of American Occupation troops. He then served as foreign minister from 1945 to 1946 and prime minister from 1946 to 1947 and 1948 to 1954. Yoshida opposed Communism strongly and favoured close links between Japan and America. Under his firm rule his defeated country rapidly regained its independence and started on its astonishing road to economic recovery. ◆

Brigham **Young**

American leader of the Mormon community
Born 1801   Died 1877 aged 76

Brigham Young was the ninth of 11 children. He had very little education and started work as a house painter.

In 1832 he became dissatisfied with the Methodist church that he had been brought up in, and became a Mormon. The Mormons are one of the many groups which have split off from other Christian Churches because of disagreements about their different beliefs.

▼ The leaders of the Mormon settlers who journeyed to Utah in 1847 were very well organized, treating the migration almost like a military operation.

In many parts of America, Mormons were disliked and were driven from their land. In 1847 Young became leader of the Mormons, and decided to find a new, peaceful home for them. He led 148 Mormon settlers to the Great Salt Lake of Utah and started what became Salt Lake City. By the time he died, 147,000 Mormons were living in Utah.

Brigham Young believed, like many Mormons, in polygamy, and had 27 wives and 56 children. ◆

Thomas **Young**

English physicist
Born *1773*   **Died** *1829 aged 55*

Thomas Young was very bright and could read when he was two. He studied medicine, but he was interested in physics, too.

Although Isaac Newton and other great scientists thought that light was a stream of particles, Young thought they were wrong. He proved that light is really a kind of wave. He also found out that our eyes can only detect three colours, and all the other colours can be made up of mixtures of these. In 1801 he was made a professor at the Royal Institution in London.

Young was also very good at languages. The famous Rosetta stone, which was over 2000 years old, was found in Egypt in 1799. It was carved in three languages: high-class Egyptian (hieroglyphics), everyday Egyptian (demotic), and Greek. Young was the first to publish an account of this important find, although it was a Frenchman, François Champollion, who first deciphered the hieroglyphics on the stone. ◆

🔍 **see also**

Huygens   Newton

Emiliano **Zapata**

Mexican revolutionary
Born *1879*   **Died** *1919 aged 40*

▼ *For eight years Zapata led his peasant armies against the haciendas and successive heads of state in his quest to give land back to the people.*

For over 30 years (1877–1911) Mexico was ruled by the dictator Porfirio Diaz. The owners of haciendas (big estates) did not treat the poor peasants well. Emiliano Zapata, son of a peasant horse-dealer, was arrested at 18 for leading a protest against an estate-owner. When the revolution broke out against Diaz in 1910, Zapata was a strong supporter. His slogan was 'Land and Liberty'. By 1911 he controlled the southern state of Morelos. While the rest of Mexico slid into chaos, Zapata used his part-time farmers' army to re-establish order, chase landowners off their estates, and divide up their lands fairly among the peasants. In 1919 he was tricked into an ambush and assassinated by corrupt political rivals. But the revolution did eventually lead to land reform and the unselfish Zapata is revered in Mexico as a national hero. ◆

> *Men of the South! It is better to die on your feet than live on your knees!*
>
> EMILIANO ZAPATA

Emil **Zatopek**

Czechoslovakian athlete
Born *1922*

Emil Zatopek was the best long-distance runner of his day and possibly of all time. At the 1948 Olympics he won the gold medal for the 10,000 m and silver for the 5000 m. Then, at the 1952 Helsinki Olympics, he won the 5000 m and 10,000 m gold medals, and entered the marathon for the first time in his life. He won by 800 m (half a mile) to complete a unique treble.

His wife, Dana Zatopkova, also added to the family celebrations by winning the gold medal in the women's javelin competition. ◆

Ferdinand von **Zeppelin**

German airship builder
Born *1838*   **Died** *1917 aged 78*

In 1870 Paris was surrounded by the Prussian army. Ferdinand von Zeppelin, a Prussian officer, saw how the French used balloons to carry supplies into the besieged city. This got him thinking about designing an airship which, unlike balloons, could be controlled.

He designed his first hydrogen-filled airship and launched it in 1900. It did not fly well but Zeppelin improved the design and, before long, his airships were making flights lasting many hours. The German government ordered a whole fleet of them, and in

▼ *This World War I German propaganda poster shows one of Zeppelin's airships flying over New York. The slogan beneath reads 'Two days to North America', implying that it would be very easy for German zeppelins to reach and bomb American cities.*

IN 2 TAGEN NACH NORD-AMERIKA!
DEUTSCHE ZEPPELIN-REEDEREI

World War I used over a hundred 'zeppelins' to bomb enemy cities, including London.

Zeppelin started the first airship passenger airline in 1909. Although he died before intercontinental airship travel became a reality, by the 1930s huge zeppelins were flying across the Atlantic. The most famous were the *Graf Zeppelin*, which flew over 1,600,000 km, and the *Hindenburg*. Then, in 1937, the *Hindenburg* burst into flames killing 36 people. This and other disasters signalled the end of the airship era. ◆

Zhou Enlai

Prime minister of Communist China from 1949 to.1976
Born *1898*   **Died** *1976 aged 77*

Zhou Enlai believed that the answer to China's economic problems was to follow socialist ideas of sharing wealth. He went to study European political ideas in France, where he formed a branch of the new Chinese Communist Party. He returned to China and worked with other Communists to build up Chiang Kai-shek's Nationalist Party, until Chiang turned against the Communists in 1927. Zhou escaped and joined up with Mao Zedong and Deng Xiaoping. He took part in the Long March of 1934–1935, and became one of Mao's chief advisers.

After the creation of the People's Republic of China in 1949, Zhou became its first prime minister, holding the post until he died. During Mao's Cultural Revolution he actively restrained extremists and helped restore order. He also played a major role in building good relations with America, which previously had been the bitter enemy of Communist China. Zhou was a charming man and was admired and trusted by both Chinese and foreigners. ◆

see also
Chiang Kai-shek   Deng Xiaoping
Mao Zedong

Emile **Zola**

French writer
Born *1840*   **Died** *1902 aged 62*

Emile Zola was one of the greatest figures in the 19th-century French literary world. He was famous not only for his novels, but also for the outspoken way in which he campaigned for social reform and other causes he believed in. His novels, of which he wrote more than 20, paint a carefully detailed panorama of French life at the time. Among the most famous are *Nana* (1880), about a prostitute, and *Germinal* (1885), about the working conditions of miners. In 1898 Zola wrote his famous letter, *J'accuse* (I accuse), to a newspaper denouncing the French justice system for wrongly convicting an army officer, Captain Dreyfus, of treason. Zola had to take refuge in England to escape imprisonment for libel; Dreyfus was later pardoned. ◆

see also
Dreyfus

Zoroaster

Persian prophet
Born *c.628 BC*
Died *c.551 BC aged about 77*

According to tradition, Zoroaster was a priest who began to have visions when he was 30. He

▲ *A Zoroastrian coin from the 2nd century showing the symbol of the Zoroastrian faith, the fire altar.*

converted a local king to his beliefs when he was 40 and it is believed that he was murdered while praying at the altar when he was 77. The religion he founded, Zoroastrianism, became the official faith of three successive Persian (Iranian) empires, from the 6th century BC to the 6th century AD. Its scriptures included the 'Gathas', 17 hymns said to have been written by Zoroaster. Its worship focused on fire as a symbol of purity.

Zoroaster taught that there is only one God, that people are free to choose between good and evil forces, and that their lives will be judged at death and lead them to either Heaven or Hell. These ideas are all fundamental to Judaism, Christianity, and Islam, though it is not clear how these religions were affected by Zoroaster. A number of people in India, known as the Parsees, still follow Zoroastrianism. ◆

Ulrich **Zwingli**

Swiss religious reformer
Born 1484   Died 1531 aged 47

Ulrich Zwingli went to university in Vienna and Basle before being ordained a Roman Catholic priest in 1506. He served in the Swiss town of Glarus (1506–1516) and then in Einsiedeln (1516–1518). Around this time, many people wanted to reform the organization and teachings of the Catholic Church. Zwingli concluded that the Church needed to be more like that of Jesus's time. This new Church was to become known as the Protestant Church.

In 1518 Zwingli moved to Zurich, where he became minister of the city's cathedral. This position gave him some influence over the city's government, and in the next ten years, he and the town council converted the city to the Protestant faith. Their aim was to simplify church rituals; they removed paintings and statues from churches, and closed down monasteries. In 1525 they declared that the Zurich Church would no longer obey the pope.

Other Swiss cities also converted to Protestantism. Rural areas, however, wanted to stay within the Catholic Church. They sent an army against Zurich and in the ensuing battle at Kappel (1531), Zwingli was killed. ◆

see also
Calvin   Luther

▼ *Swiss Protestant leader Ulrich Zwingli.*

Vladimir **Zworykin**

Russian-born American scientist
Born 1889   Died 1982 aged 93

Vladimir Zworykin graduated as an electrical engineer in Russia, and during World War I was a radio operator in the army. After the war he emigrated to America where his interest in radio led him to a career in the flourishing electrical industry.

In 1923 he invented the iconoscope, an image-scanning device. In the 1930s it was developed into the cathode-ray tube, which is at the heart of every modern television set. This all-electric system quickly replaced the relatively crude optical-mechanical system demonstrated by John Logie Baird in 1926.

Zworykin also helped to develop a device for enhancing night vision, and the electron microscope, a research instrument which gives much greater magnification than is possible with the more common optical microscopes. He earned many honours and, in 1977, he was named in the US National Inventors Hall of Fame. ◆

see also
Baird   Marconi

Special Reference Section

Thematic Directory

Famous people by subject
pages 358-370

Can you name the most famous explorers of all time? Or the most influential composers? Can you think of any artists other than Michelangelo? Or any inventors apart from Thomas Edison? In this section the 1000 people in the book have been grouped together by their area of achievement, thus making it easy to answer such questions at a glance.

Chronological Directory

Famous people through the ages
pages 371-383

Did you know that Christopher Columbus was exploring the Americas at the same time that Leonardo da Vinci was painting his masterpieces? Or that Karl Marx was developing his Communist ideas at the same time that Emily Brontë was writing *Wuthering Heights?* Get a different perspective on history by looking under the various headings in this section to find out which famous men and women in this book were born and lived at the same time.

Thematic Directory

I n this comprehensive directory, the 1000 famous men and women in this book have been divided into thematic categories, thereby linking them together by their area of achievement. For example, all the painters are grouped together, as are all the scientists, all the explorers, etc. In some cases,

categories are further divided into time periods that reflect the dates of activity for the figures listed. However, some people cannot easily be placed in just one thematic group because of the variety of skills they possessed. For this reason you might find the same person under two, or even three headings.

Artists, Composers, and Writers

Painters and illustrators

Up to 1800

Bellini, Giovanni
Blake, William
Bosch, Hieronymus
Botticelli, Sandro
Bruegel, Pieter
Canaletto, Giovanni
Caravaggio, Michelangelo Merisi da
David, Jacques-Louis
Dürer, Albrecht
El Greco
Gainsborough, Thomas
Giotto di Bondone
Hals, Frans
Hogarth, William
Holbein, Hans
Leonardo da Vinci
Michelangelo Buonarroti
Piero della Francesca
Poussin, Nicolas
Raphael
Rembrandt van Rijn
Rubens, Peter
Tintoretto, Jacopo
Titian
Van Dyck, Anthony
Van Eyck, Jan
Velázquez, Diego
Vermeer, Jan
Veronese, Paolo
Watteau, Jean-Antoine

▶ Vincent van Gogh

1800 to 1900

Cézanne, Paul
Constable, John
Degas, Edgar
Delacroix, Eugène
Gauguin, Paul
Goya, Francisco de
Manet, Edouard
Monet, Claude
Munch, Edvard
Pissarro, Camille
Renoir, Pierre Auguste
Rossetti, Dante Gabriel
Rousseau, Henri
Seurat, Georges
Toulouse-Lautrec, Henri de
Turner, J. M. W.
Van Gogh, Vincent

1900 to present

Braque, Georges
Chagall, Marc
Dalí, Salvador
Escher, M. C.
Kandinsky, Wassily
Klee, Paul
Magritte, René
Matisse, Henri
Miró, Joan
Mondrian, Piet
Nolan, Sidney
O'Keeffe, Georgia
Picasso, Pablo
Pollock, Jackson
Rivera, Diego
Roberts, Tom
Warhol, Andy

▶ Salvador Dali

Photographers

Cartier-Bresson, Henri
Daguerre, Louis
Fox Talbot, William
Muybridge, Eadweard
Niepce, Joseph

Architects

Bernini, Gianlorenzo
Brunelleschi, Filippo
Gaudí, Antoni
Griffin, Walter Burley
Gropius, Walter
Le Corbusier
Mackintosh, Charles Rennie
Michelangelo Buonarroti
Palladio

Pei, I. M.
Vitruvius
William of Sens
Wren, Christopher
Wright, Frank Lloyd

Sculptors, designers, and craftspeople

Bernini, Gianlorenzo
Brancusi, Constantin
Cellini, Benvenuto
Chippendale, Thomas
Degas, Edgar
Donatello, Donato
Epstein, Jacob
Fabergé, Peter
Giacometti, Alberto
Hepworth, Barbara

Michelangelo Buonarroti
Moore, Henry
Morris, William
Phidias
Rodin, Auguste
Stradivari, Antonio
Wedgwood, Josiah

▲ Christopher Wren

Composers

Up to 1900

Bach, J. S.
Beethoven, Ludwig van
Berlioz, Hector
Bizet, Georges
Brahms, Johannes
Bruckner, Anton
Chopin, Frédéric
Debussy, Claude
Dvořák, Antonín
Gilbert and Sullivan
Grieg, Edvard
Handel, George Frideric
Haydn, Franz Joseph
Liszt, Franz
Mahler, Gustav
Mendelssohn, Felix
Monteverdi, Claudio
Mozart, Wolfgang Amadeus
Mussorgksy, Modest
Paganini, Niccolò
Puccini, Giacomo
Purcell, Henry

Rimsky-Korsakov, Nikolay
Rossini, Gioachino
Saint-Saëns, Camille
Schubert, Franz
Schumann, Robert
Sibelius, Jean
Strauss I, Johann
Strauss II, Johann
Strauss, Richard
Tchaikovsky, Pyotr Ilyich
Verdi, Giuseppe
Vivaldi, Antonio
Wagner, Richard

▼ Ludwig van Beethoven

1900 to present

Bartók, Béla
Berlin, Irving
Bernstein, Leonard
Britten, Benjamin
Copland, Aaron
Debussy, Claude
Elgar, Edward
Gershwin, George
Holst, Gustav
Mahler, Gustav
Porter, Cole
Prokofiev, Sergei
Puccini, Giacomo
Rakhmaninov, Sergey
Ravel, Maurice
Rimsky-Korsakov, Nikolai
Rodgers, Richard
Schoenberg, Arnold
Sibelius, Jean
Strauss, Richard
Stravinsky, Igor
Vaughan Williams, Ralph

Writers

Novelists

Achebe, Chinua
Alcott, Louisa May
Angelou, Maya
Austen, Jane
Balzac, Honoré de
Brontë sisters
Bunyan, John
Camus, Albert
Carroll, Lewis
Cervantes, Miguel de
Chaucer, Geoffrey
Cocteau, Jean
Conrad, Joseph
Defoe, Daniel
Dickens, Charles
Dostoevsky, Fyodor
Doyle, Arthur Conan
Dumas, Alexandre
Eliot, George
Fitzgerald, F. Scott
Flaubert, Gustave
García Márquez, Gabriel
Gide, André
Goethe, Johann von
Golding, William
Gordimer, Nadine
Greene, Graham
Hardy, Thomas
Hawthorne, Nathaniel
Hemingway, Ernest
Hughes, Langston

Hugo, Victor
James, Henry
Joyce, James
Kafka, Franz
Kawabata, Yasunari
Kipling, Rudyard
Lawrence, D. H.
Maupassant, Guy de
Melville, Herman
Montgomery, L. M.
Nabokov, Vladimir
Orwell, George
Proust, Marcel
Rabelais, François
Sartre, Jean-Paul
Scott, Walter
Shelley, Mary
Solzhenitsyn, Alexander
Stevenson, Robert Louis
Stowe, Harriet Beecher
Swift, Jonathan
Thackeray, William
Tolkien, J. R. R.
Tolstoy, Leo
Trollope, Anthony
Twain, Mark
Verne, Jules
Voltaire
Wells, H. G.
Woolf, Virginia
Zola, Emile

◄ Mark Twain

Dramatists

Aristophanes
Barrie, J. M.
Brecht, Bertolt
Chekhov, Anton
Cocteau, Jean
Fugard, Athol
Goethe, Johann von
Havel, Vaclav
Hugo, Victor
Ibsen, Henrik
Kalidasa
Miller, Arthur
Molière
Racine, Jean
Sartre, Jean-Paul
Shakespeare, William
Shaw, George Bernard
Sophocles
Thomas, Dylan
Walcott, Derek
Wilde, Oscar
Williams, Tennessee

► Virginia Woolf

◄ Oscar Wilde

▼ William Shakespeare

▲ Beatrix Potter

▲ Lord Byron

Entertainers

Classical musicians

Bernstein, Leonard
Callas, Maria
Casals, Pablo
Liszt, Franz
Melba, Nellie
Menuhin, Yehudi
Pavarotti, Luciano
Paganini, Niccolò
Rachmaninov, Sergey
Rubinstein, Arthur
Sutherland, Joan
Suzuki, Shin'ichi
Te Kanawa, Kiri

Popular musicians (jazz, rock, and pop)

Armstrong, Louis
Berry, Chuck
Bowie, David
Brown, James
Charles, Ray
Clapton, Eric
Dylan, Bob
Ellington, 'Duke'
Fitzgerald, Ella
Franklin, Aretha
Hendrix, Jimi
Holiday, Billie
Holly, Buddy
Jackson, Michael

Jagger, Mick
John, Elton
King, B. B.
Lennon and McCartney
Madonna
Marley, Bob
Miller, Glenn
Mitchell, Joni
Presley, Elvis
Robeson, Paul
Ross, Diana
Simon, Paul
Sinatra, Frank
Wonder, Stevie

Actors

Astaire, Fred
Bernhardt, Sarah
Bogart, Humphrey
Brando, Marlon
Chaplin, Charlie
Cruise, Tom
Davis, Bette
Dean, James
De Niro, Robert
Dietrich, Marlene
Eastwood, Clint
Gable, Clark
Garbo, Greta
Grant, Cary
Hanks, Tom
Hepburn, Katherine
Irving, Henry
Kean, Edmund
Keaton, Buster
Laurel and Hardy
Marx brothers
Monroe, Marilyn
Olivier, Lawrence
Pickford, Mary
Sinatra, Frank
Taylor, Elizabeth
Temple, Shirley
Valentino, Rudolph
Wayne, John
Welles, Orson

Film makers and directors

Chaplin, Charles
Cocteau, Jean
De Mille, Cecil B.
Disney, Walt
Eastwood, Clint
Eisenstein, Sergei
Fellini, Federico
Ford, John
Goldwyn, Samuel
Griffith, D. W.
Hitchcock, Alfred
Kurosawa, Akira
Ray, Satyajit
Spielberg, Steven
Welles, Orson

▲ Marlene Dietrich

Dancers, choreographers, and other entertainers

Astaire, Fred
Blondin, Charles
De Valois, Ninette
Fonteyn, Margot
Graham, Martha
Houdini, Harry
Nijinsky, Vaslav
Nureyev, Rudolf
Pavlova, Anna
Shankar, Uday

◀ Harry Houdini

World Leaders and Rulers

Ancient leaders and rulers – before 1 AD

Alexander the Great
Antony, Mark
Asoka
Augustus, Emperor
Caesar, Julius
Chandragupta Maurya
Cicero
Cleopatra
Cyrus the Great
Darius I
David, King

Hammurabi
Hannibal
Herod
Khufu
Nebuchadnezzar II
Pericles
Pompey
Rameses II
Shi Huangdi
Solomon
Solon

Spartacus
Themistocles
Tutankhamun
Xerxes

▶ Julius Caesar

Past and present rulers – since 1 AD

Europe

Alaric
Alfred
Boudicca
Canute
Catherine the Great
Charlemagne
Charles I (of England)
Charles II (of England)
Charles V (of France)
Christina (of Sweden)
Constantine the Great
Cromwell, Oliver
Edward I
Edward II
Edward III
Edward the Confessor
Eleanor of Aquitaine
Elizabeth I
Elizabeth II
Eric the Red
Ferdinand and Isabella
Frederick I (Barbarossa)
Frederick II (the Great)
George I
George III
Gustavus Adolphus
Hadrian
Henry IV (of France)
Henry V (of England)
Henry VIII (of England)

Ivan the Terrible
James I
John
Justinian and Theodora
Llywelyn the Great
Louis XIV
Louis XVI
Macbeth
Maria Theresa
Marie Antoinette
Mary I
Mary, Queen of Scots
Napoleon I
Napoleon III
Nero
Nicholas II (of Russia)
Peter the Great
Philip II (of Spain)
Richard I
Richard III
Robert I
Suleiman I
Trajan
Victor Emanuel II
Victoria
William I
William III (and Mary II)
William the Silent

Rest of the world

Akbar
Atahualpa
Attila
Cetshwayo
Genghis Khan
Haile Selassie
Harun al-Rashid
Emperor Hirohito
Kublai Khan
Mehemet Ali
Minamoto Yoritomo
Mongkut
Montezuma II
Saladin
Shah Jahan
Sultan of Brunei
Tamerlane
Tokugawa Ieyasu

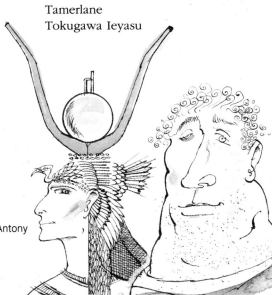

▶ Cleopatra and Mark Antony

Political leaders

Europe

Atatürk, Kemal
Attlee, Clement
Bismarck, Otto von
Blair, Tony
Borgia family
Brandt, Willy
Churchill, Winston
Clemenceau, Georges
De Gaulle, Charles
De Valera, Eamon
Disraeli, Benjamin
Franco, Francisco
Gladstone, William
Gorbachev, Mikhail
Havel, Vaclav
Hitler, Adolf
Khrushchev, Nikita
Kohl, Helmut
Lenin, Vladimir
Lloyd George, David
MacDonald, Ramsay
Mitterand, François
Mussolini, Benito
Peel, Robert
Pitt, William (the younger)
Rabin, Yitzhak
Stalin, Joseph
Thatcher, Margaret
Tito, Josip
Walesa, Lech
Walpole, Robert
Wolsey, Thomas
Yeltsin, Boris

Middle East

Arafat, Yasser
Begin, Menachem
Ben-Gourion, David
Hussein, Saddam
Khomeini, Ayatollah Ruhollah
Meir, Golda
Weizmann, Chaim

Americas and Canada

Adams, John
Bolívar, Simón
Castro, Fidel
Clinton, Bill
Davis, Jefferson
Eisenhower, Dwight

◀ Joseph Stalin

Grant, Ulysses S.
Jackson, Andrew
Jefferson, Thomas
Johnson, Lyndon B.
Kennedy, John Fitzgerald
King, William Lyon Mackenzie
Lincoln, Abraham
Macdonald, John A.
Madison, James
Monroe, James
Nixon, Richard
Pearson, Lester Bowles
Perón, Eva and Juan
Reagan, Ronald
Roosevelt, Franklin D.
Roosevelt, Theodore
Trudeau, Pierre
Truman, Harry S.
Washington, George
Wilson, Woodrow

▶ Eva Perón

Africa, Asia, and Australasia

Bhutto, Benazir
Bhutto, Zulfikar Ali
Chiang Kai-shek
De Klerk, F. W.
Deng Xiaoping
Gandhi, Indira
Gandhi, Mahatma
Haile Selassie
Hawke, Robert
Ho Chi Minh
Ito Hirobumi
Jinnah, Mohammed Ali
Kaunda, Kenneth
Kenyatta, Jomo
Lee Kuan Yew
Mandela, Nelson
Mao Zedong
Menzies, Robert
Mugabe, Robert
Nasser, Gamal Abdel
Nehru, Pandit Jawaharlal
Nkrumah, Kwame
Nyerere, Julius
Pol Pot
Qaddafi, Mu'ammar al-
Sadat, Mohammed Anwar al
Smuts, Jan
Sukarno
Verwoerd, Hendrik
Yoshida Shigeru
Zhou Enlai

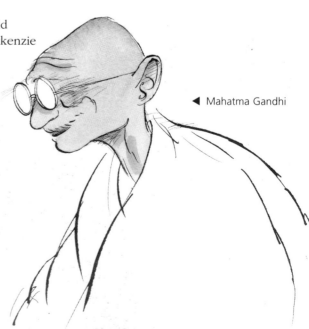

◀ Mahatma Gandhi

Other leaders and politicians

Buthelezi, Gatsha
Cavour, Camillo
Collins, Michael
Franklin, Benjamin
Goebbels, Joseph
Goering, Herman
Hardie, James Keir
Kruger, Paul
Luthuli, Albert

Masaryk, Thomas
McCarthy, Joseph
Medici family
Metternich, Klemens
O'Connell, Daniel
Parnell, Charles
Rhodes, Cecil
Richelieu, Armand Jean
Torquemada, Tomás de

▶ Joseph Goebbels

Revolutionaries and military leaders

Alexander, Earl of Tunis
Charles Edward Stuart
Clive, Robert
Crazy Horse
Cromwell, Oliver
Custer, General George A.
Danton, Georges
Eisenhower, Dwight
Garibaldi, Giuseppe
Geronimo
Glyndwr, Owain
Grant, Ulysses S.
Guevara, Che

Hereward the Wake
Joan of Arc
Lafayette, Marquis de
Lawrence, T. E.
Lee, Robert E.
MacArthur, Douglas
Marlborough, Duke of
Minamoto Yoritomo
Montgomery, Bernard Law
Nelson, Horatio
Pétain, Henri Philippe
Revere, Paul
Rizal, José
Robespierre, Maximilien

Rommel, Erwin
Saladin
San Martin, José de
Shaka the Zulu
Sitting Bull
Sun Yat-sen
Tokugawa Ieyasu
Toussaint l'Ouverture
Trotsky, Leon
Wellington, Duke of
Zapata, Emiliano

◀ Che Guevara

◀ Giuseppe Garibaldi

▶ Joan of Arc

Civil rights leaders

Biko, Steve
Douglass, Frederick
Garvey, Marcus
King, Martin Luther, Jr
Malcolm X
Mandela, Nelson

Religious Leaders, Thinkers, and Reformers

Religious founders and followers

Abraham
Abu Bakr
Ali
Andrew, Saint
Aquinas, Saint Thomas
Augustine, Saint (of Canterbury)
Augustine, Saint (of Hippo)
Becket, Saint Thomas
Bernadette, Saint
Buddha
Calvin, John
Cranmer, Thomas
Dalai Lama
David, Saint
Eddy, Mary Baker
Fox, George
Francis of Assisi, Saint
George, Saint
Gobind Singh
Gregory I
Isaiah
Jesus
John XXIII, Pope
John the Baptist
John Paul II, Pope

Joseph
Knox, John
Loyola, Saint Ignatius
Luther, Martin
Mahavira
Mary
Moses
Muhammad
Nanak, Guru
Patrick, Saint
Paul, Saint
Penn, William
Ramakrishna
Teresa of Avila, Saint
Torquemada, Tomàs de
Tutu, Desmond
Urban II, Pope
Wesley, John
Wolsey, Thomas
Wycliffe, John
Young, Brigham
Zoroaster
Zwingli, Ulrich

Social reformers

Anderson, Elizabeth Garrett
Anthony, Susan Brownell
Baden-Powell, Robert
Barnardo, Thomas
Besant, Annie
Booth, William and Catherine
Brown, John
Butler, Josephine
Fry, Elizabeth
Fukuzawa, Yukichi
Montessori, Maria
Nightingale, Florence
Paine, Thomas
Pankhurst, Emmeline and Christabel
Roosevelt, Eleanor
Schweitzer, Albert
Seacole, Mary
Sequoya
Shaftesbury, 7th Earl of
Steinem, Gloria
Stopes, Marie
Teresa, Mother
Truth, Sojourner
Tubman, Harriet
Washington, Booker T.
Wilberforce, William

▶ Karl Marx

Thinkers and philosophers

Abelard, Peter
Aristotle
Aurobindo
Averroës
Avicenna
Bacon, Francis
Cicero, Marcus
Confucius
Descartes, René
Diderot, Denis
Diogenes
Empedocles
Erasmus, Desiderius
Hegel, Georg
Hobbes, Thomas
Hume, David
Ibn Khaldun

Keynes, John Maynard
Lao Tzu
Leibniz, Gottfried
Locke, John
Machiavelli, Niccolò
Malthus, Thomas
Marx, Karl
Mencius
More, Thomas
Nietzsche, Friedrich
Pascal, Blaise
Plato
Rousseau, Jean-Jacques
Russell, Bertrand
Sartre, Jean-Paul
Smith, Adam
Socrates

Scientists, Inventors, and Engineers

Physicists

Ampère, André-Marie
Becquerel, Henri
Bernoulli family
Bohr, Niels
Boyle, Robert
Bragg, William and Lawrence
Cavendish, Henry
Curie, Marie and Pierre
Einstein, Albert
Faraday, Michael
Fermi, Enrico
Foucault, Jean
Galvani, Luigi
Gay-Lussac, Joseph
Hahn, Otto
Hawking, Stephen
Heisenberg, Werner Karl
Hertz, Heinrich
Hooke, Robert
Huygens, Christiaan
Joule, James
Kelvin, William
Maxwell, James Clerk
Meitner, Lise
Newton, Isaac
Oersted, Hans Christian
Ohm, Georg
Oppenheimer, J. Robert
Planck, Max
Röntgen, Wilhelm
Rutherford, Ernest
Salam, Abdus
Schrödinger, Erwin
Thomson, Joseph
Volta, Alessandro
Watt, James
Young, Thomas

Chemists

Dalton, John
Davy, Humphry
Haber, Fritz
Hodgkin, Dorothy
Lavoisier, Antoine
Mendelèev, Dimitri
Pauling, Linus
Priestley, Joseph

Mathematicians

Aryabhata
Boole, George
Descartes, René
Euclid
Euler, Leonhard
Gauss, Karl
Hero of Alexandria
Leibniz, Gottfried
Mandelbrot, Benoit
Pascal, Blaise
Pythagoras
Russell, Bertrand

Astronomers

Bell, Jocelyn
Brahe, Tycho
Copernicus, Nicolaus
Eddington, Arthur Stanley
Galilei, Galileo
Halley, Edmund
Herschel, Caroline and William
Hipparchus
Hubble, Edwin
Kepler, Johannes
Laplace, Pierre
Lemaitre, Georges
Ptolemy

◀ Galileo Galilei

▼ Louis Pasteur

Biologists, physicians, and psychiatrists

Banting, Frederick
Barnard, Christiaan
Best, Charles
Crick, Francis
Darwin, Charles
Fleming, Alexander
Freud, Sigmund
Galen
Harvey, William
Hippocrates of Cos
Jenner, Edward
Jung, Carl

Koch, Robert
Leakey family
Leeuwenhoek, Anton van
Linnaeus, Carolus
Lister, Joseph
Mendel, Gregor
Pasteur, Louis
Pavlov, Ivan
Vesalius, Andreas
Watson, James

Inventors, designers, and engineers

Up to 1800

Archimedes
Arkwright, Richard
Caxton, William
Crompton, Samuel
Fulton, Robert
Gutenberg, Johann
Hargreaves, James
Hero of Alexandria
Jacquard, Joseph-Marie
Leonardo da Vinci
McAdam, John
Mercator, Gerardus
Montgolfier brothers
Newcomen, Thomas
Niepce, Joseph
Telford, Thomas
Tull, Jethro
Volta, Alessandro
Watt, James

1800 to 1900

Babbage, Charles
Bell, Alexander Graham
Benz, Karl
Bessemer, Henry
Braille, Louis
Brunel, Isambard Kingdom
Colt, Samuel
Daguerre, Louis
Daimler, Gottlieb
Davy, Humphry
Diesel, Rudolf
Dunlop, John
Eastman, George
Edison, Thomas
Eiffel, Gustave
Fox Talbot, William
Hill, Rowland
Jacquard, Joseph-Marie
Krupp, Alfred
Lesseps, Ferdinand de
Lumière brothers
Marconi, Guglielmo
McAdam, John
Morse, Samuel
Niepce, Joseph
Nobel, Alfred
Otto, Nikolaus
Sholes, Christopher
Siemens family
Stephenson, George
Telford, Thomas
Zeppelin, Ferdinand von

▼ Isambard Kingdom Brunel

1900 to present

Baird, John Logie
Bardeen, John
Birdseye, Clarence
Biro, Laszlo
Braun, Wernher von
Carlson, Chester
Cockerell, Christopher
Cousteau, Jacques
Diesel, Rudolf
Eastman, George
Edison, Thomas
Ford, Henry
Hoover, William
Porsche, Ferdinand
Sikorsky, Igor
Watson-Watt, Robert
Whittle, Frank
Wright brothers
Zeppelin, Ferdinand vc
Zworykin, Vladimir

▼ Leonardo da Vinci

Explorers and Adventurers

Pioneers and adventurers

Alcock and Brown
Amundsen, Roald
Armstrong, Neil
Batten, Jean
Blériot, Louis
Byrd, Richard
Cousteau, Jacques
Earhart, Amelia
Gagarin, Yuri
Glenn, John

Heyerdahl, Thor
Hillary, Edmund
Johnson, Amy
Lindbergh, Charles
Piccard, Auguste
Scott, Robert
Smith, Charles Kingsford
Tenzing Norgay
Tereshkova, Valentina

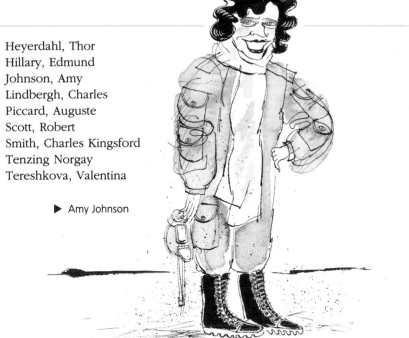

▶ Amy Johnson

Explorers and discoverers

Balboa, Vasco Núñez de
Banks, Joseph
Bering, Vitus
Bird, Isabella
Boone, Daniel
Burton, Richard
Cabot, John
Cartier, Jacques
Champlain, Samuel de
Columbus, Christopher
Cook, James
Cortés, Hernán
Dias, Bartolomeu
Drake, Francis
Eric the Red
Ericsson, Leif
Fa Hsien
Franklin, John

Gama, Vasco da
Hudson, Henry
Humboldt, Baron von
Ibn Batuta
Kingsley, Mary
La Salle, Rene
Lewis and Clark
Livingstone, David
Magellan, Ferdinand
Nansen, Fridtjof
Park, Mungo
Peary, Robert
Pizarro, Francisco
Polo, Marco
Raleigh, Walter
Tasman, Abel
Vespucci, Amerigo

◀ James Cook

◀ Marco Polo

Sports Stars

Ali, Muhammad
Beckenbauer, Franz
Bradman, Donald
Bubka, Sergey
Chiyonofuji
Comaneci, Nadia
Court, Margaret
DiMaggio, Joe
Fangio, Juan
Fraser, Dawn
Grace, W. G.
Graf, Steffi
Gretzky, Wayne
Henie, Sonja
Jordan, Michael
Kasparov, Gary
Khan, Imran
Khan, Jahangir
Killy, Jean-Claude
Laver, Rod
Lenglen, Suzanne
Lewis, Carl

Louis, Joe
Maradona, Diego
Matthews, Stanley
Merckx, Eddy
Montana, Joe
Navratilova, Martina
Nicklaus, Jack
Owens, Jesse
Palmer, Arnold
Pelé
Piggott, Lester
Prost, Alain
Ruth, Babe
Shoemaker, Bill
Sobers, Garry
Spitz, Mark
Stenmark, Ingemar
Szewinska, Irena
Thompson, Daley
Thorpe, Jim
Zatopek, Emil

◀ Joe DiMaggio

Famous Characters

Arthur, King
Billy the Kid
Branson, Richard
Buffalo Bill
Calamity Jane
Capone, Al
Carnegie, Andrew
Casanova, Giovanni
Cavell, Edith
Crockett, Davy
Diana, Princess of Wales
Dreyfus, Alfred
El Cid
Fawkes, Guy
Gates, Bill
Getty, Jean Paul
Hearst, William Randolph
Heinz, Henry
Honda, Soichiro

Hughes, Howard
James, Jesse
Keller, Helen
Kellogg, William
Kelly, Ned
Lawrence, T. E.
Murdoch, Rupert
Oakley, Annie
Phidippides
Pocahontas
Rasputin
Rockefeller, John D.
Rothschild, Mayer Amschel
Schliemann, Heinrich
Tussaud, Marie
Vanderbilt, Cornelius
Villa, Pancho
Woolworth, Frank

◀ Calamity Jane

Chronological Directory

The 1000 famous men and women in this book have been divided into groups according to their date of birth. Thus, all the people who were born over 3000 years ago are linked together, as are those people who were born in the 1950s and 1960s. The timeline at the bottom of the pages can be used for quick and easy reference. A cross-reference (*see ...*) after some names guides you to the main article in the book where these people can be found.

2700 BC – 1001 BC

Khufu 26th century BC
Abraham 20th century BC
Hammurabi 18th century BC
Joseph 18th century BC
Tutankhamun c.1370 BC–1352 BC
Rameses II 13th century BC
Moses c.13th century BC
King David 10th century BC

1000 BC – 500 BC

King Solomon c.980 BC–c.922 BC
Homer 8th century BC
Isaiah 8th century BC
Nebuchadnezzar II c.630 BC–c.562 BC
Solon c.630 BC–c.560 BC
Zoroaster c.628 BC–c.551 BC
Mahavira c.599 BC–c.527 BC
Pythagoras c.582 BC–c.497 BC
Buddha c.563 BC–c.483 BC
Darius I c.558 BC–486 BC
Confucius c.551 BC–479 BC
Themistocles c.528 BC–c.462 BC
Xerxes c.519 BC–465 BC
Aesop 6th century BC
Cyrus the Great 6th century BC
Lao Tzu 6th century BC

499 BC – 200 BC

Sophocles c.496 BC–406 BC
Pericles c.495 BC–c.429 BC
Empedocles c.494 BC–c.434 BC
Phidias c.490 BC–c.430 BC
Herodotus c.484 BC–c.424 BC
Socrates c.469 BC–399 BC
Hippocrates of Cos c.460 BC–c.370 BC
Aristophanes c.450 BC–c.385 BC
Plato 429 BC–347 BC
Diogenes c.400 BC–c.325 BC
Phidippides 5th century BC
Aristotle 384 BC–322 BC
Mencius c.371 BC–c.289 BC
Alexander the Great 356 BC–323 BC
Euclid c.330 BC–c.260 BC
Chandragupta Maurya 4th century BC
Archimedes c.287 BC–212 BC
Shi Huangdi 259 BC–210 BC
Hannibal 247 BC–183 BC
Asoka 3rd century BC

199 BC – 1 BC

Marcus Cicero 106 BC–43 BC
Pompey 106 BC–48 BC
Julius Caesar c.100 BC–44 BC
Hipparchus 2nd century BC
Mark Antony 83 BC–30 BC
Herod c.74 BC–4 BC
Virgil 70 BC–19 BC
Cleopatra c.69 BC–30 BC
Augustus 63 BC–AD 14
Jesus c.4 BC–c.AD 29
John the Baptist c.4 BC–c.AD 28
Mary, mother of Jesus c.1st century BC
Spartacus 1st century BC
Vitruvius 1st century BC

0 AD ▶

0 AD – 499

Saint Andrew 1st century
Hero of Alexandria 1st century
Boudicca 1st century
Saint Peter 1st century
Saint Paul c.3–c.65
Nero 37–68
Plutarch c.46–c.120
Ts'ai Lun c.50–118
Trajan 53–117
Hadrian c.76–138
Ptolemy 2nd century
Galen c.130–c.200
Saint George 3rd century
Constantine the Great c.274–337
Saint Augustine of Hippo 354–430
Alaric 370–410
Saint Patrick c.390–c.460
Kalidasa 5th century
Fa Hsien 5th century
Attila 406–453
Aryabhata 476–c.550
Justinian 483–565

500 – 999

Saint Augustine of Canterbury 6th century
King Arthur 6th century
Saint David 6th century
Gregory I c.540–604
Muhammad c.570–632
Abu Bakr c.573–634
Ali c.600–661
Charlemagne 742–814
Harun al-Rashid c.764–809
Alfred 849–899
Eric the Red 10th century
Avicenna 979–1037
Canute c.994–1035

1000 – 1299

Leif Ericsson 11th century
Hereward the Wake 11th century
Edward the Confessor c.1003–1066
Macbeth c.1005–c.1057
William I c.1027–1087
Pope Urban II c.1042–1099
El Cid c.1043–1099
Omar Khayyam 1048–1123
Peter Abelard 1079–1142
William of Sens 12th century
Saint Thomas Becket 1118–1170
Eleanor of Aquitaine c.1122–1204
Frederick I c.1123–1190
Averroës 1126–1198
Saladin 1137–1193
Minamoto Yoritomo 1147–1199
Richard I 1157–1199
Genghis Khan 1162–1227
King John 1167–1216
Llywelyn the Great c.1172–1240
Saint Francis of Assisi 1182–1226
Kublai Khan 1215–1294
Saint Thomas Aquinas c.1225–1274
Edward I 1239–1307
Marco Polo c.1254–1324
Dante Alighieri 1265–1321
Giotto di Bondone c.1267–1337
Robert I 1274–1329

1300 – 1449

Ibn Batuta 1304–1368
Francesco Petrarch 1304–1374
Edward III 1312–1377
John Wycliffe c.1330–1384
Ibn Khaldun 1332–1406
Tamerlane c.1336–1405
Geoffrey Chaucer c.1340–1400
Owain Glyndwr c.1354–c.1416
Filippo Brunelleschi 1377–1446
Alfonso Borgia 1378–1458
Donato Donatello 1386–1466
Henry V 1387–1422
Cosimo Medici 1389–1464

0 AD ▲

1389 ▲

Jan van Eyck c.1390–1441
Henry the Navigator 1394–1460
Thomas Malory 15th century
Johann Gutenberg c.1400–c.1468
Joan of Arc 1412–1431
Piero Medici 1414–1469
Piero della Francesca c.1415–1492
Tomás de Torquemada 1420–1498
William Caxton c.1422–1491
Giovanni Bellini 1430–1516
Roderigo Borgia 1431–1503
Sandro Botticelli c.1445–1510
Lorenzo Medici 1449–1492

1450 – 1499

Hieronymus Bosch c.1450–1516
John Cabot c.1450–c.1498
Bartolomeu Dias c.1450–1500
Christopher Columbus 1451–1506
Isabella of Spain 1451–1504 *see Ferdinand and Isabella*
Amerigo Vespucci 1451–1512
Ferdinand of Spain 1452–1516 *see Ferdinand and Isabella*
Leonardo da Vinci 1452–1519
Richard III 1452–1485
Desiderius Erasmus c.1466–1536
Vasco da Gama c.1469–1524
Niccolò Machiavelli 1469–1527
Guru Nanak 1469–1539
Albrecht Dürer 1471–1528
Nicolaus Copernicus 1473–1543
Francisco Pizarro c.1474–1541
Thomas Wolsey c.1474–1530
Vasco Núñez de Balboa c.1475–1519
Michelangelo Buonarroti 1475–1564
Cesare Borgia 1475–1507
Thomas More c.1477–1535
Lucrezia Borgia 1480–1519
Ferdinand Magellan c.1480–1521
Montezuma II c.1480–1520
Martin Luther 1483–1546
Raphael 1483–1520
Ulrich Zwingli 1484–1531
Hernán Cortés 1485–1547
Thomas Cromwell c.1485–1540
Titian c.1488–1576

Thomas Cranmer 1489–1556
Jacques Cartier 1491–1557
Henry VIII 1491–1547
Saint Ignatius Loyola 1491–1556
François Rabelais c.1494–1553
Suleiman I c.1494–1566
Hans Holbein 1497–1543

1500 – 1549

Benvenuto Cellini 1500–1571
Charles V 1500–1558
Atahualpa c.1502–1533
Michael Nostradamus 1503–1566
John Knox 1505–1572
Andrea Palladio 1508–1580
John Calvin 1509–1564
Gerardus Mercator 1512–1594
Andreas Vesalius 1514–1564
Saint Teresa of Avila 1515–1582
Mary I 1516–1558
Jacopo Tintoretto 1518–1594
Luíz vaz de Camoens 1524–1580
Pieter Bruegel c.1525–1569
Philip II 1527–1598
Paolo Veronese 1528–1588
Ivan IV 1530–1584
Elizabeth I 1533–1603
William the Silent 1533–1584
Francis Drake c.1540–1596
El Greco 1541–1614
Akbar 1542–1605
Mary, Queen of Scots 1542–1587
Tokugawa Ieyasu 1542–1616
Tycho Brahe 1546–1601
Miguel de Cervantes 1547–1616

1550 – 1599

Walter Raleigh c.1552–1618
Henry IV 1553–1610
Francis Bacon 1561–1626
Galileo Galilei 1564–1642
William Shakespeare 1564–1616
Henry Hudson c.1565–1611

1390 ▲

1565 ▲

James I 1566–1625
Samuel de Champlain 1567–1635
Claudio Monteverdi 1567–1643
Guy Fawkes 1570–1606
Michelangelo Merisi da Caravaggio 1571–1610
Johannes Kepler 1571–1630
John Donne 1572–1631
Peter Rubens 1577–1640
William Harvey 1578–1657
Frans Hals c.1581–1666
Armand Jean Richelieu 1585–1642
Thomas Hobbes 1588–1679
Shah Jahan 1592–1666
Gustavus Adolphus 1594–1632
Nicolas Poussin 1594–1665
Pocahontas 1595–1617
René Descartes 1596–1650
Gianlorenzo Bernini 1598–1680
Oliver Cromwell 1599–1658
Anthony van Dyck 1599–1641
Diego Velázquez 1599–1660

1600 – 1649

Charles I 1600–1649
Abel Tasman c.1603–c.1659
Rembrandt van Rijn 1606–1669
John Milton 1608–1674
Molière 1622–1673
Blaise Pascal 1623–1662
George Fox 1624–1691
Queen Christina 1626–1689
Robert Boyle 1627–1691
John Bunyan 1628–1688
Christiaan Huygens 1629–1695
Charles II 1630–1685
Anton van Leeuwenhoek 1632–1723
John Locke 1632–1704
Jan Vermeer 1632–1675
Christopher Wren 1632–1723
Samuel Pepys 1633–1703
Robert Hooke 1635–1703
Louis XIV 1638–1715
Jean Racine 1639–1699
Isaac Newton 1642–1727
Rene LaSalle 1643–1687

Basho 1644–1694
William Penn 1644–1718
Antonio Stradivari 1644–1737
Gottfried Leibniz 1646–1716

1650 – 1699

Duke of Marlborough 1650–1722
William III 1650–1702
Jakob Bernoulli 1654–1705
Edmund Halley 1656–1742
Henry Purcell 1659–1695
Daniel Defoe 1660–1731
George I 1660–1727
Mary II 1662–1694
Thomas Newcomen 1663–1729
Gobind Singh 1666–1708
Johann Bernoulli 1667–1748
Jonathan Swift 1667–1745
Peter the Great 1672–1725
Jethro Tull 1674–1741
Robert Walpole 1676–1745
Antonio Vivaldi 1678–1741
Vitus Bering 1681–1741
Jean-Antoine Watteau 1684–1721
J. S. Bach 1685–1750
George Frideric Handel 1685–1759
Alexander Pope 1688–1744
Voltaire 1694–1778
Giovanni Canaletto 1697–1768
William Hogarth 1697–1764

1700 – 1739

Daniel Bernoulli 1700–1782
John Wesley 1703–1791
Benjamin Franklin 1706–1790
Leonard Euler 1707–1783
Carolus Linnaeus 1707–1778
Samuel Johnson 1709–1784
David Hume 1711–1776
Frederick II 1712–1786
Jean-Jacques Rousseau 1712–1778
Denis Diderot 1713–1784

Maria Theresa 1717–1780
Thomas Chippendale c.1718–1779
Charles Edward Stuart 1720–1788
James Hargreaves c.1720–1778
Adam Smith 1723–1790
Immanuel Kant 1724–1804
Giovanni Casanova 1725–1798
Robert Clive 1725–1774
Thomas Gainsborough 1727–1788
James Cook 1728–1779
Catherine the Great 1729–1796
Josiah Wedgwood 1730–1795
Henry Cavendish 1731–1810
Richard Arkwright 1732–1792
Joseph Haydn 1732–1809
George Washington 1732–1799
Joseph Priestley 1733–1804
Daniel Boone 1734–1820
John Adams 1735–1826
Paul Revere 1735–1818
James Watt 1736–1819
Luigi Galvani 1737–1798
Thomas Paine 1737–1809
George III 1738–1820
William Herschel 1738–1822

1740 – 1759

Joseph Montgolfier 1740–1810
Thomas Jefferson 1743–1826
Antoine Lavoisier 1743–1794
Toussaint l'Ouverture c.1743–1803
Joseph Banks 1744–1820
Mayer Amschel Rothschild 1744–1812
Jacques Montgolfier 1745–1799
Alessandro Volta 1745–1827
Francisco de Goya 1746–1828
Jacques-Louis David 1748–1825
Johann von Goethe 1749–1832
Edward Jenner 1749–1823
Pierre Laplace 1749–1827
Caroline Herschel 1750–1848
James Madison 1751–1836
Joseph-Marie Jacquard 1752–1834
Samuel Crompton 1753–1827
Louis XVI 1754–1793

Marie Antoinette 1755–1793
John McAdam 1756–1836
Wolfgang Amadeus Mozart 1756–1791
William Blake 1757–1827
Marquis de Lafayette 1757–1834
Thomas Telford 1757–1834
James Monroe 1758–1831
Horatio Nelson 1758–1805
Maximilien Robespierre 1758–1794
Robert Burns 1759–1796
Georges Danton 1759–1794
William Pitt 1759–1806
Friedrich Schiller 1759–1805
William Wilberforce 1759–1833

1760 – 1779

Katsushika Hokusai 1760–1849
Sequoya 1760–1843
Marie Tussaud 1760–1850
Robert Fulton 1765–1815
Joseph Niepce 1765–1833
John Dalton 1766–1844
Thomas Malthus 1766–1834
Andrew Jackson 1767–1845
Baron von Humboldt 1769–1859
Mehemet Ali 1769–1849
Napoleon I 1769–1821
Duke of Wellington 1769–1852
Ludwig van Beethoven 1770–1827
William Clark 1770–1838 *see Lewis and Clark*
Georg Hegel 1770–1831
William Wordsworth 1770–1850
Mungo Park 1771–1806
Walter Scott 1771–1832
Samuel Coleridge 1772–1834
Klemens Metternich 1773–1859
Thomas Young 1773–1829
Meriwether Lewis 1774–1809 *see Lewis and Clark*
André-Marie Ampère 1775–1836
Jane Austen 1775–1817
Daniel O'Connel 1775–1847
J. M. W. Turner 1775–1851
John Constable 1776–1837
Karl Gauss 1777–1855
Hans Christian Oersted 1777–1851

Humphry Davy 1778–1829
Joseph Gay-Lussac 1778–1850
José de San Martin 1778–1850

1780 – 1799

Elizabeth Fry 1780–1845
George Stephenson 1781–1848
Niccolò Paganini 1782–1840
Simón Bolívar 1783–1830
Jacob Grimm 1785–1863
Davy Crockett 1786–1836
John Franklin 1786–1847
Wilhelm Grimm 1786–1859
George Ohm 1787–1854
Shaka the Zulu c.1787–1828
Lord Byron 1788–1824
Robert Peel 1788–1850
Louis Daguerre 1789–1851
Edmund Kean 1789–1833
Michael Faraday 1791–1867
Samuel Morse 1791–1872
Charles Babbage 1792–1871
Gioachino Rossini 1792–1868
Percy Shelley 1792–1822
Cornelius Vanderbilt 1794–1877
Rowland Hill 1795–1879
John Keats 1795–1821
Franz Schubert 1797–1828
Mary Shelley 1797–1851
Sojourner Truth c.1797–1883
Eugène Delacroix 1798–1863
Honoré de Balzac 1799–1850
Alexander Pushkin 1799–1837

1800 – 1809

John Brown 1800–1859
William Fox Talbot 1800–1877
7th Earl of Shaftesbury 1801–1885
Brigham Young 1801–1877
Alexandre Dumas 1802–1870
Victor Hugo 1802–1885
Hector Berlioz 1803–1869
Ralph Waldo Emerson 1803–1882

Benjamin Disraeli 1804–1881
Nathaniel Hawthorne 1804–1864
Mongkut 1804–1868
Johann Strauss I 1804–1849
Hans Christian Andersen 1805–1875
Ferdinand de Lesseps 1805–1894
Mary Seacole 1805–1881
Isambard Kingdom Brunel 1806–1859
Giuseppe Garibaldi 1807–1882
Robert E. Lee 1807–1870
Henry Wadsworth Longfellow 1807–1882
Jefferson Davis 1808–1889
Napoleon III 1808–1873
Louis Braille 1809–1852
Charles Darwin 1809–1882
William Gladstone 1809–1898
Abraham Lincoln 1809–1865
Felix Mendelssohn 1809–1847
Edgar Allan Poe 1809–1849
Alfred, Lord Tennyson 1809–1892

1810 – 1819

Camillo Cavour 1810–1861
Frédéric Chopin 1810–1849
Robert Schumann 1810–1856
Franz Liszt 1811–1886
Harriet Beecher Stowe 1811–1896
William Thackeray 1811–1863
Robert Browning 1812–1889
Charles Dickens 1812–1870
Alfred Krupp 1812–1887
Edward Lear 1812–1888
Henry Bessemer 1813–1898
David Livingstone 1813–1873
Giuseppe Verdi 1813–1901
Richard Wagner 1813–1883
Samuel Colt 1814–1862
Otto von Bismarck 1815–1898
George Boole 1815–1864
John A. Macdonald 1815–1891
Anthony Trollope 1815–1882
Charlotte Brontë 1816–1855
Ernest Werner Siemens 1816–1892
Frederick Douglass 1817–1895

Emily Brontë 1818–1848
James Joule 1818–1889
Karl Marx 1818–1883
George Eliot 1819–1880
Jean Foucault 1819–1868
Herman Melville 1819–1891
Christopher Sholes 1819–1890
Queen Victoria 1819–1901
Walt Whitman 1819–1892

1820 – 1829

Susan Anthony Brownell 1820–1906
Anne Brontë 1820–1849
Florence Nightingale 1820–1910
Harriet Tubman c.1820–1913
Victor Emmanuel II 1820–1878
Charles Baudelaire 1821–1867
Richard Burton 1821–1890
Fyodor Dostoevsky 1821–1881
Mary Baker Eddy 1821–1910
Gustave Flaubert 1821–1880
Ulysses S. Grant 1822–1885
Gregor Mendel 1822–1884
Louis Pasteur 1822–1895
Heinrich Schliemann 1822–1890
Charles William Siemens 1823–1883
Charles Blondin 1824–1897
Anton Bruckner 1824–1896
William Kelvin 1824–1907
Paul Kruger 1825–1904
Johann Strauss II 1825–1899
Cetshwayo c.1826–1884
Frederick Siemens 1826–1904
Joseph Lister 1827–1912
Josephine Butler 1828–1906
Henrick Ibsen 1828–1906
Dante Gabriel Rossetti 1828–1882
Leo Tolstoy 1828–1910
Jules Verne 1828–1905
Catherine Booth 1829–1890
William Booth 1829–1912
Geronimo 1829–1909

1830 – 1839

Emily Dickinson 1830–1886
Eadweard Muybridge 1830–1904
Camille Pissarro 1830–1903
James Clerk Maxwell 1831–1879
Louisa May Alcott 1832–1888
Isabella Bird 1832–1904
Lewis Carroll 1832–1898
Gustave Eiffel 1832–1923
Edouard Manet 1832–1883
Nikolaus Otto 1832–1891
Johannes Brahms 1833–1897
Alfred Nobel 1833–1896
Gottlieb Daimler 1834–1900
Edgar Degas 1834–1917
Dimitri Mendeléev 1834–1907
William Morris 1834–1896
Sitting Bull c.1834–1890
Andrew Carnegie 1835–1919
Yukichi Fukuzawa 1835–1901
Camille Saint-Saëns 1835–1921
Mark Twain 1835–1910
Elizabeth Garrett Anderson 1836–1917
William Gilbert 1836–1911 *see Gilbert and Sullivan*
Ramakrishna 1836–1886
Georges Bizet 1838–1875
Henry Irving 1838–1905
Ferdinand von Zeppelin 1838–1917
Paul Cézanne 1839–1906
General George A. Custer 1839–1876
Modest Mussorgsky 1839–1881
John D. Rockefeller 1839–1937

1840 – 1849

John Dunlop 1840–1921
Thomas Hardy 1840–1928
Claude Monet 1840–1926
Auguste Rodin 1840–1917
Pyotr Ilyich Tchaikovsky 1840–1893
Emile Zola 1840–1902
Georges Clemenceau 1841–1929
Anton Dvořák 1841–1904
Ito Hirobumi 1841–1909
Pierre Auguste Renoir 1841–1919

1818 ▲

1841 ▲

Arthur Sullivan 1842–1900 *see Gilbert and Sullivan*
Edvard Grieg 1843–1907
Henry James 1843–1916
Robert Koch 1843–1910
Karl Benz 1844–1929
Saint Bernadette 1844–1879
Sarah Bernhardt 1844–1923
Henry Heinz 1844–1919
Friedrich Nietzsche 1844–1900
Nikolay Rimsky-Korsakov 1844–1908
Henri Rousseau 1844–1910
Thomas Barnardo 1845–1905
Wilhelm Röntgen 1845–1923
Buffalo Bill 1846–1917
Peter Fabergé 1846–1920
Charles Parnell 1846–1891
Alexander Graham Bell 1847–1922
Annie Besant 1847–1933
Thomas Edison 1847–1931
Jesse James 1847–1882
Paul Gauguin 1848–1903
W. G. Grace 1848–1915
Crazy Horse c.1849–1877
William Hoover 1849–1932
Ivan Pavlov 1849–1936

1850 – 1859

Horatio Kitchener 1850–1916
Tomas Masaryk 1850–1937
Guy de Maupassant 1850–1893
Robert Louis Stevenson 1850–1894
Henri Becquerel 1852–1908
Calamity Jane c.1852–1903
Antonio Gaudí 1852–1926
Frank Woolworth 1852–1919
Cecil Rhodes 1853–1902
Vincent Van Gogh 1853–1890
George Eastman 1854–1932
Oscar Wilde 1854–1900
Ned Kelly 1855–1880
Sigmund Freud 1856–1939
James Keir Hardie 1856–1915
Robert Peary 1856–1920
Henri Philippe Pétain 1856–1951
Tom Roberts 1856–1931

George Bernard Shaw 1856–1950
Joseph Thomson 1856–1940
Booker T. Washington 1856–1915
Woodrow Wilson 1856–1924
Robert Baden-Powell 1857–1941
Joseph Conrad 1857–1924
Edward Elgar 1857–1934
Heinrich Hertz 1857–1894
Rudolf Diesel 1858–1913
Emmeline Pankhurst 1858–1928
Max Planck 1858–1947
Giacomo Puccini 1858–1924
Theodore Roosevelt 1858–1919
Billy the Kid 1859–1881
Arthur Conan Doyle 1859–1930
Alfred Dreyfus 1859–1935
Kenneth Grahame 1859–1932
Georges Seurat 1859–1891

1860 – 1869

J. M. Barrie 1860–1937
Anton Chekhov 1860–1904
William Kellogg 1860–1951
Gustav Mahler 1860–1911
Annie Oakley 1860–1926
Nellie Melba 1861–1931
Fridtjof Nansen 1861–1930
José Rizal 1861–1896
Rabindranath Tagore 1861–1941
William Bragg 1862–1942
Claude Debussy 1862–1918
Mary Kingsley 1862–1900
Auguste Lumière 1862–1954
Henry Ford 1863–1947
William Randolph Hearst 1863–1951
David Lloyd George 1863–1945
Edvard Munch 1863–1944
Louis Lumière 1864–1948
Richard Strauss 1864–1949
Henri de Toulouse–Lautrec 1864–1901
Edith Cavell 1865–1915
Rudyard Kipling 1865–1936
Jean Sibelius 1865–1957
W. B. Yeats 1865–1939
Wassily Kandinsky 1866–1944

Ramsay MacDonald 1866–1937
Beatrix Potter 1866–1943
Sun Yat–sen 1866–1925
H. G. Wells 1866–1946
Marie Curie 1867–1934
Frank Lloyd Wright 1867–1959
Wilbur Wright 1867–1912
Fritz Haber 1868–1934
Charles Rennie Mackintosh 1868–1928
Nicholas II 1868–1918
Robert Scott 1868–1912
Mahatma Gandhi 1869–1948
André Gide 1869–1951
Henri Matisse 1869–1954

Constantin Brancusi 1876–1957
Pablo Casals 1876–1973
Walter Burley Griffin 1876–1937
Muhammad Ali Jinnah 1876–1948
Muhammad Iqbal 1877–1938
Pancho Villa 1877–1923
Lise Meitner 1878–1968
Yoshida Shigeru 1878–1967
Albert Einstein 1879–1955
Otto Hahn 1879–1968
Paul Klee 1879–1940
Joseph Stalin 1879–1953
Leon Trotsky 1879–1940
Emiliano Zapata 1879–1919

1870 – 1879

Vladimir Lenin 1870–1924
Maria Montessori 1870–1952
Jan Smuts 1870–1950
Marcel Proust 1871–1922
Rasputin 1871–1916
Ernest Rutherford 1871–1937
Orville Wright 1871–1948
Roald Amundsen 1872–1928
Aurobindo 1872–1950
Louis Blériot 1872–1936
Piet Mondrian 1872–1944
Bertrand Russell 1872–1970
Ralph Vaughan Williams 1872–1958
Sergey Rakhmaninov 1873–1943
Winston Churchill 1874–1965
Robert Frost 1874–1963
Gustav Holst 1874–1934
Harry Houdini 1874–1926
William Lyon Mackenzie King 1874–1950
Guglielmo Marconi 1874–1937
L. M. Montgomery 1874–1942
Arnold Schoenberg 1874–1951
Chaim Weizmann 1874–1952
D. W. Griffith 1875–1948
Carl Jung 1875–1961
Ferdinand Porsche 1875–1951
Maurice Ravel 1875–1937
Albert Schweitzer 1875–1965

1880 – 1884

Jacob Epstein 1880–1959
Helen Keller 1880–1968
Douglas MacArthur 1880–1964
Christabel Pankhurst 1880–1958
Marie Stopes 1880–1958
Mustafa Kemal Atatürk 1881–1938
Béla Bartók 1881–1945
Cecil B. De Mille 1881–1959
Alexander Fleming 1881–1955
Pope John XXIII 1881–1963
Anna Pavlova 1881–1931
Pablo Picasso 1881–1973
Georges Braque 1882–1963
Eamon De Valera 1882–1975
Arthur Stanley Eddington 1882–1944
Samuel Goldwyn 1882–1974
James Joyce 1882–1941
A. A. Milne 1882–1956
Franklin D. Roosevelt 1882–1945
Igor Stravinsky 1882–1971
Virginia Woolf 1882–1941
Clement Attlee 1883–1967
Walter Gropius 1883–1969
Franz Kafka 1883–1924
John Maynard Keynes 1883–1946
Benito Mussolini 1883–1945
Auguste Piccard 1884–1962
Eleanor Roosevelt 1884–1962
Harry S. Truman 1884–1972

1866 ▶

1884 ▶

1885 – 1889

Niels Bohr 1885–1962
D. H. Lawrence 1885–1930
David Ben-Gurion 1886–1973
Clarence Birdseye 1886–1956
Arthur Brown 1886–1948 *see Alcock and Brown*
Diego Rivera 1886–1957
Marc Chagall 1887–1985
Chiang Kai–shek 1887–1975
Marcus Garvey 1887–1940
Le Corbusier 1887–1965
Bernard Law Montgomery 1887–1976
Georgia O'Keeffe 1887–1986
Arthur Rubinstein 1887–1982
Erwin Schrödinger 1887–1961
Jim Thorpe 1887–1953
John Logie Baird 1888–1946
Irving Berlin 1888–1989
Richard Byrd 1888–1957
T. S. Eliot 1888–1965
T. E. Lawrence 1888–1935
Charlie Chaplin 1889–1977
Jean Cocteau 1889–1963
Adolf Hitler 1889–1945
Edwin Hubble 1889–1953
Pandit Jawaharlal Nehru 1889–1964
Igor Sikorsky 1889–1972
Vladimir Zworykin 1889–1982

1890 – 1894

Lawrence Bragg 1890–1971
Agatha Christie 1890–1976
Michael Collins 1890–1922
Charles De Gaulle 1890–1970
Dwight Eisenhower 1890–1969
Ho Chi Minh 1890–1969
Stan Laurel 1890–1965 *see Laurel and Hardy*
Groucho Marx 1890–1977
Vaslav Nijinsky 1890–1950
Alexander, Earl of Tunis 1891–1969
Frederick Banting 1891–1941 *see Banting and Best*
Chico Marx 1891–1961
Cole Porter 1891–1964
Sergei Prokofiev 1891–1953

Erwin Rommel 1891–1944
John Alcock 1892–1919 *see Alcock and Brown*
Francisco Franco 1892–1975
Jean Paul Getty 1892–1976
Haile Selassie 1892–1975
Oliver Hardy 1892–1957 *see Laurel and Hardy*
Josip Tito 1892–1980
J. R. R. Tolkien 1892–1973
Robert Watson-Watt 1892–1973
Herman Goering 1893–1946
Mao Zedong 1893–1976
Harpo Marx 1893–1964
Joan Miró 1893–1983
Wilfred Owen 1893–1918
Mary Pickford 1893–1979
Martha Graham 1894–1991
Jomo Kenyatta c.1894–1978
Nikita Khrushchev 1894–1971
Georges Lemaitre 1894–1966
Robert Menzies 1894–1978

1895 – 1899

John Ford 1895–1973
Buster Keaton 1895–1966
Babe Ruth 1895–1948
Rudolph Valentino 1895–1926
F. Scott Fitzgerald 1896–1940
Enid Blyton 1897–1968
Joseph Goebbels 1897–1945
Lester Bowles Pearson 1897–1972
Charles Kingsford Smith 1897–1935
Bertolt Brecht 1898–1956
Ninette de Valois 1898
Amelia Earhart 1898–1937
Sergei Eisenstein 1898–1948
M. C. Escher 1898–1972
George Gershwin 1898–1937
C. S. Lewis 1898–1963
Albert Luthuli 1898–1967
René Magritte 1898–1967
Golda Meir 1898–1978
Henry Moore 1898–1986
Paul Robeson 1898–1976
Shin'ichi Suzuki 1898–1997
Zhou Enlai 1898–1976

Fred Astaire 1899–1987
Charles Best 1899–1978 *see Banting and Best*
Humphrey Bogart 1899–1957
Jorge Louis Borges 1899–1986
Al Capone c.1899–1947
Duke Ellington 1899–1974
Ernest Hemingway 1899–1961
Alfred Hitchcock 1899–1980
Yasunari Kawabata 1899–1972
Suzanne Lenglen 1899–1938
Vladimir Nabokov 1899–1977

1900 – 1904

Laszlo Biro 1900–1985
Aaron Copland 1900–1990
Ayatollah Ruhollah Khomeini 1900–1989
Uday Shankar 1900–1977
Louis Armstrong 1901–1971
Walt Disney 1901–1966
Enrico Fermi 1901–1954
Clark Gable 1901–1960
Alberto Giacometti 1901–1966
Werner Karl Heisenberg 1901–1976
Emperor Hirohito 1901–1989
Zeppo Marx 1901–1979
Linus Pauling 1901–1994
Achmed Sukarno 1901–1970
Hendrik Verwoerd 1901–1966
Langston Hughes 1902–1967
Charles Lindbergh 1902–1974
Richard Rodgers 1902–1979
John Steinbeck 1902–1968
Barbara Hepworth 1903–1975
Amy Johnson 1903–1941
Louis Leakey 1903–1972
George Orwell 1903–1950
Salvador Dalí 1904–1989
Deng Xiaoping 1904–1996
Marlene Dietrich 1904–1992
Cary Grant 1904–1986
Graham Greene 1904–1991
Glenn Miller 1904–1944
J. Robert Oppenheimer 1904–1967

1905 – 1909

Greta Garbo 1905–1990
Howard Hughes 1905–1976
Jean-Paul Sartre 1905–1980
Chester Carlson 1906–1968
Soichiro Honda 1906–1991
Dmitri Shostakovich 1906–1975
W. H. Auden 1907–1973
Laurence Olivier 1907–1989
John Wayne 1907–1979
Frank Whittle 1907–1996
John Bardeen 1908–1991
Donald Bradman 1908
Henri Cartier-Bresson 1908
Bette Davis 1908–1989
Lyndon B. Johnson 1908–1973
Joseph McCarthy 1908–1957
Jean Batten 1909–1982
Katherine Hepburn 1909
Kwame Nkrumah 1909–1972

1910 – 1914

Christopher Cockerell 1910
Jacques Cousteau 1910–1997
Dorothy Hodgkin 1910–1994
Akira Kurosawa 1910
Mother Teresa 1910–1997
Juan Fangio 1911–1995
William Golding 1911–1993
Ronald Reagan 1911
Tennessee Williams 1911–1983
Wernher von Braun 1912–1977
Sonja Henie 1912–1969
Jackson Pollock 1912–1956
Menachem Begin 1913–1992
Willy Brandt 1913–1992
Benjamin Britten 1913–1976
Albert Camus 1913–1960
Mary Leakey 1913–1996
Richard Nixon 1913–1994
Jesse Owens 1913–1980
Joe DiMaggio 1914
Thor Heyerdahl 1914
Joe Louis 1914–1981

1899 ▶

1914 ▶

Tenzing Norgay 1914–1986
Dylan Thomas 1914–1953

1915 – 1919

Billie Holiday 1915–1959
Stanley Matthews 1915
Arthur Miller 1915
Frank Sinatra 1915–1998
Orson Welles 1915–1985
Francis Crick 1916 *see Crick and Watson*
Roald Dahl 1916–1990
Yehudi Menuhin 1916
François Mitterand 1916–1996
Indira Gandhi 1917–1984
John Fitzgerald Kennedy 1917–1963
Sidney Nolan 1917–1992
I. M. Pei 1917
Leonard Bernstein 1918–1990
Ella Fitzgerald 1918–1996
Nelson Mandela 1918
Gamal Abdel Nasser 1918–1970
Mohammed Anwar el Sadat 1918–1981
Alexander Solzhenitsyn 1918
Margot Fonteyn 1919–1991
Edmund Hillary 1919
Eva Perón 1919–1952
Pierre Trudeau 1919

1920 – 1929

Federico Fellini 1920–1993
Pope John Paul II 1920
John Glenn 1921
Satayjit Ray 1921–1992
Christiaan Barnard 1922
Julius Nyerere 1922
Yitzhak Rabin 1922–1996
Emil Zatopek 1922
Maria Callas 1923–1977
Nadine Gordimer 1923
Lee Kuan Yew 1923
Marlon Brando 1924
Kenneth Kaunda 1924
Benoit Mandelbrot 1924

Robert Mugabe 1924
B. B. King 1925
Malcolm X 1925–1965
Margaret Thatcher 1925
Chuck Berry 1926
Elizabeth II 1926
Marilyn Monroe 1926–1962
Abdus Salam 1926–1996
Joan Sutherland 1926
Fidel Castro 1927
Maya Angelou 1928
Zulfikar Ali Bhutto 1928–1979
James Brown 1928
Gatsha Buthelezi 1928
Gabriel García Márquez 1928
Che Geuvara 1928–1967
Pol Pot 1928
Shirley Temple 1928
Andy Warhol 1928–1987
James Watson 1928 *see Crick and Watson*
Yasser Arafat 1929
Anne Frank 1929–1945
Robert Hawke 1929
Martin Luther King, Jr 1929–1968
Arnold Palmer 1929

1930 – 1939

Chinua Achebe 1930
Neil Armstrong 1930
Ray Charles 1930
Clint Eastwood 1930
Helmut Kohl 1930
Derek Walcott 1930
James Dean 1931–1955
Mikhail Gorbachev 1931
Rupert Murdoch 1931
Bill Shoemaker 1931
Desmond Tutu 1931
Boris Yeltsin 1931
Athol Fugard 1932
Sylvia Plath 1932–1963
Elizabeth Taylor 1932
Yuri Gagarin 1934–1968
Gloria Steinem 1934
Dalai Lama 1935
Luciano Pavarotti 1935

Lester Piggott 1935
Elvis Presley 1935–1977
F. W. de Klerk 1936
Vaclav Havel 1936
Buddy Holly 1936–1959
Margaret Mahy 1936
Garry Sobers 1936
Dawn Fraser 1937
Saddam Hussein 1937
Valentina Tereshkova 1937
Rod Laver 1938
Rudolf Nureyev 1938–1993

1940 – 1949

John Lennon 1940–1980 *see Lennon and McCartney*
Jack Nicklaus 1940
Pelé 1940
Bob Dylan 1941
Muhammad Ali 1942
Margaret Court 1942
Aretha Franklin 1942
Stephen Hawking 1942
Jimi Hendrix 1942–1970
Paul McCartney 1942 *see Lennon and McCartney*
Mu'ammar al-Qaddafi 1942
Paul Simon 1942
Jocelyn Bell 1943
Robert De Niro 1943
Mick Jagger 1943
Jean-Claude Killy 1943
Joni Mitchell 1943
Lech Walesa 1943
Richard Leakey 1944
Diana Ross 1944
Kiri Te Kanawa 1944

Franz Beckenbauer 1945
Eric Clapton 1945
Bob Marley 1945–1981
Eddy Merckx 1945
Steve Biko 1946–1977
Bill Clinton 1946
Sultan of Brunei 1946
Irena Szewinska 1946
David Bowie 1947
Elton John 1947
Steven Spielberg 1947

1950 – 1969

Richard Branson 1950
Mark Spitz 1950
Stevie Wonder 1950
Imran Khan 1952
Benazir Bhutto 1953
Tony Blair 1953
Chiyonofuji 1955
Bill Gates 1955
Alain Prost 1955
Tom Hanks 1956
Joe Montana 1956
Martina Navratilova 1956
Ingemar Stenmark 1956
Michael Jackson 1958
Madonna 1958
Daley Thompson 1958
Diego Maradona 1960
Nadia Comaneci 1961
Diana, Princess of Wales 1961–1997
Wayne Gretzky 1961
Carl Lewis 1961
Tom Cruise 1962
Sergey Bubka 1963
Michael Jordan 1963
Gary Kasparov 1963
Jahangir Khan 1963
Steffi Graf 1969

1936 ▶

1963 ▶

Picture Credits